Caribbean expert.
500 years experience.

It might surprise you to learn that Latin America has some of the most beautiful Caribbean islands off its shores.

What won't surprise you is that Iberia knows more about flying to Latin America than anyone else. After all, Spain's trade and cultural links there stretch back some five centuries.

Five decades ago, Iberia was the first airline to link Europe with Latin America.

Serving 21 cities in 19 countries, no other airline can offer more frequent flights or a wider choice of destinations between the two continents.

Should you decide to take advantage of Iberia's FREE stopover in Madrid, there's lunch or dinner plus hotel accommodation with transfers to and from the airport. If time allows there's also a free sightseeing tour of the city.

When you arrive at your chosen destination you'll be ready for all that Latin America has to offer.

Be it adventure, seeking lost cultures or just winding-down on tropical beaches, Iberia can show you how best to discover a world we've known for centuries.

For more details telephone Iberia on 071 830 0011.

SANTO DOMINGO
SAN JUAN
GUATEMALA *SAN PEDRO SULA*
SAN SALVADOR *ARUBA* *MARGARITA ISLAND*
MANAGUA *CARTAGENA*
SAN JOSE *CARACAS*
PANAMA
BOGOTA

1995

CARIBBEAN ISLANDS HANDBOOK

With Bermuda and the Bahamas

SIXTH EDITION

**Editors *Sarah Cameron & Ben Box*
Cartographer *Sebastian Ballard***

But again, again these
hot and coffee streets reclaim
my love. Carts rumble.
The long horn of a higgler's voice
painting the shadows midday
brown, cries about harvest,
and the wind calls back
blue air across the town; it tears
the thin topographies of dream, it blows me
as by old, familiar maps,
to this affectionate shore, green
and crumpling hills,
like paper in the Admiral's fist.

***Dennis Scott** From 'Homecoming'*

TRADE & TRAVEL
Handbooks

Trade & Travel Publications Ltd
6 Riverside Court, Lower Bristol Road, Bath BA2 3DZ, England
Telephone 01225 469141 Fax 01225 469461

©Trade & Travel Publications Ltd., September 1994

ISBN 0 900751 52 5   ISSN 0967-4748

CIP DATA: A catalogue record for this book is available from the British Library

In North America, published by

PASSPORT BOOKS
a division of *NTC Publishing Group*

4255 West Touhy Avenue
Lincolnwood (Chicago), Illinois 60646-1975, USA

ISBN   0-8442-8975-2

Library of Congress Catalog Card Number 94-66051

Passport Books and colophon are registered trademarks of NTC Publishing Group

**WARNING: While every endeavour is made to ensure that the facts
printed in this book are correct at the time of going to press, travellers are
cautioned to obtain authoritative advice from consulates, airlines, etc,
concerning current travel and visa requirements and conditions before
embarking. The publishers cannot accept legal responsibility for errors,
however caused, that are printed in this book.**

Cover illustration by Suzanne Evans

Printed and bound in Great Britain by Clays Ltd., Bungay, Suffolk

CONTENTS

TRADE & TRAVEL
HANDBOOKS

"*A travel guide business that looks set to sweep the world.*"
The Independent

"*The **India Handbook** (formerly the South Asian Handbook) has reminded me of how much I do not know about the sub-continent!*"
Mark Tully, BBC India correspondent

"*More info - less blah.*"
Readers's letter, Germany

"*By far the best, most comprehensive guides: in a class of their own. Unreservedly recommended - a Handbook will pay for itself many times over.*"
Journey Latin America

"*On Bible thin paper with distinctive covers. The miraculous result is that they are, at the same time, sturdy, exhaustive and light-weight.*"
Fort Lauderdale Sun Sentinel

"*Mines of information and free of pretentiousness: make other guidebooks read like Butlins brochures.*"
Bookshop review

"*Accurate and reliable down to the minutest detail. Amazingly so.*"
Reader's letter, Canada

"*By far the most informative guide to Burma published in recent years. Miraculously, the information appears to be up-to-date, rare for books in this genre.*"
Far Eastern Economic Review

PREFACE

After three difficult years in the early 1990s, Caribbean tourism experienced considerable improvement in 1993 and seemed to be continuing in the same vein as we went to print in 1994. The upswing was particularly encouraging for stayover arrivals, which the Caribbean Tourism Organization estimated grew by around 8% to 13mn in 1993, although the number of cruise ship passengers grew only slightly to 9mn. The region's main market for stayover arrivals, the USA, grew by 10% to 6.9mn as a result of rising consumer confidence and a marketing campaign jointly funded by 29 Caribbean countries, hoteliers, airlines and other companies involved in the tourist industry. Visitors from Europe showed similar growth to 2.3mn, with numbers from Germany rising by 41%, the UK by 13% and France by 8%, partly because of the promotion campaign launched by the EU-financed, 1993-96 Caribbean tourism development programme, and partly because of improved air services, particularly German charter flights.

Our mailbag has reflected the increase in travel to the region and we have received a welcome number of letters this year from all over the world. Very few have had problems while travelling or criticisms to make about where they stayed or ate, implying that standards of hospitality are good. There have been many recommendations for hotels, guest houses and restaurants which we have happily included. However, on the negative side, we must advise travellers to take security precautions in Jamaica, Trinidad and Tobago and San Juan, Puerto Rico, where muggings and theft remain a problem. As a result of the political instability in Haiti, the embargo and the cessation of flights, no one from the editorial team has visited it this year and we have not received any travellers' letters,

so the practical information unfortunately remains the same as in the 1994 edition, when the chapter was rewritten by Mike Tarr. Reports from Cuba state that it is still difficult for independent travellers to tour the island because of the dire economic situation, the shortage of foreign exchange and the lack of fuel. It is to be hoped that the mounting pressure on the USA for it to end its trade embargo will have positive results for visitors to the island.

We have added two new articles for the 1995 edition: Windsurfing in the Caribbean, by Nicolette Clifford, a journalist and expert windsurfer resident in the the British Virgin Islands, and Whale and Dolphin Watching, by Erich Hoyt, a consultant for the Whale and Dolphin Conservation Society. While we have always carried information in the country chapters on both these activities, increased interest has prompted us to give them extra space. Whale and dolphin watching received particular attention in 1994 during the meeting of the International Whaling Commission when the position of several Caribbean islands stymied Japan's attempt to reopen commercial whaling. The Bahamas chapter has been extensively updated for this edition as a result of Sarah Cameron's visit to Nassau, Freeport and several Family Islands. During her stay on the islands she experienced the wonderful Bahamian hospitality and she is particularly grateful to the Tourist Board for their willing and efficient assistance, both with travel arrangements and in updating the text.

The number of people who help us improve the *Caribbean Islands Handbook* grows steadily every year and we are grateful to the network of regular and not so regular correspondents: Dr Nicholas Saunders (University of West Indies, Jamaica), Mik and Cathy Bancroft (Baha-

6

mas), Lynda Cheetham (Cuba and the Dominican Republic), Rachel Rogers (Dominica), Susan Brazier (St Lucia), David Horwell (Aruba), Nan Elisa (Curaçao), Niki Clifford (British Virgin Islands), Louise Fletcher (Turks and Caicos Islands), Joanne James Selver (North Caicos), Dianne Erdos (Sosúa, Dominican Republic), Dania Goris (Santo Domingo), Tony Thorne (Guyana), Jorge Valle-Aguiluz (Honduras and the Bay Islands) and David Renwick (Trinidad and Tobago). Special thanks also go to John Alton (Strand Cruise and Travel Centre, London), Frank Bellamy and the staff of Transatlantic Wings (London), Rod Prince (*Caribbean Insight*) and the many Tourist Offices who gave freely of their time and expertise to check our facts. Last, but not least, we are grateful to Lorraine Horler and Celia Fletcher, who transferred all our corrections to print.

The Editors

THE EDITORS

Sarah Cameron

Sarah Cameron's interest in Latin America and the Caribbean began with a degree in Iberian and Latin American Studies, during which time she spent a year in Colombia. Following a spell with the British Council she joined Lloyds Bank International in 1977 as economist on Latin America, before rising through the ranks to become Lloyds Bank Economic Advisor on Latin America and the Caribbean. During this time she also worked as a sub-editor on the *South American Handbook* and contributed articles and chapters to many publications on the region. In 1990 Sarah decided to part company with the world of finance and debt rescheduling to devote more time to the *Handbooks*. Together with Ben Box she wrote and jointly edits the *Caribbean Islands Handbook*, is assistant editor of the *Mexico & Central American Handbook* and occasional sub-editor of the *South American Handbook*, while keeping an eye on the economic data in all three. Her travels both for the bank and the *Handbooks* have been extensive and enjoyable; she also appreciates her life in rural Suffolk, where she takes the role of mother and groom to two daughters, three horses and many other animals.

Ben Box

A doctorate in medieval Spanish and Portugese studies provided very few job prospects for Ben Box, but a fascination for all things Latin. While studying for his degree, Ben travelled extensively in Spain and Portugal. He turned his attention to contemporary Iberian and Latin American affairs in 1980, beginning a career as a freelance writer at that time. He contributed regularly to national newspapers and learned tomes, and, after increasing involvement with the *South American Handbook*, became its editor in 1989. During his frequent visits to the region he has travelled from the US/Mexico border to S Chile (not all in one go) and in the Caribbean. His own travels, and editing those of others, only whets his appetite for finding more places to explore. He also edits the *Mexico & Central American Handbook* and jointly edits the *Caribbean Islands Handbook* with Sarah Cameron. To seek diversion from a household immersed in Latin America, he plays village cricket in summer and cycles the lanes of Suffolk.

HOW TO USE THIS HANDBOOK

The Caribbean Islands Handbook is the most complete and up-to-date package of information for independent travellers on all the Caribbean islands. Its text is updated every year for the new edition which is published on 1 September. The text is based on the editors' personal travels, extensive information from correspondents living in the region, material and maps which travellers send us, contributions from national tourist authorities, and the many sources of information on the Caribbean available in the UK and elsewhere.

Editorial Logic
Users of the *Handbook* will find that we employ a logical system of arrangement, which we believe is the most convenient for travellers.

Introduction and Hints
This first section in the book gives information and hints that apply generally to all the islands we cover, including:
- ❏ Travel to and in the Caribbean
- ❏ Documents
- ❏ Language
- ❏ Money
- ❏ Travel in the Eastern Caribbean
- ❏ Further Reading

Miami
A guide to one of the major gateways to the Caribbean by Mark Wilson, teacher of geography and journalist, currently based in Trinidad. Further information has been supplied by Alyce M McDaniel of the Miami Convention and Visitors Bureau, and by Debbie Wylde of Trade & Travel.

Health Information
This major section by Dr David Snashall of St Thomas's Hospital Medical School, London, gives details of the health risks common in the Caribbean, and the sensible precautions travellers should take to combat them.

Caribbean Geology
Written by Mark Wilson.

Flora and Fauna and Responsible Tourism
These two sections have been contributed by Mark Eckstein of David Bellamy Associates, Durham, UK.

Whale and Dolphin Watching
Erich Hoyt, a marine ecologist, author and consultant for the Whale and Dolphin Conservation Society, describes the best places in the region to see these mammals and who to contact for tours.

Watersports and Sailing in the Caribbean
Rosie Mauro, an experienced sailor from Barbados, has compiled this section to give an idea of variety of the aquatic activities that can be enjoyed in the region.

Scuba Diving in the Caribbean
Martha Watkins Gilkes, a freelance diving journalist based in Antigua, outlines the best dive sites with general advice for divers.

Windsurfing in the Caribbean
Nicolette Clifford, a journalist based in the British Virgin Islands, writes about the best places and seasons for windsurfing in the region.

Walking in the Caribbean
Written by Mark Wilson.

Island Sections
Information is set out island by island in a constant sequence as follows:
- ❏ List of contents
- ❏ Description of geography and details on the people

❏ History
❏ Government
❏ The Economy
❏ Culture
❏ Flora and Fauna
❏ Diving and Marine Life
❏ Beaches and Watersports
❏ Other Sports
❏ Festivals
❏ Excursions

In smaller islands the capital is usually treated as an excursion. In larger islands, the capital and other major towns and districts are treated as separate sections, each with its own description, excursions and local information. **Local Information** sections include accommodation, where to eat, transport and other services.

In cases where a group of islands constitute a chapter, separate islands may have an **Island Information** section which will contain much the same details as the local information sections just mentioned.

Information for Visitors concludes each chapter. This section comprises how to get there, what documents are necessary, clothing, food, which is the best time to visit, currency regulations and other essential information. Where accommodation and restaurants have not been covered in the descriptive part, they will appear in Information for Visitors.

All those who have assisted in the preparation of chapters are listed with our thanks at the end of this section.

Maps

Each island chapter is accompanied by maps of the relevant islands and of the major towns.

MAP SYMBOLS

International Border	⌒‑·⌒	Capital Cities	☐
State / Province Border	—··—··—	Cities / Towns	○
Main Roads (National Highways)	⌣15—	Bus Stations	**B**
Other Roads	———	Hospitals	**H**
Jeepable Roads, Tracks, Treks, Paths, Ferries	‑‑‑‑‑‑	Key Numbers	**27**
Railways, Stations	⊢━━⊣	Airport	✈
		Bridges	⤫
Contours (approx)	⌇		
Rivers	*Rio Aruña*		
Barrier Reef	~ ~ ~	Mountains	⩙
Built Up Areas	▨	Waterfall	⥣
Lakes, Reservoirs	🝙	National Parks, Wildlife Parks, Bird Sanctuaries	◆
Sand Banks, Beaches	⸬	Archaeological Sites	▲
National Parks, Gardens, Stadiums	▨		
Fortified Walls	▲ ▲ ▲	Church / Cathedral	✝

C 0

Prices

A wide cross section of hotel rates and transport costs is listed in each chapter. Prices are either given in US dollars, or the local currency, whichever is appropriate. (A list of exchange rates is given at the end of the book.) Unless otherwise stated, hotel prices quoted are for a double room in high season; rates are subject to change without notice and therefore those given in this book should only be taken as representative. High season is normally referred to as "winter", running from roughly mid-December to mid-April. "Summer" is low season, the remainder of the year.

Certain abbreviations are used in relation to hotel prices. These are:

EP—European Plan, room only

CP—Continental Plan, room and breakfast

MAP—Modified American Plan, room, breakfast and dinner

AP—American Plan, room with three daily meals

FAP—Full American Plan, room and all meals (including afternoon tea, etc).

Other abbreviations used in the text are: pp = per person; d = double; s = single; a/c = air conditioned; T = telephone; F = fax; TCs = travellers' cheques; rec = recommended; inc = including; N = north; S = south; E = east; W = west.

We should also like to thank the following travellers who wrote to us about their experiences in the Caribbean: Fran Atkins & Alan King (Brighton, East Sussex), Barbara Bailey (Tortola, BVI), David Beardsmore, Hans & Lena Bengtsson (Güteborg, Sweden), Douglas & Anja Bousquet (Buenos Aires), Dicky Boy (London NE18), Andrew 'Taff' Kelly (Swansea), Andrew 'Father' Gillman (Sutton Coldfield), & Liz Simms (Formby), Walter Brehm (Daun, Germany), Gabriele Brudermüller (Bonn), Jeremy Cameron (London E17), Neville Chanin (Stroud, Glos), Linda Cheetham (Santo Domingo) for her most useful letters, Guy Colin (Kourou, Guyane), G K B Cullin (Poole, Dorset), Jon Einarsson (Njardvik, Iceland), Glenn & Nan Elisa (Boca Sami, Curaçao), Gerljan Essink (Curaçao), Claire & Robert Everitt (Normandy Park, WA, USA), Kit Faith (Kingston, Jamaica), Louise Fletcher (Providenciales, TCI), Richard Forsdyke (London SE1), Charles Edwin Foxwell (Dunstable, Bedfordshire), W L Gates (King Leo of Redonda), R F George (Southampton), Yvonne Gerhard & Hanspeter Gehrig (Aarau, Switzerland), Barney Gibbs (peripatetic), Valerie Gibson (Edinburgh), Angela Gordon (Grand Turk), Susan M Grady (Alexandria, VA, USA), Beate Gretz (Göppingen, Germany), Gurtman (York, Maine, USA), Judith Gysin (Liestal, Switzerland), Eva S Hansen (Prevessin-Moens, France), Luis Hernández (Winter Park, FL, USA), Norman Hildreth (Buxton, Derbyshire), Brigitte Hofler (Geneva, Switzerland), David Horwell (Bromley, Kent), Lawnae D Hunter (Lompoc, CA, USA), Gabriel Hyde (Tenbury Wells, Worcestershire), John Ickes (Baltimore, MD, USA), Renate Imhof-Grünn (Vienna, Austria), Patricia Ishmael (New York), Jürg Isler (Zurich, Switzerland), Guy Jarvi (Bondi, NSW, Australia) a most useful letter, Susan Johnson (Aptos, CA, USA), Svein-Bruno Kallkovel (Egersund, Norway), Henriette Klarskov & Mads Rosenkrans (Frederiksberg, Denmark), Lisa & Graeme Knowles (Darling Point, Sydney, Australia), Werner Kroer (Allschwil, Switzerland), Irene Bachmair and Giesela Kübler (Munich, Germany), J Andrew Kuether (Northampton, MA, USA), Terry Lowry (Tulsa, OK, USA), Henni Mariager (Aalborg, Denmark), Kate McLachlan (Horsham, Sussex), Annette Morris (Reigate, Surrey), L Müller (Dusseldorf, Germany), Agostina Murgia (London E9), Nancy J Olson (Miami Beach, FL, USA), Katherin Papadopoulos (Adelaide, Australia), Ian & Helen Parsons (Basingstoke, Hampshire), Rod Prince (London), D J Puls & R J Chapp (Amsterdam), John

availability of one-way tickets). The Horn Line has regular sailings from Hamburg on the following route: Antwerp, Le Havre, Ponta Delgada (Azores), Pointe-à-Pitre, Fort-de-France, Cayenne, Moín (Costa Rica) or Santo Tomás de Castilla (Guatemala), Le Havre, Antwerp, Hamburg. The round trip fare is £2,520-2,770; the voyage's duration is 30 days.

From the USA, Ivaran Lines' container ship, *Americana*, carries 80 passengers in luxury accommodation: New Orleans, Houston, Puerto Cabello, La Guaira, Rio de Janeiro, Santos, Buenos Aires, Montevideo, Rio Grande do Sul, Itajaí, Santos, Rio, Salvador, Fortaleza, Bridgetown, San Juan, Veracruz, Tampico, New Orleans; fare US$10,140 – 15,390pp round trip, economy season rate, one way N or S possible.

For those with 1,000 miles offshore sailing experience, a cheap way to get to the Caribbean is crewing on a yacht being delivered from Europe or the USA to the region.

Island-hopping by boats with scheduled services is fairly limited. Boat services are more common between dependent islands, eg St Vincent and the Grenadines, Trinidad and Tobago, Belize City and Caye Caulker. Again, full details are given in the relevant sections below. Windward Lines Limited run a weekly passenger and cargo ferry service: St Lucia - Barbados - St Vincent - Trinidad - Güiria or Isla Margarita - Trinidad - St Vincent - Barbados - St Lucia. For information and tickets contact Global Steamship Agencies Ltd, Mariner's Club, Wrightson Road, PO Box 966, Port of Spain, Trinidad, T (809) 624-2279/625-2547, F (809) 627-5091.

Irregular passenger services on cargo boats (with basic accommodation, usually a hammock on deck, no meals supplied), schooners, crewing or hitching on yachts can only be discovered by asking around when you are in port. Crewing on yachts is not difficult in winter (in the hurricane season yachtsmen stay away). If you are looking for a job on a yacht, or trying to hitch a ride, it will be easier to make contact if you are living at the yacht harbour. Boat owners often advertise bunks for rent, which is a very cheap form of accommodation (US$10-30); ask around, or look on the bulletin boards. If arriving by sea, make sure you are aware of the island's entry requirements before setting out.

Travel on Land

Buses are cheap, but services tend not to be very convenient, in the sense that they often involve a night away from the point of departure, even on small islands. This is because buses start in outlying towns in the early morning and return from the capital in the afternoon. Another limiting factor to public transport is a shortage of funds for spare parts, so buses may be scarce and crowded. Many smaller islands do not even have a bus service.

Taxis are plentiful, but generally not cheap. Some islands, eg Trinidad, have route taxis, which are inexpensive and travel only on set routes. On many islands, taxi fares are set by the tourist office or government.

Renting a car gives the greatest flexibility, but is also hardest on the pocket. You can expect to pay more than in the USA or Europe. A number of islands require drivers to take out a temporary, or visitor driver's licence (these are mentioned in the text), but some places will not issue a licence to those over 70 years of age without a medical certificate. In small places, to rent a motorcycle, scooter or bicycle is a good idea.

Finances

The Caribbean is not a cheap area to visit. Transport is expensive (unless you are staying in one place and using only buses), but if you book your flights in advance, taking advantage of whatever air pass or stopovers are suitable, that expenditure at least will be out of the way.

Accommodation is generally expensive, too, even at the lower end of the market. There is no shortage of luxury resorts and beach hotels throughout the price range. In a number of instances you can book all-inclusive packages which are often good value and let you know in advance almost exactly what your expenditure will be. However, you will not see much of your chosen island outside your enclave. To find cheaper accommodation you need mobility, probably a hired car. One option is renting a self-catering apartment, villa or house, the range of which is also vast, and here the advantage is that a group of people can share the cost (this is not an economical prospect for single travellers).

Since, on a number of islands, resort-type hotels form the majority, turning up at a cheaper place may not always yield a room because competition is great. The term guest house is usually applied to places at the lower end of the market; they tend, but by no means in all cases, to be basic. Note also that, if booking ahead, tourist office lists may not include the cheapest establishments, so you may have to reserve a dearer room, then look around. This is probably what you will have to do in any event, time permitting, to find the best value. In the main, tourist offices publish accurate, up-to-date lists of accommodation, which are a great help for making preliminary bookings. Remember that the Dominican Republic has the most hotel rooms in the Caribbean, so there is no real problem in finding a space there; see each island section for details. Some islands, such as the French Antilles, have well-organized camp sites, but on many camping is actually prohibited, eg Antigua.

The following tips on economizing were sent by Steve Wilson and Debra Holton of San Francisco: even if not travelling with a tent, take a cooking stove and prepare your own food; much cheaper than eating in restaurants. Look out bunk rentals on boats (see above).

"Happy Hours" in bars often have free food, couples sharing costs can often take advantage of "Ladies' Night" in a bar or nightclub, which either permits free entry or cheap drinks. If you stay in guest houses and don't eat in restaurants, the minimum you should budget for is an average of US$45 a day, not including transport between islands.

High And Low Season

High season in the Caribbean is usually called "winter"; in other words it comes in the Northern Hemisphere's colder months. Dates vary a little but the season is roughly from mid-December to mid-April. At this time air fares, room rates and other costs rise. In addition, air fares are also increased at European and US holiday times, ie July, August and September if flying from the UK, July and August from the USA, etc. Flights to the Caribbean from the UK are at a premium in the pre-Christmas period.

Money

In general, the US dollar is the best currency to take, in cash or travellers' cheques. The latter are the most convenient and, if you follow the issuer's instructions, can be replaced if lost or stolen. On the most frequently-visited holiday islands, eurocurrencies can be exchanged without difficulty but at a poor rate and US dollars are preferred. In some places, the US dollar is accepted alongside local currency (but make sure in which currency prices are being quoted). In others, only the local currency is accepted. Credit cards are widely used. Remember to keep your money, credit cards, etc, safely on your person, or in a hotel safe.

A list of currencies and exchange rates is provided, see pages 968.

Documents

Individual island entry requirements are given in the relevant chapters under Information for Visitors. North Americans, British and Commonwealth citizens in some cases need only show proof of identity. If intending to visit Puerto Rico or the US Virgin Islands, or making connections through Miami or another US gateway, a visa for the United States will not be necessary if your home country and the airline on which you are travelling are part of the US Visa Waiver Program. A US consulate will supply all relevant details. An onward ticket is a common prerequisite for entry. Australians and New Zealanders should note that many islands impose strict entry laws on holders of the above passports. Satisfying visa and other requirements, if not done at home, can take at least a day, usually involve expense, and passport photographs will be needed: be prepared.

On all forms, refer to yourself as a "visitor" rather than a "tourist".

Many islands insist that visitors have an air ticket to their home country before being allowed to enter (not just the Eastern Caribbean, see below); for non-US citizens travelling to the Caribbean from the USA, this means a ticket from the USA to their home country, not a ticket back to the USA.

You should always carry your passport in a safe place about your person, or if not going far, leave it in the hotel safe. If staying in a place for several weeks, it is worth while registering at your Embassy or Consulate. Then, if your passport is stolen or lost, the process of replacing it is simplified and speeded up. Keeping photocopies of essential documents, and some additional passport-sized photographs, is recommended.

Travel In The Eastern Caribbean

Certain conditions are common to the former British colonies, or still British dependencies, in the Leewards and Windwards, including Barbados. At immigration on arrival, say you want to stay longer than planned because getting an extension is time-consuming and difficult. If asked where you are staying and you have not booked in advance, say any hotel (they do not usually check), but do not say you are going to camp and do not say that you are going to arrange accommodation later. Do not imagine that you can go to the Eastern Caribbean to work. Make sure that you have a ticket home: in Barbados, Trinidad, St Lucia and Dominica, the immigration laws state that visitors will not be allowed to enter without a ticket back to the home country shown on the passport. Tickets to other countries will not suffice. This becomes a problem if you are not going home for 12 months since airline tickets become void after a year. Some airlines sell tickets on the 6-12 month extended payment plan; these can be credited when you have left the islands with restrictive entry requirements.

In this part of the Caribbean, including the French islands, it is difficult to buy single tickets between islands because of the entry requirements mentioned above. This is a problem if you enter the region on a one-way ticket, intending to continue to South America and fly home from there, buying the tickets en route. You may be required to buy at once all the tickets up to the point of departure for home. This would be more expensive than buying all flight tickets at home so, even if you propose to take some boat trips between islands, we recommend that you purchase flights in advance and refund those that have not been used later.

The International Student Identity Card (ISIC)

If you are in full-time education you will be entitled to an ISIC, which is distributed by student travel offices and travel agencies in 77 countries. The ISIC gives you special prices on all forms of transport (air, sea, rail, etc), and access to a variety of other concessions and services. If you need to find the location of your nearest ISIC office contact: The ISIC Association, Box 9048, 1000 Copenhagen, Denmark T (+45) 33 93 93 03.

Entering the USA

The United States Department of Agriculture informs travellers: "The US Department of Agriculture places restrictions on agricultural items brought to the United States from foreign countries as well as those brought to the mainland from Hawaii, Puerto Rico, and the US Virgin Islands. Prohibited items can harbor foreign animal and plant pests and diseases that could seriously damage America's crops, livestock, pets, and the environment."

Because of this threat, travellers are required to list on the Custom's declaration form any meats, fruits, vegetables, plants, animals, and plant and animal products they are bringing into the country. The declaration must list all agricultural items carried in baggage, hand luggage and in vehicles coming across the border.

USDA inspectors will confiscate illegal items for destruction. Travellers who fail to declare items can be fined up to $100 on the spot, and their exit from the airport will be delayed. Some items are permitted. Call 301-436-5908 for a copy of the helpful pamphlet, "Travelers Tips". The best advice is to check before purchasing an agricultural item and trying to bring it back to the United States".

Telephones

Many airport lounges and phone companies in the region have AT&T's "USA Direct" phones by which the USA and Canada may be called using a charge card (which bills your home phone account), or by calling collect. The service is not available to Europe. Public card phones have been introduced by Cable and Wireless on those islands where it operates. Phone cards usually come in several denominations, with a tax added on, and can be useful for local and international calls, particularly as you then avoid the extra charges made by hotels on phone calls. Communicating by fax is a convenient way of sending messages home. Places with public fax machines may receive messages as well as send.

Language

In the majority of cases, English is widely spoken and understood (although non-native speakers of English may have difficulty understanding some of the local dialects). In the French Antilles and Haiti, French is the main language. However, in these last, and on English islands which at one time belonged to France, Créole is spoken. On English islands the population is bilingual, so the English-speaking traveller will have no problems with communication. On the French islands, knowledge of French is of great benefit (in the French Antilles English and Spanish speakers may find assistance from the Commonwealth of Dominica and Dominican Republic citizens who work on the islands). The Netherlands Antilles speak Dutch, English and Papiamento. English and Spanish are both spoken on Puerto Rico and the Bay Islands. The principal language in the Dominican Republic, Cuba, the Mexican and Venezuelan islands is Spanish. If visiting non-English islands, a basic knowledge of the main language is a great advantage.

Sport

Information on sport is given under each island, but for those visiting the former British colonies, British dependencies and even the US Virgin Islands, an understanding of cricket is an advantage. It is more than a national game, having become a symbol of achievement and a unifying factor (baseball and basketball serve much the same function in Puerto Rico). Spectating at a match is entertaining both for the cricket itself and for the conversation that arises.

Further Reading

A number of books are suggested for further reading, these will be found in the Culture, Tourist Information and other sections. Similarly, maps that may be consulted are indicated. With regard to maps, for the British and ex-British islands the Directorate of Overseas Surveys in the UK (now merged with the Ordnance Survey, Southampton) has prepared, and sells, a wide selection at 1:25,000 or 1:50,000 scale. Similarly, the French Institut Géographique National publishes good maps of Martinique and Guadeloupe/St-Martin/St-Barthélémy.

By no means all the writers of history, fiction, poetry and other topics will be found below. There is no room to talk of the many authors who have been inspired by aspects of the Caribbean for their fiction, eg Robert Louis Stevenson, Graham Greene, Ernest Hemingway,

Gabriel García Márquez. Nor have the travellers been mentioned: Patrick Leigh Fermor, *The Traveller's Tree*, Quentin Crewe, *Touch the Happy Isles*, Trollope, *Travels in the West Indies and the Spanish Main*, Alec Waugh, *The Sugar Isles*, James Pope-Hennessy, among others. Of the histories of the region, *A Short History of The West Indies*, by J H Parry, P M Sherlock and Anthony Maingot (Macmillan, 1987) is very accessible; also *From Columbus to Castro: The History of the Caribbean 1492-1969*, Eric Williams (Harper and Row, 1970). For an introduction to the geography of the Caribbean, Mark Wilson's *The Caribbean Environment* (Oxford University Press, 1989), prepared for the Caribbean Examinations Council, is a fascinating text book. Another introductory book is *Far from Paradise, An Introduction to Caribbean Development*, by James Ferguson (Latin American Bureau, 1990). An economic study is *The Poor and the Powerless, Economic Policy and Change in the Caribbean*, by Clive Y Thomas (Latin American Bureau, 1988).

The work of a great many English-speaking poets is collected in *The Penguin Book of Caribbean Verse in English*, edited by Paula Burnett (1986); see also *Hinterland: Caribbean Poetry From the West Indies and Britain*, edited by E A Markham (Bloodaxe, 1990). For a French verse anthology, see *La Poésie Antillaise*, collected by Maryse Condé (Fernand Nathan, 1977). There are a number of prose anthologies of stories in English, eg *Stories from the Caribbean*, introduced by Andrew Salkey (Paul Elek, 1972), or *West Indian Narrative: an Introductory Anthology*, by Kenneth Ramchand (Nelson, 1966). Heinemann's Caribbean Writers series publishes works of fiction by well-established and new writers. *The Story of English*, by Robert McCrumb, William Cran and Robert MacNeil (Faber and Faber/BBC, 1986) has an interesting section on the development of the English language in the Caribbean. The Commonwealth Institute in London publishes useful checklists on Caribbean writing: No 4 on literature, 1986; No 6 on general topics, 1987, both compiled by Roger Hughes.

FT Caribbean publishes *The Caribbean Handbook*, a business and reference guide, with a useful bibliography on all Caribbean topics, and the inflight magazine of Liat *(Liat Islander)*. FT Caribbean Head Office, PO Box 1037, St John's, Antigua, or PO Box 675, St George's Grenada, or 3A Sloane Avenue, London SW3 3JD. A rival to *The Caribbean Handbook* is *The Caribbean Business Directory* and *Caribbean Yellow Pages Telephone Directory* (Antigua: Caribbean Publishing Cos, 2 vols), a good source of current information on telephone and fax numbers, key companies, economic statistics, business and government information. The *Business Directory* contains a section on each island in the Caribbean, plus Florida, North America and selected South American countries; the *Yellow Pages* volume is a listing of telephone and fax numbers for companies. BWIA's inflight magazine, *BWee Caribbean Beat*, is published quarterly by MEP, 6 Prospect Avenue, Maraval, Port of Spain, Trinidad, T (809) 622-3821, F 628-0639. *Caribbean Insight*, published monthly in London by the West India Committee in association with Caribbean Publishing Company (T 071 976 1493, F 071 976 1541) is an informative newsletter covering the entire region and Central America. Another newsletter dealing exclusively with the region is *Caribbean Focus*, PO Box 79, St Albans, Herts, AL1 3DA, UK, (T/F 0727-831381).

Finally, a generally excellent series of Caribbean books is published by Macmillan Caribbean; this includes island guides, natural histories, books on food and drink, sports and pirates, and wall maps (for a full catalogue, write to Macmillan Caribbean, Houndmills, Basingstoke, Hampshire, RG21 2XS, England).

This list is not exhaustive, concentrating mainly on books in English, published (or readily available) in the UK. For any favourites omitted, we apologize.

MIAMI

Journeys to (and between) the Caribbean Islands often involve a change of planes in Miami. A five hour transfer in the middle of a tiring journey may seem like a daunting prospect, but Miami airport is surprisingly user-friendly and there is quite a lot to do in the city if you have a longer stopover.

The airport is rather like a big, horse-shoe-shaped suburban shopping mall. The upper level has shops and airline check-in counters; the lower level has other services like car rentals and baggage claim. The airport is divided into a series of concourses labelled B to H.

On Arrival

Immigration queues are long, and can take 30-50 mins. Heavy hand luggage is more of a nuisance than at most airports, both in the queues and because of the long walk up and down the fingers which lead to the planes. Customs is crowded, but the queue moves faster.

Passengers arriving from the Bahamas pre-clear in Nassau, which saves time. Pre-clearance is also possible in Aruba. From London, through bookings of baggage is now available; ask for a suitable label.

Baggage There are baggage carts in customs, but these must be left behind when you have been cleared. From this point on there are *skycaps* (tip around US$1-2 per large bag). Skycaps can also be called from the *paging phones* which are thick on the ground in the concourses and entrances.

There are luggage lockers at all entrances to the airport and at various other points. They cost US$1 in quarters (25 cents – look for change machines, or ask information counters). After 24 hrs, bags are taken to a storage facility next to the *lost and found* office in concourse E. The charge for storage here is US$2 per day.

For very large items there is a left luggage office (baggage service office) on the lower level of concourse G and on the second level of concourse B. Charges are US$2-6 per day, depending on the size of the item.

Filling In Time

The concourses are chocabloc with snackbars, duty free shops, and gift shops selling overpriced junk. Once through Customs and into the duty free area there is one newsagent selling a limited amount of confectionery and newspapers, magazines, etc, and one poorly-stocked, overpriced Duty Free shop. Some items, such as cosmetics and perfumes, are better value in town. **Note** A 6½% sales tax is added to the marked price. Watch out if you are fine-tuning your US currency before departure. The best place to pass the time and relax is probably the *Hotel MIA*, in the middle of the horseshoe on concourse E. The Lobby Lounge, open 1000-0100, is on the same floor as flight check in. The upper floors have a sundeck (free), an open air swimming pool, gym and sauna area (US$5 per day), racquetball courts (US$8 per hour), snackbar, lounge bar (the happy hour, 1700-1900, has drinks on special and complimentary snacks). There is also the *Top of The Port* restaurant, with pleasant surroundings and much better food than on the concourses (open 0700-2300; full breakfast US$7.75, lunch specials from US$8, dinner specials from US$15). The hotel has special day rates between 0800 and 1800.

Information There are very helpful information counters in concourse E and just outside customs. They can also be contacted from any paging phone. (Counters open 0630-2230; paging phone service 24 hrs.) They will advise on ground transport, airport services,

since Hurricane Andrew), or the Seaquarium (also hurricane-damaged). Museums include Vizcaya, a Renaissance-style villa with formal gardens, and the Spanish Monastery in North Miami Beach, brought to America in pieces by William Randolph Hearst from Segovia in Spain, where it was first built in 1141. That, in a way, makes it the oldest building in the USA.

Miami Beach is probably the best place for a short stay. There are plenty of interesting Art Deco buildings, with restaurants and cafes along the sea front. Shops, hotels, nightclubs, etc are all within walking distance. Moreover, you can walk around at night without getting mugged. It also has the Bass Museum, with a good collection of European paintings. North of the Haulover channel is a section of beach where nude bathing is tolerated.

If you have a full day in Miami, there would be time to rent a car and drive to the *Everglades National Park*, a huge freshwater swamp with interesting wildlife and an excellent network of interpretative centres and nature trails (50 mins-1 hour in heavy traffic from the airport). The nearer Florida Keys would be an alternative, but are probably not so exciting if you have just been in the Caribbean.

HEALTH INFORMATION

The following information has been compiled for us by Dr David Snashall, who is presently Senior Lecturer in Occupational Health at St Thomas's Hospital Medical School in London and Chief Medical Advisor of the British Foreign and Commonwealth Office. He has travelled extensively in Central and South America, worked in Peru and in East Africa and keeps in close touch with developments in preventative and tropical medicine.

The traveller to the Caribbean is inevitably exposed to health risks not encountered in North America or Western Europe. Most of the islands have a tropical climate but this does not mean that tropical diseases as such are an enormous problem or even the main problem for visitors. The problems of infectious disease still predominate in most of the islands, but vary in severity between town and rural areas and from island to island depending on the state of economic development and the attention paid to public health. Thus there are few hard and fast rules. You will often have to make your own judgements on the healthiness or otherwise of your surroundings.

Language is not on the whole a problem and throughout the islands there are well-qualified doctors who speak good English. Medical practises vary from those you may be used to, but there is likely to be better experience at dealing with locally occurring disease.

A certain amount of self medication may be necessary and you will find that many of the drugs available have familiar names. However, always check the date stamping and buy from reputable pharmacies because the shelf life of some items, especially vaccines and antibiotics, is markedly reduced in tropical conditions.

With the following precautions and advice you should keep as healthy as usual. Make local enquiries about health risks if you are apprehensive and take the general advice of European and North American families who have lived or are living in the country.

Before You Go

Take out medical insurance. You should have a dental check-up, obtain a spare glasses prescription and if you suffer from a chronic disease such as diabetes, high blood pressure, cardio-pulmonary disease, or a nervous disorder, arrange for a check-up with your doctor who can at the same time provide you with a letter explaining details of your disability. Check the current practice for malaria prophylaxis (prevention) if you are going to the Guianas, Dominican Republic or Haiti.

Inoculations

Smallpox vaccination is no longer required. Neither is yellow fever vaccination unless you are going to or are coming from South America. As of mid-1993 the cholera epidemic in South and Central America had not spread to any of the Caribbean islands but they were all on the alert for the possibility. Although cholera vaccination is largely ineffective, immigration officers may ask for proof of such vaccination if coming from a country where the epidemic is rife. The following vaccinations are recommended: Typhoid (monovalent): one dose, followed by a booster in one month's time (an oral preparation may be recommended). Immunity from this course lasts two to three years. Poliomyelitis: this is a live vaccine generally given orally and a full course consists of three doses with a booster in tropical regions, every three to five years. Tetanus: one dose should be given with a booster at six weeks and another at six months and ten yearly boosters thereafter are recommended. Children should in addition be properly protected against diphtheria, against whooping cough, mumps and measles. Teenage girls, if they have not had the disease, should be given Rubella (german measles) vaccination. Consult your doctor for advice on tuberculosis inoculation; the disease is still present in the British Virgin Islands, Grenada, Guadeloupe, Haiti, and Martinique.

Infectious Hepatitis (Jaundice) is of some concern throughout the Caribbean, more so in Cuba, Dominica, Haiti, and Montserrat. It seems to be frequently caught by travellers. The main symptoms are pains in the stomach, lack of appetite, lassitude, and the typical yellow colour of the eyes and skin. Medically speaking there are two different types: the less serious, but more common, is Hepatitis A for which the best protection is the careful preparation of food, the avoidance of contaminated drinking water and scrupulous attention to toilet hygiene. Human normal immunoglobulin (gamma-globulin) confers considerable protection against the disease and is particularly useful in epidemics. It should be obtained from a reputable source and is certainly recommended for travellers who intend to live rough. The injection should be given as close as possible to your departure and, as the dose depends on the likely time you are to spend in infected areas, the manufacturer's instructions should be taken as to dose. At last vaccination against Hepatitis A has been developed and is generally available. Three shots over six months would seem to give excellent protection lasting up to ten years.

The other, more serious, version is Hepatitis B, which is acquired usually from injections with unclean needles, blood transfusion, as a sexually transmitted disease and possibly by insect bites. You may have had jaundice before, or you may have had hepatitis of either type before without becoming jaundiced in which case you may be immune to either Hepatitis A or B. This can be tested for before you travel. If you are not immune to Hepatitis B a vaccine is available (three shots over six months) and if you are not immune to Hepatitis A, then you should consider having gamma-globulin.

AIDS

Aids in the Caribbean is increasing in its prevalence, as in most countries, but is not wholly confined to the well known high risk sections of the population, ie homosexual men, intravenous drug abusers, prostitutes and children of infected mothers. Heterosexual transmission is now the dominant mode and so the main risk to travellers is from casual sex. The same precautions should be taken as when encountering any sexually transmitted disease. The AIDS virus (HIV) can be passed via unsterile needles which have been previously used to inject an HIV positive patient but the risk of this is very small indeed. It would however be sensible to check that needles have been properly sterilized or disposable needles used. If you take your own disposable needles, be prepared to explain what they are for. The risk of receiving a blood transfusion with blood infected with the HIV virus is greater than from dirty needles because of the amount of fluid exchanged. Supplies of blood for transfusion should now be screened for HIV in all reputable hospitals so again the risk must be very small indeed. Catching the AIDS virus does not usually produce an illness in itself; the only way to be sure if you feel you have been put at risk is to have a blood test for HIV antibodies on your return to a place where there are reliable laboratory facilities. The test does not become positive for many weeks. Presently the higher risks are probably in Haiti, Dominican Republic, Trinidad, Bahamas and Bermuda.

Common Problems

Heat And Cold Full acclimatization to high temperatures takes about two weeks and during this period it is normal to feel relatively apathetic, especially if the relative humidity is high. Drink plenty of water (up to 15 litres a day are required when working physically hard in the tropics), use salt on your food and avoid extreme exertion. Tepid showers are more cooling than hot or cold ones. Large hats do not cool you down, but prevent sunburn. Remember that, especially in the mountains, there can be a large and sudden drop in temperature between sun and shade and between night and day, so dress accordingly. Loose fitting cotton clothes are still the best for hot weather.

Intestinal Upsets

Most of the time these are due to the insanitary preparation of food so do not eat uncooked fish or vegetables or meat (especially pork), fruit with the skin off (always peel your fruit yourself) or food that is exposed to flies (especially salads.) Tap water may be unsafe outside the major cities especially in the rainy season and the same goes for stream water. Filtered or bottled water is usually available and safe. If your hotel has a central hot water supply this is safe to drink after cooling. Ice for drinks should be made from boiled water but rarely is, so stand your glass on the ice cubes instead of putting them in the drink. Dirty water should first be strained through a filter bag (available from camping shops) and then boiled or treated. Boiling water for five minutes at sea level is sufficient or you can add sterilizing tablets based on Chlorine or Iodine.

Pasteurized or heat-treated milk is now widely available as is ice cream and yoghurt. Unpasteurized milk products including cheese are sources of Tuberculosis, Brucellosis, Listeria and food poisoning germs. You can render fresh milk safe by heating it to 62 degrees centigrade for 30 minutes followed by rapid cooling, or by boiling it. Matured or processed cheeses are safer than fresh varieties.

Diarrhoea – Diagnosis and treatment

Diarrhoea is usually caused by eating food which is contaminated by food poisoning germs. Drinking water is rarely the culprit. Seawater or river water is more likely to be contaminated by sewage and so swimming in such dilute effluent can also be a cause. Infection with various organisms can give rise to diarrhoea, eg viruses, bacteria (eg Escherichia coli, probably the most common cause), protozoa (amoeba), salmonella and cholera. The diarrhoea may come on suddenly or rather slowly. It may or may nor be accompanied by vomiting or by severe abdominal pain and the passage of blood or mucus when it is called dysentery. How do you know which type you have and how to treat it?

If you can time the onset of the diarrhoea to the minute (acute) then it is probably due to a virus or a bacterium and/or the onset of dysentery. The treatment, in addition to rehydration is Ciprofloxacin 500 mgs every 12 hours. The drug is now widely available as are various similar ones.

If the diarrhoea comes on slowly or intermittently (sub-acute) then it is more likely to be protozoal ie caused by an amoeba or giardia and antibiotics will have little effect. These cases are best treated by a doctor, as is any outbreak of diarrhoea continuing for more than 3 days. Sometimes blood is passed in sub-acute amoebic dysentery and for this you should certainly seek medical help. If this is not available then the best treatment is probably Tinidazole (Fasigyn) 1 tablet 4 times a day for 3 days. If there are severe stomach cramps, the following drugs may help but are not very useful in the management of acute diarrhoea: Loperamide (Imodium, Arret) and Diphenoxylate with Atropine (Lomotil).

Any kind of diarrhoea whether or not accompanied by vomiting responds well to the replacement of water and salts taken as frequent small sips of some kind of rehydration solution. There are preparatory preparations consisting of sachets of powder which you dissolve in boiled water, or you can make your own by adding half of teaspoonful of salt (3.5 grams) and 4 tablespoonfuls of sugar (40 grams) to a litre of boiled water.

Thus the lynchpins of treatment for diarrhoea are rest, fluid and salt replacement, antibiotics such as Ciprofloxacin for the bacterial types and special diagnostic tests and medical treatment for the amoeba and giardia infections. Salmonella infections and cholera can be devastating diseases and it would be wise to get to a hospital as soon as possible if these were suspected. Fasting, peculiar diets and the consumption of large quantities of yoghurt have not been found useful in calming travellers' diarrhoea or in rehabilitating inflamed bowels. Oral rehydration has on the other hand, especially in children, been a lifesaving technique and it should be always be practised whatever other treatment you use. As there is some evidence that alcohol and milk might prolong diarrhoea they should probably be avoided during and immediately after an attack. Diarrhoea occurring day after day for long periods of time (chronic diarrhoea) is notoriously resistant to amateur attempts at treatment and again warrants proper diagnostic tests. There are ways of preventing travellers' diarrhoea for short periods of time by taking antibiotics, but this is not a foolproof technique and should not be used other than in exceptional circumstances. Doxycycline is possibly the best drug. Some preventatives such as Enterovioform can have serious side effects if taken for long periods.

Insects

These can be a great nuisance and some of course are carriers of serious diseases such as malaria, dengue fever, filariasis and various worm infections. The best way of keeping mosquitos away at night is to sleep off the ground with a mosquito net and to burn mosquito coils containing Pyrethrum. Aerosol sprays or a "flit" gun may be effective as are insecticidal tablets which are heated on a mat which is plugged into the wall socket (if taking your own, check the voltage of the area you are visiting so that you can take an appliance that will work; similarly check that your electrical adaptor is suitable for the repellent's plug-Ed) The best repellents contain a high concentration of diethyl-toluamide. Clothes impregnated with the insecticide Permethrin or Deltamethrin are now becoming available, as are wide-meshed mosquito nets impregnated with the same substance. They are lighter to carry and less claustrophobic to sleep in.

Liquid is best for arms and face (care around eyes and make sure they don't dissolve the plastic of your spectacles or watch glass), aerosol spray on clothes and ankles deter mites and ticks. Liquid DET suspended in water can be used to impregnate cotton clothes and mosquito nets. If you are bitten, itching may be relieved by baking soda baths, anti-histamine tablets (care with alcohol or driving), corticosteroid creams (great care—never use if any hint of sepsis) or by judicious scratching. Calamine lotion and cream have limited effectiveness and anti-histamine creams (Anthisan) have a tendency to cause skin allergies and are therefore not generally recommended. Bites which become infected (commonly in the tropics) should be treated with a local antiseptic or antibiotic cream such as Cetrimide (Savlon ICI), as should infected scratches. Skin infestation with body lice, crabs and scabies are unfortunately easy to pick up. Use gamma benzene hexachloride for lice, and benzyl benzoate for scabies. Crotamiton cream (Eurax CIBA) alleviates itching and also kills a number of skin parasites. Malathion lotion 5% (Prioderm) is good for lice but avoid the highly toxic full strength Malathion.

Malaria

in the West Indies is confined to the island of Hispaniola, being more prevalent in Haiti than the Dominican Republic. It also exists in parts of the Guianas (seek up-to-date advice on the type in the location to be visited). It remains a serious disease and you are advised to protect yourself against mosquito bites as above, and to take prophylactic (preventive) drugs. Start taking the tablets a few days before exposure and continue to take six weeks after leaving the malaria zone. Remember to give drugs to babies and children also. The subject of malaria prevention is becoming more complex as the malaria parasite becomes immune to some of the older drugs. However, at the present time Proguanil (Paludrine), 100 mgs two tablets a day, should give sufficient protection. You can catch malaria even when taking these drugs, though it is unlikely. If you do develop symptoms (high fever, shivering, headaches), seek medical advice immediately.

If this is not possible and the likelihood of malaria is high the treatment is Chloroquine a single dose of 4 tablets (600 mgs) followed by two tablets (300 mgs) in six hours and 300 mgs each day following. Pregnant women are particularly prone to malaria and should stick to Proguanil for prophylaxis. Chloroquine can also be used to prevent malaria on a weekly basis. The risk of malaria is obviously greater the further you move from cities and into rural areas with primitive facilities and standing water.

Sunburn

The burning power of the tropical sun is phenomenal. Always wear a wide brimmed hat and use some form of sun cream lotion on untanned skin. Normal temperate zone suntan lotions (protection factor up to 7) are not much good. You need to use the type designed specifically for the tropics or for mountaineers or skiers, with the highest protection factor. Lotions with a factor of 25 or 30 can be found on some islands. They are waterproof and well worth using for sailing or golf. Glare from the sun can cause conjunctivitis so wear sunglasses especially on tropical beaches.

Snakebite

If you are unlucky enough to be bitten by a venomous snake, spider, scorpion, centipede or sea creature, try (within limits) to catch the animal for identification. The reactions to be expected are: fright, swelling, pain and bruising around the bite, soreness of the regional lymph glands, nausea, vomiting and fever. If any of the following symptoms supervene get the victim to a doctor without delay: numbness, tingling of the face, muscular spasms, convulsions, shortness of breath and haemorrhage. Commercial snake bite or scorpion sting kits are available, but are only useful for the specific type of snake or scorpion for which they are designed. The serum has to be given intravenously so is not much good unless you have had some practice in making injections into veins. If the bite is on a limb, immobilize the limb and apply a tight bandage between the bite and the body, releasing it for ninety seconds every 15 mins. Reassurance of the bitten person is very important because death from snake bite is in fact very rare. Do not slash the bite area and try to suck out the poison because this sort of heroism does more harm than good. Hospitals usually hold stocks of snakebite serum. Best precaution: do not walk in snake territory with bare feet, sandals, or shorts; in Guyana's interior, look out for snakes in the trees as well as on the ground. If swimming in an area where there are poisonous fish, such as stone or scorpion fish (also called by a variety of local names) or sea urchins on rocky coasts, tread carefully or wear plimsoles. The sting of such fish is intensely painful and this can be helped by immersing the stung part in water as hot as you can bear for as long

WILL YOU HELP US?

We do all we can to get our facts right in the **CARIBBEAN ISLANDS HANDBOOK**. Each section is thoroughly revised each year, but the territory is vast and our eyes cannot be everywhere. If you have enjoyed a tour, trek, beach, walk, dive, sailing trip, museum or any other activity and would like to share it, please write with all the details.

We are always pleased to hear about any restaurants, bars or hotels you have enjoyed. When writing, please give the year on the cover of your *Handbook* and the page number referred to. In return we will send you details of our special guidebook offer.

Thank you very much indeed for your help.

TRADE & TRAVEL
Handbooks

Write to The Editor, *Caribbean Islands Handbook,* Trade & Travel, 6 Riverside Court, Lower Bristol Road, Bath BA2 3DZ. England

strength Malathion.

Malaria

in the West Indies is confined to the island of Hispaniola, being more prevalent in Haiti than the Dominican Republic. It also exists in parts of the Guianas (seek up-to-date advice on the type in the location to be visited). It remains a serious disease and you are advised to protect yourself against mosquito bites as above, and to take prophylactic (preventive) drugs. Start taking the tablets a few days before exposure and continue to take six weeks after leaving the malaria zone. Remember to give drugs to babies and children also. The subject of malaria prevention is becoming more complex as the malaria parasite becomes immune to some of the older drugs. However, at the present time Proguanil (Paludrine), 100 mgs two tablets a day, should give sufficient protection. You can catch malaria even when taking these drugs, though it is unlikely. If you do develop symptoms (high fever, shivering, headaches), seek medical advice immediately.

If this is not possible and the likelihood of malaria is high the treatment is Chloroquine a single dose of 4 tablets (600 mgs) followed by two tablets (300 mgs) in six hours and 300 mgs each day following. Pregnant women are particularly prone to malaria and should stick to Proguanil for prophylaxis. Chloroquine can also be used to prevent malaria on a weekly basis. The risk of malaria is obviously greater the further you move from cities and into rural areas with primitive facilities and standing water.

Sunburn

The burning power of the tropical sun is phenomenal. Always wear a wide brimmed hat and use some form of sun cream lotion on untanned skin. Normal temperate zone suntan lotions (protection factor up to 7) are not much good. You need to use the type designed specifically for the tropics or for mountaineers or skiers, with the highest protection factor. Lotions with a factor of 25 or 30 can be found on some islands. They are waterproof and well worth using for sailing or golf. Glare from the sun can cause conjunctivitis so wear sunglasses especially on tropical beaches.

Snakebite

If you are unlucky enough to be bitten by a venomous snake, spider, scorpion, centipede or sea creature, try (within limits) to catch the animal for identification. The reactions to be expected are: fright, swelling, pain and bruising around the bite, soreness of the regional lymph glands, nausea, vomiting and fever. If any of the following symptoms supervene get the victim to a doctor without delay: numbness, tingling of the face, muscular spasms, convulsions, shortness of breath and haemorrhage. Commercial snake bite or scorpion sting kits are available, but are only useful for the specific type of snake or scorpion for which they are designed. The serum has to be given intravenously so is not much good unless you have had some practice in making injections into veins. If the bite is on a limb, immobilize the limb and apply a tight bandage between the bite and the body, releasing it for ninety seconds every 15 mins. Reassurance of the bitten person is very important because death from snake bite is in fact very rare. Do not slash the bite area and try to suck out the poison because this sort of heroism does more harm than good. Hospitals usually hold stocks of snakebite serum. Best precaution: do not walk in snake territory with bare feet, sandals, or shorts; in Guyana's interior, look out for snakes in the trees as well as on the ground. If swimming in an area where there are poisonous fish, such as stone or scorpion fish (also called by a variety of local names) or sea urchins on rocky coasts, tread carefully or wear plimsoles. The sting of such fish is intensely painful and this can be helped by immersing the stung part in water as hot as you can bear for as long as it remains painful. This is not always very practical and you must take care not to scald yourself, but it does work. Avoid spiders and scorpions by keeping your bed away from the wall, look under lavatory seats and inside your shoes in the morning. In the rare event of being bitten, consult a doctor.

Other Afflictions

Remember that **rabies** is endemic in some countries including Trinidad and Tobago, Puerto Rico, Haiti, Grenada, and possibly more so in the Dominican Republic and Cuba. If you are bitten by a domestic animal try to have it captured for observation and see a doctor at once. Treatment with human diploid vaccine is now extremely effective and worth seeking out if the likelihood of having contracted rabies is high. A course of anti rabies vaccine might be a good idea before you go.

Dengue fever is present in all the islands with a higher prevalence in Barbados, Cuba, Dominican Republic, Haiti and Puerto Rico; there is no treatment, you must just avoid mosquito bites.

Intestinal worms are common and the more serious ones such as **hookworm** can be contracted from walking bare foot on infested earth or beaches.

Schistosomiasis (Bilharzia) is caused by a parasite which lurks in lakes and slow-moving rivers infested with snails and can have serious consequences later. The main problem is in St Lucia.

Leptospirosis: Various forms of leptospirosis occur in most of the Caribbean islands, transmitted by a bacterium which is excreted in rodent urine. Fresh water and moist soil harbour the organisms which enter the body through cuts and scratches. If you suffer from any form of prolonged fever, consult a doctor.

Prickly heat, a very common itchy rash, is avoided by frequent washing and by wearing loose clothing. It is helped by the use of talcum powder to allow the skin to dry thoroughly after washing. **Athletes Foot** and other fungal infections are best treated with sunshine and a proprietory preparation such as Tinaderm.

Psychological disorders First time exposure to countries where sections of the population live in extreme poverty or squalor and may even be starving can cause odd psychological reactions in visitors. So can the exceptional curiosity extended to visitors, especially women. Simply be prepared for this and try not to over-react.

When you return home Remember to take your anti-malarial tablets for 6 weeks. If you have had attacks of diarrhoea, it is worth having a stool specimen tested in case you have picked up amoebic dysentery. If you have been living rough, a blood test may be worthwhile to detect worms and other parasites. If you have been exposed to bilharzia by swimming in lakes, etc, check by means of a blood test when you get home, but leave it for 6 weeks because the test is slow to become positive. Report any untoward symptoms to your doctor and tell the doctor exactly where you have been and, if you know, what is the likelihood of diseases to which you were exposed.

Basic supplies The following items you may find useful to take with you from home: sunglasses (if you use clip-on sunglasses, take a spare pair – Ed), ear plugs, suntan cream, insect repellent, flea powder, mosquito net, coils or tablets, tampons, condoms, contraceptives, water sterilizing tablets, anti-malaria tablets, anti-infective ointment, dusting powder for feet, travel sickness pills, antacids tablets, anti-diarrhoea tablets, sachets of rehydration salts and a first aid kit.

Further information on health risks abroad, vaccinations, etc, may be available from a local travel clinic. If you wish to take specific drugs with you such as antibiotics, these are best prescribed by your own doctor. Beware, however, that not all doctors can be experts on the health problems of tropical countries. More detailed or more up-to-date information than local doctors can provide are available from various sources.

In the UK there are hospital departments specializing in tropical diseases in London, Liverpool, Birmingham and Glasgow and the Malaria Reference Laboratory at the London School of Hygiene and Tropical Medicine provides free advice about malaria, T 071-636 7921. In the USA the local public health services can give such information and information is available centrally from the Centres for Disease Control in Atlanta, T (404) 332 4559.

There are in addition computerized databases which can be accessed for a specific destination, up to the minute information. In the UK there is MASTA (Medical Advisory Service to Travellers Abroad), T 071-631 4408, Tx 895 3474, F 071-436 5389 and Travax (Glasgow, T 041-946 7120, extension 247).

Further information on medical problems overseas can be obtained from the book by Richard Dawood (Editor) – *Travellers Health, How to Stay Healthy Abroad*, Oxford University Press, 1992, £7.99. We strongly recommend this revised and updated edition, especially to the intrepid traveller heading for the more out of the way places. General advice is also available in the UK in "Health Advice for Travellers" published jointly by the Department of Health and the Central Office of Information available free from your UK Travel Agent.

32

WILL YOU HELP US?

We do all we can to get our facts right in the **CARIBBEAN ISLANDS HANDBOOK**. Each section is thoroughly revised each year, but the territory is vast and our eyes cannot be everywhere. If you have enjoyed a tour, trek, beach, walk, dive, sailing trip, museum or any other activity and would like to share it, please write with all the details.

We are always pleased to hear about any restaurants, bars or hotels you have enjoyed.

When writing, please give the year on the cover of your *Handbook* and the page number referred to. In return we will send you details of our special guidebook offer.

Thank you very much indeed for your help.

TRADE & TRAVEL
Handbooks

Write to The Editor, *Caribbean Islands Handbook,* Trade & Travel, 6 Riverside Court, Lower Bristol Road, Bath BA2 3DZ. England

PRE-COLUMBIAN CIVILIZATIONS

The recorded history of the Caribbean islands begins with the arrival of Christopher Columbus' fleet in 1492. Our knowledge of the native peoples who inhabited the islands before and at the time of his arrival is largely derived from the accounts of contemporary Spanish writers and from archaeological examinations as there is no evidence of indigenous written records.

The Amerindians encountered by Columbus in the Greater Antilles had no overall tribal name but organized themselves in a series of villages or local chiefdoms, each of which had its own tribal name. The name now used, Arawak, was not in use then. The term Arawak was used by the Indians of the Guianas, a group of whom had spread into Trinidad, but their territory was not explored until nearly another century later. The use of the generic term, Arawak, to describe the Indians Columbus encountered, arose because of linguistic similarities with the Arawaks of the mainland. It is therefore surmised that migration took place many centuries before Columbus' arrival, but the two groups were not in contact at that time. The time of the latest migration from the mainland, and consequently the existence of the island Arawaks, is in dispute, with some academics tracing it to about the time of Christ (the arrival of the Saladoids) and others to AD 1000 (the Ostionoids).

The inhabitants of the Bahamas were generally referred to as Lucayans, and those of the Greater Antilles as Tainos, but there were many sub-groupings. The inhabitants of the Lesser Antilles were, however, referred to as Carib and were described to Columbus as an aggressive tribe which sacrificed and sometimes ate the prisoners they captured in battle. It was from them that the Caribbean gets its name and from which the word cannibal is derived.

The earliest known inhabitants of the region, the Siboneys, migrated from Florida (some say Mexico) and spread throughout the Bahamas and the major islands. Most archaeological evidence of their settlements has been found near the shore, along bays or streams, where they lived in small groups. The largest discovered settlement has been one of 100 inhabitants in Cuba. They were hunters and gatherers, living on fish and other seafood, small rodents, iguanas, snakes and birds. They gathered roots and wild fruits, such as guava, guanabana and mamey, but did not cultivate plants. They worked with primitive tools made out of stone, shell, bone or wood, for hammering, chipping or scraping, but had no knowledge of pottery. The Siboneys were eventually absorbed by the advance of the Arawaks migrating from the S, who had made more technological advances in agriculture, arts and crafts.

The people now known as Arawaks migrated from the Guianas to Trinidad and on through the island arc to Cuba. Their population expanded because of the natural fertility of the islands and the abundance of fruit and seafood, helped by their agricultural skills in cultivating and improving wild plants and their excellent boatbuilding and fishing techniques. They were healthy, tall, good looking and lived to a ripe old age. It is estimated that up to 8 million may have lived on the island of Hispaniola alone, but there was always plenty of food for all.

Their society was essentially communal and organized around families. The smaller islands were particularly egalitarian, but in the larger ones, where village communities of extended families numbered up to 500 people, there was an incipient class structure. Typically, each village had a headman, called a *cacique*, whose duty it was to represent the village when dealing with other tribes, to settle family disputes and organize defence. However, he had no powers of coercion and was often little more than a nominal head. The position was largely hereditary, with the eldest son of the eldest sister having rights of succession, but women could and did become *caciques*. In the larger communities, there was some delegation of responsibility to the senior men, but economic activities were usually organized along family lines, and their power was limited.

The division of labour was usually based on age and sex. The men would clear and prepare the land for agriculture and be responsible for defence of the village, while women cultivated the crops and were the major food producers, also making items such as mats, baskets, bowls and fishing nets. Women were in charge of raising the children, especially the girls, while the men taught the boys traditional customs, skills and rites.

The Tainos hunted for some of their food, but fishing was more important and most of their settlements were close to the sea. Fish and shellfish were their main sources of protein and they had many different ways of catching them, from hands, baskets or nets to poisoning, shooting or line fishing. Cassava was a staple food, which they had successfully learned to leach of its poisonous juice. They also grew yams, maize, cotton, arrowroot, peanuts, beans, cocoa and spices, rotating their crops to prevent soil erosion. It is documented that in Jamaica they had three harvests of maize annually, using maize and cassava to make breads, cakes and beer.

Cotton was used to make clothing and hammocks (never before seen by Europeans), while the calabash tree was used to make ropes and cords, baskets and roofing. Plants were used for medicinal and spiritual purposes, and cosmetics such as face and body paint. Also important, both to the Arawaks and later to the Europeans, was the cultivation of tobacco, as a drug and as a means of exchange.

They had no writing, no beasts of burden, no wheeled vehicles and no hard metals, although they did have some alluvial gold for personal ornament. The abundance of food allowed them time to develop their arts and crafts and they were skilled in woodwork and pottery. They had polished stone tools, but also carved shell implements for manioc preparation or as fishhooks. Coral manioc graters have also been found. Their boatbuilding techniques were noted by Columbus, who marvelled at their canoes of up to 75 feet in length, carrying up to 50 people, made of a single tree trunk in one piece. It took two months to fell a tree by gradually burning and chipping it down, and many more to make the canoe.

The Arawaks had three main deities, evidence of which have been found in stone and conch carvings in many of the Lesser Antilles as well as the well populated Greater Antilles, although their relative importance varied according to the island. The principal male god was Yocahú, *yoca* being the word for cassava and *hú* meaning "giver of". It is believed that the Indians associated this deity's power to provide cassava with the mystery of the volcanoes, for all the carvings, the earliest out of shells and the later ones of stone, are conical. The Yocahú cult was wiped out in the Lesser Antilles by the invading Caribs, and in the Greater Antilles by the Spaniards, but it is thought to have existed from about 200 AD.

The main female diety was a fertility goddess, often referred to as Atabeyra, but she is thought to have had several

FLORA AND FAUNA OF THE CARIBBEAN

For many travellers, a trip to the Caribbean offers a first glimpse of the tropics, complete with luxuriant vegetation and exotic wildlife. Images of untouched beaches and rainforest form a major selling point of many travel brochures. In fact there is very little "untouched" wilderness left and what visitors see is an environment that has been affected by the activities of man (this is not the case in the interior of the Guianas, where much forest is untouched). Forestry, agriculture, fisheries and increasingly tourism have all helped to mould the modern landscape and natural heritage of the Caribbean. However, there is still much of interest to see, and it is true to say that small islands can combine a variety of habitats within a limited area. On many islands, it is possible to move between the coastal reefs and beaches through thorn scrub and plantation into rainforest within a matter of miles. Increasingly, the complexity and fragility of island ecosystems is being appreciated and fortunately most countries have recognized the value of balancing development and the protection of the natural environment and have begun to develop national parks and protected areas programmes. Many islands also have active conservation societies or national wildlife trusts (see above).

Wildlife

Over long periods of time, islands tend to develop their own unique flora and fauna. These "endemic" species add to the interest of wildlife and natural history tours. The St Lucia parrot and Dominica's sisserou have become a regular part of the tour circuit of these islands, and have undoubtedly benefited from the interest that tourists have shown in their plight. Details of National Parks and wildlife are included under the specific island chapter headings (Fauna and Flora). This section provides a broad overview of the range of animals, plants and habitats that are to be found in the region.

Mammals

Mammals are not particularly good colonizers of small islands and this has resulted in a general scarcity of species in the Caribbean. Many of the more commonly seen species (mongoose, agouti, opossum, and some of the monkeys) were introduced by man. Bats are the one exception to this rule and most islands have several native species. Again, in the forested interior of the Guianas there are many mammals associated with rain forest habitats. There are also the animals of the S savannas and mountains.

Mongoose were introduced to many islands to control snakes, they have also preyed on many birds, reptiles and other animals and have had a devastating effect on native fauna.

Of the monkeys, the green monkeys of Barbados, Grenada and St Kitts and Nevis were introduced from West Africa in the 17th century. Similarly, rhesus monkeys have been introduced to Desecheo Island off Puerto Rico. The red howler monkeys on Trinidad are native to the island as are several other mammals including the brocket deer, squirrel and armadillo. These species have managed to colonize from nearby Venezuela.

There are endemic mammals on some islands for example the pygmy racoon, a species of coati and "jabli" in Cozumel and possibly the Guadeloupe racoon.

Sailors may encounter marine mammals including dolphin, porpoise and

bean, *Butterflies and Other Insects of the Caribbean*; and the *Ephemeral Isles, a Natural History of the Bahamas*.

In Search of Flowers of the Amazon Forest, by Margaret Mee (Nonesuch Expeditions Ltd, 48 Station Rd, Woodbridge, Suffolk, UK). *A Guide to the Birds of Venezuela*, by R Meyer de Schauensee and W H Phelps Jr (Princeton).

Specialist Reading

For the more serious naturalist, there are several detailed reviews of the natural history and conservation of wildlife in the Caribbean. Among the best and most widely available are the *Floristic Inventory of Tropical Countries* (World Wide Fund for Nature) which contains a short report on the Caribbean; *Biodiversity and Conservation in the Caribbean*, Profiles of selected islands (includes Cozumel, Dominica, Grenada, Guadeloupe, Jamaica, Martinique, Montserrat, Puerto Rico, St Lucia, St Vincent, San Andrés) published by the International Council for Bird Preservation, ISBN 0 946888 14 0; *Fragments of Paradise* which covers conservation issues in the UK dependencies (Pisces Publications, ISBN 0 9508245 5 0). *A Field Guide to the Coral Reefs of the Caribbean and Florida including Bermuda and the Bahamas*, Peterson Field Guides Series no 27 (Houghton Mifflin Company). *Coral Reefs of the World*—Volume I, S Wells et al (IUCN)

The Natural History Book Service (T UK 0803 865913) holds a very large stock of wildlife and conservation books on the Caribbean.

Mark Eckstein, with additional information from Mark Wilson

WHALE AND DOLPHIN WATCHING

Whale and dolphin watching, long popular around North America, is starting to take off in the Caribbean, too. There are three main attractions: the **humpback whales**, the acrobatic whale-watchers' favourite, come to the Caribbean during the winter to mate, raise their calves and sing; the **sperm whales** are resident in various spots around the Caribbean but are easiest to see along the W coast of Dominica and Martinique; **spotted** and other **dolphin** species travel in large herds and are resident around many of the reefs, mangrove forests and offshore fishing banks.

It is possible to see whales and dolphins from land and on some regular ferries, and even on air flights between the islands, but the best way to encounter them close-up is on boat tours. Some of these are general marine nature or even birding tours that include whales and dolphins. Others are specialized tours offered by diving, sportsfishing or new eco-tourism ventures. Following is a guide to the best of whale and dolphin watching in the waters covered by this *Handbook*.

In **Bermuda**, whale-watching tours are offered to see humpback whales in April where they stop en route from the mating and calving banks off the Dominican Republic to their N feeding grounds off the E coast of New England, Canada and around Greenland. Pilot whales and various dolphins can also sometimes be seen. Since 1981, the Bermuda Zoological Society has teamed up with the Bermuda Aquarium, Natural History Museum and Zoo to offer tours.

Contact: Bermuda Zoological Society, Box 145, The Flatts, Smith's 3, Bermuda.

In the **Bahamas**, tours to meet and some-times swim with Atlantic spotted dolphins are offered May to September. The tours leave either from E Florida ports or from West End, on Grand Bahama Island. Cost is about US$1,500 for a week on the 62-foot catamaran *Stenella* and various other boats.

Two of the best tour operators are Wild Dolphin Project, PO Box 8436, Jupiter, FL 33468 USA, T 407-575-5660 or Oceanic Society Expeditions, Fort Mason Center, Building E, San Francisco, CA 94123 USA, T 415-441-1106. Others include: Bottomtime Adventures, PO Box 11919, Fort Lauderdale, FL 33339 USA, T 800-234-8464; Jennifer Marie, Royal Palm Yacht Club, 629 NE 3rd, Dania, FL 33339 USA, T 305-922-2351; Dream Team, PO Box 3271, Indialantic, FL 32903 USA, T 407-723-9312; Sea Fever, PO Box 39-8276, Miami Beach, FL 33139 USA, T 305-531-3483; Gulfstream Eagle, 278 Sussex Circle, Jupiter FL 33458 USA, T 407-575-9800; Crown Cruise Lines, Box 3000, Boca Raton, FL 33431 USA, T 407-394-7450; Coral Star, 17 Fort Royal Isle, Ft. Lauderdale, FL 33308 USA, T 305-563-1711; Innerspace Visions, 6800 SW 40th St, Suite 499, Miami, FL 33155 USA, T 305-669-0118; Shearwater Excursions, 113 Timber Run E, West Palm Beach, FL 33407 USA, T 407-842-4744.

Extended whale-watching trips with researchers and a chance to help on whale surveys to determine the abundance and distribution of large whales in the Bahamas are offered by Earthwatch out of Hope Town, Elbow Cay. Earthwatch, 680 Mount Auburn St, PO Box 403, Watertown, MA 02272 USA, T 617-926-8200.

From the **Turks & Caicos Islands**, humpbacks can be found offshore with bottlenose and other dolphins which are also seen close to shore. Boats can be chartered from Leeward Marina on Providenciales, but there are no organized tours.

In **Puerto Rico**, humpback whales and dolphins can be seen from land and occasional tours, particularly off the W coast of the island. Best lookouts are Aguadilla and from an old lighthouse near Punta Higuera, outside Rincón.

The **Dominican Republic** has the most popular and well-established whale watching in the Caribbean. The industry is centred on humpback whales, but pilot whales and spotted dolphins can also be seen in Samaná Bay, and bottlenose, spinner, and spotted dolphins, Bryde's and other whales on Silver Bank. The season for both locales is January through March. In 1994, 15,200 people went whale watching, most of them to Samaná Bay where the trips last 2 to 4 hours. The trips to Silver Bank are more educational and take a full day. In Samaná Bay, Whale Samaná is the oldest tour operator in the region and highly rated. Boats leave from the port of Samaná and cost US$50.

Contact: Kim Beddall, Whale Samaná, *Hotel Gran Bahía*, Samaná, Dominican Republic, T 538-2588. Other boats available in Samaná Bay to see humpbacks include 2 boats available for charter at the Victoria Marina in Samaná. As well, Miguel Bezi, another operator, has 6 boats over 100 feet long. Contact: Transporte Marítimo Miraniel, Samaná Bay, Dominican Republic, T 538-2556. For tours to see humpbacks on Silver Bank, some 50 miles (33 kms) N of Puerto Plata, contact: Coral Bay Cruises, 17 Fort Royal Isle, Fort Lauderdale, FL 33308 USA, T 305-563-1711, or Animal Watch, Granville House, London Road, Sevenoaks, Kent TN13 1DL, UK, T 0732-741612. It is also possible to book through travel agencies in Puerto Plata, such as Turinter, Dorado Travel or Go Caribic.

For whale watching from land from January to March, but especially in February, try Cabo Francés Viejo, E along the coast from Puerto Plata, near Cabrera, as well as Punta Balandra light and Cabo Samaná (near Samaná).

The **US Virgin Islands** and **British Virgin Islands** also have periodic trips to see the 60-100 humpback whales that winter N of the islands. There are also spinner and other dolphins to be seen. Season is October through February and a little later in the BVIs. On St Thomas, the 100-foot trimaran yacht *Wild Thing*, which operates out of Ramada Yacht Haven Marina, is used for the tours. Cost: US$45 for half a day.

Contact: Wild Thing, Suite 5, Long Bay, St Thomas, VI 08002 USA, T 774-8277. Arrangements can also be made through *Frenchman's Reef Hotel*. On Tortola in the BVIs, air tours are offered by Fly BVI, Beef Island Airport, British Virgin Islands.

On **Guadeloupe**, from November to April, there are tours to see humpback, sperm and pilot whales and dolphins offered through a fishermen's cooperative at Le Moule, a small, friendly, artisanal fishing town on the Atlantic coast. The boats are open, high-side, 21- to 25-foot "yoles" with twin outboards, which are normally used for fishing. US$50 for a day trip includes a visit to an offshore island for a swim and French/creole lunch.

Contact: Mme Mireille Prompt, La Potterie, Le Moule, 97160 Guadeloupe, T 590-23-5136.

On **Dominica**, 8-12 resident sperm whales delight visitors almost year-round. You can also see spinner and spotted dolphins, pilot whales, false killer whales, and pygmy sperm whales. Occasional sightings are made of bottlenose, Risso's and Fraser's dolphins, orcas, dwarf sperm whales and melon-headed whales. The tours are run by naturalist-diver-photographer Fitzroy Armour, his wife Sharon, and brother Andrew out of the *Anchorage Hotel*. Hydrophones are used to find and listen to the whales. The tours are US$50 for 3-4 hours.

Dominica Tours, PO Box 34, Roseau, Dominica, T 448-2638. Whale-watching tours are also offered by a well-equipped diving operator, Derek Perryman, at the *Castle Comfort Guest House* near Roseau. Cost: US$45. Dive Dominica Ltd, PO Box 63, Roseau, Dominica, T 448-2188.

For land-based whale watching of sperm whales and others, Scotts Head, at the SW tip of Dominica, overlooking Martinique Passage, is good most of the year.

On **Martinique**, sperm and the other whales and dolphins found off Dominica can also be seen off the W side. At St Pierre, whale- and dolphin-watching tours are part of the varied activities of a large diving club. Using Boston Whalers and other motor boats, they see spinner and spotted dolphins year-round and sperm whales and humpbacks mainly in the winter high season.

Contact: Carib Scuba Club, Villa Populo Bel Event, Morne Verte, Carbet, Martinique 97221, T 596-55-5944.

Off the W coast of **St Vincent**, large herds of spinner and spotted dolphins are seen regularly. Sometimes bottlenose dolphins and pilot whales are also found and, sporadically, humpback whales. Tours go aboard the 36-foot sloop, *Sea Breeze*, or on a 21-foot power boat. Snorkelling and a trip to Baleine Falls are also included. Almost year-round but avoid windy weather months of mid-December to mid-February. Best April to September when there is an 80% success rate. Trips depart from Calliaqua Lagoon on Indian Bay, SE of Kingstown and Arnos Vale Airport. Cost for tours is US$30.

Contact: Hal Daize, Arnos Vale Post Office, St Vincent, T 458-4969.

Other attractions include the island of **Petit Nevis**, off Bequia, 9 miles (15 kms) S of St Vincent, which is the site of the old whaling station once the hub of Caribbean whaling in this century. Access will require making arrangements locally as Petit Nevis is currently for sale.

From St George's Marina on **Grenada**, Mosden Cumberbach offers whale watching from his reliable 44-foot sloop or 34-foot power boat. He takes people off the S coast and to the Grenada Bank where humpbacks are often sighted from January through March, as well as up the coast to meet various dolphins and sometimes pilot whales. US$50 includes lunch and snorkelling.

Contact: Starwind Enterprise, PO Box 183, St George's, Grenada, T 440-3678.

Finally, from **Carriacou**, 23 miles (37 kms) NE of Grenada, humpbacks are often seen between December and April, as well as various dolphins and pilot whales year-round. Tours are offered aboard two catamarans by researchers working on wildlife conservation. Trips include touring bird sanctuaries, pristine coral reefs and Ile de Ronde, the submarine volcano N of Grenada. US$50 per person per day.

The catamarans, *Hokule A* and *Kido IV*, are docked in N Hillsborough Bay. Contact: Dario Sandrini, Kido Project, Carriacou, T 443-7936.

In **Belize**, spotted and bottlenose dolphins, and in E **Venezuela**, tucuxi and other tropical dolphins, can be seen close to shore on educational field trips. Oceanic Society Expeditions leads dolphin expeditions to both countries to work with researchers. Various whales are also sometimes seen.

For more information, contact Oceanic Society Eeditions, Fort Mason Center, Building E, San Francisco, CA 94123 USA, T 415-441-1106.

Colombia's whale watching opportunities include Bryde's whales which appear from February through April off Santa Marta and nearby Tairona National Park.

Other possible locales for whale and dolphin watching include Bahía Cispatá where various dolphins are reported year-round: bottlenose, tucuxi, spotted, rough-toothed dolphins and others. Further N, along the S beaches of Guajira State, tucuxi and other dolphins can be seen especially in the rainy months from May to November.

By watching whales and dolphins in the Caribbean, you can actually contribute to saving them. Many dolphins are killed mainly by fishermen, for food or fish bait. As well, pilot whales and even rare beaked whales are commonly harpooned, particularly in the E Caribbean. Whale and dolphin watching provides local people with another way to look at these intriguing animals—as well as a potentially more sustainable source of income.

Your support of whale watching may have the biggest impact in countries of the E Caribbean: Dominica, Grenada, St Lucia, and St Vincent and the Grenadines. Over the past few years, Japan has contributed to the development of these nations, by helping to build airports and adding fish docks and piers. In exchange, Japan has counted on the support of these four governments, all members of the International Whaling Commission (IWC), in its attempt to re-open commercial whaling. At the May 1994 IWC meeting in Mexico, however, these countries refrained from voting on the establishment of a S ocean sanctuary for the whales, effectively allowing this important conservation measure to pass. The credit was partly given to a tourism boycott of the four countries organized earlier in the year by a US conservation group (since lifted), and partly to local people and conservation groups who are trying to encourage responsible ecotourism, including whale and dolphin watching. You can help conservation here by simply saying you enjoy seeing whales and dolphins in local waters. However, when referring to dolphins, use the word 'porpoises'. In most parts of the Caribbean, the word "dolphin" means the dolphin fish. Best to specify that it is the mammal and not the fish that you want to see. And, in any case, if you see whales and dolphins being killed at sea, express your views to local and national tourism outlets of the country concerned.

Erich Hoyt

Erich Hoyt is a marine ecologist, conservationist and author of 6 books on whales and dolphins including *The Whale Watcher's Handbook* and *Seasons of the Whale* both of which deal partly with the Caribbean. He serves as a consultant for the Whale and Dolphin Conservation Society.

For more information about whale watching in the Caribbean and how to help whales and dolphins, contact the Whale and Dolphin Conservation Society, Alexander House, James Street West, Bath, BA1 2BT, UK.

WATERSPORTS AND SAILING IN THE CARIBBEAN

The crystal clear waters of the sunny Caribbean combined with the constant NE trade winds make the islands a paradise for watersports enthusiasts. The great increase in tourism in the area has brought a corresponding development in watersports and every conceivable watersport is now available. For a full range of watersports with all arrangements, if not at hotel reception at only a short walk down the beach, some of the best islands to head for are Barbados, Jamaica, Antigua, Martinique, the Bahamas, Cayman Islands, Puerto Rico and the Virgin Islands.

On these islands you can find hobiecats and sunfishes for rent, windsurfers, water skiing, glass-bottomed boats plying the reefs, charter yachts and booze cruises, scuba diving, snorkelling and deep sea fishing. Prices for such watersports vary from island to island and often increase by about 30% in the peak tourist season (December to April). It is worth knowing that prices can often be reduced for regular or long term rentals and that bargaining with individual beach operators is definitely worth trying.

Swimming
If all you want is sea and sand, these abound on nearly every island. The coral islands have the white postcard-perfect beaches and some of the islands of the Grenadines are nothing more than this. Swimming is safe on almost all Caribbean coasts, but do be careful on the exposed Atlantic coasts where waves are big at times and currents rip. Swimming in the Atlantic can be dangerous and in some places it is actually forbidden.

Water Skiing
This is almost always available in developed resort areas and beginners are looked after well. If you are a serious water skier it may be worth bringing your own slalom ski as many boats only cater for beginners.

Surfing
Good breaks for surfing and boogeyboarding can be found on the N shores of Puerto Rico, the Dominican Republic, Tobago and in Barbados. In both Puerto Rico and Barbados, custom-made surfboards can be bought and several competitions are organized every year. There are several good surf spots in Puerto Rico and the most consistent break in Barbados is at Bathsheba. In the Dominican Republic and Tobago, the sport is less developed. Waves tend to be bigger and more consistent in winter.

Windsurfing, Scuba Diving
See following articles by Nicolette Clifford and Martha Watkins Gilkes.

Fishing
Sportfishing is excellent in many of the islands of the N Caribbean. Almost every variety of deep-sea game fish: marlin, swordfish, tuna, mackerel and dorado abound in the waters. Over 50 world record catches have been made off the Bahamas alone. In the reefs and shallows there are big barracuda, tarpon and bonefish. There are areas for all methods of fishing: surf fishing, bottom fishing or trolling. Spearfishing, however, is banned in many islands. Although most fish seem to run between November and

March, there is really no off-season in most islands and a good local captain will always know where to find the best fishing grounds. Note, fishermen should beware of eating large predators (eg grand barracuda) and other fish which accumulate the ciguatera toxin by eating coral-browsing smaller fish.

Fishing is very well organized in such islands as the Bahamas where Bimini, lying close to the Gulf Stream, is devoted entirely to game fishing. Exciting game fishing is also available very close to the shore off Puerto Rico, especially in the area which has become known to the enthusiasts as Blue Marlin Alley. Fishing is also very good off the Cayman Islands, Jamaica and the US Virgin Islands. The barrier reef off Belize harbours a huge variety of game fish. In many islands there are annual fishing tournaments open to all, such as the Million Dollar Month Fishing Tournament held in June in the Caymans. Deep-sea fishing boats can be chartered for a half or full day and some are available on a weekly basis. Anglers can also pay individually on split charters. When arranging a charter, be careful to clarify all details in advance.

Sailing
Exploring the Caribbean has never been easier. Many of the islands have developed new facilities, new marinas and anchorages to cater for the increasing number of yachts which have made the Caribbean their home. Many of the islands, especially the gems of the Grenadines, have no airstrips and the only way to see these islands is by boat. While travelling between the islands, be careful to clear immigration, especially on arrival, as failing to do this can lead to heavy fines.

For yachts crossing the Atlantic along the trade wind route, Barbados, the most E island, is a natural first landfall. Although there is no marina yet in Barbados, mooring facilities are available at the Shallow Draft next to the Deep Water Harbour or there are calm anchorages in

Carlisle Bay. All boat needs can be met from the Boatyard on Carlisle Bay.

Following the wind, the next stop from Barbados is Grenada. Grenada Yacht Services on a sheltered lagoon next to one of the most picturesque Caribbean capitals, St George's, is one of the oldest yachting headquarters in the Southern Caribbean. There is also a friendly little marina on the S coast at Lance aux Épines.

Lying between Grenada and St Vincent over 45 miles of prime Caribbean sailing waters are the beautiful Grenadine Islands. Off the beaten track, they are a favourite cruising ground for sailors. There are few moorings or docks, but countless perfect anchorages. Many of the islands are uninhabited and you can anchor close to the shore and barbeque your own fish. Bequia is one of the two places in the world where whales are still hunted with harpoons and it is a centre for traditional boatbuilding. There are many sea oriented festivals in the Grenadines and a major one is the Bequia Regatta in April where traditional fishing boats compete.

In St Vincent, the best place to anchor is just off Young Island (which is private) opposite the Blue Lagoon. It is difficult to enter the lagoon which has a very narrow channel and should only be attempted by the experienced. An enterprising taxi-driver, Charlie Tango, can be called on the VHF and he will go and do your shopping in Kingstown.

It is an easy sail through the Windward Island chain. Land is almost always in sight. It is well worth putting into Rodney Bay in St Lucia, where an ultra modern marina has been opened. It is storm-proof, being under the shadow of Pigeon Island and there are complete services for yachts and "yachties". Several charter companies are based here including Stevens Yachts and Tradewind Yacht Charters. South of Castries there is a small marina in Marigot Bay where the Moorings charter fleet is based. Further S, one can anchor close to the impressive

Pitons. The next stop is Martinique where sailors can stock up with French goods from the hypermarkets. Charter yachts abound. Fort-de-France is one of the best places to dry dock (along with Antigua and St Martin). There is a small, relaxed marina, Trois Islets, across the bay from Fort-de-France.

The Atlantic Rally for Cruisers offers support and entertainment for any sailors contemplating an Atlantic crossing. Departure is from Gran Canaria at the end of November and the yachts arrive in St Lucia to a warm welcome for Christmas. A major regatta on the Caribbean racing circuit is held around April.

Heading further N, Les Saintes off the S tip of Guadeloupe offer peaceful anchorages. Guadeloupe has a very large marina just outside the capital, Point-à-Pitre, which is crowded with wandering French yachts. There is a slipway here with a modern 50-ton travel lift and crews can do their own work. The multi-hulls of the professional racing circuit congregate here once a year. Favourable French tax laws for boat owners have led to a proliferation of yachts and fierce competition in the charter market from the French islands of Guadeloupe, Martinique and St Martin and also St Lucia.

Antigua is the mecca of the Caribbean yachting world and it is possible that the Atlantic Rally for Cruisers may end here in the future. The hurricane-proof English Harbour is one of the most distinctive ports in the Caribbean with its restored Royal Naval Dockyard which was once the haunt of Admiral Nelson.

The major marina facilities are the Catamaran Club Marina, Crabbs Marina in the Parham Sound on the N coast, Jolly Harbour, just S of Ffryes Point and the elegant St James Club Marina in Mamora Bay. There are also dozens of coves and anchorages, a large charter fleet (home to Nicholsons Yacht Charters) and almost every spare part is available. Antigua Sailing Week in April is the biggest yachting event in the Caribbean

and the island takes on a carnival atmosphere to cater for the yachts which arrive from all over the Caribbean as well as other parts of the world.

Further N, the small island of St-Barthélémy is also worth a visit. Somewhat resembling St Tropez in the 50's, St-Barts is expensive and exclusive. Yachts can use the quay in Gustavia Harbour. Lively St Maarten, half-French and half-Dutch, with good marina facilities, is a favourite stop for sailors stocking up on duty-free goods for an Atlantic crossing.

The British Virgin Islands are home to the largest bareboat charter fleet in the world. The main sailing area between the islands, the Sir Francis Drake Channel, is protected from the open seas, making the waters calm and particularly well suited to novice sailors. There are numerous marinas with many in places that only boats can reach as at Bitter End on Virgin Gorda.

If sailing in the N Caribbean and in Bahamian waters, you should be aware of a risk of piracy by drug runners. Boats have been reported seized, crews have disappeared. Seek advice about local conditions.

Yacht Charters

Large charter fleets operate from the British Virgin Islands, Antigua, Martinique and St Lucia. Yachts can be chartered on a daily or term basis either bareboat or with skipper and crew.

Hitching Yachts

Hitching and working on yachts is an ideal way of seeing the islands for the adventurous person with time on his/her hands. The variety of yachts is endless. Many yachts charter in the Caribbean in winter and go N to the United States or Mediterranean for the charter season there. Other yachts are cruisers passing through on their way around the world. "Yachties" are friendly people and if you ask around in the right places, frequent the "yachtie" bars and put up a few notices, crew positions can be found, either on a charter yacht or a cruiser. Some of the easiest places to join boats are in Martinique (Fort-de-France and Trois Islets), St Lucia (Rodney Bay and Marigot Bay), Antigua (English Harbour) and in the Grenadines from Bequia (Admiralty Bay) and Union Island (Anchorage). The end of Antigua Week sees many boats looking for crew as does the end of the Atlantic Rally for Cruisers.

Rosie Mauro, Barbados

SCUBA DIVING IN THE CARIBBEAN

Scuba diving has become the "in sport" with the numbers of divers having increased dramatically in recent years. The epitome of a scuba dive is in clear, tropical waters on a colourful reef abounding with life. The Caribbean is a scuba diver's paradise, for there is a conglomeration of islands surrounded by living reefs providing different types of diving to suit everyone's dreams. Unfortunately, some of the islands have turned into a "diving clrcus", as in some of the more developed N Caribbean islands where 30 or 40 divers are herded onto large dive boats and dropped on somewhat packaged dive sites where "tame" fish come for handouts. Other islands in the Caribbean region are still virginal in the diving sense, which can lead to an exciting undersea adventure. Nevertheless, this can also be frustrating on a diving holiday as on the more remote islands facilities are not often available and diving can be more difficult and basic.

The **Cayman Islands** are among the most developed for scuba diving and there is a fine organization of over 20 dive operations, including liveaboard boats. There is also a well-run decompression facility on Grand Cayman, which is an added safety factor. The Caymans are very conservation minded and it is a criminal offence to take ANY form of marine life while scuba diving. In fact, it is illegal on Cayman Brac, the smaller sister island, even to wear gloves while scuba diving. This helps ensure that divers will not hold or damage the delicate coral formations and other marine life.

Belize is well-known for the spectacular diving available on its 175-mile barrier reef. Lighthouse Reef, the outermost of the three N-S reef systems, offers pristine dive sites in addition to the incredible Blue Hole, a sinkhole exceeding 400 feet. Massive stalagmites and stalactites are found along overhangs down the sheer vertical walls of the Blue Hole. This outer reef lies beyond the access of most land-based diving resorts and even beyond most fishermen, so the marine life is undisturbed. An ideal way to visit this reef is on a liveaboard dive boat. An exciting marine phenomenon takes place during the full moon each January in the waters around Belize when thousands of the Nassau groupers gather to spawn at Glory Caye on Turneffe Reef. The gathering occurs at other locations in the Caribbean also. For details on land-based diving facilities on the many cayes, see the chapter on the Belize Cayes.

The **British Virgin Islands**, with an array of some 50 coral islands, are well worth a mention as the diving is exciting and varied. Both liveaboard and land-based operations are available with well-developed facilities for divers. Popular diving sites include the wreck of the *HMS Rhone*, a 310-foot British mail ship sunk in 1867 in a hurricane. She was the site for the Hollywood movie *The Deep*, which is what really made her famous. Other interesting sites include Turtle Cave in Brewers Bay which offers a spiral arch divers can swim through beginning at a depth of 45 feet and winding up to 15 feet. Many sites lie in the string of islands to the S between Tortola and the island of Virgin Gorda. To the N lies Mosquito Island, the site of The Cousteau Society's Project Ocean Search. Hosted annually by Jean-Michel Cousteau, the expedition gives a small number of participants the chance to

The Caymans Famous for its diving, the Caymans also offers good windsurfing, the E end is popular for beginners to advanced and everything in between, flat water on the inside and bump and jump further out. Best wind Nov-Mar. Cayman Windsurfing, T (809) 947-7492, F (809) 947-7902; Sailboards Caribbean, T 949-1068, F (809) 949-1068.

Dominican Republic Voted by many top sailors as one of the most exciting places to sail in the Caribbean, Cabarete, on the N coast, offers everything a windsurfer could want: flat water for beginners and great wavesailing on the outside with thermally affected winds that mean you can take the morning off. Lots of schools and hotels on the strip of beach and some of the best gear in the Caribbean. Best wind Jan-Mar and Jun-Aug. Carib Bic Centre, T (800) 635-1155, F (809) 586-9529, Sea Horse Ranch, T (800) 635-0991, F (809) 571-2374, many more, contact the Tourist Board (see also p 348).

Grenadines Great location with no facilities, take your own gear and hire a yacht out of Grenada or St Vincent, or visit Basil at Bequia (see above) the only rental centre in the area.

Mexico Cancun is good for intermediate sailors with onshore wind and flat, waist deep water for miles. If you want to transport your own gear then there are more challenging conditions around the island. Best wind Dec-Mar. Vela Highwind Centres, T (800) 223-5443, F (415) 525-2086.

Nevis A windsurfer's paradise waiting to be discovered, good flat water and wavesailing, definitely no crowds, the island is small enough to offer all conditions for every skill level. Best wind Dec-Jan, Jun-Jul. *Mount Nevis Hotel and Beach Club*, T (800) 756-3847, F (212) 874-4276; Nevis Windsurfing, T (809) 469-9682.

Puerto Rico Great wave sailing spot, the Caribbean's answer to Maui. The location is The Shacks at Isabela on the NW point of the island. Thermal winds make this a winter spot for the committed wave sailor, gentler sailing is offered in the San Juan area and in the summer. Best waves and wind Dec-Apr, slalom Jul-Sep. Lisa Penfield Windsurfing, T (809) 796-2188, F (809) 796-2188; Windsurfing Del Caribe, T (809) 728-7526,(809) 791-1000, F (809) 728-7526.

St Barts Small exclusive island with some good windsurf spots for beginners and advanced, and it is quiet. Best wind Dec-Feb. St Barts BIC Centre, T (590) 277-122, F (590) 278-718; Wind Wave Power, T (590) 278-257, F (590) 277-276.

St Croix A great sailing spot and often overlooked, the guys here are good wave sailors and slalom racers as the island boasts all conditions at many locations. Best wind Jan-Feb and July. Mistral School at Chenay Bay, T (809) 773-4810; Off the Beaten Path Vacations, T (800) 253-0622, F (809) 773-6116.

St Lucia A beautiful destination for any visitor and for the windsurfer it offers uncrowded sailing and plenty to do on no wind days. Best to bring your own gear if you are an advanced sailor, although there is limited good gear to rent at Windsurf Cas-en-Bas. Best winds Dec-Jun. Windsurf Cas-en-Bas, T (800) 876-3941, F (804) 693-2411.

St Martin Ever fancied windsurfing naked across flat tropical waters? Orient Bay (Baie Orientale) is probably the only place in the world you can do this without getting arrested. Aside from the novelty of sailing naked, St Martin offers good learning and advanced slalom sailing. Best winds Dec-Jan and July. Surface, T (590) 879-324; Tropical Wave T (590) 873-709.

St Thomas Everything you expect from a Caribbean windsurf vacation, with shopping malls. St Thomas boasts a lively local windsurfing community, flat water and lots of races and events to attend. Best wind Dec-Jan and July, join the fun at the Caribbean Team Boardsailing Championships in July. Caribbean Boardsailing, T/F (809) 776-3486; West Indies Windsurfing T/F (809) 775-6530.

Trinidad & Tobago Situated in the prime trade wind zone, Tobago's Pigeon Point is the place to go, unexplored and beautiful with some excellent sailing spots. You will probably need to take your own gear. Best wind Dec-May. Windsurf Association of Trinidad & Tobago, T/F (809) 625-4665.

Turks & Caicos Flat turquoise waters and steady winds make this an ideal learner and intermediate destination, perfect for a family diving and windsurf vacation. Best winds Feb-Mar intermediate, Oct-Nov for beginners. Windsurfing Provo, T (809) 946-5490, F (809) 946-5936.

Nicolette Clifford (Tortola, British Virgin Islands).

WALKING IN THE CARIBBEAN

The Caribbean provides ideal conditions for medium-distance walking in the tropics. Small islands avoid the very high temperatures which are common in India, Africa, or the South American mainland. Distances are manageable; a hard day's walk will take you from coast to coast on the smaller islands, and a few days is enough for a complete circuit. The scenery is varied: peasant farms with fruit trees, rain forests, and high mountains. Mountain streams and waterfalls which would be ice-cold in temperate countries are perfect for bathing. The sea is never far away. Nor are road transport, comfortable accommodation, rum shops and restaurants. Nevertheless, the illusion of remoteness can sometimes be complete. And much of the nastier *mainland* wildlife can't swim, so there are no large carnivores and few poisonous snakes on the islands.

There are some tips to note for people more used to walking in temperate countries.

Maps Good large scale maps (1: 25,000 or 1: 50,000) are available for all the Commonwealth islands. These can be obtained from the local Lands and Surveys department on each island; and usually from Edward Stanford Ltd, 12/14 Long Acre, London WC2E 9LP, or The Map Shop, 15 High Street, Upton-upon-Severn, Worcestershire, (T 0684 593146). The Ordnance Survey (Romsey Road, Southampton, UK, T 0703 792763, F 0703 792404) publishes a series of colourful World Maps which includes some holiday destinations. They contain comprehensive tourist information ranging from hotels and beaches to climbing and climate. Each map is produced in association with the country concerned. Relevant titles so far are: Barbados, St Lucia, Cayman Islands, Belize (Ambergris Caye), British Virgin Islands, St Vincent, Dominica. There are also good large scale Serie Bleu maps of Guadeloupe and Martinique (1:25,000, 7 maps of Guadeloupe, No 4601G-4607G) issued by the Institut Géographique National, Paris, which include all hiking trails. Footpath information on maps is not always reliable, however.

The interior of Guyana is largely uncharted; beyond the coastal belt the vegetation of the rain forest can be very thick. Most maps of this area can be hard to follow as the only features are the rivers, which change according to season (ie islands becoming part of the land, etc). Always take a guide in these parts.

Clothing Lightweight cotton clothing, with a wide brimmed hat to keep off the sun. Shorts are more comfortable, but can leave the legs exposed to sunburn or sharp razor grasses; ditto short sleeved shirts. It is best to carry short and long, and change en route as appropriate. Rain comes in intense bursts. Raincoats are not particularly comfortable. A better technique is to strip down to light clothes and dry off when the rain stops. In the rainy season in the Guianas, leather footwear is of little use as it will be permanently wet. Use trainers instead.

Timing An early start is ideal, preferably just before sunrise. This will give several hours walking before the sun becomes too hot. Public transport starts running surprisingly early in most places.

Water Carry a large thermos. This can keep water ice-cold through a full day. Refilling from mountain streams is generally safe if purification tablets are used, but be careful of streams *below* villages especially in islands like St Lucia and Martinique where there is some bilharzia, and of springs in cultivated areas where generously applied pesticides may have leached into the groundwater.

Sunburn Remember that the angle of the sun in the sky is what counts, not the temperature. So you may get burnt at midday even if you feel cool, but are unlikely to have trouble before 1000 or after 1500. Forearms can get burnt, and so can the back of your legs if you are walking away from the sun. It is a good idea to walk W in the morning and E in the afternoon to avoid strong sun on the face.

Snakes The only islands where these are a worry are Trinidad, St Lucia, and Martinique. Trinidad has several dangerous species, and also has African killer bees. All three islands have the venomous Fer de Lance. This snake, however, is usually frightened off by approaching footsteps, so snakebites are rare, but they can be fatal. The Fer de Lance prefers bush country in dry coastal areas. Ask and accept local advice on where to go, and stick to well marked trails. Some other islands have boa constrictors, which can bite but are not poisonous. In Trinidad, beware of the coral snake; visitors with children should take care because the snake looks like a colourful bracelet coiled on the ground. Snakes are also found in the interior jungles of the Guianas; walk with a guide. Most snakes will only attack in the breeding season if they feel the nest is threatened. Large centipedes (sometimes found in dry coastal areas) can also give a very nasty bite.

Marijuana Farmers In remote mountain areas in most islands these people are likely to assume that outsiders have come either to steal the crop or as police spies. On most islands they are armed, and on some they set trap guns for the unwary. Again, the best way to avoid

them is to keep to well marked trails, and accept local advice about where to go.

Details of walks are to be found in each country chapter, but here is an indication of what is possible on a selection of islands:

Jamaica Spectacular scenery especially in the Blue Mountains and in the Cockpit country. Marijuana growers are a real problem in the remote areas, but the main trails in the Blue Mountains are safe. Jamaica Camping and Hiking Association and Ministry of Tourism have a useful *Hikers Guide to the Blue Mountains*.

Haiti Another story altogether. Walking is the normal means of transport in rural areas, so there are masses of well-trodden trails, but it is better to walk with a group. Maps are rudimentary and small scale. Few people speak French in remote areas—try to pick up some Créole. Make sure you carry basic supplies, particularly water. Hiring a guide should be no problem.

Guadeloupe Network of waymarked trails on the mountainous half (Basse Terre) in the Parc Naturel and up La Soufrière. Contact the Organisation des Guides de Montagne de la Caraïbe (Maison Forestière, 97120 Matouba, T 80 05 79) for a guide and/or the booklet *Promenades et Randonnées*.

Martinique The *Parc Naturel Régional* (Caserne Bouillé, Rte de la Redoute de Matouba, T 73 19 30) organizes group hikes, usually on Sundays, and publishes a useful *Guide des Sentiers Pedestres à la Martinique*. Good trails on Mont Pelée and along the N coast.

Dominica Probably has the best unspoiled mountain scenery in the Caribbean. Some of the long distance trails are hard to follow, though. Guides readily available. Try the path via Laudat to the Boiling Lake.

St Lucia Very well marked E-W trail

through Quilesse forest reserve. Other walks organized by the Forestry Department. Also a good trail up Gros Piton. See St Lucia chapter for details.

St Vincent Spectacular but sometimes difficult trail across the Soufrière volcano from Orange Hill to Richmond. Guide advisable. North coast trail past Falls of Baleine is spectacular, but hard to follow. Marijuana growers.

Grenada Very accessible mountain and rainforest scenery. Good network of signposted trails linking Grand Etang, Concord waterfall, and other points. The mountains to the SE of the Grand Étang Forest Reserve are less well marked and you may need a local guide, but the walking is spectacular with marvellous views.

Barbados Very safe and pleasant walking, especially on the E coast, but little really wild scenery. Barbados National Trust (T 426 2421) organizes regular Sunday hikes, morning at 0600, afternoon at 1500.

Trinidad Some fine scenery, but marijuana growers are a real problem, particularly in the Northern Range and you are advised always to walk in a group.

Well marked trails are safe. Those at the Asa Wright Nature Centre are recommended (T 667-4655, F 667-0493). Trinidad Field Naturalists Club (1 Errol Park Road, St Anns, Port of Spain, T 624-3321, Louisa Zuniaga) organizes long distance hikes, and visits to caves etc.

Tobago Safe and pleasant walking; distances are not too great. The scenery is varied: hills, woodland and unspoilt beaches.

Guyana The Ministry of Tourism is cautious about backpackers walking alone in the interior of the country for safety reasons. In addition, in the interests of ecotourism, visitors are asked to use local guides in order to limit damage to the rain forests.

Useful Addresses For groups organizing a serious hiking/camping expedition in the Caribbean, contact Mr David Clarke, Caribbean Regional Consultant, Duke of Edinburgh's Award, The Garrison, Bridgetown, Barbados (T 436 8954, F 431 0076). He is generally able to provide advice and to supply the address of a local organization on most islands with expedition experience.

Mark Wilson, Barbados

RESPONSIBLE TOURISM

Much has been written about the adverse impacts of tourism on the environment and local communities. It is usually assumed that this only applies to the more excessive end of the travel industry such as the Spanish Costas and Bali. However travellers can have an impact at almost any density and this is especially true in areas "off the beaten track" where local people may not be used to western conventions and lifestyles, and natural environments may be very sensitive.

Of course, tourism can have a beneficial impact and this is something to which every traveller can contribute. Many National Parks are part funded by receipts from people who travel to see exotic plants and animals, El Yunque (Puerto Rico) and the Asa Wright Centre (Trinidad) are good examples of such sites. Similarly, travellers can promote patronage and protection of valuable archaeological sites and heritages through their interest and entrance fees.

However, where visitor pressure is high and/or poorly regulated, damage can occur. This is especially so in parts of the Caribbean where some tour operators are expanding their activities with scant regard for the environment or local communities. It is also unfortunately true that many of the most popular destinations are in ecologically sensitive areas easily disturbed by extra human pressures. Eventually the very features that tourists travel so far to see may become degraded and so we seek out new sites, discarding the old, and leaving someone else to deal with the plight of local communities and the damaged environment. Fortunately, there are signs of a new awareness of the responsibilities that the travel industry and its clients need to endorse. For example, some tour operators fund local conservation pro-

jects and travellers are now more aware of the impact they may have on host cultures and environments. We can all contribute to the success of what is variously described as responsible, green or alternative tourism. All that is required is a little forethought and consideration. It would be impossible to identify all the potential impacts that might need to be addressed by travellers, but it is worthwhile noting the major areas in which we can all take a more responsible attitude in the countries we visit. These include changes to natural ecosystems (air, water, land, ecology and wildlife), cultural values (beliefs and behaviour) and the built environment (sites of antiquity and archaeological significance).

At an individual level, travellers can reduce their impact if greater consideration is given to their activities. For example in most Caribbean countries dress codes are fairly strictly adhered to; shorts and T shirts are OK on the beach but less so when shopping or cashing cheques. Avoid topless or nude bathing except where it is expressly allowed. Do not take photographs of people without permission. Recognition of these cultural cues goes a long way towards reducing the friction that can develop between host and visitor. Collecting or purchasing wildlife curios might have an effect on local ecosystems and may well be illegal under either local or international legislation (see below). Similarly, some tourist establishments have protected wildlife (especially turtle) on the menu, don't add to the problem by buying it. Some environmental impacts are caused by factors beyond the direct control of travellers, such as the management and operation of a hotel chain. However, even here it is possible to voice concern about damaging activities and an increasing number of hotels and travel operators are taking "green concerns" seriously, even if it is only to protect their share of the market.

Environmental Legislation

Legislation may have been enacted to control damage to the environment, and in some cases this can have a bearing on travellers. The establishment of National Parks may involve rules and guidelines for visitors and these should always be followed. In addition there may be local or national laws controlling behaviour and use of natural resources (especially wildlife) that are being increasingly enforced. If in doubt, ask. Finally, international legislation, principally the Convention on International Trade in Endangered Species of Wild Fauna and Flora (CITES), may affect travellers.

CITES aims to control the trade in live specimens of endangered plants and animals and also "recognizable parts or derivatives" of protected species. Sale of black coral, some hard corals, turtle shells, rare orchids and other protected wildlife is strictly controlled by signatories of the convention. The full list of protected wildlife varies, so if you feel the need to purchase souvenirs and trinkets derived from wildlife, it would be prudent to check whether they are protected. CITES parties in the Caribbean include: Dominican Republic, Trinidad and Tobago, St Lucia, St Vincent, the Bahamas, Guyana, the Central American republics and Cuba. Puerto Rico and the US Virgin Islands are included in the US ratification of CITES. The UK dependencies (Anguilla, Bermuda, British Virgin Islands, Cayman and Turks and Caicos Islands) all look to the UK government for advice and support in the implementation of international wildlife legislation and in particular CITES regulation as the UK is a party to the convention. In addition, most European countries, the USA and Canada are all signatories. Importation of CITES protected species into these countries can lead to heavy fines, confiscation of goods and even imprisonment. Information on the status of legislation and protective measures can be obtained from Traffic International (F UK 0223 277237).

Green Travel Companies and Information

The increasing awareness of the environmental impact of travel and tourism has led to a range of advice and information services as well as spawning specialist travel companies who claim to provide "responsible travel" for clients. This is an expanding field and the veracity of claims needs to be substantiated in some cases. The following organizations and publications can provide useful information for those with an interest in pursuing responsible travel opportunities.

International Organizations

Green Flag International aims to work with travel industry and conservation bodies to improve environments at travel destinations and also to promote conservation programmes at resort destinations; provides a travellers' guide for "green" tourism as well as advice on destinations, T UK 0223 893587.

Tourism Concern aims to promote a greater understanding of the impact of tourism on host communities and environments, T UK 081-878 9053.

Centre for Responsible Tourism (CRT) co-ordinates a North American network and advises on North American sources of information on responsible tourism: CRT, 2 Kensington Rd, San Anselmo, California USA.

Centre for the Advancement of Responsive Travel (CART) has a range of publications available as well as information on alternative holiday destinations, T UK 0732 352757.

Caribbean Conservation Organizations

The conservation organizations described below may also be able to provide advice on sites of historical or wildlife interest and possibly provide guides. The use of local experts as guides can of course provide an important source of income for small conservation bodies. In addition, they are often far more sensitive to the cultural taboos and ecological constraints of sites whose long term survival they can help to ensure. (**NB** Visitors should not be disappointed when a guide uses the local, rather than the technical name for wildlife; few local people know the names of animal and plant life.)

Anguilla Archeological and Historical Society, PO Box 252, The Valley, Anguilla.

Antigua Archeological and Historical Society, PO Box 103, English Harbour, Antigua.

Bahamas National Trust, PO Box N 4105, Nassau, Bahamas.

Barbados National Trust, 10th Avenue, Belleville, St Michael, Barbados.

Bermuda Audubon Society, PO Box 1328, Hamilton 5, Bermuda.

Bermuda National Trust, PO Box 61, Hamilton 5, Bermuda.

British Virgin Islands National Parks Trust, c/o Ministry of Natural Resources, Road Town, Tortola, BVI.

Caribbean Conservation Association, Savannah Lodge, The Garrison, St Michael, Barbados.

Dominican Republic National Parks office (Dirección Nacional de Parques), Av Independencia 539 esq Cervantes, Santo Domingo (Apartado Postal 2487). Ecoturisa, Santiago 203, B, Santo Domingo.

Dominica Conservation Association, PO Box 71, Roseau, Dominica.

Grenada Historical Society, St George's, Grenada.

Jamaica Conservation and Development Trust, PO Box 1225, Kingston 8, Jamaica.

Montserrat National Trust, PO Box 54, Plymouth, Montserrat.

Natural History Society of Puerto Rico Inc.

Netherlands Antilles National Parks Foundation (STINAPA), PO Box 2090, Curaçao.

Nevis Historical and Conservation Society, c/o Mr S Byron, PO Box 476, Charlestown, Nevis.

Pointe à Pierre Wildfowl Trust (Trinidad), 18 Grove Road, Valsayn Park North, Trinidad.

St Lucia National Trust, PO Box 525, Castries, St Lucia.

St Lucia Naturalists Society, PO Box 783, Castries.

Trinidad and Tobago Field Naturalists Club, 1 Errol Park Road, St Ann's, Port of Spain.

Turks and Caicos National Trust, Box 261, Grand Turk, Turks and Caicos Islands.

Union Régionale des Associations du Patrimoine et de l'Environment de Guadeloupe, BP82L, Pointe-à-Pitre, Leder 97112, Guadeloupe.

Union Régionale des Associations du Patrimoine et de l'Environment de Martinique, Centre du PNRM, Caserne Bouille, Rue Redoute de Matouba, Fort de France 97200, Martinique.

Virgin Islands Conservation Society, PO Box 12379, St Thomas, US Virgin Islands 00801 USA. Environmental Association, PO Box 3839, Christiansted, St Croix, US Virgin Islands 00822.

In Guyana there are various private organizations, see that chapter; similarly Suriname.

Publications

The Good Tourist by Katie Wood and Syd House (1991: Mandarin Paperbacks), addresses issues surrounding environmental impacts of tourism, suggests ways in which damage can be minimized, suggests a range of environmentally sensitive holidays and projects. *Independent Guide to Real Holidays Abroad* by Frank Barrett (1991: available from the *Independent* newspaper), suggestions for a range of special interest holidays.

Caribbean Festivals at a Glance

	Page	Jan	Feb	Mar	Easter	Apr	May	Jun	Jul	Aug	Sept	Oct	Nov	Dec
Aruba	865	F						F,M,W					S,A	
Anguilla	492		C							C,R				
Antigua	455					R								C
Bahamas	85		F	W					F	F		F		
Barbados	693		M	M					F	F		F	M	R,S
Bermuda	76	M							F					
Bay Islands (Honduras)	903													
Belize Cays	916			F						F	F			
Bonaire	828		C	R,W				F			F	R/F		
British Virgin Islands	423			F				W	F		F		F	
Carriacou	675		C	F						R		R/F		
Cayman Islands	202			F	C							F		
Corn Islands (Nicaragua)	885	F										M		
Cuba	158	F		F		C		F,A	U				M	
Curaçao	845		C	F					F			F,M		
Dominica	600		C									F	F	
Dominican Republic	326	A,R,S	C					A,W		F,C	M	M		F
Grenada	669		F					F		M	M	R		
Guadeloupe	547		U	F					F					
Guyana	771		F										F	
Guyane	800		C	F					F				F	
Haiti	292	F	U							F,M				
Isla de Margarita	807		U								F			
Jamaica	224				C			W	C			A		
Martinique	578	R/W	C	R		R		W					F	M
Montserrat	503			R			F							C
Nevis	473		C			F								C/U

	Page	Jan	Feb	Mar	Easter	Apr	May	Jun	Jul	Aug	Sept	Oct	Nov	Dec
Providencia	892			W										
Puerto Rico	367					C		C	F		F,A	R		F
Saba	519							F,M						F
San Andrés	892		C				M						F	
San Blas Islands (Panama)	876													
Sint Maarten	530					C,F							F	
St Eustatius	525		R						C					
St Kitts	473								C				F	C
St Lucia	619		C,F				R,M	F,W		F			F	F
St Vincent	643										R			
Bequia	650				R									
Union Island	653				S				F					
St-Barthélemy	569		C						F					
St-Martin	563		R,C						F	F				
Suriname	563			F									F	
Tobago	725		C,A						M	R			F	
Trinidad	725		C,F		F				F	F		M	F	
Turks & Caicos: Grand Turk	262													
: Providenciales	271						R		A	C,R				
: South Caicos	266								F					
: North Caicos	262									F				
: Middle Caicos	262													
USVI: St Thomas	404			W		C			W					
: St John	411		F						C					
: St Croix	416		C									M,R		
Yucatán/Mexico Islands	939												F	
Isla Mujeres	945													F

Key: C = Carnival (in Feb normally means pre-Lenten); S = other sports; R = Regatta; F = Festival; M = Music and arts festival; A = Angling tournament; W = Windsurf races
/ = two types of event combined; , = two separate events fall within same month. Where an event begins in one month and ends in another, the month of commencement is given. See Festivals, watersports, Culture and National Holidays sections in text below for precise details.

BERMUDA

ONE OF BRITAIN'S OLDEST, now self-governing, dependent territories is Bermuda. It comprises over 150 small islands and islets in the W Atlantic, 775 miles SE of New York, and 900 miles NE of Nassau, Bahamas. The ten largest islands form the main land mass of 21 square miles. They are linked by causeways and bridges to create a narrow chain which, seen from the air, takes the shape of a fish hook. Under one of its earliest governors, Daniel Tucker, Bermuda was divided into eight tribes, now called the parishes of Hamilton, Smiths, Devonshire, Pembroke, Paget, Warwick, Southampton and Sandys, with the "public land" at St George.

Bermuda sits on a cap of rock made up of tiny coral creatures, accumulated over millions of years, surmounting an extinct volcano which rises sharply from the seabed. The land is hilly, but too porous for streams to form. The mild, semi-tropical climate brings high yearly rainfall and sunshine, which sustains the attractive hedgerows and trees lining long stretches of narrow road. Most fresh water in buildings is provided by rainfall, on which all rely. The rainwater is collected from the white, furrowed roofs characteristic of Bermudian houses, channelled into underground storage tanks, then pumped into the houses. Bermuda's rural aspect is being transformed into a more urban environment as development has been fuelled by rising property values.

Around the islands are some notoriously treacherous coral reefs which are the graveyard of many seafarers and their ships. Paradoxically, the reefs protect the inshore waters, which are the feeding grounds throughout the year for a wealth of marine flora and fauna.

The civilian population in 1992 stood at approximately 60,300 about 60% of whom were of African origin, the remainder being mainly of European descent. Currently there are several thousand guest "contract" workers, whose skills are required to maintain the islands' business and environmental development. Population density is extremely high, at 2,871 per square mile, with the entire population classed as urban.

The United States, Canada and the United Kingdom have had established military bases as, for many years, Bermuda was considered strategically important. The US presence is the greatest, with its substantial Air Force base adjacent to Kindley Field Airport used by both military and commercial air transport. The station has no warships or planes but operates Bermuda's air traffic control system, rescue services and weather forecasting for the civilian airport. However, personnel at the US naval air force station were reduced from 850 to 300 by end-1993. It is proposed that all US funding for the base should cease by September 1995, leaving Bermuda to operate it on its own. The Canadian navy communications base, employing 70 people, closed in 1992. The Royal Navy's base, *HMS Malabar*, is visited regularly by NATO frigates and destroyer-class vessels, which call in for refuelling and provisioning. However, this too is to close in April 1995, although close links will remain between the Bermuda Regiment and the British Army.

History

Evidence suggests that Bermuda was first discovered by the Spanish explorer Juan Bermúdez, early in the 16th century. Apart from one or two subsequent

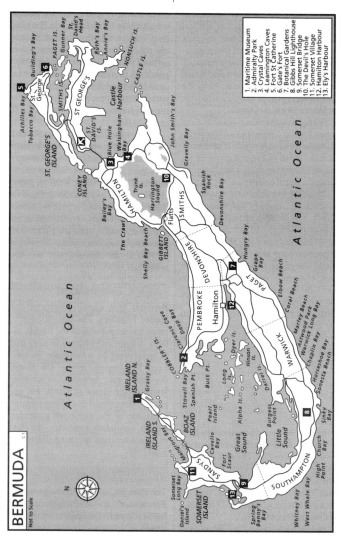

BERMUDA
Not to Scale

1. Maritime Museum
2. Admiralty Park
3. Crystal Caves
4. Leamington Caves
5. Fort St. Catherine
6. Gate's Fort
7. Botanical Gardens
8. Gibbs Hill Lighthouse
9. Somerset Bridge
10. The Devil's Hole
11. Somerset Village
12. Hamilton Harbour
13. Ely's Harbour

registered tons in 1986 to over 3.5m tons by end-1988, and is the fifth largest free flag merchant fleet in the world.

There is little agriculture on Bermuda and only 800 acres are devoted to farming for domestic consumption, market gardening and dairy produce. Pressure on land is intense and the island's size imposes development constraints. The population is close to the maximum tolerable although unemployment is low and per capita income is one of the highest in the world. Environmental issues have become important for the electorate, as have high housing costs, scarce low-cost housing, the office development boom, traffic congestion and the high level of immigration.

The lack of an export industry and scarce farming land means that Bermuda suffers from large, persistent trade deficits, as virtually all its needs are met by imports. However, this is offset by the well-developed service sector and the current account of the balance of payments usually shows a small surplus. The Gulf crisis and the downturn in the US economy was keenly felt in 1990-92 as the flow of tourists slowed, but slow growth was restored in 1993-94 as a result of improvement in both the offshore financial sector and tourism. There is no tax on income, dividends or profits in Bermuda.

Flora and Fauna

The rural parts of the island are covered by vegetation apart from breaks and rocky protrusions which pierce the thin layers of top soil. The endemic plants include olivewod bark, which is rare, and the cedar. The cedar tree with its exceptionally pleasant smelling timber once covered the island but in 1945 it was severely blighted by an insect pest. Native plants transported by natural means to the islands are the palmetto and bermudiana. Other trees introduced from different parts of the world include the pimento, the poinciana, fiddlewood, the Surinam cherry, the casuarina, the Norfolk Island pine, the coconut and royal palms. Bananas, loquats, guavas and citrus fruits which are sold from roadside stalls grow quite plentifully alongside other "allotment" type vegetable crops. The Easter Lily is cultivated for local sale. It was one of Bermuda's agricultural exports. Other shrubs include oleander and hibiscus, often grown as hedgerows. Geraniums, fennel and other herbs grow plentifully while in the sandier beach soil the prickly pear is common. Two endemic varieties of fern survive, the pretty maidenhair and the tough sword fern.

Bermuda has few wild animals, the largest are rodents and lizards and the saucer-sized toad introduced to help control pests. The whistling tree frogs have a leading voice in the continual orchestral background which reaches almost crescendo proportions after heavy rain. Other singers are the yellow kis-k-dee, the red coloured cardinal, the endemic blue bird and the European starling and sparrow. The white seagoing longtail gull is the flying favourite of the Bermudians as it glides through the summer skies during its regular visits to the islands. Jewellery models of the longtail are very popular with holiday visitors. The best months for birdwatching are November-April. There are several good areas for birdwatchers and naturalists, with trails and preserves. Spittal Pond, on South Shore Road, is the largest, and easily accessible (see below, **Excursions**). Penshurst Park covers 15 acres of the North Shore and there is the Arboretum, Middle Road, Devonshire. For further information contact the Bermuda Audubon Society, PO Box HM 1328, Hamilton HM FX, T 236 6483, the Park Ranger or Government Conservation Officer at the Department of Agriculture, Fisheries and Parks, PO Box HM 834, Hamilton HM CX, T 236 4201. Two good books on birds are *A Guide to the Birds of Bermuda*, by Eric Amos, a wildlife artist and birder (T

236 9056), and the *Check List and Guide to the Birds of Bermuda*, by David Wingate, a conservation officer (T 236 4201). Both books are available in local bookshops.

Of the insect "nasties" there are very few of the stinging variety. The principal beast to avoid is the 2- to 4-inch centipede which has poisonous pincers. These fortunately are come across very infrequently. Cockroaches, which are much more prevalent, especially near dampness or where food is stored, are relatively harmless. There is an interesting variety of spiders, moths, butterflies and the less interesting mosquito, which can irritate but does not usually pose a problem.

Diving and Marine Life

The extensive coral reef barrier combined with the warmth of the gulf stream provides excellent feeding and breeding grounds for varieties of colourful tropical and reef fish. The shallowness of some of the reef areas and rock formations in clear, relatively calm inshore waters make excellent snorkelling conditions. Beyond the reef some of the most popular game fish can be found. Although commercial fishing is restricted to holders of fishing licences, and the catching of lobster and conch is regulated, in recent years concern has been expressed, not least by the conservation organizations (Friends of Fish), that fish stocks are decreasing at an alarming rate. In 1990 the Government announced a ban on pot fishing, together with limits on permitted catches by fishing boats. Protected species include marine turtles, whales, porpoises, dolphins, corals, sea rods, sea fans, conch, helmet shells, bonnet shells, netted olive shells, Bermuda cone shells, scallops, Atlantic pearl oyster, calico clams and West Indian top shells. Spear guns are forbidden and no spear fishing is allowed within a mile of the shore. Lobsters may only be taken by licensed residents and only from 1 September-31

March. For information on fishing contact Tom Smith (T 238 0112), secretary of the Bermuda Game Fishing Association and representative of the International Game Fish Association.The Tourist Office has a list of charter boats for sport fishing.

The reefs together with the carcasses of many wrecked ships, ranging from Spanish and French galleons to more recent paddleships and steamers, provide memorable scuba-diving. A number of well trained operators run daily excursions and give guidance to novice and experienced divers. All equipment is available for hire. Among the several local diving operators are Blue Water Divers Ltd at Robinson's Marina, Somerset Bridge, Sandys (T 234 1034, F 234 3561), 2 tank dive US$60 (excluding equipment), half day snorkelling US$32 (including equipment), wet suits free of charge if necessary, and Nautilus Diving Ltd at *Southampton Princess Hotel* (T 238 2332, F 236 4284, March-December 0830-1730), 2 tank dive US$65 (including all equipment), snorkelling US$25, both dive shops offer resort courses for US$82. Other companies with similar rates include Dive Bermuda, 6 Dockyard Terrace, Sandys (T 234 0225, F 238 8564), open March-December, certified divers only. Fantasea Diving, Darrells Wharf, Harbour Road, Paget (T 236 6339 open all year), South Side Scuba Watersports, at *Grotto Bay Beach Hotel*, Hamilton Parish, and at *Sonesta Beach*, Southampton (T 293 2915 open all year).

The local branch of the British Sub Aqua Club (BSAC), based in Admiralty Park, Pembroke, has been operating and training novices since 1971. Members of BSAC visiting Bermuda are recommended to contact the dive leader for information and advice for favoured inshore and off-shore diving sites. Recommended diving sites include South West Breaker (off *Sonesta Beach Hotel*), John Smith's Bay and L'Hermione (from Somerset Bridge). There is a recompression chamber at King Edward VII Memorial Hospital, Point Finger Road, Paget.

Two operators offer helmet diving, which you do by walking, not swimming, underwater at a depth of 10 feet (the open-bottomed helmet is like a glass inverted in water, creating a vacuum, fresh air is pumped in through the top and bubbles escape at the bottom, your hair stays dry and you can reach inside, the helmet appears weightless): Bronson Hartley, Flatt's Village, Smith's (T 292 4434, 1 May-31October, daily 1000 and 1400, weather permitting) and Greg Hartley, Sandys (T/F 234 2861, 15 April-15 November, 1000 and 1330), both do 3-hour glass bottomed boat tour and half-hour shallow dive for US\$40.

Beaches and Watersports

The beach-going and water sport season for Bermudians traditionally runs from 24 May (Queen Victoria's birthday: Empire Day, now Bermuda Day) to October when sea temperatures can reach a maximum of 32°C (average in July/August 26°C). Sea temperatures rarely fall below 19°C at any time during the year. The blue and turquoise tones of the sea are striking, and the pink-tinted coral beaches of soft powdery sand are exceptional. Horseshoe Bay, Church Bay, Warwick Long Bay and Elbow Beach are favourites and are cleaned regularly. Lifeguards are on duty at certain times at Horseshoe Beach and John Smith's Bay. Unleashed dogs are not allowed on public beaches. It is important for swimmers to be aware of under-currents which can be strong. They should also watch for portuguese-man-of-war jelly fish, fortunately only a threat during February and March. The unmistakable floating 2-8 inch long cigar shaped wind bag supports up to ten foot long tentacles which can give nasty multiple stings.

Several operators, mainly in Hamilton and St George, run glass-bottomed boat tours, game fishing, snorkelling, wind surfing, parasailing (US\$45), water ski-ing (US\$50-60/30 minutes) and a host of other activities. Prices for glass-bottomed boat cruises with snorkelling are US\$30-38 for 3½-4 hours. Boardsailing rentals at Mangrove Marina (T 234 0914) are US\$15/hour, US\$50/day, while group lessons are US\$35/1½ hours pp, but at South Side Scuba Watersports at *Grotto Bay Beach Hotel*, T 293 2915 and *Marriott's Castle Harbour Resort*, T 293 2915, boards cost US\$20/hour, US\$80/day.

Sailing is one of the most popular watersports for residents. Sunfish and other craft can be rented for US\$20-35 for 2 hours from Mangrove Marina, end of Cambridge Road, Mangrove Bay, Somerset (T 234 0914), Pompano Beach Club Watersports Centre (T 234 0222, open mid-May-late October), Rance's Boatyard (T 292 1843), Robinson's Charter Boat Marina (T 234 0709), Salt Kettle Boat Rentals (T 236 4863) and South Side Scuba Watersports (T 293 2915), the last two also offering sailing instruction. Chartered yachts with licensed skippers are available from US\$250/half day. Visitors with some previous crewing experience can seek crewing opportunities at the Royal Hamilton Yacht Club and Dinghy Club. As well as casual sailing in and around the islands, there are substantial numbers of week-end racing events which take place in the Great Sound for various classes of boats.

Other Sports

The principal land sport (competitive and part time) is **golf** and there are more golf courses per square mile than anywhere else in the world. "Make your friends green with envy at one easy stroke" from a choice of eight scenic golf courses providing a stimulating variety of play for the beginner or the professional. An introduction can be arranged through the visitor's hotel or guest house. Port Royal is owned and operated by the government and the green fee is US$40 compared with US$24 at Ocean View Golf Course and US$95 at Mid Ocean Club where introduction by a member is required. Bermudians generally take a break from golf from May until September when it gets cooler again. A useful tip to bear in mind is that from 1600 green fees on some courses are reduced by fifty per cent. Caddies are available only at Mid Ocean Club, US$25 per bag; lessons are offered from US$25/½hour; a full set of clubs rents from US$10, hand golf carts from US$5, gas carts from US$26 and shoes US$5. Reseeding is done late September to early November, depending on the weather; some courses use temporary greens. There are several international tournaments held on a number of courses. The Bermuda Golf Guide published by the Bermuda Department of Tourism tells you all you need to know about the clubs, courses and fees. For schedules of tournaments (held throughout the year) contact the Bermuda Golf Association, PO Box HM 433, Hamilton HM BX, T 238 1367.

Running and **cycling** are popular and a number of marathon and triathlon events are held annually. Walking the old railway trail is a relaxing and pleasurable way of exploring the heart of Bermuda's countryside, and you can appreciate the flowers, trees, birds and small creatures in their natural setting. *The Bermuda Railway Trail Guide* is available from the Visitor's Service Bureau. The Guide describes the trail in sections of 1¾-3¾ miles, some of which are suitable for bicycles and motor bikes, but most can be walked only. Some parks are available for picnics.

The larger hotels have **tennis** courts, rates vary considerably from free to US$12 for house guests and up to US$15 for visitors. There is a Government Tennis Stadium at Pembroke (T 292 0105) with teaching pro, US$5 on clay, US$4 on asphalt, lessons US$20/½hour; the private Coral Beach and Tennis Club, South Road, Paget (T 236 2233), several pros, eight clay courts, introduction by member only; the Pomander Gate Tennis Club, Paget (T 236 5400), has four hard courts, US$10; the Port Royal Club, Southampton (T 234 0974), has four flexipave courts, US$8, pro on request. Proper tennis clothes are required everywhere. Rackets and balls can be rented. Tournaments are held throughout the year, for details contact the Bermuda Lawn Tennis Association, PO Box HM 341, Hamilton HM BX, Bermuda.

There are two English size **squash** courts at the Coral Beach and Tennis Club, South Road, Paget (T 236 2233) and four international size courts at the Bermuda Squash Racquets Club next to the National's Sports Club, Middle Road, Devonshire (T 292 6881), open 1000-2300 by reservation, US$5 pp for 40 minutes plus court fee US$4.50-6.50.

There is a strong **rugby union** following, particularly amongst British ex-patriots. The principal local teams are called the Mariners, Police, Renegades and Teachers. Bermuda has a national side that competes in a number of international fixtures at home or abroad. The Rugby Classic is held at Easter, with the Irish Invitational XV against the Bermuda Invitational XV, while the World Rugby Classic in November has teams of former international players competing. League football and cricket are also very popular, with the highlight of the **cricket** calendar being Cup Match Day between E and W end clubs, which is a national holiday. **Horse riding** is strictly controlled and you must be accompanied by a qualified instructor. Lee Bow Riding Centre, Tribe Road 1, Devonshire (T 236 4181), lessons available daily by reservation, trail rides US$25/hour. Spicelands Riding Centre, Middle Road, Warwick (T 238 8212), trail rides US$25/hour, 0645 ride along South Shore followed by breakfast US$37.50, lessons available on request. For information on horse shows, gymkhanas etc, contact the Bermuda

Equestrian Federation, PO Box DV 583, Devonshire DV BX, Bermuda.

Festivals

The principal festival is now the spring "cultural" festival running between January and March with six weeks of dance, music, drama and popular entertainment. There is an annual street festival in March on Front Street, Hamilton, with crafts, local music, exhibits. The Peppercorn ceremony (see above) in St George's is in April. May is Bermuda Heritage Month with cultural and sporting activities culminating on Bermuda Day. Sailing regattas during the summer, in particular the fitted dinghy race series, are held in Hamilton and St George harbour, Cup Match Cricket Festival (two days at end July) and Gombeys dancing are the main occasions. The military brass band adds colour to a number of celebrations and anniversary proceedings.

HAMILTON

Hamilton (population approximately 6,000), in the parish of Pembroke is the capital, located centrally in the island chain. Traditionally a harbour town, it is laid out almost geometrically, on rising ground. In recent years its development as a business centre has been phenomenal and building projects have proliferated. At the present time, there is a government restriction on the height of buildings. Most of the duty-free shops are located along Front Street facing the water.

Bermuda has the third oldest parliament in the world and the Sessions House was built in 1817, when the seat of Government was moved from St George's, where Parliament had sat for two centuries. The Golden Jubilee clocktower and terracotta colonnade were added in 1887. Open Monday-Friday 0900-1700, T 292 7408, you can watch debates from the Visitors' Gallery when Parliament meets,

October-July on Fridays at 1000. The Supreme Court, also in the Sessions House, meets most of the year. The Cabinet Building and Senate Chamber, opposite, are also open to the public Monday-Friday 0900-1700, T 292 5501, and you can watch Senate debates on Wednesdays.

The Library, Queen Street, Hamilton is a well-maintained and stocked library, in a quiet attractive building where the international press can be read freely. Open Monday-Friday 0930-1800, Saturday 0930-1700. It is situated next to the Par-la-Ville Gardens, originally the private garden to the town house, Par-la-Ville, now the Bermuda Historical Society Museum, open Monday-Saturday 0930-1230, 1400-1630, T 295 2487.

ST GEORGE

St George (population approximately 3,000) was the capital until 1815. This old harbour town is located at the N end of the island, not far from Kindley Field airport. The town with its quaint old houses, walled gardens and picturesque alleyways was said to have been the setting of Shakespeare's *The Tempest*: "the vexed Bermoothes".

Bermudians and visitors have worshipped undisturbed in the Anglican St Peter's Church, Kings Square, St George since the present church was built in 1713, which represents the longest continued use in the Western Hemisphere. The original church, built in 1612, was wooden and thatched with palmetto leaf; a stone structure replaced it in 1619. The tower was added to the 1713 building in 1814. Donations welcome.

The **State House** (open 1000-1600 Wednesdays), on Princess Street at the top of King Street, is the oldest building in Bermuda. It was built by Governor Nathaniel Butler in 1620 and while St George was the capital the House of Assembly and the principal court met here. It is currently rented to a Masonic Lodge

(Lodge St George No 200 of the Grand Lodge of Scotland) for one peppercorn a year; the Peppercorn Ceremony in April is a highlight of the town's annual festivities.

Bridge House, on Bridge Street off the King's Square, dates from the beginning of the 18th century and was the home of several governors, now owned by the Bermuda National Trust and used as an art gallery, open Monday-Saturday, 1000-1700, in summer Sun 1100-1500. Cedar furniture and Bermudan antiquities can be seen at St George's Historical Society Museum, Featherbed Alley, on Duke of Kent Street, open Monday-Friday except holidays, 1000-1600, entrance US$2, children 6-16 US$0.50, under 6 free.

Other museums include three owned by the Bermuda National Trust: Tucker House, on Water Street, containing cedar furniture and items collected by the prominent Bermudan Tucker family, open Monday-Saturday except holidays, 0930-1630 April-October, 1000-1600 November-March, entrance US$3 or by US$6 combination ticket; The Old Rectory, Broad Alley, off Church Street, open Wednesdays 1200-1700, donations welcome, T 297 0878; and the Confederate Museum, King's Square, built in 1700 by Governor Samuel Day, now housing memorabilia from the American Civil War, open Monday-Saturday, 0930-1630 April-October, 1000-1600 November-March, closed holidays, entrance US$3 or by combination ticket.

The replica of *The Deliverance* off Ordnance Island, St George's, is open for visitors 1000-1600 Monday-Saturday and most holidays, closed December-March, Good Friday, Easter Sunday, admission US$2.50, children US$0.50, proceeds in aid of local charities.

Excursions

Some of the most attractive and interesting places to visit can be reached rela-tively easily by moped (see below on moped hire). A selection of sights worth visiting are: Fort St Catherine at the NE tip of St George's. The restored fort that once defended Bermuda contains exhibits and military memorabilia covering the island's history. Open daily except Christmas Day, 1000-1600, entrance US$2.50, children under 12 free. Fort Hamilton, overlooking Hamilton, designed by the Duke of Wellington to protect the Royal Naval Dockyard from land attack. Underground passages were cut through rock in the 1870s but the moat is now a pleasant garden. Open Monday-Friday 0930-1700, admission free. There are so many fortifications on Bermuda that the Tourist Board has a leaflet just on forts, some of which are easily accessible and in good condition.

The Royal Naval Dockyard was built on Ireland Island North as a winter anchorage and major dockyard to repair Royal Naval ships used to protect trans-Atlantic shipping. Work began in 1809 and the hard labour was carried out by slaves and thousands of British convicts, many of whom died of yellow fever. H M Dockyard was opened to the public in 1951 when Royal Navy operations ceased, and there are many fine stone buildings, fortifications and wharfs, some of which have been converted for other uses. The Bermuda Maritime Museum in the fortified keep displays Bermuda's nautical heritage over the last 4 centuries (entrance US$6, children 4-12 US$2, under 4 years free, open 1000-1630 daily except Christmas Day. Other things to visit at the dockyard include the Victualling Yard and the Cooperage, a secure area for storing food that was preserved in barrels made by the cooper; the Bermuda Arts Centre, open Tuesday-Saturday 1000-1600, Sunday 1200-1700, entrance free, exhibitions change every month and feature Bermudian and foreign artists, photographers, sculptors and craftsmen; the Craft Market, open daily 1000-1700 and some holidays, demonstrations begin at 1100 in the Cooperage. Guided walking tours at 1200 and 1430, US$2 adults, children free, starting at the Cooperage.

Spittal Pond, near John Smith's Bay in Smiths parish, is the island's largest nature reserve comprising 60 acres of lush parkland, home of much of Bermuda's wildlife. November-March are the best months for birdwatching; there are many migratory and resident water fowl, herons, terns, ducks, a pair of flamingoes and in the cliff face longtails nest. At the end of the trail to Spanish Rock there is a bronze plaque of the inscription TF 1543, believed to have been carved by an early Portuguese explorer. **The Bermuda Aquarium, Museum and Zoo**, at Flatts Village, Smith's parish. Located at the seaward entrance to Harrington Sound, the aquarium has a wide selection of healthy-looking marine life in a natural environment and there is a reptile walkway, aviary, primate enclosure, petting zoo and invertebrate house (entrance US$5 per person, US$2 children 5-12 years, free under 5 years, open 0900-1700, last admission 1630, closed Christmas Day). **Crystal Leamington Caves** (T 293 0640, open 0930-1630 most days, special schedule in winter, call in advance, US$4 adults, US$2 5-11 years, under fives free) and **Leamington's Amber Caves**, both along Harrington Sound Road, Smith's Parish (T 293 1188, open 0930-1600, Monday-Saturday, closed Sundays, holidays and late November-mid-February, US$4 adults, US$2 4-12 years: stunning tours along walkways through limestone rock and salt formations in well-lit underground caves.

Botanical Gardens, South Road, Paget. This is a quiet and uncrowded 36-acre park where visitors may stroll or picnic amid sub-tropical floral gardens and bird song. There is an orchid house, an aviary, formal gardens, a hibiscus garden containing 150 varieties, a palm garden, sub-tropical fruit garden and a garden for the blind with scented plants and herbs. Open sunrise to sunset, guided tours Tuesday, Wednesday, Friday (April-October), Tuesday and Friday November-March) at 1030 from the main car park. Also in the Gardens is Camden, the official residence of the Premier, an 18th century mansion containing some superb cedar furniture and paintings, open Tuesday-Friday 1200-1400 unless there are official functions, admission free.

Gibbs Hill Lighthouse, off Lighthouse Road, Southampton. Shining since 1846, its 185 steps lead up one of the few cast-iron constructed lighthouses. It has a commanding view of the islands and the Great Sound. Open 0900-1630, closed Christmas Day, US$2 entrance, under 5 years free.

INFORMATION FOR VISITORS

● **Documents**

All visitors must be able to present a return ticket or onward ticket, or other document of onward transportation. Visitors from the United Kingdom and Western Europe are required to present a valid Passport. Visitors from the United States are required to present either a passport (if recently expired the photograph should resemble bearer) or birth certificate issued by a competent municipal authority with a raised seal (or certified copy), or a US Re-entry Permit, US Naturalization Certificate, or US Alien Registration card. Visitors from Canada are required by the Bermuda Immigration Authorities to present either a valid passport, a Birth Certificate, or a Canadian Certificate of Citizenship. Visas are required for visitors from Albania, Algeria, Armenia, Azerbaijan, Belarus, Bosnia-Hercegovina, Bulgaria, China (People's Republic of), Croatia, Cuba, Czechoslovakia (former), Georgia, Haiti, Hungary, Iran, Iraq, Jordan, Kampuchea (Cambodia), Kazakhstan, Kirgizstan, Laos, Lebanon, Libya, Macedonia, Moldova, Mongolia, Morocco, Nigeria, North Korea, Philippines, Poland, Romania, Russian Federation, Slovakia, Slovenia, South Africa, the former Soviet Union, Sri Lanka, Syria, Tajikistan, Tunisia, Turkmenistan, Ukraine, Uzbekistan, Vietnam and the former Yugoslavia.

All bona fide visitors may stay in Bermuda for a reasonable period of time, usually up to 3 or 4 weeks. Passengers arriving with an open return ticket will have a time limit imposed. Permission to stay longer may have to be sought from the Immigration Department.

Bermuda has a very strict immigration control policy over non-Bermudian workers. Only nationals who have acquired "status" can freely look for employment.

● **How To Get There**

Air links from the United Kingdom, United States and Canada are good. British Airways operates direct services 3 times a week from London (Gatwick) with a flight time of approximately 7 hours. There are also direct links and regular scheduled flights from New York, Boston, Atlanta, Baltimore, Charlotte, Cleveland, Detroit, Hartford, Chicago, Tampa/St Petersburg, Raleigh/Durham, Pittsburgh, Philadelphia, Toronto and Halifax by American Airlines, Air Canada, Delta, North West Airlines, Continental and US Air. Look out for budget-priced tours advertized in major US weekend papers.

There are connections to a number of Caribbean islands via the USA.

The international airport at Kindley Field is 12 miles (20 km) from Hamilton. A US$15 departure tax is charged on visitors and residents alike. Children under 2 years exempt, children between 2 and 11 years US$5. Be prepared for handlers who will expect a gratuity tip somewhere in the region of US$1 to US$2 for carrying baggage the short distance between the baggage collections, through customs, to the taxi rank. The cost of a taxi ride to cover the 35-min journey to Hamilton is approximately US$15. During the daytime the journey provides an excellent introduction to Bermuda's countryside and the cab driver will have the weather predictions at hand.

By Sea: The Royal Caribbean Cruise Line operates a weekly cruise service between New York and Hamilton. Additionally Celebrity Cruises and Norwegian Cruise Line visit the islands regularly throughout the summer. Other cruise lines operate occasional services from various ports, including Crystal Cruises, Cunard (QE2), Costa Line Cruises, Royal Viking Line and Regency Cruises. Some of the larger liners have to drop anchor in the Great Sound when passengers continue their journey by ferry. The government levies a US$60 tax on all visitors collected by tour operators. Passengers arriving by yacht pay a US$15 tax.

● **Customs**

Visitors may bring into Bermuda duty-free, all clothing and articles for their personal use, including sports equipment, cameras, golf bags etc. Also 50 cigars, 200 cigarettes, 1lb of tobacco, 1 quart of wine and 1 quart of spirit. You may also take in 20lbs of meat duty free for personal consumption. On all other foodstuffs duty will be charged at approximately 5½-22¼% of market value estimates. Pets will be refused entry without proper documentation.

US customs pre-clearance is available in Bermuda for all scheduled flights. Declaration forms are stocked by hotels, travel agencies and airlines.

● **Local Travel**

Motor cars were not admitted until 1947 and they are limited to size and number (one car per registered household). The official traffic speed limit is 20 mph (35 kph) and 15 mph in city limits. Vehicles drive on the left along narrow roads which, in some places, are unpaved. Serious penalties are imposed on drivers recklessly exceeding the speed limit. International Driving Licences are not valid and car users must have a valid Bermuda driver's licence which can only be obtained after taking a practical and written test. Consequently there are no car-hire facilities whatsoever.

There is a regular **bus** service network to most parts of the island along the 125 miles of road. Buses depart from the main terminal in Hamilton from approximately 0600 to 1830. The only exception being the number 8 which travels along the middle road to Dockyard.

The cost of a bus from Hamilton to the airport is US$3 (children US$0.65). Exact change (coins only), tokens or tickets are required. These can be bought from some hotels, sub-post offices and the Central Terminal on Church Street, Hamilton, next to City Hall. Some saving can be made if you purchase a booklet of 15 tickets for US$18 (14 zones) and US$10 (3 zones). Multi-day passes which provide unlimited travel on buses or ferries for 3 (US$17.50) or 7 days (US$27.50) are available from the Hamilton bus terminal and the Visitors Service Bureau. Bus timetables are readily available.

Taxis are common, but hard to find in bad weather. Radio cabs should be called in advance of important journeys. Taxis are metered and cost US$4 for the first mile and US$1.40 each mile beyond. From 2200 to 0600 there is a surcharge. Parcels carried in the boot or on the roof are US$0.25 each. Hourly/daily rates can be arranged for island tours, US$20/hr 1-4 passengers, US$30/hr 5-6 passengers. Six consecutive daylight hours constitute a full day.

Ferry boats run frequently from Hamilton to Paget (US$1.50), Salt Kettle, Warwick, Somerset, Watford Bridge and Dockyard (US$3). Bicycles may be taken on board Somerset/Dockyard ferry only, same price as passenger.

Mopeds are the most popular form of transport for residents and tourists aged 16 and over. Machines can be hired relatively easily for about US$75 per week, inclusive of helmet and insurance, and without having had previous driving experience. Gasoline stations are open 0700-1900 Mon-Sat (although a few open until 2300), with limited opening hours on Sun and holidays. Bicycles and tandems can also be hired. The charge for a horse-drawn carriage is approximately US$40 per hour.

● **Where To Stay**

There is a wide selection of hotels, guest houses, "self catering" and private houses and condominiums where visitors can make arrangements to stay. All properties taking 6 or more guests are licensed and listed by the Bermuda Department of Tourism. Most hotels are in the luxury class, but cheaper accommodation can be found. No camping facilities exist and camping on the beaches is not allowed. The peak holiday season commences in May and visitors are advised to make their bookings well in advance. High season rates for the most expensive hotels can be around US$400 per person per night plus tax and service. Accommodation at the cheaper end of the range is unlikely to be less than US$100 per night. Summer 1994 rates are quoted here. All room rates are subject to a 6% government tax and service charges will also be added to your bill. Some hotels and apartments levy an energy surcharge. In Jan, Feb, Mar 1994 many hotels offered a 20% discount on the room rate if the temperature fell below 68°F, check whether the same scheme will be continued in future springs.

In **Hamilton**, the principal hotels include the *Hamilton Princess* (US$195-285d, 456 rooms, private beach at *Southampton Princess*, fresh and salt water pools, sports facilities, convention centre, PO Box HM 837, T 295 3000, F 295 1914) and the *Rosedon* (US$144-206d EP, 43 rooms in main house or garden section, a/c, phone, fridge, fans, coffee makers, no credit cards, pool, breakfast and light meals in rooms, on verandahs or poolside,

lovely colonial building, 5-minute walk into Hamilton, PO Box HM 290, T 295-1640, F 295 5904). Out of town, along Harbour Road, Paget are *Palm Reef* (US$120-190d EP, 94 rooms, energy surcharge US$2 pp/day, use of *Elbow Beach's* private beach, salt water pool, dining room and coffee shop, PO Box HM 1189, T 236 1000, F 236 6392), Middle Road Warwick; the *White Sands Hotel and Cottages* (US$150-200d EP, overlooking Grape Bay, 32 rooms, 3 cottages on waterfront, pool, 5 mins' walk to beach, a/c, weekly barbeque, jackets after 1800, 2 miles from Hamilton, PO Box PG 174, T 236 2023, F 236 2486); the *Stonington Beach* (US$270-330d, light breakfast and service inc, 64 rooms, 1 room with facilities for handicapped, prefer no children under 5, private beach, pool, tennis, serviced by students of hotel technology, PO Box HM 523, T 236 5416, F 236 0371); and the *Belmont Hotel Golf and Country Club* (US$230-325d, BP 151 rooms, resort type hotel, shuttle bus to beach, salt water pool, rates include unlimited daytime tennis and golf, watersports arranged, PO Box WK 251, T 236 1301, F 236 6867); and on South Shore Road the *Elbow Beach* (US$265-490d BP, plus US$10.50pp service charge and US$3.18pp resort levy per day, 298 rooms and suites, resort type hotel, tennis, health club, private beach, salt water pool, games room, PO Box HM 455, T 236 3535, F 236 8043); *Sonesta* (US$198-385d EP, 403 rooms and suites, 3 private beaches, indoor and outdoor pools, health spa, games room, children's playground, tennis, croquet, scuba on site, PO Box HM 1070, T 238 8122, F 238 8463); *Coral Beach* (US$236-500d, introduction by club member required, 66 rooms and cottages, no credit cards, private beach, tennis, squash, putting green, croquet, bowls, pool, T 236 2233, F 236 1876); *Southampton Princess* (US$355-495d MAP, 600 rooms, suites available, indoor and outdoor pool, tennis, golf course, scuba diving, private beach, PO Box HM 1379, T 238 8000, F 238 8245), and *The Reefs* (US$278-340d BP, 65 rooms and cottage suites, no credit cards, tennis, scuba diving next door, pool, beach, T 238 0222, F 238 8372). *Horizons*, German-managed, main house and cottages (US$234-574d BP or cottage for four US$440-860, no credit cards, pool, tennis, pitch-and-putt golf and putting green, PO Box PG 198, T 236 0048, F 236 1981). Nearer to the Airport is the *Marriott's Castle Harbour* (US$225-350d EP, 415 rooms and suites, championship golf course, tennis, watersports, convention centre, beach, 3 pools, PO Box HM 841, T 293 2040, F 293 8288).

The larger guesthouses are often old Bermuda mansions which have been converted, some have dining rooms and pools. *Fordham Hall* on Pitt's Bay Road in Pembroke Parish, PO Box HM 692, T 295 1551, F 295 3906, within walking distance of Hamilton, US$98d CP summer, 12 rooms with bathroom, fans, suites for 4 people US$150; *Loughlands*, 79 South Road, Paget, T 236 1253, set in 9 acres in the middle of the island, a/c, tennis, pool, US$90-114d CP, 25 rooms, no credit cards, single rooms available; *Oxford House*, close to bus and ferry terminals in Hamilton, family run, a/c, US$130d CP, 12 rooms, triples, quads, PO Box HM 374, T 295 0503, F 295 0250; *Hillcrest Guest House*, Nea's Alley, off Old Maid's Lane, St George's, PO Box GE 96, T 297 1630, lovely old building, lawns and gardens, US$65d EP all year, 11 rooms, singles available, no credit cards; *Edgehill Manor*, Rosemont Avenue, near Hamilton, PO Box HM 1048, T 295 7124, F 295 3850, 9 large rooms, good breakfast, pool, US$105-120d CP, no credit cards. A full list of current tourist accommodation prices and service charges can be obtained from the Tourist Board of Bermuda and Travel Agencies. Not all hotels and guest houses accept credit cards; check beforehand.

● **What And Where To Eat And Drink**
When dining out it is advisable to dress smartly. There is a wide choice of quality restaurants serving international gourmet and Bermuda specialities. Lobster and fish chowder with sherry peppers is a special favourite, while mussel pie, conch stew, shark, wahoo and tuna steaks are also popular dishes. Local desserts include sweet potato pudding, bay grape jelly, syllabub and guava jelly. The price of a 3 course dinner for 2 will vary between US$65 and US$85 (plus gratuities of 15%) depending upon which bottle of wine is chosen from the usually comprehensive selection of US and European wines. A meal in one of the very top restaurants with a superior wine may cost up to US$150. The Department of Tourism produces a booklet, *Dining Out in Bermuda*, which includes menus from many restaurants and is published twice a year.

Some restaurant chains promote seasonal "dine about" offers which represent extremely good value, for example, vouchers can sometimes be purchased and exchanged for a 3

course evening meal exclusive of wine and service at each of *The Little Venice* lunch 1145-1430 Mon-Fri, dinner 1830-2230 daily, T 295 3503), La Trattoria (Washington Lane between Reid and Church St, T 292 7059, Mon-Sat 1130-1530, 1800-2230) and *The Harbour Front* in Hamilton. The vouchers also give free entry to the *Club* discothèque situated above *The Little Venice* restaurant, Bermudiana Road. Hotels in the scheme include *Stonnington Beach, Fourways Inn, Lantana, Colony Club, Glencoe Harbour Club, Pompana Beach Club and The Reefs*.

The Sun brunch offered by some hotels and restaurants between noon and mid afternoon is a veritable feast costing US$25 per head plus 15% service. You can eat what you like from a wide and generous selection of salads, vegetables and hot and cold meat dishes and desserts.

King Henry VIII (South Shore Road, Southampton, T 238 1977, pub and restaurant) and *The Palmetto*, near Gibbs Hill Lighthouse and the Aquarium at Flatts, respectively, are rec as good value, in pleasant surroundings and close to a place of interest to visit afterwards (keep your receipt from your meal at the *Palmetto* to gain free entry to the Aquarium).

Good restaurants are too numerous to list in full. The most expensive are *Tom Moore's Cabin, The Plantation, Norwood Room* (at the *Stonnington Beach Hotel*, T 236 5416, lunch 1200-1400, dinner 1900-2030, bar 1100-0100), *Once Upon a Table, Fourways Inn* (1 Middle Road, Paget, T 236 6517, lunch 1200-1500, afternoon tea, dinner 1830-2130), *Lantanas* and *Romanoff's* (Church St, Hamilton, T 295 0333, lunch Mon-Fri 1200-1430, dinner Mon-Sat 1900-2200.

For those who require a quick snack there are a number of cheaper, café-style places which can be found easily and where a hamburger, pizza or sandwich and a beer will cost less than US$15.

Supermarkets sell a wide selection of quality food and drinks, mainly imported from North America and Europe. Because most food is imported it is more costly than in the country of origin. As a guide, a loaf of bread costs US$2.50 and a pint of milk is US$0.75.

Tap-water is safe but it is fool-hardy to drink well-water. All kinds of rum punches and cocktails are served and bottled lager is drunk straight from the bottle. A number of bars have "happy hour" between 1700 and 1900 when the price of drinks is reduced from approximately US$4.50 to US$2.50. *The Robin*

Hood, Richmond Road in Hamilton is rec for those who like a lively environment. *The Hood's* pizzas are some of Bermuda's best (delivery service for pizza and other food, T 295 3314). The *Beer Garden*, off Washington Mall. Other "watering holes" on Front Street, Hamilton, worth a visit are *Rum Runners*, *Loquats*, *The Cock and Feather* (also restaurant, 1130-2230, T 295 2263) and, if you prefer traditional (but travelled) English real ale, *The Docksider*. For local atmosphere, try *Casey's Bar*, Queen Street.

● **Entertainment**

In Hamilton are 2 modern cinemas which show recent US and British films. There is also a cinema in Dock Yard. There are periodical theatrical and other shows performed principally at the City Hall, Hamilton, particularly during the Spring Festival when a range of shows are promoted, from jazz to opera. Every Spring programmes include the hilarious productions of the Harvard University dramatic society's *Hasty Pudding*. In November look out for the very popular satirical production of *Not the Um Um Show*, performed at the Clayhouse Inn, North Shore Road. ("Um Um" is a sort of speech impediment peculiar to many Bermudians). At Christmas there is a traditional pantomime. After dinner, many people go to the discothèque or stroll along the harbour front.

● **Best Buys**

Bermuda is famous for its local artwork. During the off season the major stores, Trimminghams, Coopers, Smiths and Pearman Watlington, Marks and Spencers have genuine reductions on a range of quality goods. Particularly popular are Italian and Scottish wool and cotton pullovers. For US visitors British and European glass, china and perfumes are good buys. At duty-free shopping outlets minimum purchase is 2 1-litre bottles of spirit or fortified wine.

● **Banks**

The majority of international banks have representation in Hamilton. The 3 Bermuda banks are The Bank of Bermuda Ltd, 6 Front Street, Hamilton HM 11 (with branches in Par-La-Ville and Church Street, Hamilton and in Somerset and St George and the Civil Air Terminal Building), which has 13 ATM machines linked to the Visa/Plus system for cash advances, of which 10 are open 24 hours; The Bank of N T Butterfield and Son Ltd, 65 Front Street, Hamilton HM 12 (with branches at the Rosebank Building, Bermudiana Road, Hamilton, Somerset

and St George and *Southampton Princess Hotel*); and Bermuda Commercial Bank Ltd, affiliated to Barclays Bank, Church Street, Hamilton HM12 (which has a cashing facility at the Airport). Bank hours are 0930 to 1500 Mon to Fri and 1630 to 1730 Fri only.

● **Currency**

The legal currency is the Bermuda Dollar (Bd$) which bears the head of Queen Elizabeth II. US dollars are accepted virtually everywhere and are interchangeable with the Bermuda dollar at par (ie 1 Bermuda dollar = US$1). Canadian currency is also accepted, but not so widely. There are exchange control regulations designed to prevent the transfer of dollars out of the country. Exchange rates for all currencies are available from any bank, US travellers' cheques can be cashed everywhere and international bank credit cards are widely accepted. Better rates of exchange currently can be obtained in Bermuda itself, although it is advisable to have some US or Bermudian currency on arrival.

● **Health**

Sanitation is good and the standard of hygiene and health care extremely high, but expensive. Medical insurance is therefore rec. King Edward VII memorial hospital in Point Finger Road just outside Hamilton is well-equipped and operates the only civilian recompression chamber. There are a number of general practitioners and clinics principally in Hamilton, but also around the island.

Mosquitoes no longer present a problem and there are very few stinging insects. Repellent sprays are not therefore essential but if needed can be purchased locally from a number of well-stocked pharmacies. The main hazards for visitors are over-exposure to the sun, moped accidents and irresponsible diving. Should you be stung by jelly fish, a solution of ammonia will relieve the pain. Rain water is collected for drinking, washing and cooking although some of the large hotels operate their own desalination plants.

● **Climate**

The climate is sub-tropical, with sunshine averaging between 7 and 8 hours a day. High rainfall of approximately 65 inches per year falls mainly between October and March. The summer season runs from May to October but in February, the coolest month, temperatures rarely drop below 60°F (15°C). The peak temperatures are in July and August when they can average 85°F (30°C). Humidity reaches a peak in August and September when sporadic winds can sometimes reach hurricane force. The last major hurricane was "Emily" in September 1987 which hit the island by surprise. In the summer months, the sun rises at approximately 0600 and sets at about 2000.

● Clothing

As a rule always dress conventionally. Bathing suits, abbreviated tops, trunks or bare feet are only appropriate on the beach or pool side. There is no nudism on the beaches. It is an offence to ride a cycle or appear in public without a shirt or just wearing a bathing suit. Casual sports-style clothes are fine for day time, but men should be prepared to wear jacket and tie in the evening in smart restaurants. Local smart and office wear, for men, is the tailored Bermuda shorts, blazer and knee-length socks. Holiday visitors should bring light-weight clothes and shower proof rain gear. An umbrella could be useful, but it's likely to be too windy to use satisfactorily.

● National Holidays

New Year's Day (1 January), Good Friday, Bermuda Day (24 May), the Queen's Birthday (12 June), Cup Match and Somer's Day (late July), Labour Day (4 September), Remembrance Day (12 November), Christmas and Boxing Day (25 and 26 December). When a public holiday falls on a Saturday, the following Monday is usually a holiday.

● Time Zone

Atlantic Standard Time, 4 hours behind GMT, 1 ahead of EST.

● Post

The Bermuda Post Office has its headquarters at Church and Parliament Streets, Hamilton 5-24. Sub-post offices can be found throughout the parishes. Airmail leaves and arrives daily; International Data Express is a 48-hour mail delivery service to most international destinations; surface mail is airlifted at regular intervals.

● Telecommunications

Bermuda has a modern automated telephone and cable system operated with the assistance of Cable and Wireless Plc which links Bermuda with the rest of the world by satellite and submarine cable to the USA. International telephone, telex, data transmission and facsimile facilities are available and most countries can be dialled directly. Cable and Wireless Plc's Administrative Office is in Church Street, Hamilton, T 295 1815. The international prefix for Bermuda is 809 followed by the local 7 digit number.

● Press

The *Royal Gazette* is the only daily (not Sun) newspaper. The *Bermudan Sun* and *Mid Ocean News* are weeklies published on Fri.

● Bermuda National Trust

The BNT owns several historical properties open to the public. Members with a valid membership card are admitted free (although several are free anyway) and there is a reciprocal agreement with National Trusts in Britain and several other countries. A BNT combination ticket is US$6 and covers entry to all properties. The National Trust headquarters is at Waterville, Harbour Road, Paget, T 236 6483, open 0900-1700 Mon-Fri, closed all holidays.

● Bermuda Department Of Tourism

For further tourist information, contact the following: **in Bermuda**, Bermuda Department of Tourism, Global House, 43 Church Street, Hamilton, Bermuda HM12, T 292 0023, F 292 7537 (PO Box HM 465, Hamilton HM BX, Bermuda); Visitors' Service Bureau, Chamber of Commerce Building, Front Street, Hamilton, Bermuda, T 295 1480. There are Visitor's Information Centres in Hamilton, St George, the Civil Air Terminal and the Naval Dockyard, open

0900-1600 Mon-Fri, 0900-1400 summer Sats. Maps and pamphlets are available for walks and cycle tours.

In the **USA**: Bermuda Department of Tourism, Suite 201, 310 Madison Avenue, New York, NY 10017, T (212) 818-9800, F (212) 983-5289; Suite 803, 245 Peachtree Center Ave, Atlanta, Georgia 30303, T (404) 524-1541, F (404) 586-9933; Suite 1010, 44 School Street, Boston, MA 02108, T (617) 742-0405, F (617) 723-7786; Suite 1070, Randolph-Wacker Building, 150 N Wacker Drive, Chicago, IL 60606, T (312) 782-5486, F (312) 704-6996; Tetley/Mayer and Associates, Suite 601, 3075 Wilshire Blvd, Los Angeles, CA 90010-1293, T (213) 388-1151, F (213) 487-5467.

In **Canada**: Bermuda Department of Tourism, Suite 1004, 1200 Bay Street, Toronto, Ontario M5R 2A5, T (416) 923-9600, F (416) 923-4840.

In the **UK** (European Representative): Bermuda Tourism BCB Ltd, 1 Battersea Church Road, London SW11 3LY T 071-734 8813, F 071-352 6501.

BAHAMAS

CONTENTS

MAPS

THE BAHAMAS is a coral archipelago consisting of some 700 low-lying islands, and over 2,000 cays (pronounced "keys"). The highest hills, on Cat Island, are less than 400 feet and most islands have a maximum height of 100 feet. The total area of the islands is about 5,400 square miles, roughly the same as Jamaica. The whole archipelago extends for about 600 miles SE from the Mantanilla shoal off the coast of Florida to 50 miles N of Haiti. Some of the smaller cays are privately owned but most of them are uninhabited. Nassau, the capital, on New Providence Island, is 184 miles by air from Miami. Freeport, on Grand Bahama island is 60 miles from Florida. The other islands, known as the "Family Islands", or "Out Islands", include Bimini, the Berry Islands, Abaco, Eleuthera (these two are particularly attractive), the Exumas, Andros, Cat Island, Long Island, San Salvador, Rum Cay, Inagua, Acklins and Crooked Island.

The islands are made up of limestone over 5,000 metres deep, most of it Oolite, laid down for more than 150 million years on a gradually sinking sea bed. New material accumulated constantly and the seas of the Bahamas Platform remained remarkably shallow, often only a few metres deep. From the air, the different shades of turquoise, ultramarine and blue in these shallow waters are spectacular. On land, the soil is thin and infertile except for a few pockets of fertile soil. In many places, bare limestone rock is exposed at the surface while much land is swampy, impenetrable and uninhabitable. There are many large cave systems, including the impressive blue holes, formed when sea levels were lower and since flooded. There are no rivers or

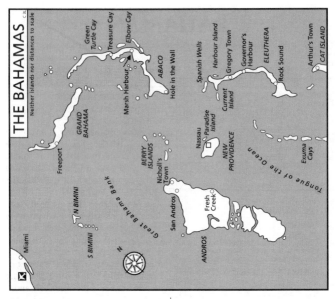

THE BAHAMAS

Neither islands nor distances to scale

Miami · S BIMINI · N BIMINI · N · Great Bahama Bank · Freeport · GRAND BAHAMA · BERRY ISLANDS · Nicholl's Town · San Andros · ANDROS · Fresh Creek · Green Turtle Cay · Treasure Cay · Elbow Cay · Marsh Harbour · ABACO · Hole in the Wall · Nassau · Paradise Island · NEW PROVIDENCE · Spanish Wells · Current Island · Harbour Island · Gregory Town · Governor's Harbour · ELEUTHERA · Rock Sound · Arthur's Town · CAT ISLAND · Exuma Cays · Tongue of the Ocean

streams on any of the islands, but there is some fresh water, found close to the surface but resting on underlying salt water. If wells are drilled too deep, they produce brackish or salt water. Andros has a surplus of fresh water, which is barged to Nassau. Most people drink bottled water.

About 15 island areas have been developed. They have a total population of about 255,000; about 175,000 live in New Providence and 41,000 in Grand Bahama. The weather can be pleasant in the winter season although cold fronts from the North American continent can bring strong N winds, heavy rain and surprisingly low temperatures. The summer months are hot, humid and often windless, with frequent thunderstorms. In August 1992 Hurricane Andrew hit the Bahamas, making over 1,200 homeless, killing four people and causing damage of over US$250m. North Eleuthera was badly damaged and although most resorts soon reopened, houses took longer

to rebuild. However, there is now little evidence of the storm and business is back to normal.

History

The first inhabitants were probably the Siboneys, fishermen who migrated from Florida and the Yucatán. The Indians Columbus found in the S Bahamas were Arawaks, practising a culture called Taínan. They called themselves Lukku-cairi, island people, and became known as Lucayans. They were primitive farmers and fishermen, but produced the best cotton known to the Arawaks. The island of Guanahani is generally credited with Columbus' first landfall in the New World on 12 October 1492. Columbus called Guanahani San Salvador but it was not until 1926 that the Bahamas Parliament officially renamed Watling Island, an island which best fitted his rather vague description, as San Salvador. Columbus visited Rum Cay, which he named Santa María de la Concepción,

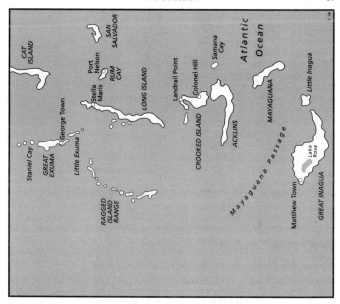

Long Island, which he called Fernandina, and several other islands and cays,
but finding no gold he set off for brighter
horizons. The lack of mineral deposits
meant that the islands held little interest
for the Spanish and there is no evidence
of permanent settlement. However, the
development of Hispaniola and Cuba led
to shortages of labour on those islands
and to the depopulation of the Bahamas
as the Lucayans were captured and carried off as slaves. By 1520 about 20,000
had been captured for use in the plantations, mines or pearl fisheries in the
Spanish colonies and the Bahamas were
uninhabited. The islands and cays became feared by navigators and many
ships were wrecked there, including a
whole fleet of 17 Spanish ships off Abaco
in 1595.

It was after founding their first colonies in Virginia that the English realized
the strategic importance of the Bahamas,
and in 1629 the islands received their
first constitution as part of the Carolinas.

In fact, the first settlers came from Bermuda with the aim of founding a colony
free from the religious and constitutional
troubles of Charles I's England. Then
William Sayle, who had been Governor
of Bermuda, published in London in
1647 *A Broadside Advertising Eleuthera
and the Bahama Islands*. As a result of this
publicity, a company of Eleutherian Adventurers was formed and a party of
about 70 settlers and 28 slaves, led by
Sayle himself, set out for Eleuthera.
Their ship was wrecked on the reefs. The
party managed to land but most of the
stores were lost and the settlers barely
managed to survive by trading ambergris.

From this time on, the life of the Bahamas was largely influenced by their
proximity to the North American mainland and their place on the sea routes.
Piracy, buccaneering and the slave trade
were features of the next two centuries.
Pirates began to make the Bahamas their
base after 1691 when they were thrown

out of Tortuga. Conditions there were perfect, with creeks, shallows, headlands, rocks and reefs for hiding or making surprise attacks. By 1715 there were about 1,000 pirates active in the Bahamas, of whom the most notorious was Blackbeard, who wore his beard in plaits and was renowned for his cruelty. The colony was very poor and survived on the fortunes of shipping, both legal and illicit. In 1739 during the War of Jenkins' Ear, privateering brought a boom in trading activity but peace returned the islands to poverty. A revival of trade during the Seven Years' War was welcomed but peace once more brought depression to Nassau. When not involved in piracy or privateering, many of the inhabitants lived off wrecks, and great was their enthusiasm when whole fleets were destroyed.

A new form of piracy began after the abolition of the British slave trade, when illegal slave traders used the Bahamas as a base to supply the S states of the mainland. This was followed during the 1861-65 American Civil War by the advent of blockade runners, shipowners and adventurers drawn by the prospect of vast profits. New, fast ships were developed which were unable to carry large cargoes and needed to find a safe, neutral port within two or three days' steaming. Nassau was again ideal, and the port prospered, the harbour and shops being packed with merchandise. The captains and pilots of the blockade running ships became as famous as their pirate predecessors. The end of the war provoked a severe and prolonged recession, with the cotton warehouses lying empty for 50 years. The inhabitants turned again to wrecking but even this livelihood was denied them when lighthouses and beacons were introduced, leaving few stretches of dangerous waters.

In 1919, with the advent of Prohibition in the United States, Nassau became a bootleggers' paradise, but with the repeal of Prohibition, this source of wealth dried up and the islands had little to fall back on. The Thirties, a time of severe depression, ended in disaster in 1939 when disease killed off the sponges which had provided some means of livelihood. Once again, it was war which brought prosperity back. This time, however, foundations were laid for more stable conditions in the future and the two bases of prosperity, tourism and offshore finance, became firmly established. Nevertheless, the Bahamas' location and the enormous difficulty in policing thousands of square miles of ocean has attracted both drug trafficking and the laundering of the resulting profits. About 11% of the cocaine entering the USA is officially estimated to pass through the Bahamas. The Bahamas Government, in full cooperation with the US anti-narcotics agencies, has stepped up efforts to eradicate the trade.

For three centuries the merchant class elite of Nassau, known as the "Bay Street Boys", influenced government and prevented universal adult suffrage until 1961. In the 1967 elections, an administration supported by the black majority came to power, led by Lynden (later Sir Lynden) Pindling, of the Progressive Liberal Party (PLP), who retained power until 1992. In the first half of the 1980s allegations were made that he was involved in the drugs trade, but they were never conclusively proven. This and subsequent scandals led to the resignation or removal of a number of public officials, and contributed, together with economic decline, to the growing distrust and unpopularity of the Government. General elections were held in August 1992 and a landslide victory was won by the Free National Movement (FNM), led by Hubert Ingraham. Mr Ingraham, a former PLP minister, had been dismissed from his post as Housing Minister after he supported a move for the resignation of Sir Lynden in 1984. Subsequently expelled from the party, he was elected as an Independent in 1987, joining the

FNM in 1990. The new Prime Minister promised an improved climate for investment and tourism and an end to political patronage. A series of inquiries are now being held into the finances of state corporations including Bahamasair, and the Hotel Corporation, where corruption and misuse of public funds were alleged.

Government

The Bahamas became independent, within the Commonwealth, in July 1973. The new Constitution provided for a Governor General to represent the British monarch who is head of state, a nominated 16-member Senate and an elected, 49-member House of Assembly, with a parliamentary life of a maximum of five years. The Free National Movement (FNM) holds 32 seats while the Progressive Liberal Party (PLP) holds 17.

The Economy

The economy of the Bahamas is based on tourism, financial services and shipping registration. Visitors are attracted throughout the year and since 1986, total arrivals have exceeded 3mn a year, mostly from the USA, of whom over half are cruise ship passengers or day trippers. In 1993, 3.7mn people visited the Bahamas, of which 2.0mn were cruise ship passengers. Also, since 1986, annual total visitor expenditure has exceeded US$1,100mn, about 13% of all tourist spending in the Caribbean region. Stopover tourists spend an average of US$794 per head while cruise ship passengers average US$60-70. In 1990 and 1991 the Gulf war and US recession took their toll on the Bahamian tourist industry with many airlines and hotels shedding staff and fiscal problems becoming more acute. Average hotel occupancy fell to 62% in 1990 and 57% in 1993 as US stopover visitors (82% of the total) declined. Room rates fell as over capacity in the hotel industry became critical. In New Providence the number of hotel

BAHAMAS : FACT FILE

Geographic

Land area	13,939 sq km
forested	32.4%
pastures	0.2%
cultivated	1.0%

Demographic

Population (1992)	264,000
annual growth rate (1987-92)	1.8%
urban	64.3%
rural	35.7%
density	18.9 per sq km
Religious affiliation	
Protestant	55.2%
Anglican	20.1%
Roman Catholic	18.8%
Birth rate per 1,000 (1990)	19.2
	(world av 27.1)
Death rate per 1,000 (1990)	4.5
	(world av 9.8)

Education and Health

Life expectancy at birth,	
male	69 years
female	76 years
Infant mortality rate	
per 1,000 live births (1990)	26.3
Physicians (1987)	1 per 809 persons
Hospital beds	1 per 243 persons
Calorie intake as %	
of FAO requirement	115%
Literacy	95%

Economic

GNP (1990 market prices)	US$2,913mn
GNP per capita	US$11,510
Public external debt (1991)	US$829.5mn
Tourism receipts (1991)	US$1,222mn
Inflation (annual av 1987-92)	5.4%
Radio	1 per 1.3 persons
Television	1 per 5.2 persons
Telephone	1 per 1.8 persons

Employment

Population economically active (1989)	
	127,400
Unemployment rate	11.7%
% of labour force in	
agriculture	3.9
trade, restaurants, hotels	28.5
manufacturing	3.3
construction	7.8
Military forces	850

Source *Encyclopaedia Britannica*

rooms grew by 48% in the 1980s, yet the number of visitor nights rose by only 20%. By 1994 prospects for the industry were improving, with an 11% increase in air arrivals in the first quarter. State-owned hotels such as the *Radisson* and *Crystal Palace* in Nassau, and the *Princess Resort* in Freeport, were kept open with government borrowings to preserve jobs and pay off their debts.

Agriculture is less important than tourism, contributing only 4.5% of gdp. Emphasis is on fruit farming, taking advantage of the lack of frost and competing with the Florida citrus growers. Economic activity is principally restricted to the two main islands although on the Family Islands tourist facilities are being developed and agriculture extended.

Some steps have been taken to encourage light industries, notably salt, pharmaceuticals, rum and beer production, and substantial investment has taken place in the free-trade zone of Freeport, Grand Bahama. The financial sector, with its banks, insurance companies and finance companies, has developed since the 1920s, but since the mid-1980s has suffered from competition from other offshore centres such as the Cayman Islands and Barbados and from pressure from US bank regulators to reduce secrecy. As far as foreign trade is concerned, exports are mostly re-exports of oil products and there are also sales of rum, pharmaceuticals, crawfish, fishery products, fruits and vegetables. Imports are of food, consumer goods and crude oil (mainly kept in bunkers for re-export).

The new government elected in 1992 aimed to reform and revive the economy. Of immediate importance was public finance and efforts were made to put the Treasury in order. Government expenditure had previously been allowed to expand unrestrained and many accounts were found to be overdrawn without proper documentation. Salaries and allowances of MPs and Senators were cut and several other reforms were instituted

into public sector pay and conditions. In an attempt to attract foreign investment, the Government joined the World Bank affiliate, the Multilateral Investment Guaranty Agency, and began studies into the establishment of a securities market to aid the divestment of state enterprises. Among the first companies to be sold were a hotel and a fish-landing complex, while inquiries were held into the loss-making Bahamasair, the Bahamas Hotel Corporation and the Bahamas Telecommunications Corporation.

Further Reading

Out-island Doctor by Evans Cottman (Hodder and Stoughton) gives a picture of the 1940s; an interesting comparison can be made with *Cocaine Wars* by Paul Eddy et al (Bantam), a fascinating study of the 1980s.

NEW PROVIDENCE

New Providence is in the centre of the Bahamas archipelago, surrounded by Andros to the W, the Berry Islands to the N, the arc of the Eleutheran cays starting off the NE tip and the Exuma Cays to the E and SE. It is one of the smallest major islands, at only 80 square miles, yet over half of the population (172,196) lives here. The centre of Nassau has some fine historic buildings and there are some good beaches, but most of the island is covered by sprawling suburbia, scrubby woodland or swamp. Tourism is the principal industry, followed by banking, with the main developments at Nassau, Cable Beach and Paradise Island. Paradise Island, just off the N coast, is 826 acres of tourist resort. Once known as Hog Island, a legacy of New Providence settlers who used it as a pig farm, it was developed in the 1950s by Huntington Hartford as a resort. The name was changed after a bridge was built to connect the island with Nassau and the first casino licence was granted. For a history of the island, read *Paradise Island Story*, by Paul Albury

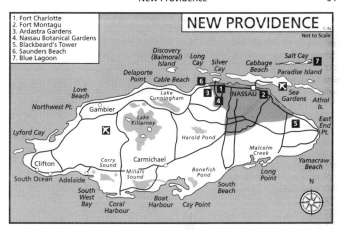

1. Fort Charlotte
2. Fort Montagu
3. Ardastra Gardens
4. Nassau Botanical Gardens
5. Blackbeard's Tower
6. Saunders Beach
7. Blue Lagoon

NEW PROVIDENCE
Not to Scale

(Macmillan Caribbean).

Diving and Marine Life

The variety of reefs and cays makes the Bahamas ideal for new or experienced divers. A great number of wrecks add spice to life underwater, including some that have been planted by film crews off the SW corner of New Providence, which attract scuba divers eager to see where the underwater scenes of James Bond films (the James Bond wreck was damaged by Hurricane Andrew and the front part collapsed, but it is still being dived), or Walt Disney's "20,000 Leagues Under the Sea", were filmed. Just off Paradise Island there is a series of caves and a 19th century wreck, while to the W of New Providence there are dramatic walls and drops leading to the mile-deep "Tongue of the Ocean". Marine conservation is not as highly developed as in some of the other Bahamian islands where dive tourism is promoted, although there are 50 permanent moorings and seven dive operations, all offering PADI certification courses and trips to wrecks, reefs and walls, as well as other activities. Shark feeding and swimming with dolphins are two popular dives. The former involves sitting on the ocean floor and watching a dive master, clad in chain mail or other protective gear, feed several large sharks. Critics claim that more sharks are attracted to the dive site than is perhaps natural and are becoming dependent upon daily handouts. On the S coast, serving the *Ramada* hotel, Stuart Cove's Dive South Ocean is particularly recommended (T 362 4171, F 362 5227), but the others include Bahama Divers Ltd (T 393 5644/6054, F 393 6078, East Bay Street), Dive, Dive, Dive Ltd (T 362 1143/1401, F 362 1994, Coral Harbour, Nitrox certification available), Sun Divers Ltd (T 325 8927, F 325 7788, at the *British Colonial Hotel*, serves the cruise ships as well as hotels, can take out 70 snorkellers or 25 divers on 55-foot boats), Diver's Haven (T 393 0869, F 393 3695, East Bay Street), Nassau Scuba Centre (T 362 1964/1379, F 362 1198, Coral Harbour, an affiliate of Neal Watson's Undersea Adventures) and Sunskiff Divers Ltd (T 361 4075, T/F 362 1979, Coral Harbour, specialty diving). A liveaboard dive boat run by Out Island Voyages was expected to start tours in 1994 (see page 154 for liveaboards). The cost of a 2 tank scuba dive with all equipment and transport included is about US$55-65. A learn-to-dive package costs much the same and enables you to dive with the same company throughout your stay on the island. Snorkelling trips for non-divers are US$20-25. Shark dives cost US$75 or more; you can see silky sharks, bull sharks and reef sharks. Stuart Cove's Dive South Ocean also offers a Shark Awareness certification course for US$210.

Beaches and Watersports

Beaches are best near the hotels where the seaweed is cleaned off. The nicest ones are Love Beach (W), the E end of Paradise Island beach (hotel security guards often try to keep people off the beach at weekends; use hotel car park and walk through hotel as if you are a guest), Ramada Beach (the sea here is very shallow) and beaches on the small islands off New Providence. One of the best and longest beaches is Lyford Cay, which is behind barriers in an exclusive housing area for the rich and famous in the W, but not impossible to enter with enough confidence. It is unwise to go to a beach where you might be on your own. Watersports include waterskiing (no tuition), parasailing, windsurfing and snorkelling. Some of the larger hotels offer full facilities to guests and non-guests. Prices about US$25 for 15 minutes for waterskiing, while windsurfing can be US$12 an hour. Parasailing is US$30 for 7 minutes and jet skiing US$25. Snorkelling equipment hire is US$10-25 for the day. For those who prefer a less active encounter with the sea, glass-bottomed boats leave several times a day from Prince George Wharf in downtown Nassau. Hartley's Undersea Walk, for those not keen to dive but wanting to see coral reefs up close, at 0930 and 1330, US$40 (T 393 8234). Check in at the houseboat, *Full Circle*, at Nassau Yacht Haven, East Bay Street, before boarding the 57-foot catamaran *Pied Piper*. You walk down a 12-foot ladder wearing a helmet into which air is pumped so you can breath normally. The *Atlantis* Submarine goes down off Lyford Cay and will tour wrecks as well as reefs,

weather permitting. The office is on Woodes Rodgers walk opposite Prince George Wharf and the cruise ships. The tour takes 3 hours, of which 50 minutes are on the submarine, Monday-Saturday, 0930-2130 on the hour, every hour, US$68 adult, US$34 child, T 356 3842/5. The *Seaworld Explorer* is a semi-submarine which descends 10-15 feet and is reached by a shuttle boat which leaves Captain Nemo's dock, then *Holiday Inn* road ferry dock. Two trips daily except Sunday and Wednesday of 1½ hours, 1100 and 1500, US$26 adults, US$18 children, T 323 8426, 356 2548. For island cruises, the Calypso Blue Lagoon trip and Rose Island excursions aboard large MVs with three decks are recommended (daily at 1000 except Wednesday, T 363 3577, US$35 for the day with lunch, although it is unlikely to be as good as in the brochure pictures, no complimentary snorkelling equipment). The Swim With The Dolphins Experience is at Blue Lagoon, Salt Cay, reached by tender from several cruise ships or on a day excursion with Calypso 1 and 11, reservations required, T 363 1653/1003. You get a 15-minute lecture on the dolphins, then you wade (US$30) or swim (US$85) with the dolphins; a full-day trip including lunch, drinks, beach, equipment, is US$59 or US$114. *Flying Cloud* catamaran cruises depart from Paradise Island West Dock for sunset, half-day, dinner or Sunday cruises for US$25-50 including snorkelling gear and transport from hotels (T 393 1957). Sea Island Adventure also do boat trips to Rose Island with lunch, snorkelling etc (T 325 3910, 328 2581), while *Yellow Bird* (250 passengers) and *Tropic Bird* (170 passengers) catamarans cater to cruise ships with 3-hour cruises. Top Sail Yacht Charters (T 393 0820/5817) have three boats and offer an all-day cruise from *British Colonial Hotel* dock 0945, Paradise Island ferry dock 1015, arriving Rose Island 1200, depart 1400, snorkelling included, US$49, private charters from US$370. Powerboat

Adventures go further in a high-speed boat; day trip departing from Captain Nemo's dock 0900, with lavish picnic to the Exuma Cays for US$149, including seeing iguanas on Allan's Cay, a nature trail walk and drift snorkelling (T 326 1936, 327 5385, Monday-Friday 0800-2000). Out Island Safaris (seaplane and boat, Captain Paul Harding, T 393 2522/1179) also offers day trips to other islands, eg Harbour Island, the Exumas, Hope Town, with scuba, snorkelling and lunch. A captained boat for fishing trips is US$300 for 4 hours or US$600 for a day for up to 6 people (T 363 2335, Captain Jesse Pinder, or T 322 8148, F 326 4140, Captain Mike Russell of Chubasco Charters, or T 393 4144, 363 2003, Captain Philip Pinder, excellent), or arranged through hotel tour desks for US$60 per person for a half day.

Other Sports

The most popular and well-developed sport on dry land is probably golf. There are four world class courses on New Providence: *Cable Beach Golf Course, Ramada, Paradise Island* and the private *Lyford Cay Golf Course*. Green fees vary but at the *Ramada South Ocean* they are US$55 for guests, US$70 non-guests including cart, US$20 for 18-hole club rental, lessons US$30 for 30 minutes, US$60 for one hour, club storage and daily cleaning US$10/week. Guests of *Crystal Palace* get US$10 off green fees.

There are over 100 tennis courts in the Nassau/Cable Beach/Paradise Island area and many of them are lit for night time play until 2200 (with an extra charge). Most of the larger hotels have tennis courts, usually free for guests. The Racquets Club, on Independence Drive (T 323 1854) has squash courts at about US$7 per hour. Very popular with Bahamians, it has European-sized squash courts. The Radisson Resort Sports Centre charges US$6 an hour for guests, US$10 for others, and has racquet-ball, squash and tennis available. Smarter, but the squash courts are smaller, being converted racquet-ball courts.

You can go horse riding for US$45 an hour, including transport, along the beach at Happy Trails, Coral Harbour (T 362 1820).

Cricket is played every Saturday and Sunday during the cricket season (5 March-27 November) at Haynes Oval, West Bay Street, Nassau. Matches begin at 1200. For further details contact Sydney Deveaux of the Bahamas Cricket Association, T 322 1875.

Gambling at Paradise Island and *Crystal Palace* casinos, 1000-0400. Enquire about lessons free of charge. Fascinating to see the massed ranks of flashing fruit machines and the many games tables. Bahamians are not allowed to gamble in the casinos.

Festivals

Junkanoo is a loud and boisterous national festivity loosely derived from African customs, celebrated on New Providence at 0300 on 26 December and 1 January (see under Grand Bahama for details of celebrations on that island). While the exact origins of Junkanoo are unknown, it is thought to have its roots in slave celebrations on their only days off in the year, at Christmas. John Canoe is said to have been a popular slave leader. Wild costumed "rushers" dance in Bay Street until dawn beating cowbells and shak-shaks, and blowing whistles. As in Carnival in many countries, local businesses sponsor groups who spend the whole year making their costumes. There is a Junkanoo Museum on Prince George Dock, by the cruise ships, open daily from 1000, closes 1300 Mon, Thur; 1600 Wed, Sun; 1800 Tues, Fri, Sat, US$2 adults, US$0.50 children, T 356 2731, where previous years' costumes are stored. Small Junkanoo displays can be seen on certain days in many of the large hotels. Parades with a military spirit and fireworks celebrate Independence Day on 10 July.

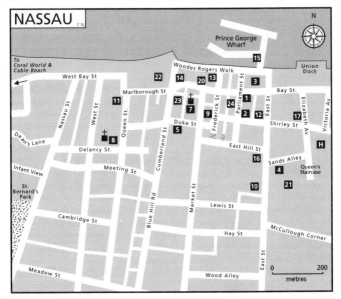

NASSAU

Nassau is the capital of the Bahamas. It looks comfortably old-fashioned with its white and pink houses: by-laws forbid skyscrapers. Bay Street is the main shopping street, which is packed with cruise ship visitors seeking duty free bargains during the day, but deserted at night. The new Government has taken steps to clean up the Bay Street area and on one occasion made the street a pedestrian mall for a day with stalls selling food and wares and lots of music. **Parliament Square** is typical of the colonial architecture with the Houses of Assembly, the old Colonial Secretary's Office and the Supreme Court clustered around a statue of Queen Victoria. On the N side of the square, more government buildings overlook the bust of Sir Milo B Butler, the first Bahamian Governor-General. To the right, surrey rides can be taken through the town for US$5 pp (horses rest 1300-1500 May-October, 1300-1400 November-April). Walking up Parliament Street you pass the Cenotaph on the left and the *Parliament Inn*, built in the 1930s, on the right. The octagonal pink building bordering on Shirley Street is the **Public Library**, built in 1798, which was once used as a prison. Inside you can climb stairs and look out from the balcony, but unfortunately the old dungeons below are no longer open to the public. Open for consulting books, records, documents and artifacts, Monday-Thursday 1000-2000, Friday 1000-1700, Saturday 1000-1600, T 322 4907.

Opposite the library is the site of the *Royal Victoria Hotel*, the first hotel in the Bahamas, built in 1859-61, which closed in 1971. It was built by the Government to accommodate the influx of visitors during the American Civil War, but sold in 1898, after when it changed hands several times. There is not much to see and it looks like a park with some lovely tall trees providing shade, while much of it is used as a car park. On Elizabeth Avenue on the corner with Shirley Street

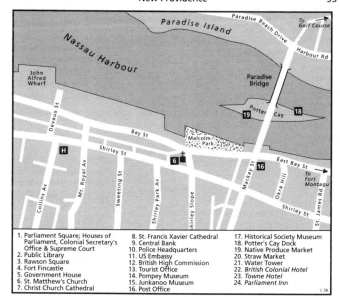

1. Parliament Square; Houses of
   Parliament, Colonial Secretary's
   Office & Supreme Court
2. Public Library
3. Rawson Square
4. Fort Fincastle
5. Government House
6. St. Matthew's Church
7. Christ Church Cathedral
8. St. Francis Xavier Cathedral
9. Central Bank
10. Police Headquarters
11. US Embassy
12. British High Commission
13. Tourist Office
14. Pompey Museum
15. Junkanoo Museum
16. Post Office
17. Historical Society Museum
18. Potter's Cay Dock
19. Native Produce Market
20. Straw Market
21. Water Tower
22. *British Colonial Hotel*
23. *Towne Hotel*
24. *Parliament Inn*

is the Bahamas Historical Society, which organizes monthly talks and houses a small museum (open Monday-Friday 1000-1600, Saturday 1000-1200, closed Thursday, T 322 4231). There is a collection of old pictures, historical documents, a few old household items and things brought up from the sea, not all of which are well-labelled; it is an old-fashioned display with little information. Nearby is the **Queen's Staircase**. The 66 steps (102-foot climb) at the end of a gorge (thought to have been cut out of the limestone by slaves in 1790, the canyon is now lined with palm trees and there is an attractive waterfall alongside the steps) lead to the ruined **Fort Fincastle**. Be careful to ignore men offering information on the history of the area unless you want to pay for it. They are very persistent, even when confronted with this text. The Fort itself was built in 1789 in the shape of a ship's bow. The Water Tower beside the fort was declared a water landmark in 1993. Take the lift

(US$0.50) or the stairs to the top to see the shape of the fort. This is the highest point on the island (216 feet above sea level) and gives some lovely views of the island. There is another guide at the top who also expects a tip. The area is heavily visited by cruise ship tours and there are lots of souvenir stalls.

Government House in traditional Bahamian pink (built 1801) is pretty. Gregory's Arch is an overpass to Government House. On alternate Saturday mornings at 1000, the Royal Bahamian Police Force Band plays in front of the **Christopher Columbus Statue** at the top of the flight of stairs. On West Hill Street is a plaque set in the rock which claims the site as being that of the oldest church in Nassau. Further along the street you pass several old houses including the Postern Gate on the left and the Sisters of Charity Convent on the right. Turning down the steps to Queen Street you pass by some of the oldest and prettiest houses in Nassau (no 16 is said to be 200 years old). The St

Francis Xavier Catholic Cathedral is on West Street and down the hill is the quaint Greek Orthodox Church in blue and white. Christ Church Cathedral (built 1837) stands on the corner of George's Street and immediately to the S is Lex House, thought to have housed the Spanish Garrison in 1782-83.

Vendue House on Bay Street, close to the *British Colonial Hotel*, was the site of slave auctions, and has now been restored (with a grant from Bacardi to commemorate 1492) and converted into the Pompey Museum. It has drawings, artifacts and documents relating to slavery and emancipation in the Bahamas. The collection is limited but well displayed and interesting. Upstairs there is a permanent art exhibition of paintings by Mr Amos Ferguson, who uses house paints. Open Monday-Friday 1000-1630, Saturday 1000-1300, adults US$1, children under 12, US$0.50. The renowned Straw Market has the offices of the Ministry of Tourism above. Almost all the straw work is imported from East Asia and is no longer native (better prices upstairs); they also sell carvings, jewellery and T-shirts. Bargain with the saleswomen but do not expect to get more than 15% off the originally stated price. Running behind the market is the enormous Prince George Wharf which can take up to 11 big cruise ships at once (peak time Saturday). A duty free shopping area is planned here and construction work to increase facilities for visitors is under way. A new Junkanoo Museum opened on the waterfront in 1993, showing the colourful costumes used in the parades, see above. Guided walking tours of old Nassau start from Rawson Square, daily at 1000 and 1400, US$2, contact the Tourist Information Centre, T 326 9772.

Excursions

Go W along Bay Street, past Nassau Street and continue to the Road Traffic Centre where you turn left to Fort Char-

lotte, built in 1787-89 out of limestone. It has a dry moat and battlements. The fort was manned during the Napoleonic Wars but never saw action. The soldiers left some interesting graffiti. Look down on the cricket field, the guns (not original cannon), Arawak Cay and the W end of Paradise Island. Guides will fill you in on the history for a small tip or just wander at leisure. The guides have Ministry of Tourism name badges and are not as pushy as at Fort Fincastle.

Coral Island (T 328 1036, entry US$16 adults, US$11 children, annual membership US$21 adults, US$15 children, under 4s free) is on the 16-acre island, Silver Cay, reached by a bridge from the man-made Arawak Cay (made when the harbour was dredged to allow cruise ships in), which is in turn reached by a bridge (where conch sellers congregate). A US$3 bus runs from Cable Beach, a US$3 boat goes from Woodes Rodgers dock (daily except Thursday, 1015, 1230, 1530, return 1200, 1500, 1700), or a US$3 bus from Paradise Island. Highlights include descending the observatory tower to view the sea below (lots of fish and masses of lobsters), wandering through the excellent indoor exhibits of reef ecology, watching sting ray and sharks feed and selecting your own oyster with a pearl inside. The only drawback is the small size of the pools housing turtles, rays and sharks. A snorkelling trail has been added, US$12 for hire of mask, snorkel and fins, and mandatory life jacket. Open 0930-1600, off a small beach overlooking Arawak Cay, where there are plenty of rest rooms and sun beds. Allow half a day for a visit. There is a restaurant, gift shops and also stands with sea biscuits and sand dollars for sale.

Going up Chippingham Road you come to the Nassau Botanic Gardens (open Monday-Friday, 0800-1630, Saturday-Sunday 0900-1600, adults US$1, children US$0.50), where there are 18 acres of tropical plants, and The Ardastra Gardens and Zoo (open daily, 0900-1700, adults US$7.50, children US$3.75, T 323 5806/7232). Trained, parading flamingoes march just after 1100, 1400, and 1600, but can be a disappointment. There are also parrots and some other animals, but not really enough to warrant the term zoo.

Going W along the coast, Saunders Beach is bordered by casuarina trees and Brown's Point looks across to the *Crystal Palace* (and *Radisson Resort*) at Cable Beach, which at night is a multi-coloured sight when the dayglo lights are switched on. Leaving Cable Beach you soon come to Delaporte Point (once a slave village) and Sandy Port residential areas. Further on are some local bars (*Nesbits* is very popular in the evenings) where you can buy drinks and native conch salad before you get to some limestone caves. There is an inscription commemorating the first visit by the British Royal Family in 1841. Just beyond is Conference Corner where Macmillan, Kennedy and Diefenbaker planted trees in 1962. At this point Blake Road leads to the airport while West Bay Street continues past Orange Hill Beach and Gambier Village (another slave village, *Travellers Rest*, bar and restaurant, overlooks sea, very pleasant to watch sunset, excellent daiquiris and minced lobster. Love Beach further on the right is probably one of the best beaches on New Providence. Park on the side of the road and walk down between the apartments, you can not see the beach from the road.

Continuing as far W as you can go you reach Lyford Cay, a private residential area for the rich, protected by barriers. Turn left at the roundabout for Clifton, a stretch of rocky coast now being developed for a power station and industry. This road leads to South West Bay where you can turn right to visit the *Ramada* hotel and beach front (a good stop for a swim and a drink) before returning E. After two miles there is a signpost for Adelaide Village. This settlement is one of the oldest, founded when illegal slave

traders were intercepted by the British Navy in the 19th century and the human cargo was taken to the Bahamas. The traditional houses are brightly painted, the beach is quite good, though the water is shallow, and the bars prepare fresh fish or conch salad. Continue E on Adelaide Road and you come to the Coral Harbour roundabout. To the right, the Bahamas Defence Force has its base. Coral Harbour was designed as a second Lyford Cay, exclusive, with security barriers, but when it was built in the 1960s there was considerable local opposition to it becoming a select ghetto. The development company went bankrupt leaving it incomplete. The shell of the hotel still stands and the area is now an upper middle class subdivision. At the roundabout you can turn off for the airport or join Carmichael Road and you will pass the Bacardi Company, open weekdays until 1600. At the end of Carmichael Road turn left to go along Blue Hill Road and join Independence Drive at the roundabout (with the cock on top). Here on the N side is the new Town Centre Shopping Mall. In this area you will see many examples of the Government's low-cost housing. Rows of rectangular houses have been painted and adapted by their owners to make each one individual. Notice also that cemeteries are built on hills, where you can dig down six feet and not hit water; elsewhere water is too close to the surface.

Continue E on Independence until you come to traffic lights with another mall. At Marathon Mall turn right on to Prince Charles Drive and follow this to the sea. Turn left and you will be on Eastern Road, which hugs the coast and has many impressive homes overlooking the sea. Blackbeard's Tower, an old lookout point, is now closed. Fort Montagu (and beach), constructed in 1741, is famous for having been captured briefly by Americans during the Revolution. It is a rather smelly area where conch and fish are sold. If you turn left into Shirley

Street and immediately left again into Village Road, you will come to **The Retreat** (opposite Queen's College), the headquarters of the Bahamas National Trust and an 11-acre botanical park. Guided tours (20 minutes) US$2, Tuesday-Thursday at 1150. Members of the BNT (PO Box N4105) are entitled to discounts at several tourist destinations locally (eg Coral Island, Power Boat Adventures, Ardastra Gardens) and free admission to National Trust properties worldwide. The BNT celebrated its 35th anniversary in 1994. It publishes a newsletter, *Currents*.

Returning to East Bay Street you will pass the *Club Waterloo* and the *Nassau Yacht Club* before reaching the toll bridge which crosses over to **Paradise Island**. Scooters cross for US$0.50, taxis and hired cars are US$2, cars with local licence plates US$0.50, pedestrians US$0.25. You pay the toll when taking a taxi across. Alternatively there is a water taxi, US$2, to the Calypso Dock on Paradise Island. Stop at the **Versailles Gardens** and **Cloisters** on the way to the golf course. The gardens with various statues were allowed to fall into disrepair for a while, but were being restored in 1994. The cloisters were brought in pieces from France and date back to the 14th century. The gazebo looking across to Nassau is a favourite spot for weddings. Paradise has some lovely stretches of beach on the N side, including Cabbage Beach and Victoria Beach to the E at the edge of the golf course.

Potters Cay, next to the Paradise Island toll bridge, has the main fish and produce market. Try freshly made conch salad or scorched conch, very spicy and fresh.

Island Information—New Providence
● Airports

Nassau International Airport, about 14 miles from Nassau. Taxi to Nassau US$15-16 and to Paradise Island US$20-21. Third and subsequent extra passengers should be charged US$2, but drivers sometimes try to charge everyone a separate full fare. This is illegal. Make sure meter is used. Paradise Island Airport is nearer to Nassau and receives flights from Miami and Fort Lauderdale. There is no public bus service to or from either airport, though some hotels have buses. For the return journey to Nassau Airport there is a bus from Nassau to Clifton (US$1.50); it leaves on the hour from Bay and Frederick Streets (Western Transportation Company) and will drop you 1½ miles from the airport, but this is not a recommended option.

The airport departure tax is US$15. US immigration and customs formalities for those going to the USA are carried out at Nassau and Paradise Island airports. Plenty of left luggage space is available in lockers outside the doors mid-way between the domestic and international ends of the terminal, they take 4 US quarter coins.

● Transport

Taxis are abundant but expensive. The rates are government-controlled: US$2 for the first ¼mile for 1-2 passengers, then US$0.30 for each subsequent ¼mile. You will be charged US$2 extra for additional passengers and for more than 2 pieces of luggage. To avoid overcharging, agree a price beforehand, or check that the meter is used. Taxi drivers in Nassau may "take you for a ride" otherwise. Tipping is not necessary but 15% is normally expected. For a limousine service, Romeo's Executive Limousine Service is highly recommended. Run by Bahamahost guide, Romeo Farrington, who has a white stretch limo and a fleet of lovely Bentleys, used for official visitors, special occasions or just sightseeing tours in style, T 327 6400/5280, PO Box GT-2280. For radio-dispatched taxis T 323 5111/4 or 323 4555. Buses called "jitneys", are good value at US$0.75, carrying from 9-44 people and going all over New Providence Island between 0600 and 1830. Make sure you have the exact fare, as by law the driver keeps the change. If you want to see some of the island catch any bus in town and it will bring you back about an hour later. They can be crowded and dirty but service is regular. Most buses run on one-way circular routes, which can be confusing. Route 10 goes out to Cable Beach along the coast road (leaving from beside *Best Western British Colonial Hotel*), route 16 goes along Eastern Road to Fox Hill and Western Transportation buses go to *Ramada* from Queen Street (US$1.75). A bus runs between hotels and the golf course on Paradise Island but no buses go over the bridge. To cross to Paradise Island from Woodes Rogers Walk take the Paradise Express boat for US$2, it leaves when full and stops at several docks on Paradise Island.

● **Car Hire**

A small car can cost US$70 a day or US$400-450 a week. Prices depend on the model and features. Avis (T 326 6380 or 377 7121 at airport); Hertz (T 327 6866); Dollar (T 325 3716) and Budget (T 377 7406) have offices at the airport and at other locations but local firms can be cheaper. Orange Creek Rent-a-Car has Suzuki runabouts for US$39 (T 323 4967). Large cash deposits can be required if you have no credit card. Scooters can be hired, Gibson's Scooter Rentals T 325 2963, US$30-45. Helmets are provided and it is mandatory that you wear them. Bicycles can be hired for US$10/day with US$10 deposit. Traffic for such a small island is busy and roads are not well maintained. Take care.

● **Where To Stay**

The 2 main resort areas on New Providence are **Cable Beach**, which stretches 3 miles W of Nassau along the N coast, and **Paradise Island**, 5 mins across Nassau harbour and reached by a toll bridge. The benefit of staying at Cable Beach is that the jitney service into town is very easy to use, while from Paradise Island you need a taxi. Other hotels are in the town and suburbs. There is a great variety of accommodation, ranging from small guest houses, offering only rooms, to luxury hotels and sprawling resorts. Prices vary according to the season. Generally standards of hotels are disappointing considering the price paid and service is slow at reception desks. Watch out for room tolls (4%), resort levies (4-6%), fuel surcharges and compulsory maid gratuities which are added to the basic price quoted. Up to date rates available at the Tourist Information Centres in Nassau, or write to the Tourist Offices listed under Information for Visitors. You can usually pick up a cheaper package deal in the USA when by arranging a hotel on arrival.

In **Nassau** the largest hotel is *Best Western British Colonial* conveniently located at the beginning of Bay Street, built in 1923 on site of Fort Nassau, the cannon outside were found when the foundations were dug (T 322 3301, 800 528 1234, F 322 2286, rooms from US$130 depending on view), economic difficulties forced the closure of 75 of its 325 rooms in 1993 with 80 staff redundancies, good

package deals year round, dive shop on site, watersports, small beach, view of cruise ships, much-needed renovation underway 1993/94; *Parliament Inn*, 18 Parliament Street (T 322 2836, F 326 7196, PO Box N-4138, US$60s, US$70d, US$81 triple inc continental breakfast), C, old wooden building, small but adequate rooms with bathrooms, *Pick-a-Dilly* Daiquiri bar and restaurant downstairs, live music some evenings; the *Diplomat Inn*, Delancey Street on top of the hill (T 325 2688) is a budget hotel in a less salubrious area; nearby on West Bay Street close to the junction with Nassau Street, are a cluster of middle range hotels along the road overlooking Long Walk Beach: *El Greco*; *Ocean Spray*; *Olympia*. A 10-min walk from the beach in the same area is the *Parthenon* on West Street (T 322 2643, US$54), clean and C. Further W off West Bay Street on St Alban's Drive is *Colony Club* (T 325 4824, F 325 1240, US$70) extra beds in room for small charge, children under 10 free. Guest houses include *Aliceanna's* on Bay Street (T 325 4974, US$23-29); *Mignon* on Market St (T 322 4771, US$34); *Towne Hotel* on George St (T 322 8451, F 328 1512, US$60-70); *Morris* on Dan's St (T 325 0195, US$25-30) and *Olive's* on Blue Hill Road (T 323 5298, US$25).

Heading away from Nassau along **Cable Beach** are *Wyndham Ambassador Beach Hotel*; *Forte Nassau Beach Hotel* (T 327 7711, F 327 7615), 6 restaurants, free tennis and non-motorized watersports, *King & Knights* native show club; *Crystal Palace Resort and Casino*, sold in 1993/94 by Carnival Corporation to Casino Management Group, of Germany (T 327 6200, F 327 6459, standard rooms US$215, suites up to US$25,000/night), this huge landmark hotel is usually lit up in dayglo orange, yellow, purple and magenta at night and contains shops, bars, restaurants and a casino the size of a football pitch, renovation is required; *Radisson Cable Beach Casino and Golf Resort*, next door, shares casino (PO Box N-4914, T 327 6000, 800-333 3333, F 327 6987), under renovation in 1993/94, 2 wings extend from C lobby and restaurant area, curving around lagoons and pools, long walk to some rooms down dark corridors, lots of packages, children's activities, all facilities but rather impersonal. Further along the beach *Le Meridien Royal Bahamian* and *Henrea Carlette Hotel* (T 327 7801) US$90 a night for 1 bedroom or US$105 for 2 bedrooms.

On **Paradise Island**, Sun International of

South Africa acquired 60% of *Paradise Island Resort and Casino* in 1993/94 and plans to invest heavily in renovation and extension. The huge resort comprises the 1,200-room *Paradise Towers* (US$140-205) and *Britannia Towers* (US$160-255), *The Ocean Club Golf & Tennis Resort* (US$235-895), 71 rooms, posh, and *Paradise Paradise Beach Resort*, 100 rooms (US$95-135, all inclusive rates for sports available), with a 30,000 sq ft casino, 18-hole golf course, 21 tennis courts, 4 pools, 14 restaurants (reciprocal dining arrangements within the resort), airport airline and 180 undeveloped acres, T 363 2845/2836, T 800-321 3000, 800-722 7466 (Paradise Island Vacations), 800-432 8807, lots of package deals available, inc golf, air fares (Paradise Island Airlines, USAir, Delta). Other large hotels include *Marriott's Paradise Island Beach Club*; *Sheraton Grand Hotel* (from US$135, all rooms with balcony and sea view, bicycles, tennis, pool, restaurants, T 363 2011, 800-325 3535; *Pirate's Cove Holiday Inn*; *Club Mediterranée*; *The Pink House* (US$80 inc breakfast) is a very small, smart hotel in the grounds of the *Club Med* (T 363 3363, F 393 1786); *Club Land'Or* (T 363 2400, F 363 3403, US$205-225), is a good villa hotel, with good restaurant. At the opposite end of the spectrum the *Yoga Retreat* (US$60, PO Box N-7550, T 363 2902, F 363 3783) charges US$25 for tent space, very strict, no onions, not allowed to skip meditation, guests cook and wash up. Paradise Island Vacations represents 10 hotels and offers air-inclusive packages from US$139 pp double occupancy, T 800-722 7466 or in Dade 891 3888.

On Silver Cay, *The Villas On Silver Cay* (PO Box N-7797, T 328 1036, 800-328 8814, F 323 3202, US$195cd, US$20 extra person on sofa bed, children under 12 free), built in a row along rocky coastline but very private and enclosed, each of the 22 suites has small pool, bed sitting room, small kitchenette/dining area, large bathroom, luxury furnishings, nice décor, leafy surroundings, unlimited access to Coral Island and the snorkelling trail, honeymoon and lovers' packages.

Ramada South Ocean Golf and Beach Resort is set in 195 acres on the S coast, with the main hotel, attractively situated in the middle of the 18-hole, PGA-rated, par 72, 6,707-yard golf course, 250 rooms, US$120-165 standard, US$174-234 ocean front in a separate section between main hotel and sea convenient for dive shop, a/c, TV, fans, ocean-front rooms have jacuzzi, several restaurants and bars, 2 pools, exercise room, games, jogging trail, watersports, tennis, golf/diving packages available, PO Box N-8191 (Adelaide Road) South Ocean, T 362 4391, F 362 4728, T 1-800-874 0027.

● **Where To Eat**

A 15% gratuity will be added to every food and drink bill although service can be very slow and poor. Lunch is always cheaper than dinner and can be taken until 1700. For al fresco dining try *Passin' Jacks* or the *Poop Deck* on East Bay, *Traveller's Rest* near Gambier Village (always enjoyable), or *Captain Nemo's* (check your bill, T 323 8394/8426, open 1200-2230). Deveaux Street on the waterfront (the last 2 specialize in good local food). Middle range places with bars and open air meals include *Coconuts* (indoors) and *Le Shack* (same place but outside), East Bay Street between Paradise Bridge and Nassau backing onto the harbour, where you can get exotic cocktails, Bahamian food and hamburgers (T 325 2148); *Tamarind Hill* on Village Road, European and Bahamian, rec, good food, live music Wed, Fri, Sat, 1930-2230 (T 393 1306) and *Pick-a-Dilly*, with live music Wed-Sat evenings, happy hour 1700-1800, on Parliament Street. *Charley Charley's*, Delancey Street serves hearty German fare while *Café Delancey*, on same street is middle range, rec. Cheap, cheerful and Bahamian are *The Shoal*, on Nassau Street, *Briteleys*, and *Three Queens* on Wulff Road, the first 2 are better than the *Three Queens*. Opposite the Central Bank, through arch down Market St is *Palm Tree*, which has very good native cooking and does takeaway. Both the *Blue Lagoon* (a trio) on Paradise Island and the *Cellar* in town have music. *The Roselawn Café* on Bank Lane, off Parliament Square serves food after 2200. *Vesuvio's* on West Bay St is a good Italian restaurant; *East Villa* on East Bay St is a Chinese restaurant (T 393 3377/3385). Most hotels have expensive and formal restaurants but they also have good value buffets (US$12-20): Sun brunch at *Café Martinique* on Paradise Island is excellent. At the *Boat House* next door you can cook your own steak, lobster etc. *Blue Marlin* is one of only 2 restaurants on Paradise Island not owned by a hotel (T 363 2660), lunch and dinner, steel band most nights, cheaper than hotels. For a special meal visitors are often encouraged to go to *Graycliff*, West Hill Street, in a colonial mansion (also a hotel, US$145-

365, T 322 2796), but service and food have declined, poor reports. *The Sun and...* (T 393 1205, closed Mon) and the *Blue Lagoon* in *Club Land'Or* (for fish) are rec (over US$50 pp). Also expensive but good are *Ocean Club* (check your bill) on Paradise Island and *Buena Vista* on Delancey St (T 322 2811/4039, reservations required, men wear jackets, popular with business people, pianist, also 10-12 guest rooms).

● **Night-life**

Some clubs have a cover charge or a 2-drink minimum. The *Paradise Island Resort & Casino* has a 30,000 square foot casino and a casino show nightly except Sun, US$30 inc 2 drinks, $48 with dinner, times of shows vary, acts are changed every few months, generally of excellent quality, good live music with large troupe of dancers and singers, well choreographed, enjoyable, T 363 2222/3000. The *King and Knights* at *Forte Nassau Beach Hotel* has a good native show, with steel drums etc. Native shows generally do not mean native to the Bahamas, but borrow from the culture of Trinidad and Jamaica with Junkanoo added. *Blue Marlin*, a restaurant/bar and night club on Paradise Island, offers a native revue similar to that at *King and Knights*, every night except Mon, starts 2115, lasts about 1½ hrs. Live bands can be heard at the *Waterloo*, East Bay, and the *Ritz*, Bay Street (popular with Bahamians). Several restaurants have live music, see above. *We Place*, Thompson Avenue, US$4, is full of Bahamians and very lively at weekends. *The Zoo*, West Bay Street, Tues-Sat, 2 restaurants, dancing areas, state of the art private lounges, theme bar, multi-faceted club caters for wide clientèle, from young parties to the sophisticated executive. Discos can be found in most of the larger hotels. Dinner cruises In the harbour leave the *Majestic Lady*, Bay Street, nightly for US$35 (T 322 2606). *The Village Lanes*, Village Road for bowling at US$2.75 a game during the day, US$3 after 1700 (T 393 2427). The *Dundas Centre for the Performing Arts*, Mackey Street, regularly has shows and plays by local groups (T 322 2728).

● **Warning**

There is a 'crack' cocaine problem in New Providence. Partly for this reason armed robberies are frequent. Targets include pedestrians out after dark, supermarkets, bars, banks and casinos; customers will be asked to hand over their valuables. Guests have been held up (or raped) in hotel rooms and on their balconies and patios. Drivers have been made to hand over car keys at knife or gunpoint. The majority of tourists are not affected by these incidents and Nassau is less dangerous than Kingston or Port of Spain. However visitors should be extremely careful, particularly at night or when venturing off the beaten track. Do not be lulled into a false sense of security.

● **Shopping**

Shops are open 0900-1700, Mon-Sat, but some close at 1200 on Thur. As there is no sales tax and many items are duty free, buying imported goods can save you about 20-50%, but shop around. *Bernard's* has some fine china, the *English Shops* and *Linen and Lace* have Irish linen. Look in the *Perfume Shop* for French perfume. Try *John Bull* for watches and cameras. For unusual gifts look in *Marlborough Antiques*, West Bay, *Coin of the Realm*, Charlotte Street, or *Best of the Bahamas*, E of the square. For clothing see the *Androsia* boutique in *Mademoiselle's*, batik fashions from Andros. There are also international names like *St Michael*, *The Body Shop*, *Benetton*, *Gucci* and *Greenfire Emeralds* from Colombia all in Nassau. In general, however, buy everything you could possibly need before you arrive as regular import duties are high. Most of the smarter, tourist-oriented shops are on (or just off) Bay Street. For everyday shopping most people use suburban centres, of which the most convenient is in the Mackey Street-Madeira Street area. Super Value supermarkets have good variety of breads and salad bar (sold by the pound). The main fish and produce market is on Potters Cay (see above). Other fresh fish markets are Montague Foreshore, next to the Sailing Club and on West Bay Street, opp Fort Charlotte and at the entrance to Coral Island. The best book shop is probably the book department of the Island Shop on Bay Street, but most cater for 'holiday reading'. Service in shops is often poor, be prepared to wait.

● **Film Developing**

Try the Island Colour Lab in the Island shop, opp the Straw Market, on Bay Street or Mr Photo chain on the Market Range off Bay Street. Others have lost films.

● **Tourist Office**

In the straw market. Ask for the monthly *What's On* and the *Tourist News*. Another, *Best-Buys*, is in your hotel or at the airport. There is also an information booth in Rawson Square (T 326 9772/9781) and at the airport

Lauderdale, FL 33335).

Other dive operators include Xanadu Dive Centre at the *Xanadu Hotel* (T 352 5856, 1-800 336 0938, F 352 4731), which offers one dive at US$32, 2 dives US$55, 3 dives US$75 or a 3-day package for US$250, including tank, weights, mask, snorkel and fins. A liveaboard is available for charter, sleeps 16, price depends on what you want to do. Certification courses and resort courses are offered. Both UNEXSO and Xanadu offer shark dives. They take it in turns to dive the same site, so the sharks are fed nearly every day with frozen fish from Canada, just like the dolphins. The fish is free of parasites, but not their natural diet. There is also the *Deep Water Cay Club* at East End, with no certification courses available. The *Deep Water Cay Club* is primarily a bone fishing lodge. Their boats fish over 200 square miles of flats and creeks. Accommodation is in cottages and cabins, there is a restaurant and private air strip, PO Box 1145, Palm Beach, Florida, 33480, T 407-684 3958, F 407-684 0959.

Beaches and Watersports

The island has several natural advantages over others in the group. It has miles of S-facing beaches sheltered from northerly winds and enjoys the full benefit of the Gulf Stream. Generally, beaches can be classed as tourist or local, the former having sports and refreshment facilities as well as security and regular cleaning. The more remote beaches, on the other hand, are usually completely empty, unspoiled by commercialism and very peaceful, their only drawback being that there is often considerable domestic waste and rubbish washed ashore, probably emanating from the garbage collection ships on their way to Florida.

Do exercise caution on the beaches as crime is common and most beaches have a security guard because of the high incidence of robbery and assault. Walking on beaches at night is definitely not a good idea and there is not necessarily safety in numbers. Also theft from parked cars is common so do not leave valuables in your car. Fortune Beach and the National Park Beach are both areas in which to be careful. Topless sunbathing is frowned upon by the Bahamians and skinny dipping is against the law.

Coral Beach, next to the hotel of the same name, is popular with windsurfers, cleaned regularly and has a small bar. Beach facilities are for hotel residents only and this policy is sporadically enforced with vigour. **Xanadu Beach** serves the *Princess Towers/Xanadu Hotel* and various watersports are available through Paradise Watersports (T 352 2887), including jet skis (US$22 for 15 mins, US$40/$\frac{1}{2}$ hr with US$50 deposit), water-skiing (US$15 for 1$\frac{1}{2}$ miles), paddle boats, catamarans, snorkelling equipment (there is a good reef here within easy reach), fishing and parasailing. Use of jet skis and boats is limited to a cordoned area. Hair braiding is done on the beach by local children who have fixed prices according to the number of plaits and length of hair (generally US$1 per plait). Watch out for scalp burn afterwards. There is a straw market and a bar which has very loud live music on Sundays. Drinks or conch salad can be bought more cheaply if you walk just beyond the boundary fence where locals bring ice boxes of cold sodas. The *Glass Bottom Boat* operates from Xanadu Marina, tickets on sale on the beach. Make sure the sea is calm, it can be very rough outside the marina and then water visibility is poor and most passengers get seasick.

The **Lucayan Beach** area includes the beaches for the *Radisson Lucaya Beach Resort, Quality Atlantik Beach Hotel* and the *Lucayan Beach Resort and Casino*, which are clean, with bar and sports facilities including parasailing. Windsurfers, hobie cats, Boston whalers, snorkelling equipment, water skis (about US$15 for 2 miles) and wave runners can all be hired here. At nearby Port Lucaya, Reef Tours operate the *Mermaid Kitty*, a glass bottomed boat which sails several times a day, US$12 for 1½ hours. They also have 2-hour snorkelling trips, US$15 pp. Various booze cruises depart daily as well as a trimaran sunset trip.

On the road to West End past Eight Mile Rock are two good beaches for shelling, Bootle Bay and Shell Bay. At West End, the beach at the *Jack Tar Holiday Village* (closed 1990) is rather small. There are good coral heads here, close enough to wade to.

One of the nicest beaches on the island with attractive palms and a few broken down old umbrellas is Taino Beach, which is over a mile long and has an excellent stretch of coral for snorkelling very close to the shore. The *Taino Beach Resort* on the first part of the beach has expensive condominiums which can be rented on a short term basis. Further along past the *Stone Crab Restaurant* is the *Surfside Bar/Restaurant*. Fortune Beach is sometimes used for tourist beach parties which are noisy and to be avoided. The main attraction of the beach is the restaurant *Blackbeards*. The beach is a bit rocky especially at low tide. Take care in this area, it is best to park near the restaurant as there have been many cars broken into in the rather lonely car park further along. The walk from William's Town along the beach is very pleasant, the vegetation being lush, mostly mangrove, sea grapes and tall grasses along the shore. The beach is used by Pinetree Riding Stables and occasionally local churches hold services here. Other beaches on the island include Smith's Point and Mathers Town just outside Freeport. Here you will find two popular bars: *Club Caribe* (Mathers Town) and the *White Wave Club* (Smith's Point).

Peterson's Cay is the archetypal one tree desert island and because of this can be crowded. Some tour companies run day trips to snorkel and eat lunch here.

You can hire a boat to get there from Port Lucaya (Reef Tours, US$75/3 hours with US$200 deposit), the approach is a bit tricky because of the reef. Directly opposite is Barbary Beach, pleasant and backed by a wide pine copse (good for hanging hammocks). An old church here called the Hermitage was built in 1901 by an ex-trappist monk,

Of the less commercial beaches, Gold Rock Beach is probably the most beautiful on the island, about 20 miles E of Freeport and part of the Bahamas National Trust. En route to it you cross the Grand Lucayan Waterway, a canal built in the 1960s when development was booming. Barely used today, the canal bisects the island and the abandoned building sites are a reminder of what Freeport could have become had the planned development taken place. Once past the canal turn right and further along this road is a deserted, never-used film studio. If you take the left turn before the studio you come to a signposted road for the crossing to Water Cay. It is not always easy to get a boat across. If you take the left turn but carry on, the road becomes overgrown and pot holed, and the area is littered with small planes shot down by drug enforcement officers or abandoned by drug traffickers. Fat Albert, a barrage balloon full of radar equipment is supposed to have put a stop to aircraft landing on the road undetected. Another detour before reaching Gold Rock is to take the first turning after the film studio to Old Free Town, where there are blue holes and Mermaid's Lair, an opening to an underwater cave system. Further inland is a sink hole, the Owl Hole. Back on the road, turn off when you see the sign for the Lucayan National Park. There is a car park and a map. The 50-acre park was set up by workers from Operation Raleigh and a subsequent expedition laid the foundations (but nothing more) for a visitors centre. A Lucayan village and burial ground have been found here. The park contains the largest charted underwater cave system in the world. You can see two caves and climb to a lookout point. As well as bromeliads and orchids there are hundreds of bats in the first cave in the breeding season; also a rare water centipede found only in these waters. Across the road from the caves is a 1,000-yard board walk through mangrove swamp which leads to Gold Rock Beach. The beach is best seen at low tide as the sea goes out a long way and there is not much room to sit when the tide is in. The beach stretches for over a mile and is usually deserted. There are dunes and a large rock sticks out of the water giving the beach its name. It is excellent for shell collecting, but horseflies are very persistent so bring insect repellent. The picnic area is often too strewn with rubbish to be pleasant. Occasionally the area is cleaned.

Another wide, beautiful beach is Pelican Point, at the E end of the island, backed by Royal Palms and a very pretty and colourful village. There are fishing boats on the beach and it is not uncommon to see people gutting or cooking fish here. Pelicans can be seen flopping by. Roads out to the East End are poor and in places 4-wheel drive is preferable.

Kayaking can be done with Mrs Moultrie from Hawksbill Creek, Queen's Cove, to a deserted Cay, US$60 for all-day trip including lunch; 16-foot kayaks, no experience necessary.

Other Sports

There is no shortage of golf courses on Grand Bahama. At the *Bahama Princess Hotel and Golf Club* there are two PGA championship courses, the 6,420-yard Emerald and the 6,450-yard Ruby, with 162 bunkers between them (also tennis courts and a 6-mile jogging trail). The length of each hole is changed daily by moving the holes on the putting green. Reservations for starting times are essential and in peak season, winter, times are often booked a month in advance. Carts are mandatory. The *Bahama Reef Golf and Country Club* offers a 6,768-yard championship course (swimming pool), and the *Fortune Hill Golf and Country Club* a 3,453-yard, 18-hole scenic course. The oldest is the *Lucaya Golf and Country Club*, where there is an 18-hole, 6,488-yard PGA-rated championship course (PO Box F-333, Lucaya, T 373 1066, F 373 7481), discounts are available through the large hotels and there is a booking booth at Port Lucaya. You can play tennis at the *Radisson*, the *Quality Atlantik Beach* (guests US$1 per day, US$100 annual membership), the *Princess Country Club* (US$5/hour daytime, US$10/hour nightime), *Princess Tower* (same rates), *Lucayan Beach* and *Lucayan Marina* (guests free, no night play) and the *Xanadu Beach Hotel* (non-guests US$5/hour). The Grand Bahama Tennis and Squash Club (T 373 4567) has courts available from 0930-2400 but you have to be a member. Horse riding is available at Pinetree Stables (T 373 3600, PO Box F-2915), US$35 for 1½-hour trail and beach ride with guide (20 horses, rider's weight limit 200lbs), lessons can also be arranged with BHS and AIRA instructor (no credit cards). There is a Rugby and Hockey Club (Pioneers Way), which organizes various social events. The YMCA next to the Rugby Club can give information about watching local basketball and softball matches. Volleyball is a popular sport and many beaches and residential street corners have nets. Aerobics classes are available at most of the major hotels. There are several jogging routes but watch out for dogs. Bowling is available at Sea Surf Lanes, Queen's Highway. There is a Super-Cross Motor Cycle dash in the autumn. The Conchman Triathlon (swim/cycle/jog) is held in November. The GB5000 road race is in February, a 5-km flat race from *Princess Country Club*, with a 1-mile fun run/walk and a run for children. Contact the Grand Bahama Island Promotion Board, T 352-8356, for information and registration. UNEXSO organizes a conch diving competition for locals at Port Lucaya.

Festivals

Junkanoo is held on 1 January in Freeport. Beginning from the Ranfurly Circle, dancing outside *Princess Hotel* 0400 onwards with drums, cowbells, whistles, brass instruments and foghorns. Scrap gangs, impromptu groups, join in with the rushin'. Much smaller than Nassau's but worth seeing. Go to Ranfurly Circle early to see the participants flame heating their goat skin drums to stretch them. The **Goombay** Summer Festival consists of a series of events at the International Bazaar or in the Lucaya area. On 10 July, **Independence Day**, a Junkanoo parade is held at 0400 in West End and also on the first Monday in August, which is a holiday to commemorate the emancipation of the slaves. A mini Junkanoo is held weekly as part of the Goombay Festival and many of the hotels include a small Junkanoo as part of their native show. Other events are also held during the festival, get a calendar of events from the Tourist Office in the Bazaar or major hotels. On **Discovery Day**, 12 October, a fair is held at McLean's Town, including a conch-cracking competition started by a British couple in the 1940s. The aim is to see who can remove the most conch from their shell in ten minutes. The women's competition has many machete-wielding experts who bring a lot of partisan support. There is also a swimming race to a nearby islet and back, which attracts a lot of local competition. The plaiting of the Maypole is an interesting Caribbean version of the English tradition, with children dancing round the pole to the beat of Reggae songs. Although much of the road to McLean's Town has been paved, the road is very poor in parts. Minibuses run regularly from Ranfurly Circle (US$2). If you rent a car it is sometimes difficult to park. Look out for details of local fairs in the Freeport News and at the Ranfurly Circle.

Freeport

Freeporters have a reputation of being less friendly than other Bahamians, but this is often blamed on the design of the town and the lack of community spirit. Avenues are large and buildings are spaced far apart, there are few corner shops or neighbourhood bars and it is hard to go anywhere without a car. In downtown Freeport there are a few small shopping malls (see under Shopping). If you take East Mall Drive out of town towards the airport you will pass the Rand Memorial Hospital and the excellent Wallace Groves Library. On the other side of the road is a bright pink pseudo classical building which is the Grand Bahama Port Authority Building. East Mall Drive connects with the Ranfurly Circle (named after 1950s British Colonial Governor) and the **International Bazaar**, a 10-acre integrated shopping complex on East Mall and West Sunrise Highway, with streets built in various assorted national styles with international merchandise and food. There is also a straw market. Open Monday-Friday 0900-1600. To the rear of the International Bazaar, the other side of the street from Colombian Emeralds (where you can tour the factory) and the Straw Market, is a perfume factory in a replica of an old Bahamian mansion, which you can tour briefly and even mix your own perfume (T 352 9391, F 352 9040, orders in USA 1-800 628 9033, PO Box F-770, Freeport), open Monday-Friday, 1000-1730. Just over a mile E of Ranfurly Circle you come to another roundabout. Turn right to get to the Lucaya area, where there is the **Port Lucaya** shopping and entertainment complex and a number of hotels (*Radisson, Quality Atlantik Beach, Lucayan Beach Resort and Casino, Port Lucaya Resort & Yacht Club*). At the Market place there is another straw and crafts market and a marina. UNEXSO is based here. In the evenings live music is played at the bandstand by the waterwalk.

plans, with many half-built plots, now mostly covered by bush, and roads which lead to nowhere. 15 miles E of Freeport, towards High Rock, is the 42-acre **Lucaya National Park**, with about 250 plant species, caves, plus a path through a Mangrove swamp, built in March 1985 by volunteers from "Operation Raleigh". Continuing E you get to High Rock (20 miles) (*Ezekiel Pinder's Restaurant* has an ocean view—almost) and Pelican Point (10 miles further), excellent deserted beach. The road on to McLean's Town (see **Festivals**, above) and East End is poor, but passable. From McLean's Town you can get a boat across to Sweetings or Deep Water Cay. Neither has vehicular traffic. It is possible to rent cottages. There is a guest house on Deep Water Cay and the *Traveller's Rest Bar* on Sweetings Cay.

Island Information—Grand Bahama
● Transport

Getting to see most of Grand Bahama without a car is difficult. Cars can be rented at the airport or in Freeport on a daily (US$70 for a compact car, plus insurance of about US$12 a day) or weekly (US$420) basis, as can jeeps (US$90/day), mopeds (US$20/day) and bicycles. Five Wheels Car Hire, T 352 7001; Hertz, T 352 3297; Dollar Rent A Car, T 352 9308. Check the telephone yellow pages for many more. Taxi fares are fixed and cabs are metered (**see page 98**), but expect additional charges for extra passengers and more than 2 pieces of luggage. Taxis are available at the airport; expect to share as they leave when full and they are big taxis. Fare to town about US$5.40. Taxis from the Harbour to the International Bazaar cost US$1 pp and to Port Lucaya US$1.50 pp, based on a full taxi. A strict rotation system is used and buses are not allowed into the harbour area. Public buses run from Freeport to Lucaya (US$0.75) and less frequently from Freeport to High Rock, Eight Mile Rock (US$1), Holmes Rock (US$2), West End (US$3) and East End. Check for timetable details. Buses drive fast and recklessly. There are routed stops but usually drivers will stop wherever you shout "bus stop coming up" loud enough to be heard over the music. Buses do not generally leave the bazaar or centre until full. Many hotels have a complimentary bus service for guests to the beach or in to Freeport.

● Where To Stay

See note on Hotels under New Providence. Price lists can be obtained from the tourist office in the Bazaar or in Lucaya. In the Lucaya area, 5 miles from the airport, 3 miles from Downtown, there are 3 large hotels in a row along the beach: the *Lucayan Beach Resort and Casino* renovated its 243 rooms in 1993, winter rates US$150-200 depending on view but gambling, diving or golf packages work out cheaper, emphasis is on the casino, T 373 7777, F 373 6916, T 1-800-772 1227, PO Box F-336, Lucaya; the nicest of the 3 is *Quality Atlantik Beach and Golf Resort*, opp the Market Place, renovated 1991-93, 123 elegant rooms and 52 luxury split-level suites of different sizes, 3 rooms for disabled, US$130-360 winter, US$115-330 summer, a/c, phone, TV, nice views, dining rooms overlook pool, beach bar, conference facilities, free use of tennis courts next door, golf, dive and other packages available, T 373 1444, F 373 7481, in USA 1-800 622 6770, in Canada 1-800 848 3315, PO Box F-42500; *Radisson Lucaya Beach Resort*, was *Holiday Inn* and looks it, needs refurbishment to compare with neighbours, 500 rooms, standard, superior, ocean front and suites, all much the same, price depends on view, from US$95 in summer, children under 12 free when sharing with adult, packages available, T 373 1333, F 373 8662/2396, PO Box F 2496; *Port Lucaya Resort, Marina and Yacht Club*, hotel adjoining existing marina opened 1993/94 with pool, jacuzzi, bars, restaurant, on reclaimed land jutting out into harbour, US$110-125d, US$196-265 suites winter, US$75-90d, US$175-196 suites in summer, slips for 50 boats of 40-125 feet surround the resort, T 373 6618, PO Box F 2452, at the marina rates are US$75-85d, US$167-225 suites in winter, US$60-75d, US$149-167 suites in summer, with slips catering for all sizes of yachts including a luxury, private dock, all services and facilities, for information on dockage call Jack Chester, T 373 9090, F 373 5884. West along the coast is the *Xanadu Beach and Marina Resort*, where Howard Hughes, the recluse, used to live on the top floors. There is a small study/library dedicated to him on the ground floor of the tower, which has a pink ring of apartments on top. Alongside is a lower rise block of rooms and restaurants. The rooms, in heavy pink paint, start from US$120, small pool, bar, 3 tennis courts with pro, dive shop and watersports centre on site, nice beach, 67 ships in marina, T 352 6782/3, F 352 5799, PO Box F-2438. Inland on West Sunrise Highway by the Ranfurly Circle are the mock-Moorish *Princess Tower*, with *Princess Casino* next door and *Princess Country Club* on the other side of the road, 400 rooms in the *Tower* with top 2 floors keyed off for gamblers, 565 rooms in the low-rise *Country Club*, where blocks of rooms and suites fan out from the large, landscaped pool with waterfalls, tunnels, rocks and hot tub, 9 restaurants, 12 tennis courts, 2 golf courses, beachshuttle, convention facilities, children's activities, rates US$140-950, packages available, children under 12 free when sharing with adults, *Tower* T 352 9661, PO Box F-2623, *Country Club* T 352 6721, PO Box F-207, both F 352 2542, 800-223 1834.

Less expensive hotels are *The New Victoria Inn* off Midshipman's Drive (40 rooms, 2-bedroom suite, pool, transport to beach, shops, casino, US$75, T 373 3040, F 373 8374, PO Box F-1261) and *Castaways* next to the Bazaar off the Ranfurly Circle (130 rooms on 4 floors, poolside or noisy roadside, TV, a/c, phone, small bathroom, US$72-98, courtesy transport to beach, T 352 6682, F 352 5087, PO Box F-42629), but none can be rec for service. Self catering apartments are available at many resorts. To stay with a Bahamian family, write to the Grand Bahama Island Promotion Board, Freeport (see below, **Tourist Office**), for details of the People To People Programme; see also under **Information for Visitors**. Vigilance is advised in Freeport. Never leave screen doors open at night, there have been a number of armed robberies and sexual assaults where intruders have just walked in through screen doors left open.

● **Where To Eat**
The hotels have several expensive restaurants which serve native/international cuisine. Buffet brunches on Sun are rec, you can eat as much as you like at *Princess Towers, Xanadu Hotel* and *Lucayan Beach Hotel* (US$18 including as much champagne as you can drink). Many restaurants, particularly those in hotels, do Early Bird Specials from 1730-1830, the EBS for US$13 at *La Trattoria* in the *Princess Towers* is good value. Beach front restaurants: *Pier One*, at Freeport Harbour, where they feed the sharks around 2100, and *The Stoned Crab* on Taino Beach are both expensive, romantic, with good views. *Surfside Restaurant* further down on Taino Beach is a wooden structure on stilts, popular with Bahamians,

cheap special most evenings; *Blackbeard's* on Fortune Beach, friendly, reasonably priced menu, mosquitos and no see'ums can be troublesome if you eat outside; *The Buccaneer Club* at Deadman's Reef has a courtesy bus (call 349 3794) but if you use it you will be presented with a higher priced menu on arrival, about 40-min drive from Freeport, Wed night specials, closed in October, interesting guest signature book. Other popular restaurants include: *Freddie's Native Restaurant* in Hunters Settlement, open 1100-2300 but phone in advance, food basic but freshly prepared, tasty and cheap with fish dishes for US$8; *The Traveller's Rest* in Williams Town has good cheap breakfasts, Johnny Cake and soused fish are popular; *The Outriggers* at Smith's Point, just outside Lucaya at the far end of Taino Beach, distinctly Bahamian flavour, phone to check menu, fish fry outdoors on Wed night, T 373 4811; nearby is *Mama Flo's*, similar, even more popular for fish fry on Wed when there is lots of loud music and barbeques; *The Native Lobster Hut*, Sergeant Major Drive, pea soup; *Scorpios*, Explorers Way, reasonably priced native food, favourable reports. For Italian food, *Silvano's* on Ranfurly Circus, *Luciano's* in Port Lucaya good, book a table outside to see fireworks over the square on Sat evenings at 2030-2100, noisy music though. *Pisces*, near *Lucayan Towers*, popular for its pizzas and cocktails, run by Bahamian George and Scottish Rosie. For oriental dishes there are at least 3 Chinese restaurants in the International Bazaar. The *Phoenix (Silver Sands Hotel)* serves kebabs and curries and has an unusual bar. The *Ruby Swiss Restaurant* on West Sunrise (seafood) is expensive but service is good. *Fat Man's Nephew* in Port Lucaya is reasonably priced, good view of bandstand, open 1200-2400 except Tues 1700-2400 and Sun 1700-2300, T 373 8520. (*Fat Man* in Pinder's Point used to be popular but the owner—Fat Man—was gunned down by an armed robber). *The Bahama Beach Club*, just W of the *Xanadu Hotel*, has a superb view of the sea, usually only bar snacks available, but watch newspapers for specials, eg Fish Fry on Fri, barbeque on Sat at 1900, nice local atmosphere; the *Brass Helmet*, upstairs at UNEXSO, a slightly different menu from normal, reasonable prices, breakfast, lunch and dinner, good and popular with divers. For sandwiches and salads at lunchtime, *Kristi's* in the Bain Building, West Atlantic Drive, Downtown, takeaway or eat in, open Mon-Sat 0800-1600, T 352

ABACO ISLANDS

To Walker's Cay
Moraine Cay
Umbrella Cay
Little Abaco Island
Pensacola Cays
Crown Haven
Wood Cay
West End Cay
Fox Town
Cedar Harbour
Spanish Cay
Cave Cay
Little Abaco Island
Cross Cays
Powell Cay
Coopers Town
Randalls Cay
Bamboo Cay
Manjack Cay
Rock Harbour Cays
Green Turtle Cay
New Plymouth
Treasure Cay Airport
No Name Cay
Whale Cay
Treasure Cay
Great Guana Cay
Guana Harbour
1
Red Bay
Man-O-War Cay
Great Abaco Island
The Marls
Marsh Harbour
Hope Town
Shallow Water Point
Spring City
Elbow Cay
Snake Cay
Tilloo Cay
Mores Island
Mastic Pt
Spencer Bight
Lynyard Cay
2
Little Harbour
Winding Bay
Cherokee
Cornwall Pt
Rolling Harbour
Gorda Cay
Big Bridge Bay
Crossing Rock
Gilpin Bay
Sandy Point
Thomas Bay
Cross Harbour
Wild Parrots
High Bank Bay
Lanthorn Head
Southwest Point
Hole in the Wall

N

0   5
miles

1. Fowl Cay, Bahamas National Trust Preserve
2. Pelican Cays Land & Sea Park

Wrecking was a profitable pastime and Abaco was ideally placed on a busy shipping route to take advantage of its reefs and sand banks. Sponge, pineapple, sisal, sugar and lumber were later developed but never became big business. Wrecking also declined after the construction of lighthouses. The lighthouse on Elbow Cay at Hope Town was built in 1863, after the wreck in 1862 of the *USS Adirondack*, despite sabotage attempts by local people. By 1900 Hope Town was the largest town in the Abacos, with a population of 1,200 engaged in fishing, sponging, shipping and boat building. The boats made in Abaco were renowned for their design and the builders became famous for their construction skills. Boats, though made of fibreglass, are still made on Man-O-War Cay today. The inhabitants of Abaco continued to live barely at subsistence levels until after the Second World War, when the Owens-Illinois Corporation revived the lumber business, built roads and introduced cars. An airport was built at Marsh Harbour and banks arrived. When the pulpwood operation ended in the 1960s sugar replaced it but was short lived. Nowadays the major agribusiness is citrus from two huge farms which export their crop to Florida. Abaco has developed its tourist industry slowly and effectively and has a high employment rate. Resorts are small and the atmosphere is casual and friendly even in the most luxurious hotels.

The 1967 elections resulted in a victory for Lynden Pindling's party the Progressive Liberal Party (PLP), which represented the black majority of the Bahamas. Abaco, which was 50% white, voted for the opposition. In the early 1970s some Abaco residents formed the Greater Abaco Council which was opposed to Bahamian independence. When independence became a reality in 1973, the Abaco Independence Movement tried to assert Abaco's independence from the rest of the Bahamas. This breakaway movement by white residents caused the islanders to split into two camps and there were bitter conflicts. According to local storytellers, there was going to be a revolution, but there was confusion over whether it was planned for Wednesday or Thursday, then some men went fishing, and well .... Support for the main opposition party, the Free National Movement (FNM), remained strong in Abaco. In 1992 it was elected to government and its Prime Minister, Herbert Ingraham, lives near Coopers Town.

The main centre on Abaco is Marsh Harbour, which is the third largest town in the Bahamas. Its name reflects the swampy nature of much of Greater Abaco. The scrub and swamp give the island a rather desolate appearance, but like many islands, life revolves around the offshore cays and the coastal settlements. The area S of Marsh Harbour owes its development and particularly its roads to lumber companies. There are miles and miles of pine forests, secondary growth after the heavy logging earlier this century. Nobody lives S of Sandy Point although there is a lighthouse at Hole in the Wall. Roads are better in the N, where they are mostly paved, while in the S they are dirt.

Guy Fawkes Day is celebrated on 5 November with parades through the streets led by the Guy to a big bonfire in the evening (no fireworks).

Flora and Fauna
Like other N Family Islands, Abaco is mostly covered by secondary growth stands of Caribbean pine, interspersed with hammocks or coppices of hardwoods such as mahogany and wild coffee. The Bahama parrot, extinct on all other islands bar Inagua, survives in these coppices, 42 breeding pairs have been counted. A captive breeding programme is now in progress and fledglings will be released back into these areas. In the wild, the parrot nests around Hole in the Wall and the area is to be made a reservation for them. Friends of the Environment, an environmental protection group, headquarters on Treasure Cay, Abaco, runs guided excursions to see the parrots (US$40 per person), and also has plenty of other, interesting information on the fauna of the Abacos, T 367 2847. A herd of wild horses roams the citrus groves and pine forests in the N. They are a hardy breed of work horses descended from those used in the sawmills which closed in the 1920s and 1930s, abandoning the animals.

Diving and Marine Life

Life revolves around the sea and Abaco is sometimes called the "sailing capital of the world", with good marina facilities at the *Treasure Cay Marina*, one of the largest tourist resorts in the Family Islands, the *Conch Inn Resort and Marina* (a 75-ship marina can accommodate boats up to 140 feet), the Boat Harbour Marina by the *Great Abaco Beach Hotel* (180 ships, boat hire, services, showers, laundromat, T 367 2736, VHF 16) and the *Green Turtle Yacht Club and Marina*. Marsh Harbour Regatta is 22 June to 4 July. Marsh Harbour is the starting place/drop off for many sailing charter companies. Charters can be arranged by the day or week, through numerous agencies (such as Sun Sail at Marsh Harbour, ABC at Hope Town or JIC Boat Rentals and Charter at Treasure Cay, T 367 2507), or more cheaply by private arrangement with boat owners. Ask at local marinas such as the *Jib Room*. Prices from $80 per day. Fishing charters are around US$200/half day, US$300/day.

The diving is good, don't miss Pelican Cay Land and Sea Park, which is an underwater wildlife sanctuary with no fishing or spear fishing allowed and Fowl Cay Bahamas National Trust Preserve with similar restrictions. Many areas are now officially protected and fish life is abundant, green turtles and porpoises numerous in and around harbour areas. Fishing is strictly controlled in reef areas although the coral still shows signs of previous damage by bleaching and careless sailors. Three of the best reefs for diving or snorkelling are Sandy Cay Reef (part of Pelican Cay Park), Johnny's Cay Reef and Fowl Cay Reef at each of which there are several dive sites and a few permanent moorings for small boats. If you like exploring wrecks, the 110-year old *USS Adirondack* with her rusting cannon is worth a visit. If it is windy or the sea rough there is unlikely to be any diving because of poor visibility in the shallow waters. Inland you can dive into Devil's Hole. Specialist dive operations include Dive Abaco at Marsh Harbour (*Conch Inn Marina*, T 367 2787, VHF 16, 800-247 5338, dives 0930, 1430, one tank US$45, 2 tanks US$60, snorkel trip US$30, resort and certification courses, one boat, one dive master, no back-up), Divers Down at Treasure Cay (T 367 2570 ext 126, one tank US$50, 2 tanks US$70, snorkelling US$30), Walker's Cay Dive Shop and Brendal's Dive Shop at Green Turtle Cay, who can offer introductory courses and a wide variety of facilities. For offshore snorkelling, Captain Nick's Tours, from the *Jib Room* marina and restaurant, runs trips out to local reefs and beauty spots, including Pelican Cay. Snorkel gear is available for hire.

Marsh Harbour lacks good beaches, but Mermaid's Cove on the road to the Point is a pretty little beach with excellent snorkelling. The best beach on Great Abaco is probably that at Treasure Cay, where there is a large, sandy bay backed by casuarina trees and a friendly beach bar. On the cays there are lots of lovely sandy beaches with few people on them, many of which are best reached by boat.

Other Sports

You can play tennis at *Bluff House* (guests free), *Great Abaco Beach Hotel* (guests free) or *Green Turtle Club* (US$5/hour). *Walker's Cay Hotel and Marina* (T 305-522 1469, US$125d EP), a 100-acre resort, has tennis courts as well as a range of water activities, including windsurfing (US$15/hour). *Treasure Cay Beach Hotel and Villas* on a 3-mile beach, has a 6,972-yard, 18-hole championship golf course (green fees US$40, cart and club rental), tennis, windsurfing (US$15/hour) and waterskiing (US$10/15 minutes). Other places where you can windsurf include *Abaco Inn* (US$30/day), at Hope Town, *Elbow Cay Club* (US$25/day), the *Green Turtle Yacht Club* (free), *Hope Town Harbour Lodge* (US$20/day), *Pinder's Cottages* (US$20/day).

Marsh Harbour

The town straggles along the flat S shore of a good and busy yachting harbour. It has the major airport about three miles from the town and is the commercial centre of Abaco. As you drive in from the airport you pass government offices, supermarkets and lots of churches and liquor stores. The town has a large white population, but at the last census 40% were found to be Haitian, most of whom live in the districts of Pigeon Pea and The Mud and work as domestic servants in the white suburbs. Many Haitians have now been repatriated however. Shops are varied and well stocked and Barclays and CIBC banks are both represented. The only traffic lights on the island are outside Barclays. BaTelCo is a yellow building off Queen Elizabeth Drive. The recently relocated Tourist Office is nearby. The two main food stores are Golden Harvest and Abaco Market. The Bahamas Family Market on Front Street sells mainly fruit and vegetables grown on Abaco. The Marsh Harbour Dental Clinic (Dr Hornaday, T 367 3167) is near Abaco Market.

Excursions

The roads are better in the N half of the island and it is easy to drive the 26 miles to Treasure Cay, a self-contained resort approached by a long drive through the grounds, past the golf course. There is a nice beach here and lots of watersports available at the marina. The main road continues past Treasure Cay airport and several small communities, where most of the workers for *Treasure Cay* live, to Coopers Town. 20 miles from Treasure Cay, it has lots of little painted wooden houses and an air of bustling importance. It is the seat of the commissioner for N Abaco and about 900 people live here. The Prime Minister, Herbert Ingraham, lives in the area. In 1993-94 a new health clinic was built, the biggest on the island with doctors, dentists and nurses work-

ing there. There is no harbour but along the waterfront are wooden jetties where fishermen clean their catch, leaving piles of conch shells. Offshore on Powell Cay (uninhabited), there are some lovely beaches, good shelling and the *Shipwreck Bar and Grill*. The paved road carries on another 15 miles to Crown Haven, the end of the island. South of Marsh Harbour it is 56 miles to Sandy Point, through citrus groves, or you can fork left to Hole in the Wall, the area where parrots breed. On the way you can visit Spencer Bight and the abandoned Wilson City, a company town founded in 1906 by the Bahamas Timber Company but closed in 1916. In its heyday there was a saw mill and dock facilities and it boasted electricity and an ice plant, both rarities at that time. At Little Harbour you find the highest point in Abaco, which is 120 feet. Little Harbour is a small, pretty and protected anchorage, famed for the Johnston family's artwork in bronze, ceramics and jewelry. Their work is on display in two galleries open 1030-1200, 1400-1500 or by appointment, closed Sundays. Pete Johnston also has *Pete's Pub*, where there are moorings and you can eat at the open air bar on the beach (hot dogs, hamburgers, lobster). There is a nice walk to the old lighthouse and snorkelling is good over the small reef at the E entrance to the harbour. There are caves where the Johnstons lived when they first came to Little Harbour. If you go on Independence Day, 10 July, there is a free for all on the beach, everyone chips in, roast wild pig a feature.

Elbow Cay

The name Elbow Cay is rarely used, people refer to the settlement of Hope Town, marked by a striped lighthouse from the top of which you can get lovely views (built by the British Imperial Lighthouse Service in 1863, it is one of the last hand-powered Kerosene-fuelled beacons still in use, open Monday-Friday 1000-1600)

weaving in the centre of the village she will show how baskets are made, and explain local culture, politics and bush medicine to visitors. Mr Russell always has plenty of sponges for sale (and illegally caught turtle and iguanas, don't buy these) and also works as a bonefishing guide. There is only one telephone in Red Bays, T 329 2369 and leave a message for the person you want to contact.

Fauna and Flora

Andros has an extensive creek system which is largely unexplored. In S Andros the 40-square-mile area beyond the $\frac{1}{2}$ mile long ridge is also uninhabited and rarely visited. The large pine forests and mangrove swamps are home to a variety of birds and animals. In the S there are wild bird reserves which allow hunting in the season (September-March). Sightings of the Bahamian parrot have been reported in S Andros, while rare terns and whistling tree ducks, roseatte spoonbills and numerous different herons have been seen in the N and C areas. Green Cay, one of the many small islands off Andros (20 miles E of Deep Creek) has the world's second largest population of white crowned pigeons. These pigeons are prey to hunters from September to March each year (hunting season). The W side of Andros is undeveloped and other than Red Bays in the NW corner there are no settlements on this side, making it ideal for wildlife; large rock iguanas up to six feet long and hundreds of flamingos live here. During May to August the Andros land crabs migrate from the pine forests to the sea. These enormous crabs are to be found everywhere during this time. Many are caught and exported to Nassau.

Beaches and Watersports

In the N, Nicholl's Town has the best beach. A wide, golden beach runs the length of the N coast, almost to Morgan's Bluff. It is ideal for swimming and excellent snorkelling spots are to be found directly off the beach. Lowe Sound, Conch Sound and Mastic Point all have good beaches. A very pleasant, 2½-mile walk from Nicholl's Town to Morgan's Bluff along a leafy overgrown road (in fact the first road built on the island) leads to the caves at Morgan's Bluff and offers beautiful views of this part of the coast. Further S near Fresh Creek is Staniard Creek where there is an attractive palm-fringed beach with white sand and pleasant settlement close by. Sand bars, exposed at the mouth of Staniard Creek at low tide, are excellent shelling spots. Somerset beach is just S of Fresh Creek, signposted from the main highway. It is a spectacular spot, especially at low tide and another excellent shelling beach. At Victoria Point in C Andros there is a graveyard right on the water's edge. In some parts of Andros on Easter Monday at 0200-0600 there is a candle-light vigil by gravesites at which Easter hymns are sung. The E side of Mangrove Cay has spectacular beaches all lined with coconut groves. In S Andros along the 28-mile stretch from Mars Bay to Drigg's Hill are beautiful palm-lined beaches with occasional picturesque settlements.

Diving and Marine Life

Visitors mostly come for the unspoiled beaches, the diving on pristine reefs in 80°F water with excellent visibility and extraordinary bonefishing. Development has been concentrated on the E coast facing one of the world's largest underwater reefs. This huge barrier reef, the second largest in the Western Hemisphere, plunges 6,000 feet to the Tongue of the Ocean, an exciting drop-off dive. Wreck dive sites include the *Lady Gloria*, an old mailboat sunk recently off Morgan's Bluff, and the *Potomac*, a steel-hulled barge which sank just after the war and is now home to many huge, friendly grouper and parrot fish, as well as some impressive barracuda. Andros has 197 blue holes, of these 50 are oceanic, the rest inland. Formed by water erosion then flooded at the end of the last ice-age, the oceanic holes actually connect to the intricate inland underwater cave system. As tide rushes in and out ideal feeding grounds are created and consequently the oceanic blue holes harbour prolific and diverse marine life and are excellent dive sites at slack tide. The inland blue holes can be very deep (up to 350 feet) and contain a lens of freshwater 40-100 feet deep floating on seawater. Beautiful to swim in: Charlie's blue hole, near Nicholl's Town is clearly signposted as is Church's blue hole, just N of Fresh Creek. Marine life in the inland blue holes is limited, though the rare crustacean *Remepedidia* and the blind cave fish *Lucifuga* have been found. Earthwatch is currently conducting a detailed study on the mosquito fish, one of the few colonists of the blue holes on North Andros. On South Andros two popular blue holes are the "Giant Doughnut" near Deep Creek, S of Kemps Bay, and "Inland Blue Hole Lissy" near the Bluff, S Andros. Legends abound about blue holes, serpents known as Luska, originally a part of Seminole Indian legends are thought to drag unsuspecting swimmers and fishermen below. Caution should be exercised at some of the holes as they are extremely deep. The underwater cave system on Andros is considered to have some of the world's longest, deepest and most stunning caves. A 1991 expedition discovered remains of a Lucayan burial site in one of the blue holes of South Andros. Intact Lucayan skulls were recovered, as well as femurs and hip bones.

Small Hope Bay Lodge is the place to go for diving, just N of Fresh Creek and a short boat journey from the barrier reef, wrecks, caves and an ocean blue hole. A well-run operation with several decades of experience in Andros, they cater for beginners as well as specialty divers and have an excellent safety record. Most guests are on all-inclusive packages, otherwise diving is US$40 for a single tank dive, US$10 for a second tank, US$50

night dive, US$10 snorkelling. Specialty diving is tailored to individual requirements. All deep dives are filmed and the videos are available from US$50, depending on how many dives you want included. This dive operation is one of the more conservation-minded in the Bahamas; no shark feeding here. A liveaboard dive boat is planned, to be based at the *Lighthouse* marina, and may start operations in 1994. Stuart Cove's Dive South Ocean occasionally come over from Nassau and dive in Andros waters. For ecological tours Forfar Field Station, at Blanket Sound N of Fresh Creek, runs guided diving, snorkelling and inland excursions, mainly for high school students or college groups from the USA, T 368 6160/6129 for details. Cheap accommodation may also be available.

Small Hope Bay Lodge also does bonefishing (US$225/day boat and guide for 2 people or US$300/day reef fishing for up to 4), but the best place for serious fishermen and women is the Cargill Creek area, where there are lots of guides. At *Charlie's Haven* rates are US$230/day including guide (T 368 4087), while at *Cargill Creek Fishing Lodge* boats and guides are US$290/day, or US$300 (2 fishermen) at Grassy Camp further S, where you can stay for US$180 pp, or do a one-day Grassy Cay trip for US$800 (maximum 5 people). At *Andros Island Bonefish Club* (known locally as Rupert's Place) a boat and guide for 2 anglers is US$300/day, deep sea fishing starting 1994, US$450/day. All sportfishing is catch and release. The usual weight of bonefish is 5-7 lbs but on most days you will find fish of 12 lbs and over. There are around 100 square miles of flats in the N and middle bights which are fished by Cargill Creek resorts. Most are fished infrequently and you see hardly anyone else. The W side of the island can also be fished, depending on the weather and tide, but it will cost an extra US$50/day for fuel as it is 1½ hours from Cargill Creek. You can still see traditional Baha-

Club has a rake'n'scrape band and traditional stepping dancing with Rosita on saw and Ben on drums.

NB: There has been an economic slump in North Andros following a crackdown on drugs trafficking and several hotels, restaurants and other businesses have closed. As a consequence, petty crime is on the increase and visitors should be vigilant. Leave your valuables at home. S and C Andros appear to be unaffected.

BERRY ISLANDS

There are 30 Berry Islands (population 634) which offer beautiful opportunities for divers and snorkellers. Most are the private homes of the wealthy or inhabited only by wildlife. **Bullock's Harbour** in **Great Harbour Cay** is the main settlement in the area, Great Harbour Cay is the largest cay in the Berry chain at just two miles across. First settled by ex-slaves in 1836, the cay proved difficult to farm. Tourism has not fared well either, a luxury resort with a golf course and sailing club is now derelict. Cruise ships drop anchor off Great Sturrup Cay and passengers can spend the day on the deserted beach there.

The only spot in the Berry Islands which caters for tourists is **Chub Cay**, which was severely damaged by Hurricane Andrew in 1992. The *Chub Cay Club* (US$150, T 325 1490, F 322 5199) has its own airstrip, tennis courts, restaurant, marina and extensive dive facilities offered by Chub Cay Undersea Adventures. There is a deep water canyon at Chub Cay where you can find a variety of colourful reef fish and open water marine life. Staghorn coral can be seen in the shallow waters near Mamma Rhoda Rock. Less natural, but still fascinating is the submarine deliberately sunk in 90 feet of water off Bond Cay, named after James himself.

Many of the cays do not welcome uninvited guests. Interesting wildlife can be found on Frozen Cay and Alder Cay. Terns and pelicans can be seen here and although they are privately owned, sailors may anchor here to observe the birds. Hoffman's Cay, now deserted, was originally home to a thriving farming settlement. Ruins of houses, a church and a graveyard still stand. Paths also lead to a deep blue hole. A golden beach runs along the length of the E coast of the island. On Little Whale Cay, Wallace Groves, the founder of Freeport, has his own home and airstrip. Great Harbour Cay has its own airport served by Airways International from Miami and Fort Lauderdale.

BIMINI

Once thought to be the site of the lost city of Atlantis, the Bimini chain of islands (population 1,638), only 50 miles from Florida, is divided into North and South Bimini and a series of cays. Ernest Hemingway lived on Bimini in 1931-37 at Blue Marlin Cottage and his novel *Islands in the Stream* was based on Bimini. A display of Hemingway memorabilia can be seen at the *Compleat Angler Hotel and Museum*. On South Bimini is the legendary site of the Fountain of Youth, sought by Ponce de León in 1512. The pool known as the Healing Hole is claimed to have some beneficial effects. There are more bars than shops on Bimini, service is minimal, car rental non-existent. It is not a glamorous resort, although there are plenty of luxury yachts moored there. The airplane wrecks at the edge of the airfield at **Alice Town** on North Bimini are mostly the results of unsuccessful drugs running attempts en route from Colombia to Miami. Bimini has been claimed as an important success in the fight against drug running to the US mainland; Gun Cay has become the centre for drug interdiction operations and is full of US DEA personnel. Bimini suffered flood damage caused by Hurricane Andrew in 1992 but soon recovered.

Alice Town is the capital of Bimini although most people live in **Bailey Town** to the N along the King's Highway. Alice Town has a lot of bars and a straw market, if little else. Heading N from Alice Town you come to *The Anchorage*, a restaurant on the highest point on the island with good views of the sea. The beach in either direction is excellent with white sand and good surfing waves. Above the beach is a pathway which passes the picturesque Methodist Church (1858) and leads to Bailey Town.

Cat Cay, to the S, was hit by Hurricane Andrew in August 1992, with winds of 180mph, gusting to 250mph. Damage to island property was estimated at US$100mn. First developed in 1932 it had a golf course, 68 houses for the rich and their staff, and lots of expensive yachts.

Diving and Marine Life

Bimini is famous for big game fishing. Fishing is excellent all year round although 7 May-15 June is the tuna season (blue fin), June and July are best for blue marlin, winter and spring for white marlin. Blue marlin are the favourite target, averaging between 150 and 500 lbs, but which can exceed 1,000 lbs. The S Biminis, Cat Cay and Gun Cay are the places to catch billfish and bluefin. There are lots of fishing tournaments and the Ministry of Tourism promotes over 40 annually, including the Bacardi Billfish Tournament, the Bimini Benefit Tournament, the Bahamas Championship Tournament and the Bahamas Billfish Championship series. *The Bimini Big Game Fishing Club* caters for most fishermen's needs and can arrange fishing trips with guides. It has 180 slips, charter/boat rental, all supplies and a large walk-in freezer for daily catches. Fishing can also be arranged through the *Compleat Angler Hotel*, Brown's Marina or Weech's Bimini Dock.

Scuba diving is recommended, particularly over the Bimini Wall to see the black coral trees, or to the lovely reefs off Victory Cay. Bimini Undersea Adven-tures, run by Bill and Nowdla Keefe, has a comprehensive list of facilities and can also offer sailing, fishing and tennis (T 347 3089, F 347 3079, in the USA 800-348 4644).

Island Information—Bimini
● How To Get There
Bahamasair does not have flights to Bimini, but Chalk International has flights from Miami, Fort Lauderdale and from Nassau to Alice Town with sea planes which land in the harbour. For mailboat details see **Information for Visitors, Inter Island Travel.**

● Where To Stay
The Bimini Big Game Fishing Club (US$148 EP all year, T 347 3391, F 347 3392, PO Box 699), owned by Bacardi, is the main hotel (cottages at US$164 rec) and social centre (beware the Beastwhacker, a cocktail of champagne and Bacardi rum) and has swimming pool and tennis courts. *Bimini Blue Water Ltd* (T 347 3166, F 347 3293, PO Box 627), rooms US$90, 3-bedroomed cottage US$285, suites US$190 also includes Hemingway's Marlin Cottage, private beach, swimming pool and 32-slip marina; *Brown's Hotel and Marina* (T 347 3227, PO Box 601), US$55, 2-bedroomed cottage US$100, near beach; *Compleat Angler Hotel* (T 347 3122, PO Box 601), US$70-80 in town, popular bar; *Admiral Hotel* (T 347 3347), US$72-80 in Bailey Town; *Sea Crest*, US$75 (T 347 3071, P O Box 654), Alice Town, managed by Alfred Sweeting; *Bimini Reef Club and Marina*, South Bimini, US$129 EP, T (901) 758 2376.

● Where To Eat
After dark activities consist of drinking and dancing. *The End of the World Bar* in Alice Town has long opening hours and the back looks out to the harbour; *Yama's Bar*, run by former boxer Billy Yama Bahama Butler; *The Red Lion Pub* is rec for its seafood, as is *Captain Bob Smith's* and *The Big Game Restaurant* on the sea front in Alice Town. The *Calypsonians* play weekly at *The Compleat Angler*, worth seeing, and *Glen Rolle and the Surgeons* provide musical entertainment at *All My Children Hotel*. Other rec nightspots are the *Hy Star Disco* and *Brown's Hotel Bar*, both in Alice Town.

CAT ISLAND

Named after Arthur Catt, a British pirate who was in league with Henry Morgan and Edward Teach (Blackbeard), Cat Island (population 1,678) boasts Lucayan Indian caves near **Port Howe**, as well as the usual underwater sites of interest and beauty. Fifty miles long, it was once called San Salvador, and is a contender for the site of Columbus' first landfall. It has rolling hills and the highest point in the Bahamas, Mount Alvernia, 206 feet above sea level. The island is a centre for the practice of Obeah, a Bahamian voodoo incorporating both bush medicine and witchcraft, which is indicated by bottles and other small objects hanging from the branches of the trees.

Most development has taken place in the S. **New Bight** is the capital and shares an impressive bay with the quaint Old Bight, the site of an early 19th century attempt to establish a cotton plantation. You can see the ruins of Pigeon Bay Cottage, an old plantation house just outside Old Bight. New Bight has a few shops. The annual regatta is held here in August. Above the village you can climb Mount Alvernia and visit Father Jerome's Hermitage. The Stations of the Cross are carved along a winding path leading to the Hermitage, built by Father Jerome, an Anglican priest who converted to Roman Catholicism and designed several churches on Cat Island and Long Island. Fernandez Bay, three miles N of New Bight and home to *The Fernandez Bay Village Resort*, has one of the island's best beaches, a secluded cove with excellent sands. On the most southerly tip of the island are two beaches with facilities: *The Cutlass Bay Club Beach* (tennis, waterskiing) has its own airstrip and a good restaurant. World famous bonefishing flats are within wading distance of the beach. Close by along the crumbling cliff tops are the impressive ruins of the Richman Hill plantation, with ruins of slave quarters, an overseer's

house and a plantation house. The original plantation stretched from the ocean to the inland lake. Another interesting ruin is Colonel Andrew Deveaux' mansion at Port Howe. Granted land on Cat Island for delivering Nassau from the Spanish, he set up a briefly prosperous cotton plantation here. Early settlers in Port Howe lured ships on to the rocks in order to loot their cargoes. Today Port Howe is famous for its coconuts and pineapples, while the bread, cooked in Dutch or Rock wood-fuelled ovens, is said to be the Bahamas' tastiest. The Cat Island Dive Centre at *Hotel Greenwood Inn*, Port Howe offers scuba diving. Run by Uwe Hinrichsen, it attracts German and other

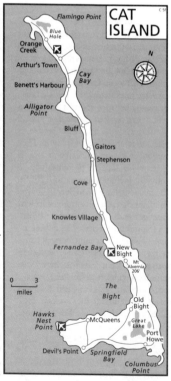

European visitors (T/F 342 3053).

The main settlement in the N of the island is **Arthur's Town**, but other than an airstrip there is not much else; there are no restaurants and only one shop which does not sell much. Local people rely on the weekly mailboat from Nassau for groceries. There are bars but none serves food. Two miles inland is a small lake surrounded by mangrove thickets. Islanders refer to it as a blue hole and tell stories of its supernatural inhabitants. The beaches in the N are excellent. Northside Beach, reached by dirt road, stretches for 20 miles but has no facilities at all and has the ubiquitous debris. Orange Creek is an attractive inlet three miles N of Arthur's Town. Along the nearby shores are the "white sand farms" with small scale farming of beets, potatoes and carrots.

Flora and Fauna

Uninhabited Conception Island and its adjoining reefs, between Cat Island and Long Island, is a land and sea park visited by migrating birds and nesting turtles, protected by the Bahamas National Trust. Many great and little blue herons can be seen at Hawksnest Creek bird sanctuary. In inland ponds it is possible to find the Cat Island turtle (*pseudyms felis*). Unfortunately, the turtles are a source of very rich meat and their numbers have recently dwindled. Near the settlement of Gaitors you can visit large caves full of bats. There are more bat caves S of Gaitors, near Stephenson. Farming is mostly subsistence, using slash and burn to grow crops such as red corn, guinea corn, cassava, okra, peas, beans, sugarcane, watermelons, pineapples, coconuts and bananas. Pot hole farming uses small amounts of soil in deep limestone holes to cultivate plants like the banana tree.

Island Information—Cat Island
● How To Get There

Bahamasair has flights to Arthur's Town from Nassau 4 times a week, 2 of which go via San Salvador. Some hotels have their own airstrips. For details on mailboats see **Information for Visitors, Inter Island Travel**. Transport is difficult in the N as there are no taxis or buses and few cars for hitching lifts.

● **Where To Stay**

There is accommodation only in the S. *Fernandez Bay Village*, New Bight, 1-3 bedroomed cottages (US$165-200), most watersports available, diving, T 342 3043, F 342 3051, 800-940 1905, PO Box 2126, flights can be arranged through Tony Ambrister (T 305-764 6945/792 1905); *Greenwood Inn*, at Port Howe on 8-mile beach, German-run, good snorkelling, scuba diving, pool, satellite TV, US$80d all year, T/F 342 3053; *The Bridge Inn*, New Bight, with disco, US$70-80, reasonable accommodation, good food, T 354 5013; *Orange Creek Inn*, 3 mins from airport, free transport, 16 rooms with kitchenettes, laundromat, store, T 354 4110/11; at Bennet's Harbour ask for Mrs Stracchan who lets rooms occasionally.

● **Where To Eat**

The Bahamas' biggest goat farm is near New Bight. Goat meat is used in a local dish called "souce stew", cooked with potatoes, onions and a lemon lookalike fruit called souce. The restaurant at the *Fernandez Bay Resort* is elegant and expensive. *Greenwood Inn* has Bahamian and European menu. *Pilot Harbour* on waterfront at Old Bight, VHF 16, Bahamian specials, cocktails. *Ambrister's Place*, Dumfries, is rec. Bars in Arthur's Town: *Miss Nelly's* (pool table), the *Hard Rock Café* and *Mr Pratt's Bar* (dominoes); also *Lovers' Boulevard Disco and Satellite Lounge* is popular and has a good local band playing Rake'n'Scrape.

CROOKED ISLAND

Crooked Island, **Long Cay** (joint population 423) and **Acklins** (population 428) comprise Crooked Island District, stretching three sides round the Bight of Acklins and bordered by 45 miles of treacherous barrier reef. At Crooked Island Passage, coral reefs can be found in very shallow water, falling sharply in walls housing sponges of every shape and colour. Although at 92 square miles, Crooked Island is larger than New Providence it is sparsely populated and the

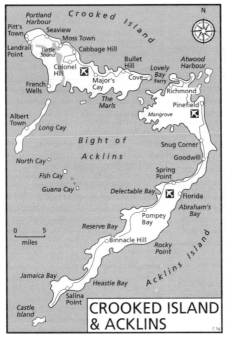

Portland Harbour
Crooked Island
N
Pitt's Town
Seaview
Moss Town
Landrail Point
Turtle Sound
Cabbage Hill
Colonel Hill
Bullet Hill
Major's Cay
Atwood Harbour
Lovely Bay Ferry
Cove
French Wells
The Marls
Richmond
Pinefield
Mangrove
Albert Town
Long Cay
Bight of Acklins
Snug Corner
North Cay
Goodwill
Fish Cay
Spring Point
Guana Cay
Delectable Bay
Florida
Abraham's Bay
Pompey Bay
Reserve Bay
Binnacle Hill
Rocky Point
Acklins Island
Jamaica Bay
Heastie Bay
Salina Point
Castle Island
0   5
miles

CROOKED ISLAND & ACKLINS

C Sg

rant of the hotel *Pittstown Point Landings* (14 rooms in cottages, US$95-110, meals US$40 pp, T 344 2507, 800-752 2322), which has its own airstrip, beaches, fishing, snorkelling, windsurfing and diving facilities. Gun Bluff, near the hotel was thought to have been a pirate's lookout, cannons have been found close by. In the surrounding area many North Americans have winter residences. Two miles away is Landrail Point, the main centre of the island, which has a hotel/restaurant and store. The people here are Seventh Day Adventists so no pork or alcohol is sold and everything closes on Saturdays. *Mrs Gibson's Lunch Room* is recommended for its freshly baked bread and simple Bahamian dishes.

Further S at Cabbage Hill are *T & S Guest Houses* run by the Rev Thompson, who also runs the *Crooked Island Beach Inn* (US$60, T 336 2096, fishing available), near the beach and airport, and is the Bahamasair representative. The capital of Crooked Island is Colonel Hill. There is a restaurant/baker's/guesthouse here run by Mrs Deleveaux, called *Sunny Lea*. Rooms have a good view of Major Cay Harbour. Close to the sheltered lagoon near Major Cay is a large cave; bromeliads can be seen at its entrance.

The airport is at Major Cay; Bahamasair has two flights a week from Nassau, one of which is via Spring Point, Acklins. The *Windward Express* mailboat docks at the harbour in Landrail Point once a week, see **Information for Visitors, Inter Island Travel**.

Acklins is a few miles from Crooked Island and a ferry operates between the

population is declining because of emigration. Tourism is not very developed and there is no electricity or running water in most of the settlements. Once as many as 40 plantations thrived here, but as in other islands, the crops failed because of poor soil and the industry declined. Nowadays, two valuable exports from the Crooked Island and Acklins District are aloe vera for use in skin preparations and the cascarilla bark which is sold to Italy for the production of Campari. Remains of the plantation era can be seen in Marine Farm and at Hope Great House in the N of the island. Bird Rock Lighthouse in the N is said to be the site of one of Columbus' original anchor spots on his first voyage. Close by is Pittstown where you can see the Bahamas' first General Post Office built in the era of William Pitt. It is now the restau-

two islands, docking at Lovely Bay twice a day. The island is 192 square miles and was named La Isabella by Columbus before being known as Acklins Cay and then just Acklins. Archaeological evidence points to a large Indian community once existing between Jamaica Cay and Delectable Bay (possibly the largest in the Bahamas). Today, Acklins is not very developed; there are roads to the settlements, but they are not paved. Atwood Bay is recommended as one of the Family Islands' most beautiful curved bays.

The main settlement on Acklins is **Spring Point**, which has an airport and Bahamasair has scheduled flights twice a week from Nassau, one flight goes via Crooked Island. The *Airport Inn* run by Curtis Hanna is a popular meeting place, with rooms to rent and a restaurant/bar. At nearby Pompey Bay it is still possible to see rock walls which were plantation demarcation boundaries. Pompey was once prosperous and busy; today most of the town is deserted and a tall church on the coast is abandoned. There is also a guesthouse at Pinefield run by the Williams family.

To the S of Acklins is a group of uninhabited cays sometimes referred to as the Mira Por Vos Cays. The most southerly is called Castle Island and is distinguished easily from afar by its tall battery operated lighthouse. There is a large seabird population here. South, North Guana and Fish Cay are all noted as havens for wildlife. **Long Cay** is the largest of the cays in this area and is inhabited. Long Cay was once known as Fortune Island and enjoyed great prosperity in the 19th century as a clearing house for ships between Europe and the Americas. The advent of the steamship made the use of Long Cay port redundant. Today you can see reminders of its former prosperity in the large unused Catholic church, various civic buildings and the relics of a railway system. On the S end of this island there is a large nesting ground for the West Indian flamingo.

ELEUTHERA

This was the first permanent settlement in the Bahamas when Eleutheran Adventurers came from Bermuda and American colonial loyalists fled the mainland during the American Revolution (see **History** above). Their descendants still live here, living in houses painted in pastel colours. The first black settlers were slaves and free Africans from Bermuda. Eleuthera (population 10,600) is only about one mile wide but 110 miles long, with lovely pink sand beaches, particularly on the Atlantic side, coves and cliffs. The main road which runs down the backbone of the island is called the Queen's Highway and makes exploring by car easy and direct. In 1992 Hurricane Andrew hit the island, causing extensive damage. Some resorts stayed closed for the winter season, some went out of business, while others soon reopened. Many homes were destroyed and they took longer than the resorts to be repaired. On Current Island 24 of the 30 houses were smashed; in Gregory Town half the settlement was left homeless; on Harbour Island most homes were badly damaged and in Bogue the storm left three dead. To a visitor now, however, there is little evidence of the hurricane although at Hatchet Bay there are still wrecked boats left high and dry some distance from the sea.

Just N of Gregory Town is the Glass Window Bridge, where you can compare the blue Atlantic Ocean with the greenish water of the Caribbean on the other side, separated by a strip of rock just wide enough to drive a car across. Nearby are two small farming communities, Upper and Lower Bogue. The Bogue was once known as the bog because of its marshy ground. During the hurricane in 1965 the sea flooded the land and now there are salt water pools where you can find barracuda, grouper and snapper which were washed there by the tide. Also in the N is The Cave, which contains some impressive stalagmites and stalactites and the Preacher's Cave, where the Adventurers took shelter. The latter is reached by a rough unpaved track about 10 miles N of North Eleuthera; there is a pulpit carved out of rock from when the cave became a place of worship. Rock Sound Water Hole Park is an ocean or blue hole well stocked with grouper and yellowtail, while the walls are encrusted with flat oysters. Swimming is dangerous. Fishing is restricted.

Fauna and Flora

Eleuthera is visited by many migrant birds. At Hatchet Bay, a few miles S of the Glass Window, there are ring necked pheasants. The Schooner and Kinley Cays in the Bight of Eleuthera are uninhabited but have large populations of white crowned pigeons. On Finlay Cay there are also sooty terns and noddy terns. The cays are protected by the Wild Bird Act. Local indigenous flowers include yellow elder, poincianas and hibiscus. Lizards, chicken snakes and feral goats and pigs are common. North of Hatchet Bay you can visit a bat cave where there are thousands of roosting leaf-nosed bats.

Diving and Marine Life

At the end of 1993, the Plateau became the sixth underwater national park in the Bahamas. It is a pretty site with mini walls and lots of fish in an area about ¾ mile by ½ mile. Funds for permanent moorings are being sought and the park will be policed by dive operators. The usual regulations apply, with no fish feeding, no reef touching, no collecting and no spear fishing. The Plateau is about a mile from the Glass Window, 7 miles from Harbour Island. If you like exciting diving, try riding the Current Cut on the incoming tide, which propels you between islands at a speed of about seven knots. Surfing is also good here. A 300-year old shipwreck at Yankee Channel lies in only ten feet of water, while on the shallow, sharp reefs to the N called the Devil's Backbone, there is the wreck of a train where a barge once sank with its cargo on its way to Cuba, and a 19th century passenger steamship. Four miles S of Royal Island is an old freighter, sunk by fire while loaded with a cargo of bat guano, now used as a landmark by sailors. The guano is an excellent fish food and the wreck is home to enormous fish, with Angel fish weighing up to 15 lbs and parrot fish of 20-30 lbs. A remarkable dive or snorkel site. Unfortunately, illegal bleach used by craw fishermen has spoiled many W side reefs.

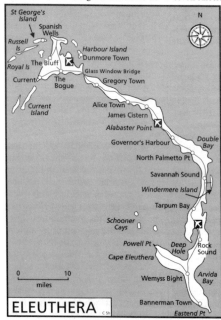

St George's Island
Spanish Wells
Russell Is
Royal Is
The Bluff
Current
The Bogue
Current Island
Harbour Island
Dunmore Town
Glass Window Bridge
Gregory Town
Alice Town
James Cistern
Alabaster Point
Governor's Harbour
North Palmetto Pt
Double Bay
Savannah Sound
Windermere Island
Tarpum Bay
Schooner Cays
Powell Pt
Deep Hole
Cape Eleuthera
Rock Sound
Arvida Bay
Wemyss Bight
Bannerman Town
Eastend Pt

0 ___ 10
miles

ELEUTHERA

Diving and other watersports can be arranged with Valentine's Dive Centre on Harbour Island, which is where *Club Med* sends its guests as the diving is not so good around Governor's Harbour. There are two boats, plenty of staff, full training courses and full service with rental, repair or purchase of dive gear (T 333 2080/2142, 800-323 5655, F 333 2135, PO Box 1, Harbour Island). Alternatively, try *Romora Bay Club* (T 333 2325, T/F 333 2324, PO Box 146, Harbour Island), where the dive operation is run by Jeff Fox and his diving dog. There are two boats taking out groups of 12-14 divers for single tank dives only, US$28 inc tank and weights, resort course US$55-65, full PADI certification available. If the wind is NNE there is no diving.

Sailing boats are recommended to use a local pilot along the notoriously dangerous stretch of coast between Harbour Island and Spanish Wells. *Valentine's Yacht Club*, Harbour Island, has a 50-slip marina taking boats of up to 160 feet and offering full services but no charter yachts. A regatta held to celebrate Discovery Day in November results in Valentine's bursting at the seams. Also on Harbour Island is the new *Harbour Island Club and Marina* with 32 slips for 50-60-foot boats. Full service facilities are gradually coming on stream, contact Roger Ironside for details (T/F 333 2427, VHF 16, PO Box 43). At Spanish Wells there is the *Spanish Wells Yacht Haven* (T 333 4255, VHF 16), with 30 slips, and several boat yards for repairs. On the W side of Eleuthera, *Marine Services* of Eleuthera (T/F 335 0186, VHF 16), with 20 slips, and *Hatchet Bay Yacht Club* are at Hatchet Bay. Round Cape Eleuthera is *Davis Harbour Marina*, with 40 slips (T 3134 6303/6101, VHF 16). This is also the centre for the deep sea and bonefishing charter companies. Harbour Island, Hatchet Bay, Governor's Harbour, Rock Sound and Cape Eleuthera are all ports of entry.

Beaches and Watersports

There are excellent beaches on the E side of South Eleuthera. The W coast, however, is a little rocky. Many of the easterly beaches are backed by coconut palms or rocky cliffs with cedars. Three miles N of Alice Town in North Eleuthera there is a bushy and bumpy road off the main road which leads to Surfers Beach. It has the best surfing waves in the Bahamas and is frequently visited by surfing enthusiasts. Harbour Island has a beautiful pink sand beach which is said to be one of the most photographed beaches in the world. Lighthouse Beach at Cape Eleuthera has three miles of good beach.

Other Sports

There is a 7,068-yard, 18-hole, par 72, championship golf course right by the sea at the *Cotton Bay Beach and Golf Club*, which also provides facilities for diving, snorkelling sailing and fishing. Green fees, US$40, carts US$25. You can play tennis at the *Club Méditerranée* (also windsurfing etc, free for guests), the *Coral Sands Hotel*, the *Dunmore Beach Club*, *Pink Sands Lodge*, *Romora Bay Club* (diving, fishing, sailing, snorkelling), *Rainbow Inn* or *Pineapple Cove* (Gregory Town).

Excursions

Gregory Town is the main settlement in the N of the island and the home of pineapple rum. A pineapple festival is held in June/July, the date changes annually. Pineapples here take 18 months to grow, making them sweeter than plants grown in six months with the help of commercial chemicals. All the farms are small and there are no large plantations. The pineapple slips were washed away by Andrew but by 1993/94 things were back to normal. Half the settlement was left homeless and water and electricity were cut off. There is a beach with good surfing. It is 20 minutes drive from the airport. Locally-made stained glass can be seen and bought at the Simba studio gallery and shop.

Governor's Harbour is one of the oldest settlements in the Bahamas with several interesting colonial period houses. The harbour is picturesque and is linked by a causeway to Cupid's Cay, the original settlement. A new cruise ship pier was built in 1991 but is unusable as no deep water channel was dredged. On 10 November a Guy Festival celebrates Guy Fawkes Day and parades are held, culminating in an evening bonfire. Tourism is dominated here by *Club Méditerranée* (T 332 2270, PO Box 80), on the Atlantic beachfront, which also runs a watersports centre on the harbour side. Keen divers are taken by *Club Med* instructors to dive with Valentine's Dive Centre at Harbour Island, where the diving is better.

In the S, **Windermere Island**, linked to the mainland by a small bridge, was an exclusive resort popular with the British Royal Family but it is closed now. **Tarpum Bay** is the home of MacMillan-Hughes' Art Gallery and Castle. It used to be a big pineapple centre and there are many examples of wooden colonial houses in good repair.

Further S is **Rock Sound**, the largest settlement on the island with a population of about 1,100. It was first known as New Portsmouth and then Wreck Sound. Rock Sound is surrounded by limey, bush covered hills. It has a large modern shopping centre, three churches and many bars.

A few farming villages exist in the extreme S with more stretches of beach and fishing. One such is **Bannerman Town**, once known as the Pearl of the South. In the 1930s it was a prosperous sponge fishing centre with 20 or more sponging schooners anchored off the W shore. Today the settlement is like a ghost town with large churches in ruins and few people. Those who have stayed eke out a living by farming goats and pineapples and catching land crabs to send to Nassau. At the most southerly point of the island, **Cape Eleuthera** and **Point Eleuthera** are sometimes likened to the opposite points on the tail of a fish. On Cape Eleuthera there is a lighthouse which was repaired by the Raleigh Expedition in 1988. At one time the keeper, Captain Finby, was also the local obeah man. Legend has it that he slept with a ghost called the White Lady, who visited him nightly. Lighthouse Beach is three miles long. At Eleuthera Point there is a good cliff top view of Cat Island and Little San Salvador. Be careful as the edges are badly eroded. From here you can also see nesting stacks of fairy terns, shark and barracuda channels and the spectacular blues, greens, yellows, reds and browns of fringing reefs. A lone tarpon known as Tommy cruises off this beach often in less than four feet of water.

Spanish Wells

On St George's Cay, an island off the N of Eleuthera (a short ferry ride), Spanish Wells gets its name from the use of the cay by Spanish ships as a water supply. $1\frac{3}{4}$ miles long and $\frac{1}{2}$ mile wide, until the hurricane disaster of 1992 it was reputed to have the highest per capita income of the Bahamas islands, with the wealth coming from fishing the spiny Bahamian lobster (known locally as bugs) as well as tourism. Most of the boats were wrecked by the storm and the fishermen lost their livelihoods. The population of 1,291 are descended from the original settlers, the Eleutheran Adventurers from Bermuda and the British Loyalists from the mainland, and are all white. The Spanish Wells Museum in a restored wooden house with shutters has exhibits of the island's history and culture, open 1000-1200, 1300-1500, Monday-Saturday. To get to Spanish Wells from North Eleuthera airport, take a Pinders Taxi to the ferry dock, then ferry to the island (about US$10 for 2 people, any other taxi will work out at least double that rate).

A number of local fishermen can be hired as fishing guides off nearby **Russell** and Royal Islands (inhabited by a group of Haitians), payment by negotiation. Royal Island was once developed as a sheep farm by an estranged English dignitary. The old house still stands and paths weave through the overgrown grounds and gardens. Visitors can hire bicycles, but there are no cars.

Harbour Island

This is the most desirable place to stay in North Eleuthera (population 1,216). From the airport it is a quick taxi ride to the dock and from there water taxis wait to take passengers on a ten minute ride to the island (US$4 pp one way or US$8 for only one person). Dunmore Town, named after Lord Dunmore, Governor 1786-1797, is a mixture of pastel coloured cottages, white picket fences and a number of small hotels and restaurants. It was the capital of the Bahamas for a time and once an important shipyard and sugar refining centre. Rum making was particularly popular during Prohibition. The three mile pink sand beach is popular. Bicycles can be rented at the dock. Fishing trips are easily arranged (US$85/half day). Reggie does taxi tours of the island for day trippers and he and his wife Jena run a regular taxi service, recommended, T 333 2116.

• **Where To Stay And Eat** A nice place to eat is *Harbour Lounge*, in an old wooden building overlooking the ferry dock with a bar and indoor or outdoor dining, good food but not cheap, bar food all day and late, Sunday brunch in high season (T 333 2031). *Arthur's Bakery* does lunch and breakfast as well as being a bakery. *Miss Mae's Tearoom* is principally a gift shop selling prints, textiles etc but you can get salads and other food in the courtyard at lunchtime, there is an ice cream parlour and also a 2-bedroom apartment to rent upstairs, US$750/week, contact through *Ocean View Club. Ma Rubie's* restaurant at *Tingum Village* is good for native food but is particularly noted for its cheeseburgers, apparently among the world's top ten, there are also 12 rooms US$75d winter, US$65d summer, and a 3-bedroom, 2-bath cottage US$150,

under 12s free, 3 mins from beach (T 333 2161, PO Box 61). *Romora Bay Club* has timeshare units for rent with a wide variety of units scattered around the property, all decorated differently, US$160-190d, dive packages available with dive shop on site, sailing, tennis, fishing available, bicycles, bar, restaurant on hill top, one sitting for dinner (T 333 2325, F 333 2324, T 800-327 8286, PO Box 146). *Valentine's Yacht Club and Inn*, in town has rooms which get heavily booked during regatta, pool side US$130, garden side US$120, pool, jacuzzi, tennis, 2 restaurants and all the facilities of the marina and dive shop, friendly (T 333 2080/2142, F 333 2135, T 800-323 5655, PO Box 1). On the other side of the island overlooking the pink sand beach, there are several lovely places to stay. *Runaway Hill Club*, built as a private home in the 1940s, now extended and run by Roger and Carol Becht, lovely bar, restaurant, pool and deck all overlooking the sea, 10 luxury rooms, all different in size and character, casual but smart, men wear jackets for candlelit dinner, US$185-200d winter, US$170 summer, US$40 pp MAP (T 333 2150, PO Box 31). *Ocean View Club*, only open for winter season, split level overlooking sea, 9 rooms, those upstairs are larger, lovely old furniture, designer decorated, US$205, lower rooms smaller, US$155, children under 12 half price, meals US$60 pp, large chessmen on patio, F/T 333 2276. *Pink Sands*, still being renovated winter 1993/94 after Hurricane Andrew, will have cottages, tennis, on the beach, lovely location (T 333 2030, F 333 2070, PO Box 86). *Coral Sands*, right on the beach with 14 acres stretching over the hill to Dunmore Town, owned by Brett and Sharon King since 1968, concrete block painted blue and yellow, cottages in gardens, 33 rooms inc 8 suites, US$150-190d, beach bar, restaurant, twice weekly evening entertainment, tennis lit for night play, watersports, games room, library (T 333 2320/2350, F 333 2368, 800-468 2799). All the major hotels close in the autumn for some weeks so plan ahead if visiting Sept-Nov.

Island Information—Eleuthera
● **How To Get There**
There are airports at Governor's Harbour (8 miles from the town, US$20 taxi fare), North Eleuthera and Rock Sound. Bahamasair have scheduled flights daily from Nassau. Airways International have flights from West Palm Beach, Miami and Fort Lauderdale to Eleuthera's 3 airports. US Air Express flies from

Fort Lauderdale to North Eleuthera and Governor's Harbour. Gulfstream International Airlines flies from Miami to all three 2 or 3 times a day (Governor's Harbour T332 2425, North Eleuthera T 333 0278, Rock Sound T 334 2344). American Eagle flies from Miami to Governor's Harbour. Island Express flies daily from Fort Lauderdale and 5 times a week from Orlando to North Eleuthera. Four mailboats call at Eleuthera. See **Information for Visitors, Inter Island Travel**, or ask the harbour master or shopkeepers about mailboat sailings. Car hire from all 3 airports and in town costs US$45-50/day, Ross Garage—U Drive It Cars (Harbour Island, T 333 2122); ASA Rent-A-Car Service (T 332 2575); Governor's Harbour Car Rental Service (T 332 2575); Hilton Johnson (near Hatchet Bay, T 332 0241/335 6241); Wendell Bullard Taxi and Car Rental (North Eleuthera, T 335 1165); also Ethel Knowles at *Ethel's Cottages*, at Tarpum Bay. You can also hire mopeds. There are some public buses.

● **Where To Stay**

Gregory Town: *Cambridge Villas*, in Gregory Town, run by Mr and Mrs Cambridge, painted yellow, 21 double rooms US$50-60, 2-bedroomed apartment US$70-100 sleep 4-8, also triple and quad rooms US$60-75 (T 335 5080, F 335 5308, PO Box 1548), pool, transport to Golden Key beach for swimming or elsewhere for surfing, bar/restaurant, music some nights, expansion started but delayed by Hurricane Andrew, rental cars available; *The Cove Eleuthera*, also known as *Pineapple Cove*, run by gregarious George Mullin, rooms in scattered cottages on headland with rocky cove one side, sandy cove the other US$89-129, triples available, children under 12 free, large airy dining room, rather spartan but relaxed, some rooms need refurbishment, small pool, tennis, snorkelling, hammocks, T 335 5142, F 335 5142, PO Box 1548) is just outside the town within walking distance. At **Hatchet Bay**, *Rainbow Inn*, US$115 a night, 3-bedroomed villa US$150, T 335 0294, PO Box EL 25053, has tennis, swimming pool and a good restaurant, 2-storey cottages became bungalows after hurricane, rocky outlook, good snorkelling, caves, fantastic view, Rainbow beach 1 mile, two beaches just other side of hill, bicycles for guests, live entertainment Wed evenings in nautical bar, popular, run by Ken Keene, friendly host; nearby is *Hilton & Elsie Island House*, 1-2 bedroom apartments US$500-700/week, rental car US$200/week,

on hill, great view of island, Rainbow beach close or walk 1 mile to Eden beach on other side if rough, good kitchens, ideal for families, food stores in nearby Hatchet Bay or Rainbow Bay, T 335 6241, 332 0241, Hilton is a taxi driver and does car rentals.

Governor's Harbour and the S: *Club Méditerrannée*, T 332 2271, US$150 adults, US$100 children; N of the town near North Palmetto Point on the ocean beach is *Unique Village*, with rooms, apartments or 2-bedroom villas US$80-168, restaurant, bar, satellite TV, children under 18 free in summer, under 12 in winter, all with sea views, T 332 1830/1288, F 332 1838; *The Cigatoo Inn* (US$63-90) (T 332 2343, PO Box 86), 6 miles from the airport, sits on top of a hill with good views of the bay, be prepared for loud music; *Laughing Bird Apartments* (US$65-80d, T 332 2012/1029, F 332 2358, PO Box EL 25076) efficiency units and a guest house US$65d, US$100 for 1-4 people, in town, overlooking the beach, managed by nurse Jean Davies. **Tarpum Bay:** *Hilton's Haven* (US$50-65) near beach and Rock Sound airport, bicycles, car rental, bar/restaurant with Bahamian specials, rec (T 334 4231/4125); *Cartwrights Ocean View* (US$70, cottage US$90-150) (T 334 4215), rec; *Ethel's Cottages*, on the waterfront (US$80), families welcome, Mrs Ethel Knowles also rents out cars (T 334 4233, PO Box 27). *Winding Bay Beach Resort* (US$280d summer, US$292d winter, all inclusive) on a secluded lagoon is a less formal resort (T 334 2020, F 334 4057, PO Box 93). **Rock Sound:** *Edwina's Place* (US$55), run by Edwina Burrows, modest accommodation but highly rec, T 334 2094, PO Box 30; *Cotton Bay Beach and Golf Club*, 77 rooms on 2two miles of sandy beach (US$250-310 winter per room, US$135-165 summer, MAP US$50pp, plus 15% service charge and 8% government tax, packages available), upmarket with its Robert Trent Jones 18-hole golf course designed by Arnold Palmer around the beach and ponds, and excellent tennis with 4 all-weather courts and pro-shop, croquet, snorkelling, most watersports are available here, inc deep sea fishing, very good food, closed Sept-Oct, T 334 6101/6156, F 334 6082, 800-334 3523, PO Box EL26028; *Club Eleuthera*, Rock Sound, all-inclusive resort, overlooks ocean, 36 rooms, US$190d all year, set in 37 acres, restaurant, bar, pool, watersports, volleyball, tennis, bicycles, ping pong, chess and other games, golf at *Cotton Bay Club* is extra, T 334

4055/56, F 334 4057, PO Box 126093; *Palmetto Shores Vacation Villas*, at South Palmetto Point, 12 miles S of the airport, 1-3 bedroom villas, US$90-180, a/c, tennis, snorkelling gear, watersports, rental cars or scooters, T/F 332 1305, PO Box EL25131.

● **Where To Eat**

The pineapples on Eleuthera are said to be the world's sweetest (see above, Gregory Town). In Gregory Town they produce a pineapple rum called "Gregory Town Special" which is highly rec. Pineapple upside down pudding is a common dish. Other local dishes include Cape Eleuthera's conch chowder, which is a substantial meal, the best is supposed to be from Mary Cambridge in Gregory Town. Hulled bonavas (a type of bean which tastes like split pea soup) or hulled corn soup with dumplings of rice. This is eaten traditionally after a special church service on Good Friday. On New Year's Eve traditional fare includes Benny Cake, pig's feet or mutton souse, or cassava/potato bread. In many of the smaller settlements such as James Cistern, outdoor or Dutch ovens are still used to bake bread. Most of the resorts have their own restaurants. Others which have been rec are *Cambridge Villas*, in Gregory Town, good seafood, fairly expensive; in Governor's Harbour, *Blue Room* (T 332 2736) is a restaurant/bar/disco, as is *Ronnie's* in Cubid's Cay, free transport to yacht or hotel at night; there are plenty of Bahamian places to eat in Governor's Harbour, fairly smart are *Buccaneer* (open Mon-Sat, no credit cards, T 332 2500, on New Bond St on top of hill) and *Sunset Inn* (on water, open daily from 0800, pool table, satellite TV, juke box), smarter is *Kohinoor*, three miles outside town on hilltop, open Tues-Sun for lunch and dinner, local and American dishes, happy hour 1600-1800, T 332 2668. *Lady Blanche's Lifesaver Restaurant* in Upper Bogue serves the best cracked conch in the area, run by hospitable family, prices reasonable; for very cheap, tasty food try a takeaway meal of barbeque ribs or chicken for less than US$5 at roadside stands in James Cistern; *Big Sally's Disco*, just N of Rock Sound, cocktails, bar snacks, dancing; *Cush's Place* (between Gregory Town and Hatchet Bay) does cookouts Sat and Sun afternoons with music and dancing, US$10; Lida Scavella in Hatchet Bay does cheap food, her pastries are rec; *Hatchet Bay Yacht Club* has good food, videos and music; outside Palmetto Point is *La Rastic*, a reasonably priced restaurant/bar with traditional fare,

no credit cards, T 332 1164; a popular bar in this area is *Mate and Jenny's Pizza*, try conch pizza, good cocktails, T 332 2504; in Rock Sound, *Edwina Burrows'* restaurant is highly rec, good food reasonably priced, popular barbeque dishes; *Sammy's Place* is another rec restaurant and bar, open daily 0800-2200, T 334 2121. *The Islander* is a popular, friendly bar; several bars in Wemyss Bight and Green Castle sell spirits in half pint glasses very cheaply; rec in Deep Creek are *Bab's Place* and *Mr Pratt's Bar*; *The Waterfront Bar* in Rock Sound is cheap, no food, while *The Ponderosa* and *The Dark Side* are bars and cheap fast food restaurants.

THE EXUMAS

The chain of 365 Exuma cays and islands stretches for 90 miles although the majority of the 3,539 inhabitants live on **Great Exuma** and **Little Exuma** at the S end. The island of Barreterre (pronounced Barra Terry) can be reached from Great Exuma by a bridge. There is a ferry to Stocking Island from Great Exuma and another to Lee Stocking Island from Barreterre. Great Exuma is long and narrow, covered with scrub and dry woodland. The soil is pitifully thin but there are aromatic shrubs, curly-tailed lizards and songbirds and a few wild peacocks. Around the villages are a few patches of what the Lands and Surveys map accurately calls 'casual cultivation'. The main industry is tourism, based on yachting and a few hundred winter visitors who own houses on the island. In 1994 the government approved a US$90mn residential and resort development covering 518 acres on Exuma. A US$35mn hotel is to be built in the first phase and there will eventually be a marina, golf course and casino as well.

The islands were virtually uninhabited until after the American Revolution, when Loyalists from the S colonies were given land and brought their slaves to grow cotton. During the late 18th century the British Crown granted Denys Rolle, an Englishman, 7,000 acres of land and he set up cotton plantations at Rolletown,

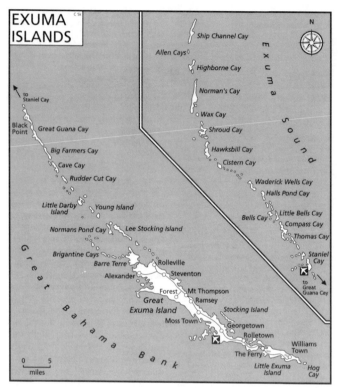

EXUMA ISLANDS

Ship Channel Cay
Allen Cays
Highborne Cay
Norman's Cay
Wax Cay
Shroud Cay
Hawksbill Cay
Cistern Cay
Waderick Wells Cay
Halls Pond Cay
Little Bells Cay
Bells Cay
Compass Cay
Thomas Cay
Staniel Cay
to Great Guana Cay

Exuma Sound

to Staniel Cay
Black Point
Great Guana Cay
Big Farmers Cay
Cave Cay
Rudder Cut Cay
Little Darby Island
Young Island
Lee Stocking Island
Normans Pond Cay
Brigantine Cays
Barre Terre
Rolleville
Alexander
Steventon
Forest
Mt Thompson
Great Exuma Island
Ramsey
Stocking Island
Moss Town
Georgetown
Rolletown
Williams Town
The Ferry
Little Exuma Island
Hog Cay

Great Bahama Bank

N

0   5
miles

Rolleville, Mt Thompson, Steventon and Ramsey. Following the emancipation of the slaves and poor cotton harvests because of the exhaustion of the soil, it was believed that Rolle's son gave away his lands to his former slaves, who were also called Rolle as was customary at the time. However, no deeds have been found confirming transfer of title and longstanding squatter's rights provide an adequate title to the land for many. Today, half the population bears the surname Rolle and two of the largest settlements are Rolleville and Rolletown.

The Exuma cays are in general isolated communities which are difficult to get to (the exception being Staniel Cay).

Their inaccessibility has attracted undesirable attention; Norman's Cay was for some time the drug smuggling centre of Carlos Lehder, the Colombian drug baron deported from the Bahamas in 1982 and now in prison in the USA. In 1993 the cay was confiscated by the Government and put up for sale. Recent attempts to control drug smuggling include mooring Fat Albert, an airship full of radar equipment, over Great Exuma, and low flying helicopters also monitor activity.

Diving and Marine Life

The Exuma Cays begin at Sail Rocks about 35 miles from Nassau. Much of the Exuma chain is encompassed in the

Exuma Cays Land and Sea Park, an area of some 176 square miles set up by the Bahamas National Trust to conserve all underwater life and for boating, diving and observation of wildlife. There is a warden's residence on Waderick Wells Cay. On the northerly Allen Cays can be seen the protected Rock Iguanas which grow up to two feet long and are known as Bahamian Dragons, but they are extremely tame. The park stretches between Wax Cay and Conch Cut, 22 miles away and offers more delights for underwater explorers, with beautiful coral and limestone reefs, blue holes and shipwrecks. Worth visiting are the underwater valley at Ocean Rock, the huge caves filled with black coral called the Iron Curtain, or Thunderball Grotto at Staniel Cay, where part of the James Bond film and the Disney film *Splash*, were made. Watch out for dangerous currents. Individual and package diving can be arranged with Exuma Fantasea, run by Madelaine and Ed Haxby, who are environmentally conscious. Ed is a marine biologist, is PADI licensed and has been researching the marine environment in the Bahamas for 20 years. He can be contacted through hotels which offer diving packages or in George Town T/F 336 3483, PO Box 29261. Get in touch with Ed Haxby for information on a stromatolite reef on the E (Atlantic) shore of Stocking Island. This is a growing reef of layered limestone, a living fossil and the oldest evidence of life on earth, dating back 3.5mn years.

Beaches and Watersports

Stocking Island is a long thin island about a mile from the mainland at Elizabeth Harbour, George Town. Its shape and position provide a natural protection for the harbour. It has good beaches and a burger bar and is famous for its Mysterious Cave, but this can only be reached by divers. A boat leaves the *Peace and Plenty Hotel* in George Town at 1000 and 1300, roundtrip US$8, free for guests, or boats can be hired from Exuma Fantasea (most watersports available) in George Town to visit the reefs off Stocking Island. The Three Sisters Rocks which rise out of the water some 100 feet from the shore, are situated between two very good beaches: Jimmy Hill, which is a long empty beach good for swimming, and the beautiful bay of Ocean Bight. Other recommended beaches are the Tropic of Cancer Beach, 15 miles E of George Town, Cocoplum Beach, 20 miles N of George Town, Jollie Hall Beach, two miles W of George Town (no land access) and Out Island Inn Beach, George Town.

The Visiting Yachts Regatta is held in early March and on the fourth Thursday in April the Family Island Regatta is held at George Town when working boats compete for the title of "Best in the Bahamas". During August there is a series of smaller regattas at Black Point, Barreterre and Rolleville. For details of sportfishing, contact Bob Hyde, Director of Sportfishing at *Peace and Plenty Hotel*, T 800 525 2210; there is a bonefishing lodge with certified guides and three areas to fish. In October the Bonefish Bonanza Tournament is held at *Peace and Plenty Hotel*, George Town. In November a second Bonefish Bonanza Tournament is held at the *Peace and Plenty*. There are several marinas in the Exumas. Exuma Fantasea Marina in George Town near *Club Peace and Plenty*, for motor boats up to 30 feet, rentals and sales of Boston Whalers, dive shop on site, T 336 3483; Exuma Docking Service, 52 ships, usual services, bar, fuel, showers etc, T 336 2578, VHF 16; Happy People Marina, Staniel Cay, 6 ships, 6 feet depth, showers, laundry, grocery, restaurant, T 355 2008; Staniel Cay Yacht Club, 4 ships, all services, tackle and bait, hotel, repairs, T 355 2024, VHF 16; Highborne Cay, fuel, electricity, supplies, restaurant, bar, VHF 16; Sampson Cay Colony, 30 ships, 7 feet depth, all services, charters and boat rentals, hotel, wet and dry storage, T 355 2034, VHF 16.

Excursions

The main town on Great Exuma is *George Town*, a pleasant little town built on a strip of land between a round lake and the sea. A narrow channel allows small boats to use the lake as a harbour but yachts moor offshore, often several hundred at a time in the peak winter months. The large and beautiful bay is called Elizabeth Harbour and is yet another contender for the site of Columbus' harbour that could "hold all the ships in Christendom." The main building is the Government Administration Building, pseudo colonial, pink and modelled on Nassau's Government House. Opposite is a large tree under which women plait straw and sell their wares. There are several pretty buildings, St Andrew's Church (Anglican), blue and white on the top of a little hill and the *Peace and Plenty Hotel* in an old cotton warehouse which was formerly the site of a slave market. There is a good range of shops and the supermarket is well stocked. The Sandpiper shop has an interesting array of clothes and souvenirs.

To the S of George Town is Rolletown, a small village on a hill overlooking the sea. Many old houses are painted in bright blues, yellows and pinks. There is a small cemetery in which women buried settlers from the 18th century in three family tombs: husband, wife and small child of the Mackay family. The Ferry is a small settlement by the beautiful strait which separates Great and Little Exuma, but there is a bridge there now, not a ferry.

North of George Town there is a thin scatter of expatriate holiday houses and a few shops along the Queen's Highway. East of the road are several fine beaches, including Hoopers Bay and Tar Bay. The airport turning is N of George Town. Small villages are Moss Town, Mount Thompson, Steventon and Rolleville. Moss Town was once an important sponging centre. Close by you can see The Hermitage, brick tombs dating back to just after the American War of Independence, not to be confused with the Hermitage or Cotton House close to Williams Town on Little Exuma. Mt Thompson was once the farming centre of Exuma and is important for its onion packing house. Some of the cottages in Rolleville, 16 miles NW of George Town, were originally slave quarters. The town overlooks a harbour and was the base of a group of rebellious slaves who attempted to escape and thereafter refused to work except in the mornings, until emancipation. Unfortunately, quite a large area of N Exuma is disfigured by roads which were laid out as part of a huge speculative land development scheme in the 1960s. Almost all the lots are still empty, but Cocoplum Beach and the coastal scenery are unspoilt. At the N end of the island is a bridge to Barreterre, with more fine scenery and places to eat lunch. At Lee Stocking Island, just offshore, the Caribbean Marine Research Centre is involved in research into the tilapia, a freshwater fish brought from Africa which can grow in salt water. This can be visited by prior appointment.

A bridge leads to Little Exuma, which is 12 miles long and one mile wide. An attractive cove is Pretty Molly Bay, next to the abandoned *Sand Dollar Hotel*. A mermaid story is based on Pretty Molly, a slave girl who sat on the rocks at night and gazed by the light of the moon towards Africa. Near Forbes Hill is the "Fort", built in 1892 and said to be haunted. On Good Friday a nearby tree is said to give off a substance the colour of blood. Williams Town is the most southerly of the settlements on Exuma. Salt used to be made in the lagoon. Perched on the cliff top here is a tall white obelisk which not only guided passing ships safely in the 19th century, but was an advertisement that salt and fresh water could be picked up here. The Cotton House, near Williams Town, is the only plantation owner's house still standing in the Exumas. It is at the end of a

driveway marked by a pair of trees, but is tiny, not grand. Slave quarters can be seen close by.

The Cays

Staniel Cay has excellent beaches with a half mile of sand dunes on the ocean side of the cay and good watersports facilities. On Staniel Cay during Bahamian Independence Day weekend on 10 July, there is a bonefishing festival, entrance fee US$20. The Staniel Cay Yacht Club provides free food in the evening and a rake'n'scrape band plays traditional music. The morning before the contest there is a sailing regatta for working Bahamian sailboats. A Bahamian sailboat regatta is held on New Year's Day. The Royal Entertainers Lounge serves food and drinks.

Farmer's Cay to the S of Staniel Cay has a lively annual festival called The Farmer's Cay First Friday in February Festival at which there are races, dancing games and the Bahamas' only Hermit Crab Race. Further S on Darby Island is an old mansion which is probably the remains of a large coconut plantation.

Forty miles off Staniel Cay on the edge of the Tongue of the Ocean is Green Cay, home to the world's second largest population of white crowned pigeons.

Island Information—Exuma
● How To Get There

There is an international airport at Moss Town with a 7,500 foot runway, 2 miles from George Town, and another airport at George Town with an 8,000 foot runway, but this is closed to commercial traffic. Confusingly the Exuma International Airport at Moss Town carries the (GT) George Town code. American Eagle flies daily from Miami into Moss Town in high season, 4 times a week in summer, Bahamasair flies from Nassau and Stella Maris, Long Island. Island Express has daily scheduled flights from Fort Lauderdale. Airways International have 4 flights daily from Miami and Fort Lauderdale and 2 flights a day from West Palm Beach in high season. Gulfstream also flies twice daily from Miami (T 345 0801 in George Town). Mr Harry Nixon runs a charter service, Nixon Avia-

tion and Harken Air (PO Box 3, Airport, George Town, T 336 2104). Bahamasair flights from Nassau through George Town to Long Island are once or twice daily, they are often booked up well in advance. For details on mailboat sailings, see **Information for Visitors, Inter Island Travel**.

● Transport

Taxis are expensive but plentiful. The fare from the airport to George Town is US$22. Hitching is easy. Cars can be rented from George Town, ask at *Peace and Plenty Hotel*. Buses run between Rolleville and George Town. Christine Rolle runs Island Tours from George Town, leaving at 1000 and 1400, including a native lunch, visits to various settlements and to Gloria, the "shark lady," on Little Exuma, who catches sharks and sells the teeth as souvenirs. Bicycles can be rented from *Two Turtles* shop or several hotels.

● Where To Stay

Coconut Cove, a mile W of George Town, newest hotel, 9 beach or garden rooms, US$128-153d, one suite US$216d EP, about 20% less in summer, diving/honeymoon/pilots packages available, a/c and fans, minibar, beach towels and robes provided, transport to town and to Stocking Island, boat rentals, pool, popular Fri barbeque, T 336 2659, F 336 2658; *Two Turtles Inn*, 200 yards from harbour in George Town, 14 rooms, US$78, rooms large enough for 4, a/c, TV, some have kitchenettes, barbeque on Fri nights (T 336 2545, F 336 2528, 800-327 0787); *Club Peace and Plenty*, T 336 2551/2, F 336 2093, 800-525 2210, PO Box 29055, dive, fishing, honeymoon packages available, 300 yards from harbour, the building was once the slave market and sponge warehouse, 35 rooms/suites US$110-140 plus US$17/day for tax and service, a/c, all rooms have balcony overlooking harbour, entertainment some evenings, pool, sailboats, bicycles, restaurant, bar. The hotel also has a quieter *Beach Inn*, 16 rooms, US$120-130, US$17 tax and service, a/c, fans, balcony, pool, sailboats, restaurant, bar, one mile out of George Town, lots of water sports, T 336 2250, F 336 2093, and a planned *Bonefish Lodge*, to have 5 rooms in a timber building close to the fishing grounds; *Regatta Point*, on a point just outside George Town, private beach, 5 apartments for 2-4 people, US$98-148, kitchens, bicycles, sunfish, dock, run by Nancy Bottomlea, T 336 2206, F 336 2046, 800-327 0787; *Pirates Point* villas,

private beach, just S of George Town, US$490/week (T 336 2554); *Marshall's Guesthouse*, US$30 (T 336 2571), John Marshall (grocery shop in George Town) has apartments to rent by week/month; also apartments at Sea Watch, an isolated position 10 miles N of George Town on fine beach, T 336 4031. *Three Sisters Beach Club and Hotel*, Mount Thompson, 12 rooms or 3 villas, US$95d, on beach, satellite TV, live music Fri, Sat nights, restaurant, T 358 4040, F 358 4043, 800-253 2711, PO Box EX 29196. *Staniel Cay Yacht Club*, has own private airstrip, accommodation in waterfront properties, 4 cottages US$195d, houseboat cottage US$195d, US$225 triple, inc all meals and use of skiff and outboard motor, larger cottage sleeps 4 US$150 EP, beach, marina, scuba diving gear available, T 355 2011/2024, F 355 2044, 800-825 5099.

● **Where To Eat**

The main hotels in George Town, *Peace and Plenty* (dance with local band Sat nights), *Two Turtles* (barbeque Fri nights, very lively and good value but take your own cutlery if you want to cut up your steak, plastic only provided, happy hour 1700-2300, US$1.50 for spirit and mixer, frequented by visitors and ex-pats), have good restaurants. For sandwiches and light meals, *Ruth's Deli*, in George Town, open Mon-Sat 0900-1700, no credit cards, T 336 2596. *Eddy's Edgewater*, T 336 2050, specializes in Bahamian food, fried conch is rec, open Mon-Sat 0730-2300, no credit cards; *Sam's Place*, run by Mr Sam Gray, manager of the marina, T 336 2579, at dock, open daily from 0730 (expensive); *La Shante*, Forbes Hill, good, open daily 1000-0200, happy hour Sun 1800-1900, 3 a/c rooms to rent, guided bonefishing, T 345 4136; *Silver Dollar*, George Town, traditional Bahamian cooking, T 336 2615, no credit cards; *Central Highway Inn*, T 345 7014, on the road 6 miles NW of George Town, Bahamian specialities; *Rodriguez Neighbourhood Bar/Restaurant & Lounge*, at Harts, a settlement 13 miles outside George Town, largest night club on Exuma, on waterfront, live band Fri, disco Sat, Sun, famous for its conch fritters. Others doing mainly peas'n'rice type dishes are *Iva Bowes* and *Three Sisters* in Mt Thompson, *Kermit Rolle's*, in Rolleville is by appointment only but he also has a good restaurant opp the airport building, *Kermit's Airport Lounge*, for breakfast, lunch or dinner, takeaway service, T 345 0002, VHF 16; and *Fisherman's Inn*, Barreterre, very good. *Staniel Cay Yacht Club*, restaurant is open to non-guests if prior notice is given, T 355 2011/2024, VHF 16, breakfast 0800, lunch 1300, dinner 1900 one sitting, box lunches available. Discos at *Cousins*, up hill from *Club Peace and Plenty*, late night music and bar; *Paramount Club* (Moss Town), *Oasis* (Queen's Highway near Mt Thompson), *Flamingo Bay* (George Town, under new management 1994).

INAGUA

Inagua (Great and Little), population 985, is the most southerly of the Bahamas Islands and the third largest. Little Inagua is uninhabited now, but the 49-square mile island is reputed to hide the treasure of Henri Christophe, one-time ruler of Haiti. On a clear day, Great Inagua is visible from both Cuba and Haiti. The highest points on the island are Salt Pond Hill at 102 feet and East Hill at 132 feet. Vegetation is sparse because of low rainfall, the buffetting trade winds and lack of fresh water, but this has granted ideal conditions for salt production leading to a development and prosperity not enjoyed by any of the surrounding islands. It is thought that the name Inagua comes from the Spanish *lleno* (full) and *agua* (water): *henagua*. This was apparently the name of the island when the first salt farmers settled there. In 1803 records show only one inhabitant, but the success of the salt industry meant that by 1871 the population had risen to 1,120. Although trade barriers in the USA caused the decline of the salt trade in Inagua for many years, the industry was revitalized in the 1930s with the establishment of the Morton Salt Company, which now utilizes 12,000 acres. Morton Bahamas Ltd installed a power plant which supplies electricity to all homes in Matthew Town. Inagua has the best telecommunications system in the Family Islands and nearly everyone has a telephone. For a while the island supported a cotton plantation; although

a shortlived enterprise, wild cotton can still be found growing on Inagua today. Outside Matthew Town you can still see the ruins of the cotton mill and the narrow plantation roads, as well as the ruins of a prison from the days when the community was large enough to need one.

Flora and Fauna

The SE side of the island is rocky and because of the effects of the sea and wind, the trees do not grow more than a foot tall. Further inland trees have a better chance of maturing. Many cactii are found in this rocky part of Inagua, in particular the dildo cactus and the woolly-nipple. On Little Inagua, although it is largely overgrown, it is possible to see some of the only natural palms in the Bahamas. The whole of Little Inagua is a Land and Sea Park and is a Bird Sanctuary.

Inagua has a restricted access National Park which is home to a wide range of birds including the world's largest flamingo colony on Lake Rosa, a 12-mile stretch of marshy wildlife sanctuary. Almost half of Great Inagua is included in the 287-square-mile park. Visitors should contact the Bahamas National Trust in Nassau (PO Box N-4105, T 393 1317). A basic but comfortable camp has been established on the W side, 23 long miles by jeep from Matthew Town. National Trust wardens will accompany you on tours of the area and it is possible to view the flamingoes close up. At certain times of the year they cannot be approached. Jimmy Nixon, one of the original wardens, is recommended as a guide. Early spring is the breeding season when large numbers of flamingoes congregate on the lake. At the Union Creek camp on the NW side of the island is a breeding and research area for Green and Hawksbill turtles, called Turtle Sound. It is ideal for observing sea turtles at close quarters. On the E side of the island are mangrove swamps which are the nesting grounds for many birds including cormorants, pelicans and the rare reddish egret. Here you can also see the white tailed tropic bird and inland, the Bahamas parrot, the most northerly species of parrot in the world.

Beaches

Apart from the rocky SE side of the island, Inagua has many deserted and unspoiled beaches. Those which are used by locals include Cartwright's beach, with bar/restaurant, within easy reach of Matthew Town, Farquharson's Beach and Matthew Town Beach, which is pleasant and conveniently located.

Sports

It is possible to play tennis and basketball in Matthew Town, but the most popular pastime is hunting. You can arrange to go on a wild boar hunt with Herman Bowe (known as the Crocodile Dundee of the Bahamas, who prefers to hunt barefoot) or Jimmy Nixon (the excellent National Trust guide). On Emancipation Day (1 August) and other public holidays, wild boar is roasted on the beach and there are wild donkey races. Rodeos take place on an ad hoc basis.

Island Information—Inagua
● How To Get There
The airport is on Great Inagua. Bahamasair have 3 scheduled flights a week from Nassau via Mayaguana. The mailboat takes 2 days from Nassau, see **Information for Visitors, Inter Island Travel**.

● **Transport**

A taxi from the airport to Matthew Town costs about US$4. There are taxis but no buses. Mr Harry Ingraham runs a fleet of 3 tour buses called Great Inagua Tours, rates negotiable. Most roads are paved, except for those leading into the interior. If you want to see the island properly you will need transport, particularly if you travel to the N side of the island. Jeeps for hire from Mr Burrows at Matthew Town Service Station, rates negotiable but expect to pay at least US$40/day. To get out to the camps arrange transport with the warden in Matthew Town (about US$10). To arrange fishing expeditions or trips around the island contact the local repair man, Cecil Fawkes (nicknamed the old Red Fox), whose boat is called "*The Foxy Lady*", or Mr Cartwright. There is no set rate, prices are negotiated. There is a marina and boats can moor here and refuel.

● **Where To Stay**

There are several guest houses in Matthew Town. The *Main House*, US$42, T 339 1267, F 339 1265, has 4 rooms. There is also the *Ford's Inagua Inn*, T 339 1277, US$35, with 6 rooms and a few small private guesthouses such as *Walkine's*, T 339 1500 (enquire locally for information). There are 2 camps, *Union Creek* in the NW and *Flamingo Camp*, 23 miles from Matthew Town, with basic accommodation. Bunks cost about US$10 a night and reservations should be made with The Bahamas National Trust, PO Box N4105, Nassau (T 323 1317 or 323 2848).

● **Where To Eat**

Eating out is cheaper than Nassau or Grand Bahama. For a typical Bahamian meal of macaroni, coleslaw, ribs or chicken and potato salad, expect to pay US$6-7. Local dishes include roast wild boar, baked box fish, crab meat 'n rice and roast pigeon and duck. A popular local drink is gin and coconut, which is made with fresh coconuts on special occasions. *Topps Restaurant and Bar*, run by the Palacious brothers is rec for its seafood dishes, fresh boiled fish is served for breakfast; also rec is *The Hide Out Club*, run by Mr Cox, which is a popular dance and drinking spot; *Pride*, run by Mr Moultry is very friendly. Nightlife revolves around the local bars, which periodically have live music and dancing.

Matthew Town has a Bank of the Bahamas Ltd (open 0930-1430 Mon-Thur, 1030-1830 Fri) and 6 churches.

NB Mosquitoes can be a problem at some times of the year, avoid May. Credit cards are not generally accepted, take plenty of cash with you.

LONG ISLAND

Long Island (population 3,107) lies SE of Little Exuma and is 57 miles long and 4 miles across at its widest. Columbus made a stop here and changed its name from the Arawak name Yuma to Fernandina, after Ferdinand, the King of Spain. The island has a variety of communities from different ethnic backgrounds, from Europe, Africa and North America. Most islanders live on the W side where the hills and dunes offer some protection from the sea. There are paths and dirt tracks to the E side, mostly used by fishermen. Villages to the S are rather neglected, with poor roads and no telephone service. The landscape is diverse, with tall white cliffs at Cape Santa Maria with caves below, old salt pans near Clarence Town, dense bush over much of the island and scattered areas of cactii. It has a rocky coastline on one side and lovely beaches and crystal clear water on the other, with the usual friendly fish and lots of convenient wrecks. One, a German freighter sunk in 1917, lies in 25 feet of water only 200 yards from the beach at Guana Cay, S of Salt Pond. Beaches in the S are good but rather hard to get to. Long Island is a major producer of vegetables and cattle and is known for its pot-hole farming which gives hearty supplies of tomatoes, bananas and onions. The *Stella Maris Resort Club* in the N is the biggest employer, but there are not enough jobs and most young people leave to work in Nassau or Grand Bahama.

The main settlements are **Deadman's Cay** and **Clarence Town** further S. Most tourists stay at Stella Maris, which is supposed to have the best yachting marina in the S Bahamas. From a lookout tower here it is possible to see right across the island and to see the nearby ruins of the Adderly Plantation House. The town of Simms is the home of the best straw work in the Bahamas, made by Ivy Simms and her workers. The mailboat calls here and there is a high school, magistrate's court and Commissioner's office. The settlement of Clarence Town in the S half of the island is very pretty and boasts two white, twin-spired churches built on opposite hilltops by Father Jerome (see under Cat Island). St Paul's is the Anglican church and St Peter's the Catholic. Both are still in use today. There are many caves to explore and ruins of old plantation houses: Adderly's near Stella Maris and the remains of a cotton gin and plantation gate posts at Dunmore. At Glenton's, N of Stella Maris, archaeologists have found the remains of an Arawak village, and at Hamilton, S of Deadman's Cay, caves have been discovered with Arawak drawings and carvings.

Diving and Marine Life

The Stella Maris Marina is the only full-service marina in the area and is a port of entry. There are 12 slips and all facilities including repairs, T 336 2106, VHF 16, and facilities for diving, snorkelling, reef, bone and deep sea fishing and boat charters. At Clarence Town dock you can get fuel, water, ice and supplies. At Harding's Supplies Center on Salt Pond you can also find showers and a laundry. There are safe anchorages at Cape Santa Maria, Salt Pond and Little Harbour. Cape Santa Maria has lovely beaches, caves and bays but do not anchor there if there is a strong N or W wind. A lagoon just beyond the W end of the cape can accommodate boats of 60 feet with depths of six feet. Diving and snorkelling are also good in this area and the Cape Santa Maria Fishing Club operates from here. On the E coast, good anchorages are at Clarence Town (groceries and other supplies) and Little Harbour (no facilities). The annual Long Island Regatta at Salt Pond is held in May. Locals compete for best seaman award, the fastest boat and the best kept boat over five years old. The Regatta is popular and accompanied by authentic Bahamian food and traditional rake'n'scrape music.

Island Information—Long Island

● How To Get There

There are 2 airports at Stella Maris and at Deadman's Cay. Island Express flies several times a week from Fort Lauderdale to Stella Maris. There are 6 Bahamasair flights a week from Nassau to Stella Maris and 6 flights to Deadman's Cay, one of which is via Moss Town. The drive from Deadman's Cay to Stella Maris is about 2 hours along a rough potholed road; there are a couple of Bahamasair flights a week. Taxis are available and private cars often negotiate to carry passengers too. Taxis are generally expensive. If you are going to Stella Maris it is better to get a flight to the airport there if possible, from where it is only 20 minutes to the resort. The main road connecting all the main settlements on the island is the Queen's Highway, which is notoriously bad, particularly in the S where the potholes are said to be the size of a car in places. Avoid night driving.

● **Where To Stay**

The *Stella Maris Resort Club* is one of the top 5 resorts in the Caribbean (T 336 2106, 800-426 0466, PO Box LI-30105). It has rooms (US$125), 1-bedroom apartments/cottages (US$139-199) and 2-bedroom villas (US$240-280). A shopping centre has a bank and post office. There are 3 pools and 5 beaches along with tennis, volley ball, table tennis, bicycles, diving, windsurfing (guests free) and waterskiing (US$25). Bicycles are free for guests; cars can be rented from US$50/day plus mileage. Free transport to Deal's Beach with use of sailboats, free daily snorkelling excursions. Glass bottom boat trips can be taken for US$20. Cave parties are held once a week and a Rum Punch party every Wed. 25 different diving areas offer a lot of variety for the experienced or the beginner and there is even a shark reef with shark feeding. Fishing trips can be arranged: during November and December huge shoals of grouper make fishing easy in the waters around Long Island. The blue hole close to the harbour at Clarence Town is good for line fishing. *Thompson's Bay Inn* at Hardings near Salt Pond (US$45, T 337 0000, PO Box 30123), rec, small and friendly, 8 rooms, pool, fishing, disco lounge, serves native food. There are also a few guest houses, *Knowles Cottages*, guest house in Clarence Town; *Hamilton's Guest House* in Hamilton; *Carroll's Guest House* (US$35, T 337 1048) at Deadman's Cay; *O and S Guest House* at Simms.

● **Where To Eat**

Two island dishes to try are wild hog with onion and spices and grouper roe with liver. *Thompson's Bay Inn* has a good restaurant but reservations essential. *The Blue Chip Restaurant and Bar* in Simms is rec. *The Harbour Bar and Restaurant* at Clarence Town has Bahamian dishes, as does *Mario's*, 7 miles S of Stella Maris, breakfast, lunch and dinner, reservations needed for dinner; *Sabrina's*, at Burnt Ground Village, is by appointment only, cheap and simple, occasional disco. In Hard Bargain in the S, the *Forget Me Not Club* has a popular bar and restaurant. In Mangrove Bush the Knowles family run the hillside tavern and bar. They also sell fresh fish at *Summer Seafood* close by.

MAYAGUANA

Mayaguana (an Arawak name), located 50 miles E of Acklins and 60 miles N of Inagua, is the least developed (population 308) and most isolated of the Family Islands although there are now three Bahamasair flights a week (Tuesday, Thursday and Saturday) from Nassau. The main settlement is **Abraham's Bay**, a small town with a few shops and one bar/restaurant run by the Brown family who also own the guesthouse. There are two other settlements, Betsy Bay and Pirate's Well, which are both very isolated. Several people will rent you a room in their homes for US$30-60; fresh water and food can sometimes be hard to come by, young coconuts are recommended if short of water. Take mosquito repellent. Most people earn their living from fishing or farming and many leave for Nassau and Freeport to look for work. In 1993 the Government approved a tourist development by a Californian group in E Mayaguana. About half of the 50,000-acre project will be a botanical garden and park. If it is implemented it will provide employment but no doubt change the island considerably.

The island is on a direct route to the Caribbean and as such is sometimes visited by yachtsmen, although it is not a port of entry. There is a very large reef around the NW side of the island and excellent diving, although a liveaboard dive boat is necessary. Twenty miles from Mayaguana are the Plana and Samana Cays, notable for their interesting wildlife, where you can

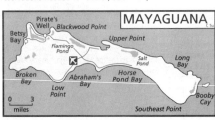

see the Bahama hutia, thought to be extinct until the mid-1960s. A cross between a rat and a rabbit, this rodent's flesh is said to be similar to pork.

RUM CAY

Some 35 miles S of San Salvador, this small island (population 53) is approximately 20 miles square. First known as Mamana by the Lucayan Indians, the cay was later renamed Santa María de la Concepción by Columbus. Spanish explorers once found a lone rum keg washed up on a shore and changed the name again to Rum Cay. In the N there is an interesting cave which has Lucayan drawings and carvings. Various artefacts from the Arawak period have been found by farmers in the fertile soil which the Indians enriched with bat guano. In common with other islands, Rum Cay has experienced a series of booms and busts. Pineapple, salt and sisal have all been important industries, but competition and natural disasters, such as the 1926 hurricane, have all taken their toll and today tourism is the main source of employment. Plantation boundaries known as "margins" can be seen all over the island, which date from the beginning of the 19th century when Loyalists settled here. Nearly everybody lives in **Port Nelson** where cottages can be rented. Settlements such as Port Boyd, Black Rock and Gin Hill are now deserted and overgrown.

This former pirates' haven is surrounded by deep reefs and drop-offs. There is staghorn coral at Summer Point Reef and good diving at Pinder's Point. At the Grand Canyon, huge 60-foot coral walls almost reach the surface.

SAN SALVADOR

Known as Guanahani by the original Lucayan inhabitants, this island (population 486) claims to be the first place that Columbus landed in the New World and is cognisant of its history. Four sites vie for recognition as the first landing place and celebrations marked the quincentennial anniversary in 1992. One of the sites where Columbus may have come ashore is Long Bay. There is a bronze monument under the sea where he was

1. Columbus Monument
2. Olympic Flame Monument
3. Cross Monument
4. Watlings Castle Ruins

SAN SALVADOR

supposed to have anchored and a white cross on the shore where he was said to have landed. Jewelry and pottery dating back to the Lucayan Indians have been found on the beach here. Close by is the Mexican Monument commemorating the handing over of the Olympic flame to the New World for the 1968 Olympics in Mexico. At Crab Cay in the E is the Chicago Herald Monument, erected in 1892 to commemorate the 400th anniversary of Columbus' landing. It is the oldest monument, but judging by the rocky setting it is the most unlikely of the putative landfall spots.

The island is about 12 miles long and six miles wide with a network of inland lakes (with names like Granny Lake and Old Granny Lake) which were once the main transport routes. For a good view, climb the lookout tower E of the airport on Mount Kerr, at 140 feet the highest point on the island. Until the 1920s San Salvador was known as Watling's Island after the legendary pirate John Watling, who was said to have built Watling's Castle on French Bay in the 17th century. Archaeologists have now proven that the ruins are the remains of a loyalist plantation. You can see the stone ruins including the master's house, slave quarters and a whipping post. Access to the ruins is via the hill to the W of the Queen's Highway near the bay. In the 1950s and 1960s, the US military leased land from the British Crown and built a submarine tracking station at Graham's Harbour in the N. Roads, an airport, a Pan American Base and a US Coast Guard Station were also built. The withdrawal of the military in the late 1960s led to unemployment and emigration. The building at Graham's Harbour is now occupied by the College of the Finger Lakes' Bahamian Field Station, a geological and historical research institute. Further development took place under the Columbus Landing Development Project, which built houses, condominiums, roads and a golf course around Sandy Point. In the 1990s,

Club Med built a resort near Cockburn Town, known as *Columbus Isle*, which has provided some jobs. The largest settlement is Cockburn in the NW, once known as Riding Rock because of the tidal movement on rocks off the bay which give the impression that the rocks are moving up and down.

Flora and Fauna

San Salvador is famous for its reefs, beautiful bays, creeks and lakes. At Pigeon Creek in the SE there is a large lagoon, edged by mangroves, which is a nursery for many different kinds of large fish, including sharks. White Cay and Green Cay, off Graham's Harbour, are designated land and sea parks. White Cay has tall white cliffs on one side where there are large numbers of Brown Boobies. They are docile and you can get very close (once making them easy prey for hunters). Green Cay also has a large bird population. Manhead Cay off the NE is home to a rare species of iguana over one foot in length. There are large rock formations on the N side of the cay, access is possible from the S but is not easy, involving a climb up a rocky hill. Frigate birds can sometimes be seen here. Some subsistence farming using old slash and burn methods is still done on San Salvador.

Beaches and Watersports

French Bay is a popular beach with excellent shelling and snorkelling. There are large reefs of elk and staghorn coral in less than 50 feet of water, some of which are exposed at low tide. Overlooking French Bay are the ruins of Watling's Castle, now better known as the Sandy Point Estate. Going S following the Queen's Highway along the bay you come to the Government Dock and further on Sandy Point. Both spots are recommended for their privacy and good reefs for scuba divers and snorkellers. The entire E coastline, with the exception of the creek areas, is uninhabited and has fine beaches of white sand. East of Dixon

Lighthouse past the sand dunes is East Beach, a mile-long stretch of excellent sands.

Diving and Marine Life

Fishing, diving and sailing are all popular. There are shallow reefs, walls, corals and several wrecks to interest scuba divers and underwater life here is said to be some of the most spectacular in the Bahamas. *Club Med Columbus Isle* has scuba diving, contact Steve Schwartz, T 331 2000/2222. Island Water Sports at *Riding Rock Inn* has a full range of watersports activities on offer, an eight slip marina and daily scuba excursions. There are facilities for taking and developing underwater colour photographs (T 332 2631). On Discovery Day, 12 October, there is a dinghies race.

Excursions

North of Cockburn on the Queen's Highway is the small settlement of Victoria Hill where the New World Museum is owned by the local historian Ruth Wolper. There are interesting Lucayan artifacts, most of which came from the remains of an Indian settlement at Palmetto Grove, named after the silver top palmettos found there. Dixon Hill Lighthouse, which was built in Birmingham in the 19th century and rebuilt in 1930 is on the NE coast, still on the Queen's Highway. Mrs Hanna, the keeper, gives tours of the lighthouse, which is run by candle power and clockwork and is one of the few remaining hand operated lighthouses. South of the lighthouse and past East Beach you get to Crab Cay and the Chicago Herald Monument (see above).

Island Information—San Salvador
● **How To Get There**
There are scheduled Bahamasair flights to Cockburn Town 4 times a week, 2 of which come via Arthur's Town. For details of mailboat sailings see **Information for Visitors, Inter Island Travel**. If you avoid the bush and water it is perfectly feasible to walk around San Salvador. The Queen's Highway encircles the

island and there are no other main roads. You can hire cars, enquire in Cockburn Town. Mopeds are not available. There is a bus tour which visits the main points of interest, ask at *Riding Rock Inn*.

● **Where To Stay**
Club Med Columbus Isle, said to be one of the nicer *Club Med* resorts, comfortable, well-integrated into surroundings, usual facilities and more, 104 rooms now, more to follow, in USA T 800 CLUB-MED, 602-948 9190, F 602-948 4562, PO Box 4460, Scottsdale, Arizona 85261. *Riding Rock Inn and Marina* (US$80), N of Cockburn Town, has 48 rooms, swimming pool and a restaurant overlooking the bay (T 367 2106), write to 1170 Lee Wagner Blvd 103, Fort Lauderdale, FL 33315 for details, T 800-272 1492, F 305-359 8254. *Ocean View Villas*, for accommodation in cottages, US$80.

● **Where To Eat**
Riding Rock Inn is considered expensive at US$30, but it has a rake'n'scrape band once a week featuring Bernie the Band Leader (also Bernie the airport manager). *Dixie Hotel and Restaurant*, Dixon Hill and *Ocean Cabin*, Cockburn Town, are both reasonable. *Harlem Square Rip Club* is rec, friendly, Fri night disco. The local dish is crab'n'rice, made from the plentiful land crabs found on the island, average cost US$5-7.

INFORMATION FOR VISITORS

● **Documents**
US citizens do not need passports or visas but for stays of up to 3 weeks they must carry a certified birth certificate or voter's registration card, along with a photo ID issued by a competent authority such as a driver's licence or military identification; for longer, a valid passport is required. Visitors may stay for up to 8 months but must have sufficient funds for their stay and an onward or return ticket. Passports are required by all other nationalities, but visas are not needed by nationals of Commonwealth and West European countries, South Korea, Israel and Japan (length of permitted stay varies between 3 and 8 months); nor by most Latin American nationals if staying no longer than 14 days. Colombians without a US visa need a Bahamian visa. Nationals of Haiti and communist countries need a visa. You will

need a certificate of vaccination against yellow fever if you are coming from an infected area. To enter the Bahamas for business purposes the permission of the Immigration Department, Nassau, must be obtained. It is advisable to apply in writing to: Director of Immigration, Immigration Department, PO Box N3002, Nassau. No expatriate can be employed in a post for which a suitably qualified Bahamian is available, nor can a permit application be considered if the prospective employee is already in the country, having come in as a visitor.

● **Air Services**

Most flights to the Bahamas originate in the USA although there are also flights from Montreal, Ottawa and Toronto in Canada to Nassau and Freeport with Air Canada. Connecting flights by Bahamasair go out from Nassau like spokes of a wheel to the Family Islands although many airlines now fly direct from the USA to the Family Islands. **From the USA to Nassau**: American Eagle from Miami; Bahamasair flies from Miami and Orlando; Carnival Air Lines from Miami and New York, Paradise Island Airways from Miami, Fort Lauderdale, Orlando and West Palm Beach to its own airport on Paradise Island (closer to Nassau than international airport); Chalk's International from Fort Lauderdale and Miami (also to Bimini); Delta and/or Comair from Atlanta, Cincinnati, Cleveland, Dallas, Fort Lauderdale, Key West, Miami, New York (La Guardia and Newark), Orlando, San Antonio (Texas) and Tampa; USAIR from Boston, Charlotte, New York, Philadelphia, Tampa/St Petersburg and Washington DC; Trinity Air Bahamas from Miami; Gulfstream International Airlines from Miami and Ft Lauderdale. **From the Caribbean**: Turks and Caicos Airways connects Grand Turk and Providenciales with Nassau, while Air Jamaica flies from Kingston.

From the USA to Freeport: Delta from Birmingham, Fort Lauderdale, Jacksonville, Miami, Orlando, Tallahassee and Tampa; American Eagle from Miami; Bahamasair from Miami. Laker Airways (Bahamas) from Chicago, Cincinnati, Cleveland, Fort Lauderdale, Hartford CT/Springfield MA, Miami, Orlando, Raleigh/Durham, Richmond and West Palm Beach; Gulfstream International Airlines from Fort Lauderdale and Miami (also flights to Cap Haitien). There are also several commuter airlines serving some of the Family Islands direct from airports in Florida including Gulfstream International Airlines (in Miami T 305-871

1200, 800-992 8532) and Airways International (T 305-887 2794, 305-359 4737, F 305-871 6522), tickets can be booked through computer systems but are normally purchased on the spot at the airport, routing and timing subject to last minute alteration depending on demand. Airways International has several daily flights Miami-Marsh Harbour, Treasure Cay, North Eleuthera, Governors Harbour and George Town, and from Ft Lauderdale to the same destinations. Walker's International flies to Walker's Cay from Fort Lauderdale. Laker Airways has charter flights to Freeport from Florida with some flights timed so that gamblers can do a day-trip to the *Princess Casino*. Charter flights to Cuba with Bahatours (T 328 7985), Mon and Fri, weekend package US$249-389 depending on hotel, including Havana city tour, Sun-Fri 5-day package is US$369-649. Departure tax is US$15 except for children under the age of 3.

● **Airlines**

American Airlines T 1-800-433 7300; US Air T 377 8888; Paradise Island T 363 2845; Air Canada T 327 8411; Bahamasair T 377 7377; Delta Airlines/Comair, T 377 1043; Gulfstream International, T 377 4314.

● **Boats From USA**

Sea Escape boat return trip to Freeport from Fort Lauderdale, including meals and entertainment, costs US$120 return. Journey is 5 hours one way; leaves from Freeport port area and carries 1,200 passengers. In 1994 a new catamaran, *Cloud 10*, owned by Party Cruise Line, was to start a high speed service from Port Everglades, Fort Lauderdale, to Freeport. The new boat, built to withstand rough seas, will hold 345 passengers (and/or freight), take 2 hrs, depart twice daily and cost only US$59 round trip inc taxes (T 305-776 9696, F 305-938 1877).

● **Inter Island Travel**

Bahamasair operates scheduled **flights** between Nassau and the Family Islands. Service is reported to be improving. Charter flights and excursions available through them and several private companies, see Prestel for details. Seaplanes fly to those islands which have no landing strip. Inter-island travel is difficult given that nearly all flights originate in Nassau. To fly from Abaco to Eleuthera with Bahamasair, for example, you have to change planes in Nassau, often with a wait of several hours and a wasted day. There is no special ticket for multiple island destinations and island hopping is time consuming. Each island is developing direct transport links with the USA rather than with each other.

The Family Islands can also be reached by regular **ferry boat** services. A car ferry service, Sea Link, sails between Nassau and Freeport, Nassau and Eleuthera and Nassau and Abaco, departing Thur 1000 for Freeport, returning Fri 0700, departing Fri 1500 for Eleuthera, returning Sun, departing Tues 1800 for Marsh Harbour, returning Wed 1800, 7 hrs. Fares in 1994 were US$250 for cars (inc return fare for 2 passengers), US$60 return adults, children half price. Reservations 3-4 days in advance needed from Island Vacation, West Bay Street; ferry docks at East Bay St, Nassau Shipyard (T 327 5444).

A colourful way of travelling between the islands is on the **mail boats**, which also carry passengers and merchandise. They leave from Potter's Cay Dock, just below the Paradise Island Bridge in Nassau, and Woodes Rogers Walk; their drawback is that they are slow and accommodation on board is very basic, but they do go everywhere. The Bahamas Family Islands Association has a helpful brochure listing fares and schedules, but do not expect the boats to leave according to the timetable. For the latest information listen to the radio on ZNS, which lists the daily schedule with last minute changes broadcast at lunchtime, or ask for information at the Dock Master's office on Potter's Cay, T 393 1064.

The following 1993/94 timetable gives the name of the boat, its destination, departure time from Nassau (dep), arrival time back in Nassau (arr), travel time and fare: *Bahamas Daybreak III*, to North Eleuthera, Spanish Wells, Harbour Island, Bluff, dep Thur 0600, arr Sun 1730, 5½ hrs, US$20; *Captain Moxey*, to South Andros, Kemp's Bay, Long Bay Cays, Bluff, dep Mon 2300, arr Wed 2100, 7½ hrs, US$30; *Central Andros Express*, to Fresh Creek, Staniard Creek, Blanket Sound, Bowne Sound, dep Tues 1200, arr Sun 1330, 3½ hrs, US$25; *Sea Hauler*, to Cat Island, Bluff, Smith's Bay, dep Tues 1400, arr Sun 1000, 10 hrs, US$35; *North Cat Island Special*, to North Cat Island, Arthur's Town, Bennet's Harbour, dep Tues 1400, arr Thurs 1000, 14 hrs, US$35; *Lady Francis*, to San Salvador, United Estates, Rum Cay, dep Tues 1200, arr Sat 1200, 18 hrs, US$40; *Grand Master*, to Exuma, George Town, Mt Thompson, dep Tues 1400, arr Fri 0700, 14 hrs, US$25-40; *Abilin*, to Long Island,

Clarence Town, dep Tues 1200, arr Thur 1000, 18 hrs, US$45; *Champion II*, to Abaco, Sandy Point, Bullock Harbour, Moore Island, dep Tues 2400, arr Fri 0800, 11 hrs, US$30; *Lisa J II*, to North Andros, Nichol's Town, Mastic Point, Lowe Sound, dep Wed 1600, arr Tues 1200, 5 hrs, US$25; *Lady Francis*, to Exuma Cays, Staniel Cay, Black Point, Farmer's Cay, Barraterre, dep Tues 1200, arr Sat 1200, US$25-30; *Deborah K*, Abaco, Marsh Harbour, Hope Town, Treasure Cay, Green Turtle Cay, Coopers Town, dep Wed 1600, arr Mon 2100, 12 hrs, US$25; *Harley & Charley*, to Governor's Harbour, Hatchet Bay, dep Mon 1900, arr Tues 2000, 5 hrs, US$20; *Mangrove Cay Express* to Mangrove Cay, Lisbon Creek, dep Thur 0700, arr Mon 1600, 5½ hrs, US$25; *Lady Gloria* to Mangrove Cay, Behring Point, Cargill Creek, dep Tues 0900, arr Sat 1200, 5 hrs, US$25-30; *Current Pride* to Current Island, Upper and Lower Bogue, Eleuthera, dep Thur 0700, arr Tues 1200, 5 hrs, US$18-20; *Emmette and Cephas* to Ragged Island, dep Tues 1400, arr Thur 1600, 21 hrs, US$50; *Bahamas Daybreak III*, to Rock Sound, Davis Harbour, South Eleuthera, dep Mon 1700, arr Tues 2000, 7 hrs, US$20; *Mia Dean*, to North Long Island, Salt Pond, Deadman's Cay, Stella Maris, dep Mon (check time), 14 hrs, US$45; *Marcella III*, to Grand Bahama, Freeport, High Rock, Eight Mile Rock, West End, dep Wed 1600, arr Sat 0800, 12 hrs, US$45; *Lady Mathilda*, to Crooked Island, Acklins, Mayaguana, Inagua, dep Wed 0700, arr Sun; *Spanish Rose*, to Spanish Wells, dep Thur 0700, arr Tues 1000, 5½ hrs, US$20; *Eleuthera Express*, to Rock Sound, dep Mon 1700, arr Tues 1900, 5 hrs, US$20; *Challenger*, to North Andros, dep Thur 0700, arr Tues 1600, US$25; *Lady Margo*, also to North Andros, dep Wed 0700, arr Sat 1200, US$25; *Eleuthera Express*, Spansih Wells, Harbour Island, dep Thur 0700, arr Sun 1200, 5 hrs, US$20; *Bimini Mack*, to Bimini, Cat Cay, (check time), 12 hrs, US$35.

● **Yacht Charter**

A pleasant way of seeing the islands is to charter your own yacht and several companies offer boats with or without crews. Abaco Bahamas Charters (ABC) is based in Hope Town. Bahamas Yachting Service (BYS) is based in Marsh Harbour, Abaco, T 305-467 8644 or toll free 800-327 2276 in North America, prices start from about US$50 per person per day. Contact the Bahamas Reservation Service (see below) for the Bahamas Marina Guide, marina reservations, known as 'book-a-slip', with details of over 50 marinas in the Bahamas and confirmation of boat slip reservations down as far as Grand Turk. Most resort islands have boats to rent.

● Scuba Diving

In addition to the land-based dive operators mentioned in the text, there are several live-aboard boats which cruise the Bahamas and offer less crowded and unspoilt sites: Black-beard's Cruises, contact Bruce Purdy, PO Box 66-1091, Miami Springs, FL 33266, T 800-327 9600, 305-888 1226, F 305-884 4214; Bottom Time Adventures Inc, contact AJ Bland, Elizabeth Longtin, PO Box 11919, Fort Lauderdale, FL 33339-1919, T 800-234 8464, 305-921 7798, F 305-920 5578; Coral Bay Cruises, contact Lori Lachnicht, Thomas Conlin, 2631 E Oakland Park Blvd 108, Fort Lauderdale, Fl 33306, T 800-433 7262, 305-563 1711, F 305-563 1811; Crown Diving Corporation, contact Edward Guirola, *M/V Crown Islander*, 2790 North Federal Hwy, Boca Raton, FL 33431, T 800-447 2290, 407-394 7450, F 407 368 5715; new in 1994, Nekton Diving Cruises, contact Lynn A Oetzman, 1057 SE 17th St, Suite 202, Fort Lauderdale, FL 33316, T 305-463 9324, F 305-463 8938; new in August 1994, the first Bahamian owned and operated boat, Out Island Voyages, contact James or Marilynn Nottage, PO Box N7775, Nassau, T 809-328 8007/6; Sea Fever Diving, contact Tom Guarino, Cynthia Herod, PO Box 398 276, Miami Beach, FL 33139, T 800-443 3837, 305 531 3483, F 305 531 3127; Sea Dragon, contact Dan Doyle, Sue Ford, SW 717 Coconut Drive, Fort Lauderdale, FL 33315, T 305-522 0161, 809-359 2058. All the above are BDA members.

● Vehicle Hire

Visitors are permitted to drive on a valid foreign licence or International Permit for up to 3 months. Beyond that they need a local licence issued by the Road Traffic Department in Nassau. Traffic keeps left, although most cars are left-hand drive. Strict speed limits: Nassau and Freeport 30 mph; elsewhere 40 mph. The roads are not in good condition and are congested in town; drivers pay scant attention to the laws.

On many of the Family Islands bicycles and mopeds are appropriate. These can be hired in Nassau, Freeport and in many other places through hotels; helmets should be worn. Approximate rates: bicycles US$10 per day, US$40 per week; mopeds: US$30-45 per day.

Scooters and light motorcycles can also be hired. Helmets are mandatory. Remember, though, that rates for car and bike hire tend to vary, according to season. Minimum age for hiring in Exuma is 25.

● Accommodation

Accommodation ranges from luxury hotels and resorts with every conceivable facility, to modest guest houses or self-catering apartments and villas. Some of the larger properties have T 800 reservations numbers in the USA and Canada. You will often get a cheaper package if you book from abroad. These packages often include restaurants, tours, day trips and airfare and are cheap enough for you to discard the bits you do not want. In restaurants, visitors on a package can pay 25-50% less than locals.

● People-to-People

The People-to-People programme is a recommended way to meet local Bahamians. Fill in a form from the Ministry of Tourism giving age, occupation and interests and you will be matched with a Bahamian. Each experience is different but it might lead to a meal in a Bahamian home, a tour of out of the way places or a trip to church. They also hold a tea party at Government House in January-August on the last Fri of each month and can arrange weddings. T 326 5371, 328 8710, 326 9772/9781 in Nassau or 352 8044, 352 6909, 352 7888 in Freeport, or ask at your hotel. The programme is also available in Eleuthera, Abaco, San Salvador, Exuma and Bimini.

● Food And Drink

Conch, crab, grouper, snapper, dolphin (not the Flipper variety) and other seafood are on all the menus. Conch is the staple diet of many Bahamians. It is considered an aphrodisiac and a source of virility, especially the small end part of the conch which is bitten off and eaten from the live conch for maximum effect. Conch is prepared in a variety of ways; conch fritters and cracked conch are both coated in batter and fried, while conch salad is made from raw, shredded conch, onion, lime, lettuce and tomatoes. It can be bought daily from vendors who let you choose your conch from their truck and will "jewk" it from the shell and prepare it for you in salad. Although delicious, conch has been linked to major outbreaks of food poisoning, so treat with caution. Bahamian cuisine is tasty, if a little predictable. The standard fare at most parties/cookouts is peas'n'rice, barbeque ribs and chicken wings, conch salad or fritters, potato salad, coleslaw and macaroni. Bahamian potato salad and macaroni are far richer than their English/Italian counterparts. The Bahamas have some good fruit: sapodilla, mango, breadfruit, sugar apple and pawpaw. Try soursop ice cream, coconut tarts and sugar bananas, which have an apple flavour. Guava duff is a popular sweet, a bit like jam roly poly pudding topped with guava sauce (often flavoured with rum). Tap water can be brackish; fresh water can be bought at the supermarket. The local beer brewed in Nassau, Kalik, is worth trying, it has won several international prizes. The local rum is Bacardi; the Anejo variety is OK. Bahama Mammas, Yellowbirds and Island Woman are all popular rum-based cocktails. Many bars have their own special cocktails.

● **Tipping**
The usual tip is 15%, including for taxi drivers. Hotels and restaurants include a service charge on the bill, sometimes a flat rate per day, or a percentage.

● **Shopping**
For those who want to pick up a bargain, prices of crystal, china and jewellery are cheaper than in the USA. You can find designer clothes and other goods from all over the world at the International Bazaar in Freeport. Local products include straw items, Androsia batik printed silk and cotton, shell jewellery and wood carvings. Bargaining is expected in the markets. Duty free shopping was introduced on 11 categories of goods on 1 January 1992; the Bahamas Duty Free Promotion Board was formed to monitor the system and ensure that merchants participating in the scheme sell authentic goods.

● **Banks**
There are several hundred banks licensed to do banking or trust business in the Bahamas. Some of the largest commercial banks include: Royal Bank of Canada at Nassau, the airport, Abaco, Andros (Fresh Creek), Bimini, Grand Bahama, Harbour Island, Long Island, Lyford Cay, and Spanish Wells; Lloyds Bank (Bahamas); Barclays Bank Plc, also at Grand Bahama, Eleuthera, Abaco; Scotiabank, also at Abaco, Grand Bahama, Exuma, Long Island; Canadian Imperial Bank of Commerce also at Grand Bahama, Andros (Nicholl's Town), Abaco; Bank of the Bahamas Ltd, Grand Bahama, Andros and Inagua; Citibank.

● **Currency**
The unit of currency is the Bahamian Dollar (B$) which is at par with the US dollar. Both currencies are accepted everywhere. There is no restriction on foreign currency taken in or out; Bahamian currency may be exported up to B$70 pp. Notes of B$ 100, 50, 20, 10, 5, 3, 1 and 50c; coins of B$5, 2, 1, 50c, 25c, 15c, 10c, 5c and 1c.

● **Credit Cards**
All major credit cards are accepted on New Providence and Grand Bahama. Not all the hotels and restaurants on the Family Islands take credit cards, although most take American Express, Mastercharge and Visa.

● **Climate**
The sunshine and warm seas attract visitors throughout the year but winter, from December to April, is the high season. Temperatures are around 20°C (68°F). Summer temperatures average 30°C (86°F). Humidity is fairly high, particularly in the summer. The rainy season is May-October, when the showers are usually short but heavy. June-November is the official hurricane season, the last major one to hit the Bahamas being Andrew in September 1992.

● **Hours Of Business**
Banks: in Nassau, Mon-Thur 0930-1500, Fri 0930-1700; in Freeport, Mon-Fri 0900-1300 and Fri 1500-1700. Shops 0900-1700 Mon-Sat. Government offices 0900-1730 Mon-Fri.

● **Public Holidays**
New Year's Day, Good Friday, Easter Monday (very busy at the airport), Whit Monday, Labour Day (first Friday in June, a parade is organized by the trade unions), Independence Day (10 July), Emancipation Day (first Monday in August), Discovery Day (12 October), Christmas Day, Boxing Day.

● **Time Zone**
Bahamas time is 5 hours behind GMT, except in summer when Eastern Daylight Time (GMT -4 hours) is adopted.

● **Diplomatic Representation**
US Embassy, Mosmar Building, Queen St, PO Box N-8197, T 322 1181/3; **British High Commission** Bitco Building, East St, T 325 7471; **Canada**, T 393 2123/4; honorary consulates: **Denmark**, T 322 1340; **France**, T 326 5061; **Germany**, T 322 8032 (office), 324 3780 (residence); **Israel**, T 362 4421; **Japan**, T 322 8560; **The Netherlands**, T 328 7671; **Sweden**, T 327 7785; **Switzerland**, T 322 8345.

There is a **Haitian** Embassy, East and Bay Streets, T 326 0325; consulate of the **Dominican Republic**, T 325 5521.

● **Electric Current**
120 volt/60 cycles.

● **Religion**
There are about 20 denominations represented in the Bahamas, of which those with the largest congregations are the Baptists, Roman Catholics and Anglicans. There is a synagogue in Freeport and a Mosque in Nassau. The Tourist Office publishes a leaflet called *Bahamas Places of Worship*, with a full list of addresses and services.

● **Post Office**
Main post office is at East Hill Street, Nassau. Letters to North America and the Caribbean US$0.55, to Europe and South America US$0.60; to Africa, Asia and Australia US$0.70. All postcards US$0.40. Air mail to Europe takes 4 to 8 days, surface mail takes a couple of months. There is no door to door mail delivery in the Bahamas, everything goes to a PO Box. Parcels must be opened at the Post Office with customs officials present. Stamp collectors can contact the Bahamas Philatelic Bureau at East Hill Street, PO Box N8302, Nassau, for current mint stamps and first day covers.

● **Telecommunications**
There is a public telephone, cable and telex exchange open 24 hours in the BaTelCo Office on East Street, near the BITCO building in Nassau. International calls can be made and faxes sent/received from here; also Prince George Dock, Shirley Street, Blue Hill Road, Mall at Marathon, Golden Gates and Fox Hill (0700-2000). BaTelCo's mailing address is PO Box N3048, Nassau (T 323 4911). Grand Ba-

hama, New Providence and most of the other islands have automatic internal telephone systems. Direct dialling is available from New Providence and most of the other islands all over the world. The code for the Bahamas is 809. International calls are expensive: US$5 a minute to the UK through the operator, US$2.50 to the Caribbean. Credit card facilities. Phone cards are now quite widely available in denominations of US$5, US$10 and US$20. A call to the UK with a phone card is US$4/min. Not all phones take cards. Facilities are available at most BaTelCo offices in Nassau and Freeport, Nassau and Freeport airports and several of the Family Islands. Videoconferencing facilities at BaTelCo's offices in the Mall at Marathon, Nassau and in Freeport.

● **Emergency Numbers On New Providence**
Police T 322 4444; Ambulance T 322 2221; Hospital T 322 2861; Med Evac T 322 2881; BASRA T 322 3877. The Police have offices at East Bay T 322 1275, Paradise Island T 363 3160, Cable Beach T 327 8800 and downtown T 322 3114.

● **Media**
There are 3 daily newspapers: the *Nassau Guardian* (circulation 12,500), *The Tribune*, published in the evening (12,500) and the *Freeport News* (4,000). There are lots of tourist magazines, eg *Dining and Entertainment Guide*, *Nassau*, *Cable Beach*, *Paradise Island*; *What-To-Do, Freeport Lucaya*; *Getaway, Bahamas Out Islands*; *The Cruising Guide to Abaco, Bahamas* (annual); *Abaco Life*. The local commercial radio stations are ZNS1, owned by the Government and covering all the Bahamas, ZNS2 and ZNS3 covering New Providence and the N Bahamas. The local commercial television station is ZNS TV 13. Transmissions from Florida

can be picked up and satellite reception is common. There is one 2-screen cinema in Freeport and a cinema in Governor's Harbour, Eleuthera.

● **Maps**

The Lands and Surveys Department on East Bay Street, Nassau, PO Box 592, has an excellent stock of maps, including a marine chart of the whole archipelago for US$10 and 1:25,000 maps covering most of the islands for US$1 per sheet (several sheets per island). These are also available from Fairey Surveys, Maidenhead, Berks, UK. A good, up-to-date street map of New Providence is available from most Bahamian bookstores for US$2.95.

● **Tourist Office**

The Bahamas Ministry of Tourism, Market Plaza, Bay Street, PO Box N3701, Nassau, Bahamas, T 322 7500, F 325 5835. There are representatives of the Bahamas Tourist Office on Abaco, Eleuthera and throughout the **USA**. In New York they are at 150 East 52nd Street, 28th floor N, NY 10022, T 212-758 2777; also in other major US cities. **See page 113** for the Grand Bahama Island Promotion Board addresses.

In the **UK** they are at 10 Chesterfield Street, London, W1X 8AH, T 071-629 5238, F 071-491 9311.

In **Canada**: 1255 Phillips Square, Montreal, Quebec, H3B 3G1, T 514-861 6797, and 121 Bloor Street E, Toronto, Ontario, M4W 3M5, T 416-363 4441.

In **France**: 7 Boulevard de la Madeleine, 75001 Paris, T 1 42 61 60 20, F 71 42 61 06 73.

In **Japan**: 4-9-17 Akasaka, Minato-Ku, Tokyo, T 813-470 6162.

In **Germany**: Morfelder Landstrasse 45, D-6000 Frankfurt am Main, T 069 62 60 51, F 62 73 11.

In **Italy**: Foro Buonaparte 68, I-20121, Milano, T 02-720 23003, F 02-720 23123.

The editor, Sarah Cameron, is most grateful to Vincent Vanderpool-Wallace, Director General of Tourism, and the staff at the Bahamas Ministry of Tourism, for all the help they gave her during a visit to the islands in 1993 and in revising the Bahamas chapter. She would particularly like to thank Sheila Cox and Carla Lockhart in Nassau, Kendy McPhee on Abaco, Tommy Thompson on Eleuthera and Felena Burrows, of the Grand Bahama Island Promotion Board. Others who deserve an especial mention are the Birch family, of *Small Hope Bay Lodge*, Andros, for their tremendous assistance, hospitality and friendliness, together with Kevin and Audrey James, for their diving encouragement. Thanks also go to Mik and Cathy Bancroft, in Nassau, for their hospitality and help in updating the text of this chapter.

CUBA

THE ISLAND OF CUBA, 1,250 km long, 191 km at its widest point, is the largest of the Caribbean islands and only 145 km S of Florida. The name is believed to derive from the Arawak word "cubanacan", meaning centre, or central. Gifted with a moderate climate, afflicted only occasionally by hurricanes, not cursed by frosts, blessed by an ample and well distributed rainfall and excellent soils for tropical crops, it has traditionally been one of the largest exporters of cane sugar in the world.

About a quarter of Cuba is fairly mountainous. To the W of Havana is the narrow Sierra de los Organos, rising to 750m and containing, in the extreme W, the strange scenery of the Guaniguánicos hill country. South of these Sierras, in a strip 145 km long and 16 km wide along the piedmont, is the Vuelta Abajo area which grows the finest of all Cuban tobaccos. Towards the centre of the island are the Escambray mountains, rising to 1,100m, and in the E, encircling the port of San-tiago, are the most rugged mountains of all, the Sierra Maestra, in which Pico Turquino reaches 1,980m. In the rough and stony headland E of Guantánamo Bay are copper, manganese, chromium and iron mines. About a quarter of the land surface is covered with mountain forests of pine and mahogany. The coastline, with a remarkable number of fine ports and anchorages, is about 3,540 km long.

Some 66% of Cubans register themselves as whites: they are mostly the descendants of Spanish colonial settlers and immigrants; 12% are black, now living mostly along the coasts and in certain provinces, Oriente in particular; 21% are mulatto and about 1% are Chinese; the indigenous Indians disappeared long ago. Some 70% live in the towns, of which there are nine with over 50,000 inhabitants each. The population is estimated at 10.9 million, of which 19% live in Havana (the city and that part of the province within the city's limits).

History

Cuba was visited by Columbus during his first voyage on 27 October 1492, and he made another brief stop two years later on his way to Jamaica. Columbus did not realize it was an island; it was first circumnavigated by Sebastián de Ocampo in 1508. Diego de Velázquez conquered it in 1511 and founded several towns, including Havana. The first African slaves were imported in 1526. Sugar was introduced soon after but was not important until the last decade of the 16th century. When the British took Jamaica in 1655 a number of Spanish settlers fled to Cuba, already famous for its cigars. Tobacco was made a strict monopoly of Spain in 1717. The coffee plant was introduced in 1748. The British, under Lord Albemarle and Admiral Pocock,

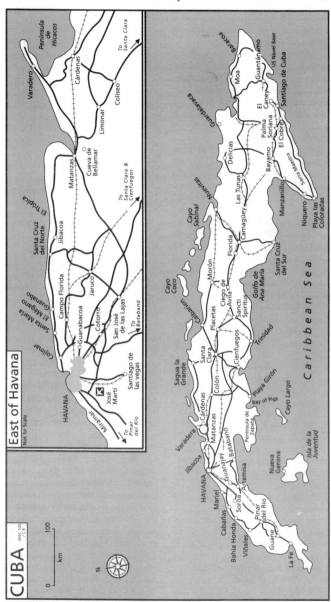

captured Havana and held the island in 1762-63, but it was returned to Spain in exchange for Florida.

The tobacco monopoly was abolished in 1816 and Cuba was given the right to trade with the world in 1818. Independence elsewhere, however, bred ambitions, and a strong movement for independence was quelled by Spain in 1823. By this time the blacks outnumbered the whites in the island; there were several slave rebellions and little by little the Créoles (or Spaniards born in Cuba) made common cause with them. A slave rising in 1837 was savagely repressed and the poet Gabriel de la Concepción Valdés was shot. There was a ten-year rebellion against Spain between 1868 and 1878, but it gained little save the effective abolition of slavery, which had been officially forbidden since 1847. From 1895 to 1898 rebellion flared up again under José Martí and Máximo Gómez. The United States was now in sympathy with the rebels, and when the US battleship *Maine* exploded in Havana harbour on 15 February 1898, this was made a pretext for declaring war on Spain. American forces (which included Colonel Theodore Roosevelt) were landed, a squadron blockaded Havana and defeated the Spanish fleet at Santiago de Cuba. In December peace was signed and US forces occupied the island. The Government of Cuba was handed over to its first president, Tomás Estrada Palma, on 20 May 1902. The USA retained naval bases at Río Hondo and Guantánamo Bay and reserved the right of intervention in Cuban domestic affairs, but granted the island a handsome import preference for its sugar. The USA chose to intervene several times, but relinquished this right in 1934.

From 1925 to 1933 the "strong man" Gerardo Machado ruled Cuba as a dictator. His downfall was brought about by Fulgencio Batista, then a sergeant. Corrupt, ineffectual governments held office in the 1940s, until Batista, by then a self-promoted general, staged a military coup in 1952. His harshly repressive dictator-ship was brought to an end by Fidel Castro in January 1959, after an extraordinary and heroic three years' campaign, mostly in the Sierra Maestra, with a guerrilla force reduced at one point to 12 men.

From 1960 onwards, in the face of increasing hostility from the USA, Castro led Cuba into communism. All farms of over 67 ha have been taken over by the state. Rationing is still fierce, and there are still shortages of consumer goods. However, education, housing and health services have been greatly improved. Infant mortality fell to 11.1 per 1,000 live births in 1989, compared with 19.6 in 1980. It is claimed that illiteracy has been wiped out. Considerable emphasis is placed on combining productive agricultural work with study: there are over 400 schools and colleges in rural areas where the students divide their time between the fields and the classroom. Education is compulsory up to the age of 17 and free.

Before the Revolution of 1959 the United States had investments in Cuba worth about US$1,000mn, covering nearly every activity from agriculture and mining to oil installations; it took 66% of Cuba's exports and supplied 70% of the imports in 1958. Today all American businesses, including banks, have been nationalized; the USA has cut off all imports from Cuba, placed an embargo on exports to Cuba, and broken off diplomatic relations. Promising moves to improve relations with the USA were given impetus in 1988 by the termination of Cuban military activities in Angola under agreement with the USA and South Africa. However, developments in Eastern Europe and the former USSR in 1989-90 provoked Castro to defend the Cuban system of government; the lack of political change delayed any further rapprochement with the USA. Prior to the 1992 US presidential elections, President Bush approved the Cuban Democracy Act (Torricelli Bill) which strengthened the trade embargo by forbidding US subsidiaries from trading with Cuba. Many countries, including EC members and Canada, said they would not allow the US bill to affect their trade with Cuba and the UN General Assembly voted in November in favour of a resolution calling for an end to the embargo. The defeat of George Bush by Bill Clinton did not, however, signal a change in US attitudes, in large part because fo the support given to the Democrat's campaign by Cuban exiles in Miami. Members of some Cuban exile groups were invited to Havana in April 1994 to discuss issues such as travel and family unification. Not included were those groups which support the US blockade. Even though a number of exiles began to press for a more flexible US line, President Clinton made no move to relax US policy and Cuban officials stated that, should any change occur, normalization of relations would be very difficult. Meanwhile, the number of Cubans fleeing to Florida by boat increased by over 40% in 1993. The defection of President Castro's daughter, Alina Fernández Revuelta, received much publicity.

In 1989 the country was shaken by the trials and executions of high-ranking officials for narcotics trafficking, abuse of power and corruption. President Castro pledged to fight against corruption and privilege and deepen the process of rectification begun in 1986. In an effort to broaden the people's power system of government introduced in 1976, the central committee of the Cuban Communist Party adopted resolutions in 1990 designed to strengthen the municipal and provincial assemblies and transform the National Assembly into a genuine parliament. In February 1993, the first direct, secret elections for the National Assembly and for provincial assemblies were held. Despite calls from opponents abroad for voters to register a protest by spoiling their ballot or not voting, the official results showed that 99.6% of the electorate voted, with 92%.6% of votes cast valid. All 589 official candidates were elected.

Economic difficulties in the 1990s brought on by the changes in the former Soviet economy and Eastern Europe, together with higher oil prices because of the Gulf crisis, forced the Government to impose emergency measures and declare a special period in peace time. Rationing was increased, petrol became scarce, the bureaucracy was slashed and several hundred arrests were made in a drive against corruption. As economic hardship continued into 1993, Cuba was hit on 13 March by a winter storm which caused an estimated US$1bn in damage. Agricultural production, for both export and domestic consumption, was severely affected, which additional disruption to food supplies increased concern over the nation's health as an outbreak of a disease attacking the nervous system, thought to have been caused in part by vitamin deficiency, affected about 50,000 people. The Cuban health services contained the illness by September, but its exact cause remained a mystery.

As the economic crisis persisted into 1994, the government adopted measures (some of which are outlined below) which opened up many sectors to private enterprise and recognized the dependence of much of the economy on dollars. The partial reforms did not eradicate the imbalances between the peso and the dollar economies, and shortages remained for those without access to hard currency. Further reforms were proposed in May 1994 aimed at giving the state greater access to the quantity of dollars in circulation and reducing the huge fiscal deficit. Great emphasis was given to the confiscation of black marketeers' illicit profits. At the time of going to press, the exact measures involved had not been published.

Government

In 1976 a new constitution was approved by 97.7% of the voters, setting up municipal and provincial assemblies and a National Assembly of the People's

Power. The membership of the Assembly was increased to 589 in 1993, candidates being nominated by the 169 municipal councils, and elected by direct secret ballot. Similarly elected are numbers of the 14 provincial assemblies. The number of Cuba's provinces was increased from six to 14 as a result of the decisions of the First Congress of the Communist Party of Cuba in December 1975. Dr Fidel Castro was elected President of the Council of State by the National Assembly and his brother, Major Raúl Castro, was elected First Vice-President.

The Economy

Following the 1959 revolution, Cuba adopted a Marxist-Leninist system. Almost all sectors of the economy are state controlled and centrally planned, the only significant exception being agriculture where some 12% of arable land is still privately owned by 192,000 small farmers. Economic pressures in 1993 brought on mainly by the US trade embargo on Cuba forced a number of reforms which, as well as permitting Cubans to hold dollars and other currencies, turned state-owned farms into semi-autonomous cooperatives, and legalized 117 categories of self-employment.

The Government has made diversification of the economy away from sugar the prime aim of economic policy. Some progress towards this has been made, but the overwhelming reliance on sugar remains and there is little expectation of achieving balanced and sustained growth in the foreseeable future. Aid from the USSR was traditionally estimated at about 25% of gnp. Apart from military aid, economic assistance took two forms: balance of payments support (about 84%), under which sugar and nickel exports were priced in excess of world levels and oil imports were indexed against world prices for the previous five years; and assistance for development projects. About 13 million tonnes of oil

CUBA : FACTFILE		
Geographic		
Land area		110,861 sq km
forested		25.1%
pastures		27.1%
cultivated		30.3%
Demographic		
Population (1992)		10,848,000
annual growth rate		1.0%
urban		72.8%
rural		27.2%
density		97.9 per sq km
Religious affiliation		
Roman Catholic		39.6%
Non religious		48.7%
Birth rate per 1,000 (1991)		18.0
		(world av 26.4)
Death rate per 1,000 (1991)		7.0
		(world av 9.2)
Education and Health		
Life expectancy at birth,		
male		73 years
female		78 years
Infant mortality rate		
per 1,000 live births (1989)		11.1
Physicians (1989)		1 per 303 persons
Hospital beds		1 per 141 persons
Calorie intake as %		
of FAO requirement		135%
Population age 25 and over		
with no formal schooling		39.6%
Literacy (over 15)		96.0%
Economic		
GNP (1990 market prices)		US$20,900mn
GNP per capita		US$2,000
Public external debt (1989)		US$6,800mn
Tourism receipts (1990)		US$246mn
Inflation		na
Radio		1 per 3.1 persons
Television		1 per 4.3 persons
Telephone		1 per 18 persons
Employment		
Population economically active (1988)		
		4,570,236
Unemployment rate		6.0%
% of labour force in		
agriculture		20.4
mining and manufacturing		21.8
construction		9.8
Military forces		175,500
Source Encyclopaedia Britannica		

were supplied a year, allowing 3 million to be re-exported, providing a valuable source of foreign exchange earnings. There is, however, a trend towards more trade credits, which are repayable, rather than trade subsidies, and all trade agreements are being renegotiated over the next few years. From 1991, trade between Cuba and the former Soviet Union has been denominated in convertible currencies. Trade agreements with the ex-USSR, involving oil and sugar, survived US pressure on Russia to end oil shipments in order to receive US aid. Other oil producers have been supplying fuel, for example Iran and Colombia, and Cuba stepped up its own production to an estimated 1.2 million tonnes in 1993, providing 30-40% of electricity generation. Foreign companies have been encouraged to explore for oil on and off-shore and investment was estimated at US$50mn in 1994. A consortium led by Total of France was to start exploratory drilling off the N coast in 1994. Two Canadian companies have found oil in Cárdenas Bay, E of Havana, in a well capable of producing 3,750 barrels a day. Cooperation is also being sought in upgrading Cuba's refining capacity. 1993 oil imports were put at 6 million tonnes, compared with 13 million in 1989. The shortage of fuel, combined with a lack of spare parts for ex-Soviet and Czechoslovakian generating plants, caused power cuts of up to 10 hours a day in Havana in 1994. Furthermore, Cuba's domestically-produced oil has corrosive effects on some machinery. A major increase in spending on installed capacity was planned for 1994.

The sugar industry (70% of export earnings) has consistently failed to reach the targets set. Cuba's dream of a 10 million tonne raw sugar harvest has never been reached and the 1991-92 crop reached only 6.2 millionn tonnes because of poor weather and shortages of oil and spare parts. The same factors further restricted the 1992-93 and 1993-94 har-

vests, exacerbated by the March 1993 storm, further torrential rain in 1993 and flooding in May 1994 covering 4,500 sq km in the E. The harvests fell to 4.2 million tonnes in 1992-93 and about 4 million in 1993-94. Under normal circumstances, Cuba would expect to be the world's second-largest producer after Brazil and the world's leading exporter, but 1993's disastrous results (little over 4 million tonnes) undermined all exports, including the sugar-for-oil trade with Russia. Earnings from sugar exports are now devoted to purchasing oil. While sugar mills now use bagasse as fuel, the canefields use large quantities of oil for machinery to cut and transport the cane. Much of the machinery was idle in 1993 owing to lack of fuel. Cuba became a member of the International Coffee Agreement in February 1985, and was allocated an export quota of 160,000 bags of 60 kg compared with production of 375,000 bags. Citrus has become the second-most important agricultural export. Production of food for domestic consumption has been encouraged as foreign exchange for imports has dwindled.

Construction and industry have been the main growth motors in recent years. A major construction project, initiated before the economic crisis, was the building of facilities for the 1991 Panamerican Games, 8 km E of Havana, including a stadium seating 35,000 spectators, a swimming complex, a cycle racetrack and housing for 8,000 visitors. Tourism is set to expand considerably with the construction of 5,000 new hotel rooms. In 1993, about 700,000 tourists visited Cuba, mostly from Western countries, generating earnings of US$220mn, compared with 460,000 visitors in 1992. Daily spending by tourists rose from US$67 per person in 1990 to US$89 in 1992, with US$100 predicted for 1995.

Commercial relations with market economies deteriorated in the late 1980s because of lack of progress in debt rescheduling negotiations. By the 1990s, however, a change in emphasis was noted following the demise of the Eastern European trading bloc, upon which Cuba was so dependent. Exports fell from US$8.1bn (1989) to US$1.7bn (1993) and since Cuba could no longer rely on trade agreements with the USSR and Eastern Europe, it began to concentrate on improving commercial relations with Western Europe, Latin America and the Caribbean. Progress was constrained by a serious lack of hard currency reserves and the US$7.5bn foreign currency debt, including substantial arrears to banks and suppliers. Trade agreements were signed with China, Iran and North Korea. The debt with the former USSR is a secret: estimates range from US$8.5bn (eq) to US$34bn (eq). In 1994 it was announced that a Mexican investment group, Domos Internacional, is to invest US$1.4bn in renovating Cuba's telephone system and purchasing 49% of the state telecommunications company, ETEC, in the first major privatization of the Castro administration. The existing system is notoriously antiquated and inadequate and the exchanges are overloaded, leading to breakdowns. In another sign of a rapprochement with the western world, Canada announced a resumption of aid programmes for Cuba, which were suspended in 1978.

Culture

The Cuban Revolution has had a profound effect on culture both on the island itself and in a wider context. Domestically, its chief achievement has been to integrate popular expression into daily life, compared with the pre-revolutionary climate in which art was either the preserve of an elite or, in its popular forms, had to fight for acceptance. The encouragement of painting in people's studios and through a national art school, and the support given by the state to musicians and film-makers has done much to foster a national cultural identity. This is not to say that the system has neither refrained from controlling what the people should be exposed to (eg much Western pop music was banned in the 1960s), nor that it has been without its domestic critics (either those who lived through the Revolution and took issue with it, or younger artists who now feel stifled by a cultural bureaucracy). Furthermore, while great steps have been made towards the goal of a fully-integrated society, there remain areas in which the unrestricted participation of blacks and women has yet to be achieved. Blacks predominate in sport and music (as in Brazil), but find it harder to gain recognition in the public media; women artists, novelists and composers have had to struggle for acceptance. Nevertheless, measures are being taken in the cultural, social and political spheres to rectify this.

The major characteristic of Cuban culture is its combination of the African and European. Because slavery was not abolished until 1886 in Cuba, black African traditions were kept intact much later than elsewhere in the Caribbean. They persist now, inevitably mingled with Hispanic influence, in religion: for instance *santería*, a cult which blends popular Catholicism with the Yoruba belief in the spirits which inhabit all plant life. This now has a greater hold than orthodox Catholicism, which lost much support in its initial opposition to the Revolution. Catholicism in Cuba today is in sympathy with the liberation theology professed elsewhere in Latin America.

Music is incredibly vibrant on the island. It is, again, a marriage of African rhythms, expressed in percussion instruments (batá drums, congas, claves, maracas, etc), and the Spanish guitar. Accompanying the music is an equally strong tradition of dance. A history of Cuban music is beyond the scope of this book, however there are certain styles which deserve mention. There are four basic elements out which all others grow.

The *rumba* (drumming, singing about social preoccupations and dancing) is one of the original black dance forms. By the turn of the century, it had been transferred from the plantations to the slums; now it is a collective expression, with Saturday evening competitions in which anyone can partake. Originating in E Cuba, *son* is the music out of which *salsa* was born. *Son* itself takes many different forms and it gained worldwide popularity after the 1920s when the National Septet of Ignacio Piñeiro made it fashionable. The more sophisticated *danzón*, ballroom dance music which was not accepted by the upper classes until the end of the last century, has also been very influential. It was the root for the *cha-cha-cha* (invented in 1948 by Enrique Jorrin). The fourth tradition is *trova*, the itinerant troubadour singing ballads, which has been transformed, post-Revolution, into the *nueva trova*, made famous by singers such as Pablo Milanés and Silvio Rodríguez. The new tradition adds politics and everyday concerns to the romantic themes.

There are many other styles, such as the *guajira*, the most famous example of which is the song "Guantanamera"; *tumba francesa* drumming and dancing; and Afro-Cuban jazz, performed by internationally renowned artists like Irakere and Arturo Sandoval. Apart from sampling the recordings of groups, put out by the state company Egrem, the National Folklore Company (Conjunto Folklórico Nacional) gives performances of the traditional music which it was set up to study and keep alive.

In Havana, a weekly guide (*La Habana*, US$1 from major hotels) appears every Thursday, with listing of concerts, theatre programmes, art exhibitions, etc. It also carries the names, addresses and programmes of the Casas de Cultura and Casas de la Trova, houses where traditional Cuban music can be heard for free, thoroughly recommended.

In Vedado, the National Folklore Company, Calle 2 entre Calzada y 5ta, sometimes stage "Rumba Saturday" at 1500, 1 peso.

Festivals of dance (including ballet), theatre, jazz, cinema and other art forms are held frequently—tickets (in dollars) from lobbies of the major hotels. Outside Havana, ask in hotels for detailed information.

NB Last-minute changes and cancellations are common.

The Cuban Revolution had perhaps its widest cultural influence in the field of literature. Many now famous Latin American novelists (like Gabriel García Márquez, Mario Vargas Llosa and Julio Cortázar) visited Havana and worked with the Prensa Latina news agency or on the *Casa de las Américas* review. As Gordon Brotherston has said, "an undeniable factor in the rise of the novel in Latin America has been a reciprocal self-awareness among novelists in different countries and in which Cuba has been instrumental." (*The Emergence of the Latin American Novel*, Cambridge University Press, 1977, page 3.) Not all have maintained their allegiance, just as some Cuban writers have deserted the Revolution. One such Cuban is Guillermo Cabrera Infante, whose most celebrated novel is *Tres tristes tigres* (1967). Other established writers remained in Cuba after the Revolution: Alejo Carpentier, who invented the phrase "marvellous reality" to describe the different order of reality which he perceived in Latin America and the Caribbean and which now, often wrongly, is attributed to many other writers from the region (his novels include *El reino de este mundo, El siglo de las luces, Los pasos perdidos*, and many more); Jorge Lezama Lima (*Paradiso*, 1966); and Edmundo Desnoes (*Memorias del subdesarrollo*). Of post-revolutionary writers, the poet and novelist Miguel Barnet is worth reading, especially for the use of black oral history and traditions in his work. After 1959, Nicolás

Guillén, a black, was adopted as the national poet; his poems of the 1930s (*Motivos de son, Sóngoro cosongo, West Indies Ltd*) are steeped in popular speech and musical rhythms. In tone they are close to the work of the *négritude* writers (see under Martinique), but they look more towards Latin America than Africa. The other poet-hero of the Revolution is the 19th-century writer and fighter for freedom from Spain, José Martí. Even though a US radio and TV station beaming propaganda, pop music and North American culture has usurped his name, Martí's importance to Cuba remains undimmed.

Flora and Fauna

The National Committee for the Protection and Conservation of National Treasures and the Environment was set up in 1978. There are six national parks, including three in Pinar del Río alone (in the Sierra de los Organos and on the Península de Guanahacabibes), the swamps of the Zapata Peninsula and the Gran Piedra near Santiago. The Soledad Botanical Gardens near Cienfuegos house many of Cuba's plants. The Royal Palm is the national tree. Over 200 species of palms abound, as well as flowering trees, pines, oaks, cedars, etc. Original forest, however, is confined to some of the highest points in the SE mountains and the mangroves of the Zapata Peninsula.

There are, of course, a multitude of flowers and in the country even the smallest of houses has a flower garden in front. The orchidarium at Soroa has over 700 examples. To complement the wide variety of butterflies that can be found in Cuba, the buddleia, or butterfly bush, has been named the national flower. In fact, about 10,000 species of insect have been identified on the island.

Reptiles range from crocodiles (of which there is a farm on the Zapata Peninsula) to iguanas to tiny salamanders. Cuba claims the smallest of a number of animals, for instance the Cuban pygmy frog (one of some 30 small frogs), the almiqui (a shrew-like insectivore, the world's smallest mammal), the butterfly or moth bat and the bee hummingbird (called locally the *zunzuncito*). The latter is an endangered species, like the *carpintero real* woodpecker, the cariara (a hawk-like bird of the savannah), the pygmy owl, the Cuban green parrot and the *ferminia*. The best place for birdwatching on the island is the Zapata Peninsula, where 170 species of Cuban birds have been recorded, including the majority of endemic species. In winter the number increases as migratory waterbirds, swallows and others visit the marshes. The national bird is the forest-dwelling Cuban trogon (the *tocororo*).

Also protected is the manatee (sea cow) which has been hunted almost to extinction. It lives in the marshes of the Zapata Peninsula. Also living in the mangrove forests is the large Cuban land crab. Many species of turtle can be found around the offshore cays.

Carnival

During July, carnivals are held in Havana and Santiago, reaching fever pitch with the 26 July festivities. Similar events are held in all Cuban cities and large towns at different times during the summer months. They generally last one-two weeks.

HAVANA

Havana, the capital, is situated at the mouth of a deep bay; in the colonial period, this natural harbour was the assembly point for ships of the annual silver convoy to Spain. Its stategic and commercial importance is reflected in the extensive fortifications, particularly on the E side of the entrance to the bay (see below). Before the Revolution, Havana was the largest, the most beautiful and the most sumptuous city in the Caribbean. Today it is rather run-down, but thanks to the Government's policy of developing the countryside, it is not ringed with shantytowns like so many other Latin American capitals. With its suburbs it has 2.1 million people, half of whom live in housing officially regarded as sub-standard. Many buildings are shored up by wooden planks. Some of it is very old—the city was founded in 1515—but the ancient palaces, plazas, colonnades, churches and monasteries merge agreeably with the new. The old city is being substantially refurbished with Unesco's help, as part of the drive to attract tourists and has been declared a World Heritage Site by the United Nations. There are good views over the city from the top floor restaurant and bar of *Hotel Habana Libre* and of the *Hotel Sevilla*.

The centre is divided into five sections, three of which are of most interest to visitors, Habana Vieja (Old Havana), Central Havana and Vedado. The oldest part of the city, around the Plaza de Armas, is quite near the docks from where you can see cargo ships from all over the world being unloaded. Here are the former palace of the Captains-General, the temple of El Templete, and La Fuerza, the oldest of all the forts. From Plaza de Armas run two narrow and picturesque streets, Calles Obispo and O'Reilly (several old-fashioned pharmacies on Obispo, traditional glass and ceramic medicine jars and decorative perfume bottles on display in shops gleaming with polished wood and mirrors). These two streets go W to the heart of the city: Parque Central, with its laurels, poincianas, almonds, palms, shrubs and gorgeous flowers. To the SW rises the domed dome of the Capitol. From the NW corner of Parque Central a wide, tree-shaded avenue, the Paseo del Prado, runs to the fortress of La Punta; at its N sea-side end is the Malecón, a splendid highway along the coast to the W residential district of Vedado. The sea crashing along the seawall here is a spectacular sight when the wind blows from the N. On calmer days, fishermen lean over the parapet, lovers sit in the shade of the small pillars, and joggers sweat along the pavement. On the other side of the six-lane road, buildings which look stout and grand, with arcaded pavements, balconies, mouldings and large entrances, are salt-eroded, faded and sadly decrepit inside.

Further W, Calle San Lázaro leads directly from the monument to General Antonio Maceo on the Malecón to the magnificent central stairway of Havana University. A monument to Julio Antonio Mella, founder of the Cuban Communist Party, stands across from the stairway. Further out, past El Príncipe castle, is Plaza de la Revolución, with the impressive monument to José Martí at its centre. The large buildings surrounding the square were mostly built in the 1950s and house the principal government ministries. The long grey building behind the monument is the former Justice Ministry (1958), now the HQ of the Central Committee of the Communist Party, where Fidel Castro has his office. The Plaza is the scene of massive parades and speeches marking important events.

From near the fortress of La Punta a tunnel runs E under the mouth of the harbour; it emerges in the rocky ground between the Castillo del Morro and the fort of La Cabaña, some 550m away, and a 5-km highway connects with the Havana-Matanzas road.

The street map of Old Havana is marked with numerals showing the places of most interest to visitors.

1. Castillo del Morro was built between 1589 and 1630, with a 20-metre moat, but has been much altered. It stands on a bold headland, it was one of the major fortifications built to protect the natural harbour and the assembly of Spain's silver fleets from pirate attack. The flash of its

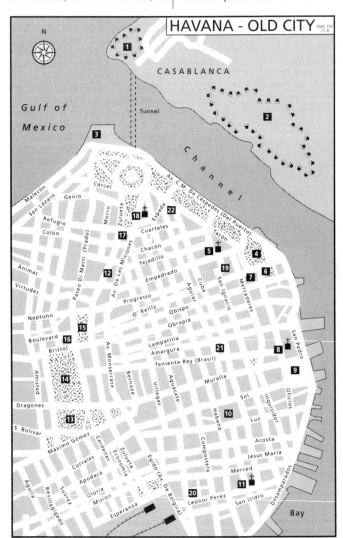

HAVANA - OLD CITY MAC 102 / C 8

lighthouse, built in 1844, is visible 30 km out to sea. The castle is open to the public, Wednesday-Sunday, 1000-1800, as a museum with a good exhibition of Cuban history since Columbus. On the harbour side, down by the water, is the Battery of the 12 Apostles, each gun named after an Apostle. It can be reached by bus through the tunnel to the former toll gates.

2. Fortaleza de la Cabaña, built 1763-1774. Fronting the harbour is a high wall; the ditch on the landward side, 12m deep, has a drawbridge to the main entrance. Inside are Los Fosos de los Laureles where political prisoners were shot during the Cuban fight for inde-

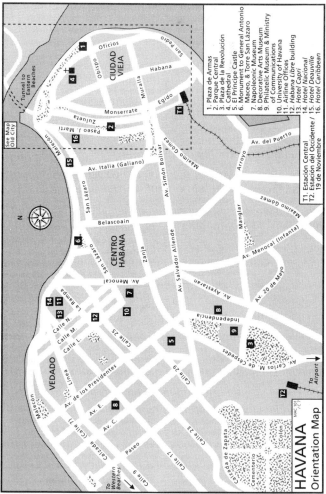

1. Plaza de Armas
2. Parque Central
3. Plaza de la Revolución
4. Cathedral
5. El Príncipe Castle
6. Monument to General Antonio Maceo, & Torre San Lázaro
7. Napoleonic Museum
8. Decorative Arts Museum
9. Philatelic Museum & Ministry of Communications
10. University of Havana
11. Airline Offices
12. Habana Libre building
13. Hotel Capri
14. Hotel Nacional
15. Hotel Deauville
16. Hotel Caribbean

T1. Estación Central
T2. Estación del Occidente / 19 de Noviembre

HAVANA
Orientation Map

pendence. Open to visitors at the same hours as El Morro.

The National Observatory and the railway station for trains to Matanzas are on the same side of the Channel as these two forts.

3. Castillo de la Punta, built at the end of the 16th century, a squat building with 2½-metre thick walls, is open to the public, daily 1400-2200. Opposite the fortress, across the Malecón, is the monument to Máximo Gómez, the independence leader.

4. Castillo de la Fuerza, Cuba's oldest building and the second oldest fort in the New World, was built 1538-1544 after the city had been sacked by buccaneers. It is a low, long building with a picturesque tower from which there is a grand view. Inside the castle is the Museo de Armas. The downstairs part is used for art exhibitions. The Castillo has reopened (1994) after renovation. **NB**: There are two other old forts in Havana: Atarés, finished in 1763, on a hill overlooking the SW end of the harbour; and El Príncipe, on a hill at the far end of Av Independencia (Av Rancho Boyeros), built 1774-1794, now the city gaol. Finest view in Havana from this hill.

5. The Cathedral, built in 1704 by the Jesuits, who were expelled in 1767. On either side of the Spanish colonial baroque façade are belltowers, the left one (W) being half as wide as the right (E). There is a grand view from the latter. The church is officially dedicated to the Virgin of the Immaculate Conception, but is better known as the church of Havana's patron saint, San Cristóbal, and as the Columbus cathedral. The bones of Christopher Columbus were sent to this cathedral when Santo Domingo was ceded by Spain to France in 1795; they now lie in Santo Domingo. The bones were in fact those of another Columbus. The Cathedral is open Monday-Friday 0900-1130 and Saturday 1530-1730. On Saturdays there is a handicraft market on the square in front of the Cathedral, and in adjacent streets.

6. Plaza de Armas, has been restored to very much what it once was. The statue in the centre is of Céspedes. In the NE corner of the square is the church of El Templete; a column in front of it marks the spot where the first mass was said in 1519 under a ceiba tree. A sapling of the same tree, blown down by hurricane in 1753, was planted on the same spot, and under its branches the supposed bones of Columbus reposed in state before being taken to the cathedral. This tree was cut down in 1828, the present tree planted, and the Doric temple opened. There are paintings by Vermay, a pupil of David, inside. On the N side of the Plaza is the Palacio del Segundo Cabo, the former private residence of the Captains General, now housing the Feria Cubana del Libro. Its patio is worth a look.

7. On the W side of Plaza de Armas is the former palace of the Captains General, built in 1780, a charming example of colonial architecture. The Spanish Governors and the Presidents lived here until 1917, when it became the City Hall. It is now the Museo de la Ciudad, the Historical Museum of the city of Havana (open Tuesday-Sunday 0930-1700, T 61-0722, entry US$2). It is best to go at 1130 when the upper floor is open. The building was the site of the signing of the 1899 treaty between Spain and the USA. The arcaded and balconied patio is well worth a visit. The museum houses a large collection of 19th-century furnishings which illustrate the wealth of the Spanish colonial community. There are no explanations, even in Spanish. Outside is a statue of Ferdinand VII of Spain, with a singularly uncomplimentary plaque. Also in front of the museum is a collection of church bells. The former Supreme Court on the N side of the Plaza is

another colonial building, with a large patio.

8. The church and convent of San Francisco, built 1608, reconstructed 1737; a massive, sombre edifice suggesting defence rather than worship. The three-storeyed tower was both a landmark for returning voyagers and a look-out for pirates. Having been restored to the Franciscan order, it is now open to the public on Sunday mornings or at other times immediately after services. Most of the treasures were removed by the government and some are in museums.

9. The Corinthian white marble building on Calle Oficinas S of the Post Office was once the legislative building, where the House of Representatives met before the Capitol was built.

10. The Santa Clara convent was built in 1635 for the Clarisan nuns. The quaint old patio has been carefully preserved; in it are the city's first slaughter house, first public fountain and public baths, and a house built by a sailor for his love-lorn daughter. You can still see the nuns' cemetery and their cells.

11. La Merced church, built in 1746, rebuilt 1792. It has a beautiful exterior and a redecorated lavish interior.

12. The Museo Nacional Palacio de Bellas Artes (T 61-2332). It also has a large collection of relics of the struggle for independence, and a fine array of modern paintings by Cuban and other artists. Its huge collection of European paintings, from the 16th century to the present, contains works supposedly by Gainsborough, Van Dyck, Velázquez, Tintoretto, Degas, et al. There are also large chambers of Greek, Roman, Egyptian sculpture and artefacts, many very impressive. Descriptions are in Spanish only and labels, on small cards, may be hard to read. The museum also has temporary exhibitions. Open Wednesday-Sunday 1030-1830—US$3.

13. Parque Fraternidad, landscaped to show off the Capitol, N of it, to the best effect. At its centre is a ceiba tree growing in soil provided by each of the American republics. In the park also is a famous statue of the Indian woman who first welcomed the Spaniards: La Noble Habana, sculpted in 1837. From the SW corner the handsome Avenida Allende runs due W to the high hill on which stands Príncipe Castle (now the city gaol). The Quinta de los Molinos, on this avenue, at the foot of the hill, once housed the School of Agronomy of Havana University. The main house now contains the Máximo Gómez museum (Dominican-born fighter for Cuban Independence). Also here is the headquarters of the young writers and artists (Asociación Hermanos Saiz). The gardens are a lovely place to stroll. North, along Calle Universidad, on a hill which gives a good view, is the University.

14. The Capitol, opened May 1929, has a large dome over a rotunda; it is a copy, on a smaller scale, of the US Capitol in Washington. At the centre of its floor is set a 24-carat diamond, zero for all distance measurements in Cuba. The interior has large halls and stately staircases, all most sumptuously decorated. Entrance for visitors is to the left of the stairway. The Capitol now houses the Museo Nacional de Historia Natural, which is open Tuesday to Saturday 1015-1745, and Sunday 0915-1245.

15. Parque Central.

16. Gran Teatro de la Habana, a beautiful building.

17. Presidential Palace (1922), a huge, ornate building topped by a dome, facing Av de las Misiones Park; now contains the Museo de la Revolución (T 62-4091). Open Tuesday-Friday 1000-1700, Saturday-Sunday 1000-1800, 1400-2000, entry US$3, no cameras either inside or in the adjoining park,

although photographs are permitted in the park in front of the building. (Allow several hours to see it all, explanations are all in Spanish.) The history of Cuban political development is charted, from the slave uprisings to joint space missions with the ex-Soviet Union. The liveliest section displays the final battles against Batista's troops, with excellent photographs and some bizarre personal momentos, such as a revolutionary's knife, fork and spoon set and a plastic shower curtain worn in the Sierra Maestra campaign. The yacht *Granma*, from which Dr Castro disembarked with his companions in 1956 to launch the Revolution, has been installed in the park facing the S entrance, surrounded by planes, tanks and other vehicles involved, as well as a Soviet-built tank used against the Bay of Pigs invasion and a fragment from a US spy plane shot down in the 1970s.

18. The Church of El Santo Angel Custodio was built by the Jesuits in 1672 on the slight elevation of Peña Pobre hill. It has white, laced Gothic towers and 10 chapels, the best of which is behind the high altar.

19. Museo de Arte Colonial, Plaza de la Catedral (in the former Palacio de los Condes de Casa Bayona), open 1000-1730 (closed Tuesday), US$2, contains colonial furniture and other items, plus a section on stained glass (T 61-1367).

20. Birthplace of José Martí, Leonor Pérez 314, opposite central railway station (Tuesday-Saturday 1315-2030, Sunday 0900-1230, T 6-8852).

21. Museu Histórico de Ciencias Carlos J Finlay, Calle Cuba 460 (Monday-Friday 0800-1200, 1300-1700, T 6-8006).

22. Palacio Pedroso, now the Palacio de la Artesanía; see **Shopping** below.

Other Museums

Museo de Alfabetización, Plaza de la Catedral, Monday-Friday 0800-1200, 1300-1600, T 20-8054; **Napoleonic Museum**,

Calle Ronda (Tuesday-Saturday 1100-1830; Sunday 0900-1300), houses paintings and other works of art, a specialized library and a collection of weaponry (T 79-1412); **Museo de Artes Decorativas**, Calles 17 y Este Vedado (Wednesday-Sunday 0900-1700 T 32-0924); **Postal Museum**, Ministry of Communications, Plaza de la Revolución (Monday-Friday 1000-1900, working Saturdays 0900-1800, T 70-5193); also **Numismatic Museum**, (Calle Oficios 8 between Obispo and Obrapía, T 63-2521, Tuesday-Saturday 1300-2100, Sunday 0900-1300). **Museo de Finanzas**, Obispo y Cuba, in the old Ministry of Finance building, has a beautiful stained-class ceiling in the foyer, Monday-Friday 0830-1700, Saturday till 1230 only. **Vintage Car Museum**, Oficios y Jústiz (just off Plaza de Armas, there are a great many museum pieces—pre-revolutionary US models—still on the road especially outside Havana, in among the Ladas, VWs and Nissans), **Casa de los Arabes** (with restaurant) opposite, on Oficios between Obispo and Obrapía, open Tuesday-Saturday 1330-2030; **Casa de Africa**, on Obrapía 157 between San Ignacio and Mercaderes (Tuesday-Sunday 1300-2000); small gallery of carved wooden artefacts and handmade costumes. **Museo de las Música**, Capdcvilla 1, Habana Vieja; small and beautifully furnished old house; interesting collection of African drums and other instruments from all around the world, showing development of Cuban *son* and *danzón* music. The *Hotel Ambos Mundos*, Calle Obispo 153, between San Ignacio and Mercaderes, has kept room 511 where Ernest Hemingway lived, as a showpiece for visitors. Hemingway lived here for 10 years before moving to La Vigía in 1939. His room has some of the finest views over the old part of the city. Always check opening times in advance.

NB In 1994 the Government introduced admission fees for museums at a nominal amount.

Suburbs

The W sections of the old city merge imperceptibly into Vedado. West of it, and reached by a tunnel under the Almendares river, lies Miramar, some 16 km W of the capital, and easily reached by bus. Miramar was where the wealthy lived before the Revolution; today there are several embassies and government buildings, and also many old, abandoned villas.

The Cuban pavilion, a large building on Calle 23, Vedado, is a combination of a tropical glade and a museum of social history. It tells the nation's story by a brilliant combination of objects, photography and the architectural manipulation of space.

The National Arts College, located in the grounds of the former Havana Country Club in Cubanacan, SW of Miramar, houses schools for different arts and was designed by Ricardo Porro. Architects will be interested in this "new spatial sensation".

The Cementerio Colón should be visited to see the wealth of funerary sculpture, including Carrara Marbles; entry US\$1.

Pabexpo completed in January 1989, a sprawling new facility SW of Havana, past Lenin Park, near the botanical gardens, features a score of pavilions showing Cuba's achievements in industry, science, agriculture and the arts and entertainment. Open weekdays Wednesday-Friday 1400-1600 and Saturday-Sunday 1000-1800 (times subject to change). Special trains leave from main terminal in Old Havana. Information on times (and special buses) from hotels.

South of the centre, in Cerro district, is the Estadio Latinoamericano, the best place to see baseball (the major league level, entrance free).

Beaches

The beaches in Havana, at Miramar and Playa de Marianao are rocky and generally very crowded in summer (transport may also be difficult and time consuming). The beach clubs belong to trade unions and may not let non-members in. Those to the E, El Mégano, Santa María del Mar and Bacuranao, for example, are much better (see also **East from Havana**). To the W of Havana are Arena Blanca and Bahía Honda, which are good for diving and fishing but difficult to get to unless you have a car.

Local Information—Havana

● **Where To Stay**

(Payment for hotels used by tourists is in US\$). Foreign tourists should obtain a reservation through an accredited Cubatur agent (see **Travel Agencies** at the end of this chapter). Always tell the hotel each morning if you intend to stay on another day. Do not lose your "guest card" which shows your name, room number and meal arrangement. Tourist hotels are a/c, with "tourist" TV (US films, tourism promotion), restaurants with reasonable food, but standards are not comparable with Europe and plumbing is often faulty or affected by water shortages. Water was rationed in 1994 and Havana residents had to use stand pipes outside some of the hotels.

The Vedado hotels (the best) are away from the old centre; the others reasonably close to it. Prices at the *Habana Libre* depend on the floor number (approx US\$90), the hotel has an ugly exterior but most facilities are here, eg hotel reservations, excursions, Post Office, airlines nearby; the buffet breakfast has been rec, as have the pizzas. Prices given for the *Nacional de Cuba* are the high season minimum; the range increases to US\$299s, US\$339d. The *Victoria* is small, quiet and pleasant, tasteful if conservative, rec. *Riviera*, comfortable, does a good breakfast. *Hostal Valencia*, Oficios 53 esq Obrapia, T 62-3801, Old Havana, joint Spanish/Cuban venture modelled on the Spanish paradores, 11 rooms, each named after a Valencian town, from US\$25-33s to US\$44-57d, tastefully restored building, nicely furnished, good restaurant; *Inglaterra*, Pascodel Prado 416 entre San Rafael y Neptuno, T 61-8351, F 33-8452, Parque Central, next to Teatro Nacional, old style, beautifully restored, highly rec, US\$60s, US\$80d with balcony overlooking Parque Central, helpful staff, several of whom speak English, lovely, old tiled dining room, also *Ristorante La Stella* (Italian), open

	Address	Tele-phone	Fax	Rates (US$)	
				Single	Double
Capri	21 y N, Vedado	32-0511	32-0525	56	75
Habana Riviera	Paseo y Malecón, Vedado	30-5051	31-1345	75	100
Nacional	21 y O, Vedado	7-8980	33-5054	155	190
Habana Libre	L y 23, Vedado	30-5011	32-8722	68	90
Presidente	Calzada y G, Vedado	32-7521	32-3577	60	80
Victoria	19 y M, Vedado	32-6531	33-3109	79	105
St John's	O, entre 23 y 25, Vedado	32-9531		32	43
Vedado	Calle O, No 244	32-6501		40	53
Colina	L y 27, Vedado	32-3535		30	40
Deauville	Galiano y Malecón	62-8051		35	46

to non-guests, snacks available in pleasant inner courtyard, piano music at meal times in *Restaurante Colonial*, the bar often has music or shows at 2200, US$5 cover. The *Colina* is popular with the airport Cubatur desk, small rooms, poor breakfast. *Sevilla*, Trocadero 55, T 33-8560, F 33-8582, US$79s, US$105d, bars, restaurant, swimming pool, Havanautos office, breakfast buffet US$3.50, rec. The *Plaza*, Zulueta y Neptuno, T 62-2006, F 63-9620, comfortable, good dinner, US$90d, street front rooms very noisy, ask for one on the inner courtyard. *Lincoln*, Galiano y Virtudes, T 62-8061, US$30s, US$40d. *Tritón*, 3 Av y Calle 74, Miramar, T 22-6081, US$50s, US$65d.

The cheaper hotels are usually hard to get into; often full. *Caribbean*, Paseo Martí 164 (bus 82 from Vedado), T 62-2071, US$18s, US$23d, hot water (sporadic supply), fan and TV, popular with travellers, clean, old city, rec, but avoid noisy rooms at front and lower floors at back over deafening water pump, and beware of petty theft from rooms, small cafe serves mostly sandwiches and eggs at a low price. *Lido*, on Consulado near corner of Animas, T 62-5231, good, choose a room away from the alley alongside, US$21s, US$28d, excellent breakfast and some food available in coffee shop, running water all day, say staff, bar on roof terrace, sometimes live music, rec. *Bruzón*, on Calle Bruzón near the Plaza de la Revolución and the bus station, US$18s, US$20d, fan, bath, TV in some rooms, no hot water, drinking water on each floor, back rooms noisy from bus station, staff from sleepy to helpful, aggressive lady in charge of breakfasts, poor restaurant. *Ambos Mundos*, Obispo 153, between San Ignacio and Mercaderes, T 61-4887, F 62-2547, US$24d with a/c, US$20d with fan, friendly, clean, retains some of its early 20th century charm, wonder-

ful location with great view of old city from roof terrace restaurant, Hemingway's room is open to visitors (see **Museums** above), rec. It is quite impossible for tourists to stay in "peso hotels" in Havana.

If you have a car, the E beaches are good places to stay for visiting Havana. The hotels are usually booked up by package tours but you can rent an apartment on the beach away from the main tourist area for US$30. The office is at the end of the main road running along the beach nearest to Havana and furthest from the main hotel area.

● **Where To Eat**

Restaurants are not cheap. The choice of food is limited to "dollar" restaurants, recognizable by the credit card stickers on the door, where meals are about US$10-15, paid only in US dollars. Check the bill carefully as overcharging is common in some Havana "dollar" restaurants, also the bill may not record what you actually ate. As a rule, in Havana, outside the hotels, the "dollar" places are the only option since, by mid-1993, there was no food on sale in pesos to foreigners (or Cubans, for that matter). In 1993-94, many private houses began operating as restaurants, charging for meals in dollars. A government clamp-down on these activities did not stop the business, but many places became caterers rather than restaurants.

The *Bodeguita del Medio*, Empedrado 207, near the Cathedral, was made famous by Hemingway and should be visited if only for a drink (*mojito*—rum, crushed ice, mint, lemon juice and carbonated water—is a must). Excellent food and wide range for vegetarians, about US$25 for 2, drinks extra, colourful atmosphere and nice roof terrace. Book in advance or go early for a meal, very popular. *Floridita*, on the corner of Obispo and Montserrate, next to the Parque Central, was another favourite haunt of Hemingway. It has had a recent face-lift and is now a very elegant bar and restaurant reflected in the prices (US$5 for a daiquiri), but well worth a visit if only to see the sumptuous decor and "Bogart atmosphere". *El Patio*, Plaza Catedral, nearby, is rec for national dishes and *La Mina*, on Plaza de Armas, traditional Cuban food but both have uneven service, waits can be long and cooking gas shortages are common; nearby, *El Oasis*, Paseo Martí 256-58, in Arab Cultural Institute, cold a/c, very good hummus and lamb dishes; and *D'Giovanni*, Italian, Tacón between Empedrado and O'Reilly, lovely old building with patio and terrace, interesting tree growing through the wall, but food very bland. Handicrafts shop in doorway specializes in miniature ornaments. *Hostal Valencia* restaurant features paella, good food, charming; *El Tocororo* (national bird of Cuba), excellent food at US$30-35 a head, old colonial mansion with nice terrace, rec as probably the best restaurant in town; *La Cecilia*, Calle 5a, Miramar, good international food, mostly in open air setting, rec. *La Divina Pastora*, fish restaurant, not far from Castillo del Morro, dollars only, expensive, food praised; *Doce Apostolos*, nearby, fish and good criollo food (but not as good as the *Bodeguita del Medio*), good views of the Malecón. *El Pacífico*, Chinese restaurant, popular with Cubans. *Las Ruinas* in Parque Lenín, Cuba's most exclusive restaurant—and aptly named for its prices—is most easily reached by taxi; try to persuade the driver to come back and fetch you, as otherwise it is difficult to get back. Reasonable cafeteria-style meals are available at *Wakamba*, opp *St John's* hotel. In Vedado, *El Cochinito*, Calle 23 (national criollo dishes); *El Conejito*, Calle North, and *La Torre* (17 y M, at top of Edificio Fosca, poor food but good view), are quite expensive. In the *Habana Libre Hotel*, try *El Barracón*, traditional Cuban with good fish and seafood at lobby level, open 1200-midnight, and *Sierra Maestra* restaurant and *Bar Turquino* on the 25th floor (spectacular views of Havana which makes the food acceptable). Also expensive, "*1830*" on Malecón. Along and near La Rampa there are some cheaper pizzerías and self-service restaurants. On Paseo Avenue and Calle 1, near the *Riviera*, there is a cafetería in the "Diploferretería" (dollar hardware store), open 1000-2200 every day for sandwiches (usual limited selection), beer and soft drinks, quicker and cheaper than hotel cafés. At Marianao beach there are also some

cheaper bars and restaurants. Inside the hard currency shopping centre, Av 5 and Calle 42 in Miramar, is an outdoor fast-foodery and an indoor restaurant, the latter with moderate dollar prices.

A visit to the *Coppelia* ice-cream parlour, 23 y L, Vedado, is rec, but even ice-cream was rationed in 1994. Open only 0800-1000, residents had to start queuing at 0500 with their ration books if it was their day for ice-cream. To get an ice-cream, pay first, collect a dish and then the ice. Alternatively, sample the Coppelia ice-cream in the tourist hotels and restaurants.

● **Bars**

Visitors find that ordinary bars *not* on the tourist circuit will charge them in dollars, if they let foreigners in at all. If it is a local bar and the Cubans are all paying in pesos, you will have to pay in US dollars. Even so, the prices in most places are not high by Caribbean standards.

The best bar in Old Havana is *La Bodeguita* (see above, also for *La Floridita*). *La Casa del Agua La Tinaja*, on SW corner of the Plaza de Armas is a nice place selling drinking water for 5 cents. Try a *mojito* in any bar.

● **Shopping**

Local cigars and rum are excellent. Original lithographs and other works of art can be purchased directly from the artists at the Galería del Grabado, Plaza de la Catedral (Mon-Fri 1400-2100, Sat 1400-1900). On Sat afternoons there are handicraft stalls in the Plaza. Reproductions of works of art are sold at *La Exposición*, San Rafael 12, Manzana de Gómez, in front of Parque Central. There is a special boutique, the *Palacio de la Artesanía*, in the Palacio Pedroso (built 1780) at Calle Cuba 64 (opp Parque Anfiteatro) where the largest selection of Cuban handicrafts is available; the artisans have their workshops in the back of the same building (open Mon-Sat 1230-1930) it has things not available elsewhere: jewellery, Cuban coffee, local and imported liqueurs, soft drinks, T-shirts, postcards and best retail selection of cigars (2 cigar-makers in attendance, lower prices than at factory); Visa and Mastercard accepted, passport required. Similar, and good, is *El Palacio del Turismo*, Obispo 252, T 63-6095, open 24 hrs, with shops, bar/café, information bureau, phones (open 0900-2100 daily) and other services (see **Travel Agents** below). The *Caracol*, formerly "Intur-shops" in tourist hotels (eg *Habana Libre*) and elsewhere, which sell tourists' requisites and other luxury items, require payment in US\$ (or credit cards: Mastercard, Visa) and will generally cash travellers' cheques and give change in US\$ cash. *La Maison* is a luxurious mansion on Calle 7 and 16 in Miramar, with dollar shops selling cigars, alcohol, handicrafts, jewellery and perfume. There is sometimes live music in the evening in lovely open-air patio, and fashion shows displaying imported clothes sold in their own boutique, free entry. The large department stores are along Galiano (Av Italia) near San Rafael and Neptuno. Large diplomatic store, Diplomercado, at Miramar (Av 5 y C 42) accepts all foreign currencies (no pesos) and has a variety of goods (including foodstuffs) at prices way below the government Intur dollar shops. Rationed goods are distinguished by a small card bearing the code number and price but a great deal is now sold freely and these articles bear only the price. Most stores are open only in the afternoon.

If buying food, go to the Diplomercado; if there is no bread, there is a good *panadería* next door. There are tourist food shops in the hotels *Habana Libre* and *Riviera*, but they do not sell fresh food.

● **Bookshops**
International bookstore at end of El Prado, near Parque Fraternidad and Capitol, English, French, German books but selection poor and payment has to be in dollars. Other good bookshops near Parque Central and La Moderna Poesía on Calle Obispo (books are very good value). *Librería La Bella Habana*, in the Palacio del Segundo Cabo, O'Reilly 4 y Tacón, open Mon-Fri 0900-1630, has both Cuban and international publications. Good art books (weighty) at the Maxim Gorky Soviet bookshop. Universal (San Rafael) and El Siglo de las Luces (Neptuno), both near Capitolio, are good places to buy *son*, *trova* and jazz (rock) records.

● **Cigar Factory**
Partagas on Calle Inglaterra behind the Capitolio, gives tours twice daily, in theory, at 1000 and 1300, US\$10 including drink and pack of small cigars. The tour lasts for about an hour and is very interesting. You are taken through the factory and shown the whole production process from storage and sorting of leaves, to packaging and labelling (explanation in Spanish only). Four different brand names are made here; Partagas, Cubana, Ramón Allones and Bolívar (special commission of 170,000 cigars made for the Seville Expo, Spain, 1992). These and other famous cigars can be bought at their

shop here, and rum, at good prices (credit cards accepted). Cigars are also made at many tourist locations (eg Palacio de las Artesanías, the airport, some hotels).

● **Photography**
Films developed at *Publifoto*, Edificio Focsa, Calle M entre 17 y 19, and *Photoservice*, Galiano 572 entre Reina y Salud (another branch in Varadero, Villa Cuatro Palmas, casa 526).

● **Night Clubs**
The *Tropicana* (closed Mon) is a must; book with Cubatur or through a tourist hotel, US\$40-55, depending on seat, entry only, transport US\$5 and drinks extra (2030-0200). Despite being toned down to cater for more sober post-revolutionary tastes, it is still a lively place with plenty of atmosphere, open-air (entry refunded if it rains). Drinks are expensive: a bottle of rum is US\$60; payment in dollars. Bringing your own bottle seems acceptable. Foreigners showing their exchange paper at the door may be admitted without booking if there is room. Next door is *Arcos de Cristal*, with live music till 0200. All the main hotels have their own cabarets, enquire at Cubatur and make a reservation. *Capri* is rec, at US\$15 and longer show than *Tropicana* but the drinks are expensive at US\$40 for a bottle of best rum. Best to reserve through Cubatur. Also *Pico Blanco* (*Rincón del Feeling*) at *Hotel St John's*; the *Commodore* disco (US\$10), crowded, Western-style, free to *Hotel Neptune* guests; *La Finca* at Playas del Este. *El Galeón* is a disco on a ship which sails at night from El Morro, 2 dance floors (one salsa, one Cuban music), US\$10. The *Cabaret Nacional*, San Rafael y Prado, costs US\$10 for 2 shows (first with dancing, second a band, with everyone dancing between the 2); you must enter with a Cuban and leave passport details at the door.

● **Theatres**
Teatro Mella, Línea entre A y B, Vedado, specializes in modern dance; more traditional programmes at *Gran Teatro de la Habana* on Parque Central next to *Hotel Inglaterra*. The Conjunto Folklórico Nacional dance company sometimes performs here, highly rec, 2 pesos (local currency accepted). Havana has some very lively theatre companies.

● **Casa De La Trova**
San Lázaro, entre Belascoán y Gervasio.

● **Jazz**

Maxim Club, Calle 10, T 33981, free entry, music starts at 2100, worth arriving early, rec but beware of 'friends' drinks appearing on your bill; *Coparrun*, *Hotel Riviera* (big names play there), jazz in the bar rec.

● **Cinemas**

Best are *Yara* (opp *Habana Libre* hotel); *Payret*, Prado 503. Many others.

● **Jardín Botánico Nacional de Cuba**

Km 3$\frac{1}{2}$, Carretera del Rocía, S of the city, beyond Parque Lenín (take Bus 4, if running, from the end of the Prado to Vivara, then take Bus 31 and ask; taxi to Varadero US$80). Open daily 0900-1700 (1000-1800 in summer), US$0.30. The garden is well-maintained with excellent collections; it has a Japanese garden with tropical adaptations. Rosa Alvarez, one of the guides, is knowledgeable and speaks some English.

● **Zoo**

Parque Zoológico Nacional Calzada de Bejucal y Avenida 200-Lenin, o Boyeros y Fontanar, Wed-Sun, 0900-1515, T 44-7614. *Parque Zoológico de la Habana*, Av 26, Vedado (open Tues-Sun 0900-1800).

● **El Bosque De La Habana**

Worth visiting. From the entrance to the City Zoo, cross Calle 26 and walk a few blocks until you reach a bridge across the Almendares. Cross this, turn right at the end and keep going N, directly to the Bosque which is a jungle-like wood.

● **Aquaria**

National Aquarium, Calle 60 and Av 1, Miramar, specializes in salt-water fish and dolphins (closed 1993 for remodelling) while the Parque Lenín aquarium has fresh-water fish on show.

● **Banks**

Banco Nacional and its branches. (See also under **Currency** below.)

● **Post Office**

There is a post and telegraph office in the *Hotel Habana Libre* building. Also on Calle Ejido next to central railway station and under the Gran Teatro de La Habana. For stamp collectors the Círculo Filatélico is on Calle San José 1172 between Infanta and Basarrata, open Mon-Fri, 1700-2000, and there is a shop on Obispo 518 with an excellent selection (Cuban stamps are very colourful and high quality).

● **Telephones and Cable Offices**

Calle Obispo 351, T 6-9901/5; Telegraph in *Habana Libre* building. Ministerio de Comunicaciones, Plaza de la Revolución, T 70-5581. The international telephone, telex and fax centre in the *Habana Libre* is open round the clock (also see **Travel Agents** below).

● **Travel Agents**

See **Excursions** in **Information for Visitors** on tours offered by *Cubatur*. Gaviota Travel, Avenida 47 No. 2821. T 294694/294528, claim to be the only private travel company in Cuba, rec. *The Palacio del Turismo*, Obispo 252, on the corner of Cuba, is also rec for arranging tours around the country (bearing in mind the warnings in **Information for Visitors**, **Excursions**); see also **Shopping** above. **Travel Assistance** Asistur, Av del Prado 254, between Trocadero y Animas, La Habana Vieja, T 62-5519/63-8284, F 33-8087, open 0830-1700, in case of emergency 24 hrs, some English spoken, maps sold, hotel and train ticket reservations, has links to many worldwide insurance companies, very helpful (cost of insurance US$1.50/day). Asistur also has a shop selling souvenirs.

● **Transport**

The economic crisis and shortage of fuel has led to severe transport problems. There is now very little local traffic, there are long queues at petrol stations and public transport has dwindled. Tourists are expected to use dollar transport, such as taxis or hired cars (when available), or not travel at all. Organized tours out of town are rarely more than day trips. Always check when booking that departure is definite, agencies will cancel through lack of passengers or fuel. A fleet of white **"Turistaxis"** with meters has been introduced for tourists' use; payment in US$: sample fare, Ciudad Vieja to Vedado US$3.50. **Panataxi** (T 81-0153/1175/7931), 24 hrs, cheaper than most as they use Ladas instead of Nissans, and are not a/c, US$1 call-out charge. If you ask your hotel to book a taxi for you they are more likely to call for the luxury variety (US$2 call-out charge). Some ordinary taxis are only allowed to operate in a restricted area (indicated by a sign in the window). If you want to go further afield look for one without a sign. The newer taxis have meters which should be set at No 1 during the daytime and at No 2 at night (2300-0700); they carry a maximum of 4 passengers (drivers may take a fifth if he/she is prepared to hide when passing the police). In the older taxis there are no meters and there is normally a fixed charge between points in or near the city. The fare should be fixed before setting out on a journey. **Ordinary taxis** are not allowed to accept US dollars; latest reports indicate that peso taxis have stopped running completely. Beware of unofficial taxis at the airport arrival gate who will overcharge. Private cars also wait at bus and train stations and will negotiate a price (their preference is for dollars).

Town buses used to be frequent and cheap but the crisis since 1993 means that they have stopped running too.

The **out-of-town bus services** leave from the Terminal de Omnibus Interprovinciales, Av Rancho Boyeros (Independencia), but practically none has run since mid-1993. See **Information for Visitors** for advance booking addresses.

Trains leave from the Estación Central in Av Egido (de Bélgica), Havana, to the larger cities. The Estación Central has what is claimed to be the oldest engine in Latin America, *La Junta*, built in Baltimore in 1842. Trains for Pinar del Río leave from the West (Occidente or 19 de Noviembre) station. It is easier to get a seat on a train than on a bus, but all public transport out of Havana is heavily booked in advance and difficult to get on. Staff at the train station have been said to be unhelpful in providing information on departures, with little interest in helping you travel. *Ferrotur*, Calles Arsenal y Egido, use side entrance for dollar tickets, is very helpful. For details of services, see below.

● **Bicycle Hire**

From **Panataxi**, car-park in corner of O'Reilly and Cuba, T 81-0153, US$1 per hour, US$12 per day. *Hotel Neptune*, charges US$3 for the first hour then US$1 for each subsequent hour. Also *Hotel Riviera* and *Palacio del Turismo*, Obispo 252. Check the bicycle carefully (take your own lock, pump, even a bicycle spanner and puncture repair kit; petrol stations have often been converted into bicycle stations, providing air and tyre repairs). Cycling is a good way to see Havana, especially the suburbs; some roads in the Embassy area are closed to cyclists. The tunnel underneath the harbour mouth has a bus designed specifically to carry bicycles and their riders. Take care at night as there are few street lights and bikes are not fitted with lamps.

● **Airport**

José Martí, 18 km from Havana. Turistaxi to airport, US$16-18 depending on time of day or night and destination. The Cubatur desk will book a taxi for you from the airport. The duty free shop at the airport is good value.

EAST FROM HAVANA

Short ferry rides across Havana Bay to Casablanca and Regla (50 centavos) are fun and a good way of looking at these "across the bay" villages and Havana itself from a different perspective. The best view of Havana is from Morro Castle.

An easy excursion is to Cojímar, the seaside village featured in Hemingway's *The Old Man and the Sea*. The coastline is dirty because of effluent from tankers, but it is a quiet, pretty place to relax. *La Terraza* is a restaurant ("dollars") with a pleasant view, reasonably priced seafood meals. Further E is Santa María del Mar, to which Cubatur runs day excursions for US$10 (min 6 people). Another easy excursion is by train to Guanabo (2 departures daily), a pleasant, non-touristy beach; no dollar facilities, few peso ones. The quietest spot is Brisas del Mar, at the E end. Taxi from Havana US$20. Hotels: *Itabo*, US$38-50, Laguna Itabo entre Santa María del Mar y Boca Ciega, T 2581, good accommodation, poor hotel, dirty pool. *Hotel Atlántico*, Av Las Terrazas, Santa María del Mar, T 3308, US$30s, US$40d, also has an *Aparthotel* (opp the hotel is the self-catering complex's shop selling fresh food, inc eggs, bread, cheese and meat). It may be possible to find "black market" apartments in Guanabo for US$15 a night with kitchen; ask around. *Villa Playa Hermosa*, 5 Av entre 472 y 474, T 2774, Guanabo, US$18s, US$23d, rents bikes (in poor condition).

Guanabacoa is 5 km to the E and is reached by a road turning off the Central Highway, or by launch from Muelle Luz (not far from No 9 on the map) to the suburb of Regla, then by bus (if running) direct to Guanabacoa. It is a well preserved small colonial town; sights include the old parish church which has a splendid altar: the monastery of San Francisco; the Carral theatre; and some attractive mansions. The Historical Museum of Guanabacoa, a former estate mansion, has an unusual voodoo collection in the former slave quarters at the back of the building, Calle Martí 108, between San Antonio and Versalles, T 90-9117. Open: Monday and Wednesday to Saturday 1030-1800, Sunday 0900-1300.

A delightful colonial town, **Santa María del Rosario**, founded in 1732, is 16 km E of Havana. It is reached from Cotorro, on the Central Highway, and was carefully restored and preserved before the Revolution. The village church is particularly good. See the paintings, one by Veronese. There are curative springs nearby.

Hemingway fans may wish to visit the house in **San Francisco de Paula**, 11 km from the centre, where he lived from 1939 to 1960 (called the **Museo Hemingway**, T 082-2515). The signpost is opposite Post Office, leading up short driveway. Closed in 1993 after storm damage in March. Visitors are not allowed inside the plain whitewashed house which has been lovingly preserved with all Hemingway's furniture and books, just as he left it. But you can walk all around the outside and look in through the windows and open doors, although vigilant staff prohibit any photographs. There is a small annex building with one room used for temporary exhibitions, and from the upper floors there are fine views over Havana. The garden is beautiful and tropical, with many shady palms. Next to the swimming pool (empty) are the gravestones of Hemingway's pet dogs, shaded by a flowering shrub. There is a bust of the author in the village of Cojímar.

Some 60 km E of Havana is **Jibacoa** beach, which is excellent for snorkelling as the reefs are close to the beach. (*Camping de Jibacoa*, cabins for 4 or 2, US$12 pp, US$16d. Food is rather expensive.)

The old provincial town of **Matanzas** lies 104 km E of Havana along the Vía Blanca, which links the capital with Varadero beach, 34 km further E (many small oilwells producing low-grade crude are passed en route). There used to be frequent buses but the journey via the Hershey Railway is more memorable (4 trains daily, 3 hrs, 1.03 pesos, from the Casablanca station, which is reached by public launch from near La Fuerza Castle, 0.50 peso). Those who wish to make it a day trip from Havana can do so, long queues for return tickets, best to get one as soon as you arrive.

The old town is on the W bank of the estuary, the new town on the E; both the rivers Yumurí and San Juan flow through the city. In Matanzas one should visit the Pharmaceutical Museum (Monday-Saturday 1400-1800, 1900-2100), the Matanzas Museum (Tuesday-Sunday 1500-1800, 1900-2200), and the cathedral, all near Parque La Libertad. There is a wonderful view of the surrounding countryside from the church of Montserrat. Bellamar Cave is only 5 km from Matanzas. (Hotel *Canimao*, Km 4 Carretera Matanzas a Varadero, T 6-1014, US$43, good restaurant.)

Varadero

From Matanzas one can continue on a good dual carriageway to **Varadero**, 144 km from Havana, Cuba's chief beach resort with all facilities. It is built on a 20-km sandspit, the length of which run two roads lined with about a dozen large hotels, some smaller ones, and many chalets and villas. Many of the villas date from before 1959. It is undergoing large scale development of new hotels and cabins and joint ventures with foreign investors are being encouraged. 5,000 rooms had been built by 1991, with the aim of expanding to 30,000 rooms by the turn of the century. A Cuban-Spanish joint venture has opened two resort hotels managed by Sol/Meliá Hotels of Spain: *Sol Palmeras* (T 566110, US$150d, room only), and the *Meliá Gran Varadero* (T 66220, US$160d, room only, 5 star). Jamaican investors have built the 160-room *Cactus* to be followed by a 250-room hotel later. In Varadero all hotels, restaurants and excursions must be paid in US dollars. Book excursions at any hotel with a Playazul Travel Agency office, or at 1 Av entre 13 y 14, T 6-2384. Cubatur office: Calle 39 entre 1 Av y Playa, T 6-4143. Despite the building in progress it is not over exploited and is a good place for a family beach holiday. The beaches are quite deserted, if a bit exposed, but there is not a lot to do. Distances are large. Avenida 1, which runs NE-SW the length of the spit, has a bus service; calle numbers begin with lowest numbers at the SW end and work upwards to the NE peninsula. There is a Municipal Museum at Calle 57 y Av de la Playa. The Centro Recreativo Josone, Av 1 y Calle 59, is a large park with pool, bowling, other activities and a café. Each November a festival is held in Varadero, lasting a week, which attracts some of the best artists in South America. Entrance US$2-10 per day.

From Varadero it is possible to explore the interesting town of *Cárdenas*, where the present Cuban flag was raised for the first time in 1850. The sea here is polluted with oil and the air smells of phosphorous. Another excursion is to Neptune's Cave (thought a more appealing name than the old one, Cepero), which is S of the town of Carboneras, half-way between Matanzas and Varadero. It has an underground lagoon, stalagmites and stalactites, evidence of Indian occupation and was used as a clandestine hospital during the war of independence.

● **Where To Stay In Varadero** (All prices high season, double. Hotels can be booked in the tourist office.) At the S end: *Paradiso*, US$140,

attached to *Puntarena*, T 6-3917 (Paradiso), 6-3919 (Puntarena), F 33-7074, also US$140, with all resort facilities, 3 pools, watersports, all shared by both hotels, good restaurants, fresh seafood, rec. *Varadero Internacional*, Carretera a Las Américas, T 6-3011, US$140, 2 grades of rooms, all facilities (including 5 restaurants), connected with *Villas Cabañas del Sol*, US$84. *Los Cactus*, US$128; *Acuazul*, Av 1 entre Calles 13 y 14, US$65; with pool; *Varazul*, Av 1 entre Calles 14 y 15, US$42, quiet; *Villa Sotavento*, dependency of *Acuazul*, US$38d, next to beach, clean, with bath, breakfast, US$5, buffet, very good. *Hotel y Villa Kawama*, Carretera de Kawama y Calle 0, T 6-3015, US$30-40. *Cuatro Palmas Resort (Four Palms)*, Av 1 y Calle 60, T 6-2893, US$120d (US$63 in bungalows and villas), very pleasant; *Villa Punta Blanca*, T 6-3916, made up of a number of former private residences with some new complexes, US$64d; *Caribe*, Av 1 y Calle 30, T 6-3310, US$42. *Pullman*, Av 1 entre Calle 49 y 50, T 6-2575, US$34, best value for the independent traveller, only 12 rooms, very popular; *Ledo*, Av Playa y C 44, T 6-3206, US$30, not rec; *Villa La Herradura*, Av Playa entre 35 y 36, T 6-3703, well-equipped suites, balcony, restaurant, bar, *Caracol* shop, etc, US$47; *Los Delfines*, Av Playa y Calle 39, T 6-3815, US$38. *Solymar* (adjacent to *Hotel Internacional*, whose facilities can be shared), US$52, rec, pool, bar and shop but no restaurant. If you need to change a little money, go to *Hotel Bellamar*.

● **Where to Eat** Recommended restaurants, all between US$9-15, are *Mi Casita* (book in advance), *La Cabañita*, *Halong*, *La Esquinita*, *El Mesón del Quijote* (Spanish) and buffets at the restaurant of hotel *Kawama*. *Albacora*, disappointing, all dishes except *pescado*, US$12-18, but if you want fish you may be told '*no hay*'; *Las Américas*, beautiful setting, food good one night, inedible the next; *Terrace* cafeteria at the *Internacional* for the best lunches; *Bodegón Criollo*, pleasant atmosphere, popular, no vegetarian food. *Coppelia*, C 46 y Av 1, in town centre, ice cream US$0.90. It is now easier to buy food in Varadero because the new Aparthotels (*Varazul*, *La Herradura*) have a small food store.

● **Car hire** Havanautos, T 6-3433, or through many hotels. **Moped rental** US$5 per hour, US$15 3 hours, US$24 for 24 hours, a good way to see the city. **Bicycle hire** from *Villa Calleta*, Av 1 y Calle 33, US$1/hour.

• **Services** Bank Banco Financiero Internacional, Av Playa y C 32, T 6-3144. **Phones,** telex and telegrams, C 64 y 1 Av, T 6-2103. **Clinic** 1 Av y C 61, T 6-2122. **Police** C 39 y 1 Av, T 116.

• **Transport** A cheap method of getting to Varadero is to take the train to Matanzas (see above), then a taxi to Matanzas bus terminal (3 pesos) from where you catch a bus, 0.40 pesos, about 1 hr (state destination, take ticket, wait for bus and then your number to be called, and run for the bus). About 5½ hrs in all, if buses are running. Bus station in Varadero is at Calle 36, but there is a wait of several days. There is an airport; bus to hotels US$10 pp.

Santa Clara, 300 km from Havana and 196 km from Varadero, is a pleasant university city in the centre of the island. It was the site of the last battle of the Cuban revolution before Castro entered Havana, and the Batista troop train captured by Che Guevara can be seen near the cathedral. There are two "dollar hotels", *Motel Los Caneyes*, Av de los Eucaliptos y Circunvalación, T 4512 (outside the city), US$32 chalet-style cabins, hot showers, good buffet, supper US$12, breakfast US$4, excellent value, and *Santa Clara Libre* (central, on Parque Vidal, T 7540), US$24, reasonable lunch. At Corralillo is *Hotel Elguea*, at the spa of that name, US$20, a/c rooms, bath, sports facilities, T 9-6240.

Cienfuegos, on the S coast, is an attractive seaport and industrial city 80 km from Trinidad and 70 km from Santa Clara. Interesting colonial buildings around the central Parque Martí. There is one "dollar hotel", 45 minutes' walk from station, *Jagua*, Punta Gorda, T 6302, US$45, comfortable, palatial restaurant next door, gorgeous decor, live piano music, simple but good food in snack bar (expensive restaurant next door). Many of the hotels are out of town or booked solid by Cubans. *Hotel Pasacaballo*, Carretera a Rancho Luna, T 96-212, US$35 and *Rancho Luna*, US$31, T 432-5929, are seaside complexes with cafeteria etc.

From Cienfuegos take a taxi to *Playa Girón* and the *Bay of Pigs* (26 pesos, 1½ hours). Ask the driver to wait while you visit the beach and tourist complex, and the site of national pilgrimage where, in 1961, the disastrous US-backed invasion of Cuba was attempted. (Hotel *Playa Girón*, T 59-7810, US$29, a/c with bath, good self-service meals.) Further W from Girón is the Zapata Peninsula, an area of swamps, mangroves, beaches and much bird and animal life. Access from Playa Larga or Guamá, inland. You can rent a cabin at Playa Larga (US$26, T 7219), or there is the *Centro Turístico Guamá*, Laguna del Tesoro, Zapata, T 2979, a/c rooms with bath, US$35, restaurant and other services. There is a crocodile farm at the Zapata Tourist Institute in Guamá, which can be visited. Varadero hotels organize day excursions for US$35 pp which includes lunch, English-speaking guide and a boat ride on the lagoon.

TRINIDAD

Trinidad, 133 km S of Santa Clara is a perfect relic of the early days of the Spanish colony: beautifully preserved streets and buildings with hardly a trace of the 20th century anywhere. It was founded in 1514 as a base for expeditions into the "New World"; Cortés set out from here for Mexico in 1518. The five main squares and four churches date from the 18th and 19th centuries; the whole city, with its fine palaces, cobbled streets and tiled roofs, is a national monument. The **Museo Romántico,** next to the church of Santíssima Trinidad on the main square, is excellent. It has a collection of romantic-style porcelain, glass, paintings and ornate furniture displayed in a colonial mansion, with beautiful views from the upper floor balconies. Admission US$3, no cameras allowed. **Museo de Historia Nacional** is on Calle Simón Bolívar, an attractive building but rather dull displays, admission US$3. The **Museo de**

Arte, on the corner of Simón Bolívar and the main square, has a small collection of works by local artists, plus a few prints of old masterpieces, such as the Mona Lisa, admission US$3. One block from the church is the *Casa de la Trova*, open weekend lunchtimes and evenings, entry free. Excellent live Cuban music with a warm, lively atmosphere. There are mostly Cubans here, of all age groups, and it's a great place to watch, and join in with, the locals having a good time. All drinks paid for in dollars. Another venue for live music is *La Canchanchara*, Calle Real 44, T 4345. Open 0900-1700, cocktails, no food. More touristy than *Casa de La Trova* (cigar and souvenir shop), but good traditional music at lunchtimes. *Restaurant El Jigue*, lunch only, live music, good food and atmosphere. Nearby are the excellent beaches of La Boca (8 km), a small fishing village, restaurant on beach, some buses or taxi.

Inland from Trinidad are the beautiful, wooded Escambray mountains. There is no public transport but day trips are organized to Topes de Collantes by the *Hotel Ancón*, for US$43 pp. Their tour includes lunch, cocktail (at 1000) and visits coffee plantations, a crystal clear swimming pond and a pretty waterfall. Half-way up the mountainside, the paved road gives way to dirt track. Passengers transfer from air-conditioned mini-bus to Russian 4-wheel drive lorry, an exhilarating experience! You can see hummingbirds and the tocororo, the national bird of Cuba. A great day out. There is also a huge hospital in the mountains, which offers special therapeutic treatments for patients from all over the world, and a hotel *Los Helechos*, US$26d—details about both places at the *Hotel Ancón*.

Local information
● **Where To Stay In Trinidad**

Hard to find, particularly in summer. *Motel Las Cuevas*, Finca Santa Ana, T 2324/2368, US$32d, on a hill 10 mins' walk from town (good road), chalets with balconies, very comfortable rooms with a/c, TV, fridge, hot water, and very clean, 2 swimming pools, bar, discotheque (most rooms are far enough away not to be disturbed by noise), dollar shop, restaurant (good self-service meals), very good value, rec. *Costa Sur*, good value, 11 km SE of town at Playa Ancón, T 2524, US$31, taxi fare approximately US$9. Pesos hotels are now closed down. Campsites at Ancón beach and La Boca (5-bed apartments). Camping at Base Manacal in the mountains: tent or small hut for US$5 per day; take No 10 bus from Cienfuegos. The only restaurant seems to be the *Mesón del Regidor* on Calle Simón Bolívar, small menu but elegant setting. There are also a couple of dollar tiendas in the centre selling souvenirs, postcards and imported snacks. On the road to Cienfuegos, *Hacienda María Dolores*, serving creole food, 0900-1600, has a collection of tropical birds, cockfighting and a fiesta on Thur, 1800-2300.

● **Transport**

From Havana: a/c buses at 0335 (arrive 0905) and 1220 (arrive 1750), if running. Train from Estación 19 de Noviembre (on Tulipán) to Cienfuegos, number 1301 departs 2146 arrives 0440, number 1303 departs 0725 arrives 1420, 7 hrs to travel 250 km, US$8. If you can get on a tour bus returning to Havana, the fare, inc lunch, will be US$25 pp. Taxi Cienfuegos-Trinidad US$75; tour US$30 pp inc lunch. From Santa Clara to Cienfuegos there are several buses daily; from Santa Clara to Trinidad only 2. Transport to the E of Cuba is difficult from Trinidad as it is not on the Carretera Central. Best to go to Sancti Spiritus (see below) and bus from there, about 1½ hrs through beautiful hilly scenery. As elsewhere, severe shortages and huge queues, trucks and tractors with trailers may be laid on as a back-up.

13 km from Trinidad is Playa Ancón (not a town as such, just two resort hotels: *Costa Sur* and *Ancón*). The *Ancón*, T 4011/3155, is US$45d with a/c, though they encourage you to take the daily package rate of US$100 inc three meals, drinks and such extras as snorkels, bicycles and horse riding. Good restaurant, snack bar and many facilities, popular for families. The beach is lovely, pure white sand and clean turquoise water, highly recommended.

Sancti Spiritus, about 80 km E of Trinidad and 90 km SE of Santa Clara, can be reached by road from Cienfuegos, Santa Clara or Trinidad (2 hours over a mountain road through the Escambray). In the San Luis valley, between Trinidad and Sancti Spiritus are many 19th century sugarmills. Among them is the 45-metre Manacas-Iznagas tower (entry US$1), with a café nearby. Daily train from Havana, 0645, 6 hours (but may take 9 or more). The train seats are very comfortable, though the journey is hot and stuffy through flat countryside, endless fields of sugar cane and a few villages. Buffet car on board (serving tinned grapefruit juice, bread with oil, rice and beans), intriguing queueing system with cards, giving priority to pregnant mothers, the elderly, the disabled and children. It is one of Cuba's seven original Spanish towns and has a wealth of buildings from the colonial period. The former is a crumbling 19th century stuccoed building in splendid baroque decay, the latter is seedy and lacks the grandeur of the *Perla*. Refreshments in town available at the *Casa de las Infusiones*. The nearest tourist hotel is the *Zaza*, US$32, T 2-6012/5334, 10 km outside the town on the Zaza artificial lake, rather run down but service and food praised by Cubans.

The next province E is Ciego de Avila, largely flat, with mangrove swamps on the coasts and cayes to the N. 2 km outside the province's capital is *Hotel Ciego de Avila*, US$39, T 2-8013, with good food. At Morón, N of Ciego de Avila, is a hotel (US$43), called *Morón*, very smart, being renovated early 1994, good a/c and food. There is also a hotel on Caya Guillermo (US$50, T 2-2352/5343), a/c, bath, restaurant, watersports, etc.

The Museo Ignacio Agramonte in the large city of **Camagüey**, half-way between Santa Clara and Santiago, is one of the biggest and most impressive museums in the country. *Hotel Camagüey*, US$35, Av Ignacio Agramonte, T 8-2490, good condition, good buffet restaurant; *Puerto Príncipe*, US$31, Av de los Mártires y Andrés Sánchez, La Vigía (in town), T 7575/78; *Gran Hotel*, US$31, Maceo 67, T 2093/4, and *Plaza*, US$34, are the "dollar" hotels.

Two tourist enclave developments have been built at Santa Lucía near Nuevitas, on the coast N of Camagüey, and at Marca del Portillo, on the coast S of Camagüey. Nuevitas was the original site of Camagüey, founded in 1514 by Diego de Velázquez as Santa María del Puerto del Príncipe. Constant pirate attacks forced the town to be moved inland.

In the province of Las Tunas there is a hotel called *Villa El Saltón*, US$35, in a wooded valley beside a river S of Contramaestra, run by Cubanacan, hard to find, rustic style, good restaurant.

Holguín, a provincial capital in the E, near Santiago, has the *Hotel Pernik*, US$41, Av Jorge Dimitrov y Av XX Aniversario, T 48-1663, plentiful food; *Motel El Bosque*, US$27, and *Motel Mirador de Mayabe*, US$24, T 4-2660. From Holguín the beautiful Atlantic resort of **Guardalavaca** (*Hotel Guardalavaca*, pool, rec, "dollar hotel", US$30), with good beach, can be reached by bus.

SANTIAGO DE CUBA

Santiago de Cuba, near the E end of the island, 970 km from Havana and 670 km from Santa Clara, is Cuba's second city and "capital moral de la Revolución Cubana". It is a pleasant colonial Caribbean city, with many balconies and *rejas* (grills), for instance on Calles Aguilera and Félix Pena. Of the several museums, the best is the Colonial Museum located in Diego de Velázquez' house (the oldest in Cuba, started by Cortés in 1516, completed 1530), at the NW corner of Parque Céspedes. It has been restored after its use as offices after the Revolution and is in two parts, one 16th century, one 18th century (each room shows a particular period; there is also a 19th-century extension; open Tuesday-Saturday 0800-2200, Sunday 0900-1300, Monday 0800-1200, 1400-1800, free). On the S side of Parque Céspedes is the Cathedral (1522). Two

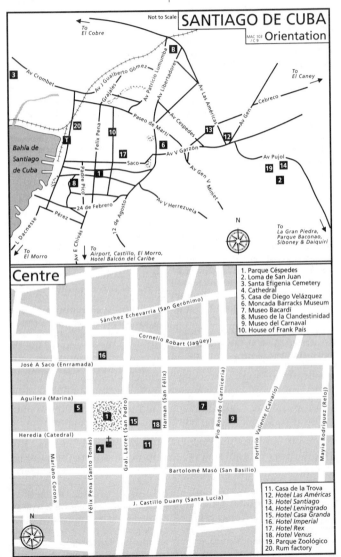

SANTIAGO DE CUBA
MAC 103 / C 9 **Orientation**

Not to Scale

To El Cobre
Av Crombet
Av J Gualberto Gómez
Grajales
Av Patricio Lumumba
Paseo de Martí
Av Libertadores
Av Céspedes
Av Las Américas
B
To El Caney
Av Gen Cebreco
Av Gen V Miniet
Av V Garzón
Av Pujol
Saco
Av V Herrezuela
Bahía de Santiago de Cuba
Félix Pena
Padre Pico
24 de Febrero
Pérez
L Dacnesse
Av E Chivás
12 de Agosto
To El Morro
To Airport, Castillo, El Morro, Hotel Balcón del Caribe
To La Gran Piedra, Parque Baconao, Siboney & Daiquirí
N

3 · 20 · T · 10 · 17 · 1 · 8 · 13 · 12 · 6 · 19 · 14 · 2

Centre

Sánchez Echevarria (San Gerónimo)
Cornelio Robart (Jagüey)
José A Saco (Enrramada)
Aguilera (Marina)
Heredia (Catedral)
Mariano Corona
Félix Pena (Santo Tomás)
Gral. Lacret (San Pedro)
Harman (San Félix)
Pío Rosado (Carnicería)
Porfirio Valiente (Calvario)
Mayía Rodríguez (Reloj)
Bartolomé Masó (San Basilio)
J. Castillo Duany (Santa Lucía)
N

16 · 5 · 1 · 15 · 18 · 7 · 9 · 4 · 11

1. Parque Céspedes
2. Loma de San Juan
3. Santa Efigenia Cemetery
4. Cathedral
5. Casa de Diego Velázquez
6. Moncada Barracks Museum
7. Museo Bacardí
8. Museo de la Clandestinidad
9. Museo del Carnaval
10. House of Frank País

11. Casa de la Trova
12. Hotel Las Américas
13. Hotel Santiago
14. Hotel Leningrado
15. Hotel Casa Granda
16. Hotel Imperial
17. Hotel Rex
18. Hotel Venus
19. Parque Zoológico
20. Rum factory

blocks E of the Parque, opposite the Palacio Provincial is the Museo Bacardí (exhibits from prehistory to the Revolution downstairs, paintings upstairs), closed indefinitely in 1993. Visit the Moncada barracks museum and the house of Frank País (General Bandera 226), leader of the armed uprising in Santiago on 30 November 1956, who was shot in July 1957. The national hero, José Martí, is buried in Santa Efigenia cemetery, just W of the city. The Museo de la Clandestinidad has an exhibition of the citizens' underground struggle against the dictatorship. It was originally the residence of the Intendente, then was a police HQ. It is at the top of picturesque Calle Padre Pico (steps), corner of Santa Rita, and affords good views of the city. Another historical site is the huge ceiba tree in the grounds of the *Leningrado* hotel, beneath which Spain and the USA signed the surrender of Santiago on 16 July 1898; at the Loma de San Juan nearby are more monuments of the Hispano-Cuban-American war (only worth visiting if staying at the *Leningrado*, or going to the zoo and amusement park behind the hotel).

The Festival de Caribe runs from 16 to 19 April, with traditional African dancing and beautiful costumes. There is daily live music, free, and singing every weekend at the Casa de la Trova at Calle Heredia 206-8 (but hope that there is no modern music at the Casa de Estudiantes Josué País García next door to drown out the more traditional thing).

For stamp and coin collectors, the *círculo filatélico* and *numismático* is held every Sunday morning on the Plaza de la Catedral near the hotel reservations office.

Local information
● Where To Stay In Santiago
Leningrado, Km 1 Carretera a Siboney, T 4-2434, too far out of town, turistaxi US$3.95, a complex with cabins, pool, bar and several restaurants for which there are always queues, water shortages, US$24; *Las Américas*,

US$35, T 4-2011, Av de las Américas y Gen Cebreco, not so far out of town, lively, rec (turistaxi US$2.35), expensive restaurant (although cheap sandwiches and spaghetti are available), non-residents may use swimming pool, bicycle hire; not far away is *Hotel Santiago*, Av Las Américas (10) y M, about US$100d a night, 5-star, clean, good service, good *A La Cubana* restaurant, highly rec, swimming pool, tennis, sauna; and *Balcón del Caribe*, next to Castillo del Morro, T 9-1011, US$32, overlooking the sea, quiet, pool, basic food, cold water in bungalows, pleasant but inconvenient for the town. *MES*, Calle L and 7 Terraza (about 5 blocks N of *Las Américas*), T 4-2398, is the cheapest dollar hotel at US$15 pp with colour TV and fan, 2 rooms share bath and fridge. *Hotel Tropical*, flats built for Russian technicians, US$25, 2 double beds, kitchen, TV, fridge, good value, reasonable restaurant. *Casa Granda* on Parque Céspedes is closed as a hotel (since 1992), but its café is open and is good. You can reserve beach accommodation in Santiago, eg a Siboney apartment, 2 rooms, 4 people, Mar Verde, crowded at weekends, a *cabaña*, basic, 3 people.

● Shopping
Diplomercado outside airport; take passport.

● Telephones
For calls outside Santiago, Centro de Comunicaciones Nacional e Internacional, Heredia y Félix Pena, underneath the cathedral.

● Train
Havana-Santiago every other day at 1659; Santiago-Havana, every other day at 1859: US$35 single for foreigners, 16 hours; train Santiago-Camagüey 1810, arrives 2300, also Tues, Thur, Sat 1000, arrive 1500, US$13 one way. No tourist taxis at the station, only local drivers, who charge, for example, US$4 to *Hotel Las Américas*.

● Bus
Terminal near Plaza de la Revolución for reservations.

For private/unofficial taxis, ask around the park at Av Victoriano Garzón and Plácido; you may be lucky.

Excursions
Excellent excursions can be made to the *Gran Piedra* (32 km E) a viewpoint from which it is said you can see Haiti and Jamaica on a clear day, more likely their lights on a clear night. It is a giant rock

weighing 75,000 tones, 1,234m high, reached by climbing 454 steps from the road ("only for the fit"). Santiago-La Gran Pedra buses are no use because daily buses leave La Gran Piedra early morning and return in the evening (the *Turismo Buró* in any hotel will arrange a tour, good value). 2 km before La Gran Piedra are the Jardines de la Siberia, on the site of a former coffee plantation, an extensive botanical garden; turn right and follow the track for about 1 km to reach the gardens. The Museo La Isabelica is 2 km past La Gran Piedra, a ruined coffee plantation, the buildings of which are now turned into a museum housing the former kitchen and other facilities on the ground floor. Upstairs is the owners' house in authentic 19th-century style. On view in the ground floor are instruments of slave torture. After the slave revolt in Haiti, large numbers of former slave owners were encouraged to settle in the Sierra de la Gran Piedra. Here they built 51 *cafetales*, using slave labour. During the Ten Years War (1868-78) the revolutionaries called for the destruction of all the *cafetales*. This influx led to the impact of Haitian/French culture on Santiago, especially in music.

The Ruta Turística runs along the shore of the Bahía de Santiago to the Castillo del Morro, a clifftop fort with a museum of the sea, piracy and local history (open all week, but only morning on Monday). Recommended, even if only for the view. Turistaxi to El Morro, US$5.50-6 round trip with wait. Transport along the road passes the ferry at Ciudadmar to the resorts of **Cayo Granma** and La Socapa in the estuary (hourly, 5 cents each way). Cayo Granma was originally Cayo Smith, named after its wealthy owner; it became a resort for the rich. Now most of its 600 inhabitants travel to Santiago to work. There are no vehicles; there is a fish restaurant and bar (try the house speciality in the restaurant) in an idyllic setting looking across the bay towards Santiago.

Another excursion can be made to **Siboney**, the nearest beach to Santiago, pleasant and unpretentious (no dollar facilities). Take bus 214 from near bus terminal. Very crowded at weekends. Even nicer is Junagua beach, bus 207, along the same road; further development is projected in this area. 12 km E of Santiago is La Granja Siboney, the farmhouse used as the headquarters for the revolutionaries' attack on the Moncada barracks. It now has a museum of uniforms, weapons and artefacts as well as extensive newspaper accounts of the attack (entry US$1). Further E is Parque Bacanao, a wonderful amusement park in which you can visit El Valle Prehistórico (with lifesize replicas of dinosaurs), an old car and trailer museum (free, recommended) and the Daiquirí Beach and Hotel, basic facilities, quiet. There are buses Nos 14, 35 & 62 (if running) to the public beaches in the park.

Ten minutes from the centre of Santiago there is a rum factory, open to visitors, US$6 for a guided tour with English-speaking guide, including free sample. From Santiago, it is possible to visit El Cobre (bus No 3) where the shrine of Cuba's patron saint, the Virgen de la Caridad del Cobre, is located (there is a hotel and reasonable restaurant). Interesting collection of personal offerings at foot of the statue, including a gold model of Fidel Castro.

Baracoa, 150 km E of Santiago, close to the most easterly point of the island, is an attractive place surrounded by a fruitful countryside. It is well worth the trip from Santiago (4 hrs drive) for the scenery of the last section of road, called La Farola, which winds through lush tropical mountains and then descends steeply to the coast. "Dollar hotel" *Castillo*, Calixto García, Loma del Paraíso, T 4-2103/2147, recommended, friendly staff, food OK, nice views, good swimming pool, US$42; *Porto Santo*, T 43512, from US$34 low season per room to US$56 in *cabaña* to US$84 in a suite, swimming pool, car hire, near runway of small airport. The Cubana office is on Plaza Martí. The taxi base is in front of the hospital. Bus to Guantánamo takes 4 hours.

Guantánamo 80 km from Santiago on the Baracoa road, is close to the US base of the same name (which cannot be easily visited from Cuba). "Dollar hotel" *Guantánamo*, Plaza Mariana Grajales, T 3-6015, US$27.

Guardalavaca (see page 183) on the N coast is a lovely drive through the mountains from Santiago. Take a day driving to Frente II (eat at *Rancho México*), down to Sagua and across to Guardalavaca. You can stay at Don Lino beach, which is small but pleasant, where there are comfortable huts (US$14) with refrigerator for cooling beer. Restaurant food is basic.

West from Santiago runs a wonderful coastal road along the Sierra Maestra with beautiful bays and beaches, completely deserted, some with black sand. It is only possible to visit by car. At La Plata, about 150 km from Santiago, is a little museum about the Cuban guerrillas' first successful battle. There is no curator so ask the local people to open it. En route you pass Las Coloradas, the beach where *Granma* landed. You can make a circular route back to Santiago via Manzanillo, **Bayamo** (both in Granma province; in Bayamo *Hotel Sierra Maestra*, on Santiago road, T 4-5013, US$41, a/c, bath, restaurant, pool and other usual facilities) and Palma Soriano.

WEST FROM HAVANA

West from Havana a dual carriage highway has been completed almost to *Pinar del Río*, the major city W of Havana. The province of Pinar del Río produces Cuba's best cigars. The city itself has many neoclassical villas with columns.

At the E entrance to the city is the modern *Hotel Pinar del Río*, Calle Martí final, T 5071/78, swimming pool, night club etc, US$32. For travel to Pinar del Río, train from Havana's Estación 19 de Noviembre/del Occidente, rather than bus, is recommended (leaves Havana 0500, book 1300 day before, leaves Pinar del Río 1702, 8 hrs); slow but comfortable.

If travelling by car on this route, you can make a detour to **Soroa** in the Sierra de Rosario, 81 km SW of the capital. It is a spa and resort in luxuriant hills. As you drive into the area, a sign on the right indicates the Mirador de Venus and Baños Romanos. Past the baths is the *Bar Edén* (open till 1800), where you can park before walking up to the Mirador (25 minutes). From the top you get fine views of the S plains, the palm-covered Sierra and the tourist complex itself; lots of birds, butterflies, dragonflies and lizards around the path; many flowers in season.

The road continues into the complex where there is an orchidarium with over 700 species (check if they are in bloom before visiting, guided tours between 0830-1140, 1340-1555 daily, US$2) and the *Castillo de las Nubes* restaurant (1130-2200, entrees US$5-6), a mock castle. Across the road from the orchidarium is a waterfall (250m, paved path, entry US$1), worth a visit if you are in the area. At the resort are cabins (T 2122, US$32 high season), restaurant *El Centro* (quite good), disco, bar, Olympic swimming pool, bike rental, riding nearby and handicrafts and dollar shops. Despite the ugly, gloomy cabins, it's a peaceful place and would be more so without the loud juke box.

Nearer Pinar del Río another detour N off the main road is to the spa of San Diego de los Baños, also in fine scenery in the Sierra de los Organos.

Viñales

North of Pinar del Río, on a road which leads to the N coast and eventually back to Havana is *Viñales*, a delightful small town in a dramatic valley. Stands of palm and tobacco fields with their drying barns (*vegas*, steep, thatch-roofed buildings which you can enter and photograph with ease) lie amid sheer and rounded mountains (*mogotes*) reminiscent of a Chinese landscape, especially at dawn and dusk. These massifs were part of a cave system which collapsed millions of years ago and, on some, remnants of stalactites can still be seen.

2 km N (27 km N of Pinar del Río) is the Mural de la Prehistoria, painted by Lovigildo González, a disciple of the Mexican Diego Rivera, between 1959 and 1976; tourist restaurant nearby. 6 km beyond Viñales is the *Cueva del Indio* which can be approached from two ends, neither far apart. Inside, though, you can travel the cave's length on foot and by boat (US$2 for foreigners), very beautiful. There is a restaurant at the cave (also at a smaller cave nearer Viñales).

Viñales itself is a pleasant town, with trees and wooden colonnades along the main street, red tiled roofs and a main square with a little-used cathedral and a Casa de Cultura with art gallery.

● **Where To Stay In Viñales** *Motel Los Jazmines*, 3 km before the town, in a superb location overlooking the valley, T 9-3265, US$31, good restaurant, bar with snacks available, shops, swimming pool, riding, easy transport, rec; *La Ermita*, US$40d, 3 km from town with good view, T 9-3204, pool (not always usable), good food, rec as beautiful; *Rancho San Vicente*, near Cueva del Indio, T 9-3200, US$31, nice pool, pleasant. Book your hotel before you arrive as everywhere is often full.

● **Transport** Turistaxi from Havana to *Motel Los Jazmines* takes 2½ hours; there may be a bus back to the capital, 3½ hours.

From Viñales to Havana along the coast road takes about 4 hours by car. It is an attractive drive through sugar and tobacco plantations, pines, the mountains inland, the coast occasionally visible. All the small houses have flower gardens in front. You pass through La Palma, Las

Pozas (which has a ruined church with a boring new one beside it), Bahía Honda and Cabañas; many agricultural collectives along the way. After Cabañas the road deteriorates; either rejoin the motorway back to the capital, or take the old coast road through the port of Mariel to enter Havana on Av 5. Near Mariel is *El Salado* beach, small, secluded, with calm, clear water, although some parts are rocky. Taxi from Havana US$25. There is a reasonably-priced restaurant, part of a small hotel used by German holidaymakers; the hotel has good value tours. Taxis back to Havana can be ordered a the hotel, but you may have to wait. Off Avenida 5 is the Marina Hemingway tourist complex, with *El Viejo y El Mar*; live music in *La Tasca Española* nightclub, entrance US$5, popular with Cubans and foreigners. There are four restaurants (*La Cora, Fiesta, Papa's* and *Los Caneyes*), bungalows for rent, shopping, car hire, watersports, facilities for yachts, sports, yacht trips (US$45, 0900-1630) and a tourist bureau. T 22-5590/93; VHF radio channels 16, 68 and 72, or 55B 2790. Also in this area is *Hotel Tritón*, US$65 operated by Cubanacán (see Havana **Where to Stay**).

THE ISLANDS

In the Gulf of Batabanó is the *Isla de la Juventud* (Isle of Youth), 97 km from the main island, reached by daily Cubana flights. At about 3,050 square kilometres, it is not much smaller than Trinidad, but its population is only 60,000. It gets its present name from the educational courses run there, particularly for overseas students. Columbus, who landed there in 1494 called the island Evangelista and, until recently, it was called the Isla de Pinos. From the 19th century until the Revolution its main function was as a prison and both José Martí and Fidel Castro served time there. Today the main activities are citrus-growing, fishing and tourism. There are several beaches and ample opportunities for water sports. The capital is Nueva Gerona, with a museum in the old Model Prison (El Presidio) and four others. Main tourist hotel is *El Colony* (US$70 high season).

Cayo Largo, E of Isla de la Juventud, is a westernized island resort reached by air from Havana (US$75 return), or by light plane or boat from Juventud, or by charter plane from Grand Cayman. There are five hotels here at present, with all facilities shared and included in the package cost (prices quoted are high season per person and include 3 meals and free use of all water sports and other activities). *Villa Capricho*, US$120, *Isla del Sur*, US$125, *Pueblito* (Villa Coral) US$120, *Hotel y Villa Pelícano*, US$140, and *Club* (Villa Iguana) US$83. The hotels and the thatched *cabañas* are low-lying and pleasantly spread out in gardens by the beach. Snorkelling and scuba diving can be done at Playa Sirena, 10 minutes' boat ride away. Very tame iguanas can be spotted at another nearby cay, Cayo Rico (day-trips available for US$37 from Cayo Largo). Cayo Largo can also be visited for the day, from Havana or Varadero, price includes return flight and lunch etc (organized in Cuba by Turcimex, 5ta Avenida No 8203, Miramar, Havana, T 22-8230). There are several restaurants attached to the hotels, including a highly recommended Italian place and a good pizzería. As with many Cuban resort hotels restaurants are run on a self-service buffet basis and food is reported to be plentiful and fresh. Hotel expansion is planned to cater for watersport tourism. Cayos Rosario and Avalos, between Juventud and Largo, have not yet been developed.

INFORMATION FOR VISITORS

● **Documents**

Visitors from the majority of countries need only a tourist card to enter Cuba, as long as they are going solely for tourist purposes. A tourist card may be obtained from Cuban embassies, consulates, or approved Cubatur agents (price in the UK £10 from the consulate, £12-13 from travel agents, some other countries US$15). From some countries (eg Canada) tourist cards are handed out on the plane and checked by visa control at the airport; the first one is free but replacements cost US$10. Nationals of other countries without visa-free agreement with Cuba, journalists and those visiting on other business must check what visa requirements pertain (in the UK a business visa costs £25, plus US$13 for any telex that has to be sent in connection with the application). The US government does not normally permit its citizens to visit Cuba. They should contact Marazul Tours, 250 West 57th Street, Suite 1311, New York City, 10107 New York, T 212-582 9570, or Miami T 305-232 8157 (information also from Havanatur, Calle 2 No 17 Miramar, Havana, T 33-2121/2318). A possibility is to go via Mexico, asking Cuban officials not to stamp any record of the visit in the passport. In the USA, the Swiss Embassy in Washington, DC now represents the Cuban interests section and will process applications for visas. Visas can take several weeks to be granted, and are apparently difficult to obtain for people other than businessmen, guests of the Cuban Government or Embassy officials. When the applicant is too far from a Cuban consulate to be able to apply conveniently for a visa, he may apply direct to the Cuban Foreign Ministry for a visa waiver. The Cuban Consulate in Mexico refuses to issue visas unless you have pre-arranged accommodation and book through a travel agent; even then, only tourist visas are available. Visitors may stay in Cuba for 72 hours in transit without tourist card or visa.

Visitors travelling on a visa must go in person to Cubatur or the Immigration Office for registration the day after arrival. The office is on the corner of Calle 22 and Av 3, Miramar. (If buses are running, take no 132 from the old city centre, get off at second stop after the tunnel; also bus 32 from La Rampa or *Coppelia* ice-cream parlour in Vedado, alight at same stop.) When you register you will be given an exit permit.

Travellers coming from or going through infected areas must have certificates of vaccination against cholera and yellow fever.

The Cuban authorities will not insist on stamping your passport in and out if you ask them not to. They will stamp your tourist card instead.

British business travellers should get "Hints to Exporters: Cuba", from DTI Export Publications, PO Box 55, Stratford-upon-Avon, Warwickshire, CV37 9GE. US citizens on business with Cuba should contact Foreign Assets Control, Federal Reserve Bank of New York, 33 Liberty St, NY 10045. Another useful leaflet "Tips For Travelers to Cuba" is available from the Passport Office, US Department of State, Washington DC 20524.

● Airport Tax
US$11 on departure.

● How To Get There
From Europe, Cubana flies Stansted-Gander-Havana once a fortnight on Sunday, returning on a Saturday. Cubana flies from Berlin, Brussels and Paris (also AOM French Airlines), Iberia and Cubana from Madrid. LTU from Dusseldorf. Cubana and Aeroflot from Moscow. Aeroflot has one route via Luxembourg and one via Shannon (Eire). Some Aeroflot flights continue on to Lima. It is essential to check Aeroflot's flights to make sure there really is a plane going. Since Havana no longer enjoys the close relationship with Moscow that it used to have, these flights are now reported to be increasingly unreliable. KLM flies from Amsterdam via Curaçao (ALM) on Wed and Sun with connections from many UK regional airports.

From the American mainland, Cubana from Montréal, Cubana and Mexicana de Aviación from Mexico City with some Mexicana flights via Mérida, Ladeco from Cancún, Viasa and Aeropostal from Caracas, Lacsa from San José, Costa Rica, Aeroflot from Managua, Cubana from Buenos Aires, Cubana from São Paulo, Cubana and Aeroflot from Panama and Cubana and Ladeco from Santiago de Chile (Ladeco via Iquique and Bogotá). Within the Caribbean Cubana flies to Kingston, Jamaica and ALM from Curaçao.

The frequency of these flights depends on the season, with twice weekly flights in the winter being reduced to once a week in the summer. Some of the longer haul flights, such as to Buenos Aires, are cut from once every 2 weeks in winter to once a month in summer. There are daily charters to Miami (US$157, but lots of restrictions on who can use this route) and twice a week to Cancún, Mexico, with ABC/Celimar, enquire at Havanatur. Weekly charter flights between Santiago de Cuba and Montego Bay, Jamaica. Regular charters between Cayo Largo and Grand Cayman. Martinair has charters from Amsterdam to Varadero

and Holguín. At certain times of year there are special offers available from Europe; enquire at specialist agents and Jamaica (see **Travel Agents** below). There are also many combinations of flights involving Cuba and Mexico, Venezuela, Colombia and the Dominican Republic; again ask a specialist agent.

Mexicana de Aviación organizes package tours. Unitours (Canada) run package tours to Cuba for all nationalities. Package tours also available from Venezuela and Jamaica (see **Travel Agencies** below). From the Bahamas, charter flights with Bahatours (T 809 328 7985), Mon and Fri, weekend package tours, see p 152. In Cuba, enquire at Havantur.

It is advisable to book your flight out of Cuba before actually going there as arranging it there can be time-consuming. Furthermore, it is essential to reconfirm onward flights as soon as you arrive in Cuba, otherwise you will lose your reservation. Independent travellers should have tickets stamped in person, not by an agent and, for Mexico, should make sure they have a Mexican tourist card and that Cuban departure tax is collected.

No passenger ships call regularly.

● Internal Air Services
Cubana de Aviación services between most of the main towns. From Havana to Camagüey (US$52 one way), Holguín (US$60), Baracoa (US$79), Guantánamo (US$73), Manzanillo (US$60), Moa (US$73), Nueva Gerona/Isla de Juventud (US$17), Bayamo (US$60), Ciego de Avila (US$44), Las Tunas (US$57), and Santiago (US$68); all have airports. Return fare is twice the single fare. Tourists must pay airfares in US$; it is advisable to prebook flights at home as demand is very heavy. It is difficult to book flights from one city to another when you are not at the point of departure, except from Havana, the computer is not able to cope. Airports are usually a long way from the towns, so extra transport costs will be necessary. Delays are common.

● Airline Offices
All are situated in Havana, at the seaward end of Calle 23 (La Rampa), Vedado: eg Cubana, Calle 23 esq, Infanta, T 70-9391; Aeroflot, Calle 23, No 64, T 70-6292. Iberia, T 7-2960; Mexicana, T 79-6615, Viasa, T 30-5011. If staying at Old Havana, allow sufficient time if you need to visit an airline office before going to the airport.

● **Customs**

Personal baggage and articles for personal use are allowed in free of duty; so are 200 cigarettes, or 25 cigars, or 1 lb of tobacco, and 2 bottles of alcoholic drinks. Many things are scarce or unobtainable in Cuba: take in everything you are likely to need other than food (say razor blades, soap, medicines and pills, insecticides against mosquitoes, tampons, reading and writing materials and photographic supplies).

● **Buses**

The local word for bus is *guagua*. In 1993-94 it was impossible to get on a bus, not many were running because of the fuel shortages, some would take you a maximum of 60 km and others refused to take foreigners. At any event, tourists could not pay in pesos. A minimum of 3 days' wait in the station for a ticket is possible. Because it is so difficult for visitors to use public buses and until the economic problems facing Cuba improve, we do not give bus fares or schedules. Some are given in the text above, but do not bank on them running. The urban bus fare throughout Cuba is 10 centavos and the exact fare is required. In 1993-94 foreigners were not allowed to pay for any bus fare in pesos. In the rush hours they are filled to more than capacity, making it hard to get off if you have managed to get on. Cubans are very helpful if you are lost or have got on the wrong bus.

● **Bus Reservations**

Tickets between towns must be purchased in advance from: Oficina Reservaciones Pasajes, Calle 21, esq 4, Vedado; Plazoleta de la Virgen del Camino, San Miguel del Padrón; Calzada 10 de Octubre y Carmen, Centro; Terminal de Omnibus Nacional, Boyeros y 19 de Mayo (all in Havana). However, the booking offices are often shut, practically no buses are running and tickets may not pay in pesos, increasing the difficulties of travelling around Cuba. Cubatur directs travellers to the office on the corner of Calles 21 and 4. This is the main booking office for buses and trains from Havana to anywhere in the country, one-way only. It is open Mon to Fri, 1200-1745, organized chaos. Look for notices in the window for latest availabilities, find out who is last in the queues (separate queues for buses and trains, sometimes waiting numbers issued), and ask around for what is the best bet. Maximum 3 tickets sold per person. If willing to pay in dollars, Asistur (see **Travel Assistance**, Havana) will

secure train tickets without too much delay.

● **Trains**

Recommended whenever possible, although delays and breakdowns must be expected. Be at station at least 30 minutes before scheduled departure time, you have to queue to reconfirm your seat and have your ticket stamped. Fares are reasonable, eg US$8 to Sancti Spiritus (for Trinidad), 6 hrs. See above for latest booking procedure. Alternatively *Ferrotur*, Calles Arsenal y Egido, near Estación Central, T 62-1770, Havana, very helpful, or at the Tourist Desk in the *Habana Libre*, *Inglaterra* and *Plaza* hotels sell train tickets to foreigners, in dollars; eg to Santiago de Cuba US$70 return, US$35 one way. Tourists will find it is only possible to pay for rail tickets in dollars. See the text above for details. Bicycles can be carried as an express item only. Food on trains can be paid for in pesos.

NB In major bus and train terminals, ask if there are special arrangements for tourists to buy tickets without queuing; payment would then be in dollars. You can waste hours queuing and waiting for public transport. Travel between provinces is usually booked solid several days or weeks in advance. If you are on a short trip you may do better to go on a package tour with excursions. Trains and some buses are air-conditioned—you may need a warm jersey.

● **Taxis**

In 1993-94 foreigners were unable to pay for any taxi ride in pesos. The best you can do is avoid the most expensive tourist taxis. See **Transport** under Havana. Dollar tourist taxis can be hired for driving around; you pay for the distance, not for waiting time. On short routes, fares start at US$1. Airport to Havana (depending on destination), US$16-18, to Playas del Este US$25, to Varadero US$71; Havana to Varadero US$65; Varadero airport to Varadero hotels US$13; Santiago de Cuba airport to *Hotel Las Américas* US$8, to *Balcón del Caribe* US$5. All other options were closed at the time of going to press because, owing to fuel shortages, Cubans are not allowed to carry foreigners in their vehicles.

● **Car Hire**

Through Havanautos at a caravan in the car park of the International Airport, *Hotels Capri* and *Victoria* in Havana, at *Tropicoco Beach Club*, Santa María del Mar (T 2531), at Varadero beach (eg *Paradiso* and *Puntarena Resort*,

Barlovento, *Villa Tortuga*, *Club Herradura* and others), *Hoteles Ancón* and *Costasur*, *Motel Las Cuevas*, *Hotel Zaza*, in Trinidad province; and *Hotel Porto Santo*, Baracoa. Maximum 4 passengers allowed; vehicles can be returned to any depot but you will be charged extra. Minimum US$55 a day (or US$60 for a/c) plus US$0.30 each km after the first 100 km, and US$5 a day optional insurance. The overall cost may work out at around US$65-70 a day. Buggies are available, mostly for use on the beach, at US$30 a day plus US$0.15 each km after the first 100 km. Visa and Mastercard accepted for the rental, or US$100-150 deposit; you must also present your passport and home driving licence. Petrol, if you can find it, costs US$0.90 per litre and must be paid for in US$. If possible, get Havanautos to fill the car with fuel, otherwise your first day will be spent looking for petrol. Get clear directions on which filling stations will serve foreigners: some accept only pesos, some do not have "Especial" fuel, some have no electricity to pump the fuel. Hiring a car is recommended, in view of difficulties of getting seats on buses and trains and you can save a considerable amount of time but it is the most expensive form of travel. Breakdowns are not unknown, in which case you may be stuck with your rented car many kilometres from the nearest place that will accept dollars to help you. Be careful about picking up hitchhikers, although it can be an interesting and pleasant way of meeting Cubans.

● **Excursions**

Cubatur, the national tourist office, offers day trips to many parts of the island as well as tours of colonial and modern Havana. Examples (one day, except where indicated): Viñales, inc tobacco and rum factories, US$39; Soroa, US$23; Varadero, US$29; Cayo Largo (by air), US$89; Trinidad (by air), US$79; Trinidad and Cienfuegos (2 days), US$109; Santiago de Cuba (by air), US$99. Tours can also be taken from Varadero, eg to Pinar del Río, 2 days, US$105. Guides speak English, French or German; the tours are generally rec as well-organized and good value. It is also possible to go on a "Vuelta a Cuba", 7-day round-trip of the island, travelling by bus to Santiago and returning by air. Details from the Cubatur office. A common complaint from individual tourists is that, when they sign up for day trips and other excursions (eg Cayo Largo), they are not told that actual departure depends on a minimum

number of passengers. The situation is made worse by the fact that most tourists are on pre-arranged package tours. They are often subject to long waits on buses and at points of departure and are not informed of delays in departure times. Always ask the organizers when they will know if the trip is on or what the real departure time will be.

In mid-1993 it was possible to hire a car with driver and English-speaking guide for 3 hrs, costing US$30 for 2 passengers; good value.

● **Hotel Reservations**

It is advisable to book hotel rooms before visiting any of the provinces otherwise you may have to return to Havana. This can be done abroad through travel agencies, accredited Cubatur agencies, or through the Cubatur office, Calle 23, No 156, Vedado, La Habana 4; telex 511243; telephone 32-4521, or through Turismo Buró desks in main hotels. It is slightly cheaper to book through Cubatur than direct at a hotel. Cubatur will only inform you about the hotels it operates. It's a good idea to book hotel rooms generally before noon. In the peak season, July and August (carnival time) and December to February, it is essential to book in advance. At other times it is possible to book at hotel reception. Prices given in the text are high season (December-April, July-August); low season prices (May-June, September-November) are about 20% lower. After 31 August many hotels go into hibernation and offer limited facilities, eg no restaurant, no swimming pool.

● **Camping**

Official campsites are opening up all over the island, charging 5-8 pesos a night (in pesos); they are usually in nice surroundings and are good value. One such is El Abra International Campsite halfway between Havana and Varadero, which has extensive facilities (car hire, bicycles, mopeds, horses, watersports, tennis etc) and organizes excursions.

● **Note**

Cuba is geared more to package tourism than to independent visitors and this has become more evident with the local petrol shortage. Camping out on the beach or in a field is forbidden. Lodging with a family is reportedly possible (at US$12 per day); enquire locally. Because of rationing it is difficult to buy food in the shops. Also be prepared for long waits for everything: buses, cinemas, restaurants, shops etc. Service has improved somewhat in Havana tourist facilities with the passage of new legislation allowing employees to be sacked if they are not up to the job. Officials in the tourist industry, tour guides, agencies and hotel staff are generally efficient and helpful "beyond the call of duty". Take care with unofficial guides or 'friends' you make; if they take you to a bar or nightclub or restaurant you will be expected to pay for them and pay in dollars. Do not take photographs near military zones. This chapter catalogues a great many difficulties for the independent traveller, but if on a package, with a couple of days in Havana and a few days on the beach, the visitor should have no problems at all. Similarly, if travelling independently in a rented vehicle, there should be no problems.

● **Eating Out**

Visitors should remember that eating is often a problem and plan ahead. It is generally impossible to have an evening meal and go on to a concert or the theatre (performances start at 2030 or 2100 in Havana).

Breakfast can be particularly slow although this is overcome in the larger hotels who generally have buffets (breakfast US$3, lunch and dinner US$10-18). If not eating at a buffet, service, no matter what standard of restaurant or hotel, can be very slow (even if you are the only customers). Look out for the *oferta especial* in small hotels which gives guests a 25% discount on buffet meals in larger hotels. Also, the "all-you-can-eat" vouchers for buffets in tourist hotels do not have to be used in the hotel where bought. Breakfast and one other meal may be sufficient if you fill in with street or "dollar shop" snacks.

In Havana the peso food situation is dire. Outside Havana, including Havana province, it is much worse according to a cyclist who found little or no food to buy. Self-catering is extremely difficult as supermarkets (as opposed to *Diplomercados*) are not accessible without ration cards and only occasionally do you find street vendors of fruit. For vegetarians the choice is very limited, normally only cheese, sandwiches, spaghetti and omelettes. Generally, although restaurants have improved in the last few years, the food in Cuba is not very exciting or enjoyable. There is little variety in the menu and menu items are frequently unavailable. Always check restaurant prices in advance and then your bill. The national dish is *arrozmoro* (rice mixed with black beans),

roast pork and yucca (manioc). Salads in restaurants are mixed vegetables which are slightly pickled and not to everyone's taste.

● **Tipping**

Tipping customs have changed after a period when visitors were not allowed to tip in hotels and restaurants. It is now definitely recommended. Tip a small amount (not a percentage) in the same currency as you pay for the bill (typically US$1-2 on a US$25 meal. At times taxi drivers will expect (or demand) a tip. Turistaxis are not tipped, but the drivers still appreciate a tip. If you want to express gratitude, offer a packet of American cigarettes. Leaving basic items in your room, like toothpaste, deodorant, paper, pens, is recommended.

● **Shopping**

Essentials—rent and most food—are cheap; non-essentials are very expensive. Everything is very scarce, although imported toiletries and camera film (Kodak print only, from Mexico), is reasonably priced. Compared with much of Latin America, Cuba is expensive for the tourist, but compared with many Caribbean islands it is not dear.

● **Language**

Spanish, with local variants in pronounciation and vocabulary. Little English is spoken.

● **Currency**

The monetary unit is the peso, US$1=1.10 peso. There are heavy penalties for Cubans caught exchanging money on the black market, though a tourist will be approached, especially on the E side of La Rampa, in front of the *Hotel Caribbean*, in the Parque Central and along the Malecón in Havana (beware muggers). These "hasslers" can be extremely persistent and even charming—at first. However their conversation soon turns to money and, once you have shown them any sign of attention, they are very hard to shake off. Do not change money where there are groups of black marketeers or where you are outnumbered, you may be tricked. Do not give them the name of your hotel. The best policy is to ignore them completely—rude but effective! Taxi drivers can be a good source of information. The extent of hustling for dollars depends on whether there is a government crackdown in operation. There has also been a reduction in activity in Havana and Varadero since it has become almost impossible for tourists to spend pesos. The going rate was 130 pesos = US$1 in May 1994, when it was still possible to change on the black market with caution, only worth changing the absolute minimum (if at all) as there is so little available to buy with pesos. Food on trains and books—but not in every shop—can be bought in pesos.) Visitors on pre-paid package tours are best advised not to change any pesos at all. Bring US$ in small denominations for spending money, dollars are now universally preferred. Watch out for pre-1962 peso notes, no longer valid. There are notes for 3, 5, 10, and 20 pesos, and coins for 5, 20, and 40 centavos and 1 peso. You must have a supply of 5 centavo coins if you want to use the local town buses (10 centavos) or pay phones (very few work). The 20 centavo coin is called a *peseta*. US dollars are accepted in all tourist establishments. Credit cards acceptable in most places are Visa, Master, Access, Diners, Banamex (Mexican) and Carnet. No US credit cards accepted so a Visa card issued in the USA will not be accepted. American Express, no matter where issued, is unacceptable.

● **Currency Control**
The visitor should be careful to retain the receipt every time money is changed officially; this will enable Cuban pesos remaining at the end of the stay to be changed back into foreign currency (to a maximum of US$10 equivalent).

Travellers' cheques expressed in US or Canadian dollars or sterling are valid in Cuba. TCs issued on US bank paper are not accepted so it is best to take Thomas Cook. Don't enter the place or date when signing cheques, or they may be refused. You can occasionally get US dollars change when paying a hotel bill with TCs, but you can not cash TCs for US dollars, nor even for Cuban pesos. Instead you receive Dinero Intur (also known as Monopoly money or funny money) which can be used at any dollar store, including the Cubatur *tiendas*. Do not get left with Dinero Intur as it cannot be changed into dollars late at night or when the airport bank is closed.

There is a branch of the Banco Nacional at the 42nd Street "diplomatic" shopping centre in Havana for changing money legally. It is useful for changing non-dollar currencies into dollars and also for changing TCs. Visitors have difficulties using torn or tatty US dollar notes.

● **Sale Of Possessions, Gifts, etc**
Tourists willing to take risks can earn extra spending money by taking along consumer goods to sell to Cubans. It has been reported that you need to guard your clothes more

closely than your camera and a T-shirt is greatly appreciated as a gift (you may be asked to sign it, to show that it *is* a gift). Cubans are now rationed to one pair of new trousers a year. Any foreigner sitting in the Parque Central with a flight bag at his side is soon approached by buyers. One can usually get about 3 times what was paid for the articles. Also appreciated as gifts are household medicines, cosmetics and, for children, pens, chewing gum and sweets. It's inadvisable to bring in too many of a single item or you may have trouble at Customs.

● **Security**
In general the Cuban people are very hospitable. The island is generally safer than many of its Caribbean and Latin neighbours, but certain precautions should be taken. Visitors should never lose sight of their luggage or leave valuables in hotel rooms (most hotels have safes). Do not leave your things on the beach when going swimming. Pickpocketing and purse-snatching on buses is quite common in Havana (especially the old city) and Santiago. Also beware of bagsnatching by passing cyclists. In the capital, street lighting is poor so care is needed when walking or cycling the city at night. Visitors should remember that the government permitting Cubans to hold dollars legally has not altered the fact that the local population will often do anything to get hard currency, from simply asking for money or dollar-bought goods, to mugging. Latest reports suggest that foreigners will be offered almost anything on the street "from cigars to cocaine to chicas." Cubans who offer their services in return for dollars are known as *jineteros*, or *jineteras* (because they "ride on the back" of the tourists). Offers to drive you around Havana in a Cadillac should be treated with suspicion. The police are very helpful and thorough, but you may have to insist on a written police report for insurance purposes. In the event of a crime, make a note of where it happened. Take extra passport photos and keep them separate from your passport. You will waste a lot of time getting new photos if your passport is stolen.

● **Health**
Sanitary reforms have transformed Cuba into a healthy country, though tap water is generally not safe to drink except in Havana; bottled and mineral water are recommended.

Medical service is no longer free for foreign visitors in Havana and Varadero, where there are clinics that charge in dollars. Visitors requiring medical attention will be sent to them. Emergencies are handled on an ad hoc basis.

Check with your national health service or health insurance on coverage in Cuba. Charges are high, but reasonable and generally lower than those charged in Western countries. According to latest reports, visitors are still treated free of charge in other parts of the country, with the exception of tourist enclaves with on-site medical services.

The Cira García Clinic in Havana (payment in dollars) sells prescription and patent drugs and medical supplies that are often unavailable in chemists.

Between May and October, the risk of sunburn is high, sun blocks are rec when walking around the city as well as on the beach. In the cooler months, limit beach sessions to 2 hours.

● **Climate**
Northeast trade winds temper the heat. Average summer shade temperatures rise to 30°C (86°F) in Havana, and higher elsewhere. In winter, day temperatures drop to 19°C (66°F). Average rainfall is from 860 mm in Oriente to 1,730 mm in Havana; it falls mostly in the summer and autumn, but there can be torrential rains at any time. Hurricanes come in June-October. The best time for a visit is during the cooler dry season (November to April). In Havana, there are a few cold days, 8°-10°C (45°-50°F), with a N wind. Walking is uncomfortable in summer but most offices, hotels, leading restaurants and cinemas are air-conditioned. Humidity varies between 75 and 95%.

NB The summers are unbearably hot and travel between Havana and Santiago is extremely difficult during Carnival (July) and also during the Christmas-New Year period.

● **Dress**
Generally informal. Summer calls for the very lightest clothing. A jersey and light raincoat or umbrella are needed in the cooler months.

● **Hours Of Business**
Government offices: 0830-1230 and 1330-1730 Mon to Fri. Some offices open on Sat morning. Banks: 0830-1200, 1330-1500 Mon to Fri, 0830-1030 Sat. The Banco Nacional de Cuba is the only bank in the country. Shops: 1230-1930 Mon to Sat, although some open in the morning one day a week. Hotel tourist (hard currency) shops generally open 1000-2100.

● **Time Zone**
Eastern Standard Time, 5 hours behind GMT; Daylight Saving Time, 4 hours behind GMT.

● **Holidays**
Liberation Day (1 January), Victory of Armed Forces (2 January), Labour Day (1 May), Revolution Day (26 July and the day either side), Beginning of War of Independence (10 October).

● **Weights And Measures**
The metric system is compulsory, but exists side by side with American and old Spanish systems.

● **Electric Current**
110-230 Volts. 3 phase 60 cycles, AC. Plugs are of the American type, an adaptor for European appliances can be bought at the Intur shop at the *Habana Libre*.

● **Post, Telecommunications**
When possible correspondence should be addressed to post office boxes (Apartados), where delivery is more certain. Telegraphic services are adequate. You can send telegrams from all post offices in Havana. Telegrams to Britain cost 49 centavos a word. The night letter rate is 3.85 pesos for 22 words. Local telephone calls can be made from public telephones for 5 centavos. A telephone call to Britain costs US$18 for the first 3 mins, US$6/min thereafter. The cost of phoning the USA is US$4.50/min from Havana, US$3 from Varadero. "Collect" calls are not permitted. Air mail rates to Britain are 31 centavos for half an ounce and 13 centavos to Canada. Postcards to North, Central America and Caribbean 20 centavos, to South America 25 centavos, Europe 30 centavos, USA, Asia, Africa 50 centavos. Stamps can only be bought in dollars at Post Offices, or at the *Habana Libre*. All postal services, national and international, have been described as appalling. Letters to Europe, for instance, take at least 4-5 weeks, up to 3 months.

● **Newspapers**
A shortage of newsprint has led to cuts in newspaper and magazine production. *Granma*, mornings except Sun and Mon; *Trabajadores*, Trade Union weekly; and *Juventud Rebelde*, now also only weekly. *Granma* has a weekly English edition (also French and Portuguese editions available, International annual subscriptions US$40, main offices: Avenida General Suárez y Territorial, Plaza de la Revolución, La Habana 6, T 70-8218, Telex: 0511 355; in UK 928 Bourges Boulevard, Peterborough PE1 2AN). *The Financial Times*, *Time*, *Newsweek* and *The International Herald Tribune* are on sale at the telex centre in *Habana Libre* and in the *Riviera* (also telex centre, open

0800-2000). The previous day's paper is available during the week. Weekend editions on sale Tues. FT costs US$2, IHT US$1.50.

● **Embassies and Consulates**

All in Miramar, unless stated otherwise: **Argentina**, Calle 36 No 511 between 5 and 7, T 33-2972/2549; **Austria**, Calle 4 No 101, on the corner with 1st, T 33-2825; **Belgium**, Av 5 No 7408 on the corner with 76, T 33-2410; **Brazil**, Calle 16 No 503 between 5 and 7, T 33-2139/2786; **Canada**, Calle 30 No 518, on the corner with 7, T 33-2516/2527; **UK**, Calle 34, No 708, T 331771, telex 511656 UKEMB CU; **Germany**, Calle 28 No 313, between 3 and 5, T 22-2560, 22-2569; **France**, Calle 14 No 312 between 3 and 5, T 33-2539/2460; **Mexico**, Calle 12 No 518 between 5 and 7, T 33-2142/2489, open 0900-1200, Mon-Fri; **Netherlands**, Calle 8 No 307 between 3 and 5, T 33-2511/2; **Peru**, Calle 36 No 109 between 1 and 3, T 33-2777; **Venezuela**, Calle 36A No 704 corner of 42, T33-2662. In Vedado, **The US Interests Section**, Calzada between L and M, T 33-3550/9; **Italy**, Paseo No 606 between 25 and 27, T 33-3378; **Japan**, Calle N No 62, on the corner with 15, T 33-3454/3598. In the old city, **Spain**, Cárcel No 51 on the corner of Zulueta, T 33-8025-6.

● **Working in Cuba**

Those interested in joining International Work Brigades should contact Cuba Solidarity Campaign, c/o The Red Rose, 129 Seven Sisters Road, London N7 7QG, or 119 Burton Road, London SW9 6TG.

● **Language Study**

Any Cuban embassy will give details, or, in Santiago, contact Cecilia Suárez, c/o Departamento de Idiomas, Universidad de Oriente, Av Patricio Lumumba, Código Postal 90500, Santiago de Cuba.

● **Travel Agents**

In the UK, agents who sell holidays in Cuba include Regent Holidays, 15 John Street, Bristol BS1 2HR, T (0117) 9211711, F (0117) 9254866, ABTA members, holding ATOL and IATA Licences; South American Experience Ltd, 47 Causton Street, Pimlico, London SW1P 4AT, T 071-976 5511, F 071-976 6908, ATOL, IATA; Progressive Tours, 12 Porchester Place, Marble Arch, London W2 2BS, T 071-262 1676, F 071-724 6941, ABTA, ATOL, IATA. Check with these agent for special deals combined with jazz or film festivals. The Cuban Consulate in London has a full list of all authorized Cubatur agents in the UK. A recommended agent in Eire for assistance with Aeroflot flights is Concorde Travel, T Dublin 763232; Cubatur agent is Cubatravel, T Dublin 713385. See above under **Documents** for Marazul Tours in the USA. If travelling from Mexico, many agencies in the Yucatan peninsula offer packages, very good value and popular with travellers wanting to avoid Mexico City. Full details are given in the **To Cuba** paragraph in the Mexico chapter, **Information for Visitors**. From Venezuela, Ideal Tours, Centro Capriles, Plaza Venezuela, T (010 582) 793-0037/1822, have 4-day package tours for US$406-517 depending on the season, 8-day tours US$500-706, flight only available. From Jamaica, UTAS Tours offer weekends in Cuba for US$199 inc flight, hotel etc, PO Box 429, Montego Bay, T (809) 979-0684, F 979-3465.

● **Tourist Information**

The main Cubatur office is at Calle 23, No 156 between N and O, La Rampa, Vedado, T 32-4521/3157 (open Mon-Fri 0800-1700, Sat 0800-1200), and reservations for all Cuban hotels, restaurants, and night clubs can be made here. Cubatur is both a tourist information bureau and an agency offering tours. In practice, staff concentrate on the latter, assuming that visitors wish to take tours (see **Excursions** above). Consequently they do not provide a great deal of information. The Oficina de Turismo Individual is in the main Cubatur office on Calle 23; all problems with pre-booked accommodation, transport, etc should be dealt with here. Most tourist hotels have a Turismo Buró, which will arrange bookings, etc; some are inefficient, but many have better information than Cubatur's main office. The magazine, *La Habana*, in Havana, weekly, US$1, lists shows, events, trips, useful addresses and has articles.

Cubatur also has offices in: **Canada**, 440 Blvd René Levesque, Suite 1402, Montréal, Quebec H2Z 1V7, T (514) 875-8004/5, F 875-8006; 55 Queen St E, Suite 705, Toronto, M5C 1R5, T (416) 362-0700/2, F 362-6799; **Spain**, Paseo de la Habana No 27, 2° izquierda T 411-3097, F 564-5804; **France**, 24 rue du 4 Septembre, Paris 75002, T 47-742-54-15, F 40-07-02-13; **Germany**, Steinweg 2, D-6000 Frankfurt am Main 1, T (069) 288322, F 296664; **UK** (Cuban Consulate, no tourist information), 15 Grape Street, London WC2H 8DR, T 071-379-1706, F 071-836-2602; **Mexico**, Insurgentes Sur 421 y Aguascalientes, Complejo Aristos, Edificio B, Local 310, México DF 06100, T 574-9651, F 574-9454; **Russia**, Hotel Belgrado, Moscow, T 2-48-2454/3262; **Argentina**, Paraguay 631, 2° piso A, Buenos Aires, F 311-4198, T 311-5820; **Italy**, Via General Fara 30, Terzo Piano, 20124 Milan, T 66981463, F 6690042.

● **Maps**

Mapa Turístico de la Habana, Mapa de la Habana Vieja, and similar maps of Santiago de Cuba, Trinidad, Camagüey and Varadero are helpful, but not always available.

We are most grateful to Christina Gibbons of Regent Holidays (Bristol), Richard Laker, South American Experience, London, Jorge Valle-Aguiluz (Tegucigalpa, Honduras) and travellers listed at the beginning of the book for their help in updating this chapter.

CAYMAN ISLANDS

THE BRITISH CROWN COLONY of the Cayman Islands consists of Grand Cayman and the sister islands of Cayman Brac and Little Cayman, in the Caribbean Sea. None of the islands has any rivers, but vegetation is luxuriant, the main trees being coconut, thatch palm, seagrape and Australian pine.

Grand Cayman, the largest of the three islands, lies 150 miles S of Havana, Cuba, about 180 miles WNW of Jamaica and 480 miles S of Miami. Grand Cayman is low-lying, 22 miles long and four miles wide, but of the total 76 square miles about half is swamp. A striking feature is the shallow, reef-protected lagoon, North Sound, 40 miles square and the largest area of inland mangrove in the Caribbean. *George Town*, the capital of the islands, is located on the W side of Grand Cayman. *Cayman Brac* (Gaelic for "bluff") gets its name from the high limestone bluff rising from sea level in the W to a height of 140 feet in the E. The island lies about 89 miles ENE of Grand Cayman. It is about 12 miles long and a little more than a mile wide. *Little Cayman* lies five miles W of Cayman Brac and is 10 miles long and just over a mile wide with its highest point being only 40 feet above sea level. *Owen Island*, an islet off the SW coast of Little Cayman, is uninhabited but visited by picnickers.

The total population of mixed African and European descent was estimated at 28,100 in 1992, of which 94% live on Grand Cayman, most of them frequented by George Town (12,972 in 1989), or the smaller towns of West Bay (5,646), Bodden Town (3,410), North Side (859) and East End (1,070). The population of Cayman Brac had fallen to 1,445 in 1989. Little Cayman is largely undeveloped with only about 33 residents, most of them frequented by sports fishermen. The Caymans are very exclusive, with strict controls on who is allowed to settle there, although the proportion of Caymanians in the total population has fallen from 79% in 1980 to 66% by 1990. Consequently the cost of living is extremely high. On the other hand, petty crime is rare and the islands are well looked after (described as "a very clean sandbank"). Drug trafficking has increased though, and it is estimated that three quarters of all thefts and burglaries are drug-related.

History

The Cayman Islands were first sighted by Columbus in May 1503 when he was blown off course on his way to Hispaniola. He found two small islands (Cayman Brac and Little Cayman) which were full of turtles, and he therefore named the islands Las Tortugas. A 1523 map of the islands referred to them as Lagartos, meaning alligators or large lizards, but by 1530 they were known as the Caymanas after the Carib word for the marine crocodile which also lived there.

The first recorded English visitor was

Sir Francis Drake in 1586, who reported that the *caymanas* were edible, but it was the turtles which attracted ships in search of fresh meat for their crews. Overfishing nearly extinguished the turtles from the local waters. The islands were ceded to the English Crown under the Treaty of Madrid in 1670, after the first settlers came from Jamaica in 1661-71 to Little Cayman and Cayman Brac. The first settlements were abandoned after attacks by Spanish privateers, but British privateers often used the Caymans as a base and in the 18th century they became an increasingly popular hideout for pirates, even after the end of legitimate privateering in 1713. In November 1794, a convoy of 10 Jamaican merchantmen was wrecked on the reef in Gun Bay, on the E end of Grand Cayman, but with the help of the local settlers there was no loss of life. Legend has it that there was a member of the Royal Family on board and that in gratitude for their bravery, King George III decreed that Caymanians should never be conscripted for war service and Parliament legislated that they should never be taxed.

From 1670, the Cayman Islands were dependencies of Jamaica, although there was considerable self-government. In 1832, a legislative assembly was established, consisting of eight magistrates appointed by the Governor of Jamaica and 10 (later increased to 27) elected representatives. In 1959 dependency ceased when Jamaica became a member of the Federation of the West Indies, although the Governor of Jamaica remained the Governor of the Cayman Islands. When Jamaica achieved independence in 1962 the Islands opted to become a direct dependency of the British Crown.

In 1991 a review of the 1972 constitution recommended several constitutional changes to be debated by the Legislative Assembly. The post of Chief Secretary was reinstated in 1992 after having been abolished in 1986. The es-

tablishment of the post of Chief Minister was also proposed. However, in November 1992 elections were held for an enlarged Legislative Assembly and the Government was soundly defeated, casting doubt on constitutional reform. The 'National Team' of government critics won 12 of the 15 seats, and independents won the other three, after a campaign opposing the appointment of a Chief Minister and advocating spending cuts. The unofficial leader of the team, Thomas Jefferson, had been the appointed Financial Secretary until March 1992, when he resigned over public spending disputes to fight the election. After the elections Mr Jefferson was appointed Minister and leader of government business; he also holds the portfolios of Tourism, Environment and Planning in the Executive Council.

Government

A Governor appointed by the British Crown is the head of Government. The present Constitution came into effect in 1993 and provides for an Executive Council to advise the Governor on administration of the islands. The Council is made up of five Elected and three Official Members and is chaired by the Governor. The former, called Ministers from February 1994, are elected from the 15 elected representatives in the Legislative Assembly and have a range of responsibilities allocated by the Governor, while the latter are the Chief Secretary, the Financial Secretary, and the Attorney General and the Administrative Secretary. The Legislative Assembly may remove a minister from office by nine votes out of the 15. There is no Chief Minister. There have been no political parties since the mid-1960s but politicians organize themselves into teams. The Chief Secretary is the First Official Member of the Executive Council, and acts as Governor in the absence of the Governor.

The Economy

The original settlers earned their living from the sea, either as turtle fishermen or as crew members on ships around the world. In 1906 more than a fifth of the population of 5,000 was estimated to be at sea, and even in the 1950s the government's annual report said that the main export was of seamen and their remittances the mainstay of the economy. Today the standard of living is high with the highest per capita income in the Caribbean. The islands' economy is based largely on offshore finance and banking, tourism, real estate and construction, a little local industry, and remittances of Caymanians working on ships abroad. Apart from a certain amount of meat, turtle, fish and a few local fruits and vegetables, almost all foodstuffs and other necessities are imported. The cost of living therefore rises in line with that of the main trading partners.

The Cayman Islands is the largest offshore centre in the world. In September 1993 there were 534 licensed banks with assets of over US$460bn, 29,298 registered companies and 370 offshore insurance companies, with assets of US$4.5bn; the banking sector employs more than a tenth of the labour force.

Tourism revenues have risen sharply in recent years. The slowdown in the US economy in 1991, however, brought a sharp drop in air arrivals and hotel occupancy fell to 60% from 68% in 1990, although cruise ship visitors soared by 31% to 474,747, with the introduction of calls by the cruise liner *Ecstasy* which carries 2,500 passengers. By 1993 cruise ship passenger arrivals were 605,715, while stopover visitors numbered a record 287,277. Tourism provides about 35% of jobs and 70% of gross domestic product.

There was a rapid rise in construction activity in the 1980s to meet demand and tourist accommodation doubled in 10 years. As a result, spectacular rates of

CAYMAN ISLANDS: FACT FILE

Geographic

Land area	264 sq km

Demographic

Population (1992)	28,100
annual growth rate (1987-92)	4.2%
urban	100%
rural	0%
density	106.4 per sq km
Religious affiliation	
Presbyterian	35.6%
Church of God	24.9%
Birth rate per 1,000 (1990)	17.9
	(world av 27.1)
Death rate per 1,000 (1990)	4.0
	(world av 9.8)

Education and Health

Life expectancy at birth	77.1 years
Infant mortality rate	
per 1,000 live births (1990)	6.1
Physicians (1990)	1 per 669 persons
Hospital beds	1 per 384 persons
Literate males (over 15)	97.5%
Literate females (over 15)	97.6%

Economic

GNP (1989 market prices)	US$357mn
GNP per capita	US$13,770
Public external debt (1988)	US$185mn
Tourism receipts (1990)	US$326mn
Radio	1 per 1.5 persons
Television	1 per 5.7 persons
Telephone	1 per 1.4 persons

Employment

Population economically active (1991)	
	16,700
% of labour force in	
agriculture	1.4
mining, manufacturing	
and public utilities	3.2
construction	16.0
trade, hotels and restaurants	30.2

Source *Encyclopaedia Britannica*

economic growth were recorded: 15.6% in 1987, 15.2% in 1988, 10.6% in 1989, slowing to 8.0% in 1990. There was full employment and labour had to be imported to meet demand. The slowdown of the 1990s brought a huge fall in public and private construction projects and unemployment rose to a record 7.6% by 1992. The government budget went into deficit, the public debt rose from US$7mn at end-1990 to US$21.3mn at end-1991, the loss-making, state-owned airline, Cayman Airways accumulated a deficit of US$32.7mn by end-1991 and the Government proposed building a US$32mn hospital. The new Government elected in 1992 called for a reduction in spending, cancelled the hospital project, cut the size of the civil service and recapitalized Cayman Airways. By 1993 Cayman Airways had reduced its debt to less than US$6mn, and by closing unprofitable routes and cutting staff and other costs it managed to reduce its loss to about US$1mn, with all routes meeting their direct costs.

Fauna and Flora

There are over 180 species of birds, including the Antillean grackle, the smooth-billed ani, the green-backed heron, the yellow-crowned night heron and many other heron species, the snowy egret, the common ground dove, the bananaquit and the Cayman parrot. If you are interested in birdwatching, go to the mosquito control dykes on the West Bay peninsula of Grand Cayman, or walk to the Cistern at East End. The Governor is a keen birdwatcher and in 1993 he set up a fund to establish the Governor Michael Gore Bird Sanctuary on 3½ acres of wetland on Grand Cayman, where you can see 60 of the 200 local species. There are booby nesting places on Little Cayman and a walk across Cayman Brac is rewarding. *Birds of the Cayman Islands*, published by Bradley, is a photographic record; it costs £22. Indigenous animals on the islands are few. The most common are the agouti, a few non-poisonous snakes, some iguana and other small lizards, freshwater turtle, the hickatee and two species of tree frogs. *Oncidium calochilum*, a rare orchid, indigenous to Grand Cayman with a small yellow

flower about half an inch long, is found only in the rocky area off Frank Sound Drive. Several other orchid species have been recorded as endemic but are threatened by construction and orchid fanciers. There is protection under international and local laws for several indigenous species, including sea turtles, iguanas, Cayman parrots, orchids and marine life. For a full description of the islands' flora see George R Proctor, *Flora of the Cayman Islands*, Kew Bulletin Additional Series XI, HMSO (1984), 834 pp, which list 21 endemic plant taxa including some which are rare, endangered or possibly extinct. The National Botanic Park, now renamed the Queen Elizabeth II Botanic Park (officially opened by the Queen in 1994), is off Frank Sound Road, Grand Cayman. A mile-long trail has been cleared and an entrance garden created. Plans have been drawn up for a Heritage Garden, with endemic plants within the park.

Several animal sanctuaries have been established, most of which are RAMSAR sites where no hunting or collecting of any species is allowed. On Grand Cayman there are sanctuaries at Booby Cay, Meagre Bay Pond and Colliers Bay Pond; on Cayman Brac at the ponds near the airport and on Little Cayman at Booby Road and Rookery, Tarpon Lake and the Wearis Bay Wetland, stretching E along the S coast to the Easterly Wetlands.

Diving and Marine Life

The Cayman Islands are world-famous for their underwater scenery. There are tropical fish of all kinds in the waters surrounding the islands, especially in the coral reefs, and green turtles (*chelonia mydas*) are now increasing in numbers, having been deliberately restocked by excess hatchings at the Grand Cayman Turtle Farm. A project at the Turtle Farm to reintroduce the endangered Kemp's ridley species of turtle has shown initial success with some reproduction in captivity.

Since 1986, a Marine Parks plan has been implemented to preserve the beauty and marine life of the islands. Permanent moorings have been installed along the W coast of Grand Cayman where there is concentrated diving, and also outside the marine parks in order to encourage diving boats to disperse and lessen anchor damage to the reefs. There are now 205 permanent mooring sites around all three islands, 119 around Grand Cayman (32 on the North Wall), 41 around Cayman Brac and 45 around Little Cayman. These parks and protected areas are clearly marked and strictly enforced by a full-time Marine Conservation Officer who has the power to arrest offenders. Make sure you check all rules and regulations as there have been several prosecutions and convictions for offences such as taking conch or lobsters. The import of spearguns or speargun parts and their use without a licence is banned. Divers and snorkellers must use a flag attached to a buoy when outside safe swimming areas. For further information call Natural Resources, T 949 8469.

Many of the better reefs and several wrecks are found in water shallow enough to require only mask, snorkel and fins; the swimming is easy and the fish are friendly. However, each island has a wall going down to extraordinary depths: the N wall of Cayman Brac drops from 60 to 14,000 feet, while the S wall drops to 18,000 feet. The deepest known point in the Caribbean is the Cayman Trench, 40 miles S of Cayman Brac, where soundings have indicated a depth of 24,724 feet. *The Cayman Divers Guide* illustrates the major dive sites on all three islands with a fish index and photo review. The dive-tourism market is highly developed in the Cayman Islands and there is plenty of choice, but is frequently described as a cattle market with dive boats taking very large parties. Many companies offer full services to certified divers as well as courses designed to introduce scuba diving to novices; there are several highly qualified instructor-guides. There is a firm limit of a depth of 110 feet for visiting divers, regardless of training and experience and the 69 member companies of the CIWOA will not allow you to exceed that. The best months for diving are April-October. A complete selection of diving and fishing tackle, underwater cameras and video equipment is available for hire. The tourist office has a full price list for all operators. There is also the liveaboard *Cayman Aggressor III*, which cruises around Grand Cayman and Little Cayman. Contact Aggressor Fleet Limited, PO Drawer K, Morgan City, LA 70381, T (504) 385 2416, F (504) 384 0817. A smaller liveaboard is the *Little Cayman Diver*, a 65-foot custom built yacht with 7 cabins, T 948 7429.

Beaches and Watersports

The beaches of the Cayman Islands are said to be the best in the Caribbean. Various companies offer glass-bottomed boats, sailing, snorkelling, windsurfing, water skiing, water tours and a host of other activities. You can hire wave runners, aqua trikes and paddlecats, take banana rides and go parasailing. When waterskiing, there must be a minimum of two people in the boat so that one person can look out for hazards. There is year-round deep sea game fishing for blue marlin, white marlin, wahoo, yellow fin tuna and smaller varieties, and shore-fishing in all three islands. There are about 12 captains offering deep sea fishing or bone fishing from their boats, rates start from US$200 for a half day bone fishing, US$325 for deep sea fishing.

Festivals

Pirates' Week is the islands' national festival and takes place in the last week of October. Parades, regattas, fishing tournaments and treasure hunts are all part of the celebrations, which commemorate the days when the Caymans were the

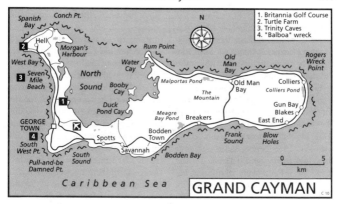

Map legend:
1. Britannia Golf Course
2. Turtle Farm
3. Trinity Caves
4. "Balboa" wreck

GRAND CAYMAN

haunt of pirates and buccaneers. **Batabano** is Grand Cayman's costume carnival weekend, which takes place in the last week of April or beginning of May. Cayman Brac has a similar celebration, known as **Brachanal**, which takes place on the following Saturday. Everyone is invited to dress up and participate, and there are several competitions. At Easter there is a **regatta** with several sailing classes, power boat races and windsurfing. The **Queen's Birthday** is celebrated in mid-June with a full-dress uniform parade, marching bands and a 21-gun salute. **Million dollar month** during June is when fishermen from all over the world come to compete in this month-long tournament. Also in June, **National Aviation Week** attracts private pilots and flight demonstrations over Seven Mile Beach.

GRAND CAYMAN

Grand Cayman is a prosperous island with a very British feel. Driving is on the left and the roads are in good order. The island is green with luxuriant vegetation, especially at the E end where there are pastures and grazing cows. North Sound is a 40-square mile lagoon with mangroves, although dredging schemes and urban growth threaten the mangrove habitat and the reefs. Some low-key but

sophisticated development has taken place along the N coast around Cayman Kai, a very attractive area with lovely beaches and good swimming and snorkelling. Most of the tourist development, however, is along Seven Mile Beach on West Bay, where there are hotels, condominiums, clubs, sports facilities, banks, restaurants and supermarkets.

Diving and Marine Life

Snorkelling and dive sites abound all round the island and include shallow dives for beginners as well as highly challenging and deep dives for the experienced. Off the W coast there are three wrecks, arches, tunnels, caves, canyons and lots of reef sites close to shore which can be enjoyed by snorkellers and divers. Along the S coast the coral reefs are rich and varied with depths ranging from 15 feet to thousands of feet. The East End wall has pinnacles, tunnels and a coral formation known as The Maze, a 500-foot coral formation of caverns, chimneys, arches and crevices. There are several wrecks here also. Along the N coast you can dive the North Wall. Near Rum Point Channel experienced divers can dive the Grand Canyon, where depths start at 70 feet. The canyons, collapsed reefs, are 150 feet wide in places. Other sites in this area towards Palmetto Point include the aptly-named Eagle Ray Pass, Tarpon Alley and Sting Ray City. Sting Ray City is a popular local phenomenon, where it is possible to swim with and observe large groups of extremely tame rays. Sting Ray City is better dived but half a mile away are the sand banks where sting rays also congregate, usually over 30 at a time. The water here is only 1-3 feet deep and crystal clear, so you hop out of your boat and the rays brush past you waiting to be fed. Their mouths are beneath their head and the rays, 3 feet across, swim into your arms to be fed on squid. The *Sandbar Taxi* leaves Rum Point every 90 minutes between 1000 and 1700 for Stingray City and Coral Gardens, US$15, T 945 1776. From Morgan's Harbour boats charge US$30. An additional refinement: Atlantis Research Submersibles Ltd, PO Box 1043G, Grand Cayman, T 949 8296, F 949 8574, operates a 20-foot research submarine, taking 2 passengers (fare US$275 pp, 5 dives a day Monday-Saturday) to the 800-foot-deep Cayman Wall or to the wreck of the *Kirk Pride* at 780 feet. A larger submarine with room for 46 passengers is operated by Atlantis Submarine, PO Box 1043, Grand Cayman, T 949 7700; fares are US$69 for a 1-hour day or night dive (children 4-12 half price), both to 150 feet along Cayman Wall. For US$25 you can take a 1-hour ride in Seaworld Explorer, an underwater observatory which feels like a submarine but you are down only 4 feet. A diver will attract fish within view by feeding them (T 949 5577).

There are at least 10 companies on Grand Cayman offering **fishing**. The Tourist Office can give you a full list with prices. Deep sea fishing boats can be chartered for a half day (US$325) or full day (US$450). Reef and bone fishing is about US$400 for a full day including all equipment, bait and lunch.

Beaches and Watersports

West Bay Beach, now known as Seven Mile Beach, has dazzling white sand and is lined by hotels and tall Australian pines. Beaches on the E and N coasts are equally good, and are protected by an offshore barrier reef. On the N coast, at the *Cayman Kai Beach Resort,* there is a superb public beach with changing facilities; from here you can snorkel along the reef to Rum Point. The beaches around Rum Point are recommended for peace and quiet, but there are also dive facilities, a restaurant and watersports. Around Rum Point at Water Cay and Finger Cay there are picnic sites on the lagoon. Take insect repellent. South of George Town there are good beaches for swimming and snorkelling at Smith's Cove and Sand Cay. In Frank Sound, Heritage Beach, just W of Cottage Point, is owned by the National Trust.

For information about sailing fixtures phone Tim Ridley (T 949 2081) of the Cayman Islands Yacht Club, PO Box 1719, Grand Cayman, T 947 4322, F 947 4432, with docking facilities for 154 boats, 8-foot maximum draft. Kaibo, PO Box 50, North Side, T 947 9064, has 12 slips, 40-foot maximum length, 7-foot maximum draft. Morgan's Harbour Marina and Restaurant, PO Box 30442 SMB, T 949 3099, F 949 3822, also offers the usual facilities.

Cayman Windsurfing is at *Morritt's Tortuga Club*, East End, T 947 7492, F 947 6773, with a full range of BiC boards and UP sails and instruction available. Lots of hotels' watersports operators offer windsurfing, sunfish, wave runners and other equipment.

Other Sports

Jack Nicklaus has designed the Britannia golf course for the *Hyatt-Regency Grand Cayman* hotel, T 949 8020 for starting times. There is a nine-hole Championship course, an 18-hole executive course and an 18-hole Cayman course played with a special short-distance Cayman ball, but it can only be laid out for one course at a time; the executive has 14 par threes and four par fours, so it is short, while the short-distance ball with local winds is a tourist gimmick. To play the executive course with hire of clubs and compulsory buggie will cost you about US$90. Links, the new 18-hole championship golf course is now open at Safehaven, with a par 71 course and a total yardage of 6,519 from the championship tees, although every hole will have five separate tee areas to accommodate all levels of players. The club house is open daily with restaurant and bar open to golfers and non-golfers. At Safehaven Driving Range, behind the Cayman Falls building on West Bay Road you can hire clubs, US$1, take lessons or just practice, US$8/100 balls, T 947 5846, open Mon-Fri 0800-2030, Saturday-Sunday 0630-2030. There are three **squash** courts at the Cayman Islands Squash Racquets Association at South Sound, also courts at Downtowner Squash Club in George Town. For information on matches contact John MacRury (T 949 2269). Most of the larger hotels have their own **tennis** courts but the Cayman Islands Tennis Club next door to the squash courts at South Sound has six floodlit tennis courts and two club pros. Again, for match information contact John MacRury (T 949 5164). For **soccer**, contact Tony Scott (T 947 2511) of the Cayman Islands Football Association. **Cricket** matches are played at the Smith Road Oval near the airport; there are five teams in the Cayman Islands Cricket Association's league, details on matches from Joan Boaden (T 949 4222) of the Cayman Islands Cricket Association. **Rugby** is played every Saturday between September and May at the Cayman Rugby Football Club at South Sound, for information phone John Law (T 949 5688).

GEORGE TOWN

The largest town and capital of the islands is George Town (population over 13,000), which is principally a business centre, dominated by modern office blocks. However, many of the older buildings are being restored and the Government is trying to promote museums and societies to complement beach and watersports tourism. The Cayman Islands National Museum, in the restored Old Courts Building in George Town, opened in 1990 and is well worth a visit. Open 0930-1730 Monday-Friday, 1000-1600 Saturday, 1300-1700 first Sunday of each month, CI$4 adults, CI$2 children aged 6-18, T 949 8368. There is a museum shop and *Jailhouse Café* for refreshments. The Cayman Maritime and Treasure Museum (T 947 5033) on West Bay Road near the *Hyatt Regency*, has a collection of gold and silver relics from sunken Spanish ships, open Monday-Saturday 0900-1700, US$5 adults, US$3 children 6-12. An archaeological dig on the waterfront on the site of Fort George has been sponsored by the Cayman National Trust. Unfortunately only a small part of the walls remains, much was demolished in 1972 by a developer who would have destroyed the lot if residents had not prevented him. The National Trust has designed a walking tour of George Town to include 28 sites of interest, such as Fort George, built around 1790, the Legislative Assembly, the war and peace memorials and traditional Caymanian architecture. A brochure and map (free) is available from the National Trust (PO Box 10, T 949 0121) or the Tourist Office.

Excursions

Some of the many things of interest to visit in Grand Cayman include a tour round **Cayman Turtle Farm**, which houses over 12,000 green turtles. Located at North West Point, this is the only commercial turtle farm in the world. Most of the turtles are used for meat locally since the USA banned the import of turtle meat, but many thousands of hatchlings and year-old turtles are released into the wild each year to replenish native stocks. Those at the farm range in

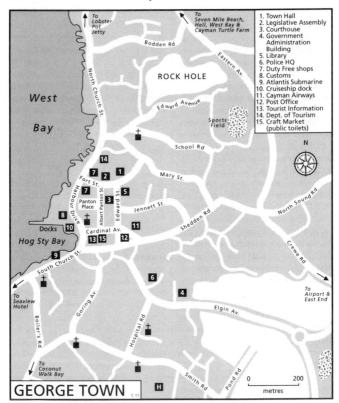

1. Town Hall
2. Legislative Assembly
3. Courthouse
4. Government Administration Building
5. Library
6. Police HQ
7. Duty Free shops
8. Customs
9. Atlantis Submarine
10. Cruiseship dock
11. Cayman Airways
12. Post Office
13. Tourist Information
14. Dept. of Tourism
15. Craft Market (public toilets)

GEORGE TOWN

size from 2-ounce hatchlings to breeding stock weighing around 400 pounds. Polished turtle shells are sold here for about US$100, but their import into the USA is prohibited. A new flora and fauna section of the farm includes three 10-foot crocodiles of the type which used to inhabit the islands and gave their name to the Caymans; there is also the Cayman green parrot, ground iguanas and agouti (known as the Cayman rabbit). Open daily 0900-1700, US$3.50 adults, US$2.50 children aged 6-12, T 949 3893/4.

Hell, situated near West Bay, is a bizarre rock formation worth visiting.

Have your cards and letters postmarked at the sub-post office there. The Post Office is open Wednesday-Friday 0830-1300, 1400-1530, Saturday 0830-1130. On the S coast at Savannah, just off the main coastal road, **Pedro St James Castle** is being excavated, restored and developed into a national landmark. The castle appears to have been a private residence (although pirate legends abound) and a variety of late 18th century artifacts have been unearthed. There are caves in **Bodden Town**, believed to have been used by pirates, where you can see bones and stocks, and a line of unmarked graves in an old cemetery on the shore opposite, said to be those of buccaneers. There are also caves on the other islands but these are not as accessible. Continuing E just after Half Moon Bay you will see blow-holes: waterspouts that rise above the coral rock in unusual patterns as a result of water being funnelled along passages in the rock as the waves come rolling in. At the E end of the island there is a good viewing point at the **Goring Bluff** lighthouse. A trip to Gun Bay at the E end of the island will show you the scene of the famous "Wreck of the Ten Sails", which took place in 1788 (see above under **History**).

For a pleasurable day's outing, arrange a boat trip to North Sound for US$35 or so. This will include snorkelling, fishing and a good look at marine life on a barrier reef. Your guide will cook fish and lobster for you by wrapping them in foil and roasting them on hot coals.

Island Information – Grand Cayman
● Transport
There is a regular **bus** service between West Bay and George Town that stops at all the hotels on Seven Mile Beach. The fare from the hotels to town is about US$1 each way. **Taxis** are readily obtainable at hotels and restaurants. You can usually find taxis stationed at the *Holiday Inn* on West Bay Road. In George Town there are always lots of taxis at the dock when the cruise ships come in, otherwise hailing a taxi is most easily done in the vicinity of the Post Office. Fares are based on a fixed place-to-place tariff rather than a meter charge and vary according to how many people there are and how much luggage there is. For going a long distance (ie across the island) they are expensive. From the airport to George Town is US$8, based on up to 4 passengers with 2 pieces of luggage each; to the *Holiday Inn*, US$12; to Governor's Harbour, US$15; to Silver Sands, US$16; to Mount Pleasant, US$19.50; to Spanish Cove and Bodden Town, US$21.50; to East End, US$39; to Rum Point US$48 and Water Cay, US$50.

For **car hire**, Avis, National and Hertz are represented and there are a number of good local companies as well. Rental firms issue visitors with driving permits on production of a valid driving licence from the visitor's country of residence. The minimum driving age is 18 at some places, 21 at other companies, check. Ace Hertz, PO Box 53, T 949 2280, standard jeep CI$40.80 a day in winter, CI$36 in summer, automatic car CI$25.60-38.40; Andy's Rent A Car Ltd, PO Box 277 WB, West Bay, T 949 8111, F 949 8385, cheapest automatic car US$35 in winter, US$25 in summer, weekly rates US$210 or US$150; Just Jeeps, North Church Street, George Town, T 949 7263, F 949 0216, US$55-65 plus US$14.95 CDW daily; Cico Avis, PO Box 400, T 949 2468, smallest standard car CI$28 winter/summer, jeeps, automatics and mini vans available, minimum 2-day rental, one day rental 25% extra, if paid in US dollars, add 25% for conversion; Coconut Car Rentals Ltd, PO Box 681, T 949 4037, from US$35/26 a day winter/summer or US$210/156 a week, jeeps US$55/50, US$330/300; National Car, PO Box 1105, T 949 4790, F 949 4795, at airport, US$51/38 a day winter/summer automatic car, standards and vans available, seventh day free summer only.

Bicycles (cheapest CI$10/day), mopeds and motorcycles (CI$20-27/day) can also be rented, from Caribbean Motors, PO Box 697, T 949 8878, F 945 1084 or Cayman Cycle Rentals, PO Box 1299, T 947 4021, at *Coconut Place*, *Hyatt Regency* and *Treasure Island*. Bicycles are also available at Rum Point, US$4/day, US$16/week. Driving is on the left. Be careful of buses whose doors open into the centre of the road. Island tours can be arranged at about US$60 for a taxi, or US$10 pp on a bus with a minimum of 20 persons. Check with your hotel for full details.

● Where To Stay
The winter season, running from 16 December to 15 April, is the peak tourist season. Visitors intending to come to the island during this period are advised to make hotel and travel arrangements well in advance. There are substantial reductions in May-November, with cut rates or even free accommodation for children under 12. Most hotels offer watersports, scuba diving and snorkelling, and many have tennis courts, swimming pools and other facilities. Accommodations are many and varied, ranging from resort hotels on the beach to small out-of-the-way family-run guest houses. There is also a wide variety of cottages, apartments (condominiums) and villas available for daily, weekly or monthly rental. A full list of tourist

accommodation and prices, including hotels, cottages, apartments and villas, is available from Cayman Islands Department of Tourism at the addresses shown at the end of this section. The Cayman Islands Hotel Reservations Service represents 52 properties in the Caymans and can be contacted abroad through the Tourist Office. A government tax of 6% is added to the room charge and most hotels also add a 15% service charge to the bill in lieu of tipping.

There are about 50 hotels along **Seven Mile Beach**. 200 yards from the beach is *Cayman Islander Hotel*, PO Box 509, T 948 0990, pool, relaxed, good value breakfast, 65 nice rooms and efficiencies, US$89-140, US$55-105 in summer, dive shop, a/c, TV, phones. Away from Seven Mile Beach, there are hotels on Grand Cayman at Spanish Bay, Conch Point, Rum Point, North Side, East End, Half Moon Bay and Bodden Bay. At East End, *Morritt's Tortuga Club* is new and upmarket, suites and town houses, US$150-325 on beach, pool with waterfalls and bar, full dive operation, packages available; on the North coast and rec for diving the N wall, *Cayman Kai Resort*, PO Box 201 Northside, T 947 9056, peaceful, on beautiful beach, dive packages available, US$135 and up for lodges or beach villa. There are lots of guest houses catering for divers in the suburbs S of George Town. A rec guest house is *Adam's Guest House*, PO Box 312G, on Melmac Ave, 3/4 mile S of George Town, T 949 2512, run by Tom and Olga Adams, excellent accommodation, 4 rooms, US$70d, US$10 additional person, a/c or fan, very helpful, about 300 yards from Parrots Landing dive shop, no credit cards, TCs accepted. A pleasant small hotel in this area is *Seaview*, PO Box 260, T 949 8804, F 949 8507, 15 rooms, US$80d winter, US$65d summer, a/c, fans, saltwater pool, piano bar, award-winning restaurant, Cayman Diving School on site, excellent snorkelling and off-shore diving, credit cards accepted. Three others in this price range (no credit cards) include *Grama's Bed and Breakfast*, PO Box 198, T 949 3798, N of Seven Mile Beach, US$80d including breakfast, tax and gratuity, a/c or fan, pool; *Ambassadors Inn*, PO Box 1789, T 949 7577, F 949 7050, 1 mile S of town, on South Church St, walking distance from Smith Cove, on site dive operation, US$80d, a/c, fans, pool, friendly, helpful, rec, and *Eldemire's Guest House*, PO Box 482, T 949 5387, F 949 6987, US$70d EP in room, US$75d studio, US$90d apartment, 1 mile from town, 1/2 mile from beach. Cottages, basic, may cost US$600-700 a week, and rates are usually by night, not per person. For longer stay visitors, a 2-bedroom, furnished house can be found away from the tourist areas in, say, Breakers or Bodden Town for US$600-1,000 a month.

● **Where To Eat And Drink**

There are dozens of restaurants on Grand Cayman ranging from gourmet standards where a jacket and tie is required, to smaller places serving native dishes. Fish, seafood and turtle meat are local specialities. In George Town, there are many restaurants catering for the lunchtime trade of the office workers and a number of fast-food places, takeaways and delicatessens. Prices obviously vary according to the standard of restaurant, but for dinner, main courses start at about US$10 and range upward to US$60 or more for a full meal including wine. Lunch prices can be around US$7-US$10 and breakfast from about US$5. During the high season it is advisable to reserve tables for dinner. People tend to eat early so if you reserve a table after 2000 you are likely to finish with the restaurant to yourself.

Good restaurants include: *The Wharf*, on the outskirts of George Town on the way to Seven Mile Beach, T 949 2231, lunch Monday-Friday, 1200-1430, dinner daily 1800-2200, beautiful waterfront setting, quite a large restaurant, reservations advisable; *Lantana's*, at the *Caribbean Club* on West Bay Road, fine, sophisticated dining, T 947 5595 for reservations; *Crow's Nest*, about 4 miles S of George Town, T 949 9366, open lunch Mon-Sat, 1130-1430, dinner daily 1800-2200, a local's favourite, small, glorious position, dining on the patio overlooking the sea or inside, moderate prices, reservations essential; *Pappagallo*, Barkers, West Bay, Italian cuisine, quite expensive, when it is windy tables are laid outside but otherwise not because of the mosquitoes, cover yourself with repellent and limit yourself to pre-dinner drinks outside and eat inside the haphazardly thatched building, excellent food but avoid the house red wine, reservations essential, T 947 3479, open daily 1800-2300; *Cracked Conch*, Selkirk Plaza, West Bay Road, T 947 5217, lively, take aways very popular; *Spanish Cove*, Barkers, West Bay, T 949 3765; *Almond Tree*, North Church Street, T 949 2893, outdoor dining, lobster specials Mon and Thur, all you can eat for US$14 on Wed and Fri, open lunch and dinner;

Grand Old House, South Church Street, T 949 9333; *Lobster Pot*, North Church Street, T 949 2736; *Welly's Cool Spot*, North Sound Road, T 949 2541, has native food at reasonable prices. *Richard Fish* at the Seven Mile Shops, deli-type restaurant serves breakfast through to 0200, inexpensive, own baked bread and local dishes. All of these restaurants are near George Town or on Seven Mile Beach on the W side of Grand Cayman. Good sandwiches from *Coconut Place Delicatessen*. Probably the best-value place to eat lunch on Grand Cayman is the *Wholesome Cafeteria* (closed Sat and Sun), located above the Wholesome Bakery on North Church Street. Others in the same price range include *Champion House*, *I* and *II*, both on Eastern Avenue, George Town, T 949 2190 (*I*), 949 7882 (*II*), cheap, local food, rec; *Dominique's*, Fort Street, T 949 5747; *Island Taste*, South Church Street, T 949 4945. Other bakeries are *Boulangerie Bakery*, Pleasant House, West Bay Road and *Caribbean Bakery and Pastry Shop*, West Bay.

For local colour visit *Farmers*, off Eastern Avenue near school. *Nelson Arms* on West Bay Road is fairly typical 'pub', popular with expatriates. Open air bars are *Sunset House* and *Coconut Harbour* on South Church Street. In down town George Town, the *Shanghai Restaurant*, T 949 5886, has a cocktail bar overlooking the harbour, jazz music; *Big Daddy's* in Seven Mile Shop, West Bay Road, T 949 8511, and *Lone Star Bar and Grill*, next to the *Hyatt Hotel*, West Bay Road, T 949 5575, are favourites with sports fans, showing international sporting events nightly.

● **Nightlife**
Monkey Business nightclub, Cayman Falls on West Bay Road, T 947 4024, popular Fri nights, dancing to disco and reggae. *Faces Nightclub* features local groups such as Cayman Edition, as well as rock, reggae and other Caribbean music, also on West Bay Road, T 949 0528. Others include *Apollo II Club*, North Side, T 947 9568; *McDoom's Club Inferno*, Hell, West Bay, T 949 3263. Many hotels have their own nightclubs. The Cayman National Theatre Company, T 949 5477, puts on plays and musicals at the Harquail Cultural Center on West Bay Road; the season runs from October to June. The Cayman Drama Society use the Prospect Play House, a small theatre on the road to Bodden Town.

CAYMAN BRAC

Settlement of Cayman Brac has been determined by the Bluff, which rises from sea level at the W end to a sheer cliff at the E end. Most building first took place on the flatter land in the W, where the sea is a little calmer, and then spread along the N coast where the Bluff gives shelter. The first three families of settlers arrived in 1833, followed by two more families in 1835. These five families, Ritch, Scott, Foster, Hunter and Ryan, are still well-represented on the island today. They made a living from growing coconuts and selling turtle shells and from the 1850s started building boats to facilitate trading. In 1886 a Baptist missionary arrived from Jamaica and introduced education and health care.

There are three roads running E-W, one along the N shore, one along the S coast and a third (unpaved) in the middle which runs along the top of the Bluff to the lighthouse. Up here it is sometimes possible to spot Cayman parrots and various orchids. From the airport the N shore road leads to Cotton Tree Bay, where in 1932 a hurricane flooded the area, killing more than 100 people and destroying virtually every house. The coconut groves were devastated and many people left the island at this time. Demand for turtle shell went into decline as the use of plastic increased and many men found that the only opportunities open to them were as sailors, travelling around the world on merchant ships.

Stake Bay is the main village on the N coast and it is well worthwhile visiting the small, but interesting Cayman Brac museum. Open Monday – Friday 0900-1200, 1300-1600, Sunday 0900-1200, T 498 4222, admission free. Further E at Creek, *La Esperanza* is a good place to stop for refreshment, in a glorious setting with good views and welcome sea breeze. At Spot Bay at the extreme E, follow a track up towards the lighthouse. Here you will find Peter's Cave and a good

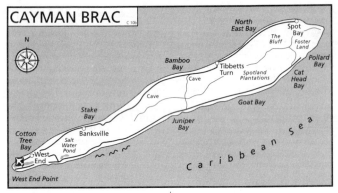

viewpoint. This can also be reached from the road which runs along the top of the Bluff. From the end of the N coast road you can walk through the almond trees to the beach, from where you get an excellent view of the Bluff from below. Little Cayman can be seen in the distance. Along the S coast, the best beaches are at the W end, where there are two dive resorts. There is a pleasant public beach with shade and toilets at South East Bay. Bat Cave and Rebecca's Cave are in this vicinity and can be visited. Holiday homes are being built along this coast. These do not seem to need the shelter of the N coast as do the locals. Tourism is now the mainstay of the economy but construction of homes for foreigners has pushed up the price of land out of the reach of many local families. Most young adults leave the island for a career in financial services in Grand Cayman or other jobs further afield.

Diving and Marine Life

Cayman Brac is also blessed with spectacular reef and wall diving with excellent visibility. Most of the sites are around the W end, with both shallow reef snorkelling and diving and deeper wall diving a bit further out. There are also a few wrecks among the 40 or so named dive sites. Two dive operations are based on Cayman Brac, offering diving at both Cayman Brac and Little Cayman sites, certification and resort courses, photo/video services and equipment rental. Brac Aquatic is at *Brac Reef Beach Resort* (T 948 7429) and Peter Hughes Dive Tiara is at the *Divi Tiara Beach Resort* (T 948 7553).

Island Information – Cayman Brac
● **Transport**

There is no bus service. An island tour by taxi costs about CI$15, Elo's Taxi and Tours, T 948 8220, rec, Hill's Taxi and Tours, T 948 8540, Maple Edward's Taxi and Tours, T 948 8448. Hertz, Avis and Four D's for car hire (about US$35-40/day for a car), B&S Motor Ventures for moped and bike hire, T 948 7546.

● **Where To Stay**

At West End Point there are the *Brac Reef Beach Resort* (PO Box 56, T 948 7323, US$120d, 40 rooms, packages available) and *Divi Tiara Beach Resort*, (T 948 7553, US$125-195, 72 rooms, packages available) both with full watersports and diving facilities, while there are also the *Brac Airport Inn*, T 948 7323, US$79-99d, 2 miles from town, 7 rooms or 3 suites with kitchenettes, a/c, TV, guests have full use of *Brac Reef* facilities and *Blackie's Seaview Hotel*, 9 rooms, a/c, fans, pool, bar, restaurant, T 948 8232. A condominium development with 22 units, *Brac Caribbean Beach Village*, on the S coast, T 948 2265, F 948 2206, a/c, fans, on beach, reef protected, credit cards accepted, 10 units all 2-bedroomed, US$150d, US$200 3-4 people, weekly rates one night free; *Seafarer Condominiums*, on SW coast, 8 beach front, one-bedroomed units, a/c, fans, verandah, daily and weekly rates, T 948 2265, no credit cards.

● **Where To Eat**

On Cayman Brac there are a few restaurants; *Blackie's*, at the Youth Centre, South Side, T 948 8232, good ice cream; *Bin's*, Watering Place, T 948 8311; *Edd's Place*, West End, T 948 7208, open from 0700, restaurant and bar, Chinese seafood and local dishes, phone for transport; *La Esperanza*, T 948 8531, seafood, transport available, open Mon-Fri, 0900-0100, Sat 0900-2400, Sun 1200-2400 and *Lagoon*, T 948 7523, both at Stake Bay; *Sonia's*, White Bay, T 948 7214; *Watering Place*, T 948 8232.

LITTLE CAYMAN

The first inhabitants of Little Cayman were turtlers who made camp on the S shore. After them, at the beginning of the 20th century, the population exploded to over 100 Caymanians living at Blossom on the SW coast and farming coconuts. Attacks of blight killed off the palms and the farmers moved to the other two islands. In the 1950s, some US sport fishermen set up a small fishing camp on the S coast known as the Southern Cross Club, which is still in operation today as a diving/fishing lodge. Since then, a handful of similar small resorts have been built but the resident population remains tiny.

Little Cayman is small and low-lying with large areas of dense mangrove swamps, ponds, lagoons and lakes. It is the ideal habitat for about 10,000 red-footed boobies and numerous iguanas. The best beach for swimming and snorkelling is at Sandy Point at the E tip of the island. Look for a red and white marker opposite a pond, a sandy path leads down to the beach. Other beaches are at Jackson's Point on the N side and on Owen Island in South Hole Sound. This privately owned island 200 yards offshore, is freely used by residents and visitors alike and is accessible by row boat. Popular with picnic parties.

Diving and Marine Life

Underwater visibility around Little Cayman averages 100-150 feet all year and diving is excellent. There are dive sites all round the island, but the most popular spot is in the Marine Park in Bloody Bay, a 2-mile stretch between Spot Bay and Jackson's Point off the N coast. Bloody Bay wall, a mile-deep vertical drop is one of the major dive sites worldwide and is highly rated by marine biologists and photographers. Unlike the walls around the other islands, which begin at a depth of about 65 feet and drop down about a mile, the Bloody Bay wall begins at only 15-20 feet, which means you can snorkel over the drop-off. Shore diving from Jackson's Point is also spectacular, with

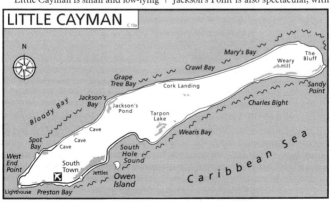

coral heads rising from a 40-foot sandy bottom to about 10 feet of the surface. *Sam McCoy's Dive Lodge* is at the W end of Spot Bay. There is also a Marine Park off the S coast opposite the airport, with *Pirate's Point Dive Resort* at one end. Diving can be arranged with *Pirate's Point*, *Sam McCoy's* or *Southern Cross Club*, all of which take out parties of no more than 16 divers.

The bonefishing around Little Cayman is some of the best and just offshore. The 15-acre Tarpon Lake is home to the game fish from which the pond gets its name. Fishing is offered at *Sam McCoy's* (T 948 4526, F 949 6821), where bonefishing and tarpon is US$15/hour and deep sea fishing is US$300/half day and US$500/full day. At *Southern Cross Club* (T 948 3255) deep sea fishing is US$150/half day and US$300/day, while a half day of bonefishing for two people with guide is US$80.

Island Information – Little Cayman
● **Transport**
The airport consists of a wooden shack and a grass runway. Jeep hire is available here with McLaughlin Rentals, T 948 4500, daily and weekly rates, best to book in advance as last minute prices can be high. Roads are unpaved.

● **Where To Stay**
Accommodation consists of diving lodges, a few private cottages and homes plus 10 rooms at the Southern Cross Club. *Sam McCoy's* (T 948 4526/949 2891, F 949 6821, US$118 pp non-diver, US$159 pp diver, 3 meals inc, deep sea fishing US$500 pp full day, small scale, low key, 8 rooms, no credit cards), *Pirates Point* (T 948 4210, F 948 4610, 10 rooms, US$200 pp double occupancy all inclusive with diving, US$140 without, owned by a cordon bleu chef, highly rec, very relaxing, friendly), *Suzy's Cottage* (US$1,295/ week winter, US$1,190 summer) *Sefton's Cottages* (US$1,295/ week for a house, US$910/ week for an apartment in winter, US$1,190 and US$805 in summer) or *Southern Cross Club* (T 948 3255, US$140 pp based on double occupancy inc 3 meals, scuba, fishing, no credit cards, all in the W end of the island. The 32-room *Little Cayman Beach Resort* opened in 1993, T/F 948 4533, US$119d all

year, a/c, TV, on beach, dock facilities, tennis, basketball, volleyball, pool, jacuzzi, diving, facilities for the handicapped, all-inclusive packages available, under same ownership as *Village Inn*, Blossom Village, by the airport, 8 apartments, US$125, a/c, fans, T 949 1064 or 948 7423. Most offer full accommodation and diving and fishing facilities.

INFORMATION FOR VISITORS

● **Documents**
No passports are required for US, British or Canadian visitors. However, proof of citizenship such as voter registration or "British Visitor's Passport" is required, as well as an outward ticket. Married women using their husband's name should also show their marriage certificate. Passports but not visas are required for citizens of West European and Commonwealth countries, Israel, Japan, Argentina, Bahrain, Brazil, Chile, Costa Rica, Ecuador, El Salvador, Guatemala, Mexico, Oman, Panama, Peru, Saudi Arabia, Venezuela and South Africa. If you are from any of these countries you may be admitted to the Cayman Islands for a period of up to 6 months providing you have proof of citizenship, sufficient resources to maintain yourself during your stay, and a return ticket to your country of origin or another country in which you will be accepted.

Visas are required by nationals of communist countries and all countries not included in the list in the foregoing paragraph. Luggage is inspected by customs officials on arrival; no attempt should be made to take drugs into the country.

● **How To Get There**
Air communications are good and there are 2 international airports, the Owen Roberts International Airport on Grand Cayman and the Gerrard-Smith Airport on Cayman Brac. The national flag carrier, Cayman Airways, has regular services between the islands and Miami, Houston, Atlanta and Tampa in the USA. With Air Jamaica it shares a service to Kingston and Montego Bay. Grand Cayman is also served from Miami by American Airlines, United Airlines and Northwest Airlines, Northwest also flies from Oklahoma, Detroit, Madison and Memphis via Miami. American Airlines also flies direct from Washington DC, Hartford, CT, Raleigh/Durham and several other cities via Miami. US Air flies from Tampa, Washington

DC, Pittsburgh, Charlotte and other US cities via Tampa or Charlotte. Islena Airlines fly between La Ceiba, Honduras and Grand Cayman. Regular charter flights also from Grand Cayman to Cayo Largo, Cuba, but you can not travel further to visit Cuba itself. Cayman Airways provides inter-island services most days from Grand Cayman to Cayman Brac and Little Cayman and return.

From Europe: From December 1994 Caledonian Airways was to start direct flights from London Gatwick on Fridays, with connections from other European cities.

Owen Roberts International Airport is situated less than 2 miles from the centre of George Town and only 10 mins' drive from most of the hotels on Seven Mile Beach. There is a departure tax of US$10 for all visitors aged 12 and over payable either in Cayman or US currency when you leave the Islands.

The islands are not served by any scheduled passenger ships but there are cargo services between the islands and Miami and Tampa in the USA, Kingston in Jamaica and Costa Rica. For boats between Grand Cayman and Honduras and the Bay Islands, see the Bay Islands chapter, **Transport to Guanaja**. The port at George Town comprises the S wharf, with a depth of 24 feet, and the W wharf, with a depth of 20 feet. The port at Creek, Cayman Brac, is equipped to handle the same class of vessels but Little Cayman has only a small facility. There is a small jetty at Spotts, Grand Cayman, which caters for cruise ships when the weather is too bad to land at George Town.

● **Airlines**
Cayman Airways, T 949 2311. For information on flights to Cayman Brac, T 948 7221. Air Jamaica, T 949 2300. American Airlines, T 949 8799. Island Air, T 949 0241/2311. Northwest Airlines, T 949 2955/6. For Sahsa Airlines flights to Central America, T 949 4979. Charter companies: Executive Air Services, T 949 7766.

● **Best Buys**
As a free port, there is duty-free shopping and a range of British glass, china, woollens, perfumes and spirits are available. US citizens are entitled to a US$400 exemption after being away from the USA for 48 hours.

Black coral carvings and jewellery are widely available. Note that since the 1978 Cayman Islands Marine Conservation Law prohibited the removal of coral from local waters, manufacturers turned to Belize and Honduras for their supply. All the Central American countries are now members of CITES, so if you must buy it it would be worth checking the source of the coral in case it has been procured illegally. Caymanite is a semi-precious gem stone with layers of various colours found only in the Cayman Islands. Local craftspeople use it to make jewellery.

The day's fish catch can be bought from the fishermen most afternoons opposite the Tower Building just outside central George Town. Otto Watler makes and sells honey in Savannah, sign on the right just after the speed limit notice. Pure Art, on South Church Street (also at *Hyatt Regency*), sells the work of over 50 local artists and craftsmen and women; paintings, prints, sculptures, crafts, rugs, wallhangings etc, open Mon-Sat 1000-1600. On Cayman Brac, NIM Things sells items made locally, including caymanite jewellery, straw bags and crochet, open 0900-1900 at Spot Bay, E end of the Main North Side Road.

The Book Nook (which sells *Caribbean Islands Handbook* among other things), is at Cayman Falls, T 947 4686, and Anchorage Centre, T 949 7392, PO Box 1551, Grand Cayman, F 947 5053.

● **Currency**
The legal currency is the Cayman Islands dollar (CI$). The exchange rate is fixed at CI$1 to US$1.20, or CI$0.80 to US$1, although officially the exchange rate is CI$0.83 to US$1. US currency is readily accepted throughout the Islands, and Canadian and British currencies can be exchanged at all banks. There is no exchange control. Personal cheques are not generally welcome and credit cards are not accepted everywhere; do not assume that your hotel will accept them. Travellers' cheques are preferred.

● **Banks**
Most of the major international banks are represented in George Town, Grand Cayman but not all are licensed to offer normal banking facilities. Those which are include Bank of Nova Scotia, Barclays Bank International, Canadian Imperial Bank of Commerce and Royal Bank of Canada. Commercial banking hours are 0900 to 1430 Mon to Thur, and 0900 to 1300 and 1430 to 1600 on Fri. Barclays Bank and the Cayman National Bank have branches on Cayman Brac.

● **Warning**
Care must be taken when walking on a high-

way, especially at night; highway shoulders are narrow and vehicles move fast.

● **Health**

Medical Care on Grand Cayman is good and readily available. There is a 52-bed government hospital in George Town (T 949 8600, out-patients appointments T 949 8601) and a 12-bed hospital in Cayman Brac. All hospital beds are in single rooms. Out-patients pay a fixed charge per visit. Primary care is provided through 4 district health centres in Grand Cayman. There is also a clinic on Little Cayman. Cayman Islands Divers, the local branch of the British Sub-Aqua Club, operates the only recompression chamber, behind Cayman Clinic, off Crew Road in George Town (T 555).

● **Note**

Although Grand Cayman is sprayed regularly, it is advisable to bring plenty of insect repellent to combat mosquitoes and sandflies, particularly when there is rain. Little Cayman has to be sprayed every 2 weeks and if the spraying aircraft is out of action you will notice the difference. Malaria does still occur occasionally although yellow fever and dengue fever appear to have been eradicated.

● **Security**

The Cayman Islands are safe to visit and present no need for extra security precautions. However, drugs related offences have increased sharply, with 894 arrests in 1993 compared with 606 in 1992 and about 80% of all thefts estimated to be drugs linked. The islands have become a major trans-shipment point.

● **Climate**

The Cayman Islands lie in the trade-wind belt and the prevailing NE winds moderate the temperatures, making the climate delightful all year round. Average temperatures in winter are about 24°C and in summer are around 26°-29°C. Most rain falls between May and October, but even then it only takes the form of short showers.

● **National Holidays**

New Year's Day, Ash Wednesday, Good Friday, Easter Monday, Discovery Day (third Monday in May), the Monday following the Queen's official birthday (June), Constitution Day (first Monday in July), the Monday after Remembrance Sunday (November), Christmas Day and Boxing Day.

● **Time Zone**

Eastern Standard Time, 5 hours behind GMT, for the whole year.

● **Telecommunications**

The Cayman Islands have a modern automatic telephone system operated by Cable and Wireless, which links them with the rest of the world by satellite and by submarine cable. International telephone, telex, telegram, data transmission and facsimile facilities are available and about 108 countries can be dialled directly. There is also a telephone route to the UK via Mercury. Public international telephone booths and a telegram counter are at the Cable and Wireless offices at Anderson Square, open from 0815-1700.

● **Postal Services**

Airmail postal rates are divided into 3 groups. Group A: the Caribbean, USA, Canada, Central America and Venezuela, first class 30 cents, second class, post cards, airletters 15 cents. Group B: Europe, Scandinavia, West Africa, South America, first class 40 cents, others 20 cents. Group C: East Africa, the Arabian subcontinent, Asia and the Far East, first class 55 cents, others 30 cents.

● **Press**

The *Daily Caymanian Compass* is published

5 days a week with a circulation of 25,000.

● **Maps**

The Ordnance Survey produces a 1:50,000 scale map of the Cayman Islands with an inset map of George Town in its World Map Series. For information contact Ordnance Survey, Romsey Road, Maybush, Southampton SO9 4DH, T 0703 792000, F 0703 792404.

● **Tourist Information**

Cable and Wireless, in conjunction with the Department of Tourism, provide a Tourist Hotline. By dialling 949 8989 you can find out this week's events and local information. Further information may be obtained from the Cayman Islands Department of Tourism at: PO Box 67, George Town, Grand Cayman, BWI, T: (809) 949 0623, F 949 4053.

USA: 6100 Blue Lagoon Drive, Suite 150, Miami, Fl 33126-2085, T (305) 266-2300, F (305) 267-2932; 9525 W Bryn Mawr Ave, Suite 160, Rosemont, Illinois 60018, T (708) 678-6446, F (708) 678-6675; Two Memorial City Plaza, 820 Gessner, Suite 170, Houston, Texas 77024, T (713) 461-1317, F (713) 461-7409; 420 Lexington Avenue, Suite 2733, New York, NY 10170, T (212) 682 5582, F (212) 986-5123; 3440 Wilshire Boulevard, Suite 1202, Los Angeles, California 90010, T (213) 738-1968, F (213) 738-1829. There are also offices in Atlanta, T (404) 934-3959; Baltimore, T (301) 625-4503; Boston, T (617) 431-7771; Dallas, T (214) 823-3838; San Francisco, T (415) 991-1836; and Tampa, T (813) 934-9078.

Canada: c/o Earl B Smith, Travel Marketing Consultants, 234 Eglinton Avenue East, Suite 306, Toronto, Ontario, M4P IK5 T (416) 485-1550, F (416) 485-7578.

UK: Trevor House, 100 Brompton Road, London SW3 1EX, T 071-581 9960, F 071-584 4463. The London office is also the European headquarters for Cayman Airways, providing air reservations and tickets as well as a hotel reservations service (free).

Germany/Austria/Switzerland: Marketing Services International, Walter Stöhrer and Partner GmbH, Postfach 170446, Liebigstr 8, 60323 Frankfurt/Main 1, T 69-726342, F 69-727714.

Italy: G & A Martinengo, Via Fratelli, Ruffini 9, 20123 Milano, T 02-4801 2068, F 02-4635 32.

Belgium/Netherlands/Luxembourg: Associated Travel Consultants, Leidsestraat 32, 1017 PB Amsterdam, Netherlands, T 20 6261 197, F 20 6274 86 9.

Japan: International Travel Produce Inc., c/o Shuwa Dai-2, Tsukiji Residence 4-3-12-201, Tsukiji, Chuo-Ku, Tokyo 104, T (03) 3546-1754, F 3545-8756.

The Cayman Islands Government Information Services (third floor, Tower Building, Grand Cayman, T 949 8092, F 949 8487) publishes a series of booklets including one on *Marine Parks Rules and Sea Code in The Cayman Islands* and several on banking, captive insurance, company registration, residential status, work permits, living in the Cayman Islands etc. The Department of Tourism publishes *Cayman Islands Rates & Facts* annually, giving hotel and transport prices as well as other useful information.

JAMAICA

JAMAICA lies some 90 miles S of Cuba and a little over 100 miles W of Haiti. With an area of 4,244 square miles, it is the third largest island in the Greater Antilles. It is 146 miles from E to W and 51 miles from N to S at its widest, bounded by the Caribbean. Like other West Indian islands, it is an outcrop of a submerged mountain range. It is crossed by a range of mountains reaching 7,402 feet at the Blue Mountain Peak in the E and descending towards the W, with a series of spurs and forested gullies running N and S. Most of the best beaches are on the N and W coasts, though there are some good bathing places on the S coast too.

Jamaica has magnificent scenery and a tropical climate freshened by sea breezes. The easily accessible hill and mountain resorts provide a more temperate climate, sunny but invigorating. In fact, it would be hard to find, in so small an area, a greater variety of tropical natural beauty.

Over 90% of Jamaicans are of West African descent, the English settlers having followed the Spaniards in bringing in slaves from West Africa. Because of this, Ashanti words still figure very largely in the local dialect, which is known as Jamaica Talk. There are also Chinese, East Indians and Christian Arabs as well as those of British descent and other European minorities. The population is approximately 2.4 million. There is considerable poverty on the island, which has created social problems and some tension.

Jamaicans are naturally friendly, easy going and international in their outlook (more people of Jamaican origin live outside Jamaica than inside; compare the Irish). The Jamaicans have a "Meet the People" programme which enables visitors to meet Jamaicans on a one-to-one basis.

History

When Columbus landed on Jamaica in 1494 it was inhabited by peaceful Arawak Indians. Evidence collected by archaeologists suggests that the tribe had not lived on the island much before the year 1000. Under Spanish occupation, which began in 1509, the race died out and gradually African slaves were brought in to provide the labour force. In 1655 an English expeditionary force landed at Passage Fort and met with little resistance other than that offered by a small group of Spanish settlers and a larger number of African slaves who took refuge in the mountains. The Spaniards abandoned the island after about five years, but the slaves and their descendants, who became known as Maroons, waged war against the new colonists for 80 years until the 1730s although there was another brief rebellion in 1795. The Cockpit Country, or "Look Behind Country," where the Leeward Maroons hid and around Nanny Town where the Windward Maroons hid is still the home of some of their descendants.

After a short period of military rule, the colony was organized with an English-type constitution and a Legislative Council. The great sugar estates, which still today produce an important part of the island's wealth, were planted in the early days of English occupation when Jamaica also became the haunt of buccaneers and slave traders. In 1833 emancipation was declared for slaves (although a system of apprenticeship remained until 1838) and modern Jamaica was born. The framework for Jamaica's modern political system was laid in the 1930s with the foundation in 1938 of the People's National Party (PNP) by Norman W Manley, and the Jamaica Labour Party (JLP) by his cousin, Sir Alexander Bustamante in 1944. These two parties had their roots in rival trade unions and have dominated Jamaican politics since universal adult suffrage was introduced in 1944.

In 1958, Jamaica joined the West Indies Federation with nine other British territories but withdrew following a national referendum on the issue in 1961. On 6 August 1962, Jamaica became an independent member of the Commonwealth.

Most of the earlier historical landmarks have been destroyed by hurricanes and earthquakes. Very few traces, apart from place names, therefore remain of the Spanish occupation. In 1692 an earthquake destroyed Port Royal which, because of being the base for English buccaneers such as Henry Morgan, had become famed as the most splendid town in the West Indies. In 1907 another earthquake damaged much of Kingston. Some of the historic buildings which are still

standing, including the 18th century churches at Port Royal, St Ann's Bay and Montego Bay, are now in the care of the National Trust Commission. The Great Houses are a reminder of the British settlers; some have been converted into hotels or museums. In September 1988, Hurricane Gilbert travelled the length of the island causing extensive damage in all areas. There is hardly any sign of Gilbert now.

After 23 years as leader of the PNP, eight of them as Prime Minister in the 1970s and three as Prime Minister from 1989, Michael Manley, son of the party's founder, retired in March 1992 because of ill health. During Manley's first two terms in office between 1972 and 1980 he endorsed socialist policies at home and encouraged South-South relations abroad. He antagonized the USA by developing close economic and political links with Cuba. State control of the economy failed to produce the desired results and Mr Manley was rejected by the electorate. The conservative JLP led by Edward Seaga, held office for the next nine years. By 1989 however, Manley's political thinking had changed dramatically and he was re-elected with policies advocating the free market. Before his retirement he oversaw the reduction in the size of the state, deregulation of the economy and close relations with the IMF. He was succeeded by the Party Chairman, former deputy Prime Minister and Finance Minister P J Patterson who overwhelmingly defeated his only rival in an election at a special party meeting. Mr Patterson promised to maintain Mr Manley's policies and deepen the restructuring of the economy.

General elections were held early on 30 March 1993 and the incumbent PNP was returned for a second term with a larger than expected majority, winning 55 of the 60 seats. Despite the landslide victory, the elections were marred by violence in which 11 people died, malpractices and a turnout of only 58%. The JLP

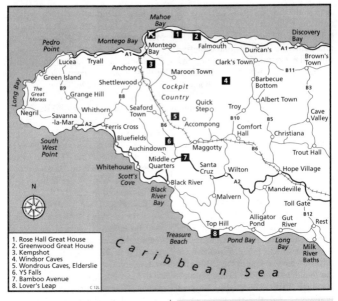

1. Rose Hall Great House
2. Greenwood Great House
3. Kempshot
4. Windsor Caves
5. Wondrous Caves, Elderslie
6. YS Falls
7. Bamboo Avenue
8. Lover's Leap

boycotted parliament for four months while it demanded electoral reform and an inquiry into the election day events. It also refused to contest by-elections, two of which were held in the next 12 months and won by the PNP. Some concessions were made by the Government. The police force is to be reorganized to remove direct political control and local government elections have been postponed pending electoral reform.

Government

Jamaica is a constitutional monarchy. A Governor-General represents the British monarch, who is Head of State, and the Government is made up of a Prime Minister, (who nominates the Cabinet), a 60-seat House of Representatives and a 21-seat Senate. All citizens over 18 are eligible for the vote. The judicial system is on British lines. There is a two-party system.

The Economy

Once one of the more prosperous islands in the West Indies, Jamaica went into recession in 1973 and output declined steadily throughout the 1970s and 1980s. Gdp per head fell considerably in real terms although by 1989-92 economic output was beginning to pick up. The average unemployment rate has improved to 16%. At the core of Jamaica's economic difficulties lay the collapse of the vital bauxite mining and alumina refining industries. Bauxite and alumina export earnings provided 46% of all foreign exchange receipts and 28% of gdp in 1980 but by 1984 these shares had fallen to 33% and 20% respectively. Nevertheless, Jamaica is the world's third largest producer of bauxite after Australia and Guinea, and higher output and prices have now improved the outlook for the industry. Figures for 1990 showed bauxite and alumina accounting for two thirds of merchandise exports, with min-

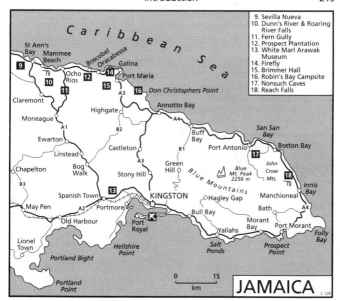

9. Sevilla Nueva
10. Dunn's River & Roaring River Falls
11. Fern Gully
12. Prospect Plantation
13. White Marl Arawak Museum
14. Firefly
15. Brimmer Hall
16. Robin's Bay Campsite
17. Nonsuch Caves
18. Reach Falls

JAMAICA

ing output increasing by nearly 18%, although their share of gdp had fallen to 10%. In 1991 output of bauxite reached 11.5mn tons, the highest level for 10 years, while alumina production hit a record 3mn tons, but export revenues fell in 1991 and 1992 because of lower prices.

By comparison with mining, agriculture is a less important sector in terms of contribution to gdp, though it generates far more employment. Sugar is the main crop, and most important export item (US$99mn in 1993) after bauxite and alumina. Four state-owned sugar mills were sold in 1993, leaving only one remaining in government hands. Other export crops include bananas (US$36mn), coffee (US$20mn), cocoa and citrus fruits (US$4mn). An agricultural development plan for 1994-2000 aims to raise agricultural exports from US$194mn in 1993 to US$400mn. Agriculture grew by 8.8% in real terms in 1993.

Tourism is the second foreign exchange earner and Jamaica is the third most popular destination in the Caribbean after the Bahamas and Cancún. Stopover arrivals grew by an annual average of 8% and cruise visitors by 14% in the first half of the 1980s until, in 1987, combined stopover and cruise arrivals passed the million mark for the first time and in 1993 the country received 978,715 stopover visitors and 626,636 cruiseship passengers. In 1993, foreign exchange earnings from tourism were an estimated US$950mn. In 1994 stopover visitors were expected to exceed 1m and earnings to rise to over US$1bn. The impact of tourism on a population of less than 2½ million is massive, both economically and socially. Bad publicity abroad or a natural disaster, such as Hurricane Gilbert, can have a devastating effect. The crime rate is high but most of the serious crime is around Kingston, principally in West Kingston. Many country districts and N coast resorts are fairly safe. Partly because of crime, all-inclusive resorts have become particularly important in Jamaica. A large proportion of tourists never leave these hotels except on an organized tour or to return to the airport.

The Government turned to the IMF for support in 1976 and has since been a regular customer. In compliance with IMF agreements, the Government had to reduce domestic demand commensurate with the fall in export earnings, by devaluing the currency and reducing the size of its fiscal deficits. Jamaica has rescheduled its debt to creditor governments and also to foreign commercial banks. Some debt forgiveness has also been granted. Debt to the IMF was US$360mn in 1990, down from US$688mn in 1986, although total official lending made up about three quarters of the total public foreign debt of around US$4.1bn. By 1994 debt had fallen to US$3.6bn, the lowest since end – 1986, through repayments, renegotiations and cancellations.

A 15-month SDR 82mn standby credit facility was agreed with the IMF in January 1990 with targets to reduce the budget and current account deficits and eliminate payment arrears. Several tax increases were announced, together with the sale of hotels and other government assets and the ending of some unprofitable Air Jamaica routes (the Government is selling 70% of Air Jamaica after several years of losses to a consortium; the state retains 25% and employees have been offered 5%). The Jamaican dollar was devalued, the foreign exchange market was deregulated, and interest rates and credit ceilings were kept high to reduce consumption, close the trade gap and rebuild foreign reserves. A further standby agreement was negotiated in 1991, together with loans from the World Bank and the InterAmerican Development Bank, which aimed to cut the budget deficit still further. In December 1992 an IMF 3-year Extended Fund Facility (EFF) replaced

JAMAICA : FACT FILE

Geographic

Land area	10,991 sq km
forested	17.2%
pastures	17.5%
cultivated	24.8%

Demographic

Population (1992)	2,445,000
annual growth rate (1987-92)	0.8%
urban	52.3%
rural	47.7%
density	222.5 per sq km
Religious affiliation	
Protestant	55.9%
Non-religious	17.7%
Other, inc Rastafarian	10.2%
Birth rate per 1,000 (1991)	24.7
	(world av 26.4)
Death rate per 1,000 (1991)	5.5
	(world av 9.2)

Education and Health

Life expectancy at birth,	
male	71.4 years
female	75.8 years
Infant mortality rate	
per 1,000 live births (1989)	27.0
Physicians (1990)	1 per 5,904 persons
Hospital beds	1 per 468 persons
Calorie intake as %	
of FAO requirement	117%
Population age 25 and over	
with no formal schooling	3.2%
Literacy (over 15)	98.5%

Economic

GNP (1990 market prices)	US$3,606mn
GNP per capita	US$1,510
Public external debt (1990)	US$3,673mn
Tourism receipts (1990)	US$764mn
Inflation (annual av 1986-91)	19.5%
Radio	1 per 1.6 persons
Television	1 per 5.0 persons
Telephone	1 per 13 persons

Employment

Population economically active (1991)	
	1,076,600
Unemployment rate	15.7%
% of labour force in	
agriculture	23.0
mining	0.5
manufacturing	8.9
construction	5.1
Military forces	3,350

Source *Encyclopaedia Britannica*

the Standby which expired in June. The economy showed signs of growth but recovery was fragile. During the political leadership handover, uncertainties caused the currency to fall rapidly, but tighter monetary policies and private business sector support enabled it to recover soon afterwards and hold steady. Inflation was cut from an annual rate of 105% at the end of 1991 to only 17% in 1992, but cuts in fiscal spending have led to a reduction in health and education services as well as in the size of the civil service and the poor have been worst hit. The lack of adequate housing is a perennial problem, commonly solved by poor Jamaicans by squatting. The police have often been accused of cruelty when trying to evict squatters at the landowners' request and no solution has yet been found. The 1993/94 budget granted wage increases to public employees, to be financed by higher taxes, including a rise in value added tax from 10% to 12.5%

DREADLOCKS TO REGGAE: JAMMIN' IN JAMAICA

Followers of the Rastafarian cult are easily recognizable by their long dreadlocks; they are non-violent and do not eat pork. They believe in the divinity of the late Emperor of Ethiopia, Haile Selassie (Ras Tafari). Haile Selassie's call for the end of the superiority of one race over another has been incorporated into a faith which holds that God, Jah, will lead the blacks out of oppression (Babylon) back to Ethiopia (Zion, the Promised Land). The Rastas regard the ideologist, Marcus Garvey (born 1887, St Ann's Bay), as a prophet of the return to Africa (he is now a Jamaican national hero). In the early part of the twentieth century, Garvey founded the idea of black nationalism, with Africa as the home for blacks, be they living on the continent or not.

The music most strongly associated with Rastafarianism is reggae. According to O R Dathorne, "it is evident that the sound and words of Jamaican reggae have altered the life of the English-speaking Caribbean. The extent of this alteration is still unknown, but this new sound has touched, *more than any other single art medium*, the consciousness of the people of this region." (*Dark Ancestor*, page 229, Louisiana State University Press, 1981). The sound is a mixture of African percussion and up-to-the-minute electronics; the lyrics a blend of praise of Jah, political comment and criticism and the mundane. The late Bob Marley, the late Peter Tosh, Dennis Brown and Jimmy Cliff are among the world-famous reggae artists, and many, many more can be heard on the island. Over the last few years, traditional reggae has been supplanted by Dance Hall, which has a much heavier beat, and instead of Marley's rather thoughtful lyrics, it is all about guns and sex, Shabba Ranks, Buju Banton and so on. Closely related to reggae is dub poetry, a chanted verse form which combines the musical tradition, folk traditions and popular speech. Its first practitioner was Louise Bennett, in the 1970s, who has been followed by poets such as Linton Kwesi Johnson, Michael Smith, Oku Onora and Mutabaruka. Many of these poets work in the UK, but their links with Jamaica are strong.

Two novels which give a fascinating insight into Rasta culture (and, in the latter, Revival and other social events) are *Brother Man*, by Roger Mais, and *The Children of Sysiphus*, by H Orlando Patterson. These writers have also published other books which are worth investigating, as are the works of Olive Senior (eg *Summer Lightning*), the poets Mervyn Morris, Andrew Salkey and Dennis Scott (who is also involved in the theatre).

and a rise in the cruise ship passengers levy from US$10 to US$15. Further tax increases were announced in the 1994/95 budget, with a rise in petrol tax and a doubling of the departure tax. The Government intends to operate without a new IMF agreement when the present EFF expires at end-1995.

Culture

The predominant religion is Protestantism, but there is also a Roman Catholic community. There are followers of the Church of God, Baptists, Anglicans, Seventh Day Adventists, Pentecostals and Methodists. The Jewish, Moslem, Hindu and Bahai religions are also practised. It is said that Jamaica has more churches per square mile than anywhere else in the world. To a small degree, early adaptations of the Christian faith, Revival and Pocomania, survive, but the most obvious local minority sect is Rastafarianism see box, p 221.

Kingston is the main cultural centre of Jamaica. There are two important institutes which can be visited: the African Caribbean Institute (ACIJ, on Little North Street) is involved in research into African traditions in Jamaica and the Caribbean; the Institute of Jamaica (East Street) has historical sections, including Arawak carvings, the National Library, science museum and occasional lectures and exhibitions. The National Gallery of Jamaica (Orange Street and Ocean Boulevard) has a large collection of Jamaican art; there are about a dozen other galleries in the city. The National Dance Theatre has an annual summer season; throughout the year plays and concerts are staged. The local press has full details of events in Kingston and other centres.

Flora and Fauna

Jamaica has been called the Island of Springs, and the luxuriance of the vegetation is striking (its Arawak name, Xaymaca, meant land of wood and water).

There are reported to be about 3,000 species of flowering plants alone, 827 of which are not found anywhere else. There are over 550 varieties of fern, 300 of which can be found in Fern Gully (see below). The national flower is the dark blue bloom of the lignum vitae. There are many orchids, bougainvillea, hibiscus and other tropical flowers. Tropical hardwoods like cedar and mahogany, palms, balsa and many other trees, besides those that are cultivated, can be seen. Cultivation, however, is putting much of Jamaica's plant life at risk. Having been almost entirely forested, now an estimated 6% of the land is virgin forest. A great many species are now classified as endangered.

This is also a land of hummingbirds and butterflies; sea-cows and the Pedro seal are found in the island's waters. There are crocodiles, but no wild mammals apart from the hutia, or coney (a native of the island and now an endangered species), the mongoose (considered a pest since it has eliminated snakes and now eats chickens) and, in the mountains, wild pig. The Jamaican iguana (*Cyclura collei*), of the lizard family Iguonidae, subspecies Iguaninae, was thought to have died out in the 1960s, but in 1990 a small group was found to be surviving in the Hellshire Hills.

Good sites for birdwatching are given in the text below; the three main areas are the Cockpit Country, the Blue Mountains and Marshall's Pen. The national bird is the doctor bird hummingbird, with a tail much longer than its body, one of Jamaica's endemic species. There are 25 species and 21 subspecies of birds which are found nowhere else. Many migratory birds stop on Jamaica on their journeys N or S. *Birds of Jamaica: a photographic field guide* by Audrey Downer and Robert Sutton with photos by Yves-Jacques Rey Millet, was published in 1990 by Cambridge University Press.

In 1989 the Government established two pilot national parks, the first in Jamaica, under the Protected Areas Resource Conservation (PARC) project. The Blue Mountain/John Crow Mountain National Park encompasses almost 200,000 acres of mountains, forests and rivers. Efforts are being made to stem soil erosion and restore woodland lost in Hurricane Gilbert, while developing the area for ecotourism and provide a livelihood for local people. The other national park is the Montego Bay Marine Park, which aims to protect the offshore reef from urban waste, over-fishing and hillside erosion leading to excessive soil deposition. All coral reefs are now protected and the sale of both black and white coral is banned. Also forbidden is the hunting of the American crocodile, the yellow- and black-billed parrot and all species of sea turtle.

Diving and Marine Life

Although established in 1989, the Montego Bay Marine Park (see above) was officially opened in July 1992. It stretches from the E end of the airport to the Great River and contains three major ecosystems, seagrass bed, mangroves and coral reefs. Non-motorized watersports such as diving, snorkelling and glass bottom boat tours are permitted, but do not touch or remove anything.

There are several conservation groups involved in marine ecology. In St Ann, Friends of the Sea is a non-profit, non-governmental organization, formed in 1992, which concentrates on education and public awareness and draws attention to what is happening on land which might affect what happens underwater. The Negril Coral Reef Preservation Society was formed in 1990. It has installed permanent mooring buoys for recreational boats and works on educational programmes with schools with slide shows, videos and environmental fun days. Together with the National Resource Conservation Authority and the Negril community, it is working on form-

ing a marine park in conjunction with protected coastal and terrestrial habitats, aimed at protecting the coral reefs and improving fish stocks for fishermen.

Around Negril there are lots of reef dive sites and there is a variety of coral, sponges, invertebrates and other marine life. Sea turtles, octopus, starfish and lots of fish can be seen here. Off Montego Bay and Ocho Rios there is wall diving quite close to shore and a few wrecks. Off Port Antonio fish are attracted to fresh water springs which provide good feeding grounds.

Nearly all dive operators are based along the N coast at hotels. They must be licensed by the Jamaica Tourist Board and most are members of the Jamaica Association of Dive Operators (JADO). They offer introductory and certification courses at all levels. Dive packages are available with the hotels where they are located. Contact the Tourist Board for a full list of operators and map of dive sites.

In 1994 the Government announced that it is to privatize 21 beaches currently owned by nine parish councils. A 'tourism action plan' will select public beaches which can be made 'commercially viable'.

Sport

Apart from the sports associated with the main resorts (tennis, riding, diving, and other water sports), golf is played at the Constant Spring (18 holes, green fee US$10, T 924-1610) and Caymanas Clubs (18 holes, green fee US$20, T 923-7538) (Kingston), the Manchester Club (Mandeville, 9-hole, first opened in the middle of the 19th century, green fee US$5, T 962-2403), Sandals Golf and Country Club, formerly known as Upton (Ocho Rios, 18 holes, green fee US$30, golf and restaurant free for Sandals guests, T 974-2528), Super Clubs Runaway Bay Country Club (18 holes, green fee US$50, free for guests at *Jamaica Jamaica*, the only golf school open to the public, T 973-2561), Ironshore Country Club (another Sandals course, free for guests, 18 holes, green fee US$40, Tel 953-2381), Half Moon Club (advance booking necessary for this championship course, 18 holes, green fee US$85, T 953-2211) and Wyndham Rose Hall Golf Club (18 holes, green fee US$60, T 953-2650) (all E of Montego Bay) and Tryall Golf and Beach Club (green fee US$125, between Montego Bay and Negril). The Tryall course is probably the best known and hosts the annual Johnny Walker World Championship. Advance bookings are essential.

The island's main spectator sport is cricket. Test matches are played in Kingston. For details on matches ring Jamaica Cricket Association, T 967-0322. **Tennis** can be played at the Eric Bell Tennis Centre, Kingston. For track and field meets phone Jam Amateur Athletics Association. **Horse racing** at Caymanas Park, T 925-7780/925-3312, every Wednesday and Saturday and most public holidays. **Polo** is played on Saturday afternoons at Drax Hall, near Ocho Rios, entrance free. International tournaments at Chukka Cove, Runaway Bay and Caymanas Polo Club, Kingston. **Riding** lessons and trail rides also available at Chukka Cove, which has probably the best facilities, T 972-2506. Hotels can arrange riding with local stables too. For **Football** phone the Jamaica Football Federation, T 929-0484.

Festivals

Carnival has come only recently to Jamaica and is held around Easter time with floats, bands and mass dances, at various locations around the islands, attended by thousands. You can get very fit dancing for six hours a night for seven nights. Byron Lee, the leading Jamaican calypsonian, spends a lot of time in Trinidad over Carnival period and then brings the Trinidad calypsoes back to Jamaica. Some Trinidadian costumes

(although not the really spectacular ones) are recycled for Jamaica's carnival. The annual reggae festival, Sun Splash, is normally held in the middle of August, usually in Montego Bay, in the Bob Marley Centre. Also in August, the celebrations around Independence Day (1 August) last a week and are very colourful. The annual International Marlin Tournament at Port Antonio in October attracts anglers from all over the world and includes festivities other than fishing. The Tourist Board publishes a twice-yearly calendar of events which covers the whole spectrum of arts and sports festivals.

KINGSTON

The capital since 1870 and the island's commercial centre, **Kingston** has a population of over 750,000 (part of St Andrew's Parish is included in the metropolitan area, which helps swell the figure). It has one of the largest and best natural harbours in the world. Following the earthquake of 1907 much of the lower part of the city (Down Town) was rebuilt in concrete. On the waterfront there are some notable modern buildings including the Bank of Jamaica and the Jamaica Conference Centre which also houses the National Gallery. Most of the new shops and offices are scattered over a wide area of N and E Kingston. Crossroads and Halfway Tree are referred to as midtown areas. Many shopping plazas are further N again along the Constant Spring Road. The old racecourse was redeveloped in the 1960's as the New Kingston district, which contains most of the big hotels and many banks and financial institutions.

Among older buildings of note in the Down Town area are Gordon House (on Duke Street), which dates from the mid-18th century and houses the Jamaican legislature. Visitors are allowed into the Strangers' Gallery but must be suitably dressed (jackets for men and dresses for women). There is also the early 18th

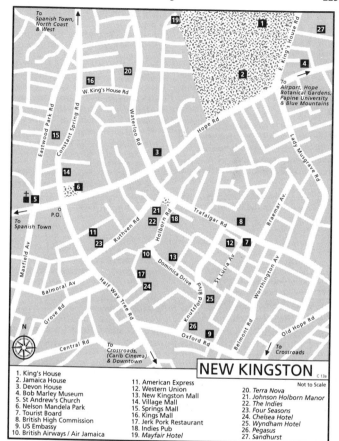

NEW KINGSTON

Not to Scale

C 13a

1. King's House
2. Jamaica House
3. Devon House
4. Bob Marley Museum
5. St Andrew's Church
6. Nelson Mandela Park
7. Tourist Board
8. British High Commission
9. US Embassy
10. British Airways / Air Jamaica

11. American Express
12. Western Union
13. New Kingston Mall
14. Village Mall
15. Springs Mall
16. Kings Mall
17. Jerk Pork Restaurant
18. Indies Pub
19. *Mayfair Hotel*

20. *Terra Nova*
21. *Johnson Holborn Manor*
22. *The Indies*
23. *Four Seasons*
24. *Chelsea Hotel*
25. *Wyndham Hotel*
26. *Pegasus*
27. *Sandhurst*

century parish church S of Parade, where Admiral Benbow is buried. Parade (Sir William Grant Park) is at the heart of the city centre; it is an open oasis amid the densely-packed surroundings. The name derives from the British soldiers' parades here during colonial rule. Now it is at the junction of the main E-W route through the Down Town area (Windward Road/East Queen Street-West Queen Street/Spanish Town Road) and King Street/Orange Street which runs N to

Cross Roads. At Cross Roads, the main route forks, left to Half Way Tree (recently renamed Nelson Mandela Park), straight on up Old Hope Road to Liguanea. These two roads encompass New Kingston.

The Parish Church at St Andrew at Half Way Tree dates from 1700. Half Way Tree, so called because it was a half-way stage on the road between the harbour and the hills, is a busy traffic junction which takes some negotiating in a car.

Hope Road, on the N edge of New Kingston, runs E from Half Way Tree. Just off it are Devon House, a former "great house", built by Jamaica's first millionaire in the 1880s, at the corner of Trafalgar and Hope Roads, now renovated, complete with antique furniture, with craft shops and refreshment stalls (small admission fee to look inside the main house, US$2 for a guided tour, but the shops and restaurants in the grounds are open to all and well worth a visit). Not far away is King's House, the official residence of the Governor-General and, nearby, Jamaica House, the Prime Minister's residence.

About 10 blocks E of Devon House, off Hope Road, is the Bob Marley Museum, entry US$3 including obligatory guided tour, which takes an hour, including 20-minute audio visual presentation. The house where Marley used to live traces back to his childhood and family, with paintings, newspaper cuttings, posters and other memorabilia. He died tragically of brain cancer at the age of 36, having survived a controversial assassination attempt (the bullet-holes in the walls have been left as a reminder). There is an Ethiopian restaurant in the garden serving some of his favourite vegetarian dishes. Marijuana plants grow profusely throughout the grounds and ganja is smoked openly in and around the restaurant and bar by staff. Photography is totally banned within the museum and grounds.

Further E, along Old Hope Road, are the Hope Botanical Gardens. The land was first acquired by Major Richard Hope in 1671 and 200 years later the Governor of Jamaica, Sir John Peter Grant, bought 200 acres and created a botanical gardens. In 1961 a zoo was opened alongside the gardens. After extensive damage in 1988 by Hurricane Gilbert, plans have been made to transform the small, traditional zoo into a showcase for the different natural habitats of Jamaica and its indigenous animals.

Local Information – Kingston

● Airport

The airport for Kingston is the Norman Manley (with restaurant, good tourist office, offering much information, maps and up-to-date hotel and guest house lists), 11 miles away, up to 30 mins' drive. There is an exchange desk in the arrivals lounge which will change cash or TCs (at a slightly lower rate than banks). You can also change back excess Jamaican dollars into US$ at the bank in the departure lounge, when you leave. There are several reasonable shops in the departure lounge which will accept Jamaican currency (except for duty free goods). Allow plenty of time to check in for a flight; there are 9 separate security, baggage or documentation checks before you board. Bus No SR8 leaves West Parade for the airport, US$0.35, but the service is infrequent, so allow for waiting time. To get to New Kingston by bus involves a change of bus (to No. 27) Down Town. The recognized service from town to airport is JUTA, taxi/minibus, which charges US$15 to New Kingston (taxi despatcher gives you a note of fare before you leave, can be shared).

● Where To Stay

A full list is available from Tourist Board: addresses in **Information for Visitors**. *Morgan's Harbour* is conveniently close to the airport (see Port Royal); all the other main hotels are in or near New Kingston: *Jamaica Pegasus* (Trust House Forte), 81 Knutsford Boulevard (PO Box 333, T 926-3690/9, F 929-5855) US$180-564 per room EP, 350 rooms; *Wyndham New Kingston*, 77 Knutsford Boulevard (PO Box 112, Kingston 10, T 926-5430/9, F 929-7439), 300 rooms, US$150-550d EP; *Terra Nova*, 17 Waterloo Road (T 926-2211, F 929-4933), US$88-99 per room EP, 20 rooms, popular with business travellers; *Mayfair*, 4 West King's House Circle (adjoining the Governor General's residence), PO Box 163, T 926-1610, F 926-7741, US$60-70d EP, beautiful setting, balconies look towards mountains, good rooms, food and service; *Four Seasons*, 18 Ruthven Road, PO Box 190, T 929-7655, F 929-5964, US$66-78, EP, run by Mrs Stocker, German, long-time knowledgeable resident, in a converted Edwardian house and gardens, good cooking, rec; and a number of others. Among the cheaper hotels is *The Indies*, 5 Holborn Road (T 926-2952), US$39-50d (television US$6 extra) EP, breakfast and lunch available, comfortable, pleasant patio, garden. Next door is the popular *Johnson Holborn Manor* (ex Mrs Johnson's Guest House), 3, Holborn Rd, US$40d with breakfast and shower, fan, clean, safe and quiet, very convenient for business in New Kingston, 3 good places to eat within 50 yards, luggage storage available, friendly, new annex, rec; *Ivy Whiteman's Guest House*, 14 Monterey Drive, T 927-5449, US$20pp bed and breakfast, very nice and helpful, clean, quiet, kitchen, beautiful garden; *Sandhurst*, 70 Sandhurst Crescent, Kingston 6 (T 927-7239), US$54-60d EP. *Retreat Guest House*, 8 Devon Road, T 926-2565, 4 rooms, US$15s, US$28d; *Chelsea Guest House*, Chelsea Ave-

nue, US$20d EP. About 25 mins from Kingston is *Ivor Guest House* and restaurant, Jack's Hill, Kingston 6, T/F 977-0033, 972-1460, high up in the hills overlooking Kingston and set in its own extensive grounds; 3 double bedrooms US$75s, US$90d CP, free transport to/from Kingston, charge for airport pickup, lunches US$12, dinners US$16 by reservation only, Helen Aitken, highly rec. About 40 minutes from Kingston is *Pine Grove*, see under Eastern Jamaica and the Mountains. The YMCA, opp Devon House on Hope Road, has a good swimming pool, many sports facilities and a cheaply priced restaurant. The Tourist Board can arrange Bed and Breakfast for you, which usually costs US$25-60 a night.

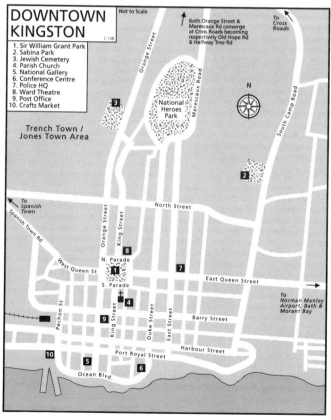

DOWNTOWN KINGSTON

C 138

1. Sir William Grant Park
2. Sabina Park
3. Jewish Cemetery
4. Parish Church
5. National Gallery
6. Conference Centre
7. Police HQ
8. Ward Theatre
9. Post Office
10. Crafts Market

Not to Scale

To Cross Roads

Both Orange Street & Marescaux Rd converge at Cross Roads becoming respectively Old Hope Rd & Halfway Tree Rd

Orange Street

Marescaux Road

National Heroes Park

N

South Camp Road

Trench Town / Jones Town Area

To Spanish Town

Spanish Town Rd

Orange Street

King Street

North Street

N. Parade

S. Parade

West Queen St

East Queen Street

To Norman Manley Airport, Bath & Morant Bay

Pechon St

King Street

Duke Street

East Street

Barry Street

Harbour Street

Port Royal Street

Ocean Blvd.

● **Where To Eat**

A great many places to eat in Down Town Kingston, New Kingston and the Half Way Tree area. There are plush establishments, inside and outside the hotels, and small places. The *Pegasus Hotel* does a good lunch and dinner special at US$5.50 and US$6.50 respectively. For the impecunious, meat patties may be had at US$0.25 each. Be warned that around the waterfront most places close at 1700. On Holborn Road, opp the *Indies Hotel* is the *Indies Pub*, which is reasonable, and next door is the *Three Little Bears* with patisserie attached, cheap cakes and coffee, excellent lobster in the main restaurant and quite palatable Jamaican wine, main course for lunch under US$4, evening meal US$8-18, buffet Fri and Sun excellent value at US$8; *Kohinoor*, 11 Holborn Road, very good Indian food, good service, nice atmosphere, US$20 for 3-course dinner and drinks for 2. On Chelsea Avenue (in the same area) is *Jerk Pork*, popular with locals. Nearby are Mexican and Indian restaurants, both very good but not cheap. The *Lychee Restaurant* in the New Kingston Shopping Mall, on Dominica Drive, serves excellent Chinese food, moderately priced, several other eating places here, from takeaway pattie bakery to upmarket restaurant, popular lunch spot for office workers; *Norma*, 8 Belmont Road, Kingston 5, T 929-4966, very good; *Heathers*, Haining Road, very pleasant to sit outside, Middle Eastern and Jamaican dishes, US$3.25-9; around the corner in Altamont Road, *Hot Pot*, very cheap, serves good Jamaican food in a pleasant patio, also a take-out box for just over US$1, difficult to find it without asking for directions. On Knutsford Boulevard there are lots of vans selling a satisfying lunch for US$1-1.50, often less, depending on what you eat. Many outlets of international takeaway chains all over the city, *Burger King* and *Kentucky Fried Chicken*, etc, as well as Jamaica's own variation, *Mothers*, also widespread. At *Devon House* (see page 226), there is a plush expensive restaurant, a reasonably-priced snack bar and delicious ice-cream at "*I Scream*".

● **Entertainment**

Amusements in Kingston include cinemas and theatres. There is a good School of Drama and several theatre and dance companies. Jamaica Dance Theatre is well known. Theatres include Ward Theatre (North Parade), Little Theatre (St Andrew), The Barn, New Kingston Playhouse, Green Gables, Creative Arts Centre. Watch the press for details of performances.

● **Night Life**

Most hotels have dancing at weekends. Clubs and discos include *Godfather's* in New Kingston, *Mingles* at *Courtleigh Hotel*, *Illusions* on Constant Spring Road, *24 Carat* at Manor Park, *Bleachers* on Constant Spring Road, all quite safe. So is *Peppers* on Waterloo Road, a good open air drinking spot, *the* place to go at night. *Devon House* is a good place for a quiet evening drink under the trees. *Centre Pole* at Mary Brown's Corner on Constant Spring Road is rowdy and raunchy but fairly safe too. Tourists are strongly advised not to try, unless they have Jamaican friends, to probe deeply into real Jamaican night life, at least in towns. For genuine local dances and songs, see the advertisements in the local press.

● **Bathing**

The swimming at Kingston is not very good. The sea at Gunboat beach, near the airport, is dirty. Better at Port Royal (see below). "Hellshire", S of Port Henderson, is a locals' favourite, but is difficult to reach. At Port Henderson is the *Rodney Arms* restaurant.

● **Shopping**

In Down Town Kingston, the Jamaica Crafts Market and many shops at W end of Port Royal Street have local crafts. Off West Queen Street is an interesting local market, selling fish, fruit and general produce. Down Town is where Jamaicans shop for bargains, but be careful, particularly in the market, it can be dangerous and you need to be thick skinned to get through, even if you do not get robbed. Most shops are in the plazas along Constant Spring Road and in Liguanea. There is a smart little shopping centre in New Kingston. Reggae music shops can be found close together along Orange Street, just N of Parade. Bookland is a good bookshop on Knutsford Boulevard, with a wide range of US magazines and newspapers and also The Times. There are various duty-free concessions for visitors. There is a laundry in Chelsea Avenue.

Port Royal and Spanish Town

Port Royal, the old naval base, lies across the harbour from Kingston, beyond the international airport, some 15 miles by excellent road. It can also be reached by boat from Victoria Pier; they leave every two hours, take 20 minutes and cost

US$0.15. On 7 June 1692 an earthquake hit E Jamaica, coursing along the Port Royal fault line and bringing with it massive tidal waves. The port, commercial area and harbour front were cut away and slid down the slope of the bay to rest on the sea bed, while much of the rest of the town was flooded for weeks. About 3,000 people died and the naval, merchant and fishing fleets were wrecked. The town was gradually rebuilt as a naval and military post. Nelson served here as a post-captain from 1779 to 1780 and commanded Fort Charles, key battery in the island's fortifications. Part of the ramparts, known as Nelson's Quarterdeck, still stands. St Peter's Church, though the restoration is unfortunate, is of historic interest, as is the Historical Archaeological Museum (admission US$0.30). The museum is little more than one room and the Fort Charles remains are more informative and substantive. *Morgan's Harbour* at Port Royal is a favourite holiday centre (T 924-8464, F 924-8562), with water ski-ing, a salt water swimming pool, beach cabins (rates US$135d, EP), a good sea-food restaurant, and dancing, closest hotel to airport. Boats may be hired for picnic bathing lunches on the numerous nearby cays or at Port Henderson.

Spanish Town, the former capital founded in 1534, some 14 miles W of Kingston by road or rail, is historically the most interesting of Jamaica's towns and in desperate need of funds for renovation. Bus S1 from Half Way Tree and S2 from Orange Street. Its English-style architecture dates from the 18th century. Well worth seeing are the Cathedral Church of St James, the oldest in the anglophone West Indies dating back to 1714; in need of renovation is the fine Georgian main square with, of special note, the ruins of the King's House built in 1762 and burnt down in 1925 (the façade has been rebuilt and now houses the Museum of Craft and Technology); a colonnade (paint peeling off) and statue commemorating Rodney's victory at the Battle of the Saints (see under Guadeloupe and Dominica); the House of Assembly and the Court House. There is a museum with interesting relics of Jamaican history and accurate portrayal of life of the country people. The park in the centre is overgrown with weeds and the gates are padlocked. Outside town, on the road to Kingston is the White Marl Arawak Museum, open Monday-Friday, 1000-1600, US$0.10. Restaurant: *Miami*, Cumberland Road, near the market area; food is delicious, especially the pumpkin soup.

EASTERN JAMAICA AND THE MOUNTAINS

Behind Kingston lie the *Blue Mountains* with Blue Mountain Peak rising to a height of 7,402 feet. This is undoubtedly one of the most spectacular and beautiful parts of Jamaica and an area which must be visited by keen bird watchers and botanists as also by those who like mountain walking. It is possible to explore some of the Blue Mountains by ordinary car from Kingston. Drive towards Papine and just before arriving there visit the Botanical Gardens at Hope with a splendid collection of orchids and tropical trees and plants. After leaving Papine and just after passing the *Blue Mountain Inn* (good restaurant and night club), turn left to Irish Town and thence to Newcastle, a Jamaica Defence Force training camp at 4,000 feet with magnificent views of Kingston and Port Royal. If energetic you may climb the road to Catherine's Peak directly behind the camp (about 1 hour for the moderately fit). Beyond Newcastle lies Hardwar Gap and Holywell National Park. This whole area is full of mountain trails with innumerable birds, some unique to Jamaica. The road then winds down to Buff Bay with a turning off to the right to Clydesdale and the Cinchona botanical garden.

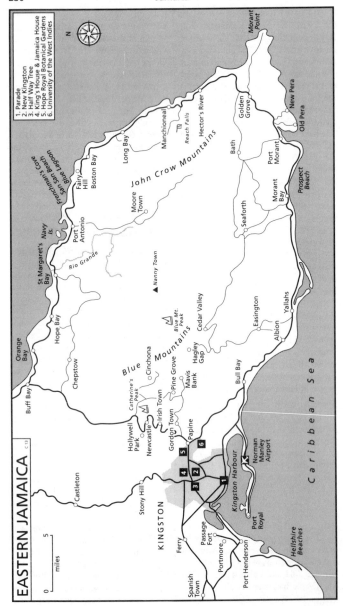

EASTERN JAMAICA C.13

1. Parade
2. New Kingston
3. Half Way Tree
4. King's House & Jamaica House
5. Hope Royal Botanical Gardens
6. University of the West Indies

miles
0   5

N

Morant Point

New Pera
Old Pera

Golden Grove

Reach Falls

Hector's River

Manchioneal

Bath

Port Morant

Long Bay

John Crow Mountains

Morant Bay

Prospect Beach

Boston Bay

Fairy Hill

Seaforth

Frenchman's Cove

San San Lagoon
Blue Lagoon

Moore Town

St Margaret's Bay

Navy Is.

Port Antonio

Rio Grande

▲ Nanny Town

Yallahs

Albion

Easington

Cedar Valley

Orange Bay

Buff Bay

Hope Bay

Chepstow

Blue Mountains

▲ Blue Mt. Peak

Cinchona

Hagley Gap

Mavis Bank

Bull Bay

Caribbean Sea

Castleton

Hollywell Park

Catherine's Peak

Newcastle

Pine Grove

Irish Town

Gordon Town

Papine

Stony Hill

KINGSTON

Kingston Harbour

Norman Manley Airport

Port Royal

Hellshire Beaches

Ferry

Passage Fort

Portmore

Port Henderson

Spanish Town

Unfortunately you are unlikely to be able to get an ordinary car past Clydesdale and perhaps not even to Clydesdale. From Clydesdale to Cinchona is about an hour's walk uphill but well worth it. If you wish to go towards Blue Mountain Peak, you drive straight on at Blue Mountain Inn (instead of turning left), through Gordon Town and on through Mavis Bank to Hagley Gap (if the Mahogany Vale ford is passable). Again, however, you will almost certainly not be able to get a car up to the starting point for the walk to the Peak. Public transport up the Blue Mountains is infrequent. There are some buses to Mavis Bank (some of which continue to Hagley Gap) from Papine on the outskirts of Kingston, but probably none on Sundays. Taxis from here to Mavis Bank about US$7.50. Four miles beyond Mavis Bank is the village of Hagley Gap, from where jeeps are available (ask for Errol) to go as far as Whitfield Hall (see below) for US$20. Only 4-wheel drive vehicles are advisable after Mavis Bank, and there are no petrol stations en route.

A much better solution is to stay at *Pine Grove Hotel* about half an hour's drive beyond Gordon Town. This consists of a series of cottages with central feeding and the atmosphere of a ski lodge. A double room with bathroom, kitchen area and couch costs about US$63 per night and meals are extra. The proprietors, Barbara and Radwick, live there and are extremely welcoming and helpful. Apart from giving advice they will also provide 4-wheel drive vehicles at very moderate cost to take guests to Cinchona and the start of the trail to Blue Mountain Peak, etc. They will also pick up guests from the airport (US$50) or from Kingston (address: *Pine Grove Hotel*, c/o 62 Duke Street, Kingston, T 922-8708, F 922-5895).

Another possible solution for the young and active is to contact Peter Bentley of SENSE Adventures at Box 216, Kingston 7, who is also President of the Jamaican Alternative Tourism, Camping and Hiking Association (JATCHA). The office is at Maya Lodge and Hiking Centre, Juba Spring, Peter's Rock Road, Jack's Hill, Kingston, T 927-2097, F 926-0727. Buses from Kingston leave from Jack's Hill Road opposite Texaco station, get off at Foxy's Pub. Contact can also be made through Stuarts Travel Service, 40 Union Square, Kingston, T 926-4291; Pauline Stuart is another pioneer of alternative tourism in Jamaica and is developing a 200-acre property on the Spanish River. SENSE Adventures specializes in hiking in the mountains, bird-watching, canoeing, rafting and camping, it lends out tents and other equipment and it is possible to stay or camp at Maya. Organized, island-wide trips range from $\frac{1}{2}$ day to 9 days (recommended for good guides, small parties and very good food). It can also provide information about all sorts of other activities, itinerary planning and cheap places to stay island wide; assistance with planning and reservations for over 150 properties is offered for US$15 including all the camping areas. A room or cabin at Maya Lodge costs US$30d, hostel style US$10pp, camping in own tent US$5pp, tent rental US$2.50 extra, restaurant, 15 acres of land in jungle setting, many paths for hikes around area, highly recommended.

Finally there is John Algrove who can be contacted at 8 Almon Crescent, Kingston 6, T 927-0986. He owns *Whitfield Hall Hostel* at the point where the Blue Mount Peak trail begins. It is a large wooden lodge with no electricity but gas for the kitchen and paraffin lamps, US$10 per person, capacity 40, some bunk beds, cold showers only. No meals but kitchen with stoves and crockery, etc, for guests' use. Very peaceful and homely with comfortable lounge, log fire and library (visitors' books dating back to the 1950's), highly recommended, staff very friendly and helpful. If the hostel is full, camping is permitted, US$5 per person.

You can either take a bus to Mount Charles from where it is a steep 4-mile walk to Whitfield Hall, or you can walk from Hagley Gap, or ask Mr Algrove to arrange transport from Mavis Bank, US$20 in a jeep for maximum 6 passengers, or US$40 all the way to/from Kingston. The hostel can also arrange mules and guide to the peak and to Cinchona, another mountain.

The walk to Blue Mountain Peak (6½ miles from Whitfield Hall) takes 3 to 4 hours up and 2 to 3 hours down. The first part is the steepest. Some start very early in the morning in the hope of watching the sunrise from the Peak. As often as not, though, the Peak is shrouded in cloud and rain in the early morning. The path winds through a fascinating variety of vegetation, coffee groves and banana plantations on the lower, S slopes, to tree ferns and dwarf forest near the summit (with some explanatory and mileage signposts). The doctor bird (national bird of Jamaica) is quite common, a beautiful swallow-tailed hummingbird. Quite hard to spot at first but recognizable by its loud buzz, especially near the many flowering bushes. You must take your own food and torch, sweater and rainproof if you set out in the darkness. There are two huts on the Peak where one can overnight in some discomfort (empty concrete buildings with no door). There is a campsite with cabins, water and a shower at Portland Gap, about one hour up.

Bath at the E end of the island is another place from which one can make attractive trips into the **John Crow Mountains** (named after the ubiquitous turkey buzzards). There is a modest but cheap hotel (*Bath Spa*) dating from 1727 whose main attraction is that it contains natural hot water spring baths which are most relaxing at the end of a long day. There are two passes above Bath, called the Cuna Cuna Pass and the Cornpuss Gap, which lead down to the source of the Rio Grande River on the N slopes of

the mountain range. Both are tough going particularly the Cornpuss Gap. It is absolutely essential to take a local guide. The N slopes of the mountain range are the home of the unique and extremely rare Jamaican butterfly, *papilio homerus*, a large black and yellow swallowtail. It can best be seen in May/June. Nearby, but not easily accessible, is the magnificent Pera beach between Port Morant and Morant Lighthouse. Near the lighthouse is another good beach but, like nearly all the beaches along the E coast round to Port Antonio, there is a dangerous undertow in certain spots. *Goldfinger's Guesthouse* in Morant Bay, US$100d, cars to rent, clean, friendly, good cooking. *Golden Shore Beach Hotel*, 2 miles E of Morant Bay, 15 rooms, 8 with a/c, 7 with fan, bathrooms, TV, hot water, bar, restaurant, T 982-9657, Windward Drive, PO Box 8 Lyssons, St Thomas. Just before reaching Manchioneal from Bath there is a road off to the left which leads to the Reach Falls or Manchioneal Falls (about 3 miles). Well worth a visit if you have a car or are prepared to walk (45 minutes with views of rolling forested hills) from the main road. No facilities at the Falls, there may be an entry charge of US$0.50. Pretty tiers of smooth boulders, the highest fall about 15 feet, through a lush, green gorge. Buses from main road to Port Antonio infrequent, every 1-2 hours. Further NW along the coast from Manchioneal are *Herman's Holiday Homes*, H Doswell, Long Bay, Portland, 3 minutes to the beach, US$15 pp, nice, clean, comfortable, helpful (also, 2 bedroom cottage, US$270 a week per couple). Several other cottages and guesthouses have been built on the beach at Long Bay, including *Rose Hill Cottage*, *Casa Pecaro*, *Seascape*, *Nirvana*, *Coconut Isle* and *Rolling Surf* (T 0993 2856, Desmond Goldbourne in Port Antonio).

Once the major banana port where many of the island's first tourists arrived on banana boats, **Port Antonio** dates back to the 16th century. Its prosperity has for many years been in gentle decline, but it has an atmosphere unlike any other town in Jamaica with some superb old public buildings. The rainfall in this part of the island is very high and in consequence the vegetation very lush. Boston Bay, Fairy Hill Beach, San San Beach, the Blue Lagoon (also known as the Blue Hole) and Frenchman's Cave Beach are notable beauty spots to the E of the town. Boston Bay is renowned for its local jerk food pits; several unnamed places by the roadside serving hot spicy chicken, pork or fish, chopped up and wrapped in paper, cooked on planks over a pit of hot coals, very good and tasty. Also worth visiting is Nonsuch Cave, a few miles to the SE, where there are fossils and evidence of Arawak occupation, Somerset Falls and Folly, an elaborate, turn-of-the-century mansion built in the style of Roman and Greek architecture, now in ruins (partly because the millionaire American's wife took an instant dislike to it). The Folly is about half an hour's walk around the bay from the town. Take a right fork off the path before going into a clump of trees on the peninsula (leading towards lighthouse inside military camp). It is a ghostly, crumbling old mansion in an open field with lovely views shared with grazing cows. A makeshift bar has been set up inside and it looks as though squatters have moved in. There is no public transport to Nonsuch Cave, return taxi fare US$10 including waiting time. Entry US$5, stalactites, gift shop and lunch area. For Somerset Falls, take a bus to Buff Bay (any westbound Kingston bus) and walk 5 minutes from there, entry US$1.

In the harbour it is possible to visit the 68-acre Navy Island, at one time owned by Errol Flynn, which has beaches (one nudist) and a moderately expensive restaurant. Return boat fare US$2, from jetty on West Street near Musgrave Market, about every hour from 0900-1800. Accommodation US$100-180d EP in rooms or individual villas. Restaurant and bar open to non-guests, open view of bay. 'Errol Flynn Gallery' has display of movie stills and screenings of his golden oldies. The beaches on the island all belong to the resort but are open to non-guests. Snorkelling available (at the nudist beach), US$2 for half-day hire, but there are strong currents and not many fish. Many other sports and other activities on offer, including a complete wedding ceremony in the resort chapel. Reservations, T 993-2667, F 993-2041.

Flynn also saw the potential as a tourist attraction for the bamboo rafts which used to bring bananas down the Rio Grande River. Expert raftsmen now take tourists on these rafts down the river. One boatman is Keith Allen, with a registered licence, who can be contacted in Port Antonio at the Huntress Marina, but if you just turn up at Berrydale there are always rafters ready and willing to take you. Each raft (US$40 per trip from the ticket office, but if you arrive before it opens at 0800 you can sometimes negotiate a fare with a rafter) takes two passengers and the trip takes $1\frac{1}{2}$-2 hours (depending on the river flow) through magnificent scenery and with an opportunity to stop en route. An unforgettable experience; a driver will take your car down from the point of embarkation to the point of arrival. This is known as Rafter's Rest and is on the main coastal road. Recommended as a place to have a moderately priced lunch or drink in pleasant surroundings even if you are not proposing to raft. The return taxi fare is US$10, there are also buses, US$0.25, to Berrydale, the setting-off point, though infrequent. Returning from St Margaret's, downstream, is easier as there are plenty of buses passing between Annotto Bay and Port Antonio. The Rio Grande valley is also well worth exploring, including a trip to the Maroons (descendants of escaped slaves) at Moore Town, but the roads are rough and public transport minimal. Ask for Colonel Harris there who is the leader of the Maroons and is recommended for guided tours. No telephone contact and no accommodation, return taxi fare US$15. To the W of the Rio Grande lie the N slopes of the Blue Mountains, many parts of which are still virtually unexplored. Nanny Town, the home of the Maroons, was destroyed by the British in 1734 and then "lost" until the 1960s. There is recent archaeological evidence at Nanny Town to suggest that the Maroons originally took to the mountains and lived with (and possibly later absorbed) Arawak peoples. There have been some dramatic discoveries of Arawak wooden carvings which are now on display at the National Gallery.

Local Information – Port Antonio
● Where To Stay
Two upmarket hotels are *Trident Villas and Hotel*, US$350-550, PO Box 118, T 993-2602/2705, F 993-2590, and *Jamaica Palace*, rates on request, PO Box 277, T 993-2020, F 993-3459. On Titchfield Hill, 5 mins' walk from the town are *De Montevin Lodge*, 21 Fort George Street (PO Box 85, T 993-2604), US$36d inc breakfast, shared bath, more expensive rooms have private bath, charming and cosy old Victorian house, restaurant serves set meals, US$8-10, very good value,no credit cards, and *Ivanhoe* nearby US$10d EP shared bath, patio with bay view. Opp the *De Montevin* also on Titchfield Hill is *Sunnyside Guest House*, US$10d EP shared bath, basic but quite clean, quiet, rec and good views of the bay. Several nearby private houses also take guests. In the town centre are *Hope View Guest House*, 26 Harbour Street, T 993-3040. US$10d EP with bath, small, friendly; *Triff's Inn*, 1 Bridge Street, T 993-2162, F 993-2062, rates on application, modern, clean, pleasant lounge area; on top of a hill overlooking both bays is *Bonnie View*, set in its own working plantation, PO Box 82, T 993-2752, F 993-2862, US$72-78d EP (depending on room and season), charming rooms, many with excellent views, bar and restaurant, very good meals, probably the best place to stay in town, horse riding and other activities also available. Outside Port Antonio on the Kingston road are *Goblin Villas*, US$45, kitchen, no restaurant; *Dragon Bay*, US$45, beach, tennis, good restaurant, rec, T 993-3281/2, F 993-3284.

Frenchman's Cove at San San, once one of the most luxurious and expensive hotels in the world, closed for refurbishment under new management since 1990, but there is still access to the beach costing about US$3.

● Where to Eat
Huntress Marina on a jetty in the harbour, mainly a bar popular with yachting fraternity, but good breakfast-evening meals also served, cold beer; *Coronation Bakery*, near Musgrave Market on West Street, good for cheap patties and spice buns; *Cream World*, good for ice-cream, cakes and cheap snacks; *Stop Group Jerk Centre* on the bay out of town towards the folly, bar and jerk pork, chicken and fish, also music and dance until late.

● Cinema
Shows recent films, 2 for US$1.

● Post Office
Located by the clock tower in town centre.

● Tourist Office
Upstairs in shopping precinct on Harbour Street, quite helpful but not knowledgeable about local buses ("soon come"), which leave regularly when full, but at uncertain hours, from sea-front behind Texaco station.

Roads into the interior

Between Port Antonio and the *Buff Bay* area there are several roads into the interior from such places as Hope Bay and Orange Bay. It's worth a detour if you have a car, but well off the beaten track and public transport is minimal. However, just to the E of Buff Bay there is a new development called Crystal Springs with beautifully laid out gardens, a variety of fish in the clear waters of the streams, an aviary, a bird sanctuary and masses of orchids. There is a moderately priced restaurant, three cottages to rent (US$100 for 4 people maximum, more one-bedroom bungalows being built) and camping sites (tent can be rented). Take any bus between Port Antonio and Kingston (US$0.40, about 45 minutes from Port Antonio), signposted at a turn-off between Orange Bay and Buff Bay (marked Spring Garden on Discover Jamaica road map). About 1½ miles along flat paved road there is a small swimming pool surrounded by palms and flowering tropical plants. An idyllic spot, not busy during the week. Admission about US$1.50 including a complimentary drink of coconut water. Well worth a visit and a good base for exploring the foothills of the Blue Mountains. Contact Pauline Stuart of Stuarts Travel Service, 40 Union Square, Kingston, T 926-4291 (or King's Plaza, Kingston 10, T 929-4222), for up to date information. From Crystal Springs the road goes on to Chepstow and thence to Claverty Cottage and Thompson Gap; spectacular scenery, waterfalls in the valleys and very remote. It is possible to walk from Thompson Gap over the Blue Mountains via Morces Gap and down to Clydesdale, but this is a full day's trip and only to be undertaken with an experienced local guide and there is a problem of getting transport to meet you at Clydesdale. It is also possible to take a bus for part of the way up the Buff Bay valley and then walk on either to Clydesdale or over the Hardwar Gap to Newcastle. Both very long trips and only for the really fit.

THE NORTH COAST

The Kingston to Port Maria road (the Junction Road) passes through Castleton Gardens (in a very tranquil setting, well worth a visit by botanists, ask Roy Bennett to be your guide if available). The journey takes about two hours and there are plenty of minibuses. *Port Maria* itself is a sleepy and decaying old banana port but not without charm and lots of goats. East of Port Maria in Robin's Bay there is a camping and cottage resort, *Sonrise Retreat* (formerly Strawberry Fields), basic cabins and tent sites, bath house, T/F 996-2351, two miles from village, transport essential. A few miles to the W of Port Maria lies the attractive looking *Casa Maria* hotel which has seen better days, US$74-93d EP, PO Box 10, T 994-2323, F 994-2324. Close by the hotel is *Firefly*, Noel Coward's Jamaican home, now owned by the Jamaican National Trust. Worth a visit if only for the magnificent view (entrance fee about US$1). Noel Coward's other property, *Blue Harbour*, is half a mile from the hotel, and is where he used to entertain film stars, royalty etc. It is now a guest house with accommodation for up to 15 in the 2-bedroomed Villa Grande, the 1-bedroomed Villa Chica and the 4-roomed Villa Rose, all much as Coward left it although there has been some hurricane damage. Prices range from US$25-60pp depending on season and number of guests, excellent Jamaican cooking or use of kitchen, fans, salt water pool, coral beach, good snorkelling and scuba, gardens, lovely views, PO Box 50, Port Maria, St Mary, T 994-2262 or in USA T 505-586-1244. At Galina, about 2 miles further W, there is the prominently signposted *Blue Rock Estate Guest House* on the cliff edge. It was badly damaged by Hurricane Gilbert and is still pretty shambolic but it has a certain charm and a friendly Jamaican atmosphere. Recommended for young, low budget visitors, US$20d with shower, food prices to match, owner's wife is Canadian. Ten minutes further on by car lies Oracabessa, another old banana port with a half completed marina and Golden Eye, the house where Ian Fleming wrote all the James Bond books. To the W of Oracabessa is Boscobel, where the air strip for Ocho Rios is located. Opposite the air strip are numerous houses for rent.

On a bay sheltered by reefs and surrounded by coconut groves, sugar cane and fruit plantations, is **Ocho Rios**, which has become increasingly popular, with many cruise ships making a stop here. It is 64 miles E of Montego Bay, and claims some of the best beaches on the island. The beach in town is safe and well-organized with facilities, 200 yards from Main Street where most of the shops and vehicle hire companies can be found. Shaw gardens are an easy walk from the town centre, being up the hill on the edge of town. Nice gardens, recommended, entrance US$2. The scenery of the surrounding area is an added attraction. Most spectacular are the beauty spots of Fern Gully, a marvel of unspoilt tropical vegetation, Roaring River Falls, which has been partially exploited for hydroelectric power, and Dunn's River Falls, tumbling into the Caribbean with invigorating salt and fresh water bathing at its foot. Worth a visit, take 5-minute bus ride, US$0.20, from Ocho Rios, or one hour's drive from Montego Bay, entry fee US$5, locker US$1, bath shoes US$5 (rental) but not necessary if you move with care. (Beware of pseudo guides who hang around and take you somewhere totally different, then try to sell you marijuana). The minibus from Kingston to Ochos Rios costs US$2 and follows a spectacular route, up the gorge of the Rio Cobre, then across Mount Diablo. Faith's Pen, right on the top, is an enormous collection of huts selling food and drink, great for a stop but you may not get on another bus as they normally pass full. The last section of road whizzes round a series of blind corners as you go through Fern Gully. Driving time is 1 hour 50 minutes once the bus has started.

Historical attractions in the area include Sevilla Nueva, some nine miles to the W, which was where the Spanish first settled in 1509. The ruins of the fort still remain. The site is being investigated by the University of California at Los Angeles and the Spanish Government and it was hoped to include it in the 1992 anniversary celebrations of Columbus' landing in the New World. Offshore, marine archaeologists, from the Institute of Nautical Archaeology at Texas A & M University, are investigating the St Ann's Bay area for sunken ships. Salvaged timbers are believed to have come from two disabled caravels, the *Capitana* and the *Santiago de Palos*, abandoned at Sevilla Nueva probably in 1503 during Columbus' last visit to Jamaica. There are numerous

plantation tours available to tourists all along the N coast. Details are widely publicized. Probably the most attractive, informative and certainly most accessible, is the Prospect Plantation Tour (T 974-2058), a short distance to the E of Ocho Rios nearly opposite the *Sans Souci Hotel*. Horseback riding also available there. Harmony Hall art gallery just E of Ocho Rios is worth a visit.

Beautifully sited, near Ocho Rios, is the *Sandals Golf and Country Club* (formerly Upton, all-inclusive, really good food and good value for people who want to be packaged): golf links (US$30 green fee), tennis, riding and swimming. The *Lion's Den* is a friendly club frequented by Rastafarians; rooms available, good food, clean. West of Ocho Rios is Mammee beach, which is beautiful and less crowded than Ocho Rios, though there is no shade there. There is much fashionable night life in and around Ocho Rios.

Local information
● Where To Stay
The Tourist Board lists many hotels and resorts: *Jamaica Inn*, PO Box 1, T 974-2514, F 974-2449, US$385-435d FAP; *Plantation Inn*, PO Box 2, T 974-5601, F 974-5912, US$191d EP, US$301d MAP, watersports; and *Sans Souci Hotel*, PO Box 103, T 974-2353, F 974-2544, US$362-616d EP. Mid-price inns include *Hibiscus Lodge*, 88 Main Street, PO Box 52, T 974-2676, F 974-1874, US$80-88d CP, pool, jacuzzi, tennis. *Jeff's House*, 10 Main Street, T 974-2664, owned by Jeffrey and Pearl McCoy, US$42-45d including tax, a/c, restaurant good, clean, cheap, kind and helpful, no credit cards; *Big Daddy's Pier View Apartment Motel*, 19 Main Street, T 974-2607, US$40-60d, clean, quiet, good service, pool with sundeck, ask to see rooms, not all same size, avoid ones near noisy fountain, close to beach and town centre; *Hunter's Inn*, 86 Main Street, T 974-5627, Swedish proprietors, rec, fan, bathroom, US$20d, clean, restaurant; about 1 mile from town centre, you can **camp** at Milford Falls, US$10-15, right by the waterfall, take Kingston road out of Ocho Rios, turn right at sign to Shaw Park Gardens then fork left up Milford Road, stop at **George Barnes' shop** on right, he will take you there and

provide you with information, food and drink, he has a tent or a rustic cabin with 1 bed to rent, nice place to get away from city hustle; the *Hummingbird Haven*, 2 miles E of Ocho Rios Clock Tower on the main highway, near White River, PO Box 95, Ocho Rios, T 974-5188, F 974-2559, a lovely campsite (US$5d, 20 bare sites) with basic cabins (US$20, twin beds, fan, hot water) and a restaurant, very relaxed, friendly, excellent food, mosquito coils necessary, available on request. There are 2 all-inclusive resorts E of Ocho Rios which are very good if you want that sort of holiday: *Boscobel Beach* is set up for family holidays (PO Box 63, T 975-7330, F 975-7370), *Couples* is for honeymooners (T 975-4271, F 975-4439). The new *Jamaica Grande* (PO Box 100, T 974-2201/9) has received lots of favourable publicity but has been described to us as a barracks and the food criticized, 720 rooms, US$205-225 EP, US$340-360 all-inclusive. *Club Jamaica Beach Resort* another all-inclusive is on Turtle Beach in Ocho Rios, US$145-165pp double occupancy winter, US$110 summer, watersports, diving, lots of games, exercise facilities, nightclub, PO Box 342, T 974-6632, F 974-6644. There are also *Sandals Ocho Rios*, Main Street, PO Box 771, T 974-5691/6, F 974-5700, US$410-500 per couple, and *Sandals Dunn's River*, Mammee Bay, T 972-0563/71, F 972-1611, US$3,035-4,600 a week. West of Ocho Rios, about 1½ miles W of St Ann's Bay town in an area called Seville Heights is *Joyce's Holiday Resort*, 40 Hibiscus Drive, T 972-1228, US$10pp for room with shared bath in family home, clean, safe, meals can be arranged, rec.

● **Where To Eat**
On Main Street are *The Lobsterpot*, US$12-15 for lobster supper, very good, and *Jerk Pork*, same price for barbequed pork, fish or chicken; *Shakey's Pizza*, Main Street, nice bar and patio, fast, friendly service, smallest pizza from US$5.50. *Bill's Place* on Main Street is good for a drink or two. *The Acropolis* night club is lively and fairly safe.

● **Watersports**
Scuba diving with Sea and Dive Jamaica, T 972-2162; Fantasea, T 974-2353; Sun Divers Watersport, T 973-3509.

West to Falmouth

Continuing W along the coast is *Runaway Bay*, an attractive and friendly re-sort. It is named for the Spanish governor Ysasi, who left quickly for Cuba in a canoe when he saw the English coming. Only five miles away is Discovery Bay where Columbus made his first landing. From Runaway Bay, the Runaway Caves can be visited with a boat ride on the underground lake in the Green Grotto. Among the hotels in this area is the *Runaway Bay HEART Country Club* (PO Box 98, T 973-2671, F 973-2693), which is a hotel training centre (US$50s, US$80d EP). The *Ambiance Jamaica*, T 973-2066, F 973-2067, US$106-160d with breakfast, has been described as adequate for fine weather but lacking in indoor facilities when it rains. Golf is available at Super Club's Runaway Bay Golf Club, where green fees are US$50. There are several all-inclusive resorts here too, including *Jamaica Jamaica*, *Eaton Hall Beach Hotel*, and *Franklyn D Resort*.

Falmouth is a charming small town about 20 miles E of Montego Bay. It has a fine colonial court house (restored inside), a church, some 18th century houses, and Antonio's, a famous place to buy beach shirts. There is good fishing (tarpon and kingfish) at the mouth of the Martha Brae, near Falmouth, and no licence is required. It is possible to go rafting from Martha Brae village. Expert rafters guide the craft for the 1-hour trip to the coast. Jamaica Swamp Safaris (a crocodile farm) has a bar and restaurant. Some 10 miles inland is the 18th century plantation guest house of Good Hope amongst coconut palms (T 954-3289): de luxe accommodation in the superb setting of a working plantation, as well as day tours and horse riding – some of the best riding in Jamaica – and its own beach on the coast.

THE COCKPIT COUNTRY

This is a strange and virtually uninhabited area to the S of Falmouth and to the SW of Montego Bay. It consists of a seemingly endless succession of high bumps made of limestone rock. The tourist office and hotels in Montego Bay organize day trips to Maroon Town (no longer occupied by Maroons) and Accompong, the headquarters of the Maroons who live in the Cockpit Country area. Older locals can accurately describe what happened at the last battle between the Maroons and the British forces. Ask to see the "Wondrous Caves" at Elderslie near Accompong. If you have a car take the road on the E side of the Cockpit Country from Duncans (near Falmouth) to Clark's Town. From there the road deteriorates to a track, impassable after a few miles even for 4WD vehicles, to Barbecue Bottom and on to Albert town. The views from Barbecue Bottom are truly spectacular (the track is high above the Bottom) and this is wonderful birding country. If you wish to go on foot into the Cockpit Country make your way, either by car or on foot (no public transport), to the Windsor Caves due S of Falmouth. They are full of bats which make a spectacular mass exit from the caves at dusk. There are local guides to hand. The underground rivers in the caves (as elsewhere in much of Jamaica) run for miles, but are only for the experienced and properly equipped potholer. There is a locally published book called *Jamaica Underground* but the local caving club seems moribund at the time of writing. Mr Stephenson is a guide who has been recommended at the town of Quick Step; many caves and good walks in the area. It is possible to walk from the Windsor Caves across the middle of the Cockpit Country to Troy on the S side (about eight hours). It is essential to have a local guide and to make a preliminary trip to the Windsor Caves to engage him. Convince yourself that he really does know the way because these days this crossing is very rarely made even by the locals. It is also vastly preferable to be met with transport at Troy because you will still be in a pretty remote area.

MONTEGO BAY AND WESTERN JAMAICA

About 120 miles from Kingston by road or rail, situated on the NW coast, is *Montego Bay*, Jamaica's principal tourist centre with all possible watersport amenities. It has superb natural features, sunshine most of the year round, a beautiful coastline with miles of white sand and deep blue water never too cold for bathing (20°-26°C average temperature) and gentle winds which make sailing a favourite sport. There are underwater coral gardens in a sea so clear that they can be seen without effort from glass-bottomed boats at the Doctor's Cave, which is also the social centre of beach life (there is an admission charge). Scuba diving can be arranged through Seaworld, T 953-2180; Poseidon Nemrod Club, T 952-3624; Montego Bay Divers, T 952-4874. A single dive costs about US$45, a snorkelling trip US$25. Montego Bay caters also for the rich and sophisticated. Visitors enjoy the same duty-free concessions as in Kingston. Gloucester Avenue, by Doctor's Cave, is one of the busiest streets for tourists, lined with duty-free shops, souvenir arcades and several restaurants and hotels. Constant importuning in the town's streets is a major problem.

Of interest to the sightseer are an old British fort (Fort Montego, landscaped gardens and crafts market) and the 18th century church of St James in Montego Bay (restored after earthquake damage in 1957). There are a few Georgian buildings, such as the *Town House Restaurant*, 16 Church Street (good local art gallery next door), and the Georgian Court at the corner of Union and Orange Streets. The centre of town is Sam Sharpe Square, named after the slave who led a rebellion in 1831-2.

If you are staying in town, rather than at the hotel strip, there are beaches close by, either public ones with no services or private (US$0.50-2.00 admission) with food, drinks, tennis, boat hire, snorkelling, shower, changing rooms etc. Walk from the traffic circle in the middle of town towards the hotels and the beach will be on your right.

Local Information – Montego Bay
● Airport

The Donald Sangster international airport is only 2 miles from the town centre. For those landing here who want to go to Kingston,

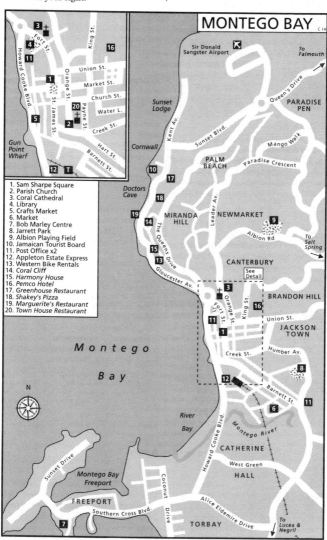

MONTEGO BAY

1. Sam Sharpe Square
2. Parish Church
3. Coral Cathedral
4. Library
5. Crafts Market
6. Market
7. Bob Marley Centre
8. Jarrett Park
9. Albion Playing Field
10. Jamaican Tourist Board
11. Post Office x2
12. Appleton Estate Express
13. Western Bike Rentals
14. Coral Cliff
15. Harmony House
16. Pemco Hotel
17. Greenhouse Restaurant
18. Shakey's Pizza
19. Marguerite's Restaurant
20. Town House Restaurant

there is a transfer service by Martins minibus which takes 5 hours. It is also possible to get to the Norman Manley airport, Kingston, by taking the minibus from the town centre to Pechon Street, Kingston, from where the airport buses leave; US$4.50, 3 hours.

● **Transport**
There is no need to take the expensive tourist buses, except that the regular buses get crowded. The regular buses are fast, very frequent and cheap, about US$2 from Montego Bay to Negril with a 30-second transfer in Lucea. Buses from Kingston depart from Pechon Street, near the railway station, roughly every hour from 0600 to 1500, US$2.80. It is possible to get to Montego Bay from Port Antonio all along the N coast, a scenic journey involving changes in Annotto Bay (then shared taxi, US$1 per person, mad rush to squeeze into clapped-out Ladas, the locals give no quarter to slow tourists), Port Maria US$1, and Ocho Rios. Ochos Rios-Montego Bay by bus takes 2 hours, US$1.50. UTAS Tours, T 952-3820, 979-0684, F 979-3465, offer 12-hr day trip to Kingston via Dunns River Falls and Ocho Rios, US$60 for driver in a/c car; also 9-hr tour to Negril, US$21, with sunset drink at Rick's Cafe, Negril. **Bicycle** rentals through Western Bike Rentals and Sales Ltd, 27 Gloucester Avenue, T 952-0185, US$8/24 hours, bikes a bit battered.

● **Where To Stay**
There are over 40 hotels, guest houses and apartment hotels listed by the Tourist Board and many more which are not. There are several large , lavish resorts in the area, including a 516-room *Holiday Inn* and the 420-room *Seawind Beach Resort*, while Sandals have 3 all-inclusive resorts, *Sandals Inn*, *Sandals Montego Bay* and *Sandals Royal Caribbean*. The weekly rate at these places often exceeds US$2,000. The *Coral Cliff*, 165 Gloucester Avenue, PO Box 253, T 952-4130, F 952-6532 (a US$7 cab ride from the airport) is rec, with a beautiful veranda, restaurant and friendly service, US$58-64d EP; also on Gloucester Avenue, *Harmony House Hotel*, proprietor Mr Mack, US$40d, friendly, basic rooms, 5 mins' walk from Doctor's Cave Beach and Duty Free shops; *The Guest House*, 29 Gloucester Avenue, T 952-3121, F 979 3176, US$60, 4 bedrooms in beautiful house with wide balcony overlooking sunset in the bay, run by Canadian consul and Englishman who also arrange villas; *Montego Bay Club*,

Gloucester Avenue, T 952-4310, F 952-4639, dominant 12-storey apartment hotel in centre of tourist area overlooking Doctor's Cave Beach, US$60, rec; *Ocean View Guest House*, 26 Sunset Boulevard, PO Box 210 (T 952-2662), 10 mins' easy walk from the airport, US$26s, US$37-39d winter, US$19s, US$27d summer, MAP US$10 on demand, many rooms overlook the bay, all clean, with bath, back-breaking mattresses (on arrival, ask tourist board to phone the hotel who will arrange free transport from the airport); *Ridgeway Guest House*, 34 Queen's Drive, PO Box 1237, (T 952-2709) 5 mins' walk from airport, US$20-27.50d CP, with bath and fan, friendly, clean, family atmosphere (cheaper rates for longer stays). The *View Guest House*, Jarrett Terrace, T 952-3175, US$30d, homely atmosphere, some rooms with excellent view over bay, very friendly staff, swimming pool, one of the cheapest, highly rec; *Mrs Craig's Guest House*, on Church Street, near Police Station, no sign, ask directions, noisy with uncomfortable mattresses and terrible showers but safe and cheap at US$25; *Linkage Guest House*, Church Street, also near the Police Station, fan, shared bath, US$15-20d, breakfast; *Pemco Hotel*, Union Street, on the way up to Brandon Hill, 20 mins' walk from Doctor's Cave Beach, can arrange accommodation at good rates (T 952-4000, Mr Samuel Clarke); *Mountainside Guest House*, Queen's Drive, near the airport, behind the *Cotton Tree Restaurant*, enquire at the restaurant, very pleasant, clean rooms, balcony, good views, private bathroom, mosquito coils provided, noisy in early evening because of restaurant, but quiet at night, US$30s, US$35d, friendly and helpful. *Datura Villa*, in hills overlooking Montego Bay, T (508) 580-9974 in USA, exquisite location, staff and food rec, ask for the master bedroom, Mr Chisholm can be contracted as guide/chauffeur at US$100/day for 2-3 couples. There is a YMCA at Mount Salem with sports facilities available to members.

● **Where To Eat**
On the way into town from the airport there are several reasonably-priced restaurants; rec is the *Pork Pit* in pleasant open-air garden on Kent Avenue, overlooks Cornwall Beach, jerk chicken, pork and ribs sold by weight, US$8/lb, service basic, and the *Toby Inn*, very good for cheap barbequed chicken and pork, cheap drinks, live band, romantic atmosphere, rec;

Cotton Tree, Queen's Drive, near airport, free pick-up service, mainly seafood but very good vegetarian food on request, T 952-5329 for reservation; *Orlan Caribe Vegetarian Restaurant*, 71 Barnett Street, tidy, comfortable, low prices, sole vegetarian restaurant. There are several restaurants along Gloucester Avenue, including *Shakey's*, for pizza and breakfasts (deliveries, T 952-2665), not too good; *Walter's Bar and Grill*, 39 Gloucester Avenue, T 952-9391, local food, nice garden, good value; *The Greenhouse*, opp St James Place shopping arcade, good food and inexpensive; *Cascade*, in the *Hotel Pelican*, (T 952-3171), seafood specialities at moderate prices; *Marguerite's*, on the sea-front, has 2 restaurants, one posh with a/c and another simpler next door on a patio; *Le Chalet*, 32 Gloucester Avenue, T 952-5240, clean, friendly, Chinese, Jamaican, European menu at ¼ price of neighbouring *Pelican* and *Marguerite's*, free hotel transfers; *Town House* (see above), T 952-2660, highly rec for mildly pungent stuffed lobster US$30, other dishes also good, US$12.50-27. Most restaurants are happy for guests to bring their own wine and will provide chillers and glasses.

● **Night Clubs**

The Cave (at *Seawinds Hotel*, drinks reasonable, beer and spirits US$2), at *Casa Montego Hotel*, *The Rum Barrel*, the *Cellar* and the *Reef Club*. Many others. Every Mon Gloucester Avenue is closed to traffic 1900-2400 for a street carnival and market. Many reggae bands and entertainers perform in the street. Vendors have stalls offering every conceivable souvenir at low prices.

Excursions

Out of town, to the E, the great houses of Rose Hall and Greenwood may be visited. The latter was built by the forefathers of the poet, Elizabeth Barrett Browning, in 1780-1800. Rose Hall was started 10 years earlier, in 1770, by John Palmer (a lively legend of witchcraft surrounds the wife of one of his descendants, Anne Palmer).

Inland, seven miles from Montego Bay off the Maroon Town road (turn off E ½ mile before the village of Johns Hall), is the recommended *Orange River Lodge*, an old Great House overlooking the Orange River Valley, which has guest rooms, US$35s, US$55d, hostel accommodation in bunk beds, US$10pp, and camping, US$5pp, bring own tent, beautiful location, excellent food, friendly staff, excursions arranged through SENSE Adventures, also shuttle service to Montego Bay. Good walking in the area, you can swim in the river or go canoeing and birdwatching is good, T 979-2688 at Lodge or PO Box 822, 34 Font Street, Montego Bay, T 952-7208, F 952-6241. Southeast of Montego Bay is the Arawak rock carving at Kempshot, while to the SW is the bird sanctuary at Anchovy (Rocklands Feeding Station, don't miss this, the doctor bird humming birds will even perch on your finger, knowledgeable guides; open to visitors after 1530, but members of birdwatching societies will be admitted any time. Children under five are not admitted). The road to Anchovy is too rough for ordinary cars. Three miles to the W of Anchovy is Lethe, the starting point for rafting down the Great River. Ten miles from Montego Bay on the Savanna-La-Mar road is the Montpelier Great House, on the site of the old Montpelier sugar factory which was destroyed during the 1831 rebellion, call Pat Ottey, T 952-4299, for bed and breakfast, US$15-25, children welcome. South of Anchovy, about 25 miles from Montego Bay, is Seaford Town, which was settled by Germans in the 1830s. Only about 200 of their descendants survive. Write to Francis Friesen, Lamb's River Post Office.

Lucea is a charming spot on the N coast where the *Tamarind Lodge* serves excellent Jamaican food. Visit the Rusea School, endowed by a refugee Frenchman in the 18th century, in a lovely location but badly damaged by Hurricane Gilbert. Between here and Montego Bay (bus, US$0.88) is Tryall, with one of the best (and certainly the most expensive) golf courses on the island. The course is home to the Jamaica Classic, an LPGA Tour event and is set in a 2,200 acre resort complex. Green fees are US$125 in winter, hire of cart US$27, clubs US$20, caddy US$15. Tennis is also available and there is a clubhouse, beach bar and restaurant. To stay at the *Tryall Golf Tennis and Beach Club* will cost you US$208-460d EP, T 956-5600/5, F 956-5673. Continuing around the island's W end, the road passes through Green Island before reaching Negril (29 miles from Lucea).

Negril

Negril, on a seven-mile stretch of pure white sand on the W end of the island, is far less formal than other tourist spots but is still a one-industry town. The town is at the S end of Long Bay; at the N is the smaller Bloody Bay, where whalers used to carve up their catch. The local Chamber of Commerce hopes to have the coastal area declared a national marine park. The main part of the town has most of the resorts and all the beaches. There is no snorkelling here, however, and you have to take a boat. In the West End of the village are beautiful cliffs and many fine caves, with great snorkelling but no beaches. In between is an area with neither beaches nor cliffs. There is clothes optional bathing at certain hotels, which is still quite rare in non-French Caribbean islands. Watersports are a particular attraction and there are facilities for tennis and riding. There is a dive shop at *Hedonism II*, T 957-4200, free for guests, and a PADI 5-star facility at *Poinciana Beach Resort*, diving lessons 0900 and 1200, resort course US$60, guided boat dives 3 times daily, US$30 single tank, US$45 – 2 tanks. By the *Poinciana Beach Resort* is the Anancy Family Fun and Nature Park with boating lake, minigolf, go-karts, fishing pond, nature trail, video arcade and historical exhibitions, open Monday-Friday 1300-2200, Saturday-Sunday 1000-2200, no admission fee, you pay for what you do. Hawkers ('higglers') are annoying and reported to be worse than at Montego Bay. They will interrupt whatever you are doing to push their drugs, hair braiding, aloe etc. Politely decline whatever they are offering (if you do not want it), they do not want to be shrugged off or ignored, but neither do they want to hold a long conversation with you. Fruit is readily available although not ready to eat; ask the vendor to cut it up and put it in a bag for you. Behind the bay is the Great Morass, which is being drained for development.

Local Information – Negril

● Transport

The orange minibuses are the cheapest way to travel around the town. There are buses to Negril from both Savanna-la-Mar (about 3/4 hour) and Montego Bay. From Montego Bay the fare is about US$2; there are also taxi and colectivo services (see under **Montego Bay** for tours). From the Donald Sangster airport minibuses run to Negril; you must bargain with the driver to get the fare to US$5-7.

● Where To Stay

There is a local rule that no hotel in Negril should be taller than the tallest palm tree to minimize the visual and environmental impact of tourism. Many Tourist Board listed establishments, ranging from the (Super Clubs) *Hedonism II* 280-room resort (T 957-4200, F 957-4289, PO Box 25) at US$275s, US$400d all inclusive; *Grand Lido* at S end of 2-mile sandy beach of Bloody Bay (P O Box 88, T 957-4010, F 957-4317), US$350s, US$500d, all inclusive, superb food, service and setting, clothes optional, pool and jacuzzi beside its nude beach area, guests can also use the facilities at *Hedonism II*, a short walk across Rutland Point, to several less expensive hotels on Norman Manley Boulevard: *Negril Gardens Hotel*, PO Box 58, T 957-4408, F 957-4374, US$125-135 EP, per room; *Negril Inn*, PO Box 59, T 957-4370, F 957-4365, US$140pp double occupancy FAP, *Foote Prints on the Sands*, PO Box 100, T 957-4300, F 957-4301, US$130-160 per room EP; *Poinciana Beach Resort*, PO Box 44, T 957-4256/4229/4100, all-inclusive from winter 1994-95, 130 rooms and villas, US$198pp double occupancy, scuba diving, bicycle rental, 2 pools, gym, jacuzzi, tennis, ping pong, basketball and lots of other sports and watersports, children's programmes, the Anancy Family Fun and Nature Park is opp the resort; *Charela Inn*, US$136-163d, on the beach (PO Box 33, T 957-4648/4650, F 957-4414), is rec.

Firefly Beach Cottages, Norman Manley Blvd, on the beach and therefore not very private (PO Box 54, T/F 925-5728), from a basic cabin for 2, US$30-40, to studios, US$70-80, or 1-3 bedroomed cottages, US$100-250, or luxury villa, US$450 in winter, cabins fall to US$10-20 in summer, luxury villa to US$270, gymnasium, min 1 week rental in winter, 3 nights in summer; *Whistling Bird Beach Cottages*, T 957-4403, or in the USA PO Box 7301, Boulder, Colorado 80306, T (303) 442-0722, family business run by Julie and Tim Boydston, 1-3 room cottages US$680-1,500/week, 25% less in summer, full service, private dining room and bar, gardens, hammocks, families welcome. Hotels to the W of centre are about 10-20 mins' walk, and are in a better area for mixing with the locals. *Tigress 1*, West End Road, US$20-40d summer, US$5 extra in winter, cheaper rooms with fan, no hot water, shared bathrooms, higher priced rooms with a/c, hot water, private bath, all with kitchen facilities, good security, nice gardens, close to water, friendly, clean, well-maintained, lots of repeat business; *Rock Cliff*, West End, PO Box 67, T 957-4331,F 957-4108, US$115-290d EP, on rocky promontory; *Ocean Edge Resort*, also on cliffs, PO Box 71, T 957-4362,F 957-4849, US$75-90d; *Addis Kobeb Guest House and Cottages* (PO Box 78, T 957-4485) US$50-110d for room in house, entire house (6 rooms) or cottages, 20% less in summer, long term rates negotiable, wooden houses, hammocks outside, shady gardens, restaurant next door. *Negril Cabins* rec by SENSE, only other accommodation on Bloody Bay, across the road from the beach, cabins on stilts, security guards keep away 'higglers', PO Box 118, T 957-4350, F 957-4381, US$96 per room EP inc tax; *Captain Nemo's*, US$20, just across the street from Joe's Caves, an excellent snorkelling area. Accommodation is available at the Yacht Club, and rooms can also be rented at Sunrise and other houses. *Lighthouse Park* on Negril's cliffs, campsite, cabins US$20-40 a night, tent site US$10, rec. The East End is the more expensive part of town, but there are a few cheap cabins: *Roots Bamboo* is very neat, US$25 a night; *Coconut International*, on the beach, US$20d, basic cabin, dirty, no fan, not rec by one traveller whose key deposit was not returned; next door is *Gloria's Sunset*, Jamaican family-run, clean, friendly, helpful, security guards at night, variety of accommodation, bar, restaurant, rec; *Mr Reynold's* (also

known as *Mr Mack's* is about US$30. This whole beach is lined with clubs and is noisy. *Mr Mack's* is at the edge of town after the craft market, and is one of the quieter places. None of the cabins has any services, nor do they provide blankets, but they are right on the beach. When choosing a cabin check to see whether it has a fan, whether there is a mesh or screen to keep out mosquitoes (if not, buy 'Destroyers', 8-hour incense to keep bugs away) and whether it looks safe (many get broken into). Locals living along the beach will often let you camp on their property.

● **Where To Eat**

For entertainment try the *White Swan*, where the locals go. *The Dolphin*, next to *New Providence Guest House*, is good. *The Yacht Club* and *Wharf Club* both have restaurants, the latter being cheaper. *Peewee's Restaurant*, in the West End of Negril, has excellent seafood and other dishes at reasonable prices. *Erica's* restaurant and *The Tigress*, both near West End; latter is cheaper than many and good. *The Hungry Lion*, on the West End road, vegetarian and fish dishes, excellent food and service, relaxing, moderately priced; *Rick's Café*, the "trendy" place to watch the sunset, full ocean view from cliff top setting but pricey with it, Red Stripe beer or cocktail US$3, plastic bead money used, full restaurant next door, expensive, even better view of sunset. *Cool Runnings*, with a chef/owner, is also rec. *The Office*, on the beach, open 24 hours, provides a good choice of Jamaican food, reasonably priced and friendly service, a good place to meet the locals. Eating cheaply is difficult but not impossible. The native restaurant-food stalls are good and relatively cheap; the local patties are delicious. Street hawkers will sell you jerk chicken for US$4-5, which is good but barely enough to whet your appetite. *The Bread Basket*, next to the banks at the mall in town is rec, but even better is the *Fisherman's Club* supermarket, just off the beach in the main part of town near *Pete's Seafood*, which is a restaurant as well as a market and serves good local, filling meals for about US$4.

● **Entertainment**

Live reggae shows in outdoor venues most nights, featuring local and well known stars. Entrance is usually US$5-7, good fun, lively atmosphere, very popular. Nice bars are located along the beach, usually with music, unnamed bar next to *Coconut International* rec, friendly service. For a pleasant drink in beautiful surroundings try the bar at the *Rock Cliff Hotel* on the West End Road, friendly barman who mixes great fruit punches and cocktails.

● **Banks**

Two banks (including National Commercial Bank) and *bureau de change* in the shopping centre in town.

East to Savanna-la-Mar

About 18 miles E of Negril, on the coast, is **Savanna-la-Mar**, a busy, commercial town with shopping, banks etc, but no major attractions for tourists. It does not have a good beach, nor good quality restaurants and accommodation. Regular concerts are held at the remodelled St Joseph's Catholic Church (T 955-2648). Talented local musicians play under the auspices of Father Sean Lavery, formerly a professor of music at Dublin University, recommended. It can easily be reached by minibus from Negril and there are hourly buses from Montego Bay (US$2). The Frome sugar refinery, five miles N of Savanna-la-Mar, will often allow visitors to tour their facilities during sugar cane season (generally November-June). Another interesting and unusual outing in this part of Jamaica is to the 6-mile long Roaring River and the Ital Herbs and Spice Farm, two miles N of Petersfield, from where it is remarkably well signposted. The Farm, owned by an American, Ed Kritzler, employs organic methods. There is a cave at Roaring River and the Farm is about half a mile further on. It is a very scenic area with interesting walks and tumbling streams suitable for bathing. A good restaurant serves fish and vegetable dishes at the Farm, best to order lunch before exploring. Totally basic accommodation in a hut available, US$28, popular but it is suggested you look before you book.

THE SOUTH COAST AND MANDEVILLE

Outside Savanna-la-Mar, the main S coast road (A2) passes by Paradise Plantation, a huge private estate with miles of frontage on Bluefields Bay, a wide protected anchorage with unspoiled reefs and wetlands teeming with birds. Just after Paradise, you come to Ferris Crossroads, where the A2 meets up with the B8 road, a well-maintained N-S connection and about 40 minutes drive to Montego Bay via Whithorn and Anchovy. For the next four miles the A2 hugs the coast along a beautiful stretch of road to *Bluefields*, where there is a lovely white sand beach mainly used by local Jamaicans and guests of the upmarket *Villas on Bluefields Bay*. This beach front resort offers exclusive, luxury, fully-staffed accommodation, US$750-2,000 per adult per week depending on season, children under 12 US$250, includes food, drinks, transfers, staff and sporting facilities, each villa has a secluded waterfront and pool. Information and bookings through the owners, Deborah and Braxton Moncure, 726 North Washington Street, Alexandria, Virginia 22314, USA (T (202) 234-4010, F (703) 549-6517). There is no mass tourism either in Bluefields or in the adjacent village of Belmont, where plenty of reggae is always playing at the numerous fishermen's bars, but there are a few expatriate homes which might sometimes be available for rent: *Oristano*, the oldest home in W Jamaica, dating back to the 1700s, owned by the Hon William Fielding, an Englishman who does beautiful drawings of the Jamaican greathouses, P O Box 1, Bluefields, Westmoreland Parish; *Two Pelicans*, built right on the side of the main road, this 1950s home is a waterfront cliffhanger with good views, contact the American owners, Steve and Linda Browne, T (301) 924-3464; *Horizon*, a cottage in Belmont, owned by American Mary Gunst, T (603) 942-7633.

The S coast is known as the best part of Jamaica for deep sea fishing and boat trips go out from Belmont to the reefs or to off-shore banks. Snorkelling is also good because the sea is almost always very calm in the morning. The Bluefields Great House, now privately owned, was the place where Philip Gosse lived in the 1830s when he wrote his famous book, *Birds of Jamaica*, and reportedly contains the first breadfruit tree planted in Jamaica by Captain Bligh after his expedition to the South Pacific. The next six miles of coast SE of Bluefields is one of the most beautiful, unspoiled coasts in Jamaica, but see it now, a 300-room *Sandals South Coast* resort is being built at Auchindown. However, much of the land is being left untouched on the resort's property. A bird sanctuary has been designated and a section of beach set aside as a turtle nesting area. Just beyond here, *Natania's*, a guest house and seafood restaurant at Little Culloden, White House, has been highly recommended. It is on the sea and has 8 rooms (16 beds) at US$50s, US$60d, food extra but good and at reasonable prices. The owner is Peter Probst; address: Natania's, Little Culloden, White House PO, Westmoreland, T/F 963-5342. Transport from Montego Bay can be arranged, as also local tours, deep sea fishing and water sports. A few miles further on, *South Sea View* guest house has 8 bedrooms at US$45s, US$50d, AP, British manager, John Ackerman, White House PO, Westmoreland, T 965-2550.

The A2 road passes through Scotts Cove, where you leave Westmoreland and enter the parish of St Elizabeth. It proceeds to the town of Black River, travelling inland from there to Middle Quarters, YS Falls and Bamboo Avenue, after which it ascends to the old hill station of Mandeville.

Black River

Black River is one of the oldest towns in Jamaica. It had its heyday in the 18th century when it was the main exporting harbour for logwood dyes. The first car imported into Jamaica was landed here. Along the shore are some fine early 19th century mansions, some of which are being restored.

At Black River, you can go by boat from across the bridge up the lower stretches of the Black River, the longest river in Jamaica (10 miles, duration 1½-2 hours, US$12 pp, drinks included, 3 boats, 25 people per boat, tours 1100, 1400, 1600 on Mon, Sat, other days 0900, 1100, 1400, 1600). You should see crocodiles (called alligators in Jamaica – most likely at midday when they bask on the river banks) and plenty of bird life in beautifully tranquil surroundings with a very knowledgeable guide (contact South Coast Safaris, Hotel Street, PO Box 129, Mandeville, T 962-0220/2513). They can also arrange for you to visit the YS Falls.

Local Information – Black River
● **Transport**
To get to Black River from Mandeville by bus involves a change in Santa Cruz.

● **Where To Stay**
Waterloo Guest House, in a Georgian building (the first house in Jamaica with electric light), US$25 for the old rooms in the main house, to US$40 in the new annex, all with showers, very good restaurant (lobster for US$7 in season), rec. *Hotel Pontio*, 49 High Street (PO Box 35, T 965-2255) US$30 a/c, US$20 without a/c, restaurant, rec. Two miles E of Black River is the *Port of Call Hotel*, 136 Crane Road, T 965-2360/2410, a bit spartan (about US$30) but on the sea. Also, *Bridge House Hotel*, on beach, US$25; *Kenchrismar Beach Cottage*, bedroom with private bath or dormitory, US$20 pp, each additional person US$8, children half price, run by Mr and Mrs Patrick Lee, Sweet Bakery, Apple Valley Farm, Maggotty, St Elizabeth (see below).

The road to Mandeville

On the S coast past Black River is *Treasure Beach*, a wide dark sand beach with body surfing waves and one of the most beautiful areas on the island. It is largely used by local fishermen as it is the closest point to the Pedro Banks. There is one small grocery shop and a van comes to the village every day with fresh fruit and vegetables. Accommodation on the beach includes the 20-room *Treasure Beach Hotel*, T 965-2305, F 965-2544, US$90-130d EP; *Old Wharf Guest House* (apartments), Sandy Bay, rates on application, *Four M's Cottage*, T/F 965-2472, T 965-0131, Box 4, Mountainside PO, 4 rooms, US$35-40d EP, and several houses you can rent: Sparkling Waters, Folichon, Caprice, and Siwind (PO Box 73, Black River), with its own cove. *Ital Rest* is a wooden guesthouse, hard to find, known to locals and bus drivers, US$40d EP, verandah decks with mountain and sea views, very clean with helpful owners, kitchen available, highly recommended. Camping is possible in the grounds and "Ital Rest II" is due to open soon. This area is quite unlike any other part of Jamaica, still relatively unvisited by tourists and well worth a visit. The local people are very friendly and you will be less hassled by higglers than elsewhere. To the E of Treasure Beach lies Lovers' Leap, a beauty spot named after the slave and his lover (his owner's daughter) who jumped off the cliff in despair, and Alligator Pond.

If you stay on the A2 instead of turning off at Black River, the road comes to Middle Quarters, on the edge of the Black River Morass (a large swamp); hot pepper shrimp are sold by the wayside, but insist that they are fresh (today's catch). Just after Middle Quarters is the left turn which takes you to the beautiful YS Falls (pronounced Why-Ess), an unspoiled spot in the middle of a large private plantation and well worth visiting. There is a 15-minute walk from where you park your car. You can bathe but there are no changing rooms or other facilities; plan a morning visit as there is no shelter in case of afternoon rain. Entrance fee about US$3. Further along the main road is the impressive 2½-mile long Bamboo Avenue (badly hit by Gilbert but now recovering). The Jamaica Tourist Board is building a travellers' halt, which will have food and toilets. North of Bamboo Avenue is Maggotty, on the (closed) railway line from Montego Bay to Kingston and close to the Appleton Estate, where tours of the rum factory are offered (for information contact Jamaica Estate Tours Ltd, T 997-6077, F 963-2243, or T 963-2210/2216, T 952-6606, Montego Bay). Regular tour parties come from Montego Bay and Negril hotels. Opposite the Maggotty train depot is the Sweet Bakery, run by Mr and Mrs Lee, who also own the *Apple Valley Guest House*, US$30d with private bath, US$25d with shared bath, US$9 camping in own tent, US$12 in rented tent, very friendly and helpful, local trips organized, Mrs Lee is an excellent cook.

After Bamboo Avenue, the A2 road goes through Lacovia and Santa Cruz, an expanding town on the St Elizabeth Plain, and on up to **Mandeville**, a beautiful and peaceful upland town with perhaps the best climate in the island. It is very spread out, with building on all the surrounding hills and no slums (population 50,000). In recent years Mandeville has derived much of its prosperity from being one of the centres of the bauxite/alumina industry (though industrial activity is outside the town).

The town's centre is the village green, now called Cecil Charlton Park (after the ex-mayor, whose opulent mansion, Huntingdon Summit, can be visited with prior arrangement). The green looks a bit like New England; at its NE side stands a Georgian courthouse and, on the SW, St Mark's parish church (both 1820). By St Mark's is the market area (busiest days are Monday, Wednesday and Friday – the market is supposed to be moved elsewhere) and the area where buses congregate. West of the green, at the corner of Ward Avenue and Caledonia Road, is the Manchester Club (T 962-2403), one of the oldest country clubs in the West Indies (1868) and the oldest in Jamaica. It has a 9-hole golf course (18 tee boxes, enabling you to play 18 holes) and tennis courts (you must be introduced by a member). Also, horse riding can be arranged, T Ann Turner on 962-2527.

Local Information – Mandeville
● **Where To Stay**
Diana McIntyre-Pyke, the proprietress of the small, family run *Astra Hotel* (62 Ward Avenue, PO Box 60, T 962-3265/3377, F 962-1461) and her staff provide a highly efficient and cheerful information service about everything to be done in the area. Rooms are US$55-110 CP, the restaurant is good and service friendly, but the highly rec hotel is some way from the town centre. Even if not staying at the *Astra*, you can seek information on the following there: community tourism (meeting the local community), tourism in central and S Jamaica, an island-wide bed and breakfast programme, villa rentals, staying with local families, and tours of Mandeville, free for guests.

In the centre is the *Mandeville Hotel*, 4 Hotel Street (PO Box 78, T 962-2138, F 962-0700), US$65-110 per room EP, TV, spacious, pool, restaurant, excursions arranged, good. Cheaper accommodation is available at *Rodan's Guest House*, 3 Wesley Avenue (T 962-2552), US$28d with bath, basic, no fan, uncomfortable beds.

● **Where To Eat**
Technically a restaurant, but also rec for its décor (of old cars and licence plates) and atmosphere is *Bill Laurie's Steak House*, 600 feet above the town, good for views, steaks, conversation (closed Sun). *Pot Pourri*, on second floor of the Caledonia Mall, just N of the Manchester Club, clean and bright, good food and service; *International Chinese Restaurant*, Newport Road; *Hunger Hut*, 45 Manchester Road, cheap, excellent food and service (owner, Fay, grew up in England and likes a chat).

● **Shopping**
Westico Health Foods, by the West Indies College, run by Seventh Day Adventists; they also run a vegetarian restaurant behind the church in the town centre, opening hours erratic. Craft Centre, sponsored by the Women's Club of Manchester, on Manchester Road.

● **Banks**
Bank of Novia Scotia; National Commercial Bank.

Excursions

Although some way inland Mandeville is a good place from which to start exploring both the surrounding area and the S coast. (In fact, by car you can get to most of Jamaica's resorts, except those E of Ocho Rios or Kingston, in two hours or less.) Birdwatchers and those interested in seeing a beautiful "great house" in a cattle property should contact Robert Sutton at Marshall's Pen (T 962-2260). Robert is the island's top ornithologist (23 of Jamaica's endemic bird species have been observed here). The *Astra Hotel* can arrange a visit. Also around the town you can visit the High Mountain Coffee and Pioneer Chocolate Factories, a factory making bammy (a delicacy from cassava root), the Alcan works, and local gardens.

There are interesting excursions N to Christiana (at about 2,800 feet, *Hotel Villa Bella*, 18 rooms and suites, restaurant, in six acres with orchard of ortaniques and bananas, nature walks, riding, special interest groups catered for, PO Box 473, Christiana, T 964-2243, F 964-2765, US$55s, US$60d, US$80 suite), SW to the Santa Cruz mountains, and S to Alligator Pond on the coast. East of Alligator Pond is Gut River, where you can sometimes see alligators and manatees; cottages can be rented near the very picturesque river flowing into the sea (contact through *Astra Hotel*). Boat and fishing trips can be made to Pigeon Island, with a day on the island for swimming and snorkelling.

From Mandeville it is about 55 miles E to Kingston on the A2, bypassing May Pen, through Old Harbour then on to Spanish Town and Kingston. Before the May Pen bypass, a road branches S to *Milk River Bath*, the world's most radioactive spa. The baths are somewhat run down, but the medical properties of the water are among the best anywhere. About three miles from the baths is a marine conservation area, Alligator Hole, where manatees (sea cows) can sometimes be seen. Local boatmen will do their best to oblige.

INFORMATION FOR VISITORS

● **Documents**

Canadian and US citizens do not need passports or visas for a stay of up to 6 months, if they reside in their own countries and have some proof of citizenship (eg a birth certificate, certified by the issuing authority with an embossed seal, together with a voter's registration card). Residents of Commonwealth countries, Austria, Belgium, Denmark, Finland, France, Iceland, Eire, Israel, Italy, Luxembourg, Mexico, Netherlands, Norway, Spain, Sweden, Switzerland, Turkey and Germany, need a passport and an onward ticket for a stay not exceeding 6 months. Citizens of all other countries must have a visa, passport and onward ticket. Immigration may insist on your having an address, prior to giving an entry stamp. Otherwise you will have to book a hotel room in the airport tourist office (friendly and helpful).

● **How To Get There By Air**

Air Jamaica has services to Kingston and Montego Bay from Canada (Toronto), the Caribbean and USA (Atlanta, Baltimore, Miami, New York, Orlando, Philadelphia). British Airways fly direct, between London and Kingston and Montego Bay. LTU International Airways has a weekly flight to Montego Bay from Dusseldorf. Martinair Holland has a weekly flight from Amsterdam. Aeroflot has a weekly flight to Kingston from Moscow via Shannon, Ireland. Air Canada flies from Toronto to Kingston and Montego Bay. American Airlines flies from Boston, New York and Miami daily to Montego Bay and from Houston, Los Angeles, New York and Miami daily to Kingston with lots of connections from other cities through Miami. The Caribbean Airline Company was to start a daily flight to Kingston from Miami in July 1994. Continental from New York and Northwest Airlines from Minneapolis and Tampa to Montego Bay. Cayman Airways and Air Jamaica connect the Caymans and Jamaica. BWIA flies to Kingston from Antigua, Barbados, Trinidad and Sint Maarten, while ALM flies to Kingston

from Curaçao. There is a twice weekly Cubana flight to Havana from Kingston. Air Jamaica fly twice a week from Kingston to Nassau. Trans Jamaica Airlines flies twice a week from Montego Bay to Santo Domingo, and in July 1994 was to begin flying to the Cayman Islands, Cancún and Belize. Copa flies Panama City-Kingston and Montego Bay 3 times a week. SAM flies to Montego Bay from Bogota via San Andrés twice a week. Ladeco flies from Santiago de Chile to Montego Bay once a week. Enquire in Florida about cheap flights from Fort Lauderdale and Orlando. There are many charter flights from Europe which change according to the season, check with travel agent. UTAS Tours, T 952-3820, 979-0684, F 979-3465, offer weekends in Havana for US$199, inc flights, hotel etc.

● **Airport Information**

Details of the 2 international airports are given under Kingston and Montego Bay.

There is an airport departure tax of J$400, payable in Jamaican or US dollars, for all those who have been in the island over 24 hours. There is no sales tax on air tickets purchased in Jamaica but there is a stamp duty which rises according to the value of the ticket.

● **Airline Offices**

Air Jamaica head office: The Towers, Dominica Drive, Kingston 5, T 929-4661 (opens at 0830), offices in Montego Bay, T 952-4300, Negril, T 957-4210, Ocho Rios, T 974-2566; British Airways is also in The Towers, T 929-9020/5, 952-3771 (Montego Bay). BWIA, 19 Dominica Drive, Kingston 5, T 929-3771/3, 924-8364 (airport), 952-4100 (Montego Bay). American Airlines, T 924-8305 (Kingston), 952-5950 (Montego Bay).

● **By Sea**

It is extremely difficult to book a passage by ship to other Caribbean islands. There are cruise ship ports in Ocho Rios, Montego Bay, Port Antonio and Kingston.

Cruise ship passengers pay a US$15 tax.

● **Local Transport**

There are **internal flights** by Trans-Jamaica Airlines (T 952-5401, Montego Bay) between Montego Bay, Kingston, Negril, Ocho Rios and Port Antonio. Charges are reasonable (US$50 Kingston-Montego Bay return) but using this method of travel is not very satisfactory unless you can arrange to be met at your destination. Montego Bay airport is the only one really within walking distance of most hotels. The

Kingston airstrip is at Tinson Pen which is only 2 miles from the centre of town on Marcus Garvey Drive, but those at Ocho Rios and Port Antonio are a long way out of town.

There was a **train**, called "The Diesel", between Kingston and Montego Bay through some spectacular hilly scenery for much of the journey, especially around the edge of the Cockpit Country. Although out of operation in 1994 the line may reopen one day. Kingston station is in a deserted, not very safe-looking area, no sign of buses, better to take a taxi. The line between Kingston and Port Antonio was damaged in a hurricane some years ago, and there are no plans to repair it.

Public road transport is mostly by **minibus**. This is cheap but overcrowded and generally chaotic and only to be recommended for the young and fit ("Step Up!" shouted by the conductors means please move down the bus, there is plenty of room at the back!). Be prepared also for a certain amount of physical abuse from the bus company front men as they compete for your custom. Country buses are slow and sometimes dangerous; they run, for instance, to Irish Town, Mavis Bank, Gordon Town and Red Hills for US$0.40. Bus X20 goes from Victoria Square to Port Henderson. There are also minibuses which ply all the main routes and operate on a "colectivo" basis, leaving (only when full) from Pechon Street in Kingston. Take a taxi to the bus station although you will still get hassled and pestered during the short walk to the bus. Colectivo to Ocho Rios costs US$2, and takes 2 hours. Crossroads and Half Way Tree are the other main bus stops. These can be preferable, less crowded and safer. Other fares from Kingston are: US$1.40 to Mandeville, US$2.75 to Montego Bay, US$1.50 to Negril, US$1.25 to Ocho Rios, US$2 to Port Antonio, 3 hrs, you are lucky if you get a seat. The buses are invaded by touts as they approach the bus station. Bus travel in Kingston costs between US$0.20 and US$0.30. A free map of Kingston bus routes is available from Jamaica Omnibus Services Ltd, 80 King Street. Travelling by bus is not safe after dark.

There are **taxis**, with red PP licence plates, in all the major resort areas and at the airports. Some have meters, some do not. Only the JUTA taxis have officially authorized charges to all destinations, with others (Yellow Cab, Checker Cab etc), the important point is to ask the fare before you get in. It can be around US$2 for a short hop, US$3-4 from New Kingstown to Down Town, US$7 from Down Town to Mona Campus. All taxis should charge the same to the airport. The tourist information centres should also be able to help in this respect. Some "non-tourist" taxis operate like minibuses, ie have a set route and can be flagged down. They will cram about 6 passengers into a small Lada, but if you do not want to share you can hire it all to yourself. Negotiate the fare in advance. To take a taxi for long distance is expensive; a JUTA taxi to Ocho Rios for example could cost US$90, rather more than a day's car hire, although you could negotiate a fare less than half that with a smaller taxi company.

Undoubtedly a **rented car** is the most satisfactory, and most expensive, way of getting about. All the major car rental firms are represented both at the airports and in the major resort areas. There are also numerous local car rental firms which are mostly just as good and tend to be cheaper. The Tourist Board has a list of members of the Jamaica U-Drive Association, Newlin Street, Ocho Rios, T 974-2852. Be prepared to pay considerably more than in North America or Europe (starting from about US$70/day plus CDW of US$9-12 and tax of $12\frac{1}{2}$%). Many companies operate a 3-day minimum hire policy. Island Car Rentals is a well known firm, airport office T 924-8075, 924-8389, Montego Bay T 925-5771, Kingston T 926-8861. Hot Tops rent neon painted jeeps in Montego Bay, Negril and Ocho Rios from US$80 plus US$9 CDW and US$11 tax, discounts after 3 days, T 979-9187, F 979-0324; UTAS Rent-a-Car, Montego Bay, T 979-0684, 979-3465, Subaru, US$60/day, US$350/week, jeeps US$99/day, bikes US$30, bicycles US$5, all credit cards accepted, rec; Prais Tours & Auto Rentals Ltd, Half Way Tree Road, Kingston 10, T 929-3580/6961/6931, F 929-3555, good deals on longer rentals, no trouble with refunds, airport transfers, rec. Driving times and distances of major routes: Kingston to Montego Bay 117 miles, 3 hours, to Ocho Rios 55 miles, 2 hours, to Port Antonio 68 miles, 2 hours; Montego Bay to Negril 50 miles, $1\frac{1}{2}$ hours, to Ocho Rios 67 miles, 2 hours; Ocho Rios to Port Antonio 67 miles, $2\frac{1}{2}$ hours. Motor scooters are widely available around Montego Bay for about US$30 a day. Watch out for sunburn. The speed limit is 30 mph in built up areas, 50 mph on highways.

Try to avoid driving outside towns at night. Roads, even on the coast, are twisty and in the mountains extremely so, add potholes and Jamaican drivers and you are an accident waiting to happen. Plan ahead because it gets dark early. Even in daylight driving is dangerous; the coastal road from Kingston to Port Antonio is in a particularly bad condition and the drivers awful. Between 1989 and 1993 there were over 42,000 accidents in which 2,441 people died. Breath tests from drunk driving are being considered. Ask car hire firms or hotels for estimates of journey times but remember that distances stretch when overtaking is difficult. Petrol stations often close on Sun; note that fuel is paid for in cash.

● **Hotels and Restaurants**

Because Jamaica is a major tourist destination there are a great many hotels and restaurants, particularly in the tourist areas. Full and up to date information is available at all tourist information centres. We only mention those which have recently been recommended for whatever reason. The brochure *Elegant Resorts* features most of the hotels in the top price-range which have reciprocal arrangements. All-inclusive resorts are extremely popular in Jamaica and development has been led by SuperClubs and Sandals, with hotels mainly along the N coast; some allow children but most are for couples. As a result of their popularity, other hotels have been forced to discount their rates, so bargains can be found.

Visitors on a low budget should aim to arrive at Montego Bay rather than Kingston because the former is the island's tourism capital with more cheap accommodation. Get hold of the Tourist Board's list of Hotels and Guest Houses, which gives rates and addresses, and also a copy of *Jamaica Today* (both free). For bed and breakfast possibilities throughout Jamaica, contact the *Astra Hotel*, Mandeville (T 962-3265/3377, telex 2426 Jamhotels, Diana McIntyre-Pike).

Information/reservations for self-catering villas and apartments can be done through the Jamaica Association of Villas and Apartments (JAVA), see below. Renting a villa may be an attractive option if you do not intend to do much travelling and there are 4/6 of you to share the costs (about US$1,000-1,500 per week for a really nice villa with private swimming pool and fully staffed). You will, however, probably have to rent a car (see **Local Transport** above) as you will have to take the cook shopping, etc.

Accommodation is subject to a 12½% value added tax called the General Consumption Tax, which may or may not be included in a quoted room rate; you have to check.

Larger hotels have introduced strict security to prevent guests being bothered by hustling.

● **Food**

Local dishes, fragrant and spicy, are usually served with rice. There are many unusual and delicious vegetables and fruits such as sweetsop, soursop and sapodilla. National specialities include codfish ("stamp-and-go" are crisp pancakes made with salt cod) and ackee; curried goat; and jerked pork, highly spiced pork which has been cooked in the earth covered by wood and burning coals. Chicken is cooked in the same way and all along the roadsides are signs advertising jerk pork or jerk chicken. Patties, sold in specialist shops and bars, are seasoned meat or lobster in pastry; normally very good value. Curried lobster is a delightful local speciality. Stew peas is chunks of beef stewed with kidney beans and spices and served with rice. Along the coast, fish tea is a hotch potch of the day's catch made into a soup, US$1 a cup.

● **Drink**

Local rum (white or brown, overproof and underproof), and the cocktails which combine it with local fruit juices, or mixed with Ting, the carbonated grapefruit soft drink; Tia Maria, the coffee liqueur and quite a lot of other liqueurs; Red Stripe lager, with which, the locals say, no other Caribbean beer compares. Try the Irish Moss soft drink. All rums are very cheap duty free at the airport, typically US$13 for a 3-pack.

● **Tipping**

Hotel staff, waiters at restaurants, barmen, taxi drivers, cloakroom attendants, hairdressers get 10-15% of the bill. In places where the bill already includes a service charge, it appears that personal tips are nonetheless expected. In some areas you may be expected to give a tip when asking for local information.

● **Entertainment**

Apart from the performance arts mentioned above, most large hotels and resorts have evening entertainment, usually including calypso bands, limbo dancers, fire eaters, etc.

● **Best Buys**

In the craft markets and stores you can find items of wood (by Rastafarians and Maroons), straw, batik (from a number of good textile companies) and embroidery; the hand-knitted woollen gold, red, green Rasta caps (with or without black dreadlocks affixed) are very cheap; jewellery from Blue Mountain Gems, near Rose Hall, Montego Bay area; for art and ceramics, Devon House gallery, Chelsea Galleries on Chelsea Road, Gallery 14, Old Boulevard Gallery, Contemporary Art Centre in Liguanea; Blue Mountain coffee is excellent, cheaper at airport duty free shop than in supermarkets or tourist shops.

Please remember to check with legislation (and your conscience) before buying articles made from tortoiseshell, crocodile skin, and certain corals, shells and butterflies. Many such animals are protected and should not therefore be bought as souvenirs. It is illegal to take or possess black or white coral in Jamaica; sea turtles are protected and you should refuse to buy products made from their shells. The closed season for lobster fishing is April-June, so if lobster is on the menu check where it has come from.

Some shopkeepers offer a 10-15% discount on all goods but in fact merely refrain from adding the tax when payment is made. Street vendors never add tax.

● **Photography**

Film is reasonably easily obtained but take spares of essentials such as Lithium batteries as they are difficult to find and expensive. Glare and UV light is constant, take suitable filters. Do not photograph Jamaicans without their permission, the men, particularly in Kingston, can get aggressive.

● **Currency**

The Jamaican dollar (J$) is the local currency but foreign currency up to US$100 is legal tender for purchases of goods and services, with change given in J$. The Jamaican dollar floats on the foreign exchange market. The only legal exchange transactions are those carried out in commercial banks, or in official exchange bureaux in major hotels and the international airports. It is illegal to buy, sell or lend foreign currency without a licence. Banks pay slightly more for US$ travellers cheques than for cash. Retain your receipt so you can convert Jamaican dollars at the end of your stay.

Note that if using credit cards the transaction will be converted from the agreed J$ rate into US$ before you sign, be sure to verify exact rate that is being used, often a 5-10% downward adjustment can be instantly obtained by this enquiry. Rates in Negril were reported 10-20% worse than in Montego Bay in 1994.

● **Banks**

The central bank is the Bank of Jamaica. National Commercial Bank of Jamaica, 77 King Street, Kingston and branches all over the island; the same applies to the Bank of Nova Scotia Jamaica Ltd (head office: Duke and Port

SECURITY

The per capita crime rate is lower than in most North American cities, but there is much violent crime in Kingston. This is particularly concentrated in downtown Kingston but you are advised not to walk any street in Kingston after dark. There are large areas of W Kingston where you should not go off the main roads even by day and even in a locked car. The motive is robbery so take sensible precautions with valuables. When in need of a taxi you are recommended to go into a shopping mall or hotel and have one ordered, rather than hail one in the street. Gang warfare increased before the 1993 elections and was exacerbated by the US policy of deporting Jamaican criminals, who returned to Kingston to shoot it out with local gangs. There were 653 murders in 1993, up from 629 in 1992, of which 366 were in the Kingston area and 123 were killed by the police.

Beware of pickpockets in the main tourist areas and be firm but polite with touts. Do not wear jewellery. Do not go into the downtown areas of the towns especially at night. Travellers have reported being threatened for refusing to buy drugs and Jamaicans can get aggressive over traffic accidents, however minor. Observe the obvious precautions and you should have no problem. The vast majority of Jamaicans welcome tourists and want to be helpful. This is particularly true in the country districts. A sense of humour and courtesy reap rich dividends.

Emergency telephone numbers: Fire/Ambulance 110, Police 119.

Royal Streets, Kingston). Citibank, 63-67 Knutsford Boulevard, Kingston; and other local banks. A string of ATM's has been installed in main centres from which you can withdraw cash from Visa and Mastercards. Immediate money transfers can be made via the Western Union Bank, behind the National Commercial Bank at the top of Knutsford Boulevard, or through American Express, at Stuarts Travel Services, 9 Cecilio Avenue (T 929-3077).

● Drugs

Marijuana (ganja) is widely grown in remote areas and frequently offered to tourists. Cocaine (not indigenous to Jamaica) is also peddled on the N (tourist) coast and in Kingston. Possession of either drug is a criminal offence and on average well over 50 foreigners are serving prison sentences in Jamaica at any given moment for drug offences. The police may stop taxis, cars etc in random road checks and search you and your luggage. Airport security is being continually tightened (sniffer dogs, etc) to prevent drug exports. You have been warned.

● Climate And Clothing

In the mountains, the temperature can fall to as low as 7°C during the winter season. Temperatures on the coast average 27°C, rising occasionally to 32° in July and August and never falling below 20°. The humidity is fairly high. The best months are December to April. Rain falls intermittently from about May, with daily short tropical showers in September, October and November.

Light summer clothing is needed all the year round, with a stole or sweater for cooler evenings. Some hotels expect casual evening wear in their dining rooms and nightclubs, but for the most part dress is informal. Bathing costumes, though, are only appropriate by the pool or on the beach.

● Time Zone

Eastern Standard Time, 5 hours behind GMT and an hour behind the Eastern Caribbean.

● Hours Of Business

Offices usually open from 0900-1700 Mon to Fri. **Shop** hours vary between 0830 and 0930 to 1600 and 1730, depending on area, Mon to Sat; there is half-day closing (at 1200) on Wed in Down Town Kingston, on Thur in uptown Kingston and Montego Bay, and on Fri in Ocho Rios. **Banking hours** are 0900-1400 Mon to Thur, 0900-1500 on Fri (there may be some local variations).

● Public Holidays

New Year's Day (1 January), Ash Wednesday, Good Friday and Easter Monday, Labour Day (4th Mon in May), Independence Day (1st Mon in August), National Heroes Day (3rd Mon in October), Christmas and Boxing Day (25-26 December).

● Electric Current

110 volts, 50 cycles AC; some hotels have 220 volts.

● Telecommunications

International cable, telephone, fax and telex services are operated by Jamaica International Telecommunications Ltd. It has main offices in Kingston and Montego Bay, but calls can easily be made from hotels. "Time and charge" phone calls overseas cost the same in hotels as at the phone company, but there is a 12½% tax and a J$2 service charge. In fact, making an international call is often easier from a hotel. Anywhere else you need a 10-digit access number, without which you cannot even make a collect call from a private phone. The only other method is a card phone, if you can find one which is working and you are prepared to queue. You can buy telephone cards at supermarkets J$50 but check that it is valid for the year you want to use it, several people have been sold out of date cards (particularly around Jan/Feb) and there is no refund. The international telephone code for Jamaica is 809.

● Post
There are post offices in all main towns. Post offices handle inland and overseas telegrams. Postcards and letters to Europe, Asia and Oceania J$1. The sorting office on South Camp Road, Down Town Kingston, has a good and helpful philatelic bureau.

● Press
The daily paper with the largest circulation is *The Daily Gleaner*, which also publishes an evening paper, *The Star* and the *Sunday Gleaner*. *The Herald* is a livelier daily than *The Gleaner*, also the *Sunday Herald*. The other daily is the *Jamaica Record*. *Money Index* is a financial weekly, *Observer* is a twice weekly, in Montego Bay *The Western Mirror* is weekly. *Lifestyle* is a monthly glossy magazine, *Jamaica Journal* is a quarterly with interesting but academic articles.

● Recommended Reading
Tour Jamaica by Margaret Morris is probably the best general guide to Jamaica for a traveller and widely available locally (US$7). The *Insight Guide to Jamaica*, besides being a general guide, delves more deeply into history, culture, etc, and is beautifully illustrated (US$14). Many other books about different aspects of Jamaica are also on sale, for example, *A to Z of Jamaican Heritage*, in the Heinemann Caribbean series. For ornithologists the standard work is *Birds of the Caribbean* by James Bond (after whom Ian Fleming named his James Bond). Ray Chen has published 2 magnificent books of photos (Periwinkle Press) and also does photos for postcards and posters. *Jamaica In focus, A Guide to the People, Politics and Culture*, by Marcel Bayer was published in 1993 as part of a series by Latin American Bureau (Research and Action) Ltd, 1 Amwell Street, London EC1R 1UL; also published in Jamaica and the Caribbean by Ian Randle Publishers, 206 Old Hope Road, Kingston 6, and in a Dutch language edition by Royal Tropical Institute, 63 Mauritskade, 1092 AD Amsterdam, and Novib, The Hague, the Netherlands.

Maps The *Discover Jamaica* road map, published by Travel Vision (1987), costs US$1. It has plans of Kingston, Montego Bay, Negril, Mandeville, Ocho Rios, Port Antonio and Spanish Town. Good clear series of 1:50,000 maps covering Jamaica in 20 sheets from Survey Department, 23½ Charles Street, PO Box 493, Kingston.

● Consulates
British High Commission is at 26 Trafalgar Road, Kingston 5, T 926-9050, F 929-7869, PO Box 575. Twenty six other countries represented. **The British Council** opened an office in 1991 in the First Life Building, 64 Knutsford Boulevard, PO Box 575, Kingston 5, T 929-6915, 929-7049, F 929-7090, with an information library, mainly on education, British newspapers available.

Jamaica Tourist Board
Circulates detailed hotel lists and plenty of other information. Head office at ICWI Building, 2 St Lucia Avenue, Kingston 5, PO Box 360, T 929-9200/19, F 929-9375. Other offices in Jamaica: at the international airports; Cornwall Beach, Montego Bay, PO Box 67, T 952-4425 or T 952-2462, airport, nights, holidays, F 952-3587; Ocean Village Shopping Centre, Ocho Rios, PO Box 240, T 974-2582/3, T 974-2570, F 974-2559; City Centre Plaza, Port Antonio, PO Box 151, T 993-3051/2587, F 993-2117; Adrija Plaza, Negril PO, Westmoreland, T 957-4243, F 957-4489; Hendricks Building, 2 High Street, Black River, T 965-2074/5, F 965-2076; 21 Ward Avenue (upstairs), Mandeville, T 962-1072.

Overseas offices: **New York**: 801 Second Avenue, 20th Floor, New York, NY 10017, T (212) 856-9727, F 856-9730; **Chicago**: 500 North Michigan Avenue, Suite 1030, Chicago, IL 60611, T (312) 527-1296, F 527-1472; **Miami**: Suite 1100, 1320 South Dixie Highway, Coral Gables, Fl 33146, T (305) 665-0557, F 666-7239; **Atlanta**: 300 W Wieuca Road, NE, Suite 100-A, Atlanta, GA 30342, T (404) 250-9971/2, F 252-7029; **Boston**: 21 Merchants Row, 5th floor, Boston, MA 02109, T (617) 248-5811/2, F 367-4866; **Detroit**: 26400 Lahser Road, Suite 114A, Southfield, MI 48034, T (313) 948-9557, F 948-1860; **Philadelphia**: 1315 Walnut Street, Suite 1505, Philadelphia, PA 19107, T (215) 545-1061, F 545-9302; **Los Angeles**: 3440 Wilshire Boulevard, Suite 1207, Los Angeles, CA 90010, T (213) 384-1123, F 384-1780; **Dallas**: 8214 Westchester, Suite 500, Dallas, TX 75225, T (214) 361-8778, F 361-7049; **Toronto**: 1 Eglinton Avenue East, Suite 616, Toronto, Ontario M4P 3A1, T (416) 482-7850, F 482-1730; **London**: 1-2 Prince Consort Road, London SW7 2BZ, T (071) 224 0505, F 224 0551; **Frankfurt**: Pan Consult, Falkstrasse 72-74, 6000 Frankfurt 90, West Germany, T (069) 70 74 065, F (069) 70 1007; **Paris**: c/o Target International, 52 Avenue des Champs Elysées, 75008 Paris, T 45 61 90 58, F 42 25 66 40; **Rome**: c/o Sergat Italia SRL, via Monte dei Cenci 207/A, 00186 Roma, T (6) 6540-1336, F 687-3644; **Barcelona**: Sergat España SL, Apdo Correos 30266, 08080 Barcelona, T 3 280 5838, F 280-4520; **Tokyo**: c/o The Carrington Club, Ginza Yomato Building, 9th floor, 7-9-17 Ginza Chuo-ku, Tokyo 104,

T 03-3289-5767, F 03-3289-5769.

The Jamaica Association of Villas and Apartments (JAVA), Pineapple Place, Ocho Rios, Box 298, T 974-2508, F 974-2967, has information on villas and apartments available for rent; also 1501 W. Fullerton, Chicago, IL60614, T (312) 883-1020, F (312) 883-5140 or toll free (800) 221-8830. In the UK, JAVA Jamaica, 21 Blandford Street, London W1H 3AD, T 071-486 3560, F 071-486 4108.

TURKS AND CAICOS ISLANDS

CONTENTS

THE TURKS AND CAICOS IS-LANDS lie some 575 miles SE of Miami, Florida, directly E of Inagua at the S tip of the Bahamas and N of Hispaniola. They comprise about 40 low-lying islands and cays covering 193 square miles, surrounded by one of the longest coral reefs in the world.

The Turks and the Caicos groups are separated by the Turks Island Passage, a 22-mile channel over 7,000 feet deep which connects the Atlantic and the Caribbean, contributing to the area's profusion of marine life. Generally, the windward sides of the islands are made up of limestone cliffs and sand dunes, while the leeward sides have more lush vegetation. The S islands of Grand Turk,

Salt Cay and South Caicos are very dry, having had their trees felled by salt rakers long ago to discourage rain. The other islands have slightly more rain but very little soil and most of the vegetation is scrub and cactus.

Only eight islands are inhabited. The main islands of the Turks group, Grand Turk and Salt Cay, shelter two fifths of the colony's 7,901 "belongers", as the islanders call themselves, but only a third of the total resident population of some 13,000. The rest of the population is scattered among the larger Caicos group to the W: South Caicos, Middle (or Grand) Caicos, North Caicos, and Providenciales, the most populous, known locally as "Provo". Pine Cay and Parrot Cay are resort islands. East and West Caicos, inhabited from 1797 to the mid-19th century, are now the private domain of wild animals. East Caicos is home to swarms of mosquitoes and wild cattle, while West Caicos harbours land crabs, nesting pairs of ospreys and flamingoes. Most of the smaller cays are uninhabited. The people of the Turks and Caicos are extremely welcoming and friendly; be prepared to say hello to anyone you pass on the road. The development of tourism on Provo has changed attitudes there, however, and friendliness is not universal.

History

The islands' first dwellers were probably the peaceful Tainos, who left behind some ancient utensils and little else. By the middle of the 16th century not one Lucayan, as Columbus named them, remained. Like the Lucayans in the Bahamas islands, they were kidnapped for use as slaves or pearl divers, while many others died of imported diseases. The dis-

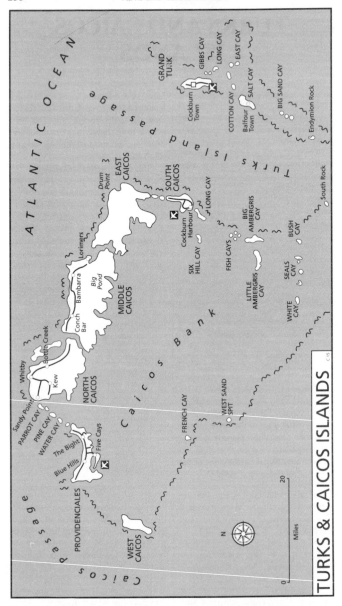

TURKS & CAICOS ISLANDS

covery of the islands, whether by Columbus in 1492 or later by Ponce de León, is hotly disputed. There is a very convincing argument that Columbus' first landfall was on Grand Turk, not Watling Island in the Bahamas, now officially named San Salvador. The infamous Caicos Banks S of the Caicos group, where in the space of 1,000 yards the water depth changes from 6,000 to 30 feet, claimed many of the Spanish ships lost in the central Caribbean from the 16th to the 18th century. The islands were named after the Turk's Head 'fez' cactus found growing on the islands. The name Caicos comes from the Lucayan, *caya hico*, meaning string of islands.

The Bermudan traders who settled the islands of Grand Turk, Salt Cay, and South Caicos in the 17th century used slaves to rake salt for sale to British colonies on the American mainland, and fought pirates and buccaneers for over 200 years. During the American Revolution, British loyalists found refuge on the islands, setting up cotton and sisal plantations with the labour of imported slaves. For a while, cotton and sisal from the islands were sold in New York and London, solar salt became the staple of the economy, and the Turks and Caicos thrived, but all these products encountered overwhelming competition from elsewhere. The thin soil was an added disdvantage and a hurricane in 1813 marked the demise of cotton plantations.

Following an alternation of Spanish, French and British control, the group became part of the Bahamas colony in 1766. Attempts to integrate the Turks and Caicos failed, rule from Nassau was unpopular and inefficient and abandoned in 1848. Links with Jamaica were more developed, partly because London-Kingston boats visited frequently. The Turks and Caicos were annexed to Jamaica in 1874. After Jamaica's independence in 1962, they were loosely associated with the Bahamas for just over 10 years until the latter became independent. At that point, the Turks and Caicos became a British Crown Colony. The Anglican Church maintained its links with the Bahamas, which is where the Bishop resides.

The main political parties are the People's Democratic Movement (PDM) and the Progressive National Party (PNP). The 1976 elections were won by the pro-independence PDM, which negotiated for independence from Britain if it won the next elections. However, when these were held in 1980 the PNP emerged victorious and talks were shelved. In 1984, the PNP, led by Norman Saunders, again won the elections and independence was not an issue.

The isolation of the Turks and Caicos and the benign neglect of the British government led to increasing use of the islands as refuelling posts by drug smugglers en route from South America to Florida until preventive action was taken in 1985. In that year the islands found themselves in the news headlines because of corruption and narcotics scandals. Norman Saunders and Stafford Missick, Minister for Development, were arrested in Miami on drugs charges and accused of accepting bribes to allow drugs planes to land and refuel. Saunders resigned as Chief Minister, was found guilty and imprisoned, although he has now returned to the islands and to politics. He was replaced by Nathaniel Francis, but the Blom-Cooper report in 1986 alleging arson and administrative malpractice, led to the resignations of Francis and two other ministers, while Oswald Skippings and two other members of the PDM were heavily criticized for incitement to commit acts of violence, although no criminal charges were ever brought. Constitutional government was suspended and direct rule from the UK was imposed while investigations continued into malpractice by other public officials.

In March 1988, general elections restored constitutional government. These were won by the PDM, and Oswald Skippings took office as Chief Minister. The PDM held 11 out of the 13 Legislative Council seats, the other two being held by the PNP, the pro-British NDA failing to win a single seat. The April 1991 elections, however, brought the PNP to power with eight seats (4,866 votes) while the PDM were reduced to five (4,542 votes). The Chief Minister is Washington Missick, who also has responsibility for Finance, Planning and Private Sector Development. In 1993 nationalist Wendal Swann, who was expelled from the PDM, founded a new party, the United Democratic Party (UDP), which may contest the next general elections to be held by 1995.

Government

The Turks and Caicos are a British Dependent Territory. The British monarch is Head of State, represented by a Governor. The Executive Council chaired by the Governor is formed by six ministers, the Financial Secretary, the Attorney General and the Chief Secretary, the last two being British government appointments.

The Economy

The traditional economic activity, salt production, ceased in 1964, and for two decades there was little to generate legal income apart from fishing, government employment and some tourism. National resources are limited, even water has to be strictly conserved. Agriculture is almost non-existent and limited to subsistence farming of corn, pigeon peas, sweet potatoes and some livestock. Small scale fishing is important for job creation, and also for export. Sales abroad of lobster and conch generate about US$2mn a year. Practically all consumer goods and most foodstuffs are imported. The lack of a manufacturing base and any major employment activities led in the 1960s and 1970s to thousands of local people emigrating to the nearby Bahamas or the USA to seek work. This trend has now been reversed as the economy has improved and the population is rising. Belongers have returned and unskilled labour, much of it illegal, comes from Haiti and the Dominican Republic.

One area of growth in the 1980s was that of offshore companies, over 12,000 of which were registered in the islands by 1993. There is no income tax, no company tax, no exchange control and no restriction on the nationality or residence of shareholders or directors. New legislation and the creation of the Offshore Finance Centre Unit (OFCU) were designed to regulate and promote the growth of offshore finance and encourage banking, insurance and trust companies. Five international banks have been granted offshore licences and some 1,350 offshore insurance companies have been licensed. A project to promote jurisdiction was started in the 1990s with several conferences to publicize the industry, which has a reputation for being well-administered and scandal-free.

Budgetary aid from the UK for recurrent expenditure was eliminated in fiscal year 1986/87 and the islands are aiming to be self-financing. Capital aid remains, augmented by financial assistance from the European Community, the European Investment Bank and the Caribbean Development Bank. In 1992 the British Government approved a capital aid package of US$43mn over three years, the largest ever awarded by the UK in the Western Hemisphere. The expansion of the airport terminal on Providenciales was the largest project on the list. Included in the aid was an award of US$2mn for 'good government'. The 1994 Public Sector Reform made sweeping cuts in the civil service and redundancies saved an estimated US$2mn a year. The Chief Minister aimed for a balanced budget in 1994/5. A deal with the USA to use Grand Turk as a processing centre for Haitian boat people was also likely to help budget revenues (see **Grand Turk**).

The main area of economic growth and revenue for the islands is tourism. Investment has taken place in infrastructure, particularly airfields, hotels and marinas. The opening of a *Club Méditerranée* in 1984 doubled the number of visitors to the Turks and Caicos in two years. By 1991, the annual number of visitors had reached 54,616, from 11,900 in 1980, but numbers declined in 1992, partly because of the collapse of Pan Am. Nevertheless, the numbers of visitors rose by 44% to 75,303 in 1993, helped by the arrival of American Airlines' daily flight to Providenciales from Miami to replace PanAm.

Fauna and Flora

The islands support 175 resident and migrant species of birds, including flocks of greater flamingoes, frigate birds, ospreys, brown pelicans, the ruby throated humming bird, the belted kingfisher, white billed tropic birds, black-necked stilts, snowy plovers, peregrine falcons, red-tailed hawks, N harriers, Baltimore orioles and scarlet tanagers and many others. There are lizards, a skink, iguanas, two species of snake, including a pygmy boa, and two species of bat. A system of National Parks, Nature Reserves and Sanctuaries has been set up; entrance to Sanctuaries is by permit only. The Turks and Caicos National Trust (Box 261, Grand Turk, T 946-1723) plans to develop and protect the Princess Alexandra National Park on Providenciales' N shore. The S parts of North, Middle and East Caicos have been designated a wetland of international importance under the Ramsar Convention to protect waterbirds, lobster, conch, flora and a fish nursery.

Diving and Marine Life

Marine life is varied and beautiful and can be enjoyed by snorkellers and sailors as well as scuba divers. Colourful fish and grouper can be seen on the coral and close to the shore you can find green turtles, loggerhead turtles and manta and spotted eagle rays. A bottle-nosed dolphin, known as Jojo, frequents the Princess Alexandra Marine Park along the N coast of Providenciales in the Grace Bay area, although he is also found occasionally in other locations. He used to be attracted by boats and humans, apparently enjoying swimming and playing with people, while often coming in very close to the shore. However he has not been seen as often as in the past and it is speculated that he may have a mate or may be getting tired of human pressure. If you are fortunate enough to see or swim with him, remember that he is a protected wild animal: do not touch him. In January-March, hump back whales migrate through the deep Turks Island Passage on their way S to the Silver and Mouchoir Banks breeding grounds N of the Dominican Republic. Beyond the reef are the game fish such as tuna, blue marlin, wahoo, snapper, bill fish and barracuda. Because there is a reef all round the islands, water visibility is excellent. Great care is being taken to conserve the reefs and the coral is in very good condition. The islands have become one of the most highly regarded diving locations in the region. Laws to conserve marine resources are strict. Do not take live coral, sea fans or other marine life. No spearguns are allowed.

There are several dive operations on Provo, offering courses and dive packages. Flamingo Divers, PO Box 322, Providenciales, T/F 946 4193, owned and operated by Jim Richardson and Karolyn Shipley at Turtle Cove, caters for small groups of experienced or novice divers. A 2-tank dive costs US$60, a 2-day resort course US$125 and full certification US$375. Provo Turtle Divers, PO Box 219, T 946 4232/4845, 1-800-328 5285, F 9415296, at Turtle Cove marina and run by the very knowledgeable and long-time resident, Art Pickering, is also recommended for small groups of experienced divers at similar prices. Other operators include Turtle Inn Divers, operating from the *Turtle Cove Inn*, a full-service dive centre with the *Caicos Cat*, accommodating 49 passengers, T 941 5389, 1-800-541 1064, F (815) 633 3993, and Dive Provo, located at the *Ramada Turquoise Reef Resort* on Grace Bay, PO Box 350, T 946 5029/5040, F 946 5936. A 2-tank dive ranges from US$55 to US$65, depending on the dive site; there have been complaints about 'cattle boat' crowding and rude instructors. *Club Med* also has a dive boat but, again, caters for large parties. There is a recompression chamber at Menzies Medical Practice on Provo, DAN insurance is accepted. Some of the best diving is off Northwest Point, where there is an underwater cliff, and West Caicos, but there are also wrecks in other areas and a coral garden reef off the N coast.

On Grand Turk there are three dive organizers. Blue Water Divers Ltd is on Front Street, next to the museum, PO Box 124, Grand Turk, T/F 946 2432. Mitch Rolling and Dave Warren offer a complete range of courses and special day trips with two small boats (no shade). Omega Divers, run by Cecil Ingham, next to the *Kittina Hotel*, T 946 2232, is a larger operation with a range of watersports on offer. Up to 20 can be taken on the dive boat, US$55 for a 2-tank dive. Off The Wall Divers, PO Box 177, T 946 2159/2517, F 946 1152 N of Cockburn Town at the *Guanahani Hotel*, uses a 42-foot customized boat taking up to 30 divers. The highlight of diving here is the wall off Cockburn Town, which drops suddenly from 40 feet to 7,000 feet only ¼ mile offshore. There are 25 moored sites along the wall where you can find coral arches, tunnels, canyons, caves and overhangs.

On Salt Cay, Porpoise Divers is based at the *Mount Pleasant Guest House*, run by Brian Sheedy, T 946 6927 (see under Salt Cay). The dive boat is an ex-landing craft and divers swim up the ramp, making it suitable for disabled divers. A 2-tank dive is US$40, but most people stay at the guest house and take a 5-day package for US$695 which includes three meals, transfers and unlimited day and night diving. There are seven moored dive sites and off Great Sand Cay there is an 18th century British shipwreck, still loaded with cannon.

On the W side of the Turks Island Passage the wall along the E shores of South Caicos and Long Cay also drops gradually or steeply from a depth of about 50 feet, with many types of coral and a variety of fish of all sizes. Grouper, barracuda, turtles, black durgeon, sharks and rays are all common. The disadvantage is that being on the windward side, the sea is sometimes rough, making boat dives difficult. Snorkelling is rewarding with several shallow reefs close to the shore. At the SE tip of Long Cay, in about 60 feet of water, are the remains of a deliberately-sunk plane to explore. No dive operator is currently established on South Caicos. On North Caicos there are no dive operators but you can make arrangements with a boat out of Provo. Your hotel or guest house on North Caicos can help you.

There are live-aboard boats for those who want to spend a week doing nothing else but diving. *Sea Dancer* (Peter Hughes Diving, 1390 S Dixie Highway, Suite 2213, Coral Gables, Fl 33146, T 800-9-DANCER or 305-669-9391) operates from the Provo shipyard, has accommodation for 18 people and offers 5 dives a day around French Cay, West Caicos and Northwest Point. Captain Bob Gascoine's *Aquanaut* (c/o See and Sea Travel, 50 Francisco St, Suite 205, San Francisco, CA 94133, T 800 DIV-XPRT 348 9778, 415-434-3400, F 415-434-3409, PO Box 113, Providenciales, F 946-4048) sleeps 4 to 6 guests. The *Ocean Outback's Island Diver* at Grace Bay or Sapodilla Bay, Provo, T 941 5810, owned and operated by Captain Bill Rattey Jr, exuberant host and excellent chef, is a 70-foot rather shabby liveaboard cruising mostly along the N reef and West Caicos (Box 1163, Dania, Fl 33004, T 305-923-3483, T/F 809-941 5810). *The Turks and Caicos Aggressor*, contact the Aggressor Fleet Limited, PO Drawer K, Morgan City, LA 70381, T (504) 385 2416, 1-800-348 2628, F (504) 384 0817.

All divers must have a valid certificate; there are plenty of training courses for novices. The best months for diving are April-November. The sea is often rough in February-March. For detailed descriptive information consult the *Diving, Snorkelling, Visitor's Guide to the Turks and Caicos Islands*, by Captain Bob Gascoine.

Beaches and Watersports

There are 230 miles of white sand beaches round all the islands surrounded by coral reefs and azure water. Grace Bay on Provo is the longest stretch of sand, at 12 miles, and despite the hotels it is possible to find plenty of empty space between them, but *no* shade. There is rarely any shade on the beaches. Most watersports can be arranged through the hotels. There are restrictions on motorized watersports in the marine park and jetskis have been banned. Turtle Tours (part of Marco Travel) at the tour desk in the *Ramada* dominates the watersports market and offers parasail rides, daytime sailing excursions and sunset cruises aboard trimarans *Tao* (US$59pp full day, US$26pp half day) and *Two Fingers* (US$59pp full day, US$35pp half day, both recommended, excellent lunch, great snorkelling, good fun) and catamarans *Beluga* (T 946 4544 direct) and *Sea 'N' Double*, which features catch and grill, island style, native crew, US$55pp (T 941 3117 direct), a trimaran *Aquanaute*, with underwater observation platform (T 946 4393 direct), and beach cruises and bonefishing aboard *Cristianna*, a motor boat,

US$35pp, (T 946 5047 direct). World famous *Kon Tiki*, offers all-day barbeque and sunset dinner cruises (US$69pp any 2 cruises, T 941 5810), excellent food, shaded lower deck, spacious upper sun deck. Classy *My Choice* sailing sloop offers lunch/sunset cruises or day cruises and private charters US$49.95pp, contact Captain Ron, T 946 4203. SV *Caicos Sol*, anchored in Sapodilla Bay at the Aquatic Centre, is a 51-foot ketch offering day sails to French Cay and West Caicos with snorkelling, swimming, lunch, guest lectures or charters, US$75pp including hotel pick up and delivery.

Fishing is popular: Provo and Pine Cay have the best bonefishing but it is also possible at South Caicos, Middle Caicos, North Caicos and Salt Cay. May is the prime time. Fishermen have not organized themselves into offering packages, so you have to find your own accommodation and fishing guide. Shop around before, committing US$250-300/day because experienced visitor fishermen have reported a lack of skill, professionalism and simple amenities among local guides. On Providenciales, choices are: Captain Barr Gardiner, of Bonefish Unlimited, PO Box 241, Provo, T 946 4874, VHF 'Light Tackle', full-day charters for US$250 for 2 people; 'Hammerhead' Joe Stubbs, on *Lights On*, T 946 5298, Provo, VHF 'Hammerhead', US$300 full day; 'Black Diamond' Earl Musgrove offers North Caicos Island Hopper from Leeward Marina, 0900-1600, US$75pp for 4 people, T 946 5225; 'Spend a day with Alan Ray', bonefishing, shelling, snorkelling, recommended, T 941 3355 daytime, 941 5288 evenings. There is sport fishing aboard the *Sakitumi* with Captain Bob Collins, T 946 4203 to leave a message, VHF Channel 16 'Sakitumi', or through the *Ramada* tour desk. On Middle Caicos fishing and boating is arranged through the District Commissioner's Office, T 946 6100, with Dotis Arthur and her husband, Cardinal. On South Caicos a bonefish specialist is Julius 'Goo the Guide' Jennings, US$20/hour, who can be contacted through Cornelius Basden at the *Club Carib*, T 946 3386/3360. A US$10 sport fishing licence is required from the Fisheries Department, Grand Turk, T 946 2970, or South Caicos, T 946 3306, or Provo, T 946 4017. Ask your guide whether the fishing licence is included in his package. An international billfishing tournament is held annually coinciding with the full moon in July, T 946 4307, F 946 4771. Over US$126,000 in Calcutta money was distributed in 1993.

Other Sports

An 18-hole championship golf course opened November 1992 (black tees 3,202 yards, white tees 2,865 yards). Owned by the water company, it is located within walking distance of the *Club Med*, *Ramada*, *Grace Bay Club*, *Ocean Club* and *Columbus Slept Here Bed & Breakfast*. Most hotels offer 3-5 day packages of green fees and mandatory carts, otherwise it costs US$80 pp, T 946 5991, F 946 5992, licensed snackbar. There are tennis courts on Grand Turk at the *Coral Reef* and on Provo at *Turtle Cove Inn*, *Club Med*, *Erebus Inn* and the *Ramada*. There are also courts on Pine Cay and North Caicos at *The Prospect of Whitby*. A small but active squash community welcomes visitors and can be contacted at Johnston Apartments, Kings Court, T 946 5683/4201/4606. Island Network sports and fitness centre with aqua/land aerobics is at *Erebus Club*, contact Darlene, T 946 4240. *Fun & Fit Health Club*, next to NAPA on Leeward Highway, offers weights and machines, aerobics, personal training and nutrition advice. There is a certified fitness trainer, T 941 3527, ask for Lisa.

Festivals

Most events are linked to the sea and land-based acitivities are tacked on to regattas or fishing tournaments. In Providenciales the billfishing tournament (see above) is a big event with lots of parties every night. Provo Day festivities follow Emancipation Day in August and a carnival procession starts in Blue Hills and ends Down Town, with floats, band and dancing. Festivities culminate in the choosing and inauguration of Miss Turks and Caicos Islands, who competes in international beauty pagents. Wooden sloops compete in the sailing regatta the following day. On Grand Turk the Cactus Fest is held at the beginning of October, with competitions for sports, costumes, bands and gospel; there is a float parade, dancing and an art exhibition. On North Caicos, Festarama is in July; on Middle Caicos, Expo is in August; on South Caicos the Regatta with associated activities is in May.

GRAND TURK

Grand Turk (population 3,691) is the seat of government and the second largest population centre, although it has an area of only seven square miles. The island was called Amuana by the Lucayans, Grand Saline by the French and Isla del Viejo by the Spanish. The E coast is often littered with tree trunks and other debris which have drifted across from Africa, lending credence to the claim that Columbus could have been carried here, rather than further N in the Bahamas chain. Grand Turk is not a resort island although there are hotels and dive operations which concentrate mostly on the wall just off the W coast. The vegetation is mostly scrub and cactus, among which you will find wild donkeys and horses roaming (there are plans to establish a donkey sanctuary with the aid of a British charity). Behind the town are old salt pans, with crumbling walls and ruined windmills, where pelicans and other waterbirds fish. More abandoned salt pans can be seen around the island, particu-

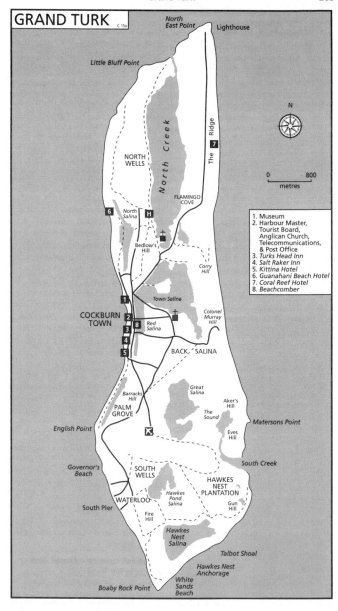

GRAND TURK C 15a

North East Point
Lighthouse

Little Bluff Point

N o r t h   C r e e k

NORTH WELLS

The Ridge

7

FLAMINGO COVE

0   800
metres

6
North Salina

H

Bedlow's Hill

Corry Hill

1. Museum
2. Harbour Master,
   Tourist Board,
   Anglican Church,
   Telecommunications,
   & Post Office
3. *Turks Head Inn*
4. *Salt Raker Inn*
5. *Kittina Hotel*
6. *Guanahani Beach Hotel*
7. *Coral Reef Hotel*
8. *Beachcomber*

Town Salina

1

COCKBURN TOWN

2

8
Red Salina

3

4

5

Colonel Murray Hill

BACK SALINA

Barracks Hill

PALM GROVE

English Point

Great Salina

Aker's Hill

The Sound

Matersons Point

Eves Hill

Governor's Beach

SOUTH WELLS

South Creek

HAWKES NEST PLANTATION

WATERLOO

Hawkes Pond Salina

Gun Hill

South Pier

Fire Hill

Hawkes Nest Salina

Talbot Shoal

Hawkes Nest Anchorage

Boaby Rock Point

White Sands Beach

larly towards the S.

Cockburn Town, the capital and financial centre, has some very attractive colonial buildings, mostly along Duke Street, or Front Street, as it is usually known. The government offices are in a nicely restored, small square with cannons facing the sea. The oldest church on Grand Turk is St Thomas' Anglican church (inland, near the water catchment tanks), built by Bermudan settlers. After a while it was considered too far to walk to the centre of the island and St Mary's Anglican church was built in 1899 on Front Street overlooking the water. The Victoria Library, built to commemorate 50 years of Queen Victoria's reign, is also an interesting building, pink, with shutters. Walking N along Front Street you come to Odd Fellows Lodge, opposite the salt pier, which is thought to be one of the oldest buildings on the island and was probably the place where the abolition of slavery was proclaimed in 1832. Continue N to the Turks and Caicos National Museum opened in 1991 in the beautifully renovated Guinep Lodge (entrance US$5 for non-residents, US$2 residents, US$0.50 students, open Monday-Friday 1000-1600, Saturday 1000-1300, for further information contact the curator, Brian Riggs, Box 188, Grand Turk, T 946 2160). The exhibition on the ground floor is of the early 16th century wreck of a Spanish caravel found on the Molasses Reef between West Caicos and French Cay in only 20 feet of water. The ship is believed to have been on an illegal slaving mission in the islands, as evidenced by locked leg irons found on the site. A guided tour is highly recommended although not essential. Upstairs there is an exhibition of local artifacts, photos, stamps, coins, a few Taino beads, figures and potsherds; expansion is planned, the museum is still growing. A local historian, the late Herbert Sadler, compiled many volumes on the theory of Columbus' landfall and local history, some of which are on sale at the museum. There is now an attractive walkway beside the salinas behind the town. There is a shaded viewing spot for birdwatchers and palm trees have been planted all along Pond Street to improve the view.

The Governor's residence, Waterloo, S of the airport, was built in 1815 as a private residence and acquired for the head of government in 1857. Successive governors and administrators have modified and extended it, prompted partly by hurricane damage in 1866 and 1945, and by the Queen's visit in 1966. In 1993 the building was again renovated and remodelled; the works were so extensive they constituted a near rebuilding of the historic residence. Further S is an ex-USAF base, known as South Base, which is now used as government offices, and beyond there some pleasant beaches on the S coast, with good snorkelling at White Sands beach by the point. US Navy, NASA and Coast Guard bases were once important for the economy of Grand Turk; John Glenn, the first American to orbit the earth, splashed down off Grand Turk in the 1960s. In 1994 a US-financed land base was built to process Haitian refugees under an agreement with the British and Turks and Caicos governments. The deal was reported to include a cash payment of US$8mn, an overhaul of air and sea port facilities and the screening of the estimated 3,000 illegal Haitian immigrants in the islands.

North of Cockburn Town a paved road leads along The Ridge up the E side of the island to the 1852 lighthouse and another abandoned US base, from where there are good views out to sea. A channel at the N point gives access to North Creek, an excellent hurricane shelter for boats. The island's carnival takes place in late August.

Island Information – Grand Turk
● How To Get There
Airlines and schedules tend to change frequently. TCA flies from Miami (rather erratic service), Cap Haitien in Haiti (suspended 1994)

and Puerto Plata in the Dominican Republic. More destinations have been applied for. TCA (T 946 2082) and Flamingo Air Services (946 2109) and Inter Island Airways (Provo, 941 5481) operate frequent inter-island flights and it is often possible to turn up on the day you want to travel and catch the next flight. Reservations are rec, however, particularly when going to Provo. For those arriving by sea, there is a safe harbour and marina at Flamingo Cove, North Creek, run by Leah and Kirk, T 946 2227. There are no buses on Grand Turk and taxis are the only form of public transport (US$4 from the airport to the *Kittina Hotel*, the nearest). Jeeps or cars can be rented from Tropical Auto Leasing, T 946 1000, or C J Car Rental, T 946 2744.

● **Where To Stay**

Rates quoted are summer-winter. In an old Bermuda-style building on Duke Street, built by Bermudan ship-wright Jonathon Glass in the 1840s, facing the beach is the very friendly, relaxed and unpretentious *Salt Raker Inn*, run by Jenny Smith, 12 rooms, US$55-125, some basic, budget rooms, others more comfortable, most with sea view, dive packages, PO Box 1, T 946-2260, F 946-2432; also rec is the *Turks Head Inn* on Duke Street, built in 1869 also by Jonathon Glass, first as a private house but later used as a doctor's dispensary, the American Consulate and once a guest house for the British Government, set back from the beach surrounded by tall trees, 6 rooms lovingly renovated in 1991/2 by the owner Xavier Tonneau (known as Mr X), with wooden floors, beds and balconies, US$50-95, fully equipped 2-bedroom apartment available, dive packages with Blue Water Divers or Omega, PO Box 58, T 946-2466, F 946 2825; *Kittina*, 43 rooms either side of Duke Street, from US$95 MAP, most face the beach or open directly onto the sand, but the cheaper rooms overlook the courtyard of the main building, suites available with kitchenette, comfortable but in need of redecoration, all watersports facilities arranged with Omega next door, small pool by the beach, PO Box 42, T 946 2232, F 946 2877; on Front Street, Angela and Douglas Gordon have a large guest suite with sea view, *Beachcomber House*, also referred to as 'The Gordons', behind the government buildings, close to beach and restaurants, superb breakfast, with homemade bread and muffins, and huge afternoon tea inc in rate of US$55s, US$75d, PO Box 110, T 946 2470, open Oct-April only;

Coral Reef, has an extensive wooden deck running all round the hotel, on the E coast away from the town, lovely colours in the sea but debris washed up frequently, rather dark studios and one-bedroom apartments with kitchenette although all sea-facing, US$75-105, PO Box 156, T 946 2055/7, F 946 2911, pool, lit tennis court, fitness centre, dive packages arranged with Off The Wall Divers; *Guanahani Beach Hotel*, on the broad, sandy Pillory Beach on the W coast N of the town, 16 functional twin-bedded rooms, 2 apartments, all with sea view, balcony, TV, a/c, fan, US$90, dive packages with Off The Wall Divers next door, pool, PO Box 178, T 946 2135, F 946 1152; *Ocean View Hotel*, 15 rooms, near beach and diving/snorkelling, restaurant popular, friendly, US$55-65, T 946 2517.

● **Where To Eat**

The best restaurants and bars are at the hotels. The outdoor *Salt Raker Inn* is rec for good food and pleasant company, it is a popular meeting place and fills up on Wed and Sun barbeque nights when Mitch and Dave, from Blue Water Divers, play the guitar and sing; the *Turks Head Inn* is also a gathering place with a friendly bar and good food; *Water's Edge*, between the two, is a reasonably priced, good restaurant open 1100-2300, closed Mon, T 946 1680; *Ocean View Hotel*, rec for good food, atmosphere, indoor or patio dining, friendly watering hole; the *Guanahani* has a rather spartan restaurant but the fish is excellent; for local food and lunch specials try *Touch of Class* on the road S, a/c, TV, bar, filling, tasty portions; the *Poop Deck* is a tiny bar, set back from the road in the centre of town by the sea, local food and hamburgers at lunchtime, chicken and chips in the evenings; local food also at *Regal Beagle* on the road N of town on the W side of North Creek; the best conch fritters are at *Peanut's* snack bar on the waterfront, not to be missed.

SALT CAY

Seven miles S of Grand Turk, Salt Cay (population 208) is out of the past, with windmills, salt sheds and other remnants of the old salt industry and little else. The island was first visited by the Bermudans in 1645; they started making salt here in 1673 and maintained a thriving salt industry until its collapse in the 1960s.

Production ceased all together in 1971. The main village is **Balfour Town**, divided into North Side and South Side, noted for its Bermudan buildings and pretty cottages with stone walls around the gardens. The White House dominates the skyline; built in the 1830s of Bermudan stone brought in as ballast, by the Harriott family during the height of the salt industry. The Methodist Church nearby, one of several churches on the island, is over 125 years old. Look into some of the ruined houses and you will find salt still stored in the cellars. Plant life was curtailed during the salt raking days to prevent rainfall but there is an iguana, known as Iggie, who lives, apparently alone, alongside the road to *Windmills Plantation*. Snorkelling is good and diving is excellent; there are seven moored dive sites along the wall, with tunnels, caves and undercuts. In January-March you can often see the humpbacked whales migrating through the channel as they pass close to the W coast.

Island Information – Salt Cay
● How To Get There
There is a paved airstrip for small aircraft, around which a fence has been erected to keep out the donkeys. The island is served by TCA, with 2 5-minute flights 3 days a week from Grand Turk, US$12 one-way, one at 0700 and one at an indeterminate time (about 1530) in the afternoon, making a day trip possible. The only public transport on the island is the taxi van run by Nathan Smith and delightful, helpful, Meglin Smith (T 946 6920); airport pickup and touring; there are very few vehicles of any sort.

● Where To Stay
The most expensive and exclusive hotel is the architect-designed and owned *Windmills Plantation* on a 2½-mile beach, which appeals to people who want to do nothing undisturbed, 8 suites, US$275-475 inc all food and drink, meals taken family style, local recipes, salt-water pool, no children, diving can be arranged with Porpoise Divers, reservations (minimum 3 nights) *The Windmills Plantation*, 440 32nd Street, West Palm Beach, FL 33407, T 800-822 7715, F 407 845 2982, on Salt Cay T 946 6962; at the other end of the scale is the cheerful *Mount Pleasant Guest House*,

owned by amiable host Brian Sheedy, who also runs Porpoise Divers, a salt raker's house built in 1830, can sleep 25 (but only take 12 on the dive boat) in 4 simple rooms in the main house, 2 with shared bath, and in a separate annex/guesthouse which has 3 basic rooms downstairs with kitchen and living room and a dormitory with 7 beds upstairs, daily rate US$85 room only but better value is the 5-night dive package at US$695, 9 nights US$895 including 3 excellent meals, transfers and unlimited diving, processing facilities for dive photos, video/TV, library, bicycles, horses for riding or driving, outdoor restaurant/bar with the best food on the island, rec as 'even on a rainy day it is a pleasure to be a guest at the *Mount Pleasant Guest House*, which has such interesting guests!' T 946 6927; Sandy Leggatt and Mrs Irene run a small **guest house** on the sea shore, 4 rooms, pleasant, clean, Sandy tells wonderful tall stories, US$35s, US$45d, good homemade breakfast US$4.50, lunch US$6.50, dinner US$8.50 by reservations, T 946 6936; the *Castaways* villas along the beach N of *Windmill Plantation* are also available for rent Oct-Apr, T 946 6921 or (315) 536-7061. Leon Wilson, the Legislative Council PDM Representative for Salt Cay, runs a small, friendly bar, *One Down And One To Go*, with iced beer and Guinness stout, dominoes, pool table, table tennis.

SOUTH CAICOS

The nearest Caicos island, 22 miles W of Grand Turk (population 1,198), South Caicos was once the most populous and the largest producer of salt, but is now the main fishing port, having the benefit of the most protected natural harbour. As a result, yachts frequently call here and there is a popular annual regatta held at the end of May. Excellent diving along the drop off to the S, snorkelling is best on the windward side going E and N. The beaches here are totally deserted and you can walk for miles beachcombing along the E shore. Boat trips can be organized with fishermen to the island reserves of Six Hill Cays and Long Cay. Further S are the two Ambergris Cays, Big and Little, where there are caves and the diving and fishing are good.

Cockburn Harbour is the only settlement and is an attractive if rather run down little place with lots of old buildings, a pleasant waterfront with old salt warehouses and boats of all kinds in the harbour. The District Commissioner's house, currently unoccupied, stands atop a hill SE of the village and can be recognized by its green roof. The School for Field Studies is in the 19th century *Admiral's Arm Inn*, and attracts undergraduate students from abroad to the island to study reef ecology and marine resources, but otherwise there are very few visitors and most of those come by boat. Wild donkeys, cows and horses can be found roaming the island and several have made their home in an abandoned hotel construction site along the coast from the Residency. The old salinas dominate the central part of the island and there is a 'boiling hole', connected to the sea by a subterranean passage, which was used to supply the salt pans. It makes an interesting walk and you may see flamingoes.

Island Information – South Caicos
● **How To Get There**
TCA connects South Caicos with Providenciales (US$40 one-way, plus tax), North Caicos (US$27), Middle Caicos (US$20) and Grand Turk (US$20). Cactus Air Ltd (T 946 3210/4152) is a charter airline based in South Caicos. There are a few taxis on the island, US$4 from the airport to *Club Carib* hotel.

● **Where To Stay**
The only hotel is the *Club Carib*, a 2-storey, functional, adequate place to sleep, 24 rooms, US$60, with a lovely sea view across to the islets offshore, you may be the only guest, maid service not always available, noisy a/c, diving is advertised but bring your own gear, there is a compressor and new tanks but little else, bonefishing can be arranged through the manager, Cornelius Basden, T/F 946 3386/3360; a few people in the town rent out rooms.

● **Where To Eat**
Club Carib will give you an excellent dinner for US$9, but it is not always open; *Muriel's* is in the front of an unprepossessing house one block from the *Club Carib*, filling native recipes, breakfast by prior arrangement, T 946 3210; *Myrna Lisa*, also local food, has been rec;

Love's has local dishes; *Dora's Lobster Pot* at the airport, known for the lobster sandwich, not always a lot of choice; *Café Columbus* for drinks and conversation with English bartender, Jack, good selection of beer, frozen yoghurt; new places are opening which are often just the dining room in a private house.

EAST CAICOS

Originally named Guana by the Lucayans, East Caicos has an area of 18 square miles, making it one of the largest islands and boasting the highest point in the Turks and Caicos, Flamingo Hill at 156 feet. A ridge runs all along the N coast, but the rest of the island is swamp, creeks, mangrove and mudflats. Jacksonville, in the NW, used to be the centre of a 50,000 acre sisal plantation and there was also a cattle farm at the beginning of the 20th century, but the island is now uninhabited. There is an abandoned railway left over from the plantation days and feral donkeys have worn paths through the scrub and sisal. Caves near Jacksonville, which were once mined for bat guano, contain petroglyphs carved on the walls and there is evidence of several Lucayan settlements. Splendid beaches including a 17-mile beach on the N coast where turtles come to lay their eggs, but accommodation for mosquitoes only. Bring repellent. There is good snorkelling and diving around Lorimer's Cut, but the reefs and banks make access difficult. Off the N coast, opposite Jacksonville, is Guana Cay, home to the Caicos iguana.

MIDDLE CAICOS

Also known as Grand Caicos (population 272), this is the largest of the islands, with an area of 48 square miles. Its coastline is more dramatic than some of the other islands, characterized by limestone cliffs along the N coast, interspersed with long sandy beaches shaded by casuarina pines or secluded coves. The S part of the island is swamp and tidal flats. There are three settlements linked by the newly paved King's Road, **Conch Bar**, where there is an airstrip, a primary school and guesthouses, **Bambarra** and **Lorimers**. Visit the huge caves in the National Park at Conch Bar where there are bats, stalactites, stalagmites and underwater salt lakes with pink shrimp, which link up with the sea. Ask in Conch Bar for a guide, for added local colour. Cardinal Arthur arranges cave tours and boat trips. There are also caves between Bambarra and Lorimers, which were used by the Lucayan Indians and were later mined for guano. Archaeological excavations have uncovered a Lucayan ball court and a settlement near Armstrong Pond, due S of Bambarra, but these are not easily accessible. Evidence of the Lucayan civilisation dates back to 750 AD. Loyalist plantation ruins can also be explored. Bambarra beach is an empty, curving sweep of white sand, fringed with casuarina trees. Middle Caicos regatta is held here and there are small thatched huts which serve as restaurants for the very popular end-August Expo (some litter remains), but otherwise there are no facilities. A sand bar stretches out to Pelican Cay, half a mile out, which you can walk at low tide, popular with wading birds. The view from Conch Bar beach is marred by a rusting barge in shallow water, but there is afternoon shade at the W end under a cliff where the reef meets the land. A pretty cove, popular with day trippers, is Mudjeon Harbour, just W of Conch Bar, protected by a sand bar and with shade under a rocky overhang. The reef juts out from the land again here before branching out westwards along the rocky coastline which can be quite spectacular in the winter months with crashing waves. South of Middle Caicos there is a Nature Reserve comprising a frigatebird breeding colony and a marine sinkhole with turtles, bonefish and shark. The blue hole is surrounded by sandy banks and is difficult to get to, but it shows up on the satellite photo of the islands on display in the museum in Grand Turk.

Ask the District Commissioner's office, T 946 6100, for information and assistance, including boat tours and cave tours.

Island Information – Middle Caicos
● How To Get There
TCA flies from Grand Turk, South Caicos, North Caicos and Providenciales. Private pilots will also stop off if flying to North Caicos, or you can charter a plane. A ferry service for cargo and passengers runs between Provo Middle and North Caicos, operated by owners of Blue Horizons Development, contact Dale T 946 6141, F 946 6139 for times and days the *Dale Marie* runs. Hired scooters may be taken on board for day trips and overnight stays on Middle Caicos. Carlon Forbes runs a taxi service and fares are based on US$2 per mile for 2 people, eg Conch Bar to Bambarra US$14, to Lorimers US$20.

● Where To Stay
In Conch Bar: **Mrs Maria Taylor** has a simple guesthouse with 4 bedrooms, communal kitchen and sitting/dining room, US$45 for twin-bedded room with private bathroom, US$40 with shared bath, US$60 for a triple room, fans, T 946 3322; *Sea View Guesthouse*, one double room US$50 with bath, or US$35s, meals available, phone for reservation, T 946 6141, airport pick up, trip to caves, Dale also runs the ferry (see above); Stacia and Dolphus Arthur run **Arthur's Guesthouse** next to Arthur's Store, US$50, one double, one twin-bedded room, private bath, kitchen; George and Martha Volz' *Villa* is a 3-bedroom house let for US$145/day, 3-day min, US$900/week May-Nov, US$1,100/week Dec-Apr, contact 1255 Carolyn Drive, Southampton, PA, 18966, T 215-322 0505, F 215-322 0593, or through District Commissioner's office, Dolphus Arthur, T 946 6100.

● Where To Eat
Most people are self-catering and buy their supplies from the few small stores in Conch Bar. Maria Taylor has milk and eggs and home made bread. Annie Taylor is known for her cooking and runs a restaurant on demand in her house, the conch stew at US$18 for 2 is rec. *Carrie's Restaurant and Bar*, next to *Seaview Guest House* in Conch Bar, lunch, dinner, picnic lunches, ask locally.

NORTH CAICOS

The lushest of the islands, North Caicos has taller trees than the other islands and attracts more rain. Like Middle and East Caicos, the S part of the island is comprised of swamp and mangrove. There is one Nature Reserve at Dick Hill Creek and Bellefield Landing Pond, to protect the West Indian whistling duck and flamingoes, and another at Cottage Pond, a fresh/salt water sinkhole, about 170 feet deep, where there are grebes and West Indian whistling duck. Pumpkin Bluff Pond is a sanctuary for flamingoes, Bahamian pintail and various waders. Three Mary's Cays is a sanctuary for flamingoes and is an osprey nesting site. Flocks of flamingoes can also be seen on Flamingo Pond, but take binoculars. There is a viewing point at the side of the road, which is the only place from where you can see them and at low tide they can be a long way off. The beaches are good along the N coast where the hotels are, although the best is a seven-mile strip W of Pumpkin Bluff, where there has been no development so far. It can be reached via a footpath from *The Prospect of Whitby*. A cargo ship foundered on the reef in the 1980s, and is still stuck fast, making it of snorkelling interest. There is also good snorkelling at Three Mary's Cays and Sandy Point beach to the W is lovely. These beaches are best reached by boat. There is a rough road to Three Mary's Cays suitable for mopeds.

The population has declined to 1,275 inhabitants living at the settlements of Bottle Creek, Whitby, Sandy Point and Kew. **Kew**, in the centre, is a pretty, scruffy but happy little village with neat gardens and tall trees, many of them exotic fruit trees, to provide shade; there are three churches, a primary school, a shop and two bars. **Bottle Creek**, in the E, has a high school, clinic and churches; the paved road ends here and a rough road requiring 4-wheel drive continues to Toby Rock. The backstreets of Bottle Creek run alongside the creek and here you can see the importance of water conservation, with people carrying buckets to and from the municipal water tap at the rain catchment area, while donkeys, goats and dogs roam around. The area is poor, but many people are building themselves bigger and better homes. **Whitby**, on the N coast, is rather spread out along the road, but this is where the few hotels are. Several expatriates have built their homes along Whitby Beach. Sandflies can be a problem in this area, particularly if there is not enough wind, take insect repellent. **Sandy Point**, in the W, is a fishing community. North Caicos is the centre of basket making in the islands and there are several women, including Clementine Mackintosh, Eliza Swan and Cassandra Gardiner, who are expert in their craft. Prices do not vary much from those in the shops in Providenciales or locally. Eliza Swan is based in Whitby and makes beautiful bags and baskets using many colours and designs. Wades Green Plantation, just to the W of Kew, is the best example of a Loyalist plantation in the islands, with many ruins, including a courtyard and a prison. Archaeologists from the University of California in Los Angeles carried out excavations in 1989. At Greenwich Creek in the NE there is a crab farm, run by West Indies Mariculture; excellent tours used to be offered but the Government did not renew their lease in 1994, check if they are still operating, T 946 7213. The King Crab will grow to 8 lbs, but is harvested at the soft shell stage when it is 7-9 months old, and sold to local restaurants. Whitby Drug and Variety Store in the Whitby Plaza sells T-shirts, crafts and non-prescription drugs at lower prices than on Provo.

You are advised to bring small denomination US dollar notes as there is no bank and it is difficult to cash US$50 or US$100.

Island Information – North Caicos

● **How To Get There**

TCA flies from Provo (US$22 plus tax one way) and there are flights via Middle Caicos (US$12) and South Caicos (US$27) to Grand Turk (US$37). Charters can be arranged from Provo, or private pilots (Blue Hills Aviation, Flamingo Air Service and Inter Island Airways, T 946-5481) have 3 or 4 flights a day US$25 one way. There is a ferry service between North and Middle Caicos, for details see above, Island Information – Middle Caicos. For day trips or overnight stays you can rent a one or 2 seater motor scooter at Whitby Plaza, island map supplied. Rates are US$25 plus US$5pp insurance per 24 hrs, for weekly rates seventh day free, credit card deposit required, T/F 946 7301/7184. There are car hire facilities on North Caicos with Saunders Rent A Car, VHF Channel 16 'Sierra 7', or Gardiners Auto Service, US$35 for half day, US$70 for full day. A taxi costs US$10 from the airport to Whitby for one person, US$12 for 2, US$15 for 3. Taxi from Sandy Point to Whitby is US$20. A tour of the island by taxi costs US$80-100, the drivers are friendly and knowledgeable but some tend to run their own errands while working.

● **Where To Stay**

All accommodation is in the Whitby beach area on the N coast. *The Prospect of Whitby*, long-established hotel now leased by Club Vacanze of Italy and nearly all guests are on an Italian package, renovated 1994, luxury accommodation, T 946 7119, F 946 7114, pool, tennis; *Pelican Beach Hotel*, down a very poor road, friendly, relaxed, few facilities, 14 rooms, 2 suites, the older rooms face the beach, US$100-150 room, US$130-160 suite, run by Clifford Gardner, T 946 7112, F 946 7139; *Ocean Beach*, 10 condominiums,

US$100-130d, T 946 7113/2876 or contact the Canadian office at PO Box 1152, Station B, Burlington, Canada, T 416-336 8276, F 416-336 1232; the only guesthouse, *Jo Anne's Bed and Breakfast*, belongs to Jo Anne James Selver, who also runs a tourist shop in Whitby, set back from the beach with purple sea fans outside, it is light and airy with a wonderful view, comfortable rooms, private bath, good breakfast included, US$80d, T/F 946 7184/7301, she also has 2 new apartments to rent 5 min walk from Whitby beach, sea view, weekly or monthly rentals, credit cards accepted, full maid service available, reservations suggested. A very basic campsite has been cleared in the bush on the hill at the corner of Kew Road and Whitby Highway, by Perry Musgrove, on his 100-acre property, there is a well and bush toilet but you need to bring all camping gear, mosquito net essential, US$25/week.

● **Where To Eat**

Good food at the *Pelican Beach Hotel*; Italian at the *Prospect of Whitby*, reservations necessary. Simple local restaurants include *Club Titter's Restaurant and Bar*, near the airport, lobster US$15, ribs, rec, and *Aquatic* restaurant and bar, lobster US$15, conch.

PARROT CAY

A luxury, 50-room hotel was built in 1992 on this 1,300-acre private island, which will offer a health club and gym, tennis, watersports and conference facilities. Its future is uncertain, however, and the opening date was not known as we went to print. Cotton used to be grown here and there are the remains of a plantation house. The wetlands and mangroves are to be preserved to protect wildlife. Information through Flagship Hotels & Resorts, T 914-214 8771 or 800-777 2022, F 914-214 6279.

DELLIS CAY

Dellis Cay is uninhabited but frequently visited for its shells. A popular excursion is to be dropped off there for the day for shelling by a local charter boat out of Leeward Marina, no facilities.

PINE CAY

Pine Cay is an 800-acre private resort owned by a group of homeowners who also own the exclusive 12-room *Meridian Club* of *Pine Cay*, US$395-575d. No children under six allowed to stay in the hotel and lots of restrictions on where they are allowed if brought to a villa. The homes, which are very comfortable, with spectacular views, can be rented from US$2,960/week to US$4,815 for 10 days, per couple. A hurricane in 1969 left Pine Cay five feet under water for a while and since then the houses have been built slightly back from the beach and many of them are on stilts. There is a fairly well-stocked commissary or you can eat in the hotel; golf carts are used to get around the island. Note that the island is on the same time as Miami. Open November-June, reservations can be made through Resorts Management Inc, The Carriage House at 201½ East 29th St, New York NY 10016, T 800-331 9154, 212-696 4566, F 212-689 1598, locally T 946 5128. Non-motorized watersports and tennis are available and excursions to other cays can be arranged. May is a popular time for bonefishing. Day trippers are not encouraged although visitors may come for lunch at the restaurant by prior reservation as long as they do not use the facilities; the homeowners value their privacy and put a ban on visitors if they feel there have been too many. Pine Cay benefits from a few freshwater ponds and wells, so water is no problem here and the vegetation is more lush than on Provo. On the other hand mosquito control is a constant problem. Nature trails have been laid out around the ponds and through the trees. Water Cay is a nature reserve and although classified as a separate island, is joined to Pine Cay by sand dunes created during the 1969 hurricane. There is an airstrip, guests usually charter a flight, and a dock if they prefer to come in with the *Meridian Club's* exclusive shuttle boat.

LITTLE WATER CAY

Little Water Cay is the nearest desert island to Provo. Iguanas live here but they have become quite aggressive because of constant pressure by people and their offerings of potato chips and lettuce. Do not feed them. Take pictures instead. Charter boats can be arranged from Leeward Going Through Marina. Many day sail charters visit regularly.

PROVIDENCIALES

"Provo" (population over 6,000 with many Haitians, Dominicans, French, Germans, Canadians, Americans) has a length of 25 miles and average width of three. Twelve-mile Grace Bay on the N shore has only seven hotels and condominiums so you can walk and snorkel without seeing another soul. The Princess Alexandra Marine Park incorporates the reef offshore along 13 miles of beach. Development of the island began in 1967 although it had been settled in the 18th century and there were three large plantations in the 19th century growing cotton and sisal. The three original settlements, The Bight(meaning Bay), Five Cays and Blue Hills, are fragmented and have not grown into towns as the population has increased. Instead there have been efforts to build shopping malls (Market Place, Plantation Hills, Central Square, retail stores, restaurants, lawyers and business offices) at points along the Leeward Highway and create new vil-

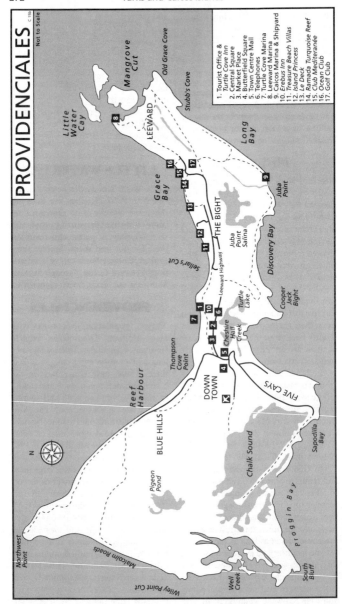

PROVIDENCIALES

C 150

Not to Scale

1. Tourist Office & Turtle Cove Inn
2. Central Square
3. Market Place
4. Butterfield Square
5. Town Centre Mall
6. Telephones
7. Turtle Cove Marina
8. Leeward Marina
9. Caicos Marina & Shipyard
10. Erebus Inn
11. Treasure Beach Villas
12. Island Princess
13. Le Deck
14. Ramada Turquoise Reef
15. Club Mediteranée
16. Ocean Club
17. Golf Club

lages. **Down Town** is where the government offices have been built and several office complexes, banks, supermarkets, church and a laundry have sprung up around Butterfield Square. **Turtle Cove** calls itself 'the heart of Provo' and is the more interesting place for tourists, with a couple of hotels, a marina, dive operators, boat charters, deep sea fishing, 28 restaurants, the Tourist Office, hairdressing and a few boutiques.

On the S side of the island, South Dock is the island's commercial port. The Caicos Marina and Shipyard on the S coast is a disappointment to sailors because the advertised facilities and major services are not available and it is many miles from shopping supplies. To the W, Sapodilla Bay offers good protection for yachts. Chalk Sound, a National Park inland from Sapodilla Bay, is a shallow lagoon of marvellous turquoise colours, dotted with rocky islets.

At the NE end, a deep channel known as Leeward Going Through is another natural harbour and a marina with fuel, water, ice and restaurant has been built here. There is a conch farm at the Island Sea Centre at Leeward, but unfortunately the main building was destroyed by fire in March 1993 and it is no longer open to the public. Baby conch are still being produced at the hatchery however.

North West Point, a marine park offshore, with a nature reserve at North West Point Pond for breeding and migrant waterfowl, has good beaches, diving and snorkelling. In 1993 a French television company shot a series of underwater game shows at North West Point and a treacherous road was bulldozed through to the beautiful beach. They left several tiki huts which offer much needed shade for a day on the beach. Two other good places to snorkel in the Grace Bay area are just to the E of Turtle Cove, where rays and turtles can be seen on Smith's reef near the entrance to the marina, and just W of *Treasure Beach Villas*, by the white house, where

there is a variety of life, including grouper, ask anybody for directions.

Inland, along Seasage Hill Road in Long Bay, is The Hole, a collapsed limestone, water-filled sinkhole next to a house called *By the Hole*. A tunnel to the right hand side gives access to the main pool. Do not attempt to descend. Ruins of Loyalist and Bermudian settlers' plantations and houses can be seen at Cheshire Hall and Richmond Hills, and along the Bight road. On the hill overlooking the *Mariner Hotel* at Sapodilla Bay a pole marks the location of stones engraved with initials and dates in the 18th century possibly by shipwrecked sailors or wreckers.

Island Information – Providenciales
● How To Get There

American Airways daily from Miami (T 800-433 7300, or locally T 941 5700), TCA has an erratic service from Miami and also from Cap Haitian and Nassau. TCA operates internal flights within the Turks and Caicos islands, see above. Charter companies at Provo airport are TCA, T 946 4255, F 946 2081; Blue Hills Aviation, T 941 5290, F 946 4644; Inter Island Airways, Lyndon Gardiner, T 941 5481, Flamingo Air Services, T 946 2109/8, is based in Grand Turk.

● Transport

Most roads are paved, contributing to fast, erratic driving by residents previously used to dirt tracks; if on a bicycle, scooter or in a rental car, particularly at night, be warned. Leeward Highway is especially risky. Hired cars are not generally well serviced, exchanges are common. An economy car, quoted at US$39/day will work out in practice at US$61.50 with taxes and insurance. Deposits are at least US$400. **Provo Rent A Car**, PO Box 137, Airport Road, T 946 4404, VHF Channel 16, F 946 4993, from US$44/day, CDW US$11.95, US$10 stamp duty, 60 miles free, at the airport only, free pick-up. **Highway Rent A Car**, Leeward Highway, Airport, T 941 5262/3, F 941 5264, smallest car US$39/day, Isuzu US$44, Ford Escort US$49. **Budget**, Down Town, Town Centre Mall, open Mon-Sat, 0800-1700, T 946 4709, at the *Ramada*, Grace Bay, 0900-1700, T 946 5400, similar prices. **Tropical Auto Rental**, Grace Bay Road at *Club Med*, T 946 5300, F 946 5456, US$49-59/day,

US$294-357/week plus insurance of US$11-95/day. **Turks & Caicos National Car Rental**, Airport Road, T/F 946 4701, US$35/day, US$210/week economy car, jeeps US$50/day, US$300/week, plus CDW US$11.95/day. Not always reliable delivery. **Turquoise Jeep Rentals**, Leeward Highway, T 946 4910, US$68/day plus US$11.95/day insurance, cash deposits 2 days US$250, 5 days US$400, tax US$10. **Rent-a-Buggy**, Suzie Turn, competitive rates, T 946 4158, US$38/day US$10.95 daily tax, 7-day rate US$315 includes insurance, fuel and pick up service. **Scooter Rental**, Central Square, Leeward Highway, T 946 4684 or VHF 'Scooter', open Mon-Sat, 0900-1700, Sun and holidays, 0900-1200, 24-hour rental starts at US$25, weekly rentals less, map supplied. Scooter rental from Honda shop, Blue Hills, T 946 4397, outlets at Sunshine Nursery, T 946 5800, and *Ramada*, T 946 5555, both near *Club Med*. Bicycle rentals also. Taxis charge US$2 per mile, a ride for one person from the airport to the *Ramada* is US$14, but is often quoted at US$12-20, and a round trip to a restaurant can be US$40. Complaints have not lowered the rates. There are usually taxis at the large hotels, otherwise phone for one. Contact Any Taxi on VHF Channel 06, or by name, or T 941 5603 at the airport.

● **Where To Stay**

Erebus Inn, on hillside overlooking Turtle Cove, 30 rooms, larger than those in other hotels, US$65-170, a few basic chalets with wonderful view liked by divers, dive packages available, all watersports at the marina, gym and fitness centre on site, pool, tennis, 2 rooms fully equipped for ham radio operators, T 946-4240, F 946-4704; *Turtle Cove Inn*, US$95-175, poolside or ocean view, smallish rooms but comfortable, suite with kitchenette available, not on beach, docking

facilities for guests, all watersports at the marina, games room, 2 lit clay tennis courts, cable TV, 2 restaurants, T 946-4203, F 946-4141; along the N shore on the beach heading E are *Treasure Beach Villas*, becoming rather run down, 18 self-catering apartments, 1-2 bedrooms, US$450-960, no restaurant, T 946-4211, F 946-4108; *Island Princess*, 80 rooms, only a few with a/c, US$80-120, rather run down, airless rooms, most on long term rental to *Sheraton* construction workers in 1994, no sports on site, T 946-4460, F 946-4666; *Le Deck Hotel and Beach Club*, 26 rooms, US$90-175, golf packages available, restaurant, lovely bougainvillea in the courtyard, watersports inc equipment rental, North Caicos cave tours, snorkel trips, beach parties, T 946-5547, F 946-5770. *Grace Bay Club*, on beach, luxury accommodation, 32 rooms, a/c, phone, TV, US$150d standard to US$500 for 2-bedroom penthouse, watersports, tennis, pool, jacuzzi, all amenities, French restaurant, beach bar, T 946 5757, F 946 5758; *Ramada Turquoise Reef Resort*, 228 rooms and suites, mostly used by North American charter package holiday business, the grounds are attractive but there is a lot of litter, service has been criticized but is friendly in bar and restaurants, US$180-425 winter, US$115-230 summer, but special deals mean most people do not pay anything like as much, several restaurants, tennis, diving, no motorized watersports, casino, conference facilities, tour desk, facilities for the disabled in a few rooms, golf packages available, condos next door under Ramada management, PO Box 205, T 946-5555, F 946-5522; *Club Méditerranée Turkoise*, Grace Bay, stays on same time as Miami all year, 298 rooms, no facilities for children, rooms stark but comfortable, keen young organizers, lots of watersports, communal dining. *Ocean Club at Grace Bay*, a beach and golf resort, condos on the beach, US$100 pp to US$450 for 3 bedroom ocean front apartment, very comfortable, well-equipped, balconies, good views the length of Grace Bay, daytime snack bar by the pool but no restaurant, next to Provo Golf Club, packages available, free transport to airport, bike rentals, PO Box 240, T 946 5880. The only bed and breakfast on the island is run by Louise Fletcher, *Columbus Slept Here*, between *Ramada* and *Le Deck*, look out for the Canadian flag, one double room in house, 2 small self-catering apartments downstairs, US$55s, US$75d all year, weekly and monthly rates, 10% discount for repeat visitors and friends of residents, comfortable, lots of hot water, use of kitchen, very friendly, knowledgeable hostess, 4-min walk to Grace Bay beach, popular, golf packages available, T 946 5878, PO Box 273. *Bed & Breakfast Hospitality Center*, Box 364, T/F 941 5860, in USA F (303) 375 0214, 3 rooms, advance booking required, no walk-ins, US$55-75s, US$65-115d, on Leeward Highway opp *Doya's Bakery*, will refer overbookings to bed and breakfast places on Provo and other islands. In the Sapodilla area there are self-catering villas: *Casuarina Cottages*, 3 houses, US$750-1,000 a week, T 946 4687, F 946 4895; *Nautilus Villas*, 10 villas, T/F 946 4069; *Club Neptune Villas*, 1-2 bedroom, from US$350/week short or long term rental, PO Box 380, T 946 4859. Other 3-5 bedroomed rental villas with pools and modest-to-luxury accommodation available through Elliot Holdings & Management, PO Box 235, T 946 5355, F 946 5176; Turks & Caicos Realty, PO Box 279, T 946 4474, F 946 4433; Prestigious Properties Ltd, PO Box 23, T 946 4379, F 946 4703; Alpha Omega, T 946 4702, F 941 5723; ASAP, T 946 4080, F 946 4081.

● **Where To Eat**

In the Turtle Cove area are *La Crêperie* at *Erebus Inn*, overlooking Turtle Cove, 1730-2230, entrée galettes and desert crêpes, T 946 4240; *Alfred's Place*, French chef, Annick Vernay, international cuisine with a flair, swordfish, lobster and fish specials, open 1100-2400, Tues-Sun, popular, T 946 4679; *Banana Boat*, colourful, cheerful, although service sometimes inattentive, T 941 5706; *Tiki Hut*, at *Turtle Cove Inn*, creative breakfasts, innovative sandwiches, open 0700-2130, fresh pasta and choice of 10 sauces, fresh fish, service inconsistent, T 946 4203, 941 5341 and *Jimmy's Dinner House and Bar*, upstairs at *Turtle Cove Inn*, open 1700-late, happy hour 1700-1900, specialities: pizza, fried chicken, delivery service home or hotel, personal, friendly service by Jimmy and Dodie, popular with residents, T 941-5575; *Mediterraneo*, Italian restaurant on the water at Turtle Cove at Admiral's Club, open from 1800, T 946 4032.

Down Town: *Tasty Temptations*, next to the dry cleaners, is a French bakery and deli, with croissants and pastries, coffee, limited seating, popular with ex-pats, open 0630-1500, closed Sun, T 946 4049; *Sweet T's Meals On Wheels*, next to Texaco service station, native dishes, soft ice cream, espresso, 0630-2300 daily, until 0300 Fri, 2400 Sat.

East along Leeward Highway: *Wilson Delight's Nibbles & Bits*, Caribbean Place, gourmet caterer and light, delightful lunches, 1000-1400, take aways open 1000-1700, Sat 1000-1500, T 941 5857 and 946 4163; *Hey José Cantina*, near tourist shops, Central Square Shopping Centre, Leeward Highway, consistently excellent service, great food, best margaritas, Mexican/American, tacos, huge pizza etc, 1200-1500, 1800-2500, closed Sun, take aways, T 946 4812; *Top O' The Cove Deli*, Leeward Highway, next to Napa auto at Suzie Turn, 'Little bit of New York-style deli', subs, bagels, order lunch by phone/fax 946 4694, beer, wine, picnic food, open 0630-1530 daily; *Dora's Restaurant and Bar*, E of Turtle Cove on Leeward Highway past Suzie Turn, open from 0730, local recipes, filling, eat in or take away, US$20pp for dinner from 1900, transport to/from hotel for Mon and Thur live band and seafood buffet, T 946 4558; *Bonnie's Kitchen*, Provo Plaza, next to satellite dishes, chef 'Bonnie' Arthur Williams, small, immaculate, reasonable prices, friendly service, local specialities and best seafood on the island, lunch 1200-1500 and dinner 1800-late, eat in or take away, closed Sun, T 946 4072; *Doya's Bakery*, T 941 5589, made to order pizza take away, fresh bread, rolls, cinnamon buns, cakes, 0800-2100 Sun-Wed, 0800-2400 Thur-Sat.

Near the *Ramada*: Off the Leeward Highway, *China Restaurant*, Ramada Road, T 946 4746, Szechuan specialities, Chinese chef, a/c, open daily 1100-1400, 1800-2200, no lunch Sun; E of the *Ramada*, *Caicos Café & Grill*, open 1100-1900, a respite from *Ramada* fare, home made pasta with French flair, grilled fish and seafood, service personal but slow, go early or late to avoid crowds, open-air, open daily 1200-2400, T 946 5278; *Bacchus Res-*

taurant & Bar, opp *Ramada*, open daily 1800-2200 for dinner, Fri disco 2300-0400, US$5 cover charge, T 946 5214; *Hong Kong Restaurant*, within walking distance of *Ramada*, a/c, Chinese eat in, take away, or delivery, moderate prices, useful if you are vegetarian as they will cook good, special meals for you, even by New Yorker standards, T 946 5678; *Fairways Bar & Grill*, opp *Ocean Club*, Provo Golf Course Clubhouse, T 946 5991, breakfast and lunch, 0700-1900, stiff not usual camaraderie among golfers; *Gilley's at Leeward*, open from 0700-2100, by the marina, breakfast, lunch specials US$3.50, beers US$2.50, sodas US$1, good food inside or under coconut palms, friendly, superb service, meet local fishermen, arrange outings, boat trips, elegant, romantic dinners, T 946 5094.

Grace Bay, W to E: *Dora's Restaurant and Bar II*, on the beach at the *Island Princess*, T 946 4260, native dishes, breakfast, lunch and dinner, Fri seafood buffet, live band, open from 0730; *Smokey's Restaurant and Bar*, no phone, next to *Island Princess*, local seafood by Smokey himself, open daily from 0900, music and dancing 2300-2400; *Sunset Restaurant* at *Le Deck*, local and French, happy hour for beer only, T 946 5547, portions small, service slow, expensive, reservations required; at the exclusive *Grace Bay Club*, its *Anacaona* restaurant and bar on the beach next to the *Ramada*, has French menu/chef, thatched roof elegance, nouvelle cuisine with Caribbean flair, exclusive and expensive, over US$50pp, waterfront dining, live music Wed, Fri, Sat, guests only, reservations rec, T 946 5050; *Ocean Club Cabana Bar & Grill*, T 946 5880, light lunch, drinks, only, 1100-1900.

In Blue Hills settlement: *Pub On the Bay*, indoor or tiki hut dining on the beach, great native dishes, T 941 5309; *Henry's Roadrunner Restaurant*, Blue Hills, everybody's favourite for seafood buffet, no phone but check VHF Channel 16 to avoid disappointment.

At or near the airport: *Gilley's* is the only place to eat at the airport, a/c, noisy, local hangout, indifferent service, daily specials, fast food, T 946 4472, within walking distance is *Fast Eddie's*, Airport Road, Wed night buffet, live music if enough reservations, US$25 inc transport, reservations required, happy hour and darts tournament 1700-1900, open 0730-2300, slot machines, T 941-3176; *Where Its At* has Jamaican specialities, T 946 4185, generous portions, daily specials, 0630-2300

WEST CAICOS

Rugged and uninhabited but worth visiting for its beautiful beach on the NW coast and excellent diving offshore. The E shore is a marine park. Once frequented by pirates, there are many wrecks between here and Provo. Inland there is a salt water lake, Lake Catherine, which rises and falls with the tides and is a nature reserve, home to migrant nesting flamingoes, ducks and waders. The ruins of Yankee Town, its sisal press and railroad are a surface interval destination for scuba divers and sailors.

FRENCH CAY

An old pirate lair, now uninhabited, with exceptional marine life on the N side. It has been designated a sanctuary for frigate birds, osprey and nesting seabirds. Visitors come almost daily aboard the *Caicos Sol* to swim, explore and snorkel. It operates out of the old Aquatic Centre, at Sapodilla Bay, enquire locally, consult newspapers, *Times of the Islands*, for the adverts.

INFORMATION FOR VISITORS

● **Documents**

US and Canadian citizens need only birth certificate or proof of identity to enter Turks and Caicos. All others need a valid passport, although a visa is not necessary except for nationals of communist countries. Onward ticket officially required. Visitors are allowed to stay for 30 days, renewable once only. The immigration office is on Grand Turk, T 946 2939.

● **How To Get There By Air**

Ports of entry for aircraft are Providenciales, South Caicos and Grand Turk, but the major international airport is on Providenciales. There are also airstrips on North Caicos, Middle Caicos, Pine Cay and Salt Cay. It is worth checking in early when returning to Miami, to avoid long queues. If travelling in a small group it is worth considering a charter to Haiti or the Dominican Republic.

Airlines and schedules have changed frequently and abruptly over the last few years and continue to do so, with passengers being stranded in airports. American Airlines flies daily from Las Vegas via Dallas/Fort Worth and Miami to Provo. Turks & Caicos Airways (TCA) flies from Miami, Nassau and Cap Haitien (also Air Metro North but flights from Haiti suspended 1994) into Provo and from Miami, Cap Haitien (suspended) and Puerto Plata (Dominican Republic) into Grand Turk and provides connecting flights between Grand Turk, Salt Cay, South Caicos, Middle Caicos, North Caicos and Providenciales. Flight time from Grand Turk to the furthest island (Provo) is 30 minutes (US$52), but TCA delays are notorious. TCA mainly uses 7-seater planes which are widely used by the islanders, rather like a bus service. Flamingo Air Service (T 946 2109) and Inter Island Airways (T 941 5481) also provide frequent flights between the islands. Private charters are readily available within the island group and can easily be arranged by asking around at Grand Turk or Provo airport, as charter pilots wait to see if they can fill a plane in the mornings. **See page 273** for telephone numbers of charter companies. On other islands they are easily arranged by phone. Airport departure tax is US$15.

● How To Get There By Sea
There is no scheduled passenger shipping service (cargo comes in regularly from Florida) and no port is deep enough to take cruise ships although some occasionally stop outside the reef and shuttle in passengers for half a day.

● Airlines
TCA, T 946 4255, domestic emergency T 941 5353, at Miami international airport, concourse E, T 800-845 2161. American Airlines T 1-800-433 7300 or locally, T 941 5700.

● Internal Transport
There are no buses. On-island transport is restricted to expensive taxi service with a basic fare of US$2/mile, although drivers are not always consistent. A trip from the airport to the *Ramada* can cost US$10, US$15 or US$20 depending on your luck. Complaints are frequent. Taxis can be hired for island tours, agree the price before hand. Rental cars are available on Grand Turk, North and South Caicos and Provo although demand often exceeds supply on Provo. Bicycles and motor scooters can be rented from some hotels but can be relatively expensive compared with cars. Most roads are fairly basic, although those on Provo have been

upgraded and paved, and all parts are easily accessible. Driving is on the left. Maximum speed in urban areas is 20 mph and outside villages 40 mph, but driving is erratic and no one (except visitors) pays heed to speed limits, not even the Traffic Department. Local drivers do not dim their headlights at night. Watch out for donkeys on Grand Turk.

● Where To Stay
There is a 10% service charge and 7% tax added to the bill. Do not expect miracles from the plumbing, even in new hotels. The hot and cold taps are frequently reversed, the toilets wobble. Hotels on Provo are aiming for North American standards and are expensive. Cheap to inexpensive, value for money accommodation is hard to find. Hoteliers may quote a price, only to forget it on check out. Rack rates will not include tax and service, be sure to check what you are quoted.

● Camping
Camping is possible on beaches on most islands, but no facilities and not encouraged. Contact the District Commissioner's office on each island for permission. If planning to stay on a deserted island take everything with you and leave nothing behind. A very basic, private campsite was started on North Caicos in 1993 but you have to take all your own gear.

● Where To Eat
Good but expensive in hotels. Restaurants and snack bars are generally of a good standard but not cheap. Seafood, mainly conch and lobster, is widely available and is an important export product, but nearly all food is imported and therefore costly. Fresh fruit and vegetables come from either the Dominican Republic or Florida. Vegetarians should order their meals in advance as there is rarely anything without meat or fish on the menu. There are no hamburger bars or fast food outlets, yet.

● Nightlife
The Port Royal Casino at the *Ramada Turquoise Reef Hotel* offers black jack, craps, roulette, money wheel, Caribbean stud poker, T 946 5508, F 946 5554.

Local bands play mostly calypso, reggae and the traditional island music with its Haitian and African influences. On Provo, ask hoteliers and residents when and where live bands and karaoke sing alongs are held at various watering holes. Bands sometimes play at the *Island Princess*, *Pub on the Bay*, *Alfred's Place* (see above, **Where To Eat**). The *Bacchus Club*, opp the *Ramada* in the 'glass house', a dance/lounge opened 1993, Thur 1900 onwards, finger food, Fri 2100-dawn, Sat 1900-2400, cover charge US$3 except Sat, ladies free Thur, no dress code but dressy is best. *Disco Elite* on Airport Road in Down Town, Provo, is a must for night hawks, good mix of Turks islanders and visitors, crowded, noisy, Fri 1500-0300, Mon-Sat 1500 onwards, canned music, pool table, slot machines. *Club Med* has nightly disco for guests and visitors who phone for reservations (which can include dinner/show). Night life does not start until 2200-2300. On Grand Turk, the *Salt Raker Inn* for music on Wed and Sun nights.

● **Security**

There is little personal security problem on most islands and it is safe to walk around at night. However, particularly on Provo, take normal precautions about leaving valuables in your room or on the beach, and be cautious at night on deserted beaches or roads.

● **Launderette**

On Provo there is a laundry/dry cleaners in Butterfield Square, Down Town, and a laundromat at *Treasure Beach Villas*.

● **Currency**

The official currency is the US dollar, although some Turks and Caicos coins are in use, including a crown (US$1) and a quarter crown. Most hotels, restaurants and taxi drivers will accept travellers' cheques, but personal cheques are not widely accepted. There are banks on Grand Turk and Providenciales. Barclays Bank is on Grand Turk, T 946 2831, F 946 2695, at Butterfield Square, PO Box 236, Provo, T 946 4245, F 946 4573, and an agency service is held on South Caicos on Thur, T 946 3268. Scotiabank is at the Town Centre Mall, PO Box 15, Provo, T 946 4750/2, F 946 4755, and at Harbour House, PO Box 132, Grand Turk, T 946 2506/7, F 946 2667. Take small denomination US dollars when visiting an island without a bank, as it is often difficult to get change from a US$50 or US$100 note.

● **Health**

There are no endemic tropical diseases and no malaria, no special vaccinations are required prior to arrival. On Provo, Menzies Medical Practice, Leeward Highway, between Suzie Turn and Down Town, open 0830-1700 Mon-Fri, 0830-1200 Sat, 2 doctors and emergency service, dental care, pharmacy and recompression chamber, T 946 4242. Provo Health Medi-

cal Centre, Down Town, open 0830-1700 Mon-Fri, 0830-1200 Sat, 2 doctors providing primary care and emergency service as well as eye and dental clinic, T 946 4201 for appointment, 946 4300 after hours. The government Blue Hills Clinic has a doctor and midwife on duty, T 946 4228. Ambulance services available and emergency medical air charter with full life support can be arranged. On Grand Turk there is a hospital on the N side of town and a government clinic in town, open 0800-1230, 1400-1630. The other islands organize emergency air evacuation to Grand Turk hospital.

● **Climate**

There is no recognized rainy season, and temperatures average 75°-85°F from November to May, reaching into the 90°s from June to October, but constant tradewinds keep life comfortable. Average annual rainfall is 21 inches on Grand Turk and South Caicos but increases to 40 inches as you travel westwards through the Caicos Islands where more lush vegetation is found. Hurricane season is normally June-October. Hurricane Kate swept through the islands November 1985; Hugo and Andrew missed in 1992.

● **Clothing**

Dress is informal and shorts are worn in town as well as on the beach. Topless sunbathing is accepted at *Club Med*, while the *Ramada* and *Le Deck* allow total nudity on their beaches. The islanders, however, find it offensive and do not look favourably on visitors who flaunt local protocol, they prefer men and women to cover up. Islanders love to dress up in the evenings when they frequent live band nights at hotels or discos.

● **National Holidays**

New Year's Day, Good Friday, Easter Monday, Commonwealth Day (last Monday in May), the Queen's birthday (second week in June), Emancipation Day (beginning of August), Columbus' Day and Human Rights Day (both in October), Christmas Day and Boxing Day.

● **Electric Current**

110 volts, 60 cycles, the same as in the USA.

● **Communications**

Grand Turk, Provo and South Caicos have a modern local and international telephone service, with Cable and Wireless offices in Grand Turk and Provo. Telephone services on the North and Middle Caicos and Salt City are improving. There are public phones but it is often best to ask at a hotel or bar; many public phones only take phonecards and it is wise to buy one for at least US$5 at the airport on arrival. The international code is 809. The small volume of international calls means that costs are high; a call to the UK costs US$3.30 a minute at peak time (US$2.70 off-peak). US 800 calls will be charged at the normal rate. The local phone book has a list of charges to anywhere in the world. Phone cards are available from Cable and Wireless and from outlets near phone booths in US$5, US$10 and US$20 denominations, The Cable and Wireless Public Sales Office in Grand Turk and Provo has a public fax service, F 946 4210.

● **Travel Agent**

Marco Travel Services, Down Town and at Turtle Cove, T 946 4393, F 946 4048, for reconfirmation of tickets, emergency check cashing, travel services, traveller's cheque sales, Amex representative. Through its Turtle Tours desk in the *Ramada* lobby it also offers watersports. Provo Travel Ltd, run by Althea Ewing, opened in 1992 at Central Square, Leeward Highway, T 946 4080, F 946 4081, helpful. Island Travel T 941 5195, Down Town, near shell station, specializes in travel and shopping packages for

TCI residents, international bookings and tours. On Grand Turk; T & C Travel Ltd, at *Hotel Kittina*, Box 42, T 946 2592, F 946 2877, run by Daphne James, friendly, reliable.

● **Tourist Information**

Turks and Caicos Islands Tourist Board, PO Box 128, Pond Street, Grand Turk, Turks & Caicos Islands, T 946 2321/2322, F 946 2733. On Provo the Tourist Office is at Turtle Cove, T 946 4970.

USA/Canada: Trombone Associates Inc, 420 Madison Avenue, New York NY 10017, T (212) 223-2323, F 223-0260.

Europe: c/o Morris Kevan International Ltd, International House, 47 Chase Side, Enfield, Middlesex, EN2 6NB, T 081-367 5175, F 081-367 9949.

We are most grateful to Louise Fletcher, *Columbus Slept Here*, Provo, for her thorough and exhaustive revision of this chapter; also to Jo Anne James Selver, *Jo Anne's Bed and Breakfast*, North Caicos, for her work on North Caicos, and other cays; to Angela Gordon, *Beachcomber House*, Grand Turk and to Brian Riggs, the Turks and Caicos National Museum, Grand Turk, for their corrections and additions to the Grand Turk section.

HISPANIOLA

ONE MIGHT EXPECT that a relatively small island such as Hispaniola (from Spanish "Isla Española" – the Spanish island) lying in the heart of the Caribbean would be occupied by one nation, or at least that its people should demonstrate ethnic and cultural similarities. This is not so. Hispaniola, with an area of just over 75,800 square km, not much more than half the size of Cuba, is shared by two very different countries, the Dominican Republic and Haiti. The original indigenous name for the island, Quisqueya, is still used in the Dominican Republic as an "elegant variation". Hispaniola is mountainous and forested, with plains and plateaux. Haiti, with 27,700 square km, has a population of 6.8 million increasing at an annual rate of 2.0%. The Dominican Republic is much larger in area, 48,443 square km, including some offshore islands, but its population is not larger to the same degree at 7.5 million, growing at 2.2% a year. In the Dominican Republic, over 60% of the population is urban, yet only 30% in Haiti live in towns.

Columbus visited the N coast of Hispaniola, modern Haiti, on his first visit to the West Indies, leaving a few men there to make a settlement before he moved on to Cuba. Columbus traded with the native Tainos for trinkets such as gold nose plugs, bracelets and other ornaments, which were to seal the Indians' fate when shown to the Spanish monarchs. A second voyage was ordered immediately. Columbus tried again to establish settlements, his first having been wiped out. His undisciplined men were soon at war with the native Tainos, who were hunted, taxed and enslaved. Hundreds were shipped to Spain, where they died. When Columbus had to return to Spain he left his brother, Bartolomé, in charge of the fever-ridden, starving colony. The latter sensibly moved the settlement to the healthier S coast and founded Santo Domingo, which became the capital of the Spanish Indies. The native inhabitants were gradually eliminated by European diseases, murder, suicide and slavery, while their crops were destroyed by newly introduced herds of cattle and pigs. Development was hindered by the labour shortage and the island became merely a base from which to provision further exploration, being a source of bacon, dried beef and cassava. Even the alluvial gold dwindled and could not compete with discoveries on the mainland. Sugar was introduced at the beginning of the sixteenth century and the need for labour soon brought African slaves to the island. In 1512 the Indians were declared free subjects of Spain, and missionary zeal ensured their conversion to Christianity.

The Haitians are almost wholly black, with a culture that is a unique mixture of African and French influences. Haiti was a French colony until 1804 when, fired by the example of the French Revolution, the black slaves revolted, massacred the French landowners and proclaimed the world's first black republic. Throughout the 19th century the Haitians reverted to a primitive way of life, indulging in a succession of bloody, almost tribal wars. Even today, nowhere else in the Caribbean do African cults, particularly voodoo, play such a part in everyday life. The standard of living is the lowest in the Caribbean and Americas.

The Dominicans are a mixture of black, Amerindian and white, with a far stronger European strain (but see **Introduction** to the Dominican Republic, below). Their culture and language are hispanic and their religion Roman Catholic. Economically, the country is much more developed, despite a stormy political past and unsavoury periods of dictatorship, particularly under Generalísimo Trujillo (1930-61). Nevertheless, in a material sense the country prospered during the Trujillo era and the standard of living is much higher than it is in Haiti.

The climate is tropical but tempered by sea breezes. The cooler months are between December and March.

HAITI

The Republic of Haiti occupies the western third of the island. Haitian Créole is the only language of 85% of its inhabitants. It evolved from French into a distinct language. The other 15% speak Créole and French. About 95% are of virtually pure African descent. The rest are mostly mulattoes, the descendants of unions between French masters and African slaves. The mulattoes became the ruling class, called the élite. In the last 50 years their economic preeminence has been weakened by Arab immigrants while an emerging black middle-class took over the state sector. Haiti is an Indian word meaning "high ground." It is the Caribbean's most mountainous country. Except for a few small, mainly coastal plains and the central Artibonite River valley, the entire country is a mass of ranges. The highest peak is the 2,674m La Selle, SE of the capital. Little remains of Haiti's once luxuriant forest cover, cut down for fuel or to make way for farming. With soil erosion and desertification far advanced, Haiti is an ecological disaster. The main regions still regularly receiving abundant rainfall are the SW peninsula and the eastern two thirds of the northern seaboard. Haiti has two rainy seasons: April-May and September-October.

History

In the 17th century the French invaded from their base on Tortuga and colonized what became known as Saint Domingue, its borders later being determined by the Treaty of Ryswick in 1697. The area was occupied by cattle hunting buccaneers and pirates, but Governor de Cussy, appointed in 1684, introduced legal trading and planting. By the eighteenth century it was regarded as the most valuable tropical colony of its size in the world and was the largest sugar producer in the West Indies. However, that wealth was based on slavery and the planters were aware of the dangers of rebellion. After the French Revolution, slavery came under attack in France and the planters defensively called for more freedom to run their colony as they wished. In 1791 France decreed that persons of colour born of free parents should be entitled to vote; the white inhabitants of Saint Domingue refused to implement the decree and mulattoes were up in arms demanding their rights. However, while the whites and mulattoes were absorbed in their dispute, slave unrest erupted in the N in 1791. Thousands of white inhabitants were slaughtered and the northern plain was put to the torch. Soon whites, mulattoes and negroes were all fighting with shifting alliances and mutual hatred.

Out of the chaos rose a new leader, an ex-slave called François-Dominique Toussaint, also known as Toussaint Louverture, who created his own roaming army after the 1791 uprising. When France and Spain went to war, he joined the Spanish forces as a mercenary and built up a troop of 4,000 negroes. However, when the English captured Port-au-Prince in 1794 he defected with his men to join the French against the English. After four years of war and disease, the English withdrew, by which time Toussaint was an unrivalled leader among the black population. He then turned against the mulattoes of the W and S, forcing their armies to surrender. Ordered to purge the mulatto troops, Toussaint's cruel lieutenant, Jean-Jacques Dessalines, an African-born ex-slave, slew at least 350. Mulatto historians later claimed that 10,000 were massacred. The same year, torrential rain broke the irri-

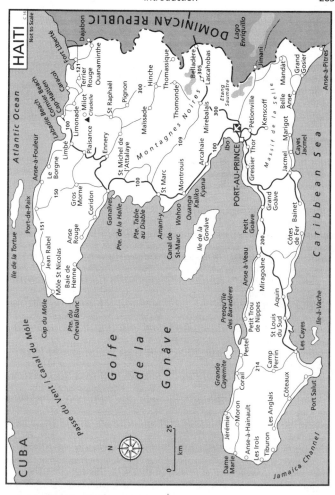

gation dams upon which the prosperity of the area depended. They were never repaired and the soil was gradually eroded to become a wilderness. By 1800 Toussaint was politically supreme. In 1801 he drew up a new constitution and proclaimed himself governor general for life. However, Napoleon had other plans, which included an alliance with Spain, complicated by Toussaint's successful invasion of Santo Domingo, and the reintroduction of the colonial system based on slavery. In 1802 a French army was sent to Saint Domingue which defeated Toussaint and shipped him to France where he died in prison. The news that slavery had been reintroduced in Guadeloupe, however, provoked another popular uprising which drove out the French, already weakened by fever.

This new revolt was led by Dessalines, who had risen to power in Toussaint's entourage and was his natural successor. In 1804 he proclaimed himself Emperor of the independent Haiti, changing the country's name to the Indian word for "high land". Dessalines was assassinated in 1806 and the country divided between his rival successors: the negro Christophe in the N, and the mulatto Pétion in the S. The former's rule was based on forced labour and he managed to keep the estates running until his death in 1820. (He called himself Roi Henri Christophe and built the Citadelle and Sans Souci near Milot – see below; for a fictionalized account of these events, read Alejo Carpentier's *El reino de este mundo – The Kingdom of This World*, arguably the first Latin American novel to employ the technique of "lo real maravilloso".) Pétion divided the land into peasant plots, which in time became the pattern all over Haiti and led to economic ruin with virtually no sugar production and little coffee. Revolution succeeded revolution as hatred between the blacks and the ruling mulattoes intensified; constitutional government rarely existed in the nineteenth century.

At the beginning of the 20th century, the USA became financially and politically involved for geopolitical and strategic reasons. Intervention in 1915 was provoked by the murder and mutilation of a president, but occupation brought order and the reorganization of public finances. Provision of health services, water supply, sewerage and education did not prevent opposition to occupation erupting in an uprising in 1918-20 which left 2,000 Haitians dead. By the 1930s the strategic need for occupation had receded and the expense was unpopular in the USA. In 1934 the USA withdrew, leaving Haiti poor and overpopulated with few natural resources. Migrants commonly sought work on the sugar estates of the neighbouring Dominican Republic, although there was hatred between the two nations. In 1937 about 10,000 Haitian immigrants were rounded up and massacred in the Dominican Republic.

In 1957 François (Papa Doc) Duvalier, a black nationalist, was elected president and unlike previous autocrats he succeeded in holding on to power. He managed to break the mulattoes' grip on political power, even if not on the economy. In 1964 he became President-for-Life, a title which was inherited by his 19-year-old son, Jean-Claude (Baby Doc) in 1971. The Duvaliers' power rested on the use of an armed militia, the "Tontons Macoutes", to dominate the people. Tens of thousands of Haitians were murdered and thousands more fled the country. However, repression eased under Jean-Claude, and dissidence rose, encouraged partly by US policies on human rights. Internecine rivalry continued and the mulatto elite began to regain power, highlighted by the President's marriage to Michèle Bennett, the daughter of a mulatto businessman, in 1980. Discontent began to grow with the May 1984 riots in Gonaïves and Cap Haïtien, and resurfaced after the holding of a constitutional referendum on 22 July 1985 which gave the Government 99.98% of the vote. Several months of unrest and rioting gradually built up into a tide of popular insistence on the removal of Duvalier, during the course of which several hundred people were killed by his henchmen. The dictatorship of the Duvaliers (father and son) was brought to a swift and unexpected end when the President-for-Life fled to France on 7 February 1986.

The removal of the Duvaliers has left Haitians hungry for radical change. The leader of the interim military-civilian Government, General Henri Namphy, promised presidential elections for November 1987, but they were called off after Duvalierists massacred at least 34 voters early on polling day with apparent military connivance. New, rigged elections were held in January 1988, and Professor Leslie Manigat was handed the presidency only to be ousted in June when he tried to remove Namphy as army commander. Namphy took over as military president, but four months later he himself was ousted in a coup that brought General Prosper Avril to power. Dissatisfaction within the army resurfaced in April, 1989, when several coup attempts were staged within quick succession and lawlessness increased as armed gangs, including disaffected soldiers, terrorized the population. Nevertheless, the USA renewed aid, for the first time since 1987, on the grounds that Haiti was moving towards democratic elections, promised for 1990, and was making efforts to combat drug smuggling. Under General Namphy, cocaine worth US$700mn passed through Haiti each month, with a 10% cut for senior army officers. However, Avril's position was insecure; he moved closer to hardline Duvalierists and arrests, beatings and murders of opposition activists increased. Foreign aid was again cut off in January 1990 when Avril imposed a state of siege and the holding of elections looked unlikely. Finally, in March, General Avril fled the country after a week of mass demonstrations and violence. Following his resignation, Haiti was governed by an interim President, Supreme Court judge, Ertha Pascal-Trouillot.

Despite poor relations between Mme Pascal-Trouillot and the 19-member Council of State appointed to assist her, successful elections were held on 16 December 1990. The presidential winner, by a landslide margin of 67% to 15%, was Father Jean-Bertrand Aristide; his nearest rival was the former finance minister Marc Bazin. The electoral campaign was marked by the candidacy of Roger Lafontant, a Duvalieriest and former "security official" of Baby Doc. A warrant for his arrest did not prevent Lafontant running

for the presidency; only the failure of his coup attempt against Mme Pascal-Trouillot in January 1991 brought him to justice.

President Aristide ("Titide"), a Roman Catholic priest who was expelled from the Salesian order in 1988 for "incitement to hatred, violence and class struggle", was sworn in on 7 February. His denunciations of corruption within the government, church and army over the previous decade had won him a vast following. Among his immediate steps on taking office were to start investigations into the conduct of Mme Pascal Trouillot and many other officials, to seek the resignation of six generals, to propose the separation of the army and police and to garner urgently-needed financial assistance from abroad for the new administration. Aristide's refusal to share power with other politicians, his attacks on the interests of the armed forces and the business elite and the actions of some of his militant supporters provoked his overthrow on 30 September 1991 by sections of the army sympathetic to Lafontant (who was murdered in his cell during the rising). Aristide fled into exile; a supreme court judge, Joseph Nerette, was made president, and Jean-Jacques Honorat, a fierce critic of Aristide and a former human rights activist was sworn in as prime minister. Harsh repression was imposed after the deposition of Aristide; at least 2,000 people were said to have died in the first six months, almost 600 during the coup itself. People began fleeing in small boats to the United States' Guantánamo naval base on Cuba in an exodus that had reached 38,000 by May 1992. The USA brought it to an end by immediately repatriating everyone without screening political asylum claims.

International condemnation of the coup was swift, with the Organization of American States, led by the USA, imposing an embargo. While the EC and other nations did not join in the embargo, they did follow the OAS in suspending aid and freezing Haitian government assets. The sanctions hurt, but not sufficiently to promote a formula for Aristide's return; this was partly because of Washington's misgivings about his radical populism. In June 1992, the army sacked President Nerette and appointed the 1990 election runner-up, Marc Bazin, as prime minister. His task of negotiating the embargo's removal was unsuccessful as he was not empowered to accept Aristide's return. At the same time, he was powerless to curb military corruption and human rights abuses.

During the 1992 US presidential election campaign, Bill Clinton promised to stop the blanket repatriation of Haitian boat people and reinstate screening of asylum claims. He also pledged to redouble efforts to get Aristide reinstated. Predictions of a new, Florida-bound refugee tidal wave forced Clinton to back down; shortly before taking office he announced that the Bush policy on repatriation would be maintained. To offset this U-turn, Clinton was obliged to seek visible progress on Aristide's return.

The prospect of more decisive US action prompted United Nations involvement. Former Argentine foreign minister Dante Caputo was appointed UN special envoy for Haiti in December 1992. With Washington making it clear it was ready to step up sanctions, Caputo persuaded Bazin and the army commander, General Raoul Cedras, to agree in February 1993 to the deployment of 250 civilian UN/OAS human rights monitors throughout Haiti. This had long been requested by Aristide. Thereafter, Caputo left Bazin out of negotiations, dealing instead directly with General Cedras. Further UN pressure was applied in June 1993 with the imposition of an oil embargo and a freeze on financial assets. As a result, an accord was reached in July whereby Aristide would return to office by 30 October, Cedras would retire and Aristide would appoint a new army chief and a prime minister.

As the 30 October deadline approached, it became clear that Aristide would not be allowed to return. In mid-October, the Haitian rulers humiliated the USA by refusing to allow a ship to dock carrying a 1,300-strong UN non-combat mission. The ship withdrew to the despair of Caputo, Canada (who provided a share of the UN force) and Robert Malval, Aristide's appointee as prime minister. Although the USA warned the régime not to harm any of Malval's cabinet, Guy Malary, the Justice Minister in charge of passing a law to separate the military and the police (part of the July accord), was murdered. Oil and arms sanctions were reimposed, yet Aristide supporters continued to be killed and harassed. Malval and his cabinet resigned in mid-December as the régime showed no signs of weakening. In fact, as smuggled fuel from the Dominican Republic flowed in, Cedras and his collaborators set their sights on staying in power until the end of Aristide's term of office, February 1996.

Meanwhile, tensions between Aristide and the Clinton administration grew as the USA appeared unable, or unwilling, to break the impasse. Pressure from the US Black Caucus and from Florida politicians eventually persuaded Clinton to take more positive action. The policy of returning boat people was stopped and asylum seekers were processed aboard two ships anchored in Jamaican waters. A land-based processing centre was built to replace the ships on Grand Turk, Turks and Caicos Islands. Tough worldwide sanctions, to include a cessation of commercial flights, were initiated in May 1994. The Dominican Republic was approached to control sanctions breaking, although the uncertainty over the presidential elections did not promise speedy action. These measures led to a state of emergency in Haiti, but not an end to defiance for, in the same month, the head of the Supreme Court,

Emile Jonassaint, was appointed provisional president, with a mandate to call elections. By June, a possible US-led invasion was given some support, but wholehearted support was not forthcoming in the USA itself. The Pentagon sent four amphibious assault ships and 2,000 Marines to the region but still General Cedras was not intimidated. Instead, he gave a team of 100 UN and OAS human rights observers 48 hours to leave the country. Finding a safe haven for the refugees (about 18,000 boat people were picked up in a month) was problematic. Panama agreed to take 10,000 but then changed its mind. Other Caribbean islands were approached but dragged their heels. By July there were 12,800 Haitians at the US base in Guantánamo, Cuba, and 3,000 more on US navy ships.

Government

At the time of going to press, Haiti was governed by a military-dominated extraconstitutional régime with two legislative houses. Seeking to end a tradition of autocratic presidents, the 1987 constitution tried to divide power between the president and a parliament consisting of a 27-seat Senate and an 83-seat Chamber of Deputies. The formula's failure on its first attempt helped pave the way for the 1991 coup.

The Economy

Haiti is the Western Hemisphere's poorest country and among the 30 poorest in the world. 75% of the people fall below the World Bank's absolute poverty level. It is overpopulated. It lacks communications, cheap power and raw materials for industry. Its mountainous terrain cannot provide a living for its rural population.

Until the embargo, the main economic problem was chronic low agricultural productivity, compounded by low world commodity prices. 1% of the population controls 40% of the wealth. The average farm size is less than 1 hectare.

HAITI : FACT FILE

Geographic

Land area	27,700 sq km
forested	1.4%
pastures	18.0%
cultivated	32.8%

Demographic

Population (1992)	6,764,000
annual growth rate (1987-92)	2.0%
urban	29.6%
rural	70.4%
density	244.2 per sq km
Religious affiliation	
Roman Catholic (inc Voodoo)	80.3%
Birth rate per 1,000 (1991)	43.0
	(world av 26.4)
Death rate per 1,000 (1991)	15.0
	(world av 9.2)

Education and Health

Life expectancy at birth,	
male	52 years
female	55 years
Infant mortality rate	
per 1,000 live births (1991)	106.0
Physicians (1989)	1 per 6,083 persons
Hospital beds	1 per 1,258 persons
Calorie intake as %	
of FAO requirement	89%
Population age 25 and over	
with no formal schooling	76.9%
Literate males (over 15)	59.1%
Literate females (over 15)	47.4%

Economic

GNP (1990 market prices)	US$2,400mn
GNP per capita	US$370
Public external debt (1991)	US$745mn
Tourism receipts (1990-91)	US$66mn
Inflation (annual av 1986-91)	6.7%
Radio	1 per 2.2 persons
Television	1 per 265 persons
Telephone	1 per 79 persons

Employment

Population economically active (1990)	
	2,679,140
Unemployment rate (1989)	60.0%
% of labour force in	
agriculture	57.3
mining	0.9
manufacturing	5.6
construction	1.0
Military forces	7,400

Source *Encyclopaedia Britannica*

Only a third of the land is arable, yet most of the people live in the country, using rudimentary tools to grow maize, rice, sorghum and coffee. Deforestation has played havoc with watersheds and agriculture. Only 1.4% of the land is now forested, yet charcoal continues to supply 70% of fuel needs. Agriculture generates only a third of the gdp but employs more than half the workforce. Coffee is the main cash crop, providing 11% of exports. Sugar and sisal output has slumped as population pressure has forced farmers to switch to subsistence crops.

Industry and commerce is limited, and heavily concentrated in Port-au-Prince. Until the embargo, assembly operations turned out baseballs, garments and electronic parts for export to the USA. Vegetable oils, footwear and metal goods are still produced for domestic consumption. Average pay in manufacturing is less than US$3 a day. Manufactured goods used to make up two thirds of total exports. Tourism all but disappeared in the 1980s, at first because of a scare about AIDS, then because of the political instability. Many hotels were forced to close. The number of hotel rooms in operation has fallen from 3,000 to 650. Cruise ships stopped coming altogether after the 1991 coup.

The 1987 aid cut-off by major donors hit the economy hard and gdp began to slip. Aid resumed in 1990 as the prospects of elections improved. By mapping out very orthodox economic policies, the Aristide government secured pledges of more than US$400mn in international aid in July and August 1991, but it never materialized because of the coup the following month.

The import embargo imposed in October 1991 caused an acute shortage of petroleum products, but the de facto government's business allies soon learned how to buy on the spot market. The telephone and power companies were starved of spare parts; the already bad phone system got much worse and blackouts got longer. The import embargo also helped drive up prices of foodstuffs and other essential goods. Among those who made fat profits from contraband imports were, it was alleged, close allies of the army high command. The most damaging sanctions were the export embargo, the aid cut-off and the freezing of assets abroad. The export assembly sector closed down, putting 35,000 out of work and depriving Haiti of 40% of its foreign currency earning (US$250mn to US$300nm a year). A few factories later reopened under special exemption licences issued by the US Treasury, but closed again after the imposition of the May 1994 sanctions. The aid cut-off stripped Haiti of another US$150mn to US$180mn a year. Virtually the only source of dollars left untouched, aside from drug smuggling (around US$500m worth of cocaine from Colombia was shipped through Haiti in 1993), was remittances by the 1.5 million Haitians living abroad, put at about US$150mn a year.

The economy contracted by 9-10% in the year after the coup. (In normal years, it used to grow by about 2.5 to 3%.) Of the 200,000 jobs in the formal sector, at least 50,000 were lost. Another 50,000 went in the informal sector. The government's revenues fell, but it was unable to curb spending, which outpaced earnings by 40%. Monetary emission soared, causing inflation to surge from 12% to an annual 45%. The Haitian gourde, more or less stable at 7.5 to the dollar during the 18 months prior to the coup, plummeted to 13 during the 18 months after the coup.

Culture

Although Haiti wiped out slavery in its 18th century revolution, its society still suffers from the racial, cultural and linguistic divisions inherited from slavery. Toussaint's tolerant statesmanship was unable to resist Napeolon's push to reimpose slavery. It took the tyranny and despotism of Dessalines and Christophe. Haitian despots stepped into the shoes of the French despots. The new, mulatto ruling class considered its French language and culture superior to the blacks' Créole language and Voodoo religion, which it despised. The corruption and despotism of the black political class created by Duvalier suggest that, despite its profession of "noirisme," it internalized the mulatto contempt for its own race.

Religion

Voodoo (French: Vaudou) is a blend of religions from West Africa, above all from Dahomey (present-day Benin) and the Congo River basin. Like Cuba's Santería and Brazil's Candomblé, it uses drumming, singing and dance to induce possession by powerful African spirits with colourful personalities. Called *loas* in Haiti (pronounced lwa), they help with life's daily problems. In return, they must be "served" with ceremonies, offerings of food and drink, and occasional animal sacrifice in temples known as *ounphors*.

The essence of Voodoo is keeping in harmony with the *loas*, the dead and nature. Magic may be used in self-defense, but those in perfect harmony with the universe should not need it. Magic in the pursuit of personal ambitions is frowned on. The use of black magic and sorcery, or the use of attack magic against others without just cause, is considered evil. Sorcerers, called *bokors*, exist but they are not seen as part of Voodoo. The *loas* punish Voodoo priests (*oungans*) or priestesses (*mambos*) who betray their vocation by practicing black magic. Many Haitians believe in the existence of *zombis*, the living dead victims of black magic who are supposedly disinterred by sorcerers and put to work as slaves.

Voodoo acquired an overlay of Catholicism in colonial times, when the slaves learned to disguise their *loas* as saints. Nowadays, major ceremonies coincide with Catholic celebrations such as Chistmas, Epiphany and the Day of the Dead. Lithographs of Catholic saints are used to represent the *loas*.

The role of attack and defence magic in Haiti's religious culture expanded during the slave revolts and the independence war. Many rebel leaders were *oungans*, such as Mackandal, who terrorized the northern plain with his knowledge of poisons from 1748 to 1758, and Boukman, who plotted the 1791 uprising at a clandestine Voodoo ceremony. Belief in Voodoo's protective spells inspired a fearlessness in battle that amazed the French. As a result, many Haitian rulers saw Voodoo as a threat to their own authority and tried to stamp it out. They also thought its survival weakened Haiti's claim to membership of the family of "civilized" nations. François Duvalier enlisted enough *oungans* to neutralize Voodoo as a potential threat. He also coopted the Catholic church hierarchy. He had less success with the Catholic grass roots which, inspired by Liberation Theology, played a key role in his son's 1986 fall and Aristide's election in 1990.

After several ruthless campaigns against Voodoo, most recently in the early 1940s, the Catholic church has settled into an attitude of tolerant coexistence. Now the militant hostility to Voodoo comes from fundamentalist Protestant sects of American origin which have exploited their relative wealth and ability to provide jobs to win converts.

Language

The origins of Haitian Créole are hotly disputed. Is Créole basically a French-derived lingua franca of seafarers in the 17th and 18th centuries that reached Haiti already evolved? Or is it the product of the transformation of French in Saint Domingue by African slaves who needed a common language, one the slave-owners were forced to learn in order to speak to their slaves? The evidence points both ways.

More important is how Créole and French are used now. All Haitians understand Créole and speak it at least part of the time. Use of French is limited to the élite and middle class. The illiterate majority of the population understand no French at all. There is almost no teaching in Créole and no attempt is made to teach French as a foreign language to the few Créole-only speakers who enter the school system. Since mastery of French is still a condition for self-advancement, language perpetuates Haiti's deep class divisions. All those pushing for reform in Haiti are trying to change this. Radio stations have begun using Créole in the last 10 years. Musicians now increasingly sing in Créole. The 1987 constitution gave Créole equal official status alongside French. Even élite politicians have begun using Créole in speeches although some speak it poorly. Aristide's sway over the people is due in part to his poetic virtuosity in Créole. A phonetic transcription of Créole has evolved over the last 50 years, but little has been published except the Bible, some poetry and, nowadays, a weekly pro-Aristide newspaper, *Libète*. Créole is famed for its proverbs voicing popular philosophy and reflecting Haiti's enormous social divisions. The best teach yourself book is *Ann Pale Kreyòl*, published by the Créole Institute, Ballentine Hall 602, Indiana University, Bloomington IN 47405, USA. It is hard to find in Haitian bookshops. **NB:** In the text below, "Cr:" means Créole version.

The Arts

Haitian handicraft and naive art is the best in the Caribbean. Even such utilitarian articles as the woven straw shoulder bags and the tooled-leather scabbards of the peasant machete have great beauty. The "rada" Voodoo drum is an object of great aesthetic appeal. Haiti is famed for its wood carvings, but poverty has pushed craftsmen into producing art from such cheap material as papier maché and steel drums, flattened and turned into cut-out wall-hangings or sculpture. Haitian naive art on canvas emerged only in response to the demand of travellers and tourists in the 1930s and 40s, but it had always existed on the walls of Voodoo temples, where some of the best representations of the spirit world are to be found. Weddings, cock-fights, market scenes or fantasy African jungles are other favoured themes. Good paintings can range from one hundred to several thousand dollars. Mass-produced but lively copies of the masters sell for as little as US$10. Negotiating with street vendors and artists can be an animated experience, offering insights into the nation's personality. (See **Where To Buy** sections below.)

Exposure to white racism during the US occupation shook some of the mulatto intellectuals out of their complacent Francophilia. Led by Jean Price Mars and his 1919 pioneering essay "Ainsi parla l'oncle" (Thus Spoke Uncle) they began to seek their identity in Haiti's African roots. Peasant life, Créole expressions and Voodoo started to appear together with a Marxist perspective in novels such as Jacques Romain's *Gouverneurs de la rosée* (Masters of the Dew). René Depestre, now resident in Paris after years in Cuba, is viewed as Haiti's greatest living novelist. Voodoo, politics and acerbic social comment are blended in the novels of Haiti's youngest successful writer Gary Victor, a deputy minister in the Aristide government before the coup.

Music and Dance

Nigel Gallop writes: The poorest nation in the western hemisphere is among the richest when it comes to music. This is a people whose most popular religion worships the deities through singing, drumming and dancing. The prime musical influence is African, although European elements are to be found, but none that are Amerindian. The music and dance (and in Haiti music is almost inseparable from dance) can be divided into three main categories: Voodoo ritual, rural folk and urban popular. The Voodoo rituals, described above, are collective and are profoundly serious, even when the *loa* is humorous or mischievous. The hypnotic dance is accompanied by call-and-response singing and continuous drumming, the drums themselves (the large Manman, medium-sized Seconde and smaller Bula or Kata) being regarded as sacred.

During Mardi Gras (Carnival) and Rara (see below), bands of masked dancers and revellers can be found on the roads and in the streets almost anywhere in the country, accompanied by musicians playing the Vaccines (bamboo trumpets). Haitians also give rein to their love of music and dance in the so-called Bambouches, social gatherings where the dancing is "pou' plaisi'" (for pleasure) and largely directed to the opposite sex. They may be doing the Congo, the Martinique or Juba, the Crabienne or the national dance, the Méringue. The first two are of African provenance, the Crabienne evolved from the European Quadrille, while the Méringue is cousin to the Dominican Merengue. Haitians claim it originated in their country and was taken to the Dominican Republic during the Haitian occupation of 1822 to 1844, but this is a matter of fierce debate between the two nations. In remote villages it may still be possible to come across such European dances as the Waltz, Polka, Mazurka and Contredanse, accompanied by violin, flute or accordion.

Haitian music has not remained impervious to outside influences during the 20th century, many of them introduced by Haitian migrant workers returning from Cuba, the Dominican Republic and elsewhere in the region (as well as exporting its own music to Cuba's Oriente province in the form of the Tumba Francesa). One very important external influence

was that of the Cuban Son, which gave rise to the so-called "Troubadour Groups", with their melodious voices and soft guitar accompaniment, still to be heard in some hotels. Jazz was another intruder, a result of the US marines' occupation between 1915 and 1934. Then in the 1950s two equally celebrated composers and band leaders, Nemours Jean-Baptiste and Weber Sicot, introduced a new style of recreational dance music, strongly influenced by the Dominican Merengue and known as Compact Directe ("compas") or Cadence Rampa. Compas (the s is not pronounced) dominated the music scene until the past few years, when it has become a much more open market, with Salsa, Reggae, Soca and Zouk all making big inroads. A number of Haitian groups have achieved international recognition, notably Tabou Combo and Coupé Cloué, while female singers Martha-Jean Claude and Toto Bissainthe have also made a name for themselves abroad. One excellent troubadour-style singer who has been well-recorded is Althiery Dorival. Also highly recommended is the set of six LPs titled "Roots of Haiti", recorded in the country, but distributed by Mini Records of Brooklyn. Finally, no comment on Haitian music would be complete without reference to the well-known lullaby "Choucounne" which, under the title "Yellow Bird", is crooned to tourists every night on every English-speaking Antillean island.

Mike Tarr adds: A musical revolution came with the emergence of "voodoo beat," a fusion of Voodoo drumming and melody with an international rock guitar and keyboard sound. Its lyrics call for political change and a return to peasant values. With two albums out on the Island label, and two US tours behind them, Boukman Eksperyans is the most successful of these bands. People who have ignored Voodoo all their lives have possessed at Boukman concerts. Other "voodoo beat" bands of note are Ram,

Boukan Ginen, Foula, Sanba-Yo and Koudjay.

Flora and Fauna

Deforestation and soil erosion have destroyed habitats. Haiti is therefore poor in flora and fauna compared with its eastern neighbour. Three sites are worth visiting. One is Lake Saumâtre, 90 minutes E of the capital. Less brackish than Enriquillo, across the Dominican border, it is the habitat of more than 100 species of waterfowl (including migratory North American ducks), plus flamingoes and American crocodiles. The N side of the lake is better, reached via the town of Thomazeau (see under **Excursions from Port-au-Prince**).

The other two are mountain parks. Relatively easy to reach is Parc La Visite, about 5 hours' hike from the hill resort of Kenscoff behind Port-au-Prince. On the high Massif de la Selle, with a mixture of pine forest and montane cloud forest, it has 80 bird species and two endemic mammals, the Hispaniolan hutia (*Plagiodontia aedium*) and the nez longue (*Solenodon paradoxus*). North American warblers winter there. It is also a nesting-place for the black-capped petrel (*Pteradoma hasitata*). See under **Excursions from Port-au-Prince**. Harder to reach is the Macaya National Park, at the tip of the SW peninsula, site of Haiti's last virgin cloud forest. It has pines 45m high, 141 species of orchid, 102 species of fern, 99 species of moss and 49 species of liverwort. Its fauna include 11 species of butterfly, 57 species of snail, 28 species of amphibian, 34 species of reptile, 65 species of bird and 19 species of bat. In addition to the hutia, nez longue and black-capped petrel, its most exotic animals are the Grey-crowned Palm Tanager (*Phaenicophilus poliocephalus*) and the Hispaniolan trogan (*Temnotrogan roseigaster*). The endangered Peregrine falcon (*Falco pergrinus*) winters in the park. From Les Cayes, it takes half a day to get to a University of Florida base on the edge of the park which has basic camping facilities. Allow another two days each way for the 2,347m Pic de Macaya. See under **Southwest from Port-au-Prince**. Paul Paryski (T 23-1400/1), a UN ecosystems expert, will give advice.

Leaf doctors, voodoo priests and sorcerers have a wealth of knowledge of natural remedies and poisons to be found in Haiti's surviving plant life. They do not share their knowledge readily. In his book *The Serpent and the Rainbow*, Harvard ethnobotanist Wade Davis gives a racy account of his attempts to discover which natural toxins sorcerers are thought to use to turn their victims into *zombis*.

Almost any tree is liable to be chopped down for firewood or charcoal; a few very large species are not because they are believed to be the habitat of *loas*. Chief among them is the silkcotton tree, "mapou" in Creole. Haiti has no poisonous snakes or insects.

Festivals

The standard of the Port-au-Prince carnival has fallen since the Duvaliers left. Nowadays few people wear costumes and the floats are poorly decorated. There is a cacophony of music blaring out from both stands and passing floats. Excitement is provided by the walking bands (*bandes-à-pied*), cousins of the "rara" bands that appear after carnival (see below). Circulating on foot, drawing a large dancing, chanting crowd in their wake, they specialize in salacious lyrics and political satire. Beware, when crowds moving in different directions pass, there is boisterous pushing and occasional knife fights. The safest place to watch is from one of the stands near the *Holiday Inn*. Carnival climaxes on the three days before Ash Wednesday, but the government lays on free open-air concerts in different parts of the city during the three or four weekends of "pre-carnival." Members of the élite prefer the carnival at Jacmel, 2-3 hours from the capital, where the tradition of elaborate, imaginative masked costumes still thrives. The music at Jacmel is unremarkable, however.

Carnival is immediately followed by Rara, dubbed the "peasant carnival." Every weekend during Lent, including Easter weekend, colourfully attired Rara bands emerge from voodoo societies and roam the countryside. They seek donations, so be ready with a few small notes. Beating drums, blowing home-made wind instruments, dancing and singing, some bands may have a thousand or more members. A good place to see it is the town of Leogane near the capital on Easter Sunday. Beware, the drinking is heavy and fights are common.

The Gede (pronounced gay-day) are *loas* who possess Voodooists on 1-2 November (All Saints and Day of the Dead). They can be seen in cemeteries or roaming the streets, dressed to look like corpses or undertakers. The lords of death and the cemetery, they mock human vanity and pretension, and remind people that sex is the source of life. They do this by dancing in a lewd fashion with strangers, causing much hilarity. For pilgrimages, see Saut d'Eau, Plaine du Nord and Limonade in the text below.

Forts

Haiti abounds with ruined forts. Those on the coast were built by the French or English in the 17th and 18th centuries. Those inland were built by the Haitians after winning independence from France in order to deter any attempt to recover the former colony. Having no navy, the Haitian strategy for an invasion was to put the plains to the torch and retreat into the mountains behind a line of fortresses. The strategy was never tested, but the Cacos guerrillas did use some of the forts during their 1918-20 fight against the US occupation.

Travel Hints

Haiti is especially fascinating for the tourist who is avid for out-of-the-way experience. In order that you may make the most of your visit, we offer the following hints. Although it is one of the poorest countries in the world, most of whose citizens suffer from one kind of oppression or another, Haiti is proud of having been the only nation to have carried out successfully a slave rebellion. Haitians at all levels are very sensitive to how they are treated by foreigners, commonly called "blanc". If you treat them with warmth and consideration, they will respond with enthusiasm and friendship. There is no hostility towards "blanc"; if you feel threatened it is probably the result of a misunderstanding.

Eye contact is very important; it is not avoided as in some other countries. Humour plays an important role in social interactions; Haitians survive by laughing at themselves and their situation. This, sadly, became a very difficult proposition during the events following the overthrow of President Aristide. Haitians are physical, touching and flirting a lot.

It is important to recognize the presence of each person in a social encounter, either with a handshake or a nod. When walking in the countryside, you usually wish "bon jour" (before 1100) or "bon soir" to anyone you meet. Coffee or cola are often offered by richer peasants to visitors (Haitian coffee is among the best in the world). Do not expect straight answers to questions about a peasant's wealth, property or income.

It is assumed that each "blanc" is wealthy and therefore it is legitimate to try to separate you from your riches. Such attempts should be treated with humour, indignation or consideration as appropriate.

Guides Young men and boys offer their services as guides at every turn and corner. It seems that it's worthwhile taking one (for about US$10-30 a day, depending where you go) just to prevent others pestering you. Most guides speak English and it is easier to get around with one than without. If you hire a guide you can also visit places off the beaten tourist track and avoid some of the frustrations of the public transport system. Max Church, a pastor who has been training English/French/Créole-speaking guides, can be called on 34-2622, Port-au-Prince. However, if you take guides you must realize that they expect you to buy them food if you stop to eat.

Secondly, and more important, the guides are often "on commission" with local shop- and stall-keepers, so that even if you ask them to bargain for you, you will not necessarily be getting a good price; nor will they necessarily go where you want to go. If you don't want a guide a firm but polite "non, merci" gets the message across. It is best to ignore altogether hustlers outside guesthouses, etc, as any contact makes them persist.

PORT-AU-PRINCE

What *Port-au-Prince* lacks in architectural grace, it makes up in a stunning setting, with steep mountains towering over the city to the S, La Gonâve island in a horsehoe bay on the W, and another wall of mountains beyond a rift valley plain to the N. Over the years the city has spilled out of its original waterfront location, climbing further into the mountains behind. A rural exodus has swollen the population from 150,000 in 1954 to 1.5 million now. The worst shantytowns (*bidonvilles*) are in a marshy waterfront area N of the centre, but most of the city is very poor. Enormous mounds of rotting garbage are a common sight. The commercial quarter starts near the port and stretches inland, to the E, about 10 blocks. It lacks charm or interest, except the area beside the port that was remodelled for the city's 1949 bicentennial. Known as the Bicentenaire (more for-

mally, Cité de l'Exposition), it contains the post office, foreign ministry, parliament, American embassy and French Institute. It is now very run down.

The central reference point for visitors is the large, irregularly-shaped park called the Champs de Mars which begins to the E of the commercial quarter. The NW corner is dominated by the white, triple-domed presidential palace. It was built in 1918 on the site of a predecessor that was blown up in 1912 with its president inside. In the 1991 coup, President Aristide made a stand inside the present building. It is still pockmarked by the bullets that were fired to make the palace guard surrender. Just to the NE is the colonnaded, white and gold army high command building, where soldiers nearly lynched Aristide after dragging him out of the palace. (He was saved by the French ambassador, the American ambassador, or General Cedras, depending on whose story you believe.) Immediately behind the palace, to the S, is a large, mustard-yellow army garrison that was once the fief of the ill-famed Colonel Jean-Claude Paul, indicted in Miami in 1987 for drug smuggling and poisoned the following year.

Immediately to the E of the palace, on Place des Héros de l'Independence, the subterranean Musée du Panthéon National (MUPANAH) houses historial relics, including the rusted anchor of Columbus' flagship, the *Santa María*. Don't miss an 1818 oil paiting of King Henri Christophe by Welshman Richard Evans, director of Christophe's Fine Arts Academy at Sans Souci. Two blocks N and two W, at the corner of rue Courte and the busy rue Pavée, the Sainte Trinité Episcopal Cathedral has astounding biblical murals by the greatest naive artists, including Philomé Obin, Castera Bazile and Riguaud Benoit. Done in 1949, they are considered the crowning achievement of Haitian art. The adjoining complex has a gift shop and a school whose students give excellent choral and classical music concerts (details from Sister Anne-Marie, T 22-5638). The pink and white stone Catholic Cathedral is four blocks to the N.

Back on the Champs de Mars, at its SE corner (intersection of rues Capois and Légitime), the Musée d'Art Haïtien (T 22-2510) has Haiti's finest naive art collection, plus a craft shop and a small restaurant in its garden. The Maison Défly, the house next door on Légitime, built by an army commander in 1896, is

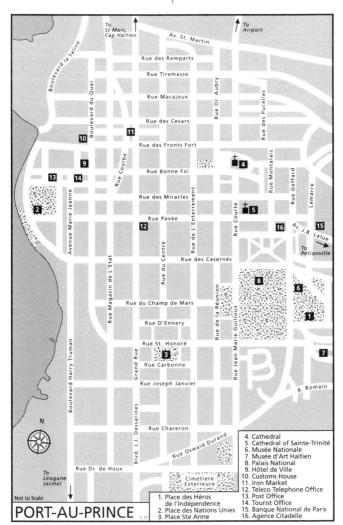

4. Cathedral
5. Cathedral of Sainte-Trinité
6. Musée Nationale
7. Musée d'Art Haïtien
8. Palais National
9. Hôtel de Ville
10. Customs House
11. Iron Market
12. Teleco Telephone Office
13. Post Office
14. Tourist Office
15. Banque National de Paris
16. Agence Citadelle

1. Place des Héros de l'Indépendance
2. Place des Nations Unies
3. Place Ste Anne

PORT-AU-PRINCE

in the Victorian "gingerbread" style, characterized by steep roofs and gables, round turrets, high ceilings, balconies and rich fretwork embellishment. Not a distinguished example, it contains a museum with period furniture, 0900-1300 Monday to Saturday. The eastern side of the Champs de Mars, formed by the Rue Capois, has several hotels, restaurants and shops. At the southern end of rue Capois, 1 km from the Champs de Mars, is the *Hotel Oloffson*, a much more imposing example of a gingerbread. West of rue Capois are leafy neighbourhoods climbing into the foothills where the well-off built residences in the 19th century, and gingerbreads abound.

Local Information
● Where To Stay

Oloffson (see above, T 23-4000/23-4102, F 23-0919), model for Hotel Trianon in Graham Greene's *The Comedians*, eccentrically managed by Haitian-American musician Richard Morse, Haiti's most charming hotel, haunt of writers, journalists and film-makers, voodoo beat or folklore 3 nights a week, pool, never lacks electricity, most rooms a/c, prices from US$49s, US$59d CP; *Holiday Inn* (T 23-9800/93, F 22-0822), 10 rue Capois, central location on Champs de Mars, jungly gardens, pool, tolerable restaurant, own generator, all rooms a/c, prices from US$58.50s, US$68.50d CP; *Visa Lodge* (T 49-1201/2/3/4, 46-2662) businessman's hotel in industrial zone near airport, pool, good restaurant, own generator, US$45s/d EP; *Villa St-Louis* (T 45-6124/6417), 95 ave John Brown, Bourdon (on busy, central avenue where it starts to climb to Pétionville) own generator but turned on only 0600-1000 and 1800-2400, rooms with bathroom and fan (a/c works only with city power), US$25s, US$35d EP; *Prince* (T 45-2764/5), corner of rue 3 and ave N, Pacot, quiet hillside neighbourhood 15 mins' walk from taxis, own generator, all rooms a/c, US$25s, US$30d CP; *Park* (T 22-4406) 25 rue Capois, near *Holiday Inn*, no generator, US$25s, US$35d; *Palace* (T 22-3344), rue Capois at SE corner of Champs de Mars, no generator, cheap, dirty and sleazy.

　　Guest Houses *Sendral's* (T 45-6502), rue Mercier, Bourdon, near *Hotel Villa St-Louis*, own generator, rooms with private bath and fan, US$25s, US$40d CP; *La Griffonne* (T

45-4095/3440), 21 rue Jean Baptiste, Canapé Vert, quiet neighbourhood 5 mins' walk from ave John Brown, own generator, rooms with private bath and a/c, US$25s, US$45d MAP; *Coconut Villa* (T 46-1691), rue Berthold, Delmas 19 (poor location in dusty, northern suburb), own generator but turned off during day, rooms with private bath and a/c, US$20s, US$30d CP; *May's Villa* (T 45-1208), 28 Debussy, quiet neighbourhood at top of ave John Paul II (Cr: Tijo), 10 mins' walk from nearest taxis, view, no generator, rooms with private bath and fan, US$8s, US$14d CP.

Note Most of the best hotels are in Pétionville, which is treated separately, although just 15 mins away. Only the most expensive hotels and guesthouses have air-conditioning plus sufficiently powerful in-house generators able to cope with the long electricity blackouts in the city. Water is also rationed, and many of the cheaper, central hotels lack both water and electricity much of the time.

Tax, service charge and even energy surcharge are sometimes added to hotel bills. These extras have been included in the prices given here, which are very approximate because of exchange rate vagaries. Some hotels have begun to quote US dollar rates to visitors and insist they pay in US$. Where possible, it is cheaper to pay in gourdes bought from money changers. Paying by credit card also works out more expensive.

Check rooms in advance in the cheaper hotels, service may be deficient.

● Where To Eat
Almost the only places to eat out at night in Port-au-Prince proper are the *Oloffson* or *Holiday Inn*, or a row of terrace cafés selling barbequed chicken at the SE corner of the Champs de Mars (starting near Rex theatre). Well-off Port-au-Princiens go up to Pétionville to dine out. The following restaurants are open during the day only: *Table Ronde*, 7 rue Capois (half block from Holiday Inn), good lunch for US$5, front veranda excellent for street watching, popular with politicians; *Café Terrasse*, rear of Air France Bldg, 11 rue Capois and rue Ducoste, excellent lunch for US$10, favoured by international aid agency staffers; *Plaisance*, 3 rue Pavée, near corner of Geffrard, créole lunch for US$3 in quiet garden on busy intersection; *Chez Nenel*, rue Pavée, a block and a half from Ave Marie Jeanne, créole lunch for US$3; *Tiffany* (T 22-3506/0993), Blvd Harry Truman, N of Tele-Haiti, 3-course meal for US$10; *Chez*

Yvane (T 22-0188), 19 Blvd Harry Truman, S of Tele-Haiti, créole lunch for US$4 in new a/c premises.

● **Where To Buy Art And Craft**

Some galleries have a near monopoly on certain artists, so don't expect to see a cross-section of all the major artists in any one, good gallery. The paintings hung at the *Oloffson* are for sale. *Galerie Carlos Jara* (T 45-7164) has a fine collection at 28 rue Armand Holly, Debussy, 10 mins' drive uphill from the *Oloffson*. The *Nader* family has 2 galleries: one at 258 rue Magasin de l'Etat, in the downtown inferno (T 22-0033/69); the other at 18 rue Bouvreuil (T 45-0565/4552) in the leafy Croix Desprez neighbourhood; *Galerie Issa* (T 22-3287), 17 ave Chile (300m from *Oloffson*) is more like a wholesale warehouse, but cheap if you know what you are looking for. Mass produced copies of the Haitian naive masters are sold very cheaply around the post office, near the port. Vendors sell first-class Voodoo flags outside the Musée d'Art Haïtien.

Gingerbread (T 45-3698), 52 ave Lamartinière (Cr: Bwa Vèna) is a gingerbread house where ironwork, papier-maché, Voodoo flags, and horn carvings are sold, 1000-1600 Monday to Friday, 1000-1300 Saturday; *Comité Artisanat Haïtien* (T 22-8440), 29 rue 3 (near *Oloffson*) is a cooperative selling handicraft from all over Haiti at good prices 0900-1600 Monday to Friday, 1000-1200 Saturday; *Ambiance*, 17 rue M, Pacot, has Haitian jewellery and pottery; *Rainbow Art Gallery* (T 45-6655/6039), 9 rue Pierre Wiener, Bourdon, sells handicraft and paintings.

● **Nightlife**

The *Oloffson* has a "voodoo beat" concert or a folklore show three nights a week. Otherwise, the best nightlife is to be found in Pétionville (see separate section). There is a red-light district on the SW Carrefour road that has been badly eclipsed by AIDS, political turmoil and the embargo. The central part of the establishments consist of spacious, breezy, outdoor discothèques. The Dominican beer on offer is excellent and cheap, but the Dominican prostitutes and loud Dominican merengue music may have scant appeal. The city's western limits, around Mariani, have several ill-lit waterfront nightclubs, such as *Le Lambi*, where couples dance groin-to-groin to live compas bands and the men eat plate after plate of spicy, fresh-caught lambi (conch) to boost their virility.

● **Caution**

Shantytown dwellers don't welcome obvious sightseers and people with cameras. The area between the Champs de Mars and the waterfront is deserted after dark and should be avoided. It is safe to go to most places by car or taxi at night, but don't go about on foot except in Pétionville's restaurant and bar district. Remember that frequent power cuts plunge entire neighbourhoods into darkness. Drivers must always carry a licence as police blocks are common at night.

Watch out for pickpockets in markets and bus terminal areas and inside buses. (See also under **Security** in **Information for Visitors**.)

● **City Public Transport**

Shared taxis, called **Publiques** or simply "taxis," are flagged down. They charge a basic fare (Cr: kous) of US$0.20 that may double or treble (de kous, twa kous) depending on how far off the beaten track you go. A red ribbon tied to the inside rear-view mirror identifies them. Language skills are needed. They stop work at about 1930.

Camionettes (minibuses) and **Taptaps** (open-backed pickups with a brightly painted wooden superstructure) have fixed routes and fares (about US$0.15). They are difficult to manage with luggage. They rarely circulate after 2030.

A regular **taxi** is hard to find. *Nick's Taxis* (T 57-7777), based in Pétionville, is the only radio taxi company. It charges according to the meter. But, at the time of writing, a shortage of spares had depleted the fleet and you could wait hours for one to arrive. A passing Publique that is empty can be persuaded to do a private job (Cr: flete). The driver removes the red ribbon.

Chauffeurs-Guides are cab drivers who cater to foreign visitors. Usually found outside the biggest hotels such as the *Holiday Inn*, or at the airport, their cars can be used like regular taxis or hired by the hour, half-day, day or for a tour. The drivers usually speak French, plus a little English. They can be booked through the Association des Chauffeurs-Guides (T 22-0330) 18 blvd Harry Truman. US$25 for 3 hrs in the capital. US$40 for a 3-hrs excursion up to Kenscoff. A one-way trip for 1-4 people to Ibo Beach would be US$25. A one-way trip for 2 to the Côte des Arcadins beaches would be US$40.

● **Street Names**

Several major Port-au-Prince thoroughfares

have two names, the official one used for maps and the telephone book, and the one commonly used in speech. Often the taxi drivers only know the second. Boulevard Jean-Jacques Dessalines is also known as Grand' Rue (Créole: Gran Ri); Avenue Lamartinière is Bois Verna (Cr: Bwa Vèna); ave Jean Paul II is Turgeau (Cr: Tijo); ave John Brown is Lalue (Cr: Lali); ave Paul VI is rue des Casernes (Cr: Ridekazèn); ave Martin Luther King is Nazon (Cr: Nazon).

● **Voodoo**

Seeing a Voodoo ceremony or dance during a short visit is not easy. They are not announced in newspapers or on the radio. Never go unless accompanied by a Haitian, or someone already known there. Most middle and upper-class Haitians do not attend ceremonies and won't know where or when they are happening. They may even be discomfitted by your interest. Befriend poor, working-class Haitians and tell them about your interest. You may strike lucky. To increase you chances, time your stay to coincide with 2 November (Day of the Dead), Christmas, New Year or Epiphany (6 January). There are many ceremonies around these dates. If invited, take a bottle or two of rum or whisky and be ready to give generously if there is a collection. Sometimes, on the contrary, a wealthy "oungan" (priest) or "mambo" (priestess) will insist on lavishing drinks and food on the visitor. Don't refuse. To take pictures with a still camera or video, ask permission. You may be asked to pay for the privilege. TV crews are usually asked to pay substantial amounts. An oungan may always be consulted in his "ounphor" (temple) even if there is no ceremony. Be ready to plead poverty if the sum requested seems exhorbitant.

Max Beauvoir (T 34-2818/3723), an oungan intellectual with fluent English, has initiated foreigners. He has a "peristyle" (Voodoo dancehall) at Mariani, on the western edge of the city. Purists questioned the authenticity of the regular voodoo dances he used to lay on for tourists, but he is unquestionably an authority and talks readily to visitors. Aboudja (T 45-8476, or through the *Oloffson*), an English-speaking TV news cameraman, has been initiated as an oungan although he does not practice regularly. He acts as voodoo consultant for visiting journalists and TV crews.

● **Cinemas**

Cheap and interesting: the best are *Imperial* (air conditioned), Delmas; *Capitol* (air conditioned), 53, rue Lamarre; *Paramount*, Champs de Mars. Popular foreign films (British, US, French) are shown; non-French films are dubbed into French.

● **Clubs**

Pétionville Club (T 57-7575/1437), near US ambassador's residence at the end of rue Métreaux, a turning off rue Panaméricaine, between Port-au-Prince and Pétionville, a social and sports club. Visitors may use 9-hole golf course. For other facilities (tennis courts, racketball, gym, pool, restaurant) a one-year temporary membership costs US$125. *Bellevue*, near Argentine Embassy on Panaméricaine, Bourdon, a social club with tennis courts. *Turgeau Tennis Club* on ave Jean-Paul II (Cr: Tijo) near corner Martin Luther King (Cr: Nazon) has a few courts. *Jotac* near airport has tennis courts, gym and restaurant.

● **Banks**

Banque Nationale de Paris, corner of Lamarre and ave John Brown; Banque de Boston, rue des Miracles (place Geffrard); Bank of Nova Scotia, route de Delmas (beneath Canadian embassy): Citibank, route de Delmas. Also several small Haitian banks such as Sogebank and Banque de L'Union Haïtienne. At the time of writing, banks were giving an exchange rate not far short of the street rate, but there are long queues in most banks for any kind of service.

● **Exchange**

Hotels give a poor exchange rate. The best rate is obtained from street money changers (Fr: cambistes), who rarely cheat or steal. Find them on rue Pavée, at the airport, or near the market in Pétionville. It is perfectly legal. Check the rate on page 2 of the daily *Le Nouvelliste* newspaper. You may prefer to go in a car and do it through the window. The cambiste hands over the agreed sum in gourdes for you to count before you surrender the equivalent US dollar amount. They take only cash.

Currency dealers working out of offices give almost as good a rate. They also take TCs. Try Daniel Fouchard (T 23-1739) 14 rue des Miracles, Banque de Boston Bldg. Many importers and big retailers give a good rate for cash, TCs and even personal cheques on US bank accounts. Try Didier Rossard (T 22-5163), upstairs at 115 Place Geffrard; M or Mme Handal at Express Market, ave John Brown, six blocks down from Villa St-Louis. (See also **Currency** in **Information for Visitors**).

● **Libraries**

Institut Haitiano-Americain (T 22-3715/2947) corner of rue Capois and rue St-Cyr, next to *Holiday Inn*, 0800-1200, 1300-1700 Monday to Friday. The director is helpful to visiting travellers. Institut Français (T 22-3720), corner of Blvd Harry Truman and rue des Casernes, Bicentenaire, 1000-1600 Tues to Fri, 0900-1700 Sat; also has art exhibitions, concerts and plays.

● **Travel Agents**

Agence Citadelle (T 22-5004 22-5494) place du Marron Inconnu, sightseeing tours in a/c buses, travel to Dominican Republic and Cuba (owner Bobby Chauvet is a leading Haitian ecologist); *Chatelain Tours* (T 23-2400/69) rue Geffrard; *Continental Travel* (T 22-0604) 105 rue Pavée; *Magic Island Tours*, 82 rue Pavée, corner of Rue du Centre; *Southerland Tours* (T 22-1600) 30 ave Marie Jeanne. Because of the collapse of tourism, sightseeing tours are set up only on request.

● **Travel To The Provinces**

Fairly conventional-looking **buses** (Cr: bis) and/or colourfully converted trucks and pick-ups (Cr: taptap) provide inter-city transport. The place where buses and taptaps leave from is called a "station". For example, to get directions to the departure point for buses to Cap Haïtien, ask for the "station Au Cap." Most of the "stations" are somewhere on or between blvd Jean-Jacques Dessalines and the water-front. There are no fixed departure times. Buses leave when they are packed. Roads are bad and journeys are long and uncomfortable. In trucks, it is worth paying more to sit up front with the driver.

There are **flights** to Jérémie, Cap and Hinche, but service was very erratic after the embargo owing to shortages of aviation fuel.

PETIONVILLE

Just 15 mins from Port-au-Prince, but 450m above sea level, *Pétionville* was once the capital's hill resort. Now it is considered a middle-to-upper-class suburb with many chic restaurants and boutiques. Three roads lead up from Port-au-Prince. The northernmost, the Delmas Road, is ugly and dusty. Prefer the Panaméricaine, an extension of Avenue John Brown (Cr: Lali), which is serviced by camionettes, and the southernmost Route Canapé Vert, which has the best views.

In Pétionville, the main streets are parallel to each other, one block apart, Lamarre and Grégoire, on the six blocks between the Panaméricaine and the place St Pierre. Most of the shops, galleries and restaurants are on or between these two streets or within a couple of blocks of them.

Local Information
● **Where To Stay**

Montana (T 57-1920/21), rue Cardozo (a turning off the Panaméricaine at the entrance to Pétionville), best views over Port-au-Prince, especially from poolside restaurant, rates from US$50s, US$60d EP all a/c; *El Rancho* (T 57-2080/1/2/3), rue José de San Martín, just off the Panaméricaine, casino, nightclub, sauna, spa, rates from US$50s, US$65d EP all a/c; *Villa Créole* (T 57-1570/1, F 57-4935), just beyond the *El Rancho* on José de San Martín, tennis court, pool, good view, rates from US$59s, US$68d EP all a/c; *Kinam* (T 57-0462 57-6525) mock Gingerbread house, pool, handy location, rates from US$40s, US$52d.

Guest houses *Doux Séjour* (T 57-1560), 32 rue Magny (quiet street five blocks from Place St Pierre) weekly rates US$100s, US$140d rooms with fan and bathroom; *Marabou* (T 57-1934), 72 rue Stephen Archer, just behind St Pierre church, haggle for good rate for long stay; *Ife* (T 57-0737), 30 rue Grégoire (a busy street), US$17s US$23d CP; *Villa Kalewes* (T 57-0817), 99 rue Grégoire (at the upper, quiet end of the street) US$15s, US$23d CP, pool.

● **Where To Eat**

Plantation (T 57-0979), impasse Fouchard (turning off rue Borno) excellent French chef, good wine US$25 pp, rec; *Souvenance*, 8 rue Gabart at the corner of Aubran, French cuisine, rec, pricey; *Chez Gerard* (T 57-1949), 17 rue Pinchinat (near Place St Pierre), French, pricey; *Les Cascades* (T 57-5704), 73 rue Clerveaux, French, US$25; *La Voile* (T 57-4561), 32 rue Rigaud between Lamarre and Faubert, good US$10-15; *La Belle Epoque* (T 57-0984), 21 rue Grégoire, good French cuisine in a pretty house US$20; *Bolero* (T 57-1929), 18 rue Louverture between Grégoire and Lamarre, salads and pastas, lively bar scene; *Coin Des Artistes* (T 57-2400), 59 rue Panaméricaine, beneath Festival Arts Gallery, grilled fish and lobster, US$15; *Steak Inn* (T 57-2153), rue Magny, beautiful, large garden, live music at weekend; *Arc-En-Ciel* (T 57-2055), 67 rue Grégoire, French and German; *Le Grégoire* (T 57-1669), 34 rue Grégoire, Viet and Thai, quiet, US$10.

● **Shopping**

Pétionville's leafy streets have many elegant boutiques, galleries, bookshops and delicatessen. Rec is La Promenade at the intersection of Grégoire and Moïse (SE corner of Place St Pierre), a garden turned into small shopping promenade with an outdoor cafe, 1000-1800.

● **Where To Buy Art And Handicrafts**

Galerie Bourbon-Lally (T 57-6321/3397), 24 rue Lamarre, corner of rue Villate, owned by Englishman Reynald Lally, good choice of naive art; *Galerie Monnin* (T 57-4430), 19 rue Lamarre, in same house as Café des Arts; *Galerie Marasa* (T 57-1977), 11 rue Lamarre, hand-painted boxes, trays: *Expressions* (T 57-0112), 75 rue Clerveaux, one of the Nader family galleries; *Festival Arts Gallery* (T 57-6233), 59 rue Panaméricaine, Haitian artists who have moved on from primitivism; *Galata* (T 57-1114), rue Faubert, mainly handicrafts, especially weavings, metalwork; *Fleur De Canne* (T 57-4266) 34 bis, rue Gabart, good quality craft in a charming store.

● **Nightlife**

Café Des Arts (T 57-7979), 19 rue Lamarre (same house as Galerie Monnin) open 1900 until late, dining and live music; *Bambu*, corner of rues Lamarre and Chavannes, especially when they have live bands; *Faces*, in the *Hotel El Rancho*, also Sat evening live jazz.

EXCURSIONS NEAR PORT-AU-PRINCE

Beaches Haiti's best beaches are far from the capital, on the Caribbean and Atlantic coasts. The Gulf of La Gonâve beaches, the only ones that can be reached within an hour's drive, are second rate. Those W of the capital are especially poor. The best of what's available is to the N. They tend to be gravelly or gritty, with a backdrop of arid, deforested mountainside, but the calm, clear, shallow water is excellent for children.

Closest is Ibo Beach, on an island near Km 30 of the Route Nationale 1. A sign painted on the side of a house shows the turnoff, which is 4 km after the flour mill and 500m before the cement works. The boat-ride is US$2. The beach is small, but it has white sand and shade. Good, basic meals are served on the beach for US$4. A hotel consisting of many chalets is closed.

The Côte Des Arcadins, a 20-km stretch of beach hotels, begins 60 km N of the capital. They all have pools, bars and restaurants, and charge US$2 admission to day visitors. They may be crowded with wealthy Port-au-Princiens at weekends. The Arcadins are three uninhabited, sandy cays 3 km offshore which are surrounded by reefs. The diving is excellent. (At the time of writing, no diving excursions were available, but check with Bobby Chauvet of *Citadelle Tours*). The first, and quietest hotel, is *Kyona Beach*; followed by *Kaliko Beach* (T 22-8040, F 23-0588), US$30s, US$40d MAP, good lunch for about US$8, horse-riding. Ouanga Bay is next, then *Wahoo Beach* (T 22-9653), clean, well-run and crowded. At Km 77, 1 km after the town of Montrouis, *Moulin sur Mer* (T 22-1844/1918) is a converted 18th century plantation house and sugar mill where people usually stay a night or two (US$35s, US$50d a/c MAP). *Club Med*, 500m beyond Moulin sur Mer, has been closed since 1987, but is ready to reopen when there is a return to democracy. Amani-Y Beach, about 5 km before St Marc, is a small, pretty beach with a restaurant and bar that have been closed for several years.

Other Excursions The asphalt road to Kenscoff, in the mountains behind Port-au-Prince, starts just to the W of the Pétionville police station, on the Place St Pierre. After 10 mins, there is a turnoff on the right at United Sculptors of Haiti, which sells good wood-carvings. It skirts a huge quarry and climbs to *Boutilliers*, a peak topped by radio and television masts that dominates the city. Next to the quarry, visit the Barbancourt rum company's mock castle to taste fruit-flavoured rum liqueurs for free. In about 20 mins, the main Kenscoff road reaches **Fermathe** where the large Baptist Mission has a snack bar with fine views S, and a store selling handicraft and souvenirs (taptaps and camionettes from near the market in Pétionville). Climb up a trail to Fermathe from Pétionville in three hours by setting off from rue Montagne Noire. A turnoff near the Mission leads to Fort Jacques and Fort Alexandre (10 minutes by car or an easy 45 minutes' walk), two forts on adjoining summits built after the defeat of Napoleon. The views N over the Cul de Sac plain are breathtaking. Fort Jacques is restored.

30 minutes from Pétionville, but 1,500m above sea level, **Kenscoff** is a hill resort where members of the élite retire to their country homes in July and August to escape the heat. (*Hotel Florville* for refreshments or meals.) Hire a guide for a 2-3 hour hike via the village of Godet to the summit above Kenscoff that is topped by a radio mast, or the summit just to the W, called Morne Zombi. The ridge just to the E of the radio mast can be reached by a surfaced road in poor condition. It offers views S over a rugged, dark massif that boasts Haiti's highest peak, the 2,674m La Selle.

From the ridge, a 5-hour hike along a trail heading towards the village of **Seguin** brings you to **Parc La Visite**, a nature park covering part of the massif. It has pine woods, montane cloud forest at higher altitudes, dozens of big limestone caves (one 10 km long), and strange karst-formation rocks locals call "broken teeth" (Cr: kase dan). See under **Flora and Fauna** for wildlife. Camp at a disused saw mill (Cr: siri) by the trail, where water is available from a fountain. Bring thick clothes and sleeping bags; temperatures can fall to freezing at night. A waterfall is a short hike away. For longer hikes and fine views, head E with a guide and climb the 2,282m Pic Cabaio or the 2,100m Pic La Visite (another camping site). The park keeper, Jean-Claude,

rents horses. Seguin lies on a sloping plateau on the massif's southern face, about 1 hour beyond the park. From Seguin, a 5-hour hike gets you to the S-coast village of Marigot, from where you can bus back to Port-au-Prince via Jacmel in 4 hours.

The lush, densely-populated coastal Leogane Plain, 45 minutes W of the capital, offers a look at rural life. E and W of the town of **Leogane**, the plain is dotted with small villages and criss-crossed by bumpy lanes. Turn right down any of the side-roads off the Route Nationale 2 after it crosses the big, stony Momance River, then wander at random.

Wildlife enthusiasts should visit **Lake Saumâtre** (see **Flora and Fauna**), at the eastern end of the Cul de Sac plain near the Dominican border. The newly improved road from Croix-des-Bouquets to the border crossing at Malpasse skirts the lake's southern side. The northern side offers more chance of seeing its wildlife. On Route Nationale 3 heading NE from Port-au-Prince towards Mirebalais, fork right at the Thomazeau turnoff to the lakeside villages of Manneville and Fond Pite. It takes 90 minutes.

SOUTH OF PORT-AU-PRINCE

Set off on the Route Nationale 2, the highway heading W toward Les Cayes, and turn S at the Carrefour Dufour intersection (Km 40) for a scenic, French-built mountain road to the lush S coast and the port of **Jacmel**, Haiti's prettiest city. Its name derives from an Indian word meaning "rich land." In Port-au-Prince, small buses leave from the "station Jacmel" near the customs house on rue du Quai and rue des Fronts Forts, taking 2-3 hours (US$3).

Quiet, with 10,000 inhabitants, Jacmel has changed little since the late 19th century when it was a booming coffee port and its wealthy merchants built New Orleans-style mansions using cast-iron pillars and balconies imported from France or the United States. The charm of its Victorian architecture is matched by a setting at the head of a 3 km wide horseshoe bay, with streets winding down three small hills to a palm-fringed, black-sand beach. Begin a visit with refreshments on the S-facing upper veranda of the *Manoir Alexandre*, a turn-of-the-century patrician home that is now a guest house. It has Jacmel's best view plus fine antiques. Two blocks to the E is an iron market built in 1895. (Saturday is market day.) The street below the *Manoir Alexandre*, rue Seymour Pradel, has another old residence, now an American-owned art gallery called *Salubria*. Closer to the beach, on rue Commerce, more 19th-century homes have been turned into galleries or handicraft stores. The Boucard family residence at the corner of Grand' Rue and Commerce, is especially fine. At the other end of Commerce, near the wharf, note the Vital family warehouse dating from 1865. The nearby prison was built in the 18th century. Members of a small expatriate community frequent *La Choubouloute*, a basic beach bar with simple meals 100m W of the wharf. Jacmel's handicraft speciality is boxes, trays, place mats and other objects covered with parrots or flowers, hand-painted in bright colours.

● **Where To Stay** *La Jacmelienne* (T 88-3451, Port-au-Prince office: 22-4899), a modern, two-storey hotel on the beach with pool, excellent cuisine, US$35s, US$60d MAP, fans, no a/c, all rooms with sea view, rec; *Manoir Alexandre* (T 88-2511), US$30d CP, lots of character but no bathroom in rooms; *Guest House Douge*, 39 Grand' Rue, character but even more basic US$10s, US$15d CP.

A hurricane swallowed up most of Jacmel's beach and what is left is dirty. A good dirt road leads E to fine white-sand beaches. The first is *Cyvadier*, a tiny cove down a side-road at Km 7. A quiet, French Canadian-run hotel, *Cyvadier Plage*, offers rooms with ceiling fans for US$20d CP. At Km 15, just

before Cayes Jacmel, is Raymond-les-Bains, a beach alongside the road. No facilities except showers. Beware, it has a slight undertow, like most beaches on the S coast. Just after Cayes Jacmel, at Ti Mouillage, the road runs beside two beaches. The first has a basic restaurant. Small beach homes can be rented at the second. From Marigot, a pretty coastal village 10 km further on, a 4WD can climb a rough trail to the village of Seguin (see under Excursions from Port-au-Prince).

A 12-km track into the hills SW of Jacmel leads to **Bassin Bleu**, a series of natural pools and waterfalls descending a limestone gorge in tiers. The big, deep, blue-green pools are framed by smooth rocks and draped with creeper and maidenhair fern. It takes 2-3 hours each way on foot or horse-back (horses for hire in Jacmel). Take a guide, fixing a price in advance. There are excellent views over Jacmel bay on the way. If it has not rained, a good driver can nurse a 2WD or 4WD three quarters of the way. The Jacmel guide hands over to a local guide for the last km which is steep and, at one point, requires the aid of a rope. This means an additional small fee.

WEST OF PORT-AU-PRINCE

The southwestern peninsula is the wettest, greenest, most beautiful part of Haiti; its rugged western tip has forests, rivers, waterfalls and unspoilt beaches.

The Route Nationale 2 to Les Cayes is asphalted all the way and very scenic. For the first 92 km it runs along the N coast of the peninsula. At Km 68 is the town of **Petit Goave** (Cr: Ti Gwav). Visit the *Relais de l'Empereur* (T 22-9557), once the residence of Emperor Faustin 1 (1849-56). The hotel is no longer operating, but the caretaker will show you around.

Just 2 km down a turn-off at Km 92 is the smugglers' port of **Miragoane**, a pretty town of narrow streets that wind around a natural harbour or climb up a hill capped by a neo-gothic church. Small, rusting freighters unload contrabrand rice, cement, bicycles, TV sets and second-hand clothes shipped from Miami. A 4WD is needed for the dirt road that continues along the N coast, fording rivers and passing fishing villages, as far as Petit Trou de Nippes. At Petite Rivière de Nippes, 15 km along this road, a 3-hour trek inland on foot or horseback (take a guide) brings you to one of Haiti's four great waterfalls, **Saut De Baril**.

After Miragoane, the main road crosses the peninsula's spine and reaches the southern, Caribbean coast at Aquin (Km 138) where you can bathe in several rivers. At *Zanglais*, 6 km farther on, there are white sand beaches near the road. (Beware of slight undertow at any beach on the S coast.) Just beyond Zanglais a ruined English fort is visible on a small offshore island, with the remains of a battery emplacement just opposite, on the mainland.

On a wet, coastal plain 196 km W of Port-au-Prince, Haiti's fourth city, *Les Cayes* (Cr: Okay), is quiet, but not without charm (*Hotel Concorde*, T 86-0277, rue Gabions des Indigènes, rooms with bath/fan US$20s US$30d EP). In Port-au-Prince, buses leave mornings from the "station Aux Cayes" near the post office for the 4-hour trip. Fare US$4. Visible from the waterfront is *Ile-à-Vache* (pop: 5,000), a 20-km-long island that was Henry Morgan's base for a 1670 raid against Panama. It has Indian remains and good beaches on the southern side near La Hatte, the biggest village. Visit it by renting a boat with outboard (about US$25 for the day) or take the daily ferry leaving at around 1600, and pay to sleep in someone's home. Or camp, after asking permission.

Fortresse des Platons, a huge ruined fortress on a 600m summit overlooking the coastal plain, can be visited in a one-day excursion from Les Cayes. It was built in 1804 at Dessalines' behest. Take the coast road SW out of the city. Just after Torbeck, a rough road heads inland up a river valley via Ducis to the village of Dubreuil (trucks from Les Cayes). From Dubreuil, the fortress is a 2-3 hour hike up a steep trail with great views. Carry on the same trail via Formond to enter the **Macaya National Park**, which has Haiti's last virgin cloud forest surrounding the 2,347m Pic Macaya. See under **Flora and Fauna** for the park's vegetation and wildlife. A University of Florida base at Plaine Durand (2 hours beyond the fortress) has basic camping facilities. Hire guides for hikes into the lower montane rain forest. Only the very fit should attempt the hike to the top of the Pic Macaya. It entails climbing a 2,100m ridge and then descending to 1,000m before tackling the peak itself. Allow at least 2 days each way and take a guide.

Beyond Torbeck, the coast road goes as far as *St Jean du Sud* where a small off-shore cay is suitable for camping. Before St Jean du Sud, fork right at L'Acul for *Port Salut*, a 90-minute drive from Les Cayes (2 buses a day). This small village has a wild, 800m-long, palm-lined beach that is one of the most beautiful in Haiti. *Arada Inn*, owned by Swiss resident Christian Deck, offers clean rooms with fans, breakfast and dinner for US$20; or rent rooms from locals. Grilled lobster lunches available in a basic restaurant near the beach.

The adventurous should take the coastal route from Les Cayes to Jérémie, around the peninsula's tip, a remote, rugged, lush region that has changed little in 200 years. It has wild rivers, sand beaches, mountains falling steeply into the sea, and some of Haiti's last rain forest. Allow four days. Les Cayes buses or taptaps may go as far as Les Anglais, depending on the state of the road. A 4WD may even get to Tiburon. Thereafter, you must hike to Anse d'Hainault or even Dame Marie before finding road good enough to be serviced by taptaps out of Jérémie. Alternatively, try getting a ride on sloops that carry merchandise and passengers along the coast. Residents in small villages all the way will cook meals and rent beds for a few dollars. "Pripri", rafts made of bamboo lashed together and steered by a pole, ply the rivers. Anse d'Hainault and Abricots (25 km W of Jérémie) have good beaches.

The scenic, hair-raising, 97-km mountain road from Les Cayes to Jérémie, across the Massif de la Hotte, can be done in 5 hours. But it may be impassable after rain. One hour's drive brings you to *Camp Perrin* (several guesthouses), a hill resort at the foot of the 2,347m Pic de Macaya. Rent horses for a 2-hour ride to **Saut Mathurine**, Haiti's biggest waterfall. It has good swimming in the deep, green pool at its base.

Fork right off the Jérémie road at the Kafou Zaboka intersection for *Pestel*, a picturesque port dominated by a French fort, 4 hours' hard drive from Les Cayes. Worth seeing any time of the year, but especially for the Easter weekend regatta, when many Rara bands come. Charter a boat to tour nearby fishing villages such as Les Basses (Cr: Obas) on the Baradères peninsula and Anse-à-Maçon on the offshore island of Grande Cayemite with its splendid view of the Massif de la Hotte and distant Pic Macaya.

With crumbling mansions overgrown by rampant vegetation, *Jérémie* (pop: 20,000) is famed for its poets, eccentrics and isolation. Two bus companies stopped services from Port-au-Prince in early 1993 because the road got so bad. Some buses are still running, however, leaving from Jean-Jacques Dessalines near rue Chareron (US$8). The 12-hour overnight ferry ride is not recommended. At least 800 (maybe as many as 1,500) Jérémie residents drowned when an overloaded ferry, the *Neptune*, sank on its way to Port-au-Prince in February 1993. Subject to aviation fuel availability, MAF and Caribintair have a total of 6 flights a week from Port-au-Prince. They may be booked up to 10 days ahead. On a hill above the town, with a shady garden, is *Hotel La Cabane* (US25d MAP). Anse d'Azur, 4 km W of the town, is a white-sand beach with, in the rocky headland at one end, a big cave into which you can swim.

NORTH OF PORT-AU-PRINCE

The seaboard N of the capital is arid or semi-arid most of the way to Gonaïves, and all round the NW peninsula as far as Port-de-Paix. From Port-de-Paix to the Dominican border, it is quite lush and green. The Route Nationale 1 is asphalted to Cap Haïtien, but is badly potholed for the 65 km between Pont Sondé and Gonaïves. It hugs the coast for most of the first 85 km, skirting the foot of the Chaine des Matheux mountains. Cabaret (Km 35) is the former Duvalierville. Its ugly, modernistic buildings and pretensions of becoming Haiti's Brasilia were lampooned in *The Comedians*. L'Arcahaie (Km 47) is where Dessalines created the blue and red Haitian flag by tearing the white out of the French tricolor. Outside L'Arcahaie, a dirt road heads E high into the Chaine des Matheux to a region where coffee and indigo was grown in colonial times. A dozen ruined plantation houses survive. The turnoff is just before the point where the highway crosses the small Mi Temps River. Sailboats leave at mid-morning from Montrouis (Km 76) for the 22-km crossing to Anse-à-Galets (one guesthouse), the main town on barren La Gonâve Island.

At Km 96, after the Côte des Arcadins beaches, the RN1 reaches the port of St Marc (*Hotel Belfort*, 166 rue Louverture, clean, basic US$6s). Several fine gingerbread houses are on streets to the E of the main street. A pretty valley runs inland SE as far as Goavier.

The highway crosses the River Artibonite at Pont Sondé, entering a region of rice paddies irrigated by canals. Fork right at the Kafou Peyi intersection, 2 km N of Pont Sondé, for **Petite Rivière de L'Artibonite** (Cr: Ti Rivyè), a picturesque town built by Christophe on a steep-sided ridge overlooking the River Artibonite. Its Palace of 365 Doors was Christophe's provincial headquarters. In 1802, there was a key battle at the Crète-à-Pierrot fort (5 minutes walk above the town) in which Leclerc sacrificed 2,000 men to dislodge a force of 1,200 led by Dessalines.

About 8 km after L'Estère, a right turn-off runs SE 25 km to Marchand, a town at the foot of the Cahos mountains that was briefly Dessalines' capital. Hike into the surrounding hills to visit seven big ruined forts built by Dessalines. Near the town is a spring with a natural swimming pool. Dessalines told his soldiers that bathing here made them immune to French bullets. The house of Dessalines' wife, Claire Heureuse, still survives in the town. You can also see the foundations of his own home. After the Marchand turnoff, the RN1 crosses a semi-desert called Savane Désolée.

Amid saltpans and arid, brackish lowlands, **Gonaïves** at Km 171 is an ugly, dusty town of 70,000 (Haïti's third largest). It is called the City of Independence because Dessalines proclaimed Haïti's independence here in 1804. The unrest that toppled Jean-Claude Duvalier in February 1986 also began here. *Chez Elias* is a safe, clean guesthouse (T 74-0318), rue Egalité opposite Teleco, rooms with fan and bathroom for U$$13s US$26d MAP. At *Chez Frantz* (T 74-0348), avenue des Dattes, the rooms are often all taken by long-term residents, but the food is Gonaïves' best. *Rex Restaurant*, rue Louverture, half a block from the market, has Créole food and hamburgers. Buses (US$3, 4 hrs) leave Port-au-Prince mornings from the intersection of Blvd La Saline and Jean-Jacques Dessalines. In Gonaïves, mopeds operate as taxis, charging US$0.20 a ride.

After Ennery at Km 201, the RN1 climbs steeply up to the Chaine de Belance watershed and enters the green, northern region. **Limbé** at Km 245, has a museum created by Dr William Hodges, a Baptist missionary doctor who runs the local hospital and supervises archaeological digs along the N coast (see La Navidad under **Excursions from Cap Haïtien**). Fort Crète Rouge, above Limbé, is one of the many fortresses built by Christophe.

A rugged side-road from Limbé down to **Le Borgne** (Cr: Oboy) on the coast offers spectacular views. The 20 km either side of Le Borgne abound with white-sand beaches. The high, green mountains right behind add to their beauty, but the coast is densely inhabited and the beaches are often used as a public latrine. From Le Borgne to St Louis du Nord, the road is very bad but not impassable for 4WD.

After Limbé, the main highway descends quickly, offering fine views over L'Acul Bay, where Columbus anchored on 23 December 1492, two days before his flagship sank.

CAP HAÏTIEN

Cap Haïtien, Haïti's second city, with 100,000 inhabitants, has a dramatic location on the sheltered, SE side of an 824m high cape, from which it gets its name. It was the capital in colonial times, when it was called Cap Français. Its wealth and sophistication earned it the title of "Paris of the Antilles." The colony's biggest port, it was also the commercial centre of the northern plain, the biggest sugar producing region. Nowadays it usually referred to simply as Cap, or Okap in Créole. It was burned to the ground three times, in 1734, 1798 and 1802, the last time by Christophe to prevent it falling intact into the hands of the French. It was destroyed again by an 1842 earthquake that killed half the population. The historic centre's architecture is now Spanish influenced, with barrel-tile roofs, porches, arcades and interior courtyards.

Vertières, an outlying district on the Port-au-Prince road, is the site of the battle at which Dessalines's army definitively routed the French on 18 November 1803, forcing them to leave the island for good 12 days later. There is a roadside monument.

Local Information

● Where To Stay

(Note: Cap Haïtien gets electricity only 1900-2300) *Mont-Joli* (T 62-0300/26, Port-au-Prince: 22-7764), on hillside above town, pool, tennis court, good restaurant, own generator runs 1000-1200 and 1730-0600, rooms with private bath and a/c, US$25s, US$35d EP; *Roi Christophe* (T 62-0414), corner of 24 and B, central location in colonial house first built in 1724 as the French governor's palace (Pauline Bonaparte stayed here) lush gardens, pool, own generator (not big enough for a/c) runs 0600 until city power comes on, US$20s, US$25d with fan, US$30s, US$35d with a/c CP; *Beck* (T 62-0001), in the mountainside, residential Bel-Air district, woodland setting, two pools, constant water, own generator, private beach at Cormier, German owner, rooms with private bath and fan US$40s, US$70d MAP; *Brise De Mer* (T 62-0821), 4 Carenage (on waterfront at northern edge of town), friendly but reportedly not very safe, own generator (but not on all the time), rooms with private bath and fan US$15s, US$25d MAP. *Columbia*, rue 5, 3-K, US$10s, US$12d, fan, clean, safe, very helpful owner speaks English.

● Where To Eat

Auberge De Madeline, a restored plantation house amid canefields 10 mins' drive toward Milot, 1200-2230, French and Créole cuisine, not too pricey for what it offers; *Hotel Universal*, rues D and 14, popular Créole food restaurant, US$4 a meal, rec; *Mezami* (T 62-0400) Italian-run take-away offering pizza, Créole food, sandwiches, 0800-0200, rues 20 and B, three blocks from cathedral; *Cap 2000*, rue 5 and Boulevard (not far from waterfront) sandwiches, icecream; *Ti Paradis*, rues D and 15, cheap and good; *Sacade*, rues 18 and B, cheap.

● Shopping

Ateliers Taggart (T 62-1931), rue 5 near Boulevard (by *Cap 2000*) all kinds of handicrafts, especially weavings and metalwork, rec, 1000-1700 Mon to Fri; *Galerie Des Trois Visages*, excellent art gallery next to *Ateliers Taggart*. A tourist market by the port has handicrafts and naive paintings. Bargain hard.

● Exchange

BNP, good for changing TCs; also Banque Union Haïtien changes TCs, open until 1800.

● Post Office

Ave B at rue 17.

● Travel Agent

Cap Travel, 84 rue 23A, T 62-0517.

● Tourist Bureau

Rue 24, Esplanade.

● Car Rental

Hertz (T 62-0369). Beware, employees are said to have given prices in Haitian dollars and then tried to charge the same figure in US dollars. Don't leave your passport as deposit.

● Transport

Buses leave Port-au-Prince from the "station Au Cap" opp the big Texaco garage at the junction of Delmas Road and Blvd La Saline between 0630 and 0830, when full. The 274 km trip usually takes 6-7 hrs. Fare US$4. It may be necessary to change in Gonaïves, 3½ hrs, US$2, then take another bus to the capital.

Subject to aviation fuel availability, MAF and Caribintair both have six **flights** a week from Port-au-Prince. A Cap-based air taxi service, Marien Air (T 62-0527/0742) offers flights to Port-au-Prince, the Dominican Republic, Turks and Caicos, Bahamas and Jamaica.

Ruins The rich, alluvial plain to the S and E of Cap boasted a thousand plantation houses during the last years of the colonial period. ISPAN (T 62-2459), rue 15 and rue B in Cap, is a good source of information on these nearby colonial ruins, as well as Sans Souci and the Citadelle.

Beaches The beaches in the town itself are dirty and lack charm. Excellent beaches on the N side of the cape can be reached in 20 minutes by car. The first is *Cormier Plage*, site of the recommended *Hotel Cormier Plage* (T 62-1000) US$45d MAP, good food, own generator turned on 0730-1100 and 1630-2330.

Scuba diving with equipment for 10. Good wrecks and coral reefs. Run by charming French couple: Jean-Claude and Kathy Dicqueman. If you call ahead, they will pick you up from airport. Book ahead, because tour groups from Dominican Republic sometimes fill the place up. Take mosquito repellent.

Five minutes further W (30 mins on foot), is *Labadie* beach, a fenced-off sandy peninsula once used by Royal Caribbean Lines as a private beach for its visiting cruise ships. The public may enter to use its facilities (pool, restaurants, water sports) for US$3. At the time of writing, no cruise ship had visited since the 1991 coup because of the embargo, but the facilities were still open.

Just beyond Labadie Beach is Belli Beach, a small sandy cove with a very basic hotel (US$5s) used as a bordello for the cruise ship crews. This is the end of the road, but boats, some with outboards, can be rented here to visit nearby Labadie village, dramatically located at the foot of a cliff, and other beaches further along the coast. Fix a price before boarding. Labadie village (about US$3 by boat, also reachable by scrambling over the rocks) has two guest houses, *Dessa Motel* and *Maison Amitié*, with basic rooms on the beach for about US$4. Employees will buy and cook food for a price that must be negotiated.

Farther still, about 10 km W of Cap, is *Club Roche Sauvage* (T 62-2765) a new, all-inclusive, 144-bed resort with its own 300m beach. Weekly rates from US$764d. Spa and diving extra. Round trip air-and-sea transfer from Port-au-Prince another US$85/person. Beyond Roche Sauvage is Labadie Shore, Crown Cruise Line's answer to Labadie Beach.

EXCURSIONS FROM CAP HAÏTIEN

The massive, mountain-top fortress of *La Citadelle* was built by King Henri Christophe between 1805 and 1820 to deter any French reinvasion (see under **History**). With walls up to 40m high and 4m thick, and covering 10,000 sq m, 20,000 people were pressed into its construction. It is dizzily perched atop the 900m high Pic La Ferrière, overlooking Cap and the entire northern plain, and controlling access to the Central Plateau. Its garrison of 5,000 soldiers (plus the royal family and its retinue) could have held out for a year. Haitians call it the eighth wonder of the world. It is indeed impressive, and has breathtaking views. Restoration work has been under way for years and is well advanced. Behind the fortress, at the end of a 1.5 km level ridge with sheer drops on both sides, is the Site des Ramiers, a complex of four small forts which controlled the rear access. Worth visiting just for the views.

To get to the Citadelle, take the 25 km asphalt road S from Cap to the village of *Milot* in a publique (US$1) or taptap (US$0.30). Taptaps leave mornings from outside the *Hotel Bon Dieu Bon*. Hotels like the *Mont Joli* offer jeep tours for about US$60 pp, but don't count on the guide's information being correct. From Milot it is a steep 5-km hike through lush countryside up to the fortress (about 90 mins, start early to avoid the heat; to find the road up to the Citadelle you need to walk through Sans Souci Palace). Wear stout shoes and be protected from the sun. Horses can be rented for about US$5 (dangerous in wet weather). Hire a guide even if you don't want one, just to stop others importuning (fix the fee in advance). Consider taking refreshments with you, because prices at the Citadelle are exhorbitant. Those with their own vehicle drive to a car park two thirds of the way up, reducing the walk to 1.5 km. Admission is US$1.

At Milot itself are the ruins of Christophe's royal palace, *Sans Souci*. More than a palace, it was an embryo administrative capital ranging over 8 hectares in the foothills beneath the Citadelle.

Christophe sited his capital inland because of the difficulty of defending coastal cities against the overwhelming naval might of France and Britain. It included a printing shop, garment factory, distillery, schools, hospital, medical faculty, chapel and military barracks. Begun in 1810, inaugurated in 1813, ransacked after Christophe shot himself in the heart with a silver bullet in 1820, it was finally ruined by the 1842 earthquake that destroyed Cap. The admission to the Citadelle covers Sans Souci. Try not to go any day there are cruise ships at Cap or the nearby beaches. If planning to visit both sites, arrive before 1300 to have enough time, as they close at 1700. There are no buses or taptaps back to Cap after 1700.

Morne Rouge, 8 km SW of Cap, is the site of Habitation Le Normand de Mezy, a sugar plantation that spawned several famous rebel slaves. (Leave Cap by the RN1 and take a dirt road running N from a point about 75m W of the turnoff to the town of Plaine du Nord.) Its ruins include two aqueducts and bits of walls. Voodoo ceremonies are held under a giant tree in the village. Among its rebel progeny was Mackandal, an African chief's son who ran away, became a prophetic oungan and led a maroon band. After terrorizing the entire northern plain by poisoning food and water supplies, he was captured and burned alive in January 1758. **Bois Caiman** was the wood where slaves met secretly on the night of 14 August 1791 to hold a Voodoo ceremony and plan an uprising. (It is near the Plaine du Nord road, about 3 km S of the RN1. Ask locals to guide you once you are in the area.) Their leader was an oungan and slave foreman from Le Normand de Mezy called Boukman. The uprising a week later was the Haitian equivalent of the storming of the Bastille. Slaves put plantation houses and cane fields to the torch and massacred hundreds of French settlers. It began the only successful slave revolt in history and led

to Haiti's independence. Little is left of the wood now except a giant ficus tree overgrowing a colonial well credited with mystic properties.

The town of **Plaine du Nord**, 12 km SW of Cap, is a pilgrimage centre every year on 24-25 July, the Catholic festival of St James, who is identified with the Voodoo spirit Ogou. Voodoo societies come from all over Haiti, camp in the streets and spend the two days in nonstop drumming and dancing. Many are possessed by Ogou and wallow in a much-photographed mud pool in one of its streets. On 26 July, the feast day of St Anne, most of the Voodoo societies at Plaine du Nord decamp to nearby **Limonade**, 15 km SE of Cap, for another day and night of celebrations. A dirt road on the NW side of Limonade leads to Bord De Mer De Limonade, a fishing village where Columbus' flagship, the *Santa María*, struck a reef and sank on Christmas Day, 1492. Columbus used wood from the wreck to build a settlement, *La Navidad*, which was wiped out by Taino Indians after he left. Its location was discovered by American archeologist William Hodges while digging at the site of Puerto Real, a city founded years later on the same spot. The untrained eye will detect nothing of either settlement now, but the Hodges museum in Limbé, 20 km SW of Cap, has relics.

Fort Liberté, 56 km E of Cap, is a picturesque, French-designed town on a large bay with a narrow entrance. It is dotted with French forts that can be reached by boat. The best is Fort Dauphin, built in 1732. The bay was the site of the Caribbean's largest sisal plantation until nylon was invented. **Ouanaminthe** (*Hotel Paradis*, basic, on main street) is northern Haiti's chief border crossing. (Taptaps for US$2 from the "station nordest" in Cap.) The Dominican frontier town, Dajabón, is just 2 km away. The crossing is easy unless there is political unrest in Haiti. Buses leave Dajabón for many Dominican cities. The River Massacre, which forms the border, had this name long before the massacre of thousands of Haitians in the neighbouring part of the Dominican Republic under Trujillo in 1937, when the river was said to have been red with blood for days.

For the rugged, the dirt road forking left 5 km before Milot could be an alternative route back to Port-au-Prince via Hinche and the Central Plateau (see under **Northeast of Port-au-Prince**). A 4WD is needed, or get a ride from Cap to Hinche in a truck. It takes 2-3 hours. The first town is Grand Rivière du Nord, where another of Christophe's fortresses, Fort Rivière, sits atop a ridge to the E. It was used by the Cacos guerrillas who fought the US occupation from 1918 to 1920. The Americans captured the Cacos leader Charlemagne Peralte near here. Dondon has caves inhabited by bats. One is close to the town. The other, 90 minutes on foot or horseback up a river bed to the W of the village, has heads carved in relief on its walls, presumably by the original Indian inhabitants. In the rainy season, cars cannot ford the river near St Raphaël, but you can walk, with locals helping for a small fee.

NORTHWEST

Except for Tortuga island and a coastal strip running E from Port-de-Paix, the NW peninsula is Haiti's driest, most barren region. In recent years, especially since the 1991 coup, it has teetered on the brink of famine.

The 86-km mountain road from Gonaïves to Port-de-Paix via Gros Morne fords several rivers and takes 4 hours in a 4WD, needed for travel anywhere in the NW. (Minibuses from Gonaïves, big buses from Port-au-Prince, leaving from beside the "station Au Cap".) *Port-de-Paix* once made an honest living exporting coffee and bananas. Now it specializes in importing contraband goods from Miami. Vendors tout the wares on all its unpaved streets. In 1992-

93, its small freighters also began ferrying illegal immigrants into Miami. Despite the smuggling, it is safe to spend a night (*Hotel Bienvenue*, T 68-5138, basic, US$8s, US$13d EP).

Half an hour's drive to the E by a good, dirt road is St Louis du Nord, a pretty coastal town from where sailing boats cross the 10-km channel to *Tortuga Island*, the Caribbean's biggest pirate base in the 17th century. Nearly 40 km long, 7 km wide and 464m above the sea at its highest point, its smooth rounded shape reminded seafarers of the back of a turtle. (Tortuga in Spanish and La Tortue, its Haitian name, in French.)

The French and English freebooters who began settling here in 1630 were drawn by the S coast's coves, beaches and small anchorages, and a protective line of reefs with few openings. Pirate raids had led Spain to withdraw from the N and W coasts of Hispaniola in 1605, leaving livestock that multiplied and was hunted by the freebooters. Because they smoked the meat on "boucans", an Indian word for spit, they became known as buccaneers.

Its present population of 30,000 is spread all over the island. The biggest S-coast villages, Cayonne and Basse-Terre, are less than 1 km apart. A ferryboat leaves Cayonne for St Louis du Nord at 0800 and returns at about 1000, charging locals US$0.50 each way. Foreigners may have to pay up to US$10, depending on their negotiating skills. Boats crossing at other times charge more. From Cayonne there is a narrow cement road up to Palmiste serviced by a single taptap, one of the four or five cars on the island. From Palmiste, the biggest village on the rounded spine, there are spectacular views of the corniche coastline stretching from Cap to Jean Rabel, and the towering mountains behind. The best view is from the home of French Canadian priest Bruno Blondeau (T 68-5138/6709), the director of a Catholic Church mission who has effectively governed the island since 1977. He runs 35 schools and has built all 55 km of its road. His order also operates a small, basic hotel (US$4s EP).

The best beach, 2 km long, is at Pointe Saline, at the western tip (34 km from Palmiste, 2 hrs by car). This is also the driest part of the island and there is little shade. La Grotte au Bassin, 6 km E of Palmiste, is a large cave with a 10m high precolumbian rock carving of a goddess. There are two other big caves: Trou d'Enfer, near La Rochelle ravine, and La Grotte de la Galerie, 1 km E of Trou d'Enfer.

The largest historic ruin on the island is a 15m high lime kiln (four à chaux), built at the end of the 18th century. Fort de la Roche, 1639, was once Tortuga's biggest fortress (70m high). Its masonry foundations can be seen at a spring where women wash clothes on the hillside above Basse-Terre. Three cannon and a bit of wall remain from Fort d'Ogeron, built in 1667.

A coast road runs W from Port-de-Paix along the N coast of the peninsula as far as Môle St Nicolas and then returns to Gonaïves via the S coast. *Jean Rabel* is a tense town that was the site of peasant massacre in July 1987. At least 150 died in the clash, said to have been engineered by local Duvalierist landlords seeking to crush the attempts of Catholic priests to organize landless peasants. From Jean Rabel round to Baie de Henne, the landscape is arid, windy and dusty. Old people say they can remember when it was still green and forested.

Columbus first set foot on the island of Hispaniola at *Môle St Nicolas*. It has several ruined forts built by the English and French. General Maitland's surrender of Môle to Toussaint in 1798 marked the end of a five-year British bid to gain a toehold on this end of the island. Strategically located on the Windward Passage, just 120 km from Cuba, Môle was long coveted as a naval base by the United States. The hinterland has Haiti's lowest rainfall and little grows. The main occupation is making charcoal and shipping it to Port-au-Prince. Because few trees are left, charcoal makers now dig up roots. The peninsula's S side, especially from Baie de Henne to Anse Rouge, is a mixture of barren rock and desert, but the sea is crystal clear. There are few inhabitants. With salt pans on either side, Anse Rouge ships sacks of salt instead of charcoal.

NORTHEAST OF PORT-AU-PRINCE

Grandly called the Route National 3, the 128-km dirt road NE from Port-au-Prince to Hinche requires a 4WD and takes at least 5 hours. It starts by crossing the Cul de Sac plain via Croix-des-Bouquets. Here, a newly improved road branches off SE through a parched, barren region, skirting Lake Saumâtre (see **Flora and Fauna** and **Excursions from Port-au-Prince**) before reaching the Dominican border at Malpasse (see **Travel to the Dominican Republic** in Information for Visitors). On the N side of the plain, the RN3 zig-zags up a steep mountainside called Morne Tapion (great views back over Port-au-Prince) to reach Mirebalais, a crossroads at the head of the Artibonite valley. It is Haiti's wettest town. The road E leads to Lascahobas and the frontier town of Belladère, the least used of Haiti's three border crossings into the Dominican Republic. The road W heads down the Artibonite valley. Before it gets too bad, a left turnoff leads up into the hills to the charming village of *Ville-Bonheur* with its church built on the spot where locals reported an appearance of the Virgin in a palm tree in 1884. Thousands of pilgrims come every 15 July. The Voodooists among them hike 4 km to visit the much-filmed **Saut d'Eau** waterfall. Overhung by creepers, descending 30m in a series of shallow pools separated by mossy limestone shelves, the fall seems enchanted. The Voodooists bathe in its waters to purify themselves and light candles to enlist the help of the ancient spirits believed to live there.

The RN3 heads N out of Mirebalais on to the Central Plateau, where the military crackdown was especially harsh after the 1991 coup because peasant movements had been pressing for change here for years. After skirting the Peligre hydroelectric dam, now silted up and almost useless, the road passes Thomonde and reaches the region's capital, **Hinche**. The *Foyer d'Accueil* is an unmarked guest house above a school that is behind the blue and white church on the E side of the main square (basic rooms with fan, rarely any power, about US$4pp EP). The *Hotel Prestige*, also unmarked, at 2 rue Cité du Peuple, near the market, has not so good rooms for the same price. In Port-au-Prince, buses leave from the "station Au Cap" at the intersection of blvd La Saline and route de Delmas. Subject to aviation fuel availability, MAF may operate two flights a week. East of Hinche, **Bassin Zim** is a 20m waterfall in a lush setting 30 minutes' drive from town (head E on the Thomassique road, then fork N at Papaye). The cascade fans out over a rounded, sloping, limestone rockface. At its foot is a 60m wide natural pool with deep, milky-blue water that is perfect for swimming.

INFORMATION FOR VISITORS

● **Documents**

All visitors need passports except Americans and Canadians, who need only proof of citizenship. At the time of writing, the de facto government had dropped visa requirements for many nations, partly because Haiti's embassies and consulates abroad were all controlled by Aristide loyalists. Visas were not needed for nationals of USA, Canada, EC and Caricom countries, Argentina, Austria, Finland, Israel, Liechtenstein, Mexico, Monaco, Norway, South Korea, Sweden and Switzerland. Caution: it was not known if some visa requirements would be reinstated if Aristide was

returned to power. Check. Visas issued at the Haitian Embassy in New York (60 East 42nd Street 1365, New York, NY 10017) take 1 hour, 2 photos required, US$18, valid for 3 months. Visitors must have an onward ticket. All visitors, except cruise ship passengers, must complete an embarkation/disembarkation card on the plane; this is valid for 90 days, and may be extended. It is no longer necessary to have a *laissez-passer* before visiting the interior, but you must have some form of identification to satisfy the many police controls. It may also be wise to obtain a letter from the Tourist Office or police in Port-au-Prince confirming that you are a tourist.

● **Customs**

Baggage inspection is thorough and drug-enforcement laws are strict. There is no restriction on foreign currency. You may bring in one quart of spirits, and 200 cigarettes or 50 cigars. There are no export limitations.

● **How To Get There**

NB Economic sanctions were imposed on Haiti in May/June 1994 and most commercial flights into Haiti ceased.

Prior to sanctions the following airlines flew from USA: American Airlines from New York and Boston; American Airlines, Haiti TransAir, Haiti National Airlines and ALM all direct from Miami. Lynx Air from Fort Lauderdale to Cap Haïtien. ALM from Curaçao. Air France from Santo Domingo once a week. A Haitian air taxi service, Caribintair, has three flights a week from Santo Domingo. Air Canada direct from Montreal. Air France links Haiti with Paris and the French Caribbean: Fort de France in Martinique, Pointe-à-Pitre in Guadeloupe and Cayenne in French Guiana. Copa twice a week from Panama City. Note that flights from Miami used to be frequently overbooked. If you are not on a tight schedule, but have a confirmed seat, you may be asked to give your seat to a passenger with no confirmation in return for credit vouchers to be used on another flight within 12 months. Your original ticket will still be valid for the next flight, or for transfer to a different flight.

● **Airport**

On the northern edge of Delmas, 13 km outside Port-au-Prince (information: T 46-410516). Arrival can be pandemonium, especially if more than one flight is being accommodated at once. Knowledge of French helps; just get on with your affairs and try not to be distracted. The so-called "supervisors" at the airport are in fact taxi-drivers, touting for business. Porters charge US$0.50 per bag. Once through the squash inside you emerge into a squash outside, of taxi drivers and people awaiting friends. Taxi into town, US$10, or a seat in a taptap (open-backed truck), US$0.10, plus US$0.10 for large bag.

Information Office at the airport is very helpful. The downstairs snackbar is cheap and friendly. Not so the upstairs restaurant at the W end of the terminal. The public area has a bookstore and a handicraft shop. Duty free goods and more crafts are on sale in the area reserved for departing passengers. In the baggage claim hall for arriving passengers, there is a *bureau de change* that gives almost as good a rate as that available from street changers outside.

Visitors must pay a US$25 departure tax and a US$2 security tax in US currency.

● **Airlines**
Air Canada (T 46-0441/2): Air France (T 22-1700/1086), 11 rue Capois, corner rue Ducoste, near *Holiday Inn*; Air Jamaica (T 22-0563), Madsen Bldg, 107 rue du Quai; ALM (T 22-0900) 69 rue Pavée, corner rue du Peuple; American Airlines (T 23-1314), ave Marie Jeanne, near post office (also T 46-0110 at the airport); Copa (T 23-2326/7), Madsen Bldg, 107 rue du Quai; Haiti Trans Air (T 23-4010/20/9258), rue Capois near *Holiday Inn*.

Lynx Air in Cap Haïtien is 62-1386.

● **Internal Air Services**
Mission Aviation Fellowship (T 46-3993) and Caribintair (T 46-0737/78, 49-0203) have flights every day except Sunday to Cap Haïtien (US$50 round trip). They also run two or three flights a week each to Jérémie (US$70 round trip). MAF additionally flies Tues, Thur and Sat to Hinche (US$40 round trip). Book and pay through travel agents. Flights leave from Aviation Générale, a small domestic airport 1 km E of the international airport.

Caribintair also operates as a charter/air taxi company, and has three flights a week to Santo Domingo. Marien Air (T 62-0527/0742), a Cap-based air taxi service run by Paul Takeo Hodges, flies anywhere in Haiti. It also offers flights to Port-au-Prince, the Dominican Republic, Turks and Caicos, Bahamas and Jamaica.

Note, at the time of writing, all regular internal services were periodically suspended because of aviation fuel shortages. Planes were still available for charter.

● **Shipping**
Cruise ships stopped calling at Port-au-Prince years ago, partly because of passenger reaction to begging. Royal Caribbean and Crown cruise lines have leased private beaches near Cap Haïtien for one-day stopovers, but they suspended visits after the 1991 coup.

● **Travel To The Dominican Republic**
See **Documents** in the Dominican Republic chapter, and check with the Dominican Consulate (see below) for those who need a visa. A *laissez-passer* from Haitian Immigration, on Avenue John Brown, is necessary to leave Haiti by land. Ask a travel agency to get it for you. Give them two days' warning, two photos and US$15. Taptaps and trucks ply the road to the border at Malpasse. Repaired and improved in 1993-94 (to transport smuggled fuel), it can be done in one hour. You should not pay anything on leaving Haiti, but travellers have been asked for anything between US$25 and US$40 before their papers will be stamped. It is US$10 to reenter Haiti. Visitors arriving in the Dominican Republic pay US$10. Mopeds ferry you between the Haitian and Dominican border posts for US$1. There are regular buses from the Dominican frontier town of Jimaní to Santo Domingo (6 hrs). Rental cars are not allowed to cross the border, but you could safely leave one at the border for a few hours during a quick excursion to Jimaní. Dominican buses leave Port-au-Prince most mornings for their return trip to Santo Domingo, but they have no fixed time or departure point (the trip can take up to 10 hrs, with 2 hrs at the border). Ask at the *Hotel Palace* on rue Capois, where many Dominicans stay. Buses also leave from *Auberge Port-au-Prince*. Haitian travel agencies sometimes offer 3 or 4 day inclusive bus tours into the Republic.

Air France has one flight a week to Santo Domingo (June 1994). Caribintair has three flights a week for US$175 round trip. No *laissez-passer* is necessary to leave by air.

● **Internal Land Transport**
See **Travel To The Provinces** under Port-au-Prince.

● **Car Rental**
A small Japanese saloon car such as a Nissan Sunny, with a/c, rents for about US$45/day, US$250/week, unlimited mileage. A 4WD such as a Nissan Pathfinder is US$65/day, US$400/week. This includes insurance, but with a high excess, ranging from US$250 to

US$750, depending on the company. It is cheaper to pay for the rental in gourdes (cash) than by credit card.

Avis (T 46-4161/2640/96), Hertz (T 46-0700/2048) and Budget (T 46-2324) all have bases near the airport, and have desks in a small, shared office just opposite the airport terminal, open 0800-1700. Smaller companies include Sunshine Jeep (T 49-1155), Secom (T 57-1913) and Sugar (T 46-3413). Hertz is the only company with a base in Cap Haïtien.

Driving in Haiti is a hazardous free-for-all, but some find it exhilarating. The streets are narrow, with many sharp bends and full of pedestrians in the towns. There are few signs. Vehicles swerve unexpectedly to avoid pot-holes. Cars often don't stop in an accident, so, to avoid paying the high insurance excess, keep a pen and paper handy to take down a number if necessary.

The embargo produced a brief fuel short-age at end-1991 but subsequently, until the time of writing, supplies were unaffected. Fuel is usually available in the big provincial towns, but power cuts may prevent stations from pumping at certain times of the day.

For driving to Cap Haïtien, Les Cayes and Jacmel, an ordinary car is fine, but for Jérémie, Port-de-Paix or Hinche, a 4WD is nessary. For-eigners may use a national driving licence for 3 months, then a local permit is required.

● **Hitchhiking**

Foreigners do not normally hitch. There are many young Haitian men who stick out a thumb asking for a "roue libre", especially from foreigners. Use your discretion.

● **Eating Out**

Most restaurants offer Créole or French cui-sine, or a mixture of both. Haiti's Créole cuisine is like its Caribbean cousins, but more peppery. Specialities include *griot* (deep-fried pieces of pork), *lambi* (conch, considered an aphrodis-iac), *tassot* (jerked beef) and rice with *djon-djon* (tiny, dark mushrooms). As elsewhere in the Caribbean, lobster is widely available.

Pétionville has many good French restau-rants. Some are French-managed or have French chefs, and are undeniably first class. Because of the fall in the gourde, they have become a bargain for visitors to Haiti.

Haiti's Barbancourt rum is excellent. Rum punch is popular. The local beer, Prestige, may be too sweet for some palates. The Dominican beer, Presidente, is the best of the foreign beers sold in Haiti, but Beck's is more widely available.

Haiti's wide range of micro-climates produces a large assortment of fruits and vegetables. It is popular to buy these in the regions where they grow and are freshest (prices can be bargained 40% below shop prices). The French influence is obvious in butcher shops where fine cuts of meat, cold cuts, paté and cheeses can be bought. The bakeries sell French crois-sants, together with Créole bread and meat pasties. American influence is felt in the super-markets. Most common are US-brand foods along with smaller amounts of Haitian, French and Middle Eastern brands.

● **Camping**

Camping in Haiti is an adventure. The dramatic scenery is very enticing but access to much of it is over rough terrain and there are no facili-ties, leaving exploring to the rugged. Campers have to take everything and create, or find their own shelter.

Peasant homes dot the countryside and it is almost impossible to find a spot where you will be spared curious and suspicious onlook-ers. It is best to set up camp or lodging before dark. To prevent misunderstanding, it is impor-tant to explain to the locals your intentions, or better yet, talk to the local elder and ask assistance or protection. Creating a relation-ship with the locals will usually ensure coop-eration and more privacy. Offer to pay a small amount for use of the land.

● **Entertainment**

Until the mid-1980s, Haiti used to be a very good place for night spots. With the drop in tourism and Haitians hesitating to be out late at night in uneasy times, many places have had to shut or curtail their level of entertainment. The few that survive offer a good evening's enjoyment and plenty of personality. Following French custom, entertaining starts late in the evening, about 2030-2100. Night clubbing starts around 2330 and continues into the small hours.

● **Tipping**

Budget travellers, particularly outside Port-au-Prince, are a rarity. Expect to be the subject of much friendly curiosity, and keep a pocketful of small change to conform with the local custom of tipping on every conceivable occa-sion. Even cigarettes and sweets are accepted. Hotels generally add 10% service charge. Bag-gage porters at hotels usually get US$0.50 per bag. Do not fail to reward good service since hotel and restaurant staff rely on tips to boost their meagre salaries. Nobody tips taxi, _publique, camionette_ or _tap-tap_ drivers, unless exceptional service has been given.

● **Shopping**

Haitians may tell you that many of the items for sale in the few tourist shops can be bought far cheaper in the markets. That may be true for them, but market vendors jack up prices for the foreigner, who will have to haggle skilfully to bring them down. The Iron Market in Port-au-Prince would be a fascinating place to visit but for the hustlers who will latch on to you and make the experience hell. Try out your bargaining skills at the Iron Markets in Jacmel and Cap Haïtien. People always ask for a discount in shops, except at food shops. All handicrafts can be bought at a discount. See above under **Culture** for best buys, and under towns for individual establishments.

Film processing services are the same as in the USA, but the price of film is high; transparency developing is considerably less.

● **Security**

Despite all the political turmoil since 1986, and the repression following the 1991 coup, security is not major a problem for the foreign visitor. In fact, Haiti has much less crime than most Caribbean countries. Take normal precautions. Carry handbags securely and do not leave belongings in sight in a parked car.

During any political unrest it is advisable to limit your movements in the daytime and not to go out at night. Streets are usually deserted by 2300. Foreigners are not normally targeted at such times, but seek local advice.

● **Currency**

The unit is the gourde (Cr: goud), divided into 100 centimes (Cr: kòb). Coins in circulation are for 5, 10, 20 and 50 centimes, notes for 1, 2, 5, 10, 25, 50, 100, 250 and 500 gourdes. The gourde was tied at 5 to the dollar during the US occupation. In the 1980s it began to trade at a slightly lower value on a parallel market, but the official rate was kept until 1991, when the Aristide government severed the tie and let the gourde float. From 7.5 to the dollar at the time of the September 1991 coup, it had fallen to 13 at the time of writing in 1993.

So far, so good. Now it gets complicated. Money changers express the rate as a percentage increase on the old official rate of 5 to 1. Thus, 6 to 1 is 20%, 7 to 1 is 40%, and 13 to 1 is 160%. Haitians routinely refer to their own money as dollars, based on the old 5 to 1 rate.

Thus, 5 gourdes is called a dollar, 10 gourdes is 2 dollars, 25 gourdes is 5 dollars, etc. Visitors must constantly clarify whether the price being quoted is in Haitian or American dollars, or gourdes, now increasingly used on bills. US coins co-circulate with local coins. They are treated as if the old 5 to 1 rate was still in force. Thus, a US penny is treated as 5 kòb, a nickel is 25 kòb, and so on.

The fall of the gourde has triggered inflation, but inflation has lagged far behind the rising value of the US dollar. This means that Haiti is currently a bargain for the visitor. The best exchange rate is obtained from money changers, whether those on the street or those working out of offices. It is perfectly legal (see **Money Exchange**, Port-au-Prince).

It is foolish to come to Haiti with any currency other than US dollars or French francs. Currencies like sterling can be changed, but only at a massive loss.

Visa, Mastercard and American Express are widely accepted. (At the time of writing, American Express was not being taken because of the embargo.) Beware, card users will not get a good rate.

● **Health**

Prophylaxis against malaria is essential. Tap water is not to be trusted (drink only filtered or treated water) and take care when choosing food. The local herb tea can help stomach troubles.

Good professional advice is available for the more common ailments. Ask friends, associates, or at the hotel desk for referrals to a doctor suited to your requirements. Office hours are usually 0730-1200, 1500-1800. A consultation costs about US$10-15.

Hospital care and comfort varies. Medical supplies were exempted from the embargo, but some doctors reported shortages in 1992-93. It was originally feared that the cutoff of most forms of international aid after the coup would trigger major epidemics, but none had materialized by the time of writing. Pharmacies/chemists can fill out prescriptions and many prescription drugs may be bought over the counter.

Recommended hospitals (all in Port-au-Prince) are Canapé Vert, rue Canapé Vert (45-1052/3/0984); Adventiste de Diquini, Carrefour Road (T 34-2000/0521), Hospital Français de Haiti, rue du Centre (T 22-2323); St Francois de Salles, rue de la Révolution (T 22-2110/0232).

A note on prostitution: there are no laws in Haiti to suppress it. Activity seems to be evident only at night with the commonly known areas being along the main roads in Carrefour and street corners in Pétionville. After hours the prostitutes move into the dive-type joints, targeting foreigners. With regard to casual sex, there is a red alert in Haiti over Aids.

● **Climate**
The climate is generally very warm but the cool on- and off-shore winds of morning and evening help to make it bearable. In coastal areas temperatures vary between 20° and 35° C, being slightly hotter in April-September. The driest months are December-March. In the hill resorts the temperature is cooler.

● **Clothing**
As in most other countries in the Caribbean beachwear should not be worn away from the beach and poolside. Dress is casual but never sloppy; Haitians appreciate good manners and style. Above-the-knee hems for women are considered risqué but acceptable. Men always wear a shirt, but a tie is not necessary in the evening.

● **Hours of Business**
Government offices: 0700-1200, 1300-1600 (0800-1200, 1300-1800 October-April); banks: 0900-1300 Mon to Fri; shops and offices: 0700-1600 (an hour later October to April).

● **Public Holidays**
New Year and Ancestors (1-2 January), Mardi Gras (the 3 days before Ash Wednesday), Americas Day (14 April), Good Friday, 1 May, Flag and University Day (18 May), Assumption (15 August), Deaths of Henri Christophe and Dessalines (8 and 17 October), United Nations Day (24 October), All Saints (1 November), Armed Forces Day (18 November), Discovery of Haiti (5 December), 25 December. Corpus Christi and Ascension are also public holidays.

● **Time Zone**
Eastern standard time, 5 hours behind GMT.

● **Embassies And Consulates**
British Consulate (T 57-3969, F 57-4048), *Hotel Montana*, rue Cardozo, Pétionville (PO Box 1032, Port-au-Prince), T 73969); **Canada** (T 23-2358/4919/9373, F 23-8720), Bank of Nova Scotia Bldg, Route de Delmas, Delmas 18; **Dominican Republic** (T 57-1650/0383), 121 rue Panaméricaine (50 m down rue José de San Martín), Pétionville; **France** (T 22-0951/2/3, F 22-0963), 51 rue Capois at the SW corner of the Champs de Mars, near *Hotel Palace*; **Germany** (T 57-3128/0456); **US Embassy** (T 22-0200), Blvd Harry Truman, Bicentenaire; **US Consulate** (T 22-0200), 22 rue Oswald Durand.

● **Weights And Measures**
The metric system is used.

● **Electric Current**
110 volt, 60 cycle AC. During the imposition of the fuel embargo, electricity production and distribution are suspended (June 1994). Only if sufficient rain falls to operate the hydroelectric facility will the capital have power and water. Only the best hotels have sufficiently powerful generators to make up the deficiency (see **Where To Stay** section). As the *Oloffson* is on the same circuit as the Presidential Palace, it is never blacked out.

● **Telephones**
Always bad, the telephone system has become even worse since the embargo. Fewer than a third of calls get through. The Haitian international operator (dial 09) is hard to raise. The *Oloffson*, *Holiday Inn*, *Montana* and *El Rancho* hotels have AT&T "USA Direct" telephones for

---

To use AT&T USADirect® Service from public telephones in Haiti, just dial **001-800-972-2883** or look for specially marked telephones. You will be connected with an AT&T Operator who will be able to place your call collect, or charge the call to your AT&T Calling Card. When calling from a hotel room, obtain an outside line before dialing the USADirect® access number. Hotel surcharges may apply.

AT&T USADirect® Service.

collect calls to the USA or calls anywhere in the world with an AT&T credit card, but even these connections were problematic in 1994.

In 1990 all telephone numbers in Haiti changed; an extra digit was added to the prefix, thus: in Port-au-Prince 2- became 22-, 3=23, 4=34, 6=46, 7=57, 8=48, 9=49 and 5 became 45 (Turgeau), or 55 (Laboule). In Cap Haïtien 2- became 62-; Port de Paix 8=68; Gonaïves 4=74; Jérémie 4=84, Jacmel 8=88.

● Media

Le Nouvelliste is the better of the two daily French-language newspapers; conservative, but tries to be impartial. Three weekly newspapers are published in French, all very one-sided, but on different sides. The pro-Aristide weekly *Libète* is the only Créole newspaper.

Radio stations use a mix of French and Créole. Metropole and Tropic are best for news. The satellite-beamed Radio France Inter is rebroadcast locally on FM 89.3. The BBC World Service can be heard on 15220 (early morning) and 7325 (evenings). Voice of America is on 11915 (mornings) and 9455 evenings.

A commercial TV station, Tele-Haiti, re-transmits American, French, Canadian and Latin American stations (including CNN) to cable subscribers, electricity permitting.

● Tourism Information

At the time of writing, the Tourist Office was temporarily located next to the commerce ministry at 8 rue Légitime (T 23-0723), half a block from the Musée d'Art Haïtien. There were tentative plans to move back to its old address at 1 ave Marie Jeanne, near the post office, Bicentenaire. Supplementary information may be sought from the Hotel and Tourism Association (T 57-4647), at the *Hotel Montana*, or from travel agencies.

ISPAN (Institute for the Protection of the Nation's Heritage) has information on ruined forts and plantation houses, corner of Ave Martin Luther King and Cheriez, Pont Morin (T 45-3220/3118). Also at Rue 15-B, Cap Haïtien (T 62-2459).

● Further Reading

History: *The Black Jacobins*, by CLR James (about Toussaint); *Papa Doc and the Tontons Macoutes*, by Bernard Diederich and Al Burt.

Voodoo: *The Drum and the Hoe*, by Harold Courlander; *Divine Horsemen* by Maya Deren; *The Serpent and the Rainbow* by Wade Davis; *Mama Lola* by Karen McCarthy Brown.

Travelogue: *Bonjour Blanc* by Ian Thomson (by a recent British visitor)

Fiction: *The Comedians* by Graham Greene (set during Papa Doc's time); *The Kingdom of This World* by Alejo Carpentier (about Mackandal and Christophe).

DOMINICAN REPUBLIC

T HE DOMINICAN REPUBLIC occupies the eastern two-thirds of Hispaniola. The country is mountainous, but despite having the highest mountain on the island and in the Caribbean, Pico Duarte (3,175m), it is less mountainous than Haiti. Within a system of widespread food production are large sugar and fruit plantations.

The Republic is building up its tourist trade, and has much to offer in the way of natural beauty, old colonial architecture, attractive beaches, modern resorts and native friendliness. Its population is mostly a mixture of black, white and mestizo, and is Spanish-speaking. These English terms should, however, be qualified: "blanco" (white) refers to anybody who is white, white/Indian mestizo, or substantially white with either or both Indian or African admixture; "indio claro" (tan) is anyone who is a white/black mixed mulatto, or a mestizo; "indio oscuro" (dark Indian) is anyone who is not 100% black (ie with some white or Indian admixture); "negro" is 100% African. "Negro" is not a derogatory term. There is a certain aspiration towards the Indian, especially after Trujillo's quest for national respectability; this can be seen not only in the use of the original name for the island, Quisqueya (and Quisqueyanos), but in place names (San Pedro de Macorís, from the Macorix tribe, the other Indian inhabitants being the Taino and the Ciguayo) and in given family names (Guainorex, Anacaona, etc). An introduction to the Indians of the region is given in the **Pre-Columbian Civilizations** chapter.

History

For the general history of the island of Hispaniola after the arrival of the Span-iards, see the beginning of this chapter.

Although the Spanish launched much of their westward expansion from Santo Domingo, their efforts at colonizing the rest of the island were desultory. Drake sacked Santo Domingo in 1586, the French gained control of the western part of the island in 1697 and, by the mid-18th century, the number of Spaniards in the eastern part of the island was about one-third of a total of 6,000. Since there was little commercial activity or population of the interior, it was easy prey for Haitian invaders fired with the fervour of their rebellion at the turn of the 19th century. Between 1801 and 1805, followers of Toussaint L'Ouverture and Dessalines plundered the territory. Sovereignty was disputed for the next 17 years, then, in 1822, Haiti took control for a further 22 years.

After the declaration of the Dominican Republic's independence in 1844, by the writer Duarte, the lawyer Sánchez and the soldier Mella, the country underwent yet another period of instability, including more Haitian incursions and, in 1861, a four-year re-annexion with Spain. Independence was regained in the War of Restoration (la Restauración), but with no respite in factional fighting or economic disorder. Apart from the dictatorship of Ulises Heureaux (1882-84, 1887-99), governments were short-lived. The country must be one of the very few where a Roman Catholic archbishop has served as head of state: Archbishop Meriño was President from 1880 to 1882.

In 1916, the USA occupied the Dominican Republic, having managed the country's customs affairs (on behalf of US and European creditors) since 1905. When the USA left in 1924, the Republic had a fully organized army, whose commander, Rafael Leonidas Trujillo

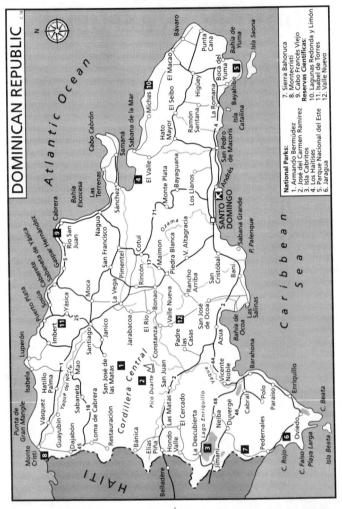

DOMINICAN REPUBLIC

National Parks:
1. Armando Bermúdez
2. José del Carmen Ramírez
3. Isla Cabritos
4. Los Haitises
5. Parque Nacional del Este
6. Jaragua
7. Sierra Bahoruca
8. Montecristi
9. Cabo Francés Viejo

Reservas Científicas:
10. Lagunas Redonda y Limón
11. Isabel de Torres
12. Valle Nuevo

Molina, became President in 1930. Thus began one of the most ruthless dictatorships ever seen in the Dominican Republic. With either himself or his surrogates at the helm (Héctor Trujillo, 1947-60, and Joaquín Balaguer, 1960-62), Trujillo embarked on the expansion of industry and public works, the introduction of the national currency and the liquidation of the country's debts. Nevertheless, his methods of government denied any form of representation and included murder, torture, blackmail and corruption. During his reign, in 1937, an estimated 10,000 Haitian immigrants were slaughtered, prolonging the hatred between the two republics which had begun in the early 19th century.

Trujillo was assassinated in 1961. President Balaguer immediately set about eradicating his family's influence, but in 1962 Balaguer was defeated in elections by Dr Juan Bosch of the Partido Revolucionario Dominicano (PRD). After seven months he was ousted by a miltary coup led by Colonel Elías Wessin y Wessin. The PRD, with the support of a group of young colonels, tried to win back constitutional government in 1965, but were prevented from doing so by the army, backed by the USA and the Organization of American States. New elections were held in 1966; they were won by Balaguer, at the head of the Partido Reformista Social Cristiano (PRSC). He remained in office until 1978, forging closer links with the USA, but not without facing coup attempts, right-wing terrorism and left-wing guerrilla incursions.

A PRD President was returned in 1978, Antonio Guzmán, whose chief aims were to reduce army power and eliminate corruption. A month before leaving office in 1982, he discovered that members of his family, who had held office under him, had been involved in corruption, so he killed himself. His successor, Dr Salvador Jorge Blanco, also of the PRD, presided over severe economic difficulties which led to rioting in 1984 in which 60 people died. The party split over the handling of the economy, helping Joaquín Balaguer to win a narrow majority in the 1986 elections giving him a fifth presidential term. The 1990 elections were contested by two octogenarians, Dr Balaguer (83) and Dr Juan Bosch (80), now of the Partido de la Liberación Dominicana (PLD). Dr Balaguer won a sixth term of office by a very narrow majority, which was subjected to a verification process after Dr Bosch alleged fraud had taken place in the capital. The May 1994 elections had the same outcome, after Balaguer had decided very late in the campaign to stand for re-election. His chief opponent was José Francisco Peña Gómez of the PRD. First results gave Balaguer the narrowest of victories. Peña Gómez, supported by many outside observers, claimed that fraud had taken place and a recount was ordered. At the time of going to press, the final result had not been announced. Among its campaigning methods, the PRSC and other parties employed attacks on Peña Gómez' colour and Haitian origins, to the extent of suggesting that the PRD candidate would succumb to international pressure to "fuse" the Dominican Republic with Haiti. Initial foreign reaction to the post-election crisis was concern in the USA and the cancellation of several tourist charter flights.

Violent demonstrations and general strikes against economic hardship occurred in 1987, 1990 and 1991, in the last instance following the signing of an IMF accord. As a result of the government's structural adjustment programme, however, improvement was recorded in most productive sectors, the level of reserves and the rate of inflation (see **Economy** below). Positive economic results did not prevent spending on health and education lagging behind other public sectors. Unemployment remained high and many Dominicans were tempted by better opportunities in the USA and Puerto Rico.

Relations between the Dominican Republic and Haiti became very strained in 1991 after President Balaguer ordered the deportation of all illegal Haitian immigrants under the age of 16 and over 60. Many from outside these age groups left, putting pressure on the resources of President Aristide's government. Attitudes to the overthrow of Aristide were ambivalent because the Dominican Republic officially supported the Organization of American States' trade embargo while politicians vocally and traders in practice defied it. In mid-1994, Balaguer assented to the presence of UN monitors who, with US support, would seek ways to end the flow of fuel and other goods by road and sea to Haiti.

For a study of contemporary Dominican politics and economics see *Dominican Republic: Beyond the Lighthouse*, by James Ferguson (London: Latin America Bureau, 1992).

Government

The Dominican Republic is a representative democracy, with legislative power resting in a bicameral Congress: a 30-seat Senate and a 120-seat Chamber of Deputies. Senators and deputies are elected for a four-year term, as is the President, in whom is vested executive power. The three main parties are the Partido Reformista Social Cristiano (PRSC), the Partido Revolucionario Dominicano (PRD) and the Partido de la Liberación Dominicana (PLD).

The Economy

There are six main agricultural regions: the N, the Cibao valley in the N central area, Constanza and Tiero, the E, the San Juan valley, and the S. Cibao is the most fertile and largest region, while the eastern region is the main sugar-producing area. Sugar is traditionally the main crop. Until 1984, the US import quota system, of which the Dominican Republic was the largest beneficiary, provided a preferential market for over half the country's sugar exports as well as a cushion against the slump in world sugar prices. Major adjustments in US consumption patterns, particularly the switch by Coca Cola and Pepsi to High Fructose Corn Syrup, prompted the USA to cut quotas drastically. By 1988, the Dominican Republic's quota had been cut to 25% of previous levels and quota cuts continued until 1994. Diversification out of sugar cane, the conversion of some cane lands into tourist resorts, the expulsion of Haitian cutters and a slump in productivity led the country to import sugar in 1992. Each season, from 1990 to 1993, the value

DOMINICAN REPUBLIC: FACT FILE

Geographic

Land area	48,443 sq km
forested	12.8%
pastures	43.2%
cultivated	29.9%

Demographic

Population (1992)	7,471,000
annual growth rate (1987-92)	2.2%
urban	60.4%
rural	39.6%
density	154.2 per sq km
Religious affiliation	
Roman Catholic	90.8%
Birth rate per 1,000 (1991)	27.0
	(world av 26.4)
Death rate per 1,000 (1991)	7.0
	(world av 9.2)

Education and Health

Life expectancy at birth,	
male	65 years
female	69 years
Infant mortality rate	
per 1,000 live births (1991)	60.0
Physicians (1988)	1 per 934 persons
Hospital beds	1 per 508 persons
Calorie intake as %	
of FAO requirement	104%
Population age 25 and over	
with no formal schooling	48.0%
Literate males (over 15)	84.8%
Literate females (over 15)	81.8%

Economic

GNP (1990 market prices)	US$5,847mn
GNP per capita	US$820
Public external debt (1990)	US$3,343mn
Tourism receipts (1990)	US$750mn
Inflation (annual av 1986-91)	43.0%
Radio	1 per 6.4 persons
Television	1 per 10 persons
Telephone	1 per 24 persons

Employment

Population economically active (1981)	
	1,915,388
Unemployment rate (1991)	30.0%
% of labour force in agriculture	22.0
mining	0.2
manufacturing	11.7
construction	4.3
Military forces	23,200

Source *Encyclopaedia Britannica*

of sugar exports has fallen.

Since 1975 gold and silver mining has been of considerable importance. The Pueblo Viejo mine's oxide ores are running out, and high productivity costs together with accumulated debts in 1992-93 forced the state mining company, Rosario Dominicana, to suspend a large part of its operations in March 1993. The country also produces ferronickel, which rivals sugar as the major commodity export earner. Reserves are estimated at 10% of total world deposits. Ferronickel mining was also suspended in the first three months of 1993 because of unfavourable market conditions. This contributed to an accumulated decline of 40% in the mining sector in 1993. Other sources of income are the industrial free zones, almost 30 in number, with 462 companies and 164,000 employees, where manufactured goods are assembled for the North American market (generating US$304mn in 1993, against US$287mn in 1992), and remittances from Dominicans resident abroad.

The largest foreign exchange earner nowadays is, however, tourism, with annual receipts exceeding US$1bn. New hotel projects brought the number of hotel rooms to 23,500 in 1992, compared with 11,400 in 1987, and this was expected to have risen to 34,000 rooms in 1993. Tourist arrivals (including Dominicans resident overseas) in 1993 were estimated at 2 million, compared with 1.6 million in 1992, when over half the visitors came from Europe.

In the first half of the 1980s, a combination of fiscal and external account problems brought about a sharp decline in the rate of gdp growth and led the Government to turn to the IMF for financial assistance. The Government agreed to reduce its fiscal deficit and take a number of other austerity measures, including a gradual devaluation of the peso. It failed to meet targets, so the programme was suspended in early 1984. Government measures to remove subsidies, as part of the austerity package agreed with the IMF, led to riots in Santo Domingo in April 1984. A one-year standby loan facility worth RD$78.5mn was eventually approved in April 1985 but not renewed because of political opposition. Despite the widespread unpopularity of policies designed to satisfy IMF demands, President Balaguer in 1990-91 negotiated a new IMF agreement. Having repaid debts worth US$81.6mn to the IMF, World Bank and other multilateral agencies, an IMF standby agreement was approved in August 1991. The terms of the accord, which included the unification of the exchange rates, an end to price controls, balancing state corporation budgets and a commitment to pay outstanding foreign debt arrears, were greeted by a series of general strikes. Agreement with the IMF did, however, permit the rescheduling of US$905mn of debt with the Paris Club group of foreign governments in November 1991, with further successful renegotiations of official debt in 1992. In February 1994, commercial bank creditors signed an agreement to reschedule US$1.04bn of debt. The IMF signed a new US$44mn standby facility in July 1993 to support the government's economic programme, and agreed to provide US$48mn in compensatory finance to cover losses in export earnings in 1992/93.

In 1990 the major problems confronting the Government were the high rate of inflation, unofficially estimated at 100% a year, and the disruptive electricity crisis, which had got steadily worse for several years. Inflation, pushed by heavy government spending on public works and increasing subsidies, was reduced to 4.6% in 1992 and 2.7% in 1993 as a result of a curtailment of spending, both in a refusal to increase public sector wages and after the completion of major public works. The introduction of a dual foreign exchange system (one rate for official transactions, and a free market rate for commercial banks) helped to stabilize the exchange rate against the dollar, although an easing of regulations on commercial bank foreign exchange transactions was necessary to reduce pressure on the peso in early 1994. In October 1991 the state electricity company, CDE, signed a management contract with Unión Fenosa of Spain to rehabilitate the generating and distribution systems. Considerable improvements in supply resulted, although power cuts were not entirely eradicated, especially outside the capital. The breakdown of a major power plant and low levels of water for hydroelectric generation in 1994 revealed the fragility of the system. Further investment and restructuring was planned for that year. Apart from mining, most sectors of the economy showed recovery in 1992, contributing to a 5% increase in GDP. Growth waned somewhat in 1993 as agriculture and manufacturing showed small declines, to add to that of mining; overall estimates for gdp growth were between 0.9 and 3%. Of growing concern was the worsening of the trade deficit as traditional exports declined, offset only by growing tourism receipts and remittances from Dominicans abroad.

Culture

Music and Dance

The most popular dance is the *merengue*, which dominates the musical life of the Dominican Republic; a great many orchestras have recorded *merengue* rhythms and are now world-famous. The traditional *merengue* is played by a 3-man group called a *perico ripiao*, or *pri-prí*, which consists of a *tambora* (small drum), an accordion and a *güira* (a percussion instrument scraped by a metal rod, or, as originally used by Indians, a gourd scraped with a forked stick). Since the 1970s the *merengue* has got much faster, with less formal steps, showing US disco influence. There is a *merengue* festival in the last week of July and the first week of August, held on the Malecón in Santo Domingo. Puerto Plata holds its *merengue* festival in the first week of October and Sosúa has one the last week of September.

Other popular dances are the *mangulina*, the *salve*, the *bambulá* (from Samaná), the *ritmo guloya* (especially in San Pedro de Macorís, see also that section below), the *carabiné* (typical of the region around Barahona), and the *chenche matriculado*. Salsa is very popular in dance halls and discos (every town, however small, has a discothèque). *Bachata* is Dominican "country music", usually songs of unrequited love, to the accompaniment of virtuoso guitar, percussion, *güira* and bass.

Literature

In the colonial period, Santo Domingo encouraged the development of literature within the framework of the first seats of learning in Spanish America. The early colonists expressed their inspiration most readily in poetry and the verses of Elvira de Mendoza and Leonor de Ovando are frequently cited as examples of that time. Among the many Dominican poets famed within the country in subsequent years are Gastón Fernando Deligne, Fabio Fiallo and the national poet, Pedro Mir, author of *Hay un país en el mundo*. The two dominant political figures of the latter half of the twentieth century, Joaquín Balaguer and Juan Bosch, are also well known for their literary output, Balaguer in many styles, especially poetry, Bosch in short stories. Of the present generation of writers, Frank Moya Pons and Bernardo Vega stand out as writers of mainly historical works.

Painting

The first major representations of the country in painting came after 1870 with the establishment of a national identity through the Restauración movement and the consolidation of independence from Haiti. The first important painter was Alejandro Bonilla while the Spaniard José Fernández Corredor is credited with the foundation of the first painting school in the country. From this period the artists Arturo Grullón, Luis Desangles (Sisito), Leopoldo Navarro and Abelardo Rodríguez Urdaneta stand out. The last named is famous as painter, sculptor and photographer. In the 1930s, Jaime Colson, Yoryi Morel and Darío Suro were precursors of *costumbrismo* (art of customs and manners). Contemporary painters have followed the various styles which have prevailed throughout the art world. Those who have gained an international reputation are Iván Tovar, Ramón Oviedo, Cándido Bidó, José Rincón Mora and Paul Giudicelli. Exhibitions of Dominican art are held frequently in Santo Domingo galleries, for example the Voluntariado de las Casas Reales, Galeria Nader, Museo de Arte Moderno, El Pincel, La Galería, and others. For additional details on Dominican painters, consult *Arte contemporáneo dominicano*, by Gary Nicolás Nader, and *Antología de la pintura dominicana*, by Cándido Gerón.

For details on theatres and other sites of cultural interest, see below under Santo Domingo, Puerto Plata and Sosúa.

Flora and Fauna

There are 13 national parks and 9 scientific reserves in the Dominican Republic, all under the control of the Dirección Nacional de Parques (DNP, address below): **Armando Bermúdez** and **José del Carmen Ramírez**, both containing pine forests and mountains in the Cordillera Central are the only remaining areas of extensive forest in the republic; it is estimated that since the arrival of Columbus, two-thirds of the virgin forest has been destroyed. The reasons for the loss are fire and the establishment of smallholdings by landless peasants. By setting up these parks the gloomy prediction of 1973, that all the Dominican Republic's

forest would vanish by 1990, has been avoided. In addition, a pilot reforestation project has been started near San José de las Matas, the Plan Sierra. The **Isla Cabritos** National Park in Lago Enriquillo is the smallest in the system; it is a unique environment, between 4 and 40m below sea level. Its original vegetation has been lost either to timber collection or to the goats and cattle which once grazed it. Now covered in secondary vegetation, 106 species of plant have been identified, including 10 types of cactus. The island has a large crocodile population, an endemic species of iguana, and other reptiles. 62 species of bird have been identified, 5 aquatic, 16 shore and 41 land birds; 45 are native to the island. Among the birds that can be seen (or heard) are the tiny manuelito (*myiarchus stolidus*) and the great hummingbird (*anthracothorax dominicus*), the querebebé (*chordeiles gundlachii*), best heard at dusk, and the cu-cú (*athene cunicularia*), which sings at night and dawn and excavates a hole in the desert for its nest.

Los Haitises, on the S coast of Samaná Bay (Bahía de San Lorenzo), is a protected coastal region, whose land and seascape of mangrove swamps, caves and strange rock formations emerging from the sea (*mogotes*) is unmatched in the republic. In Los Haitises you can visit the Cueva del Angel, cayes on which live many birds and humid tropical forest, as well as the mangroves. The **Parque Nacional del Este** is on the peninsula S of San Rafael del Yuma and includes the Isla Saona. It has remote beaches, examples of precolumbian art in a system of caves and is the habitat of the now scarce paloma coronita (crowned, or whiteheaded dove, *columba leucocephala*), the rhinoceros iguana and of various turtles. In the NW the **Montecristi** national park, on the Haitian border, contains marine and land ecosystems, the coastal Laguna de Saladillo, dry subtropical forest and the Cayos Siete Hermanos. In the SW, the **Sierra de Bahoruco** is a forested highland which has, among other plants, 52% of the orchids found in the republic; it also has many species of birds. At the southernmost tip of Barahona, also in the SW, is Jaragua national park, which includes the Isla Beata; on the mainland it is principally dry forest. Also designated national parks are a number of panoramic roads, botanical and zoological gardens (such as those in Santo Domingo, see below), aquaria and recreational parks, and sites of historic interest (La Vega Vieja and La Isabela). The Reservas Científicas include lakes, patches of forest and the Banco de la Plata (Silver Banks), to which hump-backed whales migrate from the Arctic yearly for the birth of their young. Trips are organized to see the whales; contact the DNP (see also Samaná page 349). The National Parks Office (DNP) is at Avenida Independencia 539 esquina Cervantes, Santo Domingo (Apartado Postal 2487, T 221-5340). To visit the main forest reserves you must obtain a permit from the DNP or from the authorized administration office of each park for RD$50 (US$3.95). Note that to visit Los Haitises or Isla Cabritos, prices from DNP do not include the boat fare, usually US$24 extra per boat. The DNP publishes a book, *Sistema de áreas protegidas de República Dominicana*, which describes each park and details how to reach it (US$12).

Ecoturisa (Santiago 203, B, Santo Domingo, T 221-4104/6, F 689-3703) is promoting ecotourism in the Republic; in 1992 it won the Thompson World Aware award. Part of its profits go towards the non-profit organization, Fundación Prospectiva Ambiental Dominicana. The Foundation proposes new areas for protection, education and study, while Ecoturisa sets up tours to areas already under protection or of special interest. Ecoturisa rarely sells tours direct to clients; its programmes are available through tour companies and hotels. Tours can be designed especially for small groups and all arrangements with DNP can be made.

The Jardín Botánico Nacional and the Museo de Historia Natural, Santo Domingo, have a full classification of the republic's flora. Of interest are the 67 types and 300 species of orchid found in this part of Hispaniola; there are a number of gardens which specialize in their cultivation. The most popular are *oncidium henekenii, polyradicium lindenii* and *leonchilus labiatus*. The Jardín Botánico holds an orchid show each year; in 1994 it was in March. The national plant is the caoba (mahogany). There is a wide variety of palms, some of which grow only on Hispaniola.

The Dominican Republic is becoming a popular bird-watching destination. The national bird is the cotica parrot, which is green, very talkative and a popular pet. It is, however, protected. Among other birds that can be seen, apart from those mentioned above, are other parrots, hummingbirds, the guaraguao (a hawk), the barrancolí and the flautero.

Of the island's mammals, the hutia, an endemic rodent, is endangered. Similarly in peril is the manatee, which may be seen at Estero Hondo; details from Ecoturisa.

Beaches and Watersports

According to Unesco, the Dominican Republic has some of the best beaches in the world: white sand, coconut palms and many with a profusion of green vegetation. The main ones are described in the text below. The beaches vary enormously in development, cleanliness, price of facilities, number of hawkers and so on. Boca Chica and Juan Dolio, for instance, are very touristy and not suitable for anyone seeking peace and quiet; for that, Bayahibe would be a much better bet (although development is under way here). The best-known beaches are in the E of the republic, including: Boca Chica, Juan Dolio, Playa Caribe, Guayacanes and Villas del Mar in San Pedro de Macorís; Minitas (La Romana), Bayahibe, Macao, Bávaro, Puerto Escondido (Higüey); Anadel, Cayo Levantado, Las Terrenas, Playa Rincón and Portillo in Samaná and Sánchez; Playa el Bretón at Cabrera, Playa Grande in the Province of María Trinidad Sánchez and Laguna Gri-Gri at Río San Juan, where you can also visit the beaches of Puerto Escondido, Punta Preciosa in the Bahía Escocesa and Cabo Francés Viejo. NE of Puerto Plata, recommended, although in many cases fully developed, beaches include Cabarete, Ermita, Magante, Playa Grande and Sosúa. At Puerto Plata itself are Playa Dorada, Costámbar, Cofresí, Long Beach, Boca de Cangrejos, Caño Grande, Bergantín, Playa de Copello and Playa Mariposa. Towards the NW and the Haitian border there are beaches at Bahía de Luperón, Playa de El Morro, Punta Rucia, Cayos los Siete Hermanos and Estero Hondo. The Montecristi area, outside the national park, is due for development.

In the S the best beaches are Las Salinas, Monte Río, Palmar de Ocoa, Najayo, Nigua, Palenque, Nizao and those S and W of Barahona. The majority of beaches have hotels or lodgings, but those without are suitable for camping.

Watersports such as deep-sea fishing, diving and surfing can be arranged at the Náutico Clubs in Santo Domingo and at Boca Chica beach. Güibia Beach, on the Malecón, Santo Domingo, has good waves for surfing. Demar Beach Club, Andrés (Boca Chica, T 523-4365) operates fishing, sailing, diving and water skiing charters, windsurfing, snorkelling and canoeing. All watersports can be arranged through Actividades Acuáticas, P O Box 1348, Santo Domingo, T 688-5838, F 688-5271 (you will be referred to their offices at Boca Chica, T 523-4511, or Puerto Plata, T 320-2567). There is excellent scuba diving at the underwater park at La Caleta, the small beach near the turn-off to the airport, on the Autopista de las Américas; snorkelling

and diving is good all along the S coast. Hotels on the N coast also offer diving and snorkelling facilities. For expert divers there are many sunken Spanish galleons on the reefs offshore. For full information on diving contact the Dirección Nacional de Parques, T 221-5340. Actividades Acuáticas charge US$70 for 2 dives at Boca Chica, US$217 for 6 dives at Puerto Plata (1993 prices).

Cabarete, near Sosúa, is one of the best windsurfing places in the world, attracting international competitors to tournaments there. Other centres are Boca Chica and Puerto Plata; most beach hotels offer windsurfing facilities.

Several international fishing tournaments are held each year, the catch being blue marlin, bonito and dorado. There is an annual deep-sea fishing tournament at Boca de Yuma, E of La Romana, in June. For information about fishing contact Santo Domingo Club Náutico, Lope de Vega 55, T 566-1682, or the Clubes Náuticos at Boca Chica and Cabeza de Toro. For renting boats and yachts, contact the Secretaría de Turismo. Parasailing is practised at the *Hotel Playa Dorada*, Puerto Plata, T 586-3988 (same number for deep-sea fishing), and on Sosúa beach.

Other Sports

Golf The best course is at Los Cajuiles at the *Casa de Campo Hotel* in La Romana; the *Santo Domingo* and *Hispaniola* hotels in Santo Domingo can arrange guest passes. There are also golf courses at the Santo Domingo Country Club and at Playa Dorada, near Puerto Plata. Several more golf courses are being built at new resorts around the country. Tennis can also be played at the Santo Domingo Country Club and at the tennis centre which can be found by the Autopista 30 de Mayo. Athletics facilities can be found at the Centro Olímpico Juan Pablo Duarte in the heart of Santo Domingo. Target shooting at the Polígono de Tiro on Avenida Bolívar.

The national sport is **baseball**, which is played from October to January, with national and big league players participating. The best players are recruited by US and Canadian teams; about half of the 300 professional Dominican players in the USA come from San Pedro de Macorís. There are five professional stadia, including the Quisqueya. Polo matches are played at weekends at Sierra Prieta, 25 minutes from Santo Domingo, and at Casa del Campo (T 523-3333). The **basketball** season is from June to August. **Boxing** matches take place frequently in Santo Domingo.

Festivals

In Santo Domingo, Carnival at the end of February, notable for the parade along the Malecón on 27 February; there are other parades on 16 August. The *merengue* festival in July (see **Culture** above), including festivals of gastronomy, cocktails, and exhibitions of handicrafts and fruit. Puerto Plata has a similar, annual *merengue* festival at the beginning of October on the Malecón La Puntilla, as does Sosúa, in the last week of September. In the Parque Central, there are year-end celebrations from 22 December to 3 January. Carnival in Santiago de los Caballeros in February is very colourful; its central character is the piglet, which represents the devil. On the Sundays of February in Montecristi there are the festivals of the *toros* versus the *civiles*. Each town's saint's day is celebrated with several days of festivities of which one of the most popular is the Santa Cruz de Mayo fiesta in El Seibo in May. Holy Week is the most important holiday time for Dominicans, when there are processions and festivities such as the *guloyas* in San Pedro de Macorís, the mystical-religious *ga-ga* in sugar cane villages and the *cachúas* in Cabral in the SW.

The fourth floor of the Museo del Hombre Dominicano, Santo Domingo (see below), has an excellent exhibition of the masks and costumes that feature in the various carnivals around the country. Generally the masks are of animals or devils, or a combination of the two, and are designed to be as hideous as possible. The costumes are very brightly coloured.

Throughout the year there are many festivals and events, cultural, agricultural, commercial and sporting. Most are held in Santo Domingo or Puerto Plata, although golf and polo tournaments are held at Casa de Campo, La Romana.

SANTO DOMINGO

Santo Domingo, the capital and chief seaport, population now about 2 million, was founded in 1496 by Columbus' brother Bartolomé and hence was the first capital in Spanish America. For years the city was the base for the Spaniards' exploration and conquest of the continent: from it Ponce de León sailed to discover Puerto Rico, Hernán Cortés launched his attack on Mexico, Balboa discovered the Pacific and Diego de Velázquez set out to settle Cuba. Hispaniola was where Europe's first social and political activities in the Americas took place. Santo Domingo itself holds the title "first" for a variety of offices: first city, having the first Audiencia Real, cathedral, university, coinage, etc. In view of this, Unesco has designated Santo Domingo a World Cultural Heritage site (Patrimonio Cultural Mundial). In the old part of the city, on the W bank of the Río Ozama, there are many fine early 16th century buildings.

Under the title of the **Quinto Centenario**, Santo Domingo played a prominent role in the celebration of the five hundredth anniversary of Christopher Columbus' landfall in the Caribbean (1492-1992). The Government undertook an extensive programme of public works, principally restoration work in the colonial city. A series of commemorative coins in limited editions was

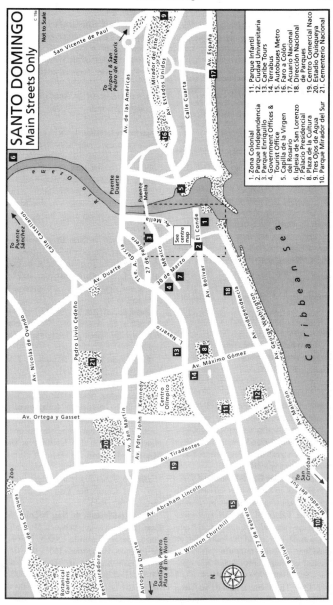

SANTO DOMINGO
Main Streets Only

Not to Scale

1. Zona Colonial
2. Parque Independencia
3. Parque Enriquillo
4. Government Offices & Tourist Office
5. Capilla de la Virgen del Rosario
6. Iglesia de San Lorenzo
7. Palacio Presidencial
8. Plaza de la Cultura
9. Tres Ojos de Agua
10. Parque Mirador del Sur
11. Parque Infantil
12. Ciudad Universitaria
13. Caribe Tours
14. Terrabus
15. Autobuses Metro
16. Faro a Colón
17. Acuario Nacional
18. Dirección Nacional de Parques
19. Estadio Quisqueya
20. Centro Comercial Naco
21. Cementerio Nacional

struck, available from the Centro de Información Numismática, Casa del Quinto Centenario, Isabel la Católica 103, T 682-0185, F 530-9164, Santo Domingo.

Buildings of the greatest interest are:
Catedral Basílica Menor de Santa María, Primada de América, Isabel La Católica esquina Nouel, the first cathedral to be founded in the New World. Its first stone was laid by Diego Colón, son of Christopher Columbus, in 1514; the architect was Alonzo Rodríguez. It was finished in 1540. The alleged remains of Christopher Columbus were found in 1877 during restoration work. In 1892, the Government of Spain donated the tomb in which the remains rest, behind the high altar, until their removal to the Faro a Colón (see below). The cathedral was fully restored for 1992, with new gargoyles and sculptures at the gates showing the indigenous people when Columbus arrived. The windows, altars and roof were all returned to their colonial splendour. Open to the public 0900-1200, 1500-1630.

Torre del Homenaje inside Fortaleza Ozama, reached through the mansion of Rodrigo Bastidas (later the founder of the city of Santa Marta in Colombia) on Calle Las Damas, which is now completely restored and has a museum/gallery with temporary exhibitions. It is the oldest fortress in America, constructed 1503-07 by Nicolás de Ovando, whose house in the same street has been restored and turned into a splendid hotel.

Museo de las Casas Reales, on Calle Las Damas, in a reconstructed early 16th century building which was in colonial days the Palace of the Governors and Captains-General, and of the Real Audiencia and Chancery of the Indies. It is an excellent colonial museum (often has special exhibits, entry US$0.50); open Tues-Sun 1000-1700; entry US$0.75, T 682-4202. The Voluntariado de las Casas Reales has exhibitions of contemporary

Dominican art.

Alcázar de Colón at the end of Las Damas and Emilio Tejera, constructed by Diego Colón in 1510-14. For six decades it was the seat of the Spanish Crown in the New World; it was sacked by Drake in 1586. Now completely restored, it houses the interesting **Museo Virreinal** (Viceregal Museum). Open 0900-1700 daily; entry US$0.75.

Casa del Cordón, Isabel La Católica esquina Emiliano Tejera, built in 1509 by Francisco de Garay, who accompanied Columbus on his first voyage to Hispaniola. Named for the cord of the Franciscan Order, sculpted above the entrance. Now the offices of the Banco Popular; free guided tours during working hours.

Monasterio de San Francisco (ruins), Hostos esquina E Tejera, first monastery in America, constructed in the first decade of the 16th century. Sacked by Drake and destroyed by earthquakes in 1673 and 1751.

Reloj de Sol (sundial) built 1753, near end of Las Damas, by order of General Francisco de Rubio y Peñaranda; by its side is

Capilla de Nuestra Señora de Los Remedios, built in the early 16th century as the private chapel of the Dávila family.

La Ataranza, near the Alcázar, a cluster of 16th century buildings which served as warehouses. Now restored to contain shops, bars and restaurants. Newly opened in La Ataranza is the **Museo del Jamón** (Museum of Ham), sponsored by several restaurants (*Catábrico, Reina de España, Tropic Snack Bar*) and Compañía Príncipe de Asturias, T 685-9644.

Hospital-Iglesia de San Nicolás de Bari (ruins), Hostos between Mercedes and Luperón, begun in 1509 by Nicolás de Ovando, completed 1552, the first stone-built hospital in the Americas. Also sacked by Drake, it was probably one of the best constructed buildings of the period, it survived many earthquakes

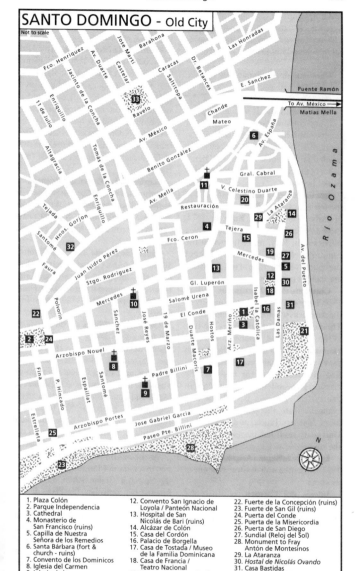

SANTO DOMINGO - Old City

Not to scale

1. Plaza Colón
2. Parque Independencia
3. Cathedral
4. Monasterio de
   San Francisco (ruins)
5. Capilla de Nuestra
   Señora de los Remedios
6. Santa Bárbara (fort &
   church - ruins)
7. Convento de los Dominicos
8. Iglesia del Carmen
9. Iglesia de la
   Regina Angelorum
10. Iglesia de las Mercedes
11. Iglesia de San Antón (ruins)

12. Convento San Ignacio de
    Loyola / Panteón Nacional
13. Hospital de San
    Nicolás de Bari (ruins)
14. Alcázar de Colón
15. Casa del Cordón
16. Palacio de Borgella
17. Casa de Tostada / Museo
    de la Familia Dominicana
18. Casa de Francia /
    Teatro Nacional
19. Museo de las Casa Reales
20. Museo de Duarte
21. Torre del Homenaje
    & Fuerte Ozama

22. Fuerte de la Concepción (ruins)
23. Fuerte de San Gil (ruins)
24. Puerta del Conde
25. Puerta de la Misericordia
26. Puerta de San Diego
27. Sundial (Reloj del Sol)
28. Monument to Fray
    Antón de Montesinos
29. La Ataranza
30. *Hostal de Nicolás Ovando*
31. Casa Bastidas
32. Mercado Modelo
33. Parque Enriquillo

C 19

and hurricanes. In 1911 some of its walls were knocked down because they posed a hazard to passers-by; also the last of its valuable wood was taken. It is now full of pigeons.

Convento de San Ignacio de Loyola, Las Damas between Mercedes and El Conde. Finished in 1743, it is now the National Pantheon. It was restored in 1955 and contains memorials to many of the country's heroes and patriots. It also contains an ornate tomb built before his death for the dictator Trujillo, the "Benefactor of the Fatherland", but his remains do not lie there.

Iglesia de Santa Bárbara, off Mella to the left near Calle J Parra, near the end of Isabel La Católica. Built in 1574, sacked by Drake in 1586, destroyed by a hurricane in 1591, reconstructed at the beginning of the 17th century. Behind the church are the ruins of its fort, where one can get good views.

Convento de los Dominicos, built in 1510. Here in 1538 the first university in the Americas was founded, named for St Thomas Aquinas; it now bears the title of the Universidad Autónoma de Santo Domingo. It has a unique ceiling which shows the medieval concept that identified the elements of the universe, the classical gods and the Christian icons in one system. The Sun is God, the four evangelists are the planetary symbols Mars, Mercury, Jupiter and Saturn. The University itself has moved to a site in the suburbs.

Iglesia de la Regina Angelorum, built 1537, contains a wall of silver near one of its altars.

Iglesia del Carmen, built around 1615 at side of Capilla de San Andrés, contains an interesting wooden sculpture of Christ.

Puerta del Conde (Baluarte de 27 de Febrero), at the end of El Conde (now a pedestrian street) in the Parque Independencia. Named for the Conde de Peñalva, who helped defend the city against William Penn in 1655. Restored in 1976, near it lie the remains of Sánchez, Mella and Duarte, the 1844 independence leaders.

Puerta de la Misericordia, Palo Hincado and Arzobispo Portes, so named because people fled under it for protection during earthquakes and hurricanes. It forms part of the wall that used to surround the colonial city, into which are now built many of the houses and shops of Ciudad Nueva. It was here on 27 February 1844 that Mella fired the first shot in the struggle for independence from Haiti.

Capilla de La Virgen del Rosario, on the other side of the Río Ozama, near the Molinos Dominicanos at the end of Avenida Olegario Vargas. It was the first church constructed in America, restored in 1943.

Museo de Duarte, Isabel La Católica 308, T 689-0326. Contains items linked with the independence struggle and Duarte, the national hero, whose home it was (open 0900-1700, Mon-Fri, US$0.75).

Other old buildings are the Iglesia de las Mercedes, dating from 1555; the Puerta de San Diego, near the Alcázar; the Palacio de Borgella, Isabel la Católica, near Plaza Colón; the ruins of Fuerte de la Concepción, at the corner of Mella and Palo Hincado, built in 1543; the ruins of Fuerte de San Gil, Padre Billini, near the end of Calle Pina; and the ruins of Iglesia de San Antón, off Mella esquina Vicente Celestino Duarte.

At the mouth of the Río Ozama, the new Avenida del Puerto gives access to the Antigua Ceiba, where Columbus moored his caravelles, the Plaza de Armas, the city's original drainage system and the old city wall. Steps lead up to the Alcázar de Colón and the Fuerte Ozama, where a square has been established. The Avenida has in a short time become an open-air discothèque, more popular than the Malecón. Together with the inauguration of the Avenida del Puerto is a boat service on the Río Ozama for sightseeing upstream (operated by Mar C por A in the vessel *Sea*, Monday-Friday 1800-2200, Saturday 1600, US$4, happy hour from 1800-2000, drinks two for the price of one). Water sports and speed-boat races can also be seen. The eastern bank of the Ozama is to be restored with a new footpath, the Vereda del Almirante, an amphitheatre and a new tourist harbour. All commercial shipping will be diverted to Río Haina.

Among the attractive parks are the Central Olímpico (see above) in the city centre, Parque Independencia (a peaceful haven amid all the traffic, with the Altar de la Patria, containing the remains of the country's founders, Juan Pablo Duarte, Francisco del Rosario Sánchez and Ramón Matías Mella), Parque Colón, Parque Mirador del Este (Autopista de las Américas, a 7 km-long *alameda*) and Parque Mirador del Sur (Paseo de las Indios at Mirador Sur, 7 km long, popular for walking, jogging, cycling, picnics). (Parque Mirador del Norte is under construction on the banks of the Río Isabela, near Guarícano and Villa Mella.) On Avenida José Contreras are many caves, some with lakes, in the southern cliff of Parque Mirador del Sur. Along this cliff the Avenida Cayetano Germosén has been built, giving access to a number of caves used at one time by Taíno Indians. One such Lago Subterráneo has been opened as a tourist attraction, entry US$0.40 (0900-1730). The road, lined with gardens, links Avenidas Luperón and Italia. The Jardín Botánico Nacional, Urbanización Los Ríos (open Tuesday-Sunday 0900-1700, admission US$0.75, children US$0.35) and the Parque Zoológico Nacional, Los Ríos (open 0900-1700, US$0.35, children US$0.25); for information T 565-2860 or 562-3149 respectively. The Botanical Gardens are highly recommended (the Japanese Garden especially); horse-drawn carriages and a small train tour the grounds (US$0.80, children US$0.55). There is an Acuario Nacional, Avenida España, on the coast E of the city, Tuesday-Sunday 0900-1700, US$0.75, very popular, very good; it has a café serving pizzas (there is a bus from Avenida Independencia, by the park). Quisqueya Park, César Nicolás Penson, is a recreational park for children, entry US$0.40. The Parque Infantil at Avenidas Bolívar y Tiradentes is to be remodelled.

The **Faro a Colón**, built at great cost (and not without controversy) in the Parque Mirador del Este, is in the shape of a cross. Where the arms of the cross intersect is the mausoleum containing the supposed remains of Columbus. The navy mounts a permanent guard over the tomb. Spotlights project a crucifix of light into the night sky, spectacular on a cloudy night, less so when it is clear. Until the lighthouse has its own solar-powered generators, the lights are lit only at weekends and on holidays. One of the rooms inside the lighthouse is a chapel, in others different countries have mounted exhibitions (the British exhibit concentrates on the entries for the competition to design the lighthouse). Many rooms are empty and the Taíno museum on the second floor has yet to be mounted. (Open daily 0900-1700; guides are free, but give a tip; shorts above the knee not allowed.) The interior of the arms of the cross are open to the sky so that when it rains the only shelter is around the mausoleum, where there are no seats. Around the building gardens have been laid out.

The modern city is very spread out because, until recently, there was no high-rise building. The outer city has fine avenues, especially Avenida George Washington (also known as the Malecón) which runs parallel to the sea; it often becomes an open-air discothèque, where locals and foreigners dance the *merengue*. The annual *merengue* festival is held here. The spectacular monument to Fray Antón de Montesinos is at the eastern end of Avenida George Washington. The continuation (Prolongación) of Avenida México, which runs parallel to Avs

Bolívar and 27 de Febrero, has many modern buildings, while Expreso Quinto Centenario, in the Villa Juana and Villa Francisca districts, is a new roadway which has rejuvenated these parts of the city. Other important avenues are Independencia, Bolívar, Abraham Lincoln, Winston Churchill, Núñez de Cáceres, 27 de Febrero, John F Kennedy, Juan Pablo Duarte, Ramón Matías Mella and General Gregorio Luperón.

Gazcue is a quiet, attractive residential area with expensive homes built in the 1930s and 1940s, stretching W of the Zona Colonial as far as Avenida Máximo Gómez. The coral pink Palacio Presidencial with a neo-classical central portico and cupola, built by Trujillo, is at the intersection of Doctor Delgado and Manuel María Castillo. It is used by the President, but guided tours of the richly decorated interior can be arranged, T 686-4771 ext 340 or 360. Opposite the Palacio's grounds, at Avenida México y 30 de Marzo, are the government offices. The 1955/56 World's Fair (Feria de Confraternidad) buildings now house the Senate and Congress. The national museum collection, which includes a wonderful display of Taino artefacts and the ethnography section mentioned under **Festivals** above, is in the Museo del Hombre Dominicano (US$0.75, 1000-1700, closed on Monday, T 687-3622), which forms part of the Plaza de la Cultura, founded by Joaquín Balaguer on Avenida Máximo Gómez. It also includes the ultra-modern national theatre and national library; the Museo de Arte Moderno (open 1000-1700, US$0.75, closed Monday, T 682-8280), the Cinemateca Nacional, the Museo de Historia Natural (T 689-4642, US$0.75, open Tuesday-Sunday 1000-1700, café open 0700-1900) and the Museo de Historia y Geografía (open 1000-1700, US$0.75, T 689-0106). The Museo de la Familia Dominicana is housed in the Casa de Tostada (Calle Padre Billini esq Arzobispo Meriño), an early 16th century mansion (Monday-Friday, 0900-1700, US$0.80, T 689-5057). The Banco Central has a Museo Numismático y Filatélico, open Mon-Fri 0830-1530, free, T 688-6512. The Fundación García Arévalo, in the 7 Up building, Avenida San Martín, near Lope de Vega, has an exhibition of pre-hispanic art and civilization, T 540-7777 for an appointment. For archaeologists there is the Instituto de Investigaciones Históricas, José Reyes 24. At José Reyes 6, in the Zona Colonial, is the Instituto de la Porcelana (T 689-1766).

Three bridges cross the Río Ozama: the nearest to the sea is Mella (originally nicknamed La Bicicleta because it is so narrow, but now with a new bridge beside it to ease congestion), next is Duarte, and further inland Sánchez. On the road to the airport are the Tres Ojos de Agua, two water-filled caves and a sunken lake which are worth a visit. To reach the last-named you must take the raft across the second cave; it is supposed to have two crocodiles in it, put there by the Botanical Gardens, but they didn't reproduce (no one bothered to check their sex). At the entrance to the airport is La Caleta Archaeological Museum (Museo Ceremonial La Caleta) with its display of Taino and Arawak ceramics and a Taino burial site (entry free). Roadside sellers offer copies of statues.

Local Information – Santo Domingo

● Where To Stay

Hotels (prices are double, high season and do not include taxes, normally 23%)

A new hotel on the Malecón is the *Quinto Centenario* (Inter-Continental), 5 stars, very well-appointed with restaurants, pools, gym, etc. A little further from the colonial centre are the *Sheraton* and the *Ramada Renaissance Jaragua*, the latter being much more glitzy than the former. The *Embajador*, a member of the Spanish Occidental chain (with other hotels in the country), is rec. Close to the *Naco* is the newer *Plaza Naco*, T 541-6226, F 541-7142, with prices from US$44s, suites with kitchenette, very comfortable, cable TV, gour-

	Address	Price US$	Telephone	Fax
Cervantes*†	Calle Cervantes 202	46	686-8161	686-5754
Comercial*	Calle El Conde esq Hostos	32	682-2814	
Comodoro†	Av Bólivar 193	43	687-7141	541-2277
Dominican Fiesta/				
Concorde†	Av Anacaona	96	562-8222	562-8938
Embajador†	Av Sarasota 65	150	221-2131	532-4494
Ramada Jaragua†	Av George Washington 367	148	221-2222	686-0528
Gran Hotel Lina*†	Av Máximo Gómez y			
	27 de Febrero	102	563-5000	686-5521
Hispaniola†	Av Independencia y			
	Av Abraham Lincoln	60	221-2131	535-4050
Hostal Nicolás de				
Ovando*†	Calle Las Damas 53	61	687-3101	
Naco†	Av Tiradentes 22	50	562-2052	544-0957
Quinto Centenario†	Av George Washington 218	160	221-0000	686-3287
Santo Domingo†	Av Independencia y			
	Av Abraham Lincoln	120	221-1511	535-1511
Sheraton†	Av George Washington 365	105	221-6666	687-8150

*Convenient to centre † Swimming pool and fully air-conditioned.

met restaurant, coffee shop (if you wish to self-cater, ask hotel for utensils and tableware and buy food in nearby supermarket), rec. *Hostal Nicolás de Ovando*, a restored 16th century mansion in the oldest part of the city, is warmly rec for comfort, quiet and atmosphere, standard of rooms varies. *Gran Hotel Lina* is also highly rec and has a good restaurant, well-equipped, 5 star. The *Santo Domingo* is colonial style, plush and charming. The *Comodoro* is reasonable, with fridges in rooms. *Cervantes* is medium-sized, family-run, with pool; the *Comercial* is central, with fans, TV, bath and a fair restaurant, friendly, clean; both are good value.

There are several apart-hotels: *Aladino*, H Pieter 34, T 567-0144, US$32d, fan and a/c; *Plaza Colonial*, Julio Verne 4, T 687-9111, F 686-2877, US$67d, big, bare apartments, close to Zona Colonial, pool; *Casa de Huéspedes Sterling*, Av Bolívar 5 y Parque Independencia, T 688-5773, next to Codetel office, self-catering apartments, weekly or monthly basis, fully equipped, friendly, clean, negotiate price, US$256/month high season, rec. *Plaza Florida*, Av Bolívar 203, T 541-3957, F 540-5582, US$40d; *Delta*, Av Sarasota 53, T 535-0800, US$50s, US$55d; *Petit Apart-Hotel Turístico*, Aníbal de Espinosa 70, T 681-5454, from US$30, with restaurant, terrace, disco.

Other hotels include: on Av George Washington, *Napolitano*, T 687-1131, F 689-2714, US$52*†; next door is *Palmeras del Caribe*, Cambronal 1, T 689-3872, US$20, nice rooms

but small, pleasant garden, use of fridge, adjoining café; *Continental*, Av Máximo Gómez 16, T 689-1151, F 687-8397, US$34 pp inc taxes and breakfast, pleasant area, pool; *Royal*, Av Duarte y 27 de Febrero, T 685-5400, US$30, fully a/c, small pool, good restaurant, *guaguas* leaving to N and W across the street. In the old city, *Hostal Nicolás Nader*, Duarte y General Luperón, T 687-6674, US$55 (inc taxes), small, old building, friendly, personal service, pleasant; *Casa Vapor*, Av Francia y Dr Delgado, US$46pp basic price, near Presidential Palace, in a house dating from Trujillo's time, in the shape of a ship, includes restaurant, *Café Francés*, *Terraza del Puerto*, *Sport Vapor* and *Cafetería La Proa*; *Palacio*, Macorís y Ureña, T 682-4730, US$52s, with fan.

Cheaper hotels include: *Alameda*, Calle Cervantes opposite *Cervantes*, T 685-5121, US$26, restaurant; *Aída*, El Conde and Espaillat, T 685-7692, US$15 a/c (less without), fairly quiet (but record shop below may be noisy in day), very central, popular, often full; *Independencia*, Estrella casi esquina Arzobispo Nouel, near Parque Independencia, US$14.50s (bargaining possible), soap, towels etc provided, clean, convenient location, rec, some rooms without windows, also has a club, bar, language school (across the street), a roof terrace and art exhibitions; *Montesino*, José Gabriel García III, Zona Colonial, T 688-3346, overlooking Malecón and Montesino's statue, 4 rooms, US$12-16 with shared bath, US$20 with bath, fan, use of kitchen, will negotiate longer stays, highly rec; *Señorial*, Av Presidente Vicini Burgos 58 (Parque Eugenio María de Hostos), T 687-4359, F 687-0600, US$27, friendly, clean and informal,good Italian food, popular with Swiss-Italian visitors, see the 1952 map on the wall; *Luna del Norte*, Benito González 89, T 687-0124/2504, US$12, clean, friendly, rec, restaurant; *Radiante*, Av Duarte between Av Mella and Benito González, US$8 with bath; *Benito*, Benito González near market, US$4 with bath, US$2.50 without, not rec; *Macau*, Benito González, near Av Duarte, US$8, basic, all rooms with bath, friendly, quiet, safe, Chinese run, as is the restaurant downstairs. There are dozens of cheap hotels, especially around the Mercado Modelo; those on Av Duarte are usually used by prostitutes; have a good look round them before making any decision. For cheap rooms in hotels or *casas de pensión*, look in the classified section of daily paper, *Listín Diario*. Rooms in the private house of Doña Hilkka, Abreu 7, near Iglesia San Carlos, central, cheap, charming. Business travellers can often get cheaper rates than posted by requesting '*la tarifa comercial*'.

● **Where To Eat**
At main hotels, eg *Alcázar* at the *Santo Domingo*; the *Lina*; *La Piazzeta* at the *Hispaniola* (Italian specialities); *Le Gourmet* at the *Comodoro*. Many of the hotels have "buffets ejecutivos" at lunch time, costing US$10.

Recommended restaurants include *Ché Bandoneón*, on El Conde between Damas y Parque Colón, Argentine owned, outdoor terrace, Argentine, criollo and French food, tangos, T 687-0023; *La Cocina*, next door at No 56, is also good, créole food, both stay open till after midnight; at No 60 is *L'Avocat* café-restaurant. *Mesón de la Cava*, Parque Mirador, situated in a natural cave, good steaks, dancing, very popular so reserve in advance, T 533-3818; *Lago Enriquillo*, also in Parque Mirador, Chinese and international. *Jai-Alai*, Av Independencia 411, for excellent seafood and local specialities, T 685-2409; also for seafood, *Sully*, Charles Summers y Calle Caoba, T 562-3389, some distance from centre, excellent. *Fonda La Ataranza*, La Ataranza 5, T 689-2900, popular for créole and international cuisine; *Café St Michel*, Lope de Vega 24, T 562-4141, good Caribbean cooking; *La Fromagière*, 27 de Febrero at Plaza Criollo, T 567-9430, French and international, reasonable; *Juan Carlos*, Av Mejía Ricart, near Olympic stadium, very good value. *Café Coco*, Sánchez 153, Zona Colonial, T 687-9624, a

small restaurant owned and run by 2 Englishmen, excellent food and service, menu changes daily.

Also worth visiting are *Vesuvio I*, Av George Washington 521, good but more touristy and less good value than *Vesuvio II*, Av Tiradentes 17, Italian and international cuisine; *Maniquí* in the Plaza de la Cultura is good. *Lucky Seven*, Av Pasteur y Casimiro de Moya, good for seafood and steaks, popular haunt for baseball fans.

Veneto Ice Cream on Av Independencia; *Las Pirámides*, Rómulo Betancourt 351, and *Il Capo del Malecón*, Av George Washington 517 (other branches at Av Tiradentes and Jardines del *Embajador*), both good for pizzas. *Aubergine*, Av Alma Mater y Av México, German food; *La Esquina de Tejas*, Av 27 de Febrero 343, offers Spanish cuisine. For good Chinese food try *Marios*, 27 de Febrero 299, very popular, or *La Gran Muralla*, Av 27 de Febrero. *Pacos Café*, El Conde, near Parque Independencia, local food at reasonable prices. For the local dish *mofongo* (see under **Food and Drink** below), *Palacio del Mofongo* Av George Washington 509, T 688-8121, or *Casa del Mofongo*, 27 de Febrero y Calle 7 Eva Mo, T 565-1778 (a long way from the centre).

Two good vegetarian restaurants are *Ananda*, Casimiro de Moya 7, T 562-4465, and *Vegetariano*, Calle Luperón 9 (open 0800-1500). Also *Ojas*, Calle Jonas Salk 2, T 682-3940 and *El Terrenal*, Malecón y Estrelleta, T 689-3161, some vegetarian dishes. *Vita Naturaleza*, Mercedes 255, sells health products (by small park at junction with Luperón).

The Village Pub, in Calle Hostos 350, opposite the ruins of Hospital San Nicolás de Bari, is a good place for snacks and drinks in a pub-type atmosphere, in the colonial city; and so is *La Taberna* (classical music) at Padre Billini with Las Damas.

There are numerous pizzerias which are good value; also try a *chimichurri* (spiced sausage), throughout the city stalls sell sandwiches, *chimichurris*, hot dogs and hamburgers. Many fast food places offer dishes for about US$1.50, which would cost US$8 in a hotel restaurant. There are also take-away places where a meal costs about US$2.50. Cheapest are probably the Chinese restaurants, but in many cases the hygiene is dubious (the same applies to other basic restaurants).

The Asociación Nacional de Hoteles y Restaurantes, Asonahores, T 688-7542, publishes a guide to the best restaurants in the capital, *Guía de Restaurantes*.

● **Shopping**

Duty-free at Centro de los Héroes, La Ataranza, shops in *Embajador*, *Sheraton* and *Santo Domingo* hotels; departure lounge at airport; all purchases must be in US dollars. The Mercado Modelo, on Avenida Mella esquina Santomé, includes gift shops and is the best place in the city for handicrafts (see **Best Buys** in Information for Visitors); you must bargain to get a good price. There are also "speciality shops" at Plaza Criolla, 27 de Febrero y Máximo Gómez. Calle El Conde, now reserved to pedestrians, is the oldest shopping sector in Santo Domingo; Avenida Mella at Duarte is a good spot for discount shopping and local colour. A flea market, Mercado de las Pulgas, operates on Sunday in the Centro de los Héroes and at the Mercado de Oportunidades, 27 de Febrero. In contrast are the modern complexes at Plaza Naco and the new US style shopping mall at the corner of Av 27 de Febrero and Av Abraham Lincoln; also Plaza Caribe, at 27 de Febrero y Leopoldo Navarro.

● **Buses**

Public transport buses (Onatrate), commonly called *guaguas*, run throughout the city, fares are RD$2 (US$0.15), but the service is very limited, therefore crowded. Exact change is needed. Private companies (eg Caribe Tours) operate on some routes, charging RD$2.

● **Taxis**

Carros públicos, or *conchos*, are shared taxis normally operating on fixed routes, 24 hrs a day, basic fare RD$2 (US$0.15). *Públicos* can be hired by one person, if they are empty, and are then called *carreras*. They can be expensive (US$2.30-3, more on longer routes); settle price before getting in. Fares are higher at Christmas time. *Públicos/conchos* also run on long-distance routes; ask around to find the cheapest. You can get to just about anywhere by bus or *público* from Parque Independencia, but you have to ask where to stand. *Conchos* running on a shared basis are becoming scarcer, being replaced by *carreras*. Radio taxis charge between US$3.50 and US$4.75 on local journeys around Santo Domingo (US$7 per hr) and are safer than street taxis, call about 20-30 mins in advance: Apolo Taxi, T 537-7772/531-3800; Tecni Taxi, T 566-0108; Hogar Taxi, T 568-2825; Alex Taxi, T 540-3311; Taxi

Bienvenido, T 686-1397 (also Raffi, Bella Vista and Anacahona). The 30-mins ride from Las Américas International airport to Santo Domingo should cost no more than US$13 in a radio taxi, but more in a *carrera*. Most hotels have a taxi or limousine service with set fares throughout the city and to the airport. There are motorcyclists who offer a taxi service, known as *motoconchos*, RD$5 (US$0.40), they sometimes take up to three passengers on pillion; they raise the noise level (in most towns) very considerably.

● **Car Rentals**

Many places at the airport, on the road to the airport and on Malecón. The prices given below are of May 1994 and are for the cheapest vehicle available at each agency. There are many more agencies than those listed: National (T 562-1444, airport T 542-0162), US$51/day, US$380/week, deposit US$435; Budget (T 562-6812), US$38/day, US$380/week; Nelly (T 544-1800), US$48-57/day, US$352/week; Dollar (T 546-6801), US$72-88/day, US$421/week; Patsy (T 686-4333); Hertz (T 221-5333), US$62/day, US$369/week; Avis (T 533-3530); Thrifty (T 687-9369), US$111/day; McDeal (T 688-6518), US$65/day, US$368/week; Auto Rental (T 685-7873), US$50/day, US$323/week. See also under **Information for Visitors**.

● **Libraries**

Biblioteca Nacional, in the Plaza de la Cultura, has a fine collection and is a good place for a quiet read. Instituto Cultural Dominico-Americano, corner of Av Abraham Lincoln and Calle Antonio de la Maza; English and Spanish books. The National Congress has a good library, as do some of the universities: Pontífica Universidad Católica Madre y Maestra, the Instituto Tecnológico de Santo Domingo and the Universidad Autónoma de Santo Domingo.

● **Concerts**

Concerts and other cultural events are often held at the National Theatre, the Casa de Francia, corner of Las Damas and El Conde, where Cortés lived for a while (run by the French Embassy, also art gallery and library, open to non-members), and the Casa de Teatro (see below).

● **Theatres**

Teatro Nacional, Plaza de la Cultura, Av Máximo Gómez; Palace of Fine Arts, Av Independencia and Máximo Gómez; Casa de Teatro, small drama workshop, Calle Padre Billini and, in Barrio Don Bosco, Teatro Nuevo (performances all year). The Anglo Dominican Theater Society, funded by the British Council and local businesses, puts on shows; details from the Honarary British Consul (address in **Information for Visitors**).

● **Night Clubs**

Salon La Fiesta in the *Jaragua Hotel*; *El Yarey* in the *Sheraton*; *Embassy Club* in the *Hotel El Embajador*; *Napolitana*; *Maunaloa Night Club* and Casino; *Hotel San Gerónimo*, Independencia; *La Azotea* in *Hotel Concorde*; *Salón Rojo*, *Hotel Comodoro*, Av Bolívar; *Night Club Herminia*; *Las Vegas*, *Babilon*, *Fuego Fuego*, *Piano Bar Las Palmas* in *Hotel Santo Domingo*, *Piano Bar Intramuros*, *Primera Clase* and *Tablao Flamenco*.

Also *Instrumental Night Club* on Autopista Las Américas; *Exodus*, George Washington 511; *Le Petit Chateau*, Av George Washington Km 11½, nude shows.

Guácara Taína, Paseo de los Indios, between Avenida Cayetano Germosén and Parque Mirador, has shows of Taino dancing in a deep cave with indigenous pictographs from 1700-0200, US$4-12 (also disco, Happy Hours and fashion shows).

To hear *pericos ripiaos*, go on Friday or Saturday night to the eating places (*colmados*) near the Malecón in Ciudad Nueva section of the city; the groups move from place to place.

● **Discothèques**

Omni in *Hotel Sheraton*, rock, merengue, salsa and ballads; *Hipocampo* in *Hotel El Embajador*; *Disco Piano* in *Hotel El Napolitano*; *Jet Set* and *Opus*, Av Independencia; *Shehara* and *Bella Blu* (next to *Vesuvio I*) on George Washington; *Punto Final*, Av Pasteur. *Tops* (*Hotel Plaza Naco*, US$2.50 entry, high above city, rec), *El Final*, *Magic Disco*, *Jet Set* and *Xappil*. *Club 60*, Máximo Gómez 60, rock, merengue and ballads; *Neon* in *Hotel Hispaniola*, upmarket, occasionally has live Latin jazz; *Sentimiento*, Hostos 99, down market with lots of merengue, very dark. For Cuban son music: *El Rincón Habanero*, Sánchez Valverde y Baltazar de los Reyes in Villa Consuelo, working class enthusiasts of Cuban son dance between tables to old records of 1940s and 1950s; *Secreto Musical Bar*, one block away, Baltazar de los Reyes and Pimentel, similar, headquarters of Club Nacional de los Soneros, rock, merengue, salsa and ballads; *La Vieja Habana*, in Villa Mella on

the northern outskirts of town, owner called Generoso.

● **Casinos**

Hotels Dominican Concorde, Santo Domingo, San Gerónimo, Sheraton, El Embajador, Naco, Jaragua, Lina and *Maunaloa* Night Club, Centro de los Héroes.

● **Exchange**

Officially possible only in banks, many along Isabel La Católica, but check which banks accept which TCs. A list of commercial banks which will change dollars can be found in the **Information for Visitors**. Do not change money on the street; you will undoubtedly be cheated and you also run the risk of imprisonment.

● **Language School**

Escuela de Idiomas de la Universidad APEC, Av Máximo Gómez 72, Apartado Postal 59-2, Santo Domingo, T 687-3181, offers Spanish courses, either 1 or 2 hrs daily, Mon to Fri, for a term.

● **Post Office**

In Zona Colonial, Arzobispo Portes 510, entre Cambronal y El Número, T 685-6920. The new Correo Central is in La Feria, Calle Rafael Damirón, Centro de los Héroes, opp *Fantasy* Night Club and Teatro Mauna Loa. Open 0700-1800, Mon-Fri; also certain hours on Sat. Lista de correo (poste restante) keeps mail for two months. There are post offices on the 2nd floor of the government building El Haucal, tallest building in the city, on Av Padre Castellanos, near Av Duarte, and in *Hotel Embajador*.

To ensure the delivery of documents worldwide, use a courier service: American Airlines (T 542-5151); DHL Dominicana (T 541-7988), Servicio de Documentos y pequeños paquetes (T 541-2119); Emery Worldwide (T 688-1855); Federal Express (T 567-9547); Internacional Bonded Couriers (T 542-5265).

● **Telephones**

International and long distance, also Telex and Fax: Codetel, Av 30 de Marzo 12, near Parque Independencia, and 11 others throughout the city (open 0800-2200); a convenient central office is at El Conde 202. Cheaper is the Tricom office on Av Máximo Gómez between Bolívar and Independencia. The Palacio de las Comunicaciones next to the Post Office (at Isabel La Católica y Emiliano Tejera) does not handle phone calls.

● **Episcopal Church**

Av Independencia 253, service in English, 0830 Sun; also Iglesia Episcopal San Andrés, on Marcos Ruiz.

● **Health**

Clínica Abréu, Av Independencia and Beller, and adjacent Clínica Gómez Patiño are rec for foreigners needing treatment or hospitalization. Fees are high but care is good. 24-hr emergency department. Other reputable clinics are Centro Médico UCE and Clínica Yunén on Av Máximo Gómez, and Clínica Abel González, Av Independencia. For free consultation and prescription, Padre Billini hospital, Calle Padre Billini y Santomé, Zona Colonial, efficient, friendly.

● **Tours**

There are several tours of the city, taking in the duty-free shops, nightlife, etc. Rec travel agents in Santo Domingo for sightseeing tours include: Metro Tours (T 544-4580), Domitur (T 544-0929), Prieto Tours (T 685-0102), Viajes Barceló (T 685- 8411). Servicio Turístico de Helicóptero Dominicano offers helicopter tours over Santo Domingo, office on the Malecón, T 687-1093/3093, US$46-110. Companies that offer tours around the republic are given in **Information for Visitors**. **NB** See warnings at the end of this chapter about unofficial guides.

● **Airport**

Aeropuerto La Américas, 23 km out of town, T 549-0450/80, has been modernized, very clean and smart. Immediately on arrival there is a tourist office on your right, and just past that an office selling tourist cards (a blackboard indicates who needs a card, see **Documents** in **Information for Visitors**). You must check if you need a card, otherwise the long queue to get through immigration will be wasted. In the customs hall is a bank for exchanging dollars; it is open at night. On leaving do not forget to fill in a departure form to present to immigration, nor that you have to pay departure tax of US$10. Pesos can be changed back into dollars, but this may involve going downstairs to the bank in the customs hall. In the departure area are lots of duty-free shops, one small café (dollars only) and limited seating.

The price of a taxi or minibus to town is given above (can be shared); it may be less if you bargain with drivers in the car park (though this is not easy) or telephone a radio taxi in advance (numbers given above). If arriving late at night it may be better to go to Boca Chica (see **East from Santo Domingo**), about 10 km from the airport, taxi US$9.50-11.50. To get to the airport cheaply take a "Boca Chica Express" bus from José Martí y París, near Parque Enriquillo, to the cargo terminal, 3-4 mins walk to the passenger terminal, US$1, buses every few minutes in either direction. Various tour agencies also run minibuses to the airport; check with your hotel. Herrera airport (T 567-3900) for internal flights to Santiago, Puerto Plata, Barahona and La Romana (allow plenty of time).

NORTH FROM SANTO DOMINGO

The Carretera Duarte runs N from Santo Domingo, first as a good highway, then becoming a crowded two-lane road. Around *Bonao* are rice paddies. The town is also known as Villa de las Hortensias. There are cheap hotels near the market and on the highway are many *paradas*, *posadas* and *plazas turísticas*.

Further N is *La Vega*, a quiet place in the beautiful valley of la Vega Real, in the heart of the Cibao. La Vega's cathedral is a modern, concrete building. The exterior looks a little like a turreted castle while the huge bell tower slightly resembles a ship's prow surmounted by a cross. The interior is spacious, with round stained-glass windows and lights suspended from a wooden ceiling. There is a Codetel office on the square. (Hotels on the highway: *América*, at the Santo Domingo end of town, looks very rundown; *Guarícano*, by the Río Camú at Santiago end of town, US$20 with a/c, a bit noisy from traffic and nearby discos, nothing special, cold water, overpriced. International artists appear at the *Astromundo* discothèque. In town: on Núñez de Cáceres, *Astral*, US$18 with a/c; opposite is *San Pedro*, no 87, T 573-2844, US$12 with a/c, cheaper without, very dirty, insecure; in the same block is *Santa Clara*, even more down market; on Restauración, near Núñez de Cáceres is *Quinta Patio*, with reasonable restaurant;

on same street near the highway is *Nueva Ilusión* restaurant and amusements.) Transport for Santo Domingo and Santiago can be caught on the highway; Expreso del Valle from Av Independencia in Santo Domingo, US$2.40, frequent. To Jarabacoa (45 mins, US$0.80) from Restauración y 27 de Febrero, opposite Ali Tours. Metrobus in La Vega, T 573-7099.

Further along the road from La Vega on the right is the turn for Santo Cerro, an old convent where the image of Virgen de las Mercedes is venerated. From there one can get a view of the valley of La Vega Real. If one continues along the road to the other side of the hill and into the valley the ruins of La Vega Vieja can be seen. It was founded by Columbus but destroyed by an earthquake in 1564; undergoing restoration.

Jarabacoa

Continuing along the highway, on the left, is the turn for Jarabacoa. The road winds through some beautiful pine forests to the town itself, which is a popular summer hill resort in a valley in the mountains. The climate is fresh, with warm days and cool nights. On the road between La Vega and Jarabacoa are several Centros Vacacionales. The town itself is quite modern, with plenty of plots of land for sale. Nearby is the good *balneario* (swimming hole) of La Confluencia, in the Río Jimenoa (nice campsite, crowded at holiday times). The Jimenoa waterfalls are worth seeing, 10 km from town; a new bridge across the river has eased access, you may need a guide to cllimb the falls (if going in your own car, the guards at the control post will look after it). Closer to town, off the Constanza road, are the Baiguate falls (3.5-4 km, an easy walk, there is a signpost to the falls, 2nd turn on the right after *Pinar Dorado*). The first turn on the right after this hotel, by the *Parada Baez*, goes into the hills through the irrigated fields where vegetables and flowers are grown (look for herons in the channels), it comes to a

dead end on private property. Horses for hire (US$3.25/hr) and bicycles from *Rancho Baiguate* (gift shop, bar, snacks), close to *Pinar Dorado*.

Local information – Jarabacoa

● Where To Stay

11 km from town on the La Vega road, *La Montaña*, T 682-8181, friendly, clean, highly rec, but need own transport to make excursions from it; *Pinar Dorado*, on road towards Constanza, about 20 mins walk from centre, US$38 inc tax, nice rooms, a/c, hot water, good atmosphere and buffet meals, dinner à la carte, well-kept grounds, pool (T 574-2820); *River Resorts*, 1 km from town on La Vega road, 3-room cabins, TV, kitchen, pool, T 574-4688, US$50 per cabin, US$16 for 1 room if available. *Plaza Ortiz*, Mario Galán entre Sánchez y Duarte, T 574-6188, US$18.50, hotel, restaurant, disco; *Doña Ligia*, on Mella, T 574-2739, US$8.50; unmarked hotel on corner of Independencia and El Carmen, US$5s without bath; *Junior*, US$7.50 with fan and shower, clean; nearby is *Dormitorio*, basic, clean, friendly, with a good *comedor*.

● Where To Eat

The town has several restaurants; try the *Rincón Montañés* on Calle Gaston F Deligne, near El Carmen; *Basilia*, not as expensive as it looks, nice food; *Don Luis*, on square; *Jarabadeli-bar-b-q*, opp Esso station, very good value, fast, rec. Several other *comedores* and *cafeterías*.

● Services

Banks on Calle Mario Galán. Codetel on road to La Vega. Market on M Galán. Tourist office opp cemetery at entrance to town, T 574-4883/4, 0800-1700 daily, very helpful.

● Transport

Conchos in town US$0.40. To Santo Domingo, Caribe Tours, T 574-4796, opp Inversiones de los Santos on Independencia, 0730 and 1500 in each direction, arrive 30 mins in advance (even earlier for the 0730 Mon bus), tickets sold only on day of departure, US$3.25, 2¾ hrs. To La Vega from Esso station, US$0.80; if you want to go to the capital or Santiago, they will let you off at the right place (coming from La Vega, *guaguas* charge an extra US$0.40 to drop you at *Hotel Pinar Dorado*). To Constanza, opp Shell station every hour or so, US$2. No transport anywhere after 1800, very little after 1500.

To Constanza is much easier via Bonao, from where the road is paved all the way; the road from Jarabacoa is very bad until El Río, the junction with the Bonao road. A new road will run from Jarabacoa to La Ciénaga, via Manabao, for access to Pico Duarte (see below).

Beyond Jarabacoa, on the same road, is **Constanza**, where the scenery is even better than in Jarabacoa, with rivers, forests and waterfalls. In winter, temperatures can fall to zero and there may be frosts. The valley is famous for food production, potatoes, garlic, strawberries, mushrooms and other vegetables, and for growing ornamental flowers. (Hotels: *Nueva Suiza*, built by Trujillo, run down, T 539-2233; *Hotel El Gran Restaurant*, without bath, good value, restaurant rather pricey; *Mi Cabaña*, good, T 539-2472; *Nacional*, T 574-2578; *Margarita* and *Casa de Huéspedes*, both on Calle Luperón; *Brisa del Valle*, simple, acceptable, meals available.) Constanza can be reached by taking a bus to Bonao from either Santo Domingo or Santiago, then *guagua*, the last 1½ hrs of the trip through the finest scenery in the Republic. Alternatively go La Vega and take a taxi from there for US$1.60. From Jarabacoa, see above.

Steve Morris recommends a route from the W to Constanza by public transport, avoiding Santo Domingo, across country and more time consuming but much more exciting. He started in Neiba, near Lago Enriquillo (see below), took a *guagua* to Cruce de Ocoa, 2½ hrs, US$1.50, and from there to San José de Ocoa (NE of Azua), 45 mins, US$0.70. (*Hotel Marien*, on the main square, without bath, clean, good value.) He writes: 'Although what could hardly be called a road exists between San José de Ocoa and Constanza, there is no regular transport connecting the two towns. Apparently a gentleman named Pepe occasionally takes his jeep through the mountains to Constanza; the only hope is to get to La Isla gas station early in the morning and let everyone know that you want to get to Constanza. There is a regular bus service to Rancho Arriba and from there you can hire a motorcyclist to take you along a horrendous road to Piedra Blanca on the Santo Domingo-Santiago highway. Once on the highway it is very easy to get to Constanza.'

In the Cordillera Central near Jarabacoa and Constanza is **Pico Duarte**, at 3,175m the highest peak in the Caribbean. Before climbing it one must inform the army in Constanza; you must also purchase a permit from the Dirección Nacional de Parques at La Ciénaga de Manabao for US$3.95. (It is advisable to take a guide, who will tell you that mules are necessary for the ascent, but it can be done without them. An organized climb with DNP, Nuevos Horizontes, Maritisant, T 585-7887, costs about US$78, September and October.) The climb takes two days and the walk from the tropical rain forest of the National Park through pine woods is pleasant. There are two huts on the path, which is clearly marked; they are lacking in "facilities". Take adequate clothing with you; it can be cold (below 0°C) and wet; also take torch, food and matches. The driest time is December to February. The last *carro* leaves Manabao for Jarabacoa at 1600, so aim to climb the peak well before lunch on the second day. The National Park itself is a 4 km walk from La Ciénaga, which is reached by a road passing through some magnificent scenery from Jarabacoa.

SANTIAGO DE LOS CABALLEROS

Santiago de los Caballeros is the second largest city in the Republic (population 308,400) and chief town of the Cibao valley in the N-central part of the country. The streets of the centre are busy, noisy, with lots of advertising signs; E of centre it becomes greener, cleaner and quieter. The Río Yaque del Norte skirts the city with Avenida Circunvalación parallel to it. In 1494 Columbus ordered a fort to be built on the banks of the Río Yaque del Norte at a place called Jacagua; the resulting settlement was moved to its present site in 1563, but was destroyed by an earthquake. It is now a centre for tobacco and rum. On Parque Duarte are the Catedral de Santiago Apóstol, a neo-classical building (19th century) containing the tombs of the tyrant Ulises Heureux and of heroes of the Restauración de la República; the Museo del Tabaco (open Tues-Sat 0800-1200, 1500-1800), the Centro de Recreo (one of the country's most exclusive private clubs) and the Palacio Consistorial. Also on Parque Duarte is the Plaza de la Cultura y Oficina Regional de Patrimonio Cultural, which holds art exhibitions (closes 1230 on Sat). Other places worth visiting are the Pontífica Universidad Católica Madre y Maestra (founded 1962, with good 50m swimming pool), the Museo Folklórico Tomás Morel, open 0900-1700 (free), and the Monumento a los Héroes de la Restauración, at the highest point in the city (panoramic views of the Cibao valley, remodelled in 1991 to include a *mirador*). Calle El Sol is the main commercial street, with both vendors and the main shops. The Instituto Superior de Agricultura is in the Herradura on the other side of the Río Yaque del Norte (km 6).

Local Information – Santiago de Los Caballeros

● **Where To Stay**

El Gran Almirante, Av Estrella Sadhalá, Los Jardines, on road N, T 580-1992, F 241-1492, US$60, popular with business visitors, quite good. Over US$30: *Camino Real*, T 581-7000, Del Sol y Mella US$50s, US$68d, has good restaurant and night club, no parking facilities; *Matum*, Av Monumental, T 581-5454, has night club, swimming pool open to non-residents US$2; *Don Diego*, Av Estrella Sadhalá, on road N, T 587-4186, has restaurant and night club. Under US$30: *Ambar*, also on Av Estrella Sadhalá, T 583-1957; *Mercedes*, Calle 30 de Marzo 18, T 583-1171, US$20, hot water, a/c or fan, phone, central so a bit noisy,

tatty, but friendly, fast laundry (5 hrs); *Delrado*, Av Salvador Cucurullo 88, T 582-7563, US$6 with bath, basic, friendly. Many other cheap hotels on S Cucurullo, 4 blocks N of Parque Duarte on 30 de Marzo (many *guaguas* start from this junction).

● **Where To Eat**

Pez Dorado, El Sol 43 (Parque Colón), T 582-2518 (Chinese and international), has a fine tradition of good quality food in generous portions. At the upper end of the price range is *El Café*, Av Texas esq Calle 5, Jardines Metropolitanos, the favourite of businessmen and upper class society. Rec for pasta and steaks is *Mezzaluna*, Av 27 de Febrero 77. Nearby is *Don Miguel*, Av 27 de Febrero 40, specializing in Cuban and local cuisine. For Spanish cuisine, try *Museo del Jamón*, Restauración esq Sabana Larga, displays of Flamenco dancing some evenings. Others include *El Sol* (upstairs in Mercado Modelo Turístico, T 583-0767); *El Diamante*, Av Circunvalación, T 583-9714; *Yaque* (Restauración), US$4 plus for a good meal; *Roma*, Juan Pablo Duarte 72, just past the Tobacco Institute, for Italian food, good pizza, salads etc. For good value, open-air eating, rec are *Mac-Selo*, Juan Pablo Duarte III, and *La Pista*, behind the monument.

The restaurants of the hotels *El Gran Almirante*, *Camino Real* and *Don Diego* are good.

For the most spectacular view across the Cibao Valley, try *Camp David Ranch*; get there by driving (or take a taxi, fare about US$10) to Km 7 on Carretera Luperón, the turn-off is on the right, unsigned, before the *El Económico* supermarket; a 10-min climb up a winding, paved road leads to the ranch. The food quality is erratic, but the view is breathtaking. Next door is *El Generalísimo*, a piano bar decorated with classic cars from the Trujillo era. (With thanks to David Beardsmore.)

● **Discothèques**

La Nuit, in *Hotel Matum*; *El Alcazar*, in basement of *El Gran Almirante* hotel; *La Mansión*, Autopista Duarte, *La Antorcha*, 27 Febrero 58; *Tempo*, El Sol, and *Las Vegas*, Autopista Navarrete Km 9, all modern. *Champion Place* is a huge disco for 2,000 people, open daily.

● **Shopping**

The Mercado Modelo Turístico is at Calle Del Sol and Avenida España. Cheap amber at Calle El Sol 60, rec. Outside town, on the main road N and S, are many potteries where ceramics can be bought very cheaply (how you get them home is another matter).

● **Services**

Banks: Scotiabank on Parque Duarte, others on El Sol between San Luis and Sánchez. Telephones: Codetel is at the junction of Estrella Sadhalá and J P Duarte; take Carro A from the Parque. **City transport**: all *carros públicos* have a letter indicating which route they are on, eg M runs on E Sadhalá to the Autopista Duarte roundabout; fare US$0.15; *carreras* US$2.70-3. Many congregate at El Sol y 30 de Marzo on Parque Duarte.

● **Buses**

Guagua to La Vega US$1.60 from the roundabout where Autopista Duarte joins Estrella Sadhalá. Caribe Tours (Av Sadhalá y Calle 10, T 583-9197) bus to Puerto Plata US$3.25; it is easier to take Caribe Tours than Metro to Puerto Plata or the capital because Metro only takes passengers on standby on their Santo Domingo-Puerto Plata route. Metro terminal Maimón y Duarte, T 582-9111, a block or so towards the centre on Duarte from the roundabout at E Sadhalá (opposite direction from Codetel); 6 buses daily Santo Domingo-Santiago. *Guaguas* to Moca leave from Autopista Duarte, near intersection with Av Estrella Sadhalá. *Guaguas* to San José de las Matas leave from the Puente Hermanos Patiño, by the river not far from the centre, US$1.20. Transporte del Cibao, Restauración casi esquina J P Duarte, runs buses up to Dajabón in the NW near the Haitian border, but no buses run to this area or to Montecristi between 1000 and 1700 (a taxi costs about US$35 after bargaining). For other services see **Information for Visitors**.

● **Tourist Information**

There is a Tourist Office in the basement of the Town Hall (Ayuntamiento), Av Juan Pablo Duarte; it has little information available, only Spanish spoken.

Excursions from Santiago de Los Caballeros

An interesting day trip is to **Moca**, E of Santiago, which is a coffee and cacao centre and one of the richer regions of the country. The Iglesia Corazón de Jesús dominates the town; the tower can be climbed. The view is well worth the recommended US$1 tip to the church official. Tourist information may be found at the Town Hall at the corner of Independencia and Antonio de la Maza. It is not recommended that you stay the night, there is only one hotel, *La Niza*, on J P Duarte towards Santiago, which does not charge by the hour. Outside Moca on the road towards the Autopista Duarte, lies El Higüerito where they make faceless dolls. Every shack is a doll factory and you can bargain for better prices than in Santo Domingo or Puerto Plata. The road leading from Moca to Sabaneta on the coast is extremely beautiful, winding through lush green hills. At the crest of the hillside, about halfway between Moca and Sabaneta is a lovely restaurant called *El Molino*, "it has the most glorious chicken crêpes and a view to match, don't forget your camera". (The restaurant *Vista del Cumbre*, higher up the hill, is not as good.) You can go from Moca to Sosúa by *guaguas*, changing at the Cruce de Veragua/Sabaneta. A very recommendable trip with a magnificent view from the summit just before you cross over the mountains, of Santiago, Moca and even La Vega. The scenery is so good it is worth taking a taxi (eg US$12 to Sabaneta), rather than squashing into a *guagua*. Metrobus has buses Santo Domingo-Moca twice daily, via La Vega (T Moca 578-2541).

To the SW of Santiago is the pleasant, mountain town of **San José de las Matas**. It has tree-lined streets, mostly modern buildings and a breezy climate. Nearby are the *balnearios* (bathing spots) of Amina, Las Ventanas and Aguas Calientes, all about 5-6 km away. There is fishing in the Represa del Río Bao.

● **Where to Stay** *La Mansión*, T 581-0393/5 or Santo Domingo 221-2131, F 532-4494 (Occidental chain), 30 mins' walk from town, set in 12 sq km of pine woods, spacious rooms with fridge, a/c and heating US$50-68, fully-equipped cabins with 2 or 3 rooms, restaurant with buffet meals, local food, plenty of salads, pool, very quiet, spa and health resort owned by Aveda of the USA with sauna, massage, gym, natural products; riding, mountain biking, walking excursions, trips to Santiago, Pico

Duarte and the coast. In town, on the main square, *Oasis*, with disco, pizzería and ice creams. On the dual carriageway into town, *Los Samanes*, T 578-8316, US$10, bath, basic, clean, local food in restaurant; nearby is *El Primitivo*. There are several restaurants and cafés.

Post Office is just uphill from *Oasis*; opp the post office is a path to a *mirador* with benches. Codetel at Padre Espinosa y Félix Saychuela.

● **Transport** For Santiago transport congregates at the bottom end of the dual carriageway (carretera a Santiago), opp Texaco (another Texaco in town centre), US$1.20 via Jánico. If driving from Santiago, the best road goes via Jánico: after crossing the Puente Hermanos Patiño, turn immediately left through Bella Vista for Jánico. The road that is signed to San José de las Matas goes towards Mao. It is paved; after about 6 km an unsigned road turns left, going over the hills through Jaqui Picado, 31 km to the junction on the Jánico-San José road, 5 km before San José; lovely views, but a very rough route.

From *Jánico*, the site of Columbus' first inland fort, Santo Tomás, can be visited, although there are no remains to be seen, just a memorial stone and a flagpole in a beautiful meadow with palms, above a little river. In Jánico seek out a *motoconcho* driver who knows the way and pay about US$4 for the trip, up and down steep hills, along narrow paths and river beds. There is a small sign in Jánico on the road.

To the NW of Santiago a Highway runs through the Yaque del Norte valley to the Haitian border. The main route to Haiti turns S to *Mao* (Hotels *Cahoba*, about US$15, T 572-3357, also *Céntrico*, T 572-2122, *San Pedro*, T 572-3134, *Marién*, T 525-3558) and continues through Sabaneta to the border town of Dajabón. South of Dajabón is the *balneario* at Loma de Cabrera, rec to visit if you are in the area. Instead of turning S to Mao, you can continue to *Montecristi*, a dusty little town at the western end of the republic's N coast. One can visit the house of Máximo Gómez, the Dominican patriot who played an important role in the struggle for Cuban independence and in the Dominican Restoration. Columbus rejected his original idea to make his first settlement here and the town was in fact founded in the 16th century, rebuilt in the 17th. In the 19th century it was a major port exporting agricultural produce. The town has an interesting old clock. Very near Montecristi is a peak named El Morro (in the national park) which has a beach (very rocky) at the foot of its E side. There are mangroves and turtles which can be seen in the clear water. The Cayos Siete Hermanos, a sanctuary for tropical birds, with white beaches, are a good excursion. There has been some destruction of the offshore reefs. Hotels: *Chic*, Benito Monción 44, T 579-2316; *Santa Clara*, Mayobanex 8, T 579-2307; *Cabañas Las Carabelas*, J Bolaños, T 579-2682. Restaurants: *La Taberna de Rafúa*, Duarte 84, T 579-2291; *Heladería y Pizzería Kendy*, Duarte 92, T 579-2386; *Mi Barrita*, Duarte 86, T 579-2487.

At the town of Navarrete on the Santiago-Montecristi Highway, a road branches N, bifurcating at **Imbert** (where there is a cheese factory and a Codetel office; Cristina Clare, Calle Ezekiel Gallardo A78, rents a hut (*bohío*) at the rear of her house, US$5, she will cook for you). The NE fork goes to Puerto Plata (see below), the NW road to the N coast at **Luperón**, which has fine beaches, suitable for water sports. It is also a good haven for yachts; the marina offers electricity and water connections for boats and there are several markets selling fish, meat and vegetables. *Hotel Luperón Beach Resort*, in Casa Marina Luperón. T 581-4153, F 581-6262, US$70-85 pp (high season), and *Hotel Luperón*, Calle Independencia, T 571-8125. *La Morena*, Calle Juan P Duarte 103, opposite Esso station, near Codetel, US$8 with bath and fan. Frequent electricity and water cuts here.

West of Luperón by a new road is **La**

Isabela. Here, on his second voyage (1493), Columbus founded the first European town in the Americas, with the first *ayuntamiento* and court, and here was said the first mass. Only the layout of the town is visible. The restoration and archaeological excavation of La Isabela is being undertaken by the Dirección Nacional de Parques. There is a hotel by the ruins. To get there either take a tour from Puerto Plata, or take a *carro público* from Villanueva y Kundhard, Puerto Plata, to La Isabela village, US$2.85, then a *motoconcho* to the ruins, US$5.65 return including wait at ruins, a lovely trip. Martisant, T 585-7887, runs group tours for US$92.

Between La Isabela and Montecristi are the beaches of Punta Rucia at Estero Hondo. Besides the beaches there are mangroves and interesting flora and fauna. Lodging at *Hotel Discovery Bay*, T 685-0151/562-7475, F 686-6741, US$139-170pp, all inclusive, no children under 16, watersports and other activities provided.

PUERTO PLATA

Puerto Plata, the chief town on the Atlantic coast (which is also known as the Amber Coast) was founded by Ovando in 1502. It is 235 km from the capital. The older scenic road from Santiago to Puerto Plata is now in poor condition. The centre of town has many old, wooden houses, some new buildings and plenty of colour. A visit to the colonial San Felipe fortress, the oldest in the New World, at the end of the Malecón is recommended. Just 1,000m past Puerto Plata, you can catch a *teleférico* (cable car) to the summit of Loma Isabel de Torres, an elevation of 779m. There is a statue of Christ that looks out over all of Puerto Plata; it also houses craft shops, a café and there are botanical gardens with a lovely view of the coast and mountains. The fare is US$0.80, daily except Wednesday (when not closed for maintenance, as it was in

early 1994); or you can take your chances with horses, bikes or even a car, but be prepared, the road is impassable at some points. *Motoconcho* from town to *teleférico* US$0.80. The Museum of Dominican Amber, Duarte 61, houses a collection of rare amber; open Monday-Saturday 0900-1700, T 586-2848. The mountains behind Puerto Plata contain the world's richest deposits of amber, which is a fossilized tree resin. The cathedral is worth a visit, as are the ruins of the Vieja Logia and the Parque Central. A new Museum of Taino Art, Beller y San Felipe, 1st floor above *artesanía* shops, only contains replicas, but is interesting (open daily, more replicas on sale in the shops below). If you are led into a shop by a local boy, tour guide or taxi driver, you will more than likely be paying a hidden commission on the price of your purchase, even after you bargain. If you want a guide, call the Association of Official Tour Guides, on 586-2866. Fishing: contact Santiago Camps (T 586-2632) for equipment and boat hire. A tourist train, the Ambar Tour Train, runs (not on rails) from Playa Dorada Plaza to San Felipe fort, The Amber Museum, a rum factory, The Parque Central and gift shops, 3 times daily, US$11.50, 2½-hr trip, safe, tickets from Discount Plaza, *Heavens Hotel* (Playa Dorada), *Bayside Hill* (Costambar, *Sand Castle* (Sosúa), or T 586-4082.

To the W is the Costambar resort area, which has not been a success (*Bayside Hill Club*, Naco group, 9-hole golf course, beach, no real centre) and Cofresí beach (several hotels, cabins, US$30 pp and more at weekends). At the E end of town is Long Beach, 2 km from the centre, US$0.15 by bus, but it is crowded at weekends, rather dirty, and it is best to be on your guard. Just E of Puerto Plata, 4 km from the airport, is the beach resort of *Playa Dorada* with an exceptional golf course, and other sporting facilities. The Playa Dorada Resort is an umbrella name for a complex of 14 large hotels. Already the resort has 3,319 rooms and there are plans to build many more. *Montellano*, to the E of Playa Dorada, about half way to Sosúa, is the town in which all the processing of sugar cane is done for the N coast. It is undeveloped as a tourist town, but there are tours of the cane processing plant. For the adventurous, it has a great discothèque called *Las Brisas*, on the river, that all the locals visit, especially on Sunday afternoons. A bottle of rum, bucket of ice and 2 colas will cost about US$4. The town is a bit primitive, but the disco is not; guaranteed to have a great time, dancing merengue, salsa and some American music.

Local Information – Puerto Plata and Playa Dorada

● **Where To Stay**

At Puerto Plata: *Puerto Plata Beach Resort and Casino*, the sort of place found in package tour brochures and so difficult to get in to, T 562-7475, F 566-2436, US$95d without meals, US$39 pp basic low season price. *Montemar*, short walk to seafront, Occidental group, PO Box 382, T 586-2800, F 586-2009, US$60-90, all facilities, taxi from centre US$4.80; *Hostal Jimessón*, John F Kennedy 41, T 586-5131/364-2024, close to Parque Central, old colonial building, US$35s or d high season, US$25 low season, lobby furnished with antiques, clean, a/c, cold water, pleasant, no restaurant; *Castilla*, US$12d with shower and fan, on José del Carmen Ariza in centre of town, T 586-2559, unhelpful staff, dirty, restaurant, not rec; around corner, and preferable is *Atlántico*, 12 de Julio 24, T 586-2503, US$12 with fan, mosquito net, clean, simple, rec; *El Condado*, Av Circunvalación Sur, T 586-3255; *Puerto Plata Latin Quarter*, on sea front, modern, T 586-2588, F 586-1828, US$40-55, pool, good value in low season. *Swedish Guest House*, Av Circunvalación Sur 15, T 586-5086, Krystyna Danielsson, 9 rooms with toilet and shower, US$10, garden, clean, backpackers welcome, rooms can be rented for long periods, decorated with Krystyna's beautiful appliqué work, opp Mercado San Luis, convenient for *guaguas*, close to hospital, good *pizzería* almost next door. At Plaza Anacaona, 30 de Marzo 94-98, are *Hotel /Restaurant El Indio*, T/F 586-1201, US$28, with breakfast and fan, clean, restaurant serves good breakfast and fish, rec, very good value,

Mexican music on Sat; a patio with native plants, palm trees and hummingbirds; and a Red Cross emergency station. Ask for Pedro Brunschwiler (who speaks German, English and Spanish) if you want to go scuba diving, horse riding or on adventure trips. Plaza Anacaona's owner, Wolfgang Wirth (who also speaks German, English and Spanish) is very helpful; he is the founder of the Dominican Red Cross.

Pensión Ilra, Calle Villanueva, T 586-2337, good food, US$8.50, friendly; *Alfa*, US$8s with shower, pleasant but watch out for mosquitoes, friendly, safe, clean, T 586-2684; *Andy's Guest House*, US$10, rec, one of many of similar price range, breakfast US$1 extra; some houses also available from US$22 a week. There are cheap hotels at Long Beach, but catering mostly for short stay.

At Playa Dorada: *Jack Tar Village* hotel, from US$57 pp basic price to US$200, all inclusive, PO Box 368, T 586-3800/530-5817, F 586-4161, US style and US prices, casino; *Heavens*, from US$36 pp basic to US$150d full board, PO Box 576, Playa Dorada, T 586-5250, F 686-6741, US$80; *Playa Dorada* (an Occidental hotel), PO Box 272, T 320-3988, from US$66s low season, casino; *Paradise Beach Resort*, formerly *Eurotel*, T 320-3663, F 320-4858, from US$65 pp (US$26 low season), also has a casino; *Dorado Naco*, PO Box 162, US$44d basic low season price, T 586-2019; *Villas Doradas Resort Hotel* (also Occidental) 207 rooms, or 5 individual houses with kitchenettes, T 320-3000, F 320-4790, from US$90 to 150 (low season); *Villas Caraibe, Playa Dorada Princess* (T 530-5871, US$40 pp low season), *Flamenco* (T 320-5084, Occidental, US$100); *Puerto Plata Village* (T 320-4012, F 320-5113), and the newest resort, *Playa Naco*, T 320-6226, touted as the most beautiful of all the hotels, it houses a fully-equipped fitness centre, from US$60 basic to US$120 for a penthouse suite. Many establishments in Playa Dorada offer all inclusive accommodation; the average price for a room is over US$100. Contact the Asociación de Proprietarios de Hoteles y Condominios de Playa Dorada, T 320-3132, telex ITT 346-0360, F 320-5301.

● **Where To Eat**

The food is superb at all the main hotels; there is every variety of cuisine. In the Playa Dorada Shopping Mall is *Hemmingway's Café*, T 320-2230, good food and music, a/c, good service, fun at night and during the day. *Los Pinos*, international cuisine, T 586-3222; *De Armando*, in city centre, near Parque Central, expensive; *Pizzería Roma*, T 586-3904; *Costa Brava*, 12 de Julio 31, Spanish, pleasant, guitarists; *La Carreta*, Calle Separación; *El Canario*, 12 de Julio; *Valter*, on Hermanas Mirabel, seafood and Italian specialities, good food and service (T 586-2329). *El Sombrero*, Playa Cofresí, Autopista Santiago-Puerto Plata. Opp the baseball stadium is *Pizzería Internacional*. *Cafetería Los Bonilla*, La Javilla, good food, *merengue* music. *La Canasta*, 2 blocks N of main square, good for lunches; *Neptuno*, on the Malecón, T 586-4243, for good seafood. *Español Pollo al Carbón*, for inexpensive and delicious roast chicken, on Calle Circunvalación. *Jade Garden*, in Villas Doradas Beach Resort, for Chinese food; *Otro Mundo*, Playa Dorada Commercial Plaza, for something different, a mini-zoo with many tropical birds, offers free transport from and to your hotel, T 543-8019; *No Name Pub*, Av Colón, very nice. *Pepe Postre* bakery chain in Puerto Plata/Montellano area, good breads, yoghurt, etc. *El Cable, La Paella, Infratur* and the *Beach Club Restaurant*, all at Long Beach.

● **Shopping**

The Playa Dorada Complex has the first real shopping mall on the N coast. Prices are slightly inflated, but the quality of all items, especially the locally-made ceramics, jewellery, and clothing, is superior to most sold by beach or street vendors. The mall includes a Benneton, a selection of Tiffany lamps and some very original jewellery. Souvenirs can also be bought on the beach, or in downtown Puerto Plata, where there is shop after shop to sell you trinkets.

● **Discothèques**

Andromeda in *Heavens Hotel, Charlie's* in *Jack Tar Village Casino* and *Crazy Moon* in *Paradise Beach Resort*; all three are popular and offer a mix of *merengue, salsa* and international pop music. All have cover charges, about US$2. *Tropimal* is very popular, good mix of locals and tourists, *merengue* music.

● **Casinos**

There are five casinos on the N coast. *Jack Tar Village, Playa Dorada Hotel, Paradise Beach Club, Playa Chiquita Resort* and *The Puerto Plata Beach Resort*. Only the last named is right in Puerto Plata, the other three are in the Playa Dorada complex, and the *Playa Chiquita* is in Sosúa. The casinos feature black jack, craps, roulette and poker. *Playa Chiquita* offers baccarat and bingo, sessions played twice nightly at 1930 and 2230. Also a game called Caribbean poker, very popular, check the rules before you begin to play. There are slot machines but these can be played **only** in US dollars. If you play other games in US dollars, you win in US dollars, if you play in pesos, you win in pesos. Do not change your foreign money to pesos in the casino, the rate given is very unfavourable. *Jack Tar Village Casino* offers novices a one hour lesson in black jack or craps at 2130 nightly, free of charge.

● **Motorcycle Rental**

US$20-30 a day, from any rental agency. Make sure to lock your motorcycle or scooter, as bike theft is big business in the area and there is no theft insurance on motorbikes.

● **Useful Phone Numbers**

Police, 586-2331; Centro Médico Antera Mota, 586-2342; Codetel (telephone office) 586-3311, on J F Kennedy, half a block E of square; association of tourist guides, 586-2866; US consular agency, 586-3676.

● **Tourist Information**

There is a tourist office on the Malecón (No 20) which has plenty of useful information.

● **Local Transport**

Públicos in the city RD$2/US$0.15; *guaguas* RD$2/US$0.15; *carreras* US$2.70-3; *motoconchos*, US$0.55. *Carreras* from Puerto Plata to Playa Dorada, US$12 (tourists), US$3.85 (Dominicans); to Sosúa, see below; from the airport to Playa Dorada US$11 (have small change handy when taking a taxi, drivers often say they have none). Bus to Nagua, US$4, 3½ hrs. *Conchos* from Puerto Plata to Playa Dorada, US$0.07, *motoconchos* between US$0.27-0.70.

A *carro público* to/from the capital costs US$4.75, but is not the most comfortable way to travel. Metrobus (T 586-6062, Beler y 16 de Agosto), 4 a day, and Caribe Tours (T 586-4544, 12 de Julio y José Carmen Ariza in centre) run a/c coaches to/from Santo Domingo, 4 hrs (for fares see **Information for Visitors**). To Samaná, there is a *guagua* daily at about 0500, passing Cabarete at 0600, 4½ hrs, US$6; at other times of day you have to change buses at least 3 times.

● **Airport**

Gregorio Luperón international airport, T 586-

0219 serves the entire N coast. It is 20 mins from Puerto Plata, 7 mins from Sosúa and 15 from Cabarete. It was extended in 1993/94, but patience is required during completion of the final stages. Taxi from airport to Puerto Plata or Cabarete US$15, to Sosúa US$7. Small bank at airport for exchange. Do not panic at the airport when approached by Dominicans in overalls attempting to take your bag. They are baggage handlers trying to make a living. Proper tipping is about US$2 per bag.

East to Sosúa and the North Coast

28 km E of Puerto Plata is **Sosúa**, a little town that has a beautiful and lively 1 km beach, perfect for diving and water sports. There is a smaller public beach on the E side of town, referred to as the "playita", where you will be less bothered by vendors. It is located by *Hotel Sosúa-by-the-Sea*. Sosúa is popular with Europeans, Americans and Canadians. The main street (correctly named Calle Pedro Clisante, but only ever referred to as Main Street, or Calle Principal in Spanish) is lined with all variety of shops, restaurants and bars. The unusual European atmosphere stems from the fact that the El Batey side of town (the side that houses most of the hotels and restaurants) was founded by German Jewish refugees who settled here in 1941. A synagogue and memorial building are open to the public. Although many of the original settlers have moved away, services are still held, and in 1991 a 50th year anniversary party brought settlers and their relatives from all over the world for a reunion. The original houses are now lost among the modern developments. The western end of the town is referred to as Los Charamicos (the two ends are separated by the beach); this is the older side of town, where the Dominicans themselves generally live, shop and party.

Note Sosúa, although crowded with tourist spots, is a small town. Little or no attention is paid to street names or numbers. The quiet road between El Batey and Playa Chiquita should be treated with caution at night. Dress is very informal. Although it is considered impolite to wander the streets in bathing attire, dress for dinner at any location is comfortable and Caribbean.

Local information – Sosúa
● Where To Stay

Casa Marina Beach Club, T 571-3690, US$70d, high season (US$42 low), but special offers may be available, located on the Little Beach, pool, restaurant, excellent value. *Sosúa-by-the-Sea*, T 571-3222, owned and operated by Austrian-Canadians, on Little Beach, immaculate, beautiful a/c rooms, good restaurant, pool, bar, US$75d high season, includes breakfast and dinner; *Playa Chiquita Beach Resort*, T 571-2800, US$54d (US$100 full board), slightly out of the way, located on own private beach, good restaurant, accommodation and service, and casino, has shuttle to town and beach. *Corallios*, unpretentious, perched on a cliff with breathtaking view of beach, US$55d in winter, US$30d in summer, T 571-2645; *Auberge du Village*, Calle Dr Rosen 8, American-run guest house 5 mins walk from beach, small pool, breakfast, rec, US$35d in winter, T 571-2569, F 571-2865 (postal address EPS – D #02-5548, Miami, FL 33102). *One Ocean Place*, El Batey, T 571-3131, US$60, restaurant, pool, 10 mins' walk to beach; *Hotel Sosúa*, T 571-2683, F 586-2442, in town centre, 3 mins from main beach, restaurant, pool, quiet; *Sandcastles Beach Resort*, T 530-5817/571-2420, F 571-2000, just outside Sosúa, private beach, restaurants, self-contained, shuttle buses into Sosúa, prices from US$56 pp in double. *Charlie's Cabañas*, 27 cabins, quiet, tropical, ocean front pool, on a cliff overlooking the sea, 5 mins to beach, US$45d, special rates for groups, T 571-2670; *Nuevo Sol*, T 571-2124, on main street, US$30-60; *La Esplanada*, T 571-3333, Spanish owned, near casino, US$50-90; *Condos Carolina*, T 571-3626, units with kitchen and sitting room, 1 and 2 bedrooms, variable prices; *Coconut Palms Resort*, T 571-1625, F 571-1725, beautiful resort, scenic hilltop view, 8 km outside Sosúa, all units with kitchen facilities, shuttle bus to town and beach, variable rates. For the budget-minded (prices between US$15-35 depending on season): *Jardín del Sol*, T/F 571-3553, family-run, clean, pool, near town; *Margaritaville*, T/F 571-3553, on hilltop, clean, scenic, shuttle to town; *Tropix*, T 571-2291, in centre of town, clean, quiet, pool, beautiful garden, good food, use of kitchen facilities, US$35-40, rec. *Koch's Guest House*, El Batey, US$25d, use of kitchen, breakfast extra. There are many other hotels, guest houses and villas for rent, ask around locally. Try in Los Cerros for rooms to rent, from US$5s to US$25d. If you are looking for a place to stay for longer than the average charter flight, or would like to get a group together to stay in a house, or have any questions regarding rentals in the Sosúa/Cabarete area, call *Sosúa Central Rental*, T/F 571-3648.

● **Where To Eat**

On the Waterfront, excellent food and a spectacular sunset overlooking the sea, all-you-can-eat barbeque on Fri night, pleasant entertainment nightly in *Charlie's Cabañas Hotel*, on the lookout point, down from the Codetel offices, T 571-3024; *The Spaghetti House*, Main Street, terrific pasta meals (especially for garlic lovers), reasonable prices, no reservations necessary, special pizza ovens; *Don Juan*, in centre of Main Street, Spanish food, *paella*, excellent seafood, tables on the boulevard; *Marco Polo Club*, La Puntilla, overlooking Sosúa beach, Italian, or set-price, 6-course French meal, great view, antipasto buffet table, T 571-3128; *El Destino*, on City Hall Street (Calle Ayuntamiento, follow the Clock Tower), vegetarian, owners read palms or cards for you with dinner, or make an appointment for a full reading; *Pavillion*, also on Calle Ayuntamiento, great European food, steaks, salad bar, and an ice cream crêpe, worth the walk, follow the signs for it all over town; *Caribbean*, Main Street, glassed-in, a/c, lovely atmosphere, good European and Caribbean cuisine. *Caribae*, seafood specialities, organically grown vegetables and a shrimp farm on the premises, El Mirador hill; *Tropix*, homestyle cooking, one special per night, friendly, tranquil, check hotels for weekly menu listings, T 571-2291 for reservations. Fast Food: *Sammy's*, good burgers and good chicken wings, in the heart of Sosúa, where the locals meet to see and be seen; *PJ's International*, satisfying breakfasts, terrific chef's salad and schnitzel burger for lunch, on corner of Main Street; *Dundee's Burgers*, Calle Alejo Martínez, in front-of-school yard, open 1900-0700, the place to go after a night of revelling, Dundee, the American-Dominican owner, is a local fixture. *Hotel Sosúa-by-the-Sea* serves the best value buffet breakfast in town. For delicious baked products go to the *German Bakery (Panadería Alemán)*, in Villas Ana

María, residential area. *The Big Squeeze* makes fresh juices out of all and any fruits and vegetables, inexpensive, delicious, on City Hall Street.

● **Bars And Nightclubs**

Tree Top Lounge, Main Street, 2nd floor, British-owned, pub atmosphere, has lots of games (backgammon, cards, scrabble, etc), rec. *Casablanca*, on Main Street, great place for dancing and partying, mostly American music. *La Roca*, last spot on Main Street before the beach, Sosúa's oldest bar/disco/eatery, recently reopened, beautiful decor, comfy couches, good food and music; *Moby Dick Disco*, by far the most popular disco, a/c, cover charge. *Barock* and *Pyramide* both in the same building at the corner of Calle Dr Rosen and Main Street, dancing until the small hours. *Tropic Disco*, on rooftop of Plaza del Fuente, biliard table, darts board, dance floor, good sound system; *Marinero*, Main Street, ground floor, local entertainment.

● **Services**

Codetel, Calle Dr Alejo Martínez, near corner with Dr Rosen. Next to the bank on the small square at Calle Dr Martínez and Duarte is the *Viva Art Gallery*. Sosúa Business Services, for all typing, faxing, phoning, photocopying needs, on Main Street, upstairs from *Casablanca Bar*, T 571-3452. *Salón Tres Hermanas*, Av Pedro Clisante 31, El Batey, very friendly hairdressers, does plaiting, uses natural cosmetics, helpful with sunburn.

● **Police**

T 571-2293.

● **Transport**

A *público* from Puerto Plata costs US$3.15, a taxi will cost about US$12 and is far more comfortable. *Guaguas*, overcrowded minibuses, charge about US$1 and leave Puerto Plata's main square or, more frequently, from the hospital on Circunvalación Sur (Caribe Tours charge US$1.25). In Sosúa, transport congregates by the Texaco station and the junction of Calle Dr Rosen and the Carretera. The most popular form of transportation within Sosúa is *motoconcho* (motorcycle taxi), pay 5 pesos during the daylight hours and 10 pesos at night, pp, to anywhere in town, not a penny more, no matter how much the driver asks. A *concho* (car) costs RD$2/US$0.15; *carreras* US$3-3.85. For organized tours by plane to Haiti, Samaná, Turks and Caicos, Santo Domingo, contact Columbus Air, T 571-2711 or 586-6991. Car and bike rentals are everywhere, shop around for prices, and once again be cautioned as to theft (eg Asociación de Renta Moto Sosúa Cabarete, US$22-28 for 1-2 days, US$4-5.65 hourly, depending on type). Several places do horse riding tours, but make sure that the group is not too large, they can be as big as 40 riders, which is not much fun.

12 km E of Sosúa is *Cabarete*, nowadays the windsurf capital of the world, having hosted the World Windsurf Championship. International competitions are held annually in June. The 2 km curving bay has a strip of hotels and guest houses catering for windsurfers' needs. Conditions vary according to season: in summer there are constant trade winds but few waves, in winter there are days with no wind, but when it comes the waves are tremendous. February and March are the best months, November and December are the worst. Boards rent for US$40/day, US$195/week, with variations, make sure insurance is available. The main places are *MB*, at *Auberge du Roi Tropical* (headquarters of the championship organizers, see below), T 571-0957; *Carib BIC*, T 586-9519, F 586-9529; Nathalie Simon; and others. There are many kilometres of white sand beach lined with coconut palms and a lagoon with many waterbirds, and waterskiing. Taxi fares: Cabarete-Sosúa US$6.45 (*guagua* US$0.40-0.80), airport US$16, Puerto Plata US$20.

● **Where To Stay And Eat** The *Punta Goleta Beach Resort* for package tours (PO Box 272, Puerto Plata, T 535-4941, basic price US$122d full board). Another development is *Camino del Sol*, T 571-2858, E of the town. *Auberge du Roi Tropical*, T 571-0770, F 571-0680, US$59d, US$49s, popular, *MB* windsurf centre, mountain bikes, pool. Opposite is *Casa Laguna*, T 571-0725, US$68-90 high season, US$44-63 low; *Cita del Sol*, T 571-0720, US$60 high season, US$30-35 low, French Canadian, *P'tit Quebec* restaurant; *Kaoba*, T 571-0837, F 571-0879, US$30 with fan and hot water, reductions for over 2 weeks, bungalows, good value, separate restaurant for breakfast and evening meal; these three are across the road from the beach. Similarly, *Banana Boat Motel*, T 571-0690, F 571-3346, US$20-35, quiet, central, kitchen facilities, laundry, rec. On beach, *Cabarete Beach Hotel*, T 571-0755, F 571-0831, US$ 80-105, good buffet breakfast, *Mariposa* restaurant. *GiGi Beach*, at Sosúa end of town, T 571-0722, US$30-35 with fan, no restaurant, windsurf shop. There are many more hotels and rooms for rent, just ask around when you arrive. Note that many places charge much more for "walk-in" customers than for tour groups. Cabarete has many restaurants, most specializing in fast food and with views of the beach.

On the NE coast, *Río San Juan*, is a friendly town with a lagoon called Gri-Grí (*guagua* from Sosúa US$2.40, 1¼ hrs, may have to change in Gaspar Hernández). Boats take visitors through the mangrove forests and to see caves and rocks, and to the natural swimming pool called the Cueva de las Golondrinas (US$16 without swim, US$24 with swim, US$1.60 pp if more than 10 people). Also worth visiting from the town is Puerto Escondido beach. You can walk beyond *Hotel Bahía Blanca* between mangroves and the sea to the mouth of Gri-Grí, many birds in the mangroves.

● **Where To Stay And Eat** Newest and nicest hotel is *Bahía Blanca*, T 589-2563, F 589-2528, lovely location right on the sea, clean, lots of balconies, US$40-60 with some meals; next best is *Río San Juan*, on main street, Duarte, at brow of hill, T 589-2379/2211, many price variations from US$25, a/c, disco, pool, good restaurant and there is a good pizzeria, *Cachalotte*, opp (the hotel offers boat trips on the lagoon). *Santa Clara*, Padre Billini y Capotillo, opp Mini Market, US$12 with bath and fan, US$5.65 without; *San Martin*, US$5, friendly but very dirty. *Cheo's Café Bar*, Padre Billini, casi Libertad, pizzas, seafood, meat; *Bar/Restaurant La Casona*, fish and creole food, good value, friendly, purified drinking water, near Laguna Gri Grí; several other eating places, mostly *pizzerías*.

Transport stops at the junction of Duarte and the main road.

Further to the E is *Playa Grande*, 60 km from Puerto Plata, another beautiful new resort which is being developed, in conjunction with Playa Dorada, at a cost of many millions of dollars (lots of hawkers on the beach). The many tour companies in Sosúa offer tours to Gri-Grí and Playa Grande. 5 km E of Playa Grande is *Club Paradise*, T (813)949-9327, F (813)949-1008, a "clothing optional" resort, with beautiful, secluded beaches, self-sufficient complex, watersports and entertainment.

Between Río San Juan and Samaná, the coast road runs through Cabrera to **Nagua**, a dirty fishing village on the shores of the Bahía Escocesa. Several small and medium-sized hotels: *Hotel San Carlos*; *Hotel Corazón de Jesús*; *Hotel Carib Caban*, 8 km S of Nagua, US$30 in studio (less in smaller room), pleasant, directly on beach, restaurant with Austrian food (hire a motorcycle to get there, US$2, T 584-3145). Puerto Plata-Nagua, three buses, 3½ hrs, US$4; Nagua-Santo Domingo, 3½ hrs, US$3 (Metrobus, T 584-2177, twice a day); Río San Juan-Nagua, US$2.40, Nagua-Samaná also US$2.40. The scenery along the N coast from Sosúa to Samaná is exceptionally beautiful. The road has been repaved all the way from Sosúa to Samaná. **Sánchez** is a pleasant, unspoilt little place with some basic accommodation. Much of the architecture is 19th century. It was at one time a prosperous sea port and had a railway which ran to San Francisco de Macorís and La Vega. Bus Santo Domingo-Sánchez, Caribe Tours 3 a day, US$3.85.

THE SAMANÁ PENINSULA

On the peninsula of **Samaná** is the city of the same name. Columbus arrived here on 12 January 1493, but was so fiercely repelled by the Ciguayo Indians that he called the bay the Golfo de las Flechas (the Gulf of Arrows). Samaná Bay, as it is now called, is very picturesque, fringed with coconut palms and studded with islets. The present town of Santa Bárbara de Samaná was founded in 1756 by families expressly brought from the Canary Islands. The city, reconstructed after being devastated by fire in 1946, shows no evidence of this past, with its modern Catholic church, broad streets, new restaurants and hotels, and noisy motorcycle taxis. In contrast to the Catholic church, and overlooking it, is a more traditional Protestant church, white with red corrugated-iron roofing, nicknamed locally "La Churcha". Traditional dances, such as *bambulá* and the *chivo florete* can be seen at local festivals (4 December, the patron saint's day; 24 October, San Rafael). An airport for the peninsula is at Arroyo Barril (8 km from town, good road, but only 25 minutes' flying time from Santo Domingo). Many Caribbean-cruising yachts anchor at Samaná, taking advantage of the calm waters.

Humpback whales return to Samaná Bay every year between December and March to mate and calve. Various tours go whale-watching (some are given under **Excursions** below), certainly worthwhile if you are in the area at that time of year.

Local Information – Samaná
● Where To Stay
Gran Bahía, T 562-6271, F 562-5232, 96-room, charming luxury resort on coast road, 10 mins, 8 km E of town, all facilities available, US$25 pp low season rising to US$185, small beach, good food and service, compact golf course, water sports, shuttle service to Cayo Levantado; *Hotel Cayo Levantado*, on the island, 10 mins by boat from Samaná, white beaches, 28 rooms, 4 *cabañas*, restaurant, beach bar, US$75-150, T 223-8704, F 538-2985; *Cayacoa*, T 538-2426, F 538-2985, from US$33 pp, on a hill overlooking the town, view of the bay, beautiful gardens, watersports, very nice; *Tropical Lodge*, on Malecón, T 538-2480, US$35, 8 rooms, basic but clean; *Nilka*, Santa Bárbara y Colón, T 538-2244, 10 rooms, US$25 with a/c (US$20 with fan), all with bath, popular; *Guest House Alcide*, T 538-2512; *Cocoloco*, near rotunda, T 240-6068, 6 rooms, clean, helpful German owner, who is also a guide to the National Park, good barbeque; *Cotubanamá*, T 538-2557, excel-

lent, US$31, breakfast US$3, good value. There are other hotels, eg *King*, T 538-2404, *Casa de Huéspedes*, T 538-2475 and *Ursula*, T 538-2402.

● **Where To Eat**

Going E along the Malecón: *Típico El Coco*, *L'Hacienda*, T 538-2383, grill and bar; *Le Café de Paris*, pizzeria, good crêperie, cocktails, loud music; *La Mata Rosada*, *Camilo* (on corner of Parque), local and not-so-local food, reasonable (takes credit cards). Also on Malecón: *La France*, T 538-2257, French owned, excellent, highly rec; *Samaná Sam's Saloon*, No 5, almost opp. *Morgan's*, on roundabout near the market place, run by American Wally, good value, good for local information. Chinese restaurant on the hill, excellent. At the dock, *El Marino* and *La Serena*.

The local cuisine is highly regarded, especially the fish and coconut dishes.

● **Other Services**

Petrol station at the dock, open 0700-2200. Banco Hispano Dominicano on Malecón. Banco del Cambio, behind Samaná Tours, changes cheques. Banco del Comercio gives cash against Visa, 5% commission, open 0830-1500 Mon-Fri. Post Office behind *Camilo*, just off Parque; Codetel, Calle Santa Bárbara; **Tourist information** at Richard Tours at *Samaná Sam's* and Samaná Information Service, T 538-2451; both on Malecón, and closed out of season; also Samaná Tours, good maps and information, closed Sunday; alternatively, T 538-2219, or 538-2206 (Ayuntamiento), or 538-2210 (provincial government).

● **Transport**

Concho or *guagua* in town RD$2/US$0.15; *carreras* between US$2.70 and US$3.50. From the capital either by bus direct, 4½ hrs via *San Francisco de Macorís*, (10-mins stop by a park with trees whose trunks are painted red, white and blue, *Hotel Joya*, near Plaza Mayor, US$4.80, quiet, clean, friendly), Nagua and Sánchez (return bus to capital, Caribe Tours on Malecón, 2-3 a day each direction; Metrobus, T 538-2851, leaves Santo Domingo 0700 daily, returns from Samaná 1400), or by bus or *público* to San Pedro de Macorís, then another to *Sabana de la Mar* (*Hotel Villa Suiza*, US$16, pool, run down; *Hotel Brisas de la Bahía*, US$7-10 range), and cross by boat (foot passengers only, 5 return trips a day, US$2.10 one way,

beware overcharging of tourists) from Sabana to Samaná at 0900, 1100, 1430, 1500, 1700 (safety conditions leave something to be desired). The road from Sabana de la Mar to Hato Mayor is good, the scenery beautiful, and from Hato Mayor to San Pedro de Macorís (see below) it is also good.

EXCURSIONS FROM SAMANÁ

There are several beautiful offshore islands. *Cayo Levantado* is a popular picnic place, especially at weekends when the beach is packed. The white sand beach is nice, though, and there are good views of the bay and the peninsulas on either side. The hotel on the island has been taken over by Occidental (see above). Good drinks and fish lunches are for sale. Public boats go there from the dock in Samaná (US$4 return, buy ticket at Malecón No 3, not from the hustlers on the pier, 2-4 trips daily outward 0900-1100, return 1500-1700); alternatively, take a *público* or *motoconcho* 8 km out of town to Los Cacaos (US$3) where two companies, Transportes José and Simi Báez, run boats to the island and will pick you up later for US$10-15 (the latter company also does fishing and whale-spotting trips). Tours with Santo Domingo agencies range from US$61.50 (Turinter, Insular) to US$77 (Martisant).

At the eastern end of the peninsula is Playa Galeras, 26 km (1 hr, US$1.20 by *guagua*), worth a visit. The 1 km beach is framed by the dark rock cliffs and forested mountains of Cape Samaná and Cape Cabrón. Hotels: *Villa Serena*, next to the shore, T 223-8703, F 538-2545, Candian-owned, 11 rooms, private terrace overlooking sea, a/c and fans, gourmet restaurant, tours organized; *Marea Beach*, French-owned, T 538-2545 and *La Marinique*, room rates range from US$32-40; several fish restaurants, good atmosphere. The area will soon be dominated by the *Cala Blanca* resort development; only 40 time share apartments so far, but there are plans for more with golf courses, sports centres etc. 20 minutes away by boat, or 40 minutes by jeep along a very rough track is the deserted Playa Rincón, dominated by the cliffs of 600m high Cape Cabrón. The whole peninsula is beautiful, but many beaches are accessible only by boat (and the Samaná boatmen charge the earth). Others are reached by a dirt road, negotiable by ordinary cars.

Visits to the Parque Nacional de Haitises, across the bay, can be arranged by launch for US$60, US$15 from Samaná, eg *Hotel Cayacoa* or from Sabana de la Mar, or ask at Samaná Tourist Information; various companies organize tours to Los Haitises and to caves in the area (eg Ecoturisa, see under Santo Domingo; Martisant, T 585-7887, US$38.50, others, eg Turinter, Prieto, T 685-0102, Insular, US$61.50; in Sabana de la Mar, Juan Julio Rodríguez, Calle Duvergé 24, or at the pier, offers trips to Los Haitises and to see whales). The DNP, from whom permits must be obtained, also organizes tours; see above, **Flora and Fauna**. Tour companies and boat owners organize whale-watching trips from mid-January to March, from about US$25 pp, an incredible experience. For reputable tour guides and people who care about the regulations which prevent boats from disturbing the whales too much, phone Kim Beddall, T 538-2494, owner of *Victoria II*, concise, interesting, friendly tours.

On the N coast of the peninsula is *Las Terrenas*, with some of the finest beaches in the country, from which, at low tide, you can walk out to coral reefs to see abundant sea life. The region is frequently visited by divers, drawn by its excellent reefs, sponges and underwater caves. Insect repellent is necessary at dawn and dusk to combat the sandflies. Many people go there by private plane, but it is reachable by a newly-paved 17 km road from Sánchez which zig-zags steeply up to a height of 450m with wonderful views before dropping down to the N coast.

● **How To Get There** *Guagua* Samaná-Sánchez US$1.20, then another to Las Terrenas, US$1, or taxi US$23 (or hire a motorbike in Samaná, US$20/day, the roads are suitable). Bus from Santo Domingo, Calle Juan B Vicini 133, opp Huacalito, 1400, 5 hrs, US$3.85; Las Terrenas-Santo Domingo at 0630; alternatively go via Sánchez; to Puerto Plata at 0700.

● **Where To Stay** *Trópico Banana*, one of the larger guesthouses, good value food, popular bar, US$50d; *Isla Bonita*, near *Trópico Banana* on beach, US$60, clean, good view, but very touristy. On Playa Bonita (see below) are *Atlantis*, US$75d, rather run down, restaurant serves Dominican food, and *Acaya*, US$40d, nice atmosphere, good breakfast and restaurant, recommended; *Palo Coco*, on main road at entrance to Las Terrenas, expensive, good. Most expensive are: *Cacao Beach*, 190 rooms, biggest hotel, T 530-5817, E of *Trópico Banana*, prices from US$43 (low season, inc 2 meals); *Plantation Club*, E of *Cacao Beach*, price inc 3 meals and drinks, and, similar, *El Portillo*, 5 km E of cemetery, T 688-5715, F 685-0457, cabins (from US$50d), no a/c, secluded, used by Spanish package holidays, own airstrip; all 3 are on beach and have swimming pools. *L'Aubergine*, T 240-6171, F 240-6070, US$8-25 depending on room and number of people, near *Cacao* and beach, very good, restaurant closed Sunday; *Papagayo*, on beach road, US$25, good, bath; *Los Pinos*, US$20, Swiss run, family atmosphere, clean, excellent, huge breakfast, helpful; *Cabañas La Esmeralda*, on beach just W of cemetery, similar price range. *Las Cayenas*, expensive; *Dinny*, on the beach, US$8-14, clean, central, noisy; *Mami*, very basic, dirty, US$4. Small hotels or guesthouses include *La Selva*, *Habitaciones*, *Louisiane* (helpful), there are several others. Ask for Doña Nina, turn right for 800m along the beach in Las Terrenas, basic cabins US$4.15, very friendly, but insecure. Each hotel has its own electricity generator and water supply. In all there are 27 places to stay.

● **Where To Eat** *Chez Paco*, French, very good; the best Spanish restaurant is in *Hotel Palo Coco*; the best Italian is in *Isla Bonita Resort*; the best German is *El Colibrí*, which also serves good beef (next to *Hotel Cacao Beach*; *Restaurante Canne à Sucre*, on beach W of cemetery, tasty pastas and crêpes; *Pizza Coca*, good, back of *Hotel Atlantis*; *El 28*, Spanish restaurant on the beach near the start of the road to *El Portillo*, poor reports received in 1993 and 1994; *Cocoloco*, cheap langosta; *La Salsa*, thatched roof restaurant on the beach near *Trópico Banana*, French-owned; *Mami*, on the main road, créole food, cheap, rec. Popular disco is *Nuevo Mundo*.

● **Services** *Agencia de Viajes Vimenca*, Remeses Vimenca, on the main road, exchanges money at the best rates in town. Codetel has a phone and fax office. Supermarket Frank will change dollars cash and TCs. Horseriding close to Supermarket Frank, good horses, US$10 for 2 hrs. There is a petrol/gasoline station. An electricity generator is being installed.

Las Terrenas village is developing rapidly to cope with the influx of tourists: the wooden houses are being replaced by concrete ones; there is a lot of traffic noise; the beaches, except Playa Bonita, are crowded and hawkers sell their wares to the visitors, but they are mostly clean and remain beautiful. Where the road reaches the shore, at the cemetery in Las Terrenas village, a left turn takes you along a sandy track that winds between coconut palms alongside the white sand beach for about 5 km, past many French and Italian-run guest-houses and restaurants. At the end of the beach, walk behind a rocky promontory to reach Playa Bonita, with hotels, guesthouses and restaurants; there are apartments beside *Hotel Atlantic*. Beyond the western tip of this beach is the deserted Playa Cosón, a magnificent 6 km arc of white sand and coconut groves ending in steep wooded cliffs (1½ hr walk or US$0.80 on *motoconcho*). A right turn at Las Terrenas takes you along a potholed road about 4 km to the largest hotel in the area, *El Portèillo* (see above). 10 km further on is El Limón, a farming village on the road across the peninsula to Samaná. From El Limón you can hike for an hour into the hills to a 50m high waterfall and swim in a pool of green water at its foot. Behind the falls is a small cave. The landscape between the village and the falls is beautiful, with many different

fruits growing in the woods. If taking a guide to the falls, fix the price in advance (the falls can be deserted, do not take valuables there). *Motoconcho* Las Terrenas – El Limón US$2, but they will try to charge US$5-10. Motorcycles can be hired in Las Terrenas for US$15-20/day, also bicycles, but they have no brakes.

EAST FROM SANTO DOMINGO

About 25 km E of Santo Domingo is the beach of *Boca Chica*, the principal resort for the capital. It is a reef-protected shallow lagoon, with many kilometres of white sand. Offshore are the islands of La Matica and Pinos. Tourist development has been intensive and, at weekends, the place is invaded by the citizens of Santo Domingo (and by attendant hawkers, disreputables and prostitutes). There are a great many hotels, aparthotels and restaurants. It is worth considering staying here if arriving at the airport late at night, rather than looking for a hotel in the capital.

● **Transport** At the W end of the beach is the marina of the Santo Domingo Club Náutico (see above, **Beaches and Watersports**). Banco Popular will change TCs at good rates.

● **Where To Stay** *Boca Chica Beach Resort*, T 563-2200, US$54s; *Sun Set*, T 523-4580, F 523-4975, US$65-85; the new, 5-star *Hotel Hamaca*, T523-4611, F 523-6767, PO Box 2973, Santo Domingo, US$115-325, vast resort hotel; on same road as *Sun Set* and *Hamaca* (Calle Duarte at eastern end of town) is *Mesón Isabela*, T 523-4224, F 523-4136, US$35 in room, US$45 in apartment without tax, French-Canadian and Dominican owned, bar, pool, family atmosphere, quiet, personal service, breakfast, light lunches on request, access to private beach, cookers in some rooms; *Villa Sans Soucy*, Juan Batista Vicini 48, T 523-4461, F 523-4136, US$40d, with tax, clean, beautiful, pool, restaurant, bar, rec; *Las Kasistas del Sol*, Primera y 2 de Junio, away from beach, T 523-4386, F 523-6056, US$30d and up, pool, restaurant, clean, beautiful setting, good service, friendly; *Don Paco*, Duarte 6, T 523-4816, central, US$14.50, clean, friendly.

● **Where To Eat** *L'Horizon* is excellent and *Buxeda* is rec for seafood, especially *centolla* – crab; also rec is *Neptuno's Club*, almost opp *Sun Set*, seafood, German-owned, 0900-2230, closed Mon. On the beach *fritureras* sell typical dishes, among them the famous *yaniqueques* – Johnny cakes. For cheaper meals go to Andrés, the next village, 2 km away. Taxi Santo Domingo-Boca Chica US$15.75, *guagua* US$0.65 from either Parque Enriquillo or Parque Independencia, but not after dark. If driving from the capital, look carefully for signposts to whichever part of Boca Chica you wish to go.

A few km SW of Boca Chica is La Caleta, with a small, often rough beach. It is right by the airport. Here is La Caleta Archaeological Museum, see under Santo Domingo.

The Guayacanes, Embassy and *Juan Dolio* beaches, E of Boca Chica, are also popular, especially at weekends when they can be littered and plagued with hawkers. The whole area is being developed in a long ribbon of hotels and resorts, but with little apparent planning. On the road between the beach and the highway are Jerry's Dive Center and Calypso Divers, also at *Punta Garza*, T 526-1242, F 526-3814, resort course US$50, PADI certification US$280, free pool lessons, also runs excursions; Diving Center Playa Caribe, also at *Hotel Talanquera*; Jungle Tours for trips all over the island. Venus Tours, rec. Buses going along the S coast will drop you, and pick you up again, at the various turn-offs to the beaches.

○ **Where To Stay And Eat** Here too are plenty of hotels: *Embassy* beach resort; *Sol-y-Mar* (Calle Central 23, Guayacanes, T 526-2514, US$36d, French-Canadian run, overpriced restaurant, overcharging reported); *Playacanes* beach resort, T 529-8516. In Juan Dolio: *Marena Beach Resort* (US$80); *Tamarindo Sol Club*, T 529-8471, prices from US$60; *Punta Garza* bungalows, US$36 and up, T 529-8331. *Metro Hotel y Marina*, T 526-2811, F 526-1808, from US$45 pp without tax, very nice, extension under construc-

tion; on the road to *Metro* are *Talanquera* (T 541-1166, US$64) and *Decámeron* (from US$52, T 685-5715, with casino). Near *Metro* is La Llave Plaza with Italian, German, Spanish restaurants, a minimarket, gift shop and travel agent. *Hotel Playa Real* (T 529-8471, US$46d) has Sunday buffets with dancing, use of pool and beach for US$9.25 pp (US$2.50 pool and beach only). The road between the beach and the highway is in poor condition; on it are *Ramada Guesthouse*, T 526-3310, F 526-2512, US$29.50, meals US$18.50 FAP, pool, disco bar, water sports; opp is *Marco's* restaurant and bar, German.

Inland from this stretch of coast, if you want a change from sea bathing, there is the recommended *balneario* at Bayaguana, some 45 km from the capital.

San Pedro de Macorís (population 86,950), on the Río Higuamo, is a quiet sea port whose economy is heavily dependent on the sugar estates which surround it. Tourist development is also under way here. Facing the river is the cathedral, by which is the bus terminus. In the city is the Universidad Central del Este and a baseball stadium. There is a marked cultural influence from immigrants from the Leeward and Windward Islands, especially in the dances called *guloyas*. Another name is *momise*, which derives from the English mummer tradition; dance-dramas known as *la danza salvaje* (the wild dance), *la danza del padre invierno* (the dance of Father Winter, which imitates the St George and the Dragon legend) and *la danza de El Codril* take place on 29 June, St Peter, and other festivals. For further information T 529-3600 (Ayuntamiento) or 529-3309 (provincial government). (Hotel: *Macorix*, T 596-3950, US$15-20.)

East of San Pedro is **La Romana**, population 101,350). The city has a large Parque Central. The church of Santa Rosa de Lima is on a little rise, fronted by a small park, close to Parque Central. On the Parque are Codetel, Ayuntamiento Municipal and Colón cinema. One block behind the church is the Mercado Modelo. The central commercial area is large, the town spread out. It is a sugar town, with railways to carry the harvest. La Romana can be reached by air (international airport) and by bus or *público* from Santo Domingo (US$3.55 and US$3.95 respectively). If driving from the capital, at the western edge of La Romana, by a large stadium, the road forks three ways: sharp right for Higüey and Parque Nacional del Este; the middle road, bearing right, for the town centre; straight on for Guaymate. *Concho* or *guagua* in town RD$2.50/US$0.20; *carrera* US$2.70-3.50.

● **Where to Stay** *Frano*, Av Padre Abreu, 21 rooms, US$14.50 with a/c, less without, inconveniently located away from main plaza and restaurants; 500m away is *Bolívar*, US$9.15, as good; *Hotel y Cabañas Tío Tom*, 4.5 km before town on road from capital, T 556-6212/5, F 556-6201, 2 standards of cabin, US$26 with fan and US$36-45 with a/c, bar, good but restaurant below average, separate pizzería, pool, hot water, disco, taxi from La Romana US$6.45; about 2 km closer to town is *Andanamay*, T 556-6102, US$18 with bath and fan; *San Santiago*, Calle Hernández, US$10s with bath; *Pensión de Aza*, Ramón Bergés y A Miranda, at plaza, US$5.65s without bath, basic; *dormitorio*, US$2, dark, basic, but OK, from SE corner of market go 2½ blocks W and it's on the right. Good restaurant, *La Pasarella*, on main plaza.

Casa de Campo, 10 km to the E of La Romana, is the premier tourist centre in the republic, P O Box 140, La Romana, T 523-3333, F 523-8548: hotel, villas, bars, restaurants and country club with many sporting facilities (on land and sea), including golf courses and polo fields, in 7,000 acres; prices start at US$85 pp, low season, rising to US$255-995, high season. The Playa Minitas beach is within the complex. An international artists' village in mock-Italian style has been established at Altos de Chavón, near La Romana, in a spectacular hilltop setting; there is a free bus every 15 mins from *Casa de Campo*. Taxi from La Romana US$10. There are sev-

eral restaurants, expensive shops, a Museo Arqueológico Regional, open 0900-1700 (free) and an amphitheatre which was inaugurated with a show by Frank Sinatra (many international stars perform there, as well as the best Dominican performers).

Off La Romana is the *Isla Catalina*, to which Costa Lines run excursions for the day (they call it Serena Cay), travel agents also run tours for US$30-68 including lunch, supper and drinks; T 585-7887, Martisant, cheapest, or Turinter, Insular, Prieto (T 685-0102), most expensive. Costa is to build a cruise ship terminal on the island.

Although inland the SE part of the island is dry, flat and monotonous, the beaches have fine, white sand with some of the best bathing in waters protected by reefs and excellent diving.

About 25 km E of La Romana is *Bayahibe*, a fishing village on a small bay. It is reached by a road which turns off the highway to Higüey (*carro público* La Romana-Bayahibe US$2, or take a Higüey bus to the turnoff and take a *motoconcho*, US$0.80). The fishing village is now accommodating tourism, with excursions, lodgings and cafés. Small wooden houses and the green wooden church of the village are on a point between the new buildings and an excellent, 1.5 km curving white sand beach fringed with palms. Plenty of fishing and pleasure boats are moored in the bay. A coral reef with sponges is popular with divers. Hotels: *Club Bayahibe*, US$28-40; *Pensión Rae*, US$16 per room, separate baths; *cabañas* for rent; at certain times almost all rooms are taken up by European tour companies. *Restaurante La Punta*, seafood; *Café Caribe*, breakfasts and other meals; *Adrian* café and restaurant. Marco's shop does boat trips to Saona and Catalina islands, US$25 pp, 5 passengers, full day, about 1 hr each way in boat. Santo Domingo travel agency trips to Saona range from US$31 (Martisant) to US$58 (Turinter, Prieto) to US$67 (Ecoturisa, T 221-4104, Insular). Sun and Fun Island Tours, T/F 223-5749, telecommunications centre, rentals, *cabañas*, excursions. Scuba Libre for diving.

About 10 km SE is *Dominicus*, an Italian-run tourist complex with its own beach, T 529-8531 (prices start at US$46 pp). Sandflies can be a nuisance.

Further E is **Boca de Yuma**, an interesting fishing village which is the scene of a deep-sea fishing tournament every June. A recently repaved road runs from Boca de Yuma inland to Higüey; along this, about 2 km N of San Rafael de Yuma, is the restored residence of Ponce de León (1505-1508).

Higüey has the Basílica de Nuestra Señora de la Altagracia (patroness of the Republic), a very impressive modern building to which every year there is a pilgrimage on 21 January; the statue of the virgin and a silver crown are in a glass case on the altar. People wearing shorts are not allowed to enter. The old 16th century church is still standing. Codetel near the Basilica. Market. (*Hotel Naranjo*, T 554-3400, F 554-5455, on road to El Seibo, US$40, a/c café, restaurant, disco, conference centre. *El Topacio*, T 554-5910. Plenty of cheap hotels on Calle Colón; also *Brisas del Este*. Buses from Santo Domingo cost US$3.55, *públicos* US$3.95; bus from La Romana US$2.40.)

Due E from Higüey, on the coast again, is **Punta Cana** which has some beautiful beaches and good diving; the all-inclusive resorts in the area are quite spread out. A good road, beside which are some pretty houses, runs to Punta Cana international airport, but some of the side roads are in bad condition. There is a *Club Méditerranée* (T 567-5228, F 565-2558, P O Box 106, Higüey, prices start at US$85 pp per day, has seen better days). Accommodation at the *Punta Cana Beach Resort* (T 686-0084, F 687-8745, P O Box 1083) costs US$85 pp (45 low season), MAP, beautiful beach, good diving, but sparse public transport. Most people staying there arrive by plane and only leave the resort on a tour bus; a taxi to Higüey costs US$6, *Club Med's* bus to Higüey US$6.40, and there is transport provided for employees. Independent visitors find it difficult to find a public beach as hotels will not allow non-residents through their property. The *Punta Cana Yacht Club* has villas and one-bedroom apartments, golf course under construction, T 565-3077. Continuing round the coast, there are many other beaches to be visited, with white sand and reefsheltered water. Another resort on the eastern tip, *Bávaro-Beach* and *Bávaro Gardens* has the largest hotel in the country with 1,000 rooms on a 2 km beach, T 686-5773, F 686-5771, P O Box 1, Higüey, to which charter flights go. Hotel rates from US$70 pp half board. There is a *Meliá* hotel at Bávaro (T 530-5817, US$90-202 per room, depending on season, good); also a guesthouse near Bávaro, *El Galeón del Pirata*, US$12d, restaurant. Take a taxi from Higüey. If exploring the eastern tip, Spanish is essential.

A road runs W from Higüey to Hato Mayor, via El Seibo. As far as Cruce El Pavón it is in very good condition, passing through cattle and agricultural land. The "living fences" are covered in pink blossom in January. After El Pavón there are huge sugar cane fields with oxen, trains, *bateyes* where the cutters live and much poverty. The road is rough either side of **El Seibo** (also spelt El Seybo). El Seibo is a quiet little town with painted houses, like many others in the region. It has an old, white church. (*Hotel Santa Cruz*, T 552-3962, on hill above road to Hato Mayor, US$15d; *Las Mercedes*, US$4.50, clean, quiet, pleasant, no generator; the town's water supply depends on the electricity supply.) A *guagua* can be taken to El Llano (US$0.50), from where you can either return to El Seibo, or continue on foot to Miches on the coast (two days, lovely scenery).

Hato Mayor (Codetel and church on square) is a junction for routes between Santo Domingo and Higüey, Sabana de la Mar and San Pedro de Macorís. 2 blocks from the square is a Shell station at Duarte y San Antonio. By the station, on Duarte, *guaguas* leave for Santo Domingo, US$1.60, and San Pedro de Macorís, US$0.75; on San Antonio they leave for Sabana de la Mar, US$1.20. Driving to Santo Domingo, either take the road to San Pedro de Macorís and turn W along the coast, or take the inland route, Ruta 4, which turns W before San Pedro. This again is sugar country; note the large steam engine in the open space at Ingenio Consuela. Ruta 4 crosses the Río Higuamo by a big bridge with traffic lights by the national cement works. The road continues through sugar cane fields to the capital.

WEST FROM SANTO DOMINGO

The far SW of the Republic is a dry zone with typical dry-forest vegetation. A new highway has been built from the capital, cutting journey times to half what they used to be. Tourist development is proceeding apace and by the mid-1990s a number of resorts should be operating. For the time being, exploring by car is the best way to enjoy this relatively untouched area.

To the W of Santo Domingo is Haina, the country's main port and an industrial zone. It has a teachers' vacation centre (with accommodation at US$1.60 a day) and a country club with swimming pool.

Further W one can visit **San Cristóbal** in the interior, 25 km from the capital, the birthplace of the dictator Rafael Leonidas Trujillo. Trujillo's home, the Casa de Caoba (now rapidly disintegrating, but open 0900-1700) may be reached by *público* from behind the market (US$4.75), or by motorcycle taxi

(US$0.25), though you may have to walk the last kilometre, uphill. You can also visit El Palacio del Cerro, the luxury residence which he built but never lived in. Both buildings are being restored. Also due for restoration are the Iglesia Parroquial and the Ingenio Diego Caballero, a colonial sugar mill at Boca de Nigua. Other attractions are the Palacio del Ayuntamiento in which the republic's first constitution was signed, the Iglesia de Piedras Vivas, the caves at El Pomier (with Taino petroglyphs) and the Santa María caves, where African-influenced stick and drum festivals are held. The local saint's day festival is from 6-10 June. Nearby are La Toma natural pools, for scenery and swimming, and the beaches at Palenque, Nigua and Najayo. At the last named are the ruins of Trujillo's beach house. Hotels: *San Cristóbal*, *Constitución*, cheaper, former has a disco, and there are others in town: *Las Terrazas*, a government-owned hotel in the centre, US$10, is best avoided, nothing works; on the road to Santo Domingo are a couple of small hotels, *La Ruta*, US$10 with small breakfast, has a helpful owner. A famous local dish is *pasteles en hojas*, made from plátano, minced meat and other ingredients. Minibus Santo Domingo-San Cristóbal from the Malecón, US$0.65, *público* US$1; radio taxi US$10.75-16.15; La Covancha company organizes group transport (27 passengers) to San Cristóbal, La Toma and Palenque Beach.

From San Cristóbal the road runs W to **Baní**, birthplace of Máximo Gómez, 19th century fighter for the liberation of Cuba. The town is a major producer of sugar cane, coffee, vegetables, bananas and salt. The parish church is Nuestra Señora de Regla (festival, 21 November). *Hotel Brisas del Sur* (T 522-3548); cheaper hotels to be found near the market on Máximo Gómez; *Disco Sur*, on three floors, in the centre; minibus from Santo Domingo, US$1.60. The local goats' milk sweets from Paya, 5km E of the town centre on main road, are renowned throughout the country, eg from *Las Marías*. Las Tablas, a village nearby, was one of the last places to conserve indigenous ways of life.

Don't bother with the Baní beach (although at Los Almendros a tourist development is being built), better to carry on to **Las Salinas**. Of the two roads W out of Baní, take the one to Las Calderas naval base for Las Salinas. There is no problem in going through the base; after it, turn left onto an unmade road for 3 km to the fishing village of Las Salinas, passing the unique sand dunes of the Bahía de Calderas. The bay is an inlet on the Bahía de Ocoa, shallow, with some mangroves and good windsurfing and fishing. In the village is *Las Salinas High Wind Center*, hotel, restaurant, windsurf centre, US$32 per room. Beyond the village are the saltpans which give it its name and then the point surrounded by a grey sand beach (one bar, calm waters, no facilities). Across the inlet are the undeveloped white sand beaches of Corbanito; fishermen will go across for US$2, apparently.

The fishing village of **Palmar de Ocoa** (99 km from Santo Domingo) hosts a fishing tournament each year; it is reached by a road branching off the Baní-Las Salinas road, going along the northern shore of the Bahía de Calderas. Poor roads go to Corbanito, no development whatsoever. Palmar has lots of summer houses, a grey sand, pebbly beach, calm waters and a newly-built, poor village behind the summer houses. There is no large-scale tourist development. The setting is beautiful, looking across the bay to the mountains inland.

The main road W, in excellent condition, carries on from Baní through Azua to Barahona. *Azua* de Compostela was founded in 1504 on the orders of Fray Nicolás de Ovando; at one time Puerto Viejo was an alternative port to Santo Domingo. An important victory by Dominican troops against the Haitian army took place here on 19 March 1844. The main beach is Monte Río. Hotels: *Altagracia*, T 521-3813; *Brisas del Mar*, T 521-3813; also *La Familiar*, T 521-3656, US$4-5.60 with shower and fan; *Hotel Restaurant San Ramón*, T 521-3529 (none is of high quality). Restaurants: *El Gran Segovia, José Segundo, Mi Bosquecito Bar, Patio Español*. Santo Domingo-Azua is 2 hrs by *guagua*, US$3.20, *público* US$2.75, and Azua has good bus connections for Barahona, under 2 hrs, US$3.20, San Juan and Padre Las Casas.

On the square in **Barahona** is the Sede Principal de la República of 1913 (being remodelled). It is a clean town with brightly painted houses. The province of Barahona produces coffee (excursions can be made to Platón or Santa Elena), sugar, grapes, salt, bananas and other fruits, also gypsum and seafood. Barahona's domestic airport is to be upgraded to international. The road which passes the airport is lined with flamboyant trees and goes to the sugar factory; see the yellow railway engine on the way.

● **Where To Stay** *Hotel Riviera Beach*, newly-built by Occidental outside town with own beach, T 524-5111, F 524-5798, good comfortable rooms, many with balconies, buffet meals, pool and poolside bar, prices from US$48 pp; *Hotel Caribe* on same road, but closer to town, US$20, T 524-2185, excellent open-air restaurant (*La Rocca*) next door; *Hotel Guaracuyá*, T 524-2211, is rec, being clean and on its own beach at Saladilla (the dawns here are spectacular), US$25 for double room with a/c, less with fan. In town, *Hotel Barahona*, Calle Jaime Mota 5, T 542-3442, US$11.50 with fan, restaurant, simple; *Micheluz*, Av 30 de Mayo 28, T 524-2358, US$20 with a/c, cheaper with fan, cold water, restaurant, opp is *Mencía*, small, central, basic, clean, friendly, fan, US$5; *Las Magnolias*, Anacaona 13, T 524-2244, US$20 with a/c, US$14 with fan; *Ana Isabel*, Anacaona y Padre Billini, T 524-5422, central, no restaurant, fan or a/c; several smaller hotels.

● **Where To Eat** *Las Mercedes* restaurant on corner of Jaime Mota and seafront road; *Brisas del Caribe* seafood restaurant near airport, excellent food and service, reasonable prices, pleasant setting, popular at lunchtime, T 524-2794 (US$6 main course); good juices on one corner of Parque Central; *José, comida criolla* and video, on Jaime Mota. 2 discos, *Imperio* next to *Riviera Beach; Costa Sur* with restaurant almost opp *Riviera Beach*.

● **Transport** Journey time from the capital is 3 hrs. Minibus fare is US$2.35, *público* US$3.15, Caribe Tours runs 2 buses a day (group transport also available with Metro Tours, La Covacha and Taxi Raffi). *Concho* or *guagua* in town RD$2/US$0.15; *carrera* US$2.30-3.

Be careful when swimming at the small, public beach at Barahona, as there are frequently stinging jelly fish, it is also filthy, as is the sea, and theft is common. About 70% of the coral reef off Barahona is reported to be dead. Those with a car can visit other, more remote beaches from Barahona (public transport is limited to *públicos*). A new road has been built S of Barahona, running down the coast through some of the most beautiful scenery in the republic, mountains on one side, the sea on the other, leading to Pedernales on the Haitian border (146 km). All along the southern coast are many white sand beaches which offer the best snorkelling and scuba diving in the Republic. The first place is the pebble beach of El Quemaito, where the river comes out of the beach, the cold fresh water mixing with the warm sea; offshore is a reef. A *parador* is under construction. The road proceeds, coming right down to the sea before San Rafael (about 40 mins from Barahona) where a river runs out onto a stony beach. The forest grows to the edge of the beach. Where the road crosses the river is a *pensión* with a swimming hole behind it (the swimming hole is safer than the sea as enormous waves surge onto the beach). Construction is under way here, too. At weekends it gets very crowded. Between San Rafael and *El Paraíso* rooms are available for rent. As the road approaches El Paraíso, see the changing colours where underground rivers flow into the sea. At El Paraíso, 31 km from Barahona, are a Texaco station and *Hotel Paraíso* (US$16d, no phone, big rooms with bath, clean, TV). At Los Patos another river flows into the sea; *comedores*, disco. Note that most of these beaches have domestic animals, so there are droppings on the sand. There are cool, fresh-water lagoons behind several of the other beaches on this stretch of coast. Limón lagoon is a flamingo reserve.

At the village of **Enriquillo**, 54 km S of Barahona, a new dock has been constructed (*Hotel Dajtra*, on main road, US$2, basic; the only place with light at night is a disco where half the village hangs out, its prices are "normal"). One must explore for oneself: the area is not developed for tourism, yet. It is scheduled for development when Punta Cana is finished. Between Enriquillo and Pedernales the beaches are all sandy.

William E Rainey, of Berkeley, California, writes: "South from Barahona between Baoruco and Enriquillo there is wet tropical forest with rushing mountain streams and fruit stands in little roadside settlements. At Enriquillo you enter the Barahona Peninsula lowlands and the terrain grows markedly drier. Continuing W from Oviedo to Pedernales the road is in good condition and the surrounding habitat, particularly near Pedernales, is tropical thorn scrub with abundant cacti growing on karstic limestone.

"The entire country is dotted with checkpoints adjacent to roadside military installations; at most of these the traffic is simply waved through. At the checkpoint in Pedernales (perhaps because gringos were an anomaly there) there were brief interrogations each time we passed (with automatic weapons pointed at us by uniformed teenagers). The last time we passed this point, one of them initiated a detailed search of our gear. Fortunately, this entertainment was cut short by a senior officer who apologized. It was, on balance, a minor aggravation, but one likely to be experienced by travellers near the Haitian border."

Pedernales is the most westerly town of the republic, on the Haitian border. Beautiful beaches include Cabo Rojo and Bahía de las Aguilas, where there is abundant fishing. Here is the Parque Nacional Jaragua in which are the islands Beata and Alto Velo; many iguanas.

Inland from Barahona, near the Haitian border, is ***Lago Enriquillo***, whose waters, 30m below sea level, are three times saltier than the sea. It has a wealth of wild life including crocodiles (best seen in the morning), iguanas and flamingoes. The crocodiles and iguanas can best be seen on the largest of the three islands in the lake, which make up the Cabritos National Park (see **Flora and Fauna** above), which is also where the crocodiles lay their eggs and spend their nights. A large colony of flamingoes overwinters at the lake. You need to purchase a Dirección Nacional de Parques (DNP) permit (US$3.95) to visit the island and only groups with a guide are permitted to go there (the boat crossing can be anything from US$25 to US$80). The two smaller islands are Barbarita and La Islita. To visit the lake it is best to have one's own transport if short of time because, even though public transport runs both on the N and S shores, there is no guarantee of travelling on (or returning) the same day.

If not in one's own car, you can either take a tour from the capital (eg Martisant, T 585-7887, US$54 pp in a group, or contact Ecoturisa or the DNP), or take a *guagua* from Av Duarte y Av 27 de Febrero to Neiba, US$2 (also reached by *guagua* from Barahona, US$1.65), and

then make a connection for La Descubierta, US$1. Alternatively take a bus from Santo Domingo to Jimaní (US$5, La Experiencia and Riviera companies; the journey takes 8 hrs) and get off at La Descubierta. Before Neiba is Galván, in a banana-growing area; the landscape is very flat (very depressing on the rare occasions that it rains). **Neiba** is known for its grapes, sold on the main square in season; *Hotel Comedor Babei* on square, *Hotel Comedor Dania* on a street off the road going E out of town. Between Galván and Neiba is Balneario Las Marías.

The road around the lake is fully paved. A portion of the Parque Nacional Isla Cabritas is on the N shore at La Azufrada, before La Descubierta. At ***La Azufrada*** is a swimming pool of sulphurous water, good for the skin. The pool is clean but the surroundings are littered. A path along the beach gives views of the lake and of Las Caritas, a line of rocks with precolumbian petroglyphs (an even better place to see them is signposted on the road). ***La Descubierta***, at the NW end, is a pleasant village with a celebrated *balneario*, Las Barías. The water is very cold; it is surprising how such an arid area can produce so much water to feed the lake. It is the best place on the lake to stay (one *pensión* can be found in the street behind the central park, no sign, it is blue, US$8, mosquito net, shared bath). After La Descubierta are the springs and *balneario* of Bocas del Chacón (a *parador* is under construction).

Jimaní, at the western end of the lake (not on the shore) is about 2 km from the Haitian border. It is a spread out town of single-storey housing; *Hotel Quisqueya*, several informal *dormitorios*, *Hotel Jimaní* on square. *Restaurant Los Lagos*, Duarte y Restauración, excellent *chivo y gandules* (goat and beans), also disco *Krystal*. Cabins are being built on the road into town from the lake's N shore. If you go to the border you will see queues of trucks waiting to cross; Haitians sell Barbancourt rum and perfumes. Customs officers in Jimaní are not above taking items from your luggage. The road around the S side of the lake goes through El Limón and La Zurza, another sulphurous *balneario*. From the lake to Barahona, the road goes through Duvergé, La Colonia (with a statue of Enriquillo, "the first fighter for independence in the New World"; he was a cacique whose land stretched from Haiti to Azua and who fought against the Spaniards) and Cabral. At Cabral is a turning marked Polo; the road climbs to a spot, with good views of Lago Rincón, where the road appears to slope upwards, but if you put your car in neutral, or place a ball or can on the road it seems to run uphill. The place is called the *Polo Magnético*; university studies have shown it to be an optical illusion, but it is a source of great discussion. Get a local to show you the best spots. From Cabral the road runs through very dry, low-lying land (there is a project to protect the dry forest, also experimental agricultural projects).

San Juan de la Maguana, in a rich agricultural area, is on the main road to the Haitian border at Comendador. Soldiers frequently patrol this route. Visit the Corral de Los Indios, an ancient Indian meeting ground several km N of the San Juan. (Hotels: *Tamarindo*, T 541-2211; *Maguana*, T 557-2244, US$15 or so.)

INFORMATION FOR VISITORS

● **Documents**

Citizens of the following countries do not need a tourist card to enter the Dominican Republic: Argentina, Austria, Denmark, Ecuador, Finland, Greece, Israel, Italy, Japan, Liechtenstein, Norway, South Korea, Spain, Sweden, UK, Uruguay. All others need a tourist card, which costs US$10, purchased from consulates, tourist of-fices, airlines on departure (eg American at Miami), or at the airport on arrival. The time limit on tourist cards is two months, but if necessary extensions are obtainable from Immigration, Huacal Building, Santo Domingo (T 685-2505/2535). The easiest method of extending a tourist card is simply to pay the fine (RD$10/US$0.80 for each month over 2 months) at the airport when leaving. Check all entry requirements in advance if possible.

All visitors should have an outward ticket (not always asked for).

● **Customs**

The airport police are on the lookout for illegal drugs. It is also illegal to bring firearms into the country.

Duty-free import of 200 cigarettes or one box of cigars, plus one litre of alcoholic liquor and gift articles to the value of US$100, is permitted. Military-type clothing and food products will be confiscated on arrival. Currency in excess of US$5,000 may not be taken out of the country without special permission.

● **How To Get There By Air**

American and Dominicana fly from Miami and New York; Continental also from New York; Apa also from Miami. American fly daily from Boston; from other US cities, connections in Miami or San Juan, Puerto Rico. Dominicana, Copa and American fly from San Juan. Iberia flies from Madrid several times a week and has connecting flights from most European and Spanish cities, eg Amsterdam, Barcelona, Bilbao, Brussels, Frankfurt, London, Milan, Rome, Zurich. Air France from Paris twice a week; also 3 times a week from Martinique, Guadeloupe, twice from Port-au-Prince (probably suspended 1994), and once a week from Cayenne. Alitalia flies from Rome once a week and TAP from Lisbon twice a week. Martinair flies from Amsterdam once a week. LTU flies once a week from Dusseldorf; Taino Airlines flies once a week from Frankfurt. ALM has flights from Curaçao, Bonaire and Sint Maarten. Aeropostal from Aruba, Curaçao and Santiago de Cuba; Trans-Jamaica Airlines from Kingston and Montego Bay twice a week (Ladeco also from Montego Bay on its route from Santiago de Chile). Copa from Panama City and Guatemala City. Flights from South America: Iberia fly Bogotá-Santo Domingo, also from Lima and Quito twice a week each (Aces also flies from Bogotá); Dominicana, Viasa and Aeropostal fly from Caracas; other capital cities are connected through Miami.

To the international airport at Puerto Plata there are flights from Miami, New Yorko and Puerto Rico by American, also from New York, and Miami Dominicana and Hispaniola Airways. From Amsterdam, Martinair; from Dusseldorf and Hamburg, LTU International; from Frankfurt and Luxembourg, Taino Airways; from Grand Turk and Providenciales, TCA.

● **Airport Information**

There is a departure tax of US$10. In 1993 President Balaguer decreed that tourists should be exempt from baggage checks on arrival. Details of airports are given in the text above.

● **Airline Offices**

In Santo Domingo: Aeropostal, Abraham Lincoln, T 541-9738; Air Canada, Kennedy y Lope de Vega, T 586-0251; Air France, Av George Washington 101, T 686- 8419; ALM, L Navarro 28, T 583-5723; American, El Conde next to Iberia, T 583-0491; Avianca, R Pastoriza 401, T 562-1797; Carnival, T 563-4691/5300/8900; Continental, Edificio IN TEMPO, T 562-6688; Copa, Edificio IN TEMPO, T 562-5824; Dominicana, on El Conde; Iberia, El Conde 401, T 686-9191; Lufthansa, George Washington 353, T 689-9625; TCA, T 586-0286; Viasa, L Navarro 28, T 687-2688.

● **By Sea**

There are cargo and passenger shipping services with New York, New Orleans, Miami and South American countries. Many cruise lines from USA, Canada and Europe call at the Dominican Republic on itineraries to various ports on Caribbean islands or the mainland. Agencies which handle cruises include Emely (T 682-2744, for Festival, Holidays, Jubilee, Sur Viking).

● **Travel To Haiti**

No special permit is needed, just a passport or visa (check if you need one, US$40, half-price if it is not your first visa, takes 3 days). Haitian Embassy, Juan Sánchez Ramírez 33, T 686-5778, Santo Domingo, 0830-1400. By plane (if flying is not suspended) to Port-au-Prince takes ½ hr, US$50 approximately. By bus, two possibilities: a bus goes once a day, sometimes twice, from outside the Haitian embassy, leaving when full, US$18 one way, US$36 return (if it leaves in the afternoon, it stops overnight in Jimaní), the second option is from *Hotel San Tomé*, Calle Santomé, beside Mercado Modelo, Santo Domingo (T 688-5100, ask for Alejandro), US$32. Alternatively, take a minibus to Jimaní from near the bridge over the Río Seco in the centre of Santo Domingo, 6-8 hrs; get a lift up to the Haitian border and then get overcharged by Haitian youths on mopeds who take you across 3 km of no-man's-land for US$3. From Haitian immigration take a lorry-bus to Port-au-Prince, 3-4 hrs, very dusty. If driving to Haiti you must get a vehicle permit at the Foreign Ministry (T 533-1424). The drive from Santo Domingo to Port-au-Prince takes about 6 hrs. Buy gourdes from money changers outside the embassy, or at the border, but no more than US$50-worth, rates are much better in Haiti. Also take US$25 for border taxes, which have to be paid in dollars cash.

● **To Cuba And Puerto Rico**

Emely Tours in Santo Domingo (T 687-7114/18, F 686-0941) run weekly excursions to Cuba, US$500. Details of other options can be found in the morning papers. There are also short cruises to Puerto Rico, eg with Diamond Cruises, for about US$120 pp. To Jamaica, Trans-Jamaican Airlines (T 567-5428/562-5454) twice weekly "Hummingbird" flights to Kingston and Montego Bay, US$250 return (1994).

● **Internal Travel**

Several companies offer **air taxi or charter** services within the Republic, all based at Herrera airport. Alas Nacionales, T 542-6688; Transporte Aéreo SA, T 567-4549; Coturisca, T 567-7211. Dorado Air flies between Santo Domingo and Puerto Plata several times a day on Fri and Sat. Flights go to Santiago, Puerto Plata, Barahona, Portillo and La Romana daily.

Hitchhiking is perfectly possible, though **bus** (*guagua*) services between most towns are efficient and inexpensive. In rural areas it can be easy to find a *guagua* (mini bus or pickup) but they are often filled to the point where you can not move your legs.

There are usually fixed *público* rates (see under Santo Domingo) between cities, so inquire first. Rates are given in the text. Many drivers pack a truly incredible number of passengers in their cars, so the ride is often not that comfortable. If travelling by private taxi, bargaining is very important.

Motorcyclists (*motoconchos*) also offer a taxi service and take several passengers on pillion. In some towns eg Samaná, motoconchas pull 4-seater covered rickshaws. Negotiate fare first. If negotiating transport by **boat**, a *canuco* is a small dugout, a *yola* is a medium-sized rowing boat taking up to 10 passengers, a *bote* takes 20 or more.

● Buses

Services from Santo Domingo: Autobuses Metro (T 566-7126) operate from Av Winston Churchill and Hatuey, near 27 de Febrero and have buses to La Vega (US$2.70), Santiago (US$4.25), Puerto Plata (US$5.75), Samaná (US$6.15), Nagua, Azua, San Juan, San Pedro de Macorís and other points. Caribe Tours (T 221-4422) operates from Av 27 de Febrero at Leopoldo Navarro; most of their services (cheaper than Metro) are in a/c buses, rec (eg US$3.85 to Puerto Plata, US$2.70 to Santiago, or Jarabacoa, US$3.45 to Samaná, US$2.40 to Barahona); they run to all parts except E of Santo Domingo. Transporte del Cibao, opp Parque Enriquillo, to Puerto Plata, cheaper than other companies. Also to Santiago, Terrabús, US$3.85, and El Expreso, cheaper. La Covacha buses leave from Parque Enriquillo (Av Duarte and Ravelo) to the E: Higüey (US$3.55), Nagua, San Pedro de Macorís, Miches, etc. Expresos Moto Saad, Av Independencia near Parque Independencia runs 12 daily buses to Bonao, La Vega and Santiago (US$2). Línea Sur (T 682-7682) runs to San Juan, Barahona, Azua and Haiti. *Guaguas* for Azua, 2 hrs US$2.35, depart from Av Bolívar near Parque Independencia; easy connections in Azua for Barahona, San Juan and Padre las Casas. For bus offices in other towns, see text above.

● Tourist Travel

A number of companies hire vehicles for group travel, which is fairly economical as long as you have a large enough number of friends. For instance Transporte Turístico Tanya, T 565-5691, 24-seat buses to Puerto Plata, US$195; Autobuses Metro, T 566-7126, 54-seaters to Puerto Plata, US$578; Compañia Nacional de Autobuses, T 565-6681, 25, 45 and 60 seaters, US$272, US$315, US$317 respectively to Puerto Plata. Other destinations also served. LC Tours and La Covacha run 30-seat minibus trips to the E of the country, including Samaná. Taxi companies (addresses under Santo Domingo) run trips to towns in the republic, again as examples, US$13.50-14.60 to Boca Chica, or US$100-120 to Puerto Plata.

Martisant, T 585-7887, has tours to the national parks, also group travel, some with overnight stops in a hotel; other companies include Tanya, T 565-5691, Nuevo Mundo, T 685-5615 and Omni Tours, T 565-6591, F 567-4710, or Punta Cana T 686-5797, F 688-0764.

In Puerto Plata, *Connex Caribe*, Plaza Turisol, T 586-6879, F 586-6099, offers a wide variety of tours in town, to Santo Domingo and all over the republic. Many other companies operate tours (some are mentioned, with prices, in the text above).

The Museo de Historia y Geografía in Santo Domingo organizes archaeological and historical tours in the republic, visiting, for example, Cotuí, Bonao, Presa de Hatillo, Sánchez, Samaná, Pozo de Bojolo in Nagua, Lago Enriquillo and other places of interest. The tour is by bus, inc lunch, US$26 pp; T 686-6668.

● Driving

A valid driving licence from your country of origin or an international licence is accepted. Dominicans drive on the right. The main road from Santo Domingo to Puerto Plata, the Carretera Duarte, is very good, but crowded. Also good are the main road from Santo Domingo to the W, as far as Pedernales and Jimaní; similarly good are the main roads to the E, coastal and inland routes to Higüey, the continuation to Punta Cana airport, Hato Mayor to Sabana de la Mar, and most of the NE coastal route from Puerto Plata to Samaná (details in the text above). Other roads and many city streets are in poor condition with lots of potholes, so avoid night driving. The speed limit for city driving is 40 kph, for suburban areas 60 kph and on main roads 80 kph. Service stations generally close at 1800, although there are now some offering 24-hr service (petrol/gasoline costs US$1.60 per gallon). Most police or military posts have "sleeping policemen", speed humps, usually unmarked, outside them. In towns there are often "ditches" at road junctions, which need as much care as humps. The operation of traffic lights depends on electricity supply, unless they are funded by a local business. In towns the lack of a right of way makes junctions difficult; proceed with caution. Local drivers can be erratic; be on the alert. Hand signals mean only "I am about to do something", nothing more specific than that. Beware motorcyclists in towns. At night look out for poorly lighted, or lightless vehicles. There are tolls on all principal roads out of the capital: US$0.08 going E, US$0.04 going W. Road signs are very poor: a detailed map is essential, plus a knowledge of Spanish for asking directions.

Drivers can expect to be stopped by the police at the entrance to and exit from towns (normally brief and courteous), at junctions in towns, or any speed-restricted area. Charges, imaginary or otherwise, are common; often an on-the-spot fine of the price of a beer or two may do the trick. At other times a more serious charge with a visit to the *tribunal* is threatened; be patient and the policeman may offer an on-the-spot fine.

If renting a car, avoid the cheapest companies because their vehicles are not usually trustworthy; it is better to pay more with a well-known agency. Car rental is expensive because of high import tariffs on vehicles (rates are given under **Car Rentals** in Santo Domingo). Credit cards are widely accepted; the cash deposit is normally twice the sum of the contract. The minimum age for hiring a car is 25; maximum period for driving is 90 days.

Mopeds and motorcycles are everywhere and are very noisy. Most beach resorts hire motorcycles for between US$20 and 30 a day. By law, the driver of a motorcycle must wear a crash helmet; passengers are not required to wear one.

● **Accommodation**

Hotels are given under the towns in which they are situated. Note that 5-star hotels charge an average of US$140, plus 23% tax. In aparthotels, the average price is US$130 for two. In more modest guest houses, a weekly or monthly rate, with discount, can be arranged. All hotels charge the 23% tax; the VAT component is 8%.

The better hotels have a high occupancy rate and it is best to book in advance, particularly at holiday times. Standards in the five-star hotels are not equivalent to those, say, in the Bahamas.

● **Food And Drink**

Local dishes include *sancocho* or *salcocho prieto* (a type of stew made of six local meats and vegetables, often including *plátanos*, *ñame* and *yautia*), *mondongo* (a tripe stew), *mofongo*, ground *plátano* with garlic and *chicharrón de cerdo* (pork crackling), usually served with a soup, a side dish of meat and avocado (very filling), *chicharrón de pollo* is small pieces of chicken prepared with lime and oregano, *locrio de cerdo* or *pollo* (meat and rice), *cocido* (a soup of chickpeas, meat and vegetables), *asopao de pollo* or *de camarones*, *chivo* (goat). Also try *pipián*, goats' offal served as a stew. Fish and seafood are good; lobster can be found for as little as US$12. Fish cooked with coconut (eg *pescado con coco*) is popular around Samaná. The salads are often good;

another good side dish is *tostones* (fried and flattened *plátanos*), *fritos verdes* are the same thing. *Plátano* mashed with oil is called *mangú*, often served with rice and beans. Sweet bananas are often called *guineo*. *Moro* is rice and lentils. *Gandules* are green beans, as opposed to *habichuelas*, very good when cooked with coconut. *Quipes* (made of flour and meat) and *pastelitos* (fried dough with meat or cheese inside) can be bought from street vendors; can be risky. *Casabe* is a cassava bread, flat and round, best toasted. *Catibias* are cassava flour fritters with meat. The most common dish is called *bandera dominicana*, white rice, beans, meat/chicken, *plátano* or *yuca* and, in season, avocado. The traveller should be warned that Dominican food is rather on the greasy side; most of the dishes are fried. Local food can often be obtained from private houses, which act as *comedores*. Basic prices, US$3-6.

Juices, or *jugos*, are good; orange is usually called *china*, papaya is *lechosa*, passion fruit is *chinola*. *Agua de coco* is coconut milk, often served cold, straight from the coconut, chilled in an ice box. Local beers, Presidente (the most popular), Quisqueya and Heineken, are excellent. There are also many good rums (the most popular brands are Barceló, Brugal, Bermúdez, Macorix and Carta Vieja). Light rum (*blanco*) is the driest and has the highest proof, usually mixed with fruit juice or other soft drink (*refresco*). Amber (*amarillo*) is aged at least a year in an oak barrel and has a lower proof and more flavour, while dark rum (*añejo*) is aged for several years and is smooth enough, like a brandy, to be drunk neat or with ice and lime. Brugal allows visitors to tour its factory in Puerto Plata, on Avenida Luis Genebra, just before the entrance to the town, and offers free daiquiris. In a discothèque, *un servicio* is a $1/3$ litre bottle of rum with a bucket of ice and *refrescos*. In rural areas this costs US$3-4, but in cities rises to US$15. Imported drinks are very expensive. Many of the main hotels have a 'Happy Hour' from 1700-1900, on a 'two for one' basis, ie two drinks for the price of one with free snacks.

● **Tipping**

In addition to the 10% service and 8% VAT charge in restaurants, it is customary to give an extra tip of about 10% in restaurants, depending on service. Porters receive US$0.50 per bag; taxi drivers, *público* drivers and garage attendants are not usually tipped.

● **Best Buys**

The native amber is sold throughout the country. Larimar, a sea-blue stone, and red and black coral are also available (remember that black coral is protected). Other items which make good souvenirs are leather goods, basketware, weavings and onyx jewellery. The ceramic *muñeca sin rostro* (faceless doll) has become a sort of symbol of the Dominican Republic, at least, as something to take home. There are excellent cigars at very reasonable prices.

● **Note**

There are well-trained guides who speak two or more languages in Santo Domingo, who are courteous and do not push themselves on you. However, outside the historic buildings in Santo Domingo, on the beaches and at other tourist attractions, visitors will be approached by unofficial English-speaking guides, sellers of rum, women or black market pesos. The last three are undoubtedly a rip-off and probably the only value in taking an unofficial guide is to deter others from pestering you (similarly, hiring a lounger chair on the beach). Beware of drug-pushers on the Malecón in Santo Domingo and near the Cathedral in Puerto Plata. Unofficial guides often refuse to give prices in advance, saying "pay what you want" and then at the end, if they are not happy with the tip, they make a scene and threaten to tell the police that the customer had approached them to deal in drugs etc. Guides also collaborate with street money changers to cheat the tourist. On no account change money on the streets. Be careful with "helpers" at the airports, who speed your progress through the queues and then charge US$15-20 for their services. Single men have complained of the massive presence of pimps and prostitutes. Be prepared to say "no" a lot.

It must be stressed that these problems do not occur in rural areas and small towns, where travellers have been impressed with the open and welcoming nature of the Dominicans.

Violent crime against tourists is rare but be careful about thieving and watch your money and valuables. The streets of Santo Domingo are not considered safe after 2300. Purse snatchers on motorcycles operate in cities. The incidence of crime on Boca Chica beach is reported to have risen.

● **Banks**

The Central Bank determines monetary policy. Among the commercial banks in the Republic are Scotiabank (Santo Domingo, Santiago, and Puerto Plata), Chase Manhattan (Santo Domingo and Santiago), Citibank (Santo Domingo

and Santiago), Banco de Reservas, Banco Popular, Banco Metropolitano, Banco Central, Bancrédito, Intercontinental, Banco Dominicano Hispano, Banco Mercantil and others. Thomas Cook Mastercard refund assistant points are Vimenca, Av Abraham Lincoln 306, Santo Domingo, T 532-7381, and the Banco del Comercio Dominicano in Puerto Plata (T586-2350, Duarte y Padre Castellanos) and La Romana (T 556-5151, Trinitaria 59).

● **Currency**

The Dominican peso (RD$) is the only legal tender. The peso is divided into 100 centavos. There are coins in circulation of 1, 5, 10, 25 and 50 centavos, and notes of 1, 5, 10, 20, 50, 100, 500 and 1,000 pesos. In 1991, new legislation outlawed all exchange transactions except those in branches of the major banks. You will be given a receipt and, with this, you can change remaining pesos back into dollars at the end of your visit (maximum 30% of dollars changed; cash obtained against a credit card does not count). Do not rely on the airport bank being open. Most European currencies can be changed at the Banco de Reservas (and some other banks); Scandinavian currencies are very hard to change. The black market usually offers rates higher than the official rate; illegal money changers on the street approach foreigners (do *not* use them, sometimes they work with a policeman who will demand a large bribe not to imprison you). Several banks will give cash against Visa or American Express cards, usually with 5% commission. The exchange rate used in the conversion of prices in this chapter was RD$13=US$1.

● **Health**

It is not advisable to drink tap water. All hotels have bottled water. The supply of drinking water in Santo Domingo was improved in 1992. The local greasy food, if served in places with dubious hygiene, may cause stomach problems. Hepatitis is common. It is also advisable to avoid the midday sun.

● **Climate**

The climate is tropical. The rainy months are May, June, August, September and November. The temperature shows little seasonal change, and varies between 18° and 32°C. Only in December does the temperature fall, averaging about 20°C. Humidity can be high, particularly in coastal areas, making physical activity difficult.

● **Clothing**
Light clothing, preferably cotton, is best all year round. It is recommended to take one formal outfit since some hotels and nightclubs do not permit casual dress.

● **Business Hours**
Offices: 0830-1230, 1430-1830; some offices and shops work 0930-1730 Mon-Fri, 0800-1300 Sat. Banks: 0830-1700 Mon-Fri. Government offices 0730-1430. Shop hours are normally 0800-1900, some open all day Sat and mornings on Sun and holidays. Most shops in tourist areas stay open through the siesta and on Sun.

● **Public Holidays**
New Year's Day (1 January), Epiphany (6 January), Our Lady of Altagracia (21 January), Duarte Day (26 January), Independence Day (27 February), Good Friday (although all Semana Santa is treated as a holiday), Labour Day (1 May), Corpus Christi (60 days after Good Friday), Restoration Day (16 August), Our Lady of Las Mercedes (24 September), Christmas (25 December).

● **Time Zone**
Atlantic Standard Time, 4 hours behind GMT, 1 hour ahead of EST.

● **Useful Addresses**
US Embassy and Consulate, César Nicolás Penson, T (embassy) 221-2171, (consulate) 541-2111; Canada, Máximo Gómez 30, T 685-1136; UK Honorary Consul, Maureen Tejada, St George School, Abraham Lincoln 552, T 586-8464, F 562-5015; Germany, J T Mejía y Calle 37, T 565-8811; France, George Washington 353, T 689-2161; Italy, Manuel Rodríguez Objío 4, T 689-3684; Netherlands, Mayor Enrique Valverde, T 565-5240; Spain, Independencia 1205, T 533-1424; Switzerland, José Gabriel García 26, T 689-4131; Denmark, Duarte Highway, Km 6.5, T 562-5244; Norway, Av Mella 468, T 689-6355; Sweden, Máximo Gómez 31, T 685-2121; Venezuela, Av Anacaona 7, T 535-0514; Colombia, Av Abraham Lincoln 502, T 562-1670; Honduras, P Herrera 9, T 566-5707; Mexico, R Hernández 11, T 565-2565; Israel, P Henríquez Ureña 80, T 686-7359; Jamaica, José Contreras 98, T 532-1079; Japan, Av Winston Churchill, Torre BHD, piso 8, T 567-3365.

● **Places Of Worship**
Roman Catholicism is the predominant religion. There are also Episcopalian, Baptist, Seventh Day Adventist, Presbyterian and Methodist churches in the main towns. There is a synagogue on Avenida Sarasota, Santo Domingo; call the Israeli Embassy (686-7359) for details of services. There is also a synagogue on Av Alejo Martínez in Sosúa, services are held every other Friday night. Voodoo, technically illegal, is tolerated and practised mostly in the western provinces.

● **Electric Current**
110 volts, 60 cycles AC current. American-type, flat-pin plugs are used. There are frequent power cuts, often for several hours, so take a torch with you when you go out at night. Many establishments have their own (often noisy) generators.

● **Weights And Measures**
Officially the metric system is used but business is often done on a pound/yard/US gallon basis. Land areas in cities are measured by square metres, but in the countryside by the *tarea*, one of which equals 624 square metres.

● **Postal Services**
Don't use post boxes, they are unreliable. The postal system as a whole is very slow. For each 10 grams, or fraction thereof, the cost to Europe is 1 peso; to North America, Venezuela, Central America and the Caribbean, 50 centavos; to elsewhere in the Americas and Spain, 70 centavos; to Africa, Australia, Asia and Oceania, RD$1.50. It is recommended to use *entrega especial* (special delivery, with separate window at post offices), for 2 pesos extra, on overseas mail, or better still a courier service (see under Santo Domingo).

● **Telephones**
Operated by the Compañía Dominicana de Teléfonos (Codetel), a subsidiary of GTE. All local calls and overseas calls and faxes to the Caribbean, European Community, US and Canada may be dialled directly from any Codetel office (no collect calls to the UK, but they are available to many other countries). Through Codetel you call abroad either person-to-person or through an operator (more expensive, but you only pay if connected). Calls and faxes may be paid for by credit card. For phone boxes you need 25-centavo coins. Phone calls to the USA cost US$7.85, to Europe US$8.50, to Australia US$9.60 and Argentina US$14.80 (3 mins). AT&T's USA-Direct is available on 1-800-872-2881, US$1.45 for the first minute, US$1.06 additional and US$2.50 service charge. Canada Direct is 1-800-333-0111. Codetel publishes a bilingual Spanish/English

business telephone directory for tourism (a sort of tourist's yellow pages), called the *Dominican Republic Tourist Guide/Guía Turística de la República Dominicana*, which contains a lot of information as well as telephone numbers. Emergency number: 711; information is 1411.

● **Newspapers**

There are 10 daily papers in all, seven in the morning, three in the afternoon. *Listin Diario* has the widest circulation; among the other morning papers are *El Caribe, Hoy, El Siglo* (has good foreign coverage). In the afternoon, *Ultima Hora* and *El Nacional* are published. The English-language *Santo Domingo News*, published every Friday, is available at hotels. It has a sister publication, *Puerto Plata News. La Información*, published in Santiago on weekdays, is a good regional paper carrying both national and international stories.

● **Broadcasting**

There are over 170 local radio stations and 7 television stations. In the N coast area, Radio Fantasia (90.5 FM) is an all-American music station. Also 1 cable TV station broadcasting in English.

● **Maps**

A map of the Dominican Republic, with plans of Santo Domingo, Santiago, Puerto Plata, La Romana, San Pedro de Macorís and Sosúa, is available from bookshops and stationers. Texaco also produce a good (Rand McNally) map of the country, capital and Santiago. Maps tend to be a little optimistic about roads and features.

● **Tourist Information**

The head office of the Secretaría de Estado de Turismo is in the Edificio de Oficinas Gubernamentales, Avenida México esquina 30 de Marzo, Ala "D", near the Palacio Nacional (PO Box 497, T 689-3655/3657, F 682-3806); it publishes a tourism guide called *La Cotica*, which is free (some places in Santo Domingo, around the cathedral, charge US$2.45 for it). There are also offices at Las Américas International Airport, La Unión Airport at Puerto Plata, in Puerto Plata (Malecón 20, T 586-3676), in Santiago (Ayuntamiento, T 582-5885), Jimaní, Samaná and Boca Chica. The Consejo de Promoción Turística (CPT), Desiderio Arias 24, Bella Vista, Santo Domingo, T 535-3276, F 535-7767, promotes the Dominican Republic abroad, under the new name of Dominicana (US mailing address EPS No A-355, PO Box 02-5256, Miami, FL 33102-5256). Asonahores (Asociación Nacional de Hoteles y Restaurantes), Av México 66, T 687-4676, F 687-4727.

Outside the Dominican Republic, there are tourist offices in the **USA**: Time Square Plaza, 11th floor, New York, NY 10036, T (212) 768-2480, F (212) 944-9937; 2355 Salzedo Street, Suite 305, Coral Gables, Miami, Florida 33134, T 444-4592/3, F 444-4845; in **Canada**: 1650 de Maisonneuve Ouest, Suite 302, Montréal, Québec, H3H 2P3, T (514) 933-9008, F 933-2070; in **Puerto Rico**: Metro Tours, Ortegón esq Tabonuco, Caparra Hills, Guaynabo, PR 00657, T (809) 781-8665, F (809) 793-7935; in **Spain**: Núñez de Balboa 37, 4° Izquierda, Madrid 1, T (01) 431-5354; in **Germany**, Voelckerstrasse 24, D-6000 Frankfurt am Main 1, T (49-69) 597-0330, F 590982.

We are most grateful to Dania Goris (Santo Domingo) and Dianne Erdos (Sosúa) for their help with updating the text.

PUERTO RICO

THE COMMONWEALTH OF PUERTO RICO, the smallest and most easterly island of the Greater Antilles, is the first Overseas Commonwealth Territory (defined as a "free and associated State") of the USA. Spanish is the first language but the citizenship is US and English is widely spoken (as is "Spanglish"). In 1993, Spanish and English were made official languages (thereby restoring a 1902 statute which had been amended in 1991 making Spanish the sole official language). *Puerto Rico* lies about 1,600 km SE of Miami between the island of Hispaniola and the Virgin Islands, which give it some shelter from the open Atlantic, and is between longitudes 66° and 67° W and at latitude 18°30 N. Almost rectangular in shape, slightly smaller than Jamaica, it measures 153 km in length (E to W), 58 km in width, and has a total land area of some 8,768 square km.

Old volcanic mountains, long inactive, occupy a large part of the interior of the island, with the highest peak, Cerro de Punta, at 1,338m in the Cordillera Central. North of the Cordillera is the karst country where the limestone has been acted upon by water to produce a series of small steep hills (*mogotes*) and deep holes, both conical in shape. The mountains are surrounded by a coastal plain with the Atlantic shore beaches cooled all the year round by trade winds, which make the temperatures of 28-30°C bearable in the summer. Temperatures in the winter drop to the range 21-26°C and the climate all the year round is very agreeable. Rain falls mainly from May to October, with most precipitation from July to October.

The population is 3.6 million, although about another 2 million Puerto Ricans live in the USA. The country is a strange mixture of very new and very old, exhibiting the open American way of life yet retaining the more formal Spanish influences. This is reflected in the architecture, not just the contrast between the colonial and the modern but also in the countryside, where older buildings sit side by side with concrete schools and dwellings. It is also found in the cuisine, a plethora of fast food restaurants together with local cuisine which has its roots in the same hybrid culture of all the Caribbean. However, if you do not stray beyond the tourist areas around San Juan, you will not experience the real Puerto Rico. Puerto Ricans are sometimes referred to as Boricuas after the Indian name of the island (see below). Second generation Puerto Ricans who were born in New York, but who have returned to the island, are called Nuyoricans. The people are very friendly and hospitable but there is crime, probably because of economic difficulties and unemployment.

History

Columbus, accompanied by a young nobleman, Juan Ponce de León, arrived in Puerto Rico on 19 November 1493. Attracted by tales of gold, Ponce obtained permission to colonize Borinquén, as it was called by the natives. Borinquén meant 'land of the great lord' and was called that because of the belief that the god, Juracan, lived on the highest peak of the island and controlled the weather from there. The word 'hurricane' is derived from this god's name. In 1508 Ponce de León established the first settlement at Caparra, a small village not far from the harbour of San Juan. A year later the Spanish Crown appointed him the first Governor. In 1521, however, the settlement was moved to the present site of Old San Juan as the former site was declared unhealthy. In that year Ponce de León was mortally wounded in the conquest of Florida.

Because of Puerto Rico's excellent location at the gateway to Latin America, it played an important part in defending the Spanish empire against attacks from French, English and Dutch invaders. After the Spanish-American war, Spain ceded the island to the United States in 1898. The inhabitants became US citizens in 1917, with their own Senate and House of Delegates, and in 1948, for the first time, they elected their own Governor, who is authorized to appoint his Cabinet and members of the island's Supreme Court. In 1952 Puerto Rico became a Commonwealth voluntarily associated with the United States.

The island's status is a matter of constant debate. The New Progressive Party (NPP) favours Puerto Rico's full accession to the USA as the 51st state. The Popular Democratic Party (PDP) favours enhancement of the existing Commonwealth status. Pro-independence groups receive less support, the Puerto Rican Independence Party (PIP) struggles to gain seats in Congress. A small guerrilla group, the Macheteros, demands that all US presence be removed from the island. A referendum on Puerto Rico's future status was held in 1991, but

voters rejected the PDP administration's proposals to guarantee that they remain citizens of the USA regardless of any change in Puerto Rico's political status. The 1991 vote was seen as a rejection of the policies of the governing party and Governor Rafael Hernández Colón subsequently decided not to seek re-election in the 1992 elections. The elections were convincingly won by the pro-statehood NPP, who secured 36 seats in the House of Representatives and 20 in the Senate. The PDP won 14 seats in the House and six in the Senate, while the PIP won one in each chamber. An extra two seats were to be added to the opposition representation under a constitutional requirement that no party may hold more than two thirds of the seats in either house. The new Governor, Pedro Rosselló, took office in January 1993. Carlos Romero Barceló, of the NPP, who was Governor 1976-84, won the office of Resident Commissioner in Washington.

In November 1993 another referendum was held on the future political status of the island. Voter turnout was high, at 73.6%, of whom 48.4% voted for Commonwealth Status, 46.2% for statehood and 4.4% for independence. Although the result was close, it was seen as a set-back for the pro-statehood government.

Government

Puerto Rico is a self-governing Commonwealth in association with the USA. The chief of state is the President of the United States of America. The head of government is an elected Governor. There are two legislative chambers: the House of Representatives, 51 seats, and the Senate, 27 seats. Two extra seats are granted in each house to the opposition if necessary to limit any party's control to two thirds. Puerto Ricans do not vote in US federal elections, nor do they pay federal taxes, when resident on the island.

The Economy

Great social and economic progress has been made in the past thirty years, as a result of the "Operation Bootstrap" industrialization programme supported by the US and Puerto Rican governments, which was begun in 1948. Accordingly manufacturing for export has become the most important sector of the economy, in place of agriculture. Until 1976, US Corporations were given tax incentives to set up in Puerto Rico and their profits were taxed only if repatriated. Industrial parks were built based on labour intensive industries to take advantage of Puerto Rico's low wages. In the mid-1970s, however, the strategy changed to attract capital intensive companies with the aim of avoiding the low wage trap. Nowadays about 70% of manufacturing income is repatriated; manufacturing produces about 40% of total output, but only 20% if remittances are excluded, about the same as in the 1950s. Investment has also fallen recently to 17% of gdp, having risen from 15% in 1950 to 30% in 1970.

The principal manufactures are textiles, clothing, electrical and electronic equipment, chemicals and pharmaceuticals. Dairy and livestock production is one of the leading agricultural activities; others are the cultivation of sugar, tobacco, coffee, pineapples and coconut. Tourism is another key element in the economy although it contributes only about 6.5% to gdp. The industry is profitable and a large employer. Visitors spend about US$1.5bn a year. In 1993, 1,189,900 visitors stayed on the island (up over 13% from 1992), while cruise ship arrivals were 968,059 (down 5%). There are several large projects designed to increase tourism. Expansion of the airport will cost US$157mn, while American Airlines is spending US$165mn on a new wing at its interchange hub in the airport. A US$173mn, 600-room hotel is being built on 590 acres

PUERTO RICO: FACT FILE

Geographic

Land area	9,104 sq km
forested	20.0%
pastures	37.7%
cultivated	14.4%

Demographic

Population (1992)	3,581,000
annual growth rate (1987-92)	0.8%
urban	70.7%
rural	29.3%
density	393.3 per sq km
Religious affiliation	
Roman Catholic	85.3%
Birth rate per 1,000 (1990)	18.3
	(world av 27.1)
Death rate per 1,000 (1990)	6.9
	(world av 9.8)

Education and Health

Life expectancy at birth,	
male	72.5 years
female	79.2 years
Infant mortality rate	
per 1,000 live births (1989)	14.3
Physicians (1984)	1 per 433 persons
Hospital beds	1 per 262 persons
Calorie intake as %	
of FAO requirement	na
Population age 25 and over	
with no formal schooling	none
Literate males (over 15)	89.7%
Literate females (over 15)	88.5%

Economic

GNP (1991 market prices)	US$22,831mn
GNP per capita	US$6,429
Public external debt (1991)	US$12,835mn
Tourism receipts (1991)	US$1,445mn
Inflation (annual av 1986-91)	3.5%
Radio	1 per 1.8 persons
Television	1 per 4.4 persons
Telephone	1 per 4.3 persons

Employment

Population economically active (1991)	1,090,000
Unemployment rate	15.2%
% of labour force in	
agriculture	2.9
manufacturing	14.2
construction	4.8
Military forces (US)	3,600

Source *Encyclopaedia Britannica.*

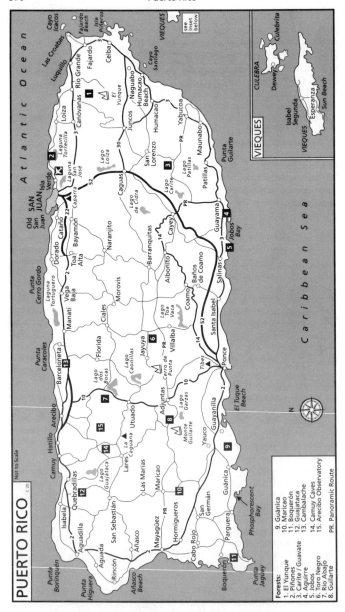

in the Rio Grande – Luquillo area E of San Juan, which will include two golf courses and other sporting facilities. A US$125mn restoration project in the waterfront district of old San Juan will include a 242-room hotel, casino and conference venue.

Despite the progress made to industrialize the country, the economy has suffered from US budget cuts. Some 30% of all spending on gnp originates in Washington and high unemployment is possible because of food stamps and other US transfers. Migration is a safety valve, and there are more Puerto Ricans living in New York than San Juan. The economy depends heavily on the tax incentives (known as Section 936) given to US mainland companies and on federal transfers. Puerto Rico is also used to channel loans to other Caribbean and Central American countries under the Caribbean Basin Initiative (CBI). President Clinton aimed to cut the Section 936 tax exemption for US companies and introduced legislation to Congress in 1993 to replace it with a more modest tax credit linked to wages paid by those companies in Puerto Rico rather than to profits. This was also likely to reduce sharply the amount of finance available to other CBI countries. It is estimated that 100,000 Puerto Ricans are employed by companies operating under Section 936 (of which 23,000 are in pharmaceuticals) and another 200,000 are indirectly employed. By 1993, Section 936 funds had been invested in nine CBI countries, with US685mn provided for 46 projects and about 13,000 jobs. President Clinton's proposals were modified by the US Senate Finance Committee after much lobbying by Caribbean and Central American governments and companies, although the outcome represented a reduction in US budgetary spending.

The negotiations between the USA and Mexico for the North American Free Trade Agreement (NAFTA) also have implications for Puerto Rico because of competition for jobs and investment. Although wage levels are lower in Mexico, Section 936 gives companies in Puerto Rico an advantage in pharmaceuticals and hi-tec industries. In low-skill labour-intensive manufacturing, such as clothing and footwear, Mexico has the advantage. Puerto Rico currently employs 30,000 in the clothing industry.

Culture

Puerto Rico may be part of the United States, but its **music and dance**, and indeed its soul, are wholly Latin American. A visitor who sticks to the hotels and beaches will be largely subjected to rock music and salsa and to hear the real Puerto Rican music you should head for the countryside and especially to the hilly interior, the "Montaña". The island was Spanish until 1898 and the oldest musical tradition is that of the nineteenth century Danza, associated particularly with the name of Juan Morel Campos and his phenomenal output of 549 compositions. This is European-derived salon music for ballroom dancing, slow, romantic and sentimental. The Institute of Puerto Rican Culture sponsors an annual competition for writers of danzas for the piano during the Puerto Rican Danza Week in May. The peasants of the interior, the Jíbaros, sing and dance the Seis, of Spanish origin, in its many varied forms, such as the Seis Chorreao, Seis Zapateao, Seis Corrido and Seis Bombeao. Other variants are named after places, like the Seis Cagueño and Seis Fajardeño. Favoured instruments are the *cuatro* and other varieties of the guitar, the *bordonúa*, *tiple*, *tres* and *quintillo*, backed by *güiro* (scraper), *maracas*, *pandereta* (tambourine) and *bomba* (drum) to provide rhythm. One uniquely Puerto Rican phenomenon is the singer's "La-Le-Lo-Lai" introduction to the verses, which are in Spanish 10-line *décimas*. The beautiful Aguinaldos are sung at Christmastime, while the words of the Mapeyé express the Jíbaro's somewhat tragic view of life. Many artists have recorded the mountain music, notably El Gallito de Manatí, Ramito, Chuito el de Bayamón, Baltazar Carrero and El Jíbarito de Lares. A popular singer is Andrés Jiménez, 'El Jíbaro', whose rustic songs of Puerto Rican folklore were honoured at Christmas 1993 by a concert with the Symphonic Orchestra of Puerto Rico and the Choir of the Conservatorio de Música de Puerto Rico, in which many traditional instruments were used.

Puerto Rico's best-known musical genre is the Plena, ironically developed by a black couple from Barbados, John Clark and Catherine George, known as "Los Ingleses", who lived in the La Joya del Castillo neighbourhood of Ponce during the years of the First World War. With a four-line stanza and refrain in call-and-response between the "Inspirador" (soloist) and chorus, the rhythm is distinctly African and the words embody calypso-style commentaries on social affairs and true-life incidents. Accompanying instruments were originally tambourines, then accordions and *güiros*, but nowadays include guitars, trumpets and clarinets. The Plena's most celebrated composer and performer was Manuel A Jiménez, known as "Canario".

There are relatively few black people in Puerto Rico and the only specifically black music is the Bomba, sung by the "Cantaor" and chorus, accompanied by the drums called *buleadores* and *subidores* and naturally also danced. The Bomba can be seen and heard at its best in the island's only black town of Loiza Aldea at the Feast of Santiago in late July. Rafael Cepeda and his family are the best known exponents.

For a modern interpretation of traditional music, recordings by the singer/composer Tony Croatto are highly recommended, while Rafael Cortijo and his Combo have taken the Plena beyond the confines of the island into the wider world of Caribbean salsa.

There are several music festivals each year, celebrating different styles and forms, including a Jazzfest in May and the Casals Music Festival in June.

The Jíbaro, mentioned above, is a common figure in Puerto Rican literature. The origin of the name is unknown, but it refers to the "campesino del interior", a sort of Puerto Rican equivalent to the gaucho, native, but with predominantly hispanic features. The Jíbaro, as a literary figure, first appeared in the 19th century, with Manuel Alonso Pacheco's *El gíbaro* emerging as a cornerstone of the island's literature. In 29 "scenes", Alonso attempted both to describe and to interpret Puerto Rican life; he showed a form of rural life about to disappear in the face of bourgeois progress. The book also appeared at a time (1849) when romanticism was gaining popularity. Prior to this period, there had been a definite gulf between the educated letters, chronicles and memoires of the 16th to 18th centuries and the oral traditions of the people. These included "coplas", "décimas", "aguinaldas" (see above) and folk tales. The Jíbaro has survived the various literary fashions, from 19th century romanticism and "realismo costumbrista" (writing about manners and customs), through the change from Spanish to US influence, well into the 20th century.

One reason for this tenacity is the continual search for a Puerto Rican identity. When, in 1898, Spain relinquished power to the USA, many Puerto Ricans sought full independence. Among the writers of this time were José de Diego and Manuel Zeno Gandía. The latter's series of four novels, *Crónicas de un mundo enfermo* (*Garduña* – 1896, *La charca* – 1898, *El negocio* – 1922, *Redentores* – 1925), contain a strong element of social protest. As the series progresses, a new theme is added to that of local economic misery, emigration to New York, which booms after 1945. For a variety of domestic reasons, many fled the island to seek adventures, happiness, material wealth in the United States. While some writers and artists in the 1930s and 1940s, eg Luis Lloréns Torres, tried to build a kind of nationalism around a mythical, rural past, others still favoured a complete separation from the colonialism which had characterized Puerto Rico's history. For a while, the former trend dominated, but by the 1960s the emigré culture had created a different set of themes to set against the search for the Puerto Rican secure in his/her national identity. These included, on the one hand, the social problems of the islander in New York, shown, for example, in some of the novels of Enrique A Laguerre, *Trópico en Manhattan* by Guillermo Cotto Thorner, stories such as "Spiks" by Pedro Juan Soto, or plays like René Marqués' *La carreta*. On the other there is the americanization of the island, the figure of the "piti-yan-qui" (the native Puerto Rican who admires and flatters his North American neighbour) and the subordination of the agricultural to a US-based, industrial economy. Writers after 1965 who have documented this change include Rosario Ferré and the novelist and playwright, Luis Rafael Sánchez. The latter's *La guaracha del Macho Camacho* (1976), an alliterative, humorous novel, revolves around a traffic jam in a San Juan taken over by a vastly popular song, "La vida es una cosa fenomenal", a far cry from the Jíbaro's world.

Flora and Fauna

Although less than 1% of the island is virgin forest, there are several forest reserves designed to protect plants and wildlife. In El Yunque Tropical Rain Forest (called The Caribbean National Forest) there are an estimated 240 types of tree (26 indigenous), and many other plants, such as tiny wild orchids, bamboo trees, giant ferns, and trumpet trees. The forest falls into four overlapping types: at the lowest level the rain forest, then thicket, palm forest and, at the highest altitudes, dwarf forest. The total area is 28,000 acres. Several marked paths (quite easy, you could walk 2-3 in a day, no guide needed), recreational areas and information areas have been set up, but note that Route 191, which some maps show traversing the forest, is closed beyond the Sierra Palma Visitors' Centre and there is no evidence of any intention to reopen it. Hurricane Hugo in 1989 did a great deal of damage to the forest and it could take 15 years before El Yunque is back to normal. It is also home to the Puerto Rican parrot, which has been saved from extinction. It is often seen around the picnic area behind the Visitors' Centre. Hurricane Hugo nearly wiped out the whole population and some say only 24 pairs are left alive. The whole forest is a bird sanctuary. Other forest areas, some of which are mentioned in the text below are Guajataca in the NW; Río Abajo, between Arecibo and Utuado; Maricao, Guilarte, Toro Negro and Carite (Guavate), all on the transinsular Panoramic Route. Mangroves are protected in Aguirre Forest, on the S coast near Salinas, at the Jobos Bay National Estuarine Research Reserve, at the W end of Jobos Bay from Aguirre, and at Piñones Forest, E of San Juan (also hit by Hurricane Hugo). Unlike the N coast mangroves, those on the S coast tend to die behind the outer fringe because not enough water is received to wash away the salt. This leaves areas of mud and skeletal trees which, at times of spring tide, flood and are home to many birds. In winter, many ducks stop on their migration routes at Jobos. Also at Jobos Bay, manatíes and turtles can be seen. A short boardwalk runs into the mangroves at Jobos, while at Aguirre a man runs catamaran trips to the offshore cays (US$4-6), and there are some good fish restaurants; take Route 7710. For Jobos Bay take Route 703, to Las Mareas de Salinas (marked Mar Negro on some maps). Before going to Jobos, contact the office at Jobos, Box 1170, Guayama, Puerto Rico 00655, T 864-0105, or 724-8774 in San Juan.

The largest number of bird species can be found at Guánica Forest, W of Ponce, which is home to several unique and endangered species. (*Las aves de Puerto Rico*, by Virgilio Biaggi, University of Puerto Rico, 1983, US$12.95, is available in San Juan, eg the bookshop in Fort San Cristóbal.) Guánica's dry forest vegetation is unique and the Forest has been declared an International Biosphere Reserve by UNESCO. Most of the trails through these and other forests are now marked, but it may be advisable to contact the wardens for directions before wandering off. One of the most notable creatures on Puerto Rico is the inch-long tree frog called a *coquí*, after the two-tone noise it makes.

Puerto Rico also has some of the most important caves in the W hemisphere. The Río Camuy runs underground for part of its course, forming the third largest subterranean river in the world. Near Lares, on Route 129, Km 9.8, the Río Camuy Cave Park has been established by the Administración de Terrenos (PO Box 3767, San Juan, T 893-3100), where visitors are guided through one cave and two sinkholes, open Wednesday to Sunday, and holidays 0800-1600, last trip 1545, US$2 for adults, US$1 for children, highly recommended, but entry is limited. There are fine examples of stalactites, stalagmites and, of course, plenty of bats. Also close is the privately-owned Cueva de Camuy, Route 486, Km 11; much smaller and less interesting, with guided tours, the area also has a swimming pool and waterslide, amusements, café, ponies, go-karts, entertainments, entry US$1, children US$0.50, open daily 0900-1700 (till 2100 Sunday). Also close is Cueva del Infierno, to which 2-3 hour tours can be arranged by phoning 898-2723. About 2,000 caves have been discovered; in them live 13 species

of bat (but not in every cave), the *coquí*, crickets, an arachnid called the *guavá*, and other species. For full details contact the Speleological Society of Puerto Rico (Sepri).

Beaches and Watersports

Swimming from most beaches is safe; the best beaches near San Juan are those at Isla Verde in front of the main hotels; Luquillo to the E of San Juan is less crowded and has a fine-sand beach from where there are good views of El Yunque. The N coast Atlantic sea is rougher than the S waters, particularly in winter; some beaches are semi-deserted. There are 13 *balneario* beaches round the island where lockers, showers and parking places are provided for a small fee. Some have cabins, tent sites or trailer sites. *Balnearios* are open Tuesday-Sunday 0900-1700 in winter and 0800-1700 in summer.

The shallow waters are good for snorkelling and while a boat is needed to reach deeper water for most scuba diving, divers can walk in at Isabela. Visibility is not quite as good as in some other islands because of the large number of rivers flowing out to the sea, but is generally around 70 feet. However, an advantage is that the fresh water attracts a large number of fish. Manatees can occasionally be seen and hump back whales migrate through Puerto Rican waters in the autumn. There are many companies offering boat dives, equipment rental and diving instruction, including Coral Head Divers, Marina de Palmas, *Palmas del Mar Resort*, Humacao (T 850-7208, F 850-4445, US$50-75), Mundo Submarino, Laguna Gardens, Isla Verde (T 791-5764, US$35-50), in San Juan, Carib Aquatic Adventures, San Juan Bay Marina, Miramar, (T 724-1882, 765-7444, F 721-3127, US$90-110). Diving also at some of the larger hotels. Check how many divers are taken on the boats, some companies cater for small groups of 6-7 divers, but several of the larger operations take out parties of 40 or 80. *Qué Pasa* lists all the operators approved by the Tourism Company.

The most popular beaches for surfing are the Pine Beach Grove in Isla Verde (San Juan), Jobos (near Isabela in the NW, not the S coast bay), Surfer and Wilderness beaches in the former Ramey Field air base at Punta Borinquén, N of Aguadilla and Punta Higuero, Route 413 between Aguadilla and Rincón on the W coast. Several international surfing competitions have been held at Surfer and Wilderness. The Condado lagoon is popular for windsurfing (there is a windsurfing school in Santurce, Lisa Penfield, 2A Rambla del Almirante, T 796-2188, with rentals at US$25 per hour and lessons starting at US$45 for 1½ hrs), as is Boquerón Bay and Ocean Park beach.

Puerto Rico's coastline is protected in many places by coral reefs and cays which are fun to visit and explore. Sloops can be hired at US$60 pp a day, with crew, and hold 6 passengers (eg Captain Jayne at Fajardo, T 791-5174).

There are three marinas at Fajardo, the Club Náutico at Miramar and another at Boca de Cangrejos in Isla Verde (both in San Juan) and one at the *Palmas del Mar Resort* near Humacao. There is a marina for fishing motor launches at Arecibo. The first phase of an ambitious marina project at Puerto del Rey, Fajardo, opened late 1988 and a second stage of expansion was under construction in 1994. Sailing is popular, with winds of about 10-15 knots all year round. Craft of all sizes are available for hire. There are several racing tournaments; a major international regatta is the Discover the Caribbean series in September and October. Power boats appeal to the Puerto Rican spirit and there are a lot of races, held mostly off the W coast from Mayagüez Bay to Boquerón Bay. A huge crowd collects for the Caribbean Offshore Race, with professionals and celebrities participating.

Deep-sea fishing is popular and more than 30 world records have been broken in Puerto Rican waters, where blue and white marlin, sailfish, wahoo, dolphin, mackerel and tarpon, to mention a few, are a challenge to the angler. An international bill fish competition is held in September, one of the biggest tournaments in the Caribbean. Fishing boat charters are available: eg Mike Benítez Fishing Charters, Inc, at the Club Náutico de San Juan, PO Box 5141, Puerta de Tierra, San Juan, PR 00906, T 723-2292 (till 2100), 724-6265 (till 1700), F 725-1336, prices from US$650 for a full day. You can also fish in the many lakes inland. Contact the Department of Natural Resources (T 722-5938) for details.

Other Sports

Golf There are 14 golf courses around the island of which six are professionally designed championship courses. The *Cerromar* and *Dorado Beach* hotels in Dorado have excellent 36-hole championship golf courses; among the 18-hole courses, *Berwind Country Club* accepts non-members on Tuesday, Thursday and Friday, *Palmas del Mar* (Humacao), Club Riomar (Río Grande), and Punta Borinquén (Aguadilla, 9 holes) all have golf pros and are open to the public. **Tennis** Over 100 tennis courts are available, mostly in the larger hotels. There are also 17 lit public courts in San Juan's Central Park, open daily, with tennis pro, T 722-1646. The *Palmas del Mar* resort, at Humacao, has 20 courts. **Cockfighting** The season is from 1 November to 31 August. This sport is held at the new, air-conditioned Coliseo Gallístico in Isla Verde, near the *Holiday Inn* (Route 37, Km 1.5). Saturday 1300-1900, T 791-1557/6005 for times. Admission from US$4 to US$10. **Horse Racing** El Comandante, Route 3, Km 5.5, Canóvanas, is one of the hemisphere's most beautiful race courses. Races are held all the year round (Wednesday, Friday, Sunday and holidays). First race is at 1430. Wednesday is

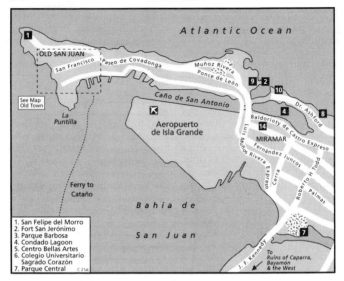

Atlantic Ocean

OLD SAN JUAN
San Francisco | Paseo de Covadonga
See Map
Old Town
La
Puntilla

Muñoz Rivera
Ponce de León

Caño de San Antonio

Aeropuerto
de Isla Grande

Baldorioty de Castro Expreso
Dr. Ashford
MIRAMAR
Fernández Juncos
Muñoz Rivera Expreso
Cerra
Roberto H. Todd
Palmas

Ferry to
Cataño

Bahía de

San Juan

To
Ruins of Caparra,
Bayamón
& the West

J. F. Kennedy

1. San Felipe del Morro
2. Fort San Jerónimo
3. Parque Barbosa
4. Condado Lagoon
5. Centro Bellas Artes
6. Colegio Universitario
   Sagrado Corazón
7. Parque Central   C 21aL

ladies' day. Children under 12 not admitted at any time. **Riding** On mountain trails or beaches, riding is a good way to see the island. Puerto Rico also prides itself on its paso fino horses. There are over 7,000 registered paso fino horses on the island and several horse shows are held throughout the year which are well worth attending. The two best known are the Dulce Sueño Fair, Guayama, the first weekend in March, and the Fiesta La Candelaria, Manatí, the first weekend in February. At Palmas del Mar, Humacao, there is an equestrian centre T 852-6000 ext 12721) which offers beach rides and riding and jumping lessons. Hacienda Carabalí (T 889-5820, 887-4954), offers beach or hill riding and has paso fino horses. **Polo** is becoming popular and the Ingenio Polo Club hosts the Rolex Polo Cup on its 25-acre grounds by the Loiza River in March.

Popular spectator sports are boxing and baseball (at professional level, also a winter league at San Juan stadium, US$4 for a general seat, US$5 box seat, Tuesday is Ladies' Night), basketball, volleyball and beach volleyball. Running, competitive and non-competitive, is also popular. Puerto Rico is a member of the Olympic Committee. The island is making a bid to host the 2004 Olympic Games.

SAN JUAN

Founded in 1510, **San Juan**, the capital (population about 1 million) spreads several km along the N coast and also inland. The nucleus is Old San Juan, the old walled city on a tongue of land between the Atlantic and San Juan bay. It has a great deal of charm and character, a living museum; the Institute of Culture restores and renovates old buildings, museums and places of particular beauty. The narrow streets of Old San Juan, some paved with small grey-blue blocks which were cast from the residues of iron furnaces in Spain and brought over as ships' ballast, are lined with colonial churches, houses and mansions, in a very good state of repair and all painted different pastel colours. Electric trolley buses, and small

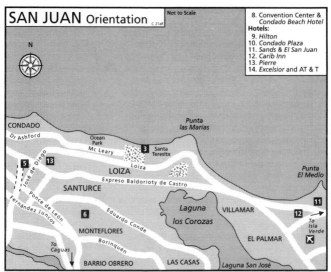

SAN JUAN Orientation

8. Convention Center & Condado Beach Hotel
Hotels:
9. Hilton
10. Condado Plaza
11. Sands & El San Juan
12. Carib Inn
13. Pierre
14. Excelsior and AT & T

yellow buses run around the old city all day, free, *paradas* (stops) are marked. They go to the forts and run every 5-8 mins from 0730-1930, reducing in frequency after then.

Some of the restored and interesting buildings to visit include La Fortaleza, the Governor's Palace, built between 1533 and 1540 as a fortress against Carib attacks but greatly expanded in the 19th century (open 0900-1600 Monday-Friday; guided tours in English every hour, in Spanish every half hour, tours of second floor 0930, 1000, 1030 and 1050, T 721-7000 ext 2211; the Cathedral, built in the 16th century but extensively restored in the 19th and 20th, in which the body of Juan Ponce de León rests in a marble tomb (open daily 0630-1700); the tiny Cristo Chapel with its silver altar, built after a young man competing in 1753 in a horse-race during the San Juan festival celebrations plunged with his horse over the precipice at that very spot (open Tuesday 1000-1600), next to it is the aptly-named Parque de las Palomas, where the birds perch on your hand to be

fed; San Felipe del Morro, built in 1591 to defend the entrance to the harbour, and the 11-hectare Fort San Cristóbal, completed in 1772 to support El Morro and to defend the landward side of the city, with its five independent units connected by tunnels and dry moats, rising 46m above the ocean—good views of the city (both open daily 0800-1800, admission free); the new Plaza del Quinto Centenario, inaugurated on 12 October 1992 to commemorate the 500th anniversary of Columbus' landing, a modernistic square on several levels with steps leading to a central fountain with hundreds of jets (good view of El Morro, the cemetery and sunsets); the restored Cuartel de Ballajá, once the barracks for Spanish troops and their families, also inaugurated 12 October 1992 with the Museum of the Americas on the second floor which will trace the cultural development of the history of the New World (open Tuesday-Sunday, 1000-1400, admission free); the Dominican Convent built in the early 16th century, later used as a headquarters by the US Army and now the office of the

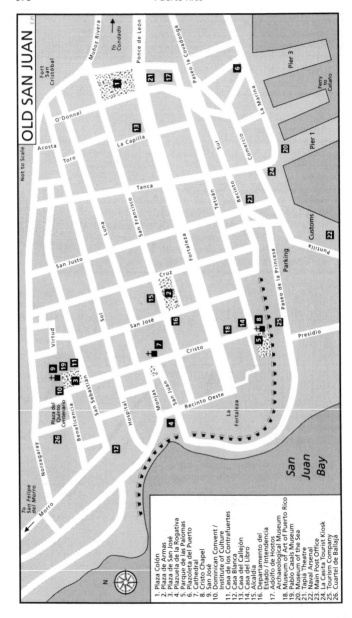

OLD SAN JUAN

Not to Scale

To Condado

To San Felipe del Morro

San Juan Bay

1. Plaza Colón
2. Plaza de Armas
3. Plaza de San José
4. Pazuela de la Rogativa
5. Parque de las Palomas
6. Plazoleta del Puerto
7. Cathedral
8. Cristo Chapel
9. San José
10. Dominican Convent / Institute of Culture
11. Casa de los Contrafuertes
12. Casa Blanca
13. Casa del Callejón
14. Casa del Libro
15. Alcaldía
16. Departamento del Estado / Intendencia
17. Adolfo de Hostos Archaeological Museum
18. Museum of Art of Puerto Rico
19. Pablo Casals Museum
20. Museum of the Sea
21. Tapiá Theatre
22. Naval Arsenal
23. Mail Post Office
24. La Casita Tourist Kiosk
25. Tourism Company
26. Cuartel de Ballajá

Institute of Culture, with a good art gallery (Chapel museum open Wednesday-Sunday, 0900-1200, 1300-1630; cultural events are sometimes held in the patio, art exhibitions in the galleries, T 724-0700); the 16th-century San José church, the second oldest church in the Western Hemisphere and once the family church of Ponce de León's descendants, Ponce was buried here until moved to the Cathedral in the 20th century (open Monday-Saturday 0830-1600, Sunday mass at 1200); the early 18th century Casa de los Contrafuertes believed to be the oldest private residence in the old city, now has periodic art exhibitions on the second floor and a small pharmacy museum with 19th century exhibits on the ground floor (open Wednesday-Sunday, 0900-1630, T 724-5949); the Casa Blanca, built in 1523 by the family of Ponce de León, who lived in it for 250 years until it became the residence of the Spanish and then the US military commander-in-chief, and is now a historical museum which is well worth a visit (open daily 0900-1200, 1300-1630, guided tours Monday-Friday by appointment, T 724-4102); the Alcaldía, or City Hall, built 1604-1789 (open Monday-Friday 0800-1600 except holidays, T 724-7171 ext 2391); the Intendencia, formerly the Spanish colonial exchequer, a fine example of 19th century Puerto Rican architecture, now houses Puerto Rico's State Department (open Monday-Friday 0800-1200, 1300-1630, T 722-2121); the naval arsenal was the last place in Puerto Rico to be evacuated by the Spanish in 1898, exhibitions are held in 3 galleries (open Wednesday-Sunday, 0900-1200, 1300-1630, T 724-5949); and the Casa del Callejón, a restored 18th-century house containing two colonial museums, the architectural and the Puerto Rican Family (both closed for restoration in 1992, T 725-5250).

Museums

Apart from those in historic buildings listed above, there are the Pablo Casals Museum beside San José church, with Casals' cello and other memorabilia (Tuesday-Saturday 0930-1730, Sunday 1300-1700, T 723-9185); the San Juan Museum of Art and History, Norzagaray y MacArthur, built in 1855 as a marketplace (closed for repairs in 1993); the Casa del Libro is an 18th century house on Calle Cristo, has a collection of rare books, including some over 400 years old (Tuesday-Saturday, except holidays, 1100-1630, T 723-0354); and the Museum of the Sea on Pier One, with a collection of maritime instruments and models (open when the pier is open for cruise ships, T 725-2532). Another museum in the old city is a military museum at Fort San Jerónimo (open Wednesday-Sunday, 0930-1200, 1300-1630, T 724-5949).

The metropolitan area of San Juan includes the more modern areas of Santurce, Hato Rey, and Río Piedras. Río Piedras was founded in 1714 but became incorporated into San Juan in 1951. On the edge of Río Piedras, the gardens and library of the former governor, Luis Muñoz Marín, are open to the public, Tuesday-Saturday 0900-1300 (T 755-7979), with a museum showing his letters, photos and speeches.

The University of Puerto Rico at Río Piedras is in a lovely area. The University Museum (open Monday-Friday, 0900-2100, weekends 0900-1500, T 764-0000, ext 2452) has archaeological and historical exhibitions, and also monthly art exhibitions. The Botanical Garden at the Agricultural Experiment Station has over 200 species of tropical and subtropical plants, a bamboo promenade, an orchid garden, and a lotus lagoon (open Tuesday-Sunday, 0900-1630, T 766-0740).

Hato Rey is the financial district of San Juan nicknamed "the Golden Mile". The Sacred Heart University with the Museum of Contemporary Puerto Rican Art (Tuesday-Saturday 0900-1600, Sunday 1100-1700, T 268-0049) is in Santurce, as is the modern Fine Arts Center, opened in 1981, which has theatres and halls at the corner of De Diego and Ponce de León (T 724-4751). The residential area Miramar has several moderately priced hotels as well as some expensive ones. Miramar is separated from the Atlantic coast by the Condado lagoon and the Condado beach area, where the luxury hotels, casinos, night clubs and restaurants are concentrated. From Condado the beach front is built up eastwards through Ocean Park, Santa Teresita, Punta Las Marías and Isla Verde. Building is expanding along the narrow strip beyond Isla Verde, between the sea and the airport. Along this road, Avenida Boca de Cangrejos, there are lots of food trucks selling barbequed specialities.

Directions

Up until the 1950s tramcars ran between Río Piedras and Old San Juan along Avs Ponce de León and Fernández Juncos. To this day directions are given by Paradas, or tram stops, so you have to find out where each one is.

Excursions

A ferry, Old San Juan (Pier Two) – Hato Rey, Cataño, crosses every half hour, 0600-2100, T 788-1155, US$0.50, to Cataño where you can catch a *público* (US$1 pp), or bus to the Bacardi rum distillery. There are free conducted tours around the plant Monday-Saturday, 0930-1530, travelling from one building to the next by a little open motor train, T 788-1500.

On Route 2, shortly before Bayamón, is the island's earliest settlement, Caparra, established by Ponce de León in 1508. Ruins of the fort can still be seen and there is a Museum of the Conquest and Colonization of Puerto Rico (open daily 0900-1600, T 781-4795).

THE INTERIOR

Out of the metropolitan area "on the island" are a variety of excursions; as it is a small island it is possible to see forested

mountains and desert-like areas in only a short time. However, because the public transport system is rather limited, it is difficult if not impossible to visit some places without a rented car. This is a highly recommended way of exploring the island. The cool climate in the mountains has caused resort hotels to be built in several towns inland.

An interesting round trip through the E half of the island, starting E from San Juan, is as follows: San Juan-Río Piedras (there are *públicos* between these two places, US$1.85) El Yunque-Luquillo-Fajardo-Vieques- Culebra-Humacao-Yabucoa-Guayama (you can get from Humacao to Guayama by a series of *públicos*, the whole journey costing about US$3.50)- Cayey-Aibonito-Barranquitas-Bayamón-San Juan. A variant between San Juan and El Yunque takes you on Route 187 from Isla Verde, outside San Juan, to Loíza along a stretch of the N coast, which includes the Piñones State Forest, sand blown and palm-lined road and much evidence of Hurricane Hugo's passing. Some parts are unspoilt, some parts pass through apartment blocks on the outskirts of towns, and the road is a popular rush-hour route. The bay at Vacía Talega is beautifully calm. The section which joins the coast to Route 3 at Río Grande is also tree-lined and attractive.

El Yunque (see also **Flora and Fauna** above) is a tropical forest and bird sanctuary. Trails (very stony) to the various peaks: El Yunque (The Anvil) itself, Mount Britton, Los Picachos. In view of the heavy rainfall, another name for the forest is Rain Forest. Visitors need not worry unduly, as storms are usually brief and plenty of shelter is provided. (No buses through the national forests, unfortunately; El Yunque is reached via Route 3 from San Juan towards Fajardo, and then right on Route 191.)

At Luquillo there is a beach in town and a *balneario* (see **Beaches and Watersports**); just by the latter is a row of restaurants on the slip road off the dual carriageway (Route 3). Fajardo is a boating centre with several marinas and a public beach at Seven Seas; beyond Seven Seas is Las Croabas beach. Offshore is an uninhabited, but much visited, coral island, Icacos. You can camp at Seven Seas Beach, but T 722-1551 first. (Bus San Juan-Fajardo US$6.) Off Humacao Beach/*Balneario* is a tiny cay called Cayo Santiago, also known as monkey island. It is inhabited by over 500 tiny monkeys, who are protected. The island is closed to the public although there are sightseeing tours which get you close enough to see the monkeys through binoculars.

One of the prettiest parts of Puerto Rico, which should be visited, lies S of Humacao, between Yabucoa and Guayama. Here are the villages of Patillas (*público* from Guayama) and Maunabo (*público* from Patillas, and from Yabucoa), where you can camp on the beach. There are a number of restaurants in this area, especially on the coast, which sell good, cheap food. Yabucoa is the E starting point of the Panoramic Route which runs the length of the island. There is an extension to the Route around the Cerro La Pandura and the Puntas Quebrada Honda, Yaguas and Toro; this affords lovely views of the Caribbean coast and Vieques island. Guayama, the cleanest town in Puerto Rico, it claims, has a delightful square, on which are the church and the Casa Cautiño, built in 1887, now a museum and cultural centre. Route 3, the coastal road around the E part continues from Guayama to Salinas (see below), where it joins Route 1 for Ponce.

A round trip through the W half of the island would take in Ponce, the second city (reached by motorway from San Juan via Caguas), Guánica, Parguera, San Germán, Boquerón, Mayagüez (the third city), Aguadilla, Quebradillas and Arecibo, with side trips to the Maricao State Forest and fish hatchery, the Río Abajo State Forest and Lake Dos Bocas, the precolumbian ceremonial ball-park near Utuado, and the Arecibo observatory (open for tours Tuesday to Friday at 1400, T 878-2612 for groups, and on Sunday pm, no tour, but there is no public transport, so you have to hitchhike from Arecibo).

Off the motorway which runs from San Juan to Ponce is Baños de Coamo, which was the island's most fashionable resort from 1847 to 1958; legend has it that the spring was the fountain of youth which Juan Ponce de León was seeking. (Take Route 153 from the motorway and then 546.) It has been redeveloped by Paradores Puertorriqueños and still has a thermal bath (see under **Where To Stay**). About 45 mins SE of Coamo is Salinas, a fishing and farming centre. There are several good seafood restaurants on the waterfront.

Ponce has a very fine art museum, donated by a foundation established by Luis A Ferré (industrialist, art historian and Governor 1968-72) in a modern building with a beautiful staircase, now famous. It contains a representative collection of European and American art from the third century BC to the present day. As well as an extensive Baroque collection and fine examples of pre-Raphaelite painting, there is a small collection of precolumbian ceramics and two cases of beautiful Art Nouveau glass. There are three gardens, one Spanish, one American and one Puerto Rican. (Open 0900-1600, Monday and Wednesday-Friday, 1000-1600 Saturday, 1000-1700 Sunday and holidays, closed Tuesday; entry US$2.50 for adults, US$1.50 for children under 12.) The cathedral is also worth a look, and so is the black and red fire-station, built for a fair in 1883. Both buildings stand back to back in the main square, Plaza Las Delicias, which has fountains and many neatly-trimmed trees. Also on the plaza is the Casa Armstrong-Poventud (or Casa de las Cariatides), facing the Cathedral, with the Instituto de Cultura Puertorriqueño (Región Sur) and tourist information centre (Monday-Friday 0800-1200, 1300-1630; the Instituto is open 0900-1200, 1300-1600 Tuesday to Sunday). East of the plaza is the Teatro La Perla, painted cream, white and gold, the city's cultural centre (19th century), restored in 1990, as was the Alcaldía on the Plaza. Much renovation has taken place in the heart of the city; the Casas Villaronga and Salazar-Zapater are being restored (the latter to accommodate the Museo de Historia de Ponce), other houses are being repainted in pastel shades, streets have been made into pedestrian areas (eg the Paseo Peotonal Atocha and Callejón Amor), and the large, air-conditioned market on Vives and Atocho (N of the plaza) has been remodelled. The city is now very pleasant to walk around. Two new museums have opened, the Museo de la Música Puertorriqueña, Calle Cristina 70, T 844-9722, open Tuesday to Sunday 0900-1200 and 1300-1600, catalogue US$3, and the Museo Castillo Serrallés, on El Vigía hill (T 259-1774), open Wednesday to Sunday 1000-1700, US$3, children US$1.50, groups must reserve in advance. This fine, 1930s mansion has been restored by the Municipio. Also on El Vigía is the Observation Tower (open Tuesday-Wednesday, 0900-1730, Thursday-Sunday 1000-2200, US$0.50). The walkway next to the Yacht and Fishing Club is a good place to be at the weekend: good atmosphere. Most *carros públicos* leave from the intersection of Victoria and Unión, 3 blocks N of the plaza (fare to San Juan US$6-7; to Guayama, either direct or via Santa Isabel, US$3).

A short drive away on Route 503, in the outskirts of the city, is the Tibes Indian Ceremonial Center. This is an Igneri (300 AD) and pre-Taino (700 AD) burial ground, with seven ball courts (*bateyes*) and two plazas, one in the form of a star, a replica of a Taino village and a good museum, open Tuesday-Sunday 0900-1600. The site was discovered in 1975 after heavy rain uncovered some of the stone margins of the ball courts. Under the Zemi Batey, the longest in the Caribbean (approximately 100 by 20m), evidence of human sacrifice has been found. Underneath a stone in the Main Plaza, which is almost square (55 by 50m), the bodies of children were found, buried ceremonially in earthenware pots. In all, 130 skeletons have been uncovered near the Main Plaza, out of a total on site of 187. All the ball courts and plazas are said to line up with solstices or equinoxes. The park is filled with trees (all named), the most predominant being the higuera, whose fruit is used, among other things, for making maracas (it's forbidden to pick them up though). Admission US$2 for adults, US$1 for children; bilingual guides give an informative description of the site and a documentary is shown.

Two other recommended excursions are: to Hacienda Buena Vista, at Km 16.8 on Route 10, N of the city. Built in 1833, converted into a coffee plantation and corn mill in 1845 and in operation till 1937, this estate has been restored by Fideicomiso de Conservación de Puerto Rico. All the machinery works (the metal parts are original), operated by water channelled from the 360-metre Vives waterfall; the hydraulic turbine which turns the corn mill is unique. Reservations are necessary for the 2-hour tour (in Spanish or English), T 722-5882 (information and at weekends 848-7020), open Friday-Sunday, tours at 0830, 1030, 1330 and 1530; groups of 20 or more admitted Wednesday to Friday; US$4 adults, US$1 children under 12. At weekends trips can be made to the beach at Caja de Muerto, Coffin Island, the ferry leaves Ponce at 0900, returns 1600, T 848-4575, US$5.50 return, children US$3.50.

Going West from Ponce is *Guánica*, the place where American troops first landed in the Spanish-American war. It has an old fort from which there are excellent views. Although Guánica has a history stretching back to Ponce de León's landing in 1508, the first of many colonist landings in the bay, the town was not actually founded here until 1914. Outside Guánica is a *balneario* with a large hotel alongside, *Copamarina*. For details on the Guánica Forest, see **Flora and Fauna**. Further W is La Parguera, originally a fishing village and now a popular resort with two *paradores*, guest houses, fish restaurants, fast food outlets. Noisy on holiday weekends. Nearby is Phosphorescent Bay, an area of phosphorescent water, occurring through a permanent population of minescent dinoflagellates, a tiny form of marine life, which produce sparks of chemical light when disturbed. One hour boat trips round the bay depart between 1930 and 0030, hourly departures, the experience is said to be rather disappointing, however.

Inland from La Parguera, off the main Route 2, *San Germán* has much traditional charm; it was the second town to be founded on the island and has preserved its colonial atmosphere. It is an excellent base from which to explore the mountains and villages of S W Puerto Rico. The beautiful little Porta Coeli chapel on the plaza contains a small, rather sparse museum of religious art. (Open Wednesday-Sunday, 0830-1200, 1300-1630.) A university town: it can be difficult to get cheap accommodation in term time.

On the S side of the W coast is *Boquerón*, in Cabo Rojo district, which has an excellent beach for swimming. It is very wide and long, admission US$1, parking for hundreds of cars, camping, changing rooms, beach and first 30 yards of sea packed with bodies on holiday weekends. About 1½ km away across the bay is a beautiful, deserted beach, but there is no road to it. The small village is pleasant, with typical bars, restaurants and street vendors serving the local speciality, oysters. This is one of the cheapest spots on the island because it is a centre for the Department of Recreation and Sports to provide holiday accommodation for Puerto Rican families. Fully self-contained apartments, with barbeques,

front the beach, and at US$40 a night they are a bargain. Foreigners are welcomed, but it is so popular with Puerto Ricans that you may have to make an application up to three months in advance. There are other hotels and a *parador* (see **Where To Stay** in **Information for Visitors**). South of the town is Boquerón Lagoon, a wildfowl sanctuary; also the Cabo Rojo Wildlife Refuge, with a visitors' centre and birdwatching trails. The Cabo Rojo lighthouse (Faro), at the island's SW tip is the most S point on the island with a breathtaking view; the exposed coral rocks have marine fossils and, closer inshore, shallow salt pools where crystals collect. Popular beaches in this area are El Combate (miles of white sand, undeveloped, but now a favourite with university students), S of Boquerón, and Joyuda (small island just offshore offers good snorkelling and swimming, but beach itself not spectacular) and Buye (camping US$8 a night) to the N.

Mayagüez has fine botanical gardens, at the Tropical Agricultural Research Station, near the University of Puerto Rico: well worth visiting, free admission, open Monday-Friday, 0730-1630. The city also has an interesting zoo; open Tuesday-Sunday, 0900-1630, adults US$1, children US$0.50. *Públicos* leave from a modern terminal in Calle Peral. The tourist office is in the Municipalidad on Plaza Colón. *Mona Island*, 80 km W of Mayagüez, is fascinating for historians and nature lovers, but can only be reached by chartered boat or plane. Originally inhabited by Taino Indians and then by pirates and privateers, it is now deserted except for its wildlife. Here you can see 3-foot iguanas, colonies of sea birds and bats in the caves. 200-foot high cliffs are dotted with caves, ascending to a flat table top covered with dry forest. The island is managed by the Department of National Resources (T 722-1726), who have cabins to rent with prior permission. Camping is allowed at Sardinera Beach, US$1 per night. There are no restaurants or facilities. Take all your food and water with you and bring back all your rubbish.

Going N from Mayagüez, you come to **Rincón**, on the westernmost point of the island. Here the mountains run down to the sea, and the scenery is spectacular. The town itself is unremarkable, but the nearby beaches are beautiful and the surfing is a major attraction. The beaches are called Steps, Dome (named after the nearby nuclear storage dome) and the Public Beach, with lifeguard. Humpback whales visit in winter. There are cottages to rent and there is also accommodation in Rincón and the neighbouring village of Puntas (see below). There are also some small bars and restaurants. Rincón can be reached by *público* from Mayagüez or (less frequent) from Aguadillas. Public transport is scarce at weekends.

Route 2, the main road in the N, is built up to some extent from Arecibo and completely from Manatí to San Juan. If you have the time it is much nicer to drive along the coast. Take Route 681 out of Arecibo, with an immediate detour to the Poza del Obispo beach, by Arecibo lighthouse. Here a pool has been formed inside some rocks, but the breakers on the rocks themselves send up magnificent jets of spray. The bay, with fine surf, stretches round to another headland, Punta Caracoles, on which is the Cueva del Indio (small car park on Route 681, US$1 charge if anyone is around). A short walk through private land leads to the cave, a sea-eroded hole and funnel in the cliff; watch out for holes in the ground when walking around. There are drawings in the cave, but whether they are precolumbian, or modern graffiti is not made clear. *Públicos* run along Route 681 from Arecibo. Rejoin Route 2 through Barceloneta. The State Forest of Cambalache is between Arecibo and Barceloneta.

The coast road is not continuous; where it does go beside the sea, there are beaches, seafood restaurants and some good views. Route 165, another coastal stretch which can be reached either through Dorado on the 693, or through Toa Baja, enters metropolitan San Juan at Cataño.

Heading E from Mayagüez is the Panoramic Route which runs the whole length of Puerto Rico, through some of the island's most stunning scenery. It passes through the Cordillera Central, with large areas of forest, and there are several excursions to various countryside resorts. Despite the fact that you are never far from buildings, schools or farms, the landscape is always fascinating. In the evening the panoramas are lovely and you can hear the song of the *coquí*. No trip to the interior should miss at least some part of the Panoramic Route, but if you want to travel all of it, allow 3 days. The roads which are used are narrow, with many bends, so take care at corners. The Maricao State Forest (Monte del Estado) is the most W forest on the Route; its visitors' areas are open from 0600 to 1800. It is a beautiful forest with magnificent views. As it approaches Adjuntas and the transinsular Route 10, the Panoramic Route goes through the Bosque de Guilarte, again with fine views, flowering trees, bougainvillaea, banks of impatiens (busy lizzie, mirame-linda in Spanish), and bird song (if you stop to listen). After Adjuntas, the road enters the Toro Negro Forest Reserve, which includes the highest point on the island, Cerro de Punta (1,338m). The Recreation Areas in Toro Negro are open from 0800-1700. After this high, lush forest with its marvellous vistas, the road continues to Aibonito, around which the views and scenery are more open (mainly as a result of deforestation). Thence to Cayey and, beyond, another forest, Carite (also known as Guavate). Finally the road descends into the rich, green valley which leads to Yabucoa.

From various points on the Panoramic Route you can head N or S; eg Route 10 goes S from Adjuntas to Ponce, or N to

Utuado and then on to Río Abajo State Forest (open 0600-1800) where there are a swimming pool and various picnic spots. It is approached through splendid views of the karst hills and the Dos Bocas Lake. Free launch trips are offered on this lake at 0700, 1000, 1400 and 1700; they last 2 hours and are provided by the Public Works Department. Route 10 reaches the N coast at Arecibo.

The Caguana Indian Ceremonial Park, W of Utuado, dates from about 1100 AD, and contains ten Taino ball courts, each named after a Taino *cacique* (chieftain). The courts vary in size, the longest being about 85m by 20 (Guarionex), the largest 65 by 50 (Aguey-bana). These two have monoliths in the stones that line the level "pitch", and on those of Agueybana there are petro-glyphs, some quite faint. None of the monoliths is taller than a man. A path leads down to the Río Tanamá. The set-ting, amid limestone hills, is very impres-sive. It is believed to be a site of some religious significance and has been re-stored with a small museum in the land-scaped park. It is on Route 111 to Lares, Km 12.3, open 0900-1700 (gate to the river closes at 1630), admission free. Fur-ther W of Utuado, Lares is a hilltop town (*públicos* go from one block from church) from where you can either carry on to the W coast at Aguadilla, or head N on one of the many routes to the Atlantic coast. Route 453 passes Lago de Guajataca, continuing as Route 113 to Quebradillas (see *Paradores* under **Where To Stay**, below). Route 455 branches W off the 453, leading via a short stretch of the 119 to the 457 and 446 (good view at the junction of these 2). Route 446 traverses, as a single track, the Bosque de Gua-jataca, which has several easy paths into the forest which are nice to walk (25 miles in all) and three recreational areas (open 0900-1800). Permission to camp must be obtained from the Departamento de Re-cursos Naturales, office in the Bosque open Monday-Friday 0700-1530 (in the-

ory). Route 129 goes to Arecibo, passing the Río Camuy Cave Park, with side trips to the Cueva de Camuy and the Arecibo Observatory (see above for all these). Driving on the country roads in the area between the Panoramic Route and the N coast is twisty but pleasant, passing conical limestone hills (*mogotes*) and farms set among patches of lush forest.

VIEQUES

Vieques, a peaceful, relaxing, low-key is-land of rolling hills, is located 11 km across the sea from Puerto Rico. Fajardo is the closest sea and air port. The island is about 34 km long by 6 km wide with a population of about 8,000 mostly concen-trated in the main town of Isabel Segunda. There is an excellent historical museum at the beautifully restored fort, El Fortin Conde de Mirasol (open week-ends 1000-1600, week days for groups by request, T 741-1717, 741-8651 evenings) and another interesting exhibit at the Lighthouse (T 741-5000 for schedule). The island was named Graciosa by Co-lumbus, after a friend's mother, but bet-ter known as Crab Island by pirates who frequented its waters. The US Military owns two thirds of the island: the E third and W third, with the civilian population living on the middle strip. Both bases are open to the public upon presentation of any photo identification except on days when the red flag is up: when manoeu-vers and/or bombing practice are under-way. The US military presence has been greatly reduced and within two years the military is expected to leave and return the land to the people. The military is heard but not much seen: planes and helicopters fly low but since only a hand-ful of personnel are permanently sta-tioned on the island, it is not a base town atmosphere. The land owned by the mili-tary is mostly untouched, creating a bird sanctuary and nature preserve. Vieques has over 52 beaches in secluded coves, the few developed beaches have people and exuberant groups of picnickers, the rest are deserted. Public Sun Beach has picnic and camping areas (no shade in camping area). Tourism is an infant industry on this island, with the small beach town of Esperanza being the main area of guest houses and tourist related restaurants, bars, dive companies, etc. The museum in Esperanza is open Tuesday-Sunday, 1100-1500, T 741-8850. The biggest 'action' on the island is Saturday night in Esperanza, when everyone promenades along the sea front dressed in their finest, talking and flirting, before going to a nightclub or bar. Small, hardy, island horses, most with paso fino blood lines (that means smooth gaits with no bouncing) are still used as transport, and wild horses roam the island. Renting a horse is an exciting way to explore the beaches and coves.

Mosquito Bay, also known as Phosphorescent Bay (the BBC broadcast a documentary about this in 1994), is a large, but very shallow bay, surrounded by mangrove trees and full of bioluminescent organisms. Sightseeing trips go at night (recommended are the tours that use non polluting electric boats or kayaks). The organisms glow when disturbed by the prop, paddle, fish or you swimming. The glow generated by a 13cm fish is about a 39cm circle of light brighter than a light bulb. Swimming in this glow is a wonderful experience.

Island information
● How To Get There

By air: Sunaire Express (T 741-4242, 800-524-2094) and Vieques Air Link (T 863-3020, 741-3266) have flights from Fajardo, San Juan, St Thomas and St Croix multiple times a day. Lapsa (T 723-4144) also has some flights from San Juan. **By sea:** from Fajardo, the car and passenger ferry runs at 0930 and 1630, returning at 0700 and 1500, Mon-Fri. Weekends the schedule to Vieques is 0900, 1500 and 1800, returning to Fajardo at 0700, 1300 and 1630, (T 863-0852), reservations needed for cars only, passenger fare is US$2.25, crossing takes 1¼ hrs. At weekends the ferries are often full and advance reservations are rec.

● Local Transport

Públicos meet you at the airport and ferry dock, posted rates (none higher than US$3.00), but some drivers will try to overcharge you, ask the price first. Jitney Taxi Service (T 741-0757) or Rafael Acevedo (T 741-4201) can be called for pick up, or let your hotel/guest house arrange transport for you. Car rentals available at Dreda Rent a Car (T 741-8397), VIAS Car Rental (T 741-8173) also has scooters, Sammy's (T 741-0106), Marco's (741-1388, 382-3054) or Island Car Rentals (T 741-1666). Horse rentals can be arranged by your guesthouse.

● Where To Stay

Esperanza: *Esperanza Beachfront Hotel*, US$60-90, (T 741-8675, 754-9810) with pool, restaurant; *Tradewinds*, US$35 and up, (T 741-8666) with bar, restaurant, rec; *Bananas Guest House*, facing the ocean, US$40-60, popular, pleasant American restaurant, (T 741-8700), some rooms a/c; *La Casa del Francés*, US$99d, winter, (T 741-3751), classical sugar plantation Great House, bar, restaurant, pool, located 5 min walk out of Esperanza. Smaller and cheaper guest houses include: *Camar*, (T 741-8604), *El Quenepo* (T 741-8541), *La Central*, (T 741-0106), *Posada Vistamar*, (T 741-8716); *La Concha*, (T 741-2733). In and around **Isabel Segunda:** *Vieques Inn*, downtown, (T 741-1500); *Casa La Lanchita*, oceanfront, (T 741-0023); *Sea Gate Hotel*, near the fort, (741-4661), US$50, pool, tennis; *Depakos Hotel*, (T 741-1126). **Inland** is *Crow's Nest*, rooms with kitchenettes, US$60d, pool, restaurant, (T 741-0033) or *New Dawn*, an unusual guesthouse built on 5 acres of land with horses grazing off the hugh veranda, is 5 km from the beach, frequently booked by women's groups for retreats, 2-storey wooden house, large deck and hammocks, rooms US$35s, US$45d, dorms US$15, and tentsite US$10, all with shared bath and outdoor showers or you can rent the entire place (sleeps 20+) with or without a cook, for US$250/day, US$3,000/month, (T 741-0495), PO Box 1512. For villa rentals contact Connections, (T 741-0023).

● Where To Eat

Almost all of the island's restaurants are part of a hotel or guesthouse listed above. There are numerous small places offering take out or eat in sandwiches, hamburgers, barbeque chicken, etc.

CULEBRA

Culebra is another quiet, unspoilt island where there is little tourism. The main village, Dewey (called Pueblo by the locals) is attractively set between two lagoons. A visitor's information centre is in the City Hall. Prices rise steeply at weekends. The Culebra National Wildlife Refuge, comprising 23 offshore islands and four parcels of land on Culebra, protects large colonies of sea birds, particularly terns and boobies. There are good, sandy beaches, clear water and a coral reef, scuba equipment, Paradise Divers (742-3569) and Gene Thomas (742-3555); snorkel rental from Kathy's (742-3112) or Jody's. Both Vieques and Culebra were heavily damaged by Hurricane Hugo.

Island information
● How To Get There
By air: from Isla Grande airport, San Juan, or Fajardo with Flamenco, T 724-7110, 725-7707. Flamenco flies between Vieques and Culebra (tickets from the airport only). **By launch**: Fajardo-Culebra, 1 hr, Mon-Thur 1600, Fri-Sat, 0900 and 1600, Sunday 0800 and 1430; Culebra-Fajardo, 0700 weekdays, Fri also 1400, 1800, Sat, 0700, 1400 and 1730, Sun 1300 and 1630. Fajardo ticket and information office is open 0800-1100, 1300-1500. (It is best to arrive in Fajardo in time for the last ferry if you are going to the islands; there is little to do in the town and it is not a cheap place). However, at weekends the ferries are usually full and it is best to reserve a ticket.

● Local Transport
Bicycles can be hired at US$2 a day from Jody's (T 742-3266) and Posada Hamaca (742-3516); cars and jeeps from George's (742-0333), Prestige (742-3141) and Stanley's (742-3575).

● Where To Stay
Bay View Villas, PO Box 775, T 742-3392/765-5711, two 2-bedroomed villas, US$1,200/week or US$1,000/week, well-equipped, good views overlooking Ensenada Honda, walking distance of Dewey; *Culebra Island Villas*, T 742-3112, or in USA 52 Marlow Ave, Bricktown, NJ 08724, T (908) 458-5591, F (203)261-7344, 10 units all with kitchen, daily rates (2 days min) from US$65-95 in a studio, US$100-150 in 2-room villa, weekly rates US$395-475, 650-775 respectively; *Posada La Hamaca*, 68 Castelar, T 742-3516, US$45-65d, well kept, only 9 units, book in advance; *Coral Island Guest House*, PO Box 396, T 742-3177, on water front near ferry terminal, 5 bedrooms, sleeps 12, living room, kitchen, fans, US$40d or US$240 weekly, group rates available, credit cards accepted, in the USA contact John Dinga, 17 Riverbank Road, Quincy, MA02169, T (617) 773-0565.

INFORMATION FOR VISITORS

● Documents
All non-US residents need a US visa, or a US visa waiver for participating countries.

● How To Get There
International: from Europe, American Airlines from Heathrow or Brussels or Paris or Madrid or Manchester via New York JFK, all via Miami with immediate connection to San Juan (T 749-1747); Lufthansa from Frankfurt via Antigua or St Maarten (T 723-9553); Iberia from Madrid (T 721-5630). British Airways is

to end its London-San Juan flight from 29 October 1994 and connections will be offered from its services to Antigua, New York, Miami and Baltimore instead.

Most South and Central American countries are connected via Miami but there are also direct flights from Caracas (American Airlines, Aeropostal, Bogotá (Aces), T 791-0580, Panama City (Iberia, Lacsa and Copa), Guatemala City (American Airlines, Copa), and San José (Iberia, Copa and Lacsa).

From other Caribbean Islands: Anguilla, Antigua, Aruba, Barbados, Dominica, Fort-de-France, Grenada, La Romana, Pointe-à-Pitre, Port of Spain, Puerto Plata, Punta Cana, St Barts, St Croix, St Kitts, St Lucia, St Maarten, St Thomas, Santiago (Dominican Republic), Santo Domingo, Tortola and Virgin Gorda, with Liat (T 791-3838), American Airlines, American Eagle, Air Guadeloupe, Caribair, United Airlines, Air St Thomas, Air St Barths, US Air, Dominicana de Aviación, T 724-7100, Copa, Sunaire Express (T 800-595-9501, F 809-773-4628), Aerolíneas Dominicanas. **Domestic**: A great many US cities are served by American Airlines and American Eagle; Delta (T 721-1144, 800-221-1212); Carnival, Northwest Airlines, Kiwi International Air Lines, Tower Air, TWA (T 753-8928), US Air and United Airlines.

Several local airlines operate services within Puerto Rico, including American Eagle, Flamenco and Vieques Air Link, and they have offices either at the Luis Muñoz Marín International Airport, or the Isla Grande airport (eg Flamenco and Vieques Air Link). There are 2 daily American Eagle flights between San Juan and Ponce. Carnival Airlines flies to Ponce and Aguadilla from New York, and American Airlines flies to Aguadilla from Miami and New York. Some charter or inter-island flights leave from the Isla Grande airport.

A number of airlines have offices at Miramar Plaza Center, Av Ponce de León 954: British Airways and Delta (9th floor), Dominicana, Aeropostal, Lufthansa, Lacsa, US Air; others can be found at Ashford 1022, Condado: American, BWIA, Liat (best to use their office at the airport for reconfirmation).

● **Airport Tax**
None is payable, although Liat demands a "security tax" of US$5.

● **Shipping**
There are no boats to other Caribbean destinations, apart from cruise ships, which call at San Juan and Ponce.

● **Airport**
There are airport limousines to a number of hotels. There is also a bus service (T1) every 45 mins, US$0.25 to and from Plaza Colón and the airport; note that people take precedence over luggage if the bus is full (it rarely is). The bus departs from the upper deck near the Departures area, the furthest corner from Arrivals. M7 bus also goes from Plaza Colón through Condado to the airport. The taxi fare to old San Juan is US$10-12, to Condado US$6 (make sure the taxi meter is used; note that drivers prefer not to go to old San Juan, the beach areas are much more popular with them).

● **Car Hire**
There are many car rental agencies, including Hertz (T 791-0840), Isla Verde International Airport and 10 other locations; National (T 791-1805), Luis M Marin Airport. Budget (T 791-3685) at the airport. Target (T 783-6592/782-6381), not at airport, among the cheapest, will negotiate rates. L & M, Condado, (main office T 791-1345/1160), free pick-up, make sure you get it even for day hire. A small car may be hired for as little as US$25 (not including collision damage waiver, US$12.50, insurance is sometimes already covered by your credit card) for 24 hrs, unlimited mileage (national driving licence preferred to international licence), but rates vary according to company and demand. The Rand McNally road map is rec (US$1.85); the Gousha road map costs US$1.50 at Texaco stations. A good map is essential because there are few signs to places, but frequent indications of Route numbers and intersections. Avoid driving in the San Juan metropolitan area as traffic can be very heavy. Car theft and burglar damage is a major problem in the San Juan area. Make sure you use all the security devices given you by the rental company. Many people actually recommend you do not stop at red lights after 2200, because of hold-ups, just pause, look and go.

● **Taxis**
All taxis are metered, charge US$1 for initial charge and US$0.10 for every additional $1/10$ mile; US$0.50 for each suitcase; US$1 is charged for a taxi called from home or business. Minimum fee US$3. Approximate fares: San Juan to Condado, US$4; Condado to Isla Verde, US$4.50-5. Taxis may be hired at US$12 an hour unmetered. Taxi drivers sometimes try to ask more from tourists, so beware, insist that the meter is used, and avoid picking up a taxi

anywhere near a cruise ship. If they refuse, tell them you will call Puerto Rico Tourist Zone Police, T 722-0738, or the Public Service Commission, T 751-5050 ext 253, 254, and complain. They can revoke a taxi licence.

There are also shared taxis, usually Ford minibuses (*carros públicos*) which have yellow number plates with the letters P or PD at the end and run to all parts of the island. Most of them leave from Río Piedras in San Juan, although some leave from the main post office and others collect at the airport; elsewhere, ask around for the terminal. They do not usually operate after about 1900. *Público* to Caguas costs US$1.25, from S side of Plaza Colón; to Ponce takes 7 hrs (US$6-7). A service referred to as *línea* will pick up and drop off passengers where they wish. They operate between San Juan, and most towns and cities at a fixed rate. They can be found in the phone book under Líneas de Carros. *Públicos* are a good way of getting around, provided you are prepared to wait up to a couple of hours for the car to fill up. It is not rec, however, if you want to get to out of the way places, such as the Arecibo Observatory, the Camuy Caves, or the Tibes Indian Ceremonial Centre, when a hired car is essential. If you hire a *público* for yourself it works out expensive, eg San Juan airport to Ponce US$75.

● **Buses**

San Juan: There is a city bus (*guagua*) service with a fixed charge of US$0.40. (No change given; make sure you have right money.) They have special routes, sometimes against the normal direction of traffic, in which case the bus lanes are marked by yellow and white lines. Bus stops are marked by white and orange signs or yellow and black notices on lampposts marked "Parada". From the terminal at Plaza Colón in old San Juan, T1 goes along Av Ponce de León, through Miramar, past the Fine Arts Center in Santurce, to Isla Verde (Route 37) and the International Airport; No 2 goes to Río Piedras via Condado, Av Muñoz Rivera and the University; No 46 goes to Bayamón along Av Roosevelt; A7 goes about every 2 hrs to Piñones, through Condado and Isla Verde (Av Ashford to Route 37); M7 goes through Condado to the airport. From behind Pier 2, No 8 goes to Puerto Nuevo and Río Piedras, No 12 to Río Piedras, and No 14 to Río Piedras via Av Ponce de León, Santurce, Hato Rey and the University. City buses run to a 30, or 45-min schedule and many do not operate after 2200.

Hitchhiking is possible, but slow.

● **Where To Stay**

Most of the large San Juan hotels are in **Condado or Isla Verde** and overlook the sea, with swimming pools, night clubs, restaurants, shops and bars. The summer season runs from 16 April to 14 December and is somewhat cheaper than the winter season, for which we give rates where possible. A 9% tax is charged on the room rate in hotels with casinos, 7% in those without casinos. A full list is given in the monthly tourist guide, *Qué Pasa*, published by the Puerto Rican Tourism Company, but listed below is a selection. To get value for money, it may be advisable to avoid the luxury hotels on the sea front. There is plenty of cheaper accommodation within walking distance of the beaches. Condado: *Radisson Ambassador Plaza*, 1369 Ashford, T 721-7300, US$145-180d, or US$185-305 for a suite, 233 rooms, casino; *Caribe Hilton*, Ocean Front, Puerta de Tierra, on the old city side of Condado bridge, T 721-0303, US$310-430d, or US$495-1,000 suites, 733 rooms, casino, set in 17 acres of gardens, many sporting facilities. On the Condado side of the bridge is the *Condado Plaza*, 999 Ashford, T 721-1000, US$365-385d, or suites US$345-1,100, 587 rooms, casino, with *Tony Roma's* restaurant, small beach, etc; *Condado Beach*, Ashford, next to the Convention Center, T 721-6888, US$190-255d, suites US$430, 245 rooms. Cheaper: *Condado Lagoon*, 6 Clemenceau, T 721-0170, US$95-110d, 44 rooms, good, with good restaurant on the premises, *Ajili-Mojili*; *Dutch Inn and Tower*, 55 Condado Av, Condado, T 721-0810, US$110-120d, 144 rooms, casino; good value are *El Canario by the Sea*, 4 Condado Av, T 722-8640, US$80-95, including continental breakfast, 25 rooms, close to beach, comfortable, and *El Canario Inn*, 1317 Ashford, T 722-3861, US$85-95d, breakfast included, 1 block from the beach, good, clean, safe.

Hostería del Mar, 1 Tapia Street, Ocean Park, T 727-3302, US$95-145, on the beach; a rec guest house in Ocean Park is *Numero Uno on the Beach*, 1 Santa Ana, T 727-9687, US$65-175d, with pool, friendly, excellent food; also rec is *Beach Buoy Inn*, 1853 McLeary, Ocean Park, T 728-8119, F 268-0037, T 800-221-8119, US$60-70d, friendly, helpful, parking, shopping close by, beach towels.

Isla Verde: *Sands*, on Route 37 (the main road

through Isla Verde), T 791-6100 (US$285-410d) and *El San Juan*, Ocean Front, T 791-1000 (US$305-450d) are the 2 poshest hotels in Isla Verde, look at the latter's lobby even if you do not stay; there is also a *Travel Lodge*, on Route 37, T 728-1300, US$135. *Holiday Inn Crowne Plaza*, T 253-2929, F 841-8085, Km 1.5 on Highway 187, resort, golf, tennis, US$215-235d. Rec is *Carib Inn*, Route 187 (T 791-3535), from US$110-140, clean, pool, 2 restaurants, near airport; *Don Pedro*, Calle Rosa 4, T 791-2838, not far from airport, close to beach, pleasant, pool, US$60s, US$65d; *La Casa Mathieson*, Uno 14, Villamar, Isla Verde T 726-8662, 727-3223, and *Green Isle Inn*, 36 Calle Uno, T 726-4330, 728-5749 are jointly owned, both charge US$48-64, both near airport, and have swimming pools, cooking facilities, friendly, free transport to and from airport, rec; between the two is *The Mango Inn*, Calle Uno 20, Villamar, T 726-5546, US$70-85, pool; *El Patio*, Tres Oeste 87, Bloque D-8, Villamar, T 726-6298, swimming pool, use of kitchen, US$50d all year, rec; *Casa de Playa*, Av Isla Verde 86, T 728-9779, on beach, US$70-90d (high season) inc continental breakfast, TV, bath, a/c, pleasant, restaurant and bar under construction; *Borinquen Royal*, Av Isla Verde 58, T 728-8400, US$70-85, also on beach.

In **Old San Juan**, *Gran Hotel El Convento*, a converted Carmelite nunnery at Cristo 100, is a charming hotel with a Spanish atmosphere and the dining room is in the former chapel, US$150-200, but cheaper rates available, eg US$89 for Caribbean residents, service not quite up to the price, swimming pool, nice garden in which to have a drink, T 723-9020. Guest houses on Calle San Francisco, information from Joyería Sol, Tanca 207, fan, cooking and washing facilities, friendly and helpful, but absolutely filthy and like cells. Also in Old San Juan are *Central*, Plaza de Armas, T 722-2751, good location, basic but rec, pleasant, satisfactory, US$15s, US$25s-35d with shower, ask for a room with fan away from a/c units, also ask for towels when checking in so you do not have to run up and downstairs again; *Enrique Castro Guest House*, Tacna 205, T 722-5436, at Relojería Suiza Mecánico Cuarzo, 2nd floor (Box 947), difficult to find, US$100d per week. *Buena Vista Guesthouse by the Sea*, Gral Valle 2218, Sta Teresita, English, French spoken, with kitchen, near beach, airport pickup for a small charge.

In **Miramar**, *Excelsior*, 801 Ponce de León, T 721-7400, US$125-151d, restaurant, bar, pool, rooms overlooking freeway are noisy; *Miramar*, 606 Av Ponce de León, T 722-6239, "not chic", but clean and friendly, longer stays possible, US$45-50; *El Toro*, 605 Miramar, T 725-5150/2647, US$38- 48d, good value, pleasant, close to bus stop.

In **Santurce**, *Pierre* (Best Western), 105 De Diego, T 721-1200, F 721-3118, from US$121d.

In **Ponce**, *Hotel Meliá* US$70-85d, a/c, TV, bath and breakfast, can be rec, friendly, roof top and garden terraces (2 Cristina, just off main plaza, PO Box 1431, T 842-0261, F 841-3602), also the *Ponce Holiday Inn*, Route 2, Km 221.2, W of the city, T 844-1200, F 841-8085, US$89-109d, where there are tennis courts, pools, and golf arrangements made; to the E of the city, on Route 1, Km 123.5, near the junction with the autopista is *Days Inn*, T 844-1200, US$90-110. Cheaper hotel near main square; *Hotel Bélgica*, 122 Villa St, T 844-3255, US$20s-40d upwards, some with a/c but not necessarily with windows, hot water but basic. There are about 5 other guesthouses. To the W of Ponce, at Guánica, *Cycle Center Youth Hostel*, cooking facilities.

On the east coast, *Las Delicias*, Fajardo Playa, on the dock, across street from post office and customs building, very good, nice staff, rec, T 863-1818, US$63d, bar; in Fajardo try *Guez House de Express*, near ferry dock, 388 Union, small, clean, US$35d, T 863-1362. *Palmas del Mar Hotel*, Humacao, T 852-6000, US$230 and up, hotel rooms or villa resort, 7 restaurants, 18-hole golf course, swimming pools and other sports. On the SE coast, near Maunabo, is *Playa Emajaguas Guest House*, off the Ruta Panorámica, Carr 901, Km 2.5, Box 834, Maunabo, T 861-6023, lovely view of the beach, owned by Victor Morales and Edna Huertos, 7 apartments with kitchens, US$50-60 all year, friendly, helpful, highly rec; near Patillas, Km 112, Route 3, is *Caribe Playa*, US$70d, right on the Caribbean, comfortable, restaurant (order dinner in advance), sea bathing and snorkelling in a small, safe area, very friendly and helpful (owner Esther Geller, manager Minerva Moreno), rec, T 839-6339 (USA 212-988-1801), Box 8490, Guardarraya, Patillas, PR 00723. Inland, N of Barranguitas is *Residencia Margarita*, US$48d, restaurant, useful for people following the Panoramic route.

At **Boquerón** in the SW, *Canadian Jack's*

Guest House, PO Box 990, Boquerón, PR 00622, T 851-2410, US$30d with private bathroom, colour tv, clean and comfortable but noisy on Fri, Sat nights when the streets are crowded with people partying, Jack also rents hammocks overlooking the water, US$6 pp per night, fantastic spot.

At **Mayagüez**, *Hilton*, casino, pool, T 831-7575, US$170-300d; *Palma*, on Méndez Vigo, T 834-3800, US$45-65d, good, TV, bathroom, a/c; *RUM Hotel* (hotel of the Recinto University of Mayagüez, only for students), US$9s, US$12d, central, safe, pool, library, T 832-4040 (similar prices at other branches of the University); *Colón*, Plaza Colón, a dump, no bath, ask for a quiet room, mainly rented by the hour; *El Embajador*, 111 E Ramos Antonini, US$33s, US$45d.

At **Rincón**, *Horned Dorset Primavera*, excellent, in US$250 range, Route 429, Km 3, T 823-4030/4050, 22 suites, restaurant, watersports. *Villa Cofresí* (US$70d) and, alongside it, *Villa Antonio*, see *Paradores* below. *The Lazy Parrot*, PO Box 430, Carrera 413, km 4.1, Barrio Puntas, T 823-5654, rooms sleep 4 in bunk beds, breakfast Tues-Sun. (At **Puntas**, Carmen's grocery store has rooms, basic, cooking facilities.)

At **Arecibo**, there are several hotels and guest houses around the main square, *Hotel Plaza*, US$27s.

At **Utuado**, *Riverside*, bargain with the manager.

There are 16 *Paradores Puertorriqueños* to put you up while touring, some old, most new, with prices starting at US$55d: the majority are to the W of San Juan; for reservations T 721-2884, or 137-800-462-7575. On the N coast, near Quebradillas are *El Guajataca* (T 721-2884, 895-3070), US$75-80, beautifully located on a beach (dangerous swimming), pool, entertainment, restaurant, bars; on the other side of the road, Route 2, Km 103.8, and higher up the hill at Km7.9, Route 113, is *Vistamar*, US$65-85, T 895-2065, also with pool, restaurant and bar. On the W coast, near Rincón, *Villa Antonio*, US$55-100 apartment (T 823-2645/2285) pool, beach, tennis courts.

In **Mayagüez**, *Sol*, rec, T 834-0303, US$55-65, 9 S R Palmer Este; S of Mayagüez are *Boquemar*, at Boquerón, T 851-2158 and *Perichi's*, Playa Joyuda, T 851-3131 (both US$60-70d, latter is well-run, with good restaurant), *Villa Parguera* and *Pargamar* at La Parguera (US$70-80 and US$55 respectively, T 899-3975 and 899-4015, the latter has a/c,

kitchen facilities), *Oasis* at San Germán, T 892-1175, not as close to the beach as it claims, but is ideal for the hills, good food and service, pool, jacuzzi, gym, sauna, a/c, US$58-60d.

Another is at **Baños de Coamo** where there are thermal water springs (maximum 15 mins) and an ordinary pool (spend as long as you like), US$60, T 825-2186, PO Box 540, Coamo, Puerto Rico 00640, rec; the *Hacienda Gripiñas*, an old coffee plantation house, US$60d, which lies in the mountains near Jayuya, N of Ponce, E of Utuado at Km 2.5, Route 527 (T 828-1717); in the same area is *Casa Grande*, Barrio Caonillas, Route 612, T 894-3939, US$55. The only paradores on the E side are *Martorell* at Luquillo, 6A Ocean Drive, close to beach, modern, US$60-70d winter (cheaper with shared bath), T 889-2710, advisable to reserve in advance here at any time; *Familia*, on Route 987, Fajardo, US$59-68d, T 863-1193.

Tourism Marketing Group, T 721-8793, arranges Fly-Drive packages, with car hire and accommodation at *paradores*; rates depend on which *paradores* you choose, but 3 days, 2 nights, starts at US$165 pp in a double room, 6 days, 5 nights US$350 pp.

See above in the main text under Boquerón for details of Dept of Recreation and Sports family accommodation; there are 3 other such centres at Punta Santiago on the E coast, Punta Guilarte near Patillas and Monte de Estado in the Marico Forest.

● **Where To Eat**

All major hotels. In **old San Juan**: *Fortaleza*, Fortaleza 252; for Puerto Rican cuisine, *La Tasca del Callejón*, Fortaleza 317; *Bistro*, Calle Cruz 152, a pleasant, small restaurant and bar with tasty local food at reasonable prices; the *Café de Armas*, Plaza de Armas, is also worth a try for their creole dishes; *La Mallorquina*, San Justo 207, T 722-3261, the oldest restaurant in the Caribbean, rec; also on San Justo: *Café de Paris*, No 256; *Szechuan*, Chinese, No 257, and other cafés and *Taco Maker*, No 255. There are several Mexican places in the city, eg *Parián* on Fortaleza; *Taza de Oro*, Luna 254, near San Justo. *La Zaragozana*, San Francisco 356, T 723-5103, some Spanish specialities, highly rec; *Bodegón de La Fortaleza*, Fortaleza 312; *La Danza*, corner of Cristo and Fortaleza, T 723-1642; *La Bombonera*, San Francisco 259, restaurant and pastry shop, good value breakfast, 1960s atmosphere, antique coffee machine; *4 Seasons Café*, in *Hotel Central*, Plaza de Armas, for good value local lunches; *Tropical Blend*, juice bar in La Calle alley on Fortaleza; *El Batey* bar, Cristo 101; *Manolin Café*, US$5 for just about anything, Puerto Rican food, lunch specials daily. *Nono's*, San Sebastián y Cristo, bar, burgers, salads, steaks, sandwiches, and nearby on San Sebastián (all on Plaza San José), *Patio de Sam* very good for local drinks (happy hour 1600-1900), and *Tasca El Boquerón*. On Av Ponce de León, *El Miramar*, good, but not cheap. *La Buena Mesa*, 605 Ponce de León, good, small, middle price range. Several bars and cafés on Plaza Colón in Old San Juan. There is a huge selection of restaurants in Condado, from the posh to all the fast food chain restaurants. Similarly, Isla Verde is well-served by the fast food fraternity; on the beach at Isla Verde is *The Hungry Sailor* bar and grill, sandwiches, tapas, burgers, with a snack bar next door. *Cecilia's Place*, Rosa St, Isla Verde.

For breakfast or lunch seek out the *fondas*, not advertised as restaurants but usually part of a private home, or a family-run eating place serving *criollo* meals which are filling and good value. Recommended in San Juan are: *Macumba*, 2000 Loíza; *Lydia's Place*, 38 Calle Sol, old San Juan, at corner of Escalera de Las Monjas, room for 20 on a rooftop terrace (pork chops, chicken, steak and daily local specials); *Casa Juanita*, 242 Av Roosevelt, Hato Rey (try chicken asopao or pork chops con mangu); *Cafetería del Parking*, 757 José de Diego, interior, Cayey (specialities include mondongo, and boronia de apio y bacalao – cod and celery root); *D'Arcos*, 605 Miramar, Santurce, speciality is roast veal with stuffed peppers and white bean sauce, also try pega'o (crunchy rice).

Outside San Juan a network of 42 restaurants, called *Mesones Gastronómicos*, has been set up. These places serve Puerto Rican dishes at reasonable prices. Most of the *Parador* restaurants are included; a full list is available for tourist offices. *Qué Pasa* magazine gives a full list of restaurants on the island.

In **Ponce**, the restaurant of the *Meliá Hotel* is good (look out for the "Breaded Lion" on the menu), there is a vegetarian restaurant in the Plaza del Mercado shopping centre, Calle Mayor, 4 blocks NE from the main plaza. Fast food places on main plaza.

In **Mayagüez** the *Vegetarian Restaurant*, Calle José de Diego, open 1100-1400; *Fuente Tropical*, same street, run by Colom-

bians, good fruit shakes and hamburgers; *Recomeni*, Calle Vigo, good inexpensive food, open all hours, eat in or take away. The area known as Joyuda, just outside the city limits, is famous for seafood restaurants on the beach; inexpensive food, good quality, nice atmosphere, whole, grilled fish is a must, especially snapper (*chillo*).

● **Camping**

Camping is permitted in the Forest Reserves; you have to get a permit (free) from the visitor centres. Camping is also allowed on some of the public beaches, contact the Recreation and Sports Department (T 722-1551 or 721-2800 ext 225). There are tent sites at Añasco, Cerro Gordo, Luquillo, Sombé, near Lake Guajataca and Punta Guilarte, cabins at Boquerón, Punta Guilarte and Punta Santiago, tent and trailer site at Seven Seas. Since Hurricane Hugo, many beach camping facilities have been closed; phone ahead to check.

● **Food And Drink**

Good local dishes are the mixed stew (chicken, seafood, etc), *asopao*; *mofongo*, mashed plantain with garlic served instead of rice, very filling; *mofongo relleno* is the *mofongo* used as a crust around a seafood stew. *Sacocho* is a beef stew with various root vegetables, starchy but tasty. *Empanadillas* are similar to South American *empanadas* but with a thinner dough and filled with fish or meat. *Pastillas* are yucca, peas, meat, usually pork, wrapped in a banana leaf and boiled. *Tostones* are fried banana slices. Rice is served with many dishes; *arroz con habichuelas* (rice with red kidney beans) is a standard side dish. Sometimes a local restaurant will ask if you want *provisiones*; these are root vegetables and are worth trying. *Comida criolla* means "food of the island", *criollo* refers to anything "native". Some local fruit names: *china* is orange, *parcha* passionfruit, *guanábana* soursop, *toronja* grapefruit; juices are made of all these, as well as guava, tamarind and mixtures. *Papaya* in a restaurant may not be fresh fruit, but *dulce de papaya* (candied), served with cheese, a good combination. Guava is served in a similar manner. Local beers are Medalla (a light beer), Gold Label (a premium beer, very good but hard to find) and Indio (a dark beer); a number of US brands and Heineken are brewed under licence. Rums: Don Q is the local favourite, also Palo Viejo, Ron Llave and the world-famous Bacardi (not so highly regarded by puertorriqueños); Ron Barrilito, a small distillery, has a very good reputation. Many restaurants pride themselves on their *piñas coladas*. *Maví* is a drink fermented from the bark of a tree and sold in many snack-bars. Home-grown Puerto Rican coffee is very good.

As most food is imported, the tourist, picknicker, or anyone economizing can eat as cheaply in a restaurant as by buying food in a grocery store.

● Tipping

Service is usually included in the bill, but where no fixed service charge is included, it is recommended that 15-20% is given to waiters, taxi drivers, etc.

● Nightclubs

Jazz at The Place, Calle Fortaleza 154 in old San Juan, no admission charge, drinks about US\$2. *Shannons Irish Pub*, Condado, T1 bus from airport passes it, live music (rock and roll), beer US\$2.50. *Caribe Hilton* is a favourite nightspot, also the other 4-5 star hotels, *Condado Beach, Regency* and *La Concha*.

● Sports

All the major hotels provide instruction and equipment for water skiing, snorkelling, boating and day trips to areas of aquatic interest. At Puerta de Tierra, near the *Caribe Hilton*, is the sports complex built for the 1979 Pan-American Games.

● Shopping

Puerto Rico is a large producer of rum, with many different types ranging from light rums for mixing with soft drinks to dark brandy-type rums (see above). Hand made cigars can still be found in Old San Juan and Puerta de Tierra. The largest shopping mall in the Caribbean is Plaza las Américas in Hato Rey, others include Plaza Carolina in Carolina, Río Hondo in Levittown, Plaza del Carmen in Caguas and Mayagüez Mall in Mayagüez. There are more traditional shops, but also many souvenir shops in Old San Juan. Imported goods from all over the world are available. Local *artesanías* include wooden carvings, musical instruments, lace, ceramics (especially model house fronts, eg from La Casa de Las Casitas, Cristo 250), hammocks, masks and basketwork. There are several shops in San Juan, but it is more interesting to visit the workshops around Puerto Rico. Contact the Centro de Artes Populares (T 724-6250) or the Tourism Company Artisan Office (T 721-2400 ext 2201) for details. Many of the tourist shops in the old city sell Andean goods.

There are a number of bookshops in the metropolitan area: The Bookstore, in Old San Juan, 257 San José, T 724-1815, has an excellent selection of English and Spanish titles. The Instituto de Cultura Puertorriqueña, Plaza de San José, has a good book and record shop with stock of all the best known Puerto Rican writers (all in Spanish). Another record shop near here is Saravá, Cristo at the corner of Sol 101, local, Caribbean, jazz and "world music".

● Banks

Banco Popular; Banco de San Juan; Banco Mercantil de Puerto Rico; and branches of US and foreign banks.

● Currency

United States dollar. Locally, a dollar may be called a *peso*, 25 cents a *peseta*, 5 cents a *bellón* (but in Ponce a *bellón* is 10 cents and a *ficha* is 5 cents). Most international and US credit cards are accepted. Currency exchange at Banco Popular; Caribbean Foreign Exchange, 201B Tetuán, Old San Juan, T 722-8222, and at the airport; Deak international at the airport; Scotia Bank exchange only Canadian currency; Western Union for cable money transfer, Pueblo Supermarket, Old San Juan.

● Warning

Crime has increased and we have received several warnings from travellers. Female tourists should avoid the Condado beach areas at night and all areas of San Juan can be dangerous after dark. Take precautions against theft from your person and your car (see **Car Hire**), wherever you are on the island. Violent car hijackings amounted to about 350 a month in 1993 and car theft was running at over 1,300 a month by 1994. Take advice locally, guided excursions or bus trips may be less hassle.

● Health

"La monga" is a common, flu-like illness, nothing serious, it goes away after a few days. Avoid swimming in rivers: bilharzia may be present.

● Water

Drought forced the imposition of water rationing in 1994 in greater San Juan and 10 other towns.

● Medical Services

Government and private hospitals. Ambulance, T 343-2500.

● Public Holidays

New Year's Day, Three Kings' Day (6 January), De Hostos' Birthday (11 January), Washington's Birthday (22 February), Emancipation Day (22 March), Good Friday, José de Diego's Birthday (16 April), Memorial Day (30 May), St John the Baptist (24 June), Independence Day (4 July), Muñoz Rivera's Birthday (17 July), Constitution Day (25 July), Dr José Celso Barbosa's Birthday (27 July), Labour Day (1 September), Columbus Day (12 October), Veterans' Day (11 November), Discovery of Puerto Rico (19 November), Thanksgiving Day (25 November), Christmas Day.

Everything is closed on public holidays. One of the most important is 24 June, though in fact the capital grinds to a halt the previous afternoon and everyone heads for the beach. Here there is loud *salsa* music and barbeques until midnight when everyone walks backwards into the sea to greet the Baptist and ensure good fortune. Every town/city has local holidays for crop-over festivals (pineapple, tobacco, sugar cane, etc) and for celebration of the town's saint. Check in *Qué Pasa* for an up-to-date listing, but call first and check in case the event has been postponed. These festivals can be great fun, especially the Carnival in Mayagüez late May. There is a festival somewhere every week.

● Places Of Worship

Roman Catholic, Episcopal, Baptist, Seventh Day Adventist, Presbyterian, Lutheran, Christian Science and Union Church. There is also a Jewish community. At the Anglican-Episcopal cathedral in San Juan there are services in both Spanish and English.

● Postal Service

Inside the new Post Office building in Hato Rey, on Av Roosevelt, there is a separate counter for sales of special tourist stamps. In Old San Juan, the Post Office is in an attractive old rococo-style building, at the corner of San Justo and Recinto Sur. *Poste restante* is called General Delivery, letters are held for 9 days.

● Telephone

Operated by Puerto Rico Telephone Co, state-owned. Local calls from coin- operated booths cost US$0.10, but from one city to another on the island costs more (eg US$1.25 Ponce-San Juan). Local calls from hotel rooms cost US$2.60 and often a charge is made even if there is no connection. The area code is 809; 800 numbers can be used. The cheapest way to phone abroad is from Phone Home (run by Sprint), 257 Recinto Sur St, Old San Juan, T 721-5431, F 721-5497, opp the Post Office by Pier 1, US$0.36/min to the USA, discounts on all other calls abroad, no 3-min minimum charge, fax, telex and telegram messages also sent and received. Overseas calls can be made from the AT&T office at Parada 11, Av Ponce de León 850, Miramar (opposite *Hotel Excelsior*, bus T1 passes outside, a chaotic place), from an office next to the Museo del Mar on Pier One, and from the airport. Three mins to New York, US$1.50 and to the UK, US$3. For Canada Direct, dial 1-800-496-7123 to get through to a Canadian operator. The blue pages in the telephone book are a tourist section in English, divided by subject.

● Broadcasting

Two radio stations have English programmes.

● Newspapers

San Juan Star is the only daily English paper. There are 3 Spanish daily papers of note, *El Mundo*, *El Vocero* and *El Nuevo Día*.

● Tourist Information

The Puerto Rico Tourism Company, PO Box 4435, San Juan 00905, with Information Centres also at the international airport (T 791-1014, F 791-8033); next to the *Condado Plaza Hotel*, T 721-2400 (ext 2280); La Casita, near Pier One, Old San Juan, T 722-1709, F 722-5208; Rafael Hernández Airport, Aguadilla, T 890-3315, T 890-0220; Citibank Building, 53 McKinley East, facing plaza, Mayagüez, T 831-5220, F 831-3210; Casa Armstrong-Proventud, Plaza Las Delicias, Ponce, T 840-5695, F 843-5958. There are also offices **New York** (T 800-223-6530, F 212-818-1866), **Los Angeles** (T 213-874-5991, F 874-7257), **Miami** (T 305-381-8915, F 381-8917), **Paris** (Express Conseil 5 bis, rue du Louvre, 75001 Paris, T 331 4477 8800, F 42 60 05 45), **Madrid** (Calle Serrano, 12 izda, 28001, Madrid, T 341-431-2128, F 577-5260), **Milan** (Via E Segre '3-20052, **Monza**, T 3939 748-820, F 749-472), **Tokyo** (Kasho Building 2-14-09, Nihombashi, Chuo-ku, Tokyo 103, T 03-3272-3060/2445), **Germany** (Kreuzberger Ring 56, D-6200 Wiesbaden 32, T 49611-744-2880, F 724-089) and **Toronto** 2 Bloor Street West, Suite 700, Toronto, Ontario, M4W 3R1, (T 416-969-9025, F 969 9478). The Caribbean Travel Service, Av Ashford 1300, Condado, is happy to help. Out in the country, tourist information can be obtained from the town halls, usually found on the main plaza. Hours are usually Mon-Fri, 0800-1200, 1300-1430.

Qué Pasa, a monthly guide for tourists published by the Tourism Company, can be obtained free from the tourist office. It is very helpful.

The Puerto Rico Tourist Zone Police are at Vieques Street, Condado (T 722-0738 and 724-5210). They can help you settle problems with taxis.

Two books which may be useful to visitors are *The Other Puerto Rico*, by Kathryn Robinson (Permanent Press, 1987), US$11.95, and *The Adventure Guide to Puerto Rico*, by Harry S Pariser (Hunter, 1989), US$13.95; they give more detail on the out of the way places than we have space for.

There is a Dominican Republic Tourist Office at Av Ponce de León 954 (Parada 10).

VIRGIN ISLANDS

CONTENTS

MAPS

THE VIRGIN ISLANDS are a group of about 107 small islands situated between Puerto Rico and the Leeward Islands; the total population is about 120,000. Politically they are divided into two groups: the larger W group, with a population of 103,000 (1992 est), was purchased from Denmark by the USA in 1917 and remains a US Territory; the smaller E group constitutes a British Crown Colony, with a population of only 17,383. Apart from their historical background, having been discovered by Columbus on the same voyage and named by him after Ursula and her 1,000 virgin warriors, the islands have little in common. The two groups share the same language, currency and cost of living, but the US group is very much more developed than the British, and tourism has been a prime source of income for much longer.

THE US VIRGIN ISLANDS

THE US VIRGIN ISLANDS (USVI), in which the legacies of Danish ownership are very apparent, contain three main islands: St Thomas, St John and St Croix, lying about 40 miles E of Puerto Rico. There are 68 islands in all, although most of them are uninhabited. They have long been developed as holiday centres for US citizens and because of that are distinct from the British Virgin Islands, which have only recently started to develop their tourist potential. The population, mainly black, has always been English-speaking, despite the long period of Danish control, although some Spanish is in use, particularly on St Croix. The West Indian dialect is mostly English, with inflections from Dutch, Danish, French, Spanish, African languages and Créole.

History

The islands were "discovered" by Columbus on his second voyage in 1493 and, partly because of their number, he named them "Las Once Mil Vírgenes" (the 11,000 virgins) in honour of the legend of St Ursula and her 11,000 martyred virgins. There were Indian settlements in all the major islands of the group and the first hostile action with the Caribs took place during Columbus' visit. Spain asserted its exclusive right to settle the islands but did not colonize them, being more interested in the larger and more lucrative Greater Antilles. European settlement did not begin until the 17th century, when few Indians were to be found. St Croix (Santa Cruz) was settled by the Dutch and the English around 1625, and later by the French. In 1645 the Dutch abandoned the island and went to St Eustatius and St Maarten. In 1650 the Spanish repossessed the island and drove off the English, but the French, under Philippe de Loinvilliers de Poincy of the Knights of Malta, persuaded the Spanish to sail for Puerto Rico. Three years later de Poincy formally deeded his islands to the Knights of Malta although the King of France retained sovereignty. St Croix prospered and planters gradually converted their coffee, ginger, indigo and tobacco plantations to the more profitable sugar, and African slavery was introduced. Wars, illegal trading, privateering, piracy and religious conflicts finally persuaded the French Crown that a colony on St Croix was not militarily or economically feasible and in 1695/6 the colony was evacuated to St Domingue.

A plan for colonizing St Thomas was approved by Frederik III of Denmark in 1665 but the first settlement failed. The Danes asserted authority over uninhabited St John in 1684, but the hostility of the English in Tortola prevented them from settling until 1717. In 1733 France sold St Croix to the Danish West India & Guinea Company and in 1754 the Danish West Indies became a royal colony. This was the most prosperous period for the Danish islands. After the end of Company rule and its trading monopoly, St Thomas turned increasingly toward commerce while in St Croix plantation agriculture flourished. St Thomas became an important shipping centre with heavy reliance on the slave trade. Denmark was the first European nation to end its participation in the slave trade in 1802. Illegal trade continued, however, and British occupation of the Virgin Islands between 1801 and 1802 and again between 1807 and 1815 prevented enforcement of the ban.

The Danish Virgin Islands reached a peak population of 43,178 in 1835, but thereafter fell to 27,086 by 1911. Sailing ships were replaced by steamships which found it less necessary to transship in St Thomas. Prosperity declined with a fall in sugar prices, a heavy debt burden, soil exhaustion, development of sugar beet in Europe, hurricanes and droughts and the abolition of slavery. In 1847 a Royal decree provided that all slaves would be free after 1859 but the slaves of St Croix were unwilling to wait and rebelled in July 1848. By the late 19th century economic decline became pronounced. The sugar factory on St Croix was inefficient and in the 20th century the First World War meant less shipping for St Thomas, more inflation, unemployment and labour unrest. The Virgin Islands became a liability for Denmark and the economic benefits of colonialism no longer existed. Negotiations with the USA had taken place intermittently ever since the 1860s for cession of the Virgin Islands to the USA. The USA wanted a Caribbean naval base for security reasons and after the 1914 opening of the Panama Canal was particularly concerned to guard against German acquisition of Caribbean territory. In 1917, the islands were sold for US$25mn but no political, social or economic progress was made for several years. The islands were under naval rule during and after the War and it was not until 1932 that US citizenship was granted to all natives of the Virgin Islands.

A devastating hurricane in 1928, followed by the stock market crash of 1929, brought US awareness of the need for economic and political modernization. Several years of drought, the financial collapse of the sugar refineries, high unemployment, low wages and very high infant mortality characterized these years. In 1931 naval rule was replaced by a civil government. In 1934, the Virgin Islands Company (VICO) was set up as a long term development "partnership programme". The sugar and rum industry benefited from increased demand in the Second World War. VICO improved housing, land and social conditions, particularly in rural areas, but the end of the wartime construction boom, wartime demand for rum and the closing of the submarine base, brought further economic recession. However, the severance of diplomatic relations between the USA and Cuba shifted tourism towards the islands. Construction boomed and there was even a labour shortage. With immigrant labour, the population increased and by 1970 per capita income reached US$2,400, five times that of the Caribbean region as a whole, with about half of the labour force engaged in tourist activities and tourism providing about 60% of the islands' revenues. With the shift from agriculture to tourism, VICO was officially disbanded in 1966, along with the production of sugarcane. Various tax incentives, however, promoted the arrival of heavy industry, and during the 1960s the Harvey Alumina Company and the Hess Oil Company began operating on St Croix. By 1970, the economy was dominated by mainland investment and marked by white-owned and managed enterprises based on cheap imported labour from other Caribbean islands.

On 17 September 1989, Hurricane Hugo ripped across St Croix causing damage or destruction to 90% of the buildings and leaving 22,500 people homeless. The disaster was followed by civil unrest, with rioting and looting, and US army troops were sent in to restore order. The territorial government, located on St Thomas, had been slow to react to the disaster on St Croix and was strongly criticized. Subsequently, a referendum endorsed the establishment of some sort of municipal government on each island which would be more responsive to that island's needs and legislation to that effect was introduced into the Legislature in July 1993. St Croix's feeling of neglect led to attempts to balance the division of power between the islands, but calls for greater autonomy grew. After some delay, a referendum was held in October 1993, which presented voters with seven options on the island's status, grouped into three choices: continued or enhanced status, integration into the USA, or independence. However, the vote was inconclusive, with only 27% of the registered voters turning out, whereas 50% were needed for a binding decision. Of those who did, 90% preferred the first option, leaving the process of constitutional change in some disarray.

In 1993 the government of the USVI reached agreement with the Danish company, the East Asiatic Company Ltd, to buy the West Indian Company Ltd (WICO), whose major holdings on St Thomas include a cruise ship dock, the Havensight Shopping Mall, a 7.2-acre landfill, the former Danish consulate, Denmark Hill, and some undeveloped land. WICO had remained in Danish hands after the 1917 purchase of the islands by the USA and had retained the right to dredge, fill and develop submerged lands in the E part of St Thomas harbour, despite local opposition. The US$54mn sale was described locally as wiping out the last vestiges of Danish colonialism.

Governor Alexander Farrelly completes his second term of office at the end of 1994. The Republican Party campaigned on the back of the unpopularity of his government to try and win the November gubernatorial election.

Government

In 1936 the Organic Act of the Virgin Islands of the United States provided for two municipal councils and a Legislative Assembly in the islands. Suffrage was extended to all residents of twenty one and over who could read and write English. Discrimination on the grounds of race, colour, sex or religious belief was forbidden and a bill of rights was in-

cluded. Real political parties now emerged, based on popular support. In 1946, the first black governor was appointed to the Virgin Islands and in 1950 the first native governor was appointed. In 1968 the Elective Governor Act was passed, to become effective in 1970 when, for the first time, Virgin Islanders would elect their own governor and lieutenant governor. The Act also abolished the presidential veto of territorial legislation and authorized the legislature to override the governor's veto by a two-thirds majority vote. The USVI is an unincorporated Territory under the US Department of Interior with a Delegate in the House of Representatives who (since January 1993) has a vote in sittings of the whole House. The Governor is elected every four years; there are 15 Senators; judicial power is vested in local courts. All persons born in the USVI are citizens of the United States, but do not vote in presidential elections while resident on the islands.

The Economy

USVI residents enjoy a comparatively high standard of living (the cost of living is the highest in the USA), unemployment is low, at around 4% (mostly on St Croix), but the working population is young and there is constant pressure for new jobs. The islands used to rely on the Martin Marietta alumina plant, and the Hess oil refinery, operating well below capacity, for employment and income, but nowadays the major economic activity is tourism. Over 1.9mn visitors come every year, of which 38% arrive by air and about 62% are cruise ship passengers. Earnings from tourism rose to US$792mn in 1992, about 70% of non-oil revenues. The number of hotel rooms is now around 5,000, generating jobs for two thirds of the labour force. There is a perennial conflict between the hotel industry, which provides employment, fixed investment and pays taxes, and the cruise ship industry, which contributes very little to the islands, but in 1993 air arrivals rose by nearly 11%, while cruise ship passengers declined by over 5%.

Industry is better developed than in many Caribbean islands and exports of manufactured goods include watches, textiles, electronics, pharmaceuticals and rum. The Hess Oil refinery operates at less than 400,000 barrels a day nowadays, compared with its previous peak capacity of 728,000 b/d, but investment of US$550mn has been made in a fluid catalytic cracking unit to produce unleaded gasoline from 100,000 b/d of heavy industrial fuel. Industrial incentives and tax concessions equivalent to those enjoyed by Puerto Rico, are designed to attract new investors with US markets to the islands. Over 30 large US corporations have set up manufacturing operations in the USVI and industrial parks are being built.

Agriculture has declined in importance since sugar production ended, and the poor soil prevents much commercial farming. Emphasis is placed on growing food crops for the domestic market and fruit, vegetables and sorghum for animal feed have been introduced. Fishing in the USVI waters is mostly for game rather than for commercial purposes. The islands' lack of natural resources makes them heavily dependent on imports, both for domestic consumption and for later re-exports, such as oil and manufactured goods. The trade account is traditionally in deficit, but is offset by tourist revenues and by US transfers. The government budget is also in deficit partly because of the high cost of public sector wages which account for 80% of spending. Revenue collections are inadequate and large sums of unpaid taxes are outstanding. In September 1993 a commission was set up to investigate ways of increasing income.

Damage from Hurricane Hugo, principally on St Croix which was declared a major disaster area, was estimated at

US VIRGIN ISLANDS: FACT FILE

Geographic

Land area	352 sq km
forested	10.3%
pastures	75.3%
cultivated	10.7%

Demographic

Population (1992)	103,000
annual growth rate (1987-92)	0.5%
urban	29.6%
rural	70.4%
density	292.6 per sq km
Religious affiliation	
Protestant	46%
Roman Catholic	34%
Birth rate per 1,000 (1988)	22.0
	(world av 27.1)
Death rate per 1,000 (1988)	5.0
	(world av 9.8)

Education and Health

Life expectancy at birth,	
male	66.7 years
female	70.7 years
Infant mortality rate	
per 1,000 live births (1988)	13.1
Physicians (1985)	1 per 622 persons
Hospital beds	1 per 505 persons
Calorie intake as %	
of FAO requirement	103%
Literacy (over 15)	90%

Economic

GDP (1987 market prices)	US$1,246mn
GNP per capita	US$11,740
Tourism receipts (1990)	US$707mn
Radio	1 per 1.1 persons
Television	1 per 3.2 persons
Telephone	1 per 1.7 persons

Employment

Population economically active (1980)	
	30,521
% of labour force in	
agriculture	1.2
mining, manufacturing	
and public utilities	10.0
construction	9.7
trade, hotels, restaurants	23.8

Source *Encyclopaedia Britannica*

US$1.25bn, equivalent to annual gnp. The islands were destined to receive US$600mn in federal assistance. Reconstruction led to improvements in infrastructure and most houses were upgraded.

Flora and Fauna

The Virgin Islands' national bird is the yellow breast (*Coereba flaveola*); the national flower is the yellow cedar (*Tecoma Stans*). Most of St John is a national park (see below). Also a park is Hassel Island, off Charlotte Amalie. The National Parks Service headquarters is at Red Hook, St Thomas. In Red Hook too is the Island Resources Foundation (T 775-6225, PO Box 33, USVI 00802; US office, 1718 P Street NW, Suite T4, Washington DC 20036, T 265-9712). This non-governmental office which is also a consulting firm, but non-profit-making, is open to serious researchers and investigators seeking information on wildlife, tourism and the environment; it has an extensive library. It may also be used as a contact base for those seeking specialist information on other islands. The Audubon Society is represented on St John by Peg Fisher at the At Your Service Travel Agency. *Virgin Islands Birdlife*, published by the USVI Cooperative Extension Service, with the US National Park Service, is available for birdwatchers. The National Park Headquarters has an excellent, reasonably priced selection of reference books for marine life, flora, fauna and island history.

On St Croix, the National Parks Service office is in the old customs building on the waterfront. Buck Island (see below) is a national marine park. In Christiansted, contact the Environmental Association, PO Box 3839, T 773-1989, office in Apothecary Hall Courtyard, Company Street. The Association runs hikes, boat trips and walks, and in March-May, in conjunction with Earthwatch and the US Fish and Wildlife Department, takes visitors to see the leatherback turtles at Sandy Point (T 773-7545 for information on trips). The association has made Salt River (see page 413) a natural park for wildlife, reef and mangroves. There are books, leaflets, etc, available at the association's office. *Exploring St Croix* by Shirley Imsand and Richard Philibosian costs US$10 and is very detailed on out of the way places and how to get to them, as is *Exploring St John* by Pam Gaffin, also US$10.

The mongoose was brought to the islands during the plantation days to kill rats that ate the crops. Unfortunately rats are nocturnal and mongooses are not and they succeeded only in eliminating most of the parrots. Now you see them all over the islands, especially near the rubbish dumps. There are many small lizards and some iguanas of up to 4 feet long. The iguanas sleep in the trees and you can see them and feed them (favourite food hibiscus flowers) at the Limetree beach. St John has a large population of wild donkeys which are pests; they bite, steal picnic lunches and ruin gardens. On all three islands, chickens, pigs, goats and cows have the right of way on the roads.

ST THOMAS

St Thomas lies about 75 miles E of Puerto Rico at 18°N, 40 miles N of St Croix. Thirteen miles long and less than 3 miles wide, with an area of 32 square miles and population of 51,000, St Thomas rises out of the sea to a range of hills that runs down its spine. The highest peak, Crown Mountain, is 1,550 feet, but on St Peter Mountain, 1,500 feet, is a viewpoint at Mountain Top. Various scenic roads can be driven, such as Skyline Drive (Route 40), from which both sides of the island can be seen simultaneously. This road continues W as St Peter Mountain Road, with a detour to Hull Bay on the N coast. Route 35, Mafolie Road, leaves the capital, Charlotte Amalie, heading N to cross the Skyline Drive and becomes Magens

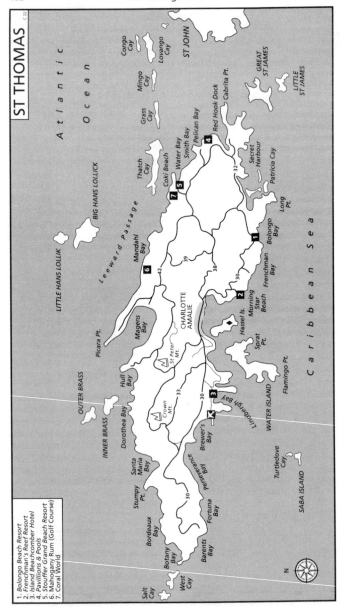

ST THOMAS

1. Bolongo Beach Resort
2. Frenchman's Reef Resort
3. Island Beachcomber Hotel
4. Pavillions & Pools
5. Stouffer Grand Beach Resort
6. Mahogany Rum (Golf Course)
7. Coral World

Bay Road, descending to the beautiful bay described below. It should be said that much of the island has been built upon, especially on its E half.

Beaches and Watersports

There are 44 beaches of which Magens Bay on the N coast is considered to be the finest on the island and wonderfully safe for small children. There are changing facilities and you can rent snorkelling equipment (but the snorkelling is not the best on the island) and loungers. Other good beaches are at Lindberg Bay (SW, close to the airport runway, good for plane spotters), Morningstar Bay (S coast near *Frenchman's Reef Hotel*, beach and watersports equipment for hire), Bolongo Bay, Sapphire Bay (E coast, good snorkelling, beach gear for rent) and Brewer's Bay (can be reached by bus from Charlotte Amalie, get off just beyond the airport). Hull Bay on the N coast is good for surfing and snorkelling. At Coki Beach (NE, showers, lockers, water skiing, jet skiing), a US$7.50 taxi ride from St Thomas, is the Coral World underwater observatory, recommended (open daily, US$12 entrance). The observatory is 20 feet under the sea and you get a good view of the reef around it. There is also a large aquarium, predator tank and other marine exhibits. On the beach snorkelling equipment can be rented for US$6, snorkelling is good just off the beach. Windsurfing lessons and rentals at Morningstar, Magens Bay, Sapphire Beach, Secret Harbour and the *Stouffer Grand*. Snorkelling gear can be rented at all major hotels and the dive shops. Sunfish sailboats for rent at Morningstar, Magens Bay and the *Stouffer Grand*. Parasailing and sea kayaking available at Blue Dolphin Water Sports, T 777-7100. Waterskiing and jet skiing at Mad Max Watersports at Lindberg Bay. There are few deserted beaches left on St Thomas, although out of season they are less crowded. The most inaccessible, and therefore more likely to be empty, are

those along the NW coast, which need 4-wheel drive to get there. Otherwise for solitude take a boat to one of the uninhabited islets offshore and discover your own beaches.

Diving and Marine Life

There is deep sea fishing with the next world record in every class lurking just under the boat. The open Atlantic Blue Marlin tournament is held in August every year; other game fish include white marlin, kingfish, sailfish, tarpon, Alison tuna and wahoo. No fishing license is required for shoreline fishing; government pamphlets list 100 good spots (T 775-6762). Deep sea boats include *Fish Hawk* (T 775-9058), *Prowler* (T 779-2515), which offers a discount if you fail to catch a fish, *Boobie Hatch* (T 775-6683), specializes in tuna, marlin, wahoo at the 100 fathom drop, *The Naked Turtle* (T 776-5506). For inshore light tackle fishing, *Ocean Quest* (T 776-5176).

Sailing of all types and cruises are available. Half day sails from US$40, full day from US$65 and sunset cruises from US$30 are offered by many boats, including *Coconuts* (T 775-5959), a 51-foot trimaran; *Independence* (T 775-1405), a 44-foot ketch; *Naked Turtle Too* (T 774-9873), a 53-foot catamaran; *Ann-Marie II* (T 771-1858), a 40-foot yacht, maximum 4 guests; *The Alexander Hamilton* (T 775-6500), a 65-foot traditional schooner; and *Spirit of St Christopher*, a 70-foot catamaran claiming to be the fastest sailboat in the Caribbean, lovely sailing, especially at sunset, half day US$45, sunset cruise US$30, T 774-7169. Power boats offering day trips are *Stormy Petrel* (T 775-7990) and *Limnos II* (T 776-4410). The *Fish N' Fool* (T 775-9500) offers a full day Sunday snorkelling cruise for US$35. Rafting Adventures (T 779-2032) offers very fast, hard bottom inflatables for tours to St John and the BVI. You can explore on your own by renting a small power boat from Nauti Nymph (T 775 5066), 21-foot runabouts; See An Ski (T 775-6265), 21-

foot makos; or Calypso (T 775-2628), 22-foot, 6 passengers, US$150/day, 27-foot, 8 passengers, US$185/day, including fuel, boats equipped with VHF radios, ice chest, stereo, fish finder, snorkelling gear, very helpful with planning a route, also scuba, waterskiing and fishing gear can be provided. Virgin Islands Power (VIP) Yacht Charters, T 776-1510, F 776-3801, PO Box 6760, has the largest power yacht charter fleet and sport fishing fleet in the Caribbean, bareboat or crewed, US$3,000-5,000 a week in summer, US$4,000-6,100 in winter.

Charter yachts available in a wide variety of luxury and size, with or without crew, cost about the same as a good hotel. Virgin Islands Charteryacht League, T 774-3944 or (800) 524-2061 has a huge number of crewed yachts from US$2,300/week in summer to US$20,000/week in winter, bareboats US$2,950-6,100; other companies include: Bajor Yacht Charters, T 776-1954; Easy Adventures, T 775-7870; Proper Yachts, T 776-6256; Sailing Vacations, T 800-922-4880 or Travel Services, T 775-9035. Note that if you plan to sail in both the US and British Virgin Islands it is cheaper to charter your boat in the BVI. To get on a yacht as crew, either for passage or paid charter jobs, try 'Captains and Crew', at *Yacht Haven* in Charlotte Amalie, a placement service which charges US$15/year and a portion of your first pay cheque.

The waters around the islands are so clear that snorkelling is extremely popular. *At-a-glance snorkeller's Guide to St Thomas* by Nick Aquilar describes 15 snorkel spots in detail. Spearfishing is not allowed and you may not remove any living things from underwater such as coral, live shells or sea fans. For divers, there are over 200 dive sites, caves, coral reefs, drop offs and lots of colourful fish to see, although be careful of short sighted barracuda if you swim into murky water. There are several wrecks of ships and even a wrecked plane to ex-

plore. Many of the resorts offer diving packages or courses and there are several dive companies. Equipment and instruction for underwater photography are available. A one-tank dive costs around US$40 while a 2-tank dive starts from US$55. Coki Beach Dive Club, T 775-4220 offers an introductory dive for US$25, cruise ships bring their guests here. Chris Sawyer Diving Centre, T 775-7320, specializes in quality service to small groups, great all day wreck of the *Rhone* trip once a week. Joe Vogel Diving Co, T 775-7610, in business since 1960, excellent night dives. Sea Horse, T 776-1987, will provide ground transport, offers lobster dives for experienced divers. The Atlantis Submarine dives to 150 feet for those who can not scuba dive but want to see the exotic fish, coral, sponges and other underwater life. Located at Building VI, Bay L, Havensight Mall, St Thomas, T 776-5650 for reservations, or 776-0288 for information (also kiosk on waterfront, usually 6 dives daily). You have to take a 4-mile launch ride on the *Yukon III* to join the submarine at Buck Island. One-hour day dives US$58, night dives US$66, children 4-12 half price.

Sports

There are a few public tennis courts (2 at Long Bay and 2 at Sub Base), which operate on a first come first served basis, but the hotel courts at *Bluebeard's Castle, Frenchman's Reef, Lime Tree Tennis Center, Mahogany Run, Sapphire Beach* and *Stouffer Grand* are mostly lit for night time play and open for non-residents if you phone in advance to book. Rates range around US$10 for 45 mins. There is an 18-hole, 6,300-yard golf course with lovely views at Mahogany Run, green fee US$60 pp, cheaper after 1400. A miniature golf course is at Smith Bay, lots of fun, $4 for 18 holes. Horse riding can be arranged at Rosendahl Riding Ring, T 775-2636. Horse racing is a popular spectator sport.

Festivals

Carnival 21-26 April. Most spectacular.

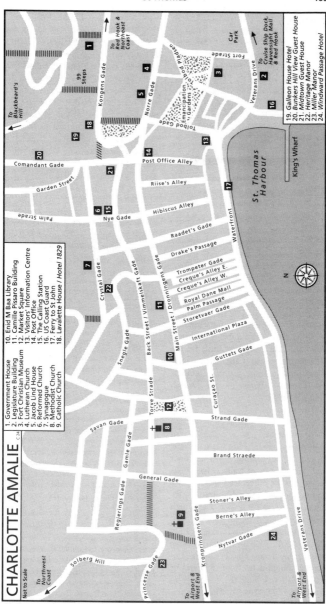

CHARLOTTE AMALIE C24
Not to Scale

1. Government House
2. Legislature Building
3. Fort Christian Museum
4. Lutheran Church
5. Jacob Lind House
6. Reformed Church
7. Synagogue
8. Methodist Church
9. Catholic Church
10. Enid M Baa Library
11. Camille Pissaro Building
12. Market Square
13. Visitors' Information Centre
14. Post Office
15. The Calling Station
16. US Coast Guard
17. Ferry to St John
18. Lavalette House / Hotel 1829

19. Galleon House Hotel
20. Bunkers Hill View Guest House
21. Midtown Guest House
22. Heritage Manor
23. Miller Manor
24. Windward Passage Hotel

To Blackbeard's Hill
To Northwest Coast
Comandant Gade
Garden Street
Palm Strade
Nye Gade
Crystal Gade
Snegle Gade
Torve Strade
Savan Gade
Gamle Gade
Reglerings Gade
General Gade
Princesse Gade
Kronprindsens Gade
Solberg Hill
To Airport & West End
Nytvar Gade
Berne's Alley
Stoner's Alley
Brand Straede
Strand Gade
Curaçao St.
Guttets Gade
International Plaza
Storetvaer Gade
Palm Passage
Royal Dane Mall
Creque's Alley W.
Creque's Alley E.
Trompeter Gade
Drake's Passage
Raadet's Gade
Hibiscus Alley
Riise's Alley
Post Office Alley
Back Street / Vimmelskaft Gade
Main Street / Dronningens Gade
Waterfront
Veterans Drive

Kongens Gade
Norre Gade
Tolbod Gade
Fort Strade
Veterans Drive
99 Steps
Emancipation Playground / Gardens
Car Park
To Reed Hook & Northeast Coast
To Cruise Ship Dock, Havensight Mall & Red Hook

St. Thomas Harbour
King's Wharf
N

Dating back to the arrival of African slaves who danced bamboulas based on ritual worship of the gods of Dahomey, the festivities have since been redirected towards Christianity. Parades with costumed bands include the J'Ouvert Morning Tramp, the Children's Parade, Mocko Jumbis on stilts and steel bands (for information on Mocko Jumbi dancing, contact Willard S John, see below under St Croix **festivals**).

CHARLOTTE AMALIE

The harbour at *Charlotte Amalie*, capital of St Thomas and also of the entire USVI, still bustles with colour and excitement, although the harbour area can be a startling contrast for the visitor arriving by sea from the British Virgin Islands. As the Fort Christian Museum (see below) puts it, "Oversized, architecturally inappropriate buildings have marred the scenic beauty of the harbour. Harbour congestion has become a major problem." One could add that the streets are congested, too. But as the museum also says, there are still a number of historical buildings. The town was built by the Danes, who named it after their King's consort, but to most visitors it remains "St Thomas". Beautiful old Danish houses painted in a variety of pastel colours are a reminder of the island's history. There are also picturesque churches: one of the oldest synagogues in the Western Hemisphere (1833) is on Crystal Gade, an airy, domed building, with a sand floor and hurricane-proof walls; it has books for sale in the office, iced spring water and visitors are given a 10-minute introduction, free, worth a visit. The Dutch Reformed Church is the oldest established church, having had a congregation since 1660 although the present building dates from 1846. The Frederick Lutheran Church dates from 1820 and its parish hall was once the residence of Jacob H S Lind (1806-27). There are several old fortifications to see: Bluebeard's

Castle Tower and Blackbeard's Castle, the latter built in 1679, now an inn and restaurant. The Virgin Islands Museum, in the former dungeon at Fort Christian (1666-80), is open Monday-Friday, 0830-1630, Saturday, 0930-1600, free, but donations welcome as much restoration work remains to be done; there are historical and natural history sections and an art gallery. In contrast to the red-painted fort is the green Legislative Building, originally the Danish police barracks (1874). Government House, off Kongens Gade, was built in 1865-87. The Enid M Baa Library and Archive is on Main Street, it is another early 19th century edifice. Two historical buildings which cannot be visited are the former Danish Consulate, on Denmark Hill and the house of the French painter, Camille Pissaro, on Main Street. The Dockside Bookshop in Havensight Mall (at the Cruise Ship Dock) has books and other publications on the Virgin Islands and the Caribbean in general. The Old Mill, up Crown Mountain Road from Sub Base traffic light is an old sugar mill open to the public. Estate St Peter Greathouse and Botanical Gardens has 500 varieties of plants, a stunning view and an art gallery for local artists.

Island Information—St Thomas
● **Transport**
Harry S Truman international airport; the taxi stand is at the far left end of the new terminal, a long way from the commuter flights from Puerto Rico and other islands. Taxi to town US$4.50 pp (US$4 for each additional passenger). There are public buses every 20 mins 0600-1900 from the terminal to the town, US$1, and hourly open-air taxi-buses which charge US$3 for the trip from Red Hook to Market Square. Bus services (US$0.75 city fare, US$1 country fare, exact change) with a new fleet of 34-passenger, a/c buses, run from town to the university, to Four Winds Plaza and to Red Hook (every hour); new routes are being added, contact Mannassah bus liners (T 774-5678). Cabs are not metered but a list of fares is published in *St Thomas This Week* and *Here's How*; fares list must be carried by each driver.

Rates quoted are for one passenger and additional passengers are charged extra; drivers are notorious for trying to charge each passenger the single passenger rate. Airport to Red Hook is US$10 for one, US$6.00 each additional passenger for extra person, town to Magens Bay is US$6.50 for one, US$4 for extra person. When travelling on routes not covered by the official list, it is advisable to agree the fare in advance. There are extra charges between 2400 and 0600 and charges for luggage. A 2-hr taxi tour for 2 people costs US$30, additional passengers US$12 each. VI taxi Radio Despatch, T 774-4550, Independent Taxi, T 776-1669, 24-hour Radio Dispatch Taxi Service, T 776-0496. Gypsy cabs, unlicensed taxis, operate outside Charlotte Amalie; they are cheaper but if you use one make sure you agree fare and route before you get in.

All types of wheels are available with rental firms plentiful. Car hire is about US$35/day, or from Budget US$42 with second day free and coupons for entry into local attractions. There are also group tours by surrey, bus or taxi. Island tours cost US$12 pp, many leave from Main Street at about 1200; complete tours only are sold.

There are a number of ferry boats to various destinations, including one from Red Hook to nearby St John (every hour from 0800 to 2400 plus 0630 and 0730 Mon to Fri, takes 20 mins, US$3 each way). Charlotte Amalie to St John, US$7, 45 mins; there is also a ferry from downtown to Frenchman's Reef Hotel and Morningstar beach, US$3 each way, leaving every hour 0900-1700, 15 mins, a nice way to go to the beach.

Helicopter To tour the islands by air, contact *Air Center Helicopters*, T 775-7335; *Antilles Helicopter*, T 776-7880; or *Seaborne Seaplane Adventures*, T 777-4491.

● **Where To Stay**

There are many hotels on St Thomas and it is possible to find somewhere to stay for US$40d a night in town or up in the hills. If you can afford it, the newer, chain hotels are comfortable, but their rates start from US$90d. Summer rates are about 33% cheaper. There is a Hotel Association counter at the airport which can help you with reservations. Please note that non-inclusion does not imply non-recommendation. Resorts, apartments and condominiums are clustered around the E end, such as the *Stouffer Grand Beach Resort* on Water Bay (PO Box 8267, T 775-1510, F 775-

3757), 290 hill or beachside suites ranging from US$295 to US$415, US$255-355 summer, well-appointed, 2 pools, 6 lit tennis courts, restaurants, bars, complimentary watersports, sailing can be arranged, lovely views over the resort's own beach to St John and the British Virgins; next to *Stouffer* is **Point Pleasant Resort**, US$240-350d winter, US$165-195 summer, children sharing parents' room free under 21, 134 rooms in villas in 15 acres of gardens, T 775-7200, F 776-5694. On the S coast is **Bolongo Bay Beach** US$200-255 (PO Box 7337, T 775-1800, F 775-3208), among others, and overlooking the entrance to Charlotte Amalie harbour and above Morningstar Beach, the huge **French-man's Reef** (a *Marriott* hotel, PO Box 7100, T 776-8500, F 774-6249), 407 rooms, 18 suites, all facilities, US$250-295d winter, US$155-200 summer, and its 96-room sister property **Morning Star Beach Resort** alongside, US$255-395 winter, US$140-235 summer. West of Charlotte Amalie are **Best Western Emerald Beach Resort**, opened in 1991, pool, bar, restaurant, 'The Palms' rooms have ocean and airport view, US$180 summer, T 777-8800, F 776-3426, and *Island Beach-comber* (PO Box 2579, T 774-5250, F 774-5615, US$125-140 winter, US$85-95 summer, poor plumbing but pleasant), both on Lindberg Bay, sheltered beach at end of airport runway. **Magens Point Resort Hotel**, T 775-5500, F 776-5524, half a mile from the sea overlooking Magens Bay, 3 miles from Charlotte Amalie, pool, tennis, adjacent to Mahogany Run Golf Course, sailing, fishing, diving packages available, 32 rooms and 23 suites, US$150-300d in winter, US$100-245d in summer; *Pavilions and Pools*, T/F 775-6110, on Sapphire Beach, offers suites and kitchens and your own private pool, very romantic, rec, US$230-255, CP winter, US$175-195 summer. Two new luxury hotels with all facilities opened in 1992: *The Grand Palazzo* on Great Bay, T 775-4444, F 775-3333, US$240 EP summer, 152 rooms, and *Sugar Bay Plantation Resort*, part of the *Holiday Inn* chain, near the *Stouffer Grand*, T 777-7100, F 777-7200, US$165-215 EP summer, children under 20 free if sharing parents' room.

In Charlotte Amalie, winter rates: *Blue-beard's Castle*, T 774-1600, F 774-5134, US$180-230, US$140 in summer, 170 rooms, sports, pool; *Blackbeard's Castle*, on Black-beard's Hill, T 776-1234, F 776-4321, US$170-190d, US$95-145 in summer, 26 rooms, restaurant. On the waterfront, Veterans' Drive heading towards the airport, is **Windward Passage** (PO Box 640, T 774-5200, F 774-1231), US$135-230 winter, US$90-135 summer, with pool, restaurant, entertainment in modern block. In the centre, on Government Hill is **Hotel 1829**, another historical building, with pool, restaurant, very comfortable (PO Box 1576, T 776-1829, F 776-4313), US$80-280 winter, US$60-190 summer; next door, behind *The Fiddle Leaf Restaurant*, is **Galleon House**, US$65-115 (PO Box 6577, T/F 774-6952), swimming pool, verandah, gourmet breakfast, but not wholly safe, missing safety bars on windows allowed theft. **Heritage Manor**, Snegle Gade (just off Back Street), T 774-3003, F 776-9585, US$70 (shared bath) to US$180 (suite), breakfast included in winter season only, US$50-95 EP summer, small pool (in old baker's oven), honour bar, clean, comfortable, helpful, each room different, rec; **Bunkers' Hill Hotel**, 7A Commandant Gade, T 776-8056, F 774-3172, from US$70, 2 sections, kitchens, TV, etc, good value; in same area but closer to centre, **Midtown Guest House** (PO Box 521, T 774-6677), US$45-75, not impressive, but reasonable rates, cash or travellers' cheques only; **Miller Manor** (PO Box 1570, T 774-1535), on the hill behind the Catholic Cathedral, clean, very friendly, a/c, from US$48-63 summer, rec; up Solberg Hill, going up from Miller Manor, is **Danish Chalet Inn**, T 774-5764, F 777-4886, US$60-80 CP summer, seventh day free, helpful, honour bar, pool, short walk to town, pleasant; **Beverley Hill Guesthouse**, US$35-60, T 774-2693, on road to airport, basic, friendly, but clean. The **Ramada Yacht Haven**, T 774-9700, F 776-3410, US$130-180 winter, US$90-110 summer, pool, restaurant, next to marina; also at the marina, check the bulletin board for boats providing overnight accommodation for US$15-30 pp.

● **Where To Eat**

There are many very good restaurants on the island, most of which are listed in **Here's How** and **St Thomas This Week**, or you can get details in your hotel. The large hotels all have their own restaurants, you will not be short of places to eat. *Hotel 1829*, on Government Hill, superb food and service; **Café Normandie** in Frenchtown, T 774-1622, for great French cuisine, or **Entre Nous** at Bluebeard's Castle, T 776-4050; **The Chart House**, at Villa Olga in Frenchtown, T 774-4262, not cheap but excellent food, rec, fish, rib, lobster, extensive salad bar, also on St Croix; *Virgilio's*, between Main and Back streets, T 776-4920, up from Store Tvaer Gade, Italian, good food and service; **Little Bopeep**, 7 Back Street, Creole specialities and pasta etc, reasonable; **Luigi's**, Back Street on corner with Snegle Gade, pizzas, Italian and bar; opposite is **Coconuts** bar and restaurant, and on same alley, **Rosie O'Grady's**; **Eat Street** on Back Street has breakfast all day plus sandwiches, pizza; **Island Reef** on Garden Street specializes in Jamaican jerk chicken for lunch, or dinner, also all you can eat spaghetti on Wed; **Zorba's**, T 776-0444, Greek, next to *The Fiddle Leaf*, T 775-2810, both across park from Post Office; **Arby's Upstairs**, on the waterfront, good, inexpensive breakfast, lunch and dinner, sometimes live music; **Hard Rock Café**, T 777-5555, next to *The Green House*, on harbour front, Veterans Drive, T 774-7998, excellent restaurant at reasonable prices, attracts younger crowd, serves drinks, happy hour 1630, in season has a band, and dancing at 2100, cover charge US$4 if no dinner ordered, ladies' night Wed, open 0700-0230 for breakfast, lunch and dinner; as does **Drake's Inn**, restaurant and bar, Drake's Passage and Trompeter Gade (good value breakfast special-best 0630 to 0900 but doesn't open that early on Sun); breakfast also at **Burger King**; there are also **Kentucky Fried Chicken**, **Baskin-Robbins** ice cream, etc. **Upper Crust Bakery** behind *The Green House*, good for continental breakfast or quick lunch. There is a **Wendy's** hamburger restaurant on Veterans Drive by the cruise ship docks, with a small Heineken bar above. The area W of the Market Square is more local, with restaurants and bars, including **Long Look** vegetarian restaurant, on General Gade. **Bavarian Restaurant and Pub** on Raphune Hill offers German cuisine and beer, live music Wed-Sat, T 775-3615; **Paradise Point** on the hill overlooking Charlotte Amalie, US$10 all you can eat buffet, happy hour 1600-1900 half price drinks, excellent view, great place to watch the sunset; **For the Birds** (T 775-6431) is a Tex-Mex style restaurant and bar outside town on the road to Red Hook, on Scotts beach, good view of Cays, Fri free buffet and happy hour 1600-1900, half price drinks, live band Thur, free drinks for ladies Thur and Sun, Sun is the big night, especially crowded during American colleges' spring break (March-early May). At Red Hook, inexpensive breakfast and lunch at *The Three Virgins*; waiting for the ferry is easy at *Piccola Marina Café-Bar*, lunch and dinner, right on the water. The *Fish Shack*, a seafood retailer, also serves lunch and dinner, T 776-7190; the *East Coast Bar and Grill* is the locals' pub with food, drinks, and conversation. At *Yacht Haven*, the *Gourmet Gallery* has excellent deli sandwiches on homemade bread to eat outside in the courtyard, also a great selection of domestic and international wines at reasonable prices (for the USVI). Award winning ribs from the *Texas Pit BBQ*, a mobile truck that shows up on the waterfront Tues-Thur 1830-2000. The *Squirrel Cage*, on Norre Gade next to World Wide Travel, cheap food, breakfast, lunch and dinner. *Wok on Water* in Frenchtown, T 777-8886 for excellent Vietnamese, Thai and Chinese food, right at the water's edge.

● **Nightlife**
St Thomas offers the greatest variety of nightlife to be found in the Virgin Islands. Bands and combos play nightly at most hotels. Several of the hotels offer limbo dancing 3 or 4 nights a week and the ubiquitous steel bands remain a great favourite with both visitors and inhabitants. At any time you will hear plenty of bass booming from the smart cars cruising the town's streets. Nightclubs include *Club Z*, *Famous*, *JP's Steak House* (also known as the *Old Mill* bar, has a progressive music night on Thur popular), *The Green House*, live rock and roll bands Mon-Sat, *Barnacle Bill's*, Frenchtown, live bands every night, some comedy, poetry reading, Mon is talent night, very popular with locals and yacht crews, *The Limetree* has 3 nightclubs, a disco, a club with West Indian bands and *Iggie's*, a bistro (cheap, good and large portions) with pool tables, darts and a sing along video machine, your chance to be a star. The Reichhold Centre for the Arts, part of the University of the Virgin Islands, has programmes with local or international performers.

Unfortunately, because of the increase in crime, you are not recommended to walk around downtown Charlotte Amalie at night, take a taxi. Between downtown and Havensight the police have put up signs advising you not to walk along the water front path.

● **Shopping**
Charlotte Amalie is packed with duty free shops of all description, and is also packed with shoppers. If you want to shop seriously, then this is the cheapest island of the 3 and has the largest selection. Nevertheless it is a good idea to have done your research at home and know what you want to buy. Local produce can be bought in the Market Square (most produce brought in by farmers on Sat 0530) and there are some small supermarkets and grocery stores. Solberg Supermart on Solberg Hill has a launderette (US$2 a load). Large supermarkets: Pueblo Grand Union, Woolworths, E end of town, K-Mart has opened near Four Winds for inexpensive clothes, sporting goods, camping equipment and household goods. Check the prices in supermarkets; what you see on the shelf and what you are charged are not always identical.

● **Telephones**
The Calling Station, Bakery Square Mall, Nye Gade, for local and international calls, Mon-Thur 0730-1930, Fri-Sat until 2130, Sun 1000-1600; also video rentals. Red Hook Mail Services, upstairs at Red Hook Plaza. VI Telecom at the West Indian Co dock.

ST JOHN

Only 16 miles square, St John is about 5 miles E of St Thomas and 35 miles N of St Croix. The population is only 3,500, mainly concentrated in the little town of Cruz Bay and the village of Coral Bay. The population of St John fell to less than a thousand people in 1950 when 85% of the land had reverted to bush and second growth tropical forest. In the 1950s Laurence Rockefeller bought about half of the island but later donated his holdings to establish a national park which was to take up about two thirds of the predominantly mountainous island. The Virgin Islands National Park was opened in 1956 and is covered by an extensive network of trails (some land in the park is still privately owned and not open to visitors). Several times a week a Park ranger leads the Reef Bay hike, which passes through a variety of vegetation zones, visits an old sugar mill and some unexplained petroglyphs and ends with a ferry ride back to Cruz Bay. The trail can be hiked without the ranger, but the National Park trip provides a boat at the bottom of the trail so you do not need to

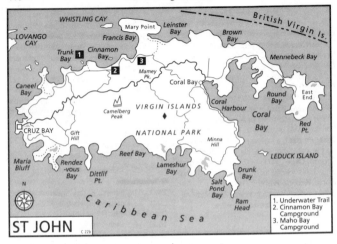

ST JOHN

1. Underwater Trail
2. Cinnamon Bay Campground
3. Maho Bay Campground

walk back up the 3-mile hill. You should reserve a place on the guided hike at the Park Service Visitors' Centre, Cruz Bay (on N side of harbour) open daily 0800-1630, T 776-6201; information on all aspects of the park can be obtained here, there are informative displays, topographical and hiking trail maps, books on shells, birds, fish, plants, flowers and local history, sign up here for activities. There are 22 hikes in all, 14 on the N shore, 8 on the S shore. The trails are well-maintained and clearly signed with interpretive information along the way. Insect repellent is essential. A seashore walk in shallow water, using a glass bottomed bucket to discover sea life, is recommended. There is a snorkel trip round St John in which the boat takes you to 5-6 reefs not accessible by land (and therefore less damaged), a good way to see the island even if you do not snorkel. An informative, historical bus tour goes to the remote East End. There are evening programmes at Cinnamon Bay and Maho Bay camps, where rangers show slides and movies and hold informal talks. For detailed information on what to do and where to find it, *Exploring St John* covers hiking trails, 39 beaches and snorkel spots,

historic sites and jeep adventures.

Beaches and Watersports

Off Trunk Bay, the island's best beach, there is an underwater snorkelling trail maintained by the National Parks Service. Not surprisingly, the beach tends to get rather crowded (especially when tour groups come in); lockers for hire, US$2 (deposit US$5), snorkelling equipment US$6 (deposit US$40) return by 1600. Other good beaches include Hawk's Nest Bay, Caneel Bay, Cinnamon Bay (there is a small museum of historical photographs and pictures here), Salt Pond (excellent beach with good snorkelling and a spectacular hike to Ram's Head), Lameshur Bay (difficult road but worth it), Maho Bay (beach is 5 feet from the road, lots of turtles, sometimes tarpon, nice and calm) and Solomon Bay (unofficial nudist beach about half an hour's walk from the road). Reef Bay has excellent snorkelling. In the National Park there are snack bars at Cinnamon Bay and Trunk Bay only. Bring water and lunch if you are hiking or going to other beaches which will not be so crowded.

Windsurfers can be rented at Cinnamon Bay and Maho Camps, sunfishes at Maho Camp. For parasailing, contact Low Key Watersports, T 776-7048, for sea kayaking contact Big Planet, T 776-6638 or Low Key for half or full day trips. Coral Bay Watersports, T 776-6850, next to *Don Carlos*, rents sail and power boats, water-skiing, sport fishing and tackle. The Coral Bay Sailing School, T 776-6922/776-6665, offers J-boat and laser rentals and group or private sailing lessons. Half and full day sails and fishing trips can be arranged by Connections, T 776-6922. For one and 2 tank scuba dives, wreck dives and night dives: Low Key Watersports at Wharfside Village, specializes in small groups, maximum 6 people; Cruz Bay Watersports, T 776-6234, across from *Joe's Diner*, offers a free snorkel map.

Sports

There is tennis at the large resorts and also 2 public courts available on a first come first served basis. Horseriding is available at Pony Express Riding Stables at Bordeaux Mountain, T 776-6494, where you can tour the sites of the National Park or go on a horticultural tour, US$40-100.

Carnival

St John's carnival is in the week of 4 July.

Island Information—St John
● **Transport**
There are only 3 roads on St John although the government map shows more roads that are barely passable 4-wheel drive dirt tracks. The island is covered with steep hills and it is hot. Mountain bicycles and long distance back-packing are not recommended ways of getting around, but you can always start walking and then catch a taxibus when it passes you. The road from Cruz Bay to Coral Bay is only 7 miles but it takes about 40 mins to drive it. There are no buses on St John, you have to use taxis or jeeps. Official taxi rates can be obtained from St John Police Department or by asking the taxi driver to show the official rate card. A 2-hour island tour costs US$30 for one or 2 passengers, or US$12 per person if there are 3 or more. Taxi from Cruz Bay to Trunk Bay, US$3; to Cinnamon Bay US$4. Vehicles may be

rented, see **Information for Visitors** below. Hitchhiking is easy. It is almost impossible to persuade a taxi to take you to Coral Bay, so hitchhike by waiting with everyone else at the intersection by the supermarket deli. There are 2 service stations, open 0800-1900, both in Cruz Bay, may be closed on holidays.

Ferry to St Thomas: hourly 0700 to 2200 and 2315 to Red Hook, every 2 hrs 0715 to 1315, 1545 and 1715 to Charlotte Amalie (fares and length of journey under St Thomas).

● **Where To Stay**
Caneel Bay Plantation, US$320-645 winter, 220-495 shoulder, 200-440 summer EP, in a variety of rooms or cottages (PO Box 720, T 776-6111, F 776-2030), 171-room resort built in the late 1950's by Laurance Rockefeller, since 1993 managed by Rosewood Hotels and Resorts, renovation due to start late 1994, several restaurants, bars, 11 all-weather tennis courts, complimentary watersports for guests inc sunfish, windsurfers, also boat rentals, fishing and diving available, ferry service between Caneel Bay and downtown St Thomas, also to sister resort of *Little Dix Bay* on Virgin Gorda, BVI; *Hyatt Regency*, US$295-475, winter, US$185-290 summer, 285 rooms and suites in 34 acres, huge pool, conference facilities, watersports, tennis etc, PO Box 8310, T 693-8000, F 693-8888; *Gallows Point*, US$225-275 winter, US$140-250 summer, 48 rooms, fans, pool, watersports, kitchen facilities (PO Box 58, T 776-6434, F 776-6520). Within walking distance of town are *Battery Hill* (PO Box 458, T 776-6152, F 776-6312), 2-bedroom villas, pools, personal service, attentive management, US$138-195d in summer; and *Caribe Havens*, lovely views, US$640-1,260/week in summer (PO Box 455, T 776-6518, F 776-6312). Cheaper places: *Cruz Inn*, T 693-8688, F 693-8590 (PO Box 566), US$50-85, CP, shared bathroom, fan, West Indian style inn, helpful advice on what to do and see, great sunsets from the Bamboo Bar, music and movies some nights, book swap; *The Inn at Tamarind Court*, T 776-6378 (PO Box 350), US$63d summer, inexpensive breakfast and dinner, bar, music and movies some nights, both are in Cruz Bay; *Raintree Inn*, also in Cruz Bay, T/F 693-8590, US$50-75 EP summer, rising in winter to US$70-95 (PO Box 566 also). At Cinnamon Bay (frequent taxibuses from Cruz Bay) there is a campground and chalet site run by the National Park Service, usually full so book in advance, maximum stay

2 weeks; space and tents, US$62d (US$44 summer), chalets US$79 (US$57), bare site US$15, a few shared showers, food reasonably priced in both the cafeteria and grocery store. Write to Cinnamon Bay Camp, PO Box 720, St John, USVI, 00830-0720, T 776 6330, F 776-6458; or to Rockresorts Reservations, 30 Rockefeller Plaza, Suite 5400, New York City, NY 10122, T 800-223-7637. At Maho Bay (8 miles from Cruz Bay, regular bus service) there is a privately run campground, write to Maho Bay Camp, Box 310, Cruz Bay, St John, USVI 00830, T 776 6240, F 776-6504. "Tent cottages" are available from US$80d (US$60 summer) a night. Tents are connected by a raised boardwalk to protect the environment, lots of steps, magnificent view from restaurant, lots of planned activities, attracts socially-conscious, environmentally-aware guests and staff, guests come back year after year, possible to work in return for your board. In Nov 1993 they also opened the Harmony Resort, (same address, phones), the world's first to operate on Sun and wind power alone and largely built from recycled materials, 8 rooms, handicap access, US$135-170 EP in summer. The St John Hostel, US$20/night, is located on Bordeaux mountain, midway between Cruz Bay, taxis don't like to go that far, but hitchhiking is easy (T 693-5544). There is a restaurant; also facilities for scuba diving and snorkelling and evening lectures on diving, sailing etc. It is possible to stay in private homes; contact Havens with Ambiance, PO Box 635, Cruz Bay. Virgin Island Bed and Breakfast Homestays (PO Box 191) T 779-4094/776-7836, also arrange rooms in private houses, US$85 and up. Serendip Apartments, PO Box 273, T/F 776-6646, fully equipped apartments, US$75-110 summer. To rent a villa contact Vacation Vistas, run by Lisa Durgin, PO Box 476, T 776-6462, about a dozen houses to rent all round the island, some with pools, nearly all over US$1,000 a week for 2, 25-50% less in summer, honeymoon specials. Catered to has rental homes and luxury villas from US$700/week in summer, US$900/week in winter for 2 people to US$4,250/week in winter for 6 people, run by Vacation Property Management Service, PO Box 704, Cruz Bay, St John, USVI 00830, T 776-6641, F 693-8191. Others include Vacation Homes, PO Box 272, Cruz Bay, T 776-6094, F 693-8455; Caribbean Villas and Resorts, T 776-6152, F 779-4044, offers 1 and 2 bedroom apartments with pools for as low as US$100/day

double, off season, US$135/day in season.

● **Where To Eat**

In Cruz Bay, *Fred's* and *Hercules* serve inexpensive, filling, delicious West Indian food. Opposite the Post Office is the *Chicken B-B-Q*. For sandwiches and light meals, *Joe's Diner*, *Jumby's*, *Dockside Pub*, *Wendy's* and *Luscious Lick's* (vegetarian meals, also has ice cream). At the *Lime Inn* restaurant, seafood, steak, excellent lobster and pasta, all you can eat shrimp night on Wed, very popular with locals and visitors; *The Barracuda Bistro* at Wharfside Village is a bakery, a deli, and a "home cooking" type restaurant for breakfast, lunch and dinner; *The Old Gallery*, West Indian and American food, 2 blocks E of ferry dock, Fri West Indian buffet, all you can eat, T 776-7544; *Morgan's Mango*, excellent seafood and steak, open air dining, great sauces; *Paradiso*, Italian; *Mongoose Restaurant*, American, also serves breakfast; *Ellington's* at Gallow's Point, continental and seafood; *Café Roma*, Italian food and good pizza; *Fish Trap*, seafood, pasta and steak; *JJ's Texas Café*, on the park, very good Tex-Mex food, hearty meat and potato type specials. For something special try the French cuisine at *Le Chateau de Bordeaux*, T 776-6611, mountain view. Breakfast is served at *Mongoose Restaurant, Wendy's, Ellington's* and *Jumby's*. In Coral Bay, *Skinny Legs* has inexpensive grilled hotdogs, hamburgers, chicken, etc, plus horse shoes and darts to play with; *Shipwreck Landing*, continental cuisine; *Don Carlos* has Mexican food; *Sea Breeze*, different menu every night, popular with locals, inexpensive; *Lucy's*, West Indian and continental. *Caneel Bay* and *The Hyatt* have several restaurants and entertainment. *The Hyatt Regency* is rec for brunch, US$25, a treat, you will not need to eat for weeks after, very lush and exquisite, super service.

● **Nightlife**

Up to date information on events is posted on the trees around town or on the bulletin board in front of Connections. In Coral Bay, *Shipwreck Landing* has jazz on Sun, a 2-day music festival in April; *Skinny Legs* has live music some nights, horse shoes, darts, and lots of special events. In Cruz Bay, the place to go and dance is *Fred's*, calypso and reggae Wed and Fri; guitar and vocals at *Pusser's* and at *JJ's*. Popular places to 'lime' (relax) are *JJ's*, the *Rock Lobster Bar*, *The Backyard* and sitting in Cruz Bay Park, watching the world go by. A disco the *Boom Boom Room* offers dancing to a DJ and videos until the small hours of the morning.

● **Shopping**

Scattered around Cruz Bay and concentrated in Wharfside Village and Mongoose Junction are shops selling souvenirs, arts and crafts and jewellery. Right in the Park is Sparkey's, selling newspapers, paperbacks, film, cold drinks, gifts. The St John Pharmacy is next to the Supermarket Deli, open 7 days a week. Small markets sell groceries, Pine Peace Market, Oscar's, the Supermarket Deli, Supernatural Foods and Marina Market. Joe's Discount Liquor has food and liquor. Food is expensive (rum is cheaper than water) and the selection is limited. If you are camping for a week, shopping at the big supermarkets on St Thomas is a good idea. Fresh produce is available at Nature's Nook, also fish and produce is sold from boats a couple of times a week at the freight dock. Love City Videos at the Boulon Centre, rents videos and VCRs, stop in and say hello to Jay, who is also the person to talk to if you want to get married, St John Weddings, PO Box 9, St John, USVI 00831, T 776-8329.

● **Bank**

Chase Manhattan in Cruz Bay is the only bank, open 0900-1500, cashes US$ travellers' cheques but will not exchange currency or process cash advances on credit cards, you must go to the St Thomas banks for that.

● **Telecommunications**

Connections (T 776-6922), as well as arranging sailing trips and villa rentals, is the place for business services, local and international telephone calls, faxes, Western Union money transfers, photocopying, wordprocessing, notary, VHF radio calls and tourist information (they know everything that is happening). Connections East (T 779-4994) does the same thing in Coral Bay.

● **Newspaper**

The St John newspaper, *Tradewinds*, is published bi-weekly, US$0.50. The funny, informative, free, St John Guidebook and map is available in shops and also at the ticket booth at the ferry dock.

ST CROIX

With 84 square miles, St Croix is the largest of the group (population 55,000), lying some 75 miles E of Puerto Rico and 40 miles S of St Thomas. The name is pronounced to rhyme with "boy". People born on the island are called Cruzans, while North Americans who move there are known as Continentals. The E of the island is rocky, arid terrain, the W end is higher, wetter and forested. Columbus thought that St Croix looked like a lush garden when he first saw it during his second voyage in 1493. He landed at Salt River on the N coast, which has now been approved as a National Park encompassing the landing site as well as the rich underwater Salt River drop off and canyon. It had been cultivated by the Carib Indians, who called it Ay-Ay, and the land still lies green and fertile between the rolling hills. Agriculture was long the staple of the economy, cattle and sugar the main activities, and today there are the ruins of numerous sugar plantations with their Great Houses and windmills. Whim Estate is restored to the way it was under Danish rule in the 1700s and is well worth a visit; it is a beautiful oblong building housing a museum of the period, and in the grounds are many of the factory buildings and implements (open Mon-Sat 0930-1600, US$4). There is a gift shop. St George Botanical Garden, just off Centreline Road (Queen Mary Highway), in an old estate, has a theatre as well as gardens amid the ruined buildings. Judith's Fancy, from the time of the French, is now surrounded by building developments and has less to see than the other two. Today agriculture has been surpassed by tourism and industry, including the huge Hess oil refinery on the S coast. Note that St Croix was badly hit by Hurricane Hugo, the effects of which are still somewhat visible in town and countryside. 90% of the buildings were damaged, but much rebuilding has been, and continues to be done; a temporary

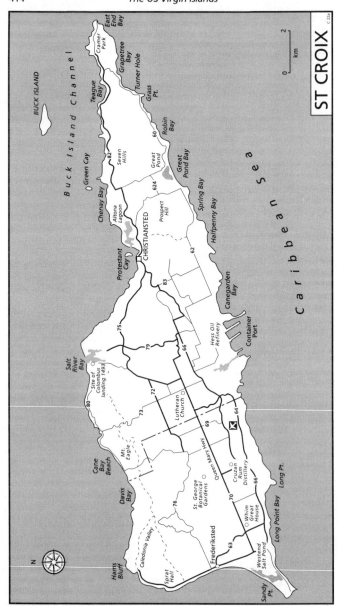

ST CROIX

cruise ship pier at Frederiksted is now being replaced by a 2-berth permanent pier and hotels, restaurants and most shops are fully operational.

Beaches and Watersports

St Croix has it all: swimming, sailing, fishing, and above all, diving. Good beaches can be found at Davis Bay, Protestant Cay, Buccaneer, the Reef, Cane Bay (good snorkelling), Grapetree Beach and Cormorant Beach. Cramer Park on the E shore and Frederiksted beach to the N of the town, both have changing facilities and showers. All beaches are open to the public, but on those where there is a hotel (*Buccaneer* - good snorkelling) which maintains the beach, you may have to pay for the use of facilities. Generally the N coast is best for surfing because there are no reefs to protect the beaches. On the NW coast, the stretch from Northside Beach to Ham's Bay is easily accessible for shell collecting (but watch out for sea urchins at Ham's Bay beach); the road is alongside the beach. The road ends at the General Offshore Sonorbuoy Area (a naval installation at Ham's Bluff), which is a good place to see booby birds and frigate birds leaving at dawn and coming home to roost at dusk. Shells can also be found on Sprat Hall beach (ask Judy or Jill at *Sprat Hall Plantation* for details). Water skiing, jet skiing, windsurfing and parasailing are all on offer. For windsurfing instruction contact Mistral School, T 773-4810. Paradise Parasailing, T 773-7060, has windsurfing, aqua bikes, waterskiing, sea kayaking, sailing, snorkelling and parasailing. The *Elinor*, a 3-masted schooner, sails between Christiansted and Frederiksted daily, from US$35 for a sunset cruise to US$60 for a day sail (PO Box 1198, Frederiksted, T 772-0919/773-7171).

The Mumm's Cup Regatta is held in October every year until 2012 to mark Columbus' arrival, with 3 days of ocean racing off the E coast. Contact the St Croix Yacht Club for details, T 773-9531.

Diving and Marine Life

At Buck Island there are guided tours on underwater snorkelling trails, the two main ones being Turtle Bay Trail and East End Trail. The fish are superb, but much of the coral is dead; it is hoped that it will come back. The reef is an underwater national park covering over 850 acres, including the island. Hawksbill turtles nest on Buck Island and, during a 1993 Buck Island National Monument Sea Turtle Research Programme, Sandy Point Leatherbacks were also observed nesting there. Half-day tours to Buck Island, including 1¼ hrs' snorkelling and ½ hour at the beach, cost between US$25 and US$35 and can be arranged through hotels or boat owners on the waterfront at Christiansted. (Mile Mark Charters, in *King Christian Hotel* complex, T 773-2628, take your own snorkelling equipment; Big Beard's, T 773-3307; Capt Heinz, T 773-3161, Llewellyn, the Calypso King, takes 6 passengers, as does Clydie; all trips, and these are, must be approved by the National Parks Service.) Another attraction is the Salt River coral canyon.

Scuba diving is good around St Croix, with forests of elkhorn coral, black coral, brain coral, sea fans, a multitude of tropical fish, sea horses under the Frederiksted pier, drop offs, reefs and wrecks. Diving trips are arranged by several companies, many of which also charter boats out and offer sailing lessons. VI Divers, T 773-6045, are located in the Pan Am Pavilion in Christiansted, they offer introductory or certification courses, equipment rentals and a full diving service. Other dive companies include: Dive St Croix, in *King Christian Hotel* complex, Christiansted, T 773-3434; Dive Experience, Christiansted, T 773-3307, good offers on prices and good equipment, including masks with prescription lenses; Cruzan Divers, 12 Strand St, Frederiksted, T 772-3701 (open 1200-1600, closed Tuesday and Thursday). Average rates start at US$35 for a pier dive, to US$45 for a 2-tank boat dive, to

US$205 for a 10-dive package. February, March and April are the months when you are likely to see hump backed whales near the islands. Boats sometimes go out to watch them.

Other Sports

Most of the large hotels have tennis courts for residents, but you can also play at the *Buccaneer Hotel* (8 courts, US$5 per person for non-guests), the *Radisson Carambola* (4 grass courts, 2 lit for night play and another 5 clay courts at the golf club, pro US$50/hour, guests offered free ½ hour clinics Tues-Fri morning), the *Hotel on the Cay* (3 courts, US$5 per person), Chenay Bay, Club St Croix, The Reef Club (2 courts, US$5/hour) and others, and there are 4 public courts at Canegata Park in Christiansted and 2 public courts near the fort in Frederiksted. Two 18-hole golf courses, one at the *Carambola* (T 778-5638), summer green fees US$230, and the other at the *Buccaneer Hotel* (T 773-2100), non-guest green fees US$20. There is also a 9-hole course at The Reef (T 773-8844), green fee US$12.50. Horse riding: Jill's Equestrian Stables (T 772-2880 or 772-2627), at Sprat Hall Plantation, 1½ miles N of Frederiksted, on Route 63, reserve one day in advance if possible for rides through the rain forest, past Danish ruins, for all levels of ability, US$50 for 2 hrs, no credit cards.

In April/May a Sports Festival Week is held, with at least three events open to all, followed the next week by the American Paradise Triathlon which attracts over 600 participants. Phone VI Pace Runners on 773-7171 for details of running courses and tours. For the Virgin Islands Track and Field Federation, contact Wallace Williams (secretary), PO Box 2720, Christiansted, T 773-5715. For swimmers, the Finmen have open water swim meetings, T Bill Cleveland 773-2153, or look in the local papers. VI Cycling organize regular monthly rides and races, T John Harper 773-0079.

Festivals

St Croix's Festival lasts from Christmas week to 6 January. There is another festival on the Saturday nearest to 17 March, St Patrick's Day, when there is a splendid parade. Mocko Jumbi dancing (on stilts) takes place at festivals and on other occasions; for information on Mocko Jumbi, contact Willard S John, PO Box 3162, Frederiksted, St Croix, USVI 00840, T 773-8909 (day), 772-0225 (evening). The St Croix Jazz and Caribbean Music and Arts Festival is held over 2 weeks in October, with lots of music and arts and cultural exhibits.

CHRISTIANSTED

The old town square and waterfront area of *Christiansted*, the old Danish capital, still retain the colourful character of the early days. Overhanging second-floor balconies designed by the Danes to shade the streets serve as cool arcades for shoppers. Red-roofed pastel houses built by early settlers climb the hills overlooking Kings Wharf and there is an old outdoor market. Old Christiansted is compact and easy to stroll. The best place to start is the Visitors' Bureau, housed in a building near the Wharf which served a century ago as the Customs Scale House. Here you can pick up brochures.

Across the way is Fort Christiansvaern, which the Danes built in 1774 on the foundations of a French fort dating from 1645. Admission is free (open 0800-1645). See the punishment cells, dungeons, barracks room, officers' kitchen, powder magazine, an exhibit of how to fire a cannon, and the battery, the best vantage point for photographing the old town and harbour. The Fort and the surrounding historic buildings are run by the National Parks Service. In front of the Fort is the old customs house, now the National Parks Service office.

The Steeple Building is a minute's walk away. Built as a church by the Danes in 1734, then converted into a military

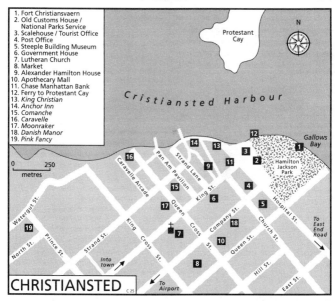

1. Fort Christiansvaern
2. Old Customs House / National Parks Service
3. Scalehouse / Tourist Office
4. Post Office
5. Steeple Building Museum
6. Government House
7. Lutheran Church
8. Market
9. Alexander Hamilton House
10. Apothecary Mall
11. Chase Manhattan Bank
12. Ferry to Protestant Cay
13. *King Christian*
14. *Anchor Inn*
15. *Comanche*
16. *Caravelle*
17. *Moonraker*
18. *Danish Manor*
19. *Pink Fancy*

Protestant Cay

Cristiansted Harbour

Gallows Bay

Hamilton Jackson Park

0   250   metres

CHRISTIANSTED C 25

Into town →

← To Airport

To East End Road

bakery, storehouse and later a hospital, it is now a museum of the island's early history. Open 0930-1200, 1300-1530.

The area here is a treasury of old Danish architecture, and many of the original buildings are still in use. The West India and Guinea Co, which bought St Croix from the French and settled the island, built a warehouse on the corner of Church and Company Streets in 1749 which now serves as a post office.

Across the way from Government House on King St is the building where the young Alexander Hamilton, who was to become one of the founding fathers of the USA, worked as a clerk in Nicolas Cruger's countinghouse. Today the building houses the Little Switzerland shop.

Government House has all the hallmarks of the elegant and luxurious life of the merchants and planters in the days when "sugar was king". The centre section, built in 1747 as a merchant's residence, was bought by the Secret Council of St Croix in 1771 to serve as a govern-

ment office. It was later joined to another merchant's town house on the corner of Queen Cross St and a handsome ballroom was added. Visitors are welcome to view the ballroom, stroll through the gardens and watch the proceedings in the Court of Justice. Across Queen Cross Street from Government House is the Dutch Reformed Church.

Queen Cross St leads into Strand and the fascinating maze of arcades and alleys lined with boutiques, handicrafts and jewellery shops. Along the waterfront there are bars, restaurant pavilions and a boardwalk, rebuilt after the Hurricane destroyed the original. Just offshore is Protestant Cay (just called The Cay), reached by ferry for US$3 return for the pleasant beach, and the *Hotel on the Cay* and restaurants, pool, tennis, watersports (T 773-2035, F 773-7046, room rates US$198 winter, US$105 summer, free ferry service).

Frederiksted, 17 miles from Christiansted, is the only other town on St Croix and although quiet, its gingerbread architecture has its own charm. Public taxis link the two towns and there are taxis from the airport to Frederiksted. Historic buildings such as Victoria House, 7-8 Straid Street, and the Customs House, have been repaired following hurricane damage. Fort Frederik (1752) is a museum; it was here that the first official foreign salute to the 13 US States was made in 1776 (see also **Sint Eustatius**). Also here was read the proclamation freeing all Danish slaves in 1848. A new pier, to accommodate at least 2 cruise ships, was built in 1993 in time for the winter season. The rain forest to the N of town is worth a visit; although Hurricane Hugo caused much damage to the forest, it is recuperating. Two roads, the paved Mahogany Road (Route 76) and the unpaved Creque Dam Road (Road 58) traverse it.

Island Information—St Croix
● **Transport**
Alexander Hamilton international airport. Boat, cycle, plane or car, the scenery is consistently beautiful (less so since Hurricane Hugo) and all methods of getting to see it are easy to arrange. Taxi airport-Christiansted US$5; airport-Frederiksted, US$4, taxi dispatcher's booth at airport exit. A taxi tour costs US$20 pp, less for groups; contact St Croix Taxi and Tours Association, Alexander Hamilton Airport, T 778-1088, PO Box 1106, Christiansted, F 778-6887. Taxi vans run between Christiansted and Frederiksted. The major car rental agencies are represented at the airport, in hotels and in both cities. Rent a 4WD car (US$40-50 a day) if you can afford it so you can drive along the scenic roads, eg to Ham's Bay or Point Udall. For scooter rental, A and B, 26 Friendensthal, Christiansted, T 778-8567. There is a distinct lack of road signs on St Croix, so if you use a car, take a good map with you.

● **Where To Stay**
The best resorts are: *Buccaneer*, from US$160d summer, US$195d winter, T 773-2100, F 778-8215, in the UK T 0800-373742, in the USA T 800-223-1108, on Gallows Bay N coast, 3 beaches, sports (see above), several restaurants, lots of packages available, and *Carambola*

Beach Resort and Golf Club, on Davis Bay, T 778-3800, F 778-1682, N coast, reopened 1993 after 2 years' closure as a Radisson resort, 150 rooms in 25 2-storey villas, rates about US$250-275d in high season, US$155-250d low season, tennis with pro, golf packages available, pool, jacuzzis; closer to Christiansted are: *Cormorant Beach* (hotel) and *Cormorant Cove* (condominium), US$260-385, first class, T 778-8920, F 778-9218. *Chenay Bay*, PO Box 24600, T/F 773-2918, secluded, private one-room cottages with kitchenettes on nice N coast beach, from US$170d winter, US$120d summer, honeymoon, family packages available, tennis, pool, snorkelling, kayaks; *St Croix by the Sea*, N coast, 3 miles W of Christiansted, T 778-8600, F 773-8002, 65 rooms, US$149-169, salt water pool, beach, etc, families welcome, restaurants and bars; just W of Christiansted is *Hibiscus Beach Hotel*, 38 beach front rooms from US$110d summer, US$180d winter, access for handicapped to beach, pool, restaurant, lots of special deals offered, T 773-4042, F 773-7668.

In **Christiansted**: *King Christian*, 59 King's Wharf, T 773-2285, F 773-9411 (PO Box 3619), with 39 superior and minimum rooms, US$90-125, honeymoon and dive packages, pool, convenient; *Caravelle*, 44A Queen Cross St, T 773-0687, F 778-7004, 43 rooms, US$95-125, also good, pool, diving, transport to other sports facilities; *The Breakfast Club*, 18 Queen Cross Street, near the Lutheran Church, T 773-7383, newly remodelled, rooms with bath and kitchenette, US$45-55d/day, US$270-330/week, gourmet breakfasts, nice view, manager is skillful golf player, highly rec; *Comanche*, Comanche Walk, Strand St, T/F 773-0210, older style, no 2 rooms alike, summer US$45-110 EP, winter US$70-129, family run, staff helpful, rec, also restaurant; *King's Alley*, on waterfront, T 773-0103, F 773-4431, summer US$73-116d EP, winter US$84-140; *Anchor Inn*, also on waterfront with watersports, fishing charters and scuba diving available on hotel broadwalk, 58 King St, T 773-4000, F 773-4408, restaurant, pool, cable TV, refrigerator, a/c, etc, US$125-160d, EP, winter, US$95-110d summer, scuba diving packages available. Slightly cheaper are *Moonraker*, Queen Cross Street, T 773-1535, US$70, small breakfast, fair but friendly; *Danish Manor*, 2 Company St, T 773-1377, F 773-1913, US$69-75 summer, pool in old courtyard, renovated rooms. *Pink Fancy*, 27 Prince Street, T 773-8460, F 773-6448, 5 mins from shopping centre and waterfront, US$125-150, bar, pool, in 18th century townhouse.

In Frederiksted: *The Frederiksted*, 20 Strand St, T 772-0500, modern, pool, restaurant, bar, good, US$115-130; ½ mile from town, *King Frederik*, on beach, pool, US$105-180, T 772-1205; *Prince Street Inn*, 402 Prince Street, T 772-9550, another historic building, small, US$44-85, charming, each room unique, rec.

North of Frederiksted: *Sprat Hall* (PO Box 695, T 772-0305), a former Great House, dating from the French Occupation, has antique furnishings, strictly no-smoking rooms in the old building, also has modern units, efficiency suites and a 2-bedroom cottage, double rates from US$100-170 in summer to US$110-240 in winter, excellent restaurant, beach bar serving lunch till 1530, highly rec, also has riding stables (see *Jill's* above) and can organize diving and fishing trips. On the N coast, *Cane Bay Reef Club*, PO Box 1407, Kingshill, T/F 778-2966, rebuilt after the hurricane, 9 suites with balconies over the sea, pool, restaurant, bar, rough sea but short walk to beach, US$80-110d summer, weekly rates cheaper, US$15 extra person; *Waves At Cane Bay*, T 778-1805, PO Box 1749, oceanfront efficiencies with balconies and cable TV, natural grotto pool, beach, good snorkelling and scuba from property, US$115-175 winter, US$85-120 summer. South of Frederiksted is *Cottages by the Sea*, US$82-102 winter, US$65-90 summer, T/F 772-0495, good beach, recently extended, good. *Ackie's Guesthouse*, US$50d, basic, kitchen facilities, in peaceful, rural location, though rather difficult to get to and from, it is a 15 min walk to the main road whence shared taxis run to Christiansted or Frederiksted, US$0.50, double after 1800. In the E, *Villa Madeleine* is a villa development, each 1/2-bedroomed villa has its own pool and terrace, US$320-420 EP, PO Box 3109, Gallows Bay, T 773 8141, F 773 7518.

● **Where To Eat**

Restaurant life on St Croix includes charcoal-broiled steaks and lobsters, West Indian Créole dishes and Danish and French specialities. Do not miss the open-air Cruzan picnics. *Club Comanche*, Strand Street, T 773-2665, popular and good for lunches and dinners; *Chart House*, on the wharf, steaks, seafood, very good salad bar, T 773-7718; *Lunchería*, Mexican food, cheap margaritas on Company Street; also on Company Street are *Harvey's Bar and Restaurant*, local cuisine, T 773-

3433; *The Captain's Table*, T 773-2026, seafood restaurant and *The Three Dolphins*; *The Smoothie Shop*, health food sandwich shop; *Stixx on the Waterfront*, Pan Am Pavilion, Sun brunch, lunch, dinner, steaks, pizzas, burgers, etc, popular bar; *Nelson's Bar and Restaurant*, in the arcade, nice, cheap; also *Hondo's Backyard*, Queen Cross St, closed 1993 but may reopen, and *Kings Alley Café*; *Ship's Galley*, deli and food store, Strand St, good. There are many other restaurants and fast food places in Christiansted. In Frederiksted, *Star of the West* (Mrs Mary Pennyfeather), Strand Street, for Créole food (Blinky and the Road Masters play local music here each Sun), *Le Crocodile* French restaurant at *The Royal Dane Hotel*. For seafood and native dishes plus music, the *Blue Moon* or the *Motown Bar and Restaurant*, rec, both on Strand Street. The out of town resorts have restaurants too. The restaurant at *Paradise Sunset Beach Hotel*, Ham's Bay, has been rec, great sunset too.

● **Food**

Local dishes include stewed or roast goat, red pea soup (a sweet soup of kidney beans and pork), callalou (dasheen soup); snacks, Johnny cakes (unleavened fried bread) and pate (pastry filled with spiced beef, chicken or salt fish); drinks, ginger beer, *mavi* (from the bark of a tree).

● **Nightlife**

Most hotels provide evening entertainment on a rotating basis, the custom of many of the Caribbean islands, so it is sometimes best to stay put and let the world of West Indian music and dance come to you. Some restaurants also provide entertainment, eg *The Captain's Table*, *Tivoli Gardens* (Queen Cross and Strand Streets), *Calabash* (Strand Street) and *The Galleon* (Green Cay Marina, piano bar). *The Wreck Bar*, Hospital Street, has crab races on Fri, folk guitar on Wed, Green Flash rock Thur-Sat. *The Blue Moon*, 17 Strand Street, has live jazz every Fri and on full moons. *Two plus Two Disco*, Northside Road, W of Christiansted (closed Mon), live entertainment Fri and Sat, US$5 cover charge; snack bar from 1200 till 1800. Most cultural events take place at the Island Centre, a 600-seat theatre with an open air amphitheatre seating another 1,600, where drama, dance and music are performed.

● **Shopping**

St Croix Leap (Life and Environmental Arts Project), on Route 76, the Paved Rain Forest

Road, is a woodworking centre, from which the artefacts may be bought direct. *Many Hands*, Pan Am Pavilion, sells only arts and crafts from the Virgin Islands. For special jewellery go to *Sonya's*, in Christiansted, and see her hand-wrought gold and silver things. The market in Christiansted is on Company Street, and has been on the site since 1735. Bookshops (all Christiansted): *Collage*, Apothecary Hall Upper Courtyard, bookshop, café and gallery, open Mon-Sat 1000-1800 (later Wed-Sat pm); *Jeltrup's* 51 ABC Company Street (on King Cross Street), both have good selection; *The Writer's Block*, King's Alley, for novels.

● **People to People Programme**

If you wish to contact someone in a similar profession to your own, contact Geri Simpson, PO Box 943, Kingshill, St Croix, USVI 00851, T 778-8007.

INFORMATION FOR VISITORS

● **Documents**

US citizens do not of course require passports for visits to the US Virgin Islands. British visitors to the US islands need passport and US visa (or waiver). Visitors of other nationalities will need passports, visas (or waiver for participating countries) and return/onward tickets.

● **How To Get There By Air**

From the USA there are flights to St Croix and/or St Thomas with American Airlines (Miami, New York, Nashville, Orlando, Philadelphia, Raleigh/Durham), Delta (Atlanta, Chicago), US Air (Baltimore, Boston, New York, Philadelphia), Private Jet Expeditions (Atlanta, Chicago, Miami), American Trans Air (Indianapolis) and Continental (New York). From Europe there are no direct flights, but connections can be made via Miami to St Thomas and there are good connections from Puerto Rico and Antigua. Airlines operating on the St Croix/St Thomas-Puerto Rico (San Juan, Vieques or Fajardo) route include American Eagle, Sunaire Express, United Express, Air St Thomas, Caribair, Vieques Air Link. Regional airlines link the USVI with other Caribbean islands and there are flights to Anguilla, Antigua, Dominica, Guadeloupe, St Barthélémy, St Kitts, Nevis, St Maarten and the BVI. There are lots of flights between St Croix and St Thomas. No departure tax at the airport (the price of US$5 is included in your ticket).

● **How To Get There By Sea**

Ocean going ships can be accommodated at Charlotte Amalie in St Thomas and Frederiksted and the South Shore cargo port in St Croix. There are regular services between the USVI and the BVI (Tortola and Virgin Gorda). Inter-Island Boat Services, *Sundance II*, between Cruz Bay, St John, and West End, Tortola, at least 3 times a day; also Water Taxi available, T 776-6597. *Native Son* between St Thomas and Road Town via West End, Tortola, or between Red Hook, St Thomas and St John to West End, several daily, T 775-4617 (Tortola). Smiths Ferry Services, T 775-7292, *M/V Daphne Elise* and *M/V Marie Elise*, between St Thomas and the BVI (both Tortola and Virgin Gorda), several daily, also between St John and Red Hook, St Thomas, and West End, Tortola, T 494-4430, 494-2355, 495-4495. *Speedy's Fantasy* and *Speedy's Delight* on the route Virgin Gorda-Road Town-St Thomas, T 774-8685. To St John: ferries run hourly from Red Hook or about every 2 hrs from the Charlotte Amalie Waterfront. For information on chartering your own boat, write to the Executive Director of the VI Charteryacht League, Homeport, St Thomas, USVI 00802.

● **Car Hire**

In St Thomas rental agencies include Budget (T 776-5774), Cowpet (775-7376), Avis (T 774-1468), Sun Island (774-3333), Discount (776-4858), VI Auto Rental (776-3616, Sub Base), Gassett (776-4600); most have an office by the airport. Rates range from US$40 to US$80 a day, unlimited mileage, vehicles from small cars to jeeps. Honda scooters, from A1's, T 774-2010, for example, range from US$25 to US$40 a day. Driving in Charlotte Amalie during business hours is a slow business. It is best to park and walk (municipal car park beside Fort Christian). Country speed limits are 35 miles an hour, in towns, 20 miles an hour, although the traffic is so heavy you will be lucky if you can go that fast. On St John: Hertz, T 776-6695; Delbert Hill's Jeep Rental, T 776-6637; Budget, T 776-7575; Avis, T 776-6374; Cool Breeze, T 776-6588, St John Car Rental, T 776-6103; rates start from US$50/day. On St John the speed limit is 20 mph everywhere. In St Croix: Avis, at the airport, T 778-9355/9365. Budget at the airport, T 778-9636, or Christiansted (*King Christian Hotel* 773-2285), also Hertz, T 778-1402, or *Buccaneer Hotel*, T 773-2100 Ext 737; Caribbean Jeep and Car Rental, 6 Hospital Street, Christiansted, T 773-4399;

Green Cay Jeep and Car Rental, T 773-7227; Berton, 1 mile W of Christiansted, T 773-1516.

NB Driving is on the left, even though the cars are lefthand drive. Donkeys, goats, chickens and cows have the right of way. There is a new seatbelt law that the police enforce with a vengeance (US$50 fine).

● **Hotels**
There is a 8% tax on all forms of accommodation in the US Virgin Islands. Hotels may also charge a US$1/night Hotel Association charge and/or a 2$1/2$-3% energy tax.

● **Tipping**
As in the mainland USA, tipping is usually 15% and hotels often add 10-15%.

● **Shopping**
The USVI are a free port and tourist related items are duty-free. Shops are usually shut on Sun unless there is a cruise ship in harbour. There are several local rums in white or gold: Cruzan (guided tours of the distillery, on St Croix, Mon-Fri 0830-1115, 1300-1615, but phone in advance, T 772-0799), Old St Croix and Brugal.

● **Banks**
US banking legislation applies. Bank of America, Citibank, Chase Manhattan, and First Pennsylvania Bank (Virgin Islands National Bank) are all represented and have several branches. Also Barclays Bank, Bank of Nova Scotia, Banco Popular de Puerto Rico, First Federal Savings and Loan of Puerto Rico.

● **Currency**
The US dollar. Credit cards are widely accepted in major tourist resorts and duty free shops, less so by local businesses.

● **Warning**
Take the usual precautions against crime, lock your car, leave valuable jewellery at home and be careful walking around at night. The Tourist Office recommends that you do not go to deserted beaches on your own, but always in a group.

● **Health**
St Thomas has a 250-bed hospital, T 776-8311, St John has a 7-bed clinic, T 776-6252, and St Croix has a 250-bed hospital, T 778-6311. All 3 have 24-hour emergency services. Mobile medical units provide health services to outlying areas.

● **Emergency**
Telephone numbers: Police 915; Fire 921; Ambulance 922; Air Ambulance 778-9177 (day), 772-1629 (night); recompression chamber 776-2686.

● **Climate**
The climate in the Virgin Islands is very pleasant, with the trade winds keeping the humidity down. The average temperature varies little between winter (25°C or 77°F) and summer (28°C or 82°F). Average annual rainfall is 40 inches.

● **Clothing**
Bathing suits are considered offensive when worn away from the beach, so cover up. There is even a law against it, you can get a fine for having your belly showing.

● **Hours Of Business**
Banks open Mon-Thur, 0900-1430, Fri 0900-1400, 1530-1700. Government offices open Mon-Thur, 0900-1700. Beware: banks, filling stations and government offices close for local holidays.

● **National Holidays**
New Year's Day, Three Kings Day (6 January), Martin Luther King Day (15 January), Presidents' Day (19 February), Holy Thursday, Good Friday, Easter Monday, Transfer Day (31 March), Memorial Day (28 May), Organic Act Day (18 June), Emancipation Day (3 July), Independence Day (4 July), Hurricane Supplication Day (23 July), Labour Day (beginning of September), Puerto Rico/Virgin Islands Friendship Day (mid-October), Hurricane Thanksgiving Day (mid-October), Liberty Day (1 November), Veterans' Day (11 November), Thanksgiving Day (mid-November), Christmas Day, 25 December.

● **Time Zone**
Atlantic Standard Time, 4 hours behind GMT, 1 ahead of EST.

● **Electric Current**
120 volts 60 cycles.

● **Consulates**
On St Thomas: Danish, T 774-1780; Dominican Republic, T 775-2640; Finnish, T 776-6666; French, T 774-4663; Norwegian, T 776-1780; Swedish, T 776-1900. On St Croix: Dutch, T 773-7100; Norwegian, T 773-7100.

● **Religion**
On St Croix: Apostolic, Baptist, Christian Scientist, Church of God, Episcopalian, Hindu,

Jehovah's Witnesses, Jewish, Lutheran, Methodist, Moravian, Moslem, Presbyterian, Roman Catholic, Seventh Day Adventist. On St John: Baptist, Christian Scientist, Episcopalian, Jehovah's Witnesses, Jewish, Lutheran, Methodist, Moravian, Moslem, Presbyterian, Roman Catholic, Salvation Army, Seventh Day Adventist. On St Thomas: Apostolic, Baha'i, Baptist, Christian Scientist, Episcopalian, Jehovah's Witnesses, Jewish, Lutheran, Methodist, Moravian, Moslem, Presbyterian, Roman Catholic, Salvation Army, Seventh Day Adventist.

It is a simple procedure to get married in the USVI and you do not need to employ wedding consultants if you do not want them. You can obtain the relevant papers from any USVI Tourist Office, send them off about 3 weeks before your visit, then pick up the marriage licence at the Territorial Court on arrival. A recommended church in which to be married is the Frederick Lutheran Church in Charlotte Amalie, contact Pastor Coleman, PO Box 58, St Thomas, USVI 00804, T 776-1315/774-9524.

● **Newspaper**
The Daily News is published daily, US$0.50, and on Fri it includes the weekend section, a complete listing of restaurants, night clubs, music and special events for the week, for all 3 islands.

● **Telecommunications**
Local telephone calls within the USVI from coin-operated phones are US$0.25 for each 5 mins. Cable, Telex, Fax, data and other business services are all available.

● **Tourist Information**
On St Thomas, the Tourist Information Centre at the airport is open daily 0900-1900. Offices at the town waterfront and at the West Indian Company dock are open 0800-1700 Mon-Fri (PO Box 6400, Charlotte Amalie, USVI 00804, T 774-8784, F 774-4390). On St Croix, there is a Tourism Booth at the airport in the baggage claim area and next to it the First Stop Information Booth. In Christiansted there is a Visitor's Bureau by the wharf in the Old Customs Scalehouse (PO Box 4538, Christiansted, USVI 00822, T 773-0495, F 778-9259), and in Frederiksted the Visitors' Centre is opposite the pier (T 772-0357). There is also an office in Cruz Bay, St John (PO Box 200, Cruz Bay, USVI 00830, T 776-6450). The publications, *St Croix This Week* and *St Thomas This Week* have regularly updated tourist information, including shopping news, ferry schedules, taxi fares, restaurants, nightlife and other tourist news. The Government offers a free road map (available at Tourist Information Offices) but considerable optimism was used in showing road classifications, especially on the St John map. Some of the 'paved highways' are really bad, unpaved roads which require hard, 4-wheel drive.

There are offices of the USVI Division of Tourism in the **USA** at: 500 North Michigan Ave, Suite 2030, Chicago, 60611, T (312) 670-8784, F 670-8788/9; 2655 Le Jeune Rd, Suite 907, Miami 33134, T (305) 442-7200, F 445-9044; 1270 Av of the Americas, Suite 2108, New York, NY 10020, T (212) 332-2222, F 332-2223; 900 17th Street NW, Suite 500, Washington DC, 20006, T (202) 293-3707, F 785-2542; 225 Peachtree St, N E, Suite 760, Atlanta, GA 30303, T (404) 688-0906, F 525-1102; 3460 Wilshire Blvd, Suite 412, Los Angeles, CA 90010, T (213) 739-0138, F 739-2005.

In the **UK**: 2 Cinnamon Row, Plantation Wharf, York Place, London SW11 3TW, T 071-978-5262, F 071-924-3171.

In **Germany**: Postfach 10-02-44, D-63002 Offenbach, T (069) 892008, F 898892.

In **Italy**: Via Gherardini 2, 20145, Milan, T (02) 33105841, F 33105827.

In **Japan**: Discover America Marketing Inc, Suite B234B, Hibiya Kokusai Bldg 2-3, Uchisaiwaicho 2-chrome, Chiyoda-ku, Tokyo 100, T (3) 3597-9451, F 3597-0385.

In **Brazil**: ITR-Representações Turisticas Internacionais Ltda, Ave São Luis, 112-13 Floor/Room 1302, São Paulo, SP, T (11) 257-9877, F 258-0206.

In **Puerto Rico**: 1300 Ashford Ave, Condado, Puerto Rico 00907, T (809) 724-3816, F 724-7223.

Hotel and restaurant lists, weekly guides and descriptive leaflets available. Texaco issues a map of the US islands, as does Phillip A Schneider, Dept of Geography, University of Illinois at Urbana-Champaign, price US$3.95.

A useful book is *The Settlers' Handbook for the US Virgin Islands*, Megnin Publishing (PO Box 5161, Sunny Isle, St Croix, USVI 00823-5161), US$7.95.

BRITISH VIRGIN ISLANDS

THE BRITISH VIRGIN IS-
LANDS (BVI), grouped around
Sir Francis Drake Channel, are
less developed than the US group, and
number some 60 islands, islets, rocks,
and cays, of which only 16 or so are
inhabited. They are all of volcanic origin
except one, Anegada, which is coral and
limestone. Most of the land was cleared
years ago for its timber or to grow crops,
and it is now largely covered by secondary forest and scrub. In the areas with
greatest rainfall there are mangoes and
palm trees, but generally the islands can
look brown and parched, or green and
lush just after rain. Mangrove and sea
grape can be found in some areas along
the shore.

The two major islands, Tortola and Virgin Gorda, along with the groups of
Anegada and Jost Van Dyke, contain
most of the total population of about
17,383, which is mainly of African descent. The resident population was only
10,985 in 1980 and most of the increase
has come from inward migration of workers for the construction and tourist industries. About half the present
population is of foreign origin. Everyone
speaks English. While there are some
large resorts in the BVI, there are no
high-rise hotels, nightclubs and casinos,
as found in some of the other islands
which depend heavily on tourism. In fact,
there is very little to do at all on land and
nearly everything happens in the beautiful water which surrounds the islands. If
you are keen on watersports and sailing
and have adequate finance (the Virgin
Islands are not cheap), you will enjoy
island hopping.

History

Although discovered by the Spanish in
1493, the islands were first settled by
Dutch planters before falling into British
hands in 1666. In 1672 the Governor of
the Leeward Islands annexed Tortola and
in 1680 planters from Anguilla moved
into Anegada and Virgin Gorda. Civil
government was introduced in 1773 with
an elected House of Assembly and a part-
elected and part-nominated Legislative
Council. Between 1872 and 1956 the islands were part of the Leeward Islands
Federation (a British Colony), but then
became a separately administered entity,
building up economic links with the US
Virgin Islands rather than joining the
West Indies Federation of British territories. In 1960 direct responsibility was
assumed by an appointed Administrator,
later to become Governor. The Constitution became effective in 1967 but was
later amended in 1977 to allow the islands greater autonomy in domestic affairs. Mr H Lavity Stoutt, of the Virgin
Islands Party (VIP), became Chief Minister in 1967. At the most recent election
in November 1990 the Virgin Islands
Party, still led by Mr Lavity Stoutt, won
another term in office with six seats. The
Independent People's Movement (IPM,
formed in 1989) won one seat and independents took two seats, but the opposition United Party (UP) lost its
representation in the Legislature. Elections were due by February 1995.

Government

A nearly self-contained community, the
islands are a Crown Colony with a Governor appointed by London, although to
a large extent they are internally self-governing. The Governor presides over the
Executive Council, made up of the Chief
Minister, the Attorney-General and
three other ministers. A 12-member Legislative Council comprises nine mem-

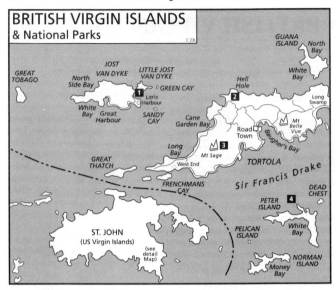

BRITISH VIRGIN ISLANDS
& National Parks

GUANA ISLAND — North Bay
GREAT TOBAGO
JOST VAN DYKE — North Side Bay
LITTLE JOST VAN DYKE
GREEN CAY
White Bay
Hell Hole
Long Swamp
White Bay — Great Harbour — Little Harbour
SANDY CAY
Cane Garden Bay
Mt Belle Vue
Road Town
Baugher's Bay
GREAT THATCH
Long Bay
Mt Sage
West End
TORTOLA
Sir Francis Drake
FRENCHMANS CAY
DEAD CHEST
PETER ISLAND
ST. JOHN (US Virgin Islands) (see detail Map)
PELICAN ISLAND
White Bay
NORMAN ISLAND
Money Bay

bers elected by universal adult suffrage, one member appointed by the Governor, a Speaker elected from outside by members of the Council, and the Attorney-General as an ex-officio member. The British Government has accepted a proposal from a constitutional review commission for the Legislative Council to be enlarged from nine to 13 seats. The four new members would represent the territory as a single constituency. This plan would create the first mixed electoral system in the UK, in which voters would have one vote for their constituency member as usual, plus four votes for the new territory-wide representatives. Although the British government intended it to come into effect before 6 December 1994, the last date for the dissolution of the current legislature, there was considerable disquiet in the BVI and in the UK at the way in which it was being rushed through without prior consultation.

The Economy

The economy is based predominantly on tourism; the islands offer up-market tourism in quiet, unspoiled surroundings and earnings are around US$125mn a year. There are approximately 1,213 hotel rooms, half of which are on Tortola and a third on Virgin Gorda, the rest being scattered around the other islands, but nearly half of those visitors who stay on the islands charter yachts and only sleep on land for their arrival and for departure nights.

Tourism in the BVI was hit badly by the recession and in 1991 stopover arrivals were down by nearly 17% while cruise ship passengers declined by almost 19%, with the fall being registered in all markets. The yacht charter business saw several closures in 1991/92 because of declining demand, higher air fares and tax changes in the USA and France, which brought greater competition from the French Caribbean. A new charter yacht strategy was announced in

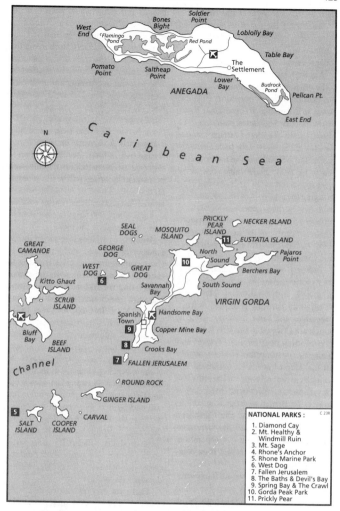

NATIONAL PARKS :

1. Diamond Cay
2. Mt. Healthy & Windmill Ruin
3. Mt. Sage
4. Rhone's Anchor
5. Rhone Marine Park
6. West Dog
7. Fallen Jerusalem
8. The Baths & Devil's Bay
9. Spring Bay & The Crawl
10. Gorda Peak Park
11. Prickly Pear

1992, removing import duty and introducing licences to encourage more business. The Government aims to attract more quality operators in a more highly structured environment with streamlined entry regulations. Crewed yachts are to be pushed rather than increasing bare boat charters. In another development to promote the islands, the British Virgin Islands Film Commission was set up to encourage film production in the islands and the previous permit fee was lifted. Film crews were expected to bring considerable economic benefit through their use of local services and labour.

Since 1991 the tourism industry has shown improvement, particularly in the numbers of cruise ships calling and passenger arrivals reached 113,245 in 1993.

A growth industry of the last few years is the offshore company business, which has benefited from uncertainty in Hong Kong and Panama. International Business Company legislation passed in 1984 allows locally-registered foreign companies tax exemptions with little currency risk as the US dollar is the national currency. In 1993, 29,000 new companies were registered as IBCs (21,000 in 1992), bringing the total to over 100,000 and fees from new licences generated substantial revenues. Diversification of the offshore financial centre is being sought; currently over one third of government revenue comes from this sector.

Industry on the islands is limited to small scale operations such as rum, sand or gravel, and desalination plants are being built. Farming is limited to fruit, vegetables and some livestock, some of which are shipped to the USVI. Fishing is expanding both for export, sport and domestic consumption. However, nearly all the islands' needs are imported. Although current revenues are healthy, the Government is still dependent for capital sources on British assistance, as well as funding from the EEC, the Caribbean Development Bank and the Commonwealth Development Corporation. Loans have also been raised from commercial banks.

1994 was election year and the government announced heavy spending plans in its budget, with US$12.6mn being spent on the new government administration buildings, the secondary school and roads on Tortola. A 5-year, US$80mn, infrastructural spending programme was also announced.

Diving and Marine Life

There is much to see around the Virgin Islands and considerable work is being done to establish marine parks and conserve the reefs. The Department of Conservation and Fisheries is in charge of the BVI's natural resources and a fisheries management plan should be in effect by 1995 to avoid overfishing and help conserve the reefs. The 17.5-km Horseshoe Reef off the S shore of Anegada is the third largest reef in the world (after the Great Barrier Reef and Belize) and now a Protected Area, with an anchor and fishing ban in force. The anchor ban is expected to remain indefinitely although permanent moorings will be put at popular dive sites. There are 80 visible wrecks around Anegada and many more covered by coral; about 300 ships are believed to have foundered on the reef.

Humpback whales migrate to the islands every year and the Department of Conservation and Fisheries is trying to estimate their numbers with the aim of designating the BVI waters as a marine mammal sanctuary. If you see any (mostly N of Tortola), let them know. Similarly, turtles are being counted with the help of volunteers in order to draw up environmental legislation to protect them. Leatherback turtles travel to N shore beaches to nest, but their numbers have been declining fast. Hawksbill and Green turtles are more common but still endangered. For several months of the year the killing of turtles or taking their eggs is prohibited and the export of turtle products is illegal. If you see turtle on the menu, or a turtle shell product, please do not buy it; even the legal killing damages the population.

There are over 60 charted dive sites, many of which are in underwater National Parks. They include walls, pinnacles, coral reefs, caverns and wrecks. The most visited wreck is that of the *Rhone*, sunk in 1867 in a storm and broken in two. The bow section is in about 80 feet of water and you can swim through the hull. The stern is shallower and you can see the prop shaft and the propeller (and an octopus). Another wreck is the 246-foot *Chikuzen* sunk in 1981 about 6 miles N of Tortola, where you will see bigger fish such as barracuda and rays. Most Caribbean and Atlantic species of tropical fish and marine invertebrates can be found in BVI waters, with hard and soft corals, gorgonians and sea fans. Watch out for fire coral, sea urchins and the occasional bristle worm. Visibility ranges from 60-200 feet and the water temperature varies from 76°F in winter to 86°F in summer. Wet suits are not essential but most people wear them.

A moorings system has been set up to eliminate anchor damage to the coral and all users of the moorings must have a National Parks permit. These are available through dive operators, charter companies, government offices and the National Parks Trust. They cost US$10-15, depending on the number of people on board, and the revenue goes towards maintenance and new moorings. As yet, there is no legislation to prohibit anchoring in areas other than in the Marine Parks, but it is actively discouraged. National Parks Trust moorings (of which there were over 200 by mid-1994) are located at The Caves, The Indians, The Baths, Pelican Island, Carrot Shoal, dive sites at Peter Island, Cooper Island, Ginger Island and Norman Island, The *Rhone's* anchor, the wreck of *The Rhone*, the wreck of *The Fearless*, Deadchest Island, Blonde Rock, Guana Island, The Dogs and other popular diving and recreational sites.

There are several dive shops around the islands which offer individual tours, package deals with hotels or rendezvous with charter boats. Rates depend on the distance to the dive site but are generally US$80-100 for 2 tanks, including equipment hire. A day's resort course and shallow dive costs about the same. Baskin in the Sun, established in 1969 and a PADI 5-star dive centre, is at *Prospect Reef* and Soper's Hole. Packages can be arranged with all the major hotels and in fact they are often full with package business so book individual diving in good time. They won the 1993 PADI award for Excellence in Resort Dive Operations. They have 3 boats, 10 certified instructors and offer full service, Box 108, Road Town, T 494-2858, 800-233-7938, F 494-4304. Dive BVI Ltd, another PADI 5-star operation (also NAUI courses) is at Virgin Gorda Yacht Harbour, Leverick Bay and Peter Island, with 5 boats, Box 1040, Virgin Gorda, T 495-5513, 800-848-7078, F 495-5347. Blue Water Divers, with 3 boats, has been at Nanny Cay since 1980, Box 846, Road Town, T 494-2847, F 494-0198. Kilbride's Underwater Tours is at the Bitter End Yacht Club, North Sound, Box 46, Virgin Gorda, T 495-9638, 800-932-4286, F 495-9369. Underwater Safaris, with 3 boats is at *The Moorings*, Road Town (PO Box 139, T 494-3235, F 494-5322), and has a small shop on Cooper Island which is used as a surface interval between dives in the area, eg *The Rhone*. Air refills are available here. Underwater Safaris (and most other companies) will take you anywhere you want to dive, even if there is only one passenger on the boat, and each dive tour location is determined by the first people to book, although they normally only go to sites within half an hour of Road Town. Underwater photography, camera rental, and film processing is offered by Rainbow Visions Photography, Prospect Reef, Box 680, Road Town, T 494-2749. They often join dive boats and take video film of you underwater. Great fun and excellent quality but expensive at US$120 for a 2-tank dive. Several companies offer snorkelling tours and there are lots of yachts offering daysails to all the little islands at around US$45-75 with snorkelling, beverages and sometimes lunch. *Patouche II* (T 494-2845), *Kuralu* (T 495-4381), *White Squall* (T 495-2564) and Ppalu (T 495-7500) all offer popular day sails, but avoid them when the cruise ships are in town as they are often packed out.

Beaches and Watersports

There are lovely sandy beaches on all the islands and many of them are remote, empty and accessible only from the sea. The clean, crystal-clear waters around the islands provide excellent snorkelling, diving, cruising and fishing. Most of the hotels offer a wide variety of watersports, including windsurfing, sunfish, scuba, snorkelling and small boats. Jet skis are banned.

"Bareboating" (self-crew yacht chartering) is extremely popular and the way most visitors see the islands. The BVI are one of the most popular destinations in the world for bareboaters. If you do not feel confident in handling a yacht, there are various options from fully-crewed luxury yachts to hiring a skipper to take you and your bareboat out for as long as you need. Navigation is not difficult, the water and weather are generally clear and there are many excellent cruising guides and charts for reference. Most of the islands offer at least one beautiful bay and it is possible even at the height of the season to find deserted beaches and calm anchorages. Bareboaters are not supposed to sail to Anegada because of the hazardous, unmarked route through the reef and generally only crewed yachts go there. If you are sailing independently, however, check the charts, ensure you approach in clear daylight when the sun is high, or call the *Anegada Reef Hotel* at Setting Point when you are within sight and they will direct you over the radio. Charter companies are too numerous to list here, there are many on Tortola and several more on Virgin Gorda. Contact the Tourist Office for a list of bareboats with prices. For crewed yachts, Caribbean Connections, T 494-3623; Virgin Islands Sailing, T 494-2774 or Paradise Yacht Vacations, T 494-0253, will be able to match your needs with the hundreds of charter yachts available. Marinas are plentiful with yard services, haul out, fuel docks, water and showers.

Sailing and boardsailing schools offer 3-hour to one-week courses. The Nick Trotter Sailing School at the Bitter End Yacht Club, North Sound, T 494-2745, has sailing and windsurfing courses for all ages with a wide variety of craft, very popular. Offshore Sailing School Ltd, at Treasure Isle Jetty, T 800-221-4326, has courses on live-aboard cruising as well as learn-to-sail on dinghies. Thomas Sailing at Nanny Cay, T 494-0333, F 494-0334, has land-based and live-aboard courses.

The annual spring Regatta is held in Sir Francis Drake's Channel, considered one of the best sailing venues in the world. It is the second stage of the Caribbean Ocean Racing Triangle (CORT) series of regattas, so international yachtsmen and women compete alongside local islanders and sailors on hired bareboats. The Regatta Village (and parties) is at Nanny Cay. Contact the BVI Yacht Club, T 494-3286, for information. A cruising permit is required by everyone cruising in the BVI: 1 December-30 April, all recorded charter boats US$2 pp/day, all non-recorded charter boats US$4 pp/day; 1 May-30 November, US$0.75 and US$4 respectively. Dive boats, sport fishing boats etc should contact the Customs Department for cruising permit regulations. Permits are required if you want to use any National Parks Trust moorings, call The Trust office at T 494-3904.

Windsurfing is popular in the islands and there is an annual Hi-Ho (hook in and hold on) race which attracts windsurfers from all over the world. The week long event involves inter-island racing with accommodation on sailing yachts (contact Ocean Promotions T 494-0337). Boardsailing BVI is at Trellis Bay, Beef Island, T 495-2447, F 495 1626, and at Nanny Cay (a BIC Centre), T 494-4022, with schools and shops. Both schools have good equipment for beginners and advanced sailors.

Sport fishing is becoming more popular with many companies offering day trips aboard sport fishing boats: *Anegada Reef Hotel*, Anegada, US$500-900, T 495-8002; *Miss Robbie*, Prospect Reef, Tortola, T 495-4870/3311, US$400-750; *Classic* at *Biras Creek*, Virgin Gorda, US$450-800, T 494-3555. A local permit is required for fishing, call the Fisheries Division for information, T 494-3429; spearfishing is not allowed, hunting on land is also banned and no firearms are allowed. There are areas known to house ciguatera (fish poisoning) around the reefs, so it is important to contact the Fisheries Division before fishing of any kind is undertaken.

Other Sports

There is a tennis club on Tortola and many hotels have their own courts. Golf has not been developed although a couple of the hotels have small practice courses. Horse riding can be arranged through the hotels, or T 494-2262, Shadow's Stables, or T 494-4442, Ellis Thomas, for riding through Mt Sage National Park or down to Cane Garden Bay, Tortola. Walking and birdwatching are quite popular and trails have been laid out in places. Spectator sports include cricket and soft ball. Horse racing is held at Sea Cow's Bay, Tortola, one Sunday a month and is a popular local event, worth seeing if you want to see the Virgin Islanders at leisure. Gyms include Bodyworks, T 494-2705, and Golden Palms, T 494-0138.

Festivals

The BVI Summer Festival is held over 2 weeks at the end of July and beginning of August. There is entertainment every night with steel bands, fungi and calypso music, a Prince and Princess show and a calypso show. During the year there are many regattas, such as the annual BVI Spring Regatta in April, Foxy's Wooden Boat Regatta in September and windsurfing events, which attract many extracurricular activities and lots of parties.

TORTOLA

The main island, with a population of about 14,000, or 81% of the total population of the BVI. Mount Sage, the highest point in the archipelago, rises to 1,780 feet, and traces of a primeval rain forest can still be found on its slopes. Walking trails have been marked through Mount Sage National Park. The S part of the island is mountainous and rocky, covered with scrub, frangipani and ginger thomas. The N has groves of bananas, mangoes and palm trees, and long sandy beaches.

Road Town, on the S shore, is the capital and business centre of the territory and is dominated by marinas and financial companies, many of which line the harbour. Main Street houses many of the oldest buildings, churches and the prison, and is the most picturesque street. Until the 1960s, Main Street was the waterfront road, but land infill has allowed another road, Waterfront Drive, to be built between it and the sea. Cruise ships now call frequently at Road Town harbour at Port Purcell, while a new dock in the Wickhams Cay area is due to open in 1995. There are many gift shops, hotels and restaurants catering for the tourist market. In 1992-93, very grand and imposing government offices were built on the waterfront overlooking the harbour entrance. Banks, offices, Cable and Wireless, the Tourist Office and a small craft village are also in this area. All these buildings are built on infilled land, called Wickhams Cay; the restaurant *Spaghetti Junction* was once a bar overlooking the water but is now some way back, divided from the sea by roads and office buildings. The Governor resides in Government House above Waterfront Drive overlooking the harbour (T 494 2345, F 494 4435). The house is in a classical style, painted white with green shutters and surrounded by beautifully tended gardens with a fine display of flamoyant trees in the front.

The 4-acre Joseph Reynold O'Neal Botanic Gardens near the Police Station in Road Town (free admission, donations welcomed) has a good selection of tropical and subtropical plants such as palm trees, succulents, ferns and orchids. There is a good booklet which gives a suggested route round the garden, pond, orchid house, fern house and medicinal herb garden. It is a peaceful place, luxuriant, with magnificent pergolas, recommended. The small BVI Folk Museum in a lovely old wooden building on Main Street behind *Pusser's Bar* closed in 1994 but may reopen late 1995.

There are also communities at East End and West End. West End has more facilities for visitors. *Sopers Hole* is a port of entry (ferries to St Thomas, St John and Jost Van Dyke leave from here) and popular meeting place for people on yachts. *Pussers* is alongside the moorings and there are several shops, including a

dive shop and some boutiques. All the buildings are painted in bright pinks and blues. It is very relaxing to sip cocktails on the dock and watch the yachts come and go. The *Jolly Roger*, on the opposite side of the bay is a popular yachtie hangout. The area is famous for being the former home of Edward Teach (Blackbeard the pirate).

The best beaches are along the N W and N coasts. Smugglers Cove and Apple Bay, West End, have fine sandy beaches. If you have no transport, Smugglers Cove is an hour's walk on a dirt road over a steep hill from West End. There is an old hotel with a bar which is often self-service; the beach is usually deserted. Cane Garden Bay is the best beach and yachts can anchor there. There are two reefs with a marked gap in between. The Callwood Rum Distillery at Cane Garden Bay still produces rum with copper boiling vats and an old still and cane crusher in much the same way as it did

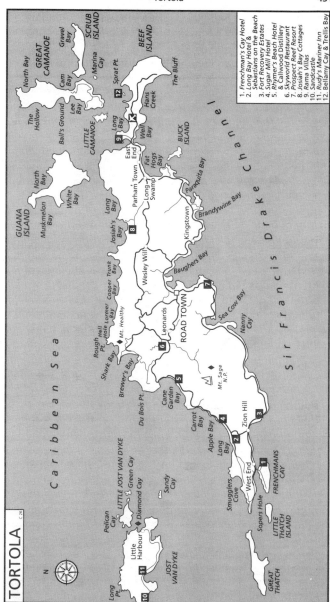

TORTOLA

N

1. Frenchman's Cay Hotel
2. Long Bay Hotel &
   Sebastians on the Beach
3. Fort Recovery Estates
4. Sugar Mill Hotel
5. Rhymer's Beach Hotel
   & Callwood Distillery
6. Skyworld Restaurant
7. Prospect Reef Resort
8. Josiah's Bay Cottages
9. Rama Villas
10. Sandcastle
11. Rudy's Mariner Inn
12. Bellamy Cay & Trellis Bay

Caribbean Sea

Sir Francis Drake Channel

GREAT CAMANOE
North Bay
Gravel Bay
SCRUB ISLAND
Cam Bay
Lee Bay
Marina Cay
The Hollow
Ball's Ground
LITTLE CAMANOE
Sprat Pt.
BEEF ISLAND
The Bluff
Hans Creek
Long Bay
Well Bay
East End
Fat Hogs Bay
BUCK ISLAND
GUANA ISLAND
North Bay
Muskmelon Bay
White Bay
Long Bay
Parham Town
Long Swamp
Paraquita Bay
Brandywine Bay
Josiah's Bay
Kingstown
Copper Trunk Bay
Wesley Will
Baughers Bay
Rough Hell Pt.
Hole Lormer
Mt. Healthy
Leonards
ROAD TOWN
Sea Cow Bay
Nanny Cay
Shark Bay
Brewer's Bay
Du Bois Pt.
Cane Garden Bay
Mt. Sage N.P.
Zion Hill
Carrot Bay
Apple Bay
Long Bay
West End
Smugglers Cove
FRENCHMANS CAY
LITTLE THATCH ISLAND
GREAT THATCH
Sopers Hole
Pelican Cay
LITTLE JOST VAN DYKE
Green Cay
Diamond Cay
Sandy Cay
Little Harbour
JOST VAN DYKE
Long Pt.

in the 18th century. Apple Bay is popular with surfers from November for a few months, as is the E end of Cane Garden Bay and Josiah's Bay. Brewers Bay is a long curving bay with plenty of shade and a small campsite in the trees by the beach. Josiah's Bay (another campsite) and Long Bay, East End, are also pleasant

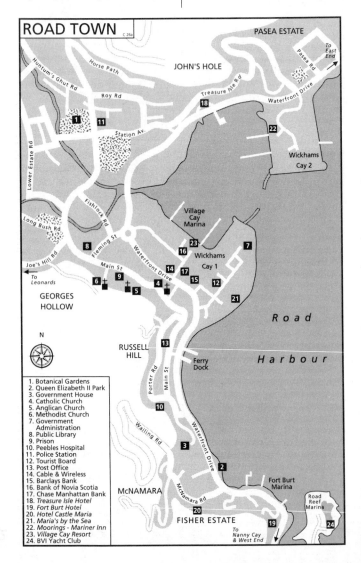

ROAD TOWN

C 26a

PASEA ESTATE

JOHN'S HOLE

Huntum's Ghut Rd

Horse Path

Roy Rd

Station Av.

Treasure Isle Rd

Pasea Rd

To East End

Waterfront Drive

Lower Estate Rd

Fishlock Rd

Long Bush Rd

Joe's Hill Rd

To Leonards

GEORGES HOLLOW

Fleming St

Main St

Waterfront Drive

Village Cay Marina

Wickhams Cay 2

Wickhams Cay 1

N

RUSSELL HILL

Ferry Dock

Porter Rd

Main St

Wailing Rd

Road

Harbour

McNAMARA

Waterfront Drive

McNamara Rd

Fort Burt Marina

FISHER ESTATE

To Nanny Cay & West End

Road Reef Marina

1. Botanical Gardens
2. Queen Elizabeth II Park
3. Government House
4. Catholic Church
5. Anglican Church
6. Methodist Church
7. Government Administration
8. Public Library
9. Prison
10. Peebles Hospital
11. Police Station
12. Tourist Board
13. Post Office
14. Cable & Wireless
15. Barclays Bank
16. Bank of Novia Scotia
17. Chase Manhattan Bank
18. *Treasure Isle Hotel*
19. *Fort Burt Hotel*
20. *Hotel Castle Maria*
21. *Maria's by the Sea*
22. *Moorings - Mariner Inn*
23. *Village Cay Resort*
24. BVI Yacht Club

beaches. Carrot Bay is stony, there is no sand, but there are lots of pelicans and the village is pleasant, having a very Caribbean feel with several bars, palm trees and banana plants. Watch out for strong rip currents at some of the N shore beaches, and seek local advice before swimming, especially if the surfers are out.

Tortola is superb, but the full flavour of the BVI can only be discovered by cruising round the other islands (see above, **Beaches and Watersports**). You can also take day trips on the regular ferry to Virgin Gorda, with lunch and a visit to The Baths included if you wish.

Island Information—Tortola
● **Where To Stay**

There is a 7% hotel tax and a 10% service charge in the BVI. Rates apply to double rooms, EP, winter/summer. **Road Town**: *Treasure Isle*, on hillside overlooking the marina and Sir Francis Drake Channel, 43 pleasant rooms, US$140-215/80-140, pool, tennis, restaurant, a/c, TV, convenient for business travellers, used by people on crewed yacht charters for first and last night, helpful staff at front desk, PO Box 68, T 494-2501, F 494-2507; under same ownership and used by *Treasure Isle* for all watersports is the *Moorings/Mariner Inn*, at the dockside for bareboat charters, 36 standard rooms with kitchenette, US$130-180, 4 suites, fan, tennis, small pool by bar, briefing room for those setting out on yachts, informal and relaxed but well organized, Underwater Safaris dive shop on site, PO Box 139, T 494-2332; *Village Cay Resort and Marina*, directly opposite on the other side of the harbour, 20 clean, bright rooms, well-furnished although a bit sterile, TV, phone, cheaper rooms face inland, US$90-125/70-90, restaurant and bar overlooking yachts, good food, buffet with steel band Fri 1800-2300, also showers, toilets and launderette for sailors, PO Box 145, T 494-2771; *Maria's By The Sea*, by new government buildings, overlooks sea but no beach, older part is simple, double rooms have kitchenette, a/c, TV, phone, 2 double beds, new wing has bigger rooms, balconies, US$85-125/70-105, conference room, friendly, Maria's cooking rec, light and airy entrance with bar, pool, PO Box 206, T 494-2595; *Sea View Hotel*, 10 studios, 6 suites, pool, US$44-160 EP all year, single or double, PO Box 59, T 494-2483; 200m further on is *Fort Burt*, on hillside opp Road Reef Marina, was fort built by Dutch, first hotel on island built 1953, 7 rooms, US$95-110/80-110, suite US$185/150, TV in some, a/c, fans, no phones, open-air dining room under canopy, conference room for 25, convenient location, good views, but rooms in need of renovation, new owners plan 14 more rooms, car rental US$40 winter, US$25 summer, PO Box 3380, T 494-2587; *Hotel Castle Maria*, up the hill overlooking Road Town, 30 rooms, US$70-130/55-100, some triple and quads, kitchenette, a/c, TV, pool, restaurant, bar, car rentals, popular with local business travellers, PO Box 206, T 494-2553, F 494-2515. About the cheapest on the island is *Wayside Inn Guest House*, Road Town, 20 rooms, US$25 double all year, basic, PO Box 258, T 494-3606.

South coast: heading W from Road Town you come to *Prospect Reef Resort*, a 15-acre resort specializing in package holidays, wide variety of rooms, studios, town houses and villas, some with sea view, some without, US$147-410/88-274, tennis, pitch and put, sea water pool, fresh water swimming lane pool, diving pool, health and fitness centre,

Baskin in the Sun dive shop, marina, sailing, fishing, café and restaurant, conference centre for 150, car rental, complimentary sports equipment, boutiques, shuttle service, PO Box 104, T 494-3311, 800-586-8937, F 494-5595; *Nanny Cay Resort and Marina*, 41 rooms, US$125-170/55-120/45-100, a/c, TV, VCRs, kitchenette, phone, deluxe rooms have 2 queen-size beds, standard rooms are darker, smaller, restaurants, bars, boutiques, tennis, Blue Water Divers dive shop, car rental, windsurfing and sailing, used by short stay people going out on bareboat charters, PO Box 281, T 800-786 4753, 494-2512; *Villas at Fort Recovery Estate*, 10 spacious and nicely furnished villas of different sizes on small beach, US$160-572/108-393 inc breakfast, built around 17th century Dutch fort, commissary, no restaurant, but à la carte room service available inc complimentary dinner for stays of over 7 nights, yoga, massage, good snorkelling offshore, car essential, PO Box 239, T 495-4467, 800-367-8455, F 495-4036; inexpensive is *BVI Aquatic Hotel*, West End, 14 rooms US$40-60, T 495-4541; *French-man's Cay Hotel*, beautiful hillside location on the cay overlooking the S coast of Tortola, 9 villas, US$190-295/135-200/115-170, all with view, fans, phone, a quiet resort with lots of repeat business, small sandy beach with reef for snorkelling, hammocks, tennis (US$10/hour for non-guests), pool, library, games, short trail out to point, Sun beach barbeque, bar, restaurant, TV in clubhouse, PO Box 1054, West End, T 495-4844, 800-235-4077; *Jolly Roger Inn*, a small inn and bar on waterfront at Sopers Hole, run by New Yorkers, live music at weekends so do not stay here if you want peace and quiet, convenient for ferries (see above), 6 brightly decorated, clean rooms, 2 with private bathroom, 4 with shared, fans, screens, US$49-79/40-60, singles, doubles, triples available, good breakfasts, busy restaurant and bar, T 495-4559, F 495-4184.

West coast: heading NE, *Long Bay Beach Resort*, 76 rooms, studios and villas spread along the beach and up the hillside, US$160-425/95-325, a/c, TV, phone, fridge, pool, tennis, pitch and put, car rental, 2 restaurants with vegetarian options, bars, surf boards, snorkelling equipment, nice beach, sandy with some rocks, level of sand can shift depending on season, PO Box 433, T 495-4252, in the USA T 800-729-9599, in the UK T 0800-373 742; *Sebastian's On The Beach*, Apple Bay, lo-

cated either side of road, informal and popular surfers' hangout, 8 comfortable beachfront rooms with balcony, 4 rear rooms which connect, 12 more rooms across the road at rear of office around patio, 2 rooms above office, US$110-180/65-110, 15% service, fans, fridge, payphones, grocery 0800-2200, restaurant/bar overlooking sandy beach, happy hour 1600-1800, blend own rum, surfboards and boogieboards for rent, PO Box 441, T 495-4212, 800-336-4870, F 495-4466; *Sugar Mill Hotel*, Little Apple Bay, 22 rooms, most with kitchenettes, US$185-578/155-450/140-390, prestigious restaurant, beach bar, pool, no children in season, PO Box 425, T 495-4355, 800-462-8834, F 495-4696; along this stretch of coast there are lots of rental villas, many of which are advertised simply with a notice outside, usually about US$90/day; at the upper end of the scale, *Rockview Holiday Homes* have several villas for rent, the cheapest in winter at US$1,280/week and the most expensive at US$14,000/week, most have daily maid service, *Sunset House* has a cook as well, PO Box 263, T 494-2559, F 494-5866; *Cliff Houses* offers various villas at a similar price, T 495-4727; private villas include *Limeberry House*, 3 bedrooms with pool, T 495-4705 and the 2-bedroom *Belmont House*, T 495-4477; *Cane Garden Bay (Rhymer's) Beach Hotel*, Cane Garden Bay, has 25 basic but clean rooms US$65-70/35-45, most with double bed and single bed, right on sandy beach, beach towels provided, store and shop, laundromat, restaurant/bar on beach, watersports companies on either side of hotel, PO Box 570, T 495-4639, 495-4215, F 495-4820; *Ole Works Inn*, Cane Garden Bay, built around 300-yr old sugar factory, on beach, 8 rooms US$60-70, honeymoon tower US$85, bar, restaurant, gift shop, T 495-4837; *Sunset Vacation Apartments*, 4 1-bed apartments US$60-80, T 495-4751; *Clyne's Beach Suites*, 5 1-bed apartments, US$100-110, 40% less in summer, T 494-2888, 495-4543.

North coast: *Lloyd Hill Villas*, Ridge Road, 2 houses, 3-4 bedrooms, US$910-2,310/week, 30% less in summer, flexible prices, will negotiate, on hillside with lovely view, lots of breeze, car essential, daily maid service, apartments being built alongside in 1993, PO Box 163, T 494-2481; *Josiah's Bay Cottages*, 4 wooden bungalows with double bed and sofa bed, kitchenette, fan, 3 older suites built of concrete in need of renovation, can sleep 4 but cramped, US$560-875/420-

650/week, gardens surrounded by trees, no breeze, take insect repellent, payphone, small pool, ½ mile to beach, PO Box 306, T 494-6186, 800-842-6260, F 494-2000; *Tamarind Club*, small hotel with pool, nestled in trees, close to 4 beaches, excellent restaurant, bar, 7 rooms with kitchenettes, US$80-100/60-80, 12 villas, US$800-1,000/600-800 a week, fans, screens, PO Box 509, East End, T 495-2477.

Camping: at *Brewer's Bay campsite* on N coast, bare site US$7, tent hire US$20 for 2 people, babysitters available, beach bar and simple restaurant, PO Box 185, T 494-3463; campground at Josiah's Bay.

There is lots of self-catering accommodation in what are variously known as houses, villas, apartments, guest houses, "efficiencies" or "housekeeping units". Prices are usually set on a weekly basis according to size and standard of luxury, and there is often a 30%-40% discount in the summer. Contact the Tourist Office for a full list and individual brochures.

● **Where To Eat**

There are lots of good restaurants across the island. The BVI Restaurant Guide, updated annually, gives menu listings of the best restaurants. Restaurants serving West Indian specialities in Road Town include: *C & F Restaurant*, Purcell Estate, very popular with visitors and locals, excellent local food, slow but friendly service, T 494-4941; *Mario's*, Palm Grove Shopping Centre, West Indian specialities, clean, a/c, good service, generous portions, T 494-3883; *Oliver's*, Waterfront Drive near roundabout, clean, a/c, good food, T 494-2177; *Beach Club Terrace*, T 494-2272, at Baughers Bay, open 0800-2200; *Butterfly Bar and Restaurant*, Main Street, open 0700-2200 except Sun; *Roti Palace*, T 494-4196, Russel Hill, East Indian specialities from Trinidad and Guyana, huge rotis, rec. Recommended restaurants include *The Fish Trap*, T 494-3626, at the Columbus Centre, behind Village Cay Marina, open 1100-2215, open air, reservations rec, good seafood, inside is a popular yachtie bar open 1630-late serving good lower-priced bar meals, and *The Captain's Table*, a French restaurant on the waterfront by Village Cay Marina, T 494-3885, lunch Mon-Fri, dinner daily except Sat from 1800; *Pusser's Co Store & Pub* on Main Street, Road Town, T 494-2467, yachties' meeting place, good pub atmosphere, open 1100-2200, on ground floor bar store and restaurant

for simple dishes such as English pies and New York deli sandwiches, first floor restaurant superior but not overpriced, reservations rec, cheap drink specials Tues and Thur nights; *Tavern in the Town*, Road Town, next to *Pussers*, traditional English pub food and atmosphere, sells Newcastle Brown Ale, garden looks out across harbour, closed Sat, T 494-2790; *Cell 5 Lounge*, next door, T 494-4629, burgers, native dishes, tropical drinks, breakfast, lunch and dinner, notice outside says 'sorry, we do not cater to persons in a hurry'; *Capriccio del Mare*, Waterfront Drive overlooking water, Italian café serving excellent coffee and delicious, if overpriced, snacks and continental lunches, T 494-5369; *Spaghetti Junction*, Waterfront Drive opp Palm Grove shopping centre upstairs in small blue building, 1800-2300, T 494-4880; *Virgin Queen*, Road Town, T 494-2310, homemade pizza plus West Indian and European food, a popular watering hole for English and American residents; *Rays of Hope*, Port Purcell, small health food store, café and take away, excellent vegetarian set lunch, Mon-Fri 1130-1530, get there early, they run out fast; *Marlene's Delicious Designs*, Waterfront Drive near Cable and Wireless, popular lunch spot for office workers serving sandwiches and local patties, cheap and delicious, open 0730-1800, T 494-4634.

Outside Road Town: *Brandywine Bay Restaurant*, East End, run by Cele and Davide Pugliese, 10 mins drive from Road Town, one of the most exclusive restaurants on Tortola, indoor and outdoor dining, grills and Florentine food, 1830-2100, closed Sun, reservations, T 495-2301, F 495-1203, Channel 16, anchorage 15-foot draft; *Bing's Drop Inn Bar and Restaurant*, at Fat Hog's Bay, East End, T 495-2627, home cooked dinners, excellent conch fritters, an after hours dance spot, late night menu, reservations; *Tamarind Club*, East End, excellent food, nice atmosphere, live music often, open 1200-1500, 1700-2130, closed Tues, T 495-2477; *The Struggling Man*, T 494-4163, Sea Cows Bay, between Road Town and Nanny Cay; *Mrs Scatliffe's*, T 495-4556, Carrot Bay, upstairs in a yellow and white building opposite the Primary School, local cuisine, home grown fruit and vegetables, family fungi performance after dinner, lunch Mon-Fri 1200-1400, dinner daily 1900-2100, reservations essential; *The Sugar Mill*, in an old mill in Apple Bay, gourmet and elegant, dinner 1900, reservations, T 495-4355, hotel attached, breakfast and lunch at beach bar. There is also *Pusser Landing* and *Jolly Roger* (fun, yachtie hangout, good pizza and burgers, good cheap breakfast, open 0700-2200, T 495-4559) at West End and many more excellent restaurants in the hotels and yacht clubs. At Cane Garden Bay you can "Jump Up" (Caribbean music), almost every night at *Rhymers* (serves breakfast, lunch and dinner; folk music at *Quito's Gazebo*, T 495-4837, restaurant and beach bar at N end of Cane Garden Bay, lunch 1100-1500, rotis and burgers, dinner 1830-2130, buffets Sun, Tues, fish fry Wed, Thur, Fri, closed Mon. There are a number of small restaurants serving excellent food along the road going towards the rum distillery ruins; check in the late afternoon to make reservations and find out what the menu will be. Ten mins' drive from Road Town or Cane Garden Bay is the *Skyworld Restaurant*, with a panoramic view of all the Virgin Islands, food and prices reasonable, open from 1000, rec for view, T 494-3567.

Fish dishes are often excellent, try snapper, dolphin (fish, not the mammal), grouper, tuna and swordfish, and don't miss the lobster. If you are self-catering, you can get reasonably priced food from K Mark's and other supermarkets at Port Purcell or at the "Rite Way" supermarkets a little closer to town, although most things are imported and will cost at least the same as in Florida. Try local produce which is cheaper; yams and sweet potatoes rather than potatoes, for example. At the entrance to the Moorings, Wickhams Cay II, is the Bon Appetit Deli, T 494-5199, where you can get cheese and wine as well as regular provisions; they also do sandwiches and lunch specials and party services. Once the centre of rum production for the Royal Navy "Pussers" (Pursers), rum is still available from *Pusser's* or supermarkets. Local rums of varying quality are also sold by hotels and restaurants.

● **Nightlife**

In Road Town, *Paradise Pub*, entertainment Mon-Sat, T 494-2608, dancing Thur-Sat, Trivial Pursuits Wed; the hotels organize live bands and movie nights. At East End is *Bing's Drop Inn Bar*, see above; *Pusser's Landing* at Frenchman's Cay has bands, Thur and Sun, T 495-4554; *Jolly Roger* at West End has live music most weekends and often has visiting bands, call for details, T 495-4559; *Bomba's Shack*, on the beach in Apple Bay has music Wed and Sun, famous full moon party every month, sleep before you go, the party goes on all night,

T 495-4148; *Quito's Gazebo*, Cane Garden Bay, has live music nightly and the beat is quickened at weekends and holidays, making it a popular beach front dance spot, T 495-4837; *Tamarind Club* at Josiah's Bay has live music Fri and Sat and often has special party nights, T 495-2477.

● **Laundry**

Sylvia's Laundromat, next to Public Library on Flemming Street, Road Town, T 494-2230; Freeman's Laundromat beside Barclays Bank, Wickham's Cay. Marinas usually have laundromats. See telephone listings for out of town laundries.

BEEF ISLAND

This island was famed as a hunting ground for beef cattle during the buccaneering days. The island is linked to Tortola by the Queen Elizabeth bridge (US$0.50 toll one way eastwards). The main airport of the BVI is here. (Taxi to Road Town, US$15) Long Bay beach is on the N shore. Also Trellis Bay which has an excellent harbour and bars. *The Last Resort*, run by Englishman Tony Snell, based on Bellamy Cay, provides a lavish buffet menu plus one-man show cabaret, happy hour 1730-1830, dinner 1930, cabaret 2130, ferry service available, reservations required, T 495-2520 or channel 16. Also Boardsailing BVI, (T 495-2447, lessons, equipment rental, US$20/hour, US$55/day) the *Conch Shell Point Restaurant* (T 495-2285) and a painting and jewellery shop. *Beef Island Guest House* has 4 rooms on the beach, US$100/65, T 495-2303, food available at its *Loose Mongoose Bar*, 0800-1600, 1800-2100, mostly burgers and sandwiches. *Rama Villas* are 3 new, elegant rental homes, very spacious, light and airy, together sleep 14 or available separately, suitable for families or corporate retreat, pool, daily maid service, fax and teleconferencing facilities, overlooks Tortola, not on beach, PO Box 663, Road Town, T 494-5972, F 494-3782.

MARINA CAY

This tiny private island of 6 acres just N of Beef Island was where Robb White wrote his book *Our Virgin Isle*, which was made into a film starring Sidney Poitier and John Cassavetes. A charming cottage hotel, *Marina Cay Hotel*, comprises most of the island, which is encircled by a reef, offering some of the best snorkelling in the BVI. Marina facilities (boats use mooring buoys and a dinghy dock), laundry, showers, diving, sailing, snorkelling etc, there are 12 rooms available, US$250/140-340 MAP, T 494-2174 or VHF channel 16, PO Box 76, Road Town. Bar, restaurant, beach barbeque on Fri. Call ahead for ferry service from Trellis Bay jetty. If sailing, enter from the N.

GUANA ISLAND

North of Tortola, Guana Island is an 850-acre private island and wildlife sanctuary as well as having a hotel, *The Guana Island Club*, 15 rooms, tennis, restaurant, watersports, US$530-2,100/395-1,575, T 494-2354, 800-544-8262, PO Box 32, Road Town. The island is available for rent. The owners discourage visitors apart from guests, in order to keep the island a sanctuary for wildlife. A few flamingoes have been introduced to the island. They live in a small pond where the salinity fluctuates widely so their diets are supplemented with food and water if they need it. The birds used to live in a zoo, so they are fairly tame.

THE DOGS

Northeast of Tortola are The Dogs, small uninhabited islands. West Dog is a National Park. On Great Dog you can see frigate birds nesting. The islands are often used as a stopping off point when sailing from North Sound to Jost Van Dyke, and are popular with divers coming from North Sound. The dive sites are not spectacular but there are some interesting rock formations, with canyons and bridges. The best anchorages are on George Dog to the W of Kitchen Point and on the S side of Great Dog.

VIRGIN GORDA

Over a century ago, Virgin Gorda was the centre of population and commerce. It is now better known as the site of the geological curiosity called The Baths, where enormous boulders form a natural swimming pool and underwater caves. The snorkelling is good, especially going left from the beach. Climbing over and around the boulders is fun for the adventurous and there is an easy trail with ladders and bridges for those not so agile. However, exploring in the water with a mask and snorkel is the recommended way to do it. Unfortunately the popularity of The Baths with tour companies and cruise ships has led to overcrowding. There are many day trips from Tortola and when a cruise ship is in port you can not move on the beach. Choose carefully which day you visit.

The island is 7 miles long and has a population of about 2,500. The N half is mountainous, with a peak 1,370 feet high, while the S half is relatively flat. There are some 20 secluded beaches; the most frequented are Devil's Bay, Spring Bay, and Trunk Bay on the W coast. North of the island is North Sound, formed to the S and E by Virgin Gorda, to the N by Prickly Pear Island, and to the W by Mosquito Island. On the SE tip is Copper Mine Point, where the Spaniards mined copper, gold and silver some 400 years ago; the remains of the mine can be seen. The rocky façade here is reminiscent of the Cornish coast of England. The amateur geologist will find stones such as malachite and crystals embedded in quartz. All land on Virgin Gorda over 1,000 feet high is now a National Park, where trails have been blazed for walking. Just off the SW tip of the island is Fallen Jerusalem, an islet which is now a National Park. There is a 3,000-

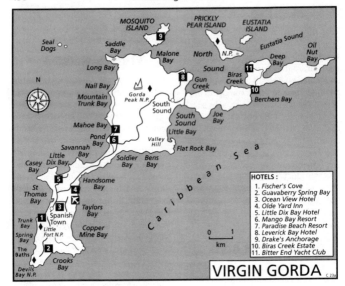

MOSQUITO ISLAND
PRICKLY PEAR ISLAND
EUSTATIA ISLAND

Seal Dogs
Saddle Bay
Malone Bay
North N.P.
Eustatia Sound
Oil Nut Bay
Deep Bay
Long Bay
Sound
Biras Creek
Gun Creek
Nail Bay
Mountain Trunk Bay
Gorda Peak N.P.
South Sound
Berchers Bay
Mahoe Bay
Joe Bay
South Sound
Little Bay
Pond Bay
Valley Hill
Flat Rock Bay
Savannah Bay
Soldier Bay
Bens Bay
Casey Bay
Little Dix Bay
Handsome Bay
St Thomas Bay
Taylors Bay
Spanish Town
Little Fort N.P.
Trunk Bay
Spring Bay
Copper Mine Bay
The Baths
Crooks Bay
Devils Bay N.P.

Caribbean Sea

HOTELS:
1. Fischer's Cove
2. Guavaberry Spring Bay
3. Ocean View Hotel
4. Olde Yard Inn
5. Little Dix Bay Hotel
6. Mango Bay Resort
7. Paradise Beach Resort
8. Leverick Bay Hotel
9. Drake's Anchorage
10. Biras Creek Estate
11. Bitter End Yacht Club

0   1
km

VIRGIN GORDA

C 23a

foot airstrip near the main settlement, Spanish Town. Bitter End and Biras Creek are good anchorages and both have a hotel and restaurant. There is no road to either of them, you have to get a hotel launch from Gun Creek or the North Sound Express from Beef Island to *Bitter End Yacht Club*.

Island Information—Virgin Gorda
● Where To Stay

In the S part of the island near The Valley and the airport are: *Little Dix Bay*, luxury 98-roomed chalet hotel, with 4 1-bedroom suites, on ½-mile beach, watersports arranged, tennis, hiking trails in surrounding hills, quiet, lovely gardens in extensive grounds, no TV or pool, strict dress code after sunset, 70% repeat guests in winter, honeymooners in summer, US$450-790/320-560/225-490, 44 rooms with a/c, suites US$1,200/930/750 EP, lots of packages available, PO Box 70, Virgin Gorda, T 495-5555, F 495-5083, under new management in 1993 (Rosewood Hotels & Resorts, same as *Caneel Bay Resort*, St John) and benefiting from a multi-million dollar renovation, also owns and operates the airport and the Virgin Gorda Yacht Harbour, a large marina in St Thomas Bay offering most facilities; at the

cheaper end of the range is *Ocean View/The Wheelhouse*, 12 rooms, close to ferry and harbour, pink building, small rooms but adequately furnished, TV, fan, a/c, functional restaurant, bar, US$70-80/50-60, PO Box 66, T 495-5230; *Fischer's Cove Beach Hotel*, St Thomas Bay, rooms upgraded in 1993, some with fan, some a/c, US$145-170/105-115, or cottages with kitchenette, less space, some beachfront, US$160-270/120-215, balcony restaurant overlooking sea open 0730-2200, beach barbeque when calm, PO Box 60, T 495-5252; *Diamond Beach*, Trunk Bay, 14 rooms, US$144-230/98-155, 1-2 bedroom villas, all with sea view, secluded location, PO Box 69, T 495-5452; *Guavaberry Spring Bay*, well-equipped wooden cottages, beautiful location, friendly, sandy beach with shade 5 mins walk through grounds, to the S are The Baths, to the N The Crawl, a National Park enclosing a natural swimming pool and more boulders, highly rec, US$125-195/85-130, EP, run by Tina and Ludwig Goschler, PO Box 20, T 495-5227; *Toad Hall*, luxury rental home, 3 bedrooms with garden showers, private access to The Baths beach along spectacular wooden walkway, pool among the boulders, caves to explore, great for agile children, US$6,000/4,800 a week, contact Stephen and Marie Green, PO

Box 7, T 495-5397, F 495-5708; *Olde Yard Inn*, convenient for airport, 14 rooms, 1 suite, a/c available, downstairs rooms rather dark, US$125-220/85-170/75-135, pleasant gardens, good food, library with piano, games room, croquet, hammocks, small shop, 10-15 mins on trail to beach, owned by Carol Kaufman, PO Box 26, T 495-5544, 800-633-7411, F 495-5968; N of The Valley up the W coast are 2 resorts which were built as one, so the villas are the same, *Mango Bay* has 5 villas which can make 12 one-bedroomed units or the apartments can be connected to provide 2 or 3 bedrooms, very clean, light and airy, tiled floors, light colours, a/c on request, pretty shrubbery, narrow sandy beach, lovely sea view, jetty, Italian management, US$135-735/95-523 EP, PO Box 1062, T 495-5672; *Paradise Beach* has 7 units in 3 houses, snorkelling and fishing gear available, dinghy, quiet, rental car inc, US$145-600/110-370, PO Box 1105, T 495-5871, 800-225-4255; on the N coast is *Leverick Bay Hotel and Vacation Villas*, offering a wide variety of spacious accommodation from hotel rooms to villas and condominiums built up a hillside with a great view of the jetty and the bay, rooms US$119-225/96-187, villas US$866-4,737/week inc tax and maid service, *Pussers* is on site and all the buildings are painted the bright multi-colours which are *Pussers'* emblem, use *Pussers'* restaurant or cross the water to *Drake's Anchorage* on Mosquito Island opposite, tennis, watersports, Dive BVI operates from here, food store, laundry, shops, beauty therapy and massage, PO Box 63, T 495-7421, 800-848-7081; perhaps the most exclusive resort on the island is *Biras Creek*, reached by launch from Gun Creek, or on the North Sound Express from Beef Island, on a spit of land overlooking both North Sound and Berchers Bay, luxury, beautifully decorated cottages and grand suites spread along the Atlantic coast, can sleep maximum 84 people, no children under 6, those under 8 are not allowed in the dining room but have early dinner and babysitter, no phones or a/c, 2 floodlit tennis courts with pro, sailing trips and other watersports arranged, free watersports instruction, small pool overlooking ocean, nice little beach in sheltered bay with mangroves, very private, beach barbeques, good menu and wonderful view from the split level restaurant, popular with honeymooners, US$445-665/325-525 MAP, sailing packages with some nights on board available, PO Box 54, T 494-3555, F 494-3557, in the UK

T 0800-373 742; *The Bitter End Yacht Club and Resort*, North Sound, reached by launch from Gun Creek or the North Sound Express from Beef Island (US$18 one way) or by yacht, lively, action-packed for water lovers with a marina, sailing in all sizes of boats for all ages, yacht charters, windsurfing, diving, anything any water lover would want, plus instruction, stay on your boat, charter one of the 8 liveaboard yachts, or use the 100 rooms and chalets, comfortable big beds, very spread out along coastal hillside (used to be 2 resorts), can be a long walk from your room to the clubhouse but taxi service available, the older, cheaper rooms are closest, busy restaurant, reserve dinner at breakfast, shops, food stores, conference room, public phone system is archaic, US$350-525/310-405 FAP, free room for children in summer, PO Box 46, T 494-2746, 800-872-2392.

● **Where To Eat**

For upmarket, elegant dining try *Biras Creek*, 5-course dinner for US$40, lobster US$45 plus 15% service, 1930-2100, dress smartly; *Little Dix Bay* has 3 full service restaurants open 0700-2100, T 495-5555; *Bitter End Yacht Club* for the sailing fraternity, champagne breakfast US$10, buffet lunch US$15, dinner US$25; *Pirate's Pub and Grill*, on Saba Rock, North Sound, burgers, barbeque and sandwiches 1200-2000, channel16, T 495-9638, F 495-9369; *Olde Yard Inn*, international food in a garden setting; *Chez Michelle*, T 495-5510, international cuisine, 1830-2130, reservations; restaurants serving West Indian recipes include *Anything Goes*, The Valley, T 495-5062, curries and seafood, 1100-2200, take away and delivery locally; *Teacher Ilma's*, in the Valley at Princess Quarters, dinner only, reservations after 1600, T 495-5355; *Fishers Cove*, international and local food and beach barbeques, T 495-5252; also *Crab Hole*, South Valley, locals eat here, inexpensive West Indian food, curries, roti, callalou, conch, entertainment on Fri 0930-2400, T 495-5307; *Lobster Pot*, at *Andy's Chateau de Pirate*, T 495-5252, beach pig roast on Mon, seafood buffet on Thur, barbeque on Sat; *The Bath and Turtle*, Virgin Gorda Yacht Harbour, standard pub fare, open 0730-2130 daily, good place to wait for the ferry; *Pusser's* Leverick Bay, T 495-7369, breakfast and lunch 0800-1800 at beach bar, dinner 1830-2200 on the veranda, steaks, seafood, pies; *Mad Dog*, next to the parking lot at The Baths, drinks, sandwiches, T-shirts and friendly conversation, open 1000-1900; there is also a bar on the beach at The Baths also selling T-shirts, not always open, be sure to bring a bottle of water just in case, toilets round the back.

● **Nightlife**

Live music at *The Bath and Turtle* and *Little Dix Bay*, live music and/or DJ at *Pirate's Pub*, *Pussers* and *Bitter End*. Check the bulletin board at the Virgin Gorda Yacht Harbour for special events and concerts.

MOSQUITO ISLAND

Mosquito Island is privately owned by *Drake's Anchorage Resort* and enjoys beautiful views over North Sound to Virgin Gorda and Prickly Pear Island. This 125-acre island is just NW of Leverick Bay and can only be reached by boat. There is a lovely beach at South Bay, sandy with boulders, and there are trails leading from the hotel to this and other quiet, sandy coves. The island can be rented in its entirety, or you can just use the hotel, which has 8 rooms, 2 villas and 2 suites, summer rate US$175-360 AP, bars, restaurant, moorings, windsurfing, very quiet and relaxed atmosphere, PO Box 2510, Virgin Gorda, T 494-2254, 800-624-6651, Restaurant open 0730-1000, 1200-1400, candlelit dinner 1900-2200, French-style menu, reservations essential for dinner.

PRICKLY PEAR ISLAND

Prickly Pear Island forms the NE edge of North Sound. It has a lovely beach at Vixen Point with a small beach bar, not always open, and a watersports centre. This is a great spot for volley ball, with a net permanently on the beach. There is no phone, call on the radio, VHF channel 16, Vixen Point.

NECKER ISLAND

This 74-acre, private island NE of Virgin Gorda is owned by Richard Branson, who wanted a Virgin island to add to his Virgin enterprise. It is available for rent, contact Necker Island (BVI) Ltd, No 5 The Lanchesters, 162-164 Fulham Palace Road, London W6 9ER, T 081-741 9980, F 081-748 9185, toll free from USA (800) 9260636. The house, in Balinese style, sleeps 20, and in winter costs US$8,250 a day, or US$6,050, if there are only 10 of you, falling to US$5,500 in summer. Lovely beaches, protected by a coral reef, all water sports provided, private.

COOPER ISLAND

In the chain of islands running SW from Virgin Gorda is Cooper Island, which has a beautiful beach and harbour at Manchioneel Bay with palm trees, crystal waters, coral reefs and *Cooper Island Beach Club* (PO Box 859, Road Town, US$60-95, T 494-3721, in USA Parlmes Enterprises Inc, T 413-659 2602, 800-542 4624, F 413-659 2514). British owned and managed, there are 4 guest rooms with kitchen and bathroom, breakfast on request, lunch 1130-1400, dinner from 1830, reservations preferred, bar all day from 1000, do your grocery shopping on Tortola, electricity generator evenings only. The supply boat leaves Road Town Mon, Wed, Sat, other days use Underwater Safaris' dive boat from *The Moorings*, Road Town; they have a small dive shop on the island and use the beach club for surface intervals or to pick up divers from yachts anchored in the bay, dive equipment for sale or rent, airfill station, photographic services.

SALT ISLAND

Very few people visit this lovely island, there are no ferries and access is only by private boat. There are two salt ponds from which salt is gathered by two ageing residents. A bag of salt is still sent to the British monarch every year as rent for the island, the remainder is sold to visitors and local restaurants. The two old men who live there welcome visitors and will show you the salt forming and packing process. They have a hut from which they sell conch shells and shell necklaces. There is a small settlement on the N side as well as a reef-protected lagoon on the E shore. The population numbers about 20. The main reason people come here is for a rest stop between dives. The British mail ship *Rhone*, a 310-foot steamer, sank off Salt Island in a hurricane in 1867 and the site was used in the film *The Deep*. Those who perished were buried on Salt Island. The wreck is still almost intact in 20-80 feet of water and is very impressive. There are moorings provided at Lee Bay, just N of the *Rhone*, for those diving the wreck, to minimize anchor damage. The dive is usually divided between the bow section and the stern section; in the former you can swim through the hull at a depth of about 70 feet, be prepared for darkness. In calm weather it is possible to snorkel part of it.

DEAD CHEST

A tiny island in Salt Island Passage, between Salt Island and Peter Island, this is reputedly the island where the pirate Blackbeard abandoned sailors: "15 men on a Dead Man's Chest—Yo Ho Ho and a bottle of rum!".

PETER ISLAND

This 1,000-acre island has a tiny population and offers isolated, palm-fringed beaches, good anchorage and picnic spots. The exclusive, luxury, *Peter Island Resort and Yacht Harbour* is built on reclaimed land jutting out into Sir Francis Drake Channel, forming a sheltered harbour with marine facilities. Built by Norwegians, there are chalet-type cottages, harbour rooms, or beach rooms US$325-475 ocean view, US$425-595 beach front, full board, a pool, tennis, horseriding, watersports, dress formally in evening, T 494-2561, in USA 800-346 4451, F 494-2313, PO Box 211, Road Town. Eight daily ferry departures from Tortola, private guest launch from Tortola or St Thomas, helicopter from St Thomas or San Juan.

NORMAN ISLAND

The island is uninhabited (apart from the converted 1910 Baltic Trader floating bar/restaurant *William Thornton*, T 494-2564 or VHF Channel 16, anchored in the Bight of Norman to the N of the island; launch service from Fort Burt Marina, Road Town, daily at 1715), but reputed to be the "Treasure Island" of Robert Louis Stevenson fame. On its rocky W coast are caves where treasure is said to have been discovered many years ago. These can be reached by small boats and there are several day trips on offer. There is excellent snorkelling around the caves and the reef in front slopes downward to a depth of 40 feet. Be careful with the wild cattle: their tempers are unpredictable. The Indians off the N W of Norman Island are pinnacles of rock sticking out of the sea with their neighbour, the gently rounded Pelican Island. Together they offer the diver and snorkeller a labyrinth of underwater reefs and caves.

JOST VAN DYKE

Lying to the W of Tortola, the island was named after a Dutch pirate. It is mountainous, with beaches at White Bay and Great Harbour Bay on the S coast. Great Harbour looks like the fantasy tropical island, a long horseshoe shaped, white sandy beach, fringed with palm trees and dotted with beach bar/restaurants. Population about 300, very friendly with lots of stories to tell. Jost Van Dyke is a point of entry and has a Customs House. In January 1991, the island was provided with electricity for the first time and a paved road. It is surrounded by some smaller islands, one of which is ***Little Jost Van Dyke***, the birthplace of Dr John Lettsome, the founder of the British Medical Society.

Island Information – Jost Van Dyke

● Where to Stay

Sandcastle, at White Bay, owned by Darrell Sanderson, 4 wooden cottages, basic amenities but great for total relaxation, hammocks between palm trees on the beach, restaurant (must reserve dinner and order in advance to your specifications), snorkelling, windsurfing, US$225-295/175-235 FAP, reservations Suite 237, Red Hook Plaza, USVI 00802, T 496-0496 or (USA) 803-237 8999, F 775 3590 or 775-5262, *The Soggy Dollar Bar* is popular at weekends, most people arrive by boat and swim or wade ashore, aspires to be the birthplace of the infamous "painkiller"; *Rudy's Mariner Inn*, Great Harbour, 3 rooms, beach bar and restaurant, kitchenettes, grocery, water taxi, US$75-220/55-180 EP, T 495-9282 or (USVI) 775 3558. *Harris' Place*, T 774-0774 (USVI) or call VHF channel 16, 2 rooms, beach bar, restaurant, grocery, water taxi, live music, Harris calls his place the friendliest spot in the BVIs, US$50-65/40-55; *Sandy Ground Estates*, T 494-3391, PO Box 594, West End, Tortola, 8 luxury villas, provisioning, free water taxi from/to Tortola, US$1,200/780 a week. Camping: *Tula's N and N Campground*, Little Harbour, T (USVI) 774 0774, 8' X 10' US$25 per day, 9' X 12' US$35 (per couple), US$15 bare site (3 people), winter rate, US$10 per day per person in summer, US$4 per person bare site, tents have hard floors with carpet, fully furnished with beds, linen, also provide insect repellent, lanterns, charcoal, pots and pans etc, restaurant, snack bar, beach, grocery, rec, T 495-9302; *White Bay Campground*, opened 1993, nice site, right on beautiful, sandy, White Bay, tents US$20s, US$35d, or bare sites US$7s, US$10d, T 495-9312.

● Where To Eat

In Little Harbour: *Harris' Place*, open daily, breakfast, lunch and dinner, happy hour 1100-1500, pig roasts with live music Tues and Thur, lobster night on Mon, ferries from Tortola and St Thomas/St John arranged for these feasts; *Sidney's Peace and Love*, Little Harbour, T 495-9271 or Channel 16, happy hour 1700-1830, pig roast Mon and Sat 1900, US$12, barbeque rib and chicken Sun, Tues and Thur, US$12.50, otherwise lunch and dinner usual steak, fish, shrimp or lobster; *Abe's By The Sea*, pig roast on Wed, call VHF channel 16 for reservations, also has 3 rooms overlooking harbour, can be one apartment, US$75-85, friendly family, T 495-9329, F 495-9529. In Great Harbour: *Ali Baba's*, run by Baba Hatchett, W of the Customs House, breakfast, lunch and dinner, happy hour 1600-1800; *Rudy's Mariner's Rendezvous*, open for dinner until 0100, US$9-20, reservations at Customs House or channel 16; *Club Paradise* open daily, Mon lobster special, Wed pig roast, live entertainment regularly, lunch 1100-1500, dinner 1900-2200, T 495-4844, F 495-9633 or VHF channel 16; *Foxy's Bar*, friendly and cheap, spontaneous calypso by Foxy, master story-teller and musician, big parties on New Year's Eve and other holidays, hundreds of yachts arrive, wooden boat regatta on Labour Day draws hundreds of boats from all over the Caribbean for a 3-day beach party, very easy to get invited on board to watch or race, special ferry service to USVI and Tortola; *Happy Laury's*, very good value for breakfast, happy hour is 1500-1700, try the Happy Laury Pain Killer. There is a pig roast on Jost Van Dyke every Fri.

For details of ferries see **Information for Visitors**.

SANDY CAY

This small uninhabited islet just E of Jost Van Dyke is owned by Laurance Rockefeller. It is covered with scrub but there is a pleasant trail set out around the whole island, which makes a good walk. Bright white beaches surround the island and provide excellent swimming. Offshore is a coral reef.

ANEGADA

Unique among this group of islands because of its coral and limestone formation, the highest point is only 28 feet above sea level. There are still a few large iguanas, which are indigenous to the island. Flamingoes were released in 1992 in the ponds and there are currently about 16, best seen from the little bridge over The Creek on the road from the *Anegada Reef Hotel* to the airport turn off. Hawksbill and Green Turtles nest all along the N shore; the Government has drawn up a conservation policy and the waters around the island are protected. The waters abound with fish and lobster,

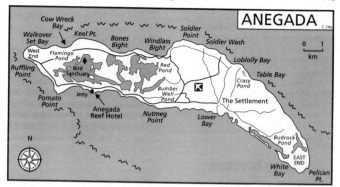

and the extensive reefs are popular with snorkellers and scuba divers who also explore wrecks of ships which foundered in years past. Some were said to hold treasure, but to date only a few doubloons have been discovered. Anegada has excellent fishing and is one of the top bone fishing spots in the world. From the wharf on the S shore, all the way round to the W end, across the entire N shore (about 11 miles) is perfect, uninterrupted, white sandy beach. Any fences on the beach are to keep out cattle, not people. Loblolly Bay is popular with day trippers, partly because it has a beach bar at either end *(The Big Bamboo* at the W end is busier and more accessible than *Flash of Beauty* at the E end), the only places where there is shade, but also for the reef just off shore where snorkellers can explore caverns and ledges and see coral, nurse sharks, rays, turtles, barracuda and shoals of colourful fish. The beach is generally deserted. Bring water and sun screen. The population numbers about 290, living mostly in *The Settlement*. This is a collection of wooden shacks and some newer houses, a smart new government building, a few bars, little shops, a bakery, jeep hire and church. A short stretch of concrete road leads from The Settlement to the airport turn off; all other roads on the island are sand. There is no public transport except

taxis and the best way to get around is to hire a jeep, bicycle or walk (take an umbrella for the sun or walk in the early evening). The island is very quiet and relaxed. There is an airstrip 2,500 feet long and 60 feet wide, which can handle light aircraft. Day trips by boat from Tortola are available. There is no regular ferry service.

Local Information – Anegada

● Where to stay

Anegada Reef Hotel, 12 rooms, where there is an anchorage, fishing packages, dive equipment, beach bar, restaurant, great service, famous lobster barbeque, rec, cash or travellers cheques only, no credit cards, US$160-215/150-205 AP, T 495-8002, F 495-9362 or by VHF Radio Channel 16, if arriving by yacht radio in advance for directions through the reef, jeep and bicycle hire, taxi service, boutique, closed Sept-Oct. *Beach Cottage* at Pomato Point, a modern, 1-bedroom cottage on beach, full kitchen, US$250/weekend, US$400/week, US$1,200/month, T 495-9236. *Anegada Beach Campground*, T 495-8038, 8'x10' tents US$20d, US$12s, 10'x12' tents US$30d, bare site US$7 a day, plus 10% service, no credit cards, beach bar, restaurant, snorkelling, windsurfing; *Neptune's Treasure* has a campsite and tents available at good rates, T 495-9439.

● Where To Eat

Pomato Point Beach Restaurant, T 495-9466, Channel 16, barbeque dinners, reserve by 1600; *Neptune's Treasure*, breakfast, lunch, dinner, camping available, delicious breads and chutneys, make sure you take some home; *Whistling Pine Restaurant*, near *Anegada Reef Hotel*, VHF channel 16; *Big Bamboo*, see above, Aubrey and his wife serve delicious lobster and conch on the beach at Loblolly Bay, VHF channel 16; *Del's Restaurant and Bar*, in The Settlement, T 495-8014, West Indian food, breakfast, lunch and dinner; *Banana Well Bar and Restaurant*, The Settlement, T 495-9461, breakfast, lunch and dinner, native dishes, seafood, sandwiches. Rec to make dinner reservations before 1600 at all restaurants.

INFORMATION FOR VISITORS

● **Documents**
An authenticated birth or citizenship certificate or voter's registration may suffice for US or Canadian citizens. All other nationalities need a valid passport and a return or onward ticket. Visitors from some countries, such as Guyana, require a visa. The Chief Immigration Officer is in Road Town, T 494-3701.

● **How To Get There By Air**
There are international airports on Tortola and Virgin Gorda, but no direct flights from Europe or from the USA. From Europe: same day connections can be made through Puerto Rico (British Airways from London, Lufthansa from Frankfurt, Iberia from Madrid) or Antigua (BWIA or Lufthansa from Frankfurt, BWIA or British Airways from London, BWIA from Zurich). From the USA: connecting flights can be arranged through Puerto Rico or the USVI; Sunaire Express, United Express, American Eagle and Liat fly to Tortola from the former, Sunaire fly from St Croix and from St Thomas. Liat flies to Tortola from Anguilla, Antigua, Barbados, Grenada, Dominica, St Kitts, St Maarten, St Lucia, Martinique, Trinidad and Tobago, Puerto Rico. Winair also flies from St Maarten to Tortola. Sunaire flies to Virgin Gorda from St Croix, Sunaire and Air St Thomas from St Thomas and Sunaire and United Express from San Juan. Within the BVI there are flights: Anegada/Tortola, Virgin Gorda/Tortola with Aero Gorda and other small airlines. Aero Gorda flies to Anegada Mon, Wed and Fri, US$27 one way, T 495-2271. Fly BVI is a small charter airline which is often cheaper and more convenient than a scheduled flight if there are a few of you, T 495-1747, 800-1-FLY BVI,

F 495-1973. Pack light, there is limited luggage space on the small aircraft.

● **How To Get There By Sea**
Port Purcell at Road Town is the principal port of entry with an 800-foot, deep water berth for cruise ships; Government Jetty, Road Town, is also used. There are others at West End, Tortola; St Thomas Bay, Virgin Gorda; and Great Harbour, Jost Van Dyke. There are frequent connections with the USVI and within the BVI. Inter-Island Boat Services, *Sundance II* between Cruz Bay, St John, and West End, Tortola, 3 times a day Mon-Thur, 4 times on Fri, 3 times on Sat and Sun, US$16 one way, US$30 return, T 495-4166; also Water Taxi available, T 776-6597. *Native Son Inc*, T 495-4617, between St Thomas and Road Town (US$35 return) via West End, or between Red Hook, St Thomas and St John to West End, several daily, Smiths Ferry Services, *M/V Daphne Elise* and *M/V Marie Elise*, from St Thomas to West End and the Government Jetty, Road Town and on to The Valley, Virgin Gorda, several daily, also to West End from St John and Red Hook, St Thomas, 4 daily, T 494-4430, 494-2355, 495-4495. *Speedy's Fantasy* and *Speedy's Delight* on the routes Virgin Gorda-Road Town-St Thomas, Virgin Gorda-Road Town, T 495-5240 Virgin Gorda, or 774-8685 St Thomas. The North Sound Express has 3 daily crossings Beef Island-North Sound (Bitter End), 30 mins, US$18, with a bus service to and from Road Town waterfront (Pussers) and Beef Island ferry dock, T 495-2271. The Virgin Gorda Ferry Service, T 495-5240/5542, between Beef Island and The Valley, has 4 daily crossings. Peter Island Boat Schedule has 8 daily crossings from the Caribbean Sailing Yachts Dock, (CSY charters ceased operations in 1992), Tortola, to Peter Island, T 494-2561. Jost Van Dyke Ferry Service, T 494-2997, 4 crossings a day between West End and Jost Van Dyke Mon-Sat, 3 on Sun.

There is a departure tax of US$8 and a security tax of US$5 if you leave by air and a US$5 departure tax by sea. There is a cruise ship passenger tax of US$7.

● **Taxis**
BVI Taxi Association, T 494-2875, island tours arranged. Taxi stands: in Road Town, T 494-2322; on Beef Island, T 495-2378. Taxis are easy to come by on Tortola but ask for a quote first. The fare from Beef Island Airport to Road Town, Tortola is US$15 or US$8 if shared.

● Buses

There is a local bus service on Tortola with cheap fares (US$1-4) but erratic timetable. Scheduled (but nowhere near actual) times are: Road Town to West End, 0700, 0835, 1000; West End to Carrot Bay, 0730, 0900, 1030. From Carrot Bay it goes to Road Town, East End and back to Road Town. In the afternoon it leaves West End at 1515 and 1645. Call Scatos Bus Service for information, T 494-5873/2365.

● Self-Drive Cars

There are only about 50 miles of roads suitable for cars. Drive on the left. Maximum speed limit 30 miles per hour, in residential areas 10-15 mph. Minimokes and jeeps can be hired on Tortola, Virgin Gorda and Anegada. Jeeps may be more useful for exploring secluded beach areas. Car rental offices (or the Police Headquarters) provide the necessary temporary BVI driving licence (US$10) but you must also have a valid licence from your home country. It is advisable to book in advance in the peak season. Rates range from US$25 a day in summer to US$45 a day in winter for a small car, US$35-60 a day for jeeps. **Tortola**: Airways Car Rentals, Inner Harbour Marina, T 494-4502, or Airport, T 495-2161, jeeps for US$35-65/day. Alphonso Car Rentals, Fish Bay, T 494-3137, US$35-65/day, 20% less in summer; Budget, Wickhams Cay I, T 494-2639, US$35-60/day; International Car Rentals, Road Town, T 494-2516, US$40-58/day; Avis Rent-a-Car, opposite Botanic Gardens, Road Town, T 494-2193, US$35-50/day winter, US$25-40 summer, cheaper weekly rates; Caribbean Car Rental, *Maria's Inn*, Wickhams Cay, T 494-2698, US$45-49/day; National Car Rental, Duffs Bottom, Road Town, T 494-3197, US$37-45/day; Rancal rent-a-car, *Long Bay Beach Resort*, T 495-4330, and Prospect Reef, T 494-4534, US$45-60/day in winter, US$36-48 in summer, package rates for resort guests; Hertz Car Rental, West End, T 495-4405, jeeps US$45 in winter, US$39 in summer; Denzil Clyne Car Rentals, West End, T 495-4900, jeeps US$45-60/day in winter, US$40-60 in summer. **Virgin Gorda**: Speedy's Car Rentals, The Valley, T 495-5235, US$35-50/day; L & S Jeep Rentals, South Valley, T 495-5297, small or large jeeps, US$35-50/day, US$210-315/week; Mahogany Car Rentals, The Valley, T 495-5469, US$42-68 includes tax and insurance; Andy's Taxi and Jeep Rental, The Valley, T 495-5511, US$50/day, guided tours US$30;

Hertz, The Valley, T 495-5803, cars US$35-55, jeeps US$35-60/day. **Anegada**: *Anegada Reef Hotel*, T 495-8002, F 495-9362, jeep rental and licence US$46/½day, US$50/day, also bicycle hire; D W Jeep Rentals, The Settlement, T 495-8018, US$40/day winter, US$35/day summer.

All bicycles must be registered at the Traffic Licencing Office in Road Town and the licence plate must be fixed to the bicycle, cost: US$5. Boardsailing BVI at Nanny Cay has a range of mountain bikes for rent by the hour, T 494-0422.

● Camping

Allowed only on authorized sites.

● Shopping

The BVI is not duty-free. There are gift shops and boutiques in Road Town, Tortola and in Spanish Town, Virgin Gorda. The BVI Philatelic Bureau or Post Offices sell stamps for collectors. You can also buy BVI coins, but they are not used as a currency. *Samarkand*, on Main St, Tortola, sells gold and silver jewellery created by the local Bibby family with nautical themes; you can buy earrings of yachts, pelicans, etc, and they will make anything to order. *Sunny Caribbee Spice Co* (PO Box 286) is on Main Street, *Skyworld Restaurant* and *Long Bay Hotel*, selling spices, herbs, preserves and handicrafts, mail order and shipping services available. *Pusser's Co Store* in Road Town and West End, Tortola, and Leverick Bay, Virgin Gorda, sells nautical clothing, luggage and accessories as well as Pusser's Rum. *Turtle Dove Boutique*, opp Public Library in Road Town, has a good selection of gifts and is the only place selling a reasonable selection of books (other than romances and thrillers stocked by hotels). *Caribbean Handprints*, Main Street, has a silk-screen studio and shop with local designs and clothing made on site. An open air market close to the Tourist Office offers a selection of T-shirts and other souvenirs.

● Banks

Barclays Bank, Road Town, T 494-2171, F 494-4315, with agencies in The Valley, Virgin Gorda; Bank of Nova Scotia, Road Town, T 494-2526; Chase Manhattan Bank, Road Town, T 494-2662; First Pennsylvania Bank, Road Town, T 494-2117; Development Bank of the Virgin Islands, T 494-3737.

● Currency

The US dollar is the legal tender. There are no exchange control restrictions. Try to avoid large denominated travellers' cheques. Credit cards are all right for most hotels and the larger restaurants, but not for the majority of the bar/restaurants. Credit cards are not accepted on Anegada. Cheques accepted rarely, cash is king. There is a 10% stamp duty on all cheques and travellers' cheques.

● **Health**
Peebles Hospital is a public hospital with x-ray and surgical facilities. There are twelve doctors on Tortola and one on Virgin Gorda, 2 dentists and a small private hospital, the Bougainvillea Clinic which specializes in plastic surgery. Be careful in the sun, always use a sunscreen.

● **Climate**
The temperature averages 84°F in summer and 80°F in winter. At night temperatures may drop about 10 degrees. Average annual rainfall is 40 inches.

● **Clothing**
Island dress is casual and only the most exclusive restaurants require formal clothes. However, bathing suits are for the beach only, it is very offensive to locals to see bare chests and bellies, so cover up.

● **Business Hours**
Banks open Mon-Fri, 0900-1400, Barclays is open until 1500, Chase Manhattan until 1600, also Chase opens on Sat 0900-1200. Shops open Mon-Fri, 0900-1700. Government offices open Mon-Fri, 0830-1630.

● **National Holidays**
New Year's Day, Commonwealth Day (2nd Monday in March), Good Friday, Easter Monday, Whit Monday in May, Queen's Birthday (2nd Monday in June), Territory Day (1 July), Festival beginning of August, St Ursula's Day (21 October), Prince Charles' Birthday (14 November), Christmas Day, Boxing Day.

● **Religion**
Methodist, Anglican (Episcopal), Roman Catholic, Seventh Day Adventist, Baptist, Church of God, Church of Christ, Jehovah's Witness and Pentecostal Churches, Hindu and Muslim.

● **Time Zone**
Atlantic Standard Time, 4 hours behind GMT, 1 ahead of EST.

● **Electric Current**
110 volts, 60 cycles.

● **Telecommunications**
Direct dialling is available locally and worldwide. The code for the BVI is 809-49 followed by a 5-digit number. All telecommunications are operated by Cable & Wireless. Telephone, telex, facsimile transmission, data transmission and telegraph facilities are all available. Phone cards are available, US$5 and US$10, discount rates in evenings at weekends. To make a credit card call, dial 111 and quote your Visa or Mastercard number. Cable & Wireless is at the centre of Road Town at Wickhams Cay I, open 0700-1900 Mon-Fri, 0700-1600 Sat, 0900-1400 Sun and public holidays, T 494-4444, F 494-2506; also in The Valley, Virgin Gorda, T 495-5444, F 495-5702. They also operate Tortola Marine Radio, call on VHF channel 16, talk on 27 or 84. The CCT Boatphone company in Road Town offers cellular telephone services throughout the Virgin Islands for yachts, US$10/day, T 494-3825. To call VHF stations from a land phone, call Tortola Radio, T 116. There is a General Post Office in Road Town, branches in Tortola and Virgin Gorda and sub-branches in other islands. Postal rates for post-cards are US$0.30 to the USA, US$0.35 to Europe and US$0,45 to the rest of the world; for aerogrammes US$0.35; for letters to the USA US$0.45, to Europe US$0.50, to the rest of the world US$0.75.

● **Press**

The Island Sun is published on Wed and Sat, while the *BVI Beacon* comes out on Thur. *The Limin' Times*, printed weekly, is a free magazine giving entertainment news: nightlife, sports, music etc. *The Restaurant Guide* is published annually and is a free menu guide. *The BVI Welcome* is a bimonthly colour tourist guide. *The Tourism Directory* is published annually and is a detailed listing of services. The Tourist Board has these and many other brochures.

● **Radio**

Radio ZBVI broadcasts on medium wave 780 KHZ. Weather reports for sailors are broadcast hourly from 0730 to 1830 every day. There are 3 FM stations: Z Wave, Z Gold and Z Hit.

● **Maps**

The Ordnance Survey publishes a map of the BVI in its World Maps series, with inset maps of Road Town and East End, Tortola, tourist information and some text; Ordnance Survey, Romsey Road, Southampton, SO9 4DH, T 0703 792792. The Tourist Office distributes a road map, updated annually with some tourist information on resorts, restaurants and what to do.

● **Tourist Office**

The BVI Tourist Board Office is in the Social Security Building, Wickhams Cay, in Tortola: PO Box 134, Road Town, T 494-3134; there is also an office at Virgin Gorda Yacht Harbour, T 495-5181; some offices overseas can help with reservations. In the **USA**: 370 Lexington Avenue, Suite 511, New York, NY 10017, T (212) 696-0400 or (800) 835-8530; 1686 Union Street, San Francisco, CA 94123, T (415) 775 0344 or (800) 232-7770; in the **UK**: 110 St Martin's Lane, London WC2N 4DY, T 071-240-4259, F 071-240-4270; in **Germany**: AM Kappelgarten 24, D 6000, Frankfurt M/60, T 069-477-223, F 069-477-235.

The editors are most grateful to Nicolette Clifford, Tortola, for updating the BVI chapter and to Keith Dawson, of the Tourist Board, Nadine Battle, of the BVI Hotel and Commerce Association and all the other people who assisted them with information for the text.

LEEWARD ISLANDS
ANTIGUA

ANTIGUA, with about 108 square miles, is the largest of the Leewards, and also the most popular and the most developed. The island is low-lying and composed of volcanic rock, coral and limestone. Boggy Peak, its highest elevation, rises 1,330 feet (399m). There is nothing spectacular about its landscape, although its rolling hills and flowering trees are picturesque, but its coast line, curving into coves and graceful harbours, with 365 soft white sand beaches fringed with palm trees, is among the most attractive in the West Indies. It had a population of around 64,000 in 1992, most of them of African origin although some are of English, Portuguese, Lebanese and Syrian descent.

History

Antigua (pronounced Anteega) was first inhabited by the Siboney (stone people), whose settlements date back to at least 2400 BC. The Arawaks lived on the island between about AD 35 and 1100. Columbus discovered it on his second voyage in 1493 and named the island Santa María de la Antigua. Spanish and French colonists attempted to settle there but were discouraged by the absence of fresh water springs and attacks by the Caribs. In 1632 the English successfully colonized the island and, apart from a brief interlude in 1666 when held by the French, the island and its dependencies, Barbuda and uninhabited Redonda, remained British. Sir Christopher Codrington established the first large sugar estate in Antigua in 1674 and leased Barbuda to raise provisions for his plantations. Barbuda's only village is named after him.

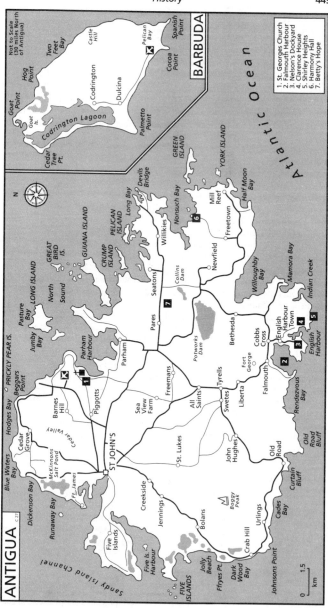

ANTIGUA C 27

BARBUDA

Atlantic Ocean

1. St. Georges Church
2. Falmouth Harbour
3. Nelson's Dockyard
4. Clarence House
5. Shirley Heights
6. Harmony Hall
7. Betty's Hope

Not to Scale
(30 miles North of Antigua)

Two Feet Bay
Castle Hill
Hog Point
Goat Point
Goat Is.
Codrington
Dulcina
Codrington Lagoon
Cedar Tree Pt.
Palmetto Point
Pelican Bay
Cocoa Point
Spanish Point

ST. JOHN'S
Ft. James
McKinnons Salt Pond
Cedar Grove
Barnes Hill
Piggotts
Parham Harbour
Parham
Freemans
Sea View Farm
All Saints
St. Lukes
Swetes
Liberta
Tyrells
Fort George
Falmouth
Cobbs Cross
English Harbour Town
English Harbour
Bethesda
Newfield
Freetown
Willikies
Seatons
Pares
Potworks Dam
Collins Dam
Mill Reef
Half Moon Bay
Nonsuch Bay
Willoughby Bay
Mamora Bay
Indian Creek
Rendezvous Bay
Old Road Bluff
Curtain Bluff
Cades Bay
Urlings
Old Road
John Hughes
Bolans
Crab Hill
Boggy Peak
Jennings
Creekside
Dark Wood Bay
Ffryes Pt.
Jolly Beach
Five Is. Harbour
FIVE ISLANDS
Johnsons Point
Sandy Island Channel
Jolly Beach
Runaway Bay
Dickenson Bay
Blue Waters
Hodges Bay
Beggars Point
PRICKLY PEAR IS.
Cedar Valley
Pasture Bay
Jumby Bay
LONG ISLAND
North Sound
GREAT BIRD IS.
GUIANA ISLAND
CRUMP ISLAND
PELICAN ISLAND
Long Bay
Devils Bridge
GREEN ISLAND
YORK ISLAND
N

0 1.5 km

Forests were cleared for sugarcane production and African slave labour was imported. Today, many Antiguans blame frequent droughts on the island's lack of trees to attract rainfall, and ruined towers of sugar plantations stand as testament to the destruction and consequent barrenness of the landscape. In the 17th and 18th centuries, Antigua was important for its natural harbours where British ships could be refitted safe from hurricanes and from attack. The Dockyard and the many fortifications date from this period. *Shirley Heights, The Story of the Red Coats in Antigua*, by Charles W E Jane, published by the Reference Library of Nelson's Dockyard National Park Foundation at English Harbour, Antigua, in 1982, gives a detailed account of the military history of the island and the building of the fortifications, price US$4.

The slaves were emancipated in 1834 but economic opportunities for the freed labourers were limited by a lack of surplus farming land, no access to credit, and an economy built on agriculture rather than manufacturing. Conditions for black people were little better than under slavery and in many cases the planters treated them worse. Poor labour conditions persisted and violence erupted in the first part of the twentieth century as workers protested against low wages, food shortages and poor living conditions. In 1939, to alleviate the seething discontent, the first labour movement was formed: the Antigua Trades and Labour Union. Vere Cornwall Bird became the union's president in 1943 and with other trade unionists formed the Antigua Labour Party (ALP). In 1946 the ALP won the first of a long series of electoral victories, being voted out of office only in 1971-76 when the Progressive Labour Movement won the general election. For a graphic account of the terrible conditions in which black people lived and worked during slavery and its aftermath, read *To Shoot Hard Labour (The Life and Times of Samuel Smith, an Antiguan Workingman 1877-1982)*, by Keithlyn B Smith and Fernando C Smith, published by Karia Press, London, and Edan's Publishers, Toronto.

Antigua was administered as part of the Leeward Islands until 1959 and attained associated status, with full internal self-government in 1967. Antigua and Barbuda, as a single territory, became independent in November 1981, despite a strong campaign for separate independence by Barbuda. Vere C Bird became the first Prime Minister and in 1989, at the age of 79, he took office for the fourth consecutive time. The general elections were marked by some irregularities and allegations of bribery, but the ALP won 15 of the 16 seats for Antigua in the 17-seat House of Representatives, the remaining seats being taken by the United National Democratic Party and the Barbuda People's Movement, for Barbuda. Mr Bird appointed a largely unchanged cabinet which included several members of his family. By-elections for seven seats were later held because of a court ruling on irregularities at the general elections. However, the ALP was returned unopposed, as the UNDP abstained in the absence of electoral reforms, and the Antigua Caribbean Liberation Movement (ACLM) could not finance a campaign.

In 1990 the Government was rocked by an arms smuggling scandal which exposed corruption at an international level when allegations were made that Antigua had been used as a transit point for shipments of arms from Israel to the Medellín cocaine cartel in Colombia. Communications and Works Minister, Vere Bird Jr, the Prime Minister's son, became the subject of a judicial inquiry, following a complaint from the Colombian Government, for having signed authorization documents. His Cabinet appointment was revoked although he remained an MP. The Blom-Cooper report recommended no prosecutions although it undermined the credibility of the Government and highlighted the rivalry between the two sons, Vere Jr and Lester Bird. The report also recommended that Vere Bird Jr be banned for life from holding public office.

Repeated calls for the resignation of Prime Minister Vere Bird were ignored although several cabinet reshuffles became necessary as ministers resigned from his Government. Demonstrations were organized in 1992 by the newly-formed three-party United Opposition Front, seeking the resignation of the Prime Minister amid allegations of his theft and corruption. Scotland Yard assistance was sought in investigating a number of fire bombs and arson attacks in 1992 and several murders in 1993. Fresh allegations of corruption were published in 1993 by the weekly opposition newspaper, *Outlet*, concerning property development contracts and misuse of public funds, resulting in a libel action issued by Lester Bird. *Outlet*, edited by Tim Hector, has for many years been the most outspoken critic of the Bird administration, frequently exposing corruption and fraud.

Vere Bird finally retired as Prime Minister in February 1994 at the age of 84. He was succeeded by his son, Lester, who led the ALP into the general elections held in March, winning its ninth out of 10 elections held since 1951. The Government's unpopularity was reflected in the vote and the ALP saw its representation cut from 15 to 11 seats in the House of Representatives. The Barbuda People's Movement retained its seat, while the United Progressive Party (formerly the United Opposition Front), led by Baldwin Spencer, won five seats, the largest number for any opposition party in the country's history. Tim Hector was appointed an opposition senator, having stood against Vere Jr in the election and lost. Vere Bird Jr, who is the chairman of the ALP, was not appointed to the new cabinet. Baldwin Spencer was nominated to chair the parliamentary Public Accounts Committee as part of the Prime Minister's aim to give credibility to his manifesto pledge of government accountability.

Freedom House, a human rights organization based in New York, claimed that the general election was not free or fair, on the basis that voting was not secret, the register contained names of people who had died or emigrated and the opposition parties had lacked access to the radio and TV networks. The new Prime Minister rejected the claims.

Government

Antigua and Barbuda is a constitutional monarchy within the Commonwealth and the British Crown is represented by a Governor General. The head of government is the Prime Minister. There are two legislative houses: a directly elected 17-member House of Representatives and a 17-member Upper House, or Senate, appointed by the Governor General, mainly on the advice of the Prime Minister and the Leader of the Opposition. Antigua is divided into six parishes: St George, St John's, St Mary, St Paul, St Peter and St Phillip. Community councils on Antigua and the local government council on Barbuda are the organs of local government.

The Economy

The economy was long dominated by the cultivation of sugar, which was the major export earner until 1960, when prices fell dramatically and crippled the industry. By 1972 sugar had largely disappeared and farming had shifted towards fruit, vegetables, cotton and livestock. The economy is now based on services, principally tourism and offshore banking. Hotels and restaurants contribute about a quarter of gross domestic product and employ about one quarter of the work force. Tourism receipts make up about 60% of total foreign exchange earnings. 505,724 tourists visited Antigua in 1993, an increase of 4.2% over 1992, of which just under half were stayover visitors. The majority came on cruise ships, Windjammer cruises or yachts. Over a third of air arrivals are from the USA, while just under a quarter come from the UK. The European market rose from 32% of the total in 1992 to 36% in 1993 and this has helped both to increase the average length of stay and to minimize seasonal fluctuations in arrival numbers, as Europeans tend to take their holidays in the summer, while Americans travel to the sun in the winter. There is some light industry which has been encouraged by tax and other incentives, but export-orientated manufacturing is hampered by high wage and energy costs. A major expansion of tourist infrastructure has taken place, with development of harbour, airport, road and hotel facilities. This investment has not yet touched the bulk of the population and in rural areas small wooden shacks still constitute the most common form of dwelling, often alongside resorts and villa developments. Economic growth slowed in the early 1990s; political instability and corruption discouraged private sector investment, while government finances were weakened by high levels of debt, wages and tax evasion.

The 1994/95 budget announced after the 1994 general elections increased taxation, notably on hotels and restaurants, and introduced a levy on incomes. Current spending was increased by 24%, partly because of wage rises in the public sector, while capital spending included expenditure on economic infrastructure, such as roads and airport works.

One of Barbuda's main sources of income is the mining of sand. In 1993 a High Court injunction against the mining led to a severe cash crisis and public employees were not paid for several months. The injunction was imposed pending the resolution of a dispute between the Government and the island council over who has authority for sand

ANTIGUA AND BARBUDA: FACT FILE

Geographic

Land area	441.6 sq km
of which Barbuda	160.6
Redonda	1.3
forested	11.0%
pastures	9.0%
cultivated	18.0%

Demographic

Population (1992)	64,000
annual growth rate (1987-92)	0%
urban	32%
rural	68%
density	144.9 per sq km
Religious affiliation	
Anglican	44.5%
Other Protestant	41.6%
Birth rate per 1,000 (1991)	18.0
	(world av 26.4)
Death rate per 1,000 (1991)	6.0
	(world av 9.2)

Education and Health

Life expectancy at birth (1991),	
male	70 years
female	74 years
Infant mortality rate	
per 1,000 live births (1987)	21.2
Physicians (1988)	1 per 1,333 persons
Hospital beds	1 per 207 persons
Calorie intake as %	
of FAO requirement	98%
Literacy (over 15)	90%

Economic

GNP (1990 market prices)	US$363mn
GNP per capita	US$4,600
Public external debt (1990)	US$268.3mn
Tourism receipts (1990)	US$258mn
Inflation (annual av 1985-90)	4.4%
Radio	1 per 0.9 persons
Television	1 per 2.3 persons
Telephone	1 per 11 persons

Employment

Population economically active (1985)	
	32,254
Unemployment rate	na
% of labour force in agriculture	9.0
trade, restaurants and hotels	22.4
manufacturing	7.4
construction	11.1
Military forces	100

Source *Encyclopaedia Britannica*

mining. Mining of sand at Palmetto Point allegedly damaged a pure water supply. The Minister of Agriculture and two businessmen were convicted of breaching the injunction, but the Minister was subsequently pardoned by the Governor General.

Many visitors regard Antigua as the ideal Caribbean holiday destination. The role of tourism in Antigua today is, however, one of the objects of a vehement attack in Jamaica Kincaid's book *A Small Place* (1988). Addressed to the foreign visitor, the essay proposes to reveal the realities underneath the island's surface. What follows is a passionate indictment of much of Antiguan government, society, the colonists who laid its foundations and the modern tourist. It is a profoundly negative book, designed to inspire the visitor to think beyond the beach and the hotel on this, or any other, island. Jamaica Kincaid was brought up on Antigua (she now lives in the USA), and memories and images from her childhood figure strongly in her other books to date, the prize-winning collection of dream-like stories, *At The Bottom Of The River* (1983) and the novel *Annie John* (1985). A new novel *Lucy* was published in 1991.

Fauna and Flora

Around 150 different birds have been observed in Antigua and Barbuda, of which a third are year-round residents and the rest seasonal or migrants. Good spots for birdwatching include McKinnons salt pond, N of St John's, where thousands of sandpipers and other water birds can be seen. Yellow crowned nightherons breed here. Potworks Dam is noted for the great blue heron in spring and many water fowl. Great Bird Island is home to the red-billed tropic bird and on Man of War Island, Barbuda, frigate birds breed. At Pasture Bay, on Long Island, the hawksbill turtle lays its eggs from late May to December. The Wide Caribbean Sea Turtle Conservation Network (Widecast) organizes turtle watches.

Beaches and Watersports

Tourist brochures will never tire of telling you that there are 365 beaches on Antigua, one for every day of the year, some of which are deserted. The nearest beach to St John's is Fort James which is sometimes rough and has a milky appearance, lots of weed and not good for swimming. At other times it can be pleasant, with palm trees and a few boulders but crowded at weekends. It is rather secluded, do not go alone, drugs-users confrontations have been recorded there. Further but better is Dickenson Bay but there are hotels all along the beach which fence off their property. Soldier's Bay, next to the *Blue Waters Hotel*, is shallow and picturesque. Instead of following the sign, park your car in the hotel car park, which has shade, walk left across the property, climb through the hole in the fence and in about three minutes you are there. Also good is Deep Bay which, like most beaches, can only be reached by taxi or car. There are several nice beaches on the peninsula W of St John's, past the *Ramada Royal Antiguan Hotel*. On Trafalgar Beach condominiums are being built on the rocks overlooking the small, sheltered bay. If you go through Five Islands village you come to Galley Bay, a secluded and unspoilt hotel beach which is popular with locals, especially joggers at sunset. The four *Hawksbill* beaches at the end of the peninsula, one of which is a nudist beach (free public entry, very secluded, security guard on duty, pleasant atmosphere), are crescent shaped, very scenic and unspoilt. Take drinks to the furthest one as there are no facilities and you may have the place to yourself. Half Moon Bay, in the E, has a resort at one end, but there is plenty of room; the waves can be rough in the centre of the bay, but the water is calm at the N end.

Near English Harbour is Galleon Beach, which is splendid, but again can only be reached by taxi or car. It has an excellent restaurant. Dark Wood Beach, on the road from St John's to Old Road round the SW coast, is very nice, quiet, with a bar and restaurant at the S end, reasonable food but not cheap.

Antigua offers sailing (sailing week at end-April, beginning of May, is a major yacht-racing event, with lots of noisy nightlife), water-skiing, snorkelling and deep-sea fishing. "Cocktail" and "barbeque" cruises are reasonably priced. From Shorty's Watersports at Dickenson Bay, glass-bottomed boats take people out to the coral reefs; there are also excursions to Bird Island, food and drink provided. Trips round the island with stops at smaller islands can be arranged on the catamarans *Siboney* (T 462 4101), *Falcon* (T 462 4792) or *Cariba* (T 462 2269), or you can charter a yacht from English Harbour or Sun Yacht Charters at Parham. *Servabo* is a Brixham fishing trawler now used for excursions and beach parties, children under 6 free, 6-12 half price, T 462 1581 for information and current rates. *Galleon Girl* can be chartered for fishing trips (T 462 2064) for a maximum of 6 people; *Lobster King*, US$450 half day, US$900 full day, maximum 6 people, special price on Wednesday US$100 pp, T 462 4363; *M/Y Nimrod*, US$500 half day, US$900 full day, T 464 0143. There is also, of course, the *Jolly Roger* (T 462 2064), a wooden sailing ship used for entertaining would-be pirates, with Wednesday lunchtime cruises from Jolly Beach, Thursday cocktail cruises from the *Royal Antiguan*, and Saturday night barbeque and dancing cruise, helped along with plentiful rum punch.

Dickenson Bay is the only beach with public hire of watersports equipment but some hotels will hire to the public especially out of season, eg the *Jolly Beach* hotel near Bolan's Village (bus from West End bus station). The *Sandals* all-inclusive resort on Dickenson Bay will admit outsiders, at EC$450 per couple 1000-1800 or EC$250 for the evening, giving you the use of all sports facilities, meals, bar etc. Patrick's Windsurfing Place at the *Lord Nelson Beach Hotel* N of the airport (no frills accommodation and food), offers package holidays for beginners or keen windsurfers (T 458 3425, F 458 3612).

A new marina was built at Jolly Harbour in 1992, just S of Ffryes Point. Several day charter boats may move there but by mid-1993 only *Kokomo* catamaran and *Franco* glass-bottom boat had done so. The marina and shopping centre is close to the *Jolly Beach Hotel*, whose facilities are available for guests at the marina or villas. For day charter bookings, water taxi and small boat rentals, T 462 7686.

Diving and Marine Life

There are barrier reefs around most of Antigua which are host to lots of colourful fish and underwater plant life. Diving is mostly shallow, up to 60 feet, except below Shirley Heights, where dives are up to 110 feet, or Sunken Rock, with a depth of 122 feet where the cleft rock formation gives the impression of a cave dive. Popular sites are Cades Reef, which runs for $2\frac{1}{2}$ miles along the leeward side of the island and is an underwater park; Sandy Island Reef, covered with several types of coral and only 30-50 feet deep; Horseshoe Reef, Barracuda Alley and Little Bird Island. There are also plenty of wrecks to explore, including the *Andes*, in 20 feet of water in Deep Bay, the *Harbour of St John's* and the *Unknown Barge*, also in Deep Bay. Diving off Barbuda is more difficult unless you are on a boat with full gear and a compressor, as facilities are very limited. The water is fairly shallow, though, so snorkelling can be enjoyable. There is little information on the island about conservation and few warnings on the dangers of touching living coral.

Dive shops are located nearly all round the island and include: Aquanaut Diving Centre, at *St James's Club*, T 460 5000 or *Royal Antiguan*, T 4621801, or *Galleon Beach Club*, T 463 1024; Dive Runaway, *Runaway Beach Club*, T 462 2626, training sessions, PADI certification courses, equipment rental; Dive Antigua, *Halcyon Cove Hotel*, T 462 0256; Jolly Dive, *Jolly Beach Hotel*, T 462 0061 and at Jolly Harbour, T 462 8305; Curtain Bluff Dive Shop, *Curtain Bluff Hotel*, T 462 8400 (certified hotel guests only); Long Bay Dive Shop, *Long Bay Hotel*, T 460 2005 (certified hotel guests only).

Other Sports

There are golf courses, including the professional 18-hole one at Cedar Valley, near St John's, T 462 0161, and a 9-hole course open to visitors at *Half Moon Bay Hotel*, T 463 2101.

Many of the large hotels have tennis courts, the most prestigious of which are probably at *Half Moon Bay Hotel*, which hosts several professional competitions during the year, T 463-2101. Also courts at the *Royal Antiguan Hotel*, T 462 3733, Deep Bay; *Hodges Bay Club*, T 462 2300; Temo Sports, T 463 1536. *St James's Club* has floodlit courts, T 463 1113. There is a tennis and squash club open to the public next to the *Falmouth Harbour Beach Apartments*. The new Jolly Harbour development includes tennis and squash courts (US$20/30 minutes).

Riding is available through the hotels. The Antigua Riding Academy has accompanied riding tours. Wadadli Riding Stables at Gambles Bluff, T 462 2721. *St James's Club* also arranges horseriding, T 463 1430.

Cricket is the national sport and Test Matches are played at the Recreation Ground. There are matches between Antiguan teams and against teams from neighbouring islands.

Horse racing takes place on public holidays at Cassada Park.

There is a sports complex overlooking Falmouth Harbour, next to the Yacht Club, which has synthetic grass tennis courts and squash courts (T 463 1781), and a Fitness Club in Hodges Bay, which offers aerobic classes, weight training rooms and other facilities (T 462 1540). The National Fitness Centre, off Old Parham Road behind the Price Waterhouse building, has a good gym, US$10 for one visit, but price negotiable for multiple visits.

Festivals

Antigua's carnival is at the end of July and lasts until the first Tuesday in August. The main event is "J'ouvert", or "Juvé" morning when from 0400 people come into town dancing behind steel and brass bands. Hotels and airlines tend to be booked up well in advance. For information contact the Carnival Committee, High Street, St John's, T 462 0194. Barbuda has a smaller carnival in June, known as "Caribana". An annual jazz festival is held, usually in late May, with concerts at Fort James, the *Sandpiper Reef Hotel*, King's Casino and on the *Jolly Roger*. Contact the Tourist Office for a programme.

ST JOHN'S

Built around the largest of the natural harbours is *St John's*, the capital, with an estimated population of about 30,000. It is rather quiet and a little run-down but parts have been developed for tourism and the town is a mixture of the old and the new. Although parts of the town are rather tatty, it is generally safe to walk around even late at night. New boutiques, duty-free shops and restaurants are vying for custom. Redcliffe Quay is a picturesque area of restored historical buildings now full of souvenir shops and the only toy shop in town. Heritage Quay, opened in 1988, is a duty free shopping complex strategically placed to catch cruise ship visitors. It has a casino and a

Antigua and Barbuda

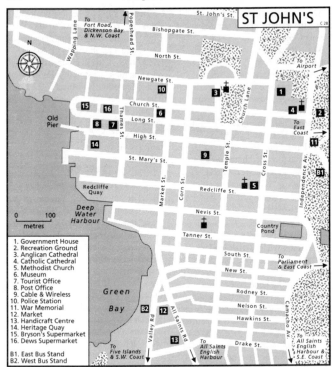

ST JOHN'S

1. Government House
2. Recreation Ground
3. Anglican Cathedral
4. Catholic Cathedral
5. Methodist Church
6. Museum
7. Tourist Office
8. Post Office
9. Cable & Wireless
10. Police Station
11. War Memorial
12. Market
13. Handicraft Centre
14. Heritage Quay
15. Bryson's Supermarket
16. Dews Supermarket

B1. East Bus Stand
B2. West Bus Stand

big screen satellite TV, a cool, pleasant place to have a drink. Most activity now takes place around these two quay developments, especially when there is a cruise ship in dock.

However, St John's does have interesting historical associations. Nelson served in Antigua as a young man for almost three years, and visited it again in 1805, during his long chase of Villeneuve which was to end with the Battle of Trafalgar. Some of the old buildings in St John's, including the Anglican Cathedral, have been damaged several times by earthquakes, the last one in 1974. A cathedral in St John's was first built in 1683, but replaced in 1745 and then again in 1843 after an earthquake, at which time it was built of stone. Its twin towers can

be seen from all over St John's. It has a wonderfully cool interior lined with pitchpine timber. Donations requested.

The Museum and Archives at the former Court House in Long Street are worth a visit, both to see the exhibition of pre-Columbian and colonial archaeology and anthropology of Antigua and for the Court House building itself, first built in 1747, damaged by earthquakes in 1843 and 1974 but now restored. There is also Viv Richard's cricket bat, with which he scored the fastest century, various 'hands on' items and games. Entrance free, although donations requested; gift shop. Open Monday-Friday 1000-1500, Saturdays 1000-1300. (T 463 1060). You can also visit Viv Richard's childhood home on Viv Richard's

Street. The Museum of Marine and Living Art, Gambles Terrace, opposite Princess Margaret School, T 462 1228, F 462 1187, exhibits of sea shells, shipwrecks and pre-Columbian history. Recommended weekly lectures, Thursday 1000, on the evolution of the earth and the formation of the continents and civilizations.

A short drive W of St John's are the ruins of Fort Barrington on a promontory at Goat Hill overlooking Deep Bay and the entrance to St John's Harbour. These fortifications were erected by Governor Burt, who gave up active duty in 1780 suffering from psychiatric disorders; a stone he placed in one of the walls at the Fort describes him grandly as 'Imperator and Gubernator' of the Carib Islands. At the other side of the harbour are the ruins of Fort James, from where you can get a good view of St John's. There was originally a fort on this site dating from 1675, but most of what can now be seen dates from 1749.

Excursions

On the other side of the island is *English Harbour*, which has become one of the world's most attractive yachting centres. Here "Nelson's Dockyard" has been restored and is one of the most interesting historical monuments in the West Indies. It was designated a National Park in 1985 (Parks Commissioner, T 463-1379). Entrance US$1.60, children under 12 free. Souvenirs and T-shirts are on sale at the entrance. See *Admiral's Inn*, with its boat and mast yard, slipway and pillars still standing but which suffered earthquake damage in the nineteenth century. The *Lumber and Copper Store* is now a hotel bar and restaurant. There is a small museum, with gift shop in the same building. *Limey's Bar* has a good view of the harbour and is a nice place for a drink. Next to it is an art centre with work by local artists including Katie Shears, who specializes in flora and fauna. The Ralph

A Aldridge shell collection in a wall case is fascinating, all the shells were found in Antiguan waters. On the quay are three large capstans, showing signs of wear and tear. Boat charters can be arranged from here; also a 20-30 minute cruise round the historic Dockyard for US$6 on *Horatio*, from outside the *Copper and Lumber Store*, depending on seasonal demand. A footpath leads round the bay to Fort Berkeley at the harbour mouth, well grazed by goats, wonderful views. Near the Dockyard, Clarence House still stands where the future King, William IV stayed when he served as a midshipman in the 1780s.

On the left of the road from English Harbour to Shirley Heights are the remains of the British Navy's magazines and a small branch road to a new cultural resource centre. There is a gift shop, restaurant, small museum with shell display and an audio visual room which puts on a display about very half hour on Antigua's history, highly recommended. Local guides also available.

At Shirley Heights, overlooking English Harbour, are the ruins of fortifications built in the 18th century with a wonderful view. Some buildings, like officers' quarters, are still standing, restored but roofless, which give an idea of their former grandeur. In 1994 it was reported rather overgrown, run down and littered. At the lookout point, or Battery, at the S end is a bar and restaurant. On Sundays a steel band plays 1500-1800, followed by reggae 1800-2200, very loud and popular, can be heard at the dockyard below. Barbequed burgers, chicken, ribs and salad US$6-11. Great fun, recommended. Antiguans as well as tourists enjoy it. There is often some activity on Thursdays too.

Great George Fort, on Monk's Hill, above Falmouth Harbour (a 30-minute walk from the village of Liberta, and from Cobb's Cross near English Harbour) has been less well preserved. There is a museum of pre-Columbian artefacts in the

Dow Hill tracking station building (formerly used in connection with the US Apollo space programme). It can be visited by prior arrangement, or on Thursday afternoons there are tours, starting from Nelson's Dockyard and taking in Dow Hill (check the details at Nicholson's travel agency). If advance notice is given, the Antigua Rum Distillery welcomes visitors.

Fig Tree Drive between Old Road and the Catholic church on the road going N from Liberta, is a steep, winding, bumpy road, through mountainous rainforest. It is greener and more scenic than most of the island, but the rainforest is scanty and can not be compared with islands like Dominica. If travelling by bicycle make sure you go *down* Fig Tree Drive from the All Saints to Liberta road, heading towards Old Road, the hill is very steep.

Boggy Peak, in the SW, is the highest point on the island and from the top you can get wonderful views over to Guadelupe, St Kitts, Nevis and Montserrat. It is a good walk up, or you can take a car. From Urlings walk (or take minibus) about ½-¾ mile in the direction of Old Town. Take the second major path to the left (the first goes to a ruined house visible from the road) which runs very straight then ascends quite steeply. When you get to the top, walk round the fence surrounding the Cable and Wireless buildings to get a good view in all directions.

A recommended excursion to the E coast, if you have a car, is to take the road out to the airport from St John's. Do not enter the airport but take the right fork which runs alongside it. After about 1½ miles take a right turn down a small road to St George's Church, on Fitches Creek Bay, built in 1687 in a beautiful location, interesting gravestones. From there, follow the rough road round the coast to **Parham**, which is interesting for being the first British settlement on the island and for having an unusual octagonal church, St Peter's, which dates from the 1840s. Lovely flamboyant trees surround the church and enhance its attractiveness. From Parham take the road due S and then E at the petrol station through Pares to Willikies. On this road, just past Pares Village, is a sign to **Betty's Hope**, a ruined sugar estate built in 1650 and once owned by the Codrington family. Restoration was started by the Antigua Museum in St John's but abandoned. The ruins are now becoming overgrown again, but there are plans for further restoration and a building has been erected for a visitors' centre. It is an extensive site with two towers, a still house and other ruined buildings, fascinating to explore, but wear stout shoes and trousers, there are long, sharp thorns. For a guided tour contact the Antigua Museum, T 462 3946 ext 14/16, or Mr Hubert Mack, of Parham Town. After Willikies the road is signed to the Pineapple Beach Club at Long Bay, but before you get there, take a right turn down a small road, which deteriorates to a bumpy track, to **Devil's Bridge** at Indian Town Point. The area on the Atlantic coast is a national park where rough waves have carved out the bridge and made blowholes, not easily visible at first, but quite impressive when the spray breaks through. Good view of Long Bay and the headland.

Returning through Willikies to Glanvilles, take a left turn shortly after St Stephen's Church down a small road S past Collins Dam. When you meet up with the main road (petrol station) turn left and then right towards St Phillips. The scenery after this village is quite attractive, there are several ruined sugar mills dotting the landscape. The road continues on to Half Moon Bay and tracks lead up the coast to Mill Reef and many small beaches and jetties. Alternatively, take a left turn through Freetown to visit **Harmony Hall** (T 460 4120), Brown's Bay Mill, at Nonsuch Bay, a restored Great House and mill which has been converted into a Caribbean art and craft exhibition centre. Open daily 1000-1800. There is a shop, bar and restaurant (Sunday barbeque, dinner by reservation only, rec), and a jetty for those arriving by sea. Moorings also available for anchoring in the bay. Harmony Hall broadcasts a daily weather service at 0900 on VHF Channel 68. There are two villas for rent with use of swimming pool. Twice a week the catamaran *Wizard* leaves from the jetty at 1000 for a snorkelling and sightseeing cruise.

Warning

Finding your way around is not easy: street names are rarely in evidence. The Ordnance Survey map, US$7.50, is recommended if you are exploring the island. It is a little dated, but there is nothing better. A map hand drawn by Brian Dyde is available from several locations and is adequate for driving around.

BARBUDA

Some 30 miles to the N is Barbuda, a flat coral island some 68 miles square, one of the two island dependencies of Antigua. The population is about 1,500 and most of them live in the only village on the island, Codrington, which stands on the edge of the lagoon.

The people of Barbuda are unusually tall, descended from the Corramante tribe in Africa and used by Codrington in his experiments in slave breeding. Barbuda has some excellent beaches and its seas are rich with all types of crustaceans and tropical fish. Palaster Reef is a marine reserve to protect the reef and the shipwrecks (there are around 60 ships documented). You can swim from the beach to the reef. This is one of the few islands in the area where there is still much wild life, although much of it introduced by man: duck, guinea fowl, plover, pigeon, wild deer, pigs, horses and donkeys.

There is an impressive frigate bird colony in the mangroves in Codrington Lagoon, particularly on Man of War Island where hundreds of birds mate and breed in August-December. Local fishermen will take you out there; you can get quite close for photography or just to watch. Popular with ornithologists working nine months of the year in Antarctica, who spend their holidays coming to see 'their' frigate birds in Codrington Lagoon. Ask the guide to drop you at Palm Bay on the W side of the lagoon, and pick you up 4-5 hours later.

Meanwhile walk the 17 miles of beaches, up N or down S, but bring a hat and sunscreen. There are no beach bars or vendors, you will probably be the only person for miles. There is no shade except around Palm Beach where there is a lot of litter. The island has a Martello Tower and fort. The tower is 56 feet high and once had nine guns to defend the SW approach. It now has a swarm of killer bees in the cellar – take care. From Codrington, River Road runs 3 miles to Palmetto Point (with beautiful pink sand beaches), past Cocoa Point and on to Spanish Point, a half-mile finger of land that divides the Atlantic from the Caribbean Sea. There is a small ruin of a lookout post here and the most important Arawak settlements found in Barbuda. Diving is excellent, bring your own gear.

Barbuda is being developed as a tourist resort with attractions for snorkellers and skin-divers such as exploring old wrecks. The elkhorn coral and staghorn coral formations are very impressive. Take your own scuba equipment or join one of the dive boats from Antigua. Snorkelling equipment is available but is more expensive than on Antigua. There are two hotels, two villas and a few guesthouses, although more are planned. *Cocoa Point Lodge*, which charges US$400 per night to include all meals and drinks, is quiet and exclusive, islanders and non-guests are not admitted. The *K-Club*, owned and designed by Italians, opened in 1991 is even more expensive, 28 rooms, from US$1,100 a night, with its own 9-hole golf course (the grass was laid on soil cleared from the mangrove swamp so there are problems now with salt) as well as water sports, welcomes islanders and non-residents, open mid-November-end-May, no children under 12, T 460 0300, in the UK T 0800 373 742. The *Sunset View Hotel* is just S of the Codrington airport, 16 rooms on 2 floors, more air upstairs, US$75d including breakfast, dining room, bar, fans, shower, in need of repairs, not always open off-season, T 460 0016/0078. *Nedd's Guest House* in Codrington, T 460 0059, US$35s, US$50d, has clean and airy rooms upstairs, call prior to arrival and fix room rate with Mr McArthur Nedd, use of kitchen, minimart downstairs, bakery just behind the guest house in the next street, no road name signs. Several small snack bars, ask locally. Houses are also available for rent at about US$35-70, phone Evans at the car rental for help. The *Lagoon Café*, at the jetty where you embark for boat trips, is a night spot run by Norris Morris Harris, who also cooks at the *Jolly Beach*. Dim table lights, food difficult to see. If you prefer to have lobster or fish with a family, ask Mr Nedd to call George for you. Fix the price beforehand and George and his family will cook. Do not expect many "mod cons" on Barbuda. The local night spot is *Jam City*, with beer cheaper than Antigua. Paradise Tours, run by Lynton Thomas, is highly recommended, T 460 0135.

Excellent 1:25,000 maps should be available from the Codrington post office, or from the map shop in Jardine Court, St Mary's, St John's (good 1:50,000 maps of Antigua as well). It is safer to get one before you arrive in Barbuda, you can not rely on anything being in stock there. It is possible to hire jeeps (US$45/day including insurance, from Williams and Thomas Car Rental, T 460 0047, on main road down S to Martello Tower) or horses in Codrington, otherwise everywhere is a long hot walk, so take liquid refresh-ment with you. Easily reached by air (taking 10 minutes), or (with some difficulty and at a high price) by boat from St John's. There are two airports. The main one is just S of Codrington, to which Liat has regular flights, US$40 return, while Four Island Airways or Carib Aviation will arrange charters and day trips. The second airport is near Cocoa Point and principally serves the two hotels nearby: *Cocoa Point* and *K-Club*.

REDONDA

Antigua's second dependency, 35 miles to the SW and at half a mile square, little more than a rocky volcanic islet, is uninhabited. Columbus sighted the island on 12 November 1493 and named it after a church in Cadiz called Santa María de Redonda. He did not land, however, and thus did not formally claim the island. Neither did anyone else until 1865 when Matthew Dowdy Shiel, an Irish sea-trader from Montserrat, celebrated the birth of a long-awaited son by leading an expedition of friends to Redonda and claiming it as his kingdom. In 1872, the island was annexed by Britain and came under the jurisdiction of the colony of Antigua, despite protests from the Shiels. The Title of King was not disputed, however, and has survived to this day. The island was never inhabited although for some years guano was extracted by the Redonda Phosphate Company until the works were blown away by a hurricane.

In 1880 MD Shiel abdicated in favour of his son, Matthew Phipps Shiel, who became King Felipe of Redonda but emigrated to the UK where he was educated and became a popular novelist. On his death in 1947 he passed the title to his friend John Gawsworth, the poet, who became Juan, third King of Redonda, but continuing to live in London. His reign was notable for his idea of an 'intellectual aristocracy' of the realm of Redonda and he conferred titles on his literary friends, including Victor Gollancz, the publisher,

JB Priestley, Dorothy L Sayers and Lawrence Durrell. This eccentric pasttime hit a crisis when declining fortunes and increasing time spent in the pub sparked a rash of new titles to all and sundry and the succession was disputed. Eventually King Juan abdicated in 1967 in favour of his friend, Arthur John Roberts, who took the title of Juan II. He formed a Shiel Society and set up a charitable trust fund to assist young writers, nevertheless, claimants to the throne continued to pop up and for many years controversy surrounded the kingdom. In 1989 King Juan II abdicated in favour of his friend and supporter, William Leonard Gates, an historian, lecturer and writer, who took the title of Leo, Fifth King of Redonda. His aim is to keep alive the Kingdom of Redonda and perpetuate the memory of M P Shiel, the novelist, while still fending off potential usurpers of his crown.

Meanwhile, on Redonda, all is much the same for the goats, lizards and sea birds, who live an undisturbed life apart from the occasional bird watcher who might come to find the burrowing owl, now extinct on Antigua.

INFORMATION FOR VISITORS

● **Documents**

A valid onward ticket is necessary. American, Canadian and British nationals need only proof of citizenship. Passports but not visas are required by nationals of other Commonwealth countries and British Dependent Territories, if their stay does not exceed 6 months. The following countries need valid passports but not visas: Argentina, Austria, Belgium, Brazil, Chile, Denmark, Finland, France, Germany, Greece, Ireland, Italy, Japan, Liechtenstein, Luxembourg, Malta, Mexico, Monaco, Netherlands, Norway, Peru, Portugal, Spain, Suriname, Sweden, Switzerland, Turkey and Venezuela. Nationals of all other countries require visas, unless they are in transit for less than 24 hours. Visitors must satisfy immigration officials that they have enough money for

their stay. You will not be allowed through Immigration without somewhere to stay. The Tourist Office can help you and you can always change your mind later. If you arrive at English Harbour by boat you must clear Customs at the Police Station.

● **How To Get There**

V C Bird airport, some 4½ miles from St John's, is the centre for air traffic in the area and is served by British Airways (4 direct flights a week from Gatwick, connections with Barbados and St Lucia, T 462 0876/9), BWIA (2 flights a week from Heathrow, one from Zurich, one from Frankfurt, 3 from Miami and 4 from New York, 4 from Toronto, 4 days a week from Guyana), Lufthansa (2 flights a week direct from Frankfurt, T 462 3142, represented by Liat), American Airlines (from New York, Miami, Puerto Rico, T 462 0950), Continental from Newark, NJ, and Air Canada from Toronto, T 462 1147.

There is an airport departure tax of EC$25.

● **Inter Island Transport**

There are frequent air services to neighbouring islands (Anguilla, Barbados, Barbuda, Dominica, Martinique, Grenada, Jamaica, Montserrat, Nevis, Guadeloupe, Trinidad and Tobago, St Croix, St Kitts, St Lucia, St Maarten, St Thomas, St Vincent, Puerto Rico, Tortola) operated by Liat (T 462 3142/3), BWIA (T 462 0262/3), Continental and American Airlines. Carib Aviation arranges charters to neighbouring islands in planes carrying 5, 6 or 9 passengers and can often work out cheaper and more convenient than using Liat. The office is at the airport, T 462 3147 0800-1700, after office hours T 461 1650. They will meet incoming flights if you are transferring to another island, and make sure you make your return connection. Also day tours. The flight to Montserrat takes 18 minutes. Montserrat Airways runs a shuttle service on a first come first served basis 0630-1830, US$33 one way.

Occasional boat services to St Kitts and Dominica; see boat captains at Fisherman's Wharf. There is a cargo boat to Dominica once a week and you can arrange a passage for EC$102 including departure tax through Vernon Edwards Shipping Company on Thames Street; very basic facilities, no toilet.

● **Local Travel**

Minivans (shared taxis) go to some parts of the island (eg Old Road) from the West End bus terminal by the market in St John's. Buses, which are banned from the tourist area (N of the line from the airport to St John's), run frequently between St John's and English Harbour, EC$2.50. There are also buses from the E terminal by the war memorial to Willikies, whence a 20 min walk to Long Bay beach and to Parham. There are no buses to the airport and very few to beaches though 2 good swimming beaches on the way to Old Road can be reached by bus. Bus frequency can be variable, and there are very few buses after dark or on Sun. Buses to Old Road are half-hourly on average, though more frequent around 0800 and 1600. There are no publicly displayed timetables, you'll have to ask for one. Buses usually go when they are full; ask the driver where he is going.

Taxis have H registration plates. In St John's there is a taxi rank on St Mary Street, or outside Dew's or Bryson's supermarkets. They are not metered and frequently try to overcharge, so agree a price first, they should have a EC$ price list so ask to see it. There is a list of government approved taxi rates posted in EC$ and US$ at the airport just after customs. From St John's to Runaway Bay, 10 mins, is US$6; to the airport, US$7 or EC$20 per car, from the airport to town EC$20 per person. If going to the airport early in the morning, book a taxi the night before as there are not many around. For excursions a knowledgeable and rec taxi driver is Mr Graham at the *Barrymore Hotel*. A day tour normally costs about US$55 for 2 people, US$10 for each extra person. Taxi: excursions advertised in the hotels are generally overpriced. Hitchhiking is easy in daylight but at night you might fall prey to a taxi driver.

● **Car Hire**
All in St John's and some at airport, most will pick you up: Avis at Jolly Harbour, T 462 7688; Antigua Car Rentals (*Barrymore Hotel*); Lapp's Rent-a-Car (Long and Cross Streets); Alexander Parris (St Mary's Street); Prince's Rent-a-Car (Fort Road); Capital Rental (High Street); Dollar Rental (Nevis Street); E J Wolfe Ltd (Long Street); National and, cheaper, Hustler Hires at The Toy Shop (Long Street). Sunshine Car Rental (T 461 2426) rec, good value compared with agencies at the airport who push up the extras (although Jacob's at the airport is reported friendly and reliable and at Oakland Rent-A-Car you can negotiate good rates, contact Ann Edwards, T 462 3021/0458). Rates are from US$40 a day, US$225 a week (no mileage charge), inc insurance charges, in summer,

more in winter.

A local driving licence, US$12, valid for 3 months, must be purchased on presentation of a foreign licence.

Renting a car or motorcycle is probably the best way to see the island's sights if you have only a short time to spend, as the bus service is inadequate. Ivor's at English Harbour has a monopoly on renting motorcycles at US$20/day (plus US$12 driving licence), bikes not in good condition. Bicycle hire from House of Vitamins, US$10/day, US$100 deposit. Sun Cycles in Hodges Bay has good bicycles, also mountain bikes, will deliver and pick up at your hotel.

Remember to drive on the left. There is a 24-hour petrol station on Old Parham Road outside St John's. Other filling stations are marked on the road map distributed by the Tourist Office, updated annually. Petrol costs US$2.25/gallon everywhere. Traffic lights were installed in St John's in 1989, but these are the only ones on the island. Be careful with one way streets in St John's. In rural areas watch out for potholes; the roads are very narrow in places. In 1994 there were a lot of roadworks and men seemed to be digging up the road all round the island. Diversion signs are inadequate; one correspondent was sent into a school playing field but not directed out again, so everyone was driving around not knowing where to go. At night people do not always dim their headlights, beware also of cows straying across the road in the dark.

● **Where To Stay**
There is a 10% service charge and 7% government tax at all hotels.

There are hotels, resorts and apartments all round the island and more are being built all the time. The greatest concentration of developments is in the area around St John's, along the coast to the W and also to the N in a clockwise direction to the airport. A second cluster of places to stay is around English Harbour and Falmouth Harbour in the SE of the island. Many may be closed September-October in preparation for the winter season. Full lists of hotels, apartments, villas and guesthouses should be available from the Tourist Office at the airport, although it is not always easy to get hold of. The Tourist Office will book you a hotel room on arrival if you have not already done so. There are lots of self-catering apartments available all round the island but a common complaint is that sufficient provisions are not available locally and you have to go into St John's for shopping.

In **St John's**: *Main Road Guest House*, near the market, EC$25-40, about the cheapest but no fan, noisy, mice visit at night. *Miami*, near market on Main Road, PO Box 300, T 462 0975, US$30d with bath, Chinese restaurant. *Joe Mike's Hotel*, in Corn Alley and Nevis St, T 462 3244 or 1142, F 462 1187, PO Box 136, US$50d, special rates can be negotiated but not by phone, nice, clean rooms, no balconies, no food but downstairs are fast food, restaurant and bar, casino, icecream parlour, cocktail lounge, beauty salon and mini-mart; *Montgomery Hotel*, Tindale Road, usually plenty of room except during carnival and cricket matches, central but not a very nice part of town, noisy roosters across the street, scruffy and basic, small rooms, shared bath, rats in downstairs rooms, no water after midnight, cable TV, US$35d, T 462 1164; *Palm View Guest House*, 57 St Mary's Street, no sign, T 462 1299, friendly, basic, good, US$30d; *Murphy's Apartments*, PO Box 491, All Saints Road, T 461 1183, run by Elaine Murphy, US$35-55, apartments somewhat aged, breakfast not always available; *Cortsland*, Upper Gambles, PO Box 403, overpriced at US$75-90d, T 462 1395. *Pigottsville Guest House*, at Clare Hall, PO Box 521, very basic, in need of repairs, but cheap, no signs, about 2 miles from the airport and within easy walking distance of St John's, 20 rooms, US$30d, T 462 0592; *Roslyn's Guest House*, Fort Road, PO Box 161, T 462 0762, 3 double rooms US$45, 1 triple room US$55, 10 mins walk to shops, 15 mins walk to beach, big garden with mango trees, friendly lady owner, rec; *Barrymore*, US$78-86d winter rate, US$63-86 summer, on Fort Road, on the outskirts of the town, get a room away from Fort Road traffic, rooms basic but clean, T 462 4062/3, F 463 4140, PO Box 244; *Barrymore Beach Club* on Runaway Bay, 2 miles from St John's, which has rooms and apartments, rec, clean, comfortable, T 462 4101, F 462 4140, US$115-235 winter rate, US$70-125 summer, on 1½ miles of white sand beach; *Runaway Beach Club*, on Runaway Bay, friendly, beachfront cabins, rooms or villas, US$80-260 winter, US$60-110 summer, 110V electricity, excellent beach restaurant, The Lobster Pot, T 462 1318/3280, F 462 4172, PO Box 874; *Siboney Beach Club*, good, small, US$230-290 winter, US$110-165 summer, T 462 0806, F 462

3356; *Time Away*, apartments, US$50-70 summer, US$75-95 winter, beach but no other facilities, a/c, PO Box 189, T 462 0775/1212; *Coral Sands* beach front cottages at Runaway Bay, US$200/night for 2-bedroomed or $250 for 3-bedroomed in winter, reservations through Mrs Sonia King, PO Box 34, St John's, T 461 0925; *Sand Haven Hotel*, PO Box 405, tiny rooms, very basic facilities, but balcony doors open onto clean, sandy beach with shade from palm trees and sea grape, US$45s, US$65d, self-catering US$80-95, T 462-4491, 5-10 min beach walk from *Barrymore Beach Apartments*, vehicle hire needed. The *Ramada Renaissance Royal Antiguan*, 3 miles from St John's, depressing drive through tatty suburbs, 270 rooms, high rise, comfortable, good facilities, quiet in summer, casino, pool, tennis etc, US$175-380d winter, US$110-250d summer, PO Box 1322, T 462 3733, F 462 3732. Further round the coast *Hawksbill Beach Resort*, 4 miles from St John's, 37 acres and 4 lovely beaches, good food, pleasant rooms, friendly staff, PO Box 108, T 462 0301, F 462 1515, tennis, table tennis, pool, watersports, 99 rooms, US$299-388 winter, US$160-200 summer BP.

At **Dickenson Bay**: *Antigua Village* has villas with free watersports from US$75-95 summer rate to US$135-170 winter rate for a studio or beach front 2-bedroomed villa, there is a small store for provisions, nothing exciting, T 462 2930, F 462 0375, PO Box 649, St John's. *Sandals Antigua*, PO Box 147, T 462 0267, F 462 4135, couples only, all-inclusive, US$510-700 winter, US$465-638 summer, 149 comfortable rooms, several restaurants, diving, waterskiing, other watersports, tennis, jacuzzi, 4 pools. *Halcyon Cove Beach Resort and Casino*, PO Box 251, T 462 0256-8, F 462 0271, US$150-310 winter rate, US$105-270 summer EP-MAP, on the beach with full watersports facilities inc diving and fishing, and tennis. On the N coast, *Blue Waters*, T 462 0290, F 462 0293, P O Box 256, US$235-285, winter, US$140-175, summer, excellent but expensive when tax and service is added to everything, tennis, pool, sailing, windsurfing, 2 mins from golf course, taxis from hotel nearly always try to overcharge.

In the **southwest**: *Jolly Harbour Beach Resort*, PO Box 1793, T 462 6166, F 462 6167, US$70-100d winter, US$60-80d EP summer rate, a/c, 30 rooms, suites, with plenty of activities, watersports, pool, tennis, squash, sports centre; *Golden Rock Studios*, at Johnson's Point are comfortable self-catering apartments with a restaurant on a pleasant beach, US$350-490/week summer, US$770/week winter for one bedroom, children sharing free, special rates for teenagers, there are also a couple of rooms without kitchen US$60d EP, Austrian run, Austrian food if you want it, highly rec, T/F 462-1442/8218.

At **English Harbour**: *Admiral's Inn*, US$104-128d winter rate, US$72-86d summer rate, PO Box 713, T 460 1027, F 460 1534, 14 rooms of varying sizes in restored 17th century building, very pleasant, transport to the beach, complimentary sunfish and snorkelling equipment, excellent location, good food. *Copper and Lumber Store* (restored dockyard building) PO Box 184, T 460 1058, F 460 1529, studios and suites available, US$80-140 summer rate, US$160-280 winter, boat transport to nearby beaches. *The Inn at English Harbour*, set in 10 acres with lovely white sand beach, watersports provided, tennis and golf nearby, US$240-340d winter rate, US$120-180d summer, PO Box 187, St John's, T 460 1014, F 460 1603.

At **Falmouth Harbour**: *Catamaran Hotel and Marina*, on narrow beach, friendly, US$65-120d winter rate, T 463 1036, F 460 1506, PO Box 958. *Falmouth Harbour Beach Apartments* (same management as *Admiral's Inn*) good value, 28 hillside or beach front studio apartments on or near private beach, US$82-86d per day in summer or US$118-130d in winter, excluding tax, very clean, friendly staff, including use of boats and other watersports equipment, all apartments have lovely view of harbour, PO Box 713, St John's, T 460 1027/1094, F 460 1534.

In the **east**: *Half Moon Bay Hotel*, good setting, not obtrusive, 9-hole golf, tennis with pro, watersports, pool etc, closed September-October, US$400-580d winter, US$280-410 summer FAP, no children under 5 in winter, PO Box 144, St John's, T 460 4300, F 460 4306.

On **Long Island**: *Jumby Bay Resort*, secluded, luxurious and incredibly expensive at US$775-975d all inclusive winter rate, US$645-775d summer, PO Box 243, St John's, T 462 6000, F 462 6020, US reservations: T 800 437 0049 or (212) 819 9490. The resort does not accept credit cards.

If you are changing planes and have to stop over, take a taxi into St John's where the accommodation is much better than near the airport. *The Airport Hotel*, T 462 1191, US$65d, where some airlines dump you if a missed connection is their fault, is grim and noisy, very depressing after the stress of missing a plane, do not rely on an early morning wake up call although transport to the airport is usually prompt. *Antigua Mill*, near the airport, T 462 3044, F 462 1500, P O Box 319, US$80-100d winter, US$60-80d summer, 22 rooms, a/c, TV, phone, pool, restaurant.

Camping is illegal.

● **Where To Eat**

If you are planning to eat out in hotels, you need to allow at least US$300 pp per week, but it is possible to eat much more cheaply in the local restaurants in St John's. A 7% tax on all meals and drinks was introduced in the 1994 budget. Restaurants tend to move, close down or change names frequently. In St John's, *18 carat* Lower Church Street, local food, light lunches and salads, popular, T 462 0016, open 1000-2200, closed Sun. *Pizzas on the Quay* (Big Banana Holding Co), at Redcliffe Quay, very popular at lunch time, salads and sandwiches as well as pizzas, rec, T 462 2621, open Mon-Sat 0830-2200, Sun 1630-2200; *La Dolce Vita* makes own pasta, 4-course dinner

EC$110, service and wine extra; *Redcliffe Tavern*, good lunch, EC$17-35, evening main course EC$25-40; *Ginger House*, also Redcliffe Quay, EC$45-75 main course, lunch EC$25, salad bar EC$30; *Hemingway's*, drink, lunch or dinner West Indian style on cool veranda overlooking Lower Mary St at entrance to Heritage Quay; *Home*, Gambles Terrace, T 461 7651, Caribbean haute cuisine, Italian pasta dishes, exotic desserts, about EC$80-100 pp, very elegant but no stiff formality, friendly atmosphere, service excellent, welcoming to families, run by Antiguan Carl Thomas and his German wife Rita, rec; *Lemon Tree*, on Long Street, also rec but management reported to be rude, T 462 1969, closed Sun; *Brother B's*, Long St and Soul Alley, opposite the Museum, open daily until 2200 for drinks and meals, live band at lunch time, slow service, local cuisine, pleasant atmosphere; *Talk of the Town*, Lower Redcliffe St, opp Benjie's Store, lively but good place for a cheap filling lunch, EC$15-20, local dishes only, popular with working Antiguans, closed from Sat pm to Mon am; *Calypso Café*, Redcliffe Street, West Indian, seafood, EC$20-30, best pumpkin soup anywhere, strong Italian coffee, lunch only, closed weekends; *Smoking Joe's*, opposite the cricket ground, for barbequed ribs, chicken, etc, Joe is a local calypsonian; *Nature's Way*, Market Street, upstairs verandah, Indian style meals, also for vegetarians, good rotis and salads; *The Island Café*, Fort Road, opp *Kentucky Fried Chicken's* suburb branch, imaginative seafood and fish dishes, but small portions; *Crazy Cactus Cantina*, All Saints Rd, excellent Mexican food, huge portions, very good quality, EC$50-80 for 2; *Fisherman's Wharf Pizza House* at Heritage Quay, good sandwiches, burgers and pizzas, pleasant setting, cheap, EC$40 for dinner for 2.

For cheap (EC$8), good set meals, go to the restaurant by the fishing boat harbour. *Dubarry's Restaurant (Barrymore Hotel)* is rec for food but overpriced. At Dickenson Bay, *Buccaneer Cove* has barbeque suppers on the beach, caters for mini-cruises, very quiet in summer. Other rec restaurants in the area are the *Lobster Pot*, *French Quarter* and *Siboney*. In the Hodges Bay area, near the airport, *Le Bistro*, excellent French food, dinner only, closed Mon (T 462 3881). At Jolly Harbour marine complex there is an excellent Italian *trattoria*, *Al Porle*, pasta, pizzas, seafood in al fresco setting, highly rec, meals from US$10. At English Harbour, there is a restaurant and bar on Shirley Heights, steel band and barbeque every Sun afternoon (See **Excursions**). *Admiral's Inn*, Nelson's Dockyard, breakfast (slow service but good value, rec), lunch and dinner (limited selection but good, slightly overpriced) every day, yachtsman's dinner EC$40, (T 463 1027). *The Copper and Lumber Store* is overpriced, you pay for the 'atmosphere', which is not to everybody's taste and the portions are small although the food is excellent. On Galleon Beach, *Colombo's* Italian restaurant, rec for good food but expensive (T 463 1452). Between English and Falmouth Harbours, *Le Cap Horn*, pizzeria, great food, for both lunch snacks and full evening meal, reasonably priced; *La Perruche*, French with regional flavour, expensive at about EC$200 each but well worth it, friendly service, tasteful decor, rec. At Falmouth Harbour the Antigua Yacht Club provides a moderately priced dinner on most nights of the week, though it is livelier at weekends, barbequed burgers, EC$20. In the E, *Harmony Hall* (see **Excursions** above), T 460 4120, superb setting, food imaginative and good, rec. If you are stuck at the airport, there is a restaurant which serves simple meals but gets very full when planes are severely delayed, often closed Sun and holidays.

● **Food**

In addition to a wide selection of imported delicacies served in the larger hotels, local specialities, found in smaller restaurants in St John's, often very reasonable, should never be missed: saltfish, pepper-pot with fungi (a kind of cornmeal dumpling), goat water (hot goat stew), shellfish (in reality the local name for trunk fish), and the local staple, chicken and rice. Oranges are green, while the native pineapple is black. Locally made Sunshine ice cream, American style, is available in most supermarkets. Imported wines and spirits are reasonably priced but local drinks (fruit and sugar cane juice, coconut milk, and Antiguan rum punches and swizzles, ice cold) must be experienced. The local Cavalier rum is a light golden colour, usually used for mixes. Beer costs US$1.25-2.00 in bars. There are no licensing restrictions. Tap water is safe all over the island. Most luxury hotels provide rain water.

● **Tipping**

Tips for taxi drivers are usually 10% of the fare. Porters expect EC$1 per bag.

● **Nightlife**

The largest hotels provide dancing, calypso, steel bands, limbo dancers and moonlight barbeques. There are cinemas, nightclubs, discothèques and casinos. *Colombo's Night Club*, English Harbour; also local dances where Burning Flames and other Antiguan musicians play, usually advertised by poster in St John's, or ask around. In St John's, *Tropix*, in Redcliffe Quay is the best disco and night club. There is also a seedy casino in the King's Building at Heritage Quay. Casinos at *Flamingo*, *Royal Antiguan* and *St James's Club* hotels. At the **Spanish Main Inn**, Independence Drive, Wed night is jazz night as well as outside on the stage across the street. You will be entertained there for free also on Thur-Sun nights, friendly, gets better the longer you stay. At *Dubarry's* bar there is jazz on Sun night, rum punch party on Tues, barbeque on Thur, take swimsuit, parties tend to end up in, not just by, the pool. At Dickenson bay, *Miller's By the Sea*, which serves lunch, dinner, or just drinks, often has live music, especially on Sun after Shirley Heights, owned by a local jazz hero, Shorty, who also has a watersports business. A free newspaper, *It's Happening, You're Welcome*, contains lots of information on forthcoming events.

● **Shopping**

Market day in St John's is Sat. The market building is at the S end of Market Street but there are goods on sale all around. Avoid the middle of the day when it is very hot. In season, there is a good supply of fruit and vegetables, which are easy to obtain on the island. The Epicurean Supermarket, on Old Parham Road outside St John's on the way to the airport, sells cheese and fresh milk, imported from the USA on Thur, stock soon sells out although the local people prefer powdered milk. The 2 main supermarkets in St John's are Dew's and Bryson's, on Long Street, not much to choose between them, imported items mostly, fresh fruit and vegetables limited and poor quality. Hutchinson's is a drive-in supermarket on Old Parham Road beyond the roundabout. Most grocery stores open 0800-1600, although many close at 1300 on Thur. You can buy fish from the fishing boats at the back of the Casino. Heritage Quay (has public toilets) and Redcliffe Quay are shopping complexes with expensive duty-free shops in the former, and boutiques. There are several shops on St Mary Street and others nearby, which stock clothing, crafts and other items from neighbouring islands, eg Caribelle Batik and Co Co shop (rec). Some tourist shops offer 10% reductions to locals: they compensate by overcharging tourists.

● **Banks**

Scotia Bank, Barclays Bank, Royal Bank of Canada, Fidelity Trust Bank, Antigua and Barbuda Development Bank, Antigua Commercial Bank. The Swiss American Bank of Antigua is the only bank at English Harbour, accepts Visa and Mastercard for cash and is open on Sat morning (also a branch in St John's). Barclays charge EC$5 to cash travellers cheques while Scotia Bank charges 10 cents per cheque. American Express is at Antours near Heritage Quay, staff helpful and friendly.

● **Currency**

Eastern Caribbean dollars are used, at a rate of EC$2.70 = US$1. It is advisable to change some currency at the airport on arrival. The airport bank is open 0900-1500, Mon-Thur, closes at 1330 on Fri just as Lufthansa and American Airlines come in, closed when BA flight comes in at 1800. US dollars are accepted in most places, but no one will know the exchange rate of other currencies. The conventional rate of exchange if you want to pay in US dollars is EC$2.50=US$1, so it is worth changing money in a bank. Credit cards are accepted, especially Visa and American Express, but small restaurants will take only cash or travellers' cheques. Always verify whether hotels, taxis etc are quoting you US or EC dollars, you can be cheated. Take care not to get left with excess EC$ on departure, you will not be able to exchange them for another currency except at a very poor rate with a taxi driver.

● **Health Warnings**

Tiny sandflies, known locally as "Noseeums" often appear on the beaches in the late afternoon and can give nasty stings. Keep a good supply of repellent and make sure you wash off all sand to avoid taking them with you from the beach.

Do not eat the little green apples of the manchineel tree, as they are poisonous, and don't sit under the tree in the rain as the dripping oil from the leaves causes blisters.

Some beaches, particularly those on the W coast, get jelly fish at certain times of the year, eg July/August.

● **Climate**

Antigua is a dry island with average rainfall of about 45 inches a year and although September-November is considered the rainy season, the showers are usually short. Temperatures range from 73°F (23°C) to 85°F (30°C) between winter and summer and the trade winds blow constantly.

● Hours Of Business

Banks: 0800-1400 Mon-Wed; 0800-1300 Thur; 1500-1700 Fri. Bank of Antigua opens Sat 0800-1200. Shops: 0800-1200, 1300-1600 Mon-Sat. Thur is early closing day for most non-tourist shops. On Sun everything closes except churches and Kings Casino, although *Kentucky Fried Chicken* opens in the afternoon.

● National Holidays

New Year's Day, Good Friday, Easter Monday, Labour Day (first Monday in May), Whit Monday (end-May), Queen's Birthday (second Saturday in June), Carnival (first Monday and Tuesday in August), Independence Day (1 November), Christmas Day and Boxing Day.

● Time Zone

Atlantic standard time, 4 hours behind GMT, 1 ahead of EST.

● Electric Current

220 volts usually, but 110v in some areas, check before using your own appliances. Many hotels have transformers.

● Post Office

At the end of Long Street, St John's, opposite the supermarkets, open Mon-Thur, 0815-1200, 1300-1600, until 1700 on Fri; also a Post Office at the airport. Federal Express is on Church Street. DHL is in the Vernon Edwards building on Thames Street.

● Telecommunications

Cable and Wireless Ltd, 42-44 St Mary's Street, St John's, and at English Harbour.

● Diplomatic Representation

The British High Commission is at the Price Waterhouse Centre (PO Box 483), 11 Old Parham Road, St Johns, T 462 0008/9, F 462 2806. The US embassy in St John's was closed in the 1993/94 fiscal year; the visa section is in Barbados.

● Tourist Office

Antigua Tourist Office on Thames Street, between Long Street and High Street. Postal address: PO Box 363, St John's, Antigua, West Indies. T 462 0480, F 462 2483. Open 0830-1600 (Mon-Fri) and 0830-1200 (Sat). Gives list of official taxi charges and hotel information. Also has an office at airport, will help book accommodation principally at the more expensive resorts.

USA: Antigua Department of Tourism and Trade, 610 Fifth Avenue, Suite 311, New York, N Y 10020, T (212) 541-4117, F 757 1607; Antigua and Barbuda Trade Mission, 121 SE 1st Street, Suite 1001, Miami, Florida 33131, T (305) 381 6762, F 381 7908; Antigua and Barbuda Trade Mission, Embassy Square, 3400 International Drive, NW Suite 4M, Washington DC, T (202) 365 5122, F 362 5225.

Canada: Antigua Department of Tourism and Trade, 60 St Clair Avenue East, Suite 304, Toronto, Ontario, M4T IN5, T (416) 961-3085, F 961 7218.

UK: Antigua Department of Tourism, Antigua House, 15 Thayer Street, London W1M 5LD, T 071-486 7073/5, F 071-486 9970.

Germany: Antigua Department of Tourism, Thomas Str 110, 61348, Bad Homburg, T 49-617221504, F 49-617221513.

ST KITTS & NEVIS

THE ISLAND OF ST KITTS (officially named St Christopher) and NEVIS are in the N part of the Leeward Islands in the Eastern Caribbean. St Kitts has an area of 68 square miles, made up of three groups of rugged volcanic peaks split by deep ravines, and a low lying peninsula in the SE where there are salt ponds and fine beaches. Nevis, separated by a two-mile channel to the S, has an area of 36 square miles. It is almost circular, rising to a peak of 3,232 feet and surrounded by beaches of coral sand. Each island is fully aware of its heritage and cares for its historical buildings; owing to the early colonization, many are of stone and are in interesting contrast with those of wood. Of the total population, estimated at 43,100 in 1992, 76% live on St. Kitts and 24% on Nevis; 86% are black, 11% mixed, 2% white and 1% Indo-Pakistani.

History

Before the islands were discovered by Columbus in 1493, there were Amerindians living there, whose relics can still be seen in some areas. As in most of the other islands, however, they were slaughtered by European immigrants, although the Caribs fought off the British and the French for many years and their battle scenes are celebrated locally. St Kitts became the first British settlement in the West Indies in 1623 and soon became an important colony for its sugar industry, with the importation of large numbers of African slaves. For a time it was shared by France and England; partition was ended by the Peace of Utrecht in 1713 and it finally became a British colony in 1783. From 1816, St Christopher, Nevis, Anguilla and the British Virgin Islands were administered as a single colony un-

til the Leeward Islands Federation was formed in 1871. From 1958, St Kitts-Nevis and Anguilla belonged to the West Indies Federation until its dissolution in 1962. In 1967 their constitutional status was changed from Crown Colony to a state in voluntary association with Britain, in a first step towards self-government. Robert L Bradshaw was the first Premier of the Associated States. Local councils were set up in Anguilla and Nevis to give those islands more authority over local affairs. Anguilla broke away from the group and was reestablished as a Crown Colony in 1971. During the 1970s independence was a burning issue but Nevis' local council was keen to follow Anguilla's lead rather than become independent with St Kitts. Negotiations were stalled because of British opposition to Nevis becoming a Crown Colony. Eventually, on 19 September 1983, St Kitts and Nevis became independent as a single nation.

The main political parties are the People's Action Movement (PAM), the St Kitts and Nevis Labour Party (SKNLP), the Nevis Reformation Party (NRP) and the Concerned Citizens Movement (CCM). Dr Kennedy Simmonds (PAM) was elected Prime Minister in 1980 and has held office ever since.

Elections in November 1993 were highly controversial when the PAM and the SKNLP each won four seats, the CCM two and the NRP one. The CCM declined to join in a coalition government to form a majority with either major party. The Governor then asked Dr Kennedy Simmonds to form a minority government with the support of the NRP, the PAM's previous coalition partner. This move was highly unpopular, given that the Labour Party had won 54.4% of votes cast in St Kitts compared with

41.7% for the PAM. A state of emergency was declared for 10 days in December because of rioting and other disturbances, a curfew was imposed for five days and a detachment of soldiers from the Regional Security System joined the local police force for a week. Negotiations between Denzil Douglas, the SKNLP leader, and Dr Simmonds, for a caretaker government for six months followed by fresh elections, failed. More clashes greeted the budget presentation in February 1994 with the SKNLP boycotting parliament (except to take the oath of allegiance in May) in support of fresh elections.

Government

St Christopher and Nevis is a constitutional monarchy within the Commonwealth. The British monarch is Head of State and is represented locally by a Governor General. The National Assembly has eleven seats, of which three are from Nevis constituencies and eight from St Kitts. There are also four nominated Senators. Under the Federal system, Nevis also has a separate legislature and may secede from the Government of the Federation. In 1992 Mr Simeon Daniel, the Premier of Nevis for 21 years, lost his assembly seat in elections which saw Mr Vance Amory (CCM) become the new leader. Mr Daniel had been in favour of secession for Nevis but his only party won two of the five seats.

The Economy

The economy is based on agriculture. Sugar is the main crop on St Kitts, accounting for about a quarter of exports and 12% of jobs. Production has been in the hands of the Government since 1975, but with low prices for sugar in the world markets, hurricane damage and recent droughts, the industry runs at a loss. Low wages deter locals from seeking jobs on the plantations and labour is imported from St Vincent and Guyana. World Bank consultants recommended policy changes, which included allowing private investment in the industry and production incentives for cane cutters. Initially, management of the state-owned Sugar Manufacturing Company was contracted to Booker Tate, of the UK, for 1991-93, with financial assistance from the World Bank. Sugar production rose by 28% in 1991 to 19,500 tonnes, to 20,159 tonnes in 1992, and again to 21,258 tonnes in 1993. In 1994 it was announced that the company was to be divested, with the Government having a minority shareholding. The Government has been encouraged to diversify away from sugar dependence and reduce food imports. More vegetables, sweet potatoes and yams are now being grown, while on Nevis, Sea Island cotton and coconuts are more common on smallholdings. Livestock farming and manufacturing are developing industries. There are enclave industries, such as data processing and garment manufacturing, which export to the USA and Caricom trading partners, while sales of sugar-based products such as pure cane spirit go mainly outside the region.

Tourism is becoming an increasingly important foreign exchange earner, while remittances of workers abroad also provide a steady source of income. In 1988 69,608 tourists arriving by air and 53,645 cruise ship passengers spent nearly US$54mn. By 1993, visitors arriving by air had risen to 86,946 while yacht and cruise ship passengers rose to 83,115. Visitors from the USA make up just under half of all stopover guests. The Government plans to increase cruise ship arrivals with a port improvement project in 1994-95 to enable four cruise liners to berth at the same time, while stopover arrivals will be encouraged by the huge development projects on the SE peninsula of St Kitts, a 275-room *Sandals Resort* in the Banana Bay/Cockleshell area, and a 250-room *Hyatt Regency Resort* at South Friar's Bay. The number of hotel beds in

St Kitts-Nevis is forecast to rise to 2,200 when all these resorts are open, giving the islands a potential annual capacity of up to 200,000 visitors.

Fauna and Flora

Both islands are home to the green vervet monkey, introduced by the French some 300 years ago, now dwelling on the forested areas in the mountains. They can be seen sometimes on Hurricane Hill. American scientists have been studying these attractive little creatures and some have been taken to the USA for experiments; a Sunday visit to the Behavioural Science Foundation at Estridge Estate in St Kitts gives visitors a chance to watch the research, and the monkeys, in action. The monkey is the same animal as on Barbados but the Kittitians used to eat them. Another animal imported by colonists, the mongoose, has outlived its original purpose (to kill now-extinct snakes) but survives in considerable numbers. There are also some wild deer on the SE peninsula. In common with other West Indian islands, there are highly vocal frogs, lots of lizards (the anole is the most common), assorted bats and butterflies, although nothing particularly rare. St Kitts and Nevis have the earliest documented evidence of honey bees in the Caribbean. Birds are typical of the region, with lots of sea fowl like brown pelicans and frigate birds to be seen, as well as three species of hummingbirds. Fish abound in local waters (rays, barracuda, king fish and brilliantly-coloured smaller species) and the increasingly rare black coral tree can be sighted in the reef of the same name.

The rainforests on the sister islands are restricted in scale but provide a habitat for wild orchids, buttress trees, candlewoods and exotic vines. Fruits and flowers, both wild and cultivated, are in abundance, particularly in the gorgeous gardens of Nevis. Trees include several varieties of the stately royal palm, the

ST KITTS AND NEVIS: FACT FILE

Geographic

Land area	269.4 sq km
St Kitts	176.2
Nevis	93.2
forested	17.0%
pastures	3.0%
cultivated	39.0%

Demographic

Population (1992)	43,100
annual growth rate (1987-92)	-0.4%
urban	48.9%
rural	51.1%
density	160 per sq km
Religious affiliation	
Protestant	76.4%
Birth rate per 1,000 (1989)	22.5
	(world av 27.1)
Death rate per 1,000 (1989)	11.0
	(world av 9.8)

Education and Health

Life expectancy at birth,	
male	64 years
female	71 years
Infant mortality rate	
per 1,000 live births (1989)	22.2
Physicians (1990)	1 per 1,593 persons
Hospital beds	1 per 167 persons
Calorie intake as %	
of FAO requirement	108%
Population age 25 and over	
with no formal schooling	1.1%
Literacy (over 15)	90.0%

Economic

GNP (1990 market prices)	US$133mn
GNP per capita	US$3,330
Public external debt (1990)	US$35mn
Tourism receipts (1990)	US$63mn
Inflation (annual av 1986-91)	2.9%
Radio	1 per 1.7 persons
Television	1 per 4.5 persons
Telephone	1 per 4.6 persons

Employment

Population economically active (1980)	
	17,125
Unemployment rate	na
% of labour force in agriculture	29.6
manufacturing	14.7
construction	2.7
Paramilitary police unit	80

Source *Encyclopaedia Britannica*

spiny-trunked sandbox tree, silk cotton, and the turpentine or gum tree. Visitors can explore the rainforests with guides on foot, horseback or by jeep, but gentle hikes through trails and estates reap many rewards in terms of plant-gazing. Several trails are clear and do not need a guide, such as Old Road to Philips, the old British military road, which connected the British settlements on the NE and SW coasts of St Kitts without going through French territory when the island was partitioned. There are also trails from Belmont to the crater of Mount Liamuiga, from Sadlers to Peak, from Lamberts to Dos d'Ane lake. St Kitts is a small island, yet it has a wide variety of habitats, with rainforest, dry woodland, grassland and a salt pond.

Beaches and Watersports

St Kitts Most of the beaches are of black, volcanic sand but the beaches known as Frigate Bay and Salt Pond fringing the S peninsula itself also has white sand beaches. Swimming is very good in the Frigate Bay area where all water sports are available.

There is also very good snorkelling and scuba diving. Most dive sites are on the Caribbean side of the islands, where the reef starts in shallow water and falls off to 100 feet or more. Between the two islands there is a shelf in only 25 feet of water which attracts lots of fish, including angelfish, to the corals, sea fans and sponges. Along the W coasts of the is-

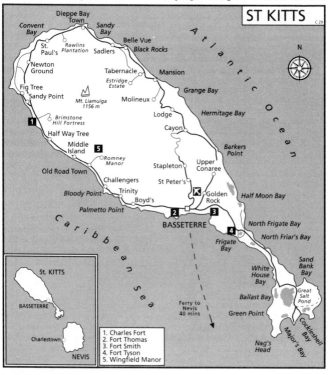

1. Charles Fort
2. Fort Thomas
3. Fort Smith
4. Fort Tyson
5. Wingfield Manor

lands there is black coral, coral caves, reefs and wrecks with abundant fish and other sea creatures of all sizes and colours. Much of the diving is suitable for novices and few of the major sites are deeper than 70 feet.

Kenneth's Dive Centre based in Basseterre (Bay Road, and also at Timothy Beach, T 465 7043/2670; Kenneth Samuel is a PADI-certified Dive Master offering courses, dive packages and all equipment and he uses a catamaran, *Lady Peggy*, or a 32-foot motor launch, *Lady Majesta*). The Pelican Cove Marina at the *Ocean Terrace Inn*, T 465 2754/2380, operates Dive St Kitts (US$30 for one-tank dive, US$50 2 tanks), offering water-skiing, fishing, hobiecat rental, windsurfer rental (US$10/hour) and boat cruises. Pro-Divers gives PADI instruction, at Fisherman's Wharf and Turtle Beach, T 465 3223, 469 9086, F 465 1057, dive gear available for rent, dive packages available, single tank dive US$30, 2 tank dive US$50, resort course US$60, snorkel pack US$10.

Leeward Island Charters' *Caona*, a 47' catamaran or *Spirit of St Kitts*, a 70' catamaran (owned by Tim and Allison Leypoldt, T 465 7474, sometimes operates in the waters around the US Virgin Islands), take visitors on a sail, snorkel and beach barbeque. *Celica III* is a catamaran used for day trips with beach barbeque lunch and open bar, run by Tropical Water Sports, T 465 4039/4167, F 465 6400. Sailing is becoming increasingly popular. The St Kitts-Nevis Boating Club organizes sunfish races on the second Sunday of every month which are fun, check the bulletin board for details at *PJ's Pizza Bar*, Frigate Bay or the *Ballahoo* in Basseterre. There are local and international regattas and even a local catamaran boatyard, Brooke's Boats. Deep sea fishing can be arranged. In summer there is a race for windsurfers and sunfish to Nevis.

Nevis has superb white sandy beaches, particularly on the leeward and N coasts. The beautiful four-mile Pin-

ney's Beach is only a few minutes' walk from Charlestown and is never crowded. However, the entire middle stretch of Pinney's Beach has been given over to a 196-room *Four Seasons Hotel*. Watersports facilities are available at *Oualie Beach Club*. Snorkelling off Oualie Beach is excellent (round the rocks to the right) and at least as rewarding, if not more than, scuba diving. Scuba Safaris, run by Ellis Chaderton, is based there, T 469 9518: diving (US$45 for a single tank dive, US$80 for 2 tanks), instruction, equipment rental and glass-bottomed boat tours. Watersports also at Newcastle Bay Marina, T 469 9373, F 469 9375, where there is the HIFLY windsurfing school. Windsurfing also at *Mount Nevis Hotel and Beach Club*, and Nevis Windsurfing, T 469 9682. On the Atlantic side of Nevis, the beaches tend to be rocky and the swimming treacherous; there is, though, an excellent beach at White Bay in the SW.

Other Sports

Horse riding, mountain climbing, tennis and golf are available. On St Kitts there is Trinity Stables, T 465 3226, on Nevis at Garners, Ira Dore, T 469 5528, and at the *Hermitage Plantation*, T 469 3422, where they also have horse-drawn carriage tours. There is an 18-hole international championship golf course at Frigate Bay and a 9-hole golf course at Golden Rock, St Kitts (T 465 8103). On Nevis, the *Four Seasons* has an 18-hole golf course. Races are held on the small, stoney race track at Black Bay, St Kitts (near White Bay beach), four times a year: Whit Monday, August Bank holiday, Independence Day and Boxing Day. On Nevis horse racing is the second most popular sport after cricket, with races held at Indian Castle Estate racetrack on New Year's Day, Easter Monday, August during Culturama and Boxing Day. Also look out for the more amusing donkey races.

Festivals

St Kitts and Nevis are very proud of their masquerade traditions. The liveliest time to visit St Kitts is for the carnival held over Christmas and the New Year. It gets bigger and better every year with parades, calypso competitions and street dancing. For details, contact the Carnival Office, Church Street, Basseterre, T 465 4151.

On Nevis, the annual equivalent is Culturama, held in end-July and August, finishing on the first Monday in August. There is a Queen show, calypso competition, local bands and guest bands and many 'street jams'. The Nevis Tourist Office has full details.

ST KITTS

The dormant volcano, Mount Liamuiga (3,792 feet, pronounced Lie-a-mee-ga) occupies the central part of St Kitts. The mountain was previously named Mount Misery by the British, but has now reverted to its Carib name, meaning "fertile land". The foothills of the mountains, particularly in the N, are covered with sugar cane plantations and grassland, while the uncultivated lowland slopes are covered with forest and fruit trees.

BASSETERRE

The small port of Basseterre is the capital and largest town, with a population of about 15,000. By West Indian standards, it is quite big and as such has a quite different feel from its close neighbour, Charlestown. It was founded some 70 years later in 1727. Earthquakes, hurricanes and finally a disasterous fire in 1867 destroyed the town. Consequently its buildings are comparatively modern. There is a complete mishmash of architectural styles from elegant Georgian buildings with arcades, verandahs and jalousies, mostly in good condition, to hideous twentieth century concrete block houses. In recent years, the devel-

opment of tourism has meant a certain amount of redevelopment in the centre. An old warehouse on the waterfront has been converted into the Pelican Mall, a duty-free shopping and recreational complex. It also houses the tourist office and a lounge for guests of the *Four Seasons Hotel* in Nevis awaiting transport. A new deep water cruise ship berth is to be built on the waterfront on 25 acres of reclaimed land in the heart of Basseterre, capable of accommodating the largest ships afloat, together with a sailing and power boat marina, berthing facilities for the inter-island ferry, the *Caribe Queen*, an expanded shopping area with space for craft vendors and small shops. Work was to start in mid-May 1994 and take about 18 months to complete.

The Circus, styled after London's Piccadilly Circus (but looking nothing like it), is the centre of the town. The clock tower is a memorial to Thomas Berkely, former president of the General Legislative Council. South down Fort Street is the imposing façade of the Treasury Building with its dome covering an arched gateway leading directly to the sea front (it is equally impressive from the bay). Next door is the Post Office (open Monday-Saturday 0800-1500, 0800-1100 on Thursdays). Head N up Fort Street, cross the main thoroughfare (Cayon Street) and you will come to St George's Cathedral, set in its own large garden, with a massive, square buttressed tower. The site was originally a Jesuit church, Notre Dame, which was rased to the ground by the English in 1706. Rebuilt four years later and renamed St George's, it suffered damage from hurricanes and earthquakes on several occasions. It too was a victim of the 1867 fire. It was rebuilt in 1856-69 and contains some nice stained glass windows. There is a fine view of the town from the tower.

Independence Square was built in 1790 and is surrounded now by a low white fence; eight gates let paths converge on a fountain in the middle of the

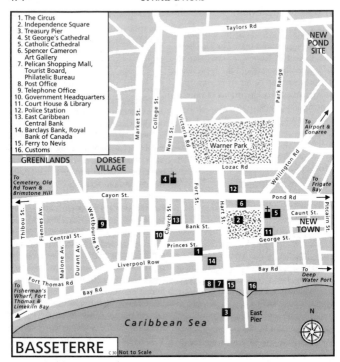

1. The Circus
2. Independence Square
3. Treasury Pier
4. St George's Cathedral
5. Catholic Cathedral
6. Spencer Cameron
   Art Gallery
7. Pelican Shopping Mall,
   Tourist Board,
   Philatelic Bureau
8. Post Office
9. Telephone Office
10. Government Headquarters
11. Court House & Library
12. Police Station
13. East Caribbean
    Central Bank
14. Barclays Bank, Royal
    Bank of Canada
15. Ferry to Nevis
16. Customs

BASSETERRE C 30 Not to scale

square (it looks like the Union Jack when seen from the air). Unfortunately the gaily painted muses on top of the fountain seem not to work at present. Originally designed for slave auctions and council meetings, it now contains many plants, spacious lawns and lovely old trees. It is surrounded by 18th-century houses and at its E end, the Roman Catholic cathedral with its twin towers. Built in 1927, the Immaculate Conception is surprisingly plain inside. At 10 North Square Street you can visit the very attractive building housing The *Spencer Cameron Art Gallery*. See Rosey Cameron-Smith's paintings, prints and leisurewear of West Indian scenes and the work of other artists too, T/F 465 1617. The Bank of Nova Scotia is housing some interesting paintings of Brimstone

Hill by Lt Lees of the Royal Engineers, circa 1783, pending the building of a museum as a permanent home: St Christopher Heritage Society, Bank Street and West Independence Square, PO Box 338, Basseterre. They are also doing a lot to preserve wildlife and are grateful for donations. Heading back towards the Circus there are lots of nice restaurants and cafés. Basseterre is very quiet on Sundays and many of the restaurants are closed.

Excursions

A clockwise route round the island will enable you to see most of the historical sites. A cheap way of touring the island is to take a minibus from Basseterre bus station in Bay Road to Dieppe Bay Town, then walk to Sadlers (there might be a minibus if you are lucky) where you can get another minibus back to Basseterre along the Atlantic coast.

The island is dominated by the SE range of mountains (1,159 feet) and the higher NW range which contains Mount Verchilds (2,931 feet) and the crater of Mount Laimuiga (3,792 feet). There are several good island tours, including excellent hiking tours to the volcano and through the rain forest with Kriss Tours (US$40 full day, US$30 half day, T 465 4042) and Greg's Safaris, recommended, pleasant and informative, (US$35-50, T 465 4121/5209, F 465 1057, PO Box 65). To climb Mt Liamuiga independently, arrange for transport from Belmont or Harris Estate. At 2,600 feet is the crater into which you can climb down, holding on to vines and roots; on the steady climb from the end of the road note the wild orchids in the forest. A full day is required for this climb. You can reach the attractive, but secluded, Dos D'Anse pond near Mount Verchilds from the Molyneux estate, a guide is recommended.

Evidence of sugar cane is everywhere on the comparatively flat, fertile coastal plain. You will drive through large fields of cane and particularly on the W coast glimpse the little railway which is now used to transport it from the fields. Disused sugar mills are also often seen. Here are situated the Great Houses: Fairview, Romney Manor, Golden Lemon, the White House, Rawlins and perhaps most famous for its colonial splendour, Ottley's. They have nearly all been converted into hotels and have excellent restaurants.

The W coast in particular is historically important. It is guarded by no less than nine forts and the magnificent Brimstone Hill Fortress. Taking the road out of Basseterre, you will pass the sites of seven of them: Fort Thomas, Palmetto Point Fort, Stone Fort, Fort Charles, Charles Fort, Sandy Point Fort and Fig Tree Fort. The remaining two are to the

S of Basseterre: Fort Smith and Fort Tyson. Little now remains of any of them. Sir Thomas Warner landed at Old Road Bay in 1623 and was joined in 1625 by the crew of a French ship badly mauled by the Spanish. Initially befriended by the local Carib chief Tegreman, as many as 3,000 Caribs, alarmed at the rapid colonization of the island, tried to mount an attack in 1626. 2,000 of them were massacred by the combined French and English forces in the deep ravine at Bloody Point (the site of Stone Fort). This is the first point of interest and is just before Old Road Town. An amicable settlement meant that the English held the central portion of the island roughly in line from Sandy Point to Saddlers in the N to Bloody Point across to Cayon in the S. French names can be traced in both of their areas of influence (Dieppe Bay Town in the N, the Parishes are called Capisterre and Basseterre in the S). The SE peninsula was neutral. This rapprochement did not last many years as following the colonization of Martinique and Guadeloupe, the French wished to increase their sphere of influence. St Kitts became an obvious target and in 1664 they squeezed the English from the island. For nearly 200 years the coast was defended by troops from one nation or another.

At Old Road Town you turn right to visit Romney Manor, one of the great houses. You drive through a deserted sugar mill and the edge of rain forest. The manor is set in beautiful gardens with pleasant views over the coast and a giant 350-year old saman tree. It is now home to Caribelle Batik, open Monday-Friday, 0830-1600, T 465 6253, F 465 3629. Apart from a well-stocked shop you can watch the artists producing the highly colourful and attractive material. A guide will explain the process. Also near here the remains of the island's Amerindian civilization can be seen on large stones with drawings and pictographs at Wingfield Manor Estate.

After a further 1½ miles, at the village of **Middle Island**, you will see on your right and slightly up the hill, the church of St Thomas at the head of an avenue of royal palms. Here is buried Sir Thomas Warner who died on 10 March 1648. The raised tomb under a canopy is inscribed "General of y Caribee". There is also a bronze plaque with a copy of the inscription inside the church. Other early tombs are of Captain John Pogson (1656) and Sir Charles Payne, "Major General of Leeward Carribee Islands" who was buried in 1744. The tower, built in 1880, has been severely damaged.

Turn right off the coastal road just before *J's Place* (a good place for a drink and local food, open 1100-2000, watch the caged green vervet monkeys: they are very aggressive) for the **Citadel of Brimstone Hill**, one of the "Gibraltars of the West Indies" (a title it shares with Les Saintes, off Guadeloupe). Sprawled over 38 acres on the slopes of a mountain 800 feet above the sea, it commands an incredible view for 70 miles around, of St Kitts and on clear days, Montserrat (40 miles), Saba (20 miles), St Eustatius (5 miles), St-Barts (40 miles) and St-Martin (45 miles) can be seen. The English mounted the first cannon on Brimstone Hill in 1690 in an attempt to force the French from Fort Charles below. It has been constructed entirely out of local volcanic stones and was designed along classic defensive lines. The five bastions overlook each other and also guard the only road as it zig zags up to the parade ground. The entrance is at the Barrier Redan where payment is made. Pass the Magazine Bastion but stop at the Orillion Bastion which contains the massive ordnance store (165 feet long with walls at least 6 feet thick). The hospital was located here and under the S wall is a small cemetery. You come next to the Prince of Wales Bastion (note the name of J Sutherland, 93rd Highlanders 24 October 1822 carved in the wall next to one of the cannons) from where there are good views over to the parade ground. Park at the parade ground, there is a snack bar and shop in the warrant officer's quarters with barrels of pork outside it. A narrow and quite steep path leads to Fort George, the Citadel and the highest defensive position. Restoration is continuing and several areas have been converted to form a most interesting museum. Barrack rooms now hold well-presented and informative displays (pre-colombian, American, English, French and Garrison). Guides are on hand to give more detailed explanations of the fortifications. The Fortress was eventually abandoned in 1852 but was inaugurated as a National Park by the Queen in October 1985. Open 0930-1730 daily, entrance EC$13 or US$5 for foreigners, EC$2 for nationals, it is highly recommended both for adults and children (half price). Allow up to 2 hours.

The remainder of the drive through the cane fields is less interesting. There is a a black sand beach at Dieppe Bay. Otherwise pass through Saddlers and stop at the **Black Rocks**. Here lava has flowed into the sea providing interesting rock formations. The road continues past Ottley Plantation, through Cayon back to Basseterre via the Golden Rock Airport. With advance notice, you can tour the sugar factory near the airport, very interesting and informative. Tours are only during harvest season, February-August.

To visit the SE pensinsula, turn S at the end of Wellington Road (just after the Texaco filling station). This leads to the narrow spit of land sandwiched between North and South Frigate Bays. This area is being heavily developed, the natural lagoons providing an additional attraction. A number of establishments, including a casino, tennis courts and an 18-hole golf course, which are international in style, but lacking in character or greenery, have been built. The new 6-mile Dr Kennedy A Simmonds Highway runs from Frigate Bay to Major's Bay. After Frigate Bay the peninsula is almost deserted and quite different from the N of the island. The road climbs along the backbone of the peninsula and overlooks North and South Friar Bays where you may see green vervet monkeys before descending to White House Bay (an abandoned jetty and wreck provides good snorkelling). Skirt the Great Salt Pond. Half way round turn left to reach Cockleshell Bay, the site of the new 5 star *Casablanca* luxury resort and beyond it the more secluded Turtle Beach (good for watersports and stunning views across to Nevis). The other branch leads to Major's bay where another large development is planned. At the moment however most of the peninsula is isolated and extremely attractive. Despite the road the majority of beaches are difficult to reach. Try to obtain local knowledge if you want to visit them.

Island Information—St Kitts

● Where To Stay

There is a wide variety of accommodation ranging from first class hotels to rented cottages, but it is advisable to book well in advance. There is a 7% occupancy tax and 10% service charge.

Ocean Terrace Inn (*OTI*, Box 65, T 465 2754, F 465-1057) a/c, TV, in winter, US$116-225d EP, apartments also available US$121-346, and *Fort Thomas Hotel* (Box 407, T 465 2695, F 465 7518), winter rates, US$75-95d, EP, are a few mins walk from Basseterre and have pools, beach shuttles and restaurants. *OTI* also organizes tours and other activities such as scuba diving, evening shows and has a fairly expensive but nice restaurant with views over Basseterre harbour; good service throughout. The *Fairview Inn* close to Basseterre is a cottage complex situated around an eighteenth century great house (double rates range from US$70-80 in summer, US$120-140 in winter, EP, MAP supplement US$30, reductions for children, a/c, fans, restaurant, pool, Box 212, T 465 2472, F 465 1056). The highly rec *Rawlins Plantation*, 16 miles from Basseterre in the NW of the island, is pricey, but beautiful, tranquil and offers grass tennis, swimming pool, horse riding and croquet, no credit cards accepted (10 cottages, rates US$225d, in summer, US$375d, in winter, MAP only, laundry service and afternoon tea included, Box 340,

T 465 6221, F 465 4954). *The White House*, British-run, PO Box 436, T 465 8162, F 465 8275, 8 rooms in the carriage house and other buildings of a plantation great house, grass tennis court, swimming pool, courtesy transport to beach 15 mins away, winter rates US$350d, US$250s, MAP inc afternoon tea and laundry service, US$250d and US$150s in summer, elegant and quiet; *Bird Rock Beach Hotel*, owned/managed by former Director of Tourism, Larkland Richards, T 465 8914, F 465 1675, 38 rooms/suites, a/c, TV, US$120-300 EP in winter, up on the cliffs overlooking the tiny black sand beach and industrial estate, inconvenient suburban location, taxi to Basseterre US$8, pool, tennis, volleyball, watersports, 2 restaurants, 3 bars; 520' above sea level in 35 acres, is the *Ottleys Plantation Inn*, PO Box 345, T 465 7234, F 465 4760, rooms in the 1832 great house or cottages, a/c, fans, winter rate, US$160-295d, EP, US$205-385d, MAP, US$110-170d EP in summer, restaurant, pool, nice walks, beach shuttle, tennis/golf shuttle; *The Golden Lemon Inn and Villas*, Dieppe Bay, T 465 7260, F 465 4019, in the UK T 0800-373 742, on black sand beach about 15 miles from Basseterre, has 36 rooms, having built some 1-2 bedroom beachfront cottages with pools next to the original great house building dating from 1610, US$225-865d, MAP, winter rate, US$175-700 in summer, pool, tennis, watersports, restaurant, owned by an interior decorator, each room is different, furnished with West Indian antiques, no children under 18.

Lots of new hotels and condominiums have now been built in the Frigate Bay area, the main tourist development area. *Frigate Bay Beach Resort*, PO Box 137, T 465 8935/6, F 465 7050, rooms and suites US$145-395, a/c, Olympic size pool, restaurant; *Gateway Inn*, PO Box 64, T 465 7155, F 465 9322, 10 self-catering apartments, a/c, phone, TV, laundry, 10 mins from beach or golf course, US$80/day, US$480/week; *Island Paradise Beach Village*, PO Box 444, T 465 8035, F 465 8236, 62 condominiums set in 5 acres of woodland on the Atlantic beach, laundry, barbeque, pool, restaurant, store, 1-3 bedrooms, US$165-380/day, US$895-1,835/week; dominating Frigate Bay with its golf course and casino is the *Jack Tar Village*, PO Box 406, T 465 8651, F 465 1031, in USA T 800-999-9182, beaches on Atlantic and Caribbean, 242 a/c rooms, all-inclusive US$160 pp double occupancy, restaurants, watersports, tennis, bicycles, lagoon fishing, disco; *Leeward Cove Condominium*, PO Box 123, T 465 8030, F 465 3476, on Atlantic Beach, 1-2 bedroom self-catering apartments, a/c, free green fees at Golf Club, mini-mart, laundry service, free car per week's stay, US$110-250; *Rock Haven Bed & Breakfast*, PO Box 821, T/F 465 5503, suite with kitchen facilities, TV, laundry facilities, US$55d, views of both coasts; *Sea Lofts on the Beach*, PO Box 813, T 465 1075, F 465 8454, condominiums in 3-acre gardens on Atlantic Beach, 2-3 bedrooms, US$125-260/day, US$850-1,800/week, pool, 2 tennis courts, barbeque, stores, free green fees; *Sun 'N Sand Beach Resort*, PO Box 341, T 465 8037/8, F 465 6745, studios or 2-bedroomed cottages on Atlantic Beach, US$160-260, a/c, fans, pool, TV, quite basic but clean, well run, lovely gardens, good food, rec; *Colony's Timothy Beach Resort*, PO Box 81, T 465 8597, F 465 7723, on Caribbean beach, studios and suites, US$140-US$360 EP, watersports, sailing, pool, a/c, TV, café.

The *Windsor Guest House* is one of the cheapest at US$35d w/o private bath but not rec, beds uncomfortable, stuffy, shared toilets (Box 122, T 465 2894). Alternatives to this are the *Parkview* (Box 64, T 465 2100), good, and *On the Square*, 14 Independence Square (Box 81, T 465 2485), US$45d, very clean, tastefully decorated, a/c, private bathroom, also single rooms available at the rear, US$29s, windows do not open and 2 larger rooms with kitchenette to sleep 3 with verandah overlooking square, prices include tax, rec. *Glimbaro Guest House*, Cayon Street and Market St, T 465 2935, F 465 9832, almost opp *Windsor Guest House*, no sign, new rooms, some with bath and patio, US$45 summer, US$55 winter, without patio US$35-45, rooms with shared bathrooms US$25-35, extra person US$10, 10% off weekly rates, fans, phone, restaurant with good food.

● **Where To Eat**

The hotels have gourmet restaurants, usually serving local specialities, with set meals of around EC$90 or à la carte entrées from EC$65. There are also many places offering snacks, light meals, ice creams and drinks in Basseterre and in the Frigate Bay area. West Indian and continental cuisine can be sampled in the elegant dining rooms of the *The OTI* (see above) and *Fisherman's Wharf* (T 465 2754) beside it offers barbequed seafood and a spicey conch sauce. The latter is lively, on the quay, open daily for dinner only from 1900, go

early. *OTI* also runs a beach bar/restaurant at Turtle Beach, T 469 9086, excellent barbeque lunch, very friendly, watersports, good snorkelling if you can ignore the seaweed, open daily 1000-1800, and late on Sat with gourmet night dinner 1900-2200, Sun buffet and steel band 1200-1500. Other good restaurants include the *Ballahoo* in town (opp the Treasury) which is very reasonable and has a nice gallery, open Mon-Sat 0800-2000, T 465 4197; also in Basseterre overlooking the harbour, *Blue Horizon*, T 465 5863, F 465 9936, run by Austrian chef Erwin Wögerbauer and his Kittitian wife Rosalinda, open evenings only;. *Chef's Place*, Church Street, T 465 6176, excellent lunchtime and evening food at reasonable price, Kittitian with a few added touches, usually choice of one fish dish and one other, all fresh ingredients, about the only non-tourist place open late, 0900-2400 Mon-Sat, no credit cards. *Coconut Café* in Frigate Bay, *Timothy Beach Resort*, T 465 3020, serves local and grilled seafood, open daily, 0730-2300, good. The *Golf View Restaurant*, Frigate Bay, T 465 1118, open for reservations only from 0700, West Indian and vegetarian dishes; *The Patio*, Frigate Bay, T 465 8666, local and international cuisine, complimentary white wine and open bar with dinner, run by Peter and Joan Mallalieu like a private dinner party so reservations essential, entrées EC$70-85, dress smartly. Small restaurants serving West Indian food, include *Tracy's Corner*, St Johnson's Village, T 465 6109, open daily 1100-2300, *Victor's*, Basseterre, T 465 2518, open 1130-1500, 1830-2200, Sun by reservation only; *Victoria's Place and Syd's Café*, Cayon St, T 465 7741, daily specials, open Mon-Sat 0800-2300.

● **Entertainment**

There is live music in the evening at *Fisherman's Wharf* at weekends, and the *OTI* has lively evenings in the week (see above). *J's Place* is a disco at the foot of Brimstone Hill; *Reflections*, above Flex Fitness Centre, open Tues-Sun from 2100, cover charge EC$10 on Thur-Sun, strict dress code, on Frigate Bay Road, T 465 7616; *Cotton House* in Canada Estate also fairly smart, open Fri and Sat 2200-0530. *Jack Tar Village* in the modern Frigate Bay development now offers a EC$50 night pass which covers all drinks, a light buffet and entertainment. There is also a casino. A more local place with free admission is on Monkey Hill on Sun nights. On Sun everything closes down in Basseterre, including the restaurants.

NEVIS

Across the two-mile Narrows Channel from St Kitts is the beautiful little island of Nevis, with a population of only 9,000. The central peak of the island is usually shrouded in white clouds and mist, which reminded Columbus of Spanish snow-capped mountains and is why he called the island "Las Nieves". (It reminds others, in the wet, of the English Lake District, as does St Kitts.) For the Caribs, it was Oualie, the land of beautiful water. Smaller than St Kitts it is also quieter. The atmosphere is civilized, but low-key and easy-going; all the same, it is an expensive island. Less fertile than St Kitts, the principal crop is cotton. Nevis was badly effected by Hurricane Hugo but despite considerable damage, nobody was killed and damage has now been repaired.

CHARLESTOWN

The main town is Charlestown, one of the best preserved old towns in the Caribbean. Situated on Gallows Bay and guarded by Fort Charles to the S and the long sweep of Pinney's Beach to the North, it is a small town with a compact centre. At first sight it would be easy to be disappointed. However there are several interesting buildings dating from the eighteenth century and an excellent, but small, museum.

Whether travelling from Newcastle airport or by sea on the *Caribe Queen* from

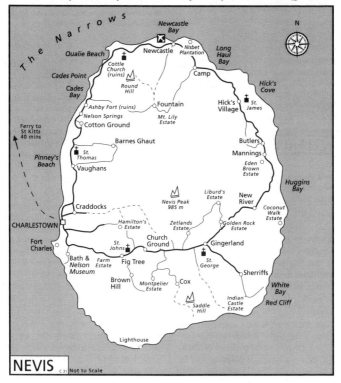

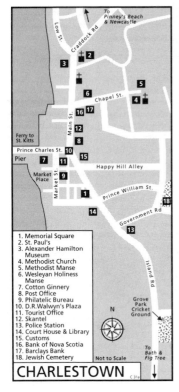

1. Memorial Square
2. St. Paul's
3. Alexander Hamilton Museum
4. Methodist Church
5. Methodist Manse
6. Wesleyan Holiness Manse
7. Cotton Ginnery
8. Post Office
9. Philatelic Bureau
10. D.R.Walwyn's Plaza
11. Tourist Office
12. Skantel
13. Police Station
14. Court House & Library
15. Customs
16. Bank of Nova Scotia
17. Barclays Bank
18. Jewish Cemetery

CHARLESTOWN

War 1914-18 Captured from the Germans". Explore the small arcade with several shops including *Caribelle Batik* before seeing the Courthouse and library above it (open Monday-Friday 0900-1800, Saturday 0900-1700). It was built in 1825 and used as the Nevis Government Headquarters but largely destroyed by fire in 1873. The curious little square tower was erected in 1909-10. It contains a clock which keeps accurate time with an elaborate pulley and chain system. Visit the library and you can see them together with the weights among the elaborate roof trusses. The courthouse is not open to the public, look in through the open windows. Along Government Road is the well-preserved Jewish Cemetery dating back to 1679, but also closed to the public. At the small market a wide range of island produce, including avocados, ginger root, yams and sweet potatoes, is on sale but go early if you want to catch the bustle. Markets are held on Tuesday, Thursday and Saturday mornings, best on Saturday. Market Street to the right houses the philatelic bureau, airconditioned and open from 0800-1600 Monday-Friday. The Cotton Ginnery is still in use during the cotton picking season (February onwards). On Chapel Street the Wesleyan Holiness Manse built in 1812 is one of the oldest stone buildings surviving on the island while the Methodist Manse (next to the prominent Church) has the oldest wooden structure, the second floor being built in 1802.

The Alexander Hamilton House Birthplace and the Museum of Nevis History (open Monday-Friday 0800-1600, Saturday 1000-1200, entrance free) is next to the sea and set in an attractive garden which contains a representative collection of Nevis plants and trees. The original house was built around 1680 but destroyed in the 1840s probably by an earthquake. This attractive two-storey house was rebuilt in 1983 and dedicated during the Islands' Independence cele-

St Kitts, you will arrive in D R Walwyn's Plaza. This is dominated by the balconied Customs House built in 1837 on a much older site, it now houses the Customs and Agricultural Ministry. Immediately to the N is the Post Office. Opposite it on the other side of the square is the Tourist Office. Apart from much useful information, it contains a plaque commemorating the landing of Captain John Smith and 143 English on 24th March 1607 – the original Virginia settlers. Memorial Square is larger and more impressive than D R Walwyn's Plaza, the War Memorial in the small garden has a German machine gun pointing at it. Inscribed on it is "In Memory The World

bration in September of that year. The Nevis House of Assembly meets in the rooms upstairs (again restored after being damaged by Hurricane Hugo), while the museum occupies the ground floor. Alexander Hamilton, Nevis' most famous son, was born in Charlestown on 11 January 1757. He lived on Nevis for only five years before leaving for St Croix with his family. About half of the museum is given over to various memorabilia and pictures of his life. There is also an excellent collection of historical documents that you can ask to see. The Museum of Nevis History is equally interesting. It contains examples of Amerindian pottery, African culture imported by the slaves, cooking implements and recipes, a rum still, and a model of a Nevis lighter. There is also a collection of 17th century clay pipes and the ceremonial clothes of the Warden which were worn on the Queen's birthday and Remembrance Day. A section is devoted to the conservation of reefs, conch and the rain forest. There is a small shop which sells local produce and some interesting books. All proceeds go to the upkeep of the museum. The Hamilton Arts Centre, next to the museum, has traditional local music and invited guest bands, also chess competitions, readings, domino tournaments etc.

Excursions

Taking the road S out of Charlestown, you can visit **Fort Charles**. Fork right at the Shell station and again at the mini roundabout, keep right along the sea shore (rough track), past the wine company building and through gates at the end of the track. The Fort was built before 1690 and altered many times before being completed in 1783-90. Nothing much remains apart from the circular well and a small building (possibly the magazine). The gun emplacements looking across to St Kitts are being badly eroded by the sea, 8 cannon point haphazardly to sea. The Nevis Council surrendered to the French here in 1782 during the siege of Brimstone Hill on St Kitts.

Back on the main road and only about ½ mile outside Charlestown lies the largely ruined **Bath Hotel** and **Spring House**. Built by the Huggins family in 1778, it is reputed to be one of the oldest hotels in the Caribbean. The Spring House lies over a fault which supplies constant hot water at 108°F. Open 0900-1600 daily, small charge for those wishing to bathe. A new building has been erected here to house the **Nelson Museum** dedicated in 1992 to commemorate the 205th anniversary of the wedding of Admiral Nelson to Fanny Nisbet. Founded by Mr Robert Abrahams, an American, the collection contains memorabilia including letters, china, pictures, furniture and books. It is well worth a visit as it contains an interesting insight into the life of Nelson and his connection with Nevis. He was not always popular having come to the island to enforce the Navigation Acts which forbade the newly independent American states trading with British Colonies. Nelson in his ship *HMS Boreas* impounded four American ships and their cargos. The Nevis merchants immediately claimed £40,000 losses against Nelson who had to remain on board his ship for eight weeks to escape being put into gaol. It was only after Prince William, captain of *HMS Pegasus*, arrived in Antigua that Nelson gained social acceptability and married the widow Fanny Woodward Nisbet (reputedly for her uncle's money: this proved a disappointment as her uncle left the island and spent his wealth in London).

More evidence of the Nelson connection is found at the **St John's Fig Tree Anglican Church** about 2 miles on from the Bath House. Originally built in 1680, the church was rebuilt in 1838 and again in 1895. The marriage certificate of Nelson and Fanny Nisbet is displayed here. There are interesting memorials to

Fanny's father William Woodward and also to her first husband Dr Josiah Nisbet. Many died of the fever during this period and taxi drivers will delight in lifting the red carpet in the central aisles for you to see old tomb stones, many connected with the then leading family, the Herberts. The graveyard has many examples of tombstones in family groups dating from the 1780s.

Slightly off the main road to the S lies **Montpelier Great House** where the marriage of Nelson and Nesbit actually took place; a plaque is set in the gatepost. The house is now a hotel with pleasant gardens. Enormous toads live in the lily ponds formed out of old sugar pans. A very pleasant place for lunch or a drink. Beyond the house lies **Saddle Hill** (1,820 feet). It has the remains of a small fort and it is reputedly where Nelson would look out for illegal shipping. You can follow several goat trails on the hill, giant aloes abound, a track starts at Clay Ghaut, but most trails beyond the fort are dense and overgrown. The *Hermitage* (another of the Great Houses) is signposted left just after the sign for the Montpelier.

The small village of **Gingerland** is reached after about 3 miles. Its rich soils make it the centre of the islands ginger root production (also cinnamon and nutmeg) but it is noteworthy for the very unusual octagon Methodist Church built in 1830. You turn right here along Hanleys Road to reach **White Bay Beach**. Go all the way down to the bottom and turn left at the Indian Castle experimental farm, avoiding Dark Bay (the site of St George's Port, little remains), past the race course (on Black Bay) and Red Cliff. There is a small shelter but no general shade. Beware, this is the Atlantic coast, the sea can be very rough and dangerous. On quieter days, the surf is fun and provides a welcome change from the quiet Leeward coast at Pinney's. There is a reef further out which is good for fishing (several fishing boats in the bay, one may take you out). There are good views

across to Montserrat. On the way back beware of the deep (and hidden) storm drain crossing the road near the church.

After Gingerland the land becomes more barren. Several sugar mills were built here because of the wind, notably **Coconut Walk Estate**, **New River Estate** (fairly intact) and the **Eden Brown Estate**, built around 1740. A duel took place between the groom and best man at the wedding of Julia Huggins. Both men were killed, Julia became a recluse and the great house was abandoned. It has the reputation of being haunted. Although government owned and open to the public, the ruins are in a poor condition and care should be taken.

The island road continues N through Butlers, past St James church (Hick's village), Long Haul and Newcastle Bays (with the *Nisbet Plantation Inn*) to the small fishing community of **Newcastle**. You can visit the Newcastle pottery where distinctive red clay is used to make among other things the traditional Nevis cooking pot. The **Newcastle Redoubt** can be seen from the road. Built in the early 17th century, it was used as a refuge from Carib attack and may have been the site of a Carib attack in 1656. The airport is situated here.

The road continues through an increasingly fertile landscape and there are fine views across the Narrows to the SE peninsula of St Kitts, looking for all the world like the W coast of Scotland. Note **Booby Island** in the middle of the channel, it is mostly inhabited by pelicans (all birds are referred to as boobies by the local population). It offers good diving. The road between here and Charlestown often passes gardens which are a riot of colour. The small hill on your left is **Round Hill** (1,041 feet). It can be reached on the road between Cardes Bay and Camps Village (there is supposed to be a soufrière along this road). Turn off the road at Fountain Village by the methodist church. There are good views from the radio station at the top over Charlestown, across to St Kitts and beyond to Antigua. Do not expect to see much wildlife however. There is a small beach at Mosquito Bay and some good snorkelling can be had under the cliffs of Hurricane Hill. The *Oualie Beach Hotel* offers a range of watersport facilities including scuba diving and snorkelling equipment. On Sunday afternoons there is often live music and festivities at Mosquito Bay.

Under Round Hill lies Cottle Chapel (1824). It was the first Anglican place on Nevis where slaves could be taught and worship with their master. Ruined now, its beautiful little font can be seen in the Alexander Hamilton museum. Nearby, just off the island road, lies Fort Ashby. Nothing remains of the Fort (it is now a restaurant on Cardes Bay although the cannons are in their original positions). It protected Jamestown, the original settlement and former capital, which was supposedly destroyed by an earthquake and tidal wave in 1680, and was originally called St James' Fort. Drive past the Nelson springs (where the barrels from *HMS Boreas* were filled) and St Thomas' Church (built in 1643, one of the oldest surviving in the Caribbean) to Pinney's Beach. There are many tracks leading down to the beach often with a small hut or beach bar (eg *Golden Rock Beach Bar* and *Mariners*) at the end of them. The *Four Seasons Hotel* lies in the middle of the beach. However the beach is so large that the hotel has had little impact on its undoubted beauty. More intrusive is the golf course which straddles the island road together with the electric cars which transport the guests from the hotel to the first tee. The manicured fairways and greens are in marked contrast with the quiet beauty of the rest of the island but the hotel's considerable efforts at landscaping will undoubtedly lessen its impact.

There are several interesting walks over old sugar plantations and through the rain forest on Mount Nevis. *Sunrise Tours* arranges trips to Nevis Peak, Saddle Hill or Water Source for US$45 pp. The Tourist Office may supply a map issued by the *Golden Rock Estate* to its guests, giving directions to reach the Water Source, a pleasant 1½ hours' walk. Part of the trail may be muddy after rain. David Rollinson of the *Nevis Academy* (T 469 2091) offers "eco rambles" over the eighteenth century Coconut Walk and New River Estates on Sundays, Mondays, Tuesdays and Wednesdays, US$10 pp.

Island Information—Nevis
● **Where To Stay**

Accommodation on Nevis tends to be up-market, in reconstructions of old plantation Great Houses, tastefully decorated in an English style (collectively called *The Inns of Nevis*). Some have reciprocal arrangements whereby you can stay at one and use the facilities of the others. They are well worth a visit. They include the *Golden Rock Estate*, St George's Parish, PO Box 493, T 469 3346, F 469 2113, 15 rooms in 18th century plantation house, 2-storey suite in old windmill for honeymooners/families, antique furniture, 4-poster beds, ocean views, US$175d, EP, US$235d, MAP, winter rate, US$100d EP, US$160d MAP in summer, family plan available, pool, tennis, beach shuttle, specialist interest tours, principally of ecological content; *Hermitage Plantation*, St John's Parish, T 469 3477, F 469 2481, in the UK T 0800-373 742, US$285-690, MAP, in winter, very friendly, beautiful cottages, 4-poster beds, tennis, pool, horse riding, stunning setting, many guests extend their stay; *Montpelier Plantation Inn*, also St John's, PO Box 474, T 469 3462, F 469 2932, a favourite with British tourists, delightful, friendly and helpful, pool, tennis, beach shuttle, US$140d inc breakfast, in summer, US$220d, in winter, child reductions, 7 cottages (16 rooms, no credit cards). The *Nisbet Plantation Beach Club*, St James, built on site of 18th century plantation on ½ mile beach, T 469 9325, F 469 9864, 38 rooms in cottages/suites with tennis, swimming pool, croquet, a beach bar and pavilion, US$315-415d MAP, winter, good food, huge breakfasts, delicious afternoon tea, excellent dinner, laundry and postage complimentary, highly rec. *Pinney's Beach Hotel* PO Box 61, T 469 5207, F 469 1088, 48 rooms, 7 cottages, pool, watersports, horse riding, US$90-110d EP, summer, US$120-140d EP, winter, on the beach, dining room has no view, food and service reported poor off season. New hotels and resorts are being built all the time. A 196-room *Four Seasons Resort* has opened on Pinney's Beach, PO Box 565, T 469 1111, F 469 1112, US$250-300 summer, US$300-350 shoulder, US$500-550 winter, has Robert Trent Jones 18-hole championship golf course, tennis, pool, watersports inc diving, sailboats, windsurfing and all entertainment inc children's activity programme and live music, particularly in high season; the *Mount Nevis Hotel and Beach Club*, PO Box 494, T 469 9373, F 469 9375, modern, 32 rooms and studios, a/c, TV, VCR, phone, pool, watersports at beach club 5 mins away inc windsurfing, US$120-150d EP in summer, US$170-210d EP in winter; *Croney's Old Manor*, PO Box 70, T 469 3445, F 469 3388, in restored 1690 sugar plantation has 14 rooms inc a cottage 800 feet above sea level, tropical gardens, beach shuttle, pool, min stay 3 nights, not rec for children under 12, US$115d EP summer, US$175d EP, US$245d MAP winter; *Oualie Beach Hotel*, on the beach, informal, comfortable, diving and other watersports, 22 rooms, US$130-145d winter EP, 1-2 bedroom studios US$170-320 winter, T 469 9735, F 469 9176.

There are also many guest houses, apartments and cottages including *Yamseed Inn*, T 469 9361, 4 rooms with private entrance, bed and breakfast US$100 in winter, on beach with view of St Kitts; *Hurricane Cove Bungalows*, T/F 469 9462, on hillside with wonderful sea view, 10 well-equipped wooden bungalows of Finnish design, swimming pool, path down to stoney beach, good snorkelling, helpful manageress, Brenda, highly rec, sports facilities nearby, US$125 for one bedroom, US$195 for 2, US$235 with pool, US$395 for 3-bedroomed villa with private pool, 3 night min stay in winter, long term discounts; *Donna's Self-Catering Apartments*, PO Box 503, T 469 3464, and *Sea Spawn Guest House*, PO Box 233, T 469 5239, in Charlestown, 1 min from town, 2 from Pinney's Beach, has 2 fishing boats, car rental and kitchen and dining facilities.

● **Where To Eat**

The best restaurants are in the hotels and it is usually necessary to reserve a table. The above hotels provide exceptional cuisine as well as barbeques and entertainment on certain nights of the week. There are very few eating places in Charlestown, but *Unellas* on the waterfront offers local dishes at very reasonable prices but with very slow service (open 0900-0400 in season, from 1900 on Sun, shuts at 2200 out of season, T 469 5574). *Miss June's*, Stoney Grove Plantation, T 469 5330, open 0800-2200, Caribbean buffet dinner, preceded by cocktails and *hors d'oeuvres*, wine, dessert, coffee and liqueurs included in price, reservations essential. The *Oualie Beach Club* does local lunches and dinners, T 469 9735, 0700-2200. Most restaurants only open in the evenings in the off season or even shut completely, the exception is *Caribbean Confections* T 469 5685, open Mon-Sat for breakfast from 0730, good for ice cream and snacks, on Sat night a special dinner is held in *The Courtyard* at the back, rec, the owner Peggy Lyman is a fountain of information, they also make excellent birthday cakes to take away. *Callaloo* on Main Street serves lunch from US$4 and dinner from US$6, local food, hamburgers, sandwiches, pizzas from 1800, open Mon-Thur 1000-2200, Fri, Sat 1000-2400, no smoking, no alocohol, friendly service; *Eddy's* on same street is a tourist favourite for local food, drinks and music with string bands, bush bands or steel bands Sat 2000-2300, Happy Hour Wed 1700-2000; *The Nook by the Waterfront*, locally popular bar with local dishes, try the conch chowder (EC$8); *Vic's Bar*, meeting place for fishermen in the morning, frequented by islanders, under new management and closed for renovations in 1994 which may change the ambience.

INFORMATION FOR VISITORS

● Documents

US and Canadian visitors do not require passports but need only produce proof of citizenship to stay up to 6 months. Other nationalities need passports and a return ticket but for up to 6 months visas are not required for Commonwealth and EEC countries, Finland, Iceland, Liechtenstein, Norway, San Marino, Sweden, Switzerland, Turkey, Uruguay, Venezuela and nationals of other member countries of the OAS, with the exception of the Dominican Republic and Haiti who do require visas.

● How To Get There

The main airport is at Golden Rock, St Kitts, 2 miles from Basseterre (the facilities for passengers are limited; there is no duty free shop). Connections to North America and Europe can be made through San Juan (American Eagle and LIAT), St Maarten (Liat and Winair) and Antigua (LIAT). There are good connections with other Caribbean Islands (Anguilla, Barbados, Grenada, St Croix, St Eustatius, St Lucia, St Thomas, Tortola) with LIAT and Windward Islands Airways (Winair). There is an airport departure tax of US$10 or EC$20 pp, not payable for stays of less than 24 hrs (or when you leave on the same flight number as you arrived the previous day, ie slightly more than 24 hrs). It is possible to get a bus to the airport and walk the last 5 minutes from the main road; some buses go up to the terminal.

There is also an airport on Nevis, at Newcastle airfield, 7 miles from Charlestown, served by LIAT, Winair, Coastal Air Transport and light charter aircraft from St Kitts, Anguilla, Antigua, St-Barthélémy, St Croix, St Eustatius and St Maarten. Expect to have your baggage searched on your way in to the island and likewise expect chaotic scenes on departure. The grander hotels on Nevis will arrange chartered air transfers from Antigua or St Kitts for their guests (for instance, Carib Aviation, US$55 pp from Antigua), this is highly rec to avoid the crush.

The following cruise ships were calling in 1994: *Yorktown Clipper, Club Mediterranée I, Cunard Countess, Sea Goddess I, Radisson Diamond, World Renaissance, Rotterdam, Freewinds, Starward, Canberra, Regent Sun, Renaissance IV, Song of America, Sun Viking, Sea Cloud, Star Clipper, Star Flyer, Sea Spirit,* *Le Ponant, Arcona, Amazing Grace, Fantome, Mandalay, Polynesia,* and *Windstar.* Basseterre has a deep water port.

● Airlines

LIAT, TDC Airline Services, PO Box 142, Basseterre, T 465 2511/2286, and Evelyn's Travel, on Main Street, Charlestown, general sales agent for BWIA, LIAT, American Airlines and British Airways, no credit cards, PO Box 211, Charlestown, T 469 5302/5238; BWIA, T 465 2286 on St Kitts, 469 5238 on Nevis; American Eagle, T 465 8490 (St Kitts); Winair, Sprott St, Basseterre, T 465 2186 on St Kitts, 469 5583 on Nevis; Carib Aviation, T 465 3055 (the Circus, Basseterre and Golden Rock airport, St Kitts), F 465 3168, T 469 9295 (Newcastle Airport, Nevis). Air St Kitts Nevis, PO Box 529, Basseterre, T 465 8571, 469 9241, F 469 9018, a charter company specializing in day excursions to neighbouring islands eg Saba, Sint Maarten, Antigua, Montserrat, USVI.

● Inter-Island Transport

A passenger ferry, the *Caribe Queen,* operates on a regular schedule between St Kitts and Nevis. The crossing takes about 45 mins and costs EC$20 round trip. Charlestown to Basseterre early morning and afternoon/evening crossing daily except Thur and Sun. Basseterre to Charlestown early morning and afternoon crossing Mon, Fri and Sat, afternoon only on Tues, 3 crossings on Wed making it a good day for a day trip, occasional service Thur and Sun. *The Spirit of Mount Nevis* runs irregularly, check schedules, T 469 9373/4, EC$15. The ferry is preferable to the LIAT flight, which is always overbooked. Island tours operate from St Kitts and there is also a water taxi service between the 2 islands (US$25 return, min 4 passengers, only 20 mins, operated by Kenneth's Dive Centre, T 465 2670 in advance). The *Four Seasons Hotel* has 2 ferry boats running up to 6 times a day for guests' flights, US$15 one-way, from Ro-Ro dock, guests have priority, T 469 1111. Nevis Express runs a shuttle air service between St Kitts and Nevis, US$20, 6 mins, also charter service.

● Road Transport

There are good main roads on St Kitts but do not expect high quality on Nevis, where storm ditches frequently cross the paved road; drive slowly and carefully. Cars, jeeps, mini mokes can be hired from US$30-35 a day from a variety of agencies on both islands, eg TDC Rentals, West Independence Square, Basseterre, T 465 2991, F 465 1099, City Drug Store, Frigate Bay, T 465 1803, or Bay Front, Charlestown, T 469 5960, F 469 1329, also at *Four Seasons*, T 469 1111, if you rent for 3-day min you can arrange for a car on the sister island if you do a day trip to St Kitts or Nevis; Caines Rent-A-Car, Princes Street, Basseterre, T 465 2366, F 465 6172; Sunshine Car Rental, Cayon Street, Basseterre, T 465 2193, Hondas and Korando jeeps. If you are arriving in St Kitts from Nevis, there are several car hire companies on Independence Square, some 3 mins walk from the ferry pier. The most convenient is Avis Car Rental, South Independence Square St, T 465 6507, F 465 1042 (Suzuki jeeps, Nissan automatics, efficient). Nisbett Rentals Ltd, 100 yards from Newcastle airport, Mini-moke US$40/day, collision damage waiver US$8/day, rec, particularly if you are flying in/out of Nevis, T 469 9211, open 0700-1900.

A local driving licence must be obtained from the Post Office or any Police Station on production of your normal driving licence (EC$30). Companies insist on you having collision damage waiver, which adds another US$5-10 to quoted rates. There is a 5% tax on car rentals. Fuel is US$4.50 per gallon.

Moped rental on Nevis through Striker's (Hermitage), T 469 2654, Skeele's (Newcastle), T 469 9458, Carlton Meade; bicycle rental on Craddock Road, T 469 5235.

Minibuses do not run on a scheduled basis but follow a set route (more or less), EC$1-3 on most routes, EC$3 from Basseterre to the N of the island, frequent service from market area. There are no minibuses to Frigate Bay. On Nevis buses start outside Chapman's supermarket next to the courthouse and go to various points, but not on a regular basis, EC$1-3, an island tour is possible, if time consuming.

Maximum **taxi** fares are set, for example: **on St Kitts**, from Golden Rock Airport to Basseterre EC$13-16 (depending on area of town), to the Deep Water Port, EC$22, to Frigate Bay, EC$25, to Old Road, EC$27, to Middle Island, EC$30. From Basseterre to Old Road, EC$24, to Frigate Bay, EC$18, to Middle Island, EC$26, to Sandy Point, EC$30. Taxis within Basseterre cost EC$8, with additional charges for waiting or for more than one piece of luggage. Between 2300-0600 prices rise by 25%. **On Nevis** a taxi from the airport to Charlestown costs EC$30, to *Pinney's Beach Hotel*, EC$30, to *Oualie Beach*, EC$20, to the *Montpelier Inn*, EC$45, to *Hermitage Inn*,

EC$40 and to *Nisbet Plantation Inn*, EC$17. Fares from Charlestown are EC$10, EC$23, EC$26, EC$23 and EC$36 respectively. A 50% extra charge is made on Nevis between 2200 and 0600. An island tour of Nevis costs US$50 for about 3 hours, but you can bargain it down if no cruise ship is in port. Complaints have been received that taxis on both islands are poor, do not stick to the regulated fares and are extremely expensive. There is no need to tip.

● **Food And Drink**

Food on the whole is good. Apart from almost every kind of imported food and drink, there is a wide variety of fresh seafood (red snapper, lobster, king fish, blue parrot), and local vegetables. The excellent local spirit is CSR—Cane Spirit Rothschild—produced in St Kitts by Baron de Rothschild. It is drunk neat, with ice or water, or with "Ting", the local grapefruit soft drink (also rec).

● **Tipping**

A 10% service charge is added to hotel bills. In restaurants about 10%-15% is expected.

● **Shopping**

The shopper has plenty of choice and is not swamped by US or British merchandise. Shops are well stocked. Local Sea Island cotton wear and cane and basketwork are attractive and reasonable. Shop opening hours 0800-1200, 1300-1600, Mon-Sat. Early closing on Thur. Pharmacies open through lunch. Walls De Luxe Record and Bookshop on Fort Street has a good selection of music and Caribbean books, open Mon-Thur 0800-1630, Fri 0800-1700, Sat 0800-1330.

The Island Hopper Boutique at the Circus, underneath the *Ballahoo* restaurant, stocks the Caribelle Batik range of cotton fashions and Rosey Cameron-Smith's fabrics but also carries clothes from Trinidad, St Lucia, Barbados and Haiti; open 0800-1600 Mon-Fri, 0800-1200 Sat, T 465 1640; also at The Arcade, Charlestown, Nevis, T 469 1491/5426. The Plantation Picture House, between Rawlins Plantation and the Golden Lemon is Kate Spencer's studio and gallery of portraits, still life and landscapes in oils and watercolours, her designs are also on silk, open 1100-1700.

Supermarkets in Basseterre include B & K Superfood on the S side of Independence Square and George Street, and Rams on Bay Road. On Nevis, there are well-stocked supermarkets: Nisbets in Newcastle and Superfood, Parkville Plaza, Charlestown. Several local craft shops in Charlestown. Next to the Tourist Office is Nevis Handicraft Cooperative, rec. On the road to the *Four Seasons Hotel* is an industrial estate with shops selling crafts and a toy shop. In Newcastle is a pottery with red clay artifacts.

There are **philatelic bureaux** on both St Kitts and Nevis which are famous (the latter more so) for their first day covers of the islands' fauna and flora, undersea life, history and carnival. The St Kitts bureau is in Pelican Shopping Mall the new development for cruise ship arrivals on the wharf; both bureaux open Mon, Tues, 0800-1630, Wed, Fri, 0800-1600, Thur, 0800-1200.

● **Laundry**
Warners, Main Street, Charlestown, inc dry cleaning.

● **Banks**
The Eastern Caribbean Central Bank (ECCB) is based in Basseterre, and is responsible for the issue of currency in Antigua and Barbuda, Dominica, Grenada, Montserrat, St Kitts and Nevis, St Lucia and St Vincent and the Grenadines. There is a local bank on St Kitts: St Kitts-Nevis-Anguilla National Bank (4 branches: on the corner of Central St and West Independence Square St; Pelican Mall; Sandy Point; Saddlers Village, T 465 2204/6331/7362 open 0830-1500 except Thur 0830-1200, Sat 0830-1100) and on Nevis, West Square St, Charlestown, T 469 5244, same hours. In addition, on Nevis, there is the Nevis Co-operative Banking Co Ltd and the Bank of Nevis. Foreign banks on St Kitts: Barclays Bank, Plc (on the Circus, Basseterre, open Mon-Thur 0800-1500, Fri 0800-1700, the other at Frigate Bay, open Mon-Thur 0800-1300, Fri 0800-1300, 1500-1700, T 465 2264/2510), Royal Bank of Canada (on the Circus, Basseterre, open Mon-Thur 0800-1500, Fri 0800-1700, T 465 2259/2389), Bank of Nova Scotia (Fort St, open Mon-Thur 0800-1500, Fri 0800-1700, T 465 4141); on Nevis, Barclays (T 469 5467/5309) and Bank of Nova Scotia (T 469 5411). Open 0800-1500 Mon-Thur, Fri until 1700. If you are in a hurry, choose a foreign bank as their queues are often shorter. Visa and MasterCard accepted by all three.

● **Currency**
East Caribbean dollar: EC2.70=US$1. US dollars accepted. When prices are quoted in both currencies, eg for departure tax, taxi fares, a notional rate of EC$2.50 = US$1 is used. There are no restrictions on the amount of foreign currency that can be imported or exported, but the amount of local currency exported is limited to the amount you imported and declared. Check which credit cards are accepted, Visa is the most widely used, Access/Mastercard and Diners Club are not so popular.

● **Health**
Mains water is chlorinated, but bottled water is available if preferred for drinking, particularly outside the main towns. Dairy produce, meat, poultry, seafood, fruit and vegetables are generally considered safe. A yellow fever or cholera vaccination certificate is required if you are arriving from an infected area.

● **Security**
Note that the penalties for possession of narcotics are very severe and no mercy is shown towards tourists. Theft has increased, do not leave your things unattended in a car or on the beach.

● **Climate**
The weather is pleasant all year round but the best time to visit is during the dry months from November to May. Locals insist that, with changing weather patterns, May to early August can be preferable. The temperature varies between 17°C and 33°C, tempered by sea winds and with an average annual rainfall of 55 inches on St Kitts and 48 inches on Nevis.

● **Public Holidays**
New Year's Day (1 January), Good Friday, Easter Monday, May Day (first Monday in May), Whit Monday (end of May), the Queen's birthday (June), August Bank Holiday Monday (beginning of the month), Independence Day (19 September), Christmas Day (25 December).

● **Time Zone**
Atlantic Standard Time, 4 hours behind GMT, 1 ahead of EST.

● **Electric Current**
230 volts AC/60 cycles (some hotels have 110V).

● **Communications**
The telephone company, Skantel, has installed new digital telecommunications systems for the 2 islands and international direct dialling is available. USA direct public phones available at Skantel office. Phone cards are sold in denominations of EC$10, 20 and 40. Coin boxes take the older, round EC$1 coins, not the mul-

tisided ones. Codes: 809-465 (St Kitts), 809-469 (Nevis). Call charges are EC$4.50 (EC$3.60 reduced rate) to the USA or the UK. The Boat Phone Company on the Frigate Bay Road offers cellular phone service for yachts. Telex and telegram facilities in the main hotels.

Post office in Basseterre is on Bay Road, open 0800-1500 except Thur when it closes at 1100; in Charlestown on Main Street. Airmail letters to the UK take up to 2 weeks.

● **Media**

Newspapers come out weekly (*The Democrat*) or twice weekly (*The Labour Spokesman*). There are 3 radio stations, 1 TV station and cable TV. AM/FM ZIZ Radio is on medium wave 555 kHz and FM 96 mHz and Radio Paradise on St Kitts. VON Radio in Nevis is on 895 kHz medium wave.

● **Diplomatic Representation**

There is a Venezuelan Embassy on St Kitts and a resident Chargé d'Affaires of the Embassy of the Republic of China. There are also Honorary Consuls of Spain, Germany, Trinidad and Tobago, France and the Netherlands. The acting British High Commissioner is in Antigua.

● **Tourist Office**

The St Kitts Department of Tourism produces very good information (Pelican Mall, PO Box 132, Basseterre, T 465 2620/4040, F 465 8794). The Nevis Tourist Office is in Main Street, Charlestown (T 469 5521, F 469 1806; it is extremely helpful, with plenty of information available.

There are tourist offices in

USA: at 414 East 75th Street, New York NY 10021, T 212-535 1234, F 212-879 4789; 1464 Whippoorwill Way, Mountainside, NJ 07092, T 908-232 6701; Presidents' Plaza II, 870 West Bryn Mawr, Suite 8005, Chicago, IL 60631, T 312-714 5015, F 312-714 4910..

Canada: 11 Yorkville Ave, Suite 508, Toronto M4W 1L3, T 416-921 7717, F 416-921 7997.

UK: c/o the High Commission for Eastern Caribbean States, 10 Kensington Court, London W8 5DL, T 071-376 0881, F 071-937 3611.

The St Kitts/Nevis Hotel Association can be reached at PO Box 438, Basseterre, St Kitts, T 465 5304.

Useful publications are *The Traveller* (biannual, the official publication of the Tourist Board); *A Motoring Guide to Nevis* by Janet Cotner and Sunny Northrup (Heidelberg Press, Burlington NJ); the Nevis Historical and Conservation Society's *Walking and Riding Tour of Nevis* pamphlet (available from Alexander Hamilton House, Charlestown).

ANGUILLA

ANGUILLA is a small island, only about 35 miles square, the most N of the Leeward Islands, five miles N of St Martin and 70 miles NW of St Kitts. The island is low lying, the highest point being Crocus Hill at 213 feet above sea level. Unlike its larger sisters it is not volcanic but of coral formation. It is arid, covered with low scrub and has few natural resources. However, it has excellent beaches and superb diving and snorkelling, protected by the coral reefs. The island's name is the Spanish word *anguilla* (eel), a reference to its long, narrow shape. Its Carib name was Malliouhana. The population numbers about 10,496, predominantly of African descent but with some traces of Irish blood. The administrative centre is *The Valley*, the largest community on the island with a population of 500. The people of Anguilla are very friendly and helpful and it is one of the safest islands in the Caribbean.

To the NW is the uninhabited Dog Island which is excellent for swimming, and beyond that is Sombrero Island, where there is an important lighthouse. Other islets include Scrub Island at the NE tip of Anguilla, Little Scrub Island next to it, Anguillita Island and Blowing Rock at the SW tip and the Prickly Pear Cays and Sail Island to the NW on the way to Dog Island.

History

The earliest known Amerindian site on Anguilla is at the NE tip of the island, where tools and artefacts made from conch shells have been recovered and dated at around 1300 BC. Saladoid Amerindians settled on the island in the fourth century AD and brought their knowledge of agriculture, ceramics and their religious culture based on the god of cassava (see page 34). By the mid-sixth century large villages had been built at Rendezvous Bay and Sandy Ground, with smaller ones at Shoal Bay and Island Harbour. Post Saladoid Amerindians from the Greater Antilles arrived in the tenth century, building new villages and setting up a chiefdom with a religious hierarchy. Several ceremonial items have been found and debris related to the manufacture of the three-pointed zemis, or spirit stones, associated with fertility rites. By the 17th century, Amerindians had disappeared from Anguilla: wiped out by enslavement and European diseases.

Anguilla was first mentioned in 1564 when a French expedition passed en route from Dominica to Florida, but it was not until 1650 that it was first colonized by the British. Despite several attempted invasions, by Caribs in 1656 and by the French in 1745 and 1796, it remained a British colony. From 1825 it became more closely associated with St Kitts for administrative purposes and ultimately incorporated in the colony. In 1967 St Kitts-Nevis-Anguilla became a State in Association with the UK and gained internal independence. However, Anguilla opposed this development and almost immediately repudiated government from St Kitts. A breakaway movement was led by Ronald Webster of the People's Progressive Party (PPP). In 1969 British forces invaded the island to install a British Commissioner after negotiations had broken down. The episode is remembered locally for the unusual presence of the London Metropolitan Police, who remained on the island until 1972 when the Anguilla Police Force was established.

The post of Chief Minister alternated for two decades between the rival politi-

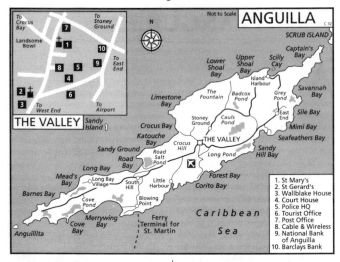

1. St Mary's
2. St Gerard's
3. Wallblake House
4. Court House
5. Police HQ
6. Tourist Office
7. Post Office
8. Cable & Wireless
9. National Bank of Anguilla
10. Barclays Bank

cians, Ronald Webster and Emile Gumbs, leader of the Anguilla National Alliance (ANA), the latter holding office in 1977-80 and 1984-94. Mr Gumbs (now Sir Emile) retired from politics at the general elections held in March 1994. These elections proved inconclusive, with the ANA, the Anguilla United Party (AUP) and the Anguilla Democratic Party (ADP) each winning two seats and an Independent, Osbourne Fleming (who was Finance Minister in the ANA government) winning the seventh. A coalition was formed by Hubert Hughes, leader of the AUP, and Victor Banks, ADP, and the former was sworn in as Chief Minister. Mr Hughes had been a Minister in the 1984 ANA government, but had been dismissed in 1985, subsequently joining the opposition AUP, then led by Ronald Webster.

Government

In 1980, Anguilla formally separated from the State and became a British Dependent Territory with a Governor to represent the Crown. A new constitution was introduced in 1982, providing for a Governor, an Executive Council comprising four elected Ministers and two ex-officio members, and an 11-member legislative House of Assembly presided over by a Speaker. In 1990 the constitution was amended to give the Governor responsibility for international financial affairs. A new post of Deputy Governor was created, to replace the Permanent Secretary for Finance as a member of the Executive Council and House of Assembly.

The Economy

The main economic activities used to be livestock raising, lobster fishing, salt production and boat building, but tourism is now the major generator of foreign exchange and employment. In 1993 stopover arrivals rose by nearly 21% to 36,729, with US visitors (65% of the total) increasing by nearly 31%. The European (13%) and Canadian (2%) markets are small but both saw growth rates of 22% and 25%. There are some 800 rooms available in guest houses, villas and apartments and hotels, although the number is steadily rising. There is also some offshore banking and the Government aims to establish a reputable offshore financial services industry. Thirty out of 43 offshore banks, who pay an annual licence fee to the Government, had their licences cancelled in 1990 following a review of the sector. At end-1991 the House of Assembly approved legislation to tighten control of offshore finance, giving the Governor complete and final authority over the granting of licences.

Previously, high levels of unemployment led to migration to other Caribbean islands and further afield, but the unemployment rate has fallen from 26% in 1985 to almost nil and shortages of labour have delayed expansion programmes, as well as putting pressure on prices and wages. Work permits have been granted to more than 1,000 non-Anguillans, but many people have two jobs. Workers' remittances are crucial, particularly since the 1984 suspension of budgetary support in the form of UK grants-in-aid, although the British Government does still provide aid for the development programme, along with other donors such as the EEC and the Caribbean Development Bank. Anguilla is to receive £10.5m in capital aid and technical assistance for 1994-97 under a Country Policy Plan agreed with the UK. The Plan details policy and programme targets up to 1996/97 and is aimed at promoting 'good government and self-sustainable growth and economic autonomy for Anguilla over the medium to long term'. There is no income tax and the Government gets its revenues from customs duties, bank licences, property and stamps.

Flora and Fauna

The island is low lying, coralline and arid. Although you will see colourful gardens with flowering hibiscus, bougainvillea and other tropical plants, the island is mostly covered with scrub. However, birdwatching is good at Little Bay, Crocus Bay's N point and at ponds and coves, T 2759 for information. 93 species of birds have been recorded on Anguilla, including the blue faced booby, Kingfisher and the great blue heron.

Diving and Marine Life

The Government is introducing a Marine Parks system, installing permanent moorings in certain areas to eliminate anchor damage. Mooring permits will be required. Do not remove any marine life from underwater. Scuba diving can be arranged through Tamariain Watersports Ltd, PO Box 247, Sandy Ground, T 2020, F 5125. Owned and run by Iain Grummit and Thomas Peabody, excellent courses are available at this 5-star PADI training centre, recommended. Retail shop open daily 0800-1630, equipment for sale or rent. All dives are guided boat dives; a single tank dive costs US$40, a 2-tank dive US$70, night dives US$50.

There are good dives just off the coast, particularly for novices or for night dives, while the others are generally in a line due W of Sandy Island, NW of Sandy Ground, and along the reef formed by Prickly Pear Cays and Sail Island. Off Sandy Island, there are lots of soft corals and sea-fans, while at Sandy Deep there is a wall which falls from 15 to 60 feet. There are also several wrecks, nine of which have been deliberately sunk as dive sites around the island, the most recent in 1993.

Further W, Paintcan Reef at a depth of 80 feet contains several acres of coral and you can sometimes find large turtles there. Nearby, Authors Deep, at 110 feet has black coral, turtles and a host of small fish, but this dive is more for the experienced diver. On the N side of the Prickly Pear Cays you can find a beautiful underwater canyon with ledges and caves where nurse sharks often go to rest. Most of the reefs around Anguilla have some red coral; be careful not to touch it as it burns.

Beaches and Watersports

There are twelve miles or 45 beaches with fine white coral sand and crystal clear water. Most of them are protected by a ring of coral reefs and offshore islands. The beaches are clean, and many of them are relatively unpopulated, but nude (or topless for women) swimming or sunbathing is not allowed. Shoal Bay is the most popular beach and claims to be one of the most beautiful in the Eastern Caribbean. There are hotels, snack bars for lunch, although only one has a toilet. The snorkelling is good, with the closest of two reefs only 10 yards from the shore and you can rent snorkelling equipment. You can also rent beach umbrellas, loungers, rafts and towels. Mead's Bay is also popular with more expensive bars, hotels and watersports. Road Bay/Sandy Ground has most nightlife and restaurants and is the starting point for most day trips, dive tours and a popular anchorage for visiting yachts. Watersports equipment rentals can be organized here. Scilly Cay is a small cay off Island Harbour with good snorkelling. A free ferry takes you to the bar on a palm-clad beach where walls are made from conch shells. Live music on Wednesdays, Fridays and Sundays. *Smitty's Bar*, across the water at Island Harbour is less sophisticated, tables made from old cable barrels, TV, popular with the locals. Captain's Bay is rougher but the scenery is dramatic and not many people go there. The dirt road is full of potholes and goats and may be impassable with a low car. At Crocus Bay the rocks on both sides have nice coral and underwater scenery. There is a bar/restaurant and toilets. At the end of Limestone Bay is a small beach with excellent snorkelling, but be careful, the sea can be rough here. Little Bay is more difficult to reach but eagle rays and turtles can be seen; turn right in front of the old cottage hospital in the Valley, after about half a mile there are some trails leading down to the water, fishermen have put up a net for the last bit. Glass bottom boats and cruise boats also come here.

Windsurfing and sailing are readily available and some of the hotels offer water skiing, paddle boats, snorkelling, fishing and sunfish sailing. There are glass bottom boats which can be hired for one or two people to operate themselves or crewed for groups. Sport fishing is available at Sandy Island Enterprises, T 5643/6395. Yacht or motorboat charters can be organized through Sandy Island Enterprises, Suntastic Yacht Services, T 3400/3699, Caribbean Concepts, T 2671, or Enchanted Island Cruises, Road Bay, T 3111, which has a 50-foot catamaran, *Wild Cat* and a 31-foot monohull, *Counterpoint*. Ocean Charters have half or full day charters to beaches, US$50 pp per day, open bar, also ½ day fishing trips, US$45/hour, T 3394. Boat racing is the national sport, the boats being a special class of wooden sloop made in Anguilla. There are frequent races, but the most important are on Anguilla Day (30 May) and during Carnival Week in August.

Other Sports

Several hotels have tennis courts. The *Malliouhana* has 4 championship courts for guests only; *Cinnamon Reef* has 2 at a cost of US$25 per hour for non-residents, free for guests; *Cap Juluca*, *Casablanca* and *Cove Castles* all have courts for guests' use only; others make a charge for non-guests: *Carimar Beach Club*, US$20/hour; *Coccoloba*, US$15/hour; *The Mariners*, US$20/hour; *Masara Resort*, US$10/hour; *Rendezvous Bay*, US$5/hour; *Spindrift Apartments*, US$5-10/hour.

Festivals

Carnival is at the beginning of August (the Friday before the first Monday), when the island comes to life with street dancing, Calypso competitions, the Carnival Queen Coronation, the Prince and

Princess Show, nightly entertainment in The Valley and beach barbeques.

Excursions

Near The Valley, Wallblake House is a restored, eighteenth-century plantation house where the priest from St Gerard's Roman Catholic Church lives. The Church itself is worth a visit to see the unusual ventilation. Several resident artists exhibit their work on Saturday mornings during the winter season in the grounds of Wallblake House. At Sandy Ground Village, you can see the salt pond, around Great Road Pond, although it is not currently in operation. Northeast of The Valley, by Shoal Village, is The Fountain national park. Its focus is in fact a cave which has a source of constant fresh water and a series of Amerindian petroglyphs. Artefacts have been found and it is hoped they will be housed in a museum at the site, but in 1994 the national park was still closed while archaeologists considered policy alternatives and was likely to remain so for a while. Anguilla awaits detailed archaeological investigation, but it is thought that the island had several settlements and a social structure of some importance, judging by the ceremonial items which have been found. Contact the Anguilla Archaeological and Historical Society for more information; the Society is involved in setting up a national museum and in several publications including a Review (PO Box 252). There is a very small museum of artefacts found on site at the *Arawak Beach Resort*, together with replicas of furnishings, pottery and baskets, T 4888, F 4498. Big Spring Cave is an old Amerindian ceremonial centre where you can see petroglyphs. It is near Island Harbour, a fishing village with Irish ancestory. Local deposits of clay have been found and pottery is now made on the island; the work of Barbadian potter and sculptor, Courtney Devonish, and his students, is on display at the

Devonish Cotton Gin Art Gallery in the Old Factory Plaza opposite the Catholic Church, T 2949. There are sometimes pottery demonstrations on Saturdays.

Day trips can be arranged to some of the neighbouring islands or to the off-shore islands and cays. Sandy Island is only 15 minutes from Sandy Ground harbour and is a pleasant desert island-type place to swim, snorkel and spend half a day or so. Motorboats or sailboats cross over hourly from 1000, US$8pp. Lunch or drinks available from a beach bar under coconut palms. There are trips to Prickly Pear, six miles from Road Bay, which is well worth a visit, where you can snorkel if you are not a scuba diver, or to some of the other cays where you can fish or just have a picnic. Enchanted Island Cruises have a boat that goes to Prickly Pear daily (except Thursday) leaving 1000 and returning 1600, US$70 including drinks, barbeque lunch and snorkelling equipment, T 3111. Scrub Island, two miles long and one mile wide, off the NE tip of Anguilla, is an interesting mix of coral, scrub and other vegetation and is worth a visit. It is uninhabited, except by goats, and can only be reached by boat. There is a lovely sandy beach on the W side and ruins of an abandoned tourist resort and airstrip. There can be quite a swell in the anchorage, so anchor well. Boats go from Road Bay, Shoal Bay or Island Harbour. Chartered yachts and motorboats leave from Road Bay or from Island Harbour for Scilly Cay, privately owned by Eudoxie and Sandra Wallace and also named Gorgeous Scilly Cay. Open 1100-1700, lunch only, live music Wed, Fri, Sun, closed Mon.

INFORMATION FOR VISITORS

● Documents

All visitors need an onward ticket. All must also have a valid passport, except US citizens who need only show proof of identity with a photograph. Visas are not required by anyone.

● How To Get There By Air

Wallblake airport is just outside The Valley, T 2514. International access points for Anguilla are Antigua, St Maarten or San Juan, Puerto Rico. LIAT has daily flights from Antigua; some flights connect with British Airways from London. Alternatively, Carib Aviation, will meet any incoming BA flight and fly you to Anguilla without you having to clear customs in Antigua. LIAT also connects Anguilla with St Kitts and Nevis, St Maarten, San Juan, Dominica, Martinique, Trinidad, St Lucia, Tortola and St Thomas (the LIAT office is at Gumbs Travel Agency, T 2238 and also at T 2748). American Eagle (T 3500) has a twice daily air link with Puerto Rico which connects with their New York flight. Winair (T 2238/2748) provides several daily flights from St Maarten (10 min, about US$15). Coastal Air Transport flies from St Croix, USVI. Air Anguilla (T 2643) and Tyden Air (T 2719, F 3079, PO Box 107, The Valley) operate charters and air taxi services to the British and US Virgin Islands, St Maarten and St Kitts.

There is a departure tax of EC$15/ US$6.

● How To Get There By Sea:

The principal port is Sandy Ground, which is being improved. Ferry between Blowing Point (departure tax EC$5/US$2) and Marigot, Saint-Martin takes at least 20 mins and costs US$9 daytime, US$11 night-time, one way (pay on board). The service starts at about 0730 and continues every 30-40 mins until 1700; (there are also 2 evening ferries in high season at 1900 and 2300 (Marigot to Anguilla) and 1815 and 2215 (Anguilla to Marigot). You pay the US$2 departure tax before boarding at Marigot but you pay the fare on the boat. The same applies when leaving from Anguilla. Have your passport and tax receipt handy when boarding.

Visiting yachts anchor at Sandy Ground, Crocus Bay and Mead's Bay on the N coast, and Blowing Point or Rendezvous Bay on the S coast. Periodic boats from St Kitts and Nevis, the British and US Virgin Islands and Puerto Rico. Immigration and customs formalities for boats are at Blowing Point. At Road Bay the customs office is at the big wharf close to the *Riviera*, the Immigration office is at the Police station behind *Johnno's*.

● Taxis

Expensive and the driver usually quotes in US dollars, not EC dollars: from Wallblake airport to The Valley costs about US$5; from The Valley to Blowing Point (ferry) US$11. Fares are fixed by the Government. To hire a taxi for a tour of the island works out at about US$40 for 2 people, US$5 for additional passengers.

● Car Rental

There are several car hire companies, including Apex, The Quarter, T 2642; H and R, The Valley, T 2656/2606; Bennie's (Avis, requires US$100 deposit one month in advance for lowest price), US$180-225/week, Blowing Point, T 2788/2360/6221; Triple K Car Rental (Hertz), on Airport Road, close to Wallblake, PO Box 219, The Quarter, T 2934, free delivery and pick up, jeeps (US$45/day), cars (US$40/day), mini mokes (US$35/day) and small buses; Budget, The Quarter, T 2217, F 5871, free pick up and delivery (to get their low price of US$167/week, reservations must be made direct to Anguilla, not through their US or European offices); Connors, South Hill, T 6433, F 6410; Island Car Rentals, T 2723, F 3723, and many others. Rates are from US$25/day off season, US$35/day high season, plus insurance, jeeps from US$40. You can normally bargain for a good rate if you rent for more than 3 days.

Driving is on the left. Speed limit 30 miles an hour. Fuel costs US$1.84 per gallon for regular, US$1.86 unleaded. Watch out for loose goats on the roads. A local driving permit is issued on presentation of a valid driver's licence from your home country and can be bought at car rental offices; US$6 for 3 months. Hitchhiking is very easy.

● Where To Stay

Anguilla has the reputation of catering for upmarket, independent travellers. This is reflected in the number of relatively small, but expensive hotels and beach clubs. Bargains can be found in the summer months, with discounts of up to 50%. An 8% tax and 10-15% service charge will be added to the bill.

The following (in anti-clockwise direction from Road Bay) have flexible accommodation in rooms, suites, studios or villas, winter 1993/94 prices quoted. *The Mariners*, Sandy Ground, T 2671/2815, F 2901, all-inclusive, 67 rooms, suites and cottages, US$170-485d, EP, in high season (US$150-305 in summer), on beach, watersports, pool, tennis; *Malliouhana Hotel*, Mead's Bay, T 6111, F 6011, PO Box 173, 54 rooms, US$480-775d, EP, no credit cards (US$250 out of season), suites up to US$1,185, every luxury, on beach, watersports, tennis, 2 pools; *Carimar Beach Club*, Meads Bay, PO Box 327, T 497 6881, F 497 6071, 1-3 bedroom apartments, US$300-600, beach, tennis; *Frangipani Beach Club*, new, luxury resort on Mead's Bay beach, 23 units, US$325-1,050, Spanish style tiled roofs, multilevel, tiled floors, fans, cool, comfortable, T 6442, F 6440; *La Sirena*, Meads Bay, T 6827, F 6829, 20 individually designed rooms, US$195-255d, villas up to US$395, beach nearby, pool; *Coccoloba Plantation*, Barnes Bay, T 6871, F 6332, 51 rooms, US$375d, suites US$375-575, villas US$475-950 including full breakfast, large reductions in summer, beach, 2 pools, tennis, colourful gardens, gingerbread verandahs round the villas; *Cove Castles Villa Resort*, Shoal Bay West, T 6801, F 6051, T 800 348 4716, PO Box 248, futuristic architecture, 4 3-bedroom villas, 8 2-bedroom beach houses, US$590-990 EP, 1994/95 rates, lowest rate US$350d or US$450 for 3 or 4 people per beach house summer 1994, housekeeper, phone, TV, beach, tennis, sunfish, bicycles included, watersports available; *Cap Juluca* at Maundays Bay (T 6666/6779, F 6617), Moorish design, bright white, luxury resort, 98 rooms, every facility here, with 2 beaches, pool, watersports, tennis, where winter rates are US$400-525d, US$650-1,500 suites and US$2,250-3,475 3-5 bedroom villas, CP, but a third less in summer, children's rooms half price in spring and summer, full children's activity programmes with watersports and tennis, 179-acre estate; *Casablanca Resort*, on Merrywing Bay, T 6999, F 6899, opulent Moorish style, rooms and villas US$315-600, all-inclusive rates US$800-1,200d, pool, tennis, health club, library, 3 restaurants, 84 rooms and still growing; *Anguilla Great House*, Rendezvous Bay, T 6061/6621, F 6019, 25 rooms, US$200-230d, falling to US$115 in summer, suites up to US$475, EP, open air restaurant and bar on beach, pool; *Rendezvous Bay Hotel*, T 6549, F 6026, 30 rooms, US$100-180, villas up to US$550, beach, tennis, family run, helpful, rooms with veranda only a few metres from the sea, moderately good snorkelling, lovely

beach, run by Jeremiah Gumbs, PO Box 31; *Cinnamon Reef*, Little Harbour, T 2727, F 3727, in the UK, T 0800 373 742, 22 rooms, US$250-350 EP in winter, beach, pool, tennis, library; *Arawak Beach Resort*, PO Box 433, T 4888, F 4898, octagonal villas on the NE coast near Big Spring ceremonial centre, overlooking Scilly Cay, US$250-450, mini museum, health bar and restaurant, T 4888, F 4898; *Shoal Bay Villas*, T 2051, F 3631, PO Box 81, 9 studios and apartments, US$210-360, pleasant setting, open air restaurant/bar, beach, pool; *Fountain Beach*, Shoal Bay, T/F 3491, 14 rooms, US$245 for a studio, US$365 for 2-bedroom suite in winter, 40% less in summer, EP, beach; *Masara Resort*, Katouche Bay, T 3200, F 3223, 13 rooms, US$175-250, beach nearby, tennis.

There are also villas and apartments to rent, among the cheapest being *Syd Ans Apartments*, Sandy Ground, T 3180, F 5381, one-bedroom apartments at US$75 day, Mexican restaurant, close to Tamariain Watersports; *Sea View*, Sandy Ground, T 2427, US$45-90, ceiling fans, kitchen facilities, beach nearby, clean, comfortable, enquire at the house next door for a room; *Viewfort Cottage*, Viewfort, T 2537, US$60, kitchen, TV; *La Palma*, Sandy Ground, T 3260, F 5381, US$60, on beach, restaurant, ceiling fans, at Lower South Hill, *Inter Island*, T 6259, F 5381, 14 rooms, US$120d, apartments US$105-125, fans, kitchen facilities, restaurant.

Anguilla Connection Ltd at Island Harbour, T 4403, F 4402, has a selection of 1-4 bedroom villas and apartments for rent, with several services on offer, US$85-500. *Select Villas of Anguilla*, Innovation Center, George Hill Road, T 5810, F 5811 has 13 villas of different sizes around the island, cheapest US$500/week in summer, most expensive US$2,200/week in winter, daily rates available.

Travellers on a lower budget can find accommodation in one of about 10 guesthouses. These include *Casa Nadine*, The Valley (T 2358), 11 rooms, US$25d all year, EP, with shower, kitchen facilities, basic but very friendly and helpful; *Florencia's*, The Valley (T 2319), 5 rooms, US$50, MAP, basic, little privacy; *Yellow Banana*, Stoney Ground (T 2626), 12 rooms, US$30-40d, EP, simple, clean, small lounge, but not very friendly; at North Side, *Norman B*, T 2242, 11 rooms, US$40d EP; and others. Anguilla under US$100 is an all-inclusive package with some meals, accommodation, ground transfers, car rental, tax and gratuities, for details contact Innovative Marketing Consultants, same company as *Select Villas of Anguilla*, above.

The Anguilla Department of Tourism has a list of all types of accommodation. Inns of Anguilla is an association of over 20 villas or small hotels at moderate prices. A brochure with pictures is available; prices are included in the Department of Tourism Rate Guide. In London there is a free reservation service on 071-937 7725. In North America, call (800) 553 4939, c/o Medhurst and Associates Inc, 271 Main Street, Northport, NY 11768.

● **Where To Eat**

Apart from hotel restaurants, where a dinner can cost US$50 and above in a 4-5 star restaurant you can find local cuisine at *Lucy's Harbour View*, Back Street, South Hill, medium prices, Tel: 6253; *Ship's Galley*, breakfast, lunch and dinner, closed Wed, T 2040, Sandy Ground; *Barrel Stay*, Sandy Ground, T 2831, overpriced because of all the charter boat tourists. *Le Fish Trap*, Island Harbour, is expensive but one of the best for seafood, T 4488; *Koalkeel*, The Valley, also expensive, in a restored 18th century Great House, the traditional home of the island's administrator, known as Warden's Place, with 100-year old rock oven, Euro-Caribbean style, T 2930; *Johnno's*, Sandy Ground, mostly barbeque, especially lively evenings are Sat and Sun, with live music, T 2728; *Riviera*, French/Caribbean restaurant on beach front in Sandy Ground, some Japanese dishes, quite expensive, T 2833, F 3663, VHF 16; *Tropical Penguin*, beach bar and restaurant, Sandy Ground, Austrian chef, pasta, seafood, salads, T 2253; *La Palma*, Sandy Ground, local food, inexpensive, T 3260; *Capers*, on Meads Bay Beach is colourful, fish, lobster, US meat, open 1800-2200, closed Mon, T 6369; *Paradise Café*, Shoal Bay West, T 6010, imaginative salads with oriental influences as well as burgers and club sandwiches; *Chillies*, Mexican, by roadside in Sandy Ground, beans, *burritos*, try the lobster tacos, veggie *tostadas*, T 3171. Most of the restaurants are small and reservations are needed, particularly in high season. For those who are self-catering, *Fat Cat*, Main Road, George Hill, T 2307, has meals to go from the freezer, picnic meals, pies and cakes. Vista Food Market, South Hill Roundabout, T 2804, good selection, cheeses, meats, pâtés, wines, beer etc, open Mon-Sat 0800-1800.

● **Nightlife**

Out of season there is not much to do during the week. On Fri the whole island changes, several bars have live music, check the local papers, try *Lucy's Palm Palm*, Sandy Ground, or *Round Rock*, Shoal Bay. On Sat go to *Johnno's Place*, Sandy Ground; on Sun to brunch at *Roy's Place*, Crocus Bay, draft beer, then around 1500 at *Johnno's Place* for a beach party. When the music dies people go to the neighbouring bar, *Ship's Galley* for the night shift. At the weekend the *Dragon Disco* opens around midnight. In high season the resort hotels have live music, steel bands etc, check in the tourist *Anguilla Life* magazine. Look for shows with North Sound, Missington Brothers the most popular bands. There is no theatre but plays are sometimes put on at the Ruthwill Auditorium. The Mayoumba Folkloric Theatre puts on a song, dance and drama show at *La Sirena* on Thur nights, T 6827.

● **Bookshop**

National Bookstore, above Lynette's Bakery, The Valley, T 3009, open Mon-Sat 0800-1700, wide selection of novels, magazines, non-fiction, children's books, tourist guides, Caribbean history and literature, managed by Mrs Kelly. A *Dictionary of Anguillian Language* has been published in a 34-page booklet, edited by Ijahnia Christian of the Adult and Continuing Education Unit following the Cultural Educational Fest.

● **Banks**

In The Valley, Barclays Bank International, T 2301/2304, F 2980, Box 140; Financial Bank (Anguilla) Ltd, Caribbean Commercial Centre, T 3890.

● **Currency**

The East Caribbean dollar. US dollars always accepted.

● **Health**

There is a new hospital with modern equipment called the Princess Alexandra. Hospital T 2551/2; Doctor T 3792/3460/6522/2882 and T 2632/3233; Pharmacy T 2366/2738; optometrist T 3700. Most people drink bottled water but there is also rainwater or desalinated water for household use.

● **Climate**

The climate is sub-tropical with an average temperature of 27°C (80°F) and a mean annual rainfall of 914 milimetres (36 inches), falling mostly between September and December.

● Clothing

Bathing costumes are not worn in public places. Nude bathing or sunbathing is not allowed.

● Hours Of Business

0800-1200, 1300-1600 Mon to Fri; banks 0800-1500 Mon to Thur, 0800-1700 on Fri. Gas stations are open in The Valley, Mon to Sat 0700-2100, Sun 0900-1300, and at Blowing Point, Mon to Sun 0700-2400.

● National Holidays

New Year's Day, Good Friday, Easter Monday, Whit Monday, 30 May (Anguilla Day), the Queen's official birthday in June, the first Monday (August Monday) and the first Thursday (August Thursday) and Friday (Constitution Day) in August, 19 December (Separation Day), Christmas Day, Boxing Day.

● Time Zone

GMT minus 4 hours; EST plus 1 hour.

● Weights And Measures

Metric, but some imperial weights and measures are still used.

● Electric Current

110 volts AC, 60 cycles.

● Telecommunications

Cable and Wireless operates internal and external telephone links (IDD available), telex and fax services. Caribbean phone cards are available throughout the islands. There are 2 AT&T USA direct telephones by Cable and Wireless office in the Valley and by the airport. The international code is 809-497, followed by a 4-digit number. **Main Post Office** is in The Valley, opposite Webster Park, open Mon-Fri 0800-1530. It has a Philatelic Bureau which sells commemorative stamps and other collections.

● Press

Chronicle daily, *The Herald* weekly, *The Light*, a local weekly. *What We Do In Anguilla* is an annual tourist magazine, *Anguilla Life* is quarterly.

● Radio

Radio Anguilla is on medium wave 1505 kHz and ZJF on FM 105 MHz, T 2218.

● Travel Agents

Malliouhana Travel and Tours, The Quarter, T 2431/2348, has been rec; Bennie's Travel Tours (address under **Car Rental**, above); Travel and Tours, Inc, The Valley, T 2788/2360. J N Gumbs' Travel Agency is the local Liat and Winair agent, T 2238/9, F 3351.

● Tourist Office

Anguilla Department of Tourism, The Valley, T 2759/2451, F 2751, open weekdays 0800-1200, 1300-1600. The office at the airport is also closed at lunchtime, but the customs officers are helpful and will often phone for a hotel reservation for you.

UK: 3 Epirus Road, London, SW6, 7UJ, T 071-937 7725, F 071-938 4793.

USA: Medhurst and Associates, 271 Main Street, Northport, NY 11768, T (800) 553-4939, F (516) 261-9606.

MONTSERRAT

ONTSERRAT, known as "the Emerald Isle", is pear-shaped and has a land area of 39 square miles. About 11 miles long and seven miles wide, its nearest neighbours are Nevis, Guadeloupe and, 27 miles to the NE, Antigua, from where frequent short-hop flights connect Montserrat with longer-haul aircraft. Three mountain ranges dominate this green-clad island, the highest, the Soufrière Hills, rising to 3,002 feet above sea level at the summit of Mount Chance. Volcanic in origin, the island has active fumaroles and hot mineral springs. Villages, linked by good roads, are situated all round the island on the slopes, but many lie on the W coast of the island at the foot of the hills. The capital, Plymouth, has the best harbour. The second largest village on the island is Harris, which is on the E side, near the airport.

The population of 11,000 has not increased throughout this century, because of emigration and birth control. The vast majority of the people are of African descent, but recent years have seen the influx of white Americans, Canadians and Britons who have purchased retirement homes on the island. In consequence, local amenities like the excellent museum and many of the cultural activities are run by expatriate volunteers with money and time to spare. Montserratians are notable for their easy friendliness to visitors, speaking English flavoured by dialect and the odd Irish expression (see History). The island is quiet all year round but visitors in search of revels should aim for the festive Christmas season, although accommodation rates peak then. The high season, in common with much of the region, is from 15 December to mid-April.

In 1989, Montserrat was devastated by Hurricane Hugo, the first hurricane to strike the island for 61 years. No part of the island was untouched by the 150 mph winds as 400-year-old trees were uprooted, 95% of the housing stock was damaged or destroyed, agriculture was reduced to below subsistence level and even the 180-foot jetty at Plymouth harbour completely disappeared, causing problems for relief supplies. However, within a few months, all public utilities were restored to service and the remaining standing or injured trees were in leaf again. Much has still to be done, but for the visitor the island is back in working order, with restaurants, hotels and cafés open and sand back on the beaches. In December 1991 a Best Kept Village competition was fiercely fought, resulting in a splendid clean-up of all the villages. This is being continued on a quarterly basis.

History

Columbus sighted Montserrat on 11 November 1493, naming it after an abbey of the same name in Spain, where the founder of the Jesuits, Ignacio de Loyola, experienced the vision which led to his forming that famous order of monks. At that time, a few Carib Indians lived on the island but by the middle of the seventeenth century they had disappeared. The Caribs named the island Alliouagana, which means "land of the prickly bush". Montserrat was eventually settled by the British Thomas Warner, who brought English and Irish Catholics from their uneasy base in the Protestant island of St Kitts. Once established as an Irish-Catholic colony, the only one in the Caribbean, Catholic refugees fled there from persecution in Virginia and, following his victory at Drogheda in 1649,

Cromwell sent some of his Irish political prisoners to Montserrat. An Irishman brought some of the first slaves to the island in 1651 and the economy became based on sugar. Slaves quickly outnumbered the original British indentured ser-

vants. A slave rebellion in 1768, appropriately enough on St Patrick's Day, led to all the rebels being executed and today they are celebrated as freedom fighters. Montserrat was invaded several times by the French during the seventeenth and

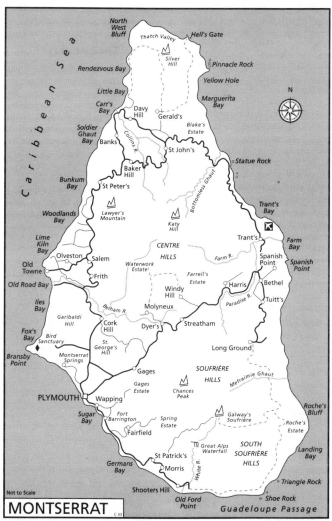

MONTSERRAT

eighteenth centuries, sometimes with assistance from the resident Irish, but the island returned to British control under the Treaty of Versailles (1783) and has remained a colony to this day.

The elections held in 1991 resulted in a resounding defeat for the Chief Minister, John Osborne. He failed to hold his seat and only one of the candidates of his People's Liberation Movement was elected and he won by only two votes. The National Development Party, previously considered the main Opposition Party also fared badly with only one candidate elected. One independent also won a seat. Success went to a new party founded by Reuben Theodore Meade called the National Progressive Party, which won four seats. Mr Meade became Chief Minister on 10 October amid general optimism that a new, young and dynamic team would secure improvements for the island. In November 1992 Mr Meade survived a vote of no confidence in the Legislative Assembly following a civil law case concerning the ownership of his car. He was one of seven people who had their cars seized by Scotland Yard detectives investigating the export of stolen cars from Britain to Montserrat.

Government

A British dependent territory, Montserrat has a representative government with a ministerial system. Queen Elizabeth II is Head of State and is represented by a resident Governor (Mr Frank Savage was appointed Governor in 1993). The Government consists of a Legislative and an Executive Council, with elections being held every five years for membership in the former. The head of Government is called the Chief Minister; a Speaker presides over the seven-member Council of Representatives. As executive authority and head of the civil service, the Governor is responsible for defence, internal security and external affairs. A constitutional reform in 1989 added financial services to the Governor's powers and recognized Montserrat's right to self-determination. Montserratians continually discuss the pros and cons of opting for independence, but the official position is that economic independence must precede political independence, so colonial status may remain for many years to come.

The Economy

Tourism contributes about 20% of gdp, it is the largest supplier of foreign exchange and the Government actively encourages investment in tourism projects. The influx of foreign residents in the 1980s saw a sharp rise in real estate deals and building construction with a parallel dependence on imports of capital and consumer goods. Gross domestic product grew rapidly at the end of the 1980s, expanding by 12.8% in 1988, although a slower rate was recorded in 1989 because of the devastation wreaked by Hurricane Hugo. 95% of the housing stock was totally or partially destroyed and overall damage was estimated at US$260mn. Production and exports were disrupted, infrastructure severely damaged and the public sector's finances were hit by reduced income and greater expenditure demands. Tourist arrivals had been rising at an annual rate of about 7.5%, with earnings by nearly twice that rate, but even after strenuous efforts at rehabilitation only half the island's hotel capacity was available at the beginning of the 1989/90 winter season. Inflation rose because of shortages of all supplies, as stocks had been wiped out and food crops destroyed, while 100-150 people lost their jobs because of the temporary closure of the offshore American Medical School (now reopened on a smaller scale), hotels and retail businesses. However, the need for skilled construction workers forced a relaxation of work permit restrictions and contractors were brought in from Dominica and other islands. In 1990 the reconstruction boom caused gdp to expand by 13.5%, but its end in 1991 brought a contraction. By 1992 the economy was back to normal and gdp growth was a healthy 4.3%. One of the two major hotels, *Montserrat Springs*, had been fully refurbished and many new villas had been built. Real estate agents mushroomed to handle property sales, rentals and villa management for owners abroad. Work on the new pier was completed in 1993, allowing Plymouth to accommodate small cruise ships as well as cargo ships. Construction activity continues to be one of the motors of growth, helped by a public sector programme of spending on infrastructure. Construction and allied services such as real estate account for about 25% of gdp. A new government headquarters building, a police station and schools are all being built with state investment.

In 1992 16,510 tourists stayed on the island and 3,197 excursionists visited. In 1993, however, a spectacular increase of 15% and 141% respectively brought the figures up to 18,992 and 7,693. This trend continued in the first quarter of 1994 with a 29% rise in the number of stayover visitors from the USA and a 110% growth in excursionists arriving by sea, ie cruise ship passengers. The Government is preparing a tourism development plan which will promote Montserrat as an upmarket destination, stressing quality, not quantity, and limiting the growth of cruise ship arrivals so as not to damage the more lucrative stayover market. Tourism earnings in 1993 were EC$40m.

Agriculture accounts for only 5% of gdp and much of this is subsistence farming. Small scale commercial farming is being encouraged. An integrated cotton industry had been developing before the hurricane, but the looms used for processing the fine Sea Island cotton were very badly damaged by Hugo. There is a small manufacturing sector (primarily electric and electronic components which has returned to pre-hurricane levels).

In 1978 an offshore banking sector was set up, initially attracting little interest, but by 1987-88 showing rapid growth with the granting of 347 banking licences. However, no bank supervision was introduced and applicants were attracted mainly by the low cost of licences, the speed with which they were granted and the relatively few checks on ownership or accounts. Evidence of fraud on a large scale was investigated by Scotland Yard and the FBI in 1989; most banks were examined and had their licences revoked after it became clear that they had been used for money laundering and fraud. The Government has now reorganized the banking industry and introduced new legislation for the sector to avoid a repetition of previous problems, providing for higher fees and greater supervision to generate foreign confidence.

The Government is still grappling with the effects of the severe economic slump in 1991 and is seeking to rebuild the economic infrastructure which was so severely affected by Hurricane Hugo in 1989. Tourism has been identified as the sector most likely to boost economic recovery and support services in tourism, construction and agriculture have been targeted for growth. There is a proposal to expand the airport and upgrade it to a full regional service capacity runway.

Culture

The Irish influence can still be seen in national emblems. On arrival your passport is stamped with a green shamrock, the island's flag and crest show a woman, Erin of Irish legend, complete with her harp, and a carved shamrock adorns the gable of Government House. There are many Irish names, of both people and places, and the national dish, goat water stew, is supposedly based on a traditional Irish recipe. A popular local folk dance, the Bamchick-lay resembles Irish step dances and musical bands may include a fife and a drum similar to the Irish bodhran.

The African heritage dominates, however, whether it be in Caribbean musical forms like calypso (the veteran Arrow is now an international superstar), steel bands or the costumed masqueraders who parade during the Christmas season. Another element in the African cultural heritage are the Jumbie Dancers, who combine dancing and healing. Only those who are intimate with the island and its inhabitants will be able to witness their ceremonies, though. Local choirs, like the long-established Emerald Isle Community Singers, mix calypso with traditional folk songs and spirituals in their repertoire, and the String Bands of the island play the African shak-shak, made from a calabash gourd, as well as the imported Hawaiian ukelele.

There are drama and dance groups in Montserrat, which perform occasionally, and a single cinema, The Shamrock, in Plymouth. At the University Centre (the local education wing of the University of the West Indies School of Continuing Studies) poetry readings and writing workshops are held. Paintings by local artists can be seen at the Montserrat Museum (National Trust), a restored sugar mill tower on Richmond Hill (open Wednesday and Sunday, 1430-1700, entrance is free but donations accepted). The museum houses permanent exhibitions on 3 floors of Arawak and Carib artefacts found on the island, a complete collection of the attractive Montserratian stamps, newspaper cuttings, maps and prints. Lots of bits and pieces of geological, anthropological and historical interest. Worth a visit. George Martin's famed recording studios, the Air Studios, used to attract rock megastars such as Elton John, the Rolling Stones and Sting to the island, but the studios were closed after Hurricane Hugo.

Note: On Montserrat a Maroon is not a runaway slave but the local equivalent of "barn-raising", when everyone helps to build a house, lay a garden, etc.

Flora and Fauna

The island is lushly green, with natural vegetation confined mostly to the summits of hills, where elfin woodlands occur. At lower levels, fern groves are plentiful and lower still, cacti, sage bush and acacias. Flowers and fruit are typical of the Caribbean with many bay trees, from which bay oil (or rum) is distilled, the national tree, the mango and the national flower, the heliconia caribaea (known locally as "lobster claw"). Montserrat cannot boast many wild animals, although it shares the terrestrial frog, known as the mountain chicken, only with Dominica. Some 30 species of land birds breed on the island. At sunset many can be seen in the Fox's Bay Bird Sanctuary (see Excursions). Unique to Montserrat is the icterus oberi, a black and gold oriole named the national bird. Agoutis, bats and lizards including iguanas which can grow to over four feet in length, can all be found and tree frogs contribute to the island's "night-music".

Beaches and Watersports

Montserrat's beaches are volcanic "black" sand, which in reality means the sand may be a silvery grey or dark golden brown colour. The single white coral beach is at Rendezvous Bay in the N of the island, most easily reached by a boat from Old Road bay. The best beaches are Woodlands (with simple beach hut facilities) where you can safely swim through caves, Fox's Bay (nice beach but pebbly and rocky just offshore, snorkelling worthwhile at N end, shower provided in a tree in the car park), Emerald Isle (near the *Montserrat Springs Hotel*), Old Road (by the *Vue Pointe Hotel*) and Little Bay in the N. Yachting can be organized through the small Yacht Club at Wapping (T 6963), outside Plymouth (temporary membership available), where they have sunfish and lasers (Sunday is the official sailing day for members) or at *Vue Pointe*, which also has facilities for snorkelling and windsurfing. Danny's Watersports on Old Road beach, run by Danny Sweeney, offers boat trips (see also below, Rendezvous Bay), fishing trips (US$40/hour, maximum 3 fishermen), waterskiing (US$10), windsurfing (US$10/hour), snorkelling (EC$20/day), pedalos (US$10/hour) etc, T 5645. For yacht charters on a trimaran, the *John Willie*, Captain Martin Haxby can be contacted through the *Vue Pointe Hotel* (US$45 pp with open bar), which can also provide picnics if ordered the previous night. The *Montserrat Springs Hotel* can also arrange yacht charters. There are two whirlpool baths, one with hot mineral spring water, at the *Montserrat Springs Hotel*, just N of Plymouth (T 2481). A regional fishing tournament is held in May, usually on Labour Day.

Diving and Marine Life

Considerable effort is now being put into promoting Montserrat as a diving destination although the sport is still relatively undeveloped with much virgin diving. There is only one dive shop noted as courteous and professional: Sea Wolf Diving School, on Strand Street, near the Post Office, Box 289, Plymouth, T 6859/7807, F 3599, open 0900-1400, closed Wednesday and Sunday, all diving by appointment. Equipment rental, PADI courses and dive packages are available. A beach dive is US$40 including tank, BCD, weights and regulator, boat diving is US$55 for one tank, again including all equipment. They also have kayaks and you can paddle to the dive site, reported great fun. If you want to go off on your own, equipment hire is US$30 for tank, BCD, regulator and weights, and US$10 for mask, fins and snorkel.

Shore diving is good from Lime Kiln Bay, where there are ledges with coral, sponges and lots of fish; Woodlands Bay, where there is a shallow reef at 25-30 feet and at Little Bay. There are toilets, showers and changing rooms at Woodlands

Beach. There are some shallow dives from boats, suitable for novices or a second dive, but also deep dives for experienced divers. Pinnacle is a deep dive, dropping from 65 to 300 feet, where you can see brain coral, sponges and lots of fish. O'Garro's is a particularly good dive, a wall with lots of sponge and coral, barracuda and loggerhead turtle. The Government and the Caribbean Conservation Association have agreed to build an artificial reef at Fox's Bay, to be made from old vehicles and items damaged by Hurricane Hugo.

Other Sports

The Belham River Valley golf course (T 5220, F 8403) covers an area of nearly 100 acres and has 11 holes that can be played as 2 9-hole courses. Beautiful location edged by flowering trees. Hazards include iguanas who sometimes take the balls mistaking them for eggs. Rates are EC$50/day, EC$250/week, full equipment rental EC$7.50. An enormously popular Annual Open Tournament is held in early March; entries open in October.

Well-maintained floodlit tennis courts exist at the *Vue Pointe Hotel*, T 5211 and at the *Montserrat Springs Hotel*, T 2481. The Golf Club has 2 tennis courts which can be rented for EC$20. The *Vue Pointe* hosts an Open Tennis Tournament in January. Cricket is the national sport and played between February and July while football or soccer dominates sporting events during the last half of the year, both at Sturge Park. Basketball is becoming increasingly popular; so, too, volleyball. Cycling events are organized, with an around the island road race at Easter and a mountain bike competition in October. A 10 km road running race is held on Whit Monday.

Festivals

Not surprisingly in the "Emerald Isle", St

Patrick's Day (a national holiday) is celebrated on 17 March with a fund-raising dinner at St Patrick's Roman Catholic Church in Plymouth, cricket matches are held, and concerts, dances and feasting at St Patrick's village. Another national knees-up is August Monday, connected to Emancipation Day on 1 August, and St Peter's Anglican Fete is held in the village rectory grounds, but the island's main festival is the Christmas season, which starts around 12 December and continues through New Year's Day. Costumed masqueraders parade around the island in small bands, culminating in a Boxing Day competition in Plymouth's Sturge Park, where the finals of the calypso competition are also held. There is a queen show, a whole series of concerts (choirs and bands) and all the night clubs are in full swing. Festival Day starts at dawn on New Year's Eve with jump-ups, and competitions are held in the afternoon in Sturge Park. On New Year's Day there is a parade through Plymouth of all the costumed bands and prize winners, followed by more jump-ups through the night. It's very small-scale and low-key compared with a carnival like Trinidad's, but great fun and visitors are made to feel welcome.

PLYMOUTH

In the capital of *Plymouth* (population 2,500) there are a lot of very attractive old wooden buildings in a variety of ornate styles and colours. Luckily the older buildings suffered less damage during Hurricane Hugo than the newer ones, many of which were totally destroyed. You can tour the grounds of the Victorian Government House (week days, except Wednesdays, 1030-1200) but not the mansion itself, now closed to visitors, which houses a painting collection, antique furniture etc, on a green hill above Wapping Village. The older part of the house was all right after Hurricane Hugo, but the newer part was badly damaged.

The gardens were back to their former glory in 1990. St Anthony's Anglican Church is white-walled, airy, with a wooden interior. On Parliament Street is the Lands and Surveys Department and the National Trust. Here you can buy the Ordnance Survey map of Montserrat (1983, EC$15), which is recommended. Also on Parliament Street, in the Empire Building, is the Lloyds Shipping Agency (Llewellyn Wall), which has a notice up of shipping sailings, cargo only. The arrival of supplies is very important in Montserrat, where so much is imported. The town is well-kept and bustling, by a quiet harbour, and with an adequate range of restaurants, bars and gift shops. The local market is at its liveliest on Friday and Saturday. Outside festive seasons like Christmas there is little nightlife in Plymouth, most of the action is in the larger hotels or discos outside town.

Excursions

Montserrat is easy to explore as distances are short, roads good, and trails well-maintained. Ask at the tourist office about expeditions organized by the local hiking group (visitors welcome). House and garden tours are organized by the Rotary Club, in season contact the Rotary Club direct, but out of season call Gary Swanston, T 2998 (home) or 2075 (work).

Little remains of the Old Fort on St George's Hill except some cannons and a recently restored powder magazine, but the site offers a commanding view over Plymouth and environs and it is very pleasant. More cannons and the ruins of a small fort are located at the Bransby Point Fortification, from where there are lovely views across the sea to Plymouth in one direction and Old Road Bay in the other (below the Point are two sandy beaches where the sea is a bit rough). The Fox's Bay Bird Sanctuary on the SW coast is best visited after 1800, when egrets and other birds return to roost at sunset. This

15-acre mangrove swamp and woodland lies next to an excellent beach, so a full day can happily be spent in the area. Trails are marked.

Popular excursions and hikes S of Plymouth include Chances Peak, Galway's Plantation, Galway's Soufrière and the Great Alps Waterfall. From St Patrick's onwards, you will be pestered by guides offering their services and insisting that you will get lost without them. They are difficult to shake off. If you have a decent map, such as the Ordnance Survey map, you will be fine on your own. However, if you have children with you it may be worth hiring a surefooted, adult guide, who can assist them over gulleys and rivers, particularly at Galway's Soufrière and the Great Alps Waterfall. If you can be at the turn-off for **Chances Peak** by 0830, the Cable and Wireless engineers, who make the ascent twice a week,

1. Methodist Church
2. National Trust & Lands and Surveys Department
3. Chamber of Commerce
4. Post Office
5. Philatelic Office
6. Barclays Bank
7. Bank of Montserrat
8. Royal Bank of Canada
9. Llewellyn Wall (Lloyds Shipping Agency)
10. CaribWorld Travel, Montserrat Airways
11. Montserrat Aviation Services
12. Montserrat Enterprises
13. Neville Bradshaw Agencies
14. Papa's Supermarket
15. Montserrat Tapestries
16. Jacquie Ryan Enterprises
17. Oriole Plaza Hotel
18. Emerald Cafe
19. Evergreen Restaurant
20. Casuarina's
21. Tourist Office

PLYMOUTH

will probably take you half way up or you can drive up to where the track starts. It's a steep, hard, hot climb, with over 2,000 steps; one to 2 hours from the end of the road to the top, go on a clear day for brilliant views all the way up. Legend has it that a mermaid lives in the shallow lake (more like a swamp) on top of the mountain. Take plenty of drinking water with you. You need a machete to hack the 50 yards from the lake through the forest to reach the crater rim. It is a stunning 500-feet drop to the bottom but with the rim covered in vegetation it is hard to tell where solid ground ends.

The ruins of **Galway's Plantation** can be reached via a paved road S out of Plymouth, which turns E at St Patrick's. This 18th-century sugar estate is the subject of an ambitious archaeological project which has identified the various stone buildings like the Great House on one side of the road, the tower mill and the boiling house on the other (entrance free). The ruins are in quite a good state of repair and are in a lovely location with the peaks above and sea views below. If you continue up the road you reach **Galway's Soufrière**. From a lookout point where you get a general view, a path leads steeply down to the bubbling, sulphurous, steaming, stinking vents and springs. The path is not difficult, although it can be a bit of a scramble in places, but if you want, a guide will take you for EC$20-30. Guides will also take you to the Bamboo Forest in the S mountains, a 1½ hour walk from the car park at Galway's Soufrière, EC$100 for 1-2 people. Another soufrière, Gages, is no longer accessible; visitors have been prohibited since the path was destroyed in an earthquake. On the other side of the island, a trail to the ruins of Roche's Estate has been reopened but this hike involves negotiating Ghaut Mefraimie and should be attempted only by the reasonably fit. Joemac of Long Ground (T 4468) is very responsible and will advise on the state of the trail and provide a guide if required.

The Great Alps Waterfall is 70 feet high and reached by a woodland trail that takes about 45 minutes to walk. From St Patrick's, drive along the coast to the White River. Just before the bridge over the river turn left towards a small hut (which sells drinks when open) and a small car park by a tree where guides congregate. Continue on foot on the track out of the car park. Cross the stream, pass a big cashew tree and a little further on is a path going left through thorn scrub, goats etc. It is an easy path to follow, crossing and recrossing the White River (a misnomer, it is yellow ochre from the sulphur in the mountains from which it springs). After a short while you get into a more enclosed, wooded ascent up the river which is cooler and more green and tropical. The waterfall drops down a sheer cliff into a small pool. Take a sulphurous shower, have a picnic, take your litter home. Guide rates are EC$15 for one person, EC$10 pp for 2, less for more.

A drive along the dramatic cliffs of the N coast is a must. Going N from Plymouth along the W side you come to **Carr's Bay** (bus from Plymouth EC$3), from where there is a little road which goes on to **Little Bay**, but it is in very bad condition and it is best to walk round Potato Hill from Carr's Bay. There are plans for a large tourist resort to be built at Little Bay, where there is a nice beach, but at the moment it is completely empty. From Little Bay you can follow a track through a gate at the end of the beach for a stiff hike along a very steep mountainous trail (not suitable for children) to the white sands of **Rendezvous Bay**. Take food and water, it is a long, hot walk. Alternatively, take a boat. Murphy's at the junction in Carr's Bay, offers boat rides to Rendezvous Bay for about EC$50 for 2 people, while Danny's at Old Road Bay by the *Vue Pointe Hotel* charges US$20 pp in a Boston Whaler, returning to pick you up whenever you wish. Two-hour sails are also on offer, but you will not get as far as Rendezvous Bay and back. Rendezvous Bay is the only white sand beach on the island and it is worth making the effort to go there. There is little shade, so take precautions. Also watch out for the spiney sea urchins among the rocks at the N end and avoid the poisonous manchineel trees.

Driving round the N of the island is twisty and steep in places but the road is good on the main route. From the Carr's Bay area you can see Redonda and beyond to Nevis; from the NE you can see Antigua and from the E Guadeloupe is just visible. There is a good view of the airport as you come round the NE coast and you can watch the small planes landing below you. Turning off the road before you get to Harris and continuing S on a paved road you come to Tuitt's, where Mr Green has a monument which is a nice place to visit for a picnic. T 2494 and ask for Mistress Green for opening hours. The paved road continues to Long Ground but thereafter becomes a trail, impassable for cars. Just the other side of Harris is Farrell's Estate, which used to be the main rum producer and made a 150° proof rum called 'Plastic'. However, the estate was bought some time ago by a US missionary who stopped sugar production and instead reared cattle.

Day excursions are offered by Montserrat Airways (T 2713/4 or UK T 0279 680453) who do charters on request (see below). Charters can also be arranged by Carib Aviation from Antigua throughout the Caribbean T Antigua 3147, F 3125.

The sites of Montserrat can be explored in two or three days, but such speed would force visitors to neglect the gentle charms of the island which can best be appreciated by leisurely strolls and unhurried meals, swimming, and encounters with the delightful local people.

INFORMATION FOR VISITORS

● Documents

A valid passport is required except for US, Canadian and British visitors, who must only show proof of citizenship for stays of up to 6 months. Visas may be required for visitors from Haiti, Cuba and Eastern bloc countries, which can be obtained from British consulate offices. Those without an onward or return ticket may be required to deposit a sum of money adequate for repatriation.

● How To Get There

By air Blackburne Airport, on the E coast some 11 miles from Plymouth, has recently been expanded and has night landing facilities. LIAT (Lower George Street, PO Box 257, Plymouth, T 2533/2362, at airport T 4200/4400) and Montserrat Airways provide about 17 flights daily from Antigua (an 18-min hop), where there are direct connections with international carriers like British Airways, BWIA, Air Canada and various American airlines. LIAT also has a daily flight from St Thomas, via Sint Maarten and St Kitts. There are connections with other islands via LIAT, the charter companies, Carib Aviation (see above) or Montserrat Airways (Box 183, reservations T 5342 or airport T 6494 or T 2713 at Carib World Travel, F 6205, or UK T 0279 680453, F 0279 680356). A flight to Montserrat from Antigua costs US$33 one way.

By sea The Atlantic Lines, Harrison Line and Nedlloyd provide regular services to the port at Plymouth. If you enquire at a shipping agent in Plymouth you may be able to arrange passage on the cargo boat which goes to Guadeloupe, but this is difficult. The Customs Department is open Mon, Tues, Thur, Fri 0800-1600, Wed and Sat 0800-1130. The jetty was washed away in the 1989 hurricane but a new 75 metre pier with berthing capacity for 2 ships was built and in operation by mid 1993. Small cruise ships can be accommodated here.

There is a departure tax of EC$20/US$8 for all aged 12 and over and a security tax of EC$5/US$2.

● Internal Travel

Driving is on the left. Roads are fairly good, but narrow. Drivers travel fast, passing on blind corners with much use of their horns. There are several **car hire** companies (the cars are mostly Japanese). Car hire rates are similar in all agencies: Montserrat Enterprises in Marine Drive, Box 58, T 2431, F 4660, hires out small cars for US$45/day or US$210/week, US$230/week with air conditioning, jeeps for US$50/day or US$40 for 2-6 days; NBA car rentals in Lime Court Building, Parliament Street, Box 270, T 2070/5270, F 5069; Jefferson's Car Rental, Dagenham, T 2126; Ethelyne's Car Rentals, Weekes Road, Box 309, T 2855; Pauline's Car Rental, Church Road, T 2345, F 2434; Edith's Car Rental, George Street, T 6696; Bennette Roach Realty Co, Parliament Street, Box 306, T 3844, F 2052; Reliable Car Rental, Marine Drive, Box 442, T 6990/2269, F 8070, for mokes and pick ups; you can also ask taxi drivers at the airport about car rental, some (eg John Roach) have cars available for US$40/day. You have to pay for half a tank of petrol and usually accept liability up to EC$2,000. With a valid driving licence, you can obtain a local 3-month licence (EC$30) at the airport immigration desk or the traffic office in the Treasury Building on Strand Street in Plymouth (open from 0830-1200, 1300-1430 Mon-Fri).

The standard fare in **minibuses** is EC$2-3. Some mini-buses to villages in the N leave from Papa's Supermarket on Church Road, those to the E go from the end of Evergreen Road and those to the S depart from opp the Royal Bank of Canada on George Street. As a general rule, buses run into town in the morning with an immediate return to source, doing the trip about 4 times a day. Outside the fixed times and routes they operate as taxis and journeys can be arranged with drivers for an extra fee.

Taxis are usually small buses, which can be shared and there is a taxi stand by the Clock Tower War Memorial at the harbour. Fares are set—the tariff list can be obtained from the tourist office (see address below), eg airport to Plymouth EC$29, Plymouth to *Vue Pointe Hotel* EC$13; a sightseeing tour is EC$30 per hour. Drivers are usually knowledgeable about historical sites and are happy to wait while passengers hike to beauty spots, or return at an appointed time. Fares from Plymouth to the Great Alps Waterfall EC$60 return, to Galways Soufrière EC$60 return, to St George's Hill EC$21, including waiting and return. John Ryner is rec, T 2190, also Adolphus Morson, T 4450, helpful, punctual and reliable.

For the fit, hire a mountain bike from Island Bikes of Harney Street, Plymouth, T 4696, F 5552, prices start at EC$280 per week, EC$54 per day or EC$11 per hour.

Hitching is safe and easy because the local people are so friendly. Similarly, don't be afraid to pick them up when you are driving. Out-of-town hotels like the *Vue Pointe* provide a free bus service into the capital for their staff, phone Carol Osborne at the hotel to see if there is space.

● **Where To Stay**

There are only a couple of large hotels and a handful of guesthouses. Most tourism is accommodated in villas and apartments and resort developments have not yet arrived on the island. By far the most welcoming of the large hotels and the centre of social activities for the island is the *Vue Pointe* (PO Box 65; T 5210, F 4813) which charges from US$126 for a double, EP, to US$166 for a rondavel (small cottage), falling to US$80d and US$106d (children under 12 sharing with 2 adults free) in summer, 10 rooms have a/c, fans, restaurant, beach bar, lounge bar, phone, cable TV, entertainment evenings, conference facilities, swimming pool, tennis courts, free transport to Plymouth. *Montserrat Springs Hotel* (PO Box 259, T 2481-2, F 4070), the other large hotel, was completely refurbished after Hurricane Hugo with 46 a/c rooms to a high standard, cable TV, phone, fans, US$145-165d winter, one-bedroomed efficiency suites US$205-215 winter, 2-bedroomed suites US$320-335 winter, 20-30% cheaper in summer, 2 tennis courts, 70-foot pool, jacuzzi, beach bar, pool bar, restaurant, conference facilities, friendly. *Providence Estate House*, St Peter's T 6476, a restored plantation house on hillside with seaview, pool, TV, gardens, large room US$80d, smaller room US$60d, with bathroom and kitchenette; *Flora Fountain* (PO Box 373, T 6092/3, F 2568) on Lower Dagenham Road, 18 rooms, a/c, private bathrooms and balconies, restaurant, US$85d winter, US$70 summer, EP. *Niggy's Bistro* at Aymers Ghaut, Kinsale, offers simple accommodation at US$15 single and US$20 double, 5 small, spartan rooms, on either side of bar, shared bathrooms, pleasant, friendly, but no peace and quiet, run by Anglo Americans Tony and Niggy Overman, T 7489/2690, F 3257; *Marie's Guesthouse*, run by Marie and Austin Bramble, PO Box 28, T 2745, F 3599, close to the road and downwind of the power plant but any noise drowned by frogs at night, US$30d, 4 bedrooms, double or single beds, bathroom, lots of towels, large, shared kitchen with starter food pack, cable TV, friendly, welcoming, highly rec. **Belham Valley Apartments**, PO Box 409, T 5553, F 3163, one and 2-bedroomed cottages overlooking Belham River and golf course, beach 5 mins walk, self-catering, kitchens, TV, stereo, phone, maid service available, US$250/week summer, US$350/week, winter, daily rates offered.

The Board of Tourism has a complete list of other smaller establishments, apartments and rooms to let, with some 9 agencies renting and selling apartments and villas. Montserrat Enterprises Ltd, PO Box 58, Marine Drive, Plymouth, T 2431, F 4660, has an extensive list of pleasant villas to rent, average price for one or 2-bedroomed villa with pool, US$400-600 low season, but the same property rents for US$550-1,000 in winter. Jacquie Ryan Real Estate, PO Box 425, Shamrock House, Marine Drive, Plymouth, T 2055, F 3257, villas available at similar rates. Neville Bradshaw Agencies, PO Box 270, Plymouth, T 5270, F 5069 has 2-bedroomed properties from US$325 in summer, highly rec. Villas of Montserrat, PO Box 421, Plymouth, T 5513, F 7850, have some very grand properties at US$1,650 in summer and US$1,950 in winter for 6 people or less, including private charter from Antigua.

Of 2 residential developments in Montserrat, Woodsville Condominiums and Town Houses, T 5119, F 5230, offer one-three-bedroomed properties to purchase from US$70,000 and also rentals from US$60/night, US$350/week in winter, US$35 and US$200 in summer. The other residential development Isles Bay Plantation offers rental of 2 of its properties to give potential purchasers a taste of elegant living; prices to purchase start at US$245,000 and rentals US$1,500 low season and US$2,000 high season per week. They all have 40-foot pools, PO Box 64, T 4842, F 4843, UK: 071 482 1418, F 071 482 1071. Agencies usually include maid service most days. **Shamrock Villas**, PO Box 221, T 2431-2, F 4660, villas on Richmond Hill, 3 mins from beach, 50 one/two-bedroomed units with fans, pool, patio, car rentals available, US$450-550/week in winter, US$350-400 summer. For cheaper self-catering accommodation without maid service, **Lime Court Apartments** in Plymouth, PO Box 250, T 69851, F 2513, F 5069, are sometimes vacant, one and 2-bedroomed apartments with balcony overlooking the sea, rather noisy, room dark but clean, about US$30-45 a day plus tax or US$150-225 a week with monthly or long term rates avail-

able, car hire offered; **Fairways Apartments**, Box 420, T 5077 3938, F 3126, overlooks golf course, one bedroom, bathroom, small living room with fridge, kettle and toaster, patio, plunge pool, US$60d winter, US$45d summer. Bennette Roach Realty Co, PO Box 306, T 3844/5495, F 2052, specialize in home rentals as well as real estate sales and car hire; also Caribbee Agencies Ltd, Box 223, T 7444, F 7426; Dream Home Realtors, Box 28, T 2883, F 6069; Pauline's Real Estate, Box 171, T 3846, F 2434; Properties Ltd, Box 495, T/F 2986; Runaway Travel Ltd Real estate, Box 54, T 2800, F 6207. Tradewinds Real Estate, Box 365, T 2004, F 6229.

There is a 7% Government tax on MAP rates, regardless of which meal plan is chosen, and a 10% service charge is usually added.

● **Where To Eat**

A large frog called mountain chicken, indigenous here and in Dominica, is the local delicacy; that and goat water stew are the most commonly found local items on the menu; most other things, like steak and sole are imported. The **Belham Valley** (PO Box 409, T 5553), which also has 4 apartments to rent, quite elegant, reservations required, lunch 1200-1400, Tues-Fri, dinner from 1830, Tues-Sun, Chinese specials Thur. On Wed nights the place to go is the **Vue Pointe Hotel**, T 5210, for a barbeque and steel band, food served from 1930, EC$66 set price includes all the salad and sweets you can eat, EC$33 for children if they eat chicken, drinks extra, good band, food from 2100 less impressive. A Sun lunchtime barbeque is US$35 in summer and US$38.50 in winter, half price for children under 10. **The Nest** at Old Road Bay, for sandwiches from EC$8, roti: EC$8.50, Caesar salad EC$11, excellent menu, quiet, pleasant, 1030-2000 every day except Mon, T 5834. Local cuisine can be found in several **Plymouth** restaurants: the **Emerald Café**, T 3821, lunch and dinner, a meal for 2 with wine US$52, pleasant, reasonable; **The Blue Dolphin**, T 3263/3388, mountain chicken, lobster, fish and steaks, lunch and dinner, catering service available, overlooks Plymouth harbour; the **Evergreen**, T 3540, fast food and pastries, daily specials, ice cream, open weekdays 0700-2200, later at weekends; **The Golden Nugget** on Lovers Lane at the foot of St George's Hill, E of Plymouth, T 7413, 3-course meal EC$35-40, book in advance and order main course choice, rec. In nearby **Wapping** the **Yacht Club**,

T 2237, open Tues-Fri for lunch and dinner for non-members, music Fri from 2200, EC$3 cover charge; the *Oasis*, T 2328, Wapping Road, open daily 1000-2400, British-run, meal for 2 with wine EC$100, basic food; the *Iguana*, meal for 2 with wine EC$140, very good, also pizzas, rec; *The Casuarina*, bar and restaurant, continental and Italian food, very popular Fri evenings with students from medical school, T 7289. Also in Wapping are bars such as *The Inn on Sugar Bay*, a restaurant/bay/nightclub with live music twice a week, snacks served at lunch and dinner, T 5067. *The Golden Apple* on the main road through Cork Hill, T 2187, serves 3-course meal for EC$35, large quantities of well-cooked vegetables, highly rec, phone the day before to book and order meat/fish course (**NB** mutton means goat, lamb means sheep). A must is *Annie Morgan's* at St John's for goat water, open Fri and Sat at lunchtime, other days by arrangement if you can arrange a party of 10 or so, T 5419. *Niggy's Bistro* in Kinsale, T 7489, bar indoors, restaurant seating on the porch, steak or pasta and salad from EC$15, wine from EC$25 a bottle, food and service highly rec, recorded jazz and blues music drowned out on Fri and Sat by Champion Sound down the road. *The Village Place*, T 5202, in the pretty hamlet of Salem is famous for its chicken, prepared in gregarious proprietor Andy's special sauce. A night club with food is the *Nepcoden* in Weekes, which serves excellent rotis.

● **Tipping**

10% service charge is usually added to bills. Taxi drivers happily accept a tip but there is no pressure to offer one.

● **Shopping**

Wed is half day closing. Sat is market day on the Plymouth waterfront. Sea Island cotton or goods manufactured from this pricey but soft, comfortable fabric; tapestries and wall hangings by local artists; glass and ceramics produced at a studio in Olveston; leather goods from locally-tanned leather; small but delightful range of post cards of naive paintings. The Sea Island Cotton shop has very little in stock, one loom has been repaired following Hugo damage to make table cloths, mats, shawls etc. Tapestries of Montserrat on Parliament Street, T 2520, F 3599, sells hand woven items. Montserrat Shirts has masses of T-shirts in attractive designs for all ages. Jus Looking, on George Street or at the airport, T 4076/4040, sells Caribelle Batiks, Haitian lacquered boxes and the Sunny Caribbee range of spices. Sea Wolf Dive Shop by Post Office sells hand made jewellery and gifts and cards. Montserrat's beautiful stamps can be bought at the Post Office (T 2996, F 2042) or at the Philatelic Bureau. Ram's Supermarket in Plymouth near Police Station, probably the best stocked and good for currency exchange (even better than the banks). Supermarkets stock a variety of expensive imported food and drink to cater for the demands of the growing expat population, but the choice is fairly limited. Captain Weekes supermarket on the road out of town going S has a good supply of drink but poor stocks of provisions. Peter & Christina's, a 24-hour bakery on George Street, beyond the Catholic Church on the way to the airport, sells excellent and varied breads and pasties, rec. Just before you get there, on the outskirts of town, a green painted house on your left sells home made ice cream in tropical fruit flavours. The local ginger beer is delicious.

● **Cost Of Living**

Middle to upmarket prices, generally speaking, so it is not an island for back-packers and the impecunious, although cheap accommodation can be found in private homes and guest houses and eating out can be reasonably priced if you stick to local foods and drink. It's cheap and easy to get around on local minibuses or by hitching.

● **Currency**

The currency is the East Caribbean dollar (EC$). The exchange rate is fixed at EC$2.67 = US$1, but there are variations depending on where you change your money (eg Ram's Supermarket gives EC$2.70).

● **Health**

With its bracing climate and clean, plentiful water, Montserrat is a healthy island. Glendon Hospital in Plymouth (T 2552, emergency 999), with 68 beds, also offers a range of services but for specialist treatment patients are sent to larger centres in the region. There is a government health service and also private practitioners. During the rainy season there are mosquitoes and "no-see-um's", but a good anti-bug repellent should suffice. Rooms that lack air-conditioning often provide mosquito nets for beds. No poisonous snakes or insects.

● **Climate**

Although tropical, the humidity in Montserrat is low and there is often rain overnight which clears the atmosphere. The average temperature is 26-27°C with little variation from one season to another. The wettest months, according to official statistics, are April and May plus July through September, although weather patterns are changing here, as elsewhere.

● Clothing

The island is not a formal place, but skimpy clothing on the streets of Plymouth and nude or topless bathing are frowned upon. Informal, lightweight clothes are suitable for virtually every occasion but evenings can be cool and require jackets, wraps or sweaters. There is a laundromat with dry cleaning facilities on Church Road.

● Banks

There are 2 international banks: The Royal Bank of Canada on Parliament Street PO Box 222, T 2426-8, F 3991 (open Mon-Thur 0800-1500, Fri 0800-1700), and Barclays Bank on Church Road PO Box 141, T 2501-3, F 3801 (open Mon-Thur 0800-1500, Fri 0800-1700). The Bank of Montserrat on Parliament Street, PO Box 10, T 3843/3188, F 3189/3163, is open Mon, Tues, Thur 0800-1500, Wed 0800-1300, Fri 0800-1700. Carib World Travel, on Parliament Street is the American Express agent, T 2713/4/2014.

● Hours Of Business

Government: 0800-1200; 1300-1600 (Mon-Fri); Business 0800-1200; 1300-1600 except Wed, 0800-1300, Sat 0800-1200, 1300-1530 (or 0800-1300).

● National Holidays

New Year's Day, St Patrick's Day (17 March), Good Fri, Easter Mon, Labour Day (first Mon in May), Whit Mon (7th Mon after Easter), first Mon in August, Christmas Day, Boxing Day (26 December) and Festival Day (31 December).

● Time Zone

Atlantic Standard Time, 4 hours behind GMT, 1 ahead of EST.

● Electric Current

Electric current is 220 volts, 60 cycles but newer buildings also carry 110 volts.

● Postal Services

The main Post Office is in Plymouth (open 0815-1555 Mon, Tues, Thur, Fri, but 0815-1125 on Wed and Sat) and there is a Philatelic Bureau, also in the capital, selling the attractive Montserrat stamps to collectors.

● Telecommunications

Cable and Wireless (West Indies) Ltd (Houston Street, T 2112, F 3599, open Mon-Thur 0730-1800, Fri 0730-2000, Sat 0730-1800) operates an excellent telecommunications system with a new digital telephone system, international dialling, telegraph, telex, facsimile and data facilities. Phone cards are available, as are credit card service, toll free 800 service and cellular phones. The international code for Montserrat is 809-491, followed by a 4-digit number.

● Media

Satellite TV Cable is operational in most areas, and stations broadcasting from nearby islands can be received. Radio Montserrat ZJB (government owned) provides daily broadcasting services, as does GEM Radio, the exclusive outlet for the Associated Press. Radio Antilles was expected to re-start in 1992 in conjunction with the BBC, who have a management contract. There is one weekly newspaper the *Montserrat Reporter*.

● Travel Agents

Montserrat Aviation Services Ltd, Lower George Street, Box 257, Plymouth, T 2533/2362, F 4632, or at airport T 4200, sales agent for Liat and BWIA, day tours on

Montserrat and to neighbouring islands. Carib World Travel, Parliament Street, Box 183, T 2713-4/2014, F 3354, sales agent for Montserrat Airways. Also Runaway Travel Ltd, Marine Drive, Box 54, T 2776/2800. Island tours can be arranged through hotels or the Tourist Office too. Ask the Board of Tourism about registered tour guides (see below).

● **Tourist Office**

Montserrat Board of Tourism, PO Box 7, Plymouth, T 2230, F 7430, on Marine Drive, helpful, plenty of information. There is a Tour Guide Association with a membership of 21 trained tour guides. The Montserrat Chamber of Commerce on Marine Drive (PO Box 384) complements the Tourist Office and offers a business directory, T 3640, F 4660. In the **USA**: Medhurst & Associates Inc, The Huntington Atrium, 775 Park Avenue, Huntington, NY 11743, T 516-425-0900, F 516-425-0903 or Caribbean Tourism Organization, 20 East 46th Street, New York, NY 10017-2417, T 212 682-0435, F 212 697-4258; in **Canada**: New Concepts - Canada, 2455 Cawthra Road Suite 70, Mississauga, Ontario L5A 3PL, T 905-803-0131, F 905-803-0132; in the **UK**: RBPR, 3 Epirus Road, London SW6 7UJ, T 071 730-7144, F 071 938-4793; in **Germany**: Montserrat Tourist Board/West India Committee, Lomer Strasse 28, 2000 Hamburg 70, T 49-40-695-88-46, F 49-40-380-51.

In the Macmillan series, *Montserrat: Emerald Isle of the Caribbean*, by Howard A Fergus, has been rec, his *History of Montserrat* was to be published by Macmillan in 1994; also *Alliouagana Folk*, by J A George Irish (Jagpi 1985), as an introduction to Montserratian language, proverbs and traditions.

CARIBBEAN ISLANDS

1:17.5M

	Relief
Metres	
5000	
3000	
2000	
1000	
500	
200	
0	Sea Level
200	
2000	
4000	
6000	
8000	
Metres	

0   100   200   300   400 km

ATLANTIC OCEAN

Tropic of Cancer

Iana Cay
Iana Cays
Mayaguana I.
Turks and Caicos Islands
(U.K.)
Caicos Is. Turks Is.

Great Inagua I.

Tortue
DOMINICAN Puerto Plata
Cap Haitien Valderro Santiago
onaives **REPUBLIC** Samana
St. Marc La Vega San Francisco
de Macoris
HAITI S. Pedro
Port-au- St. Cristobal S. Francisco
Prince Barahona **Santo** Romana Saona
Domingo
Hispaniola

Antilles

Puerto Rico Trench

8526

Anegada
San Juan Carolina Virgin Is. (U.K.)
Bayamon St. Thomas Virgin Gorda Anguilla (U.K.)
Arecibo Sint Maarten St. Martin (Fr.)
Mayaguez Caguas St. Croix (Neth.) St. Barthélemy (Fr.)
Mona Ponce Virgin Is. Sint Saba Barbuda (U.K.)
Vieques (U.S.A.) Eustatius **ANTIGUA**
PUERTO (Neth.) St. John's
RICO **ST. KITTS**
(U.S.A.) **NEVIS**
Montserrat
(U.K.) Point-à-Pitre
Guadeloupe (Fr.) Marie Galante
Basse Terre (Fr.)
Roseau **DOMINICA**

Leeward Islands

Lesser

C A R I B B E A N

S E A

Antilles

Fort-de- **Martinique** (Fr.)
France
Castries **ST.**
LUCIA

Windward Islands

Kingstown
ST. VINCENT AND **Bridgetown**
THE GRENADINES **BARBADOS**
Carriacou
C. Gallinas Aruba **GRENADA**
Paraguana (Neth.) St. George's
Castilletes Pen Bonaire Orchila
Gulf of (Neth.) La Blanquilla
Riohacha **Venezuela** Willemstad Los
Sa. Nevada Curaçao Roques
de Sta. Marta (Neth.) Tortuga Margarita I. La Asunción **TOBAGO**
S. Cristobal Punto Fijo Porlamar Scarborough
La Laguo Coro La Guaira Carúpano Paria Pen. Port of Spain
Valledupar **Maracaibo** Pto. Maracay Cumaná Güiria **Arima**
Machiques Altagracia Cabello **Caracas** Pto. La Cruz Gulf of **TRINIDAD**
Cabimas San Valencia Los Barcelona Paria Caripito San Fernando
Lago Felipe Teques Atragracia Anaco Maturín *Serpent's Mouth*
Maracaibo Yaritagua San de Urituca Cantaura *Orinoco*
La Concepción Carora Carlos El Tigre Uracoa Tucupita **Delta**
Maguin Barquisimeto Zaraza Barrancas Curiapo
Trujillo Araure Valle de San José Ciudad
Ocaña Valera Acarigua San la Pascua de Guanipa Bolívar Ciudad
Cúcuta Bocono Carlos Guayana
Merida Guanare El Baúl Calabozo Mapire Upata
Pamplona Barinas
Puerto de Nutrias Guanarito Cabruta La Paragua El Callao
Cordillera Apure
Bucaramanga San Cristobal San Fernando Ciudad Bolívar El Dorado Cuyuni Parika
Piedecuesta de Apure Bartica
San Gil Arauca

V E N E Z U E L A

Socorro 5493

WILL YOU HELP US?

We do all we can to get our facts right in the **CARIBBEAN ISLANDS HANDBOOK**. Each section is thoroughly revised each year, but the territory is vast and our eyes cannot be everywhere. If you have enjoyed a tour, trek, beach, walk, dive, sailing trip, museum or any other activity and would like to share it, please write with all the details.

We are always pleased to hear about any restaurants, bars or hotels you have enjoyed. When writing, please give the year on the cover of your *Handbook* and the page number referred to. In return we will send you details of our special guidebook offer.

Thank you very much indeed for your help.

TRADE & TRAVEL
Handbooks

Write to The Editor, *Caribbean Islands Handbook,* Trade & Travel, 6 Riverside Court, Lower Bristol Road, Bath BA2 3DZ. England

NETHERLAND ANTILLES
The 3 S's

CONTENTS

THE "3 S's", Saba, Sint Eustatius (Statia) and Sint Maarten lie 880 km N of the rest of the Netherlands Antilles group lying off the coast of Venezuela, and known as the ABC islands (Aruba, Bonaire and Curaçao). Each has a distinct character and flavour, Statia being the poorest, Saba the smallest and Sint Maarten the most developed and richest.

Lacking in natural resources, they each depend to a greater or lesser degree on tourism for their foreign exchange revenues, but are developing their potential in different ways. Saba's strength is the richness of the underwater world surrounding the island and is noted for its pristine diving locations. Sint Maarten has the best beaches and resorts, while St Eustatius is promoting its historical associations.

Although the "3 S's" precede the ABC islands in this Handbook, the introduction to the Netherlands Antilles group and much of the general Information for Visitors is contained in the ABC chapter.

SABA

SABA, pronounced "Say-bah", is the smallest of this group of islands. Only five miles square, it lies 28 miles S of St Maarten and 17 miles NW of St Eustatius. The island is an extinct volcano which seems to shoot out of the sea, green with lush vegetation but without beaches. In fact there is only one inlet amidst the sheer cliffs where boats can come in to dock. The highest peak of this rugged island is the 870-metre Mount Scenery, also known as "the Mountain", and because of the difficult terrain there were no roads on Saba until 1943, only hand-carved steps in the volcanic rock.

Although the island was once inhabited by Caribs, relics of whom have been found, there is no trace of their ancestry in the local inhabitants. The population numbers about 1,100, half of them white (descendants of Dutch, English and Scots settlers) and half black. Their physical isolation and the difficult terrain has caused them to develop their ingenuity to enable them to live harmoniously with their environment. Originally farmers and seafarers, the construction in 1963 of the Juancho E Yrausquin Airport on the only flat part of the island, and the serpentine road which connects it tenuously to the rest of the island, brought a new and more lucrative source of income: tourism. However, the island's geographical limitations have meant that tourism has evolved in a small, intimate way. About 25,000 tourists visit each year, most of whom are day trippers. Those who stay are few enough to get to know the friendliness and hospitality of their hosts, who all speak English, even though Dutch is the official language. The decision in 1993 by the Dutch Government to end 'driver licence tourism' was expected to cut stayover numbers considerably. Previously, driving tests taken in Saba were valid in Holland, where it is more difficult to secure a licence. The system brought Saba an income of about US$300,000 a year. The only other major source of income is the US Medical School, opened in 1993, which attracts students from overseas. Development is small scale; the island still merits its unofficial title, "the Unspoiled Queen".

History

Saba was first discovered by Columbus on his second voyage in 1493 but not colonized. Sir Francis Drake sighted it in 1595, as did the Dutchmen Pieter Schouten in 1624 and Piet Heyn in 1626. Some shipwrecked Englishmen landed in 1632, finding it uninhabited. In 1635 the French claimed it but in the 1640s the Dutch settled it, building communities at Tent Bay and The Bottom. However, it was not until 1816 that the island became definitively Dutch, the interregnum being marked by 12 changes in sovereignty, with the English, Dutch, French and Spanish all claiming possession.

Fauna and Flora

Vegetation on Saba changes according to altitude and a walk up Mount Scenery reveals many different types of tropical vegetation. At an altitude of 1,600-2,000 feet there is secondary rain forest with trees of between 15 and 30 feet high. Further up there are tree ferns of 13-16 feet, then palm trees, then at 2,700 feet the cloud forest begins, where you find the mountain mahogany tree (*freziera undulata*). Wildlife on the island is limited to lizards (*anolis sabanus*), iguanas and a harmless racer snake, but over 60 species of birds have been recorded, with many

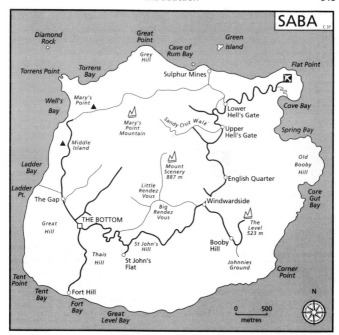

SABA
C 37

Diamond
Rock

Great
Point

Green
Island

Grey
Hill

Cave of
Rum Bay

Flat Point

Torrens Point

Torrens
Bay

Sulphur Mines

Well's
Bay

Mary's
Point

Cove Bay

Mary's
Point
Mountain

Sandy Cruz Walk

Lower
Hell's Gate

Upper
Hell's Gate

Spring Bay

Middle
Island

Old
Booby
Hill

Ladder
Bay

Mount
Scenery
887 m

English Quarter

Core
Gut
Bay

Ladder
Pt.

The Gap

Little
Rendez
Vous

Windwardside

Great
Hill

THE BOTTOM

Big
Rendez
Vous

The
Level
523 m

St John's
Hill

Booby
Hill

Thais
Hill

St John's
Flat

Johnnies
Ground

Corner
Point

Tent
Point

Fort Hill

Tent
Bay

Fort
Bay

Great
Level Bay

N

0   500
metres

migratory birds coming to nest here. The Saba Conservation Foundation preserves the environment on land and under water, developing protected areas, maintaining trails (with excellent interpretive signboards) and promoting nature conservation. The Foundation can be contacted through the Tourist Office or write to Saba Conservation Foundation, The Bottom, Saba.

Diving and Marine Life

The waters around Saba became a Marine Park in 1987 and 36 permanent mooring buoys have been provided for dive boats. The Park includes waters from the highwater mark down to 200 feet all the way around the island. Spearfishing is prohibited, as is the removal of coral or shells. Diving tourism has increased rapidly; scuba divers and snorkellers visit the Marine Park which is noted for its "virginity". Saba has no beaches so diving and snorkelling is from boats, mostly along the calmer S and W coasts. The W coast from Tent Bay to Ladder Bay, together with Man of War shoals, Diamond Rock and the sea offshore comprise the main dive sites, where line, trap, and spearfishing are prohibited. From Ladder Bay to Torrens Point is an all-purpose recreational zone which includes Saba's only beach, a pebbly stretch of coast with shallow water for swimming and areas for diving, fishing, and boat anchorage. Another anchorage is W of Fort Bay. East of Fort Bay along the S, E and N coast to Torrens Point is a multiple use zone where fishing and diving are permitted. Some of the most visited dive sites are Third Encounter, Outer Limits, Diamond Rock and Man of War. Ladder Labyrinth is a dive site which is good for snorkelling. Dive operators have been granted permits and they collect the mandatory visitor fees to help maintain the Park. The Marine Park office is at Fort Bay, PO Box 18, The Bottom, T/F 63295. The guide to the dive sites, *Guide to the Saba Marine Park*, by Tom Van't Hof, published by the Saba Conservation Foundation, is highly recommended, available at dive shops, the museum and souvenir shops, US$15. Saba now has a 4-person recompression chamber, donated by the Royal Netherlands Navy, which is administered through the Marine Park but operated by volunteers. Summer visibility is 75-100 feet with water temperatures of about 86°F, while winter visibility increases to 125 feet and water temperatures fall to 75°F. Saba's rugged, volcanic terrain is replicated underwater where there are mountains, caves, lava flows, overhangs, reefs, walls, pinnacles and elkhorn coral forests.

Not much fishing is done in these waters, so there is a wide range of sizes and varieties of fish to be seen. Tarpon and barracuda of up to 8 feet are common, as are giant sea turtles. From February to April humpback whales pass by on their migration S, while in the winter dive boats are often accompanied by schools of porpoises. Smaller, tropical fish are not in short supply and together with bright red, orange, yellow and purple giant tube sponges and different coloured coral, are a photographer's delight.

There are three dive shops on Saba. Saba Deep at Fort bay, near the pier, run by Mike Myers T/F 63347, has NAUI and PADI instructors and offers a resort course with instruction in the swimming pool at *Captain's Quarters*. They have three 25-foot boats but take out no more than 8 in a group. A 2-tank dive costs US$60. Saba Deep also offers a sunset cruise round the island, which takes about an hour, and full day excursions to nearby islands. Sea Saba Dive Centre at Windwardside, T 62246, F 62237, has two boats, one which can take groups of

14 and one which carries only 8. A 2-tank dive costs US$65. Run by Joan and Louis Bourque, who are both PADI instructors, they also offer introductory and 5-day certification courses, fishing and other non-diving excursions. They have a 40-foot cabin boat for 15 divers or a 36-foot boat for 10 divers. Wilson's Dive Shop at Fort Bay Pier has three boats taking a maximum of 5 divers each, US$60 including all equipment, even skins, for a 2-tank dive. There are also live-aboard boats: the *Caribbean Explorer*, T 800-322-3577, offers week-long trips for serious divers, usually starting in St Maarten and spending much of their time in Saban waters.

Walking

Before the road was built people got about Saba by donkey or on foot and there are still numerous steep trails and stone steps linking villages which make strenuous, yet satisfying, walking. The Conservation Foundation of Saba is preserving, upgrading and marking trails for those who like a challenge and for those who prefer a gentle stroll. All of them are accessible from the road and many can be done without a guide. Named trails include: Tent Point, Booby Hill, The Level, The Boiling House, The Sulphur Mine, The Ladder, Giles Quarter, Rendezvous, Bottom Hill, Crispeen, Mount Scenery, Spring Bay, Troy, Sandy Cruz, Middle Island and Mary's Point.

The most spectacular hike is probably the one from Windwardside up 1,064 steps to the crest of Mount Scenery, best done on a clear day otherwise you end up in the clouds. It is a hard slog, but a road goes part of the way up and drinks are available where it ends. The summit has now been cleared (the intention is to keep it cleared) and there is a spectacular view down to Windwardside and the surrounding isles. Take a sweater and waterproof jacket, it can be very rough and slippery after rain. There are lots of birds and the botanical changes are noticeable as you climb. You can get out of the rain in several shelters on the way up. The Ladder is a long path of stone steps from the shore up to The Bottom, up which all provisions used to be hauled from boats before the road was built. There is a picnic place overlooking Ladder Bay. A guide is recommended for the Sulphur Mine track; at Lower Hell's Gate, about halfway up the sharp bends on the way to the airport, a track N of the road leads to the cliffs of the N coast, with splendid scenery, and to the remains of the old sulphur mines. A very nice lookout point is from Booby Hills, up the 66 terraced steps to the Booby Hill Peak. If you want a guide, Bernard Johnson, who works in the *Chinese Family Restaurant* at night, is knowledgeable. A botanical tour can be arranged with Anna Keene, of Saba Botanico at Weaver's Cottage, Under the Hill in Windwardside, who can help you find orchids, philodendron, heliconias, ferns, begonias and other plants native to tropical rainforests or dry bushlands; highly recommended, she can also be reached through the Saba Tourist Office.

Other Sports

There is a tennis court (concrete) at the Sunny Valley Youth Centre in The Bottom which is open to the public. Basket ball and volley ball matches are held, contact the Tourist Office for a schedule.

Excursions

There are four picture book villages on Saba, connected by a single spectacular 6½ mile road which begins at the airport and ends at the pier. The road itself is a feat of engineering, designed and built by Josephus Lambert Hassell in the 1940s, who studied road construction by correspondence course after Dutch engineers said it was impossible to build a road on Saba. From the airport, the road rises to **Hell's Gate** and then on through banana plantations to **Windwardside**, a

walk of 20-30 minutes, where most of the hotels and shops are situated. There is a small museum, a bank, post office and the Tourist Office is here. On the first Sunday in each month, a 'happening' is held in the grounds of the Harry L Johnson Museum. Everyone dresses in white (including visitors), plays croquet and drinks mimosas. The museum was a sea captain's house and dates from the 1890's. It is filled with antique furniture and family memorabilia. Open 1000-1200, 1300-1530, Monday-Friday. The road goes on past Kate's Hill, Peter Simon's Hill and Big Rendezvous to St John's, which has a wonderful view of St Eustatius, then climbs over the mountain and drops sharply down to *The Bottom*, the island's seat of government, with a population of 350. The Bottom is on a plateau 800 feet above the sea, and gets its name from the Dutch words "*de botte*", meaning "the bowl". Leaving The Bottom, the road makes its final descent to Fort Bay, where small cruise ships, yachts and the ferry from St Maarten (suspended 1993, see below) arrive at the 277-foot pier. Most of the houses on the island are painted white with red roofs and some have green shutters. There are watercolour workshops for those who find the scenery picturesque.

INFORMATION FOR VISITORS

● **Documents**

See main Netherlands Antilles section under Curaçao Information for Visitors. Saba is a free port so there are no customs formalities.

● **How To Get There**

The landing strip is only 1,312 feet long, so large aircraft cannot yet be accommodated although there are plans to build a longer runway. Planes do not land in bad weather in case they skid off the end. Winair (T 62255), the only scheduled airline, has 4 daily 20-seater flights from St Maarten (20 minutes/US$62 return) and one or 2 from St Eustatius. You can also organize flights with a stopover in St Barts. It is essential to reconfirm your return flight. Saba can also sometimes be reached by boat (the regular scheduled service was suspended when the boat sank), details from Great Bay Marina, St Maarten, T 22167. A deep water pier at Fort Bay allows cruise ships to call. Airport departure tax is US$2 to Netherlands Antilles, US$5 elsewhere.

● **Local Transport**

There are no buses. There are taxis at the airport and a few others on the island. Airport to Hell's Gate, US$4; to Windwardside, US$6; to The Bottom, US$9; Hell's Gate to Windwardside, US$4. Taxis can be hired for tours round the island (US$30-35) and the drivers are knowledgeable guides. Some are also fishermen or hotel owners, so they can be valuable contacts. You can hire a jeep or car from Avis, Windwardside, for about US$30-35 a day, T 2279. Drive on the right. Hitchhiking is safe, very easy and a common means of getting about.

● **Where To Stay**

There are no resort hotels yet on Saba and even the most expensive are small and friendly. Two new luxury hotels are planned, but construction stalled in 1993 because of financial problems. There is a 5% room tax and usually a 10%-15% service charge.

Windwardside: *Captain's Quarters*, US$150d winter, US$105d summer, CP, T 62201, F 62377, best known with 10 rooms, is a handsomely decorated restored sea captain's house, with a pool, American Express not accepted, only Visa and Master; *Juliana's Apartments*, US$95d winter, US$75d summer, for room with bath, or US$100d winter,

US$80d summer for Flossie's cottage, or US$100 winter, US$75 summer for 2½ room apartment, T 62269, F 62389, the facilities of *Captain's Quarters* are available for guests; *Scout's Place*, US$55-85d, with breakfast, T 62205, F 62388, 4 rooms in former government guest house, 10 rooms with 4 poster beds in new wing, simple, relaxed.

The Bottom: *Cranston's Antique Inn*, US$57.50 all year, T 63218, 130-year old inn, some 4 poster beds, restaurant; *Caribe Guesthouse*, clean comfortable, no frills, 5 rooms, kitchen available, US$45 all year, T 63261.

The Tourist Office has a list of one-two bedroom cottages and apartments for rent from US$40-1,000 a night, which can be let on a weekly or monthly basis, and can also provide hotel rates. Saba Real Estate, PO Box 17, Saba, T/F 62299, manages property rentals, from one bedroom apartments to luxury 4 bedroom villa.

● **Where To Eat**

At *Scout's Place*, dinner is at 1930, reservations needed, slow service; the *Saba Chinese Restaurant* (open 1100-2200, closed Mon) and the *Chinese Family Restaurant* serve Cantonese food, both in Windwardside, the one higher up the hill has good food, and *Cranston's Antique Inn* has Chinese and native dishes, not open every day; *Guido's Italian Restaurant*, for pizzas and burgers; *Captain's Quarters* for more elegant dining, food average, reservations rec. In The Bottom: native specialities at *Lime Time* and *Queenie's Serving Spoon*. *Lollipop*, T 63330, is a small restaurant on the mountainside overlooking The Bottom, the owner picks up clients in her car from Windwardside or The Bottom, good food, rec for lunch, walk it off afterwards.

● **Nightlife**

Most of the nightlife takes place at the restaurants. At weekends there are sometimes barbeques, steel bands and dances at *Mountain High Club* (Windward side) and at *Boogie's* (Hell's Gate). Generally, though, the island is quiet at night.

● **Shopping**

Shops open 0900-1200, 1400-1800. Local crafts have been developed by the Saba Artisan Foundation in The Bottom and include dolls, books and silk-screened textiles and clothing. The typical local, drawn-thread work "Saba Lace" (also known as "Spanish Work" because it was learned by a Saban woman in a Spanish convent in Venezuela at the end of the last century) is sold at several shops on the island. Each artisan has his or her own style. Taxi drivers may make unofficial stops at the houses where Saba lace, dolls, pillows etc are made. Saba Spice is the local rum, very strong (150° proof) and mixed with spices, sugar and orange peel.

● **Banks**
Barclays Bank, Windwardside, T 62216, open 0830-1230, Mon-Fri. The florin or guilder is the local currency, but US dollars are accepted everywhere. Hotels and dive shops accept credit cards, but no one else does. You may be charged extra for using credit cards because of the slow processing arrangements.

● **Climate**
The average temperature is 78°- 82°F during the day but at night it can fall to the low 60°s. The higher up you get, the cooler it will be; so take a jersey, if hiking up the mountain. Average annual rainfall is 42 inches.

● **National Holidays**
New Year's Day, Good Friday, Easter Monday, Queen's Birthday (30 April), Labour Day (1 May), Ascension Day, Saba Day (7-9 December), Christmas Day, Boxing Day. Carnival is a week in July and is celebrated with jump-ups,

music and costumed dancing, shows, games and contests including the Saba Hill Climb. The first weekend in December is Saba Day, when donkey races are held, with dancing and other festivities.

● **Time Zone**
Atlantic Standard Time, 4 hours behind GMT, 1 ahead of EST.

● **Electric Current**
110 volts AC, 60 cycles.

● **Communications**
Most hotels have direct dialling worldwide, otherwise overseas calls can be made from The Bottom. The international code for Saba is 599-4, followed by a 5 digit number.

● **Churches**
There are 4 churches: Anglican, Roman Catholic, Wesleyan Holiness and Seventh Day Adventist.

● **Tourist Office**
The Saba Tourist Board is in Windwardside, T 62231. In the **USA**: Saba Tourist Information Office, c/o Medhurst & Associates Inc, 271 Main Street, Northport, NY 11768, T (800) 344-4606 or (516) 261-7474.

SINT EUSTATIUS

SINT EUSTATIUS, or STATIA, 35 miles S of St Maarten and 17 miles SE of Saba, was originally settled by Caribs and evidence of their occupation dates back to AD300. The name Statia comes from St Anastasia, as it was named by Columbus, but the Dutch later changed it to Sint Eustatius. The island is dominated by the long-extinct volcano called "The Quill" at the S end, inside which is a lush rainforest where the locals hunt land crabs at night. Visitors are advised, however, to go there only during the day. The N part of the island is hilly and uninhabited; most people live in the central plain which surrounds the airport.

Statia is quiet and friendly and the poorest of the three Windward Islands, with only 1,800 people living on the 8 square mile island. A variety of nationalities are represented, the island having changed hands 22 times in the past. Everybody speaks English, although Dutch is the official language and is taught in schools. The traditional economic activities of fishing, farming and trading have been augmented by an oil storage and refuelling facility, but the major hope for prosperity is tourism. Over half of the 17,000 visitors a year are cruiseship passengers, and the number of longer stay arrivals is likely to decline given the 1993 decision by the Dutch Government to end recognition of driving licences awarded in Statia unless the driver has lived for over 6 months in the Antilles. Investment in airport expansion and a cruiseship pier is designed to increase capacity. Nevertheless, it remains the sort of place where you will be greeted by passers by and there is no crime.

History

Statia was sighted by Columbus on his second voyage but never settled by the Spanish. The Dutch first colonized it in 1636 and built Fort Oranje, but the island changed flag 22 times before finally remaining Dutch in 1816. The island reached a peak of prosperity in the 18th century, when the development of commerce brought about 8,000 people to the tiny island, over half of whom were slaves, and the number of ships visiting the port was around 3,500 a year. Trading in sugar, tobacco and cotton proved more profitable than trying to grow them and the slave trade was particularly lucrative, gaining the island the nickname of "The Golden Rock".

The island still celebrates 16 November 1776 when the cannons of Fort Oranje unknowingly fired the first official salute by a foreign nation to the American colours. At that time, Statia was a major trans-shipment point for arms and supplies to George Washington's troops, which were stored in the yellow ballast brick warehouses built all along the Bay and then taken by blockade runners to Boston, New York and Charleston. However, the salute brought retaliatory action from the English and in 1781 the port was taken without a shot being fired by troops under Admiral George Brydges Rodney, who captured 150 merchant ships and £5 million of booty before being expelled by the French the following year.

With continuing transfers of power, the economy never recovered, many merchants were banished and the population began a steady decline. The emancipation of slaves in 1863 brought an end to any surviving plantation agriculture and the remaining inhabitants were reduced to subsistence farming and dependency

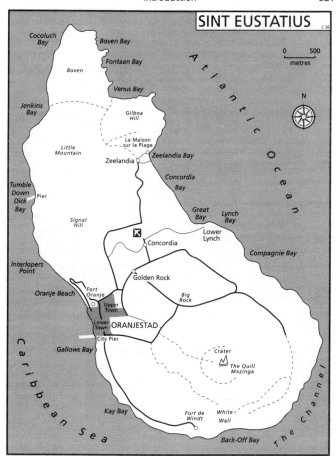

SINT EUSTATIUS

upon remittances from relatives abroad. Prosperity has returned only recently with the advent of tourism and the island is still relatively underdeveloped.

Diving and Marine Life

Statia's waters offer a wonderful combination of coral reefs, marine life and historic shipwrecks, of which there are about 200 to explore. Water visibility is over 100 feet and snorkelling is also very good. There are 16 charted dive sites, at a depth of 20-80 feet. The Supermarket, half a mile off the coast from Lower Town at a depth of 60 feet, has two shipwrecks 150 feet apart with beautiful coral, red and purple sponges, shoals of fish, sea turtles and the rare flying gurnard. The Garden is another very beautiful reef with hundreds of fish of all kinds from the smallest wrass to large barracudas and extremely tame angel fish.

There is one dive shop on the island: Dive Statia, run by Judy and Mike Brown, T 82435. Seven-night diving packages are arranged with the hotels, and it is possible to combine Saba and Statia for a diving, or non-diving package. In the USA, T 800-468 1708.

Beaches and Watersports

Oranje Beach stretches for a mile along the coast away from Lower Town. The length and width of the beach varies according to the season and the weather, but being on the Leeward side it is safe for swimming and other watersports. Following Hurricane Hugo in 1989 much of the beach disappeared and only half a mile of black sand remained, running E from the hotels to the shipwreck in a rather inconsistent manner. On the Windward side are two fine beaches but there is a strong undertow and they are not considered safe for swimming. Zeelandia Beach is 2 miles of off-white sand with heavy surf and interesting beachcombing, particularly after a storm. It is safe to wade and splash about in the surf but not to swim. There is a short dirt road down to the beach just before you get to *Maison Sur La Plage*; do not drive too close to the beach or you will get stuck in the sand. Avoid the rocks at the end of the beach as they are very dangerous. The other beach on the Windward side is Lynch Beach, which is small and a bit safer for swimming as long as you do not go out very far and pay attention to the undertow. Drive past the airport terminal entrance for about 75 yards and turn right on to a dirt road. Go past the Agricultural Experiment Station, keeping right at intersections but staying on the dirt road. Park just beyond the small white house on the left and walk for 6 minutes, not to the beach you can see, which is unsafe for swimming, but down a steep gully and then down a stony path to the smaller beach. It is often empty during the week. Take your litter home with you.

Other Sports

There is little to offer on Statia for the sporting enthusiast. At the Community Centre on Rosemary Lane: tennis (US$5), basketball, softball and volleyball; changing rooms are available. There is also a children's playground.

ORANJESTAD

Oranjestad is the capital, situated on a cliff overlooking the long beach below and divided between Upper Town and Lower Town. The town used to be defended by Fort Oranje (pronounced Orahn'ya) perched on a rocky bluff. Built in 1636, the ruins of the fort have been preserved and large black cannons still point out to sea. The administrative buildings of the island's Government are here. The fort was partly destroyed by a fire in 1990, and rebuilding work was still in progress in 1993. You can still go in and look around, but the Post Office is closed. Other places of historical interest include the ruins of the Honen Dalim Synagogue built in 1738 and the nearby cemetery. Statia once had a flourishing Jewish community and was a refuge for Sephardic and Ashkenazic Jews, but with the economic decline after the sacking of Oranjestad by Admiral Rodney, most of the Jewish congregation left. The Dutch Reformed Church, built in 1774, suffered a similar fate when its congregation joined the exodus. The square tower has been restored but the walls are open to the elements. The surrounding graveyard has some interesting tombs. Legend has it that it was here that Admiral Rodney found most of his booty after noticing that there were a surprising number of funerals for such a small population. A coffin, which he ordered to be opened, was found to be full of valuables and further digging revealed much more.

On Wilheminaweg in the centre, the 18th century Doncker/De Graaff House, once a private merchant's house and also where Admiral Rodney lived, has been

1. Fort Oranje
   & Post Office
2. Museum
3. Dutch Reform
   Church Tower
4. Old Gin House
5. Old Slave Road
6. Tourist Office
7. Police
8. Telephone Office
9. Supermarket
10. Petrol Station
11. Dive Statia
12. Cruise ship pier

ORANJESTAD (STATIA)   c.39 Rough Sketch

restored by the St Eustatius Historical Foundation and is now a museum. There is a pre-columbian section which includes an Arawak skeleton and a reconstruction of 18th century rooms at the height of Statia's prosperity. Open 0900-1600, Monday-Friday, admission US$1 or US$0.50 for children, the curator normally shows you around, explaining the history of the exhibits.

It is possible to walk round the village and see the sights in a morning. The museum or Tourist Office will provide you with a Walking Tour brochure listing the historical sites and other walking tours. In its heyday Lower Town stretched for 2 miles along the bay, with warehouses, taverns and slave markets attracting commercial traffic. Parts are now being restored as hotels or restaurants. If you like beach combing, blue, 5-sided slave beads over 200 years old can be found along the shore at Oranjestad.

Excursions

Twelve hiking trails using old donkey or farm tracks are marked and numbered. The Tourist Office has a guide book of the trails. There are several paths to the rainforest crater at the top of The Quill, which is remarkable for its contrast with the dry scrub of the rest of the island. The plant life includes mahogany and breadfruit trees, arums, bromeliads, lianas and orchids. The walk to the top is of course steep, but once there you can walk down a path to the centre. The vegetation in the crater is very dense and a local guide is recommended. The highest point, called Mazinga, affords a magnificent view. The Quill was damaged by Hurricane Hugo in 1989 and it is now not possible to walk round the rim. The crater is the breeding ground for land crabs, which Statians catch at night by blinding them with a flashlight.

A road, and then a track, leads round the lower slopes of The Quill to the White Wall, a massive slab of limestone which was once pushed out of the sea by volcanic forces and is now clearly visible from miles away across the sea. You can also see it from Fort de Windt, built in 1753, the ruins of which are open to the public, at the end of the road S from Lower Town. St Kitts can also be seen clearly from here. About 14 forts or batteries were built around the island by the end of the 18th century but the ruins of few of them are accessible or even visible nowadays. Another track affording panoramic views is that up Gilboa Hill. If you start from the Venus Bay track, turn E at post 11; you can see all across Statia.

INFORMATION FOR VISITORS

● **Documents**
See main Netherlands Antilles section under Curaçao Information for Visitors. There are no customs regulations as Statia is a free port.

● **How To Get There**
Winair has several daily 20-minute flights from St Maarten (US$62) connecting with flights from the USA, Europe and other islands. It is possible to get to Statia in a day from New York. There are other connecting Winair flights from St Kitts and Nevis, and a weekly Liat flight from St Kitts. Winair also flies to Saba (10 minutes). All flights are in small planes, although the airport has been extended to 4,290 feet to allow larger jets to land. You get an impressive view of The Quill when you come in to land. Airport departure tax is US$4. Windward Islands Airways (Winair) T 82362/82381.

Cruise ships come in at Gallows Bay, where there is a deep-water pier. Boat charters are available in the larger nearby islands.

● **Local Transport**
There are several taxi drivers who are well-informed guides and can arrange excursions, although most places are within walking distance if you are energetic. A round island tour costs US$35. To hire a car you need a driving licence from your own country or an international driver's licence. Avis at the airport rents elderly baby Daihatsus for US$36/day, cars are well-maintained, credit cards accepted. Mopeds are also available. The speed limit in the country is 50 km (31 miles) an hour and in residential areas it is 30 km (19 miles) an hour. Driving is on the right, but some roads are so narrow you have to pass where you can. Cows, donkeys, goats and sheep are a traffic hazard as they roam about freely, but if you drive slowly and carefully they will soon get out of your way.

● **Where To Stay**
The Old Gin House, Lower Town, T 82319, a reconstructed 18th century cotton gin building, using old ballast bricks, 20 rooms, the most expensive and luxurious of all the hotels, US$150d summer, US$185d winter, EP, no children under 10 accepted, all children pay full adult rate, closed September/October; *La Maison Sur La Plage*, at Zeelandia Bay, US$75s/d summer, T 82256, beautiful loca-

tion, pool, boules, particularly noted for its French cuisine, closed September; *Golden Era Hotel*, Lower Town, T 82345, on the beach, modern, 20 rooms, US$88d EP in winter. *Talk of the Town*, on road to airport a little way out of Oranjestad, 8 rooms, a/c, US$61 double, including breakfast.

There are several guest houses and apartments for rent which are much cheaper: *Henriquez Apartments*, T 82299, 2 places, one near the airport, US$40, and also in Oranjestad on Prinsesweg, near the hospital, US$30 winter, US$20 summer; also near the airport, *Alvin Courtar Apartments*, T 82218; and *Lens Apartments*, T 82226, no children; off the road towards The Quill, *Daniel's Guest House*, T 82358, De Ruyterweg 20; *Richardson Guest House*, T 82378, Union Estate 3; *Sugar Hill Apartments*, T 82305, upper end of Rosemary Lane. On the N side of The Quill, *Harry's Efficiency*, PO Box 82, no phone, good view.

Guest houses, villas and apartments are in the US$30-50 price range, double occupancy. Expect a 7% government tax, 15% service charge and sometimes a 5% surcharge. The Tourist Office also has a list of home rentals, T 82209 or 82213, ext 117.

● **Where To Eat**
The best restaurants are in the 3 hotels. *The Old Gin House* menu caters for the US market, while *La Maison Sur La Plage* serves a high standard of simple French cuisine with excellent French wine. Reservations rec for both. Cheaper meals at *Chinese Restaurant*, Prinsesweg 9, T 82389, shut Sun; *L'Etoile*, Heillegerweg, T 82299, same ownership as *Henriquez Apartments*, local style cooking, spicey pastechis rec, open from 1200-2200 Mon-Sat, closes at 1800 on Sun; *Statia Bar & Restaurant*, Paramiraweg 43, T 82280, Chinese and Caribbean dishes, closed Mon; *Stone Oven*, Faeschweg, T 82247, West Indian food, the liveliest place, on Fri open from 2100 until any time; *Talk of the Town*, Golden Rock, T 82236, varied menu, also sandwiches and cakes; you can order their specialities, lobster stew, eggplant soufflé, spiced crab backs in the morning or at lunchtime for dinner, the bar is a good meeting place. If you are self-catering and want to buy fresh fish, you have to deal direct with the fishermen as there is no fish shop. They usually come in somewhere along the shore road in Lower Town. Fresh bread is baked daily in outdoor charcoal-fired stone

ovens and best bought straight from the oven at "fresh bread time", which varies according to who makes it. Listings of fresh bread times are available.

● **Entertainment**
Statians like partying and every weekend something is always going on. Quite often you will hear a 'road block' from far away: cars stopped with huge stereos blaring and everyone jumping up in the street. Ask anybody what is going on next weekend, or just wait for the music to start in the evening.

● **Shopping**
Lots of shops or businesses are in people's homes with no visible sign of the trade from the outside, but if you ask for help it will be willingly given and you will find the right place. The Handcraft Shop is on Van Tonningenweg, next to the school, and sells gifts, clothing and furniture. Open Mon-Fri, 0800-1200, 1400-1700. Hole in the Wall, close to the telephone office, sells hand-painted T-shirts; Green and White Boutique also for clothes. Mazinga Gift Shop sells local books and a wide range of gifts. Duty free shops catering for cruise ship visitors open when there is a demand.

● **Bank**
Barclays Bank, Wilhelminaweg, T 82392, open 0830-1300, Mon-Fri, and 1600-1700 on Fri. The currency is the Netherlands Antilles florin or guilder, but US dollars are accepted everywhere. Credit cards are not widely used, although some shops do now accept them. Check beforehand at hotels and restaurants.

● **Health**
There is a hospital on Prinsesweg, T 82371 for an ambulance, or 82211 for a doctor. Outpatient hours are 0800-1100, Mon, Tues, Thur and Fri, or by appointment. A dentist comes only once a month, the nearest is on St Kitts or St Maarten.

● **Climate**
Average temperature is around 82°F with cooling trade winds from the E. Average rainfall is 45 inches a year. Average water temperature in the sea is 79°F.

● **National Holidays**
New Year's Day, Good Friday, Easter Monday, Queen's Birthday (30 April), Labour Day (1 May), Ascension Day, Statia Day (16 November), Kingdom Day (15 December), Christmas Day, Boxing Day.

Carnival is in July and is celebrated with

steel bands, picnics, sports and contests.

● **Time Zone**
Atlantic Standard Time, 4 hours behind GMT, 1 ahead of EST, all year.

● **Electric Current**
110 volts A/C 60 cycles.

● **Communications**
Public telephones, telex and cablegrams at Landsradio, Van Tonningenweg, Open Mon-Fri, 0800-1200, 1400-1700, 1800-1830. The telephone code number for Statia is 599-3. New exchanges have been introduced and some phone numbers may have changed. The **Post Office** is in Fort Oranje, still closed for renovations after the fire. There are special stamp issues and First Day Covers for collectors.

● **Churches**
Anglican, Apostolic Faith, Methodist, Roman Catholic and Seventh Day Adventist.

● **Tourist Office**
There are 3 on Statia: at the airport; in Lower Town opposite Roro Pier, operated by St Eustatius Historical society; and in the village centre, T 82433. In the **USA**: St Eustatius Tourist Information Office, c/o Medhurst & Associates Inc, 271 Main Street, Northport, NY 11768, T (800) 344-4606 or (516) 261-7474. In **Canada**: 243 Ellerslie Ave, Willowdale, Ontario, T 416-223 3501. In **Venezuela**: Edificio EXA, Oficina 804, Avda Libertador, Caracas, T 313832.

SINT MAARTEN

SINT MAARTEN (Dutch) or St-Martin (French – see under French Antilles section) lies 260 km N of Guadeloupe and 310 km E of Puerto Rico, in a cluster of islands on the Anguilla Bank. The island is amicably shared by the Dutch, who have 37 square km and the French, who have 52 square km.

The population of at least 62,000 (33,459 in St Maarten and 28,518 in St-Martin) has mushroomed with the tourist boom: the 1950 St Maarten census gave the total population at 1,484. While many of the residents were formerly ex-patriates who returned to their island, there is a large proportion who have come from other Caribbean islands to seek work. Few people speak Dutch, the official language, although Papiamento has increased with the migration of people from the ABC Dutch islands. Nearly everybody speaks English and there is a large Spanish-speaking contingent of guest workers from the Dominican Republic.

The Dutch side of the island has the main airport and seaport and most of the tourists. The French side is noticeably Gallic and few people speak English. There are no border formalities between the two parts: only a modest monument erected in 1948, which commemorates the division of the island three centuries earlier. The Dutch side occupies the S part of the roughly triangular island. The W part is low-lying and mostly taken up by the Simpson Bay Lagoon, which provides a safe anchorage for small craft. The lagoon is separated from the sea by a narrow strip of land on which the airport has been built. The rest of the Dutch part is hilly and dry and covered with scrub, although it can quickly turn green and lush after rain. The coastline is indented with sandy bays, while just inland are several salt ponds, which were what attracted the first settlers to the island.

History

The Amerindians who originally settled on the island named it Sualouiga, meaning land of salt. The belief that Columbus discovered the island on his second voyage in 1493 is disputed, with historians now claiming it was Nevis he named St-Martin of Tours, and that later Spanish explorers misinterpreted his maps. Nevertheless, the Spanish were not interested in settling the island and it was not until 1629 that some French colonists arrived in the N, and then in 1631 the Dutch were attracted to the S part by the salt ponds. By this time, there were no Caribs left on the island and the two nationalities lived amicably enough together. Spain then reconsidered and occupied St Maarten from 1633 to 1648, fending off an attack by Peter Stuyvesant in 1644 which cost him his leg.

When the Spanish left, the Dutch and French settlers returned and after a few territorial skirmishes, they divided the island between them with the signing of the 23 March 1648 Treaty of Mount Concordia. Popular legend has it that the division was settled with a race starting from Oyster Pond. The Frenchman went N and the Dutchman went S, but the Frenchman walked faster because he drank only wine while the Dutchman's penchant for Genever (a drink similar to gin) slowed him down. Since 1648, however, St Maarten has changed hands 16 times, including brief occupations by the British, but the Dutch-French accord has been peaceably honoured at least since it was last revised in 1839.

At the height of its colonial period, sugar cane and livestock were the main

SAINT-MARTIN C 35

1. Le Samanna
2. Royal Beach
3. Le Galion
4. Coralita Beach

French Side

To Anguilla & St-Barthélémy

Pt. Plum
Pointe du Bluff
Terres Basses
Baie Rouge
Baie Longue
Pt. Molly Smith
Friar's Bay
Baie Grande Base
Espérance
Grand Case
N7
Rambaud
Baie de la Potence
Baie Nettlé
MARIGOT
St James
Colombier
Simpson's Bay Lagoon
Pic du Paradis
Quartier d'Orléans
Etg. Chevrise
Anse Marcel
Bell Point
Red Rock
Cul-de-Sac
Eastern Point
Grandes Cayes
ILET PINEL
Baie Orientale
Caye Verte
Baie de l'Embouchure
Border Monument
St. Peter
Sentry Hill
Cul de Sac
Koolbaai
N7
Etang aux Poissons
Prince's Quarter
Naked Boy Hill
Babit Pond
Guana Bay
Salt Pond
PHILIPSBURG
Geneve Bay
Guana Key of Pélikan
Cole Bay
Little Bay
Great Bay
Pointe Blanche
Mullet Pond Bay
Maho Bay
Juliana
Simpson Bay

Dutch Side

Caribbean Sea

5. Oyster Pond & Dawn Beach
6. Bel Air Beach
7. Caravanserai
8. Cupecoy

SINT MAARTEN

agricultural activities, although the poor soil and lack of rain meant they were not very profitable. The emancipation of slavery in 1863 broke up the plantation system and the population began to decline as ex-slaves left to look for work elsewhere. Most of the salt produced from the Great Salt Pond behind Philipsburg was exported to the USA and neighbouring islands, but by 1949 this industry had also ended and a further exodus to other islands took place. The remaining population survived on subsistence farming, fishing and remittances from relatives abroad.

However, in 40 years the island has become unrecognizable, hotels and resorts, villas and guest houses now line the shore and there is no bay untouched by tourism. Over 1 million stopover and cruiseship tourists visit St Maarten (and French St-Martin) every year, attracted by the duty-free shopping, casinos and a wide range of accommodation, as well as the beaches and watersports. In 1993, 584 cruise ships called, bringing 659,943 passengers, a rise of 40% over 1992, while air arrivals at the Princess Juliana international airport declined by 8% to 577,659. Little of historical interest remains, except the walls of Fort Amsterdam overlooking Philipsburg, and a few other ruined fortifications, but this has not hindered the tourist industry, which is among the most successful in the region. For those who want more than sun, sand and sea, St Maarten's well-developed transport links make it an excellent jumping-off place for visiting other islands. Nearly 250,000 people were classified as in transit in 1993, making their way to other destinations with only a brief stop over in St Maarten.

Controversy arose in 1992 over the Dutch Government's decision in July to introduce 'higher supervision' of the St Maarten Island Council following an inquiry into its administration. The change meant that expenditure decisions by the island government had to be approved by the Lieutenant-Governor. In February 1993 supervision was tightened further with all major decisions requiring approval. There had been many reports of crime, corruption and financial maladministration and the USA was particularly concerned about suspected widespread drug smuggling through Juliana airport, where there are no customs controls. During 1993 several prominent members of government, including the hugely influential Dr Claude Wathey, leader of the St Maarten Democratic Party and former Prime Minister, his son Al Wathey, formerly the airport board chairman, and Ralph Richardson, the former Lieutenant Governor, as well as other influential colleagues, came under judicial investigation in connection with irregularities in the airport and Great Bay harbour expansion projects. Investigations were also carried out in France, Italy and other countries. In 1994, Dr Wathey was charged with forgery, perjury and participation in a criminal organization, together with three other people. The St Maarten executive council agreed to introduce customs checks at seaports and Juliana airport from January 1994 in an effort to control trafficking in arms, drugs and illegal immigration. The higher supervision order was extended until 1 June 1994 and France and the Netherlands agreed jointly to monitor air and sea traffic around the island.

Beaches and Watersports

The bays on the S and W shores are excellent for swimming, diving and fishing, and the beaches are of fine white sand.

The most popular beach is Mullet Bay, where you can rent umbrellas, beach chairs etc. It can get crowded in season and all weekends. On the E side is Oyster Pond, a land-locked harbour which is difficult to enter because of the outlying reefs, but which is now home to a yacht club and is a centre for bare boat charter. Dawn Beach nearby is popular with body surfers and snorkelling is good because of the reefs just offshore; Guana Bay, next to Dawn Beach, is the bodysurfers best beach. Maho Beach, by the airport, has regular Sunday beach parties with live music competitions; don't forget to duck when planes arrive. The most W beach on the Dutch side of the island is Cupecoy, where rugged sandstone cliffs lead down to a narrow sandy beach, providing morning shade and a natural windbreak.

Every conceivable form of watersports is available and the resort hotels offer all facilities. Surfing is possible all year round, from different beaches depending on the time of the year. Water visibility is usually 75-125 feet and the water temperature averages over 70°F, which makes good snorkelling and scuba diving, from beaches or boats. Wreck Alley on Proselyte Reef, has several wrecks which can be explored on one dive. *HMS Proselyte* is a 200-year-old British frigate (mostly broken up and covered in coral, although cannons and anchors are visible), while *The Minnow* and *SS Lucy* are modern ships deliberately sunk as dive sites. Training with NAUI instructors or just equipment rental is offered by Maho Watersports, at *Mullet Bay Resort*, Beach Bums and Ocean Explorers at Simpson Bay, Trade Winds Dive Center at Great Bay Marina (T 249096, ext 14, US$45 single tank 50-ft dives 0930 and 1230), Red Ensign Watersports at *Dawn Beach Hotel*, and Little Bay Watersports at *The Little Bay Beach Hotel*. They also have water skiing, jet skiing, windsurfing, para sailing, pedal boats, sunfish sailing and glass-bottomed boat trips.

There are boat charter companies

with sailing boats and motor boats, with or without a crew. You find most of them around *Bobby's Marina*, Philipsburg, from US$200 a day for bare boat. The *Eagle* and *Falcon* (US$50 pp plus tax, 0900-1700, Mon-Sat, T 22167) sail to St-Barts from Great Bay Marina. Also the 75-foot catamaran, *White Octopus*, departs 0930, returns 1700, from *Bobby's Marina*, T 22366. *El Tigre*, a 60-foot catamaran, makes day trips to St Barts and Anguilla from *Pelican Resort*, leaving 0930, returning 1730. The trip to St Barts is normally quite rough and unpleasant on the way there but more pleasant on the return journey. Check the weather, the swell and the waves can be up to 12 feet even on a nice day. *Gandalf* at Pelican Watersports goes to Tintamarre (US$70) and has dinner and sunset cruises. The schooner, *Laura Rose*, sails to Sandy Island, off Anguilla, US$50 plus tax, bring your own lunch, T 70710. Most boats offer some snacks, sodas and rum punch. Trips cost from US$50-70, plus departure tax. There are around 40 boats offering different trips around the islands, some just going out for snorkelling on the reefs or taking cruise ship passengers around. Check what is available from Marigot too. Some of the time share resorts offer free boat trips with snorkelling, lunch, taxis, (you pay departure tax), if you participate in one of their sales drives.

For fishing there are numerous boats available for a whole (US$500-750) or half (US$280-375) day from *Bobby's Marina* or *Great Bay Marina*. Arrangements can be made through the hotels. Marlin, barracuda, dolphin (not the mammal) and tuna are the best catches. Game fishing tournaments are held all year round.

The largest annual regatta takes place each February and lasts for three days with a round the island race on the Sunday. A race to Nevis and back is held in mid-June with a day for resting/parties. Other regattas held are for catamarans, match racing with charter boats, wind-surfing etc. For more information check with St Martin Yacht Club or ask Robbie Ferron at Budget Marina in Philipsburg. A half day excursion is match racing on *Canada II* or *True North*, two boats from the 1987 Americas Cup, US$60, races held when cruise ships are in port (T 43354, Bobby's Marina).

Other Sports

All the large hotels have tennis courts, many of which are lit for night play. There is an 18-hole championship golf course for guests at *Mullet Bay Resort* or *Caravanserai* at *Mullet Bay Resort & Casino*, which stretches along the shores of Mullet Pond and Simpson Bay Lagoon. **Running** is organized by the Road Runners Club, St Maarten, with a fun run of 5-10 km every Wednesday at 1730 and Sunday at 1830, starting from the *Pelican Resort & Casino* car park. On Sundays at 0700 there are two 20-km runs. There are monthly races with prizes and an annual relay race around the island to relive the legendary race between the Dutch and the French when they divided the island. Contact Dr Fritz Bus at the Back Street Clinic or Malcolm Maidwell of *El Tigre*, T 44309/22167. Crazy Acres Riding Centre takes groups horseriding every weekday morning at 0900 from the Wathey Estate, Cole Bay, to Cay Bay, where horses and riders can swim, T 42793. Make reservations two days in advance. Beach riding is also available on the French side.

Carnival

Carnival starts in mid-April and lasts for three weeks, culminating in the burning of King Mouí-Mouí. It is one of the biggest in the area, with up to 100,000 people taking part. Most events are held at the Carnival Village, next to the University.

PHILIPSBURG

Philipsburg, the capital of Dutch St Maarten, is built on a narrow strip of sandy land between the sea and a shallow lake which was once a salt pond. It has two main streets, Front and Back, and a ringroad built on land reclaimed from the salt pond, which all run parallel to Great Bay Beach, perhaps the safest and cleanest city beach anywhere. Front Street is full of shops offering duty-free goods. The Simartn Museum at Museum Arcade on 119 Front Street is open 1000-1600 Monday-Friday, 0900-1200 Saturday, closed Sundays. In a restored 19th century house, the museum exhibits the history and culture of the island. There is a museum shop. Back Street contains low cost clothes shops and low budget Chinese restaurants. The historic Townhouse (court-house and post office) dating from 1793, on De Ruyterplein, better known as Wathey Square, faces the pier. The harbour is frequented by cruise ships and a host of smaller craft and the town gets very crowded when up to eight cruise ships are in port. For information on outdoor concerts, choirs, theatre and art exhibitions, ask at the Cultural Center of Philipsburg on Back Street (T 22056). There is a zoo, opened 1991, in Madam Estate, close to New Amsterdam shopping centre, with a small exhibition of the fauna and flora from the islands, open weekdays 0900-1700, weekends 1000-1800, entrance US$4, children US$2.

Excursions

You can take a day trip round the island, visiting the ruined Fort Amsterdam overlooking Philipsburg and the French part of the island. It is well worth having lunch in one of the many French restaurants in Grand Case or the other French villages. Generally, however, there is not much of either historical or natural interest to see on the island, and most excursions are day trips to neighbouring islands: Anguilla, St-Barthélémy, Saba, St Eustatius, St Kitts or Nevis, either by boat or by plane.

INFORMATION FOR VISITORS

● Documents
See main Netherlands Antilles section, under Curaçao Information for Visitors. The local immigration officials are particularly concerned that you fill in your tourist card with a hotel address, even if you do not know whether you will be staying there.

● How To Get There
From Europe: Air France 4 times a week and AOM French Airlines twice a week from Paris, KLM twice a week from Amsterdam and Lufthansa once a week from Frankfurt. **From the USA**: Direct flights from New York (American Airlines, Continental), Phoenix, Arizona (American Airlines), Chicago (American Airlines) Baltimore (US Air), Orange County, California (American Airlines), Philadelphia (American Airlines and US Air) and Miami (American Airlines) with connecting flights from several other US cities. American Airlines flights from US cities mostly make their connections in San Juan, Puerto Rico. There are lots of flights **from other Caribbean Islands**: Anguilla, Antigua, Barbados, Curaçao, Dominica, Martinique, Grenada, Nevis, Guadeloupe, Trinidad and Tobago, Saba, St Barthélémy, USVI (St Croix and St Thomas), St Eustatius, St Kitts, Puerto Rico, St Lucia, Jamaica, Dominican Republic and the British Virgin Islands (Tortola), with a variety of regional and international carriers. Aeropostal also flies from Caracas.

Departure tax US$5 when leaving for the Netherlands Antilles, US$10 for other destinations at Juliana Airport except for French visitors returning to Guadeloupe or France. Travel agents ask for US$3 to confirm flights. Allow plenty of time on departure from Juliana airport at busy times as it can get very chaotic with several flights departing at once.

● Airport Information
Airline offices at the airport: ALM, T 54240; Air Guadeloupe, T 54212; KLM, T 52120; Liat, T 54203; American Airlines, T 52040; Aeropostal, T 53268; Air France, T 54212; Air St Barthélemy, T 53151; BWIA, T 53304;

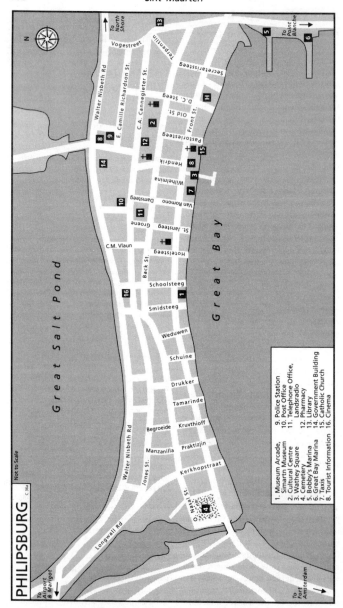

PHILIPSBURG

Not to Scale

C 26d

N

Great Salt Pond

Great Bay

To North Shore

To Point Blanche

To Airport & Marigot

To Fort Amsterdam

Vogestreet

Terpentijn

Secretarissteeg

Walter Nisbeth Rd

E. Camille Richardson St

C.A. Cannegieter St

D.C. Steeg

Old St.

Pastoristeeg

Front St.

Hendrik

Wilhelmina

Van Romono

St. Jansteeg

Groene

Damsteeg

Hotelsteeg

C.M. Vlaun

Back St.

Schoolsteeg

Smidsteeg

Weduwen

Schuine

Drukker

Tamarinde

Begroeide

Kruvthioff

Manzanilla

Praktizjin

Jones St.

Kerkhopstraat

Walter Nisbeth Rd

Longwall Rd

Nisbel St.

1. Museum Arcade,
   Simartn Museum
2. Cultural Centre
3. Wathey Square
4. Cemetery
5. Bobby's Marina
6. Great Bay Marina
7. Taxis
8. Tourist Information
9. Police Station
10. Post Office,
    Telephone Office,
    landsradio
11. Pharmacy
12. Library
13. Government Building
14. Catholic Church
15. Cinema

Lufthansa, T 52403; Winair, T 52568.

Airport flight information, T 52161.

● **Local Transport**

There are plenty of **taxis**, which are not metered so check the fare first, which is fixed according to your destination. Trips to other beaches or tours of the island can be arranged with taxi drivers: island tour US$35 plus US$2 for each additional passenger; hourly rate US$10 plus US$2.50 each additional 15 minutes. From Philipsburg to Juliana airport US$8, Dawn Beach US$10, Marigot US$8, Mullet Bay US$8, Pelican Resort US$7, all for 2 passengers, additional passengers US$2 each. Night tariffs are an extra 25% 2200-2400, an extra 50% 0001-0600. Pick up taxi at the square in Philipsburg (T 22359) or Juliana airport (T 54317). Mini-vans or tour **buses** also offer tours and are generally cheaper than taxis. Island tours from US$15; for more information ask at the Tourist Office on the square. There is a fairly regular bus service from 0600 until 2000 to Marigot (US$1.50 Philipsburg-Marigot), French Quarters and St Peters, and from Marigot to Grand Case on the French side. After 2000 there are few buses. The best place to catch a bus is on Back Street. Buses run along Back Street and Pondfill and only stop at bus stops. Outside towns, however, just wave to stop a bus. Fare price is usually US$0.80 in town, US$1 for short trips, US$1.50 for long trips. There is no regular bus service between Philipsburg and the airport although the route to *Mullet Bay Resort* passes the airport. Buses on this route run mostly at the beginning and the end of the working day (although there are a few during the day) and drivers may refuse to take you, or charge extra, if you have a lot of luggage. **Hitchhiking** is possible but allow half an hour waiting time; it is not rec for women.

● **Car Hire**

There can be a shortage of cars or jeeps for hire in high season, although there are now 15 rental companies, and it is advisable to request one from your hotel when you book the room. Many have offices in the hotels; free pick up and delivery are standard and you can leave the car at the airport on departure. Car hire companies include: Risdon's Car Rentals, Front Street, T 23578; Avis, Cole Bay, T 42322; Hertz, Juliana Airport, T 44314; Budget, Philipsburg, T 44038, Cannegie Car Rental, Front Street, T 22397; Opel Car Rental, Airport, T 44324; Speedy Car Rental, Airport, T 23893;

Roy Roger's, Airport, T 42701, US$30 plus US$10 CDW. Two-wheeled transport hire from Super Honda, Bush Road Cul-de-Sac, T 25712; Moped Cruising, Front Street, T 22330; OK Scooter Rental, at *Maho Beach Hotel* and *Cupecoy Resort*, T 42115, 44334. Foreign and international driver's licences are accepted. Drive on the right. The roads on both sides of the island are very busy and full of pot holes, making them rather unsafe for mopeds or walking, particularly at night.

● **Where To Stay**

There is a 5% Government tax on all hotel bills and a 10-15% service charge. Some add an energy surcharge. Prices are high, summer rates quoted here, winter rates can be double in the resorts. The largest resort hotels are *Mullet Bay Resort & Casino*, beach, watersports, pools, tennis, golf, casino, T 52801, F 54281, US$150-750, 600 rooms-suites; *Great Bay Beach Hotel & Casino*, convenient for Philipsburg, all resort facilities, T 22446, F 23859, US$80-195, 285 rooms-suites; *Cupecoy* perched on a cliff above Cupecoy beach, pool, tennis, casino, T 52309 F 52312, US$200-400, rooms-suites; *Dawn Beach* on Dawn Beach at Oyster Pond, watersports, tennis, pool, T 22929, F 24421, US$85-560, 155 rooms-suites with kitchenette, terrace, a/c, TV; *Maho Beach Hotel & Casino*, all facilities, T 52115, F 53018, US$110-440, 650 rooms-suites; *Pelican Resort & Casino*, pool, tennis etc, T 42503, F 42133, on Simpson Bay, huge, 654 units, US$115-450; *Divi Little Bay Beach Resort & Casino*, tennis, pool, watersports, T 22333, F 23911, 220 rooms, US$110-205; *The Towers At Mullet Bay*, watersports, disco, casino, close to airport, 5 miles from Philipsburg, T 53069, F 52147, 81 units, a/c, kitchenettes, TV, VCR etc, US$166-722.

Middle-sized hotels and resorts include *Bel Air Beach Hotel*, at Little Bay, T 23366, F 25295, US$150-275, 72 suites; *La Vista*, near *Pelican*, 24 suites and cottages, tennis, pool, horse riding, T 43005, F 43010, US$95-200; *Seaview Beach Hotel*, on Great Bay Beach, Philipsburg, casino, a/c, TV, children under 12 free, T 22323, F 24356, US$46-85; *ITT Sheraton Port de Plaisance*, on Simpson Bay, unlimited watersports, tennis, pool, fitness centre, night clubs etc, T 45222, F 42428, US$223-442, 88 units; also on Simpson Bay, *White Sands Beach Club*, PO Box 3043, T/F 54370, 1-2 bedroom suites, chalets, villas, US$109-215 high season, US$79-149 low season, special deals for cash customers, all beach front units, no restaurant but several nearby, car hire, rec, airport runway runs parallel to this part of Simpson Bay. *Oyster Pond Hotel*, near Dawn Beach, marina, fishing and water sports, tennis, pool, beach, T 22206, F 25695, US$120-200, no children under 10.

Small hotels include *Pasanggrahan*, in Philipsburg, rec, formerly the Governor's home, the oldest inn, T 23588, F 22885, no children under 12, US$68-165; *Bute*, Illidge Road 2, Philipsburg, on Great Bay Pond, 13 rooms, a/c available, US$35-50 (T 22400); *Mary's Boon*, on Simpson Bay beach, 12 studios with kitchenettes, pets welcome but no children under 16, no credit cards, US$90, T 44235.

Guesthouses on Front Street: *Marcus*, 7 rooms, US$28-35 (T 22419), *Seaside*, 5 rooms, US$25, PO Box 72; on Back Street: *Lucy's*, US$30-60, 9 rooms, no children under 6, PO Box 171, (T 22995) *Bico's*, US$30-60, extra person US$15, children welcome, no credit cards, (T 22294), PO Box 298, *Jose's*, US$20-37, US$10 extra person, prepay for 6 nights, get 7th free, 11 rooms, very basic, mosquitoes (T 22231); *Joshua Rose*, 7 Back-street, slightly better, a/c but still mosquitoes, 14 rooms, US$40-90d, extra person US$15 (T 24317, F 30080); at Simpson Bay: *The Horny Toad*, 8 studios, no children under 7, no credit cards, T 54323, F 53316, US$95, extra person US$25, *Calypso*, US$60-160, 8 efficiency apartments, Simpson Bay, PO Box 65 (T 44233); at Pointe Blanche, *Great Bay Marina*, 10 rooms, fridge, a/c, TV, grocery, pier facilities, US$70-90, PO Box 277, (T 22167), *Tamarind* 50 apartments with kitchenettes, swimming pool, US$69-109 daily, prepay for 6 nights, get 7th free, T 24359, F 25391, at Cole Bay: *Ernest*, 9 rooms in Cay Hill, 16 on Bush Road, swimming pool, a/c, TV, US$50 (T 22003), *George's*, 10 rooms in Cole Bay, 10 rooms in Philipsburg, a/c, kitchen, US$30-50, US$10 extra person (T 45363 or 22126).

The Tourist Office has a list of apartments, villas and houses to rent weekly or monthly. The best way of finding an apartment is to look in the free newspaper, *St Martin's Week*. There are several apartments for rent on Back Street, look for signs on the houses. A studio will cost about US$400-500/week in a good location. Apartments at Simpson Bay Beach cost US$350-500/week.

Camping is safe but you must seek permission from the landowner.

● **Where To Eat**

All the major hotels have restaurants with international cuisine. Pick up a free tourist guide to choose from the myriad restaurants now open on St Maarten with food from all over the world. In Mullet Bay: *The Frigate*, serves excellent charcoal-broiled steaks and lobster; *Bamboo Garden* offers some of the best Chinese dining. In Philipsburg: *Le Bec Fin*, French, highly rec, favoured by the Dutch Royal Family and winner of awards. Front Street is full of good restaurants and even a *Burger King*. *San Marco*, is an Italian restaurant, nice location overlooking sea, good for a break from shopping, T 22166; *Carri Pizza* on Pond-fill Road serves good pizza. *Callaloo*, a pleasant bar/restaurant, steaks, hamburgers and pizzas are served at reasonable prices, very popular. Indonesian rijsttafel at the hotels. Pizzas at *Portofino*. For the budget minded try Back Street where you most find Chinese and *roti* places such as *Hong Kong*, *ABC Restaurant* and *Kings Fastfood* where you can eat for US$5. *Admiral's Quarters*, Front St, interesting menu, international with Caribbean touches; *Shivsagar*, for Indian food; *Grill and Ribs*, the best ribs on the island at Old St and also Simpson Bay, all you can eat for US$12.95, reservations essential; Americanized French at *L'Escargot*, Front Street. In the Simpson Bay area: *Turtle Pier Bar and Restaurant* is reasonably priced at US$10 maximum per dish with an interesting setting in a mini zoo with parrots, monkeys, turtles etc, live music 2 or 3 times a week; *Lynette's* is a local restaurant with good seafood quite close to airport US$40 pp inc wine and tip and upstairs is *Clayton's* sport bar, where you can see most major sporting events on a big screen TV; *Don Carlos*, tasty Mexican food, US$10-15 pp for dinner, T 53112; *Ma Chance Shrimphouse* at Simpson Bay Yacht Club specializes in seafood, try the tiger shrimps; *Boat House* for drinks and food, live music several times a week, reservations essential; *The Greenhouse Bar and Restaurant*, next to Bobby's Marina at Great Bay, view over yachts, menu includes hamburgers, steak and local fish, disc jockey, dancing, harrassment of white people reported 1993, T 22941; *The Boathouse*, is rec for live music and dining or just a drink; *The News*, a '60s and '70s type of *Hard Rock Café* for late night meals, dancing, drinks, good overpriced and tasteless; at the end of Front St near the *Pasanggrahan Hotel* is a nice pastry shop, with fresh French pastries and juices; *Rembrandt*

Café at New Amsterdam shopping centre, a Dutch coffee shop/café, very popular for late drinks, best after 2100-2200. The most popular bars with nice sunsets are *Greenhouse* and *Chesterfield*, where you can find yachtsmen if you want to hitchhike by boat. Also *Paradise Café* (*Maho Resort*), *The Boat House* (*Simpson Bay*), *News Café* (*Simpson Bay*), *Turtle Pier Bar* (airport).

● **Drink**

The traditional local liqueur is *guavaberry*, made from rum and the local berries, whose botanical name is *Eugenia Floribunda*. They are not related to guavas. The berries are found on the hills and ripen just before Christmas. Used nowadays mostly in cocktails.

● **Entertainment**

Nearly all the resorts have casinos, which are a major attraction, the most popular being the casino at *ITT Sheraton Port de Plaisance*, *Pelican Casino* (*Pelican Resort*) and *Casino Royale* (*Maho/Mullet Bay*). The *Studio 7* discothèque at Grand Casino, Mullet Bay, is the most visited, entrance US$10 including one drink, can be higher if they have a special show, all drinks US$6, the disco starts late, rec to pass the time in *Cherry's* bar, a 5-min walk away, when people leave there most head for the disco. *Coconut Comedy Club* have stand up comedians Tues-Sun, 2130 and 2330, US$10 cover charge, most comedians from HBO or Carsons, well worth the price. *L'Horoscope* at Simpson Bay, opens 0100, starts to come alive only after 0200. *Caribbean Revue*, at Mullet Bay Resort, has a Caribbean show with Calypsonians and Limbo dancers, keep an eye open for King Bo Bo, the King of Calypso. Most resorts have live entertainment, such as limbo dancing, fire eating or live music, both local and international. In Philipsburg, *The Movies*, on Pondfill, has newly released films, US$5. *The News* is good for dancing, with live music every other night, extremely popular. Look out for Jack (Irish folk songs etc), G-Strings (pop-rock 1950s-70s), King Bo-Bo, the most popular bands of the last few years, whose music fills all the bars.

● **Shopping**

Duty-free shopping is a tourist attraction, but it helps if you have an idea of prices at home to compare, and shop around as prices vary. Check your duty-free allowance when returning home. Most of the shops are along Front Street. Open 0800-1200, 1400-1800.

● **Banks**

Bank of Nova Scotia, Back Street, T 22262, traveller's cheques cashed with no fee; Windward Islands Bank, T 23485, charges US$5 per traveller's cheque cashed; Barclays Bank, 19 Front Street, T 22491; Chase Manhattan Bank, Mullet Bay, T 44204; Algemene Bank Nederland, main office at Front Street, T 23505; Citco Bank Antilles, 16 Front Street, T 23471, 3 other offices on the island as well; Nederlandse Credietbank, T 22933. Open 0830-1500, Mon-Thur, 0830-1500, 1600-1700, Fri. Credit cards widely accepted.

● **Currency**

Netherlands Antilles guilders or florins are the official currency, but the most common currency is the US dollar, which one need never change at all. You will get a poor exchange rate for French francs. It is often difficult to get change from payments in any currency other than US dollars.

● **Warning**

Crime has increased on St Maarten and there have been armed robberies on the roads in the Lowland area, although the police have now clamped down with considerable force.

● **Health**

There is a new hospital on Cay Hill with 60 beds, all basic specialism, a haemodialyse department and 24-hour emergency services, T 31111, F 30116. Drinking water in the hotels is purified. Be careful of the sun. A helicopter airlift to Puerto Rico is available for extreme medical emergencies.

● **Emergency**

Police, T 22222; Fire, T 22222; Ambulance, T 22111; Hospital, T 31111.

● **Climate**

Average temperature is 80°F and average annual rainfall is 45 inches.

● **National Holidays**

New Year's Day, Carnival Monday (April), Good Friday, Easter Monday, 30 April, Labour Day (1 May), Ascension Day, St Maarten Day (11 November), Christmas Day, Boxing Day.

● **Time Zone**

Atlantic Standard Time, 4 hours behind GMT, 1 ahead of EST.

● **Electric Current**

110 volts AC. Note that it is 220 volts on the French side.

● **Telephones**

At Landsradio telecommunications office in Back Street, open until midnight. This is where you can buy telephone cards for the Dutch side of the island, open from 0700. You can also buy telephone cards at Landsradio's offices at Simpson Bay, Cole Bay and St Peter's.

● **Mail**

Two safe places for holding mail are *Bobby's Marina*, PO Box 383, Philipsburg and *Island Water World*, PO Box 234, Cole Bay. It is not possible to send a parcel by sea, only airmail which is expensive.

● **Churches**

Many denominations are represented. Seventh Day Adventist, Anglican, Baptist, Jehovah's Witness, Methodist, Roman Catholic, Church of Christ, Baha'i, The New Testament Church of God.

● **Newspapers**

Local events are noted in the free weekly newspaper, *St Martin's Week*, published in French and English every Thur afternoon on the French side and Fri morning on the Dutch side. *The Chronicle* and *The Guardian* come out 6 times a week and *Newsday* twice a week. After 1500 in the shops on Front Street or at

the airport you can find US newspapers (*New York Times*, *Miami Herald* and *San Juan Star*). American magazines (30%-40% more expensive than the USA) are especially good at Paiper Garden, Front Street.

● **Radio**

PJD2 Radio is on medium wave 1300 kHz and FM 102.7 mHz.

● **International Clubs**

The Lions, Rotary, Kiwanis, Jaycees and YMCC meet on both sides of the island.

● **Tourist Office**

Imperial building, 23 Walter Nisbeth Road, 3rd floor, T 22337, F 22734. Well supplied with brochures and guides to St Maarten, and the monthly *St Maarten Holiday*. Sightseeing tours available by bus or by car.

In the **USA**: St Maarten Tourist Bureau, 275 Seventh Avenue, 19th floor, New York, NY 10001, T 212-989 0000, F 212-242 0001.

In **Canada**: 243 Ellerslie Ave, Willowdale, Toronto, Ontario, M2N 1Y5 T 416-223 3501, F 416-223 6887.

In **Venezuela**: Edificio EXA, oficina 804, Avda Libertador, Caracas, T 31 38 32, F 416-223 6887.

FRENCH ANTILLES

Contents

THE FRENCH CARIBBEAN ISLANDS form two Départements d'Outremer: one comprises Martinique, and the other Guadeloupe with its offshore group, Marie-Galante, Les Saintes, La Désirade, and two more distant islands: Saint-Barthélémy and the French part of Saint-Martin (shared with the Dutch). Geographically, the main islands form the N group of the Windward Islands, with the ex-British island of Dominica in the centre of them. Saint-Barthélémy and Saint-Martin are in the Leeward group.

While aware of the fact that we are breaking the geographical sequence of the book, we shall deal with the French Antilles as a single entity. As the islands are politically Departments of France they have the same status as any Department in European France. Each Department sends two senators and three deputies to the National Assembly in Paris. The inhabitants are French citizens. The currency is the French franc (F). The people speak French. Visitors are often surprised by how French the islands are. The connection with France confers many benefits on the islands, which enjoy French standards of social legislation etc, but it also drives up the cost of living, which is rather higher than elsewhere in the Caribbean. There is an independence movement, whose more extremist members have been responsible for violent protests against high unemployment.

Both the main islands were sighted by Columbus on his second voyage in 1493, but no colonies were established by the Spanish because the islands were inhabited by the Caribs (who are now virtually extinct); it was not until 1635 that French settlers arrived.

Because of their wealth from sugar, the islands became a bone of contention between Britain and France; other French islands, Dominica, St Lucia, Tobago, were lost by France in the Napoleonic wars. The important dates in the later history of the islands are 1848, when the slaves were freed under the influence of the French "Wilberforce", Victor Schoelcher; 1946, when the islands ceased to be colonies and became Departments; and 1974, when they became Regions.

Culture

The cultural, social and educational systems of France are used and the official language is French. However, Créole is widely spoken on Guadeloupe and Martinique; it has West African grammatical structures and uses a mainly French-derived vocabulary. Although still not officially recognized, it is the everyday language of the Guadeloupean and Martiniquan people. English is not widely spoken, not even by hotel staff. A knowledge of French is therefore a great advantage.

Another feature common to the two main islands is the pre-Lenten Carnival, said to be more spontaneous and less touristy than most. There are also picturesque Ash Wednesday ceremonies (especially in Martinique), when the population dresses in black and white, and processions take place that combine the seriousness of the first day of the Christian Lent with the funeral of the Carnival King (Vaval).

Also shared are the African dances: the *calinda, laghia, bel-air, haut-taille, gragé* and others, still performed in remote villages. The famous biguine is a more sophisticated dance from these islands, and the mazurka can also be heard. French Antillean music is, like most other Caribbean styles, hybrid, a mixture of African (particularly percussion), European, Latin and, latterly, US and other Caribbean musical forms. Cur-

rently very popular, on the islands and in mainland France, is zouk, a hi-tech music which overlays electronics on more traditional rhythms.

Traditional costume is commonly seen in the form of brightly-coloured, chequered Madras cotton made into elegant Parisian-style outfits. It is the mixture of French and Créole language and culture that gives Martinique and Guadeloupe an ambience quite different from that of the rest of the Caribbean. An extra dimension is added by the Hindu traditions and festivals celebrated by the descendants of the 19th century indentured labourers.

The spectacles of cockfighting and mongoose versus snake are popular throughout the French Islands. Betting shops are full of atmosphere (they are usually attached to a bar). Horseracing is held on Martinique, but not Guadeloupe, but on both islands gambling on all types of mainland France track events is very keen.

The dominance of French educational and social regimes on its colonial possessions led, in the 1930s and 1940s, to a literary movement which had a profound influence on black writing the world over. This was *négritude*, which grew up in Paris among black students from the Caribbean and Africa. Drawing particularly on Haitian nationalism (1915-30), the *négritude* writers sought to restore black pride which had been completely denied by French education. The leaders in the field were Aimé Césaire of Martinique, Léopold Senghor of Senegal and Léon Damas of Guyane. Césaire's first affirmation of this ideology was *Cahier d'un retour au pays natal* (1939); in subsequent works and in political life (he was mayor of Fort-de-France) he maintained his attack on the "white man's superiority complex" and worked, in common with another Martiniquan writer, Frantz Fanon, towards "the creation of a new system of essentially humane values" (Mazisi Kunene in his introduction to the Penguin edition of *Return to My Native Land*, 1969).

INFORMATION FOR VISITORS

● **Documents**

In most cases the only document required for entry is a passport, the exceptions being citizens of Australia, South Africa, Bolivia, Dominica, St Lucia, Barbados, Jamaica, Trinidad, Haiti, Honduras, El Salvador, Dominican Republic, Turkey, when a visa is required. However, any non-EEC citizen planning to stay longer than 3 months will need an extended visa. Citizens of the United States and Canada intending a stay of less than 3 months will not need a passport, although some form of identification is required. An onward ticket is necessary but not always asked for. Vaccination certificates are not required if you are French, American or Canadian, but if you come from South America or some of the Caribbean Islands an international certificate for small pox and yellow fever vaccinations is compulsory.

● **Customs**

With the abolition of EC frontiers, Europeans are able to bring back 100 litres of rum etc. However you could run into problems if returning via Antigua, with a long, uncomfortable wait in transit. Take a direct flight if buying in bulk.

● **How To Get There**

Transport to each island is given separately. Note: as said above, French Saint-Martin has only a small airport; the international flights arrive and depart from Juliana International Airport on the Dutch side. Contact Continental Shipping and Travel, 179 Piccadilly, London W1V 9DB, T 071-491 4968, for help in arranging passage from France to the French Antilles (see also **Introduction and Hints**).

● **Accommodation And Restaurants**

Addresses for the local *gîtes* associations are also under the individual islands. In France, contact Gîtes de France, 35 Rue Godot de Mauroy, 75009 Paris, T 4742 2543. Restaurants divide fairly neatly into generally very expensive French cuisine or the more moderate créole. There is not much evidence of the *plat du jour* as there would be in France. Children may find créole food rather spicy. Fast food hamburger bars are not common.

● **Food**

A delightful blend of French, African, and Indian influences is found in Créole dishes, and the cuisine is quite distinctive. Basic traditional French and African recipes using fresh local ingredients; seafood, tropical fruits and vegetables are combined with exotic seasonings to give original results rich in colour and flavour. Here are a few local specialties not to be missed:

Ti-boudin, a soft well-seasoned sausage; *court bouillon de poisson* or *blaff* is conch (*lambis*), red snapper or sea urchin cooked with lime, white wine and onions; *ragout*, a spicy stew often made with squid (*chatrous*), or conch, or with meat; *colombo*, a recipe introduced by Hindu immigrants in the last century, is goat, chicken, pork or lamb in a thick curry sauce; *poulet au coco*, chicken prepared with onions, hot peppers (*piment*) and coconut; chunks of steakfish (usually tuna, salmon, or red snapper) marinaded and grilled; *morue* (salt cod) made into sauces and *accras* (hot fishy fritters from Africa) or grilled (*chiquetaille*), or used in *feroce d'avocat*, a pulp of avocados, peppers and manioc flour; lobster, crab and crayfish are often fricaséed, grilled or barbequed with hot pepper sauce.

Main dishes are usually accompanied by white rice, breadfruit, yams or sweet potatoes (*patate douce*) with plantains and red beans or lentils. *Christophine au gratin*; a large knobbly pear-shaped vegetable grilled with grated cheese and breadcrumbs, or a plate of fresh *crudités* are delicious, lighter side dishes.

Exotic fresh fruit often ends the meal; pineapples, papayas, soursops and bananas can be found all year round and mangos, mandarin oranges, guavas and sugar apples in season.

● **Drink**

As in other Caribbean islands the main alcoholic drink is rum. Martiniquan rum has a distinctive flavour and is famous for its strength. There are 2 main types: white rum (*blanc*) and dark rum (*vieux*) which has been aged in oak vats and is usually more expensive. *Ti punch* is rum mixed with cane syrup or sugar and a slice of lime and is a popular drink at any time of the day. *Shrub* is a delicious Christmas liqueur made from rum and orange peel. *Planteur* is a rum and fruit juice punch. There is a huge choice of Martiniquan rum, recommended brands being Trois Rivières, Mauny, Neisson and St Clément. There are different brands on Guadeloupe. French wines are available, although even red wine is usually served as a cool drink with ice. The local beer is Lorraine, a clean-tasting beer which claims to be 'brewed for the tropics'. Corsaire, made in Guadeloupe, is bitter tasting and insipid. Locally-brewed Guinness, at 7% alcohol, stronger than its Irish counterpart, is thick and rich. Malta, a non-alcoholic beverage similar to malt beer, is produced by most breweries and said to be full of minerals and vitamins. Thirst quenching non-alcoholic drinks to look out for are the fresh fruit juices served in most snack-bars and cafés. Guava, soursop, passionfruit, mandarin, and sugar cane juice are commonly seen. Tap water is drinkable.

● Tipping
Check if your bill says "Service Compris", in which case no tip is necessary.

● Time Zone
4 hours behind GMT, 1 ahead of EST in all cases.

● Holidays
New Year's Day; Carnival at the beginning of February; 8 March Victory Day; Good Friday; Easter Monday; Labour Day on 1 May; Ascension Day at the beginning of May; Whit Monday in May; National Day on 14 July; Schoelcher Day on 21 July; Assumption Day in August; All Saints Day on 1 November; Armistice Day on 11 November and Christmas Day.

● Currency Exchange
Banking hours are given under the various islands, as are the names of banks. There are money-changing offices in the big hotels and at airports. The French franc is the legal tender, but US$ are preferred in Saint-Martin and are widely accepted elsewhere. There is no limit to travellers' cheques and letters of credit being imported, but a declaration of foreign banknotes in excess of 3,500F must be made. 500F in French banknotes may be exported and 3,500F in foreign banknotes.

● Tourist Information
Les Antilles, produced by Nouvelles Frontières (Les Éditions JA, 2nd edition, Paris, 1987), contains both practical information and very interesting background information on geography, local customs and architecture, and the French Antilles' place in the Caribbean and in relation to France.

Addresses of the French Tourist Offices on the individual islands are given separately.

● Tourist Offices
Office Inter-Régional du Tourisme des Antilles Françaises, 2 Rue des Moulins, 75001 Paris, T 44 77 86 22, F 49 26 03 63.

Service Official Français du Tourisme:

UK: 178 Piccadilly, London, T 071-491 7622, F 071 493 6594.

USA: 610 Fifth Avenue, New York, NY 10020, T 212 757 0218, F 212 247 6468; 645 North Michigan Ave, Suite 630, Chicago, Illinois 60611, T 312 751 7800.

Canada: 1981 Ave MacGill College, Suite 480, Montréal PQH 3A 2W9, T 514 844 8566, F 844 8901; 30 St Patrick Street, Suite 700, Toronto, M ST 3A3, T 416 593 4723, F 979 7587.

Germany: Französisches Fremden-verkehrsamt, Post Fach 150465, 1000 Berlin 15, T 30218 2064, F 30214 1738.

Italy: 5 Via San Andrea 20121, Milan, T 2 76000268, F 278 4582.

Belgium: 21 Ave de la Toison d'Or, 1060 Brussels, T 25130762, F 25143375.

Switzerland: Löwenstrasse 59, Postfach 7226, 8023 Zurich, T 12 21 35 78, F 12 12 16 44.

Spain: Administration: Gran Via, 59-28013 Madrid, T 541 8808, F 541 2412.

GUADELOUPE

G UADELOUPE is surrounded by the islands La Désirade, Marie-Galante and Les Saintes, all of which can easily be visited from the main island, with each one offering something different. Including the two more distant islands of Saint-Barthélémy and Saint-Martin in the Leewards, the total area of the Department is 1,780 square km.

Guadeloupe (1,510 square km) is really two islands, separated by the narrow bridged strait of the Rivière Salée. To the W is mountainous egg-shaped Basse-Terre, with the volcano Grande Soufrière (1,484 metres) at its centre. It has an area of 777 square km, a total of 150,000 inhabitants, and the administrative capital of the same name on its SW coast. The commercial capital of Guadeloupe is Pointe-à-Pitre, situated in the flat half of the island, Grande-Terre. Grande-Terre, triangular in shape and slightly smaller than Basse-Terre, has a total population of 190,000. The names of the two parts shows a most un-Gallic disregard of logic as Basse-Terre is the higher and Grande-Terre is the smaller; possibly they were named by sailors, who found the winds lower on the Basse-Terre and greater on the Grande-Terre side.

Guadeloupe was badly hit by Hurricane Hugo in 1989. Much of the structural damage has been repaired or replaced with aid from the French Government, and the island's flora has recovered.

History

Christopher Columbus discovered Guadeloupe in 1493 and named it after the Virgin of Guadalupe, of Extremadura, Spain. The Caribs, who had inhabited the island, called it Karukera,

meaning "island of beautiful waters". As in most of the Caribbean, the Spanish never settled, and Guadeloupe's history closely resembles that of Martinique, beginning with French colonization in 1635. The first slaves had been brought to the island by 1650. In the first half of the seventeenth century, Guadeloupe did not enjoy the same levels of prosperity, defence or peace as Martinique. After four years of English occupation, Louis XV in 1763 handed over Canada to Britain to secure his hold on these West Indian islands with the Treaty of Paris. The French Revolution brought a period of uncertainty, including a brief reign of terror under Victor Hugues. Those landowners who were not guillotined fled; slavery was abolished, only to be restored in 1802. Up to 1848, when the slaves were finally freed by Victor Schoelcher, the island's economy was inhibited by sugar crises and imperial wars (French and English). After 1848, the sugar plantations suffered from a lack of manpower, although indentured labour was brought in from East India.

Despite having equal status with Martinique, first as a Department then as a Region, Guadeloupe's image as the less-sophisticated, poor relation persists. In common with Martinique, though, its main political voice is radical (unlike the more conservative Saint-Barthélémy and Saint-Martin), often marked by a more violent pro-independence movement.

Government

Guadeloupe is administered by a prefect, appointed by the French Ministry of the Interior. The local legislature consists of a 42-seat general council, elected by popular vote, which sits for 6 years, and a 41-seat regional council made up of the locally-elected councillors and the two senators and three deputies elected to the French parliament. Guadeloupe also sends two councillors to the Economic and Social Council in Paris. Political parties include the Socialist Party, the Communist Party, Union for French Democracy, Union for the Liberation of Guadeloupe and Rally for the Republic.

The Economy

Agriculture and, increasingly since the 1970s, tourism are the principal activities. Bananas have displaced sugar as the single most important export earner, although sugar and its by-products (rum and molasses) generate about 35% of exports. Melons and tropical flowers have been promoted for sale abroad, while many other fruits, vegetables and coffee are grown mainly for the domestic market. Wages and conditions similar to those in metropolitan France force the price of local products to levels viable only on the parent market. At the same time, the high rate of imports raises local prices above those of the island's non-French neighbours. Consequently there has been little move towards industrialization to satisfy a wider market and unemployment is high, at 31% of the labour force in 1990.

Investment in the tourism industry raised the number of hotel rooms on Guadeloupe from 3,037 in 1980 to an estimated 4,500. Nearly 90% of stopover visitors come from Europe, mostly from France. Although the US market has been growing strongly it is only about 8% of the total of about 105,000 a year. Cruise ship passengers, on the other hand, showed a spectacular 110% growth in 1993, reaching 75,202 arrivals that year.

Culture

See the general introduction to the French Antilles above.

Flora and Fauna

Guadeloupe is in some ways reminiscent

DÉPARTMENT DE GUADELOUPE: FACT FILE

Geographic

Land area	1,780 sq km
forested	40.8%
pastures	16.0%
cultivated	17.2%

Demographic

Population (1992)	400,000
annual growth rate (1987-92)	1.8%
urban	48.4%
rural	51.6%
density	234.2 per sq km
Religious affiliation	
Roman Catholic	93.2%
Birth rate per 1,000 (1990)	19.4
	(world av 27.1)
Death rate per 1,000 (1990)	6.0
	(world av 9.8)

Education and Health

Life expectancy at birth,	
male	70 years
female	77 years
Infant mortality rate	
per 1,000 live births (1990)	10.0
Physicians (1986)	1 per 682 persons
Hospital beds (1987)	1 per 99 persons
Calorie intake as %	
of FAO requirement	112%
Population age 25 and over	
with no formal schooling	10.7%
Literate males (over 15)	89.7%
Literate females (over 15)	90.5%

Economic

GNP (1987 market prices)	US$1,170mn
GNP per capita	US$3,200
Public external debt (1988)	US$41mn
Tourism receipts (1990)	US$231mn
Inflation (annual av 1986-91)	2.7
Radio	1 per 4.0 persons
Television	1 per 2.6 persons
Telephone	1 per 3.2 persons

Employment

Population economically active (1990)	
	172,418
Unemployment rate	31.1%
% of labour force in agriculture	7.2
mining and manufacturing	4.7
construction	6.8
Military forces (French troops also in	
Martinique and Guyane)	8,000

Source _Encyclopaedia Britannica_

of Normandy or Poitou, especially the farms, built in those regional styles. The comparatively low-lying Grande-Terre is mainly given over to sugar cane and live-stock-raising. Mostly a limestone pla-teau, it does have a hilly region, Les Grands-Fonds, and a marshy, mangrove coast extending as far N as Port-Louis on its W flank.

The island's Natural Park covers 30,000 hectares of forest land in the cen-tre of Basse-Terre, which is by far the more scenic part. As the island is volcanic there are a number of related places to visit. The Park has no gates, no opening hours and no admission fee. Do not pick flowers, fish, hunt, drop litter, play music or wash anything in the rivers. Trails have been marked out all over the Park, in-cluding to the dome of Soufrière volcano with its fumaroles, cauldrons and sul-phur fields (see below). Apart from the Natural Park, established in 1989, there are Les Réserves Naturelles des Pitons du Nord et de Beaugendre, La Réserve Naturelle du Grand Cul-de-Sac Marin and La Réserve Naturelle de Pigeon, or Réserve Cousteau (see below). The wa-ters after which the Caribs named the island come hot (as at the Ravine Chaude springs on the Rivière à Goyaves), tum-bling (the waterfalls of the Carbet river and the Cascade aux Écrevisses on the Corossol), and tranquil (the lakes of Grand Étang, As de Pique and Étang Zombi). One traveller has described the island as "idyllic – were it not for the noise of motorcycles".

A Maison du Volcan at Saint-Claude (open 0900-1700) and a Maison de la Fôret (0915-1700) on the Route de la Traversée give information on the vol-cano and its surrounding forest. From the Maison de la Forêt there are 10, 20 and 60-minute forest walks which will take you deep among the towering trees. The Cascade des Ecrevisses, a waterfall and small pool, is about 2 km from the Maison (easily missed) and is a good place to swim and spend the day; popular

with the locals. Also on the Route de la Traversée is the Parc Zoologique above Mahaut, which allows you to see many of the species which exist in the Natural Park, unfortunately in very small cages (entrance 25F, children 15F, open 0900-1700). It is worth a visit for the fine panoramic views from the café (free drink included in entrance ticket) and the restaurant is simple but excellent.

The Natural Park's emblem is the ra-coon (*raton laveur*) which, although pro-tected, is very rare. You are much more likely to see birds and insects in the Natural Park. On La Désirade a few agoutis survive, as well as iguana, which can also be found on Les Saintes. Much of the island's indigenous wildlife has vanished.

The vegetation of Basse-Terre ranges from tropical forest (40% of the land is forested: trees such as the mahogany and gommier, climbing plants, wild orchids) to the cultivated coasts: sugar cane on the windward side, bananas in the S and cof-fee and vanilla on the leeward. As well as sugar cane on Grande-Terre, there is an abundance of fruit trees (mango, coco-nut, papaya, guava, etc). On both parts the flowers are a delight, especially the anthuriums and hibiscus.

Beaches

Guadeloupe has excellent beaches for swimming, mostly between Gosier and St-François on Grande Terre. Petit Havre is popular with its small coves and reefs offshore. Here are mostly fishermen and locals and a small shed selling fish meals and beer. The best is at Ste-Anne where the fine white sand and crystal clear water of a constant depth of 1.5 metres far from shore make idyllic bathing; the Plage du Bourg in town is ideal for young children, the Plage de la Caravelle is excellent with access only through the *Club Med*. About 2 km from the town is the Plage de Bois Jolan, reached down a track, where the water is shallow enough

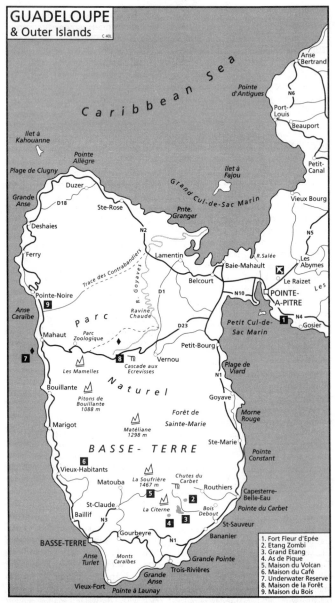

GUADELOUPE
& Outer Islands
C 40L

Caribbean Sea

1. Fort Fleur d'Epée
2. Etang Zombi
3. Grand Etang
4. As de Pique
5. Maison du Volcan
6. Maison du Café
7. Underwater Reserve
8. Maison de la Forêt
9. Maison du Bois

to walk to the protecting reef. Further E are good beaches at St-François and the 11-km road to Pointe des Colibris skirts the Anse Kahouanne with lots of tracks going down to the sea; sand is limited but there are snorkelling possibilities. At the tip of the peninsula is Plage Tarare, the island's only nude bathing beach (part of *Club Méditerranée*). Plage de l'Anse à la Gourde has good sand and is popular with campers at weekends. More deserted beaches can be found on the NE of Grande Terre. On the leeward coast of Basse-Terre are some good beaches. South of Pointe Noire on the W coast is Plage Caraïbe, which is clean, calm and beautiful, with restaurant *Le Reflet* (helpful owners), picnic facilities, toilets and a shower. A small, black sand beach, La Grand Anse, just W of Trois Rivières, has a barbeque and drinks (expensive) on the beach and a shower and toilets (which do not always work). In the NW, La Grande Anse, 30 mins walk N of Deshaies, is superb and undeveloped with no hotels, golden sand but no snorkelling except round a large rock where the current is quite strong. Body surfing is good when the waves are big. Camping sites in the area and a beach restaurant at the S end with charcoal-grilled chicken and rice. There are several snack bars half way along the beach, serving sandwiches and drinks. On Sundays local people sell hot créole food quite cheaply. The beaches on the N coast of Basse-Terre can be very dangerous and at Plage de Clugny there are warning signs not to swim as there have been several drownings.

Marine Life and Watersports

On the Leeward Coast (Côte-Sous-le-Vent, or the Golden Corniche), is the Underwater Reserve developed by Jacques Cousteau. *Nautilus*, from Malendure beach, S of Mahaut, black sand, T 98 89 08, F 98 85 66, is a glass-bottom boat which takes you round the marine park, departs 1030, 1200, 1430 and 1600, 80F adults, 40F children 5-12 years. The boat anchors for about 15 minutes off Ilet Pigeon for snorkelling, but it is rather deep to see much. In wet weather the water becomes too murky to see anything. The boat is often booked solid by cruise ship visitors. There is a créole restaurant on the beach where you can eat while waiting for the boat. Diving trips can be arranged at Les Heures Saines (T 98 86 63) at Rocher de Malendure, or Chez Guy (T 98 81 72, friendly, recommended for beginners' confidence, 140F for one dive, everything included), at Pigeon, Bouillante. Both also offer fishing trips as do Fishing Club Antilles, T 84 15 00, Le Rocher de Malendure, T 98 73 25, and Nautilus Club near Bouillante, all around 4,000-4,500 F per boat for a full day. Caraïbes Peche at Marina Bas du Fort, offers deep sea fishing or day trips with barbeques and fishing along the way, T 90 97 51, 95 67 26.

Papyrus, Marina Bas-du-Fort, Pointe-à-Pitre, T 90 92 98, is a glass-bottom boat which runs excursions through the Rivière Salée and the mangroves of Grand Cul de Sac Marin, to l'Îlet Caret and coral reef off the NE coast of Basse-Terre. The *Paoka* also does this trip through the mangroves from Lamentin at the Ginature centre at La Boucan, T 25-74-78. Alternatively, contact the National Forests Office who have an information centre behind Le Raizet airport at Abymes. Most of the hotels on the seaboard offer windsurfing for guests and visitors, and some arrange water skiing and diving courses.

Sailing boats can be chartered for any length of time from Captain Lemaire, Carénage A, Route du Gosier, 97110 Pointe-à-Pitre. With a crew of 3 the cost works out at about US$75-100 pp per day, excluding food, or US$250-300 per boat. There are two marinas between Pointe-à-Pitre and Gosier, and good, shallow-draught anchorage at Gosier. Windsurfers gather at the UCPA Hotel Club in Saint François.

Other Sports

Hiking in the Natural Park (contact the Organisation des Guides de Montagne de la Caraïbe (OGMC), Maison Forestière, 97120 Matouba, T 80 05 79, a guided hike to La Soufrière will cost around 300 F, make sure the guide speaks a language you understand, approximate hiking times, mileage and description of terrain and flora are included in the booklet *Promenades et Randonnées*); horse-riding (Le Criolo, Saint-Félix, 97190 Gosier, T 84 04 86, La Martingale, La Jaille, T 26 28 39, Ranch Caraïbes, T 82 11 54); tennis, with lighting for night games, at several hotels, including *Auberge de la Vieille Tour*, *PLM Arawak*, *Salako*, *Creole Beach*, *Novotel*, and *Village Viva* (also squash, T 90 87 66), all at Gosier, *Méridien*, *Hamak*, *Trois-Mâts* at Saint-François, and *Les Alizés* at Le Moule. There is one 18-hole, municipal golf course at Saint-François (T 88 41 87). The *Hotel Golf Marine Club* at Saint-François, T 88 60 60, has an 18-hole course designed by Robert Trent Jones, green fees 220F/day or 1,000F/week. Bullock cart racing is popular on the W coast of Grand-Terre and draws large crowds. They race along the flat, then turn sharply and charge up a steep hill. The wheels are then chocked and they have to see how far they can get, zig zag fashion, with about 10 minutes of very hard work. Much shouting, plenty of beer, food tents and an overloud PA system.

Festivals

Carnival starts on Epiphany and runs through Ash Wednesday with different events each Sunday, the main ones on the last weekend. The Festival of the Sea is in mid-August with beach parties, boat races, crab races, etc. La Fête des Cuisinières (Cooks' Festival) in early August is a lot of fun with parades in créole costumes and music.

GRANDE-TERRE

Pointe-à-Pitre, on Grande-Terre at the S end of the Rivière Salée, is the chief commercial centre, near the airport of Le Raizet and the port of entry for shipping (population is 80,000). The city lies to the S of the Route Nacional NI (the ring road) and any of the intercepts will take you to the city centre, which is quite compact, lying to the S of Boulevard Chanzy (a short stretch of dual carriageway). It is a functional city, variously described as characterless, or colourful and bustling. Its early colonial buildings were largely destroyed by an earthquake in 1843; nowadays it is an odd mixture of parts which could have been transplanted from provincial France and parts which are Caribbean, surrounded by low-cost housing blocks. The central Place de la Victoire was once the site of a guillotine, and the streets adjacent to it contain the oldest buildings. Having been refurbished in 1989 it lost several of its large trees in Hurricane Hugo but there are still some flame trees at the N end and pleasant gardens. In the middle is a statue to Félix Eboue (1884-1944), a Governor General. There is a bandstand and lots of cafés surrounding the park with tables outside, very pleasant but crowded with office workers at lunch time. The buildings around the park are a mixture of coloured tin roofs and concrete. At its S end is La Darse, where the inter-island ferries tie up. When the boats arrive/depart there is plenty of activity and chaotic scenes with buses and taxis fighting for space. At the SW corner of the Place is a war memorial dedicated to *La Guadeloupe et ses enfants, morts pour La France 1914-18*, flanked by two First World War guns. Behind it is the Tourist Office (quite helpful, some English spoken). On the E side of the Square is the Renaissance Cinema. The Place de l'Eglise lies NW of the Place de la Victoire behind the *Hotel Normandie* and contains the ochre-coloured Basilique de St Pierre et St Paul, a high modern structure held up by unusual metal columns supporting a gallery running around the top of the church with some elaborate gingerbread-style metal work. Outside there is a bubbling fountain and a statue of Admiral Gourbeyre who helped the people of Pointe-a-Pitre after the huge 1843 earthquake (see Fort Louis Delgrès, Basse-Terre). The square is flanked by the hideous Palais de Justice but looks quite attractive with florists on the street.

The colourful red-roofed central market place (between rues Peynier, Fréboult, St-John Perse and Schoelcher) is indeed bustling, with the nearest thing to local hustlers, women (some wearing the traditional Madras cotton hats) who try to sell you spices, fruit, vegetables or hats. There are other markets on the dockside in Place de la Victoire, between Blvd Chanzy and the docks and between Blvd Légitimus and the cemetery. Local handicrafts, particularly Madras cotton (from which the traditional costumes of the *doudous*, or local women, are made), are good buys. Such items are in great contrast to the French fashions, wines and perfumes available at normal French domestic prices in the shops.

There are two museums: Musée Schoelcher, 24 rue Peynier, which celebrates the liberator of the slaves (open Monday-Tuesday 0900-1230, 1400-1730, Thursday-Friday 0900-1230, 1400-1830, Saturday 0900-1230, entry 10 F), and Musée Saint-John Perse, in a lovely colonial-style house, rues Nozières et A R Boisneuf, dedicated to the poet and diplomat who was awarded the Nobel Prize for literature in 1960 (open 0900-1700, closed Sundays, entry 10F, children half price). On AR Boisneuf is the old town hall, being restored at a cost of 2m F. It has a stone/brick ground floor and a fine wooden first floor with an intricately carved gutter.

Just outside Pointe-à-Pitre on the N4 towards Gosier is Bas du Fort, the site of the large new marina, said to be the biggest in the Caribbean. The aquarium is also here, reopened December 1992 after renovation, at Place Créole, T 90 92 38, open daily 0900-1900. At the next

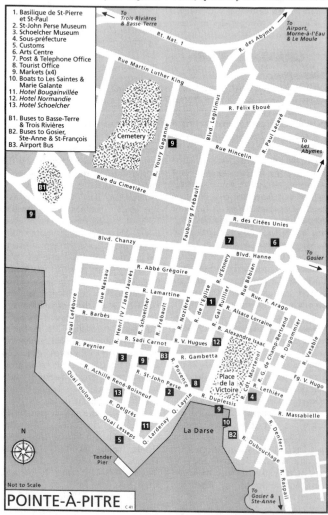

1. Basilique de St-Pierre et St-Paul
2. St-John Perse Museum
3. Schoelcher Museum
4. Sous-préfecture
5. Customs
6. Arts Centre
7. Post & Telephone Office
8. Tourist Office
9. Markets (x4)
10. Boats to Les Saintes & Marie Galante
11. *Hotel Bougainvillée*
12. *Hotel Normandie*
13. *Hotel Schoelcher*

B1. Buses to Basse-Terre & Trois Rivières
B2. Buses to Gosier, Ste-Anne & St-François
B3. Airport Bus

POINTE-À-PITRE

turing off the main road to Gosier (follow the signs to the CORA hypermarket) are the ruins of the 18th-century fortress, Fort Fleur d'Epée (open daily 0800-1800, free) which once guarded the E approaches to Pointe-à-Pitre. There are now pleasant, shady gardens within the ramparts. Art exhibitions are regularly held either in the officers' quarters or in the underground rooms. Also note the pre-war graffiti with pictures of old sailing ships. Excellent views of Pointe-à-Pitre and across Petit Cul-de-Sac Marin towards the mountains of Basse-Terre. Gosier itself is the holiday centre of Guadeloupe, with hotels, restaurants, night clubs. There has been lots of building in this area, even up into the hills above the coast road. Nevertheless, Gosier itself is a pleasant place with a marvellous picnic spot overlooking a small beach (Plage de l'Anse Canot), a little island about 100m offshore (Ilet du Gosier) and lighthouse. You could swim to it, there is a channel marked by buoys, but watch out for speed boats. There are a few old wooden houses up the hill from the church, where one or two are restaurants. The modern resort with the large hotels has been built on reclaimed mangrove marshes but the beach is nice with the usual watersports facilities. Gosier is quite sleepy but wakes up at night when the restaurants open.

The S coast between Gosier and Sainte-Anne is hilly with cliffs, making it particularly suited to development and on most headlands there are huge condominium developments looking across the sea to Marie-Galante as well as to the S tip of Basse-Terre. Sainte-Anne is a small, pleasant town and has a small church with a slightly crooked spire overlooking the square. Here you will find the Plage de la Caravelle, rated by some as the best on the island. The land gradually subsides towards St-François, originally a fishing village but now home to *Méridien* (owned by Air France), *Hamak*, *la Cocteraie* and *Plantation Ste-Marthe*

which are all luxury hotels. There is a light aircraft landing strip and eighteen hole par 71 golf course designed by Robert Trent Jones. You can catch the ferry to La Désirade from here. Watersports equipment can be hired from several companies at the marina.

The rugged Pointe des Châteaux at the easternmost tip of the island is part of the national park. From the car park, there is a small, self-guided walk to the cross (Pointe des Colibris) erected in 1951, on the point where there are two "compass" tables showing distances to various landmarks. The limestone outcrop is quite steep in places but the view over the inshore island of La Roche (housing a colony of sooty terns, *sterna fuscata*) to La Désirade in the distance, is spectacular especially on a windy day when the sea whips over the rocks. It is worth taking the slightly longer return path around the headland as you get good views of the completely flat Petite Terre with its lighthouse and on clear days Marie-Galante (30 km), Les Saintes (60 km) and Dominica (75 km). Note the Grandes Salines (salt lagoons) where flamingoes were once common. There are signs on the walk pointing out particular plants and describing features. There is a restaurant selling welcome cold drinks and exotic icecream. **NB** the beach between the two points is dangerous.

Between Saint-François and Le Moule, a colonial mansion at Zévallos can be visited. Le Moule was the original capital of Guadeloupe and there are still some cannon from the fortifications against English attack. A precolumbian Arawak village, called Morel, has recently been uncovered on the beautiful sandy beaches N of the town; the Musée d'Archéologie Précolombienne Edgar Clerc is at La Rosette (open Monday-Tuesday 0900-1230, 1400-1700, Thursday-Saturday 0900-1230, 1400-1800, free). On the Abymes road (D101) from Le Moule is the Distillerie Bellevue, makers of Rhum Damoiseau, which can be toured Monday-Friday 0800-1400. From Le Moule you can either return to Point-à-Pitre through Les Grands Fonds, or continue up the rugged, rough Atlantic coast to Pointe de la Grande Vigie in the extreme N. Take a good map as it is easy to get lost on the little roads in the sugar cane fields. After travelling through the small towns of La Rosette, Gros Cap and Campèche (small restaurant/bar), the countryside becomes more barren. At Porte d'Enfer (Hell's Gate) there are a number of barbeque places and little huts at the mouth of an inlet. You can camp here. There is not much sand and the sea can be dangerous, do not go too far out. The coastline from here is very rocky with cliffs and spectacular views.

Grande-Terre's leeward coast has beaches at Port-Louis and Petit-Canal which are the usual concrete towns with restaurant and filling station. North of Anse Bertrand there is a fine clean, sandy beach, Anse Laborde, which has plenty of shade, a restaurant, and a reef close to the beach, good for snorkelling. Inland, at Morne-à-l'Eau, there is a remarkable terraced cemetery built around a natural amphitheatre, very attractive on All Saints Day when lit by thousands of candles. Beware of large crowds.

BASSE-TERRE

Basse-Terre, on the other wing of the island, is the administrative capital of Guadeloupe and the entire Department, with a population of 20,000. There can be found in the city some very pretty and authentic old buildings of the colonial period. It is a charming port town of narrow streets and well-laid-out squares with palm and tamarind trees, in a lovely setting between the sea and the great volcano La Soufrière. Market day is Saturday. There is an interesting 17th-century cathedral, and nearby are the ruins of Fort Louis Delgrès, well-preserved and full of interesting ramparts and bastions (original building 1667, considerably enlarged in the 18th century; open daily 0900-1200, 1400-1700, free). The British occupied the fort in 1759-1763 and again in 1810-1816 when it was known as Fort Mathilde. It was fought over and renamed many times, being given its present name in 1989 in memory of the man who escaped the forces of Bonaparte after the reimposition of slavery in 1802. The Grande Caverne, formerly the billet of the non-commissioned officers, is now a cultural museum, with an exhibition of clothes and photographs of the area. In the cemetery is the tomb of Admiral Gourbeyre. The date of his tomb is not that of his death (he disappeared in 1845) but of 8 February 1843 when there was a huge earthquake; the Admiral was instrumental in disaster relief.

Saint-Claude, a wealthy suburb and summer resort 8 km into the hills, is surrounded by coffee trees and tropical gardens. Matouba, above Saint-Claude, is an East Indian village in lovely surroundings (waterfall and springs) with a good restaurant. On the outskirts of the village is a monument to Louis Delgrès on the spot where he and his companions were caught and killed by Napoléon's troops. There are hot springs a good walk above the village (1,281 m) and the bottling plant for the local mineral water.

On Basse-Terre island one of the main sights is the volcano La Soufrière, reached through a primeval rain forest. A narrow, twisty road leads up from Basse-Terre town to a car park at Savane à Mulets (1,142 m) from where the crater, 300m higher, is a 1½-hour climb up the Chemin des Dames, a fascinating trail with changing flora, but becoming eroded through overuse. Buses go to Saint-Claude from where it is a 6 km walk to Savane à Mulets. (The best clothing for the climb is the least; anoraks or coats worn against the dampness merely compound the problem; but take a sweater, it can get quite chilly. Leave

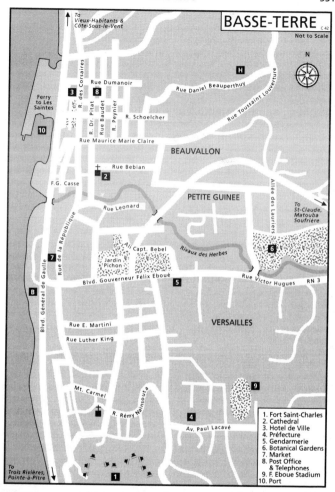

BASSE-TERRE C 42
Not to Scale

To Vieux-Habitants & Côte-Sous-le-Vent

N

Rue Daniel Beauperthuy

Rue Dumanoir

R. des Corsaires

Rue Baudet

R. Dr. Pitat

R. Peynier

R. Schoelcher

Ferry to Les Saintes

Rue Maurice Marie Claire

BEAUVALLON

Rue Toussaint Louverture

Rue Bebian

F.G. Casse

PETITE GUINEE

Rue Leonard

Allée des Lauriers

To St-Claude, Matouba Soufrière

All. Capt. Bebel

Rivaux des Herbes

Jardin Pichon

Blvd. Gouverneur Félix Eboué

Rue Victor Hugues   RN 3

Rue de la République

Blvd Général de Gaulle

Rue E. Martini

VERSAILLES

Rue Luther King

Mt. Carmel

R. Rémy Nainouta

Av. Paul Lacavé

1. Fort Saint-Charles
2. Cathedral
3. Hotel de Ville
4. Préfecture
5. Gendarmerie
6. Botanical Gardens
7. Market
8. Post Office & Telephones
9. F. Eboue Stadium
10. Port

To Trois Rivières, Pointe-à-Pitre

some spare clothes in the car.) From the top there is a spectacular view (if you are not enveloped in clouds, which is usually the case, observe the mountain for a few days to see whether early morning or mid-day is clearest, above the lush jungle foliage on the E slopes and sulphurous fumes spurting over yellow and orange rock. The summit is quite flat; the main vent is to the S (the view is more interesting than the Soufrière) and there are discs in the ground to help you find it in the fog. It is possible to come down on the Trace Micael, along a forest path, to the Chutes de Carbet waterfalls where the water becomes cool and clear. Carry on down, past more waterfalls, until you get to a car park (often full, parking can be a problem). If starting from the bottom, take a bus from Capesterre to Routhiers, 10F, then walk along the D3 road until it ends. Follow a trail and within 50 minutes you will reach the third waterfall of 20m. Go back 100m and follow the trail upwards again until you reach the 110-metre, second waterfall, 711m above sea level. The path is stony and you have to cross the Carbet on a rope bridge. You can swim in the warm, sulphuric pool below the fall but if you visit when there is rain higher up, beware of flash floods. From here you can continue climbing to the first waterfall, at 125m, or turn SE to the picnic place, Aire d'Arrivée, 15 minutes, where there are barbeque stalls (good chicken). The D4 road starts here and descends to St-Sauveur. La Citerne, a neighbouring volcano, has a completely round crater. There is a trail but part requires climbing ladders straight up the wall. There are more leisurely trails to other craters, fumaroles and lakes. Also on this side are Grand Etang and Etang Zombi. You can drive, hitchhike or walk down the D4 road from the Chutes de Carbet to the edge of Grand Etang and walk around it, about one hour through lush vegetation. Do not swim in the lake because of bilharzia. There are also marked trails to Etang de l'As de Pique, high above Grand Etang to the S on the slope of la Madeleine (2 hours) and the Trace de Moscou which leads SW to the Plateau du Palmiste (2½ hours), from where a road leads down to Gourbeyre. Walk down to St-Sauveur for fine views over banana plantations, the coast and Les Saintes. Allow at least 5 hours to walk from Capesterre to St-Sauveur via the waterfalls and Grand Etang and wear good hiking shoes.

You can walk the Trace Victor Hugues, along the main ridge of Basse-Terre (a 29-km hike), and a number of other Traces. The River Quiock trail has been recommended but take the Serie Bleu map; despite being well-marked originally, storm damage has made it difficult to find all the markers. It can be very muddy, wear good boots. You can start from the car park at the Cascade des Ecrevisses (see above) on the D23. Walk 300m along the road and take a path to the right (follow the sign to the Pathfinders camp) to Piolet, near the entrance to the Bras-David-Tropical-Parc on the other side of the road. The trail leads down to where the River Quiock meets the larger River Bras-David, carefully cross the river, then the trail heads W along the Quiock until returning to the D23. Hitchhike back to your car (if you have one). The walk will take you 3-4 hours depending on the state of the trail. Other features of the Natural Park are described under **Flora and Fauna**, above.

Besides the Maisons du Volcan and de la Fôret (see above), there are on Basse-Terre Maisons du Café at La Grivelière, Vieux Habitants (T 98 48 42), du Bois at Bourg, Pointe Noire (a cabinet-making and woodworking centre with a permanent exhibition of household implements, furniture and other things made of wood, daily hours 0915-1700, 5F) and a Centre de Broderie, Fort l'Olive, Vieux-Fort (daily 0900-1800). Vieux-Fort is on the island's SW tip, the other side of the Monts Caraïbes from the main Basse-Terre to Pointe-à-Pitre road. There are nice gardens surrounding the lighthouse, with good views. One or two cannon can be seen from the old battery. Good créole restaurant with dance hall attached.

Also visit the ancient Amerindian rock carvings dating from around 300-400 AD, at the Parc Archéologique des Roches Gravées, near Trois Rivières, on Basse-Terre's S coast; the most important is a drawing of the head of a Carib chief inside a cave where he is presumably buried. The site is now in a garden setting, with wardens (it's a good idea to consult the leaflet which comes with the 4F entry fee, children free, because some of the engravings on the stones are hard to decipher; many are badly eroded; the pamphlet also explains the garden's trees). The Parc is a 10-minute walk down from the church in Trois Rivières where the buses stop. Five minutes further down the hill is the boat dock for Les Saintes (paying car park).

Capesterre-Belle-Eau (population 18,000) is the third largest town and is an important agricultural centre with lots of shops, restaurants and a market. Above the town is the garden of Paul Lacavé, which can be visited. North of the town is the Allée de Flamboyants, a spectacular avenue of flame trees which flower May-September. South of the town is the Allée Dunmanoir, a magnificent 1-km avenue of royal palms. At Sainte-Marie, a statue erected in 1916 commemorates the site of Columbus' landing in 1493. It has now been defaced by nationalists. South of Sainte-Marie, near Carangaise, there is a Hindu temple, built in 1974 by René Komla, richly decorated with statues of Vishnu and Ganesh outside.

Between Basse-Terre town and the Route de la Traversée on the W coast are Vieux-Habitants, with a restored 17th-century church, and the underwater reserve (see **Marine Life** above). Contact the Syndicat d'Initiative de Bouillante, T 98 73 48, for information on the Bouillante area, which considers itself the capital of diving, including gîtes, restaurants and dive operators. A good hike is the Trace des Contrebandiers, 3 hours, from the Maison du Bois, Pointe Noire. A long but beautiful road takes you to the Trace. When you leave the trail on the other side you need to hitch-hike because there are no buses. North of the Traversée, on the Côte-Sous-Le-Vent are the calm, clean beaches at Ferry and Grand-Anse and the rougher ones at Deshaies. Deshaies is attractive, strung out along the beach with cliffs at each end; there are hotels, restaurants (*le Madras* and the more expensive *Le Mouillage*, offering local food such as fish, créole chicken),

basketball and tennis courts. There is an information (unmanned) centre at Batterie de Deshaies overlooking the town, with information on the vegetation of the area. All that remains of the old fort are some rusty cannons and the outline of various buildings but it is a popular, shady picnic spot and there are barbeque places. Round the N of Basse-Terre is the town of Sainte-Rose where you can visit the rum museum, Distillerie Reimonenq, Bellevue Ste-Rose (T 28 70 04, 28 79 92, open 0900-1700 Monday-Saturday, 1000-1300, 1500-1700 Sunday); the road continues S to Lamentin (visit the Grosse-Montagne distillery for guided tours and tastings) and the hot springs at Ravine Chaude.

OUTER ISLANDS OF GUADELOUPE

The outer islands of Guadeloupe are among the least visited of the West Indian islands; they can easily be reached by air or boat from Guadeloupe. One can still get on a trading schooner between the islands if patient.

LES SAINTES

On *Les Saintes* (a string of small islands named Los Santos by Columbus: only Terre-de-Haut and Terre-de-Bas are inhabited) the people are descendants of Breton fisherfolk who have survived among themselves with little intermarriage with the dominant West Indian races. Some still wear the same round hats, the salako, that Breton fisherfolk used to wear, and fishing is still the main occupation on the islands. They are a popular excursion from Guadeloupe now, but are not too spoilt, and with a good, natural harbour, many small cruise ships spend the day here. Nevertheless, to get a better idea of the islanders' traditional way of life, staying overnight is recommended so that you can appreciate it once the day trippers leave at 1600.

Terre-de-Haut is the main island visited by tourists: irregularly shaped and surprisingly barren, it is about 6 km long and 2 km wide at its widest point. Most of the 1,500 inhabitants live around the Anse Mire, looking across the Ilet à Cabrit. There are some excellent beaches including that of Pont Pierre, also known as Pompierre, where snorkelling is good and camping is possible, Marigot, L'Anse du Figuier (no shade), L'Anse Crawen (nudist) and Grand'Anse (white sand, rougher waters, swimming not allowed). The UCPA sailing school at Petit Anse offers half or full day sailing or windsurfing courses. Walking on the islands is good, either from the town to the beaches, or to the top of Le Chameau (TV mast on top) on Terre-de-Haut's W end (spectacular views of Les Saintes, Marie-Galante, Guadeloupe and Dominica). An easy trail, Trace des Crétes, starts at Terre-de-Haut. Turn right at the pier, follow the main street about 100m, turn left at the chapel and follow the road up to Le Marigot (look out for the *sentier du morne morel* sign behind the restaurant on the S side of the bay) and on to the beach of Baie de Pont Pierre, a lovely golden beach with rocks, Roches Percées, in the bay. Boats and diving equipment can be rented at the landing stage. Goats can be a nuisance if you decide to picnic here. At the end of the beach the trail leads up the hill where you have a good view of the islands, if you keep left, one branch of the trail leads to Grand'Anse beach. The 'white' cemetery, La Cimétière Rose, worth visiting, pretty, with paths bordered by shells, is close to the beach and from here you can walk back to Terre-de-Haut, about 1½ hours in total. Alternatively, you can walk along Grand'Anse and on to Pointe Rodriguez and the small cove Anse Rodriguez below it. There are beautiful views also from Fort Napoléon, high up above the town on Pointe à l'Eau, open 0900-1200 only (12F to enter, children 6 to 12 half price). The views demonstrate the stra-

tegic importance of Les Saintes (the Gibraltar of the Caribbean), and the museum in Fort Napoléon gives the French view of the decisive sea battle of Les Saintes (1782 – the English Admiral Rodney defeated and scattered the fleet of France's Commander de Grasse, who was preparing to attack Jamaica). The fort itself is rather disappointing but the exhibitions are good with interesting models of the ships and battles. A guide will give you a 30-minute tour (in French) of the main building. If not historically-minded, just sit and watch the weather. There are exhibits also of local fishing (including a *saintois*, a local fishing boat, originally with blue and white striped sail, but now diesel-powered) and crafts, a bookshop and drinks on sale. Around the ramparts is the Jardin Exotique which specializes in growing succulents and includes a wild area where plants native to Les Saintes are grown. On the Ilet à Cabrit are the ruins of Fort Joséphine.

Terre-de-Bas is home to about 1,500 people, mostly fishermen. There is a pottery which also gives some employment, but many have left for work in France.

Boats land at Grande Baie which is a small inlet guarded by a fort and two small statues. You get good views of La Coche and Grand Ilet (two of the uninhabited islands) on the way across. There is a good little information centre at the dock. Buses will meet the ferry and you can go to the main settlement at Petite Anse where there is a new fishing port as well as the secondary school for the islands and a pretty little church with a red roof (tour approx 40 mins 30F). The beach at Grand Anse is very pleasant and there are a few bars and restaurants nearby (*A La Belle Etoile* is actually on the beach). There is a track which runs from Petite Anse to Grand Anse which is a good walk. It is very quiet compared with Terre-de-Haut. Salakos and wood carvings are made by local inhabitants.

Island Information – Les Saintes

● How To Get There

There are daily boats from Trois Rivières (Guadeloupe) to Terre-de-Haut via Terre-de-Bas (40F one way, 30 mins, 70F return: depart Trois Rivières between 0800 and 0900, and 1500 and 1645, different each day; depart Terre-de-Haut 0545-0630, 1500-1615, T 92 90 30/99 53 79) and from Pointe-à-Pitre (80F one way, 160F return, children 85F, about 1 hour, daily 0800, return 1600, Trans Antilles Express from La Darse, T 83 12 45). Boat from Basse-Terre Mon, Wed, Thur and Sat 1200 and 1205, 45 mins, 50F one way (buses from Pointe Noire on W coast drop you at ferry dock). It can be a rough crossing, not suitable for those prone to seasickness. Daily flight except Sun from Pointe-à-Pitre, 180F one way, 0800, 1700, 15 mins, return 0830, 1725, Air Guadeloupe (address above); or Air Sport, Le Raizet, T 82 25 80. The ferry between Terre-de-Haut and Terre-de-Bas runs about 5 times a day (0800, 0930, 1330, 1500 and 1600, 25F, 15F for children, return) passing the pain de sucre and stopping briefly at the *Bois Joli* (except 0800 and 1500 boats).

● Island Transport

Minibuses take day trippers all over Terre-de-Haut; tour of the island 52F; bus up to Fort Napoléon, 10F (or 25 mins' walk). No transport after dark. There are few cars, unlike on Guadeloupe. Scooter rental, 200F/day, also bicycles, several central locations, 80F/day. It is not necessary to hire a scooter for the whole day, as you can walk to most places, but it may be nice to have one in the afternoon to go to the beach at Pompierre or Figuier. Scooters are banned from the town 0900-1200, 1400-1600 and have to be pushed. At the Mairie you can get some very basic information and a poor map.

● Where To Stay

On Terre-de-Haut: *Bois Joli*, reached by 10-min boat ride from town, rather inconvenient at the end of the island, hotel van transport to town or airport, 21 rooms, US$106-164/94-144 MAP, 8 bungalows, US$233-297/212-276 MAP, most have a/c, phones, pool, bar, restaurant, 2 beaches, some clothes optional, watersports, scooters, T 99 50 38, F 99 55 05, T 800 322 2223 in USA; *Kanaoa*, Pointe Coquelot, T 99 51 36, 580F, CP, a/c, but rather basic, fair restaurant used by tour groups, beautiful waterfront setting 10 mins' walk from landing jetty, very quiet; *Le Village Créole*, Pointe Coquelot, T 99 53 83, F 99 55

55, T 800 322 2223, multilingual helpful owner, Ghyslain Laps, who acts as unofficial tourist chief for the island (contact him to book villas), 22 suites, US$123-227/88-146 EP, 1-4 people, 2 bedrooms, 2-storey duplex, a/c, mosquito nets, collection from harbour, no restaurant but will provide bread etc for breakfast, yacht charter, boats to rent, private beach, bike and scooter rental; *La Saintoise*, T 99 52 50, in town (closed in November), 350F CP, *Auberge des Anacardiers*, T 99 50 99, attractive, intimate, clean, pool, good restaurant, rec and *Jeanne d'Arc*, good, T 99 50 41, at Fond de Curé village on S coast 290F single, CP (closed in November), all with 10 rooms. On Terre-de-Bas there is one hotel, *Le Poisson Volant*, 9 rooms, T 99 81 47. On both Terre-de-Haut and Terre-de-Bas there are rooms and houses to rent; tourist office has list of phone numbers. Rec are Mme Bonbon, T 90 50 52, on the road to the airfield, who has several rooms, 150F double; Mme Bernadette Cassin, T 99 54 22, clean studio under her house on road to cemetery, 200F/day, 150F for more than 5 days, 50F less without kitchen facilities, if she is full she has family and friends who offer rooms; and Mme Maisonneuve, T 99 53 38, on the same road as the *Mairie*. Reservations are generally rec in peak season, especially Christmas and New Year. The Mairie and the Gendarmerie are reported as very unhelpful regarding accommodation and will not tell you where the hotels are situated. The telephone at the jetty only takes phone cards. Not good for first impressions but otherwise idyllic. There is a shortage of water on the island.

Plenty of **restaurants** around the island, specializing in seafood and offering *menus* for about 60F, but try the *tourment d'amour* coconut sweet. Home made coconut rum punches are also rec, particularly in the little bar on the right hand side of the *gendarmerie* in front of the jetty. *Le Mouillage* restaurant has been rec, T 99 50 57. *Le Genois*, excellent and cheap pizza house on water's edge by harbour square, highly rec, but book, also does takeaways, T 99 53 01. *La Saladerie*, at top of steps on road to Fort Napoléon, popular, rec, not always open out of season. *Galerie de la Baie*, first floor overlooking harbour, snacks and very expensive ice cream. The *boulangerie* next to the *Mairie* is open from 0530, good. The supermarkets are expensive, double French prices. There are a couple of markets every morning on the road towards the Post Office, good for fresh produce.

MARIE-GALANTE

Marie-Galante, a small round island of 153 square km, is simple and old-fashioned but surprisingly sophisticated when it comes to food and drink. It was named by Christopher Columbus after his own ship, the *Santa María La Galante*, and has three settlements. The largest is Grand-Bourg (rather run down) in the SW with a population of around 8,000; Capesterre is in the SE and Saint-Louis (sugar factory, see the bullock carts delivering cane during the cutting season) in the NW. By Grand-Bourg plage try the *batterie de sirop*, selling a treacle-like sugar cane syrup mixed with rum and lime or with water. The beaches, so far almost completely untouched by the tourist flood, are superb. By Capesterre, the Plage de la Feuillère has fine sand beaches and is protected by the coral reef offshore. There is a pleasant beach at Anse de Vieux Fort, the site of the first settlement on the island in 1648 and of a series of fierce skirmishes between the French and the Amerindians. The Trou à Diable (off the D202) is a massive cave which runs deep into the earth. To visit it, it is essential to have strong shoes, a torch with extra batteries, and a guide. It is a very remote spot and there is no organized tourism. The descent requires ropes and should not be attempted unassisted. The walk from the road is striking. The D202 road meets the D201 at La Grande Barre, from where there are good views of the N end of the island and to Guadeloupe. On the coast there are limestone cliffs over 30m high which have been eroded in places to form spectacular arches with the sea splashing through them. One is at Gueule Grand Gouffre (cold drinks on sale) and another, less good example, further E at Caye Plate.

In the nineteenth century the island boasted over 100 sugar mills; a few have been restored and may be visited: Basses, Grand-Pierre, Agapit and Murat. Some are still operating. The former plantation houses of Château Murat (museum open Monday to Thursday 0900-1300, 1500-1800, Saturday and Sunday 0900-1200, free) and Brille are interesting. Murat gives a good impression of the great 18th century sugar plantations; below the sweeping lawn lies the old sugar mill with cane crushing machinery still intact. Behind the house is a walled herb garden. The Bellevue rum distillery on the D202 is a cottage industry. The rum (clear and branded as *'agricole'*) is very powerful and you will be invited to taste and buy. You may also be offered bags of brown sugar and dessicated coconut, a surprisingly nice combination. There is a cinema in Grand-Bourg, El Rancho, which has movies dubbed into French.

Island Information – Marie-Galante
● How To Get There
To get to the island there are regular flights (20 mins) from Pointe-à-Pitre, which is only 43 km away (Air Guadeloupe, as above). There are also ferries between Pointe-à-Pitre and Grand-Bourg and it is possible to do a day trip (85F one way, 160F return, children 85F, 1-1½ hours, times are posted on the booth at the dockside): *Tropic* and *Regina* sail at least 3 times a day (T 90 04 48), Trans Antilles Express 0800, 1230, 1700 Mon-Sat, 0800, 1700, 1900 Sun, returning from Grand-Bourg 0600, 0900, 1545 Mon-Sat, 0600, 1545 1800 Sun. The latter also runs a service from Saint-François to Saint-Louis, (depart Tues and Thur 0800). *Amanda Galante*, a car ferry, crosses from Pointe-à-Pitre to Saint-Louis in 1½ hrs, 560F car and driver return, 50F for each passenger, takes 22 cars and 156 passengers. Trans Antilles offer full and half-day tours to Marie-Galante from Pointe-à-Pitre, including boat trip, visits to beaches, the towns, sugar factories, rum distillery (plus tasting) and other sites (0800-1630 daily, except 0730 weekends, 230F, or 180F for half day, meals 75F extra). Generally you are better off hiring a car or scooter and doing it independently. The *Mistral* also does a Thur tour to Marie-Galante from Saint-François (210F, 0800-1600, T 88 48 74 or 88 48 63).

● Inland Transport
On the island there are buses and taxis. Self-drive cars can be hired from the airport or in the towns, eg M Seytor, rue Beaurenom,

Grand-Bourg. Rates for a full day 240F, for part of a day 190F (2,000F deposit); scooters 150F (1,000F deposit).

● **Where To Stay**

There are no deluxe hotels on Marie-Galante, prices range from 150-300F: at Grand-Bourg there are the *Soledad*, (T 97 75 45), and *L'Auberge de l'Arbre à Pain* (T 97 73 69); *Le Salut* (clean) is S of the pier at St-Louis, T 97 02 67; *Chez Hajo* at Capesterre, T 97 32 76. *Le Touloulou*, 2 km from Capesterre on the Grand Bourg road, clean, well-equipped bungalows backing directly on to the sea, discothèque and restaurant nearby, T 97 32 63, F 97 33 59. There are rooms to let (enquire at the tourist board), about 100F a day, and gîtes (175F a night, 1,250F a week). For accommodation, 24-hour advance booking is necessary.

LA DÉSIRADE

La Désirade is an attractive but rather arid island with 1,600 inhabitants, who occupy themselves in fishing, sheep-rearing and cultivating cotton and maize. A road 10 km long runs along the S coast to the E end of the island, where a giant cactus plantation can be seen. Also at the E end of the island is Pointe du Mombin where there is an outstanding view of the coastline. There are excellent beaches, such as at Souffleur. Perhaps the nicest is in the E at a village called Baie-Mahault, enhanced by a good restaurant/bar, *Chez Céce*, where you can sample dozens of different rum punches.

Island Information – La Désirade
● **How To Get There**

There are air services from Guadeloupe 4 times a week (Air Guadeloupe) and boat services from St-François, Guadeloupe (depart 0800, return 1600, 2 hours), to La Désirade, on which is found the *Hôtel L'Oasis du Désert*, T 20 02 12, 10 rooms, 160F, EP reservations advisable. The *Mistral* (as above) runs excursions from Saint-François to La Désirade daily, except Tues and Thur, 0830-1530 (1630 Sat, 1600 Sun), including minibus tour of the island and lunch, 180F. Minibuses normally meet incoming flights and boats. There are bicycles and scooters for hire.

INFORMATION FOR VISITORS

● **How To Get There**

By Air Like Martinique, Guadeloupe is on Air France's direct route from Paris (about 8 hrs) with other flights from Cayenne, Miami, Caracas, Fort-de-France, Paramaribo, Port-au-Prince and Santo Domingo; for more details, see under Martinique for Air France's services from France and elsewhere. Other services to Pointe-à-Pitre: Air Canada has direct flights from Montréal; American Eagle has flights from San Juan, with connections from the USA. Liat offers inter-Caribbean connections to Dominica, Antigua, Fort-de-France, St Vincent, and Barbados and St Lucia. Air Guadeloupe connects Pointe-à-Pitre with Dominica, Fort-de-France, La Désirade, Marie-Galante, St Barts, St Marten, St Thomas, San Juan and Terre-de-Haut. Other airlines with services to Guadeloupe include AOM French Airlines (from Paris, Marseille), Air Liberté (Bordeaux, Nantes, Paris), Linea Aeropostal Venezolana (Caracas, joint operation with Air France), Air Martinique (Martinique, St Maarten), Air St-Barthélémy (St-Barts), Air St Martin (from St Maarten).

Numerous cruise lines sail from US and French ports.

No departure tax.

● **Airport**

Le Raizet airport is large, modern and efficient with plenty of shops, a café and restaurant as well as an exchange. There is also a cash point machine which accepts credit cards with a PIN. Luggage lockers (*consigné*) are outside the terminal building in the car park, 10F for most lockers, 5F coins needed. Bus into Point-à-Pitre leaves from other side of car park, over roundabout and outside Cora (Mammouth) supermarket, 5.70F to Place de la Victoire. Food and drinks at Cora are half the price of the airport, good for sandwiches and beer, only 2 mins walk.

● **Airline Offices**

Air France, Blvd Légitimus, Pointe-à-Pitre, T 82 50 00/82 30 00, or Le Raizet airport, T 82 30 20; all others are at Le Raizet: American, T 83 62 62; Air Canada, T 83 62 49; Liat, T 82 12 26/82 00 84. Nouvelles Frontières for charter flights, T 90 36 36, Pointe-à-Pitre. Air Guadeloupe, Le Raizet, T 82 28 35, or 10 rue Sadi Carnot, Pointe-à-Pitre, T 90 12 25.

● **Inter-Island Transport**

Madikera and Caribbean Express operate a fast, scheduled ferry service between Pointe-à-Pitre, Dominica and Martinique (**see page 585** for details). Madikera agents include T-Maritimes Brudey Frères, Centre St-John Perse, 97110 Pointe-à-Pitre, T 91 60 87. You can get a small motor-sail vessel to Dominica from Pointe-à-Pitre for 240F (not much less than the flight). The boat leaves at 1300, 3 days a week, takes 2 hours, is not very comfortable and sea sickness is a distinct possibility.

● **Transport On Guadeloupe**

In Pointe-à-Pitre there are 3 main bus terminals: from La Darse (by Place de la Victoire), buses run to Gosier (4F), Sainte-Anne (11F), Saint-François (11F); for N Grande-Terre destinations, buses leave from the Mortenol station. From Blvd Chanzy (near the cemetery) they go to Trois Rivières (20F) and Basse-Terre (22F, 2 hrs). Pointe-à-Pitre to La Grande Anse, 15F, 1 hr 45 mins. Buses from Pointe-à-Pitre to Deshaies leave from Gare Routière, 1 hr 15 mins, 19F. Basse-Terre to Trois Rivières, 20 mins. The terminal in Basse-Terre is on Blvd Général de Gaulle, between the market and the sea. Buses run between 0530 and 1800, leaving for the main destinations every 15 mins or so, or when full. The airport bus leaves from 0800 from outside Renaissance Cinema, Place de la Victoire, 5.70F. It is possible to cover the whole island by bus in a day – cheap, interesting and easy. You can just stop the bus at the side of the road or wait at the bus stations in the villages. Buses are crowded and play soca music at top volume (exhilarating or deafening, depending on your mood); have your money ready when you get off.

Taxis are rather expensive; some are metered; some routes have fixed fares. All fares double at night. Taxi from the airport to Place de la Victoire costs about 50F but it may be only 45F to the airport from Place de la Victoire.

Organized bus tours and boat excursions are available but expensive, about 330-400F in a bus for about 40 people. Check with Tourist Office, Petrelluzzi Travel Agency (American Express Agents), 2 rue Henri IV, Pointe-à-Pitre, and other agencies.

Hitch hiking is no problem and if you speak French it is a rec way of meeting local people, who are very friendly. However, a bus will often come before you have been waiting long.

● **Vehicle Rental**

Self-drive hire cars are available mainly at the airport, which is inconvenient for those not arriving by air. A small, old Peugeot will cost about US$70 per day. In Pointe-à-Pitre, there is a small office above an icecream parlour on Av V Hugues, just off Place de la Victoire, which has a small selection. Rental can also be arranged through the major hotels. International and local agencies are represented. At Trois Rivières, Rosan Martin, Location de Voitures, is close to the dock, T 92 94 24, 262F a day, unlimited mileage, for a Renault B571, deposit 3,000F or credit card. Tropic-Car, 25 rue Schoelcher, 97110 Pointe-á-Pitre, T 91 84 37, F 91 31 94, evenings and weekends T 84 07 25, has a variety of models for hire. There are also mopeds for hire in Pointe-à-Pitre, Gosier, Saint-François, or through hotels. Mokes and scooters can be rented at Sainte-Anne. Bicycle rental from Velo-Vert, Pointe-à-Pitre, T 83 15 74, Le Relais du Moulin, near Sainte-Anne, T 88 23 96, Rent-a-Bike, *Meridien Hotel* Saint-François, T 84 51 00, around 50F a day. If you don't have a credit card you normally have to deposit up to 5,000F for a car; 2,000F for a scooter; and 1,000F for moped or bicycle.

● **Traffic**

Pointe-à-Pitre has a dual carriage ring road which runs from Gosier across the Rivière Salée to the industrial centre at Baie-Mahault and S towards Petit-Bourg. It is well used and the driving is very French with dead animals on the road quickly covered with lime. There can be major traffic holdups in the rush hour; expect to find slow moving traffic on the major routes for up to 20 km out of Pointe-à-Pitre. Bottlenecks include the roundabout at the university at Bas-du-Fort, the turning to Le Raizet and beyond to Abymes and the turnoff to Baie-Mahualt. In the city, parking is a nightmare in the daytime. There are no car parks, just meters. There are 2 zones, green (about 5F for max 8 hrs) and orange (cheaper). The system does not operate 1230-1400. Most traffic is one way.

● **Where To Stay**

On **Grande-Terre**: At **Pointe-à-Pitre**: top of the range is *La Bougainvillée*, 9 rue Frébault, T 90 14 14, 545-584F, EP, which is comfortable, a/c, but at that price the plumbing could be better, good expensive restaurant; *Saint John*, rue Quai Lesseps, 400Fs, 500Fd, CP, a/c, TV, balcony, comfortable, very good; *Normandie*, 14 Place de la Victoire, T 82 37 15, 300F with shower and a/c, cheaper without bath, CP, popular, best to book in advance, restaurant is good; even better, however, is the new hotel next door, *La Maison de la Marie-Galante*, T 90 10 41, 350-450F, CP; next best is *Schoelcher*, rue Schoelcher, 190-250F, EP, not very clean, reasonably-priced restaurant; *Relais des Antilles*, corner of rue Massabielle and rue Vatable, just off the Place de la Victoire, basic, noisy but friendly and cheap, 250F, EP, with toilet; *Karukera*, 15 rue Alsace-Lorraine, 200F with bath, no fan, EP, not good; *Pension Mme Rilsy*, T 91 81 71, 90 39 18, 34 Bis Rue Pegnier, rooms 120Fs, 200Fd inc breakfast, very friendly, rec.

There are a great many hotels in the **Bas du Fort Bay/Gosier** tourist area; the Tourist Board publishes full descriptions and price lists for the majority. We include a small selection: *Auberge de la Vieille Tour*, Montauban, 97190 Gosier, T 84 23 23, named after an 18th-century sugar tower incorporated into the main building, on a bluff over the sea, beach, pool, tennis, 3 2-room bungalows and 8 rooms in French colonial style, gourmet restaurant, US$120-160d (summer) inc tax and service, breakfast US$12, like a number of others this is a member of PLM-Azur group; another is *Marissol*, 15 mins from Pointe-à-Pitre, 200 rooms and bungalows, restaurants, discothèque, tennis, beach with watersports and a spa/gym with instructors and physiotherapist, 900-1,712F, CP, T 90 84 44; *Résidence de la Pergola Plage*, T 84 35 20, part of larger complex, on the beach, reasonably priced, but unfriendly, poorly equipped, not rec; better is *Chez Rosette Restaurant/Hotel*, 300F, EP, basic but clean, on other side of main road. *Arawak*, T 84 24 24, nice beach, pool, 600-700F, CP, a/c, buses 400 m away, modern, used by tour groups, comfortable rooms but poor food, not very friendly service; *Callinago* is smaller, beach, pool, 854-1,004F, T 84 25 25, also apartments at *Callinago Village*, from 795-936F for a studio or apartment, EP; *Serge's Guest House*, on seafront, T 84 10 25, 296F, CP, poor reports, very basic, not very clean, convenient for buses and beach, has nice garden and swimming pool. In the same area, *Les Flamboyants*, is clean, a/c, 360-400F, CP, T 84 14 11, pool, sea view, some kitchenettes, friendly. A smaller establishment is the *Hotel Corossol*, Mathurin, 97190 Gosier, T 84 39 89, 125F pp, CP, no towels, friendly, good meals, 50F, 20 mins walk to Gosier. Many places advertise rooms to let.

Near **Sainte-Anne** are *Relais du Moulin*, 40 a/c bungalows, 695-853F, CP, rec restaurant,

pool (T 88 23 96, F 88 03 92); *Motel Sainte-Anne*, T 88 22 40, 10 rooms, a/c, 520F, CP, *Auberge du Grand Large*, neither grand nor large, but friendly and with good restaurant on the beach, T 88 20 06, 620F, CP; and *Mini Beach*, 1 km from town, also on the beach, relaxed, good location, many restaurants nearby, T 88 21 13, 450-700F, CP, can fall to half price in summer, good restaurant, meals from 100F, excellent fish soup 15F, a meal in itself. Between Gosier and Sainte-Anne, at La Marie-Gaillarde, is *Marie-Gaillarde*, T 85 84 29, overlooking Les Grands Fonds, 2 km from Petit Havre beach, with restaurant and bar, 310F EP, 360F CP. *La Toubana*, BP63, 97180 Ste-Anne, T 88 25 78, F 88 38 90, T 800-322 2223, 32 cottages, US$136-280/124-205 CP, a/c, kitchenettes, phones, terraces, pool, private beach, tennis, pocket billiards, views of nearby Caravelle beach, *Club Med* and islands, *Toubana* is Arawak for little house. At **Saint-François**, *Méridien*, T 88 79 81, Air France's modern and conventional seaside complex, beach, pool, golf, tennis, flying school, dock, discothèque, and casino, 2,000-3,400F, CP; *Plantation Ste-Marthe* (Euro Dom Hotels), T 93 11 11, 88 43 58, F 88 72 47, 120 magnificent rooms of 42 or 65 sq m with large terrace, a/c, from 1,100F CP, restaurant, bars, 900 sq m swimming pool, close to golf course, 7-acre property; among other luxury places: *Hamak*, T 88 59 99, 1,600-2,250F, CP. *Chez Honoré*, Place du Marché, T 88 40 61, clean, simple, friendly, noisy because of the disco next door but still one of the cheapest in the French West Indies at 300F, EP. At **Le Moule**: *Les Alizés*, Canadian-owned, good horseshoe-shaped beach, pool, golf, 225-450F, T 23 17 80; *Tropical Club Hotel*, T 93 97 97, F 93 97 00, T 800-322 2223, 72 rooms, US$156-230/90-156 CP, 1-4 people, a/c, TV, kitchenette, phone, terrace, fan, pool, volley ball, ping pong, restaurant, snack bar, in coconut grove on beach, watersports, tennis and golf available.

Club Méditerranée has a hotel-village on the island (membership is required): *La Caravelle* at Sainte-Anne is on a spectacular white sand beach, perhaps the best on Guadeloupe, surrounded by a 13-hectare reserve; atmosphere strictly informal (nude bathing), all sports equipment available, gourmet dining unlimited, non-members seem to be able to get in. Apply to your local representative for rates. Bus from Pointe-à-Pitre 7F.

On **Basse-Terre**: accommodation is neither plentiful nor high class in **Basse-Terre city**: *Hotel Basse-Terre-Charlery*, 52 rue Maurice Marie Claire, T 81 19 78, central, basic, clean and cheap, 100-150F, breakfast 16F, good oriental restaurant next door; also central is *Le Drouant*, 26 rue Dr Cabre, 200F; *Le Relais d'Orléans*, rue Lardenoy; *Hotel Higuera*, 225F, on main square opp *Hotel de Ville*, T 81 11 92. At **Saint-Claude**: *Relais de la Grand Soufrière*, an elegant but rather poorly-converted old plantation mansion, a/c, attractive surroundings, old wooden furniture, friendly staff, T 80 01 27, 250-450F, EP, regular bus service to Basse-Terre, including Sun. *Fort Royal* at **Deshaies**, T 25 50 00, used to belong to *Club Med*, now Touring Hotel Club, dramatically situated on a promontory between 2 beautiful but rather rough beaches, 760-850F CP; *La Vigie*, overlooking Deshaies bay, small studios with kitchenette, bathroom, terrace, fan, cleaned daily, 1,050F for 3 nights, 2,100F 7 nights inc tax and service, T 28 42 52; rooms *chez M Eric Bernier*, T 28 40 04 or 28 42 70, about 200F double on waterfront, opp *Le Mouillage* restaurant more rooms are available; an apartment *chez Jean Memorin*, T 28 40 90, just outside town on hill in direction of Grand Anse beach, 1 bedroom, TV, 250F. *Auberge de la Distillerie*, Petit Bourg, Route de Versailles, T 94 25 91, F 94 11 91, T 800-322 2223, 12 rooms, 4 cottages, US$80-120/65-80 EP, a/c, TV, phone, mini-bar, pool, jacuzzi, pocket billiards, country inn at entrance to Parc Naturel surrounded by pineapple fields, créole restaurant, *Le Bitaco* and small pizza café, the owner also designed *Créol'Inn*, Bel'Air Des Nozières, T 94 22 56, F 94 19 28, T 800-322 2223, 20 cabins, US$170/120 EP, a/c, TV, fans, phone, kitchenette, hammocks, pool, barbeque, snack bar. At **Trois Rivières** are *Le Joyeux*, a 3F bus ride from the centre of the town (bus stop right outside) or short walk, in Le Faubourg, 100m above the sea, T 92 71 24, 6 simple rooms, kitchenettes, Créole restaurant, bar, disco, closed Mon except for reservations, rec, good views to Les Saintes, very friendly, Monsieur will drive you to the boat dock for nothing, the family also run a small supermarket and the Serie Bleu maps are sold there; *Grand'Anse*, T 92 90 47, bungalows, also has Créole restaurant and views; *Les Gîtes de l'Habitation Cardonnet*, T 92 70 55, 5 self-contained cottages.

The Tourist Board has current price lists (they run an information desk at Raizet airport but do not make reservations).

● **Gîtes**

Throughout the island there are a large number of gîtes for rent on a daily, weekly or monthly basis. Weekly rates range from 700F to 3,000F, but most are in the 1,000-1,500F bracket. The tourist offices in both Pointe-à-Pitre and Basse-Terre have lists of the properties available and should be consulted in the first instance. Gîtes are arranged by the local Syndicats d'Initiative who have an office next to the Tourist Office on rue Provence. For example, the Syndicat d'Initiative de Deshaies, T 28 49 70, lists 14 local people who let gîtes. Some gîtes are quite isolated, so choose one that is conveniently located. The Syndicats charge a 5% rental fee.

The tourist offices also have lists of villas for rent (there are a number in Saint-François, for instance); prices vary between 1,500F and 4,500F depending on number of occupants, size of villa and season.

● **Camping**

Compared with metropolitan France, camping is not well organized and the Tourist Office does not have much information. 7 km E of Ste-Anne is *Camping du Voyageur*, T/F 88 36 74, Chateaubrun 97180 Ste-Anne, cooking facilities but no washing machine, 60F for 2 people, tent rental, gîtes being built 1993, clean, beach 10 mins walk. A small campsite is *Sable d'Or*, near Deshaies, Basse-Terre, T 81 39 10. The charge is approximately 80F per tent for 2 people. Also small bungalows, 110-160F, cooking facilities, pool. Unfortunately standards deteriorated in 1993 following the death of the owner. There are buses from Pointe-à-Pitre. *Camping Traversée* is near Mahait on Basse-Terre, not suitable for tents after heavy rain, they float away. Otherwise ask mayors if you may camp on municipal land, or owners on private property. Camper vans can be arranged through Découverts et Loisirs Créoles in Abymes, T 20 55 65, from 700F.

● **Where To Eat**

Apart from the hotel restaurants mentioned above, there are a large number of restaurants, cafés and patisseries to choose from. Many are closed in the evening. In **Pointe-à-Pitre**: *Oasis*, rues Nozières et A R Boisneuf (French), T 82 02 70; *Relais des Antilles* (cheaper, but good Créole cooking); near the *Auberge Henri IV*, in a private house, good, cheap meals (ask Valentin at the *Auberge* for directions);

Krishna, 47 rue A R Boisneuf, Indian; *Le Moundélé*, rue Juan Jaurès, T 91 04 30, African. At Le Raizet airport: *Oiseau des Iles* (French), and *Godire*, self-service. On the Grande-Terre holiday coast: *La Case Créole*, Route de la Rivière; *Chez Rosette*, Av Général de Gaulle, both Créole at Gosier; *Le Boukarou*, rue Montauban, T 84 10 37, good Italian, pizza made on charcoal grill, moderately priced; lots of small restaurants in Gosier: pizzas, Vietnamese, Chinese and of course French. The local pizza house is near the park, rec, good for takeaways. The *pâtisserie* is good for an early morning coffee while collecting the *baguettes*; *Chez Gina*, in a little village cafétiére, 2½ km inland from Les Sables d'Or campsite, up the hill, excellent food, order in advance in the morning for an evening meal, 60F pp for 4 courses and apéritif, served in a sort of garage with flowers, friendly, don't be put off by the untidy surroundings; *Côté Jardin*, at Bas du Fort marina, French; *La Plantation*, same location, same cuisine. In Sainte-Anne, *Chez Yvette* is budget-priced; *La Toubana*, perched high above village overlooking *Club Med*, nice but expensive French cuisine, take swimming gear, pool and sun deck, rec; the *Relais du Moulin* has an excellent French-Créole menu, rec; and in Saint-François, *Madame Jerco* has good food in a small creaking house. At Campêche there is a small restaurant in the middle of the village, cheap and welcome relief if travelling in this area. On Basse-Terre, *Chez Paul* in Matouba has been rec for Créole and East Indian cuisine. At Bouillante, *Chez Loulouse*, Plage de Malendure, T 98 70 34, beach restaurant, créole fair; *Restaurant de la Phare*, Vieux Fort, good créole cooking, excellent fresh fish, reasonable prices, dance hall attached. In Deshaies, several reasonably priced restaurants inc *Le Madras* and *Le Mouillage*, serving créole meals; for breakfast try the *boulangerie* opp *Le Mouillage* for *croissants*, *pain au chocolat*, coffee, juice. The *Relais de la Grande Soufrière*, at Saint-Claude, used to have highly rec créole meals at reasonable prices, under reconstruction 1993, to be reopened 1994, worth checking, T 80 01 27. For a description of local cuisine, see page 539

● **Shopping**

An unusual fruit, the *carambole*, can be bought in Pointe-à-Pitre. The location of the markets is given above. Good Mamouth Supermarket near Le Raizet airport 3.50F by bus from Pointe-à-Pitre. There are lots of hypermarkets just like in France, stocked with excellent cheese counters and massive wine departments (both French only, of course). They also sell chemist sundries, toys, electrical equipment, film, cameras etc. Most have film processing facilities where prints will be ready in 24 hours or less. Generally open Mon-Sat 0800-2030. Expensive, everything imported from France. In Gosier there is a supermarket on the road to Plage de l'Anse Canot, open on Sun, otherwise not rec as hypermarkets are better value and cleaner.

● **Climate**

The temperature on the coasts varies between 22° and 30° C, but is about 3° lower in the interior. January to April is the dry season (called *carême*), July to November the wet season (*l'hivernage*), with most rain falling from September to November. Trade winds moderate temperatures the year round.

● **Business Hours**

0800-1200, 1430-1700 weekdays, morning only on Sat; government offices open 0730-1300, 1500-1630 Mon and Fri, 0730-1300 Tues-Thur. Banking hours: 0800-1200, 1400-1600 Mon to Fri.

● **Banks**

Banque Nationale de Paris (good for Visa cash advances), Banque Française Commerciale, Banque des Antilles Françaises, BRED, Crédit Agricole all have branches throughout the island. Banks charge 1% commission and 4% *dessier* (filing fee). No commission charged on French traveller's cheques. Exchange is handled up to midday so go early to avoid the late morning pandemonium. American Express is at Petreluzzi Travel, 2 rue Henri IV, English spoken, helpful. Credit cards are widely accepted, including at the hypermarkets.

● **Exchange**

Hotels give the worst rates, then banks (but their rates vary so shop around), post offices change dollars (but not all makes of travellers' cheque, slow service), and the best rates can be found in Edouard Saingolet, Bureau de Change, rues Nozières et Barbès, Pointe-à-Pitre (T 90 34 63), open daily (am only Sat and Sun). There is one exchange facility at the airport and it is closed all day Mon. There is a 24-hour automatic teller at Bas-du-Fort marina which accepts most European currencies, US, EC and Canadian dollars and yen. It can be difficult to change EC dollars.

● **Post And Telecommunications**

Post office and telephones building in Pointe-à-Pitre is on Blvd Hanne, crowded, sweltering. For local calls you must buy phone cards (*télécartes*, 40F or 96F, from a *tabac*), fairly essential when phoning ahead to book accommodation; to call abroad, you must hand over identification at the desk (calls to the USA 12.85F/minute, Europe 18.50F/minute, Australia 23.10F/minute; hotels charge twice as much). You can not make a credit card or collect call abroad from a pay phone. You can not have a call returned to a pay phone either. Post and phones in Basse-Terre is on rue Dr Pitat, between Dumanoir and Ciceron, smaller but a bit more comfortable than the Pointe-à-Pitre office. Parcel post is a problem and you can usually send parcels of up to 2 kg only. In Pointe-à-Pitre there is an office near the stadium where you can mail parcels of up to 7 kg by air but it is unreliable; one correspondent sent a tent but received a cake wrapped in the same paper. Unlike in France, stamps are not sold in bars and tobacconists, go to Post Offices in small towns to avoid the crush of the main offices.

● **Useful Addresses**

Police assistance: T 82 00 05 in Pointe-à-Pitre, 81 11 55 in Basse-Terre; nautical assistance, T 82 91 08; medical centre, T 82 98 80/82 88 88. Most diplomatic representation in the French Antilles is in Martinique; however, the Netherlands has a consulate at 5 rue de Nozières, Pointe-à-Pitre, T 82 01 16, and the Dominican Republic at rues St-John Perse et Frébault, Pointe-à-Pitre, T 82 01 87.

● **Tourist Information**

Tourist offices in Guadeloupe: 5 Square de la Banque, Pointe-à-Pitre, T 82 09 30, F 83 89 22 (very unhelpful, unlike the Gîtes office next door; Maison du Port, Cours Nolivos, Basse-Terre, T 81 24 83 (very helpful); Av de l'Europe, Saint-François, T 88 48 74. The tourist office publishes a booklet called *Bonjour Guadeloupe*, which contains descriptive and practical information; a broadsheet, *Pratique*, which gives details on concerts and exhibitions, flights, shipping, emergency numbers and all-night chemists and doctors; *Living in Guadeloupe* is a useful, free, bimonthly magazine written in English and French.

The Serie Bleu maps (1:25,000, 7 maps of Guadeloupe, No 4601G-4607G) issued by the Institut Geógraphique National, Paris, which include all hiking trails, are available at the bigger book stores in the rue Frébault in Pointe-à-Pitre, and at *Le Joyeux* hotel in Trois Rivières/Le Faubourg for 52F. National Park: Parc National de la Guadeloupe, Habitation Beausoleil, Montéran, BP13-97120, Saint-Claude, T 80 24 25, F 80 05 46.

SAINT-MARTIN

SAINT-MARTIN, the largest of Guadeloupe's outer islands, is divided between France and the Netherlands. See Netherlands Antilles section for general description and information. The French part used to be a sleepy place, but has become very Americanized since the building of the yacht marina. There is no restriction on travel between the two halves of the island.

Government and Economy

The French side is a sub-prefecture of Guadeloupe, with the sub-prefect appointed in Paris. There is an elected town council, led by a mayor. The economy is entirely dependent upon tourism, with the twin attractions of duty-free shopping and the sea (for bathers and sailors). A new harbour for cruise and cargo ships and a new international airport are planned, but nothing has happened yet.

MARIGOT

Marigot, the capital of French Saint-Martin, lies between Simpson's Bay Lagoon and the Caribbean sea. ("Marigot" is a French West Indian word meaning a spot from which rain water does not drain off, and forms marshy pools.) Shopping is good. Boutiques offer French *prêt-à-porter* fashions and St Barts batiks, and gift shops sell liqueurs, perfumes, and cosmetics at better duty-free prices than the Dutch side. At the *Marina Port La Royale* complex there are chic shops, cafés and bistros where you can sit and watch the boats. Rue de la République and Rue de la Liberté also have good shopping with fashion names at prices well below those of Europe or the USA. A fruit market is held every morning in the market place next to Marigot harbour. It is best on Wednesdays and Saturdays. On the right hand side of the market place is the Tourist Office and taxi rank; also the only public toilet on the French side (1F or US$0.25). From here it is a 10 minute walk to Fort St Louis overlooking Marigot Bay and Marigot. Follow the signs from the Tourist Office. On the waterfront the historical and archaeological Museum "On the trails of the Arawaks" open 0900-1300, 1500-1830, Monday-Saturday, may open longer during high season, has a well-presented exhibition from the first settlers of Saint-Martin around 3500 BC to 1960. Entrance US$2 (US$1 children). Carnival is held pre-Lent and most of the events are on the waterfront in Marigot. It is not as big and grandiose as on the Dutch side, where carnival is held a few weeks later, but there are calypso and beauty contests and a Grand Parade. Bastille Day (14th July) has live music, jump-ups and boat races; the celebrations move to Grand Case the weekend after (more fun). In Grand Case on New Year's Day there is a small parade with live music, while at Easter another parade is held with a lot of dancing.

Excursions

Grand Case, 13 km from the capital, is anything but grand: a quaint town between an old salt pond (which has been partially filled in to provide the Espérance airstrip) and a long sandy and secluded beach. At the far NE end is another beach, Petite Plage, delightfully *petite* in a calm bay. Every other Saturday all year round there are sailing races of old fishing boats between Anguilla and St-Martin, mostly to Grand Case. Ask for information at the *Ranch Bar* at the beach (live music every Sunday). From Grande Case pier a semi-submarine leaves Wednesday and Friday 1400, for a

1½-hour tour. You sit in the bottom of the boat, 2m under water, but the view is better than on a glass-bottomed boat, adults US$30, children US$18, call the Dutch side, T 24078, F 24079, for bookings. Anse Marcel, N of Grand Case, is a shallow beach, ideal for small children. Inland, Pic Paradise (424m) is a good lookout point from where, on a fine day, you can see Anguilla, Saba, St Eustatius, St Kitts, Nevis and St-Barts. By car, take a turn off at Rambaud on the Marigot-Grand Case road. There are also footpaths from Colombier (1½ km) and Orleans (1 km). Colombier is a small, sleepy village with some wonderful gardens, well worth a visit. In Orleans you can visit Roland Richardson, the only well-known native artist on St-Martin, whose home is open 1000-1800 on Thursdays. On the Atlantic, Cul-de-Sac, is a

traditional village, from where you may be able to hitch a ride on a fishing boat to the Île de Tintamarre. The sea here is calm and there are boat trips to Pinel Island just offshore. Baie Orientale (Orient Bay) is beautiful but rough (beware of its undertow); it's also nudist. There are several new developments along the beach and the naturist area is often overrun with day visitors and shrinking. Windsurfers (US$15/hr plus credit card deposit) and catamarans can be hired from the south end of the beach, friendly staff, good protected area for beginners and more open waters. For the intrepid, or foolhardy, depending on your point of view and courage, there is bungee jumping from a parasail at 100m, US$85, not done on very windy days. From here you can find boats to Caye Verte, just offshore. Further S, snorkelling is good at

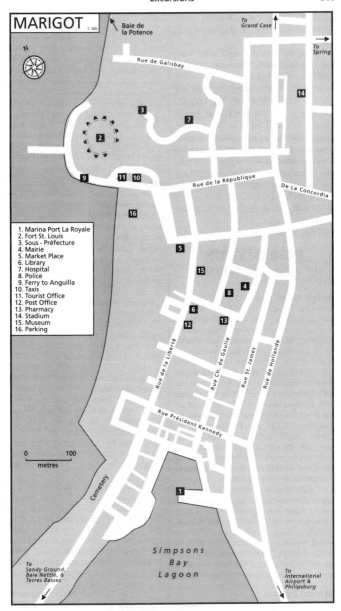

MARIGOT C 36b

Baie de la Potence

To Grand Case

To Spring

N

Rue de Galisbay

3

7

14

9

11 10

Rue de la République

De La Concordia

16

1. Marina Port La Royale
2. Fort St. Louis
3. Sous - Préfecture
4. Mairie
5. Market Place
6. Library
7. Hospital
8. Police
9. Ferry to Anguilla
10. Taxis
11. Tourist Office
12. Post Office
13. Pharmacy
14. Stadium
15. Museum
16. Parking

5

15

8   4

6

12   13

Rue de la Liberté

Rue Ch. de Gaulle

Rue St. James

Rue de Hollande

0   100
metres

Rue Président Kennedy

1

Cemetery

Simpsons Bay Lagoon

To Sandy Ground, Baie Nettlé, & Terres Basses

To International Airport & Philipsburg

Coconut Grove. Topless bathing is accepted at all beaches on the French side, but not on the Dutch.

From Marigot to Anguilla by ferry boat (20 minutes) US$18 round trip plus 10F departure tax, or with one of the many charter boats operating from the French side, US$50 (plus 10F tax), including lunch and snorkelling equipment; they tend to do it for only one tourist season, so names change quickly. Boat charter companies, with or without crew, are around *Marina Port La Royale*, about US$200/day. There are 2 squash courts at Le Privilège (T 87 37 37). Horse riding at Caid and Isa, Anse Marcel, T 87 45 70, daily rides at 0900 and 1500 if there is enough demand, US$45, reservations one day in advance.

INFORMATION FOR VISITORS

● **How To Get There**
International flights arrive at the Juliana airport on the Dutch side. On the French side is the Espèrance airport which can only take light planes. Air Guadeloupe (address under Guadeloupe above) has daily scheduled services to St Maarten from Pointe-à-Pitre, Guadeloupe and Saint-Barthélémy. CASM flies from Basse-Terre, Guadeloupe to Espérance. There is a US$10 departure tax on St-Maarten, payable only at Juliana airport, or US$5 to the Netherlands Antilles. A 5-seater helicopter run by Héli-Inter, T 87 35 86, runs day tours to St-Barths, US$700, and Anguilla, US$645, from Anse Marcel every day. Charters also available. Trans Helico Caraïbes offers helicopter tours of St-Martin; US$170 for 10 mins for 4 people, US$370 for 25 mins, T 27 40 68.

Connections with the French side by sea, besides the excursions to Anguilla (see above), can be made with Saint-Barthélémy; St Barts Express, twice daily except Sun and holidays, departs Gustavia 0815, Philipsburg 0900 and arrives Marigot 0930, returns from Marigot 1530, Philipsburg 1600, arrives Gustavia 1700. Try putting a notice up at the Capiteneri Marina Port La Royale for hitching a lift to other islands.

● **Island Transport**
Buses run from Grand Case to Marigot

(US$1.50) and from Marigot, French Quarters and St Peters to Philipsburg, normally until 2030, US$1.50. Inside town or short trip US$0.75-1. At night time fares rise by US$0.50. There are plenty of taxis, with controlled fares. You find them next to the Tourist Office in Marigot, T 87 56 54. From Marigot to Philipsburg about US$8, add 25% 2200-2400 and 50% 2400-0600. It is easy to hitchhike.

Car rental from several agencies, eg L C Fleming, Marigot, T 87 50 01 (also travel agency); Sunrise, St-James, Marigot, T 87 51 91, Saint-Martin Auto, Grand Case, T 87 50 86, or Marigot T 87 54 72; Avis, Port La Royale, Marigot, T 87 54 36; many others.

● **Where To Stay**
There are a number of luxury resorts, lesser establishments and guest houses and a building boom has raised the total number of hotel rooms to 3,000. The tourist office lists only those in the upper range, guest houses in Grand Case are rented from US$350-450/week, but for low budget accommodation you would be better in the Dutch half. *La Samanna*, Baie Longue, T 87 51 22, F 87 87 86, one of the most exclusive resorts in the Caribbean, renovated in 1992, US$550-800d (2 and 3 bedroomed villas also available, up to US$1,800, tennis, water skiing, windsurfing, sunfish sailing). *Le Galion Beach Hotel et Club* offers a private beach at Quartier d'Orléans on the NE side of the island near Baie Orientale, 510F to 960F without meals, it also has good water sport facilities (T 87 31 77); *Le Grand Saint-Martin*, 177 rooms, US$300-420d all inclusive, winter, with discothèque, T 87 57 91/2, F 87 80 34; *Le Pirate*, Marigot, a favourite with island-hoppers, studio 750-1,060F, duplex 950-1,280F, CP, T 87 78 37; *Beauséjour*, T 87 52 18, Rue de la République in centre of Marigot, US$45-50 with breakfast; *Rosely's*, 260Fs, T 87 70 17, F 87 70 20, pool in garden, kitchenette, a/c, very nice; *Fleming's*, in St-James end of Marigot, T 87 70 25, 8 rooms, some with marina view, a/c, fan, kitchenettes, clean, comfortable, nicely furnished, from US$30; *Royal Beach*, a Pullman Hotel on Nettlé Bay, modern, a/c, beachfront but not all rooms have sea view, pool, bar, restaurant, watersports nearby, US$66-104d EP (winter) inc tax and service, T/F 87 89 89, in the USA call (800) 223-9862 or (212) 719-9363; in Canada (800) 638-9699. At Grand Case: *Tackling's Beach Apartments*; *Hodge's Guest House*; *Goetz Guest House*,

apartments about US$250-335 weekly; *Bertines*, La Savane, US$75-100 inc breakfast, T 87 58 39; *Hévèa*, from 580-1,000F, EP, T 87 56 85, F 87 83 88, small colonial-style hotel, gourmet restaurant, beach across the street; *Mme Huckleman*, double apartments US$35-55, T 87 52 21; *Les Alizés*, 9 rooms with kitchenettes US$50-100, T 87 95 38; *Cagan's Guest House* and *Le Fish Pot* have a few reasonably-priced rooms; *Petite Plage* (T 87 77 83), housekeeping units on beach at US$120-150 a week, not open all year. Other hotels include the *Grand Case Beach Club*, 76 rooms, and apartments, watersports, tennis, on the beach, pre-booked by a US tour company for 1993/94, T 87 51 87, F 87 59 93; *Coralita Beach Hotel* (Quartier d'Orléans), 24 rooms, 600F EP, T 87 31 81 and *Chez Martine*, T 87 51 59, F 87 87 30, 7 rooms, 1 suite, restaurant, overlooks Grand Case Bay, US$80-96d, winter, EP. *Pavillon Beach*, T 87 96 46, F 87 71 04, in the USA T 800-322 2223, new, elegant hotel on lagoon, beautiful situation from Grand Case, 6 studios US$150-180/90-120 EP, 10 suites and 1 honey moon suite, US$220-285/135-200 EP, a/c, fans, TV, kitchenettes, phones, beach, watersports and land sports can be arranged. *Club Orient* (naturist), is 10 miles from the airport, tennis, volleyball, watersports, massage, US$175d EP, chalets for 3-4 people US$300-405, T 87 33 85, F 87 33 76.

● **Where To Eat**

French cuisine in all hotel restaurants on the French side is quite good but expensive. Picturesque gourmet dining places on the seashore are the islanders' favourites. The likelihood of finding a cheap meal is rare. In Marigot: the *Mini-Club* with its bar and dining arbour, serves a Caribbean buffet Wed and Sat, closed August and September, and *Le Boucanier* for seafood specialities. Very popular for its Créole specialities is *Cas Anny*. Traditional French in centre of Marigot is *La Calanque*. *David's Pub and Restaurant*, near the Post Office, good food, not expensive, fun bar, rec. For travellers on a small budget try the snackbars and cafés on Rue de Hollande. *La Maison sur le Port*, *L'Aventure* and *Le Poisson d'Or* offer excellent seafood. *La Fiesta*, cocktail bar/restaurant, the place to be seen at night time, live music every night except Mon; *Le Bar de la Mer*, serves lunch and dinner, good place to go before a disco; *San Remo*, not too expensive Italian, good pizza, pasta and home made ice cream; many bars on the water front next

to the tourist office serving barbeque lunch and dinner. *Jamaica* serves low budget lunch and dinner, around US$5. A Vietnamese restaurant is *Santal Thai Garden* in Sandy Ground, next to the French bridge. *Chez René* at the Lagoon Bridge, Sandy Ground, promises really gourmet fare but overpriced. *La Coupole* is French fare in 1930s ambience. Grand Case has a reputation of having more restaurants than inhabitants. Most are on the street next to the beach. *Fish Pot*, overlooking the sea, exquisite sea food. Across the street is *Rosemary's* for Créole cooking. *Chá Chá Chá*, a block away, has Brazilian food, OK but too expensive. *Coralita* offers French/Créole fare. *Don Gusano* Mexican restaurant has good food, huge servings, reasonable prices, rec. At the small snackbars near the little pier you can find barbeque fish, ribs and lobster as well as other local snacks, very popular at weekends and holidays, rec. At weekends there is usually live music in one of the bars/restaurants along the beach.

● **Entertainment**

L'Atmosphere is a disco for 'chic' French people, at Marina Port La Royale, very little English spoken, drinks US$6. *Le bar de la mer* at the waterfront is a popular meeting place for French-speaking young travellers, with live music once a week. *La Fiesta*, Marigot waterfront, South American music, Brazilian house band, popular bar for locals. Grand Case normally has live music Fri-Sun in high season with beach party style entertainment in one of the many bars. *Surf Club South*, Grand Case, a New Jersey-type bar, has beach parties every other Sun, all food and drinks US$1, with mainly 60s and 70s music, great fun. *Circus* bar in Nettlé Bay in the newly built resort area is a popular night bar, live music once in a while. *Le Privilège Disco* at Anse Marcel US$10 entrance, one drink included. Every full moon there is a beach party at Friar's Bay starting around 2100-2200.

● **Hours Of Business**

Shops open around 0900 and close between 1800-1900 with normally a 2-hour lunch break between 1200-1500, depending on the shop. Banks open 0800-1300; both slightly different from the Dutch side.

● **Currency**

The US dollar is as widely used as the franc, but watch the rate. It is sometimes difficult to get change from payments in francs. Dollars are preferred. The best place for exchange is the Post Office in Marigot where they will change all currencies and traveller's cheques, but normally only into francs. There are several exchange houses for changing from francs to dollars, one in Rue du Kennedy and one in the *Marina Royale* complex. Two banks, both on rue de la République, Marigot, Banque des Antilles Françaises and Banque Française Commerciale.

● **Electricity**

220 volts, 60 cycles (compared with 110 volts on the Dutch side).

● **Telecommunications**

There are several telephone booths on the French side but they only take telephone cards. 120 units for 90F, sold at the Post Office and at the bookshop opposite. There are 8 telephones on the square in Marigot and 2 in Grand Case in front of the little pier. To call the

Dutch side use the code 1-599-5. All Dutch side numbers have 5 digits while French side numbers have 6. The international code for St-Martin is 590. Calls from one side of the island to the other are expensive. The Post Office will hold mail, but only for 2 weeks. Letters sent c/o Capiteneri Marina Port La Royale, Marigot, will be kept 4-6 weeks.

● **Newspapers**

Le Monde, *France Soir* and *Le Figaro* from France are available 1-3 days after publication. *France Antilles*, same day. A few German and Italian magazines are sold at Maison de la Presse (opposite Post Office) and other locations.

● **Telephone Numbers**

Hospital T 87 50 07, Ambulance T 87 54 14, Gendarmerie T 87 50 10.

● **Tourist Office**

Port de Marigot, T 87 53 26.

SAINT-BARTHÉLÉMY

SAINT-BARTHÉLÉMY (St Barts or St Barth's), also in the Leewards, is 230 km N of Guadeloupe, 240 km E of the Virgin Islands, and 35 km SE of Saint-Martin. Its 25 square km are inhabited by a population of 5,043, mostly people of Breton, Norman, and Poitevin descent who live in quiet harmony with the small percentage of blacks. Thirty-two splendid white sandy beaches, most of which are protected by both cliff and reef, are surrounded by lush volcanic hillsides. The Norman dialect is still largely spoken while most of the islanders also speak English. A few elderly women still wear traditional costumes (with their characteristic starched white bonnets called *kichnottes*); they cultivate sweet potato patches and weave palm fronds into hats and purses which they sell in the village of Corossol. The men traditionally smuggled rum among neighbouring islands and now import liqueurs and perfumes, raise cattle, and fish for lobsters offshore. The people are generally known for their courtesy and honesty. Although the Rockefellers, Fords, and Rothschilds own property on the island, there is little glitter or noise.

History

Although called Ouanaloo by the Caribs, the island was renamed after Christopher Columbus' brother, Saint-Barthélémy when discovered in November 1496. It was first settled by French colonists from Dieppe in 1645. After a brief possession by the Order of the Knights of Malta, and ravaging by the Caribs, it was bought by the Compagnie des Iles and added to the French royal domain in 1672. In 1784, France ceded the island to Sweden in exchange for trading rights in the port of Göteborg. In 1801, St Barts was attacked by the British, but for most of this period it was peaceful and commercially successful. The island was handed back to France after a referendum in 1878.

Government and Economy

St Barts is administered by the sub-prefect in Saint-Martin and is a dependency of Guadeloupe. The island has its own elected mayor, who holds office for 7 years. Much the same as Saint-Martin, St Barts relies on its free port status and its anchorages and beaches for the bulk of its revenue. It is popular with both French and North American visitors and, despite the limitations of its airstrip, it is claimed that twice as many tourists as the island's population pass through each month.

Watersports and Beaches

St Barts is a popular mid-way staging post on the yachting route between Antigua and the Virgin Islands. Boat charters are available, also courses in, or facilities for, windsurfing (Toiny is the windsurfers' favourite beach), diving (in Gustavia), snorkelling (very good, particularly at Marigot), water-skiing, deep-sea fishing and sailing. Surfboard rental (not windsurfing) at Hookipa, T 27 71 31. Game fishing at La Maison de la Mer, T 27 81 00, F 27 67 29, or Marine Service, T 27 70 34, F 27 70 36, the latter also does day charters to Colombier, waterskiing, scuba rentals, speedboat rentals etc. There is excellent diving all round St Barts, especially out round the offshore rocks, like the Groupers, and islands like Ile Fourche. Dive shops are Plongée La Bulle, T 27 68 93, Daniel (PADI instructor), T 27 64 78 and Rainbow Diving in Corossol, T 27 31 29. Two submersibles, Aquarius and l'Aquascope, offer trips to the reefs around Gustavia, descending to no more than 10 feet. Tickets from La Maison de la Mer and Marine Service, US$50.

Some beaches are more accessible than others, most uncrowded. The main resort area is Baie de Saint-Jean, which is two beaches divided by Eden Rock, the most visited beach with several bars and restaurants open for lunch or a snack, watersports, but no waterskiing, small boats, snorkelling rentals, ideal for families, good windsurfing, safe swimming, some snorkelling. Motorized watersports are only allowed 150 m off the beach. Others are Lorient, Marigot, Grand Cul de Sac on the N coast, Grande Saline, Gouverneur on the S, and Colombier and Flamands at the NW tip, to name but a few. To get to Gouverneur from Gustavia take the road to Lurin. A sign will direct you to the dirt road leading down to the beach, lovely panoramic view over to the neighbouring islands, where there is

white sand with palm trees for shade. A legend says that the 17th century pirate, Montbars the Exterminator, hid his treasures in a cove here and they have never been found. Also a very good spot for snorkelling. Colombier beach is the most beautiful on St Barts. It can not be reached by car but is well worth the 20-30 minute walk during which you have majestic views of the island. Park the car at Colombier, there are several trails going down to the beach. There are also several day tours by boat from Gustavia. Flamands beach is of very clean white sand, bordered with Latania palm trees. The surf can be rough, watersports available. Sometimes in May the migrating sperm whales pass close by. From April to August female sea turtles come to Colombier, Flamands and Corossol to lay their eggs. In Corossol is the Inter Oceans Museum, a private collection of sea shells open for visitors daily 1000-1600. Petite Anse de Galet, in Gustavia, 3-5 minute

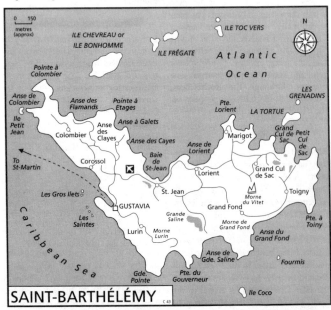

SAINT-BARTHÉLÉMY

walk from Fort Karl, is also known as Shell beach because it is covered in shells, not sand. Trees give shade and swimming is safe, shelling is of course extremely good.

Other Sports

Tennis at several hotels. Also at ASCCO in Colombier, 2 courts, T 27 61 07, AJOE in L'Orient, one court, T 27 67 63. Some opportunities for hiking. Horse riding at Flamands, Laure Nicolas, T 27 80 72. A new golf driving range has been built at Gouverneur, 100F per bucket, T 27 62 49. Body building at *St Barth Beach Hotel*, open 0730-2130, 100F, instructor on duty all the time.

Festivals

Carnival is held before Lent, on Mardi Gras and Ash Wednesday; the patron saint's day is 24 August, with celebrations on the weekends before and after.

The St Barts regatta in February is the main event for sailors. Other regattas should be checked at Lou Lou's Marine Shop, Gustavia, because none is fixed annually. The local traditional sailboats participate on all public events with their own regattas like Bastille Day, Gustavia Day and one regatta a month.

A music festival is held annually in January with 10 days of classical, folk, jazz music and ballet performed by both local school children and guest artistes and musicians from abroad.

GUSTAVIA

In *Gustavia*, the capital, there are branches of several well-known French shops (such as Cartier). The small crowd of *habitués* is mostly young, chic, and French. The food, wine, and aromas are equally Gallic. The harbour of Carénage was renamed Gustavia after the eighteenth-century Swedish king, Gustavus III, and became a free port, marking the beginning of the island's greatest prosperity. In 1852 a fire severely damaged the capital, although the Swedish influence is still evidenced in the city hall, the belfries, the Forts (Karl, Oscar and Gustave), the streetnames and the trim stone houses which line the harbour. St Barts Municipal Museum with an exhibition of the history, traditions and local crafts of the island, is at La Pointe, near the *Wall House*, open Monday-Thursday 0800-1200, 1330-1730, Friday 0800-1200, 1330-1700, Saturday 0830-1200, entrance 10F.

From Gustavia, you can head N to the fishing village of Corossol (see above), continuing to Colombier and the NW beaches; S over Les Castelets and the hills of Morne Lurin to Anse du Gouverneur; or to Saint-Jean and beaches and settlements on the E end. A hired car can manage all the roads.

INFORMATION FOR VISITORS

● How To Get There

Scheduled **flights** from St Maarten with Air Guadeloupe (Espérance airport), Air St-Barthélémy (both airports), CASM (Espérance) and Winair (Juliana airport); from Pointe-à-Pitre with Air Guadeloupe and Air St-Barthélémy from Basse-Terre with CASM; from St Thomas with Air Guadeloupe and Air St Thomas. San Juan, Puerto Rico, is served by these 2 and Air St-Barthélémy, Saint Croix by Coastal Air Transport, Anguilla by Winair and Coastal Air Transport and Dominica (Canefield) by Air Guadeloupe. Charters available locally (Air St-Barthélémy, T 87 61 20, St Barts, or 82 25 80, Pointe-à-Pitre).

Enquire locally for **boat** services between St Barts and the French and Dutch sides of Saint-Martin/Sint Maarten. St Barts Express goes to St Martin and several catamarans go to Sint Maarten, but you leave in the afternoon and return in the morning so a day trip is not possible. There are no other regular boats to other islands. Full docking facilities are available at the Yacht Club in Gustavia, and anchorplace for yachts up to 10 foot draft at Saint-Jean Bay.

● Island Transport

Minibuses (and ordinary taxis) do island tours, 2½-3 hours, US$45 for 2 people, dropping you off at Baie de Saint-Jean and collecting you later for the boat if you are on a day trip. Or hire a car from one of the many agencies at the airport. It is not easy to hire a car for only one day: ask your hotel to obtain a car if required.

● **Where To Stay**

At Saint-Jean beach: *Village St-Jean*, 21 1-2 bedroom cottages with kitchenettes, US$175-425/110-290 EP, 4 rooms with mini-fridge, US$140/80 CP, special packages available, a/c, fans, phones, pool, short walk to beach, managed by Charneau family (T 27 61 39, F 27 77 96, in the USA T 800-322 2223), reasonable lunches in *Le Beach Club* restaurant, watersports facilities; *Emeraude Plage*, similar, from 600-800F, EP (T 27 64 78, F 27 83 08); others: *PLM Azur Jean Bart*, *Tropical*,

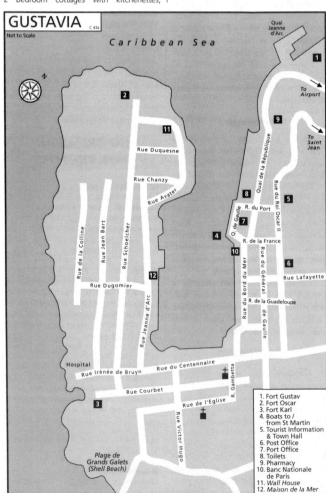

GUSTAVIA c.43a
Not to Scale

Caribbean Sea

Qual Jeanne d'Arc

To Airport

To Saint Jean

Rue Duquesne
Rue Chanzy
Rue Avater
Quai de la République
Rue du Roi Oscar II
Rue de la Colline
Rue Jean Bart
Rue Schoelcher
Q. de Gaulle
R. du Port
R. de la France
Rue du Général de Gaulle
Rue du Bord du Mer
Rue Dugomier
Rue Lafayette
R. de la Guadeloupe
Rue Jeanne d'Arc
Hospital
Rue Irénée de Bruyn   Rue du Centenaire
R. Gambetta
Rue Courbet
Rue de l'Eglise
Rue Victor Hugo
Plage de Grands Galets (Shell Beach)

1. Fort Gustav
2. Fort Oscar
3. Fort Karl
4. Boats to / from St Martin
5. Tourist Information & Town Hall
6. Post Office
7. Port Office
8. Toilets
9. Pharmacy
10. Banc Nationale de Paris
11. *Wall House*
12. *Maison de la Mer*

20 units, US\$125-150, EP (T 27 64 87, F 27 81 74) and *Filao Beach*, 30 units, US\$165-315 (T 27 64 84, F 27 62 24), all 2-, and 3-star.

At Anse des Cayes: the luxury, 4-star *Manapany Cottages*, T 27 66 55, F 27 75 28, US\$200-260, CP, 32 cottages on hillside overlooking sea, 2 gourmet restaurants, can be booked through Mondotels in New York, T 212-719 5750 or 800-847 4249 or in Canada 800-255 3393. A few hundred yards from Lorient beach is *La Banane*, owned by Jean-Marie Rivière, who owns 2 nightclubs in Paris, pastel painted bungalows, no 2 the same, beautifully furnished and decorated, 2 pools, lots of bananas, 900-2,200F CP, inc breakfast, tax and airport transfers, highly rec if you can afford it, fine dining, T 27 68 25, F 27 68 44.

At Flamands beach: *Hotel Baie des Flamands*, modern, near Anse Rockefeller, US\$116-195, CP, T 27 64 85, F 27 83 98, and *Auberge de la Petite Anse*, T 27 64 60, F 27 72 30, US\$80-140 EP. At Colombier, overlooking Flamands beach is *François Plantation*, elegant plantation style hotel with 12 bungalows, pool, good restaurant, a/c, fan, telephone, satellite TV, T 27 78 82, F 27 61 26, US\$200-220, CP. *The Christopher Hotel*, Pointe Milou, opened 1993, 40 rooms, a/c with sitting room and bathroom, terrace, balcony or patio, 3 rooms with facilities for the disabled, managed by Sofitel, shuttle service to beaches, large pool, Total Fitness Club, watersports arranged, US\$325-360d winter, inc breakfast, tax and service, US\$225-280d summer, closed in September, T 800-471 9090, T 27 63 63, F 27 92 92; *Les Castelets*, high in the hills, under US management, T 27 78 80, *Club Emmanet* restaurant (overpriced).

Least expensive: *La Presqu'île*, in Gustavia, 350 F, T 27 64 60, F 27 72 30, restaurant specializes in French and Créole cooking (closed September-October). *Carl Gustaf*, Rue des Normands, Gustavia, overlooking harbour, T 27 82 83, F 27 82 37, in the USA T 800-322 2223, in the UK T 800-373 742, 14 one or 2-bedroom suites, US\$550-660d in summer, US\$770-1,200d winter inc tax and service, breakfast and airport transfers, a/c, TV, kitchenette, private mini pool and sun deck, telefax, stereos, gym-sauna, pool side restaurant, short walk to beach.

At Anse de Grand Cul-de-Sac: *St Barths Beach Hotel*, T 27 62 73, F 27 75 57, and *El Sereno*, T 27 64 80, F 27 75 47, in USA T 800-322 2223, 20 cottages on edge of lagoon, US\$230-340/130-185 EP, a/c, TV, telephone,

fridge, large pool, superb restaurant, gardens, hammocks, private beach, the hotel also manages *El Sereno Beach Villas*, 9 villas on hillside, US\$200-295/120-170 EP, a/c, TV, phones, fans, kitchen, use of hotel facilities; *La Toque Lyonnaise*, T 27 64 80, F 27 75 47.

In the E, at Anse de Toiny, *Le Toiny*, T 27 88 88, F 27 89 30, opened 1992, 12 villa suites with a/c, fans, TV, phone, fax, plunge pools, restaurant, bar, room service, 3,500F winter, 2,200F summer. In the hills above Lorient, *Les Islets Fleuris*, Hauts de Lorient 97133, T 27 64 22, F 27 69 22, cottages US\$100-260/70-130d, pool, kitchenettes, lovely views over coastline, maid service, car rental available with room package, no credit cards. The above is just a selection. Apartments and villas may also be rented.

● **Where To Eat**

Food in St Barts is expensive, there are few bargains, expect to pay minimum US\$25 for dinner (per person). Several good ones on Saint-Jean beach; the hotel restaurants are generally good (some are mentioned above). *La New Vieille France*, beachside with dancing at Corossol. In Gustavia: *Wall House*, T 27 71 83 for reservations, for exquisite French cuisine on the waterfront with harbour view; *Au Port* also offers fine dining overlooking the harbour, T 27 62 36 for reservations, one of the most expensive restaurants on the island; there is a good restaurant on the first floor of the *Yacht Club*, overlooking the harbour, offers few but well-prepared French dishes (also has a few rooms to let); *Auberge du Fort Oscar* specializes in Créole cooking, reserve first with Mme Jacque; *La Taverne* occupies an old warehouse and is open quite late; *Côté Jardin* (T 27 70 47) for Italian food and ice creams. *Bar Le Select* is a central meeting spot, an informal bar for lunch with hamburger menu, but also one of the most popular nighttime bars and sort of general store, with a few tables in a small garden. *L'Escale*, across the harbour, a pizza, pasta place with low prices for St Bart's but still expensive, T 27 81 06. For breakfast try *Tasted Unlimited* in Gustavia, for their delicious croissants and Danish pastries. For early starters try the bakery on Rue du Roi Oscar II, they open 0600 every day except Mon (closed).

● **Nightlife**

Most of the nightlife starts around the bars at Bay Saint Jean. In Gustavia at *Bar Le Select* (closed Sun). The night club *Autour Du Ro-*

cher in Lorient opens 2200-0230, entrance US$10, one drink included, very crowded at weekends. In Saint Jean try *Pearl's Club* or *Club La Banane*.

● Hours Of Business

0800-1200, 1430-1700, morning only on Sat.

● Banks

Banque Nationale de Paris (0815-1200, 1400-1600) with an automatic bankteller that works with US and European credit cards, Visa, Mastercard and Eurocard, and Banque Française Commerciale (0800-1200, 1400-1530), both in Gustavia. Crédit Martiniquais, Port de Gustavia, and Crédit Agricole, Bord de Mer à Gustavia.

● Currency

As on Saint-Martin, dollars are widely accepted but shops, restaurants will give a bad rate of exchange.

● Telephone Numbers

Gendarmerie T 27 60 12; Police T 27 66 66; Fire T 27 62 31; Sub Prefect T 27 63 28; Radio St Barts T 27 74 74, broadcasting on FM 98 mHz; Hospital T 27 60 85; Doctor On Call T 27 76 03. The SiBarth agency on General de Gaulle in Gustavia, T 27 62 38, has a fax service and a mail holding service. There is a USA Direct phone at the airport; you can phone the USA using a phone card and have the recipient return the call to the payphone.

● Tourist Office

Rue Auguste Nyman, T 27 60 08. Open Mon-Fri until 1200.

MARTINIQUE

THE ISLAND OF MARTINIQUE is 65 km long and 31 km wide. It lies at 14°40 North and 61° West and belongs to the Lesser Antilles. The Caribbean Sea is to the W, the Atlantic Ocean to the E. Martinique's neighbouring islands are Dominica to the N and St Lucia to the S, both separated from it by channels of approximately 40 km.

Martinique is volcanic in origin and one active volcano still exists, Mount Pelée (1,397m), situated to the NW, which had its last major eruption in 1902. The rest of the island is also very mountainous; the Pitons de Carbet (1,207m) are in the centre of the island and Montagne du Vauclin is in the S. Small hills or *mornes* link these mountains and there is a central plain, Lamentin, where the airport is situated. An extensive tropical rainforest covers parts of the N of the island, as well as pineapple and banana plantations, with the rest of the island mainly used for the cultivation of sugar cane. The coastline is varied: steep cliffs and volcanic, black sand coves in the N and on the rugged Atlantic coast, and calmer seas with large white or grey sand beaches in the S and on the Caribbean coast.

The population of the island is about 369,000 of which half live in the capital, Fort-de-France. This is the main settlement located on the Baie des Flamands on the W coast, with the burgeoning town of Lamentin, slightly inland, the second largest. The rest of Martinique is fairly evenly scattered with the small towns or *communes*.

History

When Christopher Columbus discovered Martinique either in 1493 or in 1502 (the date is disputed), it was inhabited by the Carib Indians who had exterminated the Arawaks, the previous settlers of the Lesser Antilles. Columbus named the island Martinica in honour of St Martin; the Caribs called it Madinina, or island of flowers.

The Spanish abandoned the island for richer pickings in Peru and Mexico and because of their constant troubles with the Caribs. In 1635 Martinique was settled by the French under the leadership of Pierre Belain d'Esnambuc. The cultivation of sugar cane and the importation of slaves from West Africa commenced. Fierce battles continued between the Caribs and the French until 1660 when a treaty was signed under which the Caribs agreed to occupy only the Atlantic side of the island. Peace was shortlived, however, and the Indians were soon completely exterminated.

During the seventeenth and eighteenth centuries England and France fought over their colonial possessions and in 1762 England occupied Martinique, only to return it to the French in exchange for Canada, Senegal, the Grenadines, St Vincent, and Tobago. France was content to retain Martinique and Guadeloupe because of the importance of the sugar cane trade at the time.

More unrest followed in the French Caribbean colonies when in 1789 the French Revolution encouraged slaves to fight for their emancipation. Martinique was occupied by the English again from 1794 to 1802, at the request of the plantation owners of the island who wanted to preserve the status quo and avoid slave revolts.

Slavery was finally abolished in 1848 by the French and in the late nineteenth century tens of thousands of immigrant workers from India came to Martinique to replace the slave workforce on the plantations.

In 1946 Martinique became a French Department, and in 1974 a Region.

Government

Martiniquans are French citizens and Martinique is officially and administratively part of France. The President of the French Republic is Head of State and the island is administered by a Prefect, appointed by the French Government. It is represented by three Deputies to the National Assembly in Paris, by two Senators in the Senate and by one representative on the Economic and Social Council. The Legislative Council of Martinique has 36 members elected for six years, who sit on the Regional Council which includes the locally elected Deputies and Senators. Political parties include the Progressive Party of Martinique, Socialists Communists, Union for French Democracy, Rally for the Republic and several small left-wing parties. A small independence movement exists but most people prefer greater autonomy without total independence from France. In the October 1990 elections, pro-independence groups entered the Regional Council for the first time, winning nine of the 41 seats. The ruling Progressive Party lost its majority but remained in power with 14 seats.

The Economy

Martinique is dependent upon France for government spending equivalent to about 70% of gnp, without which there would be no public services or social welfare. Even so, unemployment is high at about 32% of the labour force, the economy is stagnant and the balance of payments deficit expands continuously. The economy is primarily agricultural, about 7% of the economically active population is engaged in farming and fishing, and the main export crops are bananas, sugar, rum and pineapples, while aubergines, avocados, limes and flowers are being developed. Crops

MARTINIQUE : FACT FILE

Geographic

Land area	1,128 sq km
forested	36%
pastures	19%
cultivated	19%

Demographic

Population (1992)	369,000
annual growth rate (1987-92)	1.1%
urban	80.5%
rural	19.5%
density	327.1 per sq km
Religious affiliation	
Roman Catholic	87.9%
Birth rate per 1,000 (1990)	17.8
	(world av 27.1)
Death rate per 1,000 (1990)	6.1
	(world av 9.8)

Education and Health

Life expectancy at birth,	
male	71 years
female	77 years
Infant mortality rate	
per 1,000 live births (1990)	7.1
Physicians (1990)	1 per 573 persons
Hospital beds	1 per 101 persons
Calorie intake as %	
of FAO requirement	114%
Population age 25 and over	
with no formal schooling	9.8%
Literate males (over 15)	91.8%
Literate females (over 15)	93.2%

Economic

GNP (1987 market prices)	US$1,429mn
GNP per capita	US$4,100
Public external debt (1987)	US$30mn
Tourism receipts (1990)	US$240mn
Inflation (annual av 1985-90)	3.2%
Radio	1 per 6.1 persons
Television	1 per 8.1 persons
Telephone	1 per 2.9 persons

Employment

Population economically active (1990)	
	164,870
Unemployment rate	32.1%
% of labour force in	
agriculture	7.1
mining and manufacturing	4.0
construction	4.7
Military forces (French troops also in	
Guadeloupe and Guyane)	8,000

Source *Encyclopaedia Britannica*

grown mainly for domestic consumption include yams, sweet potatoes, Caribbean cabbages, manioc, breadfruit, plantains, tomatoes and green beans. Fishing con- tributes to the local food supply but most of the domestic market is met by imports. Most manufactured goods are imported, making the cost of living very high. There

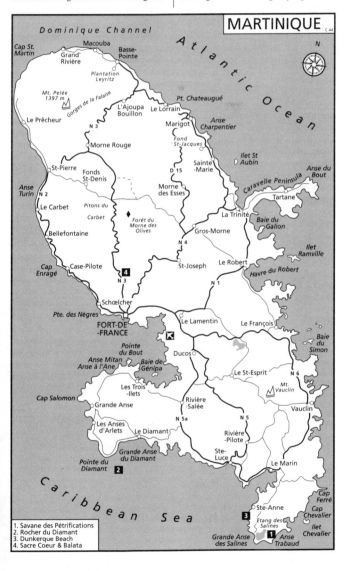

MARTINIQUE c.44

1. Savane des Pétrifications
2. Rocher du Diamant
3. Dunkerque Beach
4. Sacre Coeur & Balata

is some light industry and the major industrial plants are an oil refinery, rum distilleries and a cement works, while there is also fruit canning, soft drinks manufacturing and polyethylene and fertilizer plants. In 1994-96 the Antillean oil refinery company, SARA, is to invest 283Fmn in a new plant in Martinique to produce Kerosene and other fuels and 250Fmn on an explosion – resident control room and laboratory.

Tourism is the greatest area of economic expansion. In 1988 hotel and villa capacity was 3,274 rooms and the island received 280,000 visitors arriving by air and 385,513 cruise ship visitors, all of whom spent US$230mn. In the 5 years to 1993, stopover visitors rose by 30%, while cruise ship passenger arrivals grew more slowly, by 11%, to 428,695. Tourism income is now around US$300mn a year.

Culture

See the general introduction to the French Antilles.

Festivals

Martinique has more than its fair share of festivals. The main carnival, Mardi Gras, takes place at the beginning of February when the whole of Martinique takes to the streets in fantastic costume. On Ash Wednesday, black and white clad "devils" parade the streets lamenting loudly over the death of Vaval. At Eastertime, the children fly coloured kites which once had razors attached to their tails for kite fights in the wind. At *Toussaint* in November, the towns are lit by candlelight processions making their way to the cemeteries to sit with the dead.

Among the many other festivities there is the Martinique Food Show, in April, a culinary fair with lots of competitions; the May of St-Pierre, in May, which commemorates the eruption of the volcano Mt Pelée; the biennial International Jazz Festival, or World Crossroads of the Guitar, in December.

Watersports

Sailing and windsurfing at Club de Voile de Fort-de-France, Pointe-Simon, T 70 26 63; Club Nautique de Marin, T 74 92 48; Circle Nautique de Schoelcher, Anse Madame, T 61 15 21. There are glass bottom boats, motor boats, sailing boats for excursions and lots of craft for hire. Windsurfing is available on hotel beaches where there are board rentals. Jet skiing, sea scooters and water skiing at Pointe du Bout hotel beaches, Marouba Club (Carbet) and Pointe Marin beach in Ste-Anne. Many hotels like Bambou, La Dunette, Diamant-les-Bains organize fishing trips with local fishermen for their guests. Deep sea fishing can be arranged at Bathy's Club (*Meridien*), T 66 00 00 or Rayon Vert, T 78 80 56, for around 4,000F per boat.

Gommier races (huge rectangular sailing boats with coloured sails and teams of oarsmen) are an amazing sight at festivals all over the island from July to January. In Fort-de-France races take place in November and December from the little beach next to Desnambuc quay. Other major sailing occasions include the Schoelcher International Nautical Week in February, with sailing and windsurfing competitions; International Sailing Week in March (Yacht Club of Fort-de-France); the Aqua Festival, the Great Nautical Celebration at Robert in April; the Round Yawl Regatta Tour of Martinique in July, when over a period of 8 days about 20 round yawls set off for a colourful race.

Diving is especially good along the coral reef between St-Pierre and Le Prêcheur, over the wrecks off St-Pierre and along the S coast. A medical certificate is required unless you are a qualified diver, in which case you need your certification card. There are about 10 dive operators, most of which are based at the large hotels: Cressma, BP 574 Anse Madame, 97233 Schoelcher; Méridien Plongée, *Hotel Méridien*, T 66 00 00 ext

225; Oxygene Bleue, *Hotel Bakoua*, T 66 02 02; Topic Alizes, *Hôtel La Batelière*, T 61 49 49; Histoire d'Eau, BP1 97 227 Ste-Anne, T 76 92 98; Carib Scuba Club, BP3, 97250 St-Pierre, T 55 59 84; Club Nautique du Marin, Pointe du Marin, T 74 92 48; Club Bleu Marine Evasion, *Marine Hotel*, Pointe la Chéry, T 76 46 00; Planete Bleue, Marina Pointe du Bout, T 66 08 79/66 06 22; Sub Diamant Rock, *Hôtel Novotel*, T 76 42 42, F 76 22 87.

Sports

Tennis: courts are at many large hotels; *Bakoua*; *Club Méditerranée*; *Plantation Leyritz*; *PLM Azur Carayou*; *Novotel*; *Meridien* and *Hôtel Casino la Batelière* where visitors can play at night as well as during the day by obtaining temporary membership. For more information contact *La Ligue Regional de Tennis*, Petit Manoir, Lamentin, T 51 08 00.

Golf: At Trois-Ilets is a magnificent, eighteen-hole championship golf course with various facilities including shops, snackbar, lessons and equipment hire. Contact *Golf de la Martinique*, 97229 Trois-Ilets, T 68 32 81, F 68 38 97.

Riding is a good way to see Martinique's superb countryside; Ranch Jack, Anse d'Arlets, Galochas, T 68 37 69; Black Horse, La Pagerie, Trois-Ilets, T 66 00 04; La Caval, Diamant, T 76 22 94; and others offering schooling, hacking and other facilities. At *Plantation Leyritz* there are 2 horses for guests' use.

Cycling. Touring the island by bike is one of the activities offered by the Parc Naturel Régional. For information T 73 19 30. VT Tilt, Anse Mitan, Trois-Ilets, offers excursions by bike and cycle rallies, T 66 01 01, F 51 14 00.

Spectator Sports: Mongoose and snake fights and cockfights are widespread from December to the beginning of August at Pitt Ducos, Quartier Bac, T 56 05 60; Pitt Marceny (the most popular), Le Lamentin, T 51 28 47, and many others. Horse racing is at the Carère race-

track at Lamentin, T 51 25 09.

FORT-DE-FRANCE

Fort-de-France was originally built around the Fort St Louis in the seventeenth century. It became the capital of the island in 1902 when the former capital, St-Pierre, was completely obliterated by the eruption of Mount Pelée. The city of today consists of a bustling, crowded centre bordered by the waterfront and the sprawling suburbs which extend into the surrounding hills and plateaux. The bars, restaurants, and shops give a French atmosphere quite unlike that of other Caribbean cities. The port of Fort-de-France is situated to the E of the town centre, where cargo ships and luxury cruise liners are moored side by side.

The impressive Fort St-Louis still functions as a military base. Built in Vauban style, it dominates the waterfront. It is sometimes open to the public for exhibitions but once inside beware the low ceiling arches said to have been designed to foil the invading English who were generally taller than the French at that time. Adjacent to the fort is La Savane, a park of 5 hectares planted with palms, tamarinds, and other tropical trees and shrubs. The park contains statues of two famous figures from the island's past: a bronze statue of Pierre Belain d'Esnambuc, the leader of the first French settlers on Martinique; and a white marble statue of the Empress Josephine, first wife of Napoléon Bonaparte, who was born on the island.

The Bibliothèque Schoelcher is situated on the corner of Rue Victor Sévère and Rue de la Liberté, just across the road from the Savane. This magnificent baroque library was constructed out of iron in 1889 in Paris by Henri Pick, also the architect of the Eiffel Tower. The following year it was dismantled, shipped and reassembled in Fort-de-France where it received the extensive collections of books donated by Victor Schoelcher (responsible for the abolition of slavery in Martinique). Today it still functions as a library and regularly holds exhibitions (open 0830-1200, 1430-1800, T 40 26 67).

Just along the Rue de la Liberté towards the seafront is the Musée Départemental de la Martinique, also called Musée d'Archéologie et de Prehistoire. It contains relics of the Arawak and Carib Indians: pottery, statuettes, bones, reconstructions of villages, maps, etc. Open 0900-1700 Monday-Friday, 0900-1200 Saturday, T 71 57 05. Price of admission 12F, children 3F. Worth a visit.

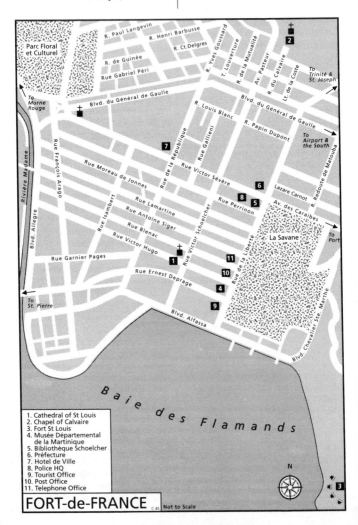

1. Cathedral of St Louis
2. Chapel of Calvaire
3. Fort St Louis
4. Musée Départemental de la Martinique
5. Bibliothèque Schoelcher
6. Préfecture
7. Hotel de Ville
8. Police HQ
9. Tourist Office
10. Post Office
11. Telephone Office

FORT-de-FRANCE C45 Not to Scale

In the centre of town, in the Square of Père Labat there is a second chance to see the baroque architecture of Henri Pick with the Cathedral of St Louis which towers above the Fort-de-France skyline. The interior is very beautiful and has stained glass windows depicting the life of St Louis.

The Parc Floral et Culturel (also called Galerie de Géologie et de Botanie or Exotarium) is a shady park containing two galleries, one of which concentrates on the geology of the island, the other on the flora. Almost 2,800 species of plants have been identified in Martinique and the Parc Floral has a very good selection. Open Tuesday-Friday, 0900-1230 and 1430-1730, Saturday, 0900-1300, 1500-1700, closed Sunday, Monday, T 70 68 41. Admission 5F. The Aquarium, on Boulevard de la Marne, has 250 species, open daily 0900-1900, 38F adults, 25F children, T 73 02 20, rather overpriced for its size.

Next to the Parc Floral are a feature of Fort-de-France not to be missed, the markets. The fishmarket is by the Madame river, where the fishermen unload from their small boats or *gommiers*. Close by is one of several markets selling fruit, vegetables and flowers as well as exotic spices. The markets are always bustling with activity from 0500 to sunset, but are best on Friday and Saturday. A fresh green coconut picked from a huge pile by the seller and hacked open with a machete, makes a refreshing drink for about 4F.

NORTH MARTINIQUE AND THE EAST COAST

The coastal road heading N from Fort-de-France passes through several fishing villages and is flanked by beaches that gradually become blacker with volcanic sand. At the popular beach of Anse Turin just N of *Le Carbet*, is the small Gauguin Museum. The artist stayed at Anse Turin during 1887 before he went to Tahiti. Open 1000-1730 every day. Admission

15F, T 78 22 66. The museum has letters, sketches and some reproductions of the artist's work as well as some pieces by local artists and examples of traditional costume.

Carbet also has a small zoo containing seventy species of animal including monkeys, lions, and ocelots, mainly from the Amazon region. Open every day 0900-1800. Admission 20F, children 10F, T 78 00 64.

To the N of Carbet is the famous *St-Pierre*. The modern village is built on the ruins of the former capital of Martinique, which was destroyed by a cloud of molten volcanic ash when Mount Pelée erupted in May 1902. As the cultural and economic capital, the town was known as the "Petit Paris" of the West Indies. Out of 26,000 inhabitants there was only one survivor, named Cylbaris, a drunkard who had been thrown into a cell for the night. Today his small cell is one of the ruins that visitors can still see. It is hidden away behind the remains of the once splendid and celebrated theatre of St-Pierre. The ruined church, originally built in the Fort of St- Pierre, also survives. In the Musée de Saint-Pierre, Museum of Vulcanology (open every day except Tuesday, 0900-1700, T 77 15 16, admission 10F) is an interesting collection of objects and documents evoking life before 1902 and remains from the disaster: household metal and glass objects charred and deformed by the extreme heat, photographs and volcanology displays. Guided tours of the Museum are available. The town of St-Pierre is well worth a visit and is an eerie reminder of destructive natural forces that dominate life in the Caribbean. For a guided tour in English or French ask at *La Guinguette* restaurant; tours about 40 minutes, Monday-Friday 0930-1300, 1430-1730, around 15F per person. You can even go in a submersible to visit the wrecks in the bay, T 78 18 18, F 78 20 84, Compagnie de la Baie de St-Pierre.

The next village on the coastal road is

the picturesque fishing village of *Le Prêcheur*. The road then continues towards the spectacular beach of Anse Ceron where the sand seems to be at its blackest. A rock called the Pearl juts out from the sea which is roughish on this beach but safe for swimming. It is a wild and beautiful beach, a pleasant change from the calm, white sand tourist beaches in the S. The coastal road ends a mile or two further on at another beach, Anse Couleuvre.

At the extreme N of the island is another small fishing village, **Grande Rivière**. There is no direct road linking Grande Rivière and Le Prêcheur but there is a coastal track through the rain forest which is a lovely 6-hour walk crossing several rivers (see **Tourist Agencies**, Island Information). The first 20 minutes on a concrete road are discouraging, but once in the forest the path is cooler and the views beautiful. Grande Rivière itself is set in breathtaking scenery characteristic of this part of the island; plunging cliffs covered with the lush vegetation of the rainforest. The island of Dominica faces the village from across the sea. Winding roads lead through the mountains to the next village, Macouba, perched on top of a cliff.

The area of **Basse-Pointe** is the pineapple cultivation area of the island, where huge fields of spikey pineapple tops cover the easternmost flanks of Mount Pelée. Inland from here is Plantation Leyritz, one of several former plantation houses (mostly in ruin). The restored eighteenth century building is now a hotel and restaurant (recommended) and anyone can stroll around the extensive grounds. There is a small exhibition of dolls made from plants and vegetables, exploiting the colours and textures of tropical leaves, which is open every day from 1000-1830, T 78 53 92.

From the road along the NE coast of the island tempting beaches with crashing waves are visible, but the Atlantic Coast is too dangerous for swimming. However, there is a safe beach at Anse Azérot, just S of **Ste-Marie**. To the N is the ancient monastery of Fond St-Jacques, built in 1658, where a restored chapel, a mill and aqueduct can be seen.

The Père Labat Museum in Ste-Marie presents the life story of the famous Dominican friar who lived in Martinique at the turn of the eighteenth century. Also, the history of the island is interestingly summarized using documents and photographs. Open 0900-1800 every day. There is a plan to transfer the museum to the slavery museum (Musée de l'Esclavage) in Fort-de-France.

Nearby, in the St James Distillery, is the Rum Museum. The free guided tour includes an explanation of the process of rum production and its history, and rum tasting. There is a collection of engraved spoons. The grounds are also very attractive. Rum is sold here but it is cheaper at the airport at the duty free shops. Open Monday to Friday, 0900-1300, 1400-1630 and Saturday and Sunday 0900-1200, T 69 30 02, admission free. A little inland is *Morne des Esses* which has a good view of Trinité and the Caravelle peninsula. There is an exhibition of Carib-style handicrafts: pottery, baskets, rugs and bags; and artisans can be seen at work.

The bustling sea front at *La Trinité* looks out onto the Caravelle Peninsula, where the vegetation is scrubby but the scenery is gently interesting. The peninsula has beaches at Tartane (the only village on the Caravelle), Anse l'Etang (the best) and Anse du Bout. It is an area protected by the Parc Naturel of Martinique; several well-marked paths criss-cross the peninsula so that visitors can enjoy the varied flora and fauna. It is also possible to visit the historic ruins of the Chateau Dubuc and various buildings that belonged to a Monsieur Dubuc, a smuggler and pirate who lived in the area. Open every day, 0830-1200 and 1400-1700, admission 5F.

The southernmost village on the Atlantic Coast is **Vauclin** where the main activity is fishing. Pointe Faula is a very safe beach here, with dazzling white sand and shallow water. To the S of Vauclin a road leads to Anse Macabou, a group of impressive white sand beaches.

THE TROPICAL RAINFOREST AND MOUNT PELÉE

La Route de la Trace winds through the tropical rainforest from Fort-de-France to Morne Rouge, Ajoupa-Bouillon and Mount Pelée. The forest itself is truly magnificent, covering the sides of the steep, inland mountains (Les Pitons de Carbet and Pelée) with a bewildering array of lush, green vegetation that stretches for miles. Giant bamboo, mountain palms, chestnut and mahogany trees, over a thousand species of fern and many climbing and hanging parasitic plants and orchids are examples of rainforest vegetation. The forest is protected as part of Martinique's Parc Naturel and makes interesting walking country (see **Tourist Agencies**).

At **Balata**, not far from the capital along the Route de la Trace is the bizarre building of Sacré Coeur, a close replica of the Parisian Cathedral, perched high up in the forest. A little further along the road is the Botanical Garden of Balata with superb views across to the capital. The gardens have a marvellous setting, though are slightly disappointing, depending on the season, when compared with the pictures in the official brochure. They are normally good in November-December. However, the gardens are well planted and the display of anthuriums, ranging from dark maroon, crimson and pink to white, is impressive. Look out for the numerous hummingbirds and brilliant green lizards. Umbrellas are provided if it is raining and the foliage gleams impressively when wet. Open 0900-1700 every day, T 64 48 73. Admission 30F, children aged 7-15, 10F. All signs are in French. A No. 7 bus goes from the rue A Aliker near the fish market, 6F each way.

As the Route de la Trace winds its way through the rainforest, the flanks of the surrounding mountains are clearly visible, covered with cultivated tropical flowers such as anthuriums and ginger lillies. The MacIntosh plantation, a 5 km steep climb from Morne Rouge, has a tourist route through its extensive fields of waxy blooms. Open Monday-Saturday, 0900-1630, adults 20F, children 8F, T 52 34 21, F 52 35 17.

Mount Pelée is reached via a track branching off the Route de la Trace, between Morne Rouge and Ajoupa-Bouillon. From the car park at the foot of the volcano there is a view of the Atlantic Coast, Morne Rouge and the bay of St-Pierre. The mountain air is deliciously fresh and cool even at the foot of the volcano. Not far away are Les Gorges de la Falaise, the dramatic waterfalls of the Falaise river, wonderful for swimming in, accessible only by following the course of the river on foot. Much of the walk is actually in the water and you clamber over waterfalls, making the carrying of cameras impractical.

SOUTH MARTINIQUE

The small village of **Les Trois-Ilets** across the bay from Fort-de-France has a charming main square and is surrounded by tourist attractions. At the Museum of La Pagerie, where Empress Josephine was born, it is possible to walk among the ruins of the old plantation house and the sugar processing plant. There is a collection of furniture, letters, and portraits which belonged to the Empress. Also on display are local works of art both contemporary and dating from the precolumbian era. Open Tuesday-Friday 0900-1730, Saturday-Sunday 0900-1300, 1430-1730, entrance 20F, children 5F, T 68 34 55, 68 38 34, F 68 38 41. Close by is the sugar cane museum (Musée de la Canne) which uses documents, machinery and superb models of sugar processing plant to illustrate the history of the Martiniquan sugar industry. Guided tours are available. Open 0900-1700 every day except Monday, entrance 15F, T 68 32 04. The pottery at Trois-Ilets has an exhibition room where traditional pottery is on sale.

A short bus ride from Trois-Ilets is the tourist complex of *Pointe du Bout*, directly opposite Fort-de-France, and linked by regular ferries. There is a marina, shops, discothèques, cafés, restaurants, sport facilities and a conglomeration of luxury hotels. The first beach after stepping off the ferry is a crowded strip of sand in front of the *Hotel Meridien*, almost completely covered with deckchairs for hire. Perhaps preferable is the beach at Anse Mitan, a 5-minute walk away, where there are numerous reasonably priced restaurants and bars. There is a direct ferry from the capital to Anse à l'Ane, a little way along the coast to the W. This beach is quieter than Anse Mitan and Pointe du Bout and has a pleasant atmosphere. Nearby, in the Musée des Coquillages (seashell museum), local scenes are depicted using seashells. Open 1000-1200 and 1500-1700 every day. Admission 15F, children 5F, T 68 34 97.

At Grande Anse is a magnificent beach, less frequented by tourists than the beaches at Pointe du Bout, although it does get more crowded at weekends. The pretty village of Anse d'Arlets is nearby.

Just S of Anse d'Arlets and around the *Pointe du Diamant* is Diamant beach. This is an idyllic beach stretching for 2½ miles along the S coast and dominated by the famous Rocher du Diamant (Diamond Rock). This huge rock, of volcanic origin, is about a mile out to sea and was occupied by the English at the beginning of the eighteenth century. They stationed cannons and about 200 soldiers there before the French reconquered it a year and a half later in 1605. British ships passing it still salute "Her Majesty's Ship Diamond Rock". The beach itself is secluded and bordered by groves of coconut palms and almond trees. The area is pleasantly unspoiled by the tourist industry. The sand is splendid but there are strong currents and it is advisable not to swim out too far, or indeed at all in rough conditions.

Inland and to the E of Diamant is the town of *Rivière-Pilote*, the largest settlement in the S of the island. The Mauny Rum distillery is located here, where free guided tours are available. The famous Cléry cock-fighting pit stages the only regular mongoose-snake fights in Martinique. These take place on Sunday afternoon. From the town of Le Marin, southwards are long white sand beaches lined with palm groves, and calm clear sea which epitomize the classic image of the Caribbean. Marin itself boasts a very fine eighteenth century Jesuit church.

At *Ste-Anne* is the extensive Club Méditerrannée complex. It has its own private beach adjacent to the long public beach, which has a spectacular view along the SW coast, including Rocher du Diamant. Ste-Anne beach is picturesque and shady with trees that overhang the sea in some places. There is a wide selection of lively bars and restaurants.

The road heading E from Marin leads to the beach at Cap Chevalier, a popular family beach at weekends. Among others along the barrier reef, the islet of Chevalier is visible from here.

At the southernmost tip of the island is the famous Grande Anse des Salines and the beaches of Dunkerque, Baham and Anse Trabaud, all of which are remarkably attractive. Inland from Anse Trabaud lies the salt marsh and the forest petrified by former lava flow. The forest is now sadly diminished thanks to the efforts of museums and souvenir hunters.

INFORMATION FOR VISITORS

● How To Get There

Scheduled direct flights from Europe are with Air France, which has flights from Paris; Air Liberté flies from Bordeaux, Nantes, Paris; AOM French Airlines from Paris and Marseilles. Air France also has direct flights to Cayenne, Miami, Paramaribo, Pointe-à-Pitre, Port-au-Prince and Santo Domingo. Ask Air France for youth fares if you are under 26, or for seasonal prices, as they vary. Nouvelles Frontières has charter flights from France. American Eagle flies from San Juan, with connections from the USA. Linea Aeropostal Venezolana flies from Caracas in a joint operation with Air France. Local airlines include SNAM (Société Nouvelle, Air Martinique), which flies to Barbados, Canouan, Guadeloupe, Mustique, St Lucia, Sint Maarten, St Vincent and Union Island, Air Guadeloupe, which flies to Pointe-à-Pitre, while Liat flies to Anguilla, Antigua, Barbados, Dominica, Pointe-à-Pitre, St Lucia, St Vincent, San Juan, Tortola and Trinidad. There are connecting flights from the UK via Antigua or Barbados, and from the USA via Miami, linked with most major North and South American airports.

● Airport

Lamentin Airport, T 59 81 81. There is a Tourist Office for hotel reservations and information, Crédit Agricole and Change Caraïbes for foreign currency exchange, car rental offices and ground tour operators. To get to the airport at Lamentin, either take a taxi, which presents no difficulties but is expensive, or take a bus marked "Ste-Anne" and ask to be set down on the highway near the airport. It is then a 100 metres' walk. The fare is 10F and the buses take reasonable-sized luggage.

● Airlines

Air France, T 55 33 00; Air Liberté, T 59 81 81; AOM French Airlines, T 70 09 16/51 74 85; Air Martinique T 51 08 09/60 00 23; Nouvelles Frontières-Corsair, T 70 59 70; American Airlines, T 51 12 29; Liat, T 51 10 00/51 21 11; Martinique Air Service (charters), T 51 51 51.

● Inter-Island Transport

Caribbean Express has a high speed catamaran service to Dominica and Pointe-à-Pitre, Guadeloupe, which runs almost daily in high season but hardly at all in the months of Sept/Oct when the sea is rough and demand low. There are also services to Les Saintes and St Lucia if warranted by demand. Contact head office: 18 rue Ernest Deproge, 97200 Fort-de-France, T 60 12 11/60 12 38, F 70 50 75, for timetable and fares. Overnight packages available with several hotels, also car hire. One way fare in 1993 from Fort-de-France to Roseau was 305F and to Pointe-à-Pitre 315F, child, youth and senior citizens' reductions. Agents for the Madikera car ferry to Dominica and Guadeloupe include T-Maritimes Brudey Frères, 108 rue Victor Hugo, 97200 Fort-de-France, T 70 08 50 (or T 91 60 87/97 77 82/90 04 48 for timetable information. Fare from Fort-de-France to Dominica 275F one way, 400F return, plus departure tax. Martinique is on the route of most Caribbean cruises. Information on travelling by cargo boat can be obtained from the travel agency next door to the CGM office at the harbour, but if going to South America it is cheaper to fly. CGM has a trans-Atlantic cargo ship from Le Havre/Dunkerque to Fort-de-France and Pointe-à-Pitre, T 55 32 00/46 25 70 00, F 46 25 78 05, cars can be brought as accompanied baggage, single or double cabins, a/c, bathroom, swimming pool, sports room (see **Introduction and Hints**).

● Yachting

The facilities are among the best in the Caribbean. The marina at Pointe du Bout is very safe, but congested and hot.

For those looking to hitch on a boat, consult the noticeboards at the Yacht Clubs, especially the bar at the W end of the Public Jetty and refuelling at the W end of Boulevard Alfassa on the Baie des Flamands.

● Tourist Agencies

Guided tours of the island by bus, trips on sailing boats and cruise ships around Martinique and to neighbouring islands, and excursions on glass-bottom boats are organized by the following companies: *STT Voyages*, 23 Rue Blénac, Fort-de-France, T 71 68 12; *Carib Jet*, Pointe du Bout, T 66 05 07, F 66 02 12; *Madinina Tours*, 89 rue Blénac, 97200 Fort-de-France, T 70 65 25, F 73 09 53; *Caribtours*, Marina Pointe du Bout, 97229 Trois Ilets, T 66 02 56, F 66 09 66; *Colibri Tours*, Hôtel La Batelière, 97233 Schoelcher, T 61 66 74, F 61 66 69.

Touring on foot: contact the *Parc Naturel Régional*, 9 Boulevard Général-de-Gaulle, T 73 19 30, for well-organized walks in the island's beauty spots such as the rainforest and the Caravelle Peninsula. The charge is 60-80F per person and includes the coach fare to the walk's starting point. Guides can be found through the tourist office, or at Morne Rouge for climbing Mount Pelée and at Ajoupa-Bouillon for the Gorge de la Falaise walk.

● **Buses**

There are plenty of buses running between Fort-de-France and the suburbs which can be caught at Pointe-Simon on the seafront and from Boulevard Général-de-Gaulle. The buses are all privately owned and leave when they're full and not before. Short journeys cost around 5F and the buses run from 0500-2000 approximately. From Fort-de- France to St-Pierre is 20F one way; to Ste-Anne 30-55F one way. To request a stop shout "arrêt"!

● **Taxis**

To go further afield the *taxi collectif* (estate cars or minibuses) are the best bet. "Taxicos", or TCs, run until about 1800 and leave Pointe Simon for all the communes; Ste-Anne 30-55F, Diamant 17-45F, St-Pierre 16-90F. It is worth noting that there are no buses to the airport, and a private taxi is the only way of getting into town from the airport, around 70F. There is a 40% surcharge on taxi fares between 1900 and 0600 and on Sun. Private taxi stands are at the Savane, along Boulevard Général-de-Gaulle and Place Clemenceau.

● **Ferries**

There are ferries running between Desnambuc quay on the sea front and Pointe du Bout, Anse Mitan and Anse à l'Ane, 17F return. These run until about 2300 to Pointe du Bout and 1830 to Anse Mitan and Anse à l'Ane and apart from a few taxis are about the only form of transport on a Sun or after 2000. The 20-min ferry from Fort de France to Trois-Ilets costs 18F return, is punctual, pleasurable and saves a 45-min drive by road. To the *Méridien* there is only one boat each hour (don't believe boatmen who say they go near, they drop you at Anse à l'Ane which is a long hot walk away). For information about ferry timetables call 73 05 53 for Somatour and 63 06 46 for Madinina.

● **Car Hire**

There are numerous car hire firms at the airport and around town; *Europcar Interent*, Aéroport Lamentin, T 51 33 33, 51 01 96, F 51 22 44, Fort-de-France T 73 33 13 and several hotels; *Hertz*, 24 Rue Ernest-Deproge, Fort-de-France, T 60 64 64. Airport, T 51 28 22; *Avis*, 4 Rue Ernest-Deproge, Fort-de-France, T 70 11 60,

Airport, T 51 26 86. Prices start from 190-230F a day for a Citroën AX or Renault 5. It will normally be cheaper to have unlimited mileage. You can get a discount if you book your car from abroad at least 48 hours in advance. An international driver's licence is required for those staying over twenty days.

One look at Fort-de-France's congested streets will tell you it's well worth avoiding driving in the city centre. Parking in central Fort-de-France is only legal with a season ticket and the capital's traffic wardens are very efficient; cars may be towed away.

Mopeds can be hired at *TS Auto*, 38 Route de Ste-Thérèse, Fort-de-France, T 63 33 05 and at Rue de Caritan, Ste-Anne, T 76 92 16. Other agencies include Funny, in Fort-de-France, T 63 33 05 and Sainte-Anne, T 76 92 16; Moppet, 3 rue Jules Monnerot Terres Sainville, Fort de France, T 60 02 88; Scootonnerre, Le Diamant, T 76 41 12; Discount, Trois Ilets, T 66 04 37; and Marquis-Moto, Sainte-Luce, opp the church. Motorcycles of 80cc and over need a licence, those of 50cc do not. Rental for all is about 170F/day. A bicycle can be hired for 50F/day, 250F/week, 350F/fortnight, from Funny, T 63 33 05; Discount, T 66 33 05; TS Location Sarl, T 63 42 82, all in Fort-de-France.

Hitching is a common way of getting around, and very easy, recommended.

● **Where To Stay**

Martinique offers a wide range of accommodation from the modest family-run *auberges* scattered over the remote and spectacular N, to the huge 5 star complexes of Pointe du Bout and Trois Ilets, the main tourist area, in the S. *Gîtes*, furnished holiday apartments and bungalows are widely available, some connected to hotels. Ste-Anne, with its attractive white sand beaches typical of the SW coast, boasts a *Club Méditerranée* and one of the island's 3 main campsites. Information and reservations can be made through Centrale de Réservation, BP823-97208 Fort-de-France Cédex, T 71 56 11, F 73 66 93. Generally, prices are high and some hotels add 10% service charge and/or 5% government tax to the bill. (Prices quoted here are for a double room, winter 1993/94 rates.)

Pointe du Bout and Les Trois-Ilets are the main tourist centres, well equipped with shops, night clubs, casinos, a marina, facilities for golf, watersports and tennis as well as several beaches. **Trois-Ilets**, benefits from the facilities of Pointe du Bout and the pleasant beaches of

Anse Mitan and Anse à l'Ane, a twenty minute ferry ride from Fort-de-France. The main hotels are *Meridien*, 97229 Trois-Ilets, T 66 00 00, F 66 00 74, where the staff show a lack of interest at this huge modern complex with 295 rooms and traditional bungalows in land-scaped grounds, the swimming is superb and it is fun to walk through the marina village (take a picnic lunch because food and drink is expensive), 1,525F, CP; *Bakoua* (named after traditional Martiniquan straw hats) with apart-ments and rooms, T 66 02 02, F 66 00 41, 986-1,974F, CP. *Hôtel la Pagerie, PLM Azur*, pool, T 66 05 30, F 66 00 99, 436F, EP; *Auberge de l'Anse Mitan*, T 66 01 12, F 66 01 05, a friendly, family-run hotel with apart-ments and rooms, 330F, CP, 500F, MAP; *Le Nid Tropical*, rents studios and has a lively beach bar and restaurant, T 68 31 30, 200-300F, EP, also camping, see below. *La Bonne Auberge Chez André*, T 66 01 55, F 66 04 50, again basic but clean, offering underwater fishing and watersports, 250F, CP, 490F, MAP.

Medium to low priced hotels in Fort-de-France include *Impératrice*, T 63 06 82, F 72 66 30, 350-450F, CP, 1950s décor and archi-tecture, apparently unchanged since it was built in 1957, friendly, and *La Malmaison*, good and clean, spacious, but some rooms smell of cigarettes, T 63 90 85, F 60 03 93, 250-375F in winter, more during Carnival, both in Rue de la Liberté opposite the Savane and both with lively bars and restaurants fre-quented by a young crowd; the *Balisier* on Rue Victor Hugo is also very centrally located with a view over the port, T/F 71 46 54, good value, 330-380F, EP. On Rue Lazare Carnot is *Un Coin de Paris*, T 70 08 52, 250-300F CP, small, friendly and cheap. *Les Hibiscus*, 11 rue Re-doute de Matouba, T 60 29 59, 170-200F. The *Blenac*, 3 Rue Blenac has small, hot, smelly rooms but is conveniently located, cheap and has a helpful proprietor, best rooms are nos 8 and 9, T 70 18 41, 180-200F, EP. *Le Gom-mier*, 3 Rue Jacques Cazotte, T 71 88 55, highly rec, has clean spacious rooms and good continental breakfasts, friendly management, 270-350F, EP. Slightly away from the crowded tourist centre of the capital, yet still centrally located near the canal is the *Palasia*, T 60 32 60, 290F, EP, 470F, CP. In the elegant suburbs of Didier is the *Victoria*, T 60 56 78, F 60 00 24, buses into town every few mins, pool, EP, 320-420F EP. At Schoelcher, on the outskirts of Fort-de-France, is *La Batelière* with pool, ten-nis courts and casino, T 61 49 49, F 61 62 29, 780-1,200F, EP.

The hotels at **Diamant** on the S coast bene-fit from miles of superb, uncrowded beach with magnificent views of coastal mountains and, of course, Diamant Rock. *Novotel* has excellent facilities, lovely pool, tennis courts, watersports, disco and it rents apartments and rooms, T 76 42 42, F 76 22 87, 870-1,690F CP. *Diamant les Bains*, rec, fine views over swim-ming pool and sea, 380-450F, CP, T 76 40 14, F 76 27 00, and *Le Village du Diamant*, T 76 41 89, F 63 53 32, 420F, EP, has 59 basic, beachside bungalows, rooms or apartments for rent.

At Ste-Luce *Aux Delices de la Mer* offers fishing amongst other activities, T 62 50 12, 300F, CP, 450F, MAP.

On the rugged **south Atlantic coast**, *Chez Julot*, T 74 40 93, a modest but pleasant hotel, one street back from foreshore road, a/c, rec, restaurant, 285F, CP, 480F, MAP, rue Gabriel Perí, Vauclin. *Les Brisants*, T 54 32 57, F 54 69 13, at François provides good Créole cuisine, 280F, CP, 520F, MAP. On the old NI, near Trinité, within easy reach of the Caravelle peninsula, *St Aubin* is a magnificent colonial-style hotel, splendid location, views and exterior, but inte-rior badly damaged by 1960s refurbishment, 380-450F, CP, T 69 34 77, F 69 41 14, and *Le Village de Tartane* is near the pretty fishing village of Tartane, T 58 46 33, F 63 53 32, 420F, EP. In Tartane, *Madras*, hotel and restaurant, on the beach, good views, spotless rooms, sea view 400F, CP, road view 300F, CP, summer rates, T 58 33 95, F 58 33 63.

Moving N through dramatic scenery to Lorrain, the *Gibsy Hotel* is very comfortable with only 6 rooms and facilities for horse riding nearby, T 53 73 46, 350-450F CP; and at Basse Pointe, rather difficult to find, *Plantation de Leyritz*, T 78 53 92, F 78 92 44, is a former plantation house set in beautiful grounds with a lot of insects because of all the fruit trees and water, glamorous accommodation, excellent restaurant serving local specialities, efficient and friendly service, pool, tennis courts, health spa, discothèque, 558F, CP. In the remote, Northern- most commune, Grand-Rivière, a small fishing village surrounded by rainforest and close to several idyllic black sand coves, *Chanteur Vacances* (formerly Les Abeilles) is a simple, clean hotel with only 7 rooms, shared facilities, restaurant, T 55 73 73, 195F, CP. In same price range is *Chez Tante Arlette*, only 2 rooms, book in advance.

One of the few hotels within easy reach of

the ruined town of **St-Pierre** is *La Nouvelle Vague*, 5 rooms only (doubles), T 78 14 34, 250F, EP, run down rooms over bar, overlooks beach, poor value. Moving inland to the foot of the volcano that destroyed St-Pierre *Auberge de la Montagne Pelée*, T 52 32 09, F 73 20 75, 8 rooms, 330F, EP, at Morne Rouge, good, an ideal base for keen walkers to explore the volcano and the surrounding countryside. There are bungalows for rent and hot water, a necessary luxury because of the cool mountain air. Book well in advance.

Also benefiting from beautiful countryside and fresh mountain air, *Chez Cecilia* at Morne Vert offers agreeable accommodation, T 55 52 83, F 75 10 74, 400F, MAP, 400-500F, AP.

On **Carbet's** enormous black sand beach are *Le Cristophe Colomb*, good value, T 78 05 38, 225F, EP, and the more upmarket *Marouba Club* which has apartments and bungalows, pool, disco, T 78 00 21, F 78 05 65, 396-536F CP.

Finally, convenient for the airport at **Ducos** in the plain of Lamentin, *Victoria Airport*, T 56 29 82, 300F EP.

Other accommodation includes *Bungalows de la Palmerie* at Ste-Anne, T 76 78 41; *Studios La Caravelle* at Tartane, T 58 07 32, 265F, EP; *Immeuble Plaisance* at Anse à l'Ane, Trois-Ilets, 5 apartments for 2 and 3 people, 1,560F for one week (2 people); *Aurore No 1 et 2* at Quartier Dizac, Diamant, 1,670F for one week (2 people).

A fuller list of hotels and other accommodation available on Martinique can be obtained from the Office Départemental du Tourism, BP 520, 97206, Fort-de-France Cédex. T 63 79 60. The tourist office at the airport is helpful and will telephone round the hotels to get you a room for your first night if you have not booked beforehand.

● **Gîtes**

To rent a gîte contact Gîtes de France Martinique, Maison du Tourisme Vert, 9 Bd du Général-de-Gaulle, BP 1122, 97248 Fort-de-France Cédex, T 73 67 92, or Centrale de Réservation Martinique, BP 823, 97208 Fort-de-France Cédex, T 71 56 11. They rent rooms in private houses, apartments, houses, in all price ranges with weekly or monthly tariffs (weekly rates between 1,500-3,000F). For information about the *Club Méditerranée* hotel village at Ste-Anne, contact Club Méditerranée, 516 Fifth Ave, New York, NY 10036 or 5 South Molton St, London W1.

● **Camping**

The most convenient campsite for Fort-de-France is at Anse à l'Ane where the *Courbaril Campsite* is situated, with kitchenette and washing facilities. They also have small bungalows to rent, 112-230F, T 68 32 30. Right next to it is *Le Nid Tropical* campsite, 70F for 2 people if you have your own tent, 100F, if you rent one, 200F EP for an apartment, T 68 31 30. A small bakery/restaurant on the beach serves cheap meals, bread and pastries. On the S coast, Ste-Luce has a good campsite with adequate facilities in the *VVF Hotel*, but the beach is not nice. There are no tents for hire. T 62 52 84. *Camping Municipal* at Ste-Anne is a popular campsite with a pleasant situation in a shady grove right on the beach, but rather dirty, 40F, cheap food available. Next to the *Club Med*, it is on the cleanest and nicest beach and was fully renovated in 1989. You can rent tents from Chanteur Vacances, 65 rue Perrinon, Fort-de-France, T 71 66 19, around 35F/day.

● **Where To Eat**

Sampling the French and Créole cuisine is one of the great pleasures of visiting Martinique. There is an abundance of restaurants, cafés, and snack bars to be found everywhere. The quality is generally very high so it is worth being adventurous and trying the various dishes and eating places. The main meal of the day is at midday and many restaurants and cafés offer very reasonable fixed price *menus du jour* ranging from 35-45F. Some worth seeking out are as follows:

La Biguine, 11 route de la Folie, T 71 47 75, closed Sat lunch time and Sun; *Le Blenac*, 3 rue Blenac, T 70 18 41, closed Sun evening; *King Creol*, 56 Av des Caraïbes, T 70 19 17, closed Sat midday and Sun; *El Chico Chico*, 29 rue Garnier Pagès, T 72 48 92, open Mon-Sat lunch only; for crêpes and salads try *La Crêperie*, 4 rue Garnier Pagès, T 60 62 09, closed Sat midday, Sun; *Espace Créole*, 8 rue Voltaire, T 70 05 95, open Mon-Sat 1100-2200; *Le Victor Hugo*, 69 rue V Hugo, T 63 61 08, closed Sun midday; *Marie Sainte*, 160 rue V Hugo, T 70 00 30, open daily except Sun. For vegetarians, *Le Second Soufflé*, 27 rue Blenac, T 63 44 11, open Mon-Fri lunchtime.

For an Italian atmosphere try *Pizza de la Savane* 28 Avenue des Caraïbes, where authentic pizza and pasta dishes are served, closed Sat, Sun lunchtimes, T 73 66 75. There are several restaurants serving Vietnamese and

Chinese food, inc *Le Cantonnais*, Marina Pointe du Bout, T 66 02 33, open daily; *Le Chinatown*, 20 rue Victor Hugo, T 71 82 62, Mon-Fri lunch; *Indo*, Vietnamese, 105 route de la Folie, T 71 63 25, closed Sun evening and Mon; *Le Jardin de Jade*, Anse Colas, T 61 15 50, closed Sun evening, *Le Kiwany's*, 2 rue Kernay, Trinité, T 58 42 44, closed Sun evening, Mon; *Le Lotus d'Asie*, Vietnamese, 24 Bd de la Marne, T 71 62 96, closed Sun lunch; *Le Xuandre*, Vietnamese, Voie No 2 Pointe des Nègres, T 61 54 70, evenings only, closed Mon. Other nationalities are also well represented: *Le Couscousser*, 1 rue Perrinon, looking out on to Bibliothèque Schoelcher, is excellent with choice of sauces and meats to accompany *couscous*, reasonably priced, interesting, rather young Algerian red wine goes well with the food, closed Sun lunch, T 60 06 42; *Les Cèdres*, Lebanese, in rue Redoute de Matouba, excellent humous, kebabs and other Lebanese meze, owner speaks English, all major credit cards accepted; *Le Salambo*, Tunisian, Patio de Cluny, T 60 47 70, closed Sun, Mon, Tues; *Le Beyrouth*, Lebanese, 9 rue Redoute de Matouba, T 60 67 45, lunch menu from 80F; *Le Méchoui*, Moroccan, Pte Simon, behind Bricogite, reservations preferred, takeaway service, T 71 58 12, open 1200-1600, 1900-2400, closed Sun; *Las Tapas de Sevillas*, Spanish, 7 rue Garnier Pagès, T 63 71 23.

Amongst the many restaurants across the Baie des Flamands at Anse Mitan is the charming *L'Amphore* where the fresh lobster is delicious, T 66 03 09, closed Mon-Tues, lunchtime. *Bambou* is a little further along the beach, specializes in fresh fish and offers an excellent *menu du jour. Chez Jojo* on the beach at Anse à l'Ane, T 68 37 43, has a varied seafood menu as does *l'Ecrevisse*. Two-star restaurants include *Auberge de l'Anse Mitan*, T 66 01 12, open every evening, reservations required; *La Bonne Auberge*, Chez André, T 66 01 55; *La Langouste*, T 66 04 99, open daily; *La Villa Créole*, T 66 05 53, closed Sun-Mon lunch. At Diamant, *La Case Créole*, Place de l'Église, T 76 10 14, French and Créole, seafood and other specialities, open daily 1100-1600, 1900-2330; *Hotel Diamant Les Bains* has a reasonable and well-situated restaurant specializing in seafood, T 76 40 14, shut Wed. There are several other restaurants in the town which front directly on to the beach, mostly offering créole cooking and seafood.

At Carbet the *Grain d'Or*, a spacious airy restaurant, is another good spot to sample Martinique's seafood specialities, T 78 06 91, open daily, and *La Guinguette* on the beach near St-Pierre is also rec. On the coast, N of St-Pierre is *Chez Ginette*, good food but overpriced, T 52 90 28, closed Thur.

The restaurant at *Plantation Leyritz* near Basse Pointe is in the restored plantation house and has waterfalls trickling down the walls giving a cool, peaceful feel to the place, elegant dining, good food and service. At Grand' Rivière, *Chez Tante Arlette* serves excellent créole food in cool, pleasant surroundings, finished off with home made liqueurs, rue Louis de Lucy de Fossarieu, T 55 75 75.

At Ste-Anne, dine in style at the *Manoir de Beauregard* or at *Les Filets Bleus*, right on the beach and lighter on the pocket, T 76 73 42, closed Sun evening, Mon. At Cap Chevalier, *Chez Gracieuse* is a good créole restaurant, choose the terrace and order the catch of the day, not too expensive, T 76 72 31, 76 93 10, open daily.

For travellers on a smaller budget wishing to eat out in the capital there are plenty of good snackbars and cafés serving various substantial sandwiches and *menus du jour*. The area around Place Clemenceau has lots of scope; *Le Clemenceau* is very good value and extremely friendly – try the *accras* or a fresh *crudité* salad; *Le Lem* on Boulevard Général-de-Gaulle has superior fast food at low prices and a young crowd. It also stays open later than many restaurants that close in the evenings and on Sun. Behind the Parc Floral on Rue de Royan is the *Kowossol*, a tiny vegetarian café which serves a cheap and healthy *menu du jour*. The pizzas are rec and the fruit juice is especially delicious – try *gingembre* (ginger) or *ananas* (pineapple). On François Arago *Los Amigos* and *Le Coq d'Or* are particularly good for substantial sandwiches for around 12F. Try *poisson* (steak fish) or *poulet* (chicken). *Le Renouveau* on Boulevard Allegre offers delicious, filling *menus du jour* for 40F, again with a warm welcome.

The place to head for in the evening when all of these eateries close (except *Le Lem* which stays open until 2100), is the Boulevard Chevalier de Ste-Marthe next to the Savane. Here every evening until late, vans and caravans serve delicious meals to take away, or to eat at tables under canvas awnings accompanied by loud Zouk music. The scene is bustling and lively, in contrast to the rest of the city at nighttime, and the air is filled with wonderful aromas. Try *lambis* (conch) in a sandwich (15F) or on a *brochette* (like a kebab) with rice and salad (30F). Paella and *Colombo* are good buys (40F) and the crêpes whether sweet or savoury are delicious. for a description of local food **see page 539**.

● **Entertainment**

For those whose visit does not coincide with any festivals, there is plenty of other entertainment. The *Ballet Martiniquais* (T 63 43 88) is one of the world's most prestigious traditional ballet companies. Representing everyday scenes in their dance, they wear colourful local costume and are accompanied by traditional rhythms. Information about performances and venues, usually one of the large hotels (*Novotel, Caritan, Carayou, Méridien, Bakoua* and *Batelière*) can be obtained from the tourist office. Every year in July, SERMAC (Parc Floral et Culturel, T 73 60 25) organizes an arts festival in Fort-de-France with local and foreign artistes performing plays and dance. CMAC (Centre Martiniquais d'Action Culturelle, Avenue Franz Fanon, Fort-de-France, T 61 76 76) organizes plays, concerts, and the showing of films and documentaries all year round.

There are several comfortable, air-conditioned cinemas in Fort-de-France and the various communes. No film is in English; tickets cost 30F. The 2 main theatres are the *Théâtre Municipal* in the lovely old Hôtel de Ville building and *Théâtre de la Soif Nouvelle* in the Place Clemenceau. Night Clubs abound and tend to be very expensive (70F to get in and the same price for a drink, whether orange juice or a large whisky). Night clubs include *Le New Hippo*, 24 Blvd Allegre, Fort-de-France, T 60 20 22; *La Vesou* at Hotel *Carayou*, *Zipp's Club*, Dumaine, Francois, T 54 65 45. There are several bars where you can listen to various types of music. At *Coco Loco*, next to the Tourist Office in Fort-de-France, regular jazz sessions are held, T 63 63 77. Others include *Chez Gaston*, rue Felix Eboué, *La Carafe*, rue Lamartine, *Le Pagayo*, Rond Point du Vietnam Héroïque, *Le Blue Cap*, 7 rue Lamartine, all in Fort-de-France. Most large hotels lay on Caribbean-style evening entertainment for tourists; limbo dancers, steelbands, etc. Hôtel Meridien has the island's main casino 2300-0300, proof of identity is required for entry. *Chouboulout*e, the local entertainments guide, is sold in most newsagents, priced 5F.

● **Shopping**

Fort-de-France has ample scope for shoppers, with an abundance of boutiques selling the latest Paris fashions, as well as items by local designers, and numerous street markets where local handicrafts are on sale. Seekers of clothing and perfume should head for Rue Victor Hugo and its 2 *galleries* (malls). Jewellery shops are mostly in Rue Isambert and Rue Lamartine, selling crystal, china and silverware, and unique gold jewellery. At markets in the Savane and near the cathedral bamboo goods, wickerwork, shells, leather goods, T-shirts, silk scarves and the like are sold. Wines and spirits imported from France and local liqueurs made from exotic fruits are readily available, and Martiniquan rum is an excellent buy. There are large shopping centres at Cluny, Dillon, and Bellevue. American and Canadian dollars are accepted nearly everywhere and many tourist shops offer a 20% discount on goods bought with a credit card or foreign traveller's cheques.

● **Cost Of Living**

Remember that the standard of living is high and expect to pay French prices or higher, which means expensive. Small beers or cokes cost around 15F, petrol 52F/litre, a nice meal at a medium priced restaurant will be at least 350F for 2.

● **Banks And Exchange**

Change Caraïbes, Airport, open 0830-1730, Mon-Fri, 0830-1300, Sat, T 51 57 91, Rue Ernest Deproge, 97200, Fort-de-France, open 0800-1900 Mon-Fri, 0800-1430 Sat, T 60 28 40; Crédit Agricole also has an office at the airport for currency exchange, open 0730-1230, 1415-1600 Tues-Fri, 0730-1230 Sat, T 51 25 99. Banque National de Paris, 72 Avenue des Caraïbes, T 59 46 00 (the best for cash advances on Visa, no commission). Banks and exchange houses charge 5% commission on travellers' cheques. Not all banks accept US dollar TCs. Always go to the bank early; by mid-morning they are very crowded. Do not change US dollars at the Post Office in Fort-de-France, you lose about 15% because of the poor exchange rate and commission. American Express at Roger Albert Voyages, 10 rue Victor Hugo, upstairs, efficient.

● **Laundry**

There are several launderettes in Fort-de-France; Laverie Automatique, Galerie des Filibustiers, rue E Deproge; Lavexpress, 61 rue Jules-Monnerot; Laverie Self-Service, Lavematic, 85 rue Jules-Monnerot, Terres Sainville, T 63 70 43.

● **Health**

In an emergency: SAMU, Pierre Zobda Quitmann Hospital, 97232 Le Lamentin, T 55 20 00. Ambulance service T 71 59 48. The Sea Water Therapy Centre is at Grand Anse, 97221 Carbet, T 78 08 78.

● **Climate**

The lushness of Martinique's vegetation is evidence that it has a far higher rainfall than many of the islands, due to its mountainous relief. The wet season lasts from June to late November and the frequency of sudden heavy showers make an umbrella or raincoat an essential piece of equipment. The cooler dry season lasts from December to May and the year round average temperature is 26°C although the highlands and Mount Pelée are quite cool.

● **Hours Of Business**

Shops are open from 0900-1800 (banks from around 0730) and until 1300 on Sat. Nearly everything closes from 1200-1500 and on Sun.

● **Diplomatic Representation**

France has responsibility for diplomatic representation; other countries with a consular service in Fort-de-France are: Belgium, Denmark, Haiti, Italy, Netherlands, Norway, Spain, Sweden, Switzerland, UK (Honorary Consul Mme Alison Ernoult, T 61 56 30), Venezuela and Germany.

● **Useful Numbers**

Fire department, T 18; Police T 17; Gendarmerie, rue Victor Sévère, 97200 Fort-de-France, T 63 51 51; Hôtel de Police, T 55 30 00; sea rescue, T 63 92 05; radio phone (international), T 10; radio taxi, T 63 63 62.

● **Weights And Measures**

The metric system is in use.

● **Electricity**

The electric current is 220 volts AC.

● **Post And Telephones**

Nearly all public telephones are cardphones except a few in bars and hotels which take coins. At the PTT office in Rue Antoine Siger, just off the Savane, there are numerous card and coin phones and *Télécartes* (phone cards) are sold. These can also be bought in most newsagents, cafés, and some shops for 36.50F upwards. Don't get caught out on arrival at the airport where there are only cardphones. Try the tourist office where they are very helpful and will phone round endless hotels to find the unprepared new arrival a room. You can not make a credit card or collect call from a public phone, nor can you have a call returned to a payphone.

Post offices are open from 0700-1800 and Sat mornings. The main post office is on Rue de la Liberté and always has long queues.

● **Tourist Offices**

Lamentin Airport, T 51 28 55; Bord de la Mer, Fort-de-France, T 63 79 60, F 73 66 93. Postal address: Office Départemental du Tourisme de la Martinique, BP 520, 97206 Fort-de-France Cédex. There are local information bureaux (Syndicat d'initiative) all round the island, many of which can be found through the town hall (mairie).

Abroad there are the Bureau Promotion Martinique, 2 rue des Moulins, 75001, Paris, T 44 77 86 22, F 49 26 03 63; the Commercial Representative Office Nordic Countries, PO Box 717 Frettvägen 14, S 1818 07 Lidingo, Sweden, T 468 765 58 65, F 765 93 60; Office due Tourisme de la Martinique au Canada, 1981 Av MacGill College, Ste 480, Montréal PQH 3A 2W9, T (514) 844 8566, F 844 8901; The French West Indies Tourist Board, 610 Fifth Av, New York, NY 10020, T (212) 757 0218, F 247 6468; La Martinique Reisen GMBH, Adel mannstrasse, 2-D 8000 Munich 82, Germany, T (089) 430 2966, F 430 7224.

WINDWARD ISLANDS

DOMINICA

DOMINICA (pronounced Domi-*neeca*) is the largest and most mountainous of the anglophone Windward Islands. The official title, Commonwealth of Dominica, should always be used in addresses to avoid confusion with the Dominican Republic. It is 29 miles long and 16 miles wide, with an area of 290 square miles. The highest peak, Morne Diablotin, rises to 4,747 feet and is often covered in mist.

Materially, it is one of the poorest islands in the Caribbean, but the people are some of the friendliest; many of them are small farmers: the island's mountainous terrain discourages the creation of large estates. In Dominica, over 2,000 descendants of the original inhabitants of the Caribbean, the once warlike Caribs, live in the Carib Territory, a 3,700-acre "reservation" established in 1903 in the NE, near Melville Hall airport. There are no surviving speakers of the Carib language on the island. The total population, which is otherwise almost entirely of African descent, is around 71,800, of whom

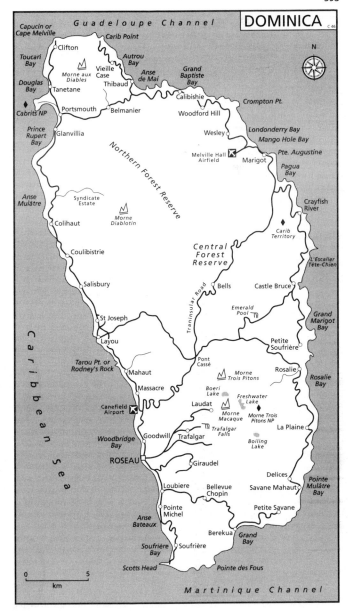

DOMINICA
C 46

Guadeloupe Channel

Capucin or Cape Melville
Toucari Bay
Douglas Bay
Cabrits NP
Prince Rupert Bay
Anse Mulâtre

Clifton
Carib Point
Morne aux Diables
Vieille Case
Autrou Bay
Anse de Mai
Thibaud
Calibishie
Belmanier
Grand Baptiste Bay
Woodford Hill
Crompton Pt.
Wesley
Londonderry Bay
Mango Hole Bay
Melville Hall Airfield
Pte. Augustine
Marigot
Pagua Bay
Tanetane
Portsmouth
Glanvillia

Northern Forest Reserve

Syndicate Estate
Morne Diablotin
Colihaut
Coulibistrie
Salisbury
St Joseph
Layou

Central Forest Reserve

Carib Territory
Crayfish River
L'Escalier Tête-Chien
Bells
Castle Bruce
Emerald Pool
Grand Marigot Bay
Petite Soufrière
Rosalie
Rosalie Bay

Traninsular Road

Tarou Pt. or Rodney's Rock
Mahaut
Massacre
Canefield Airport
Woodbridge Bay
Goodwill
Trafalgar
ROSEAU
Giraudel
Loubiere
Bellevue Chopin
Pointe Michel
Anse Bateaux
Soufrière Bay
Scotts Head

Pont Cassé
Morne Trois Pitons
Boeri Lake
Freshwater Lake
Laudat
Morne Macaque
Morne Trois Pitons NP
Trafalgar Falls
Boiling Lake
La Plaine
Delices
Savane Mahaut
Petite Savane
Pointe Mulâtre Bay
Berekua
Grand Bay
Soufrière
Pointe des Fous

Caribbean Sea

Martinique Channel

0   5
km

about 29% live in the parish of St George, around Roseau, the capital, on the Caribbean coast. Other parishes are much more sparsely populated. The parish of St John, in which Portsmouth (the second largest town) is situated contains only about 5,000 people, or 7% of the population.

Like St Lucia, Dominica was once a French possession; although English is the official tongue, most of the inhabitants also speak créole French (French-based patois). In the Marigot/Wesley area a type of English called "cocoy" is used; the original settlers of the area, freed slaves, came from Antigua and are mostly Methodists. Catholicism predominates (77%), though there are some Protestant denominations and an increasing number of fundamentalist sects, imported from the USA.

In 1979 the island was devastated by Hurricane David; 37 people were killed and 60,000 were left homeless. Much of what David left standing was felled by Hurricane Allen the next year. Since then major reconstruction has taken place, a new airport has been built at Canefield, Roseau bay front has been remodelled, new roads made, new hotels established and Dominica is developing its tourist trade.

History

The Caribs, who supplanted the Arawaks on Dominica, called the island Waitikubuli ("tall is her body"). Columbus sighted it on 3 November, 1493, a Sunday (hence the modern name), but the Spanish took no interest in the island. It was not until 1805 that possession was finally settled. Until then it had been fought over by the French, British and Caribs. In 1660, the two European powers agreed to leave Dominica to the Caribs, but the arrangement lasted very few years; in 1686, the island was declared neutral, again with little success. As France and England renewed hostilities, the Caribs were divided between the opposed forces and suffered the heaviest losses in consequence. In 1763, Dominica was ceded to Britain, and between then and 1805, it remained British. Nevertheless, its position between the French colonies of Guadeloupe and Martinique, and the strong French presence over the years, ensured that despite English institutions and language the French influence was never eliminated.

During the 19th century, Dominica was largely neglected and underdevelopment provoked social unrest. Henry Hesketh Bell, the colonial administrator from 1899 to 1905, made great improvements to infrastructure and the economy, but by the late 1930s the British Government's Moyne Commission discovered a return to a high level of poverty on the island. Assistance to the island was increased with some emphasis put on road building to open up the interior. This, together with agricultural expansion, house building and use of the abundant hydro resources for power, contributed to development in the 1950s and 1960s.

In 1939, Dominica was transferred from the Leeward to the Windward Islands Federation; it gained separate status and a new constitution in 1960, and full internal autonomy in 1967. The Commonwealth of Dominica became an independent republic within the Commonwealth in 1978. The Dominica Labour Party dominated island politics after 1961, ushering in all the constitutional changes. Following independence, however, internal divisions and public dissatisfaction with the administration led to its defeat by the Dominica Freedom Party in the 1980 elections. The DFP Prime Minister, Miss (now Dame) Mary Eugenia Charles, adopted a pro-business, pro-United States line to lessen the island's dependence on limited crops and markets. She was re-elected in 1985 and again in 1990, having survived an earlier attempted invasion by supporters of former DLP premier, Patrick John. (For a thorough history of the island, see *The Dominica Story*, by Lennox Honychurch, The Dominica Institute, 1984.)

In the general election of 1990 the Dominica Freedom Party (DFP) retained its majority by a single seat, winning 11 of the 21 seats. The official opposition is the recently-formed (1988) United Workers Party (UWP) led by Edison James with six seats, while the former official opposition party, the Dominica Labour Party (DLP) won four seats. A by-election in 1993 increased the UWP's representation to seven seats while the DLP lost one and now holds three. The next general election is due by mid-1995. The DFP will be campaigning under the leadership of Brian Alleyne, External Affairs Minister in the government of Dame Eugenia, who is to retire, having led the party since its foundation in 1968.

Government

Dominica is a fully independent member of the British Commonwealth. The single chamber House of Assembly has 31 members: 21 elected by the constituencies, nine Senators who are appointed by the President on the advice of the Prime Minister and Leader of the Opposition, and the Attorney-General. The Prime Minister and Leader of the Opposition also nominate the President, currently Crispin Sorhaindo, who holds office for five years. The Speaker is Neva Edwards, president of the Dominica National Council of Women.

The Economy

Owing to the difficulty of the terrain, only about a quarter of the island is cultivated. Nevertheless, it is self-sufficient in fruit and vegetables and agriculture contributes about 26% to gross domestic product. The main products are bananas (the principal export), coconuts (most of which are used in soap and cooking oil

production), grapefruit, limes and other citrus fruits. Bananas were badly hit by Hurricane Hugo in 1989 and over 70% of the crop was damaged, but output has since recovered. The opening up of the European market in 1992 affected Dominica's banana industry. Together with the other Windward Islands producers it had to compete with the large exporters from the US dollar areas, mainly in Latin America. Prices paid to local farmers fell while they were unable to match the economics of scale found in Latin America. Other crops are under development, such as coffee, cocoa and rice; some, like passionfruit, are being promoted to diversify away from bananas. There is a very successful aqua culture project, prawn farming. Potential areas for expansion are the exploitation of the island's timber reserves, and ornamental flowers for export. Manufacturing industry is small, but can take advantage of locally-generated hydroelectricity. Under pressure to purchase Caribbean products for their cruise ships, Royal Caribbean Cruise Lines buys 3mn bars of soap a year from Dominica Coconut Products. Labour intensive electronic assembly plants and clothing manufacturing are being encouraged for their foreign exchange earnings potential, while data processing is also growing.

Tourism is also being promoted with the emphasis officially on nature tourism. Arrivals in 1992 were 46,959, a rise of only 1.4% over 1991. The first nine months of 1993 saw a 4.9% increase in tourist arrivals, with an encouraging increase in US visitors. The authorities claim they do not wish to jeopardize the "Nature Island" image, but concern has been expressed by conservationists that mooted projects like a motorboat marina on the serene Indian River could damage the island's greatest asset, its environment. Meanwhile, the island's hotel capacity continues to expand while more hotels are planned; construction of a 250-room *Shangrila Hotel*, with Taiwanese in-

DOMINICA: FACT FILE

Geographic

Land area	750 sq km
forested	41.0%
pastures	3.0%
cultivated	23.0%

Demographic

Population (1992)	71,500
annual growth rate (1987-92)	-0.4%
density	95.3 per sq km
Religious affiliation	
Roman Catholic	76.9%
Protestant	15.5%
Birth rate per 1,000 (1990)	22.3
	(world av 27.1)
Death rate per 1,000 (1990)	7.1
	(world av 9.8)

Education and Health

Life expectancy at birth,	
male	73 years
female	79 years
Infant mortality rate	
per 1,000 live births (1990)	18.4
Physicians (1990)	1 per 1,947 persons
Hospital beds	1 per 247 persons
Calorie intake as %	
of FAO requirement	120%
Population age 25 and over	
with no formal schooling	6.6%
Literacy (over 15)	94.4%

Economic

GNP (1990 market prices)	US$160mn
GNP per capita	US$1,940
Public external debt (1991)	US$83.9mn
Tourism receipts (1991)	US$30mn
Inflation	
(annual av 1986-91)	4.6%
Radio	1 per 1.9 persons
Television	1 per 16 persons
Telephone	1 per 5.8 persons

Employment

Population economically active (1989)	
	30,600
Unemployment rate (1992)	15.0%
% of labour force in	
agriculture	25.8
mining and manufacturing	11.1
construction	9.2
trade, hotels, restaurants	12.1
Military forces	none

Source Encyclopaedia Britannica

vestment, is planned opposite the *Layou River Hotel*, now also owned by Taiwanese. The number of hotel rooms is to rise from 690 by end 1993 to over 1,000 by 1997. However, a management contact with Guinness Management Ltd for a housing and tourism development on the 800-acre Pointe Ronde estate at Portsmouth was terminated in 1993 after the company failed to find adequate finance. A new jetty for cruise ships, with related facilities, has been built at Prince Rupert Bay allowing cruise ship passenger arrivals to rise by over a third to around 90,000 a year. In Phase Two of the Roseau Seawall and Bay Front Development Project, a dedicated cruise ship berth is to be built, which will further increase passenger numbers.

There is controversy over the Government's decision in 1992 to grant economic citizenship to investors; up to 1,200 economic citizens, plus their dependents, are to be accepted and the first to be granted passports all came from Taiwan.

Culture

The best known of Dominica's writers are the novelists Jean Rhys and Phyllis Shand Allfrey. Rhys (1894-1979), who spent much of her life in Europe, wrote mainly about that continent; only flashback scenes in *Voyage in the Dark* (1934), her superb last novel, *Wide Sargasso Sea* (1966), which was made into a film in 1991, her uncompleted autobiography, *Smile Please* and resonances in some of her short stories draw on her West Indian experiences. Allfrey published only one novel, *The Orchid House* (1953); *In the Cabinet* was left unfinished at her death in 1986. Allfrey was one of the founder members of the Dominica Labour Party, became a cabinet minister in the short-lived West Indian Federation, and was later editor of the *Dominica Herald* and *Dominica Star* newspapers. The *Orchid House* was filmed by Channel 4 (UK) in

1990 for international transmission as a 4-part series.

Popular culture reflects the mixture of native and immigrant peoples. While most places on Dominica have a Carib, a French or an English name, the indigenous Carib traditions and way of life have been localized in the NE, giving way to a dominant amalgam of Créole (French and African) tradition. Dominicans are proud of their local language, which is increasingly being used in print. A dictionary was published in 1991 by the Konmité pou Etid Kwéyol (Committee for Créole Studies). Many of the costumes, dances and songs, even the Masquerade (Dominica's carnival), are being lost to more modern Caribbean influences (in Masquerade's case, to Trinidadian-style Carnival). For more detail on these, and other areas, see *Our Island Culture*, by Lennox Honychurch (Dominican National Cultural Council, 1988). Examples of arts and crafts can be seen at the Old Mill Cultural Centre, Canefield ('La Vie Dominik'), an old sugar mill converted into a museum (donations welcome), with a nearby wood carving studio run by Haitian emigré Louis Desiré (open to the public) and a new studio building for the Dominican School of Dance (director Daryl Phillip).

Flora and Fauna

Dominica is rightly known as the Nature Island of the Caribbean. Much of the S part of the island (17,000 acres) has since 1975 been designated the Morne Trois Pitons National Park. Its principal attractions include the Boiling Lake (92° celsius), the second largest of its kind in the world (the largest is in New Zealand) and reached after a six-mile, three or four-hour challenging climb. An experienced guide is recommended as the trail can be treacherous, but it is easy to follow once you are on it (guides charge about EC$100 per couple, EC$180 for 2 couples; Benjamín has been recommended,

T 448-8575, young, friendly but experienced, also Lambert Charles, T 448-3365, strong and knowledgeable). In the valley below the Boiling Lake is a region known as the Valley of Desolation, where the forest has been destroyed by sulphuric emissions. At the beginning of the trail to the Boiling Lake is the Titou Gorge, now considerably damaged by rock fall from the hydroelectric development in the area, where a hot and a cold stream mingle. A new track, the Kent Gilbert Trail, has been cut; it starts in La Plaine and is about 4½ miles long. It affords views of the Sari Sari and Bolive Falls, but avoids the spectacular Valley of Desolation. While this makes it a less strenuous route, it also renders it less impressive. Also in the Park is the Freshwater Lake; it is to the E of Morne Macaque at 2,500 feet above sea level, and can be reached by road (two miles from Laudat). Do not swim here, it is the drinking water reservoir for Roseau. A trail leads in ¾ hour on foot (follow the road where the river joins the lake about ½ mile to the pipeline, take the path to the left through the dense forest) to the highest lake in the island, Boeri, situated between Morne Macaque and Morne Trois Pitons. Work on a hydroelectric project in this area was completed in 1991. There will be lasting consequences for both the Trafalgar Falls (a diminished flow of water) and the Freshwater Lake (a raised water level).

The National Park Service has built a series of paths, the Middleham Trails, through the rain forest on the NW border of the Park. The Trails are accessible from Sylvania and Cochrane on the Laudat road, although the signs from Sylvania are not very clear. About 1½-2 hours walk from Cochrane are the Middleham Falls, about 500 feet high, falling into a beautiful blue pool in the middle of the forest (take the road out of Cochrane, which becomes a path, then fork right at the sign).

North of the Transinsular road are the

Central Forest Reserve and Northern Forest Reserve. In the latter is **Morne Diablotin**; if you wish to climb it, you must take a guide. At the highest levels on the island is elfin woodland, characterized by dense vegetation and low-growing plants. Elfin woodland and high montane thicket give way to rainforest at altitudes between 1,000 and 2,500 feet, extending over about 60% of the island. Despite the large area of forest, its protection is essential, against cutting for farm land and other economic pressures, as a water source, and as a unique facility for scientific research. It is hoped, moreover, that tourism can coexist with conservation, since any losses, for whatever reason, would be irreversible.

The **Cabrits Peninsula** in the NW is also since 1986 a National Park of 1,313 acres, its twin hills covered by dry forest, separated from the island proper by marshland (under threat from a marina development, a pier and cruise ship reception centre have been built and shops and restaurants are supposed to be opening) which is a nesting place for herons and doves and hosts a variety of migrant bird species. A walk through the woods and around the buildings of **Fort Shirley** (abandoned in 1854) will reveal much flora and wildlife (easiest to see are the scuttling hermit- or soldier- and black crabs, ground lizard—abòlò—and tree lizard).

Dominica is a botanist's paradise. In addition to the huge variety of trees, many of which flower in March and April, there are orchids and wild gardens of strange plant life in the valleys. Bwa Kwaib or Carib wood (*Sabinea carinalis*) was declared the national flower in 1978; it can be found mostly growing along parts of the W coast. It is a birdwatcher's paradise, too. Indigenous to the island are the Imperial parrot, or Sisserou (*amazona imperialis*), which is critically endangered, and its marginally less threatened relative, the Red-necked parrot, or Jacquot (*amazona arausiaca*). The Sisserou

has been declared the national bird. They can be seen in the Syndicate area in the NW which is now a protected reserve and the site of a future information and research centre for visitors and scientists. There is a nature trail but signs are difficult to spot. The parrots are most evident during their courting season, in April and early May. To get the best from a parrot-watching trip, it is worth taking a guide. Bertrand Jno Baptiste, of the Forestry Division (T 448-2401) is highly recommended and charges EC$80 a group. While there are other rare species, such as the Forest Thrush and the Blue-headed hummingbird, there are a great many others which are easily spotted (the Purple-throated Carib and Antillean-crested hummingbirds, for instance), or heard (the Siffleur Montagne). Waterfowl can be seen on the lakes, waders on the coastal wetlands (many are migrants). There are various bat caves, most particularly at Thiband on the NE coast.

There are fewer species of mammal (agouti, manicou-opossum, wild pig and bats), but there is a wealth of insect life (for example, over 55 species of butterfly) and reptiles. Besides those mentioned above, there is the rare iguana, the crapaud (a large frog, eaten under the name of mountain chicken) and five snakes, none poisonous (including the boa constrictor, or tête-chien). Certain parts of the coast are used as nesting grounds by sea turtles (hawksbill, leatherback and green).

The Forestry Division in the Botanical Gardens, Roseau, has a wide range of publications, trail maps, park guides, posters and leaflets (some free) on Dominica's wildlife and National Parks, T 448-2401, F 448-7999.

Diving and Marine Life

Dominica is highly regarded as a diving destination. Features include wall dives, drop-offs, reefs, hot, freshwater springs under the sea, sponges, black coral, pinnacles and wrecks, all in unpolluted water. Visibility is excellent, at up to 30m depending on the weather. Many drop-offs are close to the beaches but access is poor and boats are essential. There is a marine park conservation area in Toucari Bay and part of Douglas Bay, N of the Cabrits where an underwater trail for snorkellers is marked by white buoys, but the most popular scuba sites are S of Roseau, at Point Guignard, Soufrière Bay and Scotts Head. An unusual site is Champagne, with underwater hot springs where you swim through bubbles, fascinating for a night dive, lots of life here. This area in the SE, Soufriére-Scotts Head, is now a marine park without moorings so that all diving is drift diving and boats pick up divers where they surface. Areas may be designated for diving and other areas for fishing. Along the S and SE coast there are more dive sites but because of the Atlantic currents these are for experienced, adventurous divers only. Note that the taking of conch, coral, lobster, sponge, turtle eggs etc is forbidden and you may not put down anchor in coral and on reefs; use the designated moorings.

Whale watching tours are offered when whales migrate past Dominica to mate and calve. Several different types of whales have been spotted not far from the W shore where the deep, calm waters are ideal for these mammals. Calves and dolphin are often attracted to dive boats. Fitzroy Armour of the Anchorage Dive Centre has an 85% success rate and charges US$80 per person.

Scuba diving is permitted only through one of the island's registered dive operators or with written permission from the Fisheries Division. Dive Dominica Ltd, at the *Castle Comfort Guest House* (PO Box 63, Roseau, T 448-2188, F 448-6088), offers full diving and accommodation packages, courses, single (US$40) or multiple (US$70) day dives, night dives (US$45) and equipment rental as well as whale watching (US$45pp inc rum punch, no guarantees). Owned by Derek Perryman who has three fast, well-equipped dive boats, this company is recommended for its professional service. Dive Dominica is represented in the UK by Traveller's Tree (see under **Tours** section). The Anchorage Dive Centre (T 448-2638, F 448-5680, US$80 2-tank dive inc weights and belt) is based at the *Anchorage Hotel*, Castle Comfort, with other outlets at *Picard Beach Cottage Resort* and *Portsmouth Beach Hotel*. This is another long established operation with a good reputation. Other dive companies are Dive Castaways at the *Castaways Beach Hotel* (T 449-6244, F 449-6246, US$40 one dive, US$55 with full equipment), East Carib Dive at Salisbury (T 449-6602, F 449-6603) and Windward Island Divers at Portsmouth (T 445-5104).

Beaches and Watersports

Compared with other Caribbean islands, Dominica has few good beaches, but does have excellent river bathing. The best beaches on the W coast are immediately S of Portsmouth and Prince Rupert Bay in the Picard area. Other beaches on the Caribbean coast, such as at Mero, where the *Castaways Hotel* is located, are of "black" (really a silver-grey) sand. Although there are no beaches near Roseau, Scotts Head can be reached in about 20 mins by bus, EC$3, excellent snorkelling and a few small stretches of sandy beach. There are smaller, mostly white sand beaches on the NE coast, suitable for bathing and snorkelling, for example at Woodford Hill (near Melville Hall airport, the best beach on the island but entirely lacking facilities) and Hampstead. Beware of strong undercurrents on the Atlantic Coast. Pointe Baptiste (see under **Where To Stay**), has a fine golden beach featured in the TV series "The Orchid House".

The Dive Centres at the *Anchorage*, *Portsmouth Beach* and *Picard Cottage Re-*

sort and *Castaways Hotel* offer sailing and the *Anchorage* has deep-sea fishing. They also offer water-skiing and windsurfing, as does James Water World at *The Shipwreck* in Canefield, T 449-1059.

The best harbour for yachts is Portsmouth (Prince Rupert Bay), but there are no facilities and yachtsmen have complained about the hostile attitudes of some locals. This may change with the opening of the new cruise ship jetty, but guard your possessions. Stealing from yachts is quite common. The new jetty in Roseau (see below) is designed for small craft, such as yachts, clearing for port entry. Both the *Reigate Waterfront* and *Anchorage Hotels* have moorings and a pier, and yachtsmen and women are invited to use the hotels' facilities.

Other Sports

Football and cricket are among the most popular national sports; watch cricket in the beautiful setting of the Botanical Gardens. Basketball and netball are also enthusiastically played. There are hard tennis courts at the privately-owned Dominica Club, *Reigate Hall* and *Castaways*. *Anchorage Hotel* has squash courts. Cycling is growing in popularity and the island's roads, although twisty, are good. Hiking in the mountains is excellent, and hotels and tour companies arrange this type of excursion. Mountain climbing can be organized through the Forestry Division in the Botanical Gardens, Roseau, T 448-2401. Guides are necessary for any forays into the mountains or forests, some areas of which are still uncharted.

Festivals

The main one is Carnival, on the Monday and Tuesday before Ash Wednesday; it is not as commercialized as many in the Americas (see above, under **Culture**). During Carnival, laws of libel and slander are suspended. Independence celebrations (3/4 November) feature local folk dances, music and crafts. On Créole Day, the last Friday in October, the vast majority of girls and women wear the national dress, 'la wobe douillete', to work and school and most shop, bank clerks etc speak only Créole to the public. Domfesta, The Festival of the Arts, takes place during July and August and includes exhibitions by local artists (notably Kelo Royer, Earl Etienne, Arnold Toulon), concerts and theatre performances, (see local papers, *The New Chronicle* or *The Tropical Star*, for details or ask at hotel.)

ROSEAU

Roseau is small, ramshackle and friendly, with a surprising number of pretty old buildings still intact. Quite a lot of redevelopment has taken place over the last few years, improving access and making the waterfront more attractive. The Old Market Plaza has been made into a pedestrian area, with shops in the middle. Between the Plaza and the sea is the old Post Office, currently painted cream and green, but awaiting renovation to accommodate the Tourism Division of the National Development Corporation. The new Post Office is on the Bay Front at the bottom of Hillsborough Street. It has a colourful mural depicting the development of Dominica's postal service, and a Philately Counter. The new market, at the N end of Bay Street, is a fascinating sight on Saturday mornings from about 0600-1000; it is also lively on Friday morning, closed Sundays. The new sea wall was completed in late 1993, which has greatly improved the waterfront area of town, known as the Bay Front. A promenade with trees and benches, a road from the Old Jetty to Victoria Street, and parking bays take up most of the space. New facilities promised include new restaurants and shops, public conveniences, and eventually another cruise

ROSEAU

Not to Scale

C 47

To Canefield Airport, Portsmouth & Transinsular Rd

Federation Drive

Roseau (Queen's) River

Windsor Park

To Trafalgar Falls

Elliot Av.

Piveteau St.

Goodwill Rd

East Bridge

Bath Rd

7

Cricket Ground

26

B3

Botanical Gardens

St John's Av.

River St.

West Bridge

Hillsborough St.

Kennedy Av.

8

B1

Great George St.

15

Laing Lane

5

Ship St.

11

Kings Lane

16

Gt. Marlborough St.

14

23

25

6

Queen Mary St.

Drury Lane

Old St.

22

24

12

Cork St.

19

Fields Lane

10

17

Hanover St.

9

Long Lane

King George V St.

Virgin Lane

2

Roseau Jetty

Bay Street

18

B2

13

1

Cross St.

3

Turkey Av.

Long Acre

N

21

Castle St.

Jewel St.

4

20

To Morne Bruce & Reigate Hall Hotel

High St.

Glover L.

Bath Rd

Caribbean

Cornwall St.

Victoria St.

To South West & South Coasts

Sea

1. Old Market Plaza & Tourist Office
2. Roman Catholic Cathedral
3. Methodist Church
4. Anglican Church
5. New Market
6. LIAT
7. Government Headquarters
8. Police Headquarters
9. Customs
10. Post Office
11. Cable & Wireless
12. Barclays Bank
13. Royal Bank of Canada
14. Banque Française Commerciale
15. National Commercial Bank
16. Scotiabank
17. Whitchurch Travel
18. Paperbacks
19. Cee-Bee's Bookshop

20. *Fort Young Hotel*
21. *The Garraway Hotel*
22. *Kent Anthony's Guesthouse*
23. *Continental Inn*
24. *Cherry Lodge*
25. *Vena's Guesthouse & The World of Food*
26. Division of Tourism
B1. Northbound Buses
B2. Southbound Buses
B3. Buses to Trafalgar & Laudat

ship berth. Although small, you may need to ask for directions around Roseau. One correspondent claims he has never been so consistently misinformed, even by the police; the inhabitants appear to be unaware of street names. The 40-acre Botanical Gardens are principally an arboretum, although seriously damaged by Hurricane David in 1979; they have a collection of plant species, including an orchid house. Three bored Jacquot parrots and one Sisserou live in cages in the park, thanks in part to the Jersey Wildlife Preservation Trust. Breeding programmes are underway and it is hoped that some of the offspring will be released to the wild. In honour of its centenary in 1990, trees and plants lost in the hurricane were replaced. The town has no deep-water harbour; this is at Woodbridge Bay over a mile away, where most of the island's commercial shipping is handled, and tourist vessels are accommodated. The Roseau jetty, destroyed by

Hurricane David in 1979, was rebuilt in the Seawall and Bay Front Development Project for the use of yachts and other small craft. In Phase Two a cruise ship berth is to be built with a reception area for cruise ship passengers, while a ferry passenger reception building will be built on the new jetty.

Excursions

The Trafalgar waterfalls are in the Roseau Valley, five miles from the capital. Hot and cold water flows in two spectacular cascades in the forest, but the volume of the hot fall has been sharply diminished by a hydroelectric scheme higher up (see **Flora and Fauna**). The path to the falls is easy to follow. Trying to cross over the falls at the top is very hazardous; bathing should be confined to pools in the river beneath the falls. The Trafalgar Falls are crowded because they are close to the road (bus EC$3 from Roseau) and children pester to be your guide. There is a one-hour trail from the sulphur springs of the tiny settlement of Wotten Waven through forest and banana plantations across the Trois Pitons River up to the Trafalgar Falls.

South of Roseau are the villages of Soufrière and Scotts Head. There are plenty of buses (EC$3) to Scotts Head, over the mountain with excellent views all the way to Martinique. Ask around the fishing huts if you are hungry, and you will be directed to various buildings without signs where you can eat chicken pilau for EC$6 and watch draughts being played. There is a new, clean and friendly café on the main road just across from the most active fishing area (this boasts the only lavatories for the use of visitors). On the S coast is Grand Bay, where there is a large beach (dangerous for swimming), the 10-foot high Belle Croix and the Geneva Estate, founded in the 18th century by the Martinican Jesuit, Father Antoine La Valette, and at one time the home of the novelist Jean Rhys. From Grand Bay, it is a two-hour walk over the hill, past Sulphur Spring to Soufrière.

The Leeward coastal road, N from Roseau, comes first to Canefield, where are the new airport, the Old Mill Cultural Centre with La Vie Dominik museum, open Monday-Friday, 0800-1600, and the junction with the Transinsular Road. The coast road passes through Massacre, reputed to be the settlement where 80 Caribs were killed by British troops in 1674. Among those who died was Indian Warner, Deputy Governor of Dominica, illegitimate son of Sir Thomas Warner (Governor of St Kitts) and half-brother of the commander of the British troops, Colonel Philip Warner. From the church perched above the village there are good views of the coast.

The road continues to *Portsmouth*, the second town. Nearby are the ruins of the 18th-century Fort Shirley on the Cabrits, which has a museum in one of the restored buildings (entry free). Clearly marked paths lead to the Commander's Quarters, Douglas Battery and other outlying areas. The colonial fortifications, apart from the main buildings which have been cleared, are strangled by ficus roots, and cannon which used to point out to sea now aim at the forest. From the bridge just S of Portsmouth, boats make regular, one-hourly trips up the Indian River (EC$20 pp), a peaceful trip through a tunnel of vegetation as long as you are not accompanied by boatloads of other tourists. Competition for passengers is keen. Negotiate with the local boatmen about price and insist they use oars rather than a motor, so as not to disturb the birds and crabs. There is a tiny bar open at the final landing place on this lovely river. You can then continue on foot through fields and forest to the edge of a marsh where migrating birds come in the winter months. The river and the swamps and marshes are being considered for inclusion in the national parks system.

From Portsmouth, one road carries on

to the Cabrits National Park and the island's N tip at Cape Melville. An unpaved road leads off this at Savanne Paille; if you have a 4-wheel drive vehicle, and are there when it is definitely not the rainy season, it is a beautiful drive over the mountain, through a valley with sulphur springs, to Penville on the N coast, from where you can pick up the road heading S. Allow several hours. Another road from Portsmouth heads E, winding up and down to the bays and extensive coconut palm plantations of the NW coast, Calibishie, Melville Hall airport and Marigot.

The shortest route from Roseau to Marigot and Melville Hall is via the Transinsular Road, which climbs steeply and with many bends from Canefield. Along this road you will see coconut and cocoa groves; look out for the land crabs' holes, the orange juveniles come out in the daytime, the white adults at night. There are banana plants all along the gorge, together with dasheen, tannia, oranges and grapefruit. At Pont Cassé, the road divides three ways at one of the island's few roundabouts. One branch turns left, down the Layou Valley, to join the Leeward coast at Layou; the Transinsular Road goes straight on (the path up the Trois Pitons is signed on the right just after the roundabout), through Bells, to Marigot; the third branch goes E, either to Rosalie and La Plaine on the SE Windward coast, or to Castle Bruce and the Carib Territory.

The Emerald Pool is a small, but pretty waterfall in a grotto in the forest, 15 mins by path from the Pont Cassé-Castle Bruce road. Unfortunately, visitors walking alone or in couples to the pool have been mugged and cameras have been stolen from parked cars; also avoid the area on days when cruise ships have docked, as hundreds of passengers are taken to visit the Pool, with resulting damage to its delicate ecology. There is a picnic area, and toilet facilities are being built. There are no buses from Roseau

but you can catch a minibus to Canefield and wait at the junction for a bus going to Castle Bruce.

The Atlantic coast is much more rugged than the Caribbean, with smaller trees, sandy or pebbly bays, palms and dramatic cliffs. Castle Bruce is a lovely bay and there are good views all around. After Castle Bruce the road enters the Carib Territory, although there is only a very small sign to indicate this. At the N end there is another sign, but it would still be easy to drive through the Territory without seeing anything of note except a few small souvenir shops selling basket work. In fact, there is much to see; to appreciate it fully, a guide is essential. Horseback Ridge affords views of the sea, mountains, the Concord Valley and Bataka village. At Crayfish River, a waterfall tumbles directly into the sea by a beach of large stones. The Save the Children Fund has assisted the Waitikubuli Karifuna Development Committee to construct two traditional buildings near Salybia: a large oval *carbet* (the nucleus of the extended Carib family group), and an A-frame *mouina*. The former is a community centre, the latter a library and office of the elected chief. The Carib chief is elected for five years and his main tasks are to organize the distribution of land and the preservation of Carib culture. In 1994, Hilary Frederick was re-elected to the post after serving in 1979-84, defeating Irvince Auguiste, who had been chief since 1984. The dilapidated Church of the Immaculate Conception at Salybia is being restored as a Carib Museum (opening date uncertain; it has been replaced by the new church of St Marie of the Caribs, which opened in May 1991), its design is based on the traditional *mouina* and has a canoe for its altar, murals about Carib history both inside and out. Outside is a cemetery and a three-stone monument to the first three Carib chiefs after colonization: Jolly John, Auguiste and Courriett. L'Escalier Tête-Chien, at Jenny Point in Sineku is a line of rock climbing out of the sea and up the headland. It is most obvious in the sea and shore, but on the point each rock bears the imprint of a scale, circle or line, like the markings on a snake. It is said that the Caribs used to follow the snake staircase (which was made by the Master Tête-Chien) up to its head in the mountains, thus gaining special powers. However, there are more prosaic, geological explanations.

Taking the road from Pont Cassé to the SE part of the island, you come to Rosalie. Cross the River Rosalie and go S to Pointe Daniel and Delices. You can see the Victoria Falls from the road. The Forestry Division plans to improve the rugged trail to the Falls. Be sure to take an experienced guide if you attempt the steep hike to these Falls and avoid it in the rainy season. The White River falls in to the Atlantic at Savane Mahaut, reached by a steep road from Victoria Laroche down to the sea. There are delightful places to picnic, rest or swim in the river. At the weekend local families picnic and wash their cars here. If it has not rained much the previous day you can follow the river up, jumping from one to another of the big stones in the river bed. Be wary of flash floods and do not attempt to cross the river if there has been heavy rainfall as you might not be able to get back. Sea bathing here is very dangerous.

INFORMATION FOR VISITORS

● Documents

All visitors entering Dominica must be in possession of an outward ticket and a valid passport. Proof of citizenship only is required for US and Canadian citizens. A *Carte identité* allows French nationals to visit for up to 2 weeks. Visas are required by nationals of communist countries: they can be obtained from the Ministry of Home Affairs, Government Headquarters, Roseau.

● Warning

The police are strict in their enforcement of anti-narcotic laws. The present Government takes a strong stand on "moral" issues.

● How To Get There By Air

There are no direct flights from Europe or North America to Dominica. Connections must be made in St Maarten, Antigua, St Lucia or the French Leewards. LIAT flies from Antigua, Anguilla, Martinique, Guadeloupe, Port of Spain, St Lucia, St Maarten, San Juan and Tortola, BVI; Air Guadeloupe from Guadeloupe, St-Barts; LIAT has special day return flights to/from Antigua, St Maarten and Guadeloupe. Winair flies daily from St Maarten into Canefield using 19-seater Twin Otters and offers connections with other islands or international airlines through St Maarten, St Lucia, St Thomas and San Juan, Puerto Rico.

There is a departure tax of EC$25 and a security service charge of EC$5, or US$10 if you pay in dollars. Day trippers pay EC$5; under 12s are free.

● How To Get There By Sea

Antilles-Trans-Express and Caribbean Express merged in 1992 and in 1993 introduced a 300-seat catamaran on the route from the French Antilles to Dominica (EC$212 return Dominica-Guadeloupe, EC$253 Dominica-Martinique), see p 585 for details. The Caribbean Express agency office is upstairs in the Whitchurch Centre, T 448-2181, F 448-5787. Also on this route, Madikera, a fast, scheduled car and 352 passenger service, 275 F one way Roseau-Pointe-à-Pitre or Fort-de-France, 400 F return plus departure tax; the agent is Trois Pitons Travel, 5 Great Marlborough Street, T 448-6977.

● Airports

Dominica has 2 airports, the older **Melville**

Hall (DOM), which handles larger planes, and Canefield (DCF), which can only take small aircraft. Check which your flight will be using. Melville Hall, in the NE is 36 miles from Roseau; taxis cost EC$42pp on the Transinsular Road, but they can go via the East Coast Road or the West Coast Road and charge more. From Melville Hall to Portsmouth by taxi is EC$30. These rates are per seat; find someone to share with, or it will be assumed you want the vehicle to yourself, which is much more expensive. Canefield is only a 10-mins' drive from Roseau; taxi fare to town is EC$20, per car of up to 4 passengers. Minibus (public transport) fare from Canefield to Roseau is EC$1.50. (You must flag one down on the highway passing the airport.)

● **Airlines**

LIAT, 8 Fort Lane, Roseau, T 448-2421, Canefield airport T 449-1421, Melville Hall T 445-7242. Agent for Air Guadeloupe, Air Martinique and Winair is Whitchurch Travel, Old Street, Roseau, T 448-2181, or Canefield Airport, T 449-1060.

● **Internal Transport**

Minibuses run from point to point. Those from Roseau to the NW and NE leave from between the East and West bridges near the modern market; to Trafalgar and Laudat from Valley Road, near the Police Headquarters; for the S and Petite Savane from Old Market Plaza. They are difficult to get on in the early morning unless you can get on a 0630 bus out to the villages to pick up schoolchildren and return in similar fashion. Apart from the Soufrière/Scotts Head route, it is difficult to get anywhere on the island by public transport, and return to Roseau, in one day. This is because buses leave Marigot, or wherever, to arrive in Roseau around 0700, then return at about 1300. It is just possible to get to Portsmouth and return in one day, the first bus is at 1000, returning at 1600. Many buses pass the hotels S of Roseau (eg *Anchorage*). Fares are fixed by the Government. Roseau to Salisbury is EC$3.50, to Portsmouth EC$7.50, to Woodford Hill EC$9, to Marigot EC$9, to Castle Bruce EC$7, Canefield EC$1.50, Laudat EC$3, Trafalgar EC$2.25.

Hitchhiking rides in the back of the ubiquitous pick-up trucks is possible. It is often difficult at weekends.

● **Taxis**

A sightseeing tour by taxi will cost EC$45 per hour, per car (4 people), but it is wise to use experienced local tour operators for sightseeing, particularly if hiking is involved. Fares on set routes are fixed by the Government (see above for rates to the airports). Ask at your hotel for a taxi; in Roseau, Mally's Taxi Service, 64 Cork Street, T 448-3360/3114 (if planning a day trip out of town on public transport, you can sometimes arrange to be picked up and returned to Roseau by their airport taxi service), Eddie, 8 Hillsborough St, T 448-6003, and others.

● **Car Rental**

Rates are about US40 per day for a small Hyundai, plus US$8 for collision damage waiver; unlimited mileage for hiring for 3 days or more. It may be preferable to rent a car or jeep as the taxi service is expensive and buses take a lot of planning. Jeep rental is about US$50-60 a day including collision insurance of US$600-700. Failing that, get a bicycle from D & A's Bike Rental, 21 Winston Lane, T 448-5075 or a moped from Francis Scooter Rental, 5 Cross St, T 448-5295, US$25/day. On either hand, Dominicans drive fast in the middle of the road and many visitors prefer to take a taxi so that they can enjoy the views. Companies: ACE Car Rentals, 8 Castle Street, T 448-4444, jeeps, some with bikini tops, free pick up and delivery; Anselm's, 3 Great Marlborough St, T 448-2730, refund difficulties reported after breakdown; Budget, Canefield Industrial Estate, T 449-2080, rec as cheaper, more reliable and informative than some other companies, cars in good condition; Wide Range Car Rentals, 81 Bath Road, T 448-2198, rents out old Lada cars for US$30 a day, not rec for smaller roads, also Suzuki jeeps, US$60 a day including 80 miles and collision protection free; Valley, PO Box 3, T 448-3233, on Goodwill Road, next to Dominican Banana Marketing Corporation, or in Portsmouth, T 445-5252, free delivery to Canefield and within 2 miles of Roseau or Portsmouth offices, cars in need of maintenance but in the cheaper category; also on Goodwill Road, S T L, US$387/10 days inc EC$20 licence and insurance, PO Box 21, T 448-2340, free deliveries as for Valley, but only in Roseau area; Shillingford, 10 Winston Lane, T 448-3151; C N C, 37 Kennedy Ave, T 448-5888. No car rental at the airports. It is extremely difficult to hire a vehicle between Christmas and New Year without prior reservation.

Driving is on the left. The steering wheel

may be on either side. You must purchase a local driving permit, valid for one month, for EC\$20, for which a valid international or home driving licence is required; the permit may be bought from the police at airports, or at the Traffic Dept, High Street, Roseau or Bay Street, Portsmouth (Mon to Fri). Main roads are fairly good; the Portsmouth-Marigot road built in 1987 is excellent, but in towns and S of Roseau, roads are very narrow and in poor condition. There are no road signs, but with a good map finding your way is not difficult. The Tourism Office in the Old Market, Roseau, sells Ordnance Survey maps.

You have nothing to fear if you offer local people a lift and men, women and children are unfailingly courteous; the carrying of machetes is not an indication of likely violence, the bearer is probably just on his way home from his banana field.

● **Where To Stay**

There are a number of small, informal hotels, guest houses and apartment facilities on the island. 1994 rates are quoted here and are therefore subject to change. Always verify whether tax and service are included in the quoted rate. The are now 2 large hotels in Roseau: the *Fort Young Hotel*, within the old fort (P O Box 519, T 448-5000, F 448-5006), which has been attractively renovated, very good food and service, international-type atmosphere. Weekdays it is occupied by businessmen and visiting politicians, the atmosphere is more relaxed on weekends, special events like concerts and barbeques and a popular Happy Hour every Fri and Sat, 1800-1900, dive packages with Dive Dominica, 33 rooms, US\$115d, EP; also the *Garraway*, Place Heritage, Bay Front, T 448-3247, F 448-3962, 31 rooms, a/c or fans, TV, phones, conference facilities, restaurant, cocktail bar, US\$105-170d. Otherwise, lodging in town is in guesthouses: *Continental Inn*, 37 Queen Mary Street, T 448-2214/6, F 448-87022, US\$60d, EP, 11 rooms, a/c, fans, TV, bar, restaurant, entertainment, used by travelling salesmen and visiting sailors, adequate, good food but very slow service; *Kent Anthony Guesthouse*, 3 Great Marlborough Street, T 448-2730, F 448-7559, 19 rooms, US\$30d, EP, with fan and bath, cheaper rooms without, good food, rooms of varying standard, brusque but friendly landlady, mice and cockroaches; *Vena's Guesthouse*, 17 rooms, US\$20d, EP, prices higher during carnival, 48 Cork Street,

T 448-3286, Jean Rhys' birth place, interesting, rather inefficient, rooms small and grim, rooms without bath more spacious and comfortable but noisy as on the corner of the 2 main streets, *The World of Food* restaurant is next door; *Wykies Guesthouse*, 51 Old Street, T 448-8015, F 448-7665 US\$35d, 6 rooms, shared shower, no fan, clean, rats and cockroaches but not in the rooms, basic, friendly, rec, good bar but noisy at night so do not plan an early night. *Cherry Lodge Guesthouse*, 20 Kennedy Ave, T 448-2366, historic and quaint, US\$37d, some rooms with bath, rooms can be noisy and mosquitoes abundant, coils provided but no fans, good value meals available to order (EC\$15 for 3-course meal); *Bon Marché Guest House*, 11 Old Street, PO Box 449, T 448-2083/4194, 4 rooms, US\$25-35d, EP, fans, bar, souvenir shop and boutique on site. Apartments are available to rent in and around Roseau, check at the Tourist Office, look in the *New Chronicle*, *Tropical Star* or ask a taxi driver. The *Honychurch apartment*, 5 Cross Street, T 448-3346, US\$60/day, US\$360/week.

Outside Roseau, up a steep and windy hill (King's Hill), is *Reigate Hall*, with a splendid location but laid back management T 448-4031/2/3, F 448-4034, US\$95d, suite US\$140-180, 16 rooms, fans, service in restaurant sloppy and slow, pricey, bar, swimming pool, tennis courts, dive packages with Dive Dominica. A short distance S of Roseau, at Castle Comfort on the way to Soufrière, are: *Anchorage*, on seafront, T 448-2638/9, F 448-5680, US\$85-105d EP, US\$155-175d MAP, waterfront restaurant, some rooms rather tatty, bar, friendly service, food nothing special, swimming pool and diving facilities, a 7-night, 10-dive package available, good squash court; friendly and a delightful place to stay, family-run, with good restaurant and excellent service is *Evergreen*, P O Box 309, T 448-3288/448-3276, F 448-6800, 16 rooms, US\$98-113d with breakfast, a/c, TV, bar, pool; *End of Eden Guest House*, Copthall, Roseau Valley, c/o 2 Princess Lane, Goodwill, T 448-8272, US\$30d, fans, shared bathroom; *Reigate Waterfront*, P O Box 134, T 448-3111, F 448-3500, US\$85d EP, pool, restaurant with well-known barbeque Wed night, 24 rooms, recently refurbished; *Castle Comfort Lodge*, highly rec, very friendly, professional, excellent local food, good service, P O Box 63, T 448-2188, F 448-6088, US\$115d MAP, a 7-night 10-dive package available inc transfers, unlimited shore diving, tax and service, (see above under **Diving and Marine Life**); *Sans Souci Manor*, St Aroment, 2 miles from Roseau, PO Box 373, T 448-2306, F 448-6202, self catering, 11 rooms in 4 units, sparsely furnished but very clean, fans, phones, TV, pool, tours arranged, dive packages with Dive Dominica, US$105/day, US$650/week, breakfast and dinner can be provided.

Also close to Roseau is *Ambassador*, within walking distance of Canefield airport, P O Box 41, T 449-1501/2, F 449-2304, from US$75d EP to US$121d MAP, reasonable restaurant, comfortable, but can be noisy, good for business visitors. *The Hummingbird Inn*, Morne Daniel, PO Box 20, Roseau, T/F 449-1042, US$65d EP, US$105d MAP, US$110 for a suite, run by Mrs Finucane who is very knowledgeable on Dominica,peaceful, simple, comfortable, good food, stunning views down the hill over the sea, 5 mins N of Roseau. *Itassi Cottages*, self-catering, on Morne Bruce, spectacular view of S coast, one studio, 2 cottages, attractively furnished, phone, TV, US$60-90, US$380-570 weekly, contact Mrs U Harris, PO Box 319, T 448-4313, F 448-3045, who also has a cottage to rent, *Lydia Villa*, in Scotts Head, on the most southerly part of the island, US$25-40/day, US$150-220/week; on the road to Trafalgar and Papillotte, the Honychurch family rents a one-bedroom apartment on their lovely estate, *D'Auchamps*, US$40/day, US$240/week, PO Box 89, T 448-3346, this and *Itassi* can be booked through Travellers Tree in the UK, see **Tours** below. Near the Trafalgar Falls (15 mins' walk) is *Papillotte Wilderness Retreat*, PO Box 67, T 448-2287, F 448-2285, US$50-60d EP, suite with kitchenette, US$70, several complimentary reports, in beautiful gardens with hot mineral pool and geese, good terrace restaurant but soon to be for residents only; new restaurant for non-residents to open nearer road. Lunch 1000-1600, except Sun, (avoid days when cruise ship passengers invade, reservations required) but menu does not change frequently enough if you are staying there, not for those who are afraid of insects, no window screens in chalet-type rooms, noise from hydroelectric plant, ask for cottage by the waterfall when the plant's noise is drowned by water. Bad road from the nearby village of Trafalgar because of heavy traffic for hydroelectric scheme and heavy rains, but being improved, spectacular setting. *Roxy's Mountain Lodge* in Laudat, PO Box 265, T 448-4845, US$24-30d EP, US$54-62

MAP, good breakfast and hearty supper, basic rooms, good beds, hot showers, also apartment, 4-6 people, US$120/day, US$750/week, convenient for visiting Boiling Lake, Boeri Lake, Middleham Falls, Trafalgar Falls and Freshwater Lake, all within walking distance, guides arranged if required, transport into Roseau 0700 except Sun, returning 1615, EC$3. *Springfield Plantation*, in the interior but only 6 miles N from Roseau, PO Box 456, T 449-1401, F 449-2160, has a magnificent setting 1,200 feet above sea level, overlooking a lush valley, lovely rooms, apartments, suites, cottages, modernized and enlarged wooden plantation house, but now also an agricultural research centre so periodically overrun by students, erratic management, but food can be good, US$80d EP, US$130 MAP.

On the extreme S coast E of Scotts Head, reached from Soufrière, are **Petit Coulibri Guest Cottages**, PO Box 331, Roseau, T 446-3150, F 449-8182, on the Petit Coulibri Estate which used to grow sugar, cacao, and until recently aloe vera, but still grows citrus. The 3 cottages have 2 bedrooms, pool, maid service, US$100-150d, built 1,000 feet above sea, overlooking Martinique, isolated setting, solar powered, home grown food and locally caught fish, run by Barney and Loye Barnard. In Scotts Head is *Gachette's Seaside Lodge*, Bay St, T 448-4551, 10 rooms, US$60d, fans, a/c, TV, fish restaurant, watersports, diving, fishing arranged; also *Lydia Villa*, see above, *Itassi Cottages*. Other self-catering apartments include *Castille Apartment*, Scotts Head, T 448-2926, US$50/day, US$200/week; Gallion-On-Sea, Scotts Head, PO Box 85, T 448-3031, F 448-6007, US$50-70/day, US$250-300/week; *Hilfrance Cottage*, Scotts Head, PO Box 133 (Roseau), T 448-2937, F 448-3404, US$80 summer, US$125 winter, weekly rates US$500 and US$ 750.

Castaways, Mero, PO Box 5, T 449-6244/5, F 449-6246 conveniently located, just N of St Joseph, for visiting all parts of the island, on large, black sand beach, US$96 (summer), US$120d (winter) EP, restaurant, beach barbeque on Sun, good food, staff slow but friendly, reasonable rooms all with balcony and sea view but over-priced, get a receipt for safety box deposits, watersports and dive shop attached, German spoken, 7-night dive package available. *Lauro Club*, Grand Savanne, PO Box 483, Roseau, T 449-6602, F 449-6603, opened 1992, self-contained bungalows sleep 1-4, half-way between Roseau and Portsmouth, multi-lingual Swiss owners, pool, bowls, small shops and snack bar in central building, built on cliff top overlooking sea, access to sea but no beach, US$105d EP, US$169d MAP, inc taxes, all year.

In **Portsmouth** are *Casa Ropa*, on Bay Street, T 445-5492, F 445-5277, rooms for rent for US$35-40d EP with bath, single downstairs US$30-35, friendly, clean, rec; *Douglas Guest House*, Bay Street, T 445-5253, US$12s, US$24d, US$30 triple, EP, ask for fan, clean, next to noisy disco and cinema; *Mamie's On The Beach*, Prince Rupert's Bay, T/F 445-4295, has pleasant, modern rooms, fans, bathroom, no mosquito screens, adjoining restaurant, US$35-40d EP. Ask around for low budget rooms/huts to let. **Southern Prince Rupert Bay**, *Portsmouth Beach Hotel* is primarily used by students at the nearby Ross Medical School (PO Box 34, T 445-5142, F 445-5599), US$40s EP, US$50d, US$60 triple, half price for children, there is a pool, restaurant, diving packages available. On the beach is a sister establishment, *Picard Beach Cottage Resort* (also PO Box 34, T 445-5131, F 445-5599) which has an attractive open-sided restaurant and bar, self-catering cottages which, at a pinch, can sleep 4 (US$140d EP), good sea bathing with coral reef just beside jetty, 7-night, 10-dive, package available. *Coconut Beach Hotel* has apartments and bungalows for US$75d CP, US$110d MAP, a/c, fans, bar, restaurant, beach, car hire, tours arranged, PO Box 37, T 445-5393, F 445-5693, reported chaotic but improvements are now under way. Further apartments are being built on the beach. *Sango's Sea Lodge*, Prince Rupert's Bay, beach bar, fresh fish and 6 apartments set in lovely gardens, spacious, self-contained, insect nets, 2 double beds, bathroom, US$50d, US$80 for 4, run by Willie (who catches the fish) and Harta (German) Sango, T 445-5211, rec, yachts can moor in the bay, sandy outside beach bar.

On the N coast near the charming fishing village of Calibishie, *Pointe Baptiste* estate rents out the Main House, sleeping 6, US$160 a night including cook and maid, US$960 a week, spectacular view from the airy verandah, house built in 1932, wooden, perfect for children, cot, welcoming staff, very popular, also smaller house sleeping 3, self-catering, US$55-60 a night, reduced weekly rates, book locally through the housekeeper Geraldine Edwards,

T 445-7322, or in the UK through Traveller's Tree, see **Tours** below. Next door are 3 new self-catering villas *Red Rock Haven*, T 448-2181, F 448-5787, tastefully decorated, expensive, meals can be provided, share beach with guests from *Pointe Baptiste*, US$140-200d.

In Marigot, *Thomas's Guest House*, W end of main street, T 445-7264, US$40d EP, clean, basic, near Melville Hall airport (check in advance if it is open); *Paul Carlton's Guest House*, E end of main street, 6 clean, basic rooms, cooking facilities, US$18pp EP, cheaper for longer than 1 night, Paul also runs taxi service.

Away from the Leeward Coast: *Layou River*, PO Box 8, T 449-6281, F 449-6713 US$50s, US$60d, US$70 triple EP, add US$20 pp MAP, nice location, pool, restaurant, bar, river bathing, may be noisy if construction of neighbouring *Shangrila* hotel goes ahead; *Layou Valley Inn*, 5 rooms, rather bossy landlady at times but very comfortable, excellent cuisine, high in the hills with superb views, need a car to get there, US$55-66d EP, add US$30 pp MAP, T 449-6203, F 448-5212, PO Box 196. *Emerald Bush Hotel* and *Carib Cottages*, about 1 mile from Emerald Pool, A-frame cottages without electricity, a few small rooms, simple bar and restaurant, river swimming, suitable for the fit and adventurous, accommodation very basic, US$18 to stay in the bush 'camp', US$28d for room, or US$120/week self-catering, US$68-78d MAP, T 448-4545, F 448-7954, P O Box 277. *Floral Gardens*, Concord Village, at the edge of the Carib Territory, T/F 445-7636, comfortable rooms, US$40s, US$55d, with breakfast, apartments, US$90, 10% discount for stays of 5 days and over, dinner, excellent food but expensive and service very slow, lovely gardens by the Pagua River where you can swim, 15 mins away from beaches of Woodford Hill, electrics basic, ask for a mosquito coil for your room, many minibuses in the morning, easy to get a pick-up, bus to Roseau EC$9, 1 hour, bus to airport and Woodford Hill Beach, lovely walks in the area, either into the Carib territory or around Atkinson further N, rec. Charles Williams and his wife, Margaret, run the *Carib Territory Guest House*, Crayfish River, on the main road, T 445-7256, US$35-45d EP, she cooks if meals are ordered in advance but there are no restaurants nearby as an alternative and you may go hungry, water intermittent, he also does island-wide tours but is better on his own patch. About a mile away, *Olive's Guest House* at Atkinson, slightly set back off the road, has been rec, bamboo huts, comfortable, friendly, EC$18, meals extra, T 445-7521. Also in the Carib Territory, exceptionally cheap and basic, *Bionics Co-Op*, T 445-7167, US$10s, US$15d, kitchen and laundry facilities but little else, river swimming nearby.

There are a 10% service charge and 5% government tax on hotel bills. A sales tax of 3% may be added to meal charges.

Camping is not encouraged and, in the National Parks, it is forbidden. Designated sites may be introduced in the future.

● **Where To Eat**

(Not including hotels.) In Roseau, *La Robe Créole*, Victoria Street, créole and European, good but expensive, service inattentive; with same ownership is the *Mouse-Hole Café*, underneath, which is excellent for little pies and local pasties; *Pearl's Cuisine*, 19 Castle Street, good local food and service, reasonable prices, also mobile wagon in town centre catering for lunchtime takeaway trade; *Restaurant Paiho*, Castle Street, good chinese food, delicious fruit punch, uncrowded, slightly pricey; *The World of Food*, next to *Vena's Guesthouse*, local dishes but unexciting, good breakfast about EC$10, lunch and dinners EC$20-30, drink your beer under a huge mango tree which belonged to writer Jean Rhys's family garden. *Guiyave*, 15 Cork Street, for midday snacks and juices, patisserie and salad bar, popular, crowded after 1300. *Cartwheel Café*, Bay Street (next to Royal Bank of Canada), clean, on waterfront, good place to stop for a coffee, and *Green Parrot*, same street, small, family-run, good value creole food, daily specials for US$4-5; *Orchard*, corner of Great George and King George V Streets (friendly yet slow service, but food OK, good callaloo). Lots of "snackettes", eg *Hope Café*, 17 Steber St, good local dishes and snacks, lively, open till late. *Cathy's Pizzeria*, opp the Old Market Plaza, food all right but report received of rather bold rat in hall way; *Erick's Bakery* has opened a small patisserie on Old Street for 'tasty island treats'. *Wykie's*, 51 Old Street, caters for serious drinkers; the *Pina Colada Bar*, 30 Bath Road, is lively, popular with the young crowd, light meals.

Near Canefield, The *Shipwreck* offers simple barbeque meals, occasional live music, a seafront bar on Donkey Beach and Sun beach party (see under Entertainment). *Good Times*, an old house next to the *Warehouse Disco*, offers a good barbeque and loud music from Wed-Sun, opening at 1830, convivial proprietor, Ian Georges. *E George Chicken Shack*, on roadside between Emerald Pool and Pont Cassé, small bar, cold beer and great fried chicken. *La Flambeau Restaurant* at Picard Cottage, near Portsmouth, is comfortable, has an attractive beachside setting and a varied menu. *The Almond Beach Bar and Restaurant* at Calibishie on the N coast has been rec, it has very good food and fresh fish.

On weekdays in the capital the lunch hour begins at 1300 and places fill up quickly. Dominicans eat their main meal at lunch time and it is often hard to get anything other than takeaways after 1600 or on Sun except at hotels. If you have a car, try different hotel restaurants on different nights and check when the barbeque specials etc are being held. Generally, Dominicans eat in restaurants at lunchtime and in hotels at night.

● **Food And Drink**

There is little in the way of international or fast food on the island, but plenty of local fruit and vegetables, fish and "mountain chicken" (crapaud, or frog) in season. Try the seedless golden grapefruit, US$1 for 6 in the market. The term 'provisions' on a menu refers to root vegetables: dasheen, yams, sweet potatoes, tannia, pumpkins, etc. To buy fresh fish listen for the fishermen blowing their conch shells in the street; there is no fish shop or fish market. Try the sea-moss drink, rather like a vanilla milk shake (with a reputation as an aphrodisiac), also drunk on Grenada, see page 682.

● **Entertainment**

Mid-week entertainment at *Anchorage* and *Reigate Waterfront* hotels. Weekends at *Fort Young Hotel*. Discos at Canefield: *Warehouse* on Sat, in converted sugar mill by the airport; *Aqua Cade* on Fri; *The Shipwreck*, restaurant, bar, live entertainment at weekends, on waterfront, screened from industrial area by tall trees, before you get to the airfield, turn left after the bottling plant and twin bridges opp car sales garage, turn left at end of road.

● **Shopping**

Straw goods are among the best and cheapest in the Caribbean; they can be bought in the Carib Territory and in Roseau. Best shops for crafts in Roseau are the Caribana, 31 Cork St and, for the famous vetiver-grass mats, Tropicrafts, Queen Mary Street, where you can see the women making the mats. It takes 4 weeks to complete a 10-foot mat. Note 4% extra charged on VISA. Portsmouth has a sizeable craft shop at the Cruise Ship Berth on the Cabrits. Other good buys are local Bay rum (aftershave and body rub) and candles. Bello 'Special' or 'Classic' pepper sauce is a good souvenir. The public market is lively and friendly. Try a jelly coconut. Cee-Bee's Bookshop, 20 Cork Street and Paperbacks at 6 Cork Street, for Caribbean and other English books and magazines. Front Line Cooperative Services Ltd, 78 Queen Mary Street, T 448-8664, has books, CDs, cassettes, stationery, photography etc.

● **Banks**
Royal Bank of Canada, Bay Street, Roseau, T 448-2771; Barclays Bank Plc, 2 Old Street, T 448-2571 (branch in Portsmouth, T 445-5271); National Commercial Bank of Dominica, 64 Hillsborough Street, T 448-4401 (opens lunchtime, branch at Portsmouth, T 445-5430); Banque Française Commerciale, Queen Mary Street, T 448-4040; Scotia Bank, 28 Hillsborough Street, T 448-5800. American Express agent is Whitchurch Travel, T 448-2181, efficient and helpful for emergency cheque cashing. Visa and Mastercard well accepted with cash advances from all banks.

● **Currency**
East Caribbean dollar.

● **Emergency**
T 999 for Police, Fire and Ambulance.

● **Climate And Clothing**
Daytime temperatures average between 70° F and 85° F, though the nights are much cooler, especially in the mountains. The rainy season is from July to October though showers occur all through the year. (Note that the mountains are much wetter and cooler than the coast, Roseau receives about 85 inches of rain a year, while the mountains get over 340 inches.) Clothing is informal, though swimsuits are not worn on the streets. A sweater is rec for the evenings. When hiking take a raincoat and/or a pullover; a dry T-shirt is also a good idea. Take good walking shoes.

● **Hours Of Business**
Government offices: Mon, 0800-1300, 1400-1700, Tues to Fri, close one hour earlier in the afternoon; the only government offices open on Sat are the tourist kiosk in Old Market Plaza,

and the tourist office at Canefield airport (open daily 0615-1115, 1415-1730—or last flight); the Melville Hall tourist office is only open at flight arrival times. Shops: 0800-1300, 1400-1600, Mon-Fri, 0800-1300 Sat. Some of the larger supermarkets in Roseau stay open until 2000 and tiny, local shops may still be open at 2200 even on Sun. Banks: 0800-1300 Mon-Fri, plus 1400-1600 Fri.

● **National Holidays**
1 January; Carnival; Good Friday and Easter Monday; 1st Monday in May; Whit Monday; 3/4 November (Independence); Christmas Day and Boxing Day. 2 January is a merchant's holiday, when all shops and restaurants are closed, although banks and hotels remain open; Government offices will in most cases not be open.

● **Time Zone**
Atlantic Standard Time, 4 hours behind GMT, 1 ahead of EST.

● **Electric Current**
220/240 volts AC, 50 cycles. There is electricity throughout the island, but many places lack running water, especially in the villages between Marigot and La Plaine.

● **Post Office**
Hillsborough Street and Bay Street, Roseau, 0700-2000 Mon to Sat. A mural depicts the development of the postal service in Dominica. This Post Office opened in 1993; it has a list of other stamp sellers around the island. Paperbacks on Cork St and other stationers or gift shops. A postcard to Europe costs EC$0.55. Parcels go airmail only. Post your mail at the main Post Office if possible, post boxes around the country are not all in operation and there is no indication of which ones have been taken out of service. DHL is in the Whitchurch Centre, represented by Whitchurch Travel Agency, T 448-2181, F 448-5787.

● **Telecommunications**
Telephone, fax and telex services at Cable and Wireless, Mercury House, Hanover Street, Roseau, open 0700-2000, Mon-Sat. Phone cards are available for EC$10, 20 and 40 from Cable and Wireless and some shops. The international telephone code for Dominica is 809.

● **Radio**
DBS broadcasts on medium wave 595 kHz and FM 88.1 MHz. There are 2 religious radio stations (one Protestant and one Catholic) as well

as a repeater for St Lucian Radio Caribbean International on FM 98.1 MHz.

● **Tours**

Island tours can be arranged through many of the hotels, for instance Dominica Tours at the *Anchorage Hotel*, T 448-2638, F 448-5680, PO Box 34 (an 8-day, 7 night package including accommodation, all meals, transfers, plus a photo safari, hiking, birdwatching, boating and sailing, costs US$1,028d per person). The most knowledgeable operators are Antours (Anison's Tour and Taxi Service), Woodstone Shopping Mall, Roseau. T 448-6460, F 448-6780, Ken's Hinterland Adventure Tours and Taxi Service, rec, 62 Hillsborough St, Roseau, PO Box 447, T 448-4850, F 448-8486 and Lambert Charles, strong on conservation and hiking, no office but T 448-3365. Other operators include Paradise Tours, 4 Steber Street, Pottersville, Roseau, T 448-5999/448-4712, F 448-4134 and Ivor Rolle's Rainbow Rover Tours, T/F 448-8650. Check beforehand which tours are offered on a daily basis or once or twice a week. You may have to wait for the tour you want or be offered an alternative. German, French, Spanish and English are offered at different agencies. In the UK, Traveller's Tree specializes in holidays in Dominica, 116 Crawford Street, London W1H 1AG, T 071-935 2291, 0703 671312, F 071-486 2587. BA Holidays and Caribbean Connection organize individual, personalized tours through La Robe Créole Tours and Travel, PO Box 270, T 448-4436/2896, F 448 5212, who can also offer tours, excursions, transfers, hotel reservations and car rentals. The Whitchurch Travel Agency, PO Box 71, Old Street, Roseau, T 448-2181, F 448-5787, handles local tours as well as foreign travel and represents American Express Travel Related Services, several airlines and Caribbean Express.

● **Maps**

The Ordnance Survey, Romsey Road, Southampton, SO9 49H, UK, T 0703 792792, publishes a 1:50,000 colourful map of Dominica, with a 1:10,000 street map insert of Roseau, including roads, footpaths, contours, forests, reserves and National Parks. This can be bought at the Old Market tourist office in Roseau.

● **Consulates**

The **British** Honorary Consul is Mr Robert Duckworth, general manager of Cable & Wireless in Dominica.

● **Tourist Information**

The Dominica Division of Tourism has its headquarters in the National Development Corporation, in a converted Rose's Lime Juice factory, Valley Road, Roseau (PO Box 73, T 448-2045, F 448-5840). There is a Dominica Information Desk in the arrival section of VC Bird International Airport, Antigua, open daily. A useful brochure is *Discover Dominica*. **USA**: In New York information can be obtained from the Caribbean Tourism Association, 20 East 46th St, New York, NY 10017-2452, T 212-682 0435, F 212-697 4258, or the Dominica Consulate Office, Suite 900, 820 2nd Avenue, New York, NY 10017, T 212-599 8478, F 212-808 4975. **UK**: Contact the Caribbean Tourism Organization, Suite 3, 15 Vigilant House, 120 Wilton Road, Victoria, London SW1V 1JZ, T 071-233 8382, F 071-873 8551. **Belgium**: OECS Embassy, Rue des Aduatiques 100, 1040 Brussels, T 322-733-4328, F 322-735-7237. **Canada**: OECS Mission in Canada, Suite 1050, 112 Kent St, Ottawa, Ontario KIP 5P2, T 613-236-8952, F 613-236-3042.

The editors are very grateful to Rachel Rogers, formerly resident in Portsmouth, for a thorough updating of the Dominica chapter.

ST LUCIA

S T LUCIA is the second largest of the Windwards, lying between St Vincent and Martinique. Its total population is 135,000 (1992), and the area is about 238 square miles. St Lucia (pronounced "Loosha") has become a popular tourist destination, with sporting facilities, splendid beaches, a clear, warm sea and sunshine. (The island was the scene of the films *Dr Doolittle*, *Water*, and *Superman Two*.) It also has some of the finest mountain scenery in the West Indies.

The highest peak is Morne Gimie (3,118 feet); the most spectacular are the Gros Piton (2,619 feet) and the Petit Piton (2,461 feet) which are old volcanic forest-clad plugs rising sheer out of the sea near the town of Soufrière on the W coast. A few miles away is one of the world's most accessible volcanoes. Here you can see *soufrières*: vents in the volcano which exude hydrogen sulphide, steam and other gases and deposit sulphur and other compounds. There are also pools of boiling water. The mountains are intersected by numerous short rivers; in places, these rivers debouch into broad, fertile and well-cultivated valleys. If you are staying in one of these valleys on the W coast (eg Marigot Bay) expect to be hot, they are well-sheltered from the breeze.

The scenery is of outstanding beauty, and in the neighbourhood of the Pitons it has an element of grandeur. Evidence of volcanic upheaval can be found in the layers of limestone and even sea shells in the perpendicular cliffs on the W coast and which occur at about 100 to 150 feet just N of Petit Piton above Malgretout and in other areas. An uplift of from 50-100 feet is supposed to have occurred comparatively recently and is thought to explain the flat plain of Vieux Fort district in the S and the raised beaches of the N Gros Islet district.

History

Even though some St Lucians have claimed that their island was discovered by Columbus on St Lucy's day (13 December, the national holiday) in 1502, neither the date of discovery nor the discoverer are in fact known, for according to the evidence of Columbus' log, he appears to have missed the island and was not even in the area on St Lucy's Day. A Vatican globe of 1520 marks the island as Santa Lucía, suggesting that it was at least claimed by Spain. In 1605, 67 Englishmen en route to Guiana touched at St Lucia and made an unsuccessful effort to settle though a Dutch expedition may have discovered the island first. The island at the time was peopled by Caribs. There are Amerindian sites and artefacts on the island, some of which are of Arawak origin, suggesting that the Caribs had already driven them out by the time the Europeans arrived, as no trace of the Arawaks was found by them. The Indians called their island Iouanalao, which may have meant: where the iguana is found. The name was later changed to Hiwanarau and then evolved to Hewanorra. In 1638 the first recorded settlement was made by English from Bermuda and St Kitts, but the colonists were killed by the Caribs about three years later.

In 1642 the King of France, claiming sovereignty over the island, ceded it to the French West India Company, who in 1650 sold it to MM Houel and Du Parquet. There were repeated attempts by the Caribs to expel the French and several governors were murdered. From 1660, the British began to renew their claim to the island and fighting for pos-

ST LUCIA C 48
Not to scale

Pointe du Cap
Pointe Hardy
Pigeon Island Historic Park
Cap Estate
Anse Lavoutte
Cas-en-Bas
Gros Islet
Anse Lapins
Rodney Bay
Reduit
Espérance Harbour
Labrellotte Point
Monchy
Cap Marquis
Marisule Estate
Choc Bay
Grande Rivière
Cassimi Point
Rat Is.
Mt. Monier
Tanti Point
Vigie Beach
D'Estrées Point
CASTRIES
Paix Bouche
Grande Anse
La Toc Bay
Babonneau
Tortue Point
Coubaril Point
Fond Cacao
Fond Assor
Cul de Sac Bay
Anse Massacré
Hess Oil Terminal
La Sorcière
Louvet Point
Marigot Bay
Anse Louvet
Roseau Bay
La Croix Maingot
Povert Pt.
Massacré
Bexon
Piton Flor
Pointe La Ville
Anse La Raye
Ravine Poisson
Grande Rivière
La Caye
Mamelles Pt.
Dennery
Fond D'Or Bay
Barre de l'Isle
Dennery Bay
Canaries
Linnis Point
Blanche Point
Fregate Is. Nature Reserve
Praslin Bay
Grand Caille Point
Anse Chastanet
Mt. Tabac
Quillesse Forest Reserve
Mon Repos
Patience
Trou Gras Point
Soufrière
Mt. Gimie 3118 ft
Anse Chapeau
Soufrière Bay
Diamond
Sulphur Springs
Fond St Jacques
Fond Bay
Port Volet
Anse des Pitons
Petit Piton
Etangs
Mt. Grand Magazin 2022 ft
Micoud
Troumassé Bay
Victoria Jnct.
Monzie
Blanchard
Ti Rocher
Gros Piton
Dacretin
Desruisseaux
Anse L'Ivrogne
Industry
Belle Vue
Anse Ger
Point Lamarre
Banse
Pierrot
Anse L'Islet
Gertrine
Augier
Savannes Bay Nature Reserve
Choiseul
Sauzay
Laborie
Maria Islands Nature Reserve
Piaye
Laborie Bay
Black Bay
Vieux Fort
Anse de Sables
N
Caesar Point
Cap Moule à Chique

session began in earnest. The settlers were mostly French, who developed a plantation economy based on slave labour. In all, St Lucia changed hands 14 times before it became a British Crown Colony in 1814 by the Treaty of Paris (more historical details can be found in the text below).

From 1838, the island was included in a Windward Islands Government, with a Governor resident first in Barbados and then Grenada. Universal adult suffrage was introduced in 1951. The St Lucia Labour Party (SLP) won the elections in that year and retained power until 1964. The United Workers' Party (UWP) then governed from 1964-79. In 1958 St Lucia joined the West Indies Federation, but it was short-lived following the withdrawal of Jamaica in 1961-62 (see Jamaica, **History**). In 1967, St Lucia gained full internal self-government, becoming a State in voluntary association with Britain, and in 1979 it gained full independence.

Government

St Lucia is an independent member of the Commonwealth and the British monarch is the Head of State, represented by a Governor General. The Government is led by Mr John Compton, of the UWP, who held power in 1964-79 and who has since won elections in 1982, 1987 and 1992. The UWP holds an 11-6 seat majority in the 17-member House of Assembly. The third political party, the left wing Progressive Labour Party (PLP), has failed to win any seats since 1987. The 11 members of the Senate are appointed by the Governor General, six on the advice of the Prime Minister, three on the advice of the Leader of the Opposition and two of his own choice.

The Economy

St Lucia's economy has historically been based on agriculture, originally sugar, but since the 1920s particularly on bananas and also cocoa and coconuts. It has

the largest banana crop in the Windward Islands, banana exports rose from 99,000 tonnes in 1991 to 135,000 tonnes in 1992 but fell back to 108,830 tonnes in 1993; Geest boats call weekly to take them to the UK. The industry has suffered because of low prices; a strike by farmers in 1993 caused further damage, and in 1994 the St Lucia Banana Growers Association was put into receivership with debts of EC$44 mn. Greater competition in the European banana market, particularly after EC unification in 1992, is leading to diversification away from bananas; dairy farming, flowers and fisheries are being encouraged. There is also some industry, with data processing and a diversified manufacturing sector producing clothing, toys, sportswear and diving gear, and 20% of the workforce is now engaged in manufacturing. The island is promoted as a location for industrial development within the US Caribbean Basin Initiative. An oil transshipment terminal has been built and the Government has set up several industrial estates. There are plans to establish a free zone at Vieux Fort, where a new deep water container port was opened in 1993. Public sector investment in large scale infrastructure projects includes electricity expansion and road construction.

Tourism is now a major foreign exchange earner, and in 1993 192,339 visitors stayed on the island, an increase of 9.4% over 1992. St Lucia is one of the few Caribbean islands to show consistent growth in tourism, particularly from Europeans, who stay longer than Americans. Air arrivals from Europe rose by over a third in 1991 and then by a further 25% in 1992 and 5.5% in 1993 to become the largest market with over 49% of the total. In 1993 there were 2,932 hotel rooms, of which the eight all-inclusive resorts of the 12 major hotels accounted for almost half. Further expansion is taking place with new hotels being built in the N of the island and a 350-room hotel and marina to be built by the Jamaican

SAINT LUCIA: FACT FILE

Geographic

Land area	617 sq km
forested	13.0%
pastures	5.0%
cultivated	30.0%

Demographic

Population (1992)	135,000
annual growth rate (1987-92)	0.8%
urban	46.4%
rural	53.6%
density	218.8 per sq km
Religious affiliation	
Roman Catholic	79.0%
Birth rate per 1,000 (1990)	23.2
	(world av 27.1)
Death rate per 1,000 (1990)	5.6
	(world av 9.8)

Education and Health

Life expectancy at birth,	
male	68.6 years
female	74.4 years
Infant mortality rate	
per 1,000 live births (1989)	17.7
Physicians (1990)	1 per 2,521 persons
Hospital beds	1 per 283 persons
Calorie intake as %	
of FAO requirement	107%
Population age 25 and over	
with no formal schooling	17.5%
Literacy (over 15)	80.0%

Economic

GNP (1990 market prices)	US$286mn
GNP per capita	US$1,900
Public external debt (1990)	US$58mn
Tourism receipts (1991)	US$174mn
Inflation	
(annual av 1986-91)	4.5%
Radio	1 per 1.7 persons
Television	1 per 6 persons
Telephone	1 per 11 persons

Employment

Population economically active (1980)	
	42,200
Unemployment rate (1990)	13.0%
% of labour force in	
agriculture	33.9
manufacturing	10.4
construction	3.2
trade, restaurants	18.5
Paramilitary police unit	80

Source *Encyclopaedia Britannica*

Superclubs chain, is planned for the S, near Hewanorra airport. Small hotels and restaurants have suffered a reported 75% drop in business since the growth of all-inclusives. The Atlantic Rally for Cruisers was changed from Barbados, its normal venue, to St Lucia in 1990 and this brings revenue of about US$2mn to the tourist industry. Tourists are estimated to have spent over US$208mn in the island in 1992.

Culture

There is still a good deal of French influence: most of the islanders, who are predominantly of African descent (though a few black Caribs are still to be found in certain areas), speak a French patois, and in rural areas many people, particularly the older generation, have great difficulty with English. There is still a French provincial style of architecture; most place names are French; about 79% of the population are Roman Catholics. The French Caribbean also has an influence on music, you can hear zouk and cadance played as much as calypso and reggae.

One of the Caribbean's most renowned poets and playwrights in the English language, Derek Walcott, was born in St Lucia in 1930. He has published many collections of poems, an autobiography in verse (*Another Life*), critical works, and plays such as *Dream on Monkey Mountain*. Walcott uses English poetic traditions, with a close understanding of the inner magic of the language (Robert Graves), to expose the historical and cultural facets of the Caribbean. His books are highly recommended, including his latest work, the narrative poem *Omeros*, which contributed to him winning the 1992 Nobel Prize for Literature. Another St Lucian writer worth reading is the novelist Garth St Omer (for instance *The Lights on the Hill*).

Fauna and Flora

The fauna and flora of St Lucia is very similar to that on Dominica, the Windwards chain of islands having been colonized by plants and animals originally from South and Central America, with endemic species such as sisserou and jacquot. Rainforest would have covered most of the island prior to European colonization but the most dramatic loss has been in the last 20 years. Much of the remaining forest is protected, mainly for water supply, but also specifically for wildlife in places. There are many orchids and anthurium growing wild in the rain forests, while tropical flowers and flowering trees are found everywhere. To date, 1,179 different species of flowering plants have been documented. There are several endemic reptile species including St Lucia tree lizard, pygmy gecko, Maria Island ground lizard and Maria Island grass snake. The only snake which is dangerous is the Fer de Lance which is restricted to dry scrub woodland on the E coast near Grande Anse and Louvet and also near Anse La Raye and Canaries in the W. The agouti and the manicou are present throughout the island, but rarely seen. The national bird is the colourful St Lucian parrot (*Amazona versicolor*), which is most frequently seen in the dense rain forest around Quillesse. A successful conservation programme established in 1978 probably saved the species from extinction and has allowed numbers to rise from 150 birds in 1978 to over 400 today. Other endemic birds are the St Lucia oriole, Semper's warbler and the St Lucia black finch. Several other species such as the white breasted thrasher are rare and endangered. Measures are being taken to protect these birds and their habitats.

In the N of the island, Pigeon Island, Pointe du Cap and Cap Hardy are worth visiting for their landscapes, seabird colonies and interesting xerophytic vegetation, including cactus, thorn scrub etc.

Union is the site of the Forestry Department headquarters, where there is a nature trail, open to the public, a medicinal garden and a small, well-organized zoo (free, but donations welcome). The Forestry Department also organizes a strenuous seven-mile trek across the island (franchized to several local tour operators and booked only through them, US$39, Mondays and Wednesdays, with pickup from your hotel) through rainforest and mature mahogany, Caribbean pine and blue mahoe plantations which will give you the best chance of seeing the St Lucia parrot, as well as other rainforest birds: thrashers, vireos, hummingbirds, flycatchers etc. Wear good shoes and expect to get wet and muddy. The isolated E coast beaches are rarely visited and have exceptional wildlife. Leather backs and other turtles nest at Grand Anse and Anse Louvet and the Fisheries Department/Naturalists Society organize nocturnal vigils to count nesting females and discourage poachers. This area is also the main stronghold of the white-breasted thrasher and St Lucia wren; there are also iguanas (although you will be lucky to see one) and unfortunately the fer de lance snake, although attacks are extremely rare. The bite is not always fatal but requires hospitalization (it is extremely painful). Avoid walking through the bush, especially at night, and wear shoes or boots and long trousers. La Sorcière and Piton Flor are densely forested mountains in the N with excellent rainforest vegetation. Piton Flor can be walked up in 40 mins although it is a strenuous climb and you will need to ask how to get to the top, from where there are spectacular views. It is the last recorded location of Sempers warbler, an endemic bird now probably extinct.

In the S, Cap Moule à Chique has spectacular views and good bird populations. The Maria Islands, just offshore, are home to two endemic reptiles, a colourful lizard and small, rare, harmless snake, the Kouwes snake (see page 41).

The National Trust (T 452 5005/453 2479) and Eastern Caribbean Natural Areas Management Programme (EC-NAMP) run day trips with a licensed guide. All participants must be capable swimmers. Interpretive facilities are on the mainland at Anse de Sables, where you can arrange boat transport. Unauthorized access is not allowed. Good beach, excellent snorkelling. From 15 May to 31 July public access is not permitted while the birds are nesting. However, you can visit the Fregate Islands Nature Reserve, handed over to the National Trust by the Government in 1989. Frigate birds nest here and the dry forest also harbours the trembler, the St Lucian oriole and the ramier. The reserve includes a section of mangrove and is the natural habitat of this boa constrictor (tête chien). There is a major SE coast conservation programme being coordinated by ECNAMP.

Some of these areas are very isolated and you are recommended to get in touch with the relevant organizations before attempting to visit them.

The St Lucia Naturalists Society meets every month at the Castries Library and often has interesting talks and slide shows on St Lucia. Visitors welcomed. Details in local press or from Library.

Diving and Marine Life

There is some very good diving off the W coast, although this is somewhat dependent on the weather, as heavy rain tends to create high sediment loads in the rivers and sea. Diving on the E coast is not so good and can be risky unless you are a competent diver. Several companies offer scuba diving with professional instructors, catering for the experienced or the novice diver. One of the best beach entry dives in the Caribbean is directly off Anse Chastanet, where an underwater shelf drops off from about 10 feet down to about 60 feet and there is a good dive over Turtle Reef in the bay, where there are over 25 different types of coral. Below the Petit Piton are impressive sponge and coral communities on a drop to 200 feet of spectacular wall. There are gorgonians, black coral trees, huge barrel sponges and plenty of other beautiful reef life. Other popular dive sites include Anse L'Ivrogne, Anse La Raye Point and the Pinnacles (an impressive site where four pinnacles rise to within 10 feet of the surface), not forgetting the wrecks, such as the *Volga* (in 20 feet of water N of Castries harbour, well broken up, subject to swell, requires caution), the *Waiwinette* (several miles S of Vieux Fort, strong currents, competent divers only), and the 165-foot *Lesleen M* (deliberately sunk in 1986 off Anse Cochon Bay in 60 feet of water). Scuba St Lucia operates from Anse Chastanet, PO Box 7000, Soufrière, T 459 7000, F 459 7700, three dive boats, photographic hire and film processing, day and night dives, resort courses and full PADI certification; Buddies Scuba at Vigie Marina, T 452 5288/7044, two-tank day dives, one tank night dives, camera rental, open water certification or resort course, dive packages available; Dolphin Divers at *The Moorings*, Marigot Bay, T 451 4357, day and night dives, equipment rental, certification courses and underwater camera hire, they also have a branch at the Rodney Bay Marina, where you can be picked up and taken down to Marigot in the boat, Rodney Bay T 452 9485 or turn up at 0815, alternatively arrange a beach pick up from your hotel. The St Lucia Tourist Board can give help and advice on sites and the dive companies. A single tank dive costs around US$55, introductory resort courses are about US$65. The Fisheries Department is pursuing an active marine protection programme; divers should avoid taking any coral or undersized shellfish. Corals and sponges should not even be touched. It is also illegal to buy or sell coral products on St Lucia.

Beaches and Watersports

All the W coast beaches have good swimming but many are dominated by resort hotels. The Atlantic E coast has heavy surf and is dangerous but with very spectacular and isolated beaches (difficult to get to without local knowledge or the Ordnance Survey map and 4-wheel drive) which make a pleasant change from the W coast. Many are important habitats and nesting places for the island's wildlife (see **Fauna and Flora**, above). Cas en Bas Beach can be reached from Gros Islet (45-mins' walk), it is sheltered, shady and a bit dirty. Donkey Beach can be reached from there by taking a track to the N (20-mins' walk), the scenery is wild and open and it is windy. To the S of Cas en Bas Beach are Anse Lavoutte, Anse Comerette and Anse Lapins, follow the rocks, it is a 30-mins' walk to the first and an hour to the last. Access is also possible from Monchy. They are deserted, wind-swept beaches and headlands. Grande Anse, further S, is a long windy beach, reached from Desbarras. If the road is all right you can drive, or walk (1 hour down, 1½ hours back). Anse Louvet is a sheltered beach in a stunning setting, reached from Desbarras (three hours' walk or drive if possible) or Au Leon (two hours' walk or drive if possible). Ask locally about the state of the roads, which change frequently (with thanks to Henry Augustin, *La Panache Guesthouse*, for this information).

The beaches on the W coast N of Castries can be reached by bus, with a short walk down to the sea. Vigie (1½ miles from Castries) is a lovely strip of sand with plenty of shade and popular. Its only drawback is that it runs parallel to the airport runway. Choc Bay (Palm Beach) has good sand and shade (get off the bus after *Sandals Halcyon*). Marisule is a small beach, but popular with the locals. La Brelotte Bay is also popular and you can get lunch at *East Winds* or *Windjam-*

mer Landing. Bois d' Orange is a deserted bay (except on public holidays), best reached on foot or 4-wheel drive. Rodney Bay has another excellent beach at Reduit, dominated by the *St Lucian* (parasailing) and *Royal St Lucian* hotels, where you can use their bars and sports hire facilities but it is crowded with their guests. The northern part of the bay is cut off by the marina and it is now a 45-mins' walk or 5-10 mins' bus ride into Gros Islet, but there is no resort near the beach. There are more beaches on the way to Pigeon Island, with ample shade, where snorkelling equipment can be hired for EC$10 for 2 hrs, and two small beaches on Pigeon Island itself.

Heading S from Castries there are beaches at all the small towns but they are not generally used by tourists and you may feel an oddity. Marigot Bay is a popular tourist spot. Anse Chastanet is well used and claims to have the best snorkelling on the island. The trade winds blow in to the S shore and the sandy beach of Anse de Sable near Vieux Fort offers ideal windsurfing. Many hotels hire out hobbycats, dinghies, windsurfing equipment, jet bikes and small speedboats.

At Marigot Bay and Rodney Bay you can hire any size of craft, the larger ones coming complete with crew if you want. Many of these yachts sail down to the Grenadines. Rodney Bay has been developed to accommodate 1,000 yachts (with 232 berths in a full-service boatyard) and hosts the annual Atlantic Rally for Cruisers race, with over 150 yachts arriving there each December. Charters can be arranged to sail to neighbouring islands. At Rodney Bay Marina is: Trade Winds Yachts, T 452 8424, F 452 8442, an extensive range of services on offer, bareboat or crewed charters, liveaboard sailing school, trips to Martinique or St Vincent (one-way available); Sunsail Stevens Yachts, T 452 8648, bareboat or crewed charters, one-way cruises to the Grenadines. At Marigot Bay: The Moorings,

T 451 4357/4246, bareboat fleet of 38'-50' Beneteaus and crewed fleet of 50'-60' yachts, 45-room hotel for accommodation prior to departure or on return, watersports, diving, windsurfing. There is a yacht basin at Gros Islet. Soufrière has a good anchorage, but as the water is deep it is necessary to anchor close in. There is a pier for short term tie-ups. Fishing trips for barracuda, mackerel, king fish and other varieties can also be arranged. Several sport fishing boats sail from Rodney Bay Marina. There is an annual billfish tournament, at which in 1993 a 549-lb blue marlin was landed, breaking the record.

As some of the best views are from the sea, it is recommended to take at least one boat trip. There are several boats which sail down the W coast to Soufrière, where you stop to visit the volcano, Diamond Falls and the Botanical Gardens, followed by lunch and return sail with a stop somewhere for swimming and snorkelling. The price usually includes all transport, lunch, drinks and snorkelling gear; the *Unicorn*, a 140-foot replica of a 19th century brig (used in the filming of *Roots*) sails on Tuesday, Thursday and Friday in low season, more often in high season, and has been recommended, US$65 pp including lunch and the inevitable rum punch, can only be booked through Sunlink International, T 452 0842 (*Unicorn* is based at Vigie Marina, T 452 6811). Other excursions on catamarans and private yachts can be booked with tour operators in Castries or through the hotels. At the swimming stop on the return journey local divers may try to sell you coral. Don't buy it, it is illegal, and what is more, a reef dies if you do.

Other Sports

There is a 9-hole golf course, at Cap Estate (green fee US$20, club hire US$9, trolley hire US$3, T 450 8523) and a private course for guests at La Toc. The larger hotels usually have tennis courts,

or there is the St Lucia Tennis Club. *Club St Lucia* has nine floodlit tennis courts, T 450 0551 for bookings. The *St Lucian Hotel* also has courts available for public use and lessons can be arranged. **Squash** is available at Cap Estate golf clubhouse and the St Lucia Yacht Club (T 452 8350). The St Lucia Raquet Club at *Club St Lucia* also has a court and optional instruction, T 450 0551.

Horses for hire at Trim's Stables, Cas-en-Bas (PO Box 1159, Castries, T 450 8273), riding for beginners or advanced; also offers lessons and picnic trips to the Atlantic, US$45. Laborde's Gym, Old La Toc Road, exercise equipment and body building, open Monday-Friday 0600-2000, T 452 2788, no credit cards. Jazzercise Fitness Centre at Gablewoods Mall offers fitness classes, step, stretch and weights on a walk-in basis, T 451 6853. *Hotel Le Sport* specializes in health and fitness, with tennis, cycling, weight training, volley ball etc, all inclusive packages. Jogging is organized by The Roadbusters, who meet outside JQ's Supermarket, La Clery, on Tuesdays and Thursdays at 1700 and on Sundays at 0800, call Jimmie James for details, T 452 5142 daytime, T 452 4790 evenings. Cricket and football are the main spectator sports.

Festivals

Carnival is held in the days leading up to Shrove Tuesday and Ash Wednesday and is a high point in the island's cultural activities, when colourful bands and costumed revellers make up processions through the streets. 22 February is Independence Day. The annual St Lucia Jazz Festival in May is now an internationally recognized event, drawing large crowds every year. On 29 June St Peter's Day is celebrated as the Fisherman's Feast, in which all the fishing boats are decorated. Street parades are held for the Feast of the Rose of Lima (La Rose), on 30 August, and for the Feast of St Margaret

Mary Alacoque (La Marguerite), on 17 October, which are big rival flower festivals. 22 November is St Cecilia's Day, also known as Musician's Day (St Cecilia is the patron saint of music). The most important day, however, is 13 December, St Lucy's Day, or the National Day, on which cultural and sporting activities are held throughout the island. This used to be called Discovery Day, but as Columbus' log shows he was not in the area at that time, it was renamed (see **History**). St Lucy, the patron saint of light, is honoured by a procession of lanterns accompanied by traditional music and mouth watering local foods. For details contact Castries City Council, T 452 2611 ext 7071. Some processions start around 0400 and are all over by midday.

CASTRIES

The capital, *Castries*, (population 60,000) is splendidly set on a natural harbour against a background of mountains. The town was originally situated by Vigie and known as Carenage (the dock to the W of Pointe Seraphine is still referred to as Petit Carenage). An area of disease and defensively vulnerable, it was moved in 1768 and renamed Castries after the Minister of the French Navy and the Colonies, Marechal de Castries. It was guarded by the great fortress of Morne Fortune (Fort Charlotte and Derrière Fort). There is a spectacular view from the road just below Morne Fortune where the town appears as a kaleidoscope of red, blues, white and green: it promises much. However it can be a disappointment as, close to, the town is thoroughly modern but this is more than compensated by the bustle of its safe streets. Castries is twinned with Taipei, in China, who have provided all of the town's litter bins (most of which are not used, full, or destroyed).

Largely rebuilt after being destroyed by four major fires, the last in 1948, the commercial centre and government offices are built of concrete. Only the buildings to the S of Derek Walcott Square and behind Brazil Street were saved. Here you will see late 19th and early 20th century wooden buildings built in French style with three storeys, their gingerbread fretwork balconies overhanging the pavement. *Chez Paul* restaurant, 1885, is a fine example as is Marshalls pharmacy further along the street. The other area which survived was the market on the N side of Jeremie Street. Built entirely of iron in 1894, it was conceived by Mr Augier, member of the Town Board, to enhance the appearance of the town and also provide a sheltered place where fruit and produce could be sold hygienically. Covered with rather flaky red paint, the fine old clock has been repaired and now tells the exact time. The foodstalls sell cold drinks and bottled Guinness. Other items include basket work, T-shirts, leeches, spices and hot pepper sauce. A new market is being built next door to house the many fruit sellers who currently sell their huge selection on Jeremie Street and the market steps.

Derek Walcott Square was the site of the Place D'Armes in 1768 when the town transferred from Vigie. Renamed Promenade Square, it then became Columbus Square in 1893. In 1993 it was renamed Derek Walcott Square in honour of Derek Walcott, the poet (see above, **Culture**). It was the original site of the Courthouse and the market. The library is on its W side. The giant Saman tree is about 400 years old. On its E side lies the Cathedral which, though sombre outside, bursts into colour inside. Suffused with yellow light, the side altars are often covered with flowers while votive candles placed in red, green and yellow jars give an almost fairy tale effect. The ceiling, supported by delicate iron arches and braces is decorated with large panelled portraits of the apostles. Above the central altar with its four carved screens, the apse ceiling has paintings of five female saints with St Lucy in the centre. The walls have murals of the work of the church around the island painted by Dunstan St Omer, probably the most famous of St Lucia's artists.

As you wander around the town, note the Place Jean Bapiste Bideau (a sea captain who dedicated his life to freedom and heroically saved the life of Simón Bolívar) and the mural on Manoel Street by the St Lucia Banana Growers Association building. It was painted in 1991 by Dunstan St Omer and two of his sons and depicts scenes of St Lucian life: banana boats, tourism, 18th century sea battles, the king and queen of the flower festivals and Carib indians.

On the outskirts of Castries is **Pointe Seraphine**, a duty-free complex (see below, **Shopping**), near the port. From Cas-

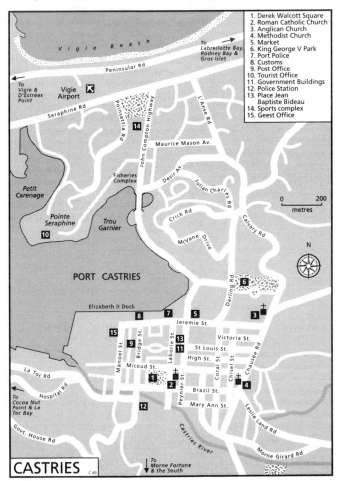

1. Derek Walcott Square
2. Roman Catholic Church
3. Anglican Church
4. Methodist Church
5. Market
6. King George V Park
7. Port Police
8. Customs
9. Post Office
10. Tourist Office
11. Government Buildings
12. Police Station
13. Place Jean Baptiste Bideau
14. Sports complex
15. Geest Office

CASTRIES C 49

tries take the John Compton Highway N towards Vigie airport and branch off just past the new fish market. All of the goods are priced in US dollars and it consists largely of chic boutiques. The Tourist Board head office is here, open 0800-1630 Monday-Friday, and there is an information desk serving the cruise ship passengers. NB There are plenty of people who will "mind your car" here. Ignore them. The rather curious pyramid-shaped building is the Alliance Française, the French cultural centre built in conjunction with the St Lucia Ministry of Education. If you continue on the John Compton Highway past the sports complex and at the traffic lights turn left to go to the airport, you are sandwiched between the runway on your left and the beautiful Vigie beach on your right. There is a small war cemetery here mostly commemorating those from the British West Indies regiment who lost their lives. You can drive around Vigie point, there is much evidence of the colonial past. The St Lucia National Trust has its headquarters here in an old barrack.

Just S of Castries you can walk (unfortunately only on the main road, allow about one hour each way) or drive to the Governor's Mansion with its curious metalwork crown, at the top of Mount Morne. From here carry on to **Fort Charlotte**, the old Morne Fortune fortress (now Sir Arthur Community College). You will pass the Apostles' battery (1888) and Provost's redoubt (1782). Each has spectacular views, but the best is from the Inniskilling Monument at the far side of the college (the old Combermere barracks) where you get an excellent view of the town, coast, mountains and Martinique. It was here in 1796 that General Moore launched an attack on the French. The steep slopes give some idea of how fierce the two days of fighting must have been. As a rare honour, the 27th Inniskillings Regiment were allowed to fly their regimental flag for one hour after they took the fortress before the Union Jack was raised. The college is in good condition having been carefully restored in 1968. On returning to Castries, branch left at the Governor's mansion to visit La Toc point with its luxury *Sandals* hotel. Take the road to the hotel through its beautiful gardens and take the path to the right of the security gate if you want to visit the beach. Further on is the road leading to Bagshaws studio. Down a long leafy drive, you can buy attractive prints and visit the printshop to watch the screen printing process. Max, a blue green Guyanese Macau, has been in residence for 17 years. Open Monday-Friday 0830-1600, Saturday 0830-1200.

North to Pointe du Cap

The part of the island to the N of Castries is the principal resort area, it contains the best beaches and the hotels are largely self contained. It is the driest part of the island with little evidence of the banana plantations or rain forest. The John Compton highway leaves Castries past Vigie airport and follows the curves of Vigie Beach and Choc Bay. Where the road leaves the bay and just before it crosses the Choc river, a right turn to Babonneau will take you past the **Union Agricultural station** (about one mile) where there is a nature trail and interpretive centre. A mini zoo boasts a pair of St Lucian parrots. The trail goes through a nursery and herbal garden before going through Caribbean pine trees, latanier palms and cinnamon and bay trees. It takes about 20 mins.

Back on the main highway, the road passes the turning to **Labrellotte Bay** (dominated by the *Windjammer Hotel*) before reaching Rodney Bay and the town of Gros Islet. Here is the site of the US Naval Air Station of **Reduit**. Built in February 1941, the swamps were reclaimed and the bay dredged. It was the first of a chain of bases established to protect the Panama Canal. Acting as a communications centre (code name "Peter Item"), it supported a squadron of sea planes. The base was eventually closed in 1947. The whole area now supports a mass of tourist facilities including the *St Lucian* and *Royal St Lucian* hotels, restaurants and sport facilities. You can pass through the entrance gates of the old Naval Air Station or take the next left turn off the main road to reach the hotels and restaurants. If you drive past them all to the end of the road there is good access to the beach. Rodney Bay is an excellent base for watersports; it is ideal for windsurfing. At the back of the development is a 1,000-boat marina. Development is still taking place and at Rodney Heights a huge area has been set aside for condominiums. The normally sleepy fishing village of Gros Islet holds a popular jump-up in the street each Friday night, from 2200, music, dancing, bars, cheap food, rather touristy but still highly recommended for night owls. Try the grilled conch from one of the booths selling local dishes.

About ¾ mile after Elliot's Shell filling station on the outskirts of Gros Islet, turn left to Pigeon Island National Landmark (see also above, **Fauna and Flora**), once an island, now joined to the mainland by causeway. The park was opened by Princess Alexandra on 23 February 1979 as part of St Lucia's Independence celebrations. It has two peaks which are joined by a saddle. The higher rises to a height of about 360 feet. Owned and managed by the National Trust, the island is of considerable archaeological and historical interest. Amerindian remains have been found, the French pirate François Leclerc (known as Jamb de Bois for his wooden leg) used the large cave on the N shore and the Duke of Montagu tried to colonize it in 1722 (but abandoned it after one afternoon). From here, Admiral Rodney set sail in 1782 to meet the French navy at the Battle of Les Saintes (see under Guadeloupe). It was

captured by the Brigands (French slaves freed by the leaders of the French revolution) in 1795 but retaken in 1798 by the English. Used as a quarantine centre from 1842 it was abandoned in 1904 but became an US observation post during World War ll. The island finally became the home of Josset Agnes Huchinson, a member of the D'Oyly Carte Theatre who leased the island from 1937 to 1976. The bay became a busy yacht haven and "Joss" held large parties to entertain the crews. Her abandoned house can still be seen on the S shore of the island. On the lower of the two peaks lies Fort Rodney. There is a steep climb but well worth it for the 360° panorama. The museum (located in the Officers' Mess and recently rebuilt to the original design) contains an interesting display of the work of the National Trust as well as a comprehensive interpretive exhibition. There is a small entrance fee (EC$3, open every day 0900-1800; museum closed Sundays). The park also contains *Les Pigeones* restaurant which is recommended for snacks and a cool drink (open 0900-1600, closed Saturdays). You can swim off the small beach, although sandy, it has a lot of broken coral. The park is a good place for watching sea birds. Four peacocks also roam freely over the park. Offshore are the remains of the Castries telephone exchange, donated to the Fisheries Department by Cable and Wireless to make an artificial reef. You can walk to Pigeon Island along Rodney Bay. Take plenty of sun creams and protective clothing as there is no shade on the walk.

The road N passes through the Cap estate (golf course and the *Club St Lucia*) to Pointe du Cap, a viewpoint some 470 feet high with a splendid panorama along the coast. If you wish to explore further the N part of the island contact Safari Adventures Ltd (T 452 8778) who run all terrain vehicles to Cas-en-Bas beach. A good circular walk from Gros Islet can be done to Cas-en-Bas taking the road past *La Panache Guesthouse* (ask the owner, Henry Augustin for directions if necessary, he is always willing to help) down to the beach (sheltered, shady, a bit dirty), then following tracks N until you reach the golf course, from where you return along the W coast to Gros Islet. You will see cacti, wild scenery, Martinique and no tourists. The sea is too rough to swim. If exploring the Atlantic beaches by vehicle, make sure it is 4-wheel drive, check your spare tyre and tools, take OS map and water, be prepared to park and walk, and if possible take a local person with you. Always take local advice on the state of the roads, which change quickly. For more details, see above, **Beaches and Watersports**.

The road to Monchy from Gros Islet is a pleasant drive inland through several small villages. You gradually leave the dry N part of the island and climb into forest. The ridge between Mount Monier and Mount Chaubourg gives particularly impressive views over the E coast. You will also pass through Paix Bouche where it is thought that Napoleon's empress Josephine was born. There are no road signs. Watch out for the names on schools and if in doubt at junctions bear W. At the larger village of Babonneau, you can turn right to follow the river down to the coast at Choc Bay or go straight on to Fond Cacao where a W turn will take you back to Castries. The road to Forestière is the access point for the climb to Piton Flor (1,871 feet).

East Coast to Vieux Fort

The transinsular highway from Castries to Vieux Fort has been completely repaved for most of the 33 miles to the S. Leaving Castries, one gets an increasingly good view of the town and harbour as the road climbs to the "top of the morne", over a thousand feet. The road goes through extensive banana plantations with the occasional packaging plant through the village of Ravine Poisson before climbing steeply over the Barre de l'Isle, the mountain barrier that divides the island. There is a short, self-guided trail at the high point on the road between Castries and Dennery, which takes about 10 mins and affords good views of the rainforest and down the Rouseau valley. There is a small picnic shelter. It is neglected and can be slippery after rain. The experience is rather spoilt by the noise of traffic. A longer walk to Mount La Combe can also be undertaken from this point although it is overgrown and easy to get lost. The Forestry Department may provide guides for the day for a fee. Unfortunately there have been incidents of tourists being robbed here, so caution is advised.

The road descends through Grande Rivière to Dennery where the vegetation is mostly xerophytic scrub. Dennery is set in a sheltered bay with Dennery Island guarding its entrance and dominated by the Roman Catholic church. Here you can see the distinctive St Lucia fishing boats pulled up on the beach. Carved out of single tree trunks, the bows are straight and pointed rather than curved and are all named with phrases such as "God help me". A US$6mn fishing port has been built with improved moorings, cold storage and other facilities, with Japanese assistance. There are lots of small bars but no other facilities. You can follow the Dennery River inland towards Mount Beaujolais. At Errard there is a photogenic waterfall. Permission should be obtained from the estate office before attempting this trip. A plantation tour with lunch and hotel transfers costs US$50. You will be driven around the estate by the owner who explains how cocoa is processed and points out different fruits.

Fregate Island Nature Reserve, on the N side of Praslin Bay has a small but interesting visitor centre. The two small islands provide nesting sites for the frigate bird and the N promontory of Praslin bay gives a good vantage point. The reserve is closed from May-July during the breeding season. At other times call the National Trust, T 452 5005 for a guide. The area is also of some historical interest as there was an Amerindian lookout point in the reserve. It was also the site of a battle between the English and the Brigands. It used to be known as Trois Islet and the nearby Praslin River is still marked as Trois Islet river on maps today.

Praslin is noted as a fishing community with traditional boat building. The road leaves the coast here and goes through banana plantations and the villages of Mon Repos and Patience. Mon Repos is a good area to witness the flower festivals of La Rose and La Marguerite. The coast is regained at Micoud. There are one or two restaurants (including *Palm*, simple and clean), a department store, post office and a branch of Barclays bank. Between here and Savannes is the proposed site of Ivan Lendl's tennis camp, the *Troumassee Resort Hotel*. It is also the centre of St Lucia's wine industry: banana, guava, pineapple and sugar cane brewed and bottled under "Helen Brand".

Mangrove swamps can be seen at Savannes Bay Nature Reserve. The bay is protected by a living reef and is a very active fishing area. The shallow bay is excellent for the cultivation of sea moss, an ideal breeding ground for conch and sea eggs. Scorpion island lies in the bay and to the N are more archaeological sites on Saltibus Point and Pointe de Caille (the latter excavated by the University of Vienna in 1983 and 1988).

After about three miles you reach **Vieux Fort** (population 14,000), the island's industrial centre, where the Hewanorra international airport is situated. It is a bustling town with a good Saturday market, a lot of traditional housing and gaily-painted trucks for transport, although they are gradually being replaced by the ubiquitous Toyota vans. The area is markedly less sophisticated than the N of the island. The town boasts lots of supermarkets. The post office is on Theo-

dore Street which with the police station is right in the middle of the town. Fishing boats are pulled up on the small beach but there is no proper beach here. On Clarke Street you will pass the square with a war memorial and band stand. The bus terminal is being relocated to a site at the end of Clarke Street near the airport. Vieux Fort makes a good base for exploring the S of the island.

The perimeter road skirts Anse de Sables beach (no shade), the base for *Club Med* watersports and looks across to the Maria Islands. The interpretive centre on the beach is not always open. If you want to visit Cap Moule à Chique, turn left at the T junction and follow the road to the banana loading jetty (you will pass truck after truck waiting to be weighed). Bear left and go up a badly maintained track. Finally go left again through the Cable and Wireless site up to the lighthouse. The duty officer will be glad to point out the views including the Pitons, Morne Gomier (1,028 ft) with Morne Grand Magazin (2,022 ft) behind it. Unfortunately Morne Gimie ((3,118 ft) is largely obscured. Further to the E is Piton St Esprit (1,919 ft) and Morne Durocher (1,055 ft) near Praslin. The lighthouse itself is 730 feet above sea level and also has good views over the Maria islands and SW to St Vincent.

The West Coast to Soufrière and the Pitons

Take the transinsular highway out of Castries and instead of branching left at Cul de Sac bay carry straight on. The road quickly rises to La Croix Maingot where you get good views of the Roseau banana plantation. On reaching the Roseau valley take the signposted road to Marigot Bay (plenty of "guides" waiting to pounce). A good place to stop for a drink, the *Marigot Bay Resort* dominates both sides of the valley. In between is a beautiful inlet which is a natural harbour and provided the setting for *Dr Doolittle*. It supports a large marina and not surprisingly a large number of yachts in transit berth here to restock with supplies from the supermarket and chandler. You will notice a small strip of land jutting out into the bay. This has a small beach (not particularly good for swimming) and can be reached by the *gingerbread express* (a small, complimentary water taxi) either from the hotel or the customs post. It is a good place for arranging watersports and the staff of the resort are most helpful. There is a police station and immigration post here. High above the bay are *JJ's* and *Albert's* bars, popular alternatives to Gros Islet on Friday nights. You can also eat well at *JJ's*, a much cheaper alternative to the expensive restaurants at Marigot Bay. The main road continues to Soufrière and passes through the fishing villages of **Anse La Raye** and **Canaries** (no facilities).

NOTE that this road is spectacular with lots of bends, panoramic views of the Pitons and the coast and many ups and downs through lush valleys. In 1992/93 it was completely reconstructed as far as Canaries. From there to Soufrière work continues and the road is only open after 1800 in the week and all day on Sundays when the men are not working; very slow but beautiful driving. The work was expected to be completed mid-1995. Check with the tourist authorities to make sure that it is open.

After Canaries the road goes inland and skirts Mount Tabac (2,224 ft) before descending into **Soufrière** (population 9,000). This is the most picturesque and interesting part of the island, with marvellous old wooden buildings at the foot of the spectacular Pitons, surrounded by thick vegetation and towering rock formations looming out of the sea. Note that Petit Piton is dangerous to climb (several people have fallen off in recent years) and also that it is restricted Crown Lands. This does not stop local guides offering to show visitors up, though. Because of its location, the town is a must for tourists although it is not geared for people want-

ing to stay there and nobody seems bothered about visitors. It can help to have an hotel guide or dayboat skipper with you. In any event it is not cheap, expect to be charged for everything (see warnings under **Information for Visitors**). A stay in this town within view of the majestic Pitons is well worth while. Indeed, it is essential if you have no transport of your own and want to see the volcano and the Pitons, as there are no buses back to Castries after midday (particularly while the road is up) unless you make a roundabout journey via Vieux Fort. To do this, leave Castries at 0800, the ride can take 2 hrs. After visiting Soufrière, wait at the corner opposite the church and ask as many people as possible if they know of anyone going to Vieux Fort; you will get a lift before you get a bus. It is important to get off at Vieux Fort 'crossroads', where there are many buses returning to Castries by another route, 1¼ hrs. Buses to Castries leave from the market area. If you arrive by boat head for the N end of the bay, you will find plenty of help to tie up your yacht (EC$5) and taxis will appear from nowhere. It is a much cheaper alternative to tying up at the jetty. Organized tours are available from the hotels further N, by sea or road, from around US$65 including lunch, drinks, transfers and a trip to Soufrière, Diamond Gardens and the Sulphur Springs (see below).

Soufrière is a charming old West Indian town dating back to 1713 when Louis XIV of France granted the lands around Soufrière to the Devaux family. The estate subsequently produced cotton, tobacco, coffee and cocoa. During the French Revolution, the guillotine was raised in the square by the Brigands but the Devaux family were protected by loyal slaves and escaped. It is situated on a very picturesque bay totally dominated by the pitons. The water here is extremely deep and reaches 200 feet only a few yards from the shore, which is why boats moor close in. To reach Anse Chastanet from here take the rough track at the N end of the beach (past the yacht club) about one mile. This is an absolute must if you enjoy snorkelling (the S end near the jetty is superb but keep within the roped off area). The hotel has a good and inexpensive restaurant (although if you are on a budget you may prefer to take a picnic) and the dive shop is extremely helpful, they will hire out equipment by the hour. The *Unicorn* and day boats often stop here for a brief swim in the afternoon on their return to Castries.

Most visitors come to the town to see the Diamond Gardens and Waterfall and the Sulphur springs. There are no road signs in Soufrière and locating these two places can be difficult (or expensive if forced to ask). From the square take the road E past the church and look for a right hand turning to reach the **Diamond Gardens**. These were developed in 1784 after Baron de Laborie sent samples taken from sulphur springs near the Diamond river to Paris for analysis. They found minerals present which were equivalent to those found in the spa town of Aix-la-Chapelle and were said to be effective against rheumatism and other complaints. The French King ordered baths to be built. Despite being destroyed in the French Revolution, they were eventually rebuilt and can be used by members of the public for about EC\$6.50. The gardens are well maintained and many native plants can be seen. Only official guides are allowed in, do not accept offers from those at the gates. Entrance EC\$5 (children EC\$2.25), open daily 1000-1700, T 452 4759.

To get to the **Sulphur Springs** take the Vieux Fort road between wooden houses about half way along the S side of Soufrière square. Originally a huge volcano about eight miles in diameter, it collapsed some 40,000 years ago leaving the W part of the rim empty (where you drive in). The sign welcomes you to the world's only drive-in volcano, although actually you have to stop at a car park and enter with a guide. The sulphur spring is the only one still active, although there are seven cones within the old crater as well as the pitons which are thought to be volcanic plugs. Tradition has it that the Arawak deity *Yokahu* slept here and it was therefore the site of human sacrifices. The Caribs were less superstitious but still named it *Qualibou*, the place of death. There is a small village of about 40 inhabitants located inside the rim of the volcano. Water is heated to 180°F and in some springs to 275°F. It quickly cools to about 87°F below the bridge at the entrance. There has been much geothermal research here since 1974. From the main viewing platform, you can see over a moonscape of bubbling, mineral rich, grey mud. It is extremely dangerous to stray onto the grey area. The most famous "crater" was formed a few years ago when a local person fell into a mud pocket. He received third degree burns. There are good, informative guides (apparently compulsory) on the site but you must be prepared to walk over uneven ground. Allow approximately ½ hour. Entrance EC\$3, open every day 0900-1700. South of Soufrière, in the valley between Petit Piton and Gros Piton, a luxury all-inclusive resort, *Jalousie Plantation*, has been built despite complaints from ecological groups and evidence from archaeologists that it is located on a major Amerindian site. An important burial ground is believed to be under the tennis courts and there have been many finds of petroglyphs and pottery.

The road from Soufrière to Vieux Fort takes about 40 mins by car. The branch of the road through Fond St Jacques runs through lush rain forest and a track takes you to the W end of the rain forest trail. In a few miles the road rapidly descends from Victoria Junction (1,200 ft) to the coastal plain at Choiseul. Choiseul is a quaint old West Indian village – there is a fish market and church on the beach. You can visit Caraibe Point from here: the last place on St Lucia where Caribs still survive, living in simple thatched houses. On the S side of Choiseul is the Art and Craft development centre sponsored by China. Experts from Taiwan are teaching St Lucians skills in bamboo handicrafts and you can buy pottery and carvings, as well as baskets. Bigger pieces of furniture are made from mahogany in the workshops at the back of the complex. There is a snack bar.

INFORMATION FOR VISITORS

● Documents
Citizens of the UK, USA and Canada may enter with adequate proof of identity, as long as they do not intend to stay longer than 6 months. A British Visitors Passport is valid. Citizens of the Organization of Eastern Caribbean States (OECS) may enter with only a driving licence or identity card. Visas are not required by nationals of all Commonwealth countries, all EEC countries except Eire and Portugal, all Scandinavian countries, Switzerland, Liechtenstein, Turkey, Tunisia, Uruguay and Venezuela. Anyone else needs a visa; check requirements, duration of validity, cost, etc at an embassy or high commission. Without exception, visitors need a return ticket. You also need an address for where you are staying.

On arrival you will be given a 42-day stamp in your passport. The immigration office at the central police station in Castries is very bureaucratic about extensions; they cost EC$40 per period and it is worth getting one up to the date of your return ticket.

● How To Get There
The only direct scheduled services from Europe are with BWIA or British Airways from London, or BWIA once a week from Frankfurt. From the USA, Leisure Air and American Airlines have direct flights from New York, American Airlines and BWIA direct from Miami. American Airlines connects with other US cities through San Juan, Puerto Rico, from where there are daily flights. Air Canada flies from Toronto, Leisure Air flies from Georgetown, Guyana, and LIAT flies from Caracas. There are excellent connections with other Caribbean islands: from Anguilla (LIAT), Antigua (LIAT, BWIA and British Airways), Barbados (LIAT and British Airways),

Carriacou (LIAT), Dominica (LIAT), Grenada (LIAT, BWIA), Guadeloupe (LIAT), Martinique (LIAT, Air Martinique), Tortola, BVI (LIAT), St Vincent (LIAT, Air Martinique), Trinidad and Tobago (BWIA and LIAT) and Union Island (LIAT, Air Martinique).

St Lucia has 2 airports: Vigie Airport, for inter-island flights only (2 miles from Castries, taxi for EC$12, no exchange facilities), and Hewanorra International Airport in the Vieux Fort district, where international flights land; there is an air shuttle to Vigie by helicopter, 12 mins. Alternatively a taxi to Castries costs EC$120 (though, out of season, you can negotiate a cheaper rate) and it will take you 1½-2 hrs to reach the resorts N of Castries. If you are travelling light you can walk to the main road and catch the minibus or route taxi to Castries, or if you are staying in Vieux Fort you can walk there. No baggage storage yet available at Hewanorra. Try to arrange it with one of the Vieux Fort hotels. Porters expect a tip of EC$0.50 at Vigie and EC$0.75 at Hewanorra.

At both airports there is a departure tax of EC$27 and a security charge of EC$10; if you leave with LIAT you will be charged EC$37 departure tax.

● Airline Offices
The following airlines have offices on Brazil Street, Castries: LIAT (T 452 3051, or at Hewanorra airport T 454 6341, or Vigie airport T 452 2348, F 453 6584), Air Canada (T 453 1517, at Hewanorra T 454 6249) and BWIA (T 452 3778/3789 and at Hewanorra T 454 5075, F 454 5223); British Airways is at Cox and Co Building, William Peter Boulevard (T 452 3951, F 452 2900 and at Hewanorra T 454 6172); Air Martinique, Vigie Airport (T 452 2463); Air France, c/o Minvielle and Chastanet, Bridge St, T 452 2811; Air Guadeloupe, T 452 2216; American Airlines, Hewanorra Airport (T 454 6777, 454 6779, 454 6795, F 454 5953). Eagle Air Services, at Vigie, T 452 1900. Helenair, at Vigie, T 452 7196, F 452 7112.

● Shipping
The island is served by several shipping lines, including Geest Industries: cargo and passenger vessels; Harrison Lines: cargo vessels only; West Indies Shipping Corporation; also local trading schooners. Windward Lines Ltd operate a weekly passenger and cargo ferry service linking Venezuela (Guiria or Pampatar, Margarita), Trinidad, St Vincent, Barbados and St Lucia, arriving St Lucia 0800 Sat, departing

0800 Sun, fare St Lucia to Venezuela US$100 one way, rate does not include port taxes, embarcation fees, transfers or food; child reductions, restaurant on board, rec for good way to see lots of islands at reasonable price. For information contact Windward Lines Ltd, Mendes Shipping, Valco Building, Cadette St, Castries, T 452 1364, or Global Steamship Agencies Ltd, Mariner's Club, Wrightson Road, PO Box 966, Port of Spain, Trinidad, T 809-624 2279, F 627 5091. Many cruise lines call. There is a US$10 pp tax on cruise ship passengers.

● **Car Hire**

Cars and Suzuki jeeps can be rented. They are more expensive than on some islands because of all the extras which are included. Car hire starts at about US$50 a day, jeep rental is US$60 a day, US$295-390 a week; if you hire for 8 days you will be charged for one week and one day. Collision Damage Waiver is US$12/day, personal accident insurance US$12 a day, deposit US$250-400, or credit card. A 5% tax is added to everything. Car rental agencies include Avis, Vide Bouteille (T 452 2700, F 453 1536); Hertz headquarters at Rodney Bay (T 452 0680); National, Gros Islet Highway (T 452 8721, F 450 8577); also at Pointe Seraphine (T 453 0085), Le Sport (T 452 9066), Vigie airport (T 452 3050), Hewanorra airport (T 454 6699) and Club Med, Vieux Fort (T 454 6547); Royal (T 452 8833/452 0117); Budget, Marisule T 452 0233/452 8021, F 452 9362. Most have offices at the hotels, airports and in Castries. Check for charges for pick-up and delivery. If dropping off a car at Vigie airport you can sometimes leave the keys with the Tourist desk if there is no office for your car hire company. If you have an international driving licence a temporary licence can be obtained for free; if you only have a national permit, a temporary licence costs EC$30. If arriving at Vigie airport, get your international licence endorsed at the immigration desk (closed 1300-1500) after going through Customs. Car hire companies can usually arrange a licence. You can only hire a car if you are aged 25 or over. Drive on the left. Although there are about 500 miles of roads on the island only 281 are paved so be prepared for some rough driving. Filling stations are open Mon-Sat 0630-2000, selected garages open Sun and holidays 1400-1800. Leaded fuel costs EC$6, unleaded EC$6.50.

Water taxis and speedboats can be rented. Waynes Motorcycle Centre, Vide Bouteille, rents bikes; make sure you wear a helmet and have adequate insurance, potholes are everywhere.

● **Taxi**

Fares are supposedly set by the Government, but the EC$95 Castries-Soufrière fare doubles as unlucky tourists discover that there are no buses for the return journey. *Club St Lucia*, in the extreme N, to Castries, about 10 miles away, costs EC$40 one way. Fare to or from Gros Islet (for Fri evening street party), EC$30; to Pigeon Island National Park, EC$35 one way; to Vigie airport, EC$12; to Hewannora airport, EC$120; Vigie airport to Gros Islet and Rodney Bay EC$40. If in doubt about the amount charged, check with the tourist office or hotel reception. You can see a copy of the fixed fares at the airport. A trip round the island by taxi, about US$20 per hour for 1-4 people, can be arranged. Many agencies operate tours of the island. Coach tours are cheaper and are usually daily in high season, falling to once or twice a week off season, ask in hotels. Coach tours of the S of the island can be frightening, however, as the roads are narrow and extremely bad. Alternatives are to go by boat (quicker and easy between Castries and Soufrière, some hotels have their own boats: *Anse Chastanet, Jalousie Plantation, Windjammer Landing* and *Sandals*) or by helicopter (rec for a spectacular view of the sulphur springs). From Pointe Seraphine a N island helicopter tour costs US$40, 10 mins; S island US$80, 20 mins; helicopters can also be hired for airport transfers, US$85 from Pointe Seraphine to Hewanorra, also pick-up from some hotels, St Lucia Helicopters, PO Box 2047, Gros Islet, T 453 6950 and Eastern Caribbean Helicopters, PO Box 1742, Castries, T 453 6952 at Vigie airport.

● **Buses**

It is much cheaper to go by bus. The service has been described as tiresome by some, but in 1994 one correspondent found it 'amazingly reliable', managing to get to Soufrière via Vieux Fort on a Sun and back the same day. St Lucia's buses are usually privately-owned minibuses and have no fixed timetable. The N is better served than the S and buses around Castries and Gros Islet run until 2200, or later for the Fri night Jump-up at Gros Islet. There are several bus stands in Castries: those going to Gros Islet and Rodney Bay leave from behind the market on Darling Road; to Dennery from the Customs shed on Jeremie Street; to Jacmal, Marigot (be prepared to walk over steep hill as few buses turn off into the bay), Bois D'Inde and Roseau Valley from Mongiroud Street (between Bridge and Micoud Streets); to Vieux Fort from Jno Baptiste Street off Darling Road. From Castries to Vieux Fort, EC$7; to Choc Beach, EC$1; to Soufrière, EC$6; to Dennery EC$2.25; to Gros Islet EC$1.50; to Morne Fortune EC$0.75. The road to Soufrière is very bad because of roadworks and buses take 2 hrs and leave before 1000. Check with the Tourist Board to ensure the road is open past Canaries before setting out. Ask the driver to tell you when your stop comes up, they are usually cooperative.

● **Where To Stay**

Many of the hotels are resorts, providing everything their guests need. Apart from those around Rodney Bay they are remote and you will have to arrange car hire or expensive taxis to get around the island or go to restaurants. All-inclusive resorts are usually, but not always booked from abroad. There is a 10-15% service charge and a 8% government tax on all hotel bills.

Working roughly N to S down the W coast, hotels include: *Club St Lucia*, T 450 0551, F 452 0281/450 9544, with 372 rooms, making it the island's largest hotel, rooms and family suites, an all-inclusive resort including free membership of the St Lucid Racquet Club on site, 7 tennis courts, gymnasium, squash court and swimming pool; *Le Sport*, in the N at Cap Estate, T 450 8551, F 450 0368, is for health and fitness lovers, lots of sporting facilities, massage, beauty salon, all-inclusive, rec; *Wyndham Morgan Bay Hotel*, T 450 2511, F 450 1050, all-inclusive, 240 rooms N of Castries on the beach, pool, watersports, tennis; *Rex St Lucian* (Reduit Beach, T 452 8351, F 452 8331), on the beach, 260 a/c rooms, 6 miles from Castries, diving, watersports, tennis, discotheque, restaurants; the *Royal St Lucian*, its sister property, next door, T 452 9999, F 452 9639, 98 luxury suites, interconnecting pools, swim up bar and waterfalls, restaurants, watersports, all facilities, very elegant. *Islander Hotel*, T 452 0255, F 452 0958, short walk to Reduit beach, or complimentary bus, 60 rooms or apartments, no watersports offered, but close to all Rodney Bay facilities; *Harmony Marina Suites*, on Rodney Bay lagoon, close to beach, T 452 8756, F 452 8677, recently modernized watersports inc canoeing; *East Winds Inn* (La Brelotte, T 452 8212, F 452 5434), 26 hexagonal

bungalow rooms, in tropical gardens close to the beach, all-inclusive; *Windjammer Landing*, Labrelotte Bay, (PO Box 1504, T 452 0913, F 452 0907, in the UK T 0800-373 742), probably the best villa complex with hotel facilities, 1-bedroomed suites clustered together, 2/4-bedroomed villas US$240-350d more spread out with own plunge pool, luxury resort, tennis and all watersports available, on the beach, honeymoon, family, diving packages available, rec; *Sandals Halcyon*, Choc Beach, T 453 0222, F 451 8435, all-inclusive, opened 1994, couples only, all facilities interchangeable with *La Toc*, transport between 2 sites; *Rendezvous* (Vigie Beach, T 452 4211, F 452 7419), couples only, all inclusive, top quality, has some self-catering cottages, many facilities, tennis, gym, jacuzzi, sauna, scuba, yacht cruises, lots of sports equipment, rec despite the noise of aircraft landing and taking off; *Green Parrot Inn*, The Morne (T 452 3399/452 3167, F 453 2272); *Top of the Morne Apartments*, Morne Fortune, T 452 3603/2531, F 453 1433, 1-2 bedrooms for 1-5 people, no credit cards, discounts given on car rental, food; *Sandals St Lucia La Toc*, T 452 3081/9, F 452 1012), luxuriously appointed, couples only, all-inclusive, tennis courts, golf course, watersports; *Hurricane Hole*, 9 miles S of Castries, where much of the *Dr Doolittle* film was made, and nearby *Oasis Marigot* comprise the *Marigot Bay Resort* (T 451 4357/451 4246, F 451 4353), a Club Mariner resort, dive shop, sailing, yacht chartering and watersports, there is a pleasant beach 300 yds away by ferry, also by ferry you can get to *Doolittle's bar and restaurant*, excellent but expensive, the swimming pool and bar (happy hour 1730-1830) overlook the marina; *Anse Chastanet Hotel* (Soufrière, T 459 7000, F 459 7700), 36 hillside and 12 beachside rooms, the best scuba diving on the island, diving packages available, watersports, tennis, lovely beach setting, isolated; *Humming Bird Beach Resort*, T 459 7232, F 459 7033 only 10 rooms and a hillside cottage, nice gardens, near Soufrière; *Jalousie Plantation*, Soufrière T 459 7666, F 459 7677, all inclusive, 115-room luxury resort built in 1991 amid much controversy over its location at the foot of the Pitons but very popular with guests, programmes include massage, sauna, jacuzzi and most sports, diving also available at extra cost; *Ladera Resort* (PO Box 225, Soufrière, T/F 459 7323, 459 0756), in spectacular setting between Gros Piton and Petit Piton, 1,000 ft up, 1-3 bedroomed villas and suites, an interesting design feature is the lack of a W wall in each unit to take maximum advantage of the wonderful view, every luxury here, plunge pools, swimming pools, maximum 50 guests, used to film *Superman II*, good restaurant; There is also a *Club Méditerranée* at Vieux Fort, T 454 6548, F 454 6017.

Several other apartment hotels and villas for rent. Full details from tourist offices. *Cloud's Nest Apartments* (Vieux Fort, T 454 6711), US$45-60 1-3 bedroom apartments; *Harmony Apartel* (Rodney Bay Lagoon, Reduit, T 452 8756, F 452 8677), studios, apartments, mini-mart, windsurfing, canoeing; *Villa Beach Cottage* (Choc Beach, T 450 2884/452 2691), no credit cards.

Guesthouses Castries: *Damascus*, 20 Victoria St, very good, EC$40s, EC$80d; *Lee's*, Chauseé Road, T 452 4285, noisy and no fan, US$24d EP with bath; *Chateau Blanc*, on Morne du Don Road 300m away, US$33d, not as good as its brochure implies, grubby, too few toilets etc for number of rooms, frequently no water or fans but good central location, food available, T 452 1851, F 452 7967; *Thelma's Guesthouse*, near Courts Store on Morne du Don Road, T 452 7313, US$20, pay cash in advance, TCs not accepted, fan, TV in rooms, private bathroom, kitchen, laundry, popular, clean and central, hot and noisy, recognizable by its bright red awnings; *Chesterfield*, Bridge St, T 452 1295, US$20-50, central.

Above the town on Morne Fortune are: *Dubois Guesthouse*, T 452 2201, F 452 7967, 4 rooms, US$20-40, a long way from anything but on bus route, wins prizes for cleanliness; *Hotel Bon Appetit*, nearby, T 452 2757, F 452 7967, beautiful view, clean, friendly, cable TV, restaurant, US$37-42 including breakfast, rec, book early for evening meal, popular.

Tapion Reef Apartment Hotel, just off La Toc road, T 452 7470, pool, access to beach, US$55-75, rec; *Tropical Haven*, La Toc, 10 mins by car from town, T 452 3505, F 452 5476, US$50d, 10 rooms and 2 apartments (negotiable), no credit cards, more than adequate, excellent food.

Sunset Lodge Guesthouse, near Vigie Airport T 452 2639, John Compton Highway, US$25-60, convenient, a/c, TV, restaurant, bar, nothing special, ask for a room away from the road; *Summersdale Hideaway*, 20 mins walk N of Vigie airport, off the main road and bus route, T 452 1142 for directions, US$17-20,

cheap restaurant.

Vide Bouteille (just outside Castries): *Beach Haven*, Vide Bouteille, 10 rooms, US$40-85, clean, comfortable, a/c, TV, 100m to sandy beach, restaurant with expensive food and breakfast, inexpensive fast food, public phone inside hotel, T 453 0065, F 453 6891; *E's Serenity Lodge*, 3 miles from Castries overlooking Choc Bay, T 452 1987, F 451 8600, 7 rooms, US$25-65, few facilities but good; *Modern Inn*, on the main road N of Castries, 3 km from Vide Bouteille, T 452 4001, US$18-40, friendly, good rooms, very clean and pleasant, breakfast available. In the hills at **Marisule**, a 15 mins' walk from La Brelotte Bay, the Zephirin family has cottages to let, self-catering, highly rec.

At **Gablewoods Mall**, *Sundale Guest House*, T 452 4120 is very popular, US$25-35 inc breakfast, own bathroom, check availability; nearby the *Friendship Inn*, T 452 4201, has rooms with kitchenette and baby sitting services, small pool, restaurant, from US$55; further N, *The Golden Arrow*, T 450 1832, clean, pleasant rooms from US$40, no single rooms, walking distance from beach and bus, friendly host; recently renovated, the *Orange Grove Hotel*, T 452 8213, is set in the hills of Bois d 'Orange, US$58-78, very comfortable, pool, complimentary bus to beach; *Parrots Hideaway*, T 452 0726, US$27-35, discounts for long stays, bar, restaurant, charming hostess.

At **Gros Islet**: *Alexander Guesthouse*, T 450 8610, a new building on Mary Thérèse St, 1 min from beach, US$20-30s, US$20-30, highly rec, clean, safe, friendly, helpful, kitchen, credit cards accepted; *Bay*, mini guest house, Bay Street, on village beach, T 450 8956, US$25s, US$35d, spacious rooms, fan, kitchen, fridge, bathroom, run by Klaus Koef: *La Panache*, PO Box 2074, T 450 0765, F 450 0453, on Cas-en-Bas Road, run by Henry Augustin, helpful and friendly, who can give information on Atlantic beaches and coastal walking, US$25s, US$35d inc tax and service, own bathroom, hot water, insect screens, clean, fans, good meals, créole dinners US$9 or dinners can be ordered from outside, snacks during day, bar with excellent alcoholic and non-alcoholic cocktails, laundry EC$10 per load, no food Fri nights when everyone goes to *Jump-up*, highly rec; *Nelson's Furnished Apartments* on Cas-en-Bas Rd, T 450 8275, US$25-38; opp Reduit beach, *Tuxedo Villas*, popular location, T 452 2418, US$70-100. Others include *B&B Guesthouse*, on Gros Islet highway, T 452 8689, F 452 1971, walking distance of Marina, beaches and Pigeon Island causeway, US$24-48, pizza restaurant attached; *Scott's Café/Bar*, EC$25, friendly but noisy location; *Daphil's*, US$25s.

Soufrière: there is a lack of good accommodation for the budget traveller, all guesthouses appear to charge about US$30d for a basic room without private facilities; *Soufrière Sailing Club Guest House*, T 459 7194, 4 rooms, US$30 room only, US$35 with breakfast, US$45 with dinner too, no credit cards; *Home Guesthouse*, US$25-35, T 459 7318, on the main square, clean, pay cash, TCs not accepted; *Tropical Palm Inn*, near hospital, US$18-35, it is possible to bargain cheaper rates for longer stays, friendly, basic, helpful, T 459 7487; *Claudina's*, very basic rooms with shower and toilet in courtyard of boutique of same name, kitchen facilities, cheaper than some. Mrs Mathurin, 18 Church Street, Soufrière, has rooms to rent, EC$40 for bed and cooking facilities, reduction for long stay.*The Still Plantation*, T 459 7261, from US$50, popular, pool, restaurant, some consider it overpriced for what you get; *Khayere Pann B+B*, T 459 7441, walking distance from shops and beach, US$45s, US$65d inc airport transfers, quiet, friendly, rec. There is an apartment to rent on the edge of Soufrière, new, basic but good, rates negotiable but competitive, PO Box 274, T 459 7269.

Vieux Fort: *St Martin*, on main street, clean, friendly, cooking and washing facilities, rec; *Kimatrai Hotel* (Vieux Fort, 5 mins from Hewanorra, T 454 6328), US$30-45, also has self-catering apartments; *Sky Way Inn*, T 454 7111, from US$85, 2 restaurants, night club, pool, shuttle service to airport and beach; *Il Pirata*, US$50, clean, welcoming motel, 5 mins from airport, restaurant, good breakfast, on beach.

Villa rentals for short or long terms can be arranged, usually with maid service and car hire: *Barnard Sons & Co*, Bridge St, Castries, T 452 2216, F 453 1394, PO Box 169; *Property Shop*, Rodney Bay, T 450 8288, F 450 0318; *Tropical Villas*, Cap Estate, Box 189, Castries, T 450 8240, F 450 8089; *Marlin Quay*, on the waterfront in Rodney Bay, is a villa resort offering rentals or purchases with a 37' yacht for combination holidays, currently 9 villas (opened late 1993), with plans for another 72 smaller units, luxurious, restaurant attached, pool, T 452 0393, F 452 0383, PO Box 2204 Gros Islet.

● **Camping**

Allowed on most beaches, but not rec, no facilities, lots of sandflies and very strong land crabs which could break into your tent. There are no official campsites.

● **Where To Eat**

All the large hotels have a selection of restaurants and there are snack bars and restaurants all along the W coast. Most places add on a 10% service charge, the menu usually specifies and it is rarely left to your discretion.

In **Castries** *Kimlans*, Derek Walcott Square, upstairs café and bar with verandah, cheap, serves local food, open 0700-2300 Mon-Sat, T 452 1136; on the opp side of the square on Bridge Street is *Chez Paul*, in a lovely old wooden mansion, several recs, pleasant balcony for lunchtime refreshment, from EC$18-30 (lunch is cheaper), open for breakfast, lunch and dinner from 0900-2300 Mon-Fri and 1100-2330 on Sun, T 453 1588; vegetarian and health foods are available from *The Natural Café* on Chauseé Rd, T 452 6421, open 0830-1800 Mon-Fri and 0900-1400 on Sat; there are several roti houses on Chauseé Rd, especially at S end, rec. **South of Castries** on The Top of the Morne, *Bon Appetit*, is rec for its daily specials and spectacular views, but is not cheap, meals from EC$35, T 452 2757; also on the Morne, *San Antoine*, is a plantation great house, lovely gardens, elegant dining room, open for lunch and dinner, expensive, T 452 4660, reservations requested; in the same area *The Green Parrot*, T 452 3399, 4-course dinner EC$95, serves excellent lunches daily for around EC$20, but waiters rather annoying, constantly seeking praise. **North of Castries** is *D's Restaurant*, on Vide Bouteille, indoor or on patio, special 3-course set menu at EC$25, rec, T 453 7931; *Jimmie's*, tucked away at Vigie Cove, great views of harbour at sunset, excellent for fresh fish and to sample the local vegetables, open for lunch and dinner, but expect to spend about EC$150 for 2 people in the evening, highly rec, T 452 5142; *Vigie Beach Bar*, beside *Rendezvous Hotel* serves good rotis and inexpensive cold beers; in Gablewoods Mall there are a selection of fast food outlets open from 0800-2100 daily. You can expect to pay just EC$30 for 2 people at *Chungs* Chinese restaurant at Choc Bay, service is often poor, but the food is delicious, closed from about 2100 and on Sun, T 452 4795.

Further N in the **Rodney Bay** area, *The Lime*

serves good meals and snacks at moderate prices, open from 1100 till late, closed Tues, T 452 0761; *The Ginger Lily* nearby is rec for its Chinese food, open 1130-1430 and 1830-2330, special lunch menu at EC$20, Tues-Sat, T 452 8303; *Capones* is a restaurant in the speakeasy style of the 1920s, open for dinner only and quite expensive, but attached to a *pizzeria*, open from 1100, with prices starting at EC$12, T 452 0284. Further along the road and directly on the beach at Reduit is *Spinnakers*, T 452 8350, lunch and dinner daily, with full English breakfast on Sat and Sun for EC$20, excellent location, though food and service suffer when it is busy, good too for coffee and deserts, they also hire out loungers for EC$5 a day. In the marina complex at Rodney Bay is *Key Largo*, T 452 0282, delicious, authentic, huge Italian pizzas, reasonably priced; call in also to *The Bread Basket* for lunch.

In the far N **Cap Estate** is *The Great House Restaurant*, traditional tea from 1430-1730 is worthwhile for watching the sunset, and affordable, dinner is extravagantly priced, T 450 0450; *Portias* on the road to Corinth is a fairly new restaurant with a large selection of affordable meals.

South of Castries, **Marigot Bay** has several hotels for lunch and dinner, but *JJ's Restaurant and Bar* on the road down to the bay is a cheaper alternative, specializes in fresh local dishes and seafood, open from 1000 till late, T 451 4076, Fri night jam session.

In **Soufrière**, *The Still* specializes in authentic St Lucian dishes, open daily 0800-1700 it is not cheap but serves local vegetables grown on site, T 459 7224; *Spotlight* near *Home Guesthouse* and Barclays Bank, good local food, tuna and kingfish rec, lunches and dinners EC$16-25; *The Humming Bird* is a good place to eat and take a swim, French, Créole and seafood, daily specials, reasonable food but reported overpriced, good views, open from 0700, T 454 7232; *Dasheene*, at *Ladera Resort*, good food, Austrian chef cooks with local produce, T 454 7850, wonderful views, rec, worth coming here even if only for a drink just for the views; The *Purity Bakery* near the church in the main square serves breakfast with good coffee, rolls and cakes; *Le Haut Plantation* on the W coast road serves excellent meals for about EC$20, very welcoming; at Étangs Soufrière, on the road to Vieux Fort, is *The Barbican* restaurant and bar, T 459 7888,

run by the very welcoming Mr and Mrs Smith, local food at local prices, good home cooking, not sophisticated, but clean, popular, rec.

Vieux Fort, *Il Pirata* is rec, Italian restaurant on the beach, prices from EC$25, attached to a motel, T 454 6610; close to Hewanorra airport is the *Chak Chak Café*, open from 0900 to midnight, T 454 6260.

● **Entertainment**

Most of St Lucia's night life revolves around the hotels, while some restaurants host live bands. The choice varies from steel bands, jazz groups, folk dancing, crab racing, fire eating and limbo dancers. The hotels welcome guests from outside and advertize the month's activities in *The Tropical Traveller*. In May, nightlife is dominated by the annual jazz festival with lots of outdoor concerts. *Splash Disco* at the *St Lucian Hotel* is the only European style disco on the island. At other places, but particularly around Rodney Bay, venues like *The Lime* and *The A Pub* are popular places for those who just want to hang out. The highlight of the week, for locals and visitors however, is Friday night's jump up at Gros Islet, where it is hard to resist getting involved (see above, **Gros Islet**). For a more cultural evening, tours are available to La Sikwi, patois for sugar mill, at Anse La Raye. There is a visit to the 150 year-old mill, followed by a full costume play reliving life in the village on a stage set into the hills with jazz bands and local acts. There is no cinema on the island.

● **Laundry**

There are no self-service launderettes on St Lucia, but there are dry cleaners at Rodney Bay, Gros Islet and Gablewoods Mall in the N of the island.

● **Shopping**

Pointe Seraphine, next to the main port in Castries, is a designer-built, duty-free shopping centre, with many tourist-oriented outlets, restaurants, entertainment and tour operators. Goods bought here can be delivered directly to the airport. Cruise ships can tie up at the complex's own berths. Batik fabrics and cotton clothing from Caribelle Batik on Old Victoria Rd, The Morne and Bridge St; Bagshaw's silk screening workshops at La Toc, T 452 2139, are very popular, studio open Mon-Fri 0830-1630, Sat 0830-1200, also shops at *Marigot* and *Windjammer*; souvenirs from Noah's Arkade, Jeremie Street, Castries, T 452 2523 and other branches at Rodney Bay opp *St Lucian Hotel*, Pointe Seraphine, Hewanorra duty free and Soufrière; local crafts and paintings from Artsibit, corner of Brazil and Mongiraud Streets, open Mon-Fri 0900-1700, Sat 0930-1300. Eudovics Art Studio, T 452 2747, in Goodlands, coming down from the Morne heading N, sells local handicraft and beautiful large wood carvings. Perfume from Caribbean Perfumes, by *Green Parrot*, T 453 7249. Sunshine Bookshop, Gablewoods Mall, books, foreign newspapers and magazines, open Mon-Fri 0830-1630, Sat half day; Book Salon, Jeremie Street on corner of Laborie Street, good selection of paperbacks, several books on St Lucia, also stationery. Rodney Bay Shipping Services runs a book exchange, 2 for one, mostly spy thrillers and light novels, not a huge selection, but useful.

Market day in Castries is Sat, very picturesque (much quieter on other days, speakers of Patois pay less than those who do not). In 1993 a contract was awarded for the construction of a new public market on the Castries waterfront, with the old market building to be renovated and turned into a craft market. There is a new Fisherman's Cooperative Market on the John Compton Highway at the entrance to Pointe Seraphine. Many fishermen still sell their catch wherever they can. Fish is cheap and fresh. JQ's supermarket at the traffic lights at the end of the Vigie runway, open Mon-Fri 0800-1900, Sat 0800-1600, bank next door, fair range of goods, also supermarket on Jeremie Street opp the Fire Station and on the William Peter Boulevard. Wholesale meat from Chicken Galore behind Shell station on Manoel Street. Gablewoods shopping Mall opened in 1992 in the N part of Castries with a selection of boutiques, gift shops, open air eating places and Julie N's Supermarket, open Mon-Thur until 2000, Fri, Sat until 2100. Next door is a delicatessen with a choice of frozen and defrosted foods. Rodney Bay Marina has a variety of shops: Pieces of Eight has a good choice of gifts, although few are made in St Lucia; Le Marché de France Supermarket is one of the few to open on Sun morning; the Bread Basket sells excellent fresh loaves, sandwiches and cakes. Soufrière has a market on the waterfront. At Choiseul, on the SW coast, there is an art and craft centre, T 459 3226. In Castries cold drinks are sold on street corners, EC$1 for a coke, drink it and return the bottle. Snokone ice cream vendors roam the beach and streets, a cup of ice cream should cost EC$2.

● **Banks**

Bank of Nova Scotia (T 452 2292), Royal Bank of Canada (T 452 2245), Canadian Imperial Bank of Commerce (T 452 3751), all on William Peter Boulevard, Castries; Barclays Bank (T 452 3306), and the St Lucia Cooperative Bank (T 452 2880), on Bridge Street, National Commercial Bank, Waterfront (T 452 3562), Castries. All have branches in Vieux Fort, and Barclays and National Commercial Bank in Soufrière; Barclays and Royal Bank of Canada at Rodney Bay marina. Royal Bank of Canada is reported better than Barclays for cash advances on credit cards. It is better to change currency at a bank than in a hotel where you can get 5-10% less on the exchange. There is no rate quoted for many currencies, such as Deutsch Marks; if you insist, Canadian banks will convert them first into Canadian dollars and then into EC dollars, but you get a poor rate. The Thomas Cook representative is on Brazil Street.

Banks opening hours vary, but most are open 0830-1500 Mon-Thur, 0830-1700 Fri. Barclays Bank at Rodney Bay opens Sat until 1200, as do the National Commercial Bank and Royal Bank of Canada in Castries.

● **Currency**

East Caribbean dollar.

● **Warnings**

When visiting the waterfalls and sulphur springs on Soufrière note that "guides" might expect large payments for their services. Be prepared to say no firmly, they are persistent and bothersome. Reports from St Lucia of harassment and hostility towards tourists declined in 1993/94 and personal safety has improved. However, you may still encounter problems on the West Road between Marigot Bay and Soufrière, on the Soufrière beaches and in other remote areas. The use and sale of narcotics is illegal and penalties are severe. Most readily available is marijuana, or 'wacky backy', which is frequently offered to tourists, but hard drugs are a problem. People staying at well-protected resorts and using organized tours generally have no problem. Be careful taking photographs, although everybody seems to be accustomed to cameras in the market.

● **Health**

Drinking water is safe in most towns and villages. Many rivers, however, cannot be described as clean and it is not recommended that you swim or paddle in them unless you are far upstream. There is bilharzia (see **Health Information**). The AIDS hotline is T 452 7170. Despite the breeze, the sun is strong. Take precautions, wear a hat and use high factor sun tan lotion (Banana Boat is a local range) or sun screens. There is a doctor's surgery on Manoel Street, Castries, Mon-Thur 0800-1330, 1715-1815, Fri 0800-1330. Dr King at Gablewoods Mall holds a morning surgery, appointments cost about EC$50, T 451 8688. Most villages have health centres. For emergency T 999; Victoria Hospital, Castries, T 452 2421/453 7059; St Jude's , Vieux Fort, T 454 6041, Soufrière Casualty, T 459 7258, Dennery, T 453 3310. Larger hotels have resident doctors or doctors 'on call', visits cost about EC$50. If given a prescription, ask at the Pharmacy whether the medication is available 'over the counter', as this may be cheaper.

● **Climate**
There is a dry season roughly from January to April, and a rainy season starting in May, lasting almost to the end of the year. The island lies in latitudes where the NE trade winds are an almost constant, cooling influence. The mean annual temperature is about 26°C. Rainfall varies (according to altitude) in different parts of the island from 60 to 138 inches.

● **Clothing**
Lightweight clothing all year; a summer sweater may be needed on cooler evenings. Short shorts and swimming costumes are not worn in town. An umbrella or light mac may be handy in the wet season.

● **Business Hours**
Shops: 0800-1230, 1330-1700 Mon-Fri (shops close at 1200 on Sat); banks: 0800-1300 Mon-Thur, although some are open until 1400-1500, plus 1500-1700 on Fri; government offices: 0830-1230, 1330-1600 Mon-Fri.

● **National Holidays**
New Year's Day, Carnival, Independence Day on 22 February, Good Friday, Easter Monday, Labour Day on 1 May, Whit Monday, Corpus Christi, Emancipation Day in August, Thanksgiving Day, National Day on 13 December, Christmas Day and Boxing Day.

● **Time Zone**
Atlantic Standard Time, 4 hours behind GMT, 1 ahead of EST.

● **Electric Current**
220v, 50 cycles.

● **Weights and Measures**
Most often imperial, though metric measurements are gradually being introduced.

● **Communications**
The island has an adequate telephone system, with international direct dialling, operated by Cable and Wireless, Bridge Street, Castries. There is a sub-office on New Dock Road, Vieux Fort. Telex and Fax facilities at both offices. Hotels do not generally allow direct dialling, you will have to go through the operator, which can be slow and costly. Intra-island calls are EC$0.25, no limit if on the same exchange, EC$0.25 for 90 seconds to another exchange. Pay phones use EC$0.25 and EC$1 coins. Cable and Wireless phone cards are sold for EC$10, EC$20 or EC$40; with these you can phone abroad. There is a credit card phone at Vigie airport operated via the boat phone network, open daily 0800-2200. The International code for St Lucia is 1809. Main Post Office is on Bridge Street, Castries, open Mon-Fri, 0830-1200, 1300-1630, Sat, 0800-1200, poste restante at the rear. Postcards to Europe EC$0.45, to the USA EC$0.45; letters to Europe EC$0.95, to the USA EC$0.85-0.90. The DHL office is on Bridge Street.

● **Media**
The Voice is a thrice-weekly paper (Tues, Thur and Sat), and *The Crusader* and *The Star* appear weekly. There is a commercial radio station, Radio Caribbean, which broadcasts daily in Patois and English, and a government-owned station, Radio St Lucia. A commercial television service operates in English only. There is lots of cable TV.

● **Tours**
Most hotels will arrange tours to the island's principal attractions either by road, boat or helicopter. Tours can also be arranged to coconut oil and other craft shops, fabric manufacturers, and so on. Local tour operators offer plantation tours; Errard, Marquis and Balembouche offer fascinating insights into colonial history and local environments. You can take a carriage ride through the N of the island, or spend an evening cruising into the sunset with as much champagne as you can drink.

● **Maps**
Maps of the island may be obtained from the Land Registry building on Jeremie Street. Ordnance Survey, Romsey Road, Southampton, UK (T 0703 792792), produce a map of St Lucia in their World Maps series which includes tour-

ist information such as hotels, beaches, climbing and climate. The Tourist Board map is free.

● **Diplomatic Representation**

UK: British High Commission, 24 Micoud Street, Derek Walcott Square, PO Box 227, Castries, T 452 2484, F 453 1543, open Mon-Fri 0830-1230. **Venezuelan** Embassy, Casa Vigie, PO Box 494, Castries, T 452 4033. **French** Embassy, Vigie, T 452 2462, open Mon-Fri 0800-1230, 1330-1600. **German** Consul, Inland Revenue Dept, Govt Building, Castries, T 452 2611, open Mon-Fri 0800-1230, 1330-1630. **Italian** Vice Consul, Reduit, PO Box GM 848, T 452 0865. **Embassy of the Republic of China**, Reduit, T 452 0643. **Organization of American States**, Vigie, T 452 4330. **Organization of Eastern Caribbean States**, Morne Fortune, T 452 2537.

● **Tourist Information**

St Lucia Tourist Board, Pointe Seraphine, PO Box 221, Castries, St Lucia, T 452 5968, Telex 6380 LC, F (809) 453 1121. There are Tourist Board information centres at the Pointe Seraphine Duty Free Complex; Vigie Airport (most helpful but closed for lunch 1300-1500), T 452 2596; Hewanorra Airport (very helpful, particularly with hotel reservations, only open when flights are due or leave), T 454 6644 and Soufrière (very helpful, local phone calls free), T 459 7419. *The Tropical Traveller* is distributed free to hotels, shops, restaurants etc every month and contains some extremely useful information. *Visions of St Lucia*, a quarterly magazine produced by the St Lucia Hotel and Tourism Association is also of a high standard and widely available.

USA: 9th Floor, 820 2nd Avenue, New York, NY 10017, T (212) 867-2950, Telex 023-666762, F (212) 370-7867.

Canada: 4975 Dundas Street West, Suite 457, Etobicoke D, Islington, Ontario, M9A 4X4, T 800 456 3984, F 416 2360937.

UK: 421a Finchley Road, London NW3 6HJ, T 071 4314045, F 071 4377920.

Germany: Postfach 2304, D-61293 Bad Homberg 1, T (06172) 30-44-31, Telex 041-411806, F (06172) 30-50-72.

France: ANI, 53 Rue François Ler, 7th floor, Paris 75008, T 47-20-3966, F 47-23-0965.

The editors would like to express their thanks to Susan Brazier, formerly resident in St Lucia, for a thorough updating of the St Lucia chapter.

ST VINCENT

ST VINCENT, and its 32 sister islands and cays which make up the Grenadines, were, until fairly recently, almost unknown to tourists except yachtsmen and divers, and are still uncrowded. St Vincent is very picturesque, with its fishing villages, coconut groves, banana plantations and fields of arrowroot, of which the island is the world's largest producer. It is a green and fertile volcanic island, with lush valleys, rugged cliffs on the leeward and windward coasts and beaches of both golden and black volcanic sand. The highest peak on the island is La Soufrière, an active volcano in the N rising to about 4,000 feet. It last erupted in 1979, but careful monitoring enabled successful evacuation before it blew. The steep mountain range of Morne Garu rises to 3,500 feet and runs southward with spurs to the E and W coasts. Most of the central mountain range and the steep hills are forested. St Vincent is roughly 18 miles long and 11 miles wide and has an area of 133 square miles, while the Grenadines contribute another 17 square miles all together.

About a quarter of the people live in the capital, **Kingstown** and its suburbs. 8% live on the Grenadines. 66% of the population is classed as black and 19% as mulatto, while 2% are Amerindian/black, 6% East Indian, 4% white and the remainder are 'others'.

History

By the time Columbus discovered St Vincent on his third voyage in 1498, the Caribs were occupying the island, which they called Hairoun. They had overpowered the Arawaks, killing the men but interbreeding with the women. The Caribs aggressively prevented European settlement until the 18th century but were more welcoming to Africans. In 1675 a passing Dutch ship laden with settlers and their slaves was shipwrecked between St Vincent and Bequia. Only the slaves survived and these settled and mixed with the native population and their descendants still live in Sandy Bay and a few places in the NW. Escaped slaves from St Lucia and Grenada later also sought refuge on St Vincent and interbred with the Caribs. As they multiplied they became known as "Black Caribs". There was tension between the Caribs and the Black Caribs and in 1700 there was civil war.

In 1722 the British attempted to colonize St Vincent but French settlers had already arrived and were living peaceably with the Caribs growing tobacco, indigo, cotton and sugar. Possession was hotly disputed until 1763 when it was ceded to Britain. It was lost to the French again in 1778 but regained under the Treaty of Versailles in 1783. However, this did not bring peace with the Black Caribs, who repeatedly tried to oust the British in what became known as the Carib Wars. A treaty with them in 1773 was soon violated by both sides. Peace came only at the end of the century when in 1796 General Abercrombie crushed a revolt fomented the previous year by the French radical Victor Hugues. In 1797, over 5,000 Black Caribs were deported to Roatán, an island at that time in British hands off the coast of Honduras. The violence ceased although racial tension took much longer to eradicate. In the late 19th century, a St Vincentian poet, Horatio Nelson Huggins wrote an epic poem about the 1795 Carib revolt and deportation to Roatán, called *Hiroona*, which was published in the 1930s. Nelcia Robinson, above Cyrus Tailor shop on Grenville Street, is an authority on Black

ST VINCENT C 50

Caribbean Sea

Baleine Bay
Fancy
Commantawana Bay
Salt Pond
Owia
Owia Bay
Sandy Bay

Falls of Baleine

Waterloo Mountains

Sandy Bay

Larikai Bay

La Soufrière 4173 ft

Overland Village

Wallibou Beach
Wallibou
Orange Hill

Petit Wallibou

Rabacca Dry River

Chateaubelair Island
Richmond
Morne Garu Mountains

Rose Bank
Chateaubelair
Richmond Peak 3523 ft
Mt. Brisbane 3058 ft
Georgetown

Troumaka Bay
Troumaka
Chester Cottage

Cumberland Bay
Rose Hall
Black Point

Coco
Spring Village
Colonarie Basin
South Rivers
Friendly

Wallilabou Bay
Hermitage

Barrouallie
Sans Souci
Colonarie Bay
North Union

Mt Wynne Bay
Petroglyph
6
Greiggs

Buccament Valley
Vermont
Mount St. Andrew 2413 ft
Biabou
Grant's Bay

Buccament Bay
Questelles
Camel
Mesopotamia
Peruvian Vale

Anse Cayenne
Camden Park
3
5
Evesham
Belmont
Petroglyph
Argyle Beach

Lowmans Bay
KINGSTOWN
Yambou Head
Mt Pleasant Beach

Johnson Pt
1
Stubbs
4

Kingstown Bay
Arnos Vale
Brighton Village
Stubbs Bay

Cane Garden Point
Villa
Calliaqua
Brighton Beach

Indian Bay
2
Sharp's Bay
Milligan Cay

N

1. Fort Charlotte
2. Young Island & Fort Duvernette
3. Botanical Gardens
4. Kings Hill Forest Reserve
5. Queen's Drive
6. Vermont Nature Trail

Caribs/Garifuna and is the coordinator of the Caribbean Organization of Indigenous People on St Vincent.

In the 19th century labour shortages on the plantations brought Portuguese immigrants in the 1840s and East Indi-ans in the 1860s, and the population today is largely a mixture of these and the African slaves. Slavery was abolished in 1832 but social and economic conditions remained harsh for the majority non-white population. In 1902, La Soufrière erupted, killing 2,000 people, just two days before Mont Pelée erupted on Martinique, killing 30,000. Much of the farming land was seriously damaged and economic conditions deteriorated further. In 1925 a Legislative Council was inaugurated but it was not until 1951 that universal adult suffrage was introduced.

St Vincent and the Grenadines belonged to the Windward Islands Federation until 1959 and the West Indies Federation between 1958 and 1962. In 1969 the country became a British Associated State with complete internal self-government. Government during the 1970s was mostly coalition government between the St Vincent Labour Party (SVLP) and the People's Political Party. In 1979 St Vincent and the Grenadines gained full independence, but the year was also remembered for the eruption of La Soufrière on Good Friday, 13 April. Fortunately no one was killed as thousands were evacuated, but there was considerable agricultural damage. In 1980 Hurricane Allen caused further devastation to the plantations and it has taken years for production of crops such as coconuts and bananas to recover. Hurricane Emily destroyed an estimated 70% of the banana crop in 1987.

The general elections held in February 1994 were won for the third successive time by the National Democratic party (NDP), which has held power under Prime Minister James Mitchell since 1984. The NDP won 12 of the 15 seats in the House of Assembly, compared with all 15 previously, and its share of the vote fell. The three remaining seats were won by an alliance of the opposition SVLP, led by Stanley John, and the Movement for National Unity (MNU), led by Ralph Gonsalves. Stanley John failed to win a seat, but a former SVLP leader, Vincent Beache did and was subsequently endorsed as parliamentary opposition leader. The two parties agreed on the alliance only shortly before the elections, having previously disagreed over the leadership of such an alliance. The Prime Minister appointed a largely unchanged cabinet but for the first time named a deputy prime minister, Parnel Campbell, who is also the Attorney General and Minister of Justice, Information and Ecclesiastical Affairs.

Government

St Vincent and the Grenadines is a constitutional monarchy within the Commonwealth. The Queen is represented by a Governor General. There is a House of Assembly with 15 elected representatives and six senators.

The Economy

The St Vincent economy is largely based on agriculture and tourism, with a small manufacturing industry which is mostly for export. In 1992 unemployment was estimated at 25-50% of the labour force. The main export is bananas, the fortunes of which fluctuate according to the severity of the hurricane season; in 1990 the volume rose to 79,586 tonnes, the highest ever, but the 1991 output was reduced because of drought and by 1993 exports had plummeted to 58,642 tonnes and earnings were down to US$23.1mn. Drought again affected the 1994 crop. The sector contributes about 60% of export revenues and the fall in prices brought about by the new European banana policy has hit hard. The Banana Growers Association is in debt and has been attempting to cut costs, but has launched a EC$50 mn programme to rehabilitate and improve 3,200 acres of banana land by 1997. Nevertheless, the Government is encouraging farmers to diversify and reduce dependence on bananas with incentives and land reform. About 7,000 acres of state-owned land is being split up into 1,500 small holdings.

Arrowroot starch is the second largest export crop, of which St Vincent is the world's largest producer; the Government plans to increase production by

ST VINCENT AND THE GRENADINES : FACT FILE

Geographic
Land area	389.3 sq km
forested	36.0%
pastures	5.0%
cultivated	28.0%

Demographic
Population (1992)	109,000
annual growth rate (1987-92)	0.8%
urban	24.7%
rural	75.3%
density	280 per sq km
Religious affiliation	
Protestant	77.3%
Roman Catholic	19.3%
Birth rate per 1,000 (1990)	23.9
	(world av 27.1)
Death rate per 1,000 (1990)	6.4
	(world av 9.8)

Education and Health
Life expectancy at birth,	
male	68 years
female	72 years
Infant mortality rate	
per 1,000 live births (1988-90)	21.3
Physicians (1989)	1 per 2,650 persons
Hospital beds	1 per 258 persons
Calorie intake as %	
of FAO requirement	102%
Population age 25 and over	
with no formal schooling	2.4%
Literacy (over 15)	85%

Economic
GNP (1990 market prices)	US$184mn
GNP per capita	US$1,610
Public external debt (1990)	US$52mn
Tourism receipts (1991)	US$53mn
Inflation (annual av 1986-91)	3.6%
Radio	1 per 2.0 persons
Television	1 per 6.2 persons
Telephone	1 per 6.4 persons

Employment
Population economically active (1980)	
	34,739
Unemployment rate (1992)	25-50%
% of labour force in agriculture	25.7
mining	0.3
manufacturing	5.1
construction	10.2
Paramilitary police unit	80

Source *Encyclopaedia Britannica*

raising the area sown from 140 acres in 1990 to 1,200 acres by 1996. Output increased from 139,342lbs in 1990 to 209,875 in 1991, with a rise in sales from EC$0.2 mn to EC$0.4 mn. However, the Arrowroot Association incurred a net loss of EC$1 mn. Arrowroot is now used as a fine dressing for computer paper as well as the traditional use as a thickening agent in cooking. Other exports include coconuts and coconut oil, copra, sweet potatoes, tannias and eddoes. Over half of all exports are sold to the UK. Fishing has received government promotion and substantial aid from Japan, which in 1994 looked unsuccessfully to St Vincent for support in the dispute over whaling. In 1993 Japan gave the island a grant of 72mn yen (about US$7mn) for a coastal fisheries development project, having previously given 916mn yen for the national fisheries development plan. St Vincent emerged as the largest flag of convenience in the Caribbean, with 521 ships on its register in 1990. In 1991 about 100 more were added as a direct result of the Yugoslav conflict, most of which came from Croatia and Slovenia. However, ships carrying the Vincentian flag have a poor record for safety, second only to Romania. Between 1990-92, 16.5% were detained by European port officials for unseaworthiness.

Tourism has grown steadily in St Vincent and the Grenadines and is important as a major employer and source of foreign exchange. Expansion is limited by the size of the airport and the Government has encouraged upmarket, often yacht-based tourism. In 1993 stopover tourists rose by 6.4% to 56,558 of which over 30% came from Europe and 27% form the USA. Tourist accommodation expanded rapidly in the 1980s, reaching 1,157 rooms in hotels, villas, apartments or guest houses in 1988. Visitor expenditure was estimated at US$53mn in 1991 and also in 1992. Plans to expand tourist capacity include the construction of a US$100mn resort on Union Island, including a hotel, 300-berth marina, golf course and villas. A US$75mn shipyard and marina is planned, to be built near Kingstown, St Vincent.

Healthy economic growth was recorded in the 1980s: government receipts grew faster than spending, investment in infrastructural development was promoted and social development projects such as schools and hospitals received foreign concessionary financing. In the 1994 budget, Prime Minister Mitchell cut income tax and banana export tax as part of a tax reform programme, but increased hotel guest tax. The large tourism development project on Union Island, was expected to boost the rate of economic growth, which had slowed since 1990 as the difficulties faced by the banana industry had grown.

Flora and Fauna

St Vincent has a wide variety of tropical plants, most of which can be seen in the Botanical Gardens, where conservation of rare species has been practised since they were founded in 1765. There you can see the mangosteen fruit tree and one of the few examples of *spachea perforata*, a tree once thought to be found only in St Vincent but now found in other parts of the world, as well as the famous third generation sucker of the original breadfruit tree brought by Captain Bligh of the *Bounty* in 1793 from Tahiti. Other conservation work taking place in the gardens involves the endangered St Vincent parrot, *Amazona guildingii*, which has been adopted as the national bird. An aviary, originally containing birds confiscated from illegal captors, now holds 12 parrots. In 1988 the first parrot was hatched in captivity and it was hoped that this was the first step towards increasing the number on the island, estimated at down to only 500. This mostly golden brown parrot with a green, violet, blue and yellow-flecked tail, spectacular in flight, is found in the humid forests in the lower and middle hills on the island. The main colonies are around Buccament, Cumberland-Wallilabou, Linley-Richmond and Locust Valley-Colonarie Valley. Their main enemy is man, who has encroached into the forest for new farming land and exploited the bird's rarity in the illegal pet trade, but they have also suffered severely from hurricanes and volcanic eruptions such as in 1979. They are protected now by the Wildlife Protection Act, which covers the majority of the island's birds, animals and reptiles and carries stiff penalties for infringements. A parrot reserve is being established in the upper Buccament Valley.

Another protected bird unique to St Vincent is the whistling warbler, and this, as well as the black hawk, the cocoa thrush, the crested hummingbird, the red-capped green tanager, green heron and other species can be seen, or at least heard, in the Buccament Valley. There are nature trails starting near the top of the Valley, passing through tropical forest, and it is possible to picnic. The Vermont Nature Trail can be reached by bus, from the market square in Kingstown to the road junction in Peniston near the *Emerald Valley Hotel and Casino*; the sign for the trail is clearly marked. If travelling by car, look for the Vermont Nature Trail sign about one mile past Questelles. The car park, at 975 feet, is close to the Vermont Nature Centre. Get a trail map from the information hut on the right. There is a rest stop on the trail, at 1,350 feet, and a Parrot Lookout Platform at 1,450 feet. It is a beautiful trail, through thick forest and is probably the best place to see the St Vincent parrot. Be prepared for rain, mosquitoes and chiggars, use insect repellent. Anyone interested in nature trails should visit the Forestry Department (in the same building as the Land and Survey Department), who have prepared official trail plans, published in conjunction with the Tourism Department. A pamphlet details the Vermont Nature Trails, Wallilabou Falls, Richmond Beach, Trinity Falls, Falls of Baleine, Owia Salt Pond and La Soufrière Volcano Trails. The Tourist Office may also have a supply of pamphlets.

Diving and Marine Life

The underwater wildlife around St Vincent and the Grenadines is varied and beautiful, with a riot of fish of all shapes and sizes. There are many types and colours of coral, including the black coral at a depth of only 30 feet in places. There is reef diving, wall diving, drift diving and wrecks to explore. On the New Guinea Reef you can find all three types of black coral in six different colours. The coral is protected so do not remove any. Bequia has a leeward wall which is a designated marine park where no spearfishing, traps, nets or anchors are allowed. There are 10 marine protected areas scattered throughout St Vincent and the Grenadines, of which the Tobago Cays are the most visited.

There are facilities for scuba diving, snorkelling, deep sea fishing, windsurfing and water ski-ing, with experienced scuba diving instructors for novices. The St Vincent reefs are fairly deep, at between 55 to 90 feet, and there is a great deal of colourful marine life to see, so scuba diving is more rewarding than snorkelling. Bequia is also considered excellent, with 35 dive sites around the island and nearby, reached by boat within 15 minutes. There is no shore diving. Snorkellers will prefer the Tobago Cays and Palm Island. No licence is needed for gamefishing, but spearfishing is illegal. Contact the Fisheries Department for more information on rules and regulations, T 456-2738. As well as the specialist companies, many of the hotels offer equipment and services for their guests and others.

There is a network of dive shops: Dive St Vincent (Bill Tewes) at Young Island Dock, PO Box 864, T 457-4714/457-4928, F 457-74948, links up with other dive operators in Wallilabou Bay, Bequia and Union Island to offer a 10-dive package throughout the area; also on St Vincent are St Vincent Dive Experience at the Lagoon marina, also waterskiing with instruction and trips to Bequia and Baleine Falls, T 456-9741, F 457-2768, and there is diving at Petit Byahaut Bay organized by the hotel there, T/F 457-7008. On the other islands are: Dive Bequia, a full service PADI/NAUI dive shop at the *Plantation House Hotel*, near Port Elizabeth, PO Box 16, Bequia, T 458-3504, F 458-3886; Sunsports at the *Gingerbread* complex has diving, windsurfing, sailing and tennis (T 458-3577, F 457-3031). Dive Paradise, *Friendship Bay Hotel*, Bequia, T/F 458-3563, 3 dive boats, German and English speaking staff, no credit cards; Bequia Dive Resort, Friendship Bay, can accommodate up to 16 people on the boat but groups are normally smaller, T 458-3248, F 458-3689; Dive Anchorage on Union Island, T 458-8221; Grenadines Dive (Glenroy Adams), at *Sunny Grenadines Hotel*, Clifton, Union Island, T 458-8138/8122, F 458-8122; Dive Canouan, at *Canouan Beach Hotel*, instruction, rentals, boat trips and rendezvous service, T 458-8648, F 458-8875. You can organize packages of 10 dives with or without certification course, combining Dive St Vincent on Young Island, Dive Canouan and Grenadines Dive, Union Island, a good way of diving throughout the islands.

Beaches and Watersports

St Vincent has splendid, safe beaches on the leeward side, most of which have volcanic black sand. The windward coast is more rocky with rolling surf and strong currents. All beaches are public. Some are difficult to reach by road, but boat trips can be arranged to the inaccessible beauty spots. Sea urchins are a hazard, as in many other islands, especially among rocks on the less frequented beaches.

Sailing is excellent, indeed it was yachtsmen who first popularized the Grenadines; St Vincent has a good yacht marina and boats can be chartered from several companies on St Vincent, Young Island, Bequia or Union Island. Yacht races include the Bequia Easter Regatta, in which there are races for all sizes and types of craft, even fishing boats. There are other contests on shore. The centre of activities is the *Frangipani Hotel*, which fronts directly on to Admiralty Bay. The Canouan Yacht Race is in August.

The Lagoon Marina and Hotel, Blue Lagoon, has crewed or bareboat yacht charters (PO Box 133, T 458-4308), as does the *Anchorage Yacht Club* on Union Island (T 458-8221). There are a number of other yacht charterers. On Bequia, Captain Danny with his 43-foot yacht, *Prospect of Whitby*, has been recommended for tailor-made charters. A 2-day sail to the Tobago Cays via Mayreau costs about US$50 pp, food US$15 extra, contact through Frangipani Yacht Services, T 458-3244, F 458-3824, or on VHF 68 'Prospect'.

Other Sports

Many of the more expensive hotels have tennis courts but there are others at the Kingstown Tennis Club and the Prospect Racquet Club. On Bequia, tennis is offered at four hotels: *Friendship Bay*, *Spring*, *Plantation House* and *Frangipani*. Squash courts can be found at the Cecil Cyrus Squash Complex (St James Place, Kingston, reservations T 456-1805), the *Grand View Beach Hotel* and the Prospect Racquet Club. Horse riding can be arranged at the *Cotton House Hotel*, Mustique. Spectator sports include cricket (Test Match cricket ground at Arnos Vale, near the airport), soccer, netball, volleyball and basketball. Pick up games of basket ball are played on St Vincent after 1700, or after the heat has subsided, at the Sports Complex behind the Arnos Vale airport. Everyone is welcome, although it can get very crowded and there is only one court, arrive early. There is also a court in Calliaqua (same times), but it is right on the street. Players beware, fouls are rarely called, although travelling violations are. No one is deliberately rough but overall the game is unpolished, unschooled but spirited.

Festivals

St Vincent's carnival, called Vincy Mas, is held in the last week of June and the first week of July. Mas is short for masquerade, and the three main elements of the carnival are the costume bands, the steel bands and the calypso. Thousands of visitors come to take part, many of whom come from Trinidad. From 16 December, for nine mornings, people parade through Kingstown and dances are held from 0100. At Easter on Union Island there are sports, cultural shows and a calypso competition. Also on Union Island, in May, is the Big Drum Festival,

---

CRICKET GRENADINE STYLE

Cricket is played throughout the Grenadines on any scrap of ground or on the beach. In Bequia, instead of the usual three stumps at the crease, there are four, while furthermore, bowlers are permitted to bend their elbows and hurl fearsome deliveries at the batsmen. This clearly favours the fielding side but batsmen are brought up to face this pace attack from an early age and cope with the bowling with complete nonchalance. Matches are held regularly, usually on Sundays, and sometimes internationals are staged. In Lower Bay v England, which Lower Bay usually wins, the visitors' team is recruited from cricket lovers staying in the area. Ask at *De Reef*; it is best to bat at number 10 or 11.

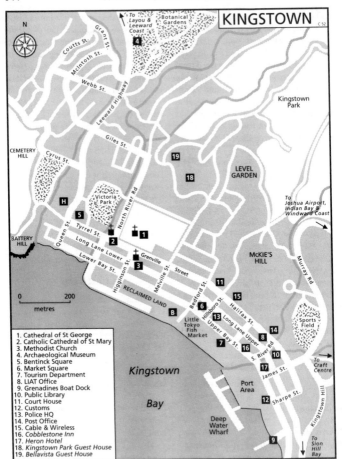

KINGSTOWN

C 52

Legend:

1. Cathedral of St George
2. Catholic Cathedral of St Mary
3. Methodist Church
4. Archaeological Museum
5. Bentinck Square
6. Market Square
7. Tourism Department
8. LIAT Office
9. Grenadines Boat Dock
10. Public Library
11. Court House
12. Customs
13. Police HQ
14. Post Office
15. Cable & Wireless
16. *Cobblestone Inn*
17. *Heron Hotel*
18. *Kingstown Park Guest House*
19. *Bellavista Guest House*

an event which marks the end of the dry season, culminating in the Big Drum Dance.

Kingstown

The capital, **Kingstown**, stands on a sheltered bay where scores of craft laden with fruit and vegetables add their touch of colour and noisy gaiety to the town. However, much land has been reclaimed and continuing dock works shield the small

craft from sight, except at the N end of the bay.

The market square in front of the Court House is the hub of activity. Market day is Friday and Saturday and very colourful with all the produce spread out on sacks or on makeshift tables. The shopping and business area is no more than two blocks wide, running between Upper Bay Street and Halifax Street/Lower Bay Street and Grenville

Street. There are quite a lot of new buildings, none of them tall. A new Fish Market, built with Japanese aid, was opened in 1990 near the Police Headquarters. This new complex, known as Little Tokyo, has car parking facilities and is the new point of departure for minibuses to all parts of the island. Looking inland from the bay, the city is surrounded on all sides by steep, green hills, with houses perched all the way up.

Kingstown has two cathedrals, St George's (Anglican) and St Mary's (Catholic). St George's, parts of which date from 1820, has an airy nave and a pale blue gallery running around the N, W and S sides. There is an interesting floor plaque in the nave, commemorating a general who died fighting the Caribs. St Mary's is of far less sober construction, with different syles, all in dark grey stone, crowded together on the church, presbytery and school. Building was carried out throughout the 19th century, with renovation in the 1940s. The exterior of the church is highly decorated but the interior is dull in comparison. The Methodist church, dating from 1841, also has a fine interior, with a circular balcony.

At the jetty where the boats for the Grenadines berth, you can see island schooners loading and unloading, all of which is done by hand. The men throw crates from one to the other in a human chain; the whole business is accompanied by much shouting and laughter. When the Geest boat is in dock, the farmers queue in their pick-ups to unload their boxes of bananas, and the food and drink stalls on the road to the Reception Depot do good business.

In Kingstown the Botanical Gardens just below Government House and the Prime Minister's residence are well worth a visit (for a description see above under **Fauna and Flora**). Established in 1765, they are the oldest in the Western Hemisphere. In the Gardens, there is a very interesting Archaeological Museum of Amerindian artefacts, some of which date from about 4,000 BC. The most spectacular exhibit is the bat effigy. Outside is a collection of shrubs which may have been planted in a Carib garden. Anyone interested in St Vincent history, flora or fauna should talk to the curator, Dr Earle Kirby (Doc); he is very knowledgeable and friendly. Unfortunately, the museum is only open Wednesday morning 0900-1200 and Saturday afternoon 1500-1800. Dr Kirby is elderly and not always at the museum. Occasionally he will open the museum and give a personal tour for especially interested visitors. The Gardens themselves are open 0600-1800 daily. They are about a 20-minute walk from the market square: go along Grenville Street, past the cathedrals, turn right into Bentinck Square, right again and continue uphill to the gate. Or take a bus, EC$1 from the terminal. You will be approached by guides who can explain which plant is which. There are notices specifying the official tour rates (in US$), so make sure you agree a price beforehand. Some guides can be persistent and bothersome, and have been known to get aggressive and demand payment for unrendered services. You do not have to have a guide.

Fort Charlotte (completed 1805) is on the promontory on the N side of Kingstown Bay, 636 feet above sea level, 15 minutes' drive out of town (EC$1.50 from bus terminal to village below, if you ask the driver he might take you into the fort for EC$1-2, worth it if it is hot). The views of Kingstown and surroundings are spectacular, and on a clear day the Grenadines and even Grenada are visible. Although the fort was designed to fend off attacks from the sea, the main threat was the Black Caribs and many of its 34 guns (some of which are still in place) therefore faced inland. In the old barrack rooms, a series of paintings shows the early history of St Vincent. There is also a coast guard lookout which controls the comings and goings of ships entering the port. Below, the ruins of a military hospital can be seen, as well as a bathing pool at sea level on the end of the point, used when the fort housed people suffering from yaws. The National Trust and the Caribbean Conservation Association (CCA) are proposing to develop Fort Charlotte as part of an Eastern Caribbean plan for historic military sites, with an Interpretive Centre, gift shop and museum. The National Trust of St Vincent and the Grenadines, PO Box 752, T 456-2591, has further information.

Excursions

The highest peak on the island, La Soufrière volcano, rises to about 4,000 feet. In 1970 an island reared itself up out of the lake in the crater: it smokes and the water round it is very warm. Hiking to the volcano is very popular, but you must leave very early in the morning and allow a full day for the trip. About two miles N of Georgetown (van from Kingstown to Georgetown EC$4) on the Windward side you cross the Dry River, then take a left fork and walk/drive through banana plantations to where the trail begins. A local guide is recommended, although not essential, always useful for carrying food and water as well as ensuring you do not get lost. It takes about three hours to reach the crater edge and it is a strenuous hike along a marked trail, the first three miles are through the Rabacca plantation, then up, along Bamboo Ridge and all the way to the crater's magnificent edge; the top can be cloudy, windy, cold and rainy, take adequate clothing and footwear. There is an alternative, unmarked and even more challenging route from the Leeward side starting from the end of the road after Richmond, but you will need a guide. After crossing a river delta, turn right into a ravine and climb; it will take about four hours. Guided tours usually on Tuesdays and Thursdays, about US$20-35, guides provide

and carry drinks. If you want to avoid organized tours, a guide can be obtained in Georgetown. One such is Benjamin Hudson, who lives opposite Sadoo's Grocery. Leave an extra set of clothes in the van in case you get wet through. Take water and insect repellent.

An easier climb is up Mount St Andrew, near Kingstown. A tarmac track runs up to the radio mast on the summit of the peak, at 2,413 feet, passing first through banana and vegetable gardens and then through forest. There are no parrots but otherwise virtually all the species of birds which can be found on the Vermont Nature Trail. It is particularly good for the Antillean crested hummingbird and black hawks. The view from the summit covers the Grenadines and the Vermont and Mesopotamia valleys. To reach the summit take either a van running along the Leeward Highway and ask to be put down at the junction with the Mt St Andrew road, or start your walk in Kingstown.

There are few good roads, but cars, including self-drive, can be hired and most of the beauty spots are accessible by road (but see below under **Car Rental**). The Leeward Highway is a dramatic drive, passing through Questelles and Layou. Much of this road is in very poor condition N of Barrouallie (pronounced Barrelly), a small whaling village. This drive along the W coast towards La Soufrière should not be missed; it has been described as a "tropical corniche". There are lush valleys and magnificent sea views. On the Leeward coast 14 miles N of Kingstown and two miles N of Barrouallie, are the Wallilabou Falls (Wallyla-boo), 15-20 feet high with a pool at the bottom which you can bathe in. There are changing rooms, toilets and a picnic site. On the opposite side of the road is a nutmeg plantation. You can get there by car or by bus from Little Tokyo Fish Market to Barrouallie and walk from there. Another set of falls, also on the Leeward side, is 20 miles N of Kingstown; Petit Wallibou Falls are a double waterfall in a very remote region and you can bathe at the bottom of the second waterfall. To get there, go through Richmond and turn right up the side road beside the Richmond Vale Academy; follow this road for one mile, in then turns into a track for two miles. At the river the top of the waterfall is on your left. There is a steep climb on the left hand side of the waterfall to reach the pool where you can swim. Trinity Falls are 45 minute's walk from Richmond in the Wallibou Valley, set deep in a canyon in the rainforest. The only known hot springs are in the canyon, having appeared since the last volcanic eruption.

A boat trip to the falls of Baleine (on the NW coast) is recommended. Wading ashore and for a few minutes up a river which originates on Soufrière, you come to the falls. At their base are natural swimming pools. It is possible to reach the falls on foot, but the easiest way is to take an excursion by motor boat (eg with Dive St Vincent, or Grenadine Tours), which includes a stop for snorkelling, and a picnic lunch, for US$35-40. Sea Breeze Boat Service uses a 36-foot auxiliary sloop, not recommended if you get seasick, otherwise nice, includes snorkelling stop, rum punch but no lunch, for US$25 pp, Captain Al is an authority on the bottle-nosed dolphin and will probably find a school of them to watch, recommended, T 458-4969.

The Queens Drive takes you into the hills S of Kingstown and gives splendid views all around. The Marriaqua Valley with its numerous streams is particularly beautiful. In the Valley, beyond Mesopotamia (commonly known as Mespo), the lush, tropical gardens of Montreal are worth a visit; anthuriums are grown commercially there. The drive along the Windward coast to Georgetown offers good views of rocks, black sand beaches and rolling breakers. The road to Sandy Bay (beyond Georgetown), where St Vincent's remaining Black Caribs live, is now good, however you have to cross the Dry River, which sometimes is not dry and therefore not passable. Sandy Bay is poor but beyond it is an even poorer village along a rough dirt road, Owia. Here is Salt Pond, a natural area of tidal pools filled with small marine life. The rough Atlantic crashes around the huge boulders and lava formations and is very picturesque. The villagers have planted flowers and made steps down to the Salt Pond area. There is also an arrowroot processing factory which can be visited. Past Owia is Fancy, the poorest village on the island, also Black Carib and very isolated, reached by a rough jeep track which makes a pleasant walk. Baleine Falls (see above) are a two-mile hike from here around the tip of the island, rugged and not recommended for the unadventurous. Fishing boats can be hired in Fancy to collect you (do not pay in advance).

The SE of the island is drier and has different vegetation and birdlife. Take a van running to Stubbs and alight at the Post Office by the Brighton road junction. Walk into Brighton village and find a guide who can lead you to see, among others, the mangrove cuckoo, smooth-billed ani, broad-winged hawk and green heron. When tidal conditions are right it is possible to cross to Milligan Cay. To see seabirds in the bay visit early morning or late afternoon.

There are some interesting petroglyphs and rock carvings dating back to the Siboney, Arawak and Carib eras. The best known are just N of Layou, carved on a huge boulder next to a stream. They can only be visited on payment of US$2 for the owner, Mr Victor Hendrickson to open the gate to the fenced off area. Ask the local children to show you his house and then the petroglyphs for a tip, well worth a visit.

Island Information - St Vincent
● **Where to Stay**

In Kingstown: on Upper Bay Street, *Cobblestone Inn* (PO Box 867, T 456-1937), upstairs in a building which used to be a sugar and arrowroot warehouse, US$70d, CP, including tax, a/c, very quiet, rooms good; nearby, at junction with South River Road, is **Heron** (PO Box 226, T 457-1631, F 457-1189), also once above a warehouse (now above a screenprinting shop and bookshop), popular with business visitors, spotlessly clean, good, set-menu food in restaurant, a/c, TV lounge, rec, US$55-60d CP, the place for a well-earned bacon and egg breakfast after crossing from Bequia on the early boat; **Haddon**, Grenville Street (PO Box 144, T 456-1897, F 456-2726) good food, helpful, US$50d EP, a/c, tennis courts nearby, car hire available. Two guest houses close to each other are **Kingstown Park** (PO Box 41, T 456-1532, F 457-4174), the oldest guest house on the island with a certain old-fashioned colonial ambience (originally the governor-general's residence), US$17d without bath, US$23d with bath, EP, also modern flats, clean, basic, very helpful and friendly staff, haphazard management, breakfast overpriced, but dinner at good value, bar in basement, no credit cards and **Bella Vista** (T 457-2757), smaller, more modern, US$17-21d EP, good location and rec except for bed bugs.

At **Villa Point** and Beach, and **Indian Bay**, 3 miles from town, **Grand View Beach**, Villa Point (PO Box 173, T 458-4811, F 457-4174), refurbished 1993/94, first class, pool, tennis, squash, fully-equipped gym, snorkelling, excursions arranged, restaurant, US$210-270d winter, US$130-190d summer CP; **Villa Lodge**, Villa Point (PO Box 1191, T 458-4641, F 457-4468) US$115d EP, US$185d MAP, 10 rooms overlooking Indian Bay, a/c, fans, TV, pool, restaurant, bar, 10 mins from airport, rec; **Brownes**, on the water in Villa, 24 a/c rooms, phone, TV, restaurant, free shuttle to Kingstown, US$115d winter, US$90d summer, T 457-7000, F 457-4040; **Umbrella Beach** (P O Box 530, T 458-4651, F 457-4930), US$48 for double room with kitchen, bath, balcony, nice, simple, opp Young Island. Also at Villa Beach is **Sunset Shores**, PO Box 849, T 458-4411, F 457-4800, US$110-130d EP, 32 rooms, a/c, TV, sunfish, snorkelling gear, pool, table tennis, dining room, bar; **Tranquility Beach Apartment Hotel**, Indian Bay (PO Box 71, T/F 458-4021), US$50 EP, excellent view, kitchen facilities, fans, TV, laundry service, clean, friendly, rec, very helpful owners, Mr and Mrs Providence, delicious meals if given a few hours' notice; **Coconut Beach Inn**, US$50d, nice, clean, comfortable rooms, beautiful

seaview, very friendly people, highly rec, T 457-4900, good restaurant (see below); **Indian Bay Beach Hotels and Apartments** (PO Box 538, T 458-4001, F 457-4777) hotel on beach, nice verandah, good snorkelling just outside the hotel, US$65d EP, US$390d/week all year, 2 bedroomed apartments available, sleep 3-4, a/c, kitchenettes, restaurant, watersports nearby. **The Lagoon Marina and Hotel**, Blue Lagoon (PO Box 133, T 458-4308, F 457-4716) US$95d with a/c, US$85 without, winter, US$90-80d summer EP, formerly *CSY Hotel*, 19 rooms with lovely view, run by Vincentians, Richard and Nancy Joachim, yacht charter US$200-400/day, US$1,400-2,800/week, full service marina, bar, restaurant, pools, scuba diving, windsurfing. Other guest houses: **Sea Breeze Guest House**, Arnos Vale, near airport (T 458-4969), US$22d EP, cooking facilities, 6 rooms with bath, no credit cards, noisy, friendly, helpful, bus to town or airport from the door.

On the Leeward coast, **Petit Byahaut**, set in a 50-acre valley, no TV or phones, 10 x 13-ft tents with floors, queen-sized bed, shower and hammock in each tent, US$105-115 pp double occupancy, US$495-545 for 5 days, inc all meals, snorkelling, sail and row boats, trips, scuba, packages available, you can hire the whole resort for 14 people for US$1,200/day, T/F 457-7008, VHF 68, access only by boat, diving and snorkelling good in the bay, ecological and conservation emphasis, solar powered.

● **Where to Eat**
There is a shortage of good restaurants in Kingstown, the better ones, eg the *French Restaurant*, are in the beach area several miles E. **Vee-Jay's** restaurant on Lower Bay Street is friendly and offers local food; open Mon-Sat 1000-1900, Fri until late, also **Vee-Jay's Rooftop Diner & Pub** on Upper Bay St, T 457-2845/1395, above Roger's Photo Studios, open Mon-Sat from 0900, sandwiches, rotis etc for lunch, good local juices, dinner by reservation only, cocktail bar, entrés EC$12-45, great steel band. For genuine West Indian food and local company **Aggie's Bar and Restaurant** on Grenville St, T 456-2110, is superb; **Sid's Pub** is a great bargain, good native food, main course from EC$10, friendly, clean, good service, sports on satellite TV, open Mon-Sat from 1100, Sun from 1900, T 456-2315. **Basil's Bar and Restaurant** (see below) has a branch underneath the *Cobblestone Inn*, in

Upper Bay Street, buffet 1200-1400 for hungry people, open from 1000, rather overrated, T 457-2713. *Cobblestone Roof Top Restaurant*, belonging to the *Cobblestone Inn*, T 456-1937, West Indian lunches and hamburgers, open Mon-Sat 0730-1500, good place for breakfast, as is the *Heron Hotel* (see above).

At the bus station (Little Tokyo) you can buy freshly grilled chicken and corn cobs, good value and tasty. Cafés on the jetty by ferry boats serve excellent, cheap, local food, eg salt cod rolls with hot pepper sauce. On market days fruit is plentiful and cheap, great bananas. Take away food from *Pizza Party*, T 456-4932/9, in Arnos Vale by the airport, delivery and takeaway until 2300, no credit cards; *Chung Wua*, Upper Bay Street, T 457-2566, open Mon-Sat 1100-2230, Sun 1700-2200, Chinese eat in or take away, no credit cards, from EC$10.

In the **Villa** area, *The French Restaurant*, T 458-4972, VHF Channel 68, open daily for lunch and dinner, very good food, lobster from the tank, rec, superb service and lovely beach view, the place for a treat. The *Lime'n' Pub* on the waterfront at Villa has a casual menu and a dinner menu, reasonable prices, T 458-4227, open 1000-2400; *Beachcombers* on Villa Beach has light fare and drinks, very casual, or à la carte menu, open air, food 1000-2200, bar open later, happy hour 1700-1830, T 458-4283; The *Coconut Beach Inn* on Indian Bay has a good restaurant and rooms to let (see above), West Indian specialities, sandwiches, fish and chips etc, open daily from 1000, dinner by reservation only before 1500, entrées, EC$10-45. *Villa Lodge Hotel* is a good place to eat, not cheap but wonderful piña colada. *Sugar Reef*, at the *Lagoon Marina and Hotel*, Blue Lagoon, T 456-9847, run by Americans, Janet and Neil Becker, breakfast, lunch and dinner with daily specials, pleasant for happy hour watching the sunset, reasonable prices.

Stephens Hideout, Cumberland Bay, T 458-2325, West Indian and seafood, restaurant on Leeward Highway, Beach Bar on the bay, call ahead for made to order meals or picnic on beach, open 0900-2230, no credit cards, tours also arranged; *Wallilabou Anchorage*, T 458-7270, caters mainly to yachties, mooring facilities, West Indian specialities.

● **Entertainment**

Several hotels have live music some evenings. In Kingstown, *Touch Entertainment Centre* opened its dance hall in 1993, run by the Vincentian band, *Touch*, T 457-1825. *The Attic*, T 457-2558, at the corner of Melville and Grenville Streets, nightly live entertainment, jazz, karaoke, dancing, large screen video, music bar open 1200 till late, restaurant open Mon-Sat for lunch 1100-1430.

THE GRENADINES

THE GRENADINES, divided politically between St Vincent and Grenada, are a string of 100 tiny, rocky islands and cays stretching across some 35 miles of sea between the two. They are still very much off the beaten track as far as tourists are concerned, but are popular with yachtsmen and the "international set".

YOUNG ISLAND

A tiny, privately-owned islet, 200 yards off St Vincent. Pick up the phone at the crossing to see if you will be allowed over. Fort Duvernette, on a 195-foot high rock just off Young Island, was built at the beginning of the 19th century to defend Calliaqua Bay. To visit it, arrangements must be made with the hotel or ask around the dock for a boat to take you out: approximately EC$20 to be dropped off there and picked up later; wonderful view, inspires imagination, recommended. There is a lovely lagoon swimming pool, surrounded by tropical flowers. *Young Island Resort*, P O Box 211, T 458-4826, F 457-4567, in UK T 0800-373742; all accommodation in cottages, double-occupancy rates (MAP) range from US$260-400 a day in summer to US$410-550 in winter, yachts are US$500-650 a day, no children 15 January – 15 March, part sailing and honeymoon packages available. The Thur noon buffet for US$12 is highly rec.

BEQUIA

Named the island of the clouds by the Caribs, (pronounced Bek-*way*) this is the largest of the St Vincent dependencies with a population of 4,874 (1991 census). Nine miles S of St Vincent and about seven miles square, Bequia attracts quite a number of tourists, chiefly yachtsmen. The island is quite hilly and well-forested with a great variety of fruit and nut trees. Its main village is **Port Elizabeth** and here Admiralty Bay offers a safe anchorage. Boat building and repair work are the main industry. Experienced sailors can sometimes get a job crewing on boats sailing on from here to Panama

ST VINCENT and the GRENADINES

Waterloo Mountains

Georgetown

Barrouallie

KINGSTOWN

ST VINCENT

N

PORT ELIZABETH   *Bequia*

Isle à Quatre   Petit Nevis   Battowia
Balliceaux

The Pillories

LOVELL VILLAGE

Mustique

Petit Mustique

Petit Canouan   Savan Is.

Canouan

Catholic Is.   CHARLESTOWN

Union Island   Mayreau

Tobago Cays

Palm (Prune) Is.

CLIFTON

Petit St Vincent

The GRENADINES

0   10
km

and other destinations. For maps and charts (and books) go to Iain Gale's Bequia Bookshop, which is very well stocked. The nearest beach to Port Elizabeth is the pleasant Princess Margaret beach which shelves quickly into the clear sea. There are no beach bars to spoil this tree-lined stretch of soft sand. At its S end there is a small headland, around which you can snorkel to Lower Bay, where swimming is excellent and the beach is one of the best on the island. Local boys race their homemade, finely finished sailing yachts round the bay. In the village is *Kennedy's Bar*, a good place to watch the sunset with a rum punch. Further along is *De Reef*, whose bar and restaurant are the hub of much local activity.

Away from Port Elizabeth the beaches are empty. Take a taxi through coconut groves past an old sugar mill to Industry Bay, a nice beach surrounded by palms with a brilliant view across to Bullet Island, Battowia and Balliceaux where the Black Caribs were held before being deported to Roatán. Some luxury homes have been built at the N end of the bay. Food and drink available at the somewhat run down *Crescent Beach Inn*, T 458-3400, which has a taxi to get you back to Port Elizabeth. A short walk along the track leads to Spring Bay, to the S, where there is a beach bar (maybe be closed). Both beaches are narrow with shallow bays and a lot of weed, making them less good for swimming and snorkelling. The walk up Mount Pleasant from Port Elizabeth is worthwhile (go by taxi if it is too hot), the shady road is overhung with fruit trees and the view of Admiralty Bay is ever more spectacular. There is a settlement of airy homes at the top, from where you can see most of the Grenadines. By following the road downhill and S of the viewpoint you can get to Hope Bay, an isolated and usually deserted sweep of white sand and one of the best beaches. At the last house (where you can arrange for a taxi to meet you afterwards), the road becomes a rough track, after ½ mile

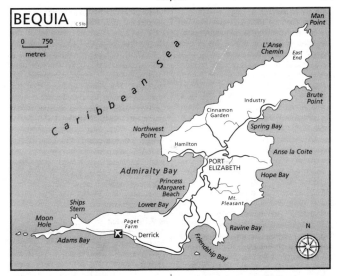

BEQUIA C 51b

Caribbean Sea

Man Point

L'Anse Chemin — East End

Brute Point

Industry

Cinnamon Garden

Northwest Point

Spring Bay

Hamilton

Anse la Coite

PORT ELIZABETH

Admiralty Bay

Princess Margaret Beach

Hope Bay

Ships Stern

Lower Bay

Mt. Pleasant

Moon Hole

Paget Farm — Derrick

Ravine Bay

Adams Bay

Friendship Bay

N

0   750
metres

turn off right down an ill-defined path through cedar trees to an open field, cross the fence on the left, go through a coconut grove and you reach the beach. The sea is usually gentle but sometimes there is powerful surf, a strong undertow and offshore current, take care. Friendship Bay is particularly pleasant, there is some coral but also quite a lot of weed, a taxi costs EC$12, or you can take a dollar bus (infrequent) in the direction of Paget Farm, get out at Mr Stowe's Store (EC$1.50) and walk down to the bay (you may have to ring for a taxi at one of the hotels to get back, though).

The Tourist Office by the jetty (very helpful) can help you arrange a visit to the cliffside dwellings of Moon Hole at the S end of the island, where a rocky arch frames the stone dwelling and the water comes up the front yard. At Paget Farm, whale harpooning is still practised from February to May by a few elderly fishermen who use two 26-foot long cedar boats, powered by oars and sails. They do not catch much. If you can arrange a trip to **Petit Nevis**, to the S, you can see the whaling station and find out more about Bequia's whaling tradition.

Island Information - Bequia
● Transport

An airport named the J F Mitchell Airport, after the Prime Minister, has been built on reclaimed land with a 3,200-foot runway, a terminal and night landing facilities, at the island's SW tip. Residents view it as a mixed blessing, some not wanting the island's peace and tranquility disturbed by an influx of visitors. The island's infrastructure and hotel accommodation is inadequate to handle greater numbers of tourists.

For about $30, you can take a taxi around the island. You can also rent Honda scooters (and bicycles) from an agency between the bookstore and the National Commercial Bank for US$10/hour or US$30/day, but you need to get the police to verify your licence. Water taxis scoot about in Admiralty Bay for the benefit of the many yachts and people on the beach, whistle or wave to attract their attention, fare EC$10 per trip. There are day charters to other islands. Bart has trips to the Tobago Cays and one other island with snorkelling, swimming, breakfast, lunch and all drinks on the *Island Queen*, US$75 pp, attentive, friendly service, hotel pick-up, beautiful scenery, rec.

● Where to Stay

The Old Fort, on Mount Pleasant, a 17th century French built fortified farmhouse, probably oldest building on Bequia, magnificent views, idyllic restaurant (dinner only, must book), animals in spacious grounds inc donkeys, kittens, peacocks, talking parrot, 4 apartments and a cottage, US$120d EP winter, US$100 summer, T 458-3440, F 458-3824, excursions, diving, boat trips arranged, highly rec, German run; *Friendship Bay* (PO Box 9, T 458-3222, F 458-3840), US$125-175d winter, US$92-145d summer, CP, lovely location, boat excursions, water and other sports facilities, friendly, refurbished in 1991/92, jump-up at beach bar, Sat night; *Blue Tropic Hotel*, Friendship Bay, T 458-3573, F 457-3074, US$92d winter, US$72d summer, CP; *Bequia Beach Club*, Friendship Bay, T 458-3248, F 458-3689, 10 rooms, US$50d winter, US$75d MAP, restaurant, bar, diving, windsurfing, tennis nearby, day sails, weekly barbeques; *Spring on Bequia* (T 458-3414), on a bay to the NE of Port Elizabeth, 10 rooms, US$130-175d EP in winter, US$90-130d in summer, pool, tennis, bar, restaurant, beach bar. In Port Elizabeth itself, *Frangipani* (PO Box 1, T 458-3255, F 458-3824), US$40-80d EP in summer, US$50-120d EP in winter, cheaper rooms share bathroom, on beach, pleasant, bar, terrible sandflies and mosquitoes in wet season, mosquito net provided; *Gingerbread Apartments*, PO Box 1, T 458-3800, F 458-3907, one-bedroomed with kitchen and bathroom, no children, US$65/day, US$400/week in summer, US$90 and US$550 in winter, also restaurant and bar upstairs, café downstairs, dive shop, tennis, water skiing, international phone calls 0700-1900 in upstairs office of restaurant, attractive, friendly, rec, run by Mrs Mitchell, Canadian, ex-wife of Prime Minister; *Mitchells*, overlooking harbour (above Bookshop, go round the back and seek out the owner), EC$50d, inc morning coffee, but 10% more if you are staying only one night, cooking facilities available, good, cheap, basic; *Julie's Guest House*, 19 rooms with bath and shower, turn right by the police station, T 458-3304, F 458-3812, mosquito nets in rooms, US$48-54d MAP year round, rec, good local food, good cocktails in noisy bar downstairs, meeting place for travellers to form boat charter groups; *'Sunny Caribbee' Plantation House Hotel*, rebuilt after 1988 fire, on beach at Admiralty Bay, tennis, swimming pool, watersports, Dive Bequia dive shop, cottages or rooms, US$305-335d winter, US$190-200d summer, all MAP, PO Box 16, T 458-3425, F 458-3612, entertainment at weekends; *The Old Fig Tree*, by *Sunny Caribbee*, PO Box 14, T 458-3201, restaurant with basic rooms at US$25d shared bath, US$30d private bath, meals extra (good), friendly, on extremely narrow beach. *The Village Apartments* in Belmont, overlooking Admiralty Bay above *Sunny Caribbee Hotel*, studio, one or 2-bedroomed apartments US$40-70 all year, T 456-4960, F 456-2344, PO Box 1621, Kingstown. *Keegan's Guesthouse* (T 458-3254), US$60-75d MAP, lovely position, 11 rooms, also 2-bedroom apartment US$340/week, and *Creole Garden Hotel* at Lower Bay above Corner Bay and Lower Bay beach, new, US$86d MAP, bath, porch, refrigerator, T/F 458-3154. There are also apartments to rent.

● Where to Eat

Apart from hotel restaurants, *Mac's Pizza* on Belmont Beach, is rec, very popular, get there early or reserve in advance, even in low season, also takeaways, T 458-3474; *Le Petit Jardin*, Back Street, T 458-3318, French and international, open daily 1130-1400, 1830-2130, reservations preferred, EC$30-85 for entrées; *Daphne's*, just off the main street, cooks excellent créole meals to eat in or take away, T 458-3271, no credit cards; *Dawn's Créole Tea Garden*, Lower Bay, at the far end, open from 0900, breakfast, lunch and dinner, good home cooked food, fairly expensive, must book, T 458-3154; the *Gingerbread House* has sandwiches and snacks all day; *De Reef*, Lower Bay, if you rent a locker note that all keys fit all locks, lovely position, popular with yachties, set meals and bar snacks, the place for Sun lunch; the *Frangipani* has sandwiches and snacks all day, slow service but friendly and you have a good view to look at. Thur night barbeque and jump up with steel band is well-organized, with excellent food, rec. There is something going on most nights either at Admiralty Bay or Friendship Bay, check locally. Bands play reggae music in the gardens of several hotels, popular with residents and tourists.

There are two supermarkets in Port Elizabeth (limited choice of meat), fish is sometimes on sale in the centre by the jetty although a new fish market is being built, fruit and vegetable stalls by the jetty daily, frozen food and homemade bread from *Doris's*, also *Daphne's* for homemade bread.

MUSTIQUE

Lying 18 miles S of St Vincent, Mustique is three miles long and less than two miles wide. In the 1960s, Mustique was acquired by a single proprietor who developed the island as his private resort where he could entertain the rich and famous. It is a beautiful island, with fertile valleys, steep hills and twelve miles of white sandy beach, but described by some as "manicured". It is no longer owned by one person and is more accessible to tourists, although privacy and quiet is prized by those who can afford to live there. There is no intention to commercialize the island; it has no supermarkets and only one petrol pump for the few cars (people use mopeds or golf carts to get around). House building will be limited to thirty. All house rentals are handled by the Mustique Company (Jeanette Cadet), which organizes activities such as picnics and sports, especially at Easter and Christmas. Radio is the principal means of communication, and the airstrip, being in the centre of the island is clearly visible, so check-in time is five minutes before take off (ie after you've seen your plane land).

There is sailing, diving, snorkelling, and good swimming (very little water-skiing), while riding can also be arranged or you can hire a moped to tour the island. Take a picnic lunch to Macaroni Beach on the Atlantic side. This gorgeous, white sand beach is lined with small palm-thatched pavilions and a well-kept park/picnic area. It is isolated and wonderful. *Basil's Bar and Restaurant* is *the* congregating spot for yachtsmen and the jet set. From it there is a well-beaten path to the *Cotton House Hotel*, which is the other congregating point.

Since the island has no fresh water, it is shipped in on Mustique Boats *Robert Junior* (T 457-1918) and the *Geronimo*. Both take passengers and excursions on Sunday (EC$10, 2 hrs trip).

Island Information - Mustique
● Where To Stay

Mustique hotels: *Cotton House*, a 20-room refurbished cotton plantation house built of rock and coral, is the only hotel and is expensive (US$325-550d in summer, winter US$550-730d, FAP), pool, tennis, riding available, windsurfers, sailfish, snorkelling, T 456-4777, F 456-5887, in UK T 0800-373 742; smaller, less expensive *Firefly House*, T 458-4621 (all rooms with view overlooking the bay), bed and breakfast in US$70-85 range. 43 of the private residences are available for rent, with staff, from US$2,800/week in summer for a 2-bedroomed villa to US$13,000/week in winter for a villa sleeping 10. Contact Pauline Wilkins of Mustique Villa Rentals, Chartam House, 16a College Avenue, Maidenhead, Berkshire, SL6 6AX, UK, T 0628 75544, F 0628 21033, or the Mustique Company Renters Office by the airstrip on Mustique, mailing address PO Box 349, T 458-4621, F 456-4565, or Resorts Management Inc, The Carriage House, 201½ East 29th Street, New York, NY 10016, T (212) 696-4566, (800) 225-4255, F (212) 689-1598.

● Where To Eat

Basil's Bar and The Raft, for seafood and night life, T 458-4621 for reservations, open from 0800, entrées EC$10-75. Locals' night on Mon with buffet for EC$35 excluding drinks and dancing, Wed is good, on Sat go to the *Cotton House*. Up the hill from *Basil's* is the local *Piccadilly* pub, where rotis and beer are sold, and pool is played; foreigners are welcome, but it is best to go in a group and girls should not go on their own.

UNION ISLAND

40 miles from St Vincent and the most S of the islands, it is three miles long and one mile wide with two dramatic peaks, Mount Olympus and Mount Parnassus, the latter being 900 feet high. Arrival by air is spectacular as the planes fly over the hill and descend steeply to the landing strip. The runway and airport building are new and in good order, having been completed in 1993. The road from the airport to Clifton passes a mangrove swamp which is being used as a dump prior to filling it in to get rid of mosquitoes and enable building to take place. A walk around the interior of the island

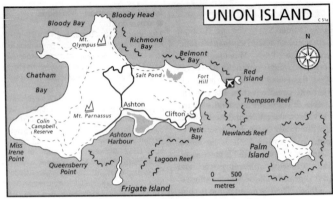

UNION ISLAND C 51a

Bloody Bay / Bloody Head / Mt. Olympus / Richmond Bay / Belmont Bay / Salt Pond / Fort Hill / Red Island / Chatham Bay / Thompson Reef / Mt. Parnassus / Ashton / Clifton / Newlands Reef / Colin Campbell Reserve / Ashton Harbour / Petit Bay / Palm Island / Miss Irene Point / Queensberry Point / Lagoon Reef / Frigate Island / N

0   500
metres

(about two hours Clifton-Ashton-Richmond Bay-Clifton) is worth the effort, with fine views of the sea, neighbouring islands, pelicans and Union itself. It has two settlements, Clifton and Ashton (minibus between the two, EC$2), and the former serves as the S point of entry clearance for yachts. The immigration office is opposite the harbour, but they may send you to the airport to get your passport stamped and your bags checked. The *Anchorage Yacht Club* seems to be full of French people. The barmen are slow and sometimes rude. You can make phone calls from here (there are no pay phones) but expect a charge of about EC$17 per minute to the UK compared with a pay phone price of EC$5. A good reason to visit Union Island is to arrange day trips to other islands or to find a ride on a yacht to Venezuela towards the end of the season (May-June). Day trip boats leave around 1000 and are all about the same price, EC$100, including lunch. Ask at the *Anchorage Yacht Club* or Park East, across the airport runway, about boats going to the **Tobago Cays** (see below), you may be able to join a group quite cheaply. A large catamaran, *Typhoon*, runs a charter service, well worth while. An old sailing vessel, *Scaramouch*, also sails to the Tobago Cays, stopping additionally at Mayreau and Palm Island. The

Clifton Beach Hotel arranges tours of Palm Island, Petit St Vincent and other small islands. The beach at Chatham Bay is beautiful and deserted (very good mangoes grow there), but not particularly good for swimming as there is a coral ledge just off the beach. An area at the N end of the bay has been cleared for a hotel development and a road has been cut over the mountain from Ashton to Chatham Bay. A large tourist development is planned for Union Island, with a luxury hotel, 300-berth marina, golf course and villas. Work began in 1994 on the US$108mn project, with investment from Europe and the Middle East. The Government has a 14% shareholding.

Island Information - Union Island
● **Where To Stay**
Anchorage Yacht Club, Clifton, full marina service, French restaurant, US$100/room, US$160 cabana or bungalow, in winter, T 458-8221, F 458-8365; *Clifton Beach Hotel and Guest House* (T/F 458-8235), US$29-48d EP winter, US$25-44d summer, a bit run down; *Sunny Grenadines* (T 458-8327, F 458-8398), US$85d CP, reductions sometimes offered if business is slack, 5 mins' walk from airport, adequate rooms, bar quite lively, food very good, boats can tie up at jetty; *Lambis Guest House*, Clifton, T 458-8549, F 458-8395, 14 rooms, US$22d summer, US$30d winter.

● **Where To Eat**
Food is expensive; *Clifton Beach* and *Sunny*

Grenadines hotels both have good restaurants and bars. The *Anchorage* restaurant has been criticized for serving bland, overpriced food, the occupants of the shark pool are given food rejected by customers.

CANOUAN

A quiet, peaceful, crescent-shaped island 25 miles S of St Vincent, with very few tourists and excellent reef-protected beaches. The beach at the *Canouan Beach Hotel* is splendid with white sand and views of numerous islands to the S. There are no restaurants outside the hotels and only basic shops. The main anchorage is Grand Bay, although anchorages exist all round the island. A recommended day trip is to the Tobago Cays, Mayreau or Petit St Vincent, depending on the weather and conditions, on the *Canouan Beach Hotel* 35-foot catamaran, EC$100 with lunch and drinks, non-hotel guests are permitted to make up numbers if the boat is not fully booked. There is an airstrip. A Swiss company, Canouan Resorts Development Ltd, has leased 1,200 of the island's 1,866 acres in a US$100mn development plan.

Island Information - Canouan
● **Where To Stay**
Canouan: *Canouan Beach Hotel* has developed the S part of the island with de luxe bungalows as well as the main building, nudist beach, refurbished 1993, reopened 1994, call for rates (T 458-8888, F 458-8875, PO Box 530); *Villa le Bijou* (Mme Michelle de Roche, T 458-8025), US$140d MAP, on hill overlooking town, superb views, friendly, helpful, showers, water and ice for yacht visitors, no credit cards; George and Yvonne at the *Anchor Inn Guest House* in Grand Bay, T 458-8568, offer clean and basic accommodation, for double rooms, US$80 MAP, packed lunches available, no credit cards; also possible to rent houses. You are recommended to phone in advance to book rooms as there is so little accommodation on the island.

MAYREAU

A small privately-owned island with deserted beaches and only one hotel, *Salt Whistle Bay Club* (contact by radio, VHF Ch 16, boatphone 493 9609, T 613-634 7108, in UK T 0800-373742, 10 rooms from US$300-490 MAP yacht charters and picnics on nearby islands), and one guest house, *Dennis' Hideaway*, (3 rooms, US$70d winter, US$50d summer, EP, T 458-8594), though there is a plan to develop tourism. You can reach it only by boat. Once a week, however, the island springs to life with the arrival of a cruise ship which anchors in the bay and sends its passengers ashore for a barbeque and sunburn. In preparation for this, local women sweep the beach and the manchineel trees (poisonous) are banded with red. Good food and drinks at reasonable prices can be found at *Dennis' Hideaway*. The **Tobago Cays** are a small collection of islets just off Mayreau, protected by a horseshoe reef and surrounded by beautifully clear water. The beaches are some of the most beautiful in the Caribbean. Unfortunately their popularity has caused considerable destruction. You may find about 30 boats anchored, and anchor damage, together with over-fishing and removal of black coral has led to the death of some of the reef. Coral eating fish, such as parrot fish, are rare and hard coral lies broken on the bottom. Snorkelling is not what it was but it is still a popular trip. The cays have now been declared a wildlife reserve and visitors are asked to take care not to damage marine resources. There are day charters out of St Vincent, Bequia and Union Island.

PETIT ST VINCENT

Locally referred to as PSV, this is a beautiful, privately-owned, 113-acre island with one of the Caribbean's best resorts, the *Petit St Vincent* (rates vary during the year from US$340s to US$680d, FAP, closed September/October, no credit cards). Accommodation is in 22 secluded cottages, there is a tennis court, fitness track and a wide range of watersports (sunfish, hobie cats, windsurfers, yacht day sails, snorkelling) is available, T 458-8801, F 458-8428. You can have room service (especially nice for breakfast) or eat in the central building. Once a week dinner is moved to the beach with music from a local band. Communication with the administration is done with coloured flags hoisted outside your cottage. Picnics can be arranged on the tiny islet Petit St Richardson. US reservations: PSV, PO Box 12506, Cincinnatti, Ohio 45212; T (513) 242-1333 or 800-654-9326, F (513) 242-6951. The island can be reached by the resort's launch from Union Island. The resort will charter a flight from Barbados to Union Island for US$113 pp one way, children half price.

PALM ISLAND

Also known as *Prune Island*, is another privately-owned resort, about a mile from Union Island, with coral reefs on three sides. There are four beaches, of which the one on the W coast, Casuarina, is the most beautiful. *Palm Island Beach Club*, individual bungalows, T 458-8824, F 458-8804 (US$245-345d full board, depending on season, no credit cards). Sailing, windsurfing, scuba diving, snorkelling, fishing, tennis, healthclub all available. There is a 10-minute launch service from Union Island. Shared charter flights can be arranged on Mustique Airways from Barbados to Union Island, where you will be met.

INFORMATION FOR VISITORS

● **Documents**
All visitors must have a passport and an onward, or return, ticket. Nationals of the UK, USA and Canada may enter for up to 6 months on proof of citizenship only. As well as the 3 countries already mentioned, citizens of the following countries do not need a visa: all Commonwealth countries, all the EC countries (except Eire and Portugal), Chile, Finland, Iceland, Liechtenstein, Norway, Switzerland, Swe-

den, Turkey, Uruguay, Venezuela. You will be asked where you will be staying on the island and will need a reservation, which can be done through the Tourist Office at the airport, before going through immigration. If you are only given entry of a few days and want to stay longer, extensions are easily obtained for EC$20.

● **How To Get There By Air**
There are no direct services out of the Caribbean but same day connecting flights with BWIA, British Airways, Air France, Air Canada, American Airlines are available through Barbados, St Lucia, Martinique, Trinidad and Grenada. The only carriers with scheduled services are LIAT, which connects **St Vincent** with Antigua, Barbados, Carriacou, Dominica, Guadeloupe, Martinique, Trinidad, St Lucia, Grenada, Bequia and Union Island, and Air Martinique, with flights to Union Island, St Lucia and Martinique (linking with Air France to Paris). **Bequia** has scheduled service connections with Carriacou, Grenada, St Vincent, Mustique and Union Island, using LIAT and Mustique Airways. **Union Island** is reached by LIAT and/or Air Martinique from Carriacou, Fort de France, Grenada, Mustique, Bequia, St Lucia and St Vincent. Mustique is served by Air Martinique from Fort-de-France and by Mustique Airways from St Vincent via Bequia. Inter island charters are also operated by SVGAIR, Mustique Airways and Aero Services.

Flights within the Grenadines are cheap but prices rise if travelling to or from another country, eg Carriacou or St Lucia. If economizing it is worth considering a boat to travel internationally, eg from Union Island to Carriacou. Inter-island flights operated by Air Martinique are erratic and sometimes leave early, while LIAT often fails to appear at all, but do not expect the ferry to be any different. Check in for flights a good hour before departure.

● **How To Get There By Sea**
Windward Lines Ltd operates a passenger and cargo ferry service on the *MV Windward* from Trinidad on Thur 1600, arriving St Vincent Fri 0700, departing 1000 for Barbados-St Lucia-Barbados arriving back in St Vincent Mon 0700 and leaving for Trinidad at 1600 with a following service to Guiria, Venezuela or Pampatar, Margarita, round trip fare from St Vincent to St Lucia US$60, Barbados US$60, Trinidad US$90, Venezuela US$138, cabins US$20-50, one way fares 65% of return. For information

contact Global Steamship Agencies Ltd, Mariner's Club, Wrightson Road, PO Box 966, Port of Spain, Trinidad, T 809-624-2279, 625-2547, F 627-5091. The Geest Line calls weekly at St Vincent en route from and to Southampton (passengers are taken; T 456-1718 in St Vincent, (0446) 700 333 in UK). Several flour ships ply between St Vincent and St Kitts via Montserrat, and it is possible to hitch a lift on these, T 457-1918. There is a regular boat service to Grenada and the Grenadines (see below).

If arriving by yacht, ports of entry are at Wallilabou, on the NW coast, Kingstown, Bequia, Mustique and Union Island. Yachtsmen often anchor at Blue Lagoon or Young island and taxi to Kingstown to complete customs and immigration formalities.

● Airlines

LIAT, Halifax Street, Kingstown, T 457-1821 for reservations, airport office T 458-4841, on Union Island T 458-8230; Air Martinique T 458-4528, F 458-4187, or T 458-8826 on Union Island; Mustique Airways, PO Box 1232, T 458-4380, F 456-4586; SVGAIR, PO Box 39, Blue Lagoon, St Vincent, T 456-5610, F 458-4697; British Airways, T 458-4841; Airlines of Carriacou, Point Salines Airport, Grenada, T 444-2898/4101 ext 2005/2035; St Vincent Airways, T 456-4176 at the airport.

● Airport

Arnos Vale, 2 miles from Kingstown. Taxi fare to town EC$15 (with other fares ranging from EC$10-35 for nearer or more distant hotels set by government); minibus to Kingstown EC$1.50, 10 mins. On Union Island there is an airport fee of EC$6 on both arrival and departure as it is private property. Check in is at the Anchorage by the gate to the airfield, no signs, you have to carry your own luggage over to the airport building.

There is a departure tax of EC$20.

● Customs

200 cigarettes, or 50 cigars, or 250 grams of tobacco, and 40 fluid ounces of alcoholic beverage may be imported duty free.

● Boat Services

From Kingstown to Bequia, MV *Admiral 1* sails at 0900 and 1900 Sun-Fri, returning 0730 and 1700; 0700 returning 1700 on Sat, 1 hour; MV *Admiral II* (passengers and cars) sails at 1030 and 1630 Mon-Fri (1230 on Sat), returning 0630 and 1400 (0630 on Sat), 1 hour journey, EC$10, EC$12 on Sun (both vessels run by

Admiralty Transport Co Ltd, T 458-3348 for information); if you travel under sail, be prepared to get wet from the spray as the crossing is often rough, *Friendship Rose* (a mailboat until 1992, now passengers only) and *Maxann O* (island schooners) sail at 1230, returning 0630 Mon-Fri, 1¼ hrs.

MV *Snapper* sails on Mon and Thur from Bequia (0600) for Kingstown, then returns (1030) to Bequia, continuing (1145) to Canouan, Mayreau, arriving in Union Island at 1545; on Tues and Fri she returns to St Vincent via Mayreau, Canouan and Bequia, leaving Union Island at 0530, arriving St Vincent 1200. On Sat she departs St Vincent at 1030 for Canouan, arriving 1400, then sails via Mayreau to Union Island, returning to St Vincent at 2230. All times are approximate, depending on the amount of goods to be loaded. There are 3-4 cabins, 2 of which are used by the crew but you can negotiate for one quite cheaply if you need it. The *Snapper* is the islands' main regular transport and carries everything, families and their goods, goats and generators; she rolls through the sea and is very cheap, eg Bequia-Union EC$15, Union-Canouan EC$12, Canouan-Mayreau EC$8; the trip can be highly entertaining but note that the timetable is highly unreliable.

MV *Obedient* sails twice a week (Mon and Thur) between Union Island, departs 0745 approximately, and Carriacou, arriving 1300. Two fishing boats sail Carriacou-Union Island from Hillsborough Pier, Mon 1300, 1 hour, EC$10. Frequent boat trips are organized, ask at hotels, take your passport even though not strictly necessary. For other services, check at the Grenadines dock in Kingstown. There are often excursions from Kingstown to Bequia and Mustique on Sun. Fares from Kingstown to Bequia EC$10, EC$12 at night and weekends, Canouan EC$13, Mayreau EC$15 and Union Island EC$20. From Bequia you can take a boat trip to Mustique for US$40 pp by speedboat from Friendship Bay or by catamaran from Port Elizabeth, ask at Sunsports at *Gingerbread*. Throughout the Grenadines local power boats can be arranged to take small groups of passengers almost any distance. If possible try to ensure that the boat is operated by someone known to you or your hotel to ensure reliability. Prices are flexible. Do not expect a dry or comfortable ride if the sea is rough.

For possibilities of crewing on yachts, check the notice board at the Frangipani Yacht Services, Bequia.

For an exit stamp, go to the airport customs and immigration one day before departure.

● **Buses**

Minibuses from Kingstown leave from the new Little Tokyo Fish Market terminal to all parts of the island, including a frequent service to Indian Bay, the main hotel area; they stop on demand rather than at bus stops. At the terminal they crowd round the entrance competing for customers rather than park in the bays provided. They are a popular means of transport because they are inexpensive and give an opportunity to see local life. No service on Sun or holidays. Fares start at EC$1, rising to EC$2 (Layou), EC$4 (Georgetown on the Windward coast), to EC$5 to the Black Carib settlement at Sandy Bay in the NE (this is a difficult route, though, because buses leave Sandy Bay early in the morning for Kingstown, and return in the afternoon). The number of vans starting in Kingstown and running to Owia or Fancy in the N is limited. The best way is to take the early bus to Georgetown and try to catch one of the 2 vans running between Georgetown and Fancy (EC$10). To get to Richmond in the NW take a bus to Barrouallie and seek onward transport from there. It is worthwhile to make a day trip to Mesopotamia (Mespo) by bus (EC$2.50). On Bequia, buses leave from the jetty at Port Elizabeth and will stop anywhere to pick you up, a cheap and reliable service.

● **Car Rental**

If you do want to travel round St Vincent, it is better to rent a car, or hire a taxi with driver for EC$30 per hour. Note that the use of cars on the island is limited, so that only jeeps may be used to go right up Soufrière or beyond Georgetown on the E coast. Charges at Kim's (T 456-1884) for example are: EC$100/day for a car, with restrictions on where you drive in the N, EC$125 for a jeep, 60 miles free a day, EC$1/mile thereafter, weekly rental gives one day free, EC$1,000 excess deposit in advance, delivery or collection anywhere on the island, phone from airport for collection to save taxi hassle, credit cards accepted. Among other agencies (all offering similar rates and terms) are Avis (T 456-9334/4945), Davids (T 457-1116), Star Garage (Hertz, T 457-1169), Johnsons (T 458-4864), and others. Bicycles from Sailors Cycle Centre, T 457-1712. On Bequia, Handy Andy's rents motorbikes and bicycles, T 458-3722/3370.

Driving is on the left. A local driving licence, costing EC$40, must be purchased at the airport, the police station in Bay Street, or the Licensing Authority on Halifax Street, on presentation of your home licence. However, there is no need to pay if you have an International Driving Permit and get it stamped at the central police station. There are limited road signs on St Vincent.

● **Taxis**

Taxi fares are fixed by the Government but drivers are rarely prepared to make a journey at the official price and you may have to pay double the rates quoted here: Kingstown to Airport EC$15, Indian Bay EC$20, Mesopotamia EC$35, Layou EC$35, Orange Hill EC$75, Blue Lagoon EC$30. Hourly hire EC$35 per hour. On Bequia, taxis are pick-up trucks with benches in the back, brightly coloured with names like 'Messenjah', call them by phone or VHF radio.

● **Accommodation**

All prices quoted in the text above are for a double room, 1994 rates. There is a government tax of 7% on hotel rooms, and most add a 10% service charge. Air conditioning is not generally available. If there is no fan in your room, it is often worth asking for one.

● **Camping**

Camping is not encouraged and there are no organized camp sites. Exceptions are made for groups such as Boy Scouts or Girl Guides.

● **Food and Drink**

The national dish is fried jackfish and breadfruit. The island's rum is called Captain Bligh, and the local beers are Hairoun and EKU.

● **Tipping**

10% of the bill if not already included.

● **Shopping**

The St Vincent Philatelic Society on Bay Street, between Higginson Street and River Road, sells stamps in every colour, size and amount for the novice and collector alike. Service is helpful but slow in this second floor warehouse, complete with guard. The St Vincent Craftsmen's Centre is on a road to the right off James Street, heading towards the airport; all local handicraft items are on display here. *Crab Hole* on Bequia, overlooking Admiralty Bay is a boutique where silk screened fabrics are made downstairs and sewn into clothes upstairs, open 0800-1700 Mon-Sat in season, closing earlier out of season, T 458-3290. For handi-

crafts and books, Noah's Arkade, Blue Caribbean Building, Kingstown (T 457-1513, F 456-
9305), and at the *Frangipani* and *Plantation
House* Boutique on Bequia (T 458-3424).
Other bookshops: Wayfarer, beneath the
Heron Hotel, and the Bequia Bookshop in Port
Elizabeth, run by Iain Gale, who keeps an
excellent stock of books, maps and charts, T
458-3905. A map of St Vincent, 1:50,000 (and
Kingstown, 1:10,000), EC$15, is available
from the Ministry of Agriculture, Lands and
Survey Department, Murray Road (on the road
to Indian Bay, or if walking, go through the
alleyway at the General Post Office and turn
right at the Grammar School). In 1992 the
Ordnance Survey (Southampton, UK) brought
out a new tourist map of St Vincent, 1:50,000,
with insert of Kingstown, 1:10,000, double
sided with Grenadines on the reverse, with text
panels giving information, walks etc.

● **Banks**
Barclays Bank plc, Scotia Bank, Canadian Im-
perial Bank of Commerce, National Commer-
cial Bank of St Vincent, all on Halifax Street,
Caribbean Banking Corporation, 81 South
River Road, Kingstown, and at Port Elizabeth,
Bequia. Barclays Bank has a branch on Bequia;
National Commercial Bank has branches at
Arnos Vale airport, on Bequia and Union Island.
There is no bank on Canouan, but the National
Commercial Bank at Grand Bay opens every
alternate Wed from 1000-1400. When you
cash traveller's cheques you can take half in US
dollars and half in EC dollars if you wish.

● **Currency**
The East Caribbean dollar, EC$.

● **Security**
The S end of the waterfront in Kingstown
should be avoided at night as there are no lights
and is an area frequented by drugs users.

● **Health**
Kingston General Hospital, T 456-1185. Emer-
gency T 999. Bequia Casualty Hospital, Port
Elizabeth, T 458-3294.

● **Climate And Clothing**
Temperatures the year round average between
77°F and 81°F (25-7°C), moderated by the
trade winds; average rainfall is 60 inches on
the coast, 150 inches in the interior, with the
wettest months May to November. Best
months to visit are therefore December to May.
You can expect a shower most days, though.
Low season is June to mid-December.

Wear light, informal clothes, but do not
wear bathing costumes or short shorts in shops
or on Kingstown's streets.

● **Hours Of Business**
Shops: 0800-1200, 1300-1600 Mon-Fri
(0800-1200 only, Sat); government offices:
0800-1200, 1300-1615 Mon-Fri; banks:
0800-1200 or 1300 Mon-Fri, plus 1400/1500-
1700 on Fri. The bank at the Airport is open
Mon-Sat 0700-1700.

● **Public Holidays**
1 January, St Vincent and the Grenadines Day
(22 January), Good Friday and Easter Monday,
Labour Day in May, Whit Monday, Caricom Day
and Carnival Tuesday (first or second Monday
and Tuesday in July), August Bank Holiday first
Monday in August, Independence Day (27
October), Christmas Day and Boxing Day.

● **Time Zone**
Atlantic Standard Time, 4 hours behind GMT,
1 hour ahead of EST.

● **Electric Current**
220/240 v, 50 cycles.

● **Post Office**
Halifax Street, open 0830-1500 (0830-1130
on Sat, closed Sun). St Vincent Philatelic Services Ltd, General Post Office, T 457-1911, F
456-2383; for old and new issues, World of
Stamps, Bay 43 Building, Lower Bay Street,
Kingstown.

● **Telecommunications**
are operated by Cable and Wireless, also on
Halifax Street; there is a 5% tax on international phone calls. Phone cards, fax, telex and
telegraph available. Portable phones can be
rented through Boatphone or you can register
your own cellular phone with them upon arrival, T 456-2800. The international code for St
Vincent is 809, followed by a 7-digit local
number beginning with 45.

● **Radio**
NBC Radio is on 705 kHz.

● **Press**
Two newspapers, *The Vincentian* and *The
News*, are both published every Fri.

● **Diplomatic Representation**
UK British High Commission, Grenville St, Box
132, Kingstown, T 457-1701 (after hours
T 458-4381), F 456-2750; **Netherlands** Con-
sulate, St Clair House, 1 Melville St, Box 354,
Kingstown, T 457-2677; **China,** Murray Road,

T 456-2431; **Venezuela**, Granby St, T 456-1374; **France**, Middle St, Box 364, Kingstown, T 456-1615; **Italy**, Queen's Drive, T 456-4774.

● **Tourist Offices**

St Vincent and the Grenadines Department of Tourism, Finance Complex, Bay Street, PO Box 834, Kingstown, T 457-1502, F 456-2610 open Mon-Fri 0800-1200, 1300-1615; helpful desk at Arnos Vale airport, T 458-4685, hotel reservation EC$1; on Bequia (at the landward end of the jetty), T 458-3286, open Sun-Fri 0900-1230, 1330-1600, Sat morning only; on Union Island, T 458-8350, open daily 0800-1200, 1300-1600.

There is a desk in the arrivals hall at the Grantley Adams airport on Barbados, open daily from 1300 until 2000 or the last flight to St Vincent (T 428-0961). This is useful for transfers to LIAT after an international flight.

UK: 10 Kensington Court, London W8 5DL, T 071-937 6570, F 071-937 3611. **USA**: 801 2nd Avenue, 21st floor, New York, NY 10017, T (212) 687-4981, 800-729-1726, F (212) 949-5946 and 6505 Cove Creek Place, Dallas, Texas, 75240, T (214) 239 6451, 800-235-3029, F (214) 239 1002. **Canada**: 32 Park Road, Toronto, Ontario M4W 2N4, T (416) 924-5796, F (416) 924-5844. **Germany**: Bruno Fink, Wurmberg Str 26, D-7032, Sindelfingen, T 49-7031 806260, F 49-7031 805012.

GRENADA

G RENADA, the most southerly of the Windwards, is described as a spice island, for it produces large quantities of cloves and mace and about a third of the world's nutmeg. It also grows cacao, sugar, bananas and a wide variety of other fruit and vegetables. Some of its beaches, specially Grand Anse, a dazzling two-mile stretch of white sand, are very fine. The majority of the tourist facilities are on the island's SW tip, but the rest of the island is beautiful, rising from a generally rugged coast to a spectacular mountainous interior. The highest point is Mount St Catherine, at 2,757 feet. The island seems to tilt on a NE-SW axis: if a line is drawn through ancient craters of Lake Antoine in the NE, the Grand Étang in the central mountains and the Lagoon at St George's, it will be straight. NW of that line, the land rises and the coast is high; SE it descends to a low coastline of rias (drowned valleys). The island is green, well forested and cultivated and is blessed with plenty of rain in the wet season.

Grenada (pronounced "Gren*ay*da") has two dependencies in the Grenadines chain, Carriacou and Petit (often spelt Petite) Martinique. They, and a number of smaller islets, lie N of the main island. The group's total area is 133 square miles. Grenada itself is 21 miles long and 12 miles wide.

The population of some 90,900 (of which 4,595 live on Carriacou and 720 on Petit Martinique) is largely (82%) of African descent. In contrast to other Windward Islands which have had a similar history of disputed ownership between the French and English, the French cultural influence in Grenada has completely died out. Nevertheless, it is a predominantly Catholic island (59%), though there are Protestant churches of various denominations, and a Baha'i Centre. Many people who emigrated from Grenada to the UK are returning to the island and are building smart houses for their retirement which are in stark contrast to the tiny, corrugated iron shacks which are home to many of their countrymen. The population is very young; 36% are under 15 years old and nearly 29% are in the 15-29 years' age bracket.

History

When Columbus discovered the island on his third voyage in 1498, it was inhabited by Caribs, who had migrated from the South American mainland, killing or enslaving the peaceful Arawaks who were already living there. The Amerindians called their island Camerhogue, but Columbus renamed it Concepción, a name which was not to last long, for shortly afterwards it was referred to as Mayo on maps and later Spaniards called it Granada, after the Spanish city. The French then called it La Grenade and by the 18th century it was known as Grenada. Aggressive defence of the island by the Caribs prevented settlement by Europeans until the 17th century. In 1609 some Englishmen tried and failed, followed by a group of Frenchmen in 1638, but it was not until 1650 that a French expedition from Martinique landed and made initial friendly contact with the inhabitants. When relations soured, the French brought reinforcements and exterminated the Amerindian population. Sauteurs, or Morne des Sauteurs, on the N coast, is named after this episode when numerous Caribs apparently jumped to their death in the sea rather than surrender to the French.

The island remained French for about one hundred years, although possession was disputed by Britain, and it was a period of economic expansion and population growth, as colonists and slaves arrived to grow tobacco and sugar at first, followed by cotton, cocoa and coffee. It was during the Seven Years' War in the 18th century that Grenada fell into British hands and was ceded by France to

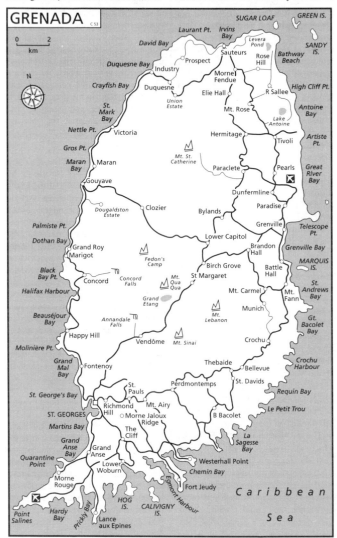

GRENADA

0   2
km

Caribbean Sea

Britain as part of a land settlement in the 1763 Treaty of Paris. Although the French regained control in 1779, their occupation was brief and the island was returned to Britain in 1783 under the Treaty of Versailles. The British introduced nutmeg in the 1780s, after natural disasters wiped out the sugar industry. Nutmeg and cocoa became the main crops and encouraged the development of smaller land holdings. A major slave revolt took place in 1795, led by a free coloured Grenadian called Julian Fedon, but slavery was not abolished until 1834, as in the rest of the British Empire.

In 1833, Grenada was incorporated into the Windward Islands Administration which survived until 1958 when it was dissolved and Grenada joined the Federation of the West Indies. The Federation collapsed in 1962 and in 1967 Grenada became an associated state, with full autonomy over internal affairs, but with Britain retaining responsibility for defence and foreign relations. Grenada was the first of the associated states to seek full independence, which was granted in 1974. Political leadership since the 1950s had alternated between Eric (later Sir Eric) Gairy's Grenada United Labour Party (GULP) and Herbert Blaize's Grenada National Party. At the time of independence, Sir Eric Gairy was Prime Minister, but his style of government was widely viewed as authoritarian and corrupt, becoming increasingly resented by a large proportion of the population. In 1979 he was ousted in a bloodless coup by the Marxist-Leninist New Jewel (Joint Endeavour for Welfare, Education and Liberation) Movement, founded in 1973, which formed a government headed by Prime Minister Maurice Bishop. Reforms were introduced and the country moved closer to Cuba and other Communist countries, who provided aid and technical assistance. In 1983, a power struggle within the government led to Bishop being deposed and he and many of his followers were murdered by a rival faction shortly afterwards. In the chaos that followed a joint US-Caribbean force invaded the island to restore order. They imprisoned Bishop's murderers and expelled Cubans and other socialist nationalities who had been engaged in building a new airport and other development projects. An interim government was set up until elections could be held in 1984, which were won by the coalition New National Party, headed by Herbert Blaize. Since the intervention, Grenada has moved closer to the USA which maintains a large embassy near the airport. Further reading on this era of Grenada's history includes: *Grenada: Whose Freedom?* by Fitzroy Ambursley and James Dunkerley, Latin America Bureau, London, 1984; *Grenada Revolution in Reverse* by James Ferguson, Latin America Bureau, London, 1990; *Grenada: Revolution, Invasion and Aftermath* by Hugh O'Shaughnessy, Sphere Books, London, 1984; *Grenada: Revolution and Invasion* by Anthony Payne, Paul Sutton and Tony Thorndike, London, Croom Helm, 1984; *Grenada: Politics, Economics and Society*, by Tony Thorndike, Frances Pinter, London 1984, and many others.

After the New National Party (NNP) coalition's victory at the polls, with an overwhelming majority, Herbert Blaize became Prime Minister. The NNP won 14 of the 15 seats in the legislature while GULP, led by Sir Eric Gairy, won one. In 1987, the formation of a new opposition party, the National Democratic Congress, led to parliamentary changes. Defections reduced the NNP's representation to nine seats while the NDC gained six. Further divisions within the NNP preceded Mr Blaize's death in December 1989; his faction, led by Ben Jones, became the National Party, while the New National Party name was retained by Keith Mitchell's faction. In general elections held on 13 March 1990, each of these parties won two seats while the NDC, led by Nicholas Brathwaite (formerly head of the interim administration), won seven. The GULP gained four seats, but one of its members joined the Government of Mr Brathwaite in a gesture of solidarity after the fire on the Carenage in April 1990 (see below, under **St George's**), another subsequently joined the NDC and a third left GULP to become an Independent. The fourth was expelled from the party in 1992. By mid-1991 the NDC Government could count on the support of 10 of the 15 MPs. Another opposition party, the left wing Maurice Bishop Patriotic Movement (MBPM), led by Terry Marryshow, failed to win a seat in the elections.

In 1991 the Government decided to commute to life imprisonment the death sentences on 14 people convicted of murdering Maurice Bishop after world wide appeals for clemency. The decision set an important precedent in the region, where the death penalty is still practised. Soon afterwards, Grenada was readmitted to the OECS court system, which it had left in 1979, and which allows for final recourse to the Privy Council. Amnesty International and other organizations have appealed for the release of Mrs Phyllis Coard, one of the 14 convicted, on grounds of ill-health following years of solitary confinement, but so far the Government has refused.

Government

Grenada is an independent state within the Commonwealth, with the British monarch as Head of State represented by a Governor General. There are two legislative houses, the House of Representatives with 15 members. and the Senate with 13 members. The Government is elected for a five year term.

The Economy

Agriculture accounts for about 14% of gdp and employs about 6,000 people. The major export crops are nutmeg, bananas and cocoa; nutmeg and mace together account for about 40% of all exports and Grenada is a leading world producer of this spice. However, prices tumbled following the collapse of the minimum price agreement with Indonesia. At end-1993 prices had fallen to US$0.30/lb, compared with US$1.50/lb four years before. Stocks of nutmeg have been burnt in both Grenada and Indonesia. There are now signs of an improvement in the industry and an informal agreement on price stability has been reached with Indonesia; new projects are coming on stream (eg nutmeg oil distillation) and sales are growing. Banana exports have been falling because of labour shortages and inconsistent quality and quantity. Cocoa exports fluctuate according to the volume of rainfall but the fine flavour of Grenadian cocoa allows it to command a premium of 40%-50% over the world price. Nevertheless, both cocoa and nutmeg growers receive funds from the European Community commodity price funds (Stabex). There is also some cotton grown on Carriacou and limes are grown on both Carriacou and Grenada. Sugar cane is grown in the S of Grenada but efficiency is not high. Most of the rest of farming land is devoted to fruit and vegetables for domestic consumption, such as yams, eddoe, sweet potatoes, tannia, pumpkin, cassava, pigeon peas and maize.

Manufacturing is also mostly processing of agricultural produce, making items such as chocolate, sugar, rum, jams, coconut oil, honey and lime juice. There is also a large brewery (now majority owned by Guinness following the sale of the Government's shares in 1994) and a rice mill. There are 10,000 acres of forest, of which three-quarters are owned by the Government which is undertaking a re-afforestation programme to repair hurricane damage. Fishing is a growing industry, involving about 1,500 people, and there are plans for new fisheries complexes at Halifax Harbour, Gouyave and Grenville.

GRENADA: FACT FILE

Geographic

Land area	348 sq km
forested	8.8%
pastures	3.0%
cultivated	38.2%

Demographic

Population (1992)	90,900
annual growth rate (1987-92)	0.2%
urban	32.2%
rural	67.8%
density	261.2 per sq km
Religious affiliation	
Roman Catholic	59.3%
Protestant	34.5%
Birth rate per 1,000 (1989)	33.0
	(world av 27.1)
Death rate per 1,000 (1989)	8.3
	(world av 9.8)

Education and Health

Life expectancy at birth,	
male	69 years
female	74 years
Infant mortality rate	
per 1,000 live births (1991)	29.0
Physicians (1990)	1 per 1,617 persons
Hospital beds	1 per 279 persons
Calorie intake as %	
of FAO requirement	110%
Population age 25 and over	
with no formal schooling	2.2%
Literacy (over 15)	85.0%

Economic

GNP (1990 market prices)	US$199mn
GNP per capita	US$2,120
Public external debt (1990)	US$82.1mn
Tourism receipts (1990)	US$38.5mn
Inflation (annual av 1985-90)	2.7%
Radio	1 per 1.1 persons
Television	1 per 3.0 persons
Telephone	1 per 8.3 persons

Employment

Population economically active (1988)	
	38,920
Unemployment rate (1992)	+30%
% of labour force in	
agriculture	14.3
quarrying	0.3
manufacturing	7.3
construction	9.1
trade, restaurants	13.9
Police inc paramilitary unit	632

Source *Encyclopaedia Britannica*

The economy suffered from the uncertainties surrounding the Bishop murder and the US invasion, but confidence has gradually returned and investment has picked up. The main area of expansion has been tourism, which has benefited from the airport expansion started with Cuban assistance by the Bishop administration. Air arrivals grew every year in the decade 1983-93 by an annual average of 10%. In 1993 Grenada received 93,919 tourists by air, a 7.3% increase over 1992, with US visitors recording a growth of 24.4%. An even greater rise was expected for 1994 following the opening, in late 1993, of two large new hotels on the S coast, the *Rex Grenadian* and *La Source*, which between them raised room capacity by 28% to 1,428 rooms. 8,639 people visited Carriacou in 1993, a huge increase of 62% over 1992. The yacht charter business has expanded considerably, attracting over 7,000 sailors in 1993 compared with under 5,900 in 1992. The number of yachts calling at Grenadian harbours fluctuates annually, but in 1993 rose to 4,267 from 3,373 in 1992. The greatest increase, however, has been in cruise ship visitors, although they are low spending and do not generate so much foreign exchange. In 1984 only 65 cruise ships called, but have now risen to 382 in 1993, with the number of passengers rising from 34,166 in 1984 to 200,061 in 1993. The Government elected in 1990 announced an arrival tax of US$1 per cruise ship passenger, to raise EC$350,000 per year for improving tourist facilities and this is now likely to rise to US$15 in line with other OECS countries. Grenada currently earns about EC$120 mn from stayover visitors, but only EC$10 mn from cruise ship passengers.

Despite bouyant tourism, Grenada has considerable financial imbalances and unemployment is estimated at 30% of the labour force. Imports are three times the value of exports and tourism revenues are insufficient to cover the trade deficit. Total debt was EC$285.5

mn at the end of March 1990, of which EC\$152.5 mn was external debt, most of which was contracted on concessionary terms to finance infrastructure and other development projects. The need to repay the IMF loans contracted in 1979-83 and reduce the growing budget deficit led the Government to increase levies and fees in the 1991 budget. Income tax was abolished in 1985/86 but there were problems in collecting the value added tax which replaced it; a 10% levy introduced on higher incomes to help service the debt was criticized as reintroducing a form of income tax. Poverty increased because of the worldwide recession, the high cost of imported goods and the introduction of indirect taxation. The World Bank called for direct taxation to be reintroduced. A five-year economic programme announced in 1991, called for fiscal balance to be achieved in 1993. It envisaged selective debt rescheduling, a reduction in the number of public employees, the sale of certain state assets and an overhaul of the tax system. The IMF approved a structural adjustment programme to allow Grenada to seek credits from other multilateral agencies. Economic output declined in 1992 but grew slightly by 0.7% in 1993. In the 1994 budget income tax was reintroduced and VAT was downgraded to a consumption tax. The fiscal position had improved, allowing the Government to consider greater capital spending, which fell from 10% of gdp in 1990 to 2% in 1993. A major programme of road and sea defence improvement was to be financed by the Kuwait Development Fund, Opec, the European Community and the Caribbean Development Bank. After three years of structural adjustment the Government announced a new economic programme aimed at producing annual growth of 3% in 1994-96. Fiscal policy is to remain tight, but public sector investment will rise and the sale of state land will finance the elimination of external debt arrears (EC\$54mn at end-1993) and reduce overall debt.

Flora and Fauna

A system of national parks and protected areas is being developed. Information is available from the Forestry Department, Ministry of Agriculture, Archibald Avenue, St George's. To date, the focal point of the system is the **Grand Étang National Park**, eight miles from the capital in the central mountain range. It is right on the transinsular road from St George's to Grenville. The Grand Étang is a crater lake surrounded by lush tropical forest. A series of trails has been blazed which are well worth the effort for the beautiful forest and views, but can be muddy and slippery after rain. The Morne Labaye nature trail is only 15 mins' long, return same route; the shoreline trail around the lake takes 1½ hrs and is moderately easy; much further, 1½ hrs walk, is Mount Qua Qua. The trail then continues for an arduous three hours to Concord Falls, with an extra ½ hour spur to Fedon's Camp (see p 673) if you wish. From Concord Falls it is 25 mins' walk to the road to get a bus to St George's. These are hard walks (Mount Qua Qua, Fedon's Camp, Concord): wet, muddy, it rains a lot and you will get dirty. Take food and water. A guide is not necessary. An interpretation centre overlooking the lake has videos, exhibitions and explanations of the medicinal plants in the forest. Leaflets about the trails can be bought here for EC\$2 each. There is a bar, a shop and some amusing monkeys and parrots. The Park is open 0830-1600, entrance US\$2. There is overnight accommodation at Lake House, T 442-7425 or enquire at forest centre, also for camping.

The high forest receives over 150 inches of rain a year. Epiphytes and mosses cling to the tree trunks and many species of fern and grasses provide a thick undergrowth. The trees include the gommier, bois canot, Caribbean pine and blue mahoe. At the summit, the vegetation is an example of elfin woodland, the trees stunted by the wind, the leaves adapted with drip tips to cope with the excess moisture. Apart from the highest areas, the island is heavily cultivated. Of interest to the visitor is the variety of spices harvested, many of which can be seen (and samples purchased) at the Dougaldston Estate (see below): nutmeg and its secondary product, mace, cloves, cinammon, allspice, bay, tumeric and ginger. In addition there are calabash gourds, cocoa and more common crops, bananas and coconuts.

In the NE, 450 acres around Levera Pond was opened as a National Park in 1994. As well as having a bird sanctuary and sites of historic interest, Levera is one of the island's largest mangrove swamps; the coastal region has coconut palms, cactus and scrub, providing habitat for iguana and land crabs. There are white beaches where turtles lay their eggs and, offshore, coral reefs and the Sugar Loaf, Green and Sandy islands (boat trip to the last named on Sunday, see **Inter-Island Transport**). You can swim at Bathway but currents are strong at other beaches. The coast between Levera Beach and Bedford Point is eroding rapidly, at a rate of several feet a year. South of Levera is Lake Antoine, another crater lake, but sunken to only about 20 feet above sea level; it has been designated a Natural Landmark.

On the S coast is **La Sagesse Protected Seascape**, a peaceful refuge which includes beaches, a mangrove estuary, a salt pond and coral reefs. In the coastal woodland are remains of sugar milling and rum distilleries. Accommodation and restaurant facilities have been set up at the plantation house (see **Where To Stay** below). To get there turn S off the main road opposite an old sugar mill, then take the left fork of a dirt road through a banana plantation. Close to the pink plantation house, a few feet from a superb sandy beach, is *La Sagesse* bar and restaurant, good food, nutmeg shells on the ground outside. Walk to the other end of the beach to where a path leads around a mangrove pond to another beach, usually deserted apart from the occasional angler, fringed with palms, good snorkelling and swimming, reef just offshore.

Marquis Island, off the E coast, can be visited; at one time it was part of the mainland and now has eel grass marine environments and coral reefs. Nearby is La Baye Rock, which is a nesting ground for brown boobies, habitat for large iguanas and has dry thorn scrub forest. It too is surrounded by coral reefs.

To see a good selection of Grenada's flowers and trees, visit the Bay Gardens at Morne Delice (turn off the Eastern Main Road at St Paul's police station, the gardens are on your left as you go down). It's a pleasant place with a friendly owner; the paths are made of nutmeg shells. In the capital are the rather run down Botanic Gardens.

Grenada is quite good for birdwatching. The only endemic bird is the Grenada Dove, which inhabits scrubby woodland in some W areas. In the rainforest you can see the emerald-throated hummingbird, yellow-billed cuckoo, red-necked pigeon, ruddy quail-dove, cocoa thrush and other species, while wading and shore birds can be spotted at both Levera and in the S and SW. Watch also for the chicken hawk. Yellow-breasted bananaquits are very common. There is little remarkable animal life: frogs and lizards, of course, and iguana, armadillo (tatoo) and manicou (possum), all of these are hunted for the pot. One oddity, though, is a troop of Mona monkeys, imported from Africa over 300 years ago, which lives in the treetops in the vicinity of the Grand Étang. Another import is the mongoose.

The Foundation for Field Research, a US non-profit organization, has four projects on Grenada: an archaeological excavation of an Amerindian village near La Sagesse, which is believed could date back to 500 AD; a sea turtle conservation effort to protect eggs and prevent extinction of the leatherback; a monkey observation programme to study the social behaviour of the Mona monkey; and the underwater excavation of a shipwreck at the mouth of St George's Harbour. Volunteers are welcomed to support the work of the scientists for a day or a week. Contact the Foundation at PO Box 771, St George's, or T 440-8854, F 440-2330, office hours Mon-Fri, 1000-1800.

Diving and Marine Life

Some of the reefs around Grenada have been mentioned above; they and other reefs provide excellent sites for diving. A popular dive is to the wreck of the Italian cruise liner, *Bianca C* which went down in 1961. A number of diving companies operate from Grand Anse, eg Dive Grenada by the *Grenada Renaissance*, T 444-4371 ext 638, evenings T 440-5875, F 444-4800. A basic scuba dive costs about US$40 pp, a 2-tank dive is US$60, resort course US$50, snorkelling trips US$16; dive packages and open water certification are available. Other companies on Grenada offering scuba diving include Scuba World, T 444-3333, at the *Rex Grenadian*. On Carriacou, Silver Beach Diving, attached to the *Silver Beach Hotel*, provides courses and a variety of dive locations. German-run, the equipment is new. Windsurfing and waterskiing also available, T/F 443-7882. Tanki's Watersport Paradise is on L'Esterre Bay, T 443-8406, F 443-8391, also offers instruction and modern equipment.

Snorkelling equipment hire costs about US$12 for 3 hrs, sometimes for a day; again, there are plenty of opportunities for this. Glass-bottomed boats make tours of the reefs.

Humpback whales can be seen off Grenada and Carriacou during their migrations in December-April. Contact Mosden Cumberbatch (see below) for whale watching tours. Pilot whales and dolphins are also found in Grenadian waters (see **Whale and Dolphin Watch-** **ing** by Erich Hoyt at the beginning of this *Handbook*.

Beaches and Watersports

There are 45 beaches on Grenada. The best are in the SW, particularly Grand Anse, a lovely stretch of white sand which looks N to St George's. It can get crowded with cruise passengers, but there's usually plenty of room for everyone. Watch your bags, petty theft has been reported and vendors can be bothersome. Morne Rouge, the next beach going SW, is more private, has good snorkelling and no vendors. There are other nice, smaller beaches around Lance aux Épines. The beaches at Levera and Bathway in the NE are also good, and since the construction of a new road are much easier to get to.

Windsurfing, waterskiing and parasailing all take place off Grand Anse beach. Windsurf board rental about US$7 for ½ hour, waterskiing, US$15 per run, parasailing US$25. The Moorings' Club Mariner Watersports Centre at *Secret Harbour*, T 444-4439, F 444-4819, has small sail boats, sunfish, windsurfing, waterskiing, speedboat trips to Hog Island including snorkelling.

Sailing in the waters around Grenada and through the Grenadines, via Carriacou, is very good; sheltered harbours, such as Halifax Bay on the Leeward coast, can be found and there are two marinas: Grenada Yacht Services in St George's harbour (T 440-2508) and Spice Island Marina in Prickly Bay (Lance aux Épines, T 444-4257/4342). There are no port dues or fees for visiting yachts. Grenada Yacht Services, Lagoon Road, St George's, T 440-2508/2883, Go Vacations, T 444-4924, and others charter boats for cruises. *Starwind Enterprise*, skippered by Mosden Cumberbatch, T 440-3678 or at Grenada Yacht Services, US$50 pp day sail, snorkelling included, US$15 sunset cruise. The Moorings Club Mariner Watersports Centre at *Secret Harbour* has a 43-foot yacht for charter with skipper only at US$25 pp half day, US$40 pp whole day, minimum 4 people, T 444-4548/9.

On the first weekend in August the Carriacou Regatta is held, which has developed into a full-scale festival, with land as well as watersports and jump-ups at night. On Grenada yacht races are held at New Year and Easter (another big regatta). In 1994 the First Sailing Festival was held in the last week of January in what is expected to be an annual event, with feeder races from Trinidad and Bequia, Match Racing and other races and on-shore activities. In October an end-of-hurricane-season yacht regatta sponsored by Carib Beer is timed to coincide with Beach Fest, a weekend of beach parties and watersports. Inshore sailing on sunfish, sailfish and hobiecats is offered by Grand Anse and Lance aux Épines hotels and operators. Rates are about US$10 for ½ hour for sunfish rental. If you want someone else to do all the work, take a booze cruise on the *Rhum Runner* (T 440-2189/3422), daytime or evening.

Deep-sea fishing can be arranged through Grenada Yacht Services. Fishermen with charter boats include Captain Peters (T 440-1349), Evans Chartering Services (T 444-4422) and Tropix (T 440-4961). At the end of January each year, Grenada hosts The Spice Island Game Fishing Tournament, which had its 25th anniversary in 1994.

Other Sports

Cricket, the island's main land sport, is played from January to June. There is a large stadium at Queen's Park, just outside St George's, but the locals play on any piece of fairly flat ground or on the beaches. Soccer is also played. Hotels have tennis courts and the Richmond Hills and Tanteen Clubs welcome guests to use their courts. A recommended tennis pro is Richard Hughes, an ex-Davis Cup player who teaches at Richmond Hills and goes round the hotels giving

basic tuition and advanced level sessions, contact him through the *Grenada*, T 444-4371. There is a 9-hole **golf** course at the Grenada Golf and Country Club, Woodlands, above Grand Anse; the club is open daily 0800 to sunset, but only till 1200 on Sunday (green fee EC$15, club hire EC$5, T 444-4128). **Hiking** is excellent, if muddy, in the Grand Étang National Park (see above, **Flora and Fauna** and below, **Around the Island**). An annual triathlon is held in January, with a 1½ km swim along the Grand Anse beach to the *Grenada Renaissance*, a 25-km bicycle race to the aiport, St George's and back to the hotel, then a 5-km run to the Carib brewery and back. For information, contact Paul Slinger, PO Box 44, St. George's, T 444-3343. **Horseriding** can be arranged with The Horseman, St Paul's, St George's, for lessons or trail riding, T 440-5368.

Festivals

Carnival takes place over the second weekend in August, although some preliminary events and competitions are held from the last week in July, with calypsos, steelbands, dancing, competitions, shows and plenty of drink. The Sunday night celebrations continue into Monday, J'Ouvert; Djab Djab Molassi, who represent devils, smear themselves and anyone else (especially the smartly dressed) with black grease. On Monday a carnival pageant is held on the stage at Queen's Park and on Tuesday the bands parade through the streets of St George's to the Market Square and a giant party ensues. Also in August, over the first weekend, are the Carriacou Regatta (see above) and the Rainbow City cultural festival in Grenville which goes on for three days and nights. Carriacou celebrates its carnival at the traditional Lenten time, unlike Grenada. It is not spectacular but it is fun and there is a good atmosphere.

Throughout the island, but especially

at Gouyave, the Fisherman's Birthday is celebrated at the end of June (the feast of Saints Peter and Paul); it involves the blessing of nets and boats, followed by dancing, feasting and boat races. Independence Day is 7 February.

During Carnival it is difficult to find anywhere to stay and impossible to hire a car unless booked well in advance.

ST GEORGE'S

The island's capital, *St George's*, with its terraces of pale, colour-washed houses and cheerful red roofs, was established in 1705 by French settlers, who called it Fort Royale. Much of its present-day charm comes from the blend of two colonial cultures: typical 18th century French provincial houses intermingle with fine examples of English Georgian architecture. Unlike many Caribbean ports, which are built around bays on coastal plains, St George's straddles a promontory. It therefore has steep hills with long flights of steps and sharp bends, with police on point duty to prevent chaos at the blind junctions. At every turn is a different view or angle of the town, the harbour or the coast.

St George's is one of the Caribbean's most beautiful harbour cities. The town stands on an almost landlocked sparkling blue harbour against a background of green and hazy blue hills. The Carenage runs around the inner harbour, connected with the Esplanade on the seaward side of Fort George Point by the Sendall Tunnel, built in 1895. There is always plenty of dockside activity on the Carenage, with food, drinks and other goods being loaded and unloaded from wooden schooners. It is planned to redevelop St George's harbour, moving the cruise liner dock from the mouth of the Carenage to a point further down the SW coast. The Carenage would then be left to small shipping and all the shopping would be duty-free. So far, a small promenade and shelter have been built.

The small National Museum, in the cells of a former barracks, in the centre of town (corner of Young and Monckton Streets) is worth a visit; it includes some items from West Africa, exhibits from the sugar and spice industries and of local shells and fauna (entry US$1, open Mon-Fri 0900-1600, Sat 1030-1300). Fort George (1705) on the headland is now the police headquarters, but public viewpoints have been erected from which to see the coast and harbour. Photographs are not allowed everywhere. Some old cannons are still in their positions; tremendous views all round. Just down from the Fort is St Andrew's Presbyterian Kirk (1830) also known as Scot's Kirk. On Church Street are a number of important buildings: St George's Anglican Church (1825), the Roman Catholic Cathedral (tower 1818, church 1884) and the Supreme Court and Parliament buildings (late 18th, early 19th century). St George's oldest religious building is the Methodist Church (1820) on Green Street. The Post Office and the Public Library are examples of old government buildings on the Carenage (the Library has been renovated and is being stocked with foreign assistance). In this part of the city are many brick and stone warehouses, roofed with red, fish tail tiles brought from Europe as ballast. A serious fire on 27 April 1990 damaged six government buildings on the Carenage, including the Treasury, the Government Printery, the Storeroom and the Post Office. They were still not repaired in early 1994, but funds have now been made available and work was due to commence. Also on the Carenage is a monument to the Christi Degli Abbissi, moved from the entrance to the harbour, which commemorates "the hospitality extended to the crew and passengers of the ill-fated liner", *Bianca C* (see **Diving and Marine Life** above). It stands on the walkway beside Wharf Road. The Market Square, off Halifax Street (one of the main streets, one steep block from the

Esplanade), is always busy. It is the terminus for many minibus routes and on Saturday holds the weekly market.

Just N of the city is Queen's Park, which is used for all the main sporting activities, carnival shows and political events. It is surrounded by a turquoise palisade. From Richmond Hill there are good views (and photo opportunities) of both St George's and the mountains of the interior. On the hill are Forts Matthew (built by the French, 1779),

1. St George's Anglican Church
2. St Andrew's Presbyterian Kirk
3. Roman Catholic Cathedral
4. National Museum
5. Public Library
6. Parliament
7. Botanical Gardens
8. Market Sq, Bus terminal & National Commercial Bank
9. LIAT
10. Grenada Yacht Club
11. Department of Tourism

12. Post Office
13. Old Post Office
14. Cable & Wireless / Telephone Office
15. Barclays Bank
16. Scotia Bank
17. Police Headquarters
18. Tourist Bureau
19. The Nutmeg

ST. GEORGE'S

Frederick (1791) and Adolphus (built in a higher position than Fort George to house new batteries of more powerful, longer range cannon), and the prison in which are held those convicted of murdering Maurice Bishop.

The Southwest

From the Carenage, you can take a road which goes round the Lagoon, another sunken volcanic crater, now a yacht anchorage. It is overlooked by the ruins of the *Santa Maria Hotel*, which was taken over by the revolutionary government and subsequently destroyed in the intervention. Several plans have been submitted for the rehabilitation of the hotel. Carrying on to the SW tip you come to *Grand Anse*, Grenada's most famous beach. Along its length are many hotels, but none dominates the scene since, by law, no development may be taller than a coconut palm. A side road leads round to the very pleasant bay and beach at Morne Rouge, which is away from the glitz of Grande Anse. There is a good view across Grande Anse to St George's from the little headland of Quarantine Point. From Grand Anse the road crosses the peninsula to the new Point Salines airport and the Lance aux Épines headland. The road to Portici and Parc à Boeuf beaches leads to the right, off the airport road; follow the signs to *Groomes* beach bar on Parc à Boeuf (food and drink available). Portici beach is virtually deserted, with good swimming despite a steeply shelving beach and excellent snorkelling around Petit Cabrits point at its NE end. On Prickly Bay (the W side of Lance aux Épines) are hotels, the Spice Island Marina and other yachting and watersports facilities. Luxury homes take up much of Lance aux Épines down to Prickly Point. There is a glorious stretch of fine white sand, the lawns of the *Calabash Hotel* run down to the beach, very nice bar and restaurant open to non-residents, steel bands often play there.

From the Point Salines/Lance aux Épines crossroads you can head E along a road which snakes around the S coast. At Lower Woburn, a small fishing community, you can see vast piles of conch shells in the sea, forming jetties and islets where they have been discarded by generations of lambie divers. Any number of turn-offs, tracks and paths, go inland to join the Eastern Main Road, or run along the rias and headlands, such as Calivigny (which is being developed, together with neighbouring Calivigny and Hog Islands, into a resort), Fort Jeudy, Westerhall Point or La Sagesse with its nature reserve (see above). Many of Grenada's most interesting and isolated bays are in the SE, accessible only by jeep or on foot; taxi drivers can drop you off at the start of a path and you can arrange to be picked up later.

Around the Island

The W coast road from St George's has been rebuilt with funds from the government, the Caribbean Development Bank, the EEC and USAID. It is good all the way to Industry. Only the section from Industry to Sauteurs has particularly rough patches but it is fine in an ordinary car with care.

Beauséjour Estate, once the island's largest, is now in ruins (except for the estate Great House). On its land are a Cuban-built radio station, a half-completed stadium and squatters; the owners and the government cannot agree on the estate's future. Beyond Beauséjour is Halifax Bay, a beautiful, sheltered harbour.

At Concord, a road runs up the valley to the First Concord Falls (45 mins hot walk from the main road or go by car, driving slowly, children everywhere), where you can pay US$1 to go to a balcony above the small cascade. The Second Concord Falls are a 30-mins' walk (each way), with a river to cross seven times; a guide will charge EC$20 but there is no need for one, the path has been improved and security at the lower falls has stopped occasional thefts. Three hours further uphill is Fedon's Camp, at 2,509 feet, where Julian Fedon (see **History** above) fortified a hilltop in 1795 to await reinforcements from Martinique to assist his rebellion against the British. After bloody fighting, the camp was captured; today it is a Historical Landmark. It is possible to hike from Concord to Grand Étang in five hours, a hard walk, wet and muddy but rewarding (see **Flora and Fauna**). The trail is hard to spot where it leaves the path to the upper falls about two thirds of the way up on the left across the river. There is no problem following the trails in the opposite direction.

North of Concord, just before Gouyave, is a turn-off to Dougaldston Estate. Before the revolution 200 people were employed here in cultivating spices and other crops. Now there are only about 20 workers, the place is run down, the buildings in disrepair, the vehicles wrecked. Still, you can go into a shed where bats fly overhead and someone will explain all the spices to you. Samples cost EC$3 for a bag of cinammon or cloves, EC$2 for nutmeg, or there are mixed bags; give the guide a tip.

Gouyave, "the town that never sleeps", is a fishing port, nutmeg collecting point and capital of St John's parish. At the Nutmeg Processing Station, you can see all the stages of drying, grading, separating the nutmeg and mace and packing (give a tip here too). The husks are used for fuel or mulch and the fruit is made into nutmeg jelly (a good alternative to breakfast marmalade). The Station is a great wooden building by the sea, with a very powerful smell. A tour for EC$1 is highly recommended. Gouyave is the principal place to go to for the Fisherman's Birthday festival (see above).

Just outside Victoria, another fishing port and capital of St Mark's Parish, is a rock in the sea with Amerindian petroglyphs on it (best to know where to look

over the parapet). The road continues around the NW coast, turning inland before returning to the sea at *Sauteurs*, the capital of St Patrick's parish, on the N coast. The town is renowned as the site of the mass suicide of Grenada's last 40 Caribs, who jumped off a cliff rather than surrender to the French (see **History** above). Behind Sauteurs is McDonald College from whose gate there are marvellous views out to sea, with the Grenadines beyond the town's two church towers, and inland to cloud-covered mountains. In March Sauteurs celebrates St Patrick's Day with a week of events, exhibits of arts and crafts and a mini-street festival.

From Sauteurs a road approaches Levera Bay (see above) from its W side. Turn left at *Chez Norah's* bar, a two-storey, green, corrugated iron building (snacks available); the track rapidly becomes quite rough and the final descent to Levera is very steep, suitable only for 4-wheel drive. A better way to Levera approaches from the S. The road forks left about two miles S of Morne Fendue, passes through River Sallee and past Bathway Beach. Swimming is good at the beautiful Levera Beach and there is surf in certain conditions. Do not swim far out as there is a current in the narrows between the beach and the privately-owned Sugar Loaf Island. Further out are Green and Sandy Islands; you may be able to arrange a trip there with a fisherman who keeps his boat on Levera Beach.

Morne Fendue plantation house offers accommodation (4 rooms, US$35s, US$40-75d including meals), and serves lunch for EC$40, including drinks; good local food and all you can drink, T 440-9330, reservations essential. The house, owned by Betty Mascoll MBE, is full of atmosphere (although some of the plaster and stucco work is in poor shape), and the driveway ends in a flowerbed full of poinsettias. St Patrick's is an agricultural region, comparatively poor and marginal.

On the E side of the island, Amerindian remains can be seen on rock carvings near Hermitage (look for a sign on the road) and at an archaeological dig near the old Pearls airport. Apparently it's so unprotected that lots of artefacts have been stolen. An excursion can be made to Lake Antoine (see above) with, nearby, the River Antoine Rum Distillery, driven by a water mill.

Grenville is the main town on the E coast and capital of St Andrew's Parish, the largest parish in Grenada with a population of about 25,000. It is a collection point for bananas, nutmeg and cocoa, and also a fishing port. There are some well-preserved old buildings, including the Court House, Anglican Church, police station and Post Office. The Rainbow City Festival is held here at the beginning of August, with arts and crafts displays, street fairs, cultural shows and a 10 km road race. Funds are being raised to restore and convert the old Roman Catholic church into a library, museum, art gallery and cultural centre. Construction of the church began in 1841 and was used as a church until 1915, when mosquitoes finally triumphed over worshippers. From 1923-1972 it was used as a school, but then abandoned. Two miles S of Grenville are the Marquis Falls, also called Mt Carmel Falls, the highest in Grenada. Trails are being improved, with sign posts and picnic areas. Marquis village was the capital of St Andrew's in the 17th and 18th centuries. Nowadays it is the centre of the wild pine handicraft industry. Historical sites nearby are Battle Hill and Fort Royal. From here boats go to Marquis Island (see above).

Mount St Catherine can be climbed quite easily, contrary to popular opinion, although in places it is a climb rather than a walk. There are several routes, the easiest reported to be from the village of Mt Hope (minibuses go there from Grenville), from where a 4-wheel drive can take you to within an hour of the summit

or you can walk along the track, 30 mins. A guide is not essential but you will need someone to point out the route. Do not go alone and do not go if you suffer from vertigo. Do not take chances with daylight. For information on this and anything else, contact Mr and Mrs Benjamin at Benjamin's Variety Store, Victoria Street, Grenville. If they do not know the answer they will know someone who does. Mrs Benjamin is on the Tourist Board. Telfer Bedeau, from Soubise, is the walking expert, and can be contacted on T 442-6200.

The transinsular, or hill road, from Grenville to St George's used to be the route from the Pearls airport to the capital, which all new arrivals had to take. Now it is well-surfaced, but twisty and narrow. The minibus drivers on it are generally regarded as "maniacs". To give an idea of the conditions, one bend is called "Hit Me Easy". The road rises up to the rain forest, often entering the clouds. If driving yourself, allow up to $1\frac{1}{2}$ hours from Levera to St George's and avoid the mountain roads around Grand Étang in the dark, although the night time sounds of the dense jungle are fascinating. Shortly before reaching the Grand Étang (full details above), there is a side road to the St Margaret, or Seven Sisters Falls. They are only a $\frac{1}{2}$-hour walk from the main road, but a guide is essential, or else get very good directions. After Grand Étang, there is a viewpoint at 1,910 feet overlooking St George's. A bit further down the hill is a detour to the Annandale Falls which plunge about 40 feet into a pool where the locals dive and swim. If coming from St George's on Grenville Road, fork left at the Methodist Church about half way to Grand Étang.

The peaks in the SE part of the Grand Étang Forest Reserve can be walked as day trips from St George's. **Mount Maitland** (1,712 feet), for instance, is a pleasant morning out. Take a bus from the Market Place to Mardigras, or if there is none, get off at the junction at St Paul's and walk up. At the Pentecostal (IPA) church, turn left and immediately right. The paths are reasonably clear and not too muddy, but shorts are not recommended and long sleeves are preferable. The walk takes less than an hour each way and there are good views from the top over both sides, with some humming-birds.

Mount Sinai (2,306 feet) is not as spectacular as Mount St Catherine, nor as beautiful as Mount Qua Qua, but is is not as muddy either. Take a bus from St George's to Providence, then walk up (two hours) the particularly lovely (and friendly) road to Petit Étang and beyond, where the road turns into a track in the banana fields. The path up the mountain is hard to spot; it begins behind a banana storage shed and must be closely watched. The terrain is a bit tricky near the top. There is a path down the other side to Grand Étang. Local opinions differ over how badly you would get lost without a guide as the paths are no longer maintained.

The highest point in the SE is known on the Ordnance Survey map as South East Mountain (2,348 feet), but to locals as Mount Plima (Plymouth?). You can get up to the ridge, from where there are fine views, but both this summit and the nearby Mount Lebanon are inaccessible without a guide and machete. Here too it used to be possible to descend to Grand Étang but it is difficult now. For this area take a bus from St George's to the junction for Pomme Rose and walk up through the village. Mayhe Hazard lives near the top of the village and is the local expert on the trails (traces). He is good company and may be prepared to guide in the area; he will certainly show you the trail to the ridge, which you could never find alone.

CARRIACOU

Carriacou (pronounced *Carr*-yacoo) is an attractive island of green hills descending to sandy beaches. It is much less mountainous than Grenada, which means that any cloudy or rainy weather clears much quicker. With an area of 13 square miles, it is the largest of the Grenadines. It lies 23 miles NE of Grenada; 2½ miles further NE is Petit Martinique, which is separated by a narrow channel from Petit St Vincent, the southernmost of St Vincent's Grenadine dependencies. Efforts are being made by the Government to curb contraband and drug smuggling in Carriacou. An opposition proposal has been put forward to make the island a free trade zone, or to allow it to secede from Grenada.

Carriacou's population is under 5,000, less than 600 of whom live in the capital, **Hillsborough**. On the one hand, the islanders display a strong adherence to their African origins in that the annual Big Drum Dances, which take place around Easter, are almost purely West African. The Tombstone Feasts are unique. On the other hand, French traditions are still evident at L'Esterre and there is a vigorous Scottish heritage, especially at **Windward**, where the people are much lighter skinned than elsewhere on the island as a result of their Scottish forebears. Windward used to be the centre for the craft of hand-built schooners but in recent years the boat builders have moved to Tyrrel Bay. Begun by a ship-builder from Glasgow, the techniques are unchanged, but the white cedar used for the vessels now has to be imported from Grenada or elsewhere. The sturdy sailing vessels are built and repaired without the use of power tools in the shade of the coconut palms at the edge of the sea. To demonstrate the qualities of these local boats, the Carriacou Regatta was initiated in 1965. It has grown into the major festival described above.

The local painter, Canute Calliste, has

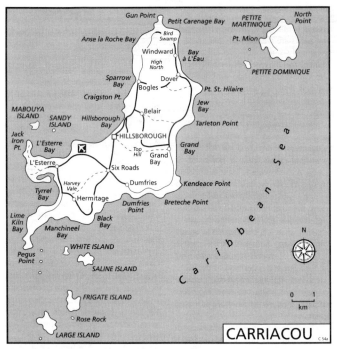

Gun Point
Petit Carenage Bay
PETITE MARTINIQUE
North Point
Anse la Roche Bay
Bird Swamp
Pt. Mion
Windward
High North
Bay à L'Eau
PETITE DOMINIQUE
Sparrow Bay
Dover
Bogles
Pt. St. Hilaire
Craigston Pt.
Belair
Jew Bay
MABOUYA ISLAND
SANDY ISLAND
Hillsborough Bay
Tarleton Point
Jack Iron Pt.
L'Esterre Bay
HILLSBOROUGH
Top Hill
Grand Bay
Grand Bay
L'Esterre
Six Roads
Harvey Vale
Dumfries
Kendeace Point
Tyrrel Bay
Hermitage
Dumfries Point
Breteche Point
Lime Kiln Bay
Black Bay
Manchineel Bay
Pegus Point
WHITE ISLAND
SALINE ISLAND
Caribbean Sea
N
FRIGATE ISLAND
Rose Rock
LARGE ISLAND
0   1
km
CARRIACOU C 54a

his studio at L'Esterre. His naive style captures the scenes of Carriacou (kite flying, launching schooners, festivals); a collection of his paintings have been published in a book by MacMillan, he is also an accomplished violinist and performs the quadrille, a dance which is part of the island's cultural heritage. The Carriacou Historical Society Museum on Paterson Street in Hillsborough has exhibits from Amerindian settlements in the island and from later periods in its history; the woman who runs it is the daughter of Canute Calliste, and can tell you about the Arawak ruins on the island, open Monday-Friday, 0930-1600, Sat 1000-1600. There are also ruined plantations. On Hospital Hill, Belair, NE of Hillsborough, there is an overgrown old sugar Mill, stunning views. There is good

walking on the back roads and the woods are teeming with wildlife such as iguanas.

Off the island are interesting underwater reefs and sandy islets with a few palms on them, ideal for snorkelling and picnicking. **Sandy Island** is a tiny, low-lying atoll in Hillsborough Bay off Lauriston Point, with a few palm trees for shade, safe and excellent swimming and snorkelling, take food, drink and plenty of suntan lotion. Boat from Hillsborough EC$60, 30 mins each way, pick a day when the islet is not swamped with boat loads of cruise ship visitors. Alternatively try **White Island**, a similar islet in Manchineel Bay off the S coast, ask for boats at *Cassada Bay Hotel*. Visitors should see the oyster beds at **Tyrrel Bay** where "tree-oysters" grow on mangrove roots. Tyrrel

Bay is a favourite anchorage for the many yachts which visit the island.

A recommended beautiful beach is **Anse La Roche**, which faces W and has a spectacular view across the strait to the mountains of rugged Union Island. Snorkelling is good, particularly among the rocks at the side. Walk from Bogles along the dirt road heading northwards, past the *Caribbee Inn* and forking right at Honey Hill House; after about 30 mins the road starts to rise, turn left at the large tree which overhangs the track and follow a narrow path through the woods to a ruined farmhouse. The path leads to the right, through bushes; keep to the downhill side of the open slope, bear right down a steep slope leading through more trees to the beach. Take food and drink, there are no facilities and few people, about 45 mins' walk each way. Very peaceful, watch the yachts rounding the headland on their way to anchorage; at night turtles swim ashore to lay their eggs. If instead of turning off the track to Anse La Roche, you carry on walking northwards, the well-shaded, grassy road rounds Gun Point with lovely views of the Grenadines. A path leads down (opposite a mauve-painted house) to the beach at *Petit Carenage Bay*, which has coarse, coral sand, good swimming and modest surf in some conditions. Returning to the road, Windward is a few mins walk further on, a few shops and local bars.

Buses go from Hillsborough to Bogles, Windward (EC$2) and to Tyrrel Bay. A bus also goes from the airport to Windward (EC$1.50). The normally excellent service goes to pieces if it is wet. There are also plenty of taxis, or you can hire a car. Alternatively, just walk around. Fishing and sailing trips from Hillsborough pier or ask at hotels. Yachts can be hired by the day from Tanki's diving base near the airport; ask for Captain Dennis. Out of season the island is quiet, and not all the hotels are open.

Barclays Bank and National Commercial Bank have branches on Carriacou. These, the government and customs offices, post office and the commercial centre are around the pier in Hillsborough. The market is here too; it comes alive on Monday when the produce is brought in. Food is limited in variety, especially fresh vegetables. "Jack Iron" rum (180° proof) is a local hazard, it is so strong that ice sinks in it. It is distilled in Barbados but bottled in Carriacou; it costs around EC$10 per bottle and is liberally dispensed on all high days and holidays (fairly liberally on other days too).

It is advisable to use insect repellent on the beaches, especially in the rainy season. At night it is best to use a mosquito net.

Island Information - Carriacou
● **Where To Stay**

Silver Beach Resort, US$90-105d off season, US$100-120 winter, depending on room or apartment, though for a longer stay a cheaper rate can be negotiated with the owner, good, helpful, child-friendly, T 443-7337, F 443-7165, scuba diving on site; *Cassada Bay Resort*, 9 cabins, 14 double rooms, use of private island, fitness room, use of watersports equipment, mini-cinema room, US$80d summer, US$90d winter, T 443-7494, F 443-7672; *Caribbee Inn*, Prospect, T 443-7380, F 443-8142, lovely setting, pricey US$80-110d for small room, US$120-150 for a suite, US$800-1,250/week for 4-person villa, expensive food, snorkelling off stoney beach, 40-mins walk to excellent beach, out of town.

● **Guesthouses**

Peace Haven Guest House, S of pier, Main Street, Hillsborough, T 443-7475, family and bachelor units from US$24-55, basic but good rooms, share small kitchen and bathroom, contact Lucille Atkins, very friendly and helpful, on the sea front a few hundred yards S of the jetty, rooms rather small, sometimes water shortages, more rooms being built; *Ade's Dream*, T 443-7317, N of pier, Main Street, Hillsborough, US$20-40d, newly extended with 16 rooms share large kitchen, very clean, run by hard-working and friendly Mrs Mills (good reports); *The Sand*, T 443-7100, between Hillsborough and the airport, quiet, basic but clean, across the road is a nice beach, 6 rooms, US$25d with shared kitchen and bathroom, US$21 rooms without kitchenette, US$35d apartment; *Scraper's*, Tyrrel Bay, T 443-7403, local restaurant and 5 rooms US$40d all year, 2-bedroomed cottages available, close to bay, cheaper for locals; *Constant Spring*, T 443-7396, overlooks Tyrrel Bay, 3 double rooms with shared bathroom and kitchen, comfortable, attractive, US$90d.

There are many fully equipped houses to rent, costing about US$100 a month. See Mr Emmons or Mrs Joseph, or ask at the tourist office on the quay.

● **Where To Eat**

There are some basic local bar/restaurants but they often run out of food quite early or close in the evenings, check during the day if they will be open; finding meals is particularly difficult at weekends. *Barba's Oyster Bar*, at Tyrrel Bay above a supermarket, is new and clean but has slow service; *L'Aquilone*, above Tyrrel Bay, 15 mins' walk from bus stop, T 443-7197, marvellous view, small restaurant serving good Italian food at moderate prices, is also coast-guard station with radio contact and has takeaway/delivery service to boats; *Constant Spring*, Tyrrel Bay, does takeaway chicken; *Love Knott*, Tyrrel Bay, French food, moderate prices; *Scraper's*, Tyrrel Bay, very good lunch, Mr Scraper and his family are very hospitable; *Roof Garden*, misleading name, near Market Hall, Hillsborough, T 443-7204, clean and friendly but limited choice; *Hillsborough Bar*, Main Street, attractive place for a drink, meals can be ordered the day before; *Callaloo*, Hillsborough, T 443-8004, EC$30 for dinner, plenty of choice, highly rec; *Talk of the Town*, in Hillsborough, cheap and good; *Turtle Dove* snack bar in Hermitage, T 443-7194; *Cassada Bay Resort* in the SE is good for a meal or drink, good food and wonderful sunset view, friendly.

PETIT MARTINIQUE

Petit Martinique is the only offshore island from Carriacou on which people live (about 600 of them). Its area is 486 acres, rising to a pointed peak. The principal occupations are boatbuilding and fishing. There are no hotels.

INFORMATION FOR VISITORS

● **Documents**

Citizens of the UK, USA and Canada need only provide proof of identity (with photograph) and an onward ticket (but note that if you go to Grenada via Trinidad, a passport *has* to be presented in Trinidad). For all others a passport and onward ticket are essential, though a ticket from Barbados to the USA (for example) is accepted. Departure by boat is not accepted by the immigration authorities. Citizens of certain other countries (not the Commonwealth, Caribbean—except Cuba—, South Korea, Japan and most European countries) must obtain a visa to visit Grenada. Check before leaving home. When you arrive in Grenada expect to have your luggage examined very thoroughly. It may take you at least 45 mins to get through passport control and customs. You must be able to give an accommodation address when you arrive.

● **Airport Tax**

For stays of over 24 hrs, departure tax is EC$25 (EC$12.50 for children aged 10 to 16) and a security supplement is EC$10. There is a EC$5 tax on airline tickets purchased in Grenada. No tax payable on flights from Grenada to Carriacou.

● **How To Get There By Air**

Scheduled flights from London, Gatwick, once a week with British Airways, or connections via Antigua with LIAT; BWIA flies once a week from Frankfurt; Caledonian and Air Europe fly from London and Milan respectively; from the USA, BWIA flies daily from Miami. American Airlines fly daily from the USA via San Juan, Puerto Rico.

Within the Caribbean BWIA connects Grenada with St Lucia, Trinidad and Barbados. LIAT flies to Grenada from Antigua, Barbados, Trinidad, St Lucia, St Vincent and Union Island. LIAT connects Grenada with Carriacou, flying 6 or 7 times a day from 0640 to 1715. (The airline is sometimes forgetful where luggage is concerned, so make sure yours is loaded on and off the plane. Also be sure to reconfirm your flights.) Airlines of Carriacou also flies to Carriacou, and to Bequia, St Vincent and Union Island.

Several companies operate charters to Grenada from the Caribbean and North America.

● **Airport**

The Point Salines airport is 5 miles from St George's: taxis only, EC$30 to St George's, 15 mins; EC$25 to Grand Anse and Lance aux Épines. Journeys within a one-mile radius of the airport EC$7. Add EC$10 to fares between 1800 and 0600. However, if you start walking down the road towards St George's, you will find that the taxi changes into a bus and will pick you up for EC$10 (only feasible with light luggage). If you are energetic, it takes an hour to walk to Grand Anse, longer to St George's. Returning to the airport you can take a bus from St George's market to Calliste (EC$1.50) then walk, 20 mins downhill. Another route is by bus to the 'Sugarman', EC$1, then catch another minibus or collective taxi to the airport, EC$5. Alternatively, when reconfirming your ticket with LIAT ask about taxis, they offer a reliable taxi service for EC$25 if paid in advance. There are no exchange facilities at the airport.

Carriacou's airport is Lauriston, a EC$10 taxi ride from Hillsborough, EC$15-20 from Windward. Disconcertingly, the main road goes straight across the runway. A fire engine drives out from Hillsborough to meet incoming flights, bringing the Immigration Officer, who clings to a platform at the back in Keystone Cops fashion.

● **Airline Offices**

LIAT, The Carenage, St George's, T 440-2796/7 (444-4121/2 Point Salines, 443-7362 Carriacou); same number in St George's for British Airways and ALM; BWIA, The Carenage, St George's, T 440-3818/9 (T 444-4134 at airport); American Airlines, T 444-2222; Aereotuy, T 444-4732/6.

● **How To Get There By Sea**

A large number of North American cruise lines call, including Chandris American Line and Royal Caribbean Cruise Line. Geest Line stops at the island on its Barry, South Wales/Windward Islands run. T Isaac Joseph, St Andrew's 7512, for information about sailing on the *Fazeela* to Trinidad. The *Eastward* sails about once a month to Isla de Margarita, Venezuela, US$60 one way but you have to buy a return to satisfy Venezuelan entry requirements (the captain will refund your return fare, less 10%, on arrival).

● **Inter-Island Transport**

Every day LIAT flies between Grenada and Carriacou: US$62 return, half that one way (flying time is 12 mins).

On Wed and Sat at 1000 the trading schooners *Alexia II* and *Adelaide B* sail from The Carenage, St George's to Carriacou (4 hrs, EC$20 one way, EC$30 return), returning on Thur and Mon. A larger, steel ferry was added in 1994, schedule currently unknown. In heavy seas you may be better opting for a schooner, which despite being smaller, ride the waves better than the larger boats which may make you seasick. Be prepared for incredibly loud reggae/rap music. The *MV Edna David* sails on Sun 0700, arriving Carriacou 1030, returning 1700, arriving in St George's 2030, EC$35. Times are subject to change and you must check. There are also unscheduled schooner services between these islands; by asking around you might be able to get a passage on one. *Eagle Quest* sails from Grenada to Sandy Island and back on Sun, departing 0930, return 1700.

Carriacou is one hour by schooner from Union Island; scheduled service by MV *Obedient* twice a week, EC$10. Two small fishing boats sail Mon 1300 from Hillsborough pier, one hour, EC$10.

● **Local Transport**

Buses run to all parts of the island from the Market Square and the Esplanade in St George's; on the Esplanade look for the signs, in the Square, ask around. Fares are EC$0.50-1 within St George's, EC$3 to Grand Étang, and EC$4.50 to Grenville and EC$5 to Sauteurs. There is also a regular bus service between Grenville and Sauteurs. The last buses tend to be in mid-afternoon and there are very few on Sun.

Taxi fares are set by the Tourist Board. Fares from the airports are given above. On Grenada, taxis charge EC$4 for the first 10 miles outside St George's, then EC$3 per mile thereafter (an additional charge is made after 1800, EC$10 per journey). A minibus taxi tour of Grenada costs about US$85, 0900-1800, worth it if you can get a group together. Island tours of Carriacou cost between EC$100 and EC$140 by taxi.

Taxis and buses are heavily 'personalized' by the drivers with brightly coloured decorations and names like 'Rusher with Love' or 'Danny Boy', while large speakers blast out steel bands or reggae music; taxi drivers will adjust the volume on request. A water taxi service runs from in front of the *Nutmeg* restaurant, St George's to the Grand Anse beach.

Hitchhiking is quite easy though the roads are not very good.

● **Car Rental**

Cars can be rented from a number of companies for about US$55 or EC$150 a day, plus US$2,500 excess liability and 5% tax (payable by credit card). You must purchase a local permit, on presentation of your national driving licence, for EC$30/US$12; a local permit is not required if you hold an international driving licence. Driving is on the left. When driving, be prepared for no road signs, no indication which way the traffic flow goes (just watch the other cars), and few street names. Maps are often not accurate, so navigation becomes particularly difficult. Also be careful of the deep storm drains along the edges of the narrow roads.

Companies in St George's include Spice Island Rentals (Avis), Paddock and Lagoon Road, T 440-3936; David's, Archibald Avenue, T 444-3399 (has an office at the airport); Mc Intyre, Lagoon Road, T 444-3944; Maitland's (who also rent motorcycles), Market Hill, T 440-4022, also an office at the airport which is often open for late arrivals when others, eg Budget, are closed; C Thomas and Sons, cars, minibuses, jeeps, T 444-4384, mixed reports.

We have received reports that daily rates quoted over the phone are not always honoured when you pick up the car; check that the company does not operate a 3-day minimum hire if you want a rate for one day only, this often applies in high season. On Carriacou: Barba Gabriel, T 443-7454; Leo Cromwell, T 443-7333; Martin Bullen, T 443-7204; *Silver Beach Resort*, T 443-7337.

Bike rentals can be arranged with Ride Grenada, T 444-1157.

● **Where To Stay**

Hotel rooms are subject to a 10% service charge and an 8% tax on accommodation, food and beverages. Rates quoted here are 1994/95. The majority of hotels are in the Grand Anse area, with several around Lance aux Épines. In St George's there are more guesthouses than hotels.

Hotels St George's: *Balisier*, Richmond Hill, PO Box 335, T 440-2346, F 440-6604, out of town, double rooms US$104, excellent views, restaurant, swimming pool, rec; ask here about 1-day walking tours to plantations and other areas of interest.

On Grand Anse: *Coyaba*, PO Box 336, St George's, T 444-4129, F 444-4808, popular with package tours, but very comfortable, lots of facilities, double rooms US$95 to US$165 depending on season; *Grenada Renaissance*, PO Box 441, St George's, T 444-4375, F 444-4800, 186 rooms and suites, a/c, US$150 garden view, US$210 beachfront, suites US$300-500 winter 1994/95, many facilities, restaurant pricey, open 0700-2300; *Spice Island Inn*, PO Box 6, St George's, T 444-4258, F 444-4807, US$270 garden view, US$300 beach suite, US$425 pool suite, US$325-460 all inclusive, lots of sports and other facilities on offer but service needs improvement; *Hibiscus*, PO Box 279, St George's, T 444-4233, F 440-6632, cottages US$85, rec, car hire available; *Blue Horizons Cottage Hotel*, PO Box 41, St George's, T 444-4316, F 444-2815, US$95-110 summer, US$135-165 winter, its *La Belle Créole* restaurant is one of the island's best. *The Flamboyant*, PO Box 214, St George's, T 444-4247, F 444-1234, 39 units in rooms, suites and cottages, US$80-130d summer, US$105-215 winter, EP, TV, phone, pool, free snorkelling equipment, at the end of Grand Anse, lovely views, steep walk down to beach, rec but food nothing special, quite a walk to bus stop; *South Winds Holiday Cottages and Apartments*, Grand Anse, PO Box 118, St George's, T 444-4310, F 444-4847, from US$40 to US$65 per day in summer, US$50-80 in winter, monthly rates on request, 5-10 mins walk from beach, good view, rec (also car hire).

At **Morne Rouge**: *Gem Holiday Beach Resort*, PO Box 58, T 444-4224, F 444-1189, US$60-85 summer to US$80-125d winter, depending on quality, 2-bedroomed apartments US$105-140 for 4, lovely beach, good position but hot, a/c nice and cool, enjoyable beachside lounge also popular with locals, restaurant limited. *True Blue Inn*, P O Box 308, St George's, T 444-2000, F 444-1247, between Grand Anse and Point Salines airport, owner-managed cottages and apartments, kitchenettes, pool, US$110-165 winter, US$70-100 summer, dock facilities, boat charter available, restaurant and bar. *Rex Grenadian*, Point Salines, PO Box 893, St George's, T 444-3333, F 444-1111, opened 1993, 212 rooms, US$140-310 winter, the largest on the island, a/c, fans, gym, pool, tennis, 2 beaches, watersports, scuba diving, 4 restaurants and bars, conference facilities, 5 rooms for handicapped guests; also at Point Salines, *La Source*, PO Box 852, T 444-2556, F 444-2561, opened 1993, 100 rooms, all-inclusive, pool, 9-hole golf course, health and leisure facilities,

US$240-295 winter.

Lance aux Épines: *Calabash*, PO Box 382, St George's, T 444-4334, F 444-4804, winner of a prestigious Golden Fork award for quality of food and hospitality, probably the poshest hotel on Grenada, 28 rooms, expensive, US$180-245 BP, US$230-295 MAP double in summer, US$395-495 in winter, MAP, on beach, nice grounds, pool suites, tennis, games room; *Secret Harbour*, PO Box 11, St George's, T 444-4548, F 444-4819, 20 luxury rooms, chalets built into the rock face overlooking the harbour, private, wonderful views, US$125 EP in summer, US$208 EP in winter, pool, friendly, steel band at times, no children under 12 accepted, this is a Club Mariner Resort and bareboat or crewed yacht charters are available from the marina; *Horse Shoe Beach*, PO Box 174, St George's, T 444-4244, F 444-4844, rooms US$100d, suites US$150d, villas US$130d, cheap rates for children under 18; *Holiday Haven*, above a cove on Prickly Point, 2-3 bedroomed villas US$500-600/week in summer, US$600-700 in winter, 1-2 bedroomed apartments also available, contact Dr John Watts, T 440-2606, 444-4325.

On the S coast: *Petit Bacaye*, on bay of same name, PO Box 655, St George's, T/F 443-2552, T 443-2902, thatched self-catering cottages, 1-bedroom US$65-85, 2-bedroom US$95-125, inc tax and service, breakfast and snacks at beach bar, fisherman call daily, catch can be cooked to order, reef and own Islet 200m offshore, jeep and guide hire arranged, sandy beach round the bluff; *La Sagesse Nature Centre* (see **Flora and Fauna** above), St David's, PO Box 44, St George's, Grenada, T 444-6458, F 444-4847, 4 rooms in winter cost US$100 d, in summer US$60, small, excellent, perfect setting, an old plantation house on a secluded, sandy bay (the sea may be polluted in the rainy season, seek the hotel's advice), child-friendly, good restaurant, excursions, highly rec. On the E coast: near Grenville, *St Martins Catholic Retreat Centre*, Mount St Ervans, PO Box 11, Grenville, T 442-7348, spectacular views, lovely surroundings, good spot for lunch, open to non-residents.

Guesthouses (all prices year round) St George's: *Mitchell's Guest House*, Tyrrel Street, T 440-2803, US$26s, US$34d inc breakfast with grandchildren, central, spotless, home made bread, town noises, ability to sleep through cock crowing essential; *Simeons*, Green Street, T 440-2537, 9 rooms, US$35d including breakfast, central, clean, friendly, rec, view over Carenage; *St Ann's Guest House*, Paddock, beyond Botanic Gardens (some distance from centre), T 440-2717, US$31d, inc excellent breakfast, friendly, entrance forbidden to "prostitutes and natty dreds", meals (communal), EC$20, good value, a bit difficult to sleep because of dogs and roosters, take ear plugs; *Yacht's View*, Lagoon Road, T 440-3607, US$22d, cheap but noisy and frequently without water or fans, if you complain they may throw you out; *Mamma's Lodge*, PO Box 248, Lagoon Road, T 440-1459, F 440-7788, good value, 6 double, 4 single rooms, pleasant, friendly, very clean, nice view, US$25 s, US$35 d, inc breakfast, no credit cards, now managed by a daughter after Mama's death in 1991; *Lakeside*, at the end of Lagoon Road going towards Grand Anse, T 440-2365 (Mrs Ruth Haynes), view over yacht marina, helpful, cooking facilities, US$10pp without meals, drinks available, mixed reports. *Skyline*, Belmont, between St George's and Grand Anse Beach, T 444-4461, US$15s, mixed reports. At **Grand Anse**: *Roydon's*, T 444-4476, US$40-50d EP, US$80-85d MAP, helpful staff, fans, very nice even if a bit overpriced, rec but next to a busy street, good restaurant, 10 mins' walk from beach, access through *Grenada Renaissance*; *Windward Sands Inn*, PO Box 199, T 444-4238, US$55d CP winter, US$50 summer, apartments US$290-370/week, friendly, helpful, tours arranged, nice place, walk to the beach, good cooking. **Grenville**: *Rainbow Inn*, PO Box 923, T 442-7714, US$30s, US$45d, 15 rooms.

There are also many furnished villas and apartments available for rent from various agents, with prices for daily or weekly rental. *RSR Apartments* on Lagoon Road, Springs PO, St George's, T 440-3381, has been rec for good value, US$20 for 1-bedroom apartment, US$28 for 2 bedrooms, US$32 for 3 bedrooms, kitchen, living room, bathroom, veranda, guard at night, also cockroaches, bus into town.

● **Where To Eat**

There is quite a wide choice of restaurants, apart from the hotels mentioned above, and you are recommended to eat the local dishes, which are very good. Tax of 8% and service of 10% is usually added to the bill. Unless stated otherwise, restaurants below are in **St George's**. *Nutmeg*, on the Carenage (T 440-2539), delicious local dishes and its own famous rum punch, very popular, but avoid if you do not want to see turtle on the menu; **Rudolph's**, also on the Carenage, (T 440-2241), expensive, but good, local and international food, in friendly pub atmosphere, excellent rum punch; **Sand Pebble**, T 440-2688, the Carenage too, cheap and clean, good rotis EC$5, excellent sea moss, take away or eat in, bar snacks only, also taxi service; **Portofino**, on the Carenage, Italian, about US$20 for meal and drink, nice place, witty proprietor, T 440-3986; **Delicious Landing**, on the Carenage, local and international food, good; **Tropicana**, on the Lagoon, T 440-1586, popular, Chinese and local food, good, meals from EC$6, excellent egg rolls, rec, seating inside or out on covered patio, barbeques, Fri and Sat, closed Sun; **Mamma's Bar**, Lagoon Road, try multifarious local foods (famous for wild meat dishes when in season but you don't always know what you are getting, you may not be told until you've finished that there is no wild game that night), need to book, T 440-1459, quite commercialized now, owned by Mamma's daughter and not as good as it was; **Bobby's Health Stop**, Gore Street, daytimes, also at Morne Rouge shopping centre, vegetable rotis; also **Snug Corner** near the Market Square; on Melville Street, **Deyna's**, new, modern, good local food at local prices, excellent coffee, open daily 0730-2200, T 440-6795, rec; **Pitch Pine Bar**, fun place on the sea for a drink.

At the St George's end of Grand Anse is **The French Restaurant**, T 444-4644, with excellent food and fruit juices and punches. **The Bird's Nest** at Grand Anse has good Chinese food, very reasonable, quick service, friendly, clean, opp Grenada Renaissance, T 444-4264; **Southwinds**, Grand Anse, about 20 mins' walk from Grenada Renaissance, is rec as probably the best seafood restaurant on the island, on top of a hill with magnificent view, friendly and expertly-trained staff. T 444-4310; the little **Beach Bar** on Grand Anse in front of Coyaba has a couple of tables and can produce good burgers for about US$2, locals drink here from morning onwards and are keen conversationalists; **Canboulay**, Morne Rouge, T 444-4401, rec, upmarket and very good but not cheap. **Tabanca**, near The Flamboyant, excellent food, a mixture of Grenadian and international, run by an Austrian, her coffee is superb. **The Green Parrot**, rec but take plenty of insect repellent, you eat on little islands connected by walkways, lots of croaking frogs and mosquitoes at night, T 444-1087. **Aquarium Beach Club and Restaurant**, T 444-1410, Balls Beach, run by Ollie and Rebecca, rec, bar open from 1000, kitchen 1200-2200, Sat volleyball, Sun barbeque, showers toilets, snorkelling offshore, good food, lobster, fish, steak, sandwiches, closed Mon.

See above for **Morne Fendue** plantation house restaurant, said to serve the best Caribbean food on the island and the best rum punch in the Caribbean, T 444-9330. **La Sagesse** (see above, **Where To Stay** and **Flora and Fauna**) rec for lunch, fresh lobster, grilled tuna, outdoor restaurant, beautiful location, walk it off afterwards, good hiking over the mountain, T 444-6458 for reservations.

● **Food And Drink**

To repeat, Grenada's West Indian cooking is generally very good. Lambi (conch) is very popular, as is callaloo soup (made with dasheen leaves), souse (a sauce made from pig's feet), pepper pot and pumpkin pie. There is a wide choice of seafood, and of vegetables. Goat and wild meat (armadillo, iguana, manicou) can be sampled. Nutmeg features in many local dishes, try nutmeg jelly for breakfast, ground nutmeg comes on top of rum punches. Of the many fruits and fruit dishes, try stewed golden apple, or soursop ice cream. There is limited food or choice on Carriacou.

Rum punches are excellent, and be sure to try the local sea-moss drink (a mixture of vanilla, algae and milk). There are 2 makes of rum, whose superiority is disputed by the islanders, Clarke's Court and River Antoine. Westerhall Plantation Rum, made by Westerhall Distilleries has also been endorsed by readers. The term "grog", for rum, is supposed to originate in Grenada: taking the first letters of "Georgius Rex Old Grenada", which was stamped on the casks of rum sent back to England. Grenada Breweries brew Carib Lager, Guinness and non-alcoholic malt beers.

● **Entertainment**

The resort hotels provide evening entertainment, including dancing, steelband and calypso music, limbo, etc. There are not a great many discothèques and night clubs outside the hotels; La Sucrier, Panache, Fantazia 2001 and Club Paradise at Lance aux Épines are some examples. On Carriacou there is a good jump-up every Fri after mass at Liz' Refreshment, Tyrrel Bay, with excellent DJ. The Regal Cinema is off Lagoon Road, next to Tropicana.

● **Security**

On the Carenage in St George's, you may be pestered for money, particularly after dark, but it is no more than a nuisance. Lagoon Road, however, does appear to be unsafe at times. Unemployment and drug abuse are serious problems; more than three quarters of the prison population have been sentenced for drug related crimes. Night police patrols in hotels and beach areas were introduced in 1993. In the countryside people are extremely helpful and friendly and there is no need anywhere for anything other than normal precautions against theft.

● **Shopping**

The Yellow Poui Art Gallery sells Grenadian paintings and is worth a visit, above Noah's Arkade souvenir shop on Cross Street. Spice Island Perfumes on the Carenage sells perfumes and pots pourris made from the island's spices, as well as batiks, T-shirts, etc (it has a branch at the *Spice Island Inn*, Grand Anse). Arawak Island factory and retail outlet on the Upper Belmont Road between Grand Anse and St George's, T 440-4577, open Mon-Fri 0830-1630, perfumes, body oils, spices, syrups, cocoa bars etc. Grencraft on the Esplanade; Blind People's Work Shop at Delicious Landing, and others. You can purchase straw and palm wares, and items in wood. Spices are cheaper in the supermarket than on the street or in the market. There is duty-free shopping at the airport and on the Carenage for cruise ship passengers.

St George's Bookshop is on Halifax Street; The Sea Change Book and Gift Shop is on the Carenage, beneath the *Nutmeg* bar. Good supermarkets include one opp the *Grenada Renaissance* and one also on Lagoon at Belmont end.

● **Laundry**

Tangie's Laundry & Dry Cleaning Service, Sugar Mill Roundabout, St George's, T 444-4747, next to the *Sugar Mill Night Club*, pick up and delivery service.

● **Currency**

The currency is the East Caribbean dollar: EC$2.70 = US$1.

● **Banks**

Barclays Bank (branches in St George's-Halifax Street, Grand Anse, Grenville and Carriacou), T 440-3232; National Commercial Bank of Grenada, (Halifax Street, St George's, Grand Anse, Grenville, Gouyave, St David's, Carria-cou), T 440-3566; Scotiabank (Halifax Street, St George's), T 440-3274, branch at Grand Anse; Grenada Bank of Commerce (Halifax and Cross St, St George's, and Grand Anse), T 440-4919; Grenada Co-operative Bank (Church St, St George's, Grenville and Sauteurs), T 440-2111. They do not exchange European currencies other than sterling.

● **Climate**

The average temperature is 26°C. December and January are the coolest months. The rainy season runs from June to November.

● **Clothing**

Dress is casual, with lightweight summer clothes suitable all year. Bathing costumes are not accepted in hotel dining rooms, shops or on the streets.

● **High Season**

Winter (high) season prices come into effect from 16 December to 15 April. The tourist season is at its height between December and March, although visitor numbers also pick up in July and August.

● **Health**

St George's has a general hospital, there is a smaller one in Mirabeau, on the E coast and clinics all round the island. For an ambulance, T 434 in St George's, T 724 in St Andrew's and T 774 on Carriacou.

● **Business Hours**

Banks: 0800-1200 or 1400 Mon-Thur; 0800-1200 or 1300, 1430-1700 Fri. Shops: 0800-1145, 1300-1545 Mon-Fri, 0800-1145 Sat; government offices the same, but closed all day Sat.

● **Holidays**

New Year's Day (1 January), Independence Day (7 February), Good Fri and Easter Mon, Labour Day (1 May), Whit Mon (in May/June), Corpus Christi (June), August holidays (first Mon and Tues in August) and Carnival (second weekend in August), Thanksgiving (25 October), 25 and 26 December.

● **Time Zone**

Atlantic Standard Time, 4 hours behind GMT, 1 ahead of EST.

● **Electric Current**

220/240 volts, 50 cycles AC.

● **Postal Services**

The General Post Office in St George's is on the Carenage, open 0800-1530 Mon to Thur, and

1630 on Fri (operating from a temporary building near the cruise ship dock after the fire of May 1990). Villages have sub-post offices.

● **Telecommunications**

Cable and Wireless Ltd, the Carenage, St George's (open 0700-1900 Mon- Sat; 1600-1800 Sun), operates fax and telex services; Grenada Telephone Company (Grentel, a joint venture with Cable and Wireless), T 440-1000, with offices behind Cable and Wireless, operates telephone services, including "USA Direct" and calls to USA on Visa card, etc, at a fee, facsimile, telex, telegraph and cellular phones. Payphones take coins or phone cards issued by Grentel, available at outlets near payphones. Home Direct Service can be made from any phone, if you have a credit or telephone charge card, and is available to the UK through BT Direct and to Canada through Teleglobe. Credit card holders and Visaphone card holders' access number is 1-800-877-8000 for domestic and international calls. If you dail 872 at any public phone (no coin required), you get through to AT and T. A call to the UK costs approximately EC$37.50 for 5 mins.

● **Newspapers**

There are no daily papers, only weeklies, including *Grenadian Voice*, *Indies Times*, *Grenada Guardian*, *The National*, and *The Informer*. There is a state-run radio station (Radio Grenada) and one television station.

● **Religion**

Roman Catholic, Anglican, Presbyterian, Methodist, Scots Kirk, Seventh Day Adventist, Jehovah's Witnesses, Islam, Salvation Army, First Church of Christian Scientists, Church of Christ and Baha'i.

● **Travel Agents**

All in St George's: Grenada International Travel Service, of Church Street (American Express representative), T 440-2945; Huggins Travel Service, the Carenage, T 440-2514; McIntyre Brothers, Lagoon Road, T 440-2901; Grenada Tours and Travel, the Carenage, T 440-3316 (PO Box 46, operates a people-to-people scheme in which visitors may meet locals with similar interest or professions). Otway's, also on the Carenage, T 440-2558; and many others. Edwin Frank, from the Tourism Department, T 443-5143, does guided tours at weekends, US$20 pp island tour, very knowledgeable on history, politics, geography, people, fauna, hiking etc, rec and much better than an untrained taxi driver. Henry, of Henry Tours (T 443-5313) conducts tours of the island and is very well informed on all aspects of Grenada. Arnold's Tours, Grenville Street, T 440-0531, F 440-4118, offers similar services to Henry's, also rec, but in German as well. Clinton 'Guava' George, of Clinton's Taxi Service, T 444-4095, 441-9648, knows a lot about Grenadian geography, politics and biology and gives a well-informed, fun tour of the island. Q and K Sunsation Tours is very knowledgeable and rec, bilingual guides are available for half or full day tours, PO Box 856, St George's, T 444-1656, 444-1594, F 444-4819. Mrs Pat Walcott, of Tours R Us, T 444-1785, uses 3 old, open-sided buses with wooden seats, rec. In the UK, Carriacou Travel Service, 81 Askew Road, London W12, organizes trips, T (71) 743 4518, ask for Mr Harroo, helpful.

● **Hiking**

For guided hikes contact Telfer Bedeau in the village of Soubise on the E coast; you must ask around for him (or T 442-6200 or see if the Tourism Department can put you in touch). Grenada National Parks publishes a series of map and trail guides, worth having for the Grand Étang National Park and related walks. The Overseas Surveys Directorate, Ordnance Survey **map** of Grenada, published for the Grenada Government in 1985, scale 1:50,000, is available from the Tourist Office, from the Lands and Surveys Department in the Ministry of Agriculture (at the Botanic Gardens) and from shops for EC$10.50-15 (it is not wholly accurate). Also available from Ordnance Survey, Southampton, are 2 separate sheets, North (1979) and South (1988) at 1:25,000 scale.

● **Diplomatic Representation**

The **British** High Commission is at 14 Church St, St George's, T 440-3222, F 440-4939. The **Venezuelan** Embassy is at Archibald Avenue, St George's, T 440-1721/2. **USA**, T 444-1173/1179; **Republic of China**, T 440-3054; **Netherlands**, T 440-2031; **Guyana**, T 440-2189; **Sweden**, T 440-1832; **France**, T 440-2547; **European Community**, T 440-3561.

● **Tourist Information**

Grenada Tourism Department, the Carenage,

St George's (PO Box 293), T 440-2279/2001/3377/2872, F 440-2123. Its hours are 0800-1600 and it is very helpful. There is also a tourist office at the airport, helpful, hotel reservation service, T 444-4140.

In the **USA**: Grenada Tourism Office, 820 2nd Avenue, Suite 900D, New York, NY 10017, T (212) 687-9554, (800) 927 9554, F (212) 573 9731; in **Canada**: Grenada Tourism Office, Suite 820, 439 University Avenue, Toronto, Ontario M5G 1Y8, T (416) 595-1339, F (416) 595 8278; in the **UK**: 1 Collingham Gardens, London SW5 0HW, T (071) 370 5164/5, F (071) 370 7040; in **Germany**: Grenada Board of Tourism-Europe, Liebigstrasse 8, 60323 Frankfurt/Main, T 069-726-908, F 069-727-714.

BARBADOS

BARBADOS is 21 miles long and 14 miles wide, lying E of the main chain of the Leeward and Windward islands. It is flatter, drier, and more prosperous and tourists who come here looking for the "untouched" Caribbean are in for a disappointment. There are no volcanoes or rain forests, and hardly any rivers, but there are plenty of white sand beaches and lots of pleasantly rolling countryside with fields of sugar cane, brightly painted villages, flowering trees and open pastures. The island is probably better equipped with infrastructure and reliable tourist services than anywhere else to the S of Miami on this side of the Atlantic.

Most of the island is covered by a cap of coral limestone, up to 600,000 years old. Several steep inland cliffs or ridges run parallel to the coast. These are the remains of old shorelines, which formed as the island gradually emerged from the sea. There are no rivers in this part of the island, although there are steep-sided gullies down which water runs in wet weather. Rainwater runs through caves in the limestone, one of which, Harrison's Cave, has been developed as a tourist attraction. The island's water supply is pumped up from the limestone. In the Scotland District in the NE, the coral limestone has been eroded and older, softer rocks are exposed. There are rivers here, which have cut deep, steep-sided valleys. Landslides make agriculture and construction hazardous and often destroy roads.

Barbados has a population of 259,000. This is more than any of the Windwards or Leewards, and is considered enough to make the island one of the "big four" in the Caribbean Community. With population density of 1,560 per square mile in 1992, Barbados is one of the most crowded countries in the world.

History

There were Amerindians on Barbados for upwards of a thousand years. The first Europeans to find the island were the Portuguese, who named it "Os Barbados" after the Bearded Fig trees which grew on the beaches, and left behind some wild pigs. These bred successfully and provided meat for the first English settlers, who arrived in 1627 and found an island which was otherwise uninhabited. It is not clear why the Amerindians abandoned the island, although several theories exist. King Charles I gave the Earl of Carlisle permission to colonize the island and it was his appointed Governor, Henry Hawley, who in 1639 founded the House of Assembly. Within a few years, there were upwards of 40,000 white settlers, mostly small farmers, and equivalent in number to about 1% of the total population of England at this period. After the "sugar revolution" of the 1650s most of the white population left. For the

BARBADOS C 55

1. Garrison
2. Clapham, Harry Bailey Observatory
3. Harrisons Cave
4. Welchman Hall Gully
5. Flower Forest
6. Andromeda Gardens
7. Cotton Tower
8. Gun Hill Signal Station
9. Villa Nova
10. St John's Church
11. Codrington College
12. East Point Lighthouse
13. Oughterson & Barbados Zoo Park
14. Sam Lord's Castle
15. Sunbury Plantation House
16. Farley Hill House & Wildlife Reserve
17. St Nicholas Abbey
18. Morgan Lewis Windmill
19. Mount Gay Distillery
20. Animal Flower Cave
21. Folkestone Marine Museum & Underwater Park
22. Portvale Sugar Factory
23. Turners Hall Woods

rest of the colonial period sugar was king, and the island was dominated by a small group of whites who owned the estates, the "plantocracy". The majority of the population today is descended from African slaves who were brought in to work on the plantations; but there is a substantial mixed-race population, and there has always been a small number of poor whites, particularly in the E part of the

island. Many of these are descended from 100 prisoners transported in 1686 after the failed Monmouth rebellion and Judge Jeffrey's "Bloody Assizes".

The two principal political parties are the Barbados Labour Party (BLP) and the Democratic Labour Party (DLP). The Democratic Labour Party has been in office since 1986, and was re-elected in 1991, when it won 18 seats in a general election. The Prime Minister is Mr Erskine Sandiford. The BLP is led by Mr Owen Arthur, previously its economic affairs spokesman, who took over the leadership in 1993 from Mr Henry Forde, when he resigned on health grounds. Economic difficulties in the 1990's eroded support for the DLP and by 1994 the Government's popularity was low. Mr Sandiford was criticized for his autocratic style and the resignation of three ministers was seen as damaging the party's hopes for the general election, due by January 1996. In June he lost a vote of no-confidence by 14-12 votes and soon afterwards called a general election for 6 September 1994.

Government

Barbados has been an independent member of the Commonwealth since November 1966. The British Monarch is the Head of State, represented by a Governor General. There is a strong parliamentary and democratic tradition. The House of Assembly is the third oldest parliament in the Western Hemisphere and celebrated its 350th anniversary in 1989, although voting was limited to property owners until 1950. There are 21 senators appointed by the Governor General, of whom 12 are on the advice of the Prime Minister, two on the advice of the Leader of the Opposition and seven at his own discretion to reflect religious, economic and social interests. 28 single-member constituencies elect the House of Assembly.

The Economy

Barbados is now officially a "middle income" country, with a per capita gnp higher than that of European countries like Portugal, or Greece. There are few natural resources and sugar is still the main crop, but there is some export-oriented manufacturing and an expanding offshore financial sector. At the end of 1993 there were 1,171 international busi-

BARBADOS : FACT FILE

Geographic
Land area	430 sq km
forested	0.0%
pastures	9.0%
cultivated	77.0%

Demographic
Population (1992)	259,000
annual growth rate (1987-92)	0.3%
urban	37.9%
rural	62.1%
density	602.3 per sq km
Religious affiliation	
Anglican	39.7%
Other protestant	25.6%
Birth rate per 1,000 (1991)	16.4
	(world av 26.4)
Death rate per 1,000 (1991)	8.8
	(world av 9.2)

Education and Health
Life expectancy at birth (1990-95),	
male	72.9 years
female	77.9 years
Infant mortality rate	
per 1,000 live births (1991)	11.8
Physicians (1986)	1 per 1,042 persons
Hospital beds	1 per 121 persons
Calorie intake as %	
of FAO requirement	134%
Population age 25 and over	
with no formal schooling	0.8%
Literacy (over 15)	98.0%

Economic
GNP (1990 market prices)	US$1,680mn
GNP per capita	US$6,540
Public external debt (1991)	US$948mn
Tourism receipts (1990)	US$500.2mn
Inflation (annual av 1986-91)	4.7%
Radio	1 per 1.3 persons
Television	1 per 3.7 persons
Telephone	1 per 2.4 persons

Employment
Population economically active (1991)	
	122,500
Unemployment rate	17.2%
% of labour force in	
agriculture	5.4
trade and restaurants	16.7
manufacturing	10.7
construction	8.3
Military forces	154

Source *Encyclopaedia Britannica*

ness companies, 926 foreign sales corporations, 250 exempt insurance companies and 19 off-shore banks, all showing steady growth. There is a well-established service sector, and a wide range of light industries which produce mainly for the local, regional, and North American markets. More than half the households own a car, and almost all have a piped water supply and a telephone. By far the main foreign exchange earner is now tourism. In 1993, 395,979 tourists, over 40% of whom came from Europe, stayed in Barbados and 439,572 cruise ship passengers also visited, spending about US$550 mn. There are about 6,650 rooms available in hotels, guest houses and apartments.

The sugar industry has been in the hands of the receivers since 1992 and many producers have abandoned the land, while trying to get planning permission for golf courses or housing developments. The industry is under the management of Booker Tate, through the Barbados Agricultural Management Co established in 1993. Under a restructuring plan production is to be restored to 75,000 tonnes by 1999. Production was over 100,000 tonnes a year in the early 1980s but by 1994 was only about 49,000 tonnes, all of which was exported under the Lomé Convention. Domestic consumption is Guatemalan or Guyanese sugar.

The slowdown in the USA and other industrialized countries has had a negative affect on the Barbadian economy. Stopover arrivals declined by over 7% in 1990, nearly 9% in 1991 and a further 2.2% in 1992, while construction and agriculture also declined, leading to an overall gdp contraction of 4.2% in 1991 and 4.0% in 1992. The Government's budget deficit rose to 8.9% of gdp in 1990, while foreign reserves declined and unemployment rose to 14.7%. The 1991 budget sought to close the gap by raising taxes and the deficit fell to 2.9% of gdp but at the cost of rising unemployment with 20% of the labour force out of work. In 1992 the IMF approved a loan package of US$65mn over 15 months; inflation was 6.5% and unemployment rose to 25% but results for 1993 were more positive with public finances and the external accounts showing improvement. The economy grew by 1.0% after 3 years of decline and was expected to expand by over 2% in 1994. Tourism, distribution and construction were the leading growth sectors. A tight budget was set for 1994 as the Government continued its austerity policies, although some tax cuts were made. A value added tax system is to be introduced in April 1995 which will replace several indirect taxes.

Culture

Because Barbados lies upwind from the main island arc, it was hard to attack from the sea, so it never changed hands in the colonial wars of the 17th and 18th centuries. There is no French, Dutch, or Spanish influence to speak of in the language, cooking or culture. People from other islands have often referred to Barbados as Little England, and have not always intended a compliment. Today, the more obvious outside influences on the Barbadian way of life are North American. Most contemporary Barbadians stress their Afro-Caribbean heritage and aspects of the culture which are distinctively "Bajan". There are extremes of poverty and wealth, but these are not nearly so noticeable as elsewhere in the Caribbean. This makes the social atmosphere relatively relaxed. However, there is a history of deep racial division. Although there is a very substantial black middle class and the social situation has changed radically since the 1940s and 50s, there is still more racial intolerance on all sides than is apparent at first glance.

Two Barbadian writers whose work has had great influence throughout the Caribbean are the novelist George Lamming and the poet Edward Kamau Brathwaite. Lamming's first novel, *In The Castle Of My Skin* (1953), a part-autobiographical story of growing up in colonial Barbados, deals with one of the major concerns of anglophone writers: how to define one's values within a system and ideology imposed by someone else. Lamming's treatment of the boy's changing awareness in a time of change in the West Indies is both poetic and highly imaginative. His other books include *Natives Of My Person*, *Season Of Adventure* and *The Pleasures Of Exile*.

Brathwaite too is sensitive to the colonial influence on black West Indian culture. Like Derek Walcott (see under St Lucia) and others he is also keenly aware of the African traditions at the heart of that culture. The questions addressed by all these writers are: who is Caribbean man, and what are his faiths, his language, his ancestors? The experience of teaching in Ghana for some time helped to clarify Brathwaite's response. African religions, motifs and songs mix with West Indian speech rhythms in a style which is often strident, frequently using very short verses. His collections include *Islands*, *Masks* and *Rights Of Passage*. Heinemann Caribbean publish the *A to Z of Barbadian Heritage* which is worth reading. Macmillan publish *Treasures of Barbados*, an attractive guide to Barbadian architecture.

Beaches

There are beaches along most of the S and W coasts. Although some hotels make it hard to cross their property to reach the sand, there are no private beaches in Barbados. The W coast beaches are very calm, and quite narrow, beach erosion is a serious worry and the Government's Coastal Conservation Unit is trying to sort it out. A swell can wash up lots of broken coral making it unpleasant underfoot. The S coast can be quite choppy. The SE, between the air-port and East Point, has steep limestone cliffs with a series of small sandy coves with coconut trees, and waves which are big enough for surfing. Be careful on the E side of the island, currents and undertow are strong in places. Don't swim where there are warning signs, or where there are no other bathers, even on a calm day. Bathsheba, on the E coast, is quite spectacular, with wonderful views. Some hotels sell day passes, eg *Hilton*, US$10 pp, for the use of their facilities: pool, showers, deck chairs, etc.

Beach vendors now have a licence, plastic stalls, and a blue and yellow uniform shirt. Unscrupulous cocaine and sex vendors still operate but are more subtle in their approach than in the past.

Watersports

There are a large number of motor and sailing boats available for charter by the day or for shorter periods. These include *Irish Mist*, T 436 9201, *Station Break*, T 436 9502, *Tiami*, T 436 5725, *La Paloma*, T 427 5588, *Cap'n Jack*, T 427 5800, *Calypso Charters*, T 426 7166, *Secret Love*, T 432 1972, *Jolly Jumper*, T 432 7090. Others are moored in the Careenage in Bridgetown, with a telephone number displayed. Most are equipped for fishing and snorkelling, and will serve a good meal on board. Rates and services offered vary widely.

Glass-bottomed boats can be hired from several private operators along the W coast. In December, the Mount Gay International Christmas Regatta for yachts is held.

The S coast is good for windsurfing and the International Funboard Challenge is held in March. Club Mistral at the Barbados Windsurfing Club Hotel, Maxwell, Christ Church, T 428 9095, and at *Silver Sands Hotel*, T 428 6001, ext 4227, rent equipment at US$13 an hour, US$40 a day, US$165 a week. Lessons are extra. Easy windsurfing for beginners with private operators near *Sandy Beach*

Hotel. There is also windsurfing at *Hilton Hotel*, T 427 4350. Skyranger Parasail, Holetown, T 432 2323 or 424 5687 for parasailing. The best surfing is on the E coast and the Barbados International Surfing Championship is held at the Soup Bowl, Bathsheba, in early November.

Scuba diving to the reefs or the wrecks around the coast can be arranged with Jolly Roger Watersports at Sunset Crest, St James, T 432 7090 and at Colony Club, St James, T 422 2335; Dive Boat Safari, *Hilton Hotel*, Needham's Point, T 427 4350; Underwater Barbados, *Sand Acres Hotel*, Maxwell, T 428 9739; Exploresub, St Lawrence Gap, T 435 6542; Willie's Watersports, Black Rock, St Michael, T 425 1060; Shades of Blue at Coral Reef, St James, T 422 3215; Blue Reef Watersports, *Royal Pavilion Hotel*, St James, T 432 7090; The Dive Shop, T 426 9947. These companies also offer diving courses, equipment rental and other facilities such as snorkelling. The first two also offer waterskiing, as do several other W coast operators. The BSAC meets at 0800 on Saturday and Sunday at the *Boatyard Pub* on the waterfront on Bay Street, Bridgetown. They do not hire out equipment but if you have your own they are most welcoming to members from other branches. One of their groups dives for old bottles on a reef just offshore where ships have anchored for some 350 years. There is a recompression chamber at St Anne's Fort, T 427 8819, or tell the operator if there is an emergency. For those who want to see the underwater world without getting wet, the Atlantis Submarine near the Careenage in Bridgetown (1st floor, Horizon House, McGregor Street), T 436 8929, has day and night dives at US$58, children aged 4-12 half price. The tour starts with a short video and then you go by bus to the deep water port or join the launch at the Careenage. The boat takes about 10 minutes to get to the submarine, sit at the back to be first on the sub, an advantage as then you can see out of the driver's window as well as out of your own porthole. Booking is necessary, check in half an hour before dive time, whole tour takes 1½ hrs.

Sports

Ask the Tourist Office for the Sports and Cultural Calendar, which has lots of information about what is on and who to contact in all possible areas of sport.

Cricket Lots of village cricket all over the island at weekends. A match here is nothing if not a social occasion. For information about the bigger matches at Kensington Oval phone the Barbados Cricket Association, T 436 1397.

Horseracing At the Garrison on Saturdays for most of the year. Again, this is something of a social occasion. The Cockspur Gold Cup Race, held in March, features horses from neighbouring islands. For information on race meetings phone Barbados Turf Club, T 426 3980.

Golf There are three courses, the best and most prestigious of which is Sandy Lane, 18 holes, T 432 2946/432 1311/432 1145. *Rockley* has no clubhouse and is not highly rated, 9 holes, T 435 7880. *Heywoods*, 9 holes, T 422 4900. A new course at Royal Westmoreland Golf and Country Club, St James, is associated with the *Royal Pavilion* and *Glitter Bay Hotels*. Planning applications have been lodged for many more. The Barbados Open Golf Championship is held in December.

Polo Barbados Polo Club near Holetown, St James, T 432 1802. **Water Polo** is played at the Barbados Aquatic Centre, where visitors are welcome to join in practice sessions with the team, which is sponsored by the local beer company, Banks. Confirm practice times, T 429 7946.

Squash *Rockley Resort* has two courts, T 435 7880, Barbados Squash Club, T 427 7193, *Casuarina Hotel*, T 428 3600, *Marine House* has three courts. **Tennis** The best courts are at *Paradise Beach*

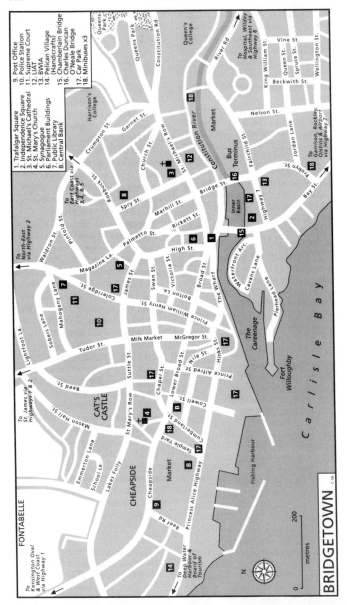

BRIDGETOWN

FONTABELLE

1. Trafalgar Square
2. Independence Square
3. St. Michael's Cathedral
4. St. Mary's Church
5. Synagogue
6. Parliament Buildings
7. Public Library
8. Central Bank
9. Post Office
10. Police Station
11. Supreme Court
12. LIAT
13. BWIA
14. Pelican Village (Handicrafts)
15. Chamberlain Bridge
16. Charles Duncan O'Neale Bridge
17. Car Park
18. Minibuses x3

Carlisle Bay

CHEAPSIDE

CAT'S CASTLE

Queen's Park

Queen's College

Harrison's College

Constitution River

Market

Bus Terminus

The Careenage

Fort Willoughby

Fishing Harbour

0   200
metres

To North-East via Highway 2

To East Coast via Highways 3, 4 & 5

To St. James via Highways 1 & 2

To Kensington Oval & West Coast via Highway 1

To Deep Water Harbour & Board of Tourism

To Garrison, Rockley, Oistins & Airport via Highway 7

To Hospital, Wildey & Southeast via Highway 6

Hotel; they are also good at *Royal Pavilion* and *Glitter Bay*. *Paragon*, T 427 2054, *Hilton*, T 426 0200, *Rockley Resort*, T 435 7880, *Sam Lord's*, T 423 7350, *Crane Hotel*, T 432 6220.

Athletics In November 1992 a multipurpose gymnasium was opened as part of the Wildey Sporting Complex at Wildey, St Michael, T 436 6284. It has facilities for badminton, bodybuilding, boxing, basketball, gymnastics, handball, judo, karate, netball, table tennis, volleyball and weightlifting, with plenty of changing rooms and showers. There are also sauna and massage rooms, a medical room and warm-up/practice area. Within the complex there is an Olympic-size swimming pool and tennis courts and there are plans for hockey, football and cricket pitches outside. The Universal Gym in Hastings is good, with reasonable equipment, aerobic classes and weights at moderate prices.

Motor racing on the circuit in St Philip. **Riding** There are 8 riding schools offering beach and/or country rides. Some do not give instruction and cater for pleasure riding only. Congo Road Riding Stables, T 423 6180, one hour ride including lift to and from hotel is US$25, beginners or advanced; also Brighton Stables on W coast, T 425 9381; Beau Geste Stables, St George, T 429 0139, Tony's Riding School, St Peter, T 422 1549, Caribbean International Riding Stables, St Joseph, T 433 1453, Trevena Riding Stables, St James, T 432 6404 and Big C Riding Stables, Christ Church, T 437 4056.

Running The Run Barbados Series is held in December and is comprised of a 10 km race and a marathon. 1993 was the 10th anniversary of the race.

Walking The most beautiful part of the islands is the Scotland District on the E coast. There is also some fine country along the St Lucy coast in the N and on the SE coast. Walking is straightforward. There is a good 1:50,000 map available from the Public Buildings in Bridge-town, from the museum, in the airport and from some bookstores in town. The Ordnance Survey, Southampton, UK, produces a map of Barbados in its tourist map series, 1:50,000 scale with 1:10,000 inset of Bridgetown. There is a particularly good route along the old railway track, from Bath to Bathsheba and on to Cattlewash. The National Trust, together with the Duke of Edinburgh Award Scheme, T 426 2421, organizes walks at 0600 on a Sunday morning and sometimes at 1530 or 1730 (depending on season) on Sunday afternoon. Details are usually printed in the *Visitor* magazine. Their walk to Chalky Mount in the Scotland District has been recommended.

Festivals

Cropover is the main festival, with parades and calypso competitions over the weekend leading up to Kadooment Day (the first Monday in August), and calypso "tents" (mostly indoors though) for several weeks beforehand. The celebrations begin with the ceremonial delivery of the last canes on a brightly-coloured dray cart pulled by mules, which are blessed. There is a toast to the sugar workers and the crowning of the King and Queen of the crop (the champion cutter-pilers). The bands and costumes are a pale imitation of what Trinidad has to offer but even Trinidadians now take Barbadian calypso seriously. The big crowd is on the Spring Garden Highway outside Bridgetown Monday afternoon. Baxters Road Mall runs for a couple of weekends beforehand; the road is closed off for fried fish, music and beer. Some related activities take place in July.

The Holetown Festival in February, commemorating the first settlers' landing in February 1627, and the Oistins Fish Festival at Easter, celebrating the signing of the Charter of Barbados and the history of this fishing town, are much less elaborate. There are competitions and a big street party with music goes on until late at night. Many villages will also hold a "street fair" from time to time.

NIFCA, the National Independence Festival of Creative Arts, is a more serious affair, with plays, concerts and exhibitions in the weeks before Independence on 30 November.

BRIDGETOWN

The capital, *Bridgetown*, is on the SW corner of the island. The city itself covers a fairly small area. It is busy, and full of life. There are no really large buildings except the central bank. The suburbs sprawl most of the way along the S and W coasts, and quite a long way inland. It is houses and hotels almost all the way along the coastal strip between Speightstown in the N and the airport in the SE, but many of the suburban areas are very pleasant, full of flowering trees and 19th century coral stone gingerbread villas. There are two interesting areas, downtown Bridgetown with Trafalgar Square on the N side of the Careenage and the historic area at Garrison.

Trafalgar Square has a statue of Lord Nelson, sculpted by Sir Richard Westmacott and predating its London equivalent by 36 years. It has recently been the subject of some controversy as it was thought to link Barbados too closely with its colonial past. There were plans to remove it but instead Nelson was turned through 180° and now no longer looks down Broad Street, the main shopping area. There is a memorial to the Barbadian war dead and the fountain commemorates the piping of water to Bridgetown in 1861. To the N is the Parliament Building. Built in 1872, the legislature is an imposing grey building with red roof and green shutters. Built in gothic style, the clock tower is more reminiscent of a church. You can walk between the buildings (providing you are correctly dressed). Take the NE exit out of Trafalgar Square along St Michael's Row to reach the 18th century **St Michael's Cathedral**. It has a fine set of inscriptions and a single-hand clock. The first building was consecrated in 1665 but destroyed by a hurricane in 1780. The present cathedral is long and broad, with a balcony. It has a fine vaulted ceiling and some tombs (1675) have been built into the porch. Completed in 1789, it suffered hurricane damage in 1831. If you contine W, you reach Queen's Park, a pleasant, restful park just outside the city centre. **Queen's Park House** is now a small theatre and art gallery. There is a small restaurant and bar, which does a good lunch and a buffet on Fridays.

The **Synagogue** is an early 19th century building on the site of a 17th century one, one of the two earliest in the W hemisphere. Built in the late 1660s by Jews fleeing Recife, Brazil, who heard that Oliver Cromwell had granted freedom of worship for Jews and gained permission to settle in Barbados. The tomb of Benjamin Massiah, the famous circumciser of 1782 lies on the left hand side of the graveyard, just inside the entrance. The original synagogue was destroyed in 1831, the present one was dedicated in 1838. Recently painstakingly restored, it is now used for religious services again although some work still needs to be done on the ceiling and cemetery. It is supported by only 16 families now.

The area S of James Street is good for street markets. A whole range of goods can be bought along Swan Street and Boulton Lane, good fruit and vegetables as well as leather goods. Street music is sometimes performed. This is in marked contrast to the large shopping malls and department stores on Broad Street. Here you will find a whole range of sophisticated shops catering for tourists (see **Shopping** below). More developments are planned along by the Careenage where old warehouses are being converted into restaurants, discos, smart shops.

Further out, to the S of the Constitution river is **Ronald Tree House** on Tenth Avenue, Belleville (T 426 2421), the headquarters of the Barbados National Trust. Nineteenth century suburban house with furniture, photographs and objets d'art. Useful source of information on historical and natural sites. The National Trust (T 426 2421/436 9033) runs an Open House programme of visits to interesting private houses on Wednesday afternoons from January to April every year. A National Trust passport is US$25, which admits you to all National Trust properties and several privately-owned places like Sunbury Plantation House. National Trust properties admit children under 12 for half price and children under 6 free. The Duke of Edinburgh Award Scheme (Bridge House, Cavans Lane, Bridgetown, T 436 9763) and National Trust joint scheme also arrange early Sunday morning walks to places of historical and natural interest.

The **Harry Bailey Observatory** in Clapham (T 426 1317/422 2394) is open Friday nights 2030-2230. It is in Wildey, not far from Banks Brewery. A chance for northern visitors to look at the Southern hemisphere stars.

The Mount Gay Visitor Centre at Brandons, St Michael, does a 30-minute tour of the blending and bottling plant, weekdays and Saturday morning, B$8, with an exhibition of rum, rum tasting and shop. For their distillery tour, see page 698.

THE GARRISON AREA

Cross the Careenage by the Charles Duncan O'Neale Bridge (one of the bus terminals and market area are just to the W) and follow Bay Street around the curve of Carlisle Bay. You will pass St Patrick's Cathedral (Roman Catholic), the main government offices with St Michael's Hospital behind it before reaching the historic Garrison area. From here you can visit **Fort Charles** on Needham Point (turn right at the Pepsi plant). The Fort was the largest of the many which guarded the S and W coasts. It now forms part of the gardens of the *Hilton Hotel*. Only the ramparts remain but there are a number of 24 pounder cannons dating from 1824. There is a military cemetery here and the Mobil oil refinery was the site of the naval dockyard. Built in 1805, it was subsequently moved to English Harbour, Antigua. The buildings were then used as barracks before being destroyed in the 1831 hurricane.

Carry on up the hill to the **Garrison Historical Area**, which contains many interesting 19th century military buildings, grouped around the Garrison Savannah. There are numerous buildings surrounding the parade ground, now the 6 furlong race course. These were built out of brick brought as ballast on ships from England. They are built on traditional colonial lines, the design can be seen throughout the Caribbean but also in India. Painted bright colours, some now contain government offices. There are several memorials around the oval shaped race course, for instance in the SW corner, the "awful" hurricane which killed 14 men and one married woman and caused the destruction of the barracks and hospital on 18 August 1831 and outside the Barbados Museum in the NE corner to the men of the Royal York Rangers who fell in action against the French in Martinique, Les Saintes and Guadeloupe in the 1809/10 campaign. Across the road is St Anne's fort which is still used by the Barbados defence force. You cannot enter but look for the crenellated signal tower with its flag pole on top. It formed the high command of a chain of signal posts, the most complete of which is at Gun Hill (see below). The long, thin building is the old drill hall. **The Main Guard**, overlooking the savannah, has a nice old clock tower and a fine wide verandah. It has been turned into an information centre and houses exhibits about the West Indian Regiment. The Garrison Secretary of the Regiment, Major Michael Hartland, T 426 0982, is here. Outside is the **National Cannon Collec-**

tion which he created, an impressive array of about 30 cannon, some are mounted on metal "garrison" gun carriages (replaced with wooden ones during action as they were prone to shatter). There are also a number of newer howitzers, dating from 1878. Major Hartland welcomes visitors but he is still creating a Regimental museum, so make an appointment first.

The **Barbados Museum** (T 427 0201/436 1956; Monday-Saturday 1000-1800, B$6 for adults, B$1 for children) is housed in the old military prison on the NE corner of the savannah. Based on a collection left by Rev N B Watson (late rector of St Lucy Parish), it is well set out through a series of 10 galleries. It displays natural history, local history (in search of *Bim*), a fine map gallery including the earliest map of Barbados by Richard Ligon (1657), colonial furniture (Plantation House Rooms), military history (including a reconstruction of a prisoners cell), prints and paintings which depict social life in the West Indies, decorative and domestic arts (17-19th century glass, china and silver), African artefacts, a children's gallery and one to house temporary exhibits. The museum shop has a good selection of craft items, books, prints, and cards. Library available for research purposes. The *Cafe Musée* under the trees in the museum courtyard is a delightful place for a drink or for lunch. The popular review *1627 and all that* takes place here in the evenings. Allow at least 1 hour.

Nearby there are stables for the race course. The Barbados Turf Club holds meetings on Saturdays during three seasons (January to March, May to October and November to December). The biggest one being the Cockspur Gold cup held in March. Races go clockwise. A good place to watch is from the Main Guard. At other times, it is used as a jogging course for people in the mornings, when you can see the horses being exercised, or on weekday evenings. There

is also rugby, basketball, etc, played informally in the Savannah, go and see what is going on on Sunday afternoons. There is a small children's playground in one corner. Later, at night, prostitutes parade here.

EXCURSIONS

Being the most E island and extremely difficult to attack, there are few defensive forts on Barbados. Instead the great houses of the sugar growing plantocracy give the island its historic perspective and most of its tourist attractions. Many parish churches are also impressive buildings. The island is not large but it is easy to get lost when driving. There are deep gullies cut in the coral limestone which is the surface rock over most of the island. These are often full of wildlife and plants but make travelling around very confusing. It sometimes helps to remember that the island is divided into 11 parishes named after 11 saints. A good map is essential. The bus service is cheap and efficient and recommended even for families with small children.

THE WEST COAST

The mass development of the W coast was carried out only recently. The beaches are easily eroded and can be covered with broken coral after storms. Pre-war, the area was regarded by the local Bajans as unhealthy. They preferred to go for their holidays to the E coast. Nowadays, the road N of Bridgetown on Highway 1 is wall to wall hotels. Highway 2a runs parallel inland and goes through the sugar cane heartland, with small villages and pleasant views.

Holetown today is a thoroughly modern town but was the place where the earliest settlers landed on 17 February 1627. The Holetown monument commemorates Captain John Powell claiming the island for England. Initially named Jamestown, it was renamed Holetown because of a tidal hole near the beach. It was quite heavily defended until after the Napoleonic Wars. Little trace of the forts can be seen now. Well worth visiting is **St James Church**. Originally built of wood in 1628, it was replaced by a stone structure in 1680. This building was extended 20 feet W in 1874 when columns and arches were added and the nave roof raised. You can see the original baptismal font (1684) under the belfry and in the N porch is the original bell of 1696. Many of the original settlers are buried here (although the oldest tombstone of William Balston who died in 1659 is in the Barbados Museum). Church documents dating to 1693 have been removed to the Department of Archives. It was beautifully restored between 1983-86.

On the beach at the back of the church is the post office and also the **Folkestone Marine Museum** and **Underwater Park**. Here you can snorkel in a large area enclosed by buoys. The reef is not in very good condition but there are some fish. The small museum is open Monday-Friday 1000-1700. Slide shows are held about every hour. Entrance B\$1. Snorkelling equipment (eg mask and snorkel B\$5) for hire as are glass bottomed boats which will take you over the reef to two small wrecks further down the coast opposite the *Gold Palm Hotel*. A diving platform about 100 yards offshore allows you to snorkel over the wrecks. Expect to pay B\$20 pp (children B\$10) but be prepared to bargain. There are toilets and a shower here.

The **Portvale Sugar Factory** (best in the crop season, February to May) and Sugar Machinery Museum inland has an exhibition on the story of sugar and its products. Closed temporarily in 1993. Open usually 0900-1600, Monday-Friday, T 432 1100 to check.

Follow the coast road and glimpse the sea at Gibbes and Mullins Bays to reach *Speightstown* where William Speight once owned the land. An important trading port in the early days, when it was known as Little Bristol. Speightstown

(pronounced Spitestown, or Spikestong in broad dialect) is now the main shopping centre for the N of the island. There are several interesting old buildings and many two-storey shops with Georgian balconies and overhanging galleries (although sadly many have been knocked down by passing lorries). The Lions Club building (Arlington) is 17th century, built very much on the lines of an English late mediaeval town house. No longer occupied, it is rapidly becoming derelict, but well worth a look. In 1989, the Barbados National Trust launched an appeal for funds to help restore the town.

ST LUCY

The road N of Speightstown is mercifully free of buildings and there is a good sandy beach on Six Men's Bay. Go through Littlegood Harbour and notice the boat building on the beach. The jetty you can see is at Harrison Point. You are now entering the almost unspoilt (apart from the Arawak Cement Plant) parish of St Lucy. Almost any of the roads off Highway 1b will take you to the N coast, at first green and lush around Stroud Point but becoming more desolate as you approach North Point. The NW coast, being slightly sheltered from the Atlantic swells, has many sandy coves (for example Archers Bay). The cliffs are quiet and easy to walk. You may spot turtles swimming in the sea.

The **Animal Flower Cave** at **North Point** is a series of caverns at sea level which have been eroded by the sea. The animals are sea anemones. There are various "shapes" in the rock which are pointed out to you. The main cave can be closed due to dangerous seas, so T 439-8797 around 0930 to enquire. Entrance B\$3 (B\$2 if you cannot see full cave). The floor of the cave is very stony and can be slippery. Following the rocky coast, turn into the semi-abandoned *North Point Surf Resort* (park outside the wall to avoid being charged for parking, the buildings are half ruined now, and there is an enormous empty swimming pool) where you can walk around the Spout, which has lots of blow holes and a small, rather dangerous beach. Good walks along the cliffs can be enjoyed, for instance from River Bay to Little Bay along the Antilles Flat, but beware as there is no shade and there are shooting parties during the season. If driving, several back roads go through the attractive communities of Spring Garden and St Clements. At Pie Corner you can rejoin the coast and visit Little Bay. This is particularly impressive during the winter months with the swell breaking over the coral outcrops; lots of blowholes. Note the completely circular hole on the N edge of the Bay. If you climb through this natural archway in the cliff, there is a big, calm pool, just deep enough to swim, between the cliffs and a line of rock on which the enormous waves break and send up a wall of spray. Wear shoes to stop your feet getting cut to pieces on the sharp rock. At Paul's Point is a popular picnic area. If the ground looks wet park at the millwall by the Cove Stud Farm as it is easy to get bogged down. You will get a good view of Gay's Cove with its shingle beach (safe to swim in the pools at low tide) and beyond it the 240-feet high Pico Teneriffe, a large rock (almost in the shape of Barbados and named by sailors who thought it looked like the mountain on Teneriffe in the Canaries) on top of a steeply sloping cliff. The white cliffs are oceanic rocks consisting of myriad tiny white shells or microscopic sea creatures. The whole of the coast to Bathsheba is visible and it is easy to see the erosion taking place in Corben's Bay. Indeed you get an excellent impression of the Scotland District, where the coral limestone has been eroded. The whole of this coast between North and Ragged Points has been zoned, no further development will be allowed along the seafront.

The Mount Gay Rum Distillery is reached off the road between the St Lucy church junction and Alexandra. There are tours Monday-Friday at 1100 and 1400. They also have a visitor's centre in St Michael (see page 695). This makes an alternative to Cockspur's West Indian Rum Refinery (see **Entertainment**, page 709).

THE SCOTLAND DISTRICT

Heading S, you get excellent views from Cherry Tree Hill. Just to the NW is St Nicholas Abbey which is approached down a long and impressive avenue of mahogany trees. Dating from around 1660, it is one of the oldest domestic buildings in the English-speaking Americas (Drax Hall, St George, open once a year under the National Trust Open House programme, is probably even older). Three storied, it has a façade with three ogee-shaped gables. It was never an abbey, some have supposed that the "St" and "Abbey" were added to impress, there being lots of "Halls" in the S of the island. Visitors are given an interesting tour of the ground floor and a fascinating film show in the stables behind the 400-year-old sand box tree. Narrated by Stephen Cave, the present owner and son of the film maker, its shows life on a sugar plantation in the 1930s. You will see the millwall in action and the many skilled workers from wheelwrights to coopers who made the plantation work. The importance of wind is emphasized. If the millwall stopped the whole harvest came to a halt as the cane which had been cut would quickly dry out if it was not crushed straight away. The waste was used to fuel the boilers just as it is today in sugar factories. There is a collection of toy buses and lorries in the stables.

Going back down the steep Cherry Tree Hill you come to the National Trust-owned **Morgan Lewis Mill**, a restored millwall with original machinery. You can climb to the top of it. Note the 100-

foot tail, this enabled the operators to position the mill to maximize the effect of the wind. It is on a working farm. Open Monday-Friday 0800-1600, entrance B$2. On the flat savannah at the bottom of the hill is a cricket pitch, a pleasant place to watch the game at weekends.

The **Barbados Wildlife Reserve**, established with Canadian help in 1985, is set in 4 acres of mature mahogany off Highway 2. It is an excellent place to see lots of Barbados green monkeys close up. Most of the animals are not caged, you are warned to be careful as you wander around the shady paths as the monkeys can bite. They have a collection of the large red-footed Barbados tortoise. Also (non-Barbadian) toucans, parrots and tropical birds, hares, otters, opossums, agoutis, wallabies, porcupines, and iguanas. You can observe pelicans and there is a spectacled caiman (alligator) in the pond. The primate research centre helps to provide farmers with advice on how to control the green monkeys who are regarded as a pest. The animals are fed near it at about 1600. Café and shop. Open daily 1000-1700. Admission B$10, children half price. T 422-8826. Can be reached by bus from Bridgetown, Holetown, Speightstown or Bathsheba. The centre has also developed a nature trail in the neighbouring Grenade Hall Forest, ask for further details. An early 19th century signal station next to Grenade Hall Forest has been restored and is open for visitors, daily 1000-1700, admission B$10, children half price. The wonderful panoramic view gives you a good idea of its original role in the communications network.

Farley Hill House, St Peter (T 422 3555), is a 19th century fire-damaged plantation house; a spectacular ruin on the other side of the road from the Wildlife Reserve, set in a pleasant park with views over the Scotland District. There is a large number of imported and native tree species planted over 30 acres of woodland. Open daily 0830-1800. US$1

per vehicle.

From Farley Hill it is possible to walk more or less along the top of the island as far as Mt Hillaby, through woods and then canefields. However, it helps to know where you are going as the paths have a mind of their own and losing them can be uncomfortable. You will see plenty of monkeys on the way and good views.

THE ATLANTIC PARISHES

The five-mile East Coast Road, opened by Queen Elizabeth on 15 February 1966 affords fine views. From Belleplaine, where the railway ended, it skirts Walker's Savannah to the coast at Long Pond and heads SE to Benab, where there is Barclays Park, a good place to stop for a picnic under the shady casuarina trees (a walk up Chalky Mount has been recommended for the magnificent views of the E coast, easily reached at the end of the bus line from Bridgetown, ask locally for the exact path and stop at Barclays Park for a drink when you come down). It continues through Cattlewash, so named because Bajans brought their animals here to wash them in the sea, to Bathsheba.

The tiny hamlet of **_Bathsheba_** has an excellent surfing beach (see **Watersports** above). Guarded by two rows of giant boulders, the bay seems to be almost white as the surf trails out behind the Atlantic rollers. Surfing championships are often held here. A railway was built in 1883 (but closed in 1937) between Bridgetown and Bathsheba. Originally conceived as going to Speightstown, it actually went up the E coast to a terminus at Belleplaine, St Andrew. The cutting at My Lady's Hole, near Conset Bay in St John is spectacular, with a gradient of 1:31, which is supposed to have been the steepest in the world except for rack and pinion and other special types of line. The railway suffered from landslides, wave erosion, mismanagment and underfunding so that the 37 miles of track was in places in very bad condition. The crew would sprinkle sand on the track, the first class passengers remained seated, the second class walked and the third class pushed. Above the bay at Hillcrest (excellent view) are the **Andromeda Gardens**. Owned by the Barbados National Trust, the gardens contain plants from all over Barbados as well as species from other parts of the world. There are many varieties of orchid, hibiscus and flowering trees. Open every day. Admission B$10. The *Hibiscus Café* at the entrance is a useful place to stop for refreshment. The *Atlantis Hotel* is a good place for lunch especially on Sunday (1300 sharp) when an excellent buffet meal containing several Bajan dishes is served. Almost an institution and extremely popular with Bajans, so book ahead.

From Bathsheba you can head inland to **Cotton Tower signal station** (also National Trust owned but not so interesting as Gun Hill). Then head S to Wilson Hill where you find Mount Tabor Church and **Villa Nova**, another plantation Great House (1834), which has furniture made of Barbadian mahogany and beautiful gardens. It is worth a visit not least as it was owned by the former British Prime Minister, Sir Anthony Eden (open Monday-Friday, 0900-1600, entrance B$6, children B$3). You can continue from here via Malvern along the scenic Hackleton's Cliff (allegedly named after Hackleton who committed suicide by riding his horse at full gallop over the cliff) to Pothouse, where **St John's Church** stands with excellent views over the Scotland District. Built in 1660 it was another victim of the great hurricane of 1835. There is an interesting pulpit made from six different kinds of wood. You will also find the curious grave of Fernando Paleologus "descendant of ye imperial line of ye last Christian emperors of Greece". The full story is in Leigh Fermor's *The Traveller's Tree*.

At the satellite tracking station turn off to **Bath**. Here you will find a safe beach, popular with Barbadians and a recreation park for children. It makes a good spot for a beach barbeque and a swim.

Codrington College is one of the most famous landmarks on the island and can be seen from Highway 4b down an avenue of Cabbage Palm trees. It is steeped in history as the first Codrington landed in Barbados in 1628. His son acted as Governor for three years but was dismissed for liberal views. Instead he stood for parliament and was elected speaker for nine years. He was involved in several wars against the French and became probably the wealthiest man in the West Indies. The third Codrington succeeded his father as Governor-General of the Leeward islands, attempted to stamp out the considerable corruption of the time and distinguished himself in campaigns (especially in taking St Kitts). He died in 1710, a batchelor aged 42, and left his Barbadian properties to the Society for the Propagation of the Gospel in Foreign Parts. It was not until 1830 that Codrington College, where candidates could study for the Anglican priesthood, was established. From 1875 to 1955 it was associated with Durham University, England. Apart from its beautiful grounds with a fine avenue of Royal Palms, a huge lily pond (flowers close up in the middle of the day) and impressive façade, there is a chapel containing a plaque to Sir Christopher Codrington and a library. There are plans to develop it as a conference centre. You can follow the track which drops down 360 feet to the sea at the beautiful Conset Bay. You can take the Sargeant Street bus as far as Codrington College, then walk 7 miles back along the Atlantic Coast to Bathsheba.

At **Ragged Point** is the automatic East Point lighthouse standing among the ruined houses of the former lighthouse keepers. There are good views N towards Conset Point, the small Culpepper island, and the S coast. Note the erosion to the 80-foot cliffs caused by the Atlantic sweeping into the coves.

THE CENTRE

NE of Holetown and reached from St Simon's Church are Turners Hall Woods, a good vantage point. Some think that the wood would have been very similar to the one covering the island before the English arrived. This 50-acre patch of tropical mesophytic forest has never been clear-felled (although individual trees were often taken out). You can walk over the steep paths here and see many species, ranging from the sandbox tree to Jack-in-the-box and the 100-foot locust trees supported by massive buttresses. The island's first natural gas field was here and the main path through the wood is the remains of the old road.

On Highway 2, take the Melvin Hill road just after the agricultural station and follow the signs to the Flower Forest, a 50-acre, landscaped plantation, opened in 1983 with beautifully laid out gardens. Dropping downhill, the well-maintained paths afford excellent views over the valley to the E coast. To the W you can see Mount Hillaby, at 1,116 feet the island's highest point (see above for walking from Farley Hill). It too contains species not only from Barbados but also from all over the world, they are beautifully arranged with plenty of colour all year round. There is a *Best of Barbados* shop, cafeteria and toilets. Good information sheet. Open daily 0900-1700, entrance B$10, T 433 8152.

Roads in this area are often closed by landslides and circuitous routing may be necessary.

Close by and to the S on Highway 2 is Welchman Hall Gully, a fascinating walk through one of the deep ravines so characteristic of this part of Barbados. You are at the edge of the limestone cap which covers most of the island to a depth of about 300 feet. There is a small car park

opposite the entrance (despite the sign to the contrary). Maintained by the National Trust, a good path leads for about half a mile through six sections, each with a slightly different theme. The first section has a devil tree, a stand of bamboo and a judas tree. Next you will go through jungle, lots of creepers, the "pop-a-gun" tree and bearded fig clinging to the cliff (note the stalactites and stalagmites); a section devoted to palms and ferns: golden, silver, macarthur and cohune palms, nutmegs and wild chestnuts; to open areas with tall leafy mahogany trees, rock balsam and mango trees. At the end of the walk are ponds with lots of frogs and toads. Best of all though is the wonderful view to the coast. On the left are some steps leading to a gazebo, at the same level as the tops of the cabbage palms. Open daily, 0900-1700, B$5, children B$2.50.

Harrison's Cave nearby has an impressive visitors' centre which has a restaurant (fair), shop and a small display of local geology and Amerindian artefacts. You are taken into the cave on an electric "train". The visit takes about 20 minutes and you will see some superbly-lit stalactites and stalagmites, waterfalls and large underground lakes. There is a guide to point out the interesting formations and two stops for photo-opportunities. Interesting as it is, it is all rather overdone, you even have to wear hard hats and serviettes on your head despite claims that the caves are totally stable. Open daily 0900-1600, admission B$15, children half price, T 438 6640.

If you take Highway 2 heading to Bridgetown you will pass Jack-in-the-Box gully, part of the same complex of Welchman Hall Gully and Harrison's Cave. Coles Cave (an "undeveloped" cave nearby, which can easily be explored with a waterproof torch or flashlight) lies at its N end.

At Gun Hill is a fully restored signal tower. The approach is by Fusilier road and you will pass the Lion carved by

British soldiers in 1868. The road was built by Royal Scot Fusiliers between September 1862 and February 1863 when they were stationed at Gun Hill to avoid yellow fever. The signal station itself had its origins in the slave uprising of 1816. It was decided that a military presence would be maintained outside Bridgetown in case of further slave uprisings. It was also intended for advance warning of attack from the sea. The chain of six signal stations was intended to give very rapid communications with the rest of the island. The hexagonal tower had two small barrack rooms attached and would have been surrounded by a pallisade. They quickly lost importance as military installations but provided useful information about shipping movements. Informative guides will explain the workings of the signal station and point out interesting features of the surrounding countryside. You will not necessarily get the same story from all the guides. Entrance B$5 (children B$2.50), guide book B$2.

THE SOUTH COAST

The area around Six Cross Roads was where the Easter Rebellion of 1816 took place, an uprising by slaves who thought (incorrectly) that William Wilberforce had introduced a bill in the English parliament granting slaves their freedom. It was thought by the slaves that the Barbados plantation owners were denying them this freedom. Despite destroying a large acreage of cane fields, no owners or their families were killed and the uprising was quickly crushed by the West Indian Regiment. Several hundred slaves were killed in battle or hanged afterwards, including the best-known leader, an African called Bussa, and Washington Francklyn, a free man of mixed race who was thought, probably erroneously, to have planned the rebellion. 123 slaves were exiled to Sierra Leone. You can visit two of the great

houses. Turn N at Six Cross Roads for Sunbury Plantation. Some 300 years old, the house is elegantly furnished in Georgian style, much of it with mahogany furniture, and you can roam all over it as, unusually, there is access to the upstairs private rooms. In the cellars, you can see the domestic quarters. There is a good collection of carriages. Open 1030-1630 every day. There is a restaurant in the courtyard.

Take the road to Harrow and Bushy Park to reach Oughterson Plantation House and the Barbados Zoo Park. Although not as extensive as Sunbury, the entrance to the Wildlife Park takes you through the ground floor of the house which is quite interesting. There is a self-guided nature trail. The zoo is very small but has expanded from a bird garden and more animals have slowly been added. Vikki, a small monkey, is a great favourite with children as she will stroke their hands. You are given bread and encouraged to feed the ducks.

Sam Lord's Castle on the SE coast is the site of the *Marriott Hotel*. It is high on the list of tourist attractions because of the reputation of Sam Lord who reputedly lured ships onto Cobbler's Reef where they were shipwrecked. There is supposed to be a tunnel from the beach to the castle's cellars to facilitate his operation. The proceeds made him a wealthy man although the castle was supposed to have been financed from his marriage to a wealthy heiress. The castle is not particularly old or castle-like, being in fact a regency building. Unfortunately the rooms are poorly lit making it difficult to appreciate the fine mahogany furniture or the paintings. Note the superb staircase, you are not allowed upstairs. Wander down to the cove where there is a good example of a turtlecrawl, a salt water pond enclosed by a wall. Here turtles were kept alive until wanted for the kitchen. Today the *Marriott Hotel*, in conjunction with the Barbados Wildlife park, keeps a few hawksbill turtles, a shark and a congor eel. There is a B$7 entrance charge (children free) even though the hotel reception forms part of the two rooms open to the public.

Crane Bay, SW of Sam Lord's Castle, is worth a detour. It is a pleasant cove overlooked by 80-foot cliffs.

INFORMATION FOR VISITORS

● **Documents**

Visitors from North America, Western Europe, Venezuela, Colombia, and Brazil need a passport but no visas. Visitors from most other countries are usually granted a short stay on arrival, and tourist visas are not necessary. Officially, you must have a ticket back to your country of origin as well as an onward ticket to be allowed in.

State the maximum period you intend to stay on arrival. Overstaying is not rec if you wish to re-enter Barbados at a later date. Extending the period of stay is possible at the Immigration Office on the Wharf in Bridgetown but costs US$12.50 and is fairly time consuming. When visiting the Immigration Office, which is open from 0830-1630, you will need to take your passport and return ticket. Tickets are inspected quite carefully.

You will need an accommodation address on arrival, they do not check your reservation but if you say you do not know where you will be staying, you will be sent to the back of the queue and 'helped' to select a hotel (which may be more expensive than you wanted) at least for one night.

Work permits are extremely difficult to obtain and the regulations are strictly enforced.

● **How To Get There**

By Air From North America BWIA and American Airlines fly from New York and Miami daily, American Airlines also flies daily from Orlando, Florida; BWIA and Air Canada fly from Toronto and Air Canada from Montreal. From Europe British Airways and BWIA have several flights a week from London and BWIA has twice-weekly flights from Frankfurt and once a week from Zurich. From South America Liat and Surinam Airways from Georgetown, Guyana; Surinam Airways and Gonini Air Service from Paramaribo, Suriname. There is no longer a direct flight from Venezuela, but Aeropostal

comes in from Porlamar, Isla Margarita. Connections with Caribbean islands are good, from Antigua (Liat, British Airways, BWIA), Dominica (Liat), Fort-de-France, Martinique (Liat, Air Martinique), Grenada (BWIA, Liat), Kingston, Jamaica (BWIA), Pointe-à-Pitre, Guadeloupe (Liat), Port of Spain, Trinidad (BWIA, Liat, British Airways), St Lucia (Liat, British Airways), St Maarten (Liat, BWIA), St Vincent (Liat), San Juan, Puerto Rico (Liat, American Airlines), Tobago (Liat, BWIA) and Tortola, BVI (Liat). Check different airlines for inter-island travel, the Trinidad route is particularly competitive, British Airways often has good offers between Barbados, Antigua, St Lucia and Trinidad and a comfortable plane. Air tickets bought in Barbados, and tickets bought elsewhere for journeys starting in Barbados, have a 20% tax added. It is usually worth organizing ticketing at the start of your journey so that Barbados appears as a stopover rather than as the origin for any side trips you make. Note that flights to Barbados are heavily booked at Christmas and for Cropover.

There is a departure tax of B$40, not payable if your stay is for less than 24 hrs.

By Sea Barbados is not well served by small inter-island schooners. Information and tickets from the shipping agents, Eric Hassell & Son, 2nd floor, Citibank building, Bridgetown (T 436 6102). If you buy a one-way ticket, you will need to show passport and onward ticket when paying for your passage. You may be able to get a passage to another island on a yacht, ask at the harbour or at the *Boatyard*.

Windward Lines Limited run a weekly passenger/car/cargo ferry service: Trinidad – St Vincent – Barbados – St Lucia – Barbados – St Vincent – Trinidad – Guiria (or every other week to Pampatar, Margarita). Arriving Fri 1930 from St Vincent, departing 2200, coming back from St Lucia on Sun at 0800, arriving in Barbados 1900 and departing 2200. Information from Global Steamship Agencies Ltd, Mariner's Club, Wrightson Road, PO Box 966, Port of Spain, Trinidad, T (809) 624-2279, F 627-5091. To Venezuela is especially good value as you see several islands and have somewhere to sleep on the way. Restaurant on board. Fare Barbados-Venezuela round trip US$148, cabins US$20-50, reservation fee for bunks US$5, seats US$2.50.

There are several companies running mini-cruises based on Barbados. Caribbean Safari Tours (T 427 5100, F 429 5446), organize day trips to St Lucia, Dominica, Grenada,

Martinique and the Grenadines; they also do 2 and 3 night packages to these islands and to Trinidad, Tobago, St Vincent and Caracas. Some of these are quite competitively priced. The cruise ship passenger tax is to be raised.

Geest Lines run a fortnightly service for bananas from Britain (Southampton) to the Windwards via Barbados. This is a cheap and efficient method of freighting bulky items. There is also room for a few luxury passengers, but it is expensive, and booking is up to 18 months in advance. Thos and Jas Harrison Ltd's MV *Author* also calls at Bridgetown on its 6-week round trip from Liverpool; details are given in **Introduction and Hints**, Travel to and in the Caribbean—By Sea.

● **Airport Information**

The airport is modern and well equipped. Clearing immigration can be a problem and it can take an hour to clear a 747. If three 747s arrive together expect delays. There is a Liat connection desk before immigration. There is a helpful Tourism Authority office, Barbados National Bank (very slow), bureau de change in the arrivals and departure areas is open from 0800-2200), a post office, car hire agencies and quite a wide range of shops (good for stocking up on film or alcohol even if just going on a day trip) including an Inbound Duty Free Shop (very useful, saves carrying heavy bottles on the plane). *The Voyager* restaurant is fairly expensive. Taxis stop just outside customs, and there is a bus stop just across the car park, with buses running along the S coast to Bridgetown, or (over the road) to the *Crane* and *Sam Lord's Castle*. But you may have a long wait for a bus, and they often pass full in the rush hour.

● **Airlines**

The Liat office is at St Michael's Plaza, St Michael's Row (T 436 6224). BWIA (T 426 2111); British Airways (T 436 6413), Aeropostal (T 427 7781) are all on Fairchild Street. American (T 428 4170) and Cubana (T 428 0060) have offices at the airport.

● **Helicopters**

For those who want to make a lot of noise buzzing round the island, Bajan Helicopters do tours from US$130/20 mins, US$200 right round the coastline. The heliport is near the deep water harbour at Bridgetown, T 431 0069.

● **Road Transport**

The island is fairly small (just over 21 miles from N to S) but it can take a surprisingly long time to travel from A to B as the rural roads are narrow and winding. Note that a new Adams Barrow Cummins highway has been built from the airport to a point between Brighton and Prospect, N of Bridgetown. This road (called the ABC, or industrial access highway) skirts the E edge of the capital, giving access by various roads into the city.

Buses are cheap and frequent, but also crowded and unreliable. There is a flat fare of B$1.50 which will take you anywhere on the island. Around Bridgetown, there are plenty of small yellow privately-owned minibuses and route taxis with ZR numberplates; elsewhere, the big blue buses (exact fare required or tokens sold at the bus terminal) belong to the Transport Board. Private companies tend to stick to urban areas while the public buses run half empty in rural areas. Almost all the routes radiate in and out of Bridgetown, so cross-country journeys are time-consuming if you are staying outside the city centre. The main Fairchild Street bus terminal, serving the S coast, is clean and modern. Other terminals at Lower Green and Princess Alice Highway serve the N and centre of the island. During the rush hour, all these terminals are chaotic, particularly during school term. Terminals for minibuses and route taxis are close to the bus terminals (River Road for S coast, Cheapside for W, others by Treasury building on Careenage). Don't rely on a bus to the airport (Route 12 to *Sam Lord's Castle*) if you have a plane to catch as this route is notorious, although reportedly better than it used to be. On most routes, the last bus leaves at midnight and the first bus at 0500.

However, travelling by bus can be fun. There are some circuits which work quite well; for example:

1. Any S coast bus to Oistins, then cross country College Savannah bus to the E coast, then direct bus back to Bridgetown.

2. Any W coast bus to Speightstown, then bus back to Bathsheba on the E coast, then direct bus back to Bridgetown.

Out of town bus stops are marked simply 'To City' or 'Out of City'. For the S coast ask for Silver Sands route.

Bus Tours L E Williams (T 427 1043, has a sign up in the bus: 'no 10% service charge is paid with the tour price'), Bartic tours (T 428 5980), Sunflower Tours (T 429 8941), International Tour Services (T 428 4803) and Blue Line (T 423 9268) do round-the-island tours for US$25-55, including entrance fees to sites visited. Longer tours generally include lunch at the *Atlantic Hotel* in Bathsheba. A criticism of the tours with some companies is that it can take 1½ hrs to pick up everyone from hotels, depending on who has booked.

Taxis are expensive. There are plenty at the airport, the main hotels, and in Bridgetown. There are standard fares (Airport to Bridgetown US$15, or to Worthing US$12 for example). Maximum standard fare US$27.50, airport to any point N of St Lucy church. These are displayed just outside "arrivals" at the airport, and are also listed in the *Visitor* and the *Sunseeker*. Fares are quoted also by mile or kilometre (the latter slightly cheaper) but there are no taxi meters. Up to 5 people can travel for one fare. You may have to bargain hard for tours by taxi but always agree a fare in advance. Vehicles which look like route taxis but with ZM numberplates, are taxis plying for individual hire, and will charge accordingly.

● **Motoring**
Car Hire is efficient and generally reliable. There is a car hire company stand at the airport outside Arrivals, but they are often fully booked. Costs range upwards from B$100 per day for an open Mini Moke (not rec in the rainy season). Small cars are often cheaper. Weekly rates work out lower. Sunny Isle Motors, Dayton, Worthing, T 435 7979, car hire B$147/day or B$522/week, collision damage waiver B$20/day, B$70/week. Stoutes Car Rentals (T 435 4456/7, F 435 4435) are particularly helpful, and will arrange to meet you at the airport if you telephone in advance, minimokes B$100/day, B$435/week, small car B$110/day, B$530/week, Suzuki B$150/day, CDW B$15/day, B$70/week. L E Williams (T 427 1043) has slightly lower rates for some vehicles. Other companies are listed in the Yellow Pages. There are often discounts available and tourist magazines frequently contain 10% vouchers.

It is also possible to hire a light **motorcycle** or a **bicycle**. Fun Seekers, Rockley Main Road, T 435 8206, have motor scooters B$58/day, B$298/week, bicycles B$17/day, B$63/week. Deposit B$200 on scooter, B$100 on bicycle.

Drivers need a visitor's driving permit from Hastings, Worthing, or Holetown police stations (cost US$5). You will need this even if you have an International Driving Licence. Petrol costs B$1.64 per litre.

VIP Limo Services (T 429 4617) hire a vehicle with driver for a whole-day tour at a cost of US$150 for up to 4 persons.

● **Where To Stay**
There are over 175 hotels, although the Board of Tourism lists only 85 hotels and guest houses, and 53 apartment complexes. Rates in the larger hotels almost double in the peak season, which is from mid December to mid April. A 5% government tax and 10% service charge are generally added to the published rates and these rates are often quoted in US currency, which can be a pitfall for the unwary. The Barbados Hotel Association introduced a new charge in 1990, ranging from B$1 to B$4 per room per night.

Most of the accommodation offered is very pleasant to stay in, if not particularly cheap.

Super Luxury Most of these are on the W coast. *Sandy Lane*, US$495-750 summer, rises in winter to US$720-1,600 MAP, is Trust House Forte, extensively renovated in 1991 and quite nice of its type. Has a golf course. Watch out for extras on top of the astronomical room rate, golf, honeymoon packages available (T 430-1311, F 430 2954). *Glitter Bay*, US$345-485 winter, US$195-330 summer EP, (T 422 4111, F 422 3940), and *Royal Pavilion*, US$445-485 winter, US$230-325 summer EP (T 422 4444, F 422 3940), are newer and just as smart, next to each other and under the same management. One is "Spanish Colonial Style", the other a pink palace. Perhaps better value to stay elsewhere and visit for a drink or afternoon tea, but well worth looking at, the guests as spectacular in some cases as the (faultless) interior design and landscaping. *Settlers Beach*, St James, T 422 3052, F 422 1937, US$500-550d winter, US$220-260d summer EP, no children in Feb, pool, on beach, and *Treasure Beach*, Paynes Bay, T 432 1346, F 432 1094, US$325-440 winter, US$150-220 summer CP, both Unique Hotels, in UK T 0800-373742. *Coral Reef Club*, St James (T 422 2372, F 422 1776), US$310-541d winter MAP, US$126-225d summer EP, member of Elegant Resorts of Barbados and Prestige Hotels, London, very highly regarded; also in St James, *Sandpiper Inn*, T 422 2231, F 422 1776, US$275-567d winter, US$138-322d summer EP, family-run, with award-winning restaurant. Also on the W coast, good but not as luxurious, *Kings Beach Hotel*, US$120-140d EP, summer US$220-240d winter, (T 422 1690, F 422 1691 or 0932 849 462 in the UK or 800 223 1588 in the USA), at Mullins Bay, facilities for children and the handicapped.

Convenient for Bridgetown *Barbados Hilton*, US$218-484 winter, US$137-266 summer EP, good location on a nice beach with gentle surf, good pool, concrete structure showing its age, good buffet breakfast and lunch, (T 426 0200, F 436 8946); *Grand Barbados*, US$140-600d winter, US$100-300d summer EP rooms and suites, (T 426 0890, F 436 9823); an all-inclusive *Sandals Barbados Resort* is to open shortly on Paradise Beach; *Blue Horizon*, Rockley, large hotel with pool, bar, restaurant, 100 yards from beach across main road, US$90-110d winter, US$55-75d summer EP with kitchenette, 10 mins from Bridgetown, T 435 8915, F 435 8153; *Ocean View Hotel*, S coast, US$75-150d EP winter rate, US$55-95 summer, very old fashioned, with mahogany furniture and a dining terrace overlooking the sea but no beach (T 427 7821, F 427 7826), mediocre food.

Near the Airport *Shonlan Inn Airport Hotel*, T 428 0039, F 428 0160, 16 rooms, 9 bathrooms, US$35-45d EP, some rooms with kitchenette, very mixed reports, noisy, nowhere near a beach, but only a mile from the terminal, although the taxi fare makes it no cheaper than a guest house further away. *Crane Beach*, US$137-297d winter, US$77-177d summer CP, fairly near the airport, but definitely a taxi ride away, spectacular cliff top setting, good beach, and good pool, tennis, luxury prices and usually fairly quiet with only 18 rooms, but they are planning an extra 250 units (T 423 6220, F 423 5343); *Silver Sands Resort*, Christ Church, (T 428 6001, F 428 3758), 20 mins drive from airport, on the sea at South Point, rooms spacious and well-equipped, US$120-155d winter, US60-75d summer EP, good service, food dull, good beach but take care swimming, waves strong and high, good for surfing but children and weak swimmers should use the pool.

Good Value Rec are *Sandridge*, 1 mile from Speightstown, good-sized rooms or family apartments with cooking facilities, N-facing balconies overlook the sea, friendly staff and management, watersports free for guests, good value barbeque evenings, excellent for families, US$85-165d winter, US55-75d summer EP, T 422 2361, F 422 2965. *Woodville Apartments*, Worthing, T 435 6694, F 435 9211, US$70-125 winter, US$43-85 summer for studio apartment, 1-bedroom or, 2-bedroom. *Worthing Court Apartment Hotel*, Worthing, T 435 7910, F 435 7374, studios or 1-bedroom connecting apartments, US$80-100d winter, US$55-75d summer and *Casuarina Beach Club*, Dover, US$150-300 winter, US$75-170 summer EP, T 428 3600, F 428 1970, on beach, pool, tennis. *Pegwell Inn*, US$20-24, Oistins (T 428 6150). Good for shops and airport buses, not brilliant for beaches. *Bona Vista*, on a side road off Golf Club Road, US$20s, US$40d, rec, T 435 6680. *Summer Place on Sea*, run by George de Mattos, US$20s, US$30d winter rate, US$15-25 summer EP, Rydal Water, Worthing (T 435 7417), rooms basic but clean, 2 rooms with cooking facilities available, very pleasant and good value, right on the beach, friendly, bus to/from airport, get off at Star Discount Supermarket, but both always seem to be booked up well in advance. Ring ahead. Lots of pubs, nightlife and other small hotels in the area. *Rydal Waters Guest House*, 3rd Ave in Worthing, US$20s, US$30d winter rate, US$15-25 summer EP, with private bath and fan, breakfast US$4 extra, payment in cash preferred, rec, good value, pleasant beach (T 435 7433), Chinese restaurant next door, quite good. *Chateau Blanc Apartments*, T 435 7518, 50m from *Rydal Waters*, good value studios, US$35-50 summer, US$65-85 winter, well-equipped but old kitchen facilities, friendly management, also has 1/2 bedroom apartments on beach front, US$105-140 winter, US$75-100 summer. *Shells Guest House*, First Avenue, Worthing, T 435 7253, US$35d winter, US$25d summer with breakfast, 6 rooms, 5 bathrooms, excellent food in restaurant, rec. *Set Set's Guest House*, on corner of 4th Ave, Worthing, small, friendly, family atmosphere, use of kitchen, clean, US$15d, rec; *The Nook Apartments*, Dayrells Road in Rockley has 4 excellent 2-bedroom apartments for US$62 winter, US$50 summer, with pool, maid service, clean, secure, convenient for shops and restaurants, highly rec, discounts for airline staff and Caricom residents (T 436 6494 0800-1600 Mon-Fri, 428 1033 evenings and weekends, F 425 4975, Mr Harold Clarke). *Tree Haven*, Rockley, a short bus ride from the centre of town, US$35 low season, US$50 high season, excellent apartment opp the beach, very clean, helpful and friendly owner. *Fred La Rose Bonanza*, Dover, from US$30 for a studio, US$35 1 bedroom, US$50 for 2 bedrooms (winter), US$25-42 in summer, helpful, quite convenient but not too clean, T 428 9097. There are several other cheap places to stay in this area, all within walking distance of each other. *Woodbine*, very pleasant, hot shower, use of kitchen, rec but a short walk away from the beach (T 427 7627 or 428 7356). All these are well served by the S coast bus routes. *Romans Beach Apartments*, Enterprise, studio US$45-65 winter rate, US$35-60 summer, T 428 7635, friendly, comfortable, on beautiful beach. *Miami Beach Apartments*, Enterprise Drive, Christ Church, T 428 5387, US$36-50d, all year, kitchen, 1-2 bedroom, living room, veranda, TV, phone, 2 min from small, clean beach, 3 min to main road and minibus route. *Travellers Palm*, 265 Palm Ave, Sunset Crest, St James (T 432 6666/7722), US$55 for 1-bedroom apartment with kitchen, winter rate, US$35 summer, roomy apartments, pool, 10 mins walk to the beach, close to the underwater sea park. *Tower Hotel* in Paradise Village, Black Rock, N of Bridgetown on Princess Alice Highway, US$50-60 for 1-bedroom apartment, winter rate, US$40 summer, US$80-50 winter/for 2 bedrooms, a/c, fridge, very pleasant (T 424 3256).

Away from the main tourist areas *Atlantis*, Bathsheba, US$55-65d MAP winter, US$50-60d summer, T 433 9445, and *Kingsley Club*, Cattlewash, US$101d winter EP, US$84d summer rate, T 433 9422, F 433 9226, both on the E coast, with a spectacular setting. Both do good food, pleasant, family-run hotels but the former is a little run down. *Edgewater Hotel*, Bathsheba, T 433 9900, F 433 9902, US$50-200 EP, pool overlooking sea, quiet and out of the way, popular with Venezuelans. *Sam Lord's Castle*, Marriott's fun-factory, US$195-220d EP winter (T 423 7350, F 423 5918). Lots of new stuff round a cliff-top plantation house with some fairly spurious pirate legends attached. Good Sun buffet, 3 swimming pools, and outdoor bars where they serve the drinks in plastic cups.

Villa Rental agents and property managers include Realtors Limited, Riverside House, River Road, St Michael, T 426 4900, F 426 6419; Bajan Services Ltd, Seascape Cottage, Gibbs, St Peter, T 422 2618, F 422 5366. Weekly rates for a small villa on the beach start at US$800 in the summer but can be twice the price in the winter, plus 8% tax. If staying for a while, try the small ads in the *Advocate* and *Nation*. Ordinary apartments to let can be rented furnished for about US$400 a month which could work out cheaper even if you do not stay that long. If possible get a Bajan who knows the island well to help you.

● **Youth Hostel**

The YMCA has a hostel at Pinfold St, Bridgetown, T 426 3910/1240 which can accommodate 24 people, dormitory beds B$20, single rooms B$35, breakfast B$6.50, lunch B$7.50.

● **Where To Eat**

Barbados has a very wide range of places to eat. There is a good listing in the *Visitor*. Good places include:

Low prices fast food from Chefette chain, Pizza House chain or Del's chain. *Chicken Barn*, Broad Street and Rockley (big portions if you're hungry), *China Garden* (Bay Street). For those who like that sort of thing there are several *Kentucky Fried Chickens*, although for vegetarians the salad bars here and at the *Chefettes* have been rec. In St Lawrence Gap is the *Duke of Edinburgh Pub*. In Worthing on the main road opp the Plantation supermarket, the *Roti Hut* is cheap but nasty, nothing like rotis on Trinidad. *Granny's* in Oistins is more traditional and good value. *The Hotel School* in Marine House (T 427 5420) does an excellent lunch at certain times of year, and a smarter evening meal on Tues. Also drinks and snacks in the evening when they are running courses for bar staff. You could also try the canteens in the Light and Power Company on Bay Street and at Spring Gardens which are open to the public and do a huge traditional lunch. Good reports about *Kingsley Inn*, Cattlewash and *Little Edge*, Bathsheba (T 433 9900), for breakfast and lunch. *Mangoes*, Holetown, on balcony overlooking beach, view spoilt by enormous satellite dish, better bet is small beach bar next door, delicious flying fish and good club sandwiches. There is a good cheap café in Mall 34, just behind Atlantis Submarine office in Bridgetown. The *Pirate's Bar* at the Animal Flower Caves has the best value coke on the island, B$1.75 for ½ litre. Most sightseeing attractions have some kind of food available, eg Harrison Cave, fair snacks.

Middle price range *Waterfront Café* on the Careenage, interesting food, plenty to look at and a good social centre in the evenings. *39 Steps*, T 427 0715, on the coast road near the Garrison is well run and lively, lunchtimes and evenings, imaginative blackboard menu and choice of indoors or balcony, opened by Josef, previously of restaurant of that name, see below, popular, so book at weekends. There are some good beach bars, which do light meals and sometimes have a lively atmosphere; *Carib Beach Bar* at Worthing, near

Rydal Waters Guest House, has inexpensive meals and drinks, barbeque and music twice a week, excellent rum punches, happy hour 1700-1800 Mon-Fri, great fun even if you are not eating; even better is the Fri night barbeque at *Stowaways Beach Bar* at the *Sheringham Hotel* in Maxwell; *Sandy Banks* in Rockley; *The Boatyard* in Bay Street, full of divers and friends at weekends, food unimportant. In Holetown, *Rumours Beach Bar* is a nice place to sit and drink, but do not bother to eat there; *Garden Grill* has an imaginative menu and is good value. *Nico's Wine Bar* also pleasant. *Coach House* and *Bamboo Beach Bar* in St James, sometimes have live bands in the evenings. *Mango Café* in Speightstown is good value; *Mullins Beach Bar* just S of Speightstown has good menu and worth a visit to see the *trompe l'oeil* monkey murals. *The Ship/Captain's Carvery*, St Lawrence, has a good lunchtime buffet; in the evening there is usually a big crowd in the bar and often a live band. *Boomers* in St Lawrence Gap has quite good fast-food type dishes in a restaurant-type setting. *Sam's Lantern* and the *Pot and Barrel*, good inexpensive pizzas, just outside *Sam Lord's Castle* are worth a try. *Barclays Park Beach Bar* on the E coast does light meals (closed after 1900).

More expensive but worth it *The Treasure Beach Hotel* has the best food on the island, but at US$50 a head. *Kokos* (T 424 4557) has an interesting menu and a waterfront setting on the W coast. They will also do a good vegetarian meal if they have advance warning. *Brown Sugar* (T 426 7684), Aquatic Gap, Bay Street, St Michael, buffet lunch B$22, dinner, regional specialities, is good. So is *Reid's* (T 432 7623) on the W coast (but they are quite capable of producing an already-opened bottle of wine at the table). *Josef's* (T 435 6541/428 3379) on St Lawrence Gap, small, delightful, is well used by Barbadians, you need to book well ahead, arrive early and have pre-dinner drinks on the lawn with the sea lapping the wall a few feet below you. *Pisces* (T 428 6558), much larger, also on St Lawrence Gap, has some excellent and original fish dishes, an excellent vegetarian platter and a perfect waterfront setting; *David's*, also on waterfront, in Worthing, very good with better service and friendlier. *Ile de France* in Worthing is French managed and very good. Another fish restaurant is *Fisherman's Wharf* (T 436 7788), upstairs, on the Careenage in Bridgetown. *Da Luciano's* (T 427 5518) is a good Italian restaurant. *Luigi's*, Dover Woods, Christ Church, T 428 9218, run by Miles and Lisa Needham, Italian cuisine, reservations preferred. Also good: *La Cage aux Folles*, St James; *Carambola*, St James; *Schooner* and *Golden Shell* in Grand Barbados.

Generally, eating out in Barbados is not cheap. There are some good places, but even the best are apt to fall down over some detail like the coffee, which can be annoying after an expensive meal.

Buffets are good value. Unlimited food for a fixed price, usually lunchtime only, certain days only. Try *Hilton, Colony Club* (buffet by the beach on Sun B$25) or *Sam Lord's*. *Atlantis Hotel* in Bathsheba has an enormous Sun buffet, which is the place to try for traditional Barbadian cooking at its best (filling). Get up early and do a National Trust Sun morning walk to work up an appetite.

● **Food And Drink**

Fresh fish is excellent. The main fish season is December to May, when there is less risk of stormy weather at sea. Flying fish are a speciality and the national emblem, 2 or 3 to a plate. Dolphin (dorado, not a mammal in spite of its name) and kingfish are larger *steak-fish*. Snapper is excellent. Sea eggs are the roe of the white sea urchin, and are delicious but not often available. Fresh fish is sold at the fish markets in Oistins, Bridgetown and elsewhere in the late afternoon and evening, when the fishermen come in with their catch.

Cou-cou is a filling starchy dish made from breadfruit or corn meal. *Jug-jug* is a Christmas speciality made from guinea corn and supposedly descended from the haggis of the poor white settlers. Pudding and souse is a huge dish of pickled breadfruit, black pudding, and pork.

Barbados rum is probably the best in the English-speaking Caribbean, unless of course you come from Jamaica, or Guyana or ... It is worth paying a bit extra for a good brand such as VSOP or Old Gold, or for Sugar Cane Brandy, unless you are about to drown it in Coca Cola, in which case anything will do. *Falernum* is sweet, slightly alcoholic, with a hint of vanilla. *Corn and oil* is rum and falernum. *Mauby* is bitter, and made from tree bark. It can be refreshing. *Sorrel* is a bright red Christmas drink made with hibiscus sepals and spices; it is very good with white rum. Water is of excellent quality, it comes from inland springs.

● **Entertainment**

Nightclubs There are quite a selection. Most

charge US$10 for entry. It's worth phoning in advance to find out what is on offer. There are live bands on certain nights in some clubs, and on other nights drinks may be included in the cover charge. Most do not get lively until almost midnight, and close around 0400. Some have a complicated set of dress codes or admission rules, which is another reason for phoning ahead.

After Dark, St Lawrence Gap, recently re-decorated, huge selection at the bar, very lively. *Frontline* on Cavans Lane in Bridgetown is another but lacks adequate fire exits and attracts a rough crowd. *The Warehouse*, across the road has reopened after a fire and has a pleasant open air balcony to cool off, it gets overcrowded, particularly Mon when entry covers drinks, and Thur. Others are *Harbour Lights* (lots of tourists and expats, open air on the beach, local and disco music, crowded on Wed, entry covers drinks, Fri, Sat) and *Septembers* on Bay Street (lots of Barbadians). *The Boatyard* is the sailor's pub in front of the anchorage at Carlisle Bay, Bay Street. *The Ship Inn* in St Lawrence has a big outdoor area and is often packed, especially at weekends and when there is a live band. The beach bars can be lively (see listings above), but pick your night. Cheap bars in St Lawrence Gap are *Harry's* and *Colonnade*. At *Shakey's Pizza Parlour* in Rockley they have a Karaoke sing-along machine nightly from 2100.

Dances For something less glossy and more Bajan, it might be worth trying one of the dances which are advertized in the *Nation* newspaper on Fri. People hire a dance hall, charge admission (usually B$5), provide a disco, and keep the profits. There are very few foreigners, but the atmosphere is friendly, and the drinks a lot cheaper than in the smarter nightclubs. Unfortunately, there have been a few fights at 'Dub' fêtes and they are no longer as relaxed as they were.

Baxters Road in Bridgetown is another place to try. The one-roomed, ramshackle, rumshops are open all night (literally), and there's a lot of street life after midnight, although you might get pestered by cocaine addicts. Some of the rumshops sell fried chicken (the *Pink Star* is rec, it has a large indoor area where you can eat in peace and the place also has clean lavatories) and there are women in the street selling fish, seasoned and fried in coconut oil over an open fire. Especially rec if you are hungry after midnight.

If you drink in a rumshop, rum and other drinks are bought by the bottle. The smallest size is a mini, then a flask, then a full bottle. The shop will supply ice and glasses, you buy a mixer, and serve yourself. The same system operates in dances, though prices are higher; night clubs, of course, serve drinks by the glass like anywhere else. Wine, in a rumshop, usually means sweet British sherry. If you are not careful, it is drunk with ice and beer.

Shows The *Visitor* has a fairly full listing. Some of the better ones are: *The Off Off Off Broadway Revue*, Ocean View Hotel. Hollywood music with a twist. *Barbados Barbados*, Balls Plantation Tues, dinner with musical show based on Barbadian history and culture. *1627 And All That*, Barbados Museum, Sun and Thur. Buffet dinner, folkdance drama, and museum tour, B$80, B$5 extra for hotel pickup, starts 1830, T 435 6900 to book. *Where the Rum Comes From*, guided tour of the Cockspur West India Rum Refinery near the deep water port in Bridgetown on the Spring Garden Highway, with buffet lunch, free rum drinks and steel band entertainment every Wed, B$55, inc transport to/from hotels, B$50 without transport. The last 3 shows can be booked, T 435 6900. All 3 provide transport to and from hotel.

Cinemas There are 2 cinemas in Bridgetown and a drive-in not far from the S coast. Fairly second-rate selection of features.

Theatres There are several good semi-professional theatre companies. Performances are advertized in the press. It is usually wise to buy tickets in advance. Most people dress quite formally for these performances.

Party Cruises The *Jolly Roger* (T 436 6424) and *Bajan Queen* (T 436 2149/2150) run 4-hour daytime and evening cruises along the W coast to Holetown, near the Folkestone Underwater Park (where the fun and games take place) from the deepwater harbour. The drinks are unlimited (very). There is also a meal, music, dancing, etc. On daytime cruises, there is swimming and snorkelling.

● **Security**

Bridgetown is still much safer than some other Caribbean cities but crime rates have increased and both the UK and USA have raised a Travel Advisory on Barbados. Local people are now more cautious about where they go after dark and many no longer go to Nelson Street or some other run-down areas. Baxters Road, however, is generally quite safe although the former attracts prostitutes while the latter attracts cocaine addicts (paros). Unlike Jamaica, where crime is concentrated mainly in Kingston, crime has become prevalent in Barbados where tourists congregate, particularly at night. Care should be taken not to go for romantic walks along deserted beaches and to watch out for pickpockets and bag snatchers in tourist areas. Families with small children to care for at night rarely notice any crime and have commented on how secure they felt on Barbados. If hiring a car, watch out for people who wash the vehicle unasked and then demand US$5. Police have patrols on beaches and plain clothes officers around some rural tourist attractions.

● **Shopping**
Prices are generally high, but the range of goods available is excellent. Travellers who are going on to other islands may find it useful to do some shopping here. If coming from another Caribbean island you can bring fresh fruit and vegetables, but no mangoes from St Lucia, Dominica or Martinique, no fruit from Latin America, no soft fruit from Guyana or Trinidad (you can bring pineapples and citrus), no bananas or plantains from Grenada.

The best stocked supermarket is JB's Mastermart in Wildey. Big B in Worthing and Supercentre in Oistins and Holetown are also good, and are easier to reach by public transport. Food is not cheap but generally most things are available and good quality except items like tinned pâté or good quality salami, which you might like to bring with you.

Duty-free shopping is well advertized. Visitors who produce passport and air ticket can take most duty-free goods away from the store for use in the island before they leave, but not camera film or alcohol. Clothing for example is significantly cheaper duty-free, so don't go shopping without ticket and passport. But cameras and electrical goods may be much cheaper to buy in an ordinary discount store in the USA or Europe than duty free in Barbados. A new duty-free shopping centre for cruise ship passengers opened in Bridgetown in 1994.

The *Best of Barbados* shops (plus Walkers' Caribbean World, Mount Gay Visitor Centre Shop and Great Gifts) sell high quality items made or designed by Jill Walker, including paintings and designs by Jill Walker, pottery, basketwork, island music and dolls. Locations include *Sandpiper Inn*, *Sam Lord's Castle*, Mall 34, Broad Street, St Lawrence Gap, Flower Forest, Andromeda Gardens, Quayside Centre, Rockley. Other good displays of craft items are at Pelican Village on the Harbour Road. Origins on the Careenage in Bridgetown is a gallery with well-designed but expensive clothing, jewellery and ceramics. There is also a street market in Temple Yard where Rastafarians sell leather and other goods.

Street Vendors are very persistent but generally friendly even when you refuse their wares.

Bookshops are much better stocked than on other islands. The Cloister on the Wharf probably has the largest stock. The Book Place on Probyn Street specializes in Caribbean material and has a good secondhand section. Brydens and Cave Shepherd also have a good selection. Also Roberts Stationery, The Book Shop, The Bookstop.

Camera repairs Skeetes Repair Service on Milkmarket is a small workshop which repairs most brands of camera. Louis Bailey in Broad Street is well-equipped but more expensive. Professional Camera Repair, Bolton Lane, Bridgetown, T 426 7174.

Film Processing Graphic Photo Lab in Worthing is quick and efficient. Rec for slides and enlargements. Be prepared to wait a day or 2 for slides wherever you go.

● **Banks**
Barclays Bank, the Royal Bank of Canada, Canadian Imperial Bank of Commerce, Scotiabank, Caribbean Commercial Bank, Barbados Mutual Bank and Barbados National Bank all have offices in Bridgetown. The first 5 also have branches in the main S and W coast tourist centres. Opening hours for banks are 0800-1500 Mon to Thur, and 0800-1200 and 1500-1700 on Fri. Caribbean Commercial Bank in Hastings and Sunset Crest is also open on Sat from 0900 to 1200. The Barbados National Bank has a branch and a bureau de change at the airport; the latter is open from 0800-2200, but inaccessible unless you are actually arriving or departing. Barclays Bank and Royal Bank of Canada in Bridgetown both have cash machines which you can use with a credit card after hours.

● **Currency**
The currency unit is the Barbados dollar, which is pegged at B$2.00 for US$1.00. Banks will of course charge a small commission on this rate. Many tourist establishments quote prices in US dollars, if you are not careful a hotel room may end up costing twice as much as you bargained for. Rates offered by the banks for currencies

other than the US dollar, sterling, and Deutschmark are not good. Credit cards are accepted in the large resorts, but their use is not widespread.

● National Holidays

New Year's Day, 21 January (Errol Barrow Day), Good Friday, Easter Monday, 1 May, Whit Monday, Kadooment Day (first Monday in August), United Nations Day (first Monday in October), Independence Day (30 November), Christmas Day; Boxing Day.

● Time Zone

Atlantic Standard Time, 4 hrs behind GMT, 1 ahead of EST.

● Electric Current

120 volts (American standard) and 50 cycles per second (British standard). Some houses and hotels also have 240-volt sockets for use with British equipment.

● Telephone Service

Calls from a pay phone cost 25 cents for 3 mins. Otherwise local calls are free. Many business places will allow you to use their telephone for local calls. International calls can be made from most hotels or (more cheaply) from Barbados External Telecommunications (Wildey). Telexes and Faxes can be sent from and received at BET's office by members of the public. BET has a public office on the Wharf in Bridgetown for international calls, facsimile and telex. Phone cards are available for B$10, 20, 40, 60 from phone company offices, Cave Shepherd or Super Centre supermarkets; a cheaper way of making overseas calls than using hotel services, and can be used on most English-speaking islands except Trinidad, Jamaica, Guyana, Bahamas.

● Religion

Barbadians are a religious people and although the main church is Anglican, there are over 140 different faiths and sects, including Baptists, Christian Scientists, Jews, Methodists, Moravians and Roman Catholics. Times of services can be found in the *Visitor*.

● Newspapers

The Advocate, which also publishes *The Sunday Advocate* and *Sunseeker* tourist magazine; *The Nation* (publisher also of *Sun on Saturday*, *Sunday Sun* and *The Visitor* tourist weekly); *Caribbean Contact*, irregularly published by the Caribbean Conference of Churches. *Caribbean Week*, a newspaper covering the whole of the Caribbean, is published in Barbados, rec.

● Radio Stations

CBC Radio, medium wave 900 kHz; Voice of Barbados, medium wave 790 kHz; BBS, FM 90.7 MHz; Yess-Ten 4, FM 104.1 MHz; Radio Liberty, FM 98.1 MHz.

● Diplomatic Representation

British High Commission, Lower Collymore Rock, St Michael, PO Box 676, T 436 6694, F 436 5398. Canadian High Commission, Bishop Court, Hill Pine Road, T 429 3550. FDR Hon Consul, T 427 1876. US Embassy, Broad Street, T 436 4950; Brazilian Embassy, Fairchild Street, T 427 1735; Venezuelan Embassy, Worthing, T 435 7619.

● Tourist Information

The Barbados Tourism Authority has its main office in Harbour Road, Bridgetown (PO Box 242, T 427 2623/4, F 426 4080). There are also offices at the deepwater harbour (T 426 1718) and the airport (T 428 0937). The airport office has been criticized for directing travellers only to expensive hotels, claiming that the cheaper places have closed down. The BTA publishes a useful annual Sports and Cultural Calendar, which gives information on what to see throughout the year and the addresses of sporting organizations. Two good sources of information are *Visitor* and the *Sunseeker*, published weekly and distributed free by Barbados's 2 daily newspapers. *Ins and Outs of Barbados*, also free, is published annually, a glossy magazine with lots of advertising and distributed by hotels. *Exploring Historical Bar-*

---

bados, by Maurice Bateman Hutt, is quite good but perhaps slightly out of date as it was published in 1981.

Overseas the BTA has offices in:

UK: 263 Tottenham Court Road, London W1P 9AA, T 071-636 9448/9, F 637 1496. **USA**: 800 Second Avenue, New York, NY 10017, T 212-986 6516 or toll-free 800-221 9831, F 212-573 9850; 3440 Wilshire Boulevard, Suite 1215, Los Angeles, CA 90010, T 213-380 2198, toll free 800-221 9831, F 213-384 2763).

Canada: 5160 Yonge Street, Suite 1800, North York, Ontario M2N GL9, T 416-512 6569-71 or toll free 800-268 9122, F 416-512 6581; 615 René Lévéque Boulevard, Suite 460, Montreal H3B 1P5, T 514- 861 0085, F 514-861 7917). **Germany**: Rathenau Platz 1A, 6000 Frankfurt 1, T 280 982/3, F 49-69-294-782. **Sweden**: Target Marketing of Scandinavia, Kammakargatan 41, 11124 Stockholm, T (8) 11 3613, F (8) 20 6317. **France** c/o Caraibes 102, 102 Ave des Champs- Élysées, 75008 Paris, T 45 62 62 62, F 331-4074-0701.

The Barbados Embassy in Caracas (Quinta Chapaleta, 9a Transversal, Entre 2 y 3 Avenidas, Altamira, T 582-39 1471, F 32 3393) can also provide tourist information.

Ordnance Survey Tourist Maps include Barbados in the series, 1:50,000 scale with inset of Bridgetown 1:10,000.

TRINIDAD AND TOBAGO

TRINIDAD, the most S of the Caribbean islands, lying only seven miles off the Venezuelan coast, is one of the most colourful of the West Indian islands. It is an island of 1,864 square miles, traversed by two ranges of hills, the N and S ranges, running roughly E and W, and a third, the central range, running diagonally across the island. Apart from small areas in the northern, forested range which plunges into the sea on the N coast, of which the main peaks are Cerro del Aripo (3,083 feet) and El Tucuche (3,072 feet), all the land is below 1,000 feet. The flatlands in central Trinidad are used for growing sugar cane. There are large areas of swamp on the E and W coasts. About half the population lives in the urban E-W corridor, stretching from Chaguaramas in the W through Port of Spain to Arima in the E. Trinidad is separated from the mainland of South America by the Boca del Dragón strait in the NW (Dragon's Mouth) and Boca del Serpiente in the SW (Serpent's Mouth, both named by Columbus).

Tobago (116 square miles) is only 21 miles by sea to the NE. It is 26 miles long and only nine miles wide, shaped like a cigar with a central 18-mile ridge of hills in the N (the Main Ridge, highest point 1,890 feet) running parallel with the coast. These NE hills are of volcanic origin; the SW is flat or undulating and coralline. The coast itself is broken by any number of inlets and sheltered beaches. The population is concentrated in the W part of the island around Scarborough. There are small farms, but the main ridge is forested and quite wild. The climate is generally cooler and drier, particularly in the SW, than most parts of Trinidad.

Trinidad has one of the world's most cosmopolitan populations. The emancipation of the slaves in 1834 and the adoption of free trade by Britain in 1846 resulted in far-reaching social and economic changes. To meet labour shortages over 150,000 immigrants were encouraged to settle from India, China and Madeira. Of today's population of approximately 1,261,000, about 43% are black and 36% East Indian. The rest are mixed race, white, Syrian or Chinese. French and Spanish influences dominated for a long time (Catholicism is still strong) but gradually the English language and institutions prevailed and today the great variety of peoples has become a fairly harmonious entity, despite some tension between blacks and those of East Indian descent. Spanish is still spoken in small pockets in the N mountains and French patois here and there. Catholics are still the largest religious group (32%) but the Anglican Church and Methodists (28%) are also influential. There are many evangelical groups. Spiritual Baptists blend African and Christian beliefs; the women wear white robes and head ties on religious occasions. They can be seen performing the sea ceremony on the coast to the W

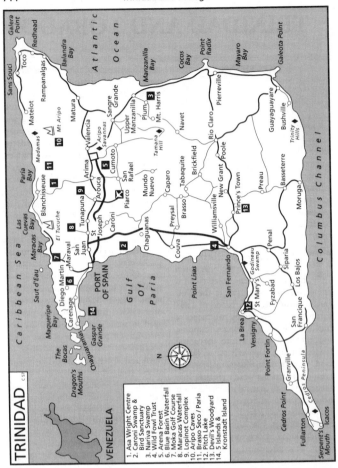

TRINIDAD

1. Asa Wright Centre
2. Caroni Swamp & Bird Sanctuary
3. Nariva Swamp
4. Wild Fowl Trust
5. Arena Forest
6. Blue Basin Waterfall
7. Moka Golf Course
8. Maracas Waterfall
9. Lopinot Complex
10. Aripo Caves
11. Brasso Seco / Paria
12. Pitch Lake
13. Devil's Woodyard
14. 5 Islands & Kronstadt Island

of Port of Spain late on Sunday nights. Most East Indians are Hindu, some are Muslim, others have converted to Christianity, particularly Presbyterianism (Canadian Presbyterian missionaries were the first to try converting the Indian population). Unlike most other Caribbean islands tourism plays a small role in Trinidad's economy. In the 1960's and 1970's the official policy was to discourage tourism, and although this has now

changed, visitors are still a rarity in some parts of the island, big hotels are set up for business visitors and some tourist services may be lacking. Nevertheless, Trinidadians are genuinely welcoming to strangers.

Tobago's population, mainly black, numbers about 51,000. The crime rate is much lower than on Trinidad and the people are noticeably helpful and friendly. Tourism is a major source of income here and considerable investment has gone into hotels and infrastructure in the last few years.

History

Trinidad was discovered by Columbus and claimed for Spain on his third voyage in 1498. Whether he named the island after the day of the Holy Trinity, or after a group of three hills that he spied from the sea is in dispute. At that time there were at least seven tribes of Indians living on the island: the Arawaks, Chaimas, Tamanaques, Salives, Chaguanes, Quaquas and Caribs, the last being divided into four sub-groupings, the Nepoios, Yaios, Carinepagotos and Cumanagotos. The peaceful Arawaks were the majority and lived in the S part of the island, having originally come from the upper regions of the Orinoco river. The N part was populated by Indians of the Carib strain from the Amazon area who were aggressive and warlike. It was their hostility which prevented successful colonization until the end of the 17th century when Catalan Capuchin missionaries arrived. However, European diseases and the rigours of slavery took their toll of the Indian population; by 1824 there were only 893 Indians left on Trinidad and today there are none.

The first Spanish governor was Don Antonio Sedeño who arrived in 1530, but failed to establish a permanent settlement because of Indian attacks. In 1592 the governor, Don Antonio de Berrio y Oruna, founded the town of San José de Oruna (now St Joseph), but it was destroyed by Sir Walter Raleigh in 1595 and not rebuilt until 1606. In 1783 a deliberate policy to encourage immigration of Roman Catholics was introduced, known as the Royal Cedula of Population, and it was from this date that organized settlement began with an influx of mostly French-speaking immigrants, particularly after the French Revolution. Many also came from St Lucia and Dominica when these islands were ceded to Britain in 1784, others came with their slaves from the French Caribbean when slavery was abolished and from Saint Domingue after the war of independence there (eg the Compte de Lopinot, whose house in Lopinot has been restored, see page 729).

British rule in Trinidad began in 1797 when an expedition led by Sir Ralph Abercromby captured the island. It was later ceded to Britain by Spain in 1802 under the Treaty of Amiens. (VS Naipaul's *The Loss of El Dorado* is a fascinating, if pessimistic, account of the early Spanish settlement, Sir Walter Raleigh's raid, and the early years of British rule). At this time large numbers of African slaves were imported to work in the sugar fields introduced by the French until the slave trade was abolished in 1807. After the abolition of slavery in 1834, labour became scarce and the colonists looked for alternative sources of workers. Several thousands of immigrants from neighbouring islands came in 1834-48, many Americans from Baltimore and Pennsylvania came in 1841, Madeirans came seeking employment and religious freedom and were joined by European immigrants, namely the British, Scots, Irish, French, Germans and Swiss. There was also immigration of free West Africans in the 1840s, but by 1848 this had ceased as conditions improved in their own countries. In 1844 the British Government gave approval for the import of East Indian labour and the first indentured labourers arrived in 1845. By 1917, when Indian immigration ceased, 141,615 Indians had arrived for an indentured period of five years, and although many returned to India afterwards, the majority settled. The first Chinese arrived in 1849 during a lull in Indian immigration. Initially these were men only and this naturally encouraged intermarriage, but later arrivals included women. In 1866 the Chinese Government insisted on a return passage being paid, and this put an end to Chinese immigration. Persistent labour shortages led to higher wages in Trinidad than in many other islands and from emancipation until the 1960s there was also migration from Barbados, Grenada and St Vincent.

Tobago is thought to have been discovered by Columbus in 1498, when it was occupied by Caribs. He is said to have called the island "Bella Forma"; the present name is a corruption of tobacco, which the Caribs used to grow there. In 1641 James, Duke of Courland (in the Baltic), obtained a grant of the island from Charles I and in 1642 a number of Courlanders settled on the N side. In 1658 the Courlanders were overpowered by the Dutch, who remained in possession of the island until 1662. In this year Cornelius Lampsius procured Letters Patent from Louis XIV creating him the Baron of Tobago under the Crown of France. After being occupied for short periods by the Dutch and the French, Tobago was ceded by France to Britain in 1763 under the Treaty of Paris. But it was not until 1802, after further invasions by the French and subsequent recapture by the British, that it was finally ceded to Britain, becoming a Crown Colony in 1877 and in 1888 being amalgamated politically with Trinidad. By some reckonings Tobago changed hands as many as 29 times because of its strategic importance and for this reason there are a large number of forts.

The first political organizations in Trinidad and Tobago developed in the 1930s, when economic depression spurred the formation of labour movements. Full adult suffrage was introduced in 1946 and political parties began to develop. In 1956, the People's National Movement (PNM) was founded by the hugely influential Dr Eric Williams, who dominated local politics until his death in 1981. The party won control of the new Legislative Council, under the new constitutional arrangements which pro-

vided for self-government, and Dr Williams became the first Chief Minister. In 1958, Trinidad and Tobago became a member of the new Federation of the West Indies, but after the withdrawal of Jamaica in 1961 the colony was unwilling to support the poorer members of the Federation and Dr Williams sought the same rights for Trinidad and Tobago. The country became an independent member of the Commonwealth on 31 August, 1962 and became a republic within the Commonwealth on 1 August, 1976. Dr Williams remained Prime Minister, his party drawing on the support of the majority African elements of the population, while the opposition parties were supported mainly by the Indian minority.

In 1986, the National Alliance for Reconstruction (NAR) ended 30 years' rule by the PNM which had been hit by corruption scandals, winning 33 of the 36 parliamentary seats in the general election. Six NAR members defected in 1989 to form the United National Congress (UNC), led by former Deputy Prime Minister, Basdeo Panday. The popularity of the Prime Minister, A N R Robinson, was extremely low and he was seen as heading an uncaring administration which alienated voters by its economic policies of cutting the public sector and other costs.

General elections were held on 16 December 1991, bringing another about turn in political loyalties. Patrick Manning, of the PNM, led his party to victory, winning 21 seats, while the UNC won 13 and the NAR was left in the cold with only two Tobago seats. Elections for Tobago's House of Assembly, in December 1992, gave the NAR 11 seats and the PNM one seat, the same as in the previous assembly. By mid-term the Government was suffering from unpopularity and lack of confidence. Its economic policies were blamed for higher unemployment, lack of growth and rising crime. However, the opposition was not strengthened by the formation of three new parties, which were likely to split any anti-Government vote. The National Development Party (NDP) was launched in 1993 by Carson Charles, former leader of the NAR, after he failed in a second bid for the party's leadership. The Republic Party (RP) was formed by Nello Mitchell, a former general secretary of the PNM, after he was expelled from the PNM for gross disrespect of the party. Third, Yasih Abu Bakr, leader of the Jamaat-al-Muslimeen, formed the National Vision Party in 1994. Two PNM MPs and one UNC MP died, causing by-elections to be held in 1994. One seat was won by the PNM, a second by the UNC and the third by-election was pending as we went to press.

In 1992 Scotland Yard detectives began investigations into allegations of corruption in the police force and its links with the drugs trade. A number of senior officers were implicated. Confidence in the police was low and deteriorated as the crime rate rose. The Government announced reforms in recruitment, inspection of the police force and police management.

Government

Trinidad and Tobago became a republic within the Commonwealth on 1 August 1976 under a new constitution which provides for a President and a bicameral Parliament comprising a 31-seat Senate and a 36-seat House of Representatives. Noor Mohammed Hassanali took office as President in March 1987. Tobago has its own 12-seat House of Assembly, which runs many local services. There are plans to improve Tobago's constitutional status, possibly by establishing an executive council and appointing an independent senator for Tobago.

The Economy

The soil in Trinidad is remarkably rich and the first settlers had no difficulty in raising a variety of crops, with tobacco, sugar and cocoa being the major exports. Today, however, agriculture contributes 2.6% of gross domestic product and employs only 10.8% of the labour force. Agricultural exports have been broadened to include citrus fruits, coconut oils and flowers, and diversification of the traditionally sugar-based agriculture of the Caroni area with rice, pawpaw, other fruit and vegetables has led to improvements in supplies for the domestic market. Sugar production and exports grew in 1992 and 1993, exceeding targets and enabling Trinidad to meet its export quotas to the EU and USA.

JAMAAT-AL-MUSLIMEEN

On 27 July 1990 Trinidad was shaken by an attempted overthrow of the Government by a Muslim fundamentalist group, the Jamaat-al-Muslimeen, led by the Imam Yasin Abu Bakr. The rebels held the Prime Minister, A N R Robinson, eight of his Cabinet and other hostages, until their unconditional surrender on 1 August. A total of 23 people were killed in the disturbances and about 500 were injured (including the Prime Minister) during the bombing of the police headquarters, the takeover of the parliament building and TV station and subsequent rioting. Despite a promise of an amnesty 114 Jamaat members were arrested and charged with a number of offences, including murder and treason. After taking their case to the courts their appeal was heard in 1992 and the amnesty was reinstated, leading to the release of prisoners. The Government's appeal against the decision was turned down by the High Court in 1993. It then turned to the Privy Council, which heard its case in mid-1994 but a decision had not yet been announced at the time of going to press.

Trinidad is rich in mineral deposits including asphalt from the pitch lake at La Brea on the SW coast, gypsum, limestone, sand, gravel, argillite and fluorspar, but apart from the asphalt, which is used for road surfacing, they are not well developed. Petroleum and petroleum products dominate the economy, providing about a quarter of gdp, one third of government current revenue and two thirds of foreign exchange earnings. Three quarters of oil production comes from marine fields. Production in 1994 was expected to be around 110,000 barrels a day with some new wells being drilled. There are two oil refineries, at Pointe-a-Pierre and Point Fortin. The island has substantial proven reserves of natural gas of 9 trillion cubic feet, producing around 612mn cubic feet a day, and these are used to power several heavy industries such as an iron and steel mill, urea, methanol and ammonia plants. In addition to the Point Lisas industrial estate, a new industrial site is planned for the Brighton/La Brea area with the focus mainly on gas and methanol. New methanol plants will raise annual capacity to 1.01mn tonnes by end-1996.

Dependence on oil has led to wide fluctuations in the rate of economic growth, with the 1970s a period of rapid expansion and rising real incomes as oil prices soared and the 1980s a decade of declining output and falling wages as the oil market retrenched. The recession in the oil industry exposed structural imbalances in the rest of the economy and the inability of agriculture, manufacturing or services to counter its effects.

Assistance was sought from the IMF in the context of debt rescheduling agreements with the Paris Club of creditor governments and with commercial banks. The Government also turned to the World Bank, the Inter American Development Bank and Japan for the new lending to support structural adjustment of the economy. Debt service was projected to absorb 28% of export revenue

TRINIDAD AND TOBAGO: FACT FILE

Geographic

Land area	5,128 sq km
forested	43.1%
pastures	2.1%
cultivated	23.4%

Demographic

Population (1992)	1,261,000
annual growth rate (1987-92)	1.2%
urban	69.1%
rural	30.9%
density	245.9 per sq km
Religious affiliation Roman Catholic	32.2%
Protestant	27.6%
Hindu	24.3%
Moslem	5.9%
Birth rate per 1,000 (1989)	20.7
	(world av 27.1)
Death rate per 1,000 (1989)	6.8
	(world av 9.8)

Education and Health

Life expectancy at birth, male	69.7 years
female	74.7 years
Infant mortality rate per 1,000 live births (1989)	10.2
Physicians (1990)	1 per 1,543 persons
Hospital beds	1 per 318 persons
Calorie intake as % of FAO requirement	120%
Population age 25 and over with no formal schooling	7.1%
Literacy (over 15)	96.1%

Economic

GNP (1990 market prices)	US$4,458mn
GNP per capita	US$3,470
Public external debt (1990)	US$2,508mn
Tourism receipts (1990)	US$95mn
Inflation (annual av 1985-90)	9.7%
Radio	1 per 1.8 persons
Television	1 per 5.0 persons
Telephone	1 per 5.7 persons

Employment

Population economically active (1990)	467,700
Unemployment rate (1991)	18.8%
% of labour force in	
agriculture	10.8
mining and petroleum	4.5
manufacturing	10.1
construction	13.9
Military forces	2,650

Source *Encyclopaedia Britannica*

in 1993, falling to 20% in 1996. Proceeds from the sale of state enterprises were to be used to reduce the outstanding external debt of US$2.4bn. The second standby agreement expired on 31 March 1991 and the Government did not seek a third IMF programme.

From 1990 the economy did begin to grow slowly after seven consecutive annual declines in gdp but it contracted again in 1992 and 1993. A liberalization of some foreign exchange controls in 1992 led to an easing of liquidity constraints and a return of some capital held overseas. In April 1993 the TT dollar was floated, with an initial depreciation of 26% to TT$5.75 = US$1, and a consequent rise in the rate of inflation, but then stabilized and by mid-1994 had not crossed the TT$6=US$1 threshhold. Oil prices in 1994 were low, about 20% lower in the first six months than had been budgeted, leading to a loss of about 5% of projected government revenue. Government bond issues consequently became less attractive and there was difficulty in raising finance to meet debt servicing payments. To counter lower income, the Government increased taxation, reduced employment in state companies and speeded up the divestment of many state corporations as a source of foreign exchange, as well as raising output of oil and gas.

The Government's difficulties in meeting its debt servicing commitments and a large public sector wage bill led to arrears in salary payments. In 1993 and 1994 strikes and demonstrations by public sector workers intensified as the Government struggled to cope with deteriorating labour relations. Unemployment is at least 19% of the labour force and is most acute in the 15-19 age group, where about 43% are out of work. The crime rate has increased noticeably, particularly serious crimes and murders, many of which are related to drugs and gang killings.

A concerted attempt is being made to diversify the economy and lessen the dependence on petroleum. Tourism is becoming an important source of foreign exchange and the Government is actively promoting both islands abroad. Expenditure by Trinidadians abroad still exceeds earnings from incoming tourism but only by a narrow margin, thanks to a recession-induced slowdown in holidays abroad and increased visitor revenues. Stayover arrivals rose by nearly 6% in 1993 to 248,033, of which North American visitors made up 52% and Europeans 19%. Tobago now has over 1,000 hotel rooms available, following an expansion in construction and more are planned, notably a 250-room Hilton hotel. A new cruise ship complex was opened in August 1989 at Port of Spain. A similar terminal has been constructed in Tobago as part of the Scarborough harbour re-development project. Cruise ship passenger arrivals increased by nearly 2% in 1992 to 26,948, but then by 21% in 1993 to 32,572 visitors.

Culture

The most exciting introduction to the vivid, cosmopolitan culture of this Republic is, of course, Carnival, or "De Mas", as locals refer to the annual "celebration of the senses". Background reading is a help for a visit at any time of the year. It is sensible to purchase books before departure, as prices are much higher in Trinidadian shops, even for locally produced reading matter. Some authors to investigate are the late C L R James, Samuel Selvon, Shiva Naipaul, V S Naipaul, the historian and past prime minister Dr Eric Williams, Earl Lovelace and newcomer Valerie Belgrave (whose *Ti Marie* has been described as the Caribbean *Gone with the Wind*). Although the tradition of performance poetry is not as strong here as in, say, Jamaica (calypso fulfils some of its role), the monologues of Paul Keens-Douglas (not so active nowadays), some of which are on album or cassette, are richly entertaining and a great introduction to the local dialect or patois.

Alongside a strong oral/literary tradition goes a highly developed visual culture, reflecting the islands' racial melange. The most obvious examples are the inventive designs for the carnival bands, which often draw on craft skills like wire bending, copper beating, and the expressive use of fibreglass moulds. Fine painters and sculptors abound, too, although the only good galleries are small and commercial and located primarily in Port of Spain. Michel Jean Cazabon, born 1813, was the first great local artist (an illustrated biography by Aquarela Gallery owner Geoffrey MacLean is widely available). Contemporary work to look out for, often on the walls of the more enlightened hotels, restaurants and banks, includes paintings by Emheyo Bahabba, Pat Bishop, Isaiah Boodhoo, Francisco Cabral, LeRoy Clarke, Kenwyn Crichlow, Boscoe Holder and the fabled, controversial Mas' designer Peter Minshall, who designed the opening ceremony for the Barcelona Olympic Games (thousands twirled silk squares in one sequence).

Jewellery and fashion designers also figure strongly in the life of these islands, with exceptionally high standards of work demonstrated by jewellers like Barbara Jardine, Gillian Bishop and Rachel Ross. The doyenne of the fashion business is the gifted Meiling, but attractive original clothing by a growing number of native fashionmakers can be found in boutiques and shopping centres.

Carnival This extraordinary fete (see **Festivals** for dates and details) is considered by many to be safer, more welcoming to visitors and artistically more stimulating than its nearest rival in Rio de Janeiro. Commercialization is undermining many of the greatest Mas' traditions, and only some of the historical characters like the Midnight Robber and the Moko Jumbies can be glimpsed on J'Ouverte (pro-

nounced joo-vay) morning and in small, independent bands of players. But it's a great party, enlivened by hundreds of thousands of costumed masqueraders and the homegrown music, calypso and steelband (usually referred to as "pan").

Calypsonians (or kaisonians, as the more historically-minded call them) are the commentators, champions and sometime conscience of the people. This unique musical form, a mixture of African, French and, eventually, British, Spanish and even East Indian influences dates back to Trinidad's first "shantwell", Gros Jean, late in the 18th century. Since then it has evolved into a popular, potent force, with both men and women (also children, of late) battling for the Calypso Monarch's crown, in a fierce competition that climaxes on Dimanche Gras, the Sunday immediately before the official beginning of Carnival. Calypsonians band together to perform in "tents" (performing halls) in the weeks leading up to the competition and are judged in semifinals, which hones down the list to six final contenders. The season's calypso songs blast from radio stations and sound systems all over the islands and visitors should ask locals to interpret the sometimes witty and often scurrilous lyrics, for they are a fascinating introduction to the state of the nation.Currently, party soca tunes dominate although some of the commentary calypsonians, like Sugar Aloes, are still heard on the radio. There is also a new breed of "Rapso" artistes, fusing calypso and rap music.

Pan music has a shorter history, developing this century from the tamboobamboo bands which made creative use of tins, dustbins and pans plus lengths of bamboo for percussion instruments. By the end of World War II (during which Carnival was banned) some ingenious souls discovered that huge oil drums could be converted into expressive instruments, their top surfaces tuned to all ranges and depths (eg the ping pong, or soprano pan embraces 28 to 32 notes, including both the diatonic and chromatic scales). Aside from the varied pans, steelbands also include a rhythm section dominated by the steel, or iron men. For Carnival, the steelbands compete in the grand Panorama, playing calypsoes which are also voted on for the Road March of the Year. Biennally, the World Steelband Festival highlights the versatility of this music, for each of the major bands must play a work by a classical composer as well as a calypso of choice. On alternate years the National Schools Steelband Festival is held, similarly in late October/early November.

Other musical forms in this music-mad nation include **parang** (pre-Christmas). Part of the islands' Spanish heritage, parang is sung in Castillian and accompanied by guitar, cuatro, mandoline and tambourine. For the Hindi and Muslim festivals, there are East Indian drumming and vocal styles like chowtal, which is particularly associated with Phagwa in early March.

The national **Best Village** competition, which runs from September to November, gives the smallest community a chance to display its finest drama, dance, music and crafts (price of tickets in the Queen's Park Savannah Grand Stand, TT$3 per night). Throughout the year, there are regular performances of plays and musicals, often by Caribbean dramatists, and concerts by fine choirs like the Marionettes Chorale, sometimes accompanied by steelbands. There is a lot of comedy but some serious plays too, see press for details. Theatres include the Little Carib Theatre (T 622-4644), Space Theatre (T 623-0732), the Central Bank Auditorium (T 623-0845) and Queen's Hall (624-1284).

In short, Trinidad and Tobago boast some of the most impressive artists to be found anywhere in the region, and visitors can enjoy that art throughout the year, although many of the now internationally recognized performers tour abroad during the summer months.

Fauna and Flora

The Forestry Division of the Ministry of Agriculture, Land and Marine Resources (Long Circular Road, St James, Port of Spain, T 622-7476, contact them for information on guided tours and hikes) has designated many parts of Trinidad and Tobago as national parks, wildlife reserves and protected areas. On Trinidad, the national parks are the Caroni and Nariva Swamps, Chaguaramas, and Madamas, Maracas and Matura in the N range of hills. The Nariva Swamp, an area of 3,840 acres, contains hardwood forest, home to red howler monkeys and the weeping capuchin as well as 55 other species of mammal. Birds include the savannah hawk and the red-breasted blackbird. Access is by boat only. The Northern Range Sanctuary, Maracas, or El Tucuche Reserve, is a forest on the second highest peak, at 3,072 feet, covering 2,313 acres. It contains some interesting flora, such as giant bromeliad and orchids, as well as fauna, including the golden tree frog and the orange-billed nightingale-thrush. There are several hiking trails, the most popular of which is from Ortinola estate; guides can be hired. Walking alone is not recommended in the N hills, join a group to avoid robbery. There are seven natural landmarks, three of which are described below (Blue Basin, the Pitch Lake and the Devil's Woodyard) and others include Tamana Hill in the central range, and Galera Point in the NE. Twelve areas are scientific reserves (eg Trinity Hills, Galeota Point and the Aripo Savannas); twelve are nature conservation reserves: the Asa Wright Centre is described below, but also Cedros Peninsula and Godineau Swamp in the SW, Manzanilla in the E and Valencia. The Valencia Wildlife Sanctuary covers 6,881 acres and contains at least 50 species of birds including antbirds and tanagers. Several mammals live here: deer, wild pig, agouti, tatoo. Near Valencia is the Arena Forest, one of ten recreation parks, while five areas have been designated scenic landscapes (Blanchisseuse, Maracas and Toco-Matelot on the N coast, Cocos Bay on the Atlantic, and Mount Harris on the Southern Road, S of Sangre Grande). Although about 43% of the island remains forested, there is much concern about the loss of wildlife habitats.

On Tobago, apart from two national parks (Buccoo Reef and the virgin and secondary forests of E Tobago), there are the Goldsborough natural landmark, the Kilgwyn scientific reserve, the Grafton nature conservation area, the Parlatuvier-Roxborough scenic landscape, and three recreation parks (including Mount Irvine). Many of the small islands off the coasts of the two larger ones are reserves for wildlife and are important breeding grounds for red-billed tropic birds, frigate birds, man-o-war and other sea birds (for instance Saut d'Eau, Kronstadt Island and Soldado Rock off Trinidad, and Little Tobago, see below, St Giles and Marble Islands off Tobago).

Many flowering trees can be seen: pink and yellow poui, frangipani, cassia, pride of India, immortelle, flamboyant, jacaranda. Among the many types of flower are hibiscus, poinsettia, chaconia (wild poinsettia—the national flower), ixora, bougainvillea, orchid, ginger lily and heliconia. The Horticultural Society of Trinidad and Tobago (PO Box 252) has its office on Lady Chancellor Road, Port of Spain, T 622-6423.

The islands boast 60 types of bat, and other mammals include the Trinidad capuchin and red howler monkeys, brown forest brocket (deer), collared peccary (quenk), manicou (opossum), agouti, rare ocelot and armadillo. Caymans live in the swamps.

Trinidad and Tobago together have more species of birds than any other Caribbean island, although the variety is South American, not West Indian. No species is endemic, but Tobago has 13 species of breeding birds not found on Trinidad. Most estimates say that there are 400 species of bird, including 41 hummingbirds (the aboriginal name for the island of Trinidad was Ieri, the land of the hummingbird). There are also 622 recorded species of butterfly. The most accessible bird-watching sites are the Caroni Bird Sanctuary, the Asa Wright Centre, the Caurita Plantation and the Wild Fowl Trust, all described elsewhere in this chapter.

Recommended is *A Guide to the Birds of Trinidad and Tobago*, by Richard Ffrench (Macmillan Caribbean). Those interested can also contact the Trinidad Field Naturalists Club, 1 Errol Park Road, St Anns, Port of Spain (T 624-3321 evenings or weekends, walks on Sundays), secretary Miss Luisa Zuniaga. *The Trinidad and Tobago Field Naturalists' Club Trail Guide*, by Paul Comeau, Louis Guy, Ewoud Heesterman and Clayton Hull, was published in 1992, 288 pages on 48 trails, difficult to obtain. French and Bacon's *Nature Trails of Trinidad*, first published in 1982 has been revised by Victor Quesnel and reissued by Mohammed Publishers, TT$49.95. Each October Trinidad and Tobago hold Natural History Festivals to foster understanding of the islands' flora and fauna.

Beaches and Watersports

The nearest beach to Port of Spain is Carenage, but it is badly polluted. To the NW there are one or two pleasant swimming places in Chaguaramas Bay, with windsurfing and yachting, though you have to pay to use the beach here. Maqueripe Bay has a sheltered beach. Maracas Bay on the N coast over the hills, 10 miles/16 km from the capital, has a sheltered sandy beach fringed with coconut palms; despite small waves there can be a dangerous undertow here and at other beaches and drownings have occurred, there is a lifeguard watching the beach, but do not swim far out and watch the markers (try "bake and shark", shark meat in a heavy fried dough, a Maracas speciality, or the "shark and bread," a roll with shark meat in it, very tasty, especially after a drinking session at 0300, sold all along the beach for TT$5). Maracas Bay Village is scheduled for development. At present a few people rent out basic rooms in the village, ask at the small shop. There are buses to Maracas Bay running every 4 hours (but they can be irregular) from the bus terminal. Difficulties in catching the bus have led travellers to recommend taxis: from Port of Spain costs US$25 or there is a pick-up "route taxi" service from the centre of town, TT$10. Another method is maxitaxi to Maraval then 4-wheel drive jeep to Maracas, irregular, get back in good time. The jeep may go right into Port of Spain but do not rely on it. Next to Maracas Bay is Tyrico Bay (surfing, lifeguard, another beach with a dangerous undertow and sandflies). Las Cuevas, also on the N coast (like Maracas Bay, surfing is good here but beware of the sandflies in the wet season), and Blanchisseuse have lovely beaches but are more difficult to reach (see below, under Arima). Blanchisseuse beach has a sweet water lagoon and the place is kept clean by a friendly man who appreciates a few pennies. At the NE end, near Toco, are a number of bays, including Balandra for good bathing. For Toco, get an express bus or highway maxi to Arima, then route taxi to Sangre Grande, then taxi to Toco. Further down, the Atlantic coast from Matura to Mayaro is divided into three huge sweeping bays, with palm trees growing as high as 200 feet in some places. Of these bays Mayaro and Manzanilla both have beautiful sandy beaches; there are several beach houses to rent at Mayaro, heavily booked in peak holiday periods, some are poor, check beforehand. In the SW, near La Brea and the Pitch Lake is the resort of Vessigny. The SW, or Cedros, peninsula is a 3-hour car trip from Port of Spain along often atrocious roads, but is worth it for the unspoilt beaches and miles of coconut palm plantations. Generally, the beaches are difficult to get to except by taxi or hired car.

For boat trips to the islands N and W of Port of Spain T 622-8974, Elton Pouchet, US$75 for 1-3 people.

Yachting has become big business in Trinidad and there are now two marinas: Trinidad Yacht Club at Bayshore and Yachting Association Marina at Chaguaramas.

BRIAN LARA - CENTURION AND MILLIONAIRE

Brian Lara, the West Indies Test cricketer, is currently the most famous Trinidadian. In 1994 he beat Sir Garfield Sobers' record of 365 runs in an innings when he scored 375 in the Test Match against England in Antigua. Records have continued to tumble during the English County season. Playing for Warwickshire, he made 501 (the highest total in an innings during a county match and a world record) and has also achieved the highest consecutive number of first class hundreds. He is also famous for having caused the unions to cancel a general strike on the day he arrived home; it was renamed a Day of Achievement and declared a public holiday in his honour by the Government.

At the end of July, Mercury Asset Management (a leading investment company) announced that it had signed Lara in a sponsorship deal thought to be in the region of £500,000. UK papers were splashed with pictures of Lara padded up in a pinstripe suit and bowler hat. However, this, together with other sponsorship deals also worth £500,000, make Lara one of the highest paid cricketers ever.

Every July/August, there is a power boat race from Trinidad to Store Bay, Tobago. Each year Tobago has a sailing week; many crewing possibilities. The annual International Game Fishing Classic is held in February/March.

Diving and Marine Life

The waters around Tobago are gradually becoming known as an unspoilt diving destination and several dive shops have started operations in the last few years. Coral reefs flourish almost all round the island. Every known species of hard coral and lots of soft corals can be found, and there is a huge brain coral, believed to be one of the world's largest, off Little Tobago. The Guyana current flows round the S and E shores of Tobago and supports a large variety of marine life. Dive sites are numerous and varied, there are walls, caves, canyons, coral gardens and lots of fish. Snorkelling is also excellent almost everywhere, with good visibility. Some of the most popular sites are Arnos Vale, Pirates Bay, Store Bay, Man O'War Bay and Batteaux Bay.

Tobago Dive Experience (Sean Robinson/Derek Chung) at the *Blue Waters Inn*, Batteaux Bay, Speyside, T 660-4341, F 660-5195 (or the *Grafton*, T 639-0191, F 639-0030), offers exciting drift diving, not recommended for novices although they will teach you. The only thing better than racing past dancing sea fans at 3 knots is to do it again at 5 knots. You are swept along the coral reef while, high above, manta rays flap lazily to remain stationary in the current as they sieve out the plankton. (*Blue Waters Inn* tends to be full throughout the year so book early.) *Man Friday Diving* (Finn Rinds), Charlotteville, T/F 660-4676, covers the area from Charlotteville to Speyside. A fully-equipped, new dive shop has a classroom for PADI training, lockers for rent and equipment for hire. Diving is from two 28-foot, custom-built piroques one operating from Speyside (transport to boat included) and one from Charlotteville, taking one to six in a group (must be 2 or more for night dives), single dive US\$35, plus VAT, five dives US\$150, hire of BCD, regulator, mask, snorkel and fins US\$11/day, night dives US\$50, lots of courses on offer, accommodation can be arranged. Other dive operators include Go Ran Quarsordt, Viking Dive, opposite *Crown Point Hotel*, Crown Point, T/F 639-9209/0414; Dive Tobago Ltd (Jimmy Young), Pigeon Point, PO Box 53 (Scarborough), T 639-0202, F 639-2727 and *Tobago Marine Sports* (Keith Darwent), Store Bay, T 639-0291, F 639-4416, also at *Blue Waters Inn* and *Crown Point Beach Hotel*. There are several more people involved in diving, fishing and other watersports, who are not listed here.

The only really safe place for diving off Trinidad is in the channels called the Bocas, between the islands off the NW peninsula (The Dragon's Mouth). However, the currents are cold, so protective gear is essential. Contact the Diving Association of Trinidad, or Twin-Island Dives, Maraval.

Other Sports

Cricket is very popular. Test matches are played at Queen's Park Oval, W of Queen's Park Savannah, Port of Spain; take a cushion, sunhat/umbrella, whistle (!) and drinks if sitting in the cheap seats. It is a private club but a friendly gate guard might let you in for a look around. For information, ring Queen's Park Cricket Club, T 622-2295/3787. Hockey and soccer are also played at the Oval (Football Association T 624-5183/7661). Also played are rugby, basketball, cycling and marathon running. There is horse-racing at Port of Spain (Queen's Park Savannah—see the horses exercising in the park), San Fernando and Arima. Horse-hire near Fort George. Swimming at the *Hilton Hotel*, US\$4 (US\$2 children), *Valley Vue Hotel* or *La Joya* at St Joseph, check first for availability, T 662-

1184; see below for swimming and golf at St Andrews (Moka) Golf Club (T 629-2314); there are 6 other golf clubs on Trinidad, including a 9-hole public course at Chaguaramas (T 634-4349); squash, Long Circular Mall, T 622-1245, 0600-2200 (0900-1700 Saturday), US$3 for 40 minutes, advance booking essential; tennis, Trinidad Country Club Maraval, T 622-3470/2111/2113, temporary membership, advance booking necessary, also at *Hilton Hotel*, Tranquility Square Lawn Tennis Club (T 625-4182) and public tennis courts at Princes Building Grounds (T 623-1121). The *Valley Vue Hotel*, Ariapita Road, St Ann's has 2 squash courts with seating for 100 spectators per court, T 624-0940, 627-8058/60, F 627-8046. Squash also at *La Joya*, Pelican Squash Club, St Ann's, T 633-2087, and others.

On Tobago, golf and lawn tennis at Mount Irvine Bay, T 639-8871: green fee US$20/day, tennis US$3 in day, US$6 at night. For hiking, bird-watching on- and off-shore, contact David Rooks, PO Box 58, Scarborough, T 639-9408.

Festivals

Carnival (see also above, **Culture**) takes place officially each year on the two days before Ash Wednesday which marks the beginning of the Christian season of Lent. In practice, the festivities start well in advance, with the Mas' camps abustle, the calypsonians performing most nights of the week and the impressive Panorama finals taking place with the competing steelbands at the Queen's Park Savannah stadium the week before Mas' proper. Band launching parties, where band leaders show off their costume designs, are held before Christmas. Calypso "tents", where calypsoes are played, start in January. Try Roxy Theatre, St James, SWWUT Hall on Wrighton Road, NUGFW Hall on Henry Street, Spektakula on Henry Street. Panyards start practising even earlier; visiting one is

usually no problem. Amoco Renegades are in Oxford Street, Port of Spain; Exodus is on Eastern Main Road, St Augustine; Witco Desperadoes is at Champs Fleurs. There are parties most of the time from then on. The biggest public fetes at Spectrum, previously Soca Village near the National Stadium, may have a crowd of 20,000 or more. Getting a ticket in advance or arriving early (eg 2130) saves a struggle at the door; most go on until 0400-0500.

Panorama steel band finals are at the Savannah on Carnival Saturday night. Parties on Sunday start early; then there is the Dimanche Gras show at the National Stadium, W of the city centre. The children's carnival takes place on Sunday afternoon. On Carnival Monday, the festivities start with "J'Ouverte" at 0200. ("Mud Mas", with bands dressed up in paint, wear old clothes, be ready to be painted and plastered with mud). This followed by "Ole Mas" which lasts until 0900. In the afternoon is "Lil Mas" when the bands start moving, followed by their lively and brightly dressed supporters. Tuesday is the more important day, however, when the bands all have their own troops of followers, there is a procession of floats and everyone is "jumping up" in the street (beware of pickpockets). For the stadium parades and band play-offs, try the North Stand which is cheaper, rowdier and more fun than the Grand Stand. Tickets for all National Carnival Commission shows (about TT$20 for most events) are sold at the Queen's Park Savannah, where the shows are held. You can join one of the Mas' camps by looking in the newspaper for the times and locations of the camps. If you are early enough you can get a costume which will allow you to participate in one of the "tramps" through town. The Tourism Development Agency has a list of names and addresses of the bands to whom you can write in advance to organize a costume. Fair-skinned visitors should avoid the skimpy costumes. You will be two full days in the hot sun and sun block lasts about five minutes. There is a lot of alcohol consumed during the road marches but there are no drunken brawls. Police are much in evidence on the streets. Note that it is illegal to sell tapes of carnival artists but "bootleg" tapes are inevitably sold on the streets.

The Hosay, or Hosein Festival, commemorating the murder of two Moslem princes, starts ten days after the first appearance of the new moon in the Moharrun month of the Moslem calendar. Colourful processions, hauling 10-to 30-foot-high miniature temples of wood, paper and tinsel, start the next day, heralded by moon dancers and accompanied by drum-beating. The main celebrations are in St James, W of Port of Spain. There is also a Hosay celebration in Cedros in S Trinidad. Many strict Muslims disapprove; lots of beer and rum is consumed. Also celebrated is the Moslem festival of Eid-ul-Fitr, to mark the end of Ramadan. Two principal Hindu festivals are Phagwa, or Holi, the colour, or spring, festival on the day of the full moon in the month of Phagun (February/March), and Divali, the festival of lights, usually in the last quarter of the year. At Phagura everyone gets squirted with brightly coloured dyes (abeer); strict Hindus have their doubts about some of the dancing styles. Divali is more of a family affair and involves a lot of rather good food in Indian homes. On 29 August in Arima the feast of St Rose of Lima is celebrated; the parish church is dedicated to her. Descendants of the original Amerindians come from all over the island to walk in solemn procession round the church (see below, *Arima*).

On Tobago there is a carnival, but it is very quiet compared with Trinidad's. On Easter Monday and Tuesday, there are crab, goat and donkey races at Buccoo Village. The Tobago Heritage Festival lasts for the second fortnight of July, with historical re-enactments, variety shows and parades.

TRINIDAD

PORT OF SPAIN

With a population of 51,000 (350,000 including suburbs), lies on a gently sloping plain between the Gulf of Paria and the foothills of the Northern Range. The city has a pleasant atmosphere, but the streets and buildings are not well maintained. It is also full of life and an exciting city to spend time in. The streets are mostly at right-angles to one another; the buildings are a mixture of fretwork wooden architecture and modern concrete, interspersed with office towers and empty lots. Within easy reach of the port (King's Wharf and its extension) are many of the main buildings of interest. On the S side of Woodford Square, named after the former governor, Sir Ralph Woodford, is the fine Anglican Cathedral Church of the Holy Trinity (consecrated 1823), with an elaborate hammer-beam roof festooned with carvings. It was built during Woodford's governorship (1813-28) and contains a very fine monument to him. The Red House (completed 1907) contains the House of Representatives, the Senate and various government departments. It was the scene of an attempted overthrow of the Robinson Government by armed black Muslim rebels in July 1990. The rebels held the Prime Minister and several of his Cabinet captive for five days before surrendering to the Army. On the W side of the Red House, at the corner of St Vincent and Sackville Streets, can still be seen the skeletal remains of the former Police Headquarters, which the rebels firebombed before launching their assault on the Red House. The first Red House on this site was, ironically, destroyed by fire in 1903 during riots over an increase in water rates. On the opposite side of the Square to the Cathedral are the modern Hall of Justice (completed 1985), Central Library and City Hall (1961), with a fine relief sculpture on the front. The Square

PORT OF SPAIN

1. Woodford Square
2. Victoria Square
3. Lord Harris Square
4. Adam Smith Square
5. Memorial Park
6. Jackson Square
7. Anglican Cathedral
8. Catholic Cathedral
9. Red House
10. Hall of Justice
11. National Museum
12. President's Residence
13. White Hall
14. Queen's Royal College
15. Financial Complex
16. Queen's Hall
17. BWIA Office
18. LIAT Office
19. Port Authority / boats to Tobago
20. Tourist Board
21. TSTT (Telecommunications)
22. *Holiday Inn*
23. *Hilton*
24. *Normandie Hotel*
25. *Kapok Hotel*
26. *Queen's Park Hotel*

is Trinidad's equivalent to Speaker's Corner in London's Hyde Park.

On Independence Square (2 blocks S of Woodford Square) are the Roman Catholic Cathedral of the Immaculate Conception, built on the shore-line in 1832 but since pushed back by land reclamation, the modern TSTT (Telecommunications) and Twin Towers complex at the W end of the square and the Salvatori building at the junction with Frederick Street. Behind the Cathedral is Columbus Square, with a small, brightly-painted statue of the island's discoverer. South of Independence Square, between Edward and St Vincent Streets is the financial centre, two tall towers and Eric Williams Plaza, housing the Central Bank and Ministry of Finance. Also, a little to the S of the square is the old neo-classical railway station, now used for buses. At the back, outside, is an old engine, worth a look.

To the N of the city is Queen's Park Savannah, a large open space with many playing fields, a racecourse with grandstands, and plenty of joggers. In the middle of the Savannah is the Peschier cemetery, still owned and used by the family who used to own the Savannah and sold it to the city. Below the level of the Savannah are the Rock Gardens, with lily ponds and flowers. Opposite are the Botanic Gardens, founded in 1818 by Sir Ralph Woodford. There is an amazing variety of tropical and sub-tropical plants from SE Asia and South America, as well as indigenous trees and shrubs.

Adjoining the Gardens is the small Emperor Valley Zoo, which specializes in animals living wild on the island. (Open 0930-1800, no tickets after 1730, adults TT$3, children 3-12, TT$1.50). Also next to the Gardens is the presidential residence: a colonial style building in an "L" shape in honour of Governor James Robert Longden (1870-74). Just off the Savannah (on St Ann's Road) is Queen's Hall, where concerts and other entertainments are given.

There are several other Edwardian-colonial mansions along the W side of Queen's Park Savannah, built in 1904-10 and known as the Magnificent Seven (after the film of the same name). From S to N, they are Queen's Royal College; Hayes Court, the residence of the Anglican Archbishop; Prada's House, or Mille Fleurs; Ambard's House, or Roomor; the Roman Catholic Archbishop's residence; White Hall, formerly the Prime Minister's office, now housing a few government departments; and Killarney, Mr Stollmeyer's residence (now owned by the Government). Apart from Hayes Court, which was built in 1910, all were built in 1904. A walk along the N and W sides of the Savannah can be made in the early morning (before it gets too hot), arriving outside Queen's Royal College as the students are arriving and the coconut sellers are turning up outside. The Anglican Church of All Saints at 13 Queen's Park West is also worth a visit; its stained glass windows are recently restored. Knowsley, another 1904 building, and the *Queen's Park Hotel* (1895), both on the S side of the Savannah, are interesting buildings too.

Just off the Savannah, at the corner of Frederick and Keate Streets, is the small National Museum, in the former Royal Victoria Institute. It has sections on petroleum and other industries, Trinidad and Tobago's natural history, geology, archaeology and history, carnival costumes and photographs of kings and queens, and art exhibitions (including a permanent exhibition of the work of the 19th-century landscape artist, M J Cazabon, see **Culture** above). Entry free.

Away from the city centre, to the W of Port of Spain, is the suburb of St James where in Ethel Street is a large new Hindu temple, the Port of Spain Mandir. On the waterfront is the San Andres Fort built about 1785 to protect the harbour.

EXCURSIONS

There are pleasant drives in the hills around with attractive views of city, sea, and mountain: up Lady Young Road about two miles from Savannah to a look-out 563 feet above sea level (not on a taxi route, but some cars take this route from the airport); by Lady Chancellor Road to a look-out 600 feet above sea level (not always safe, even by car) and to the Laventille Hills to see the view from the tower of the shrine of Our Lady of Laventille. From Fort George, a former signal station at 1,100 feet, there are also excellent views; to reach it take the St James route taxi from Woodford Square and ask to get off at Fort George Road; from there it is about one hour's walk uphill passing through some fairly tough residential territory. From Fort George you can also continue on foot on a rough road up to the telecommunications masts at the top of the hill, from where there are views down to Port of Spain, over to Venezuela and across the N hills. Midway along the Western Main Road to Chaguaramas a road runs off to the N, through the residential area of Diego Martin. The Blue Basin waterfall and natural landmark, on the Diego Martin river, is off this road, about a five-minute walk along a path from the town. (If you do leave your car to visit the fall, leave nothing of value in it. Also, you are advised to visit the falls in a group of five or six people if possible to avoid being robbed.) At River Estate, by Diego Martin, is a waterwheel which was once the source of power for a sugar plantation. The Western Main Road, with many pretty views, especially of the Five Islands, runs on to Carenage, where there is a remarkable little church, St Peter's Chapel, on the waterside, and to Chaguaramas, on the bay of the same name. From here you can take a launch (known locally as a pirogue) to Gaspar Grande, one of the islands, on which are the Gasparee Caves. Also here is the Calypso Beach Resort (Gasparee Island).

North of Port of Spain is Maraval, just beyond which is the 18-hole St Andrews golf course at Moka (green fees US$16 for fewer than five people, cheaper for larger groups; there is also a swimming pool, US$3 for non-members). The North Coast Road branches off Saddle Road (which runs through Maraval back over the hills to meet the Eastern Main Road at San Juan), leading to Maracas Bay and Las Cuevas (see **Beaches** page 723).

The E corridor from Port of Spain is a dual carriageway and a priority bus route through the industrial and residential suburbs. At *St Joseph*, which was once the seat of government, is the imposing Jinnah Memorial Mosque. North of St Joseph is the Maracas Valley (nothing to do with Maracas Bay), which has a 300-foot waterfall about two miles from the road. Get a Maracas Valley taxi from St Joseph and ask where to get off. Further E, high on a hill, is Mount St Benedict monastery, reached through Tunapuna. The monastery has a retreat, and a guest house, US$45 (MAP)s, US$75d. There are marvellous views over the Caroni Plain to the sea. A minibus from Port of Spain to Tunapuna takes at least 40 minutes, TT$5. There are several good, cheap Chinese restaurants in Tunapuna and a wide variety of fruits in the market. A little further along the Eastern Main Road, the Golden Grove Road branches S to Piarco international airport. If you turn N at this point (Arouca) a road winds 10 km up into the forested mountains to the Lopinot Complex, an estate built by the Comte de Lopinot (see page 715) at the turn of the 19th century. Originally called La Reconnaissance, it is now a popular picnic spot and destination for school trips; there is a small museum. Bar across the road, open "anyday, anytime".

High on a ridge in the Maracas Valley are the only known Amerindian rock drawings (petroglyphs) in Trinidad, known as the Caurita drawings. They are probably Arawak and show a series of faces with curving lines indicating limbs. To get there it is a stiff climb of 1-1½ hours in the valley, with access from the main cross roads between San Juan and Tunapuna.

Arima is the third largest city, 16 miles/25 km E of Port of Spain, reached by bus or route taxi, population 26,000. It has a small but interesting Amerindian museum at the Cleaver Woods Recreation Centre, on the W side of town housed in a reproduction Amerindian long house, entrance free but donations welcome. In Arima there is a group of people who regard themselves as descendants of the original Amerindians of the area, although there are none left of pure blood. They have a figure head Carib queen and call themselves the Santa Rosa Carib Community, although it is not clear whether they are of Carib, Arawak or other Amerindian descent. West of the church in the centre of town is the Santa Rosa Carib Community Crafts Centre selling traditional crafts: cassava squeezers, serving trays, carvings etc. The political leader of the community is Ricardo Hernández, who is very helpful and knowledgeable. The Catholic church has good stained glass windows. At the end of August there is an annual religious procession where the image of Santa Rosa de Lima is carried from the church and paraded through the streets, very picturesque and interesting.

From Arima the road runs either to Toco at Trinidad's NE tip (which is well worth a visit though its rocky shore defies bathing) or, branching off at Valencia, to the E coast. At Galera Point, reached off the road which goes to Toco, over a rickety wooden bridge, there is a small, pretty lighthouse. If you arrive before 1530 it is often open and you can climb to the top for a breathtaking view from the ramp.

About eight miles N of Arima, off the Blanchisseuse Road, you can get (by car

or taxi, TT$40, the driver should wait for you, or warm 2½-hour walk up hill through lovely forests) to the **Asa Wright Nature Centre**, an old plantation house overlooking a wooded valley and a must for bird-lovers. 23 rooms and full board are provided at the Asa Wright Centre, US$97.50-105pp double occupancy for foreign tourists although it seems to vary, (PO Box 4710, Arima, T 667-4655, F 667-0493 for booking). There is swimming in a beautiful man-made pool, a network of trails and guided tours. Sit on the verandah and watch the hummingbirds. The rare oil-birds in Dunstan Cave (also called Diablotin Cave) cannot at present be seen as the caves are closed indefinitely to visitors because the birds had been leaving. The centre is open daily 0900-1700; entrance charge TT$25.50 (US$6, US$4 children). It is wise to give 48 hours notice of your visit. This road carries on to Blanchisseuse (restaurant close to beach where the surfers are). A 9-mile (14 km) walk from the road are the Aripo Caves (the longest system in Trinidad) with spectacular stalagmites and stalactites (in the wet season, June to December, a river runs through the caves).

From Arima you can take a (rare) bus, or hitchhike, to Brasso Seco and Paria (though the latter does not appear on some maps). From here the trail runs to Paria Bay, which is possibly the best beach on the island, about 8 miles/13 km, ask directions, or see the Tourism Development Authority's *Sites (trail guide)* book for the route. There is a primitive shelter on the beach but no other facilities so take provisions with you. At the beach, turn right to get to the bridge over the Paria River, from where it is a five-minute walk inland to the spectacular Paria waterfall. Another path from the beach leads W to Blanchisseuse (7 miles/11 km), where the track forks; take the fork closer to the shore. A road continues W from Blanchisseuse to Las Cuevas.

Driving S you see Indians in the rice fields, herds of water buffalo, buffalypso (bigger animals, selectively bred for meat), Hindu temples and Moslem mosques. There are boat trips to the **Caroni Bird Sanctuary**, the home of scarlet ibis, whose numbers are dwindling as the swamp in which they live is encroached upon. The boats leave around 1600 so as to see the ibis returning to their roost at sunset. A spectacular sight, recommended even for those who do not consider themselves bird watchers. Egrets, herons and plovers can also be seen. Bus or route taxi from Port of Spain or San Fernando to Bamboo Grove Settlement no 1, on the Uriah Butler Highway, from where the boats leave, TT$2.50 or TT$5 respectively. Maxi taxi (green bands) from Independence Square. Ask to be dropped off at the Caroni Bird Sanctuary. Arrange return transport in advance, it is difficult to hail a bus in the dark. Authorized boat operators in the swamp are Mr Winston Nanan (T 645-1305), TT$40 for adults, TT$20 for children 15 and under, group rates available, and Mr David Ramsahai (T 663-2207/645-4706), TT$25, children 12 and under TT$15; also enquire at the Asa Wright Centre for more detailed tours. Tour operators in Port of Spain offer tours. Take mosquito repellent and if possible a cold bag with drinks.

San Fernando on the SW coast is a busy, hot city (population 60,000), as yet not spoilt by tourism but spoilt by just about everything else and not especially attractive. An expressway connects Port of Spain with San Fernando, making it a half hour drive (one hour by taxi). In its neighbourhood are the principal industrial-development area of Point Lisas and the Pointe-a-Pierre oil refinery. Within the oil refinery is the 26-hectare Wild Fowl Trust, a conservation area with two lakes and breeding grounds for many endangered species (open 1000-1700, closed Saturday; entry TT$4,

children TT$3. T 637-5145, Ms Molly Gaskin or Mrs K Shepard on T 662-4040, you must call 48 hours in advance to get permission to enter the compound (there are many entrances, it can be confusing).

A famous phenomenon to visit on the SW coast near San Fernando is **Pitch Lake**, about 47 hectares of smooth surface resembling caked mud but which really is hot black tar; it is 41m deep. It has been described by disappointed tourists, expecting something more dramatic, as looking like a parking lot, although others have pointed out that it is parking lots that look like the Pitch Lake. If care is taken it is possible to walk on it, watching out for air holes bubbling up from the pressure under the ooze. The legend is that long ago the gods interred an entire tribe of Chaima Indians for daring to eat sacred hummingbirds containing the souls of their ancestors. In the place where the entire village sank into the ground there erupted a sluggish flow of black pitch gradually becoming an ever-refilling large pool. It provides a healthy, though recently decreasing, item in Trinidad's export figures. It can be reached by taking a bus from Port of Spain to San Fernando (TT$6 by air-conditioned express, by route taxi it costs TT$10) and then another from there to La Brea (TT$4). Official tours have been stopped but the former tour guides offer their services. Agree on a price in advance as there are no fixed rates any more. Sometimes there are crowds of guides who are difficult to avoid and travellers have complained about hassling, but on the other hand it is difficult to understand the lake without their explanation.

East of San Fernando, near Princes Town, is the Devil's Woodyard, one of 18 mud volcanoes on Trinidad, this one considered a holy site by some Hindus (it is also a natural landmark).

On the S coast is the fishing village of Moruga, which is reached by a fascinating drive through the Trinidad countryside. Every year around the middle of July they have an unusual celebration of Columbus' 1498 landing on the beach. Fishing boats are decked out as caravels, complete with red Maltese cross. Columbus, a priest and soldiers are met by Amerindians (local boys, mostly of East Indian and African extraction); after the meeting everyone retires to the church compound where the revelry continues late into the night.

It is quite difficult to get beyond Arima and San Fernando by bus, but there are route taxis, privately-operated maxi taxis, or you can hire a car or motorcycle.

Island Information—Trinidad

● Airport

Piarco International, 16 miles SE of Port of Spain. Allow plenty of time to get there. The taxi fare to Arouca is TT$40 and to the centre of Port of Spain is TT$120, (50% more after 2200). Taxi despatchers find taxis for new arrivals, ask to see the rate card for taxi fares to different places. Unlicensed taxis outside the main parking area charge less, depending on the volume of business. If you are not loaded with luggage public transport is much cheaper. To get to Port of Spain walk out of the airport and cross the road to catch a route taxi (see **Information for Visitors, Taxis**), destination Main Road, or, rather better if slower, go a bit further to Arouca (TT$2). Then take a route taxi or maxi taxi from the junction into Port of Spain (TT$5). Coming back to the airport do the same in reverse. People are very helpful if you need to ask. There is a direct bus, TT$2, 45 minutes-1 hour, from the airport to Port of Spain bus station, officially departing from a shelter 100m to the right as you come out of the airport, on the hour every hour, but in practice it runs irregularly or not at all, ask the Tourist Office to find out; buy tickets at the left luggage office at airport entrance. From the central bus terminal at the old railway station you will have to walk to Independence or Woodford Square for a route taxi for your ultimate destination. This is not advisable at night, especially if carrying luggage (ie take a taxi from the airport at night). If intending to take the bus to the airport, allow plenty of time to ensure arriving in time for checking in.

To eat at the airport, go to the food stalls

beside the bus shelter. Excellent cheap local food, airport staff buy their lunches there.

● Transport

In Trinidad, the word "taxi" includes most forms of public transport. The word "travelling" means going by bus or taxi rather than by private car. **Buses** are run by the PTSC. They are big and cheap, also slow, irregular and dirty. However, the PTSC also has newer air-conditioned buses on main routes from Independence Square to Arima, Chaguanas and San Fernando. These are not quite so cheap, faster and more comfortable, TT$6 to San Fernando. On all routes, you must purchase your ticket at the kiosk before boarding the bus; you may have to tender the exact fare. At the PTSC office in the old railway station on South Quay, you can get information showing how to reach the various sights by bus. **Taxis** Most sedan taxis (saloon cars, often rather beat up) set off from Independence Square, but those for St Ann's and St James leave from Woodford Square, for Carenage from St Vincent and Park Streets, for the Diego Martin area from South Quay, and for Maraval, Belmont and Morvant from Duke and Charlotte Streets. Fares in town TT$2-3, further out TT$4-5. If you are in a hurry you can pay for any remaining empty seats and ask the driver to go. They will also go off-route for a little extra but going off route to the *Hilton* costs TT$40. They are the only means of transport on some suburban routes, such as to St Ann's, and in rural areas away from main roads. Travelling to remote areas may involve 3 or more taxis, not really a problem, just ask where the next one stops. Major routes run all night and are amazingly frequent during the day, others become infrequent or stop late at night. St Christopher's taxis or airport taxis are taxis as understood in most countries. Some are smarter and more comfortable than route taxis. St Christopher's operates from the main hotels. Take a taxi if you have a complicated journey, or you have heavy baggage, or it is raining. At night it can be a lot cheaper than getting robbed. **Maxitaxis** are minibuses which cover longer distances than route taxis; they are frequent and go as fast as the traffic will allow, often a bit faster. Prepare for ear-blasting music. They are colour coded (yellow for Diego Martin and W, red for E, green for San Fernando, brown or black for maxis which start in San Fernando and travel S from there) and they set off mostly from Independence Square except the Carenage and Chaguaramas maxis, which start from Green corner on St Vincent and Park Streets (Globe cinema) and Maraval maxis, which start from Duke and Charlotte Streets. Check exact route before starting, eg E taxis are either "San Juan" or "all the way up" the Eastern Main Road to Arima, or "highway", which is faster and runs closer to the airport but misses places like Tunapuna and Curepe. Fares start at TT$2 and run to Arima, TT$6; to Chaguanas, TT$6; to San Fernando, TT$10. If you are worried about being overcharged, pay with TT$10 and look as though you know how much change to expect, but drivers are usually very helpful and friendly.

● **Where To Stay**

If you intend to stay in Trinidad for Carnival, when prices rise steeply, you must book a hotel well in advance. Some are booked a year ahead. If arriving without accommodation arranged at Carnival time, the tourist office at the airport may help to find you a room with a local family, though this like hotels will be expensive. You will be lucky to find anything. Prices are for 16 December 1992 to 15 April 1993, for a double room. VAT of 15% will be added to your bill.

Hotels in the upper bracket in the **Port of Spain** area include: *Bel Air Piarco*, by the airport, T 664-4771/3, F add ext 15, US$70-89d for a small room, overpriced, typical airport hotel, swimming pool, good bar and restaurant but noise from planes; *Holiday Inn*, Wrightson Rd (PO Box 1017), T 625-3361, F 625-4166, in the business centre, US$105d, all facilities very nice but has cockroaches, good buffet lunch for US$15; *Hilton*, on a rise at the corner of Lady Young and St Ann's Rds, NE Queen's Park Savannah (PO Box 442), T 624-3211, F ext 6133, US$135-161, public areas and pool deck are on top and rooms on lower levels, view and breeze from pool level excellent, all facilities, restaurant excellent if pricey, including wide variety of lunch buffet, eating by the pool is not expensive, non-residents can eat/swim there, *Aviary Bar* for drinking and dancing; off St Ann's Rd, at the end of Nook Av (No 10) is *Normandie* (PO Box 851), T 624-1181/4, 52 rooms, a/c, US$70-95, but reduced rates for businessmen, swimming pool, in a complex with craft and fashion shops and restaurants, comfortable, good restaurant; *Kapok*, a Golden Tulip hotel, 16-18 Cotton Hill, St Clair (NW Queen's Park Savannah, T 622-6441, F 622 9677), 71 rooms, a/c, TV,

phone etc, good, friendly, try to get room on upper floors away from traffic noise, US$82, restaurants, pool, shopping arcade; *Valley Vue*, 67 Ariapita Road, St Ann's, T 623-3511/13, F 627-8046, 68 rooms, US$80-100, children under 12 free, good hotel, nice pool with waterslide (TT$25 for non-guests to use pool), sports facilities, special day rate for couples; *Royal Palm Hotel*, 7 Saddle Rd, Maraval, T 628-6042, US$57-145d, kitchenette, pool; *Chaconia Inn*, 106 Saddle Rd, Maraval, in receivership but still operating, US$75-85d, (T 628-8603/5, F 628-3214); *Tropical Hotel*, 6 Rookery Nook Road, Maraval, T 622-5815/4249, F 628-3174, US$55-60, a/c, pool, maid service, bar and restaurant attached, short walk from the Savannah, friendly, helpful, rec. *Hosanna Hotel*, 2 Santa Margarita Circular Rd, St Augustine, US$75-85d CP, pool, all credit cards. See **Excursions** above for accommodation at the St Benedict Monastery and Asa Wright Centre.

Guesthouses below US$20 a night are few and far between in the capital. Several of these listed here are not recommended by the TDA. The *Hillcrest Haven Guesthouse* is in this price range (7A Hillcrest Rd, Cascade, T 624-1344) but prices rise to US$30 during Carnival, minimum stay 6 nights, use of kitchen facilities, mixed reports. *Zollna House*, 12 Ramlogan Development, La Seiva, Maraval, T 628 3731, owned by Gottfried and Barbara Zollna, small guest house, food varied with local flavour, special diets catered for, US$50, breakfast and dinner per person US$5 and US$12 respectively. *Copper Kettle Hotel*, 66-68 Edward Street, T 625-4381, central, good, clean but hot and dingy rooms with shower, US$20-36, depending on whether you have a/c, friendly and helpful staff, good restaurant; *Schultzi's Guest House and Pub*, 35 Fitt Street, Woodbrook, T 622-7521, US$25 inc breakfast, kitchen, hot shower, good; *Five Star Guesthouse*, 7 French St, Woodbrook, US$30-50d, kitchenette, T 623-4006; *Pelican Inn*, 2-4 Coblentz Avenue, Cascade, US$40d EP, T 627-6271; *Halyconia Inn*, 7 First Avenue, Cascade, US$40 CP; *La Calypso Guest House*, 46 French Street, Woodbrook, T 622-4077, US$25-30, clean, safe, efficient, Kitchen, helpful, car hire available; under same management is *Alicia's Guest House*, 7 Coblentz Gardens, St Ann's, T 623-2802, F 623-8560, US$45-58d, inc breakfast; *Trini House*, 5A Lucknow Street, St James, T/F 638-7550, 4 rooms, US$30d inc breakfast, English, German, Italian and French spoken by owners Michael Figuera and Margrit Lambrigger; *Valsayn Villa*, 34 Gilwell Road, Valsayn North, T/F 645-1193, very large, modern, private house with beautifully furnished rooms and lovely garden, US$40, in one of the safest residential areas, close to university, 15 mins from airport, 20 mins by bus from down town Port of Spain, excellent home-cooked Indian meals available, rec; *Par-May-La's Inn*, 53 Picton St, T 628-2008, F 628-4707, convenient for carnival and cricket, US$25s, US$50d, US$65 triple, full American breakfast, or local cuisine with roti, tax and service inc, credit cards accepted; *Kitty Peters*, 26 Warren Street, US$15pp, breakfast extra, immaculately clean, hot water showers, fans, quiet area, friendly; *Mardi Gras Guest House*, 134A Frederick Street, next to TDA building, T 627-2319, from US$15s, US$18d (except carnival week), with private bath, dining room, bar; *The New City Cabs Guesthouse*, 93 Frederick St, T 627-7372, cheap, but expect rats and intermittent water (US$10 without meals), "nutrition house" in basement with fruit and vegetable juices; *Royal Guest House*, 109 Charlotte Street, T 623 1042, in front of gas station, coffee shop next door owned by same family, US$10d, shared bathroom, good beds, friendly, safe, but do not walk down Charlotte Street towards the harbour area which is dangerous; *Bullet Guest House*, 6 Park Street, central, clean and safe, does not raise prices during carnival; *YMCA*, 8a Cipriani Blvd, under US$20. *Monique's Guest House*, 114 Saddle Road, Maraval, T 628-3334, on road to Maracas Beach, US$45-60, clean, attractive, facilities for the disabled, Monique is helpful and hospitable. *Carnetta's House*, 28 Scotland Terrace, Andalusia, Maraval, T 628-2732, F 628-7717, US$40-50d EP (children under 12 free), US$129 during carnival, a/c, 5

rooms; *Jirah's Guesthouse*, 109 Long Circular Road, Marawal, US$30d EP, kitchenette, T 628-2337. *Naden's Court Guesthouse*, 32 St Augustine Circular Road, Tunapuna, T 645-2937 (15-30 minutes to Port of Spain by bus on the priority route), US$35 with bath, less without, friendly, comfortable, safe and clean, laundry facilities, breakfast room where you can also get sandwiches in the evening, highly rec; *Pax Guesthouse*, Mt St Benedict, Tunapuna, T 662-4084, US$75d, simple but wholesome food, good view of central Trinidad as well as of occasional monk. Halfway between the airport and Port of Spain near the St John's Road bus stop in the Saint Augustine district on East Main Road is the *Scarlet Ibis Hotel*, T 662-2251, US$25 without shower, once upmarket, restaurant, pool, but now run down with mostly short stay visitors although rec have been received for its cleanliness. *S & D Bed and Breakfast*, run by Savitri and Dinesh Bhola, Waterpipe Road, Five Rivers, Arouca, T 642-3659, F 642-1076, close to airport, US$30s, US$40d, weekly and group rates available, a/c; *Airport View Guesthouse*, St Helena Junction, Piarco, US$35. At Longdenville, near Chaguanas, is the *Unique Hotel*, corner of Dam Road and Nelson Street, good service, TT$80 with bathroom, excellent meals, ask for the local Indian food, even at breakfast, recommended.

At mile post 23 on the Toco Main Road, N of Balandra Bay is Mr Hugh Lee Pow's *Green Acres Guest House*, TT$80, on a farm backed by the ocean, 3 good meals a day inc, very kind and restful. At **Blanchisseuse** at Paradise Hill, Upper Village, Mrs Cooper offers bed and breakfast, not cheap but very good. Jeanette Holder, lamp post 191 or PO Box 995, Port of Spain, T 623-8827, has one double room and one cottage available, US$50d. *Surf's Country Inn*, in the same village, is a good restaurant and the owners plan to add some rooms, T 669-2475. It can be hard to get a hotel room on the N coast in the low season when many places shut; self-catering may be difficult with few shops, no bank, no car rental.

In **San Fernando**, not a lot of choice, *Royal Hotel*, 46-54 Royal Road, T 652-4881, F 652-3924 US$64-90, a/c, kitchenette, lovely hilltop garden; *Farrell Guest Hotel*, Southern Main Road, Claxton Bay, near San Fernando, T 659-2230, F 659 2204, a/c, swimming pool, kitchenette, restaurant, good view of the Gulf of Paria, popular with visiting oil men, US$130. At Pointe-a-Pierre, near Guaracara cricket ground, *Blue Gardenia Guest House*, above a bar, basic, "a real bargain", not much to do in the area but take-away food places and at *Mario's* nearby, prostitutes in the bar. At La Brea near the pitch lake is a hotel called *The Hideaway*, some rooms a/c, OK but not for the faint hearted, rooms available for 3, 12 or 24 hours.

At **Mayaro** on the SE coast there are beach houses to rent but check their condition, some are unacceptable; the *Queen's Beach Hotel* is pleasant, US$28, friendly, rec, meals around US$10. Inland, the Victoria Regia Research Station, La Gloria Rd, Talparo, Mundo Nuevo, central Trinidad, T 662-7113 or 662-5678, for all-inclusive accommodation and airport transfers, US$35 pp, or 7-night package including 5 guided tours, US$595 pp.

The Bed and Breakfast Association of Trinidad and Tobago, Diego Martin Post Office, Box 3231, Diego Martin (Miss Grace Steele T 637-9329, F 627-0856, or Mrs Barbara Zollna 628-3731, F 625-6980), lists a number of establishments in Port of Spain, the suburbs, Carenage, Tunapuna, Arima and Blanchisseuse; prices from US$20-35s, US$40-60d, inc breakfast. It has a desk at the airport before immigration, very helpful.

If arriving by boat, the Seaman's Mission, opp the immigration office, has been helpful in finding hotel rooms.

● **Where To Eat**

In **Port of Spain**: at the main hotels where you can expect to pay TT$90 for a full meal in a nice setting with imaginative menus, eg *Tiki Village* in the *Kapok Hotel*, T 622-6441, serves good Polynesian and Chinese food; next door and owned by the *Kapok* is the *Café Savannah*, T 622-6441, small and intimate (creole seafood, steak, quality unreliable); The *Hilton* Sun brunch buffet is good value at TT$150 inc tax and service and use of pool; *Rafters*, 6 Warner Street, Newtown, T 628-9258, local and seafood, good; in the **Normandie** complex, Nook Av, *La Fantasie*, T 624-1181, and *Café Trinidad*, both pricey. *Michael's*, 143 Long Circular Road, T 628-0445, Italian. Smart, but good value restaurants include *Monsoon*, 72 Tragarete Road, T 628-7684, Indian dishes recommended, good selection, large meal for about TT$15; *Wazo Deyzeel*, T 623-0115, the name is a corruption of the French word for bird, perched on steep hill above St Ann's, spectacular views over city lights, ask for a table on edge of verandah, food is simple and cheap, nice place for late meal and a drink, closed Wed; at Nook Av is *Solimar*, T 624-1459, international, reasonable prices, good service, outdoor dining, excellent food, reservations advisable and essential at weekends; *Ali Baba*, T 622 5557, on first floor level in Royal Palm Plaza shopping mall on Saddle Road, Maraval, open air dining with a roof, Arabic and other dishes, TT$25-100, excellent service, popular, run by a Lebanese, Joe; *Gourmet Club*, Ellerslie Plaza, Maraval, T 628-5113, Italian and international, lunch TT$35-55, dinner TT$45-165; *Une Cachette*, Dheine's Bay, Carenage, T 637-

5954, Caribbean-style food, TT$20-100 lunch and dinner. If you've a yen for the best pepper shrimps in the Caribbean, the *Hong Kong City Restaurant*, 86A Tragarete Road, Chinese is the place. Fast food outlets include *Mario's Pizza Place*, Tragarete Rd and other outlets, average to awful; *Joe's Pizza*, St James, good, also other Italian dishes; *Pizza Burger Boys*, Frederick St, and Ellerslie Plaza, Boissiere Village, Maraval (for take away T 628-2697, best of its type). The first *Pizza Hut* has opened in Curepe and more are to come. *Kentucky Fried Chicken* in most cities and towns, better than you might expect; *Royal Castle*, 49 Frederick St and other locations throughout Trinidad, chicken and chips with a local flavour. All along Western Main Road in St James there are lots of cafes, snack bars and restaurants, all reasonably priced, lots of choice. The *Pelican Inn*, Coblenz Av, Cascade, serves food, but is mainly a pub, hugely popular (late arrivals at the weekend have to park 600 m away); *New Shay Shay Tien*, 81 Cipriani Blvd, T 627-8089, rec; *De Backyard*, 84 Picton Street, local dishes; *Golden Palace*, 212 Southern Main Road, Marabella, T 658-6557, also Chinese, very good. *Imperial Garden*, Highland Plaza, Glencoe, T 663-6430, 'authentic' Chinese food. For Chinese food in San Fernando, try *Soongs Great Wall*, 97 Circular Rd, T 652-2583, round the corner from the *Royal Hotel*, very good, the distinctive, Trinidadian version of Chinese food. At the cruise ship harbour, *Coconut Village*, good food, cheap; *Breakfast Shed*, opposite *Holiday Inn* and sometimes called *Holiday Out*, a big hall with several kitchens where locals eat, TT$15 for very substantial lunch with juice; *Hot Shoppe* has by far the best rotis, see *Food*; next to the Maraval Road branch, the jerk chicken/jerk pork places have good, spicey Jamaican-style food; the Town Centre Mall and Voyager Mall on Frederick Street have indoor halls with a varied and good selection of stands selling food, seating in the middle. Colsort Mall is similar but not so good.

At **Chaguaramas Anchorage**, Point Gourde Road, T 634-4334, for seafood, at **Blanchisseuse**, *Surf's Country Inn*, North Coast Road, T 669-2475, good value, delicious meals.

● **Entertainment**
Trinidad abounds in evening entertainment, with calypso dancing eg *Sparrow's Hideaway*, limbo shows and international cabaret acts.

Monday's local song and dance at the *Hilton* is less authentic in atmosphere than the steel band concerts on Fri at the same venue. Entrance TT$10. For those wishing to visit the places where the local, rather than tourist, population go, anyone in the street will give directions. Though the atmosphere will be natural and hospitality generous, it will not be luxurious and the local rum is likely to flow. *Chaconia* on Saddle Rd has live music on Fri and Sat. *Moon Over Bourbon Street*, West Mall, has a cocktail lounge and live local entertainment at weekends. The *Bel Air* near the airport has live entertainment on Sat night. Other discos and clubs include the **Upper Level Club**, West Mall, Westmoorings; *Ramparts*; *The Attic Pub*, Shoppes of Maraval, Saddle Road; *Club Coconut* in Valley Vue Hotel, St Ann's; *Genesis* in Diego Martin; *The Tunnel*, 89 Union Road, Marabella near San Fernando and in Chaguanas. For spicier entertainment, go to the *International* (Wrightson Rd). *Mas Camp Pub* in Woodbrook has nightly entertainment including calypso and steel band, the best place to see live calypso out of season (cover charge usually TT$10). *007 Club* nearby is good, open late (but lots of prostitutes who can be ignored). The Silver Stars Steel Orchestra (formed in the 1950s) can occasionally be seen in rehearsal (check beforehand) at the Panyard, 56 Tragarete Road, Newtown, Woodbrook, Port of Spain. Silver Stars plays at local parties, cruise ships or on the beach, workshops for individuals or groups can be arranged, contact Michael Figuera, T/F 628-7550. For late drinking and music, *Pelican* (down hill from Hilton), Coblentz Avenue, Cascade, is lively; so are *Smokey* and *Bunty* in St James, an area which is normally livelier at night than Port of Spain.

Theatres: Queen's Hall, 1-3 St Ann's Rd; Little Carib, White and Roberts Sts; Central Bank Auditorium, Eric Williams Plaza, Edward St. In San Fernando, Naparima Bowl reopened after a lengthy period of renovation; the folk theatre of the South National Institute of Performing Arts (T 653-5355). See press for details of performances.

Cinemas: 3 cinemas are grouped near Park Plaza on Park Street and Tragarete Road. They are very cheap and occasionally show something good. Audiences are audibly enthusiastic, particularly for sex and violence.

TOBAGO

Tobago is not as bustling as Trinidad but tourism is booming. The end of the oil boom in Trinidad and the growth of tourism in Tobago has narrowed the gap in living standards between the two islands. Nevertheless, it is ideal for those in search of relaxation. The tourist area is concentrated on the SW end, near the airport, and about six miles from the capital, *Scarborough*.

SCARBOROUGH

In Scarborough itself there are interesting Botanic Gardens. Above the town is Fort King George (1770), which is well-maintained and has good views along the coast. At the Barrack Guard House is the Tobago museum, with an excellent display of early Tobago history including Amerindian pottery, shells, military relics, maps and documents from the slave era. Open Mon-Fri, 0900-1700, adults TT$3, children TT$1. At the same location is a hospital. The town itself is pleasant but perhaps not worth an extended visit. Although there are some interesting buildings, such as the House of Assembly on James Park (built in 1825), and Gun bridge, with its rifle-barrel railings, the claim that "Except for the recently built Scarborough Mall there has been very little significant change in its appearance over 200 years" (Joan Bacchus-Xavier, *A Guide to Touring Tobago*) is exaggerated. There is plenty of new development with a new deep water harbour and cruise ship terminal. (NB The *Guide* is a handy book on the features of Tobago, it costs TT$20.)

EXCURSIONS

If you are driving around Tobago, the 1:50,000 map, usually available from the TDA office in Scarborough, at TT$20, is adequate, although note that many of the minor roads are only suitable for 4-wheel drive. If you are hiking, get the three 1:25,000 sheets, not currently available in Tobago but you can get them from the Lands and Survey Division, Richmond Street, Port of Spain, or a good map shop abroad. You can walk anywhere as long as you can get there. There is a book of trails. East from Scarborough, on the Windward coast, is Bacolet Bay. Off the coastal road you can go to the Forest Reserve by taking a bus from Scarborough to Mount St George and then walking or hitching to Hillsborough Dam (the lake is the drinking water supply for the island, no swimming, you may find a man to take you on the lake in a rowing boat, lovely forest setting); from there continue NE through the forest to Castara or Mason Hall on an unpaved, rough road. Directions, compass and supplies, including water, are essential. Bird-watching is excellent, but look out for snakes (none of them poisonous). By Mount St George (Tobago's first, short-lived principal town, then called George Town) is Studley Park House and Fort Granby which guards Barbados Bay. The road continues through Pembroke and Belle Garden, near where is Richmond Great House, now a hotel. Roxborough, the island's second town, also on the Windward coast, is worth a visit. The Argyll River waterfalls near Roxborough comprise four beautiful falls with a big green pool at the bottom, a 10-minute walk upstream from the road which can be very muddy. You can't miss them because of all the rather overpriced and pushy guides standing in the road. A good walk is the road from Roxborough to Parlatuvier and Bloody Bay. There is hardly any traffic and you go through singing forests with masses of birds. After the 5-mile marker is a semi-circular trail in the forest called Gilpin's Trace. Great views from the hut at the top of the road.

Beyond Roxborough is King's Bay, with waterfalls near the road in which you can swim. From the fishing village of Speyside you can visit *Little Tobago*, a forested islet off the NE coast, and sanc-

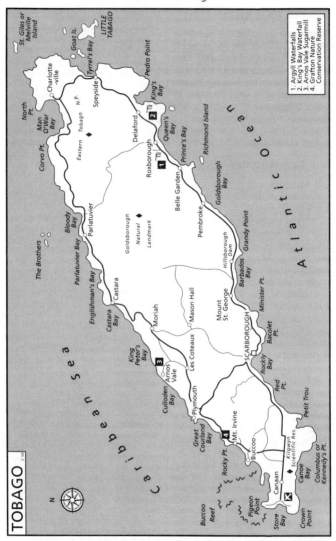

TOBAGO

1. Argyll Waterfalls
2. King's Bay Waterfall
3. Arnos Vale Sugarmill
4. Grafton Nature Conservation Reserve

St. Giles or Melville Island
Goat Is.
LITTLE TABAGO
Tyrrel's Bay
Pedro Point
King's Bay
North Pt.
Man O'War Bay
Charlotteville
Speyside
Queen's Bay
Prince's Bay
Richmond Island
Corvo Pt.
Delaford
Eastern Tobago N.P.
Roxborough
Belle Garden
Goldsborough Bay
Bloody Bay
Parlatuvier Bay
Parlatuvier
Goldsborough Natural Landmark
Pembroke
Grandy Point
The Brothers
Englishman's Bay
Castara
Hillsborough Dam
Barbados Bay
Minister Pt.
Castara Bay
Moriah
Mason Hall
Mount St. George
Rockly Bay
Bacolet Pt.
King Peter's Bay
Les Coteaux
SCARBOROUGH
Culloden Bay
Arnos Vale
Plymouth
Red Pt.
Petit Trou
Great Courland Bay
Mt. Irvine
Buccoo
Kilgwyn Scientific Res.
Columbus or Kennedy's Pt.
Rocky Pt.
Canoe Bay
Buccoo Reef
Pigeon Point
Canaan
Store Bay
Crown Point

Atlantic Ocean

Caribbean Sea

N

tuary for birds. There are wild fowl and 58 species of other birds, including the red-billed tropic bird found here in the largest nesting colony in the N Atlantic. Boats across cost TT$50 (bargain; make sure the price includes return and a guided tour of the islet, some also include snorkelling). Go early in the morning to see the birds. If you want to camp, you are supposed to have prior permission

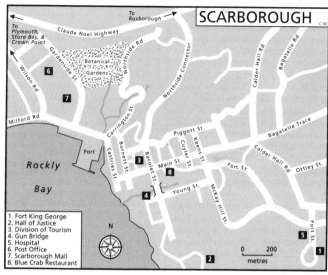

SCARBOROUGH

1. Fort King George
2. Hall of Justice
3. Division of Tourism
4. Gun Bridge
5. Hospital
6. Post Office
7. Scarborough Mall
8. Blue Crab Restaurant

from the Forestry Division at Studley Park, T 639-4468. They also have a rudimentary camp on the main ridge by the Roxborough-Parlatuvier road, which can be used by arrangement. At Speyside, you can sling a hammock near the government centre on the beachfront: well-lit, a night-guard may keep your belongings under lock, but it may be windy. Buses from Scarborough to Charlotteville rarely go past Speyside even though the road is paved, because drivers do not like negotiating the hairpin bends.

A trip to Charlotteville in the NE (2 hours by bus from Scarborough, TT$2, be sure to check there is a bus back to Scarborough in the afternoon, the timetable is unreliable; a route taxi is easier, TT$10, but not on Saturdays, when the Adventist drivers do not work) is recommended; there are magnificent views on the way and the village itself is on a fine horse-shoe bay with a good beach; swimming and snorkelling. On 29 June, the village celebrates St Peter's day with a festival. From Charlotteville, it is a 15-minute walk to Pirate's Bay, which is

magnificent and unspoilt. Also adjacent is Man O'War Bay. It is fairly easy to hitch a ride from Charlotteville to Speyside. The road from Charlotteville to Plymouth along the Caribbean coast is bad and 4-wheel drive is needed for part of the way. The views are worth the trouble with lots of lovely bays beneath you. It is not advisable to drive this road when it is raining.

At the SW/tourist end of the island, many hotels and resorts are within walking distance of the airport. At Store Bay are the ruins of small Milford Fort, and brown pelicans frequent the beautiful beach, which is kept spotlessly clean and is a good place to watch the sunset. *Pigeon Point* has the island's most beautiful beach, clean and with calm water, though TT$10 is charged for adults and TT$3 for children for admission as the land is private; a wall has been built to stop you walking along the foreshore and groynes built by the owners have caused beach erosion. There are huts, tables and benches, lockers, bars, shopping, boat hire and water sports. It is another good place to watch the sunset. From Mount Irvine Bay (further N on the Caribbean coast), where there is an attractive, palm-fringed championship golf course (the hotel of the same name has a good beach—surfing) you can walk up to Bethel (about 2 miles), the island's highest village, for excellent views across the island. Another beach which is well worth a visit is Turtle Bay. The main town on this coast is Plymouth, with Fort James overlooking Great Courland Bay (site of the Courlander settlement in the 17th century). A much-quoted attraction in Plymouth is the enigmatic tombstone of Betty Stevens (25 November, 1783), which reads: "She was a mother without knowing it, and a wife, without letting her husband know, except by her kind indulgences to him." Hidden in the forest some miles from Arnos Vale is the Arnos Vale Sugarmill, dating from 1880; a recommended excursion, it is possible to hitchhike. It is difficult to continue along this coast by bus, Plymouth to Parlatuvier is not a recognized route. You have to go instead via Roxborough, with a lovely journey from there through the forest. Check that there is a bus back in the afternoon as there is nowhere to stay in Parlatuvier.

Buccoo Reef Glass-bottomed boats for visiting this undersea garden leave from Pigeon Point, Store Bay and the larger hotels nearby. Boats may be cheaper if hired from Buccoo Village. The charge is TT$35 for 2-2½ hours, with shoes and snorkel provided; wear swimming costume and a hat. The dragging of anchors and greed of divers have tarnished the glory of this once marvellous reef, though. Elkhorn and other corals have been badly damaged by snorkellers and divers walking on them. The reef is now protected by law; it is forbidden to remove or destroy the corals or other marine life. Boat trips also include the Nylon Pool, an emerald-green pool in the Caribbean. Boats leave between 0900 and 1430, depending on the tide. Be selective

in choosing which boat—and captain— you take for the trip; some are less than satisfactory (Selwyn's *Pleasure Girl* has been recommended, so has Archie and Mala's *Come to Starcheck*, others include Hew's Tours, Hewlett Hazel, T 639-9058, F 639-7984, Kenneth Christmas, Buccoo Reef Cooperative, Buccoo Point, T 639-8582, or after 1900, T 639-8746). From Scarborough to Buccoo by bus is TT$0.75. Taxis also go to Buccoo.

Island Information—Tobago
● Transport To Tobago

Almost all **flights** to Trinidad with BWIA can have a Tobago coupon added at no extra charge, dates can be open, worth booking on any trip. A new airline, Air Caribbean, took over the Trinidad-Tobago route in 1993 offering 9 daily flights; the crossing takes 12 mins and costs TT$200 return, (adults), cheaper for children. Departures, however, are often heavily booked at weekends and holidays, particularly Christmas and afterwards (at other times tickets can be bought the day before, even standby). Tobago's Crown Point airport has been extended to take international flights direct. There is a tourist office and a bank at the airport.

Boats from Port of Spain to Tobago go once a day at 1400 Mon-Fri and 1100 on Sun, no crossings on Sat; all return crossings from Scarborough at 0200, but the schedule is modified monthly and departure times are unreliable. The crossing is supposedly 5 hours. Hammocks can be slung at night. The trip can be rough. There are 2 vessels: M/F *Tobago*, on which all tickets cost TT$25 one way; and M/V *Panorama*, on which a cabin is TT$80 one way, tourist class TT$30 and economy TT$25. Tickets are sold at the Port Authority on the docks, office hours Mon-Fri 0700-1500, 1600-1800, 1900-2200 (buy passage in advance, everyone will recommend you to queue at 0800, but 1000 is usually early enough). You need a boarding pass and not just a ticket before you can board. A faster ferry service has been approved, which will take 4 hours, but at time of going to press no company had been awarded the contract.

On Tobago (as on Trinidad), buy **bus** tickets in advance as drivers will not accept money. All buses originate in Scarborough. Schedules are changed or cancelled frequently. Buses every ½ hour between Crown Point (airport) and

Scarborough, TT$1.25. Buy tickets from the grey hut outside the airport building where timetable is posted. Also an express bus to Scarborough, TT$2, ticket from souvenir shop, not hut as for the other bus. Route taxis charge TT$4. **Taxi** fares are clearly displayed as you leave the airport: to Scarborough TT$25, the longest journey, to Charlotteville is TT$125. The Crown Point Airport route is the best, every 15-30 mins, 0530-1830; Black Rock route is fair, every 30 mins Mon-Fri 0530-2030, every 60-75 minutes Sat and Sun until 2000. There are less frequent and less reliable routes to Parlatuvier and Charlotteville. The route taxi system is difficult for the foreigner, being based on everyone knowing every car and therefore where it is going.

● **Where To Stay**

In the vicinity of Crown Point: *Tropikist*, (T 639-8512, F 628-1110), US$50, a/c rooms with balcony, pool, rocky beach, has been rec; *Crown Point Beach Hotel*, PO Box 223, (T 639-8781/3, F 639-8731), studios and cabins, pool, US$50-75; *Arthur's On-Sea*, Crown Point, T 639-0196, F 639-4122, kind and helpful, a/c, pool, 4 mins' walk from safe beach, US$45, US$57 triple, rec; *Jimmy's Holiday Resort*, Store Bay, T 639-8292, F 639-3100, US$60 per apartment, bars, eating places, shops nearby. If you turn right out of the airport, and take the first right, you come to *Store Bay Holiday Resort*, T/F 639-8810, 5 mins' walk, do not be fooled by taxi drivers who will charge US$5 for the ride, at US$29 about the cheapest in this area, but self-catering only, 16 apartments, clean, well-furnished, kitchen, gardens, night time security guard, small pool, friendly, good value, rec; next door is *Kariwak Village*, US$60, very nice, cabins, restaurant with excellent food, no beach, pool,

PO Box 27 (T 639-8545/8442, F 639-8441); *Jetway Holiday Resort*, 100m from airport terminal, can be noisy until after 2200, pleasant self-contained units with cooking facilities, friendly, helpful, US$30d, a few mins' walk to Pigeon Point and Store Bay, T 639-8504; a bit further from the main road is *Golden Thistle* (T/F 639-8521) US$40d, US$50 triple summer, US$65 winter, quiet location; *James Holiday Resort*, Crown Point, T/F 639-8084, US$40 winter, US$35 summer for standard room, US$50-40 apartment, US$170 3-bedroom apartment max 12 people, MAP US$16, CP US$5.50, car and jeep rental US$30-35, credit cards accepted, 2 mins' walk from airport, a/c, shower, TV, patio or balcony, restaurant; *Conrado Beach Resort*, Milford Extension Rd, Pigeon Point, T 639-0145, beach front, US$45-60, family owned, excellent service, highly rec. There are lots of guesthouses and small hotels along the road between the airport and Pigeon Point. *Anjo's Villa*, PO Box 148, Crown Point, T 639-7963, 15 mins' walk from airport, use of kitchen, from US$15; *Lewis Villa*, T 639-8022, small units with kitchen, US$10pp, good value; *Classic Resort Guest House*, turn left out of airport and walk along track, US$18 for double room with kitchen and lounge with TV, friendly; *Spence's Terrace*, Crown Point, T 639-8082, US$25-30 per room, kitchenette, bathroom, balcony, new and fresh, rec, near beach and airport, Spence is helpful, car rental available.

Accommodation in **Scarborough** is either in guesthouses or bed and breakfast (contact the *Association* c/o Mr Lloyd Anthony, *Tony's House*, Carnbee, T 639-8836, or the Tourism Development Authority on Tobago; the brochure lists 14 properties, mostly in the SW or near Scarborough, about US$20d). Highly rec is *Glenco Guest House*, Glen Road, Scarborough (rates negotiable according to length of stay), clean, basic, mosquitoes, no fans, breakfast TT$2-3, T 639 2912. *Jacob's Guesthouse*, Scarborough, in a bad area for drugs, no longer rec, US$30d, T 639-2271; *Hope Cottage*, Fort Street, US$11 b&b; several others, eg *Della Mira Guest House*, Windward Rd, T 639-2531, US$35-42; *Miriam's Bed and Breakfast*, or *Federal Villa*, Crooks River, T 639-3926, 6 rooms, US$35d, shared bath, fan, modest but clean and comfortable, 7 mins' walk to harbour, run by friendly and helpful Miriam Edwards, secretary of the Bed and Breakfast Association. *Arnos Vale Hotel*, PO Box 208, T 639-2881, F 639-4629, 30 rooms, US$180, beautiful surroundings, hospitable, dive shop. Ten mins' drive from Scarborough is *Ocean View*, John Dial, T 639-6796, US$30 pp, rec; under same management is *Windy Edge*, Concordia, 12 minutes drive from the harbour, 600 feet above sea level overlooking the Atlantic and the Caribbean, spacious grounds, quiet, highly rec, US$30 pp inc breakfast, evening meals by arrangement US$25-30, route taxis pass by, T 639-5062.

On the **Windward coast**, *Richmond Great House*, T 660-4467, F 639-2213, (see page 737) rates on request, about US$120-165, overlooking Richmond Bay, lovely, airy, quiet, only 3 suites and 2 family rooms; one guest house in Roxborough, ask for Mrs Carter, Police Station Road, TT$25pp, 2 rooms, kitchen, shower, quiet, friendly; *Blue Waters Inn*, Batteaux Bay, Speyside, T 660-4341, F 660-5195, an isolated and delightfully unsophisticated hotel, US$56, 28 rooms, 4 self-catering units for 4 people each, US$80-100 caters for people who want to sit on the beach, bird watchers and divers; *The Speyside Inn*, Windward Road, Speyside, T/F 660-4852, opened 1993 on outskirts of village, 3 rooms with bathroom and fan, US$65d winter, US$50d summer, and 1 self-catering studio apartment, more rooms planned, breakfast inc with home made breads, dinner by reservation only. At **Charlotteville** are *Man O'War Bay Cottages*, T 660-4327, F 660-4328, cottages US$55-105 a night, sleep 4, minimum 2 nights, spacious, well-equipped kitchen, right on beach with tropical gardens behind, barbeque facilities, expensive shop with limited range, check your shopping bill carefully; *Cholson's Chalet* has 1-3 bedroom apartments separated from the beach by the road, TT$60-80,

contact Hewitt Nicholson (T 639-2847) or Pat Nicholson (T 639-8553). *Alyne*, TT$50, very friendly, clean, comfortable; *Venizia*, TT$60-80, new, clean. Ask around for private accommodation, it is available, eg Mrs McCannon's house in Bellaire Road, not luxury but OK; for small houses to rent try asking in *Phebe's Ville View* restaurant. At **Plymouth**, *Tante Loo*, old place but friendly; *Cocrico Inn*, T 639-2961, F 639-6565, US$45, swimming pool; *Mount Irvine Bay Hotel and Golf Course* (see page 725, PO Box 222, T 639-8871, F 639-8800) charges from US$150-510, some deluxe suites, reported badly run and overpriced; *Grafton Beach Resort*, PO Box 25, Black Rock, T 639-0191/9444, F 639 0030, luxury, highly rec, a/c, pool, TV, friendly and efficient service, excellent beach front location in Stonehaven Bay, US$162-550; *Plantation Beach Villas*, Stonehaven Bay, T 639-0455, US$240, 6 villas, pool; *Palm Tree Village Hotel*, Little Rockly Bay, Milford Road, T 639-347/9, F 623-5776, a/c, kitchenette, beach, better beach 500 yards away, US$150, US$240 2-bedroom villa, US$450 4-bedroomed villa, no stores nearby for buying food; *Turtle Beach Hotel*, PO Box 201, Plymouth, T 639-2851, F 639-1495,125 rooms, pool, on beach, tennis, a/c, US$68, double in winter; *Bougainvillea Beach Towers*, Studley Park, swimming pool, a/c, kitchenette, on beach, US$80-200; *Coral Reef Guest House and Apartments*, T 639-2536, F 639-0770, a/c, pool, US$40; *La Belle Creole*, Mt Irvine, PO Box 372,T 639-0908, run by Mrs Gerhild Oliver, English, German, French and Italian spoken, right by golf course, 5 mins' walk from beach, US$70d, US$50s, bed and breakfast, dinner on request, queen sized beds; *Old Grange Inn*, PO Box 297, Buccoo, Mt Irvine, T/F 639-0275, a/c, US$40; in Buccoo on Battery St, *Aunty Flo's*, T 639-9192, TT$40pp, nice, friendly, run by Mrs Flora Howie; *Golf View Apartments*, Buccoo Junction, Mt Irvine, T 639-0979, US$35-45, 7 apartments, 5 rooms, kitchenette; *Blue Horizon*, Jacamas Drive, Mt Irvine, T 639-0432/3/, US$45-50 EP, kitchenette, pool; *Plaza 2*, Milford Road, Canaan, US$14d, no kitchen facilities, away from the beach but buses stop outside; *Samada Guest House*, Milford Road, a/c, kitchenette, US$32; *Credit Union Guest House*, Black Rock, clean, kitchen, bath, 5 mins' walk to the beach, US$10, contact office in Scarborough, Bacolet Street.

There are many cheap guesthouses throughout Tobago and many people take in visitors: ask at any village store (prices for room only).

● **Where To Eat**

The *Beach Bar* at Store Bay has music all day on Sat, and a barbeque from 2000-2400, for TT$100 per head for drinks and small portions of fish and chicken, poor value unless you drink a lot. At the *Store Bay Resort* there are a number of restaurants, including *John Grant's*, many have tables outside near the beach, rec is *Miss Jean's*, US$2 and less for all kind of 'ting', a full meal with drinks for 2 costs less than US$10, crab and dumplings are a speciality but the crabs are woefully small because of overfishing; the restaurant at the *Kariwak Village* has excellent food, well served; nearby is *Golden Spoon* (junction of roads to Scarborough and Pigeon Point, T 639-8078, open for breakfast, lunch and dinner, local dishes) and *Columbus Snackette* (at the crossroads near Crown Reef Hotel). *La Tartaruga*, Buccoo Bay, T 639-0940, Italian restaurant café-bar, PO Box 179, excellent Italian food, reservations essential. The *Papillon Restaurant* at the *Old Grange Inn*, T 639-0275, and the *Sugar Mill* at *Mt Irvine Bay Hotel* have both been rec for excellent meals. *Le Beau Rivage* at the Mt Irvine Golf Course, French and international cuisine; the *Conrado Beach Hotel*, T 639-0145, has local dishes. *Phebe's Ville View*, Charlotteville, nice view of the bay, very good and cheap meals, try the prawns if available, dumplings and curried crab also rec. The *Blue Crab*, Robinson Road, Scarborough, T 639-2737, specializes in local food, good lunch, as do *Gemma's Sea View*, Speyside, T 660-4066, on a tree top platform by the beach, good, filling lunch or dinner, TT$40, good service, nice atmosphere, closed Sat (Adventists) and *Rouselles*, Bacolet Street, T 639-4738; *Joy's*, in Buccoo, small, friendly, good local food for TT$20, barbeque on Wed for TT$15pp; *Old Donkey Cart*, Bacolet, T 639-3551, German wines, closed Wed; *Dillon's Seafood Restaurant*, Crown Point, T 639-8765, fresh fish, good service, but expensive, lobster has been reported as too small ie it should not have been caught. The bar/restaurant at Pigeon Point is good value, but closes at 1700. *Buddies Café* in the Mall, Scarborough, Tobago, is reasonable, T 639-3355; *The Cabin Pub*, opposite the Customs House near the port in Scarborough, a favourite "liming" spot for locals and yachties, owned by Gus, a Tobagonian who is full of stories, open from

0900, lots of happy people, rec. The *Black Rock Café* on Black Rock main road, T 639-7625, has been rec for very good food, reservations essential.

Crown Point Supermarket is well-stocked but expensive; small huts along Store Bay Road are cheaper.

● **Entertainment**

Though not as lively as Trinidad, Tobago offers dancing in its hotels. The Buccoo Folk Theatre gives an attractive show of dancing and calypso every Thur at 2100. There is a Tobago Folk Performing Company. In Scarborough, *El Tropical* is a club frequented mostly by locals; it has a live show every Sat night at about 2330. Also *JG's Disco*, nightly. The *Starting Gate Pub*, Shirvan Road, is rec.

INFORMATION FOR VISITORS

● **Documents**

Passports are required by all visitors aged 16 and over. **Visas** are not required by nationals of most Commonwealth countries, West European countries, Brazil, Colombia, Israel, Pakistan and Turkey; for US citizens for visits up to 2 months; and for Venezuelans for stays of up to 14 days. Some Commonwealth citizens do need visas, however; these include Australia, New Zealand, India, Sri Lanka, Nigeria, Uganda, Tanzania, and Papua New Guinea. A visa normally requires 48 hours' notice. A waiver for those with no visa can be obtained at the airport, but it costs TT$100, double the ordinary visa price. **Entry permits** for one month are given on arrival; they can be extended at the immigration office in Port of Spain (at 67 Frederick Street) for TT$5. This is a time-consuming process, so try and get a 3-month entry permit if planning a long stay.

After 6 weeks visitors must get a tax clearance from the Inland Revenue office on Edward St. Even though you may not get asked for it all travellers need a return ticket to their country of origin, dated, not open-ended, proof that they can support themselves during their stay, an address at which they will be staying in Trinidad (the tourist office at the airport can help in this respect). A ferry ticket to Venezuela has often satisfied immigration officials instead of a full return ticket to your own country. Only those coming from an infected area need a yellow fever inoculation certificate. People going to Venezuela can obtain a tourist card (free of charge) at the Aeropostal office; this means buying a return ticket but this can be refunded or changed if an alternative ticket out of Venezuela is later purchased.

● **How To Get There By Air**

BWIA and Air Caribbean link Trinidad with Tobago (several daily flights). **USA**: United Airlines (from Denver, Miami, Orlando, San Francisco and some other cities in high season); BWIA (Miami, New York); American Airlines (Philadelphia, Miami, Washington DC in high season, Puerto Rico). **Canada**: Air Canada and BWIA from Toronto. **Europe**: British Airways (shared route from London with BWIA via Barbados or Antigua); BWIA (from Frankfurt, London, Zurich). British Airways is to end flights on 28 October 1994. The Tobago route will be serviced by its subsidiary, Caledonian Airways on a weekly basis. **Venezuela**: United Airlines and Aeropostal from Caracas (book as far in advance as possible, ticket valid 7-17 days, you cannot buy it at Caracas airport, Liat also sometimes stops here on its Caracas-Barbados flight, worth checking). **Guyana**: BWIA, Suriname Airways and ALM, daily flights from Georgetown. **Suriname**: Gonini Air Service and Suriname Airways from Paramaribo. **Inter-Island**: BWIA, Liat and ALM airlines connect Trinidad with other Caribbean islands including Anguilla, Antigua, Barbados, Curaçao, Dominica, Grenada, Jamaica (Kingston), Martinique, St Lucia, St Maarten, St Vincent, San Juan, Puerto Rico (also American Airlines) and Tortola (BVI). There are flights to Tobago (Crown Point Airport) with Liat and/or BWIA from Barbados, Frankfurt, Grenada, St Lucia, London and Miami, eliminating the need to change planes at Piarco airport. BWIA (and possibly other airlines) is reluctant to let you leave unless you have an onward ticket from your immediate destination to the next one.

There is a TT$75 exit tax. Passengers in transit do not have to pay, but are required to obtain an "exempt" ticket from the departure tax window before being allowed through to the immigration officers on the way to the departure lounge.

Try to avoid overnight connections at Piarco airport. Airline schedules ensure that it is possible to arrive at Piarco after the check-in counters have closed until next morning, so you cannot go through to the departure lounge. There is nowhere safe to leave baggage. There is a restaurant upstairs and a bar but they close

at 2330. By then the benches in the observation deck are occupied, the seats downstairs are uncomfortable and open to the elements, leaving you and your bags the only safe option of a locked toilet cubicle. If you are in transit always check that your bags have not been off-loaded at Piarco, most are not checked through despite assurances.

● **Airline Offices**

BWIA is at 30 Edward Street (T 625-1010/1, 625-5866/8), opens for reservations at 0800; there is a separate desk for Tobago flights (take a number and wait in the queue; be prepared for a long wait, particularly for international tickets). BWIA at Piarco airport, T 664-4871/3400 (open later than Edward Street office for reservations for Tobago); also at Carlton Centre, San Fernando, T 657-9712/1359, and at Crown Point airport, Tobago, T 639-3130. Aeropostal, 13 Pembroke Street, T 623-8201/6522. The following are at 90 Independence Square: American Airlines (T 625-1661), British Airways (T 625-1816); Air Canada is at 88 Independence Square (T 625-2195). KLM and ALM, 1 Richmond Street, T 625-1719. Guyana Airways, 44-48 Edward Street, T 627-2753/625-1171. LIAT, CIC Building, 122-124 Frederick Street, T 623-1837/4480, on Tobago T 639-0484. There is a 15% VAT on airline tickets purchased in Trinidad and Tobago.

● **How To Get There By Sea**

The Geest Line started a service to Trinidad from Barry, South Wales, UK, in 1992, see page 13. A weekly passenger and cargo ferry service run by Windward Lines Limited sails from Trinidad to Güiria, Venezuela on Tues 1700, arriving 2130, returning from Güiria on Wed 2300, arriving Trinidad Thur 0700. This service alternates with a ferry to Margarita (Pampatar), every other week, with 12 hours in Margarita. On Thur 1600 it sets off for St Vincent, Barbados and St Lucia, arriving there Sat 0800, returning Sun 0800, getting back to Trinidad Tues 0800. Check in 2 hours before departure in Trinidad (1 hour in other ports). The schedule is printed in 2 daily newspapers. For information and tickets contact Global Steamship Agencies Ltd, Mariner's Club, Wrightson Road, PO Box 966, Port of Spain, T 624-2279, 625-2547, F 627-5091. For a round trip to St Lucia the fare is US$95 (one-way fares are 65% of return), cabins are US$20-50/night, TT$621, return fare to Güiria US$60. Every Fri morning a boat carrying racing pigeons leaves for Güiria, Venezuela. Contact Francis Sagones, T 632-0040; or talk to Siciliano Bottini in the Agencia Naviera in Güiria for sea transport in the other direction. Fishing boats and trading vessels ply this route frequently and can often be persuaded to take passengers. Be careful to get your passport stamped at both ends of the journey. A Trinidadian, Adrian Winter Roach, travels at least once a week with his boat *El Cuchillo*, and charges US$60 one way, US$100 return, he can be contacted in Venezuela through the Distribuidora Beirut, Calle Valdez 37, Güiria, T/F 81677.

● **Customs**

Duty-free imports: 200 cigarettes or 50 cigars or ½lb tobacco, 1 quart wine or spirits, and TT$50-worth of gifts. Perfume may not be imported free of duty, but may be deposited with Customs until departure. Passengers in transit, or on short visits, can deposit goods such as liquor with Customs at the airport and retrieve it later free of charge.

● **Taxis**

Look for **cars with first letter H** on licence plates (no other markings). Agree on a price before the journey and determine whether the price is in TT or US dollars. Taxis are expensive, although **route taxis** (similar to colectivos) are very cheap. These cannot be distinguished from ordinary taxis, so ask the driver. They travel along fixed routes, like buses, but have no set stops, so you can hail them and be dropped anywhere along the route. During rush hour it is not easy to hail them, however, and in general it takes time to master how they work. Be warned that route taxis are not covered by insurance so you cannot claim against the driver if you are involved in an accident. There are also **"pirate" taxis** with the P registration of a private car, which cost the same as the ordinary taxis, although you can sometimes bargain with the drivers. "Ghost" taxis accept fares and drive off with your luggage as well— be warned. Be careful if hitching on Tobago as the cars that stop often prove to be pirate taxis.

● **Car Rentals**

Car rental can be difficult on Trinidad, particularly at weekends, because of heavy demand from Trinidadians, many of whom cannot afford to buy but rent on a long term basis. Best to make reservations in advance. Several companies do not accept credit cards, but require a considerable cash deposit. Small cars can be rented from TT$160 a day upwards, unlimited mileage, check tyres before driving off. Deposit TT$500-1,000 (varies from company to company, as does method of payment), book in advance. Insurance costs TT$6-7. Many car rental companies have offices at the airport. Car rental firms are numerous and include Auto Rentals Ltd, Uptown Mall, Edward Street, Port of Spain (623-3063), Piarco (T 669-2277), and at Cruise Ship Complex, 1 D Wrighton Road (T 624-8687); Bacchus Taxi and Car Rental, 37 Tragarete Rd (622-5588); Lord Calloo, 100 la Paille Village, Caroni (T/F 645-5182), helpful, check tyres; Singh's, 7-9 Wrightson Rd (625-4247) and at airport (T 645-5417, F 664-3860). Also on Tobago: Auto Rentals Ltd, Crown Point Airport (T 639-0644, F 639-0313); Banana Rentals at *Kariwak Village*, cars and jeeps, TT$125/day, scooters TT$56/day (deposit TT$350), bicycles TT$25/day (T 639-8441/8545); Suzuki Jeep Rental (and small cars), and Cherry Scooter Rental at *Sandy Point Beach Club* (scooters and deposit cheaper than Banana); Tobago Travel, P O Box 163, Store Bay Road, Crown Point (639-8778/8105, F 639-8786); Baird's, Lower Sangster Hill Road (639-2528) and other agencies. Bicycles can be hired at the *Mount Irvine Bay Hotel*. Some companies only rent for a minimum of 3 days.

Driving is on the left and the roads are narrow and winding. A major re-surfacing programme brought considerable improvement in the roads in 1994. On Tobago the roads are good in the S but badly maintained further N. There are lots of pot holes in Scarborough and traffic weaves about all over the place to avoid them. The road between Charlotteville and Bloody Bay is for 4-wheel drive vehicles only. Mountain bikes are fine on these roads if you can stand the hills and the heat. International and most foreign driving licences are accepted for up to 90 days, after that the visitor must apply for a Trinidad and Tobago licence and take a test. Visitors must always carry their driving document with them. Do not leave anything in your car, theft is frequent.

● **Where To Stay**

There are many hotels on the islands and the better known ones are expensive, but there are very good guest houses and smaller hotels which are reasonable. Information about accommodation can be obtained from Trinidad and Tobago Tourism Development Authority (TDA) at 134-138 Frederick Street, Port of Spain. Their office at Piarco airport is helpful.

A 15% value added tax is charged at all hotels and in most a 10% service charge is added to the bill. Some, like the *Hilton*, add a 2% surcharge. See **Island Information** sections for details of hotels.

● Camping

Camping on Trinidad is unsafe and is not rec. Try the Boca Islands to the W. On Tobago, it is possible near the Mt Irvine beach. Ask the taxi drivers for advice on where to camp. *Canoe Bay Resorts* has 50 camp sites available, TT$20 per adult and TT$5 for children per night, includes toilet and shower but use of kitchen costs extra, T 639-4055. At Store Bay and on the road to *Kariwak Village*, etc, there are small stores selling provisions.

● Food

A wide variety of European, American and traditional West Indian dishes (these include pork souse, black pudding, roast sucking pig, sancoche and callaloo stews, and many others) is served at hotels and guest houses. Some also specialize in Créole cooking. There is also, of course, a strong East Indian influence in the local cuisine. Seafood, particularly crab, is excellent. Do not eat local oysters: their habitat has become polluted. Turtle meat is sold even though turtles are protected, do not buy it. The many tropical fruits and vegetables grown locally include the usual tropical fruits, and sapodillas, eddoes and yam tanias. The variety of juices and ice creams made from the fruit is endless. For those economizing, the *roti*, a chapatti pancake which comes in various forms, filled with peppery stew, is very good. The best place for *roti* is the *Hot Shoppe for Hot Roti*, on Mucurapo St, W of downtown Port of Spain. *Buss up shut* (shut means shirt) is a paratha, or Indian bread accompaniment to curries. *Pelau*, savoury rice and meat, is also good, but when offered pepper, refuse unless you are accustomed to the hottest of curries or *chili* dishes. Try also *saheena*, deep-fried patties of spinach, dasheen, split peas and mango sauce. *Buljol* is a salt fish with onions, tomatoes, avocado and pepper. *Callaloo* is a thick soup based on dasheen leaves. *Doubles* are curried chick peas (channa) in a tiny roti case. *Pastelles*, eaten at Christmas, are maize flour parcels stuffed with minced meat, olives, capers and raisins, steamed in a banana leaf (known as *hallacas* in Venezuela). A hops is a crusty bread roll. Dumplings are a must on Tobago, particularly good with crab. The shopping malls offer a variety of places to eat, including Créole, Indian, Chinese, etc. On Tobago there are lots of small eating places, clean and nice, where you can get a freshly cooked meal and a beer for US$3-4pp.

A local drink is mauby, like ginger beer, and the rum punches are rec. Fresh lime juice is also rec; it is sometimes served with a dash of Angostura bitters. Local beers are Carib ("each bottle tastes different") and Stag ("the recession fighter"), both owned by the same company which also brews Heineken and Guinness. A nice place to drink Guinness is the *Cricket Wicket*, in Tragarete Road, opp the Queen's Park Oval.

● Tipping

If no service charge on bill, 10% for hotel staff and restaurant waiters; taxi drivers, 10% of fare, minimum of 25 cents (but no tip in route taxis); dock-side and airport porters, say 25 cents for each piece carried; hairdressers (in all leading hotels), 50 cents.

● Shopping

The main Port of Spain shopping area is in Frederick Street, less exciting but pleasanter are Long Circular Mall at the junction of Long Circular Rd and Patna Street, St James, West Mall, Cocorite, Port of Spain, Ellerslie Plaza on the way to Maraval, close to Savannah, considered to be the best in the country. Purchases can be made at in-bond shops in Port of Spain and at the airport. There is a huge selection of duty-free shops, accessible to both arriving and departing passengers, selling everything, including computers. Markets offer wide varieties of fruit. Handicrafts can also be purchased at markets. In Port of Spain there is a craft market in Independence Square with leather, hand painted T-shirts etc. There are also street vendors on Frederick Street and elsewhere. Crafts also at East Mall on Charlotte Street. Good quality local pottery in a variety of designs is available from Ajoupa Pottery, owned by Rory and Bunty O'Connor. You can get it in Port of Spain but a wider selection can be viewed at their kiln at Freeport, central Trinidad; T 622-5597 at Port of Spain shop, or T 673-0604 at kiln/factory. The Tourism Development Authority has a list of suppliers of traditional items such as batik and fabrics, straw and cane work, wood carvings, leather, ceramics, copper work and steelpans. The Central Market is on the Beetham Highway. Do not purchase turtle shell, black coral, or other protected, shell items. For music, try Crosby's Music Centre, 54 Western Main Road,

St James, or Rhyner's, 54 Prince Street, Port of Spain. Production costs are a problem and despite being the main music outlets in this island of music they frequently have no stock.

● **Bookshops**
Metropolitan Books, Colsort Mall, good selection; R I K Services Ltd, Queen Street, Port of Spain, and 104 High Street, San Fernando; Cosmic Book Services, West Mall; Inprint Bookstore, 35 Independence Square; St Aubyns Book Services, Palm Plaza, Maraval. There are second hand bookshops in Town Centre Mall and various side streets. Generally the selection is poor, particularly for Caribbean novels which is disappointing in a country with such a long literary tradition.

● **Banks**
In Port of Spain: Republic Bank Ltd (formerly Barclays, gives cash on Visa card), 11-17 Park St, T 625-4411, F 623-0371; Royal Bank of Trinidad and Tobago, 3B Chancery Lane, T 623-4291; Bank of Commerce, 72 Independence Square, T 625-9325; Bank of Nova Scotia, Park and Richmond Streets, T 625-3566; Citibank, 74 Independence Square, T 625-1040; Citicorp Merchant Bank, same address, T 623-3344. In 1993 3 banks which had been brought under Central Bank control were merged; the Trinidad Cooperative Bank, the National Commercial Bank of Trinidad and Tobago, and the Workers' Bank merged to become the First Citizens Bank. All banks charge a fee for cashing travellers' cheques, some more than others, so check first. Banks generally will not change Venezuelan or other South American currencies.

● **Currency**
The Trinidad and Tobago dollar, fixed at TT$2.40 = US$1 since 1976, was devalued to TT$3.60 = US$1 in December, 1985, then to TT$4.25 = US$1 in August, 1988 and finally floated in April 1993. The rate moved initially to TT$5.75, a depreciation of 26%, but then stabilized at around TT$5.90. Notes are for TT$1, 5, 10, 20 and 100. Coins are for 1, 5, 10, 25 and 50 cents. A maximum of TT$200 may be taken out of the country. When changing money keep the receipt so that what remains unspent can be changed back, as long as there is no more money taken out than was brought in. Travellers' cheques and major credit cards are accepted almost everywhere.

● **Warning**
The people of both islands are, as a rule, very friendly but several areas are no longer safe at night, especially for women. To the E of Charlotte Street, Port of Spain becomes increasingly unsafe. Laventille and East Dry River are to be avoided. Central Port of Spain is fairly safe, even at night, as there are plenty of police patrols. Care must be taken everywhere at night and walking on the beach is not safe. Stick to main roads and look as if you know where you are going. The incidence of theft has risen sharply. Avoid the area around the port or bus terminal except when making a journey. A favourite local saying is "Tobago is Paradise, Trinidad is New York". Take care accordingly but do not underestimate crime in Tobago. We have received reports of theft and muggings on the Pigeon Point road and parts of Scarborough are known to have crack houses.

● **Health**
There are hospitals in Port of Spain, San Fernando, Scarborough (T 639-2551) and Mount Hope, as well as several district hospitals and community health centres. The Port of Spain General Hospital is at 169 Charlotte Street, T 623-2951.

● **Climate**
The climate on the islands is tropical, but, thanks to the trade winds, rarely excessively hot. Temperatures vary between 21° and 37°C, the coolest time being from December to April. There is a dry season from January to mid-May and a wet season from June to November, with a short break in September. It can rain for days at a stretch but usually falls in heavy showers. Humidity is fairly high.

● **Clothing**
Beachwear should be kept for the beach. In the evening people dress more smartly but are less formal than, for example, the Bahamians.

● **Business Hours**
Government offices 0800-1600, Mon-Fri. Banks: 0900-1400, Mon-Thur, 0900-1200, 1500-1700, Fri. Some banks have extended hours until 1800. Businesses and shops: 0800-1600/ 1630, Mon-Fri (shops 0800-1200 on Sat). Shopping malls usually stay open until about 2000, Mon-Sat.

● **Public Holidays**
New Year's Day, Carnival Sunday, Monday and Tuesday, before Ash Wednesday (not officially holidays but everyone regards them as such), Good Friday, Easter Monday, Whit Monday,

Corpus Christi, Eid ul-Fitr (8 or 9 March in 1995), Labour or Butler's Day (19 June), Emancipation Day (1 August), Independence Day (31 August), Republic Day (24 September); Divali (23 October in 1995), Christmas Day, Boxing Day.

Special Events: All Souls' Day (2 November) is not a holiday, but is celebrated. The Hindu festival of Divali is a holiday, but Phagwah (Feb/March) is not. Similarly, of the Moslem festivals, Eid ul-Fitr is a public holiday, but Eid ul-Azha and Yaum um-Nabi are not (all fall 10-11 days earlier each year).

● **Time Zone**

Atlantic Standard Time, 4 hours behind GMT, 1 hour ahead of EST.

● **Useful Addresses**

(Port of Spain) **Canadian** High Commission, Huggins Building, 72 South Quay, T 623-7254, F 624-4016); **US** Embassy, 15 Queen's Park West (T 622-6371/6, F 628-5462), 0700-1700; **British** High Commission, will be moving in late 1993 to a new building on Elizabeth St at the NE corner of Queen's Park Oval, but until then is at the 3rd floor, Furness House, 90 Independence Square (PO Box 778), T 625-2861-6, F 623-0621, 0730-1530; **New Zealand** Consulate, Goe F Huggins Building, 233 Western Main Road, Cocorite, opp Community Hospital (PO Box 823), T 622-7020, F 622-6673; **German** Embassy, 7-9 Marli St, PO Box 828 (T 628-1630/2, F 628-5278); **French** Embassy, 6th floor, Tatil Bldg, Maraval Rd, T 622-7446/7, F 628-2632; **Danish** Consulate General, 72-4 South Quay, PO Box 179, T 623-4700, F 624-4981; **Brazilian** Embassy, 18 Sweet Briar Rd, St Clair (T 622-5779/5771, F 622-4323; **Venezuelan** Embassy, 16 Victoria Av (T 627-9823/4), 0900-1300, 1400-1600, Consulate at same address, T 627-9773/4. Changes of address, and other representatives, can be checked at the Ministry of External Affairs, T 623-4116/60.

● **Weights And Measures**

Trinidad and Tobago have gone metric, so road signs are given in kilometres.

● **Electric Current**

110 or 220 volts, 60 cycles AC.

● **Post And Telephones**

The main Post Office is on Wrightson Road, Port of Spain, and is open 0700-1700, Mon-Fri. Stamps for Europe TT$2. The main Telecommunications Services of Trinidad and Tobago Ltd (TSTT) office on Frederick St operates international telephone, cable, telex and fax. There is a TSTT telephone office in Scarborough, Tobago. The service for international calls has improved greatly, with direct dialling to all countries but from anywhere other than the TSTT office it can be difficult and expensive. The fax, telex and telegraph service shuts from 2300 Sat to 2300 Sun and on public holidays except for "life or death" messages. This means no faxes for 3 days over Carnival. The internal telephone system is being improved. Phone cards are available for TT$15, 30 or 60, plus 15% VAT, from TSTT offices, banks, airport, cruise ship complex etc.

● **Press**

The main daily papers are the *Trinidad and Tobago Express* and the *Trinidad Guardian*, both good. A third newspaper, *Newsday*, was launched in 1993. The *Mirror* on Fri and Sun has interesting investigative journalism. *Trinidad and Tobago Review* is a serious monthly. *Tobago News* is weekly. *Galerie* is an excellent arts glossy. There are several racier weekly papers which appear on Fri or Sat. *Punch*, *Bomb*, *Heat* and *Blast* are sensational tabloids, not to be missed by the visitor who wants the gossip. The official visitor's guide, *Discover Trinidad and Tobago* is published twice a year and distributed free to all visitors by the TDA and through hotels. There are 3 book-length guides including *Trinidad and Tobago, An Introduction and Guide*, by Jeremy Taylor (Macmillan 1991).

● **Travel Agency**

The Travel Centre Limited, Level 2, Uptown Mall, Edward Street, Port of Spain, T 625-1636/4266, F 623-5101 (P O Box 1254) is an American Express Travel Service Representative. The Davemar Reservations Agency, 2 Aylce Glen, Petit Valley, T 637-7583, run by Marjorie Cowie, can arrange accommodation in hotels, guesthouses or self-catering and organize sightseeing tours. On Tobago, Peter Gremli is a rec tour guide, friendly, knowledgeable and popular. On Trinidad, in Arima, ask for Matthew, an elderly taxi driver who knows a lot about everything in the region (TT$140 day tour, 1993).

● **Trinidad And Tobago Tourism Development Authority (TDA)**

The TDA is now the tourism division of a new government agency called the Tourism and Industrial Development Company Trinidad and Tobago Ltd (TIDCO). The address was due to be changed in September 1994 but no one knew where as we went to press. Until the move, the TDA was at 134-138 Frederick Street, Port of Spain, PO Box 222, T 623-1932/4, F 623-3848. Lists of hotels, restaurants, tour operators, monthly schedule of events, maps for sale etc. Piarco Tourist Bureau (at the airport), T 664-5196, helpful with hotel or guest house reservations for your first night. You can also buy maps of Trinidad and Port of Spain here. In Tobago the Division of Tourism is in Scarborough, NIB Mall, there is a kiosk, and the head office is on the third level, next to *Buddy's Restaurant* (T 639-2125/3566, F 639-3566), or at Crown Point airport, T 639-0509.

Overseas offices all have up-to-date hotel lists: **USA**: Suite 1508, 25 West 43rd St, New York, NY 10036, T (212)719-0540, F (212)719-0988. **UK**: 8a Hammersmith Broadway, London W6 7AL, T 081-741-4466, F 081-741-1013.

Our warmest thanks go to David Renwick of Port of Spain for updating this chapter.

THE GUIANAS

L IKE the West Indians, the people of the three Guianas, Guyana (formerly British Guiana), Suriname (formerly Dutch Guiana) and French Guyane, are not regarded as belonging to Latin America. The explanation of these three non-Iberian countries on the South American continent goes back to the early days of the Spanish conquest of the New World. There was no gold or any other apparent source of wealth to attract the attention of the Spanish discoverers. This part of the coast, which Columbus had first sighted in 1498, seemed to them not only barren but scantily populated and seemingly uninhabitable. The English, the French and the Dutch, anxious to establish a foothold in this part of the world, were not so fastidious.

All three countries are geographically very similar: along the coast runs a belt of narrow, flat marshy land, at its widest in Suriname. This coastland carries almost all the crops and most of the population. Behind lies a belt of crystalline upland, heavily gouged and weathered. The bauxite, gold and diamonds are in this area. Behind this again is the massif of the Guiana Highlands. They reach a height of 3,000 feet (915m), in the Tumuc-Humac range, the divide between French Guyane and Suriname, and Brazil, and 9,219 feet (2,810m) at flat-topped Mount Roraima, where Guyana, Venezuela and Brazil all meet.

GUYANA

G UYANA has an area of 83,000 square miles, nearly the size of Britain, but only about 2.5% (or 1,328,000 acres) is cultivated. About 90% of the population lives on the narrow coastal plain, either in Georgetown, the capital, or in villages along the main road running from Charity in the W to the Suriname border. Most of the plain is below sea level. Large wooden houses stand on stilts above ground level. A sea wall keeps out the Atlantic and the fertile clay soil is drained by a system of dykes; sluice gates are opened to let out water at low tide. Separate irrigation channels are used to bring water back to the fields in dry weather. In several places fresh water is supplied by reservoirs, known as conservancies. Most of the western third of the coastal plain is undrained and uninhabited. The strange cultural mix: Dutch place names and drainage techniques, Hindu temples, mosques, coconut palms and calypso music, reflect the chequered history of the country.

Four major rivers cross the coastal plain, (from W to E) the Essequibo, the Demerara, the Berbice, and the Courantyne (which forms the frontier with Suriname). Only the Demerara is crossed by bridges. Elsewhere ferries must be used. At the mouth of the Essequibo river, 21 miles wide, are islands the size of Barbados. The lower reaches of these rivers are navigable (75 miles up the Demerara to Linden and 45 miles up the Essequibo to the mouth of the Cuyuni River); but waterfalls and rapids prevent them being used by large boats to reach the interior.

Inland from the coastal plain most of the country is covered by thick rain forest, although in the E there is a large area of grassland. Some timber has been extracted, but the main economic activity is mining: principally bauxite, but gold and diamonds are sifted from the river beds by miners using mercury (at considerable environmental cost). The largest goldmine in the western hemisphere has been opened by Omai Goldmines of Canada on the W bank of the Essequibo river. It is located in a fairly remote area and is planned to produce 250,000 ozs of gold for ten years. Large areas of rain forest are still undisturbed and even the more accessible areas have varied and spectacular wildlife, including brightly-plumaged birds. The timber industry has been based primarily on Greenhart, a wood renowned for its resistance to sea water. It is used in piers and piles around the world and, until the introduction of carbon fibre fishing rods, was a favourite with fishermen and women. When the Duke of Edinburgh visited Guyana in 1992 he was presented with two Greenhart rods. Also in 1992, however, a tract of land totalling between 7 and 8% of Guyana's land area was granted to a Korean/Malaysian consortium for logging (in 1993 the concession was under investigation for its likely environmental impact). At any event, general timber exports are increasing, although Guyana's loggers practise selective; as opposed to clear felling in an effort to foster a sustainable timber industry. Towards the Venezuelan border the rain forest rises in a series of steep escarpments, with spectacular waterfalls, the highest and best-known of which are the Kaieteur Falls on the Potaro river. In the southwest of the country is the Rupununi Savanna, an area of open grassland more easily reached from Brazil than from Georgetown.

The area W of the Essequibo river, about 70% of the national territory, is claimed by Venezuela. Another area in

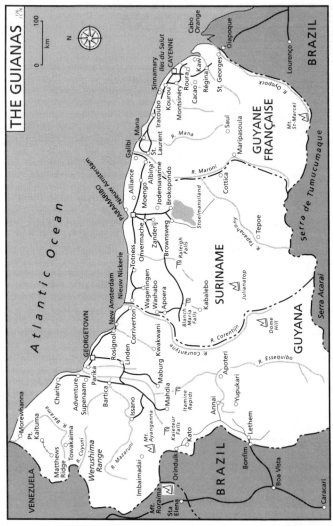

the SE, between the Koeroeni and New rivers, is claimed by Suriname.

Until the 1920s there was little natural increase in population, but the eradication of malaria and other diseases has since led to a rapid growth in population,

particularly among the East Indians (Asian), who, according to most estimates comprise over 50% of the population. The 1980 census showed the following ethnic distribution: East Indian 51.4%; black (African Negro and

Bush negro) 30.5%; mixed 11%; Amerindian 5.3% (Carib 3.7%, Arawak 1.4%); Chinese 0.2%; white (mostly Portuguese) 0.1%; other 1.5%. Descendants of the original Amerindian inhabitants are divided into nine ethnic groups, including the Akawaio, Makuxi and PeMonday. Some have lost their isolation and moved to the urban areas, others keenly maintain aspects of their traditional culture and identity.

History

The country was first partially settled between 1616 and 1621 by the Dutch West India Company, who erected a fort and depot at Fort Kyk-over-al (County of Essequibo). The first English attempt at settlement was made by Captain Leigh on the Oiapoque River (now French Guyane) in 1604, but he failed to establish a permanent settlement. Lord Willoughby, famous in the early history of Barbados, founded a settlement in 1663 at Suriname, which was captured by the Dutch in 1667 and ceded to them at the Peace of Breda in exchange for New York. The Dutch held the three colonies till 1796 when they were captured by a British fleet. The territory was restored to the Dutch in 1802, but in the following year was retaken by Great Britain, which finally gained it in 1814, when the three counties of Essequibo, Berbice and Demerara were merged to form British Guiana.

During the 17th century the Dutch and English settlers established posts up-river, in the hills, mostly as trading points with the Amerindian natives. Plantations were laid out and worked by slaves from Africa. Poor soil defeated this venture, and the settlers retreated with their slaves to the coastal area in mid-18th century: the old plantation sites can still be detected from the air. Coffee and cotton were the main crops up to the end of the 18th century, but sugar had become the dominant crop by 1820. In 1834 slavery was abolished. Many of the slaves scattered as small landholders, and the plantation owners had to look for another source of labour. It was found in indentured workers from India, a few Chinese, and some Portuguese labourers from the Azores and Madeira. At the end of their indentures many settled in Guyana.

The end of the colonial period was politically turbulent, with rioting between the mainly Indo-Guyanese People's Progressive Party (PPP), led by Dr Cheddi Jagan, and the mainly Afro-Guyanese People's National Congress (PNC), under Mr Forbes Burnham. The PNC, favoured over the PPP by the colonial authorities, formed a government in 1964 and retained office until 1992. Guyana is one of the few countries in the Caribbean where political parties have polarized along racial lines. As a result, tensions between the ethnic groups have persisted.

On 26 May 1966 Guyana gained independence, and on 23 February 1970 it became a cooperative republic within the Commonwealth, adopting a new constitution. Another new constitution was adopted in 1980; this declared Guyana to be in transition from capitalism to socialism. Many industries, including bauxite and sugar, were nationalized in the 1970s and close relations with the USSR and Eastern Europe were developed. Following the death of President Forbes Burnham in August 1985, Mr Desmond Hoyte became President. Since then, overseas investors have been invited back and relations with the United States have improved.

Elections to the National Assembly and to the Presidency have been held regularly since independence, but have been widely criticized as fraudulent. The main opposition parties were the PPP, still led by Dr Jagan, and the Working People's Alliance, which attracts support from both East Indian and African communities. Having been delayed since May 1991, national assembly and presidential elections were finally held on 5 October 1992. The polling was monitored by both the Carter Center and a team from the Commonwealth, who declared the elections free and fair even though the campaign was not free of incidents. The PPP/Civic party, led by Dr Jagan, won power after 28 years in opposition, and the installation of a government by democratic means was greeted with optimism. The result also prompted foreign investors to study potential opportunities in Guyana. Recovery has to some extent begun, with two years of positive gdp growth recorded, but many feel that the government has not been quick enough in making important decisions. The economic recovery programme which aided economic improvement also seriously eroded workers' real income and hit the middle classes very hard. The first half of 1994 was marked by protests and strikes for more pay.

Government

A Prime Minister and cabinet are responsible to the National Assembly, which has 65 members elected for a maximum term of five years. The President is Head of State. The country is divided into ten administrative regions.

The Economy

Apart from instant, temporary prosperity brought about by the brief non-oil commodities boom in the mid-1970s, which raised gdp growth to 10.4% in 1975, Guyana's economy was in almost permanent recession between 1970 and 1990, despite considerable, unexploited potential in hydroelectric power, minerals and forestry. While Venezuela's long standing claim to the Essequibo region, within which most of these resources are situated, discouraged investment, other factors were more to blame. Inefficient management in the dominant state sector covering vital sugar and bauxite in-

dustries, an investment climate which discouraged both domestic and foreign savings, and an acute foreign exchange shortage, resulted in poor performances from the key agricultural and mining sectors, and a largely moribund manufacturing sector.

In 1991, the economy experienced a dramatic turn around, with improvements in almost every sector, especially rice, sugar and gold, promoting 6.1% growth in gdp. An even higher level, 7.7%, was recorded in 1992, rising to 8.3% in 1993. Under an IMF-approved Economic Recovery Programme, a number of state-owned companies were privatized, with others earmarked for divestment. Major foreign investment in gold and timber were expected to increase these industries' foreign exchange earnings. Inflation was cut from a rate of 75% in 1991 to 7% in 1993.

Most agriculture is concentrated on the coastal plain. Sugar is the main crop, and has vied with bauxite and alumina as the most important source of export earnings. Rice is the second most important crop, and a useful foreign exchange earner, though significant quantities of rice production are bartered or export proceeds are undeclared through trade with South American neighbours, especially Suriname and Brazil.

Guyana is the world's largest producer of calcined bauxite, the highest grade of the mineral, and currently has roughly half the world market, though competition from China is becoming stronger.

A series of devaluations of the Guyana dollar between January 1987 and February 1991 culminated in the alignment of the official exchange rate with that of licensed exchange houses. These and other adjustment measures proved beneficial both for the current account and for government finances. The Government struggled to come to terms with the IMF, which declared Guyana ineligible for further assistance in May 1985 because of payment arrears. It was rewarded in June 1990 when the Bank for International Settlements and a group of donor countries provided funds to clear the country's arrears to the IMF and other creditors. This opened the way for lending from a variety of sources, including World Bank support for a Social Impact Amelioration Programme aimed at easing the hardship inflicted on lower income groups by the Economic Recovery Programme.

Breaking with the doctrines he espoused in opposition, President Jagan continued his predecessor's free market policies. After the 1992 elections, Guyana benefitted from substantial debt cancellations (eg from Britain and from the Paris Club creditor countries) and debt reschedulings. The election result also opened the way for renewed overseas aid. In January 1994, the government's efforts to reform the economy were rewarded by international financial institutions and foreign governments with funds to cover Guyana's financing requirements until end-1996 and for infrastructure projects. Guyana entered negotiations for closer cooperation with Barbados and Trinidad and Tobago. Rebuilding the economy, however, remained a monumental task as an estimated 75 cents in every dollar still had to be used for debt repayment.

Guyana has suffered from serious economic problems for over 15 years. Wages are very low and many people depend on overseas remittances or "parallel market" activities to survive. There are frequent shortages of many basic items, although the country is basically self-sufficient for its food supply. Many foreign goods are readily available. The country's infrastructure is seriously run down. There are many electricity blackouts, sometimes lasting for several hours, but not necessarily every day. Increased generating capacity has eased the situation and in mid-1994 the government was tendering for electricity supply from international companies. During power cuts no

GUYANA : FACT FILE

Geographic

Land area	215,083 sq km
forested	83.2%
pastures	6.2%
cultivated	2.5%

Demographic

Population (1992)	748,000
annual growth rate (1987-92)	-0.2%
urban	34.5%
rural	65.5%
density	3.5 per sq km
Religious affiliation	
Christian	42.4%
Hindu	37.1%
Muslim	8.7%
Birth rate per 1,000 (1991)	23.0
	(world av 26.4)
Death rate per 1,000 (1991)	7.0
	(world av 9.2)

Education and Health

Life expectancy at birth,	
male	61 years
female	68 years
Infant mortality rate	
per 1,000 live births (1991)	51.0
Physicians (1989)	1 per 6,809 persons
Hospital beds	1 per 341 persons
Calorie intake as %	
of FAO requirement	110%
Population age 25 and over	
with no formal schooling	8.1%
Literate males (over 15)	97.5%
Literate females (over 15)	95.4%

Economic

GNP (1990 market prices)	US$293mn
GNP per capita	US$370
Public external debt (1991)	US$1,112mn
Tourism receipts (1990)	US$30mn
Inflation (annual av 1983-88)	22.9%
Radio	1 per 2.4 persons
Television	1 per 19 persons
Telephone	1 per 47 persons

Employment

Population economically active (1987)	
	270,074
Unemployment rate (1991)	13.5%
% of labour force in agriculture	20.4
mining	3.9
manufacturing	11.8
construction	2.8
Military forces	4,000

Source *Encyclopaedia Britannica*

running water is available, except in larger hotels and businesses which have emergency generators and water pumps. (Remember to take a good torch/flashlight with you, or buy candles locally.)

GEORGETOWN

Georgetown, the capital, and the chief town and port, is on the right bank of the River Demerara, at its mouth. Its population is roughly 200,000. The climate is tropical, with a mean temperature of 27°C, but the trade winds provide welcome relief. The city is built on a grid plan, with wide tree-lined streets and drainage canals following the layout of the old sugar estates. Despite being located on the Atlantic coast, Georgetown is known as the "Garden City of the Caribbean". Parts of the city are very attractive, with white-painted wooden nineteenth century houses raised on stilts and a profusion of flowering trees. In the evening the sea wall is crowded with strollers and at Easter it is a mass of colourful paper kites. Although part of the old city centre was destroyed by fire in 1945, there are some fine nineteenth century buildings, particularly on or near the Avenue of the Republic. The Gothic-style City Hall dates from 1887; its interior has been restored and may be viewed. St George's Anglican Cathedral, which dates from 1889 (consecrated 1894), is 44m (143 feet) high and is reputed to be the tallest wooden building in the world (it was designed by Sir Arthur Blomfield). The Public Buildings, which house Parliament, are an impressive neo-classical structure built in 1839. State House on Main Street is the residence of the president. Much of the city centre is dominated by the imposing tower above Stabroek market (1880). At the head of Brickdam, one of the main streets, is an aluminium arch commemorating independence. Nearby is a monument to the 1763 slave rebellion, surmounted by an impressive statue of Cuffy, its best-known leader. Near the *Guyana Pegasus Hotel* on Seawall Road is the Umana Yana, a conical thatched structure built by a group of Wai Wai Amerindians using traditional techniques for the 1972 conference of the Non-Aligned Movement (it was rebuilt in 1994 after collapsing in a storm in 1993).

The National Museum, opposite the post office, houses an idiosyncratic collection of exhibits from Guyana and elsewhere, including a model of Georgetown before the 1945 fire and a good natural history section on the top floor (free, 0900-1700 Mon-Fri, 0900-1200 Sat). The Walter Roth Museum of Anthropology has a good collection of Amerindian artefacts (still under development).

The Botanical Gardens (entry free), covering 50 hectares, are beautifully laid out, with Victorian bridges and pavilions, palms and lily-ponds (run-down, but undergoing continual improvements). Near the SW corner is the former residence of the President, which now houses the National Art Collection, and there is also a large mausoleum containing the remains of the former president, Forbes Burnham, which is decorated with reliefs depicting scenes from his political career. Look out for the rare cannonball tree (Couroupita Guianensis), named after the appearance of its poisonous fruit. The zoo (being upgraded) has a fine collection of local animals and the manatees in the ponds will eat grass from your hand. It has a new aquarium and a recently-constructed Arapaima pond near the entrance, which houses Guyana's largest fresh water fish. The zoo also boasts a breeding centre for endangered birds which are released into the wild. The zoo is open 0800-1800, US$0.05 for adults, half-price for children. The police band gives a free concert on Thursdays, 1730-1830. There are also beautiful tropical plants in the Promenade Gardens on Middle Street and in the National Park on Carifesta Avenue. The National Park

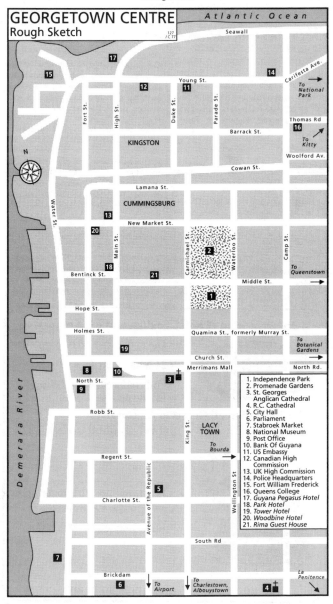

GEORGETOWN CENTRE
Rough Sketch

127
I C 77

Atlantic Ocean

Seawall

Carifesta Ave.

To National Park

Young St.

Fort St.

High St.

Duke St.

Parade St.

Barrack St.

Thomas Rd

To Kitty

Woolford Av.

KINGSTON

Cowan St.

N

Water St.

Lamana St.

CUMMINGSBURG

New Market St.

Main St.

Carmichael St.

Waterloo St.

Camp St.

To Queenstown

Bentinck St.

Middle St.

Hope St.

Holmes St.

Quamina St., formerly Murray St.

To Botanical Gardens

Church St.

Merrimans Mall

North Rd.

North St.

Robb St.

LACY TOWN

To Bourda

Regent St.

Avenue of the Republic

Charlotte St.

King St.

Wellington St.

South Rd

Demerara River

Brickdam

To Airport

To Charlestown, Albouystown

La Penitence

1. Independence Park
2. Promenade Gardens
3. St. Georges Anglican Cathedral
4. R.C. Cathedral
5. City Hall
6. Parliament
7. Staebroek Market
8. National Museum
9. Post Office
10. Bank Of Guyana
11. US Embassy
12. Canadian High Commission
13. UK High Commission
14. Police Headquarters
15. Fort William Frederick
16. Queens College
17. *Guyana Pegasus Hotel*
18. *Park Hotel*
19. *Tower Hotel*
20. *Woodbine Hotel*
21. *Rima Guest House*

has a good public running track.

The Georgetown Cricket Club at Bourda has one of the finest cricket grounds in the tropics. Near the SE corner of the Botanic Gardens is a well-equipped National Sports Centre. Nearby is the Cultural Centre, an impressive air-conditioned theatre with a large stage. Performances are also given at the Playhouse Theatre in Parade Street.

Local Information – Georgetown
● Warning
Despite the delights of this beautiful city precautions must be taken. Don't walk the streets at night. Check where it is safe to go with your hotel and in particular avoid Albouystown (S of the centre). Leave your valuables in your hotel.

● Where To Stay
There is a 10% room tax on all hotels with more than 16 rooms. *Guyana Pegasus*, Seawall Road, PO Box 101147, T 52853-9, F 60532, US$100-290d, recently renovated and extended with new Kingston wing, very safe, a/c, comfortable, fridge, cable TV, lovely swimming pool, poolside barbeque every night, 2 bars, 2 restaurants, gym, tennis, business centre, 24-hr back up electricity, organizes tours to the interior; *Tower*, 74-75 Main St, T 72011-5, F 65691, US$75 EP standard to US$120 for a suite, a/c, lively bar, excellent restaurant, *The Cazabon*, 24-hour restaurant, *Main Street Café*, nightly buffets, swimming pool, gym, business centre, boutique, beauty salon, in-house tour company (see below) 24-hr electricity back up; *Park*, 37-38 Main St, T 54914/16/70312-3, F 60351, US$27-65, a/c, secure, beautiful Victorian ballroom (worth a visit), beautiful restaurant too, but food could be better (average meal US$4.80); *Woodbine*, 41-42 New Market St, T 59430-4, F 58406, just off Main St, US$50-85, a/c, bar, restaurant, health club, rec; *Campala*, Camp St, T 52951, 61920/51620, US$57-67 inc breakfast, very clean, modern, a/c, near prison (other meals: lunch US$2, dinner US$2.50-6); *Queenstown Inn*, 65 Anira St, Queenstown, T 61416, F 61411, US$65-100, 6 self-contained rooms with a/c, gourmet breakfast included, US-style family-run, clean, friendly, safe, afternoon tea, laundry, non-alcoholic drinks.

There are also many smaller, cheaper hotels. Recommended are: *Waterchris*, Waterloo St, between Murray and Church Streets, T 71980, US$14-38, a/c, US$8 pp with fan, good restaurant, friendly; *Ariantze*, 176 Middle St, T 70115/70210, US$21, simple, clean, fans, US$40-50d in a/c deluxe rooms and suites, dining room with TV and a/c, *Side Walk Café* and *Jazz Club* night club; *Demico*, near Stabroek Market, T 56372, US$15, with a/c, US$11 without; *Friends*, 82 Robb St, T 72383, US$10-19, safe, fan, mosquito net, shower, bar, restaurant, travel agency; *Rima Guest House*, 92 Middle St, T 57401, good area, modernised, well-run, US$10.60 pp, good value, central, clean, safe, mosquito nets, restaurant (breakfast US$3.40, lunch and dinner US$$3.80); *Van Ross*, North Rd and Camp St, US$4.80, same management, very basic. Others include: *Belvedere*, Camp St, on the same block as the hospital and thereby benefiting from constant electricity, US$8; opposite is *Alpha Guest House*, 203 Camp St, T 54324, US$11, all rooms with double beds and mosquito nets, bar downstairs; *Trio La Chalet*, corner of Camp St and Hadfield St, T 56628, US$5.30-11.60, (US$15.50 in self-contained unit with a/c), popular with locals, 24-hr bar (breakfast US$1.30, other meals US$1.60). *Dal-Jean's Guest House*, Albert St, Queenstown, noisy but friendly, under US$3; *German's*, 81 Robb St, T 53972, with bath, no fan, US$5.30-7.60. *Tropical*, Waterloo and Middle Sts, US$5, very basic. Many small hotels and guest houses are full of long-stay residents, while some are rented by the hour. Try to book in advance. If in doubt, go to a larger hotel for first night and look around next day in daylight.

● **Apartments**

N and R, 246 Anaida Ave, Eccles, East Bank Demerara, T 60921 (reservations through N and R Apartment Rentals, 301 Church and Thomas Sts, Georgetown, T 58079/664040), US$45 a day, one bedroom, a/c, TV, maid service, washer, dryer, guard service, generator; *Blue Wave*, 3 locations, office at 8-9 North Rd, Bourda, T 64295, fully-furnished, kitchenette, TV, a/c, hot water, 24-hr electricity and security, US$45-75.

● **Where To Eat**

Eating out is very cheap at present because of the favourable exchange rate. 10% service may be added to bill. Many restaurants are closed on public holidays. Prices given below are for an average main course. At Hotels:

Pegasus, *El Dorado*, good atmosphere, Caribbean, Continental and Guyanese, *flambé* menu US$8, good breakfasts; *Brown's Brasserie*, lunch special US$4.70, main course from menu US$5.50. *Tower*, *Cazabon*, very good food, US$7.50-9.20; very good breakfast at *Waterchris*. Best in town are *Del Casa* (good food and atmosphere) and *Caribbean Rose* (very good indeed, up 4 flights of stairs and on the roof, the open sides will cool you down, credit cards not accepted but will accept US or Guyanese dollars, booking required), both on Middle St, (US$7.50-9.20); also rec are *Palm Court*, Main St (many Chinese dishes, good food, poor service), and *Arawak Steak House*, in roof garden above *Demico Hotel* (casual atmosphere, good value, average price US$4.80, closes 2200). Good lunches for around US$4-5 at the *Rice Bowl* in Robb St, the *Coalpot* in New Town (no shorts allowed, cheaper cafeteria) and *Hack's Hallal*; *Country Pride* in Robb St serves lunch and dinner, US$4-5. Good Chinese: *Orient*, Camp and Middle Sts, nice atmosphere US$4-5, 10% service in VIP lounge, service at bit poor; has a much better new branch on Lamaha St, just off Camp St. Many Chinese restaurants (all pretty rough), including *Double Dragon*, Av of the Republic; and *Diamond Food House*, 9 Camp St. For late night eating there are several Chinese restaurants on Sheriff St including *Double Happiness*. For fast food, try *Red Rooster*, Regent St; *Arapaima*, Main St; *Idaho*, Brickdam; *Forest Hills*, Camp St; *Calypso*, Regent St; *Demico House*, Stabroek Market, convenient but poor service, try the roof garden above *Demico House* for a quiet daytime drink. Cheaper counter lunches at *Guyana Stores*, Main St. Excellent fruit juices at *Organic Juices*, Croal St, Bourda.

● **Night Life**

Georgetown is surprisingly lively at night, mainly with gold miners, traders and overseas Guyanese throwing US$ around. Liveliest disco is *Hollywood*, Camp St (entrance US$0.80, expensive); *The Library*, Camp St, very popular Wed night (ladies free), barbeque, beer garden, dance floor, bar (entrance US$0.80); *Blue Note*, Camp St, disco and beer garden; *Palm Court*, Main St, popular bar/café (French style) very lively Fri pm and holidays, no entrance fee; *Mingles*, corner of Vlissengen Rd and Duncan St, is a good small club with excellent live music and dancing (entrance US$0.80, take a taxi there, US$1); *Jazz Club* at *Ariantze Hotel*, Middle St, good atmosphere, excellent live band every Thur; *Trump Card*, Church St, near St George's, sometimes has a live band. Near the Kitty Market are *Jazzy Jacks*, Alexander St (open till 0400 at weekends), and *Wee Place*, Lamaha St, but this area is unsafe unless you go with locals. Sheriff St is some way from the centre but is "the street that never sleeps" full of late night Chinese restaurants and has some good bars including *Tennessee Lounge*, *Burns Beat* and *Sheriff*. Most nightclubs sell imported, as well as local Banks beer; many sell drinks by the bottle rather than shot, this works out cheaper. You can visit the steel pan yards and watch practice sessions. There are two theatres in Georgetown.

● **Shopping**
Normal shopping hours are 0800-1600, Mon-Thur, 0800-1700 Fri, 0800-1200 Sat Market hours 0800-1600, Mon-Sat, except Wed 0900-1200. The main shopping area is Regent St. The two main department stores are *Guyana Stores* in Church St, and *Fogarty's*, but neither has a wide range of goods. Most Guyanese do their regular shopping at the four big markets: Stabroek, Bourda, La Penitence and Kitty. Craft items are a good buy; Amerindian basketwork, hammocks, wood carvings, pottery, and small figures made out of Balata, a rubbery substance tapped from trees in the interior. *Houseproud*, 6 Avenue of the Republic, has a good selection of craftwork, but there are many other craft shops including *Creation Craft*, Water St. Good T-shirts are sold at Guyana Stores and in the markets. Gold is also sold widely, often at good prices but make sure you know what you are buying. Do not buy it on the street. Films over ASA200 are normally not available; bring your own stock. 24-hr developing is now available: *Risans* on Main St (top end) and Ave of the Republic recommended as efficient, sells slide film (photocopying, too), also *Guyana Stores* and a 1-hr photo print service in Quamina St, near Main St.

● **Bookshops**
Some interesting books in *Houseproud*. Try also *GNTC* on Water St, *Argosy* and *Kharg* both on Regent St, *Dimension* on Cummings St, as well as *Guyana Stores* and *Fogarty's*; *Universal Bookstore* on Water St, nr Forgarty's has a good selection of books and greetings cards. *Newsweek* is sold at *Hotel Tower*.

● **Vehicle Rental**
Car hire is available through numerous companies (page 15 of Guyana Telephone Book gives details). Prices range from US$42/day to US$65/day for a new Nissan Sentra. Better companies are *N and R Rentals*, 301 Church and Thomas Sts, T 58079/66404, Toyota Camry and Corolla, Nissan Station Wagon, and Transportation Services Ltd, T 68491/5. Scooters can be hired from Addis Scooter Enterprise Ltd, 38 Sussex St, Charlestown, T 66789. a permit is needed from local police; rental agencies can advise.

● **Local Transport**
Minibuses run regularly to most parts of the city, mostly from Stabroek market or Avenue of the Republic, standard fare US$0.20, very crowded. It is difficult to get a seat during rush hours. **Taxis** charge US$1.25 for short journeys, US$2.20 for longer runs, with higher rates at night and outside the city limits. Minibuses and taxis have "H" on their number plate. Normal ones ply set routes at a fixed fare; they stop at any point on request. Certain hand signals are used on some routes to indicate the final destination (ask). Special taxis at hotels and airports, also with "H" and marked "special" on the windscreen, charge US$1.25 around town, stops and waiting time extra, or you can negotiate a "by the hour" deal, usually US$6.

● **Exchange**
National Bank of Industry and Commerce; Guyana Bank of Trade and Industry; Bank of Baroda; Bank of Nova Scotia will give cash advance on Visa card. Bank hours are 0800-1230 Mon-Fri, plus 1500-1700 on Fri. **Exchange houses** (*cambios*) in shops may be open longer hours. A good, safe *cambio* is Joe Chin Travel on Main St. The *cambio* opp the *Tower Hotel* accepts Thomas Cook travellers' cheques, but not at the best rates. There is a *cambio* next to *Rima Guest House*, Middle St.

● **Post Office**
Main one on North St, slow service.

● **Churches**
Anglican: St George's Cathedral, Christ Church, Waterloo Street; St Andrew's (Presbyterian), Avenue of the Republic; Roman Catholic Cathedral, Brickdam; Pentecostal, Full Gospel Fellowship, South Rd corner of Albert Rd, welcoming.

● **Sport**

The national indoor sport is dominoes. There are sports clubs for cricket, tennis, football, rugby, hockey, riding, swimming, cycling, athletics, badminton, volley ball, netball, snooker, pool, golf, boxing, ballroom dancing and rifle shooting. At Easter there are kite flying competitions.

● **Travel Agencies**

Try Mr Mendoza at *Frandec Travel Service*, Main St, repeatedly rec (no tours to the interior); *Wieting and Richter*, 78 Church and Carmichael Sts, very helpful, ask for Onassis Stanley (has Tourism Association of Guyana information desk). *H and R Ramdehol*, 215 South Rd, Lacytown, T 70639/73183/73486; *Joe Chin Travel*, rec (see **Exchange**, above). For **Tour Operators**, see below.

● **Bus Services**

There are regular services by minibuses and collective taxis to most coastal towns from the Stabroek Market. To **Rosignol** (for New Amsterdam, Springlands and Suriname), 2 hrs, US$1.60; to **Parika** US$1; to **Linden** US$1.50.

● **Tour Operators**

The tourism sector is promoting ecotourism in the form of environmentally friendly resorts and camps on Guyana's rivers and in the rainforest. There is much tropical wildlife to be seen.

Wilderness Explorers, 27-28 Queen St, Kitty, Georgetown, T 54929, offers ready-made itineraries and specialize in custom-designed, personal itineraries for any group size. Tours available to all of Guyana's interior resorts, day and overland tours to Kaieteur Falls, horse trekking, hiking and general tours in the Rupununi and rainforest. Specialists in nature,

adventure and bird-watching tours. Free tourism information and advice available. *Tropical Adventures*, c/o Guyana Pegasus, Seawall Road, Georgetown, T 52853-9, F 60532, offer day trips to Kaieteur and Orinduik Falls, Kamuni Creek and Santa Mission, Timberhead (see below), Double 'B' Exotic Gardens (see below) and city tours. Overnight tours to Timberhead, Shanklands (see below) and Essequibo River. Individual itineraries catered for. Also 7 and 14 night itineraries travelling around Guyana, fully inclusive rates, 7 nights US$950 pp, 14 nights US$1,750. *Wonderland Tours*, 65 Main St, Georgetown, T 65991, AH65991, day trips to Kaieteur and Orinduik Falls, Santa Mission, Essequibo and Mazaruni Rivers (developing own camp on the Mazaruni river), city tours; special arrangements for overnight stays available. *Torong Guyana*, 56 Coralita Avenue, Bel Air Park, Georgetown, T 65298, trips to Kaieteur and Orinduik Falls and three-day Rupununi Safaris, including Kaieteur (US$450). *Discover Tours*, Hotel Tower, 74-75 Main St, Georgetown, T 72011-5/58001, F 65691/56021, custom-designed itineraries to inland resorts, day and overland trips to Kaieteur Falls and other locations, rates fully inclusive, 4-14 day tours US$450-2,0000 pp, group sizes 8-15. *Cattleya Rainforest Tours*, 225 South Rd, Georgetown, T 76590, F 70944, overland trips to Kaieteur. *Shell Beach Adventures*, 22A Wight's Lane, Kingston, Georgetown, T 58578/61767, F 66046, trips to Shell Beach in NW Guyana to see nesting turtles in season and scarlet ibis roosting, 2-day trip US$250 pp using light aircraft and camping on beach. *Rainbow River Safari Ltd*, c/o Allison, Guyenterprise Agency, 234 Almond St, F 2-56959 or phone Allison 2-69874; can provide tours into the interior, to its campsite on

the Mazaruni River (see below), arranges overland tours to Kaieteur Falls, director Miss L Prowell, resident at the campsite (London office, Mr Sabat, T 081-671 1414, F 071-703 5500).

● **Resorts**

Timberhead, operated by Tropical Adventures (see above) in the Santa Amerindian Reserve, situated on a sandy hill overlooking Savannah and the Pokerero Creek, 3 beautifully appointed native lodges with bath and kitchen facilities, well-run, good food, lovely trip up the Kamuni River to get there, much wildlife to be seen, 91 species of bird have been recorded, activities include swimming, fishing, jungle treks, visit to Santa Mission Amerindian village, volley ball, US$80 pp for a day trip, US$120 pp for one night and two days, plus US$85 per night from second night on (includes all transport, meals, bar, guide, accommodation), highly rec. *Shanklands*, contact Joanne Jardim, Residence No 3, Thirst Park, Georgetown, T/F 51586, (or through *Tropical Adventures*) on a cliff overlooking the Essequibo, 3 colonial style cottages with verandah and kitchen, activities include swimming, walking, bird watching, croquet, fishing, water sports, about

US$95 pp, not including transport. *The Gazebo*, on Kaow Island, contact Bibi Zackeryah, Willems Timber and Trading Co Ltd, PO Box 10443, Georgetown, T 72046/7, 69252, F 60983, the country home of the Willems family on 136-acre Kaow Island in the Essequibo River, facilities include a jungle walk, tennis, swimming, water sports, trekking, bird watching, room rates US$190d full board, most activities included, transport from Georgetown not included (air, 30 mins, US$200; minibus and boat via Parika, 2 hrs, US$125 or US$275, latter in cabin cruiser). *Double 'B' Exotic Gardens*, 58 Lamaha Gardens, Georgetown, T 52023, F 60997, contact Boyo Ramsaroop, near Timehri Airport, good birdwatching, gardens specializing in heliconias, day tours US$35. *Emerald Tower*, Madewini Rainforest Lodges, T 72011-5, F 65691, on the Demerara River, reached by minibus from Georgetown, 8 private tree-level cabins, activities include swimming, bicycle and nature trails, croquet, putting green, sauna, birdwatching, archery, all inclusive rates US$195d regular, US$235d deluxe; organizes custom itineraries, including other interior resorts, Kaieteur and Orinduik Falls. For *Rock*

View Ecotourism Resort, Karanambu Ranch and *Dadanawa Ranch*, see under Rupununi, below.

● **Camps**

Rainbow River Safari, a 17,000 acre conservation site on the Mazaruni River, dormitory style accommodation in 3 large tented camps (chalets planned), pit latrines, washing in river, cooking over wood fire, US$60-90 pp all inclusive, day trips with 3 different jungle trails US$3.75, swimming, whitewater rafting, wildlife walking, birdwatching, hill climbing, gold panning, no music unless requested, no caged animals. Day trippers pay a landing fee of G$500. See above for contact addresses, which should be approached for all latest details. Agent in Bartika, Bell Boats, Monti Bell, T 05-2405, or Stephen Bell, T 05-2414, or Attack, T 05-2484.

● **Note**

For visiting many parts of the interior, particularly Amerindian districts, permits are required in advance from the Ministry of Home Affairs and/or the Public Works, Communications and Regional Development in Georgetown. If venturing out of Georgetown on your own, you must check beforehand whether you need a permit for where you intend to visit.

SOUTHEAST TO SURINAME

Linden (pop 60,000), the second-largest town in Guyana, is a bauxite mining town 70 miles/112 km S of Georgetown on the Demerara river. A good road connects the two towns; the police checks are to stop drug and gun running. On the W bank of the river Linden is a company mining town. The opencast mine is 200-300 feet deep and is said to have the world's longest boom walking dragline. Across the river (bridge or ferry, G$5) are the poorer suburbs of Wismar and Christianburg. The town is dominated by a disused alumina plant and scarred by old bauxite pits. Accommodation is scarce (in town *Crescent* and *Chez Docs*, cheap basic; *Hotel Star Bonnett*, three-quarters of a mile out of town on Georgetown road, clean, good lunches; nearby *Summit Hotel*, US$10).

From Linden rough roads suitable for four-wheel drive vehicles run S to the bauxite mining towns of Ituni and Kwakwani. The road S to the logging centre at Mabura Hill is in excellent condition; it continues to Kurupukari in extremely bad condition, even for 4WD trucks. Money for upgrading the road is not currently available. A good road goes W from Linden to Rockstone ferry on the Essequibo river. From Rockstone very bad roads run N to Bartica and S to Issano.

New Amsterdam (pop 25,000) is 65 miles/104 km southeast of Georgetown on the E bank of the Berbice river, near its mouth. From Georgetown, take a minibus or collective taxi to Rosignol on the W bank of the Berbice, then cross the river by launch rather than the ferry, 15 mins (US$0.10; also takes vehicles). The town is picturesque.

●**Hotels** *Church View Guest House*, 3 Main and King St, T (03) 2880, F 3927, US$15-23, inc meals; *Hotel Embassy*, at Rose Hall; *Astor*, 7 Strand, T (03) 3578, verandah with lounge chairs, rec, US$7-15.

From New Amsterdam, it is sometimes possible to get a lift on a bauxite barge up the Berbice river to the small mining town of Kwakwani (there is a guesthouse, reasonable, check for vacancies at Guymine in Georgetown).

The road continues E from New Amsterdam (minibus, US$1.45), to **Springlands** and Skeldon at the mouth of the Courantyne river. The two towns are officially known as **Corriverton** (Courantyne River Town, pop about 31,000).

●**Hotels in Springlands**: *Ambassador*, near point for ferry to Nieuw Nickerie; *Swiss Guest House*, T (039) 2329, US$4-6, Pakistani run, rough but helpful. In Skeldon: *Parapak*, US$10, no fan, no mosquito net, poor value; *Mahogony*, US$6, fan, clean, friendly, rec; *Arawak*, under US$3, rough, avoid. Several good Chinese restaurants within a few blocks of Springlands town centre.

● **Exchange** National Bank of Industry and

Commerce; Guyana National Commercial Bank. *Cambio* (National Bank of Industry and Commerce) at Skeldon for arriving ferry passengers. Suriname guilders can officially be changed into Guyanese dollars.

Crossing to Suriname

Before you leave Georgetown, check with the Suriname embassy whether you need a visa (without one, if required, you may be imprisoned before being sent back to Georgetown). See **Documents**, Suriname, **Information for Visitors**. From Springlands there is a daily ferry (not Sunday or national holidays of either country) to Nieuw Nickerie (foot passengers only). Queue at the booking office near the jetty from 0700, office opens 0800, booking fee US$0.25, all passports must be presented when booking, tickets are sold later on the ferry, Sf45 one way, payable in Suriname guilders only. Immigration and customs formalities (very slow and thorough) take place from 0900, ferry sails in the afternoon depending on tides and weather, crossing time normally 2 hrs. If not 'in transit' through Suriname you are obliged to change US$175 at the local bank, if it is closed your passport is retained (see **Suriname**, **Currency**). In this instance, travel on to Paramaribo, change currency at the Central Bank and with receipt given at border retreive your passport from Fort Zeelandia.

NB This ferry was not running in March 1994. Small boats ferried people across. Check the situation in advance.

WEST FROM GEORGETOWN: ROUTES TO VENEZUELA

Travelling W from Georgetown, the road crosses the 1¼-mile long floating Demerara bridge (toll, pedestrians free) and continues to *Parika*, a small town on the E bank of the Essequibo river (minibus US$1). If you need accommodation, there are two small guesthouses where you can stay fairly safely. From here ferries cross the river to *Adventure* on the W bank at 1700 daily and 0830 Wednesday and Friday, returning at 0300 daily and 1330 Wednesday and Friday; alternatively take a speedboat US$2.40. (See *Three Singles to Adventure* by Gerald Durrell). There are also three ferries a day to Leguan Island (½ hour, US$0.25); accommodation available at the *Hotel President*.

From Parika the Sherry Express runs tours to nearby Fort Island (with a ruined Dutch fort), which has a beach. A popular trip with Guyanese, it costs US$4 pp. Drinks and food are available. Departures are irregular, normally on Sunday; check at Kwality Centre, Hinks St, Georgetown, T 54075/58313.

The NW coastal area is mainly accessible by boat only. From Adventure a road runs N through Anna Regina. Nearby is Lake Mainstay, a small resort (due for renovation), reached by taxi; it is also known as the hot and cold lake because it varies in temperature from one place to another. Then the road goes on to *Charity*, a pleasant little town with two small hotels and a lively market on Mondays.

Near the border with Venezuela is the small port of *Morawhanna* (Morajuana to the Venezuelans), which may be reached by an unreliable ferry from Georgetown. The journey is surprisingly rough and "you will have to fight for hammock space and watch your possessions like a hawk". From Morawhanna boats sail up the river to Port Kaituma, 40 miles/ 64 km inland, from where a small passenger railway connects with the isolated settlement of Matthews Ridge (more easily reached by chartered aircraft from Georgetown). The site of the Jonestown mass-suicide is nearby.

● Near Marrthews Ridge, at Mabaruma, is *Kamaka Tourist Resort*; bookings can be made in Georgetown at 116 Waterloo St, T 73378. Guyana Airways Corporation fly to this area once a week; book at their Georgetown office on Main Street.

The Venezuelan border can be crossed at the River Cuyuni (at least from Venezuela into Guyana). On the Venezuelan side is San Martín, from which a narrow road goes to El Dorado on the road S to Brazil. It is possible to reach this border by boat from Georgetown (very infrequent), or by military plane, about 4 or 5 times a week, no schedule, US$60.

From Parika there is also a ferry up the Essequibo river to Bartica on Mon, Thur and Sat, returning next day, US$1.50 one way. The 36 mile/ 58 km journey takes 6 hrs, stopping at Fort Island; small boats come out from riverside settlements to load up with fruit. Local people generally prefer to take a speedboat, US$5.30 pp, 1-2 hrs, depending on horsepower.

SOUTHWEST FROM GEORGETOWN: TO BRAZIL

Bartica, at the junction of the Essequibo and Mazaruni rivers, is the "take-off" town for the gold and diamond fields, Kaieteur Falls, and the interior generally. Here an Amazon-like mass of waters meets, but with an effect vastly more beautiful, for they are coloured the "glossy copper" of all Guyanese rivers and not the dull mud-brown of most of the Amazon. Swimming very good. The *stelling* (wharf) and market are very colourful.

● **Where To Stay** *Main Hotel*, 19 Second Ave, T (05) 2243, rooms from US$6, meals: breakfast US$2.30, lunch US$4.20, dinner US$4.60; *The Nest* on Fifth Avenue, US$10, unsafe, very noisy, meals to be had from disco after 1730, or "Robbie's". *Modern*, near ferry, US$4.50, bath and fan, rec, good food, noisy disco; *Pink House*, (Mrs Phil's), Second Ave, US$3, clean, without bath, basic, secure, quiet, family-run. Book ahead if possible. Mrs Payne's, near Hospital, basic, clean. *Sea View*, condominium-style resort, under construction.

The Essequibo is navigable to large boats for some miles above Bartica. The Cuyuni flows into the Mazaruni 3 miles above Bartica, and above this confluence the Mazaruni is impeded for 120 miles by thousands of islands, rapids and waterfalls. To avoid this stretch of treacherous river a road has been built from Bartica to Issano, where boats can be taken up the more tranquil upper Mazaruni.

At the confluence of the Mazaruni and Cuyuni Rivers are the ruins of the Dutch stronghold Kyk-over-al, once the seat of government for the Dutch county of Essequibo. Nearby are the Marshall Falls (35 mins by boat from Bartica, US$38 per boat, return) where you can swim in the falls themselves ("a natural jacuzzi"), or the nearby bay, part of the Rainbow River Safari conservation area, GS$500 landing fee.

The *Kaieteur Falls*, on the Potaro river, rank with the Niagara, Victoria, and Iguazú Falls in majesty and beauty, but have the added attraction of being surrounded by unspoilt forest. The Falls, nearly five times the height of Niagara, with a sheer drop of 228m, are nearly 100m wide. They are unspoilt because of their isolation.

The Kaieteur Falls lie within the **Kaieteur National Park**, where there is a variety of wildlife: tapirs, ocelots, monkeys, armadillos, anteaters, and jungle and river birds. In 1994 the government was considering extending the national park. At the Falls themselves, one can see the magnificent silver fox, often near the rest house, the cock-of-the-rock and the Kaieteur swift, which lives behind the falls. At dusk the swifts swoop in and out of the gorge before passing through the deluge to roost behind the water. Permission to enter the national park must be obtained from the National Parks Commission in Georgetown, T 59142. In the dry months, April and October, the flow of the falls is reduced; in January and June/July the flow is fullest, but in June, the height of the wet season, the overland route is impassable.

A trip to the Kaieteur Falls costs US$130-140; (eg with GAC, T 64011, from Timehri airport, Sun, inc lunch, drinks and guide, also goes to Orinduik Falls; see below, sit on left for best views, take swimming gear). Most agencies include the Orinduik Falls as well, US$170, including ground and air transport, meal, drinks, US$5 national park entrance fee and guide. Trips depend on the charter plane being filled; there is normally at least one flight per week. Cancellations only occur in bad weather or if there are insufficent passengers. Operators offering this service are *Tropical Adventures* at the *Guyana Pegasus Hotel* (T 52853-9, F 60532), Richard Ousman (T 72011-5) *Wilderness Explorers* (T 54929), trips to both falls in light aircraft, *Discover Tours* at *Hotel Tower* (T 72011-5) spends longer at each falls, US$195, *Wonderland Tours* (T 65991), and *Torang Guyana*, Mrs Chan-A-Sue in Georgetown, T 65298. You may get very little time at the Falls. Flights from Timehri or Ogle airport cost US$40. To charter a plane privately costs US$900 to Kaieteur and Orinduik. The overland route to the falls takes 4-7 days. *Tropical Adventures, Wilderness Explorers, Discover Tours* and *Cattleya Rainforest Tours*, all in Georgetown offer overland trips, as does *Rainbow River Safari* (7-10 days, not including rest days).

To go independently overland to Kaieteur:

Take any truck from Bartica to Mahdia (they usually run at night after the ferry has arrived from Parika). They carry stores for miners; passengers sit on planks on top. The 100 very uncomfortable miles (160 km) take at least 14-16 hrs; make sure the truck has a good cover against rain. Fare US$12. No food or drink is available en route, so take your own. Leave the truck at the Kangaruma junction, 2 miles after Garraway Stream,

which has a fine suspension bridge over the Potaro River.

It is also possible to get a mining truck direct from Georgetown, eg Rhaman Trucks to Mahdia, or Danny, Victoria St, Albouystown, to Garraway Stream, with speedboat connections to Tukeit (see below). Another alternative from Georgetown is to take a bus to Linden, then another bus (unreliable) to Mabura. After Mabura, take the road that follows the river upstream to Yaya on the Essequibo (also reached by bus from Linden) and then a speedboat to Chomach on the Potaro (US$6 for 15, 2 hrs; there is a road Yaya-Chomach). From Chomach take a boat to Garraway Stream, US$4 for 6 people, 2 hrs (the bridge between Chomach and Garraway Stream was down in 1994, so trucks cannot go between the two). Gorgeous waterfalls in Chomach. The Anglican priest is a nice man. Direct trucks go from Georgetown to Chomach Tues-Sat. From Chomach walk to Kangaruma junction.

Kangaruma ($1\frac{1}{2}$ hrs walk) is a very small village ("12 people, 6 prostitutes", beware theft and overcharging); the first house on the right acts as a hostel for workers, with food and hammock space. There is also a bar and store. Speedboats (1-2 a day) go from Kangaruma to Tukeit via Amatok falls (1 hr) and Waratok falls ($1\frac{1}{2}$ hrs); walk around each fall and then get a new boat. From Tukeit you walk to Kaieteur in about 2 hrs in the dry season; not rec in the rainy season. There is no public speedboat service, they belong to companies working in the area. Company speedboats apparently will not ask for money, but to hire a boat is beyond a budget traveller's means.

In the dry season you can walk from Kangaruma to Kaieteur: 8-10 hrs to Amatok, very rough and swampy, with many streams to cross; then 4-5 hrs to Waratok; then 7-9 hrs to Tukeit. 2-3 hrs after Amatok is a deserted mining camp where you can camp; there are many other flat places suitable for camping. The whole route is very hard going and it would seem that there is much more chance of being near people if you go by boat. On the boat route you can sling a hammock at any of the camps if stuck and each camp has ham radio for emergency use. Nevertheless, boats are very unreliable. A speedboat is preferable to going in a paddled boat, which cannot cope with the strong currents.

Once at Kaieteur, you can walk to the top of the falls, at least 2 hrs, but worth it to watch the blue, white and brown water tumbling into the stupendous gorge.

From Lethem to Kaieteur, take a truck to Annai, Saruma, Cupucari, then a truck to Mabura, via Amerindian villages of Icowaw and Frenchman. From Mabura, as above. (We are grateful to Piero Scaruffi, Redwood City, CA, and Yoav Berkovich, Ramat Efal, Israel, for the above information.)

● **Where To Stay** The rest house at the top of the Falls was not open in mid-1994, ask in the house next door or enquire first at the National Parks Commission, Georgetown, T 59142 (if planning to stay overnight, you must be self-sufficient, whether the guesthouse is open or not; take your own food and a hammock, it can be cold and damp at night. It is nearly impossible to get down the gorge below the falls; the path is completely overgrown, a guide is essential and it takes a full day.

● **When to go** Avoid April and October, which are the dry months when the flow of the falls is reduced, and June, which is the height of the wet season when the route is impassable.

The Pakaraima Mountains stretch from Kaieteur westwards to include the highest peak in Guyana, Mount Roraima, the possible inspiration for Conan Doyle's *Lost World*. Roraima is very difficult to climb from the Guyanese side.

There are several other spectacular waterfalls in the interior, including Imbaimadai and Orinduik, but none is very easy to reach. *Orinduik Falls* are on the Ireng River, which forms the border with Brazil; the river pours over steps

and terraces of jasper, with a backdrop of the grass-covered Pakaraima Mountains. There is good swimming at the falls.

● **Precautions** If going on your own, detailed planning and a guide are essential. Take adequate supplies of food and drink, a sleeping bag, a sheet and blanket, a mosquito net, and kerosene for Tilley lamps.

The *Rupununi Savanna* in the SW is an extensive area of dry grassland with scattered trees, termite mounds and wooded hills. The freshwater creeks, lined with Ite palms, are good for swimming. The region is scattered with occasional Amerindian villages and a few large cattle ranches which date from the late nineteenth century: the descendants of some of the Scots settlers still live here. Links with Brazil are much closer than with the Guyanese coast; many people speak Portuguese and most trade, both legal and illegal, is with Brazil.

Avoid visiting the Rupununi in the wet season (mid-May to August) as much of the Savanna is flooded and malaria mosquitoes widespread. The best time is October to April. River bathing is good, but watch out for the dangerous stingrays. Wild animals are shy, largely nocturnal and seldom seen. Among a wide variety of birds, look out for macaws, tocan, parrots, parakeets, hawks and jabiru storks. Note that a permit from the Ministry of Home Affairs is required to visit Rupununi. A separate permit to visit Amerindian villages is needed from the Ministry of Public Works, Communications and Regional Development in Georgetown. Without them you will be sent straight back to Georgetown or on to Brazil.

Lethem, a small but scattered town on the Brazilian frontier, is the service centre for the Rupununi and for trade with Brazil. There are a few stores, a small hospital, a police station and government offices which have radio telephone links with Georgetown. Prices are about twice as high as in Georgetown. About 1½ miles/ 2½ km S of town at St Ignatius there is a Jesuit mission dating from 1911. In the nearby mountains there is good birdwatching and there are waterfalls to visit.

● **Where To Stay** A number of places take guests, full board, organize tours and transport. **Accommodation** in Lethem at *Casique Guest House* (OK) and *Regional Guest House*. The *Manari Ranch Hotel*, 7 miles/11 km N of Lethem, also *Pirara Ranch*, 15 miles further N, both on creeks for swimming, both US$50 pp per day. Duane and Sandy de Freitas at the *Dadanawa Ranch*, 60 miles/80 km S of Lethem, one of the world's largest ranches, US$75 pp per day. Dianne McTurk at *Karanambo Ranch*, 60 miles/80 km NE of Lethem, on the Rupununi River, US$100 per day (unique old home with cottages for visitors, fishing, birdwatching and boat rides). At the village of Annai on the road to Georgetown, some 70 miles from Lethem *The Rock View Ecotourism Resort* has opened; with 4 rooms and cheaper rooms in the main ranch house; it is located in the Pakaraima foothills where the savannah meets the Iwokrama rainforest project; contact Colin Edwards, Trans Guyana Aviation, T 60605/65128 (in Georgetown contact Charlene, T 73010/73188, F 51171), pony treks to nearby foothills, nature tours with opportunities for painting, photography and fishing, regional Amerindian and other local cooking, US$95 per day full board, rec. All can be contacted at the Airport Shop in Lethem, where Don and Shirley Melville provide the most comprehensive information and assistance service in the Rupununi. In Georgetown contact Wendella Jackson, T 53750, (for *Karanambo*), or Tony Thorne at *Wilderness Explorers*, T 54929. Eat at *Foo Foods*, *Savannah Inn* or the Airport Shop in Lethem.

● **Exchange** Changing money is unlikely to be much better on the Brazilian side of the frontier.

●**Transport** At *Foo Foods* bicycles can be hired for US$8/day; also available at the Airport Shop, as are horses for US$8/hour. The Airport Shop can arrange landrovers and trucks at US$3 per mile. For birdwatching trips and transport contact Loris Franklin through the Airport Shop.

Transport around the Rupununi is difficult; there are a few four-wheel drive vehicles, but ox-carts and bicycles are more common on the rough roads. From Lethem trucks can be hired for day-trips to the Moco-Moco Falls and the Kamu Falls and to the Kanuku Mountains. Trucks may also be hired to visit Aishalton, 70 miles/110 km S along a very bad road, 6-hr journey, US$300; and to Annai, 60 miles/96 km NE along a better road, 3-hr journey, US$200. Samuel Hawker near the police station has 5 trucks; nice fellow, he may let you sling your hammock in his backyard (he also changes money). All trucks leaving town must check with the police so the police know all trucks that are departing.

A road link between Georgetown and Lethem via Linden, Mabura Hill and Kurupakari was opened in early 1991. Once completed it will provide a through route from Georgetown to Boa Vista (Brazil), which will have a major impact on Guyana. As said above, the funding for the final section has not been found, and it remains virtually impassable.

Truck Georgetown-Lethem: contact Ministry of Regional Development, Georgetown, Eddie Singh, 137 Herstelling, T (065) 2672, or Borderline, Belvair Court, Georgetown; Ng-a-fook, on Church St, between Camp St and Waterloo St. Trip takes 48 hrs, US$25 pp one way, no seat but share truck with load, take food, water and hammock. (Care is needed on this route, but it is exciting, through savannah and rainforest.) Guyana Airways Corporation flies from Georgetown to Lethem and back Tues, Wed, Fri and Sat, US$53 one way (reliable; diversions available to Annai and Karanambu Ranch for extra US$91 per flight); book well in advance at the GAC office on Main St, Georgetown. Regular charter planes link the town with Georgetown, about US$200 return.

Crossing to Brazil

Formalities are generally reported to be very lax on both sides of the border, but it is important to observe them as there are reports of people being refused entry to Guyana for not having the correct papers, including visa. In Lethem all procedures are dealt with at the police station (there is also immigration at the airport); report there also with a visa if arriving from Brazil. The Takutu river, the frontier between the two countries, is about 1 mile N of Lethem (taxis available, or pick-ups, US$1). There are small boats for foot passengers (US$0.25) and a pontoon for vehicles (temporarily out of action in mid-1994). Vehicles can drive across the river in the dry season. Just over the river is a shop and the Brazilian customs post. From here it is 1½ mile/2½ km walk to the village of Bonfim, from where a bus leaves for Boa Vista at 0800 Tuesday, Thursday and Saturday (from Boa Vista to Bonfim at 1630 Monday, Wednesday and Friday), 3½ hrs, US$5. Colectivo US$15, 3 hrs. It is possible to cycle across to Bonfim with minimum formalities (5 km), but if you want to take a bus on to Boa Vista full passport/visas (if necessary) are required.

INFORMATION FOR VISITORS

● **Documents**

Visa requirements have been relaxed; as of 15 February 1993, the following countries do not need a visa to visit Guyana: USA, Canada, Belgium, Denmark, France, Germany, Greece, Ireland, Italy, Luxembourg, the Netherlands, Portugal, Spain, UK, Norway, Finland, Sweden, Australia, New Zealand, Japan, Korea, and the Commonwealth countries. Visitors are advised to check with the nearest Embassy, Consulate or travel agent for further changes. All visitors require passports and all nationalities, apart from those above, require visas. To obtain a visa, two photos, an onward ticket and yellow fever certificate are required. Visas are charged strictly on a reciprocal basis, equivalent to the cost charged to a Guyanese visitor to the country concerned. Visitors from those countries where they are required arriving without visas are refused entry. To fly in to Guyana, an exit ticket is required, at land borders an onward ticket is usually not asked for.

● **Customs**

Baggage examination can be very thorough. Duties are high on goods imported in commercial quantities.

International Air Services There are no direct flights to Guyana from Europe, but BWIA's flights from London, Frankfurt and Zurich to Antigua or Port of Spain connect; from North America BWIA flies 4 times a week from New York, 6 times a week from Miami; most BWIA flights involve a change of planes in Port of Spain. Guyana Airways fly 3 times a week from New York and once from Miami, all direct; it also has flights from Toronto. Leisure Air flies once a week from New York via St Lucia. BWIA flies to Guyana from Trinidad 18 times a week (Surinam Airways 3 a week, ALM once). LIAT flies daily from Barbados; BWIA flies 4 times a week from Antigua. LIAT have connecting flights with British Airways in Barbados to/from London and Air Canada from Toronto. Surinam Airways flies 5 times a week from Paramaribo, while Gonini Air flies daily, but these flights are difficult to book from outside the Guianas and are subject to cancellation at short notice. ALM twice a week from Curaçao. There are no direct flights to Caracas, Venezuela, which can be reached via Port of Spain with an overnight stop.

Flights are often booked weeks in advance, especially at Christmas and in August when overseas Guyanese return to visit relatives. Flights are frequently overbooked, so it is essential to reconfirm your outward flight, which can take some time, and difficult to change your travel plans at the last minute. A number of travel agents are now computerized, making reservations and reconfirmations easier. Foreigners must pay for airline tickets in US$ (most airlines do not accept US$100 bills), or other specified currencies. Luggage should be securely locked as theft from checked-in baggage is common.

● **Airport Information**

The international airport is at Timehri, 25 miles/40 km S of Georgetown. There is an exit tax of G$1,500, payable in Guyanese dollars, or US dollars at US$13. It can be paid when reconfirming your ticket at least 3 days before expected departure, in Georgetown, or at the airport after check-in. There is also a 15% tax on international airline tickets for flights leaving Guyana, no matter where bought. The terminal building was being rebuilt in 1994 with various services coming on stream all the time. Check in two hours before most flights, listen to the local radio the day before your flight to hear if it has been delayed, or even brought forward. Minibus No 42 to Georgetown US$1.50 (from Georgetown leaves from next to Parliament building); for a small charge they will take you to your hotel (similarly for groups going to the airport). Taxi US$20. There are two duty-free shops, one selling local and imported spirits, the other local handicrafts and jewellery. There is also an exchange house, open usual banking hours; if closed, plenty of parallel traders outside (find out from fellow passengers what the rate is). It is difficult to pay for flight tickets at the airport with credit cards or TC's. The exchange desk will change TCs for flight ticket purchases. Internal flights go from Ogle airport; minibus from Market to Ogle US$0.20.

● **Internal Air Services**

Guyana Airways has scheduled flights between Georgetown and Lethem on Tues, Wed, Fri and Sat. There are several charter companies, including Masaharally, Trans Guyana Airways (Correia) and Kayman Sankar. Ask the charter companies at Ogle airport for seats on cargo flights to any destination, they will help you to get in touch with the charterer. Prices vary, up to US$0.80 per pound. Returning to Ogle can be cheaper, even, if you are lucky, free.

● **Road Transport**

Most coastal towns are linked by a good 185 mile road from Springlands in the E to Charity in the W; the Berbice and Essequibo rivers are crossed by ferries, the Demerara by a toll bridge, which, besides closing at high tide for ships to pass through (2-3 hrs), is subject to frequent closures (when an alternative ferry service runs). Apart from a good road connecting Georgetown and Linden, continuing as good dirt to Mabura Hill, most other roads in the interior are very poor. Car hire is available from several firms, see under Georgetown. There are shortages of car spares. Gasoline costs about US$1.40 a gallon. Traffic drives on the left. Minibuses and collective taxis, an H on their numberplate, run between Georgetown and most towns in the coastal belt.

● **River Transport**

There are over 600 miles of navigable river, which provide an important means of communication. Ferries and river boats are referred to in the text, but for further details contact the Transport and Harbours Department, Water St, Georgetown. Note that there is no vehicle ferry across the Courantyne to Suriname.

● **Accommodation**

The largest hotels in Georgetown have their own emergency electricity generators and water pumps to deal with the frequent interruptions in supply. Other hotels usually provide

a bucket of water in your room, fill this up when water is available. When booking an air-conditioned room, make sure it also has natural ventilation.

● **Food And Drink**

The blend of different national influences (Indian, African, Chinese, Creole, English, Portuguese, Amerindian, North American) gives a distinctive flavour to Guyanese cuisine. One well-known dish, traditional at Christmas, is pepper-pot, meat cooked in bitter cassava juice with peppers and herbs. Seafood is plentiful and varied, as is the wide variety of tropical fruits and vegetables. Staple foods are rice and long thin bora beans. The food shortages and import ban of the early 1980s have ended, but they did have the positive effect of encouraging experimentation with local ingredients, sometimes with interesting results. In the interior wild meat is often available, eg wild cow, or else labba (a small rodent).

Rum is the most popular drink. There is a wide variety of brands, all cheap, including the best which are very good and cost less than US$2 a bottle. Demerara Distillers 12-year old *King of Diamonds* premium rum won the *Caribbean Week* (Barbados) Caribbean rum tasting for two years running (1992, 1993). High wine is a strong local rum. There is also local brandy and whisky (Diamond Club), which are worth trying. The local beer, Banks, made partly from rice is acceptable and cheap. There is a wide variety of fruit juices.

● **Currency**

The unit is the Guyanese dollar. There are notes for 1, 5, 10, 20, 100 and 500 dollars, though devaluation and inflation mean that even the largest of these is worth very little. Coins for amounts under a dollar exist but are of little practical use.

The devaluation of the Guyanese dollar in February 1991 aligned the official exchange rate with that offered by licensed exchange houses (known as *cambios*). Since that date the exchange rate was to be adjusted weekly in line with the market rate. In June 1994, this stood at G$145 = US$1. At present *cambios* only buy US or Canadian dollars and pounds sterling. Most *cambios* accept drafts (subject to verification), travellers' cheques and telegraphic transfers, but not credit cards. Rates vary slightly between *cambios* and from day to day and some *cambios* offer better rates for changing over US$100. Rates for changing travellers' cheques are good in *cambios* or on the black market. A few banks accept Thomas

Cook travellers' cheques. Note that to sell Guyanese dollars on leaving the country, you will need to produce your *cambio* receipt. The illegal black market on America St ("Wall Street") in Georgetown still operates, but the rates offered are not significantly better than the *cambio* rate and there is a strong risk of being robbed or cheated. The black market also operates in Springlands, the entry point from Suriname.

● **Cost Of Living**

The devaluation to the *cambio* rate means that, for foreigners, prices are low at present. Even imported goods may be cheaper than elsewhere and locally produced goods such as fruit are very cheap.

● **Health**

There is a high risk of both types of malaria in the interior, especially in the wet season. Recommended prophylaxis is chloroquine 500 mg weekly plus paludrine 200 mg daily. Reports of chloroquine-resistant malaria in the interior (seek advice before going). If travelling to the interior for long periods carry drugs for treatment as these may not be available. Sleep under a mosquito net. Although there are plenty of mosquitoes on the coast, they are not malarial.

There is some risk of typhoid and waterborne diseases (eg cholera – 1993) owing to low water pressure. Purification is a good idea. Tapwater is usually brown and contains sediment. It is not for drinking; bottled water should be bought for drinking. The Georgetown Hospital is run down, understaffed and lacking equipment, but there are a number of well-equipped private hospitals, including St Joseph's on Parade St, Kingston; Prasad's on Thomas St, doctor on call at weekends; and the Davis Memorial Hospital on Lodge Backlands. Charges are US$2 to US$8 per day and medical consultations cost US$2 to US$4. If admitted to hospital you are expected to provide your own sheets and food (St Joseph's and Davis provides all these). Rec doctor, Dr Clarence Charles, 254 Thomas St, surgery hours 1200-1400.

In the interior, travellers should examine shower pipes, bedding, shoes and clothing for snakes and spiders. Also, in most towns there is neither a hospital nor police. If travelling independently, you are on your own.

● **Climate**

Athough hot, is not unhealthy. Mean shade temperature throughout the year is 27°C; the mean maximum is about 31°C and the mean minimum 24°C. The heat is greatly tempered by cooling breezes from the sea and is most felt from August to October. There are two wet seasons, from May to June, and from December to the end of January, although they may extend into the months either side. Rainfall averages 2,300mm a year in Georgetown.

● **Time Zone**

4 hours behind GMT; one hour ahead of EST.

● **Public Holidays**

1 January, New Years' Day; 23 February, Republic Day and Mashramani festival; Good Friday, Easter Monday; Labour Day, 1 May; Caricom Day, first Monday in July; Freedom Day, first Monday in August; Christmas Day, 25 December, and Boxing Day, 26 December.

The following public holidays are for Hindu and Muslim festivals; they follow a lunar calender, and dates should be checked as required: Phagwah, usually March; Eid el Fitr, end of Ramadan; Eid el Azah; Youm un Nabi; Deepavali, usually November.

Note that the Republic Day celebrations last about a week: during this time hotels in Georgetown are very full.

● **Weights And Measures**

Although Guyana went metric in 1982, imperial measures are still widely used.

● **Voltage**

100 v in Georgetown; 220 v in most other

places, including some Georgetown suburbs.

● **Postal And Telephone Services**

Overseas postal and telephone charges are very low. Telecommunications are rapidly improving. It is possible to dial direct to any country in the world. Blue public telephones in Georgetown only allow collect calls overseas; each phone booth has country codes printed in it. Yellow public phones are for free calls to local areas. Some businesses and hotels may allow you to use their phone for local calls if you are buying something, usual charge about US$0.05. Overseas calls can be made from the Guyana Telephone and Telegraph Company office in the Bank of Guyana building (arrive early and be prepared for a long wait), or from the *Tower Hotel* (more expensive but more comfortable). Travel agencies may allow you to make overseas collect calls when buying tickets. To use Canada Direct, dial 0161. Fax rates to Europe under US$1 per page. Most hotels have Fax service.

● **Press**

The Chronicle, daily except Mon; *The Mirror*, weekly PPP-run; *The Stabroek News*, daily, independent; *The Catholic Standard*, weekly, well-respected and widely read. Street vendors charge more than the cover price, this is normal and helps them make a living.

● **Embassies And Consulates**

There is a large number of embassies in Georgetown, including: **British High Commission** (44 Main St, PO Box 10849, T 592-2-65881/4); **Canadian High Commission** (Young St) and the Embassies of the **United States** (Young St, Kingston, near *Guyana Pegasus Hotel*), **France** (7 Sherriff St, T 65238), **Venezuela** (Thomas St), **Brazil** (308 Church St, Queenstown, T 57970, visa issued next day, 90 days, 1 photo,

US$12.75), **Cuba** (Main St) and **Suriname** (304 Church St, T 56995; 2 passport photos, passport, US$20 and 5 days minimum needed).

● **Tourist Information**

The combination of incentives, the stabilization of the economy and government recognition of the foreign exchange earning potential of tourism has led to many new ventures since 1990. The Ministry of Trade, Tourism and Industry has a Tourism Department which can provide information through its office on South Rd near Camp St, Georgetown, T 62505/63182, F 02-544310. The Ministry has a booth at Timehri Airport. Substantial private sector growth has led to the formation of the Tourism Association of Guyana (TAG – office at 225 South Rd, next to Ministry of Trade, Tourism and Industry), which covers all areas of tourism (hotels, airlines, restaurants, tour operators, etc). The TAG produced a 36-page, full-colour booklet on Guyana; the *Tourist Guide* may be obtained by writing to the Association at PO Box 101147, Georgetown, or by phoning 592-2-70267. This is also the Association's information number.

Maps of country and Georgetown (US$6) from Department of Lands and Surveys, Homestreet Ave, Dorban Backland (take a taxi). T 60524-9 in advance, poor stock. Rivers and islands change frequently according to water levels, so maps can only give you a general direction. A local guide can be more reliable. City maps also from *Guyana Store*, Water St, next to the ice house (take a taxi).

We are grateful to Tony Thorne (Georgetown) for an update of the Guyana chapter, also, for her assistance, to Dianne McTurk. Thanks are also due to Mr E Sabat (MD) of Rainbow River Safari (Guyana).

SURINAME

SURINAME has a coast line on the Atlantic to the N; it is bounded on the W by Guyana and on the E by French Guyane; Brazil is to the S. The principal rivers in the country are the Marowijne in the E, the Corantijn in the W, and the Suriname, Commewijne (with its tributary, the Cottica), Coppename, Saramacca and Nickerie. The country is divided into topographically quite diverse natural regions: the northern part of the country consists of lowland, with a width in the E of 25 km, and in the W of about 80 km. The soil (clay) is covered with swamps with a layer of humus under them. Marks of the old seashores can be seen in the shell and sand ridges, overgrown with tall trees. There follows a region, 5-6 km wide, of a loamy and very white sandy soil, then a slightly undulating region, about 30 km wide. It is mainly savannah, mostly covered with quartz sand, and overgrown with grass and shrubs. South of this lies the interior highland, almost entirely overgrown with dense tropical forest and intersected by streams. At the southern boundary with Brazil there are again savannahs. These, however, differ in soil and vegetation from the northern ones. A large area in the SW is in dispute between Guyana and Suriname. There is a less serious border dispute with Guyane in the SE.

The 1980 census showed that the population had declined to 352,041, because of heavy emigration to the Netherlands. By 1992 it was estimated to have grown to 404,000. The 1983 population consisted of Indo-Pakistanis (known locally as Hindustanis), 37%; Creoles (European-African and other descent), 31%; Javanese, 14%; Chinese, 3%; Bush Negroes, called locally "bosnegers" (retribalized descendants of slaves who escaped in the 17th century, living on the upper Saramacca, Suriname and Marowijne rivers), 8.5%; Europeans and others, 3%; Amerindians, 3% (some sources say only 1%). About 90% of the existing population live in or around Paramaribo or in the coastal towns; the remainder, mostly Carib and Arawak Indians and bosnegers, are widely scattered.

The Asian people originally entered the country as contracted estate labourers, and settled in agriculture or commerce after completion of their term. They dominate the countryside, whereas Paramaribo is racially very mixed. Although some degree of racial tension exists between all the different groups, Creole-Hindustani rivalry is not as fundamental an issue as in Guyana, for example. Many Surinamese, of all backgrounds, pride themselves on their ability to get along with one another in such a heterogeneous country.

The official language is Dutch. The native dialect, called negro English (Sranan Tongo), usually referred to as Taki-Taki) originally the speech of the Creoles, is now a *lingua franca* understood by all groups, and standard English is widely spoken and understood. The Asians still speak their own languages among themselves.

History

Although Amsterdam merchants had been trading with the "wild coast" of Guiana as early as 1613 (the name Parmurbo-Paramaribo was already known) it was not until 1630 that 60 English settlers came to Suriname under Captain Marshall and planted tobacco. The real founder of the colony was Lord Willoughby of Parham, governor of Barbados, who sent an expedition to

Suriname in 1651 under Anthony Rowse to find a suitable place for settlement. Willoughbyland became an agricultural colony with 500 little sugar plantations, 1,000 white inhabitants and 2,000 African slaves. Jews from Holland and Italy joined them, as well as Dutch Jews ejected from Brazil after 1654. On 27 February 1667, Admiral Crynssen conquered the colony for the states of Zeeland and Willoughbyfort became the present Fort Zeelandia. By the Peace of Breda, 31 July 1667, it was agreed that Suriname should remain with the Netherlands, while Nieuw Amsterdam (New York) should be given to England. The colony was conquered by the British in 1799, and not until the Treaty of Paris in 1814 was it finally restored to the Netherlands. Slavery was forbidden in 1818 and formally abolished in 1863. Indentured labour from China and the East Indies took its place.

On 25 November 1975, the country became an independent republic, which signed a treaty with the Netherlands for an economic aid programme worth US$1.5bn until 1985. A military coup on 25 February 1980 overthrew the elected government. A state of emergency was declared, with censorship of the press, radio and TV. The military leader, Colonel Desi Bouterse, and his associates came under pressure from the Dutch and the USA as a result of dictatorial tendencies. After the execution of 15 opposition leaders on 8 December 1982, the Netherlands broke off relations and suspended its aid programme, although bridging finance was restored in 1988.

The ban on political parties was lifted in late 1985 and a new constitution was drafted. In 1986 guerrilla rebels (the Jungle Commando), led by a former bodyguard of Colonel Bouterse, Ronny Brunswijk, mounted a campaign to overthrow the government, disrupting both plans for political change and the economy. Nevertheless, elections for the National Assembly were held in November 1987. A three-party coalition (the Front for Democracy and Development) gained a landslide victory over the military, winning 40 of the 51 seats. In January 1988, Mr Ramsewak Shankar, was elected President by the Assembly for a 5-year term. Conflicts between President Shankar and Colonel Bouterse led to the deposition of the government in a bloodless coup on 24 December 1990 (the "telephone coup"). A military-backed government under the presidency of Johan Kraag was installed and elections for a new national assembly were held on 25 May 1991. The New Front of four traditional parties won 30 National Assembly seats. Twelve went to the army-backed National Democratic Party and nine to the Democratic Alternative, which favours closer links with The Netherlands. Ronald Venetiaan of the New Front was elected president on 6 September 1991. Both the Netherlands and the USA suspended aid after the coup, but meetings between Suriname and Netherlands ministers after the 1991 elections led to the renewal of aid in the second half of 1992. Although a basis for peace was drawn up in mid-1989 (the Kourou Accord), it was not until March 1991 that Colonel Bouterse and Brunswijk stated publicly that hostilities had ceased (Brunswijk had declared an end to his campaign in June 1990). A peace treaty was signed between the government and the Jungle Commando in August 1992. The different factions, however, retained control of their respective areas in the interior and violence breaks out occasionally. Col Bouterse resigned as chief of the armed forces in December 1992 to found a political party, the New Democratic Party (NDP). He remains a prominent, powerful national figure.

By 1993, the New Front's popularity had slumped as its handling of the economy failed to reap any benefit from the 1992 Structural Adjustment Programme and corruption scandals undermined its claim to introduce "clean politics." Both

Bouterse's NDP and Democratic Alliance strengthened their opposition to government policies, calling for strikes and protests, but as these two parties have wide ideological differences, no concerted campaign against the New Front was mounted.

Government

There is one legislative house, the National Assembly, which has 51 members. The President is both head of state and government. Suriname is divided into ten districts, of which the capital is one.

The Economy

Agriculture is restricted to some districts of the alluvial coastal zone, covering about 0.8m hectares. At least two-thirds of permanent crop and arable land is under irrigation. Farming (including forestry) accounts for 11.1% of gdp and about 15% of exports. The main crops are rice (the staple), bananas, sugar cane and citrus fruits, all of which are exported to Europe, along with small quantities of coffee. Apart from rice, Suriname is a net importer of food; priority is being given to rice and livestock. Between 1981 and 1983, the sector registered annual declines in output, but after 1984, positive growth was restored with the rice and shrimp sectors receiving new incentives. Suriname has vast timber resources, but exports account for less than 1% of the total and development has been hampered by a lack of investment. There is a small fishing industry, the chief catch being shrimps.

Manufacturing's contribution to gdp is 10.1%. Import substitution, using both imported goods and local raw materials, is the main activity, with food processing accounting for 60% of the total.

Suriname is the world's sixth largest producer of bauxite, with reserves estimated at 1.9% of the world's total. The country has the capability to process the extracted ore into alumina and alu-

SURINAME : FACT FILE

Geographic
Land area	163,820 sq km
forested	95.3%
pastures	0.1%
cultivated	0.4%

Demographic
Population (1992)	404,000
annual growth rate (1987-92)	0.6%
urban	65.2%
rural	34.8%
density	2.5 per sq km
Religious affiliation	
Hindu	26.0%
Roman Catholic	21.6%
Muslim	18.6%
Protestant	18.0%
Birth rate per 1,000 (1988)	23.2
	(world av 27.1)
Death rate per 1,000 (1988)	6.1
	(world av 9.8)

Education and Health
Life expectancy at birth,	
male	67.1 years
female	72.1 years
Infant mortality rate	
per 1,000 live births (1985)	27.6
Physicians (1985)	1 per 1,798 persons
Hospital beds	1 per 200 persons
Calorie intake as %	
of FAO requirement	108%
Literate males (over 15)	95.1%
Literate females (over 15)	94.7%

Economic
GNP (1990 market prices)	US$1,365mn
GNP per capita	US$3,050
Public external debt (1986)	US$70mn
Tourism receipts (1990)	US$11mn
Inflation (annual av 1985-90)	19.1%
Radio	1 per 1.7 persons
Television	1 per 10 persons
Telephone	1 per 8.4 persons

Employment
Population economically active (1985)	
	99,240
Unemployment rate (1989)	15.6%
% of labour force in	
agriculture	16.8
mining	4.7
manufacturing	11.1
construction	2.8
Military forces	1,800

Source Encyclopaedia Britannica

minium ingot. The bauxite/aluminium industry accounts for 72% of exports, while the mining sector as a whole contributes 3.6% of gdp. Two companies control the industry, the Suriname Aluminium Company (Suralco), a subsidiary of Alcoa, and Billiton Maatschappij, part of Royal Dutch Shell. Their progressive merging of operations to improve competitiveness on world markets began to yield positive results in 1986 until the industry was severely disrupted by the civil war which started in that year.

Oil production from the Tambaredjo heavy oil deposit, operated by the state oil company, Staatsolie, is about 4,700 bpd. Exploratory wells in the Saramacca district have also yielded oil. Installed electricity generating capacity is 415 MW, of which 19% is thermal, 81% hydroelectric.

After five years of decline and a fall in gdp of 8.1% in 1987 alone, the economy began to recover, helped by resumption of activity in the bauxite industry, the attenuation of the domestic insurgency and the resumption of aid from the Dutch Government. Consistent improvement was not maintained and The Netherlands, the IMF and World Bank urged Suriname to unify the official and parallel exchange rates, reduce state involvement in the economy and cut the huge budget deficit to attract overseas investment. These issues began to be addressed after a new economic crisis in 1991 when the export price of alumina fell by 25% and Dutch aid was again cut after the 1990 coup. In 1992 a Structural Adjustment Programme was drawn up as a forerunner to a Multi-Year Development Programme (for 1994-98). The unification of official and market exchange rates was achieved in July 1994 and a floating rate of Sf183 was established, replacing complex exchange rate system. By 1994, little progress had been made in complying with the Structural Adjustment Programme. Inflation rose sharply; prices of staple items also rose; petrol

rationing was introduced in September 1993 as the government could not pay suppliers' bills. The EC suspended balance of payments support in 1993 pending Suriname seeking renewed assistance from the IMF or World Bank in monitoring the economy. However, it did grant aid of G88 mn in 1994 for the development of rural areas, social projects and the reconstruction of the E-W road.

Nature Reserves

Stinasu, the Foundation for Nature Preservation in Suriname, Jongbawstraat 14, T 75845/71856, PO Box 436, Paramaribo, offers reasonably priced accommodation and provides tour guides on the extensive nature reserves throughout the country. One can see "true wilderness and wildlife" with them, recommended.

Many reserves were badly damaged during the civil war. At present only *Brownsberg* has any organized infrastructure. Located atop hills overlooking the van Blommensteinmeer reservoir, it features good walking and 3 impressive waterfalls. There are all-inclusive tours from Paramaribo with Stinasu (3 days Sf650, 1 day Sf195, including transport, accommodations, food, and guide). One can also make an independent visit. Buses for Brownsweg leave Paramaribo daily at approx 0830 from Saramacastraat by BEM shop, Sf10, trucks at the same time Sf50. Go to Stinasu at least 24 hrs in advance of your visit to reserve and pay for accommodation in their guest houses (approx Sf40 double) and to arrange for a vehicle to pick you up in Brownsweg (Sf80 for up to 8 people, Sf100 for up to 10). Take your own food.

Raleighvallen/Voltzberg Nature Reserve (57,000 hectares) is rainforest park, including Foengoe Island and Voltzberg peak; climbing the mountain at sunrise is unforgettable. The Coppename Estuary is also a national park, protecting many bird colonies.

Two reserves are located on the NE coast of Suriname. Known primarily as a major nesting site for sea turtles (five species including the huge leatherback turtle come ashore to lay their eggs) **Wia-Wia Nature Reserve** (36,000 hectares), also has nesting grounds for some magnificent birds. The nesting activity of sea turtles is best observed February-August (July and August are good months to visit as you can see both adults coming ashore to lay eggs and hatchlings rushing to the sea at high tide). Since the beaches and consequently the turtles have shifted westwards out of the reserve, accommodation is now at **Matapica** beach, not in the reserve itself. (After a visit to the reserves please send any comments to Hilde Viane at Stinasu. Your support is needed to keep the reserve functioning.) There may also be mosquitoes and sandflies, depending on the season. A riverboat leaves Paramaribo daily at 0700 (buy ticket on board) and arrives in Alliance by way of the Commewijne River at 1100. You then transfer to a Stinasu motorboat for a one-hour ride to Matapica. The motorboat costs US$50 for 4 people, round trip. Suitable waterproof clothing should be worn. Fishermen make the crossing for US$3-4. The beach hut accommodates 18 people in 4 rooms, and costs US$4 pp. Take your own bedding/food. Cooking facilities provided. Book the hut and boat through Stinasu and keep your receipts or you will be refused entry. Early booking is essential as the closure of the other reserves has made Matapica very popular.

The **Galibi Nature Reserve**, where there are more turtle-nesting places, is near the mouth of the Marowijne River. There are Carib Indian villages. From Albina it is a 3-hour (including ½ hour on the open sea) boat trip to Galibi.

PARAMARIBO

Paramaribo, the capital and chief port, lies on the Suriname river, 12 km from the sea. It has a population of about 192,000. There are many attractive colonial buildings.

The Governor's Mansion (now the Presidential Palace) is on Eenheidsplein (formerly Onafhankelijkheidsplein, and before that, Oranjeplein) ; it was being renovated in 1993. Many beautiful 18th and 19th century buildings in Dutch (neo-Normanic) style are in the same area. A few have been restored but much of the old city is sadly decaying. The restored Fort Zeelandia used to house the Suriname Museum, but the fort has been repossessed by the military (the whole area is fenced off); very few exhibits remain in the old museum in the residential suburb of Zorg-en-Hoop, Commewijnestraat, 0700-1300. Look for Mr F Lim-A-Po-straat if you wish to see what Paramaribo looked like only a comparatively short time ago. The nineteenth-century Roman Catholic Peter and Paul cathedral (1885), built entirely of wood, is said to be the largest wooden building in the Americas, and is well worth a visit (closed indefinitely for repairs in 1993). Much of the old town, dating from the nineteenth century, and the churches have been restored. Other things to see are the colourful market and the waterfront, Hindu temples in Koningstraat and Gravenstraat 31, the Caribbean's largest mosque at Keizerstraat (magnificent photos of it can be taken at sunset). There are two synagogues: one next to the mosque on Keizerstraat, the other (1854) on the corner of Klipstenstraat and Heerenstraat (services on Sat morning, alternating monthly between the two – to visit when closed T 498944 and ask for Dennis Kopinsky). A new harbour has been constructed about 1½ km upstream. Two pleasant parks are the Palmentuin, with a stage for concerts, and the Cultuurtuin (with well-kept zoo,

US$1.20, busy on Sunday), the latter is a 20-mins walk from the centre. National dress is normally only worn by the Asians on national holidays and at wedding parties, but some Javanese women still go about in sarong and klambi. A university was opened in 1968. There is one public swimming pool at Weidestraat, US$0.60 pp. There is an exotic Asian flavour to the market and nearby streets. Cinemas show US, Indian and Chinese movies, with subtitles.

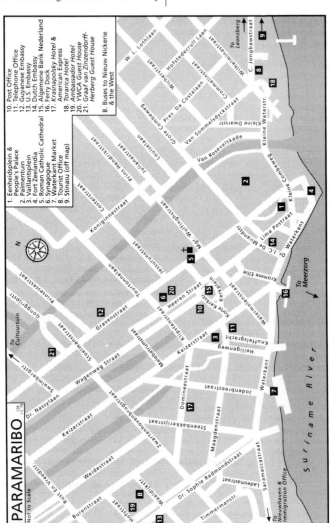

PARAMARIBO
Not to Scale

1. Eenheidsplein & People's Palace
2. Palmentuin
3. Vaillantsplein
4. Fort Zeelandia
5. Roman Catholic Cathedral
6. Synagogue
7. Waterkant Market
8. Tourist Office
9. Stinasu (off map)
10. Post Office
11. Telephone Office
12. Guyanese Embassy
13. U.S. Embassy
14. Dutch Embassy
15. Algemene Bank Nederland
16. Ferry Dock
17. Krasnapolsky Hotel & American Express
18. Torarica Hotel
19. Ambassador Hotel
20. YWCA Guest House
21. Graaf van Zinzendorff-Herberg Guest House

B. Buses to Nieuw Nickerie & the West

An interesting custom practised throughout Suriname is the birdsong competitions. These are held in parks and public plazas on Sundays and holidays. People carrying their songbird (usually a small black tua-tua) in a cage are a frequent sight on the streets of Paramaribo at any time; on their way to and from work, off to a "training session", or simply taking their pet for a stroll!

Local Information – Paramaribo
● Where To Stay
Prices are at the parallel rate unless stated otherwise. Service charge at hotels is 10-15% *Krasnapolsky* Domineestraat 39, T 475050, F 478524, Telex 142 BH-KR, US$60-85 run down, poor quality, central but unpleasant location, ugly, swimming pool and shops, good breakfast, launderette on 1st floor, and bank (open until 1430); much nicer is *Torarica* (T 471500, F 411682) PO Box 1514, Telex 167 SURTOR, best in town, US$60-85, very pleasant, book ahead, swimming pool, casino, nightclub, tropical gardens, fully air conditioned, central, superb breakfast US$6-12; *Ambassador* 66-68 Dr Sophie Redmonstraat, PO Box 15, (T 477555, F 477903), Telex 295 HOTAM SN, renovated in 1993, US$31; *River-club*, at Leonsberg (8 km from city), T 451959, F 452981, same prices, many very-short-stay customers, swimming pool.

For budget travellers, best is the recently refurbished *YWCA Guesthouse* at Heeren-straat 14-16, T 476981 (under US$10), cheaper weekly rates, clean, full of permanent residents, essential to book in advance (office open 0800-1400); if it's full try the *Graaf Van Zinzendorff-Herberg* at Gravenstraat 100, T 471607, the same price as the YWCA, large rooms, TV lounge. Advance booking advisable. Otherwise, try *Continental Inn*; *Fanna*, Princessestraat 31, T 476789, about US$2-7, from basic to a/c with bath, breakfast extra, safe, clean, friendly, family run, English spoken, rec, can book in advance; *Au Soleil Levant*. *La Vida* on the way in from the airport is "cheap but nice". *Mivimost*, Anamoestraat 23, 3 km from centre, T 451002, US$9 with a/c, US$6 with fan and toilet, clean, safe, friendly, rec; *Lisa's Guest House*, Buren Straat, noisy, over-priced. *Mrs Robles' Guesthouse*, Roseveltkade 20, T 474770, family run, organizes tours. *Balden*, Kwathweg 183, 2 km from centre on the road to Nickerie is probably the cheapest available accommodation; its Chinese restaurant serves cheap meals. Beware: many cheap hotels not listed above are "hot pillow" establishments. A religious organization, Stadszending, Burenstraat 17-19, T 47307, good location, clean, friendly, best to reserve. The *Salvation Army*, Saramaccastraat, will give the hard up a bed for Sf4.50 a night.

● Where To Eat
Main meals cost Sf60-100 pp. There are some good restaurants, mainly Indonesian and Chinese dishes. Try a *rijsttafel* in an Indonesian restaurant, eg *Sarinah* (open-air dining), Verlengde Gemenelandsweg 187. *La Bastille*, Kleine Waterstraat, opp *Torarica*, good, T 473991; also *Golden Dragon*, Anamoestraat 22, *New Korean*, Mahonylaan, *Golden Crown*, David Simmonstraat and *New China*, Verlengde Gemenelandsweg. *Fa Tai*, Maagdenstraat 64, a/c; for the best Chinese food, but not cheap, try *Iwan's*, Grote Hofstraat. *Oriental Foods*, Gravenstraat 118, for well-prepared Chinese food. Many other Chinese restaurants. Cheap lunches and light meals at *Chindy's*, Keizerstraat opp TeleSur, lunch only, try *pom*, also ice cream; *Hofje*, Wagenwegstraat, and *Chalet Swiss*, Heerenstraat (more Chinese than Swiss). *Natura*, Rust-en-Vredestraat between Keizerstraat and Weidestraat, whole-grain bread and natural foods. Meat and noodles from stalls in the market costs at least Sf20. Javanese foodstalls on Waterkant are excellent and varied, lit at night by candles. Try *bami* (spicy noodles) and *petjil* (vegetables); no dish costs less than Sf10. Especially recommended on Sun when the area is busiest. In restaurants a dish to try is *gadogado*, an Indonesian vegetable and peanut concoction. Good places for lunch include *Hola's Terrace*, Domineestraat. For breakfast, try *Klein Maar Fijn*, Watermolenstraat. Local beer, Parbo, is worth a try.

● Shopping
Crafts of Amerindian and Bush Negro origin. *Arts & Crafts*, Neumanpad 13a. Amerindian goods, batik prints, carvings, basket work, drums are attractive. *Cultuurwinkel*, Anton de Kom Straat, bosneger carvings, also available at *Hotel Torarica*. Carvings are better value at the workshops on Nieuwe Dominee Straat and the Neumanpad. *Peet* woodworks have been rec for hardwood pieces. Local ceramics are sold on the road between the airport and Paranam, but they are rather brittle. *Disco*

Amigo sells local and international music on cassette (no CDs of national music, which is heavily influenced by Caribbean styles). Old Dutch bottles US$10-25. **Bookshops** The two main bookshops are *Fahco* (opp *Krasnapolsky*) and *Kersten*, both on Domineestraat, and both sell English-language books. Also *Hoeksteen* (Gravenstraat 17) and the kiosk in *Krasnapolsky Hotel*. *Boekhandel Univers NV*, Gravenstraat 61, is rec for nature, linguistic and scholarly books on Suriname. Second hand books, English and Dutch, are bought and sold in the market. Maps are hard to find, although *Fahco* sells a good country map.

● Local Transport

There are very few regular buses; the few services that are left leave from Waterkant or Dr Sophie Redmondstraat. There are privately run "wild buses", also known as "numbered buses" which run on fixed routes around the city; they are minivans, severely overcrowded, charging Sf0.75. **Taxis** generally have no meters. The price should be agreed on beforehand to avoid trouble. A trip inside the city costs about Sf20-35, rising to Sf50 from one side of the city to the other. Rec is Ally's Taxi service, T 479434, English spoken. If hiring a taxi for touring, beware of overcharging.

● Long Distance Transport

To **Nickerie** from Dr Sophie Redmondstraat, nr *Hotel Ambassador*, minibuses leave when full between 0500 and 1000; there are also buses after 1000, but the price then depends on the driver, 4-5 hrs (depending on ferry crossing), Sf25-45 (extra for large bag). Taxis from the same area, slightly faster, Sf200 pp or Sf1,000-1,500 for the trip. To **Albina** from near ferry dock or from Meerzorg, 3-4 hrs, Sf100, large bag extra. Taxis also available (Sf200). There are irregular bus services to other towns. For full details ask drivers or enquire at the tourist office.

Verify all fares in advance and beware of overcharging. There is much jostling in the queues and pure mayhem when boarding vehicles. They are all minivans and have no luggage space. Try to accommodate baggage under your seat or you will have to hold it in your lap.

● Exchange

Algemene Bank Nederland (Kerkplein 1), Surinaamse Bank and Hakrin Bank, 0700-1400. Surinaamse branch in *Hotel Krasnapolsky* open 0700-1430; 0800-1200 Sat, charges Sf6 flat rate commission on each TC exchanged. Amex agent is C Kersten and Co, NV, in *Hotel Krasnapolsky*, T 477148. Be very wary of money changers in the market and on the street, who approach you calling "whistle" (exchange). Many visitors have been robbed or cheated and, as the black market is illegal, you have no recourse. Many shop keepers will change cash at parallel rates and this is a much safer option. Ask around for best rates (see **Currency** in Information for Visitors).

● Church

The Anglican Church is St Bridget's, Hoogestraat 44 (Sunday 0900 service in English). Roman Catholic Cathedral on Gravenstraat. Dutch Reformed Church and many other denominations.

● Tourist Agencies

Mrs W J Robles-Cornelissen, *Independent Tours*, Rosenveltkade 20, T 474770, and *Suriname Safari Tours* organize excursions to the interior. Trips take 3-5 days and cost about US$120 (parallel exchange), all inclusive. *CTM Travel*, Sophie Redmondstraat opp Hakrin Bank building, 0730-1600, helpful. *Ram's Tours*, Neumandpad 30 Ben, T 476011/476223. *Does Travel Service*, Domineestraat. *Saramaccan Jungle Safaris* (John Ligeon), PO Box 676, Zwartenhovenbrugstraat 19, Paramaribo, for visits by canoe to Saramaccan Bush Black villages and wildlife tours. *NV Mets Tourism*, PO Box 9080, Paramaribo, organizes trips to the interior at reasonable rates.

NB If intending to take a tour to the jungle and either Amerindian or Bush Black villages, check how much time is spent in the jungle itself and on the conditions in the villages. One such is to Paloemeu, an Amerindian village due S of Paramaribo, not far from the Brazilian border. A 3-day trip costs US$150, inc flights, food, accommodation, jungle hikes and river trips. We have received two reports of this trip, one recommending it and one disappointed.

Excursions

Powaka, about 90 mins outside the capital, is a primitive village of thatched huts but with electric light and a small church. In the surrounding forest one can pick mangoes and other exotic fruit. An interesting half, or full day excursion is to take minibus 4, or taxi, to Leonsberg on the

Suriname river (restaurant *Rusty Pelikan* on waterfront; at *Leonsberg* restaurant try *saoto* soup and other Javanese specialities, overlooking the river), then ferry to **Nieuw Amsterdam**, the capital of the predominantly Javanese district of Commewijne. There is an open-air museum inside the old fortress (badly rundown, open only in mornings except Friday, 1700-1900, Sfl5), which guarded the confluence of the Suriname and Commewijne rivers. There are some old plantation mansions left in the Commewijne district which are of interest; Mariënburg is the last sugar estate in operation in Suriname. The return trip can be made by bus to Meerzorg on the river, taking the vehicle ferry back to Paramaribo.

By private car to **Jodensavanne** (Jews' Savanna, established 1639), S of Paramaribo on the opposite bank of the Suriname river, where a cemetery and the foundations of one of the oldest synagogues in the Western Hemisphere has been restored. There is no public transport and taxis won't go because of the bad road. It is still only 1½ hrs with a suitable vehicle. There is a bridge across the Suriname River to Jodensavanne. Mrs Robles, T 474770, organizes tours if there are enough people. **Blakawatra** is said to be one of the most beautiful spots in all Suriname. This was the scene of much fighting in the civil war. A full day trip to Jodensavanne and Blakawatra, returning to Paramaribo via Moengo, has been recommended if one can arrange the transport. Some 4 km from the International Airport there is a resort called Cola Creek, so named for the colour of the water, but good swimming.

Approximately 30 km SW of Paramaribo, via **Lelydorp** (*Hotel De Lely*, Sastrodisomoweg 41), is the Bush Negro village of **Santigron**, on the E bank of the Saramaca River. Mini-buses leave from Saramacastraat in front of BEM store at approx 0700 and 1030, Mon-Sat, one afternoon bus on Sat, 1 hr, Sf5, crowded. They return as soon as they drop off passengers in the village, so make sure you will have a bus to return on, no accommodation in Santigron. Nearby is the Amerindian village of **Pekein Poika**. The two make a good independent day trip. Tour agencies also visit the area about twice month, including canoe rides on the Saramaca River and a Bush Negro dance performance.

By bus or car to **Afobakka**, where there is a large hydro-electric dam on the Suriname river. There is a government guesthouse (price includes 3 meals a day) in nearby **Brokopondo**. Victoria is an oil-palm plantation in the same area. The Brownsberg National Park is one hour by car from here.

Stoelmanseiland, headquarters of Ronnie Brunswijk, on the Lawa River (guest house with full board) in the interior, and the *bosneger* villages and rapids in the area can be visited on excursions organised by tour operators. Price US$150 pp for 3 days (5 persons, minimum). They are, however, more easily reached by river from St-Laurent du Maroni and Maripasoula in Guyane. Excursions also to Tepoe, up the Tapanahony river in the S, where one can visit the Trio and Wayana Indians.

WEST OF PARAMARIBO

Leaving Paramaribo, a narrow but well paved road leads through the citrus and vegetable growing districts of Wanica and Saramaca, connected by a bridge over the Saramaca River. At Boskamp (90 km from Paramaribo) the Coppename River is reached. Daytime only ferry to Jenny on the W bank (passengers Sfl0.25) takes about 20 mins.

A further 50 km is **Totness**, where there was once a Scottish settlement. It is the largest village in the Coronie district, along the coast between Paramaribo and Nieuw Nickerie on the Guyanese border. There is a good government guesthouse. The road (bad, liable to flooding) leads through an extensive forest of coconut palms. Bus to Paramaribo at 0600. 40 km further W, 5 km S of the main road is **Wageningen**, a modern little town, the centre of the Suriname rice-growing area. The road from Nickerie has recently been renewed. One of the largest fully mechanized rice farms in the world is found here (*Hotel de Wereld*). The **Bigi-Pan** area of mangroves is a bird-watchers' paradise; boats may be hired from local fishermen.

Nieuw Nickerie, on the S bank of the Nickerie River 5 km from its mouth, opposite Guyana is the main town and port of the Nickerie district and is distinguished for its ricefields and for the number and voraciousness of its mosquitoes. The town has a population of more than 8,000, the district of 35,000, mostly East Indian. Paramaribo is 237 km away by road. For bus services, see under Paramaribo. Sit on the left-hand side of the bus to get the best views of the birdlife in the swamps. The coastal ferry service has been discontinued, but once a week the SMS company makes an interesting water trip, using inland waterways, to Nieuw Nickerie taking 36 hrs; it leaves Paramaribo on Mondays at 0800, departs Nieuw Nickerie 1200 Wednesday (times subject to 2 hrs variation due to tides), no cabins, only slatted seats, but there is hammock space; take food and drink; lots of mosquitoes.

● **Where To Stay** Prices converted at parallel rate of exchange: *Americali*, US$10, a/c, clean, friendly, good; *Moksie Patoe*, Gouverneurstraat 115, T 232219, US$7, restaurant, owner rents a 2-bedroom house 93 beds) next door; *De-Vesting*, similar quality, Balatastraat 6, T 031265; *De President*, Gouverneurstraat, US$5 with bath, US$3 without, a/c, good value, friendly; *Luxor*, Jozefstraat 22, T 231365, US$3.65, private bath, friendly; *Diamond*, Balatastraat 29, T 232210, US$2, some rooms with bath, close to ferry, basic; *Tropical*, Gouverneurstraat 114, T 231796, US$2, noisy bar downstairs.

● **Where To Eat** *Moksie Patoe*, Gouverneurstraat 115, run by Frenchman, Jean Amar, provides European and Indian dishes with items rarely found elsewhere in friendly atmosphere. *Ella*, Javanese food. *Incognito*, Gouverneurstraat 44, Indondesian; *Pak-Hap*, Gouverneurstraat 101, Chinese. Many others on same street.

● **Exchange** The bank at the immigration office is reported to close at 1500 Mon-Fri, whether or not the ferry has arrived.

● **Air** SLM to/from Paramaribo Tues and Thur, US$29, office on main square on river, helpful, can book international flights, no credit cards, open till 1600.

Ferry to Springlands, Guyana

Normally operates Mon to Sat (except public holidays of either country), foot passengers only, Sf65 one way, heavy luggage extra. Booking office at Landenstraat 26, open Mon-Sat, 0630-0645, 0900-1200, 1600-1700, essential to book the day before travelling, booking fee Sf2.50, must show passport.

All immigration and customs formalities take place at the ferry dock. Queue up at gate at 0600, expect about 3 hrs of waiting before sailing. The trip takes at least 2 hrs, Guyanese immigration and customs forms handed out on board, cold drinks are sometimes sold. There may be up to another 3 hrs of queuing for Guyanese formalities. Visa requirements have been relaxed (see Guyana, **Documents**) and a return ticket is not always asked for. Ferry returns to Nickerie the same afternoon (bookings in the am).

Note The ferry was not running in March 1994. Suriname officials were giving exit stamps and small boats ferried people across for US$20. On arrival in Guyana it was essential to go to immigration and, probably, pay a bribe. Not a recommended route at that time.

From Springlands, there are minibuses to New Amsterdam, thence ferries and launches to Rosignol, and minibuses to Georgetown. Entire journey (Nickerie-Georgetown) takes 10-12 hrs, 2 days from Paramaribo including overnight in Nickerie.

Vast reserves of bauxite were discovered

in the Bakhuis Mountains, S of Nickerie District in the NW of Sipaliwini District. A road once ran as far as Lucie on the Corantijn River, but it is now mostly overgrown. The infrastructure developed for the bauxite industry in the 1970s was subsequently abandoned or destroyed. *Apoera* on the Corantijn; it can be reached by sea-going vessels. *Blanche Marie Falls*, 320 km from Paramaribo on the Apoera road, is a popular destination. There is a guesthouse, *Dubois*, US$35, contact Eldoradolaan 22, Paramaribo T 76904/2. Camping is Sf30 tent/day. There is a good guesthouse at Apoera (US$25 with 3 meals, advance booking from Paramaribo advisable). *Washabo* near Apoera, which has an airstrip, is an Amerindian village. There is no public transport from Paramaribo to the Apoera-Bakhuis area, but there are frequent charter flights to the Washabo airstrip. Irregular small boats go from Apoera to Nieuw Nickerie and to Springlands (Guyana). Try to rent a canoe to visit the Amerindian settlement of Orealla in Guyana or Kaboeri creek, 12 km downstream, where giant river otters may possibly be seen in October or March.

EAST OF PARAMARIBO TO GUYANE

Eastern Suriname was the area most severely damaged during the civil war, and its effects are still evident. A paved road connects Meerzorg (vehicle ferry from Paramaribo, every 30 min, passengers Sf0.25) with Albina, passing through the districts of Commewijne and Marowijne. There is little population or agriculture left here. *Moengo*, 160 km up the Cottica River from Paramaribo, is a bauxite mining and loading centre for the Suriname Aluminium Company (Suralco) a subsidiary of Alcoa (*Government Guesthouse*). Paranam, another loading centre, is on the left bank of the Suriname River. It can be reached by medium draught ships

and by cars. Near Paranam is Smalkalden, where bauxite is loaded by the Billiton company on the road to Parimaribo.

East of Moengo, the scars of war are most obvious. Temporary wooden bridges replace those that were blown up, shell craters dot the road, and many abandoned or destroyed houses are seen. *Albina* is on the Marowijne River, the frontier with Guyane. Once a thriving, pleasant town, it is today a bombed-out wreck. No services whatsoever were available here in Feb 1993.

A passenger and vehicle ferry leaves Albina for St Laurent du Maroni Mon, Tues, Wed, Thur, 4 times a day, $1/2$ hr voyage, free. Motorized canoes charge 30F/Sf100, lots of competition. Changing money on the Suriname side of the border is illegal; see **Currency**, below, on currency control. Customs and immigration on both sides close at 1900. Be wary of local information on exchange rates and transport (both the free ferry and buses to Paramaribo). Money can be changed on the Guyane side.

INFORMATION FOR VISITORS

● **Documents**

Visitors must have a valid passport (one issued by the Hong Kong government, and a few others, will not be accepted), a visa, or tourist card. Visas must be obtained in advance by citizens of all countries except Great Britain, Japan, Israel, The Gambia, South Korea, Denmark, Finland, Sweden, Switzerland, Netherlands Antilles, Brazil, Ecuador, Canada, Chile and Guyana (these require a tourist card, obtainable at the airport, US$14). There are consulates in Caracas, Brasília, Georgetown and Cayenne. Visas issued at the consulate in Cayenne normally take 15 days and cost F150 (US$28), but may be obtained the same day (an extra charge for this is sometimes made). Take a photocopy of your ticket out of South America. In Georgetown a visa takes 5 days minimum and costs US$20. On entry to Suriname (by land or air) your passport will be stamped by the military police indicating a brief period (usually 7 days) for which you can re-

with spicy potatoes and vegetables), and *phu-lawri* (fried chick-pea balls). Among the many tropical fruits of Suriname, palm nuts such as the orange coloured awarra and the cone shaped brown maripa are most popular.

● **Health**

No information has been made available about the incidence of cholera in Suriname. Since the disease is almost certainly present, take the appropriate precautions. Boil or purify water, even in the capital. Otherwise, no special precautions necessary except for a trip to the malarial interior; for free malaria prophylaxis contact the Public Health Department (BOG, 15 Rode Kruislaan), but better to take your own. Suriname Safari Tours provides malaria prophylaxis on its package tours. Chloroquine-resistant malaria in the interior. Mosquito nets should be used at night over beds in rooms not air-conditioned or screened. In some coastal districts there is a risk of bilharzia (schistosomiasis). Ask before bathing in lakes and rivers. Vaccinations: yellow fever and tetanus advisable, typhoid only for trips into the interior. Swim only in running water because of poisonous fish. There is good swimming on the Marowijne river and at Matapica beach and on the Coppename river. There are 5 hospitals in Paramaribo, best is St Vincentius.

● **Climate And Clothing**

Tropical and moist, but not very hot, since the NE trade wind makes itself felt during the whole year. In the coastal area the temperature varies on an average from 23° to 31°C, during the day; the annual mean is 27°C, and the monthly mean ranges from 26° to 28°C, only. The mean annual rainfall is about 2,340mm for Paramaribo and 1,930mm for the western division. The seasons are: minor rainy season, November-February; minor dry season, February-April; main rainy season, April-August; main dry season, August-November. None of these seasons is, however, usually either very dry or very wet. The degree of cloudiness is fairly high and the average humidity is 82%.

The climate of the interior is similar but with higher rainfall.

Except for official meetings, informal tropical clothing is worn, but not shorts. An umbrella or plastic raincoat is very useful.

The **high seasons**, when everything is more expensive, are 15 March-15 May, July-September and 15 December-15 January.

● **Hours Of Business**

Shops and businesses: Mon-Fri 0730-1630, Sat 0730-1300. Government departments: Mon-Thur 0700-1500, Fri 0700-1430. Banks are open Mon-Fri 0730-1400. The airport bank is open at flight arrival and departure times.

● **Public Holidays**

1 January, New Year; Holi Phagwa (Hindu festival, date varies each year, generally in March, very interesting but watch out for throwing of water, paint, talc and coloured powder); Good Friday; Easter (2 days); 1 May (Labour Day); 1 July (National Unity); 25 November (Independence Day); Christmas (2 days). For Moslem holidays see note under Guyana.

● **Time Zone**

3 hours behind GMT.

● **Weights And Measures**

The metric system is in general use.

● **Electricity Supply**

127 volts AC, 60 cycles. Plug fittings are usually 2-pin round (European continental type). Lamp fittings are screw type.

● **Post, Telegraph, Telephone**

Overseas phone calls must be booked anywhere between ½ hr to several days in advance, specifying the exact duration of the call. Rates are higher if you request more than 5 mins. Calls can be booked up to 2200, Mon-Sat, no operator assisted calls on Sun. Overseas calls can also be direct dialled from some public phones using tokens, but there are only 4 such phones (just outside TeleSur, often broken) and the queues get very long. USA direct available at both *Torarica* and *Krasnapolsky* Hotels, as well as from private phones. The public fax number from overseas is +597-410-555, good service.

The postal service is remarkably quick and reliable. Both postal and telecommunications charges are very low at the black market exchange rate. Airmail costs US$3 for 1 kg, surface mail US$1.30. Post office in *Hotel Krasnapolsky*, Paramaribo; a shop next door sells mediocre postcards. **NB** Postcard rate for postcards means only 5 words.

● **Newspapers**

in Dutch, *De Ware Tijd* (morning) and *DeWest* (evening).

● **Embassies And Consulates**

USA (Dr Sophie Redmondstraat 129, PO Box 1821, T 477881), Netherlands, Belgium, Brazil, Cuba, France, Mexico, Venezuela, South Korea, India, Indonesia, Guyana, India, Japan, China (People's Republic). There are consuls-general, vice-consuls or consular agents for Canada, Denmark, Dominican Republic, Ecuador, Finland, Germany, Haiti, UK, Mexico, Norway, Spain, and Sweden, all in Paramaribo. British Honorary Consul, Mr James Healy, T 472870 office/474764 house, is very helpful.

● **Suriname Representatives Abroad**

USA: Embassy, Van Ness Center, 4301 Connecticut, NW Suite 108, Washington DC, 20008, T 202-244-7488, F 202-244-5878; Consulate, 7235 NW 19th St, Suite A, Miami, FLA 33126, T 305-593-2163. **Belgium**, Avenue Louise 379, 1050 Brussels, T 640- 11-72. **Netherlands**: Embassy, Alexander Gogelweg 2, 2517 JH Den Haag, T 65-08-44; Consulate, De Cuserstraat 11, 1081 CK Amsterdam, T 642-61-37. **Brazil**, SCS Quadra 2 Lotes 20/21, Edif, OK, 2e Andar, 70457 Brasília, T 244-1824; **Venezuela**, 4a Av de Altamira 41, entre 7 y 8a Transversal, Altamira, Caracas 1060A, PO Box 61140, Chacao, T 261-2095. **Guyana**, 304 Church St, Georgetown, PO Box 338, T 56995. **Guyane**, 38 TER, rue Christoph Colomb, Cayenne, T 30-04-61.

● **Information**

about Suriname can be had from: Cornelius Jongbawstraat 2, T 471163, F 420425, Telex 118 ALBUZA SN, Paramaribo, useful handouts on lodgings and restaurants, free map of Paramaribo, English spoken; open Mon-Thur 0700-1500, Fri 0700-1430. Stinasu, address under **Nature Reserves**; or from embassies.

The *Surinam Planatlas*, out of print, can be consulted at the National Planning office on Dr Sophie Redmondstraat; maps with natural environment and economic development topics, each with commentary in Dutch and English.

GUYANE

GUYANE, an Overseas Department of France, has its eastern frontier with Brazil formed partly by the River Oiapoque (Oyapoc in French) and its southern, also with Brazil, formed by the Tumuc-Humac mountains (the only range of importance). The western frontier with Suriname is along the River Maroni-Itani. To the N is the Atlantic coastline of 320 km. The area is estimated at 86,504 square km, or one-sixth that of France. The land rises gradually from a coastal strip some 15-40 km wide to the higher slopes and plains or savannahs, about 80 km inland. Forests cover some 8 million hectares of the hills and valleys of the interior, and timber production is increasing rapidly. The territory is well watered, for over twenty rivers run to the Atlantic.

There are widely divergent estimates for the ethnic composition of the population (123,000). Calculations vary according to the number included of illegal immigrants, attracted by social benefits and the high living standards. (The prefect stated in 1994 that Guyane had 30,000 illegal residents.) By some measures, over 70% of the population are Créoles, with correspondingly low figures for Europeans, Asians and Brazilians (around 17% in total). Other estimates put the Créole proportion as low as 35%, with Haitians 26%, Europeans 9.7% (of whom about 95% are from France), Brazilians 8.8%. Asians 8.1% (6.1% from Hong Kong, 1.5% from Laos), about 4.4% each from Suriname and Guyana. The Amerindian population is put at 3.6% (over 4% by some estimates). The main groups are Galibis (1,700), Arawak (400), Wayanas (600), Palikours (500), Wayampis-Oyampis (600) and Emerillons (300). There are also bush negroes

(Bonis, Djukas, Bosh, Paramakas), who live mostly in the Maroni area. The language is French, with officials not usually speaking anything else. Créole is also widely spoken. The religion is predominantly Roman Catholic.

●Note The Amerindian villages in the Haut-Maroni and Haut-Oyopoc areas may only be visited with permission from the Préfecture in Cayenne *before* departure to Guyane.

History

Several French and Dutch expeditions attempted to settle along the coast in the early 17th century, but were driven off by the native population. The French finally established a settlement at Sinnamary in the early 1660s but this was destroyed by the Dutch in 1665 and seized by the British two years later. Under the Treaty of Breda, 1667, Guyane was returned to France. Apart from a brief occupation by the Dutch in 1676, it remained in French hands until 1809 when a combined Anglo-Portuguese naval force captured the colony and handed it over to the Portuguese (Brazilians). Though the land was restored to France by the Treaty of Paris in 1814, the Portuguese remained until 1817. Gold was discovered in 1853, and disputes arose about the frontiers of the colony with Suriname and Brazil. These were settled by arbitration in 1891, 1899, and 1915. By the law of 19 March, 1946, the Colony of Cayenne, or Guyane Française, became the Department of Guyane, with the same laws, regulations, and administration as a department in metropolitan France. The seat of the Prefect and of the principal courts is at Cayenne. The colony was used as a prison for French convicts with camps scattered throughout the country; Saint-Laurent was the port of entry. After serving prison terms convicts spent an equal number of years in exile and were usually unable to earn their return passage to France. Those interested should read *Papillon* by Henri Charrière. Majority opinion seems to be in favour of greater autonomy: about 5% of the population are thought to favour independence.

Government

The head of state is the President of France; the local heads of government are a Commissioner of the Republic, for France, and the Presidents of the local General and Regional Councils. The General Council (19 seats) and the Regional Council (31 seats) are the two legislative houses. In regional council elections in March 1992, the Parti Socialiste Guyanais won 16 seats, while the other major party, the Front Democratique Guyanais, won 10. Guyane is divided into two *arrondissements*, Cayenne and St-Laurent du Maroni.

The Economy

Guyane has renewable natural riches in its timber forests (about 75,000 sq km) with 15 sawmills and mineral resources. Farming employs only 11.4% of the population and the country is very sparsely populated. An estimated 42 mn tons of extractable bauxite have been located in the Kaw mountains to the SE of Cayenne by Alcoa and Pechiney. Some 40mn tonnes of kaolin have been located at St-Laurent du Maroni and gold is again being mined.

Guyane imports most of its foodstuffs and manufactured goods, of which about 60% come from France. The value of exports, mainly shrimps, rum, essence of rosewood, hardwoods and gold, is very low; France buys just under 50%, the remaining EC about 20%.

At end-1982 the French Government announced plans to step up the Department's development in consultation with local parties: the so-called Green Plan

FRENCH GUYANE : FACT FILE

Geographic

Land area	86,504 sq km

Demographic

Population (1992)	123,000
annual growth rate (1987-92)	4.5%
urban	73.4%
rural	26.6%
density	1.4 per sq km
Religious affiliation	
Roman Catholic	79%
Birth rate per 1,000 (1990)	31
	(world av 27.1)
Death rate per 1,000 (1990)	5.1
	(world av 9.8)

Education and Health

Life expectancy at birth (1991),	
male	63.4 years
female	69.7 years
Infant mortality rate	22.7
per 1,000 live births (1985-88)	
Physicians (1988)	1 per 374 persons
Hospital beds	1 per 109 persons
Calorie intake as %	
of FAO requirement	119%
Literate males (over 16)	82.5%
Literate females (over 16)	81.3%

Economic

GNP (1987 market prices)	US$179mn
GNP per capita	US$1,820
Public external debt (1988)	US$45mn
Radio	1 per 2.1 persons
Television	1 per 18 persons
Telephone	1 per 2.9 persons

Employment

Population economically active (1985)	
	48,700
% of labour force in	
agriculture	11.4
mining & manufacturing	5.9
Construction	8.8

Source *Encyclopaedia Britannica*

(Plan Vert), backed by the Société Financière de Développement de la Guyane. Under the plan local production of basic foodstuffs, such as meat and eggs, was to be raised, and areas of timber plantations doubled to 22,000 hectares. The Plan Vert notwithstanding, the vast majority of consumer goods (including staples such as milk, sugar, rice, even bananas) continue to be imported from France or the French Caribbean. There is little agriculture, no manufacturing and consumer prices are extraordinarily high. One exception is the market gardening of Laotian Hmong immigrants, near Cacao, who produce the only fresh vegetables in the department. Having virtually no developed, independent economic base, Guyane is perpetually concerned about the consequences of any decrease in French financial support (an estimated US$1 bn a year).

Gold prospecting, much of it carried out by teams of Brazilian garimpeiros, is causing ecological damage through the silting of rivers and the indiscriminate use of mercury. Major ecological impact will also be felt with the completion in 1994 of a 120-mw hydroelectric scheme at Petit Sant on the Sinnamarie river. It is estimated that the habitat for 1 mn animals and 1.5 mn birds will be lost.

The Phèdre Plan assists Guyane with infrastructure projects: bridges across the Mana and Mahuri rivers (the latter for access to Roura); renewal of Rochambeau airport; a road from Régina to St-Georges de l'Oyapoc is planned for completion in 1995-96.

CAYENNE

Cayenne, the capital and the chief port, is on the island of Cayenne at the mouth of the Cayenne River. It is 645 km from Georgetown (Guyana) and 420 km from Paramaribo (Suriname) by sea. Population 42,000. There is an interesting museum, the Musée Departemental, in rue de Remire, near the Place de Palmistes (Mon and Wed 0900-1330, Tues and Fri 0900-1330, 1630-1830, Sat 0900-1200; US$2, students US$1). It contains quite a mixture of exhibits, from pickled snakes to the trunk of the "late beloved twin-trunked palm" of the Place de Palmistes; there is a good entomological collection and excellent paintings of convict

life. Next door is the municipal library. The Musée de L'Or, Impasse Buzaré (Mon-Fri 0800-1200) has been restored. L'Ostrom (scientific research institute), Route de Montabo, Mon and Fri 0700-1330, 1500-1800, Tues-Thur 0700-1300, has a research library and permanent exhibits on ecosystems and archaeological finds in Guyane. Also worth a visit are Crique, the colourful but dangerous area around the Canal Laussat (built by Malouet in 1777); the Jesuit-built residence (circa 1890) of the Prefect (L'Hôtel-de-Ville) in the Place de Grenoble; the Place des Amandiers (also known as the Place Auguste-Horth) by the sea; the Place des Palmistes, with assorted palms; a swimming pool and five cinemas. The fruit and vegetable market on Monday, Wednesday and Friday mornings has a Caribbean flavour, but it is expensive.There are bathing beaches (water rather muddy) around the island, the best is Montjoly, but watch out for sharks. Minibuses run from terminal to Rémire-Montjoly for beaches. They leave when full – check when the last one returns. There is a walking trail called "Roronta" which follows the coastline and can be reached from Montjoly or the Gosselin beaches. Another trail, "Habitation Vidal" in Rémire, passes through former sugar cane plantations. Remains of sugar mills can be seen on the way.

Local Information – Cayenne
● Where To Stay
Novotel Cayenne, Chemin Hilaire-route de Montabo, T 30-38-88, F 31-78-98, not central, US$110 on beach, restaurant, a/c, very good; *Hotel des Amandiers*, Place Auguste Horth, T 30-26-00, F 30-74-84, US$90, a/c, excellent restaurant; *Phigarita Studios*, US$80, 47 bis, rue F Arago, T 30-66-00, F 30-77-49, spacious apartments with kitchenette, a/c, rec, friendly, helpful, breakfast 40F; *Amazonia*, 26 Av Gen de Gaulle, good, friendly, a/c, luggage stored, central location, T 31-00-00, F 31-94-41, US$68-74; *Le Coin d'Or*, PK 5.5, route de Montabo, T 30-21-77, F 30-46-28, take bus No 1 from Place des Palmistes, to Carefour de Soussini about 4 km from centre,

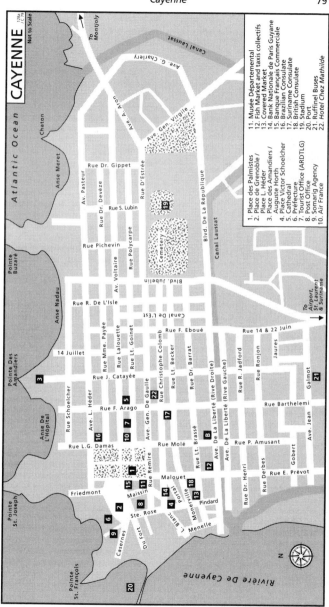

128a
/ C.79

CAYENNE
Not to Scale

Atlantic Ocean

To Montjoly

Canal Laussat

Ave. G. Charlery

Ave. A. Aron

Ave. Gen Virgile

Rue D'Estrée

Chaton

Anse Meret

Rue Dr. Gippet

Av. Pasteur

Rue Dr. Deveze

Rue S. Lubin

Blvd. De La République

Pointe Buzaré

Rue Pichevin

Av. Voltaire

Rue Polycarpe

Cemetery

Canal Laussat

Anse Nadau

Rue R. De L'Isle

Blvd. Jubelin

Pointe Des Amandiers

14 Juillet

Canal De L'Est

Rue F. Eboué

Rue 14 & 22 Juin

To Airport, St. Laurent & Suriname

Rue Mme. Payée

Rue Lalouette

Rue Lt. Goinet

Rue Christophe Colomb

Rue Lt. Becker

Rue Dr. Barrat

Rue R. Jadford

Rue Ronjon

Jaures

Rue J. Catayée

Rue Schoelcher

Ave. L. Héder

Rue F. Arago

Ave. Gen. De Gaulle

Ave. De La Liberté (Rive Droite)

Ave. De La Liberté (Rive Gauche)

Rue Barthelemi

Ave. Jean

Galmot

Anse De L'Hôpital

Rue L.G. Damas

Rue Molé

Rue Lt. Brassé

Rue P. Amusant

Gobert

Rue Derbes

Rue E. Prévot

Friedmont

Maison

Malouet

Pointel

Pindard

Rue Dr. Henri

Pointe St. Joseph

Casernes

Du Fort

Ste. Rose

L. Blanc

Moneville

Menelle

Pointe St. Francois

Rivière De Cayenne

N

1. Place des Palmistes
2. Place de Grenoble / Place L. Héder
3. Place des Amandiers / Auguste Horth
4. Place Victor Schoelcher
5. Cathedral
6. Préfecture
7. Tourist Office (ARDTLG)
8. Post Office
9. Somaroi Agency
10. Air France
11. Musée Départemental
12. Fish Market and taxis collectifs
13. Covered Market
14. Bank Nationale de Paris Guyane
15. Banque Français Commerciale
16. Brazilian Consulate
17. Suriname Consulate
18. British Consulate
19. Stadium
20. Port
21. Ruffinel Buses
22. Hotel/ Chez Mathilde

with bath, US$48, US$12 in adjacent gîtes, shared bath, clean, friendly, rec, breakfast 40F, full board 180F; *Central Hotel*, corner rue Molé and rue Becker, T 31-30-00, F 31-2-96, US$76, downtown, a/c; *Le Grillardin*, PK6 Route Matoury, 4 km from airport, T 35-63-90, US$54, a/c, restaurant; *Ket-Tai*, Ave de la Liberté, corner Blvd Jubelin, new, clean, modern, overpriced; *Guyane Studios*, 16 rue Molé, T 30-25-11, US$60, a/c; *Le Baduel*, Route de Baduel, T 30-51-58, F 30-77-76, US$40, a/c, TV, cooking facilities; *Ajoupa*, T 30-33-08, F 30-12-82, Route Camp de Tigre, 2 km from town, helpful. *Chez Mathilde/Hotel du Palais*, 42 Av Gen de Gaulle, T 30-25-13, hammock space, friendly, clean, noisy, not safe for left luggage, always full; *Madeleine*, T 30-17-36, US$42.50, a/c, basic, clean, breakfast, will book Raffinel bus to St Laurent, 1 km out of town, friendly (good Surinamese snackbar nearby). *Neptima*, rue F Eboué 21, T 30-11-15, F 37-98-60 (15 rooms), US$46, best value, a/c, clean, friendly. Cheapest in town is *Foyer Paul VI*, rue des Mangues, 10-15 mins walk from centre, T 30-04-16, under US$10, cheap meals. About 10 km from Cayenne is the *Beauregard*, route de Rémire, T 35-41-00, F 35-44-05, rec for business visitors, pool, tennis, squash, sauna, restaurant *Cric Crac*, US$70, or US$72 in bungalow with cooking facilities. Also *Hotel M*, a motel with a/c rooms and a small swimming pool; the owner hires out small cars, rec for business visitors, breakfast, T 35-41-00, Telex 010 310, and *Motel du Lac*, T 38-08-00, F 38-10-34, Chemin Poupon, Montjoly, US$90, 10 km from centre, pool, bar, restaurant, good business hotel. *Mme Romieu*, PK 5.5 Route de Montabo, T 31-06-55; *Mme Martin*, 19 rue Euloge Jean Elie, T 38-24-27; *Residence Vetulie*, 12 Lot Cogneau Lamirande, T 35-82-89; *Mme Mirta*, 35 Lot Alexandre, T 31-47-78; *M Roques*, 2 Lot Amarillys, T 38-18-20; *Mme Stanistlas*, Villa Sonia PK 0.4 Route de Rémire, T 38-22-13; *Mme Anastase*, 59 Av de Gaulle, T 35-17-70; *Jacqueline Barranco*, 42 Av de Gaulle, T 30-25-13, US$36, no a/c; *Mme Castor*, 4 rue du Dr Gippet, T 31-27-38; *Mme de Chadirac*, Route de Montjoly PK6, T 38-23-01; *Mme Girard*, Route de Montabo PK3.5, T 30-61-28; *M Benoit*, 117 rue Ch Colomb, T 31-42-81; *Mme Kong*, 41 Av de la Liberté, T 30-13-98. Prices range from US$20 at Romieu and Roques, to US$60 at Kong; most are in the US$30-40 range. Most hotels do not add tax and service to their bill, but stick to prices posted outside or at the desk. Hotel rooms are expensive, it is hard to find a room under 200F a night double. Bed and breakfast accommodation (gîtes) is available for about 150F a night (breakfast is usually at extra cost), contact the tourist office for details. Ask the Catholic Fathers at Cité Messaih, near *Hotel Madeleine*, about sleeping possibilities. Amex cards often not accepted but Visa OK.

● **Restaurants And Bars**

Main hotels. *L'Auberge des Amandiers*, Place Auguste-Horth, excellent, the most famous French, expensive (US$38) *Au Vieux Genois*, 89 rue Christophe Colomb, very good, French with local products, fish specialities, good business lunches; *Armand Ti A Hing*, Place des Palmistes, French, excellent, 180F pp; *Cap St Jacques*, rue Docteur E Gippet, excellent Vietnamese food, reasonable. *Maxim'um*, Av Estrée. *La Croix du Sud*, 80, Av de Gaulle; *Tournesol*, rue Lt Goinet, real French food, fine wines, expensive, highly rec; *Le Grillardin* (see **Hotels**), very good Créole; *Paris-Cayenne*, 59 rue Lallouette, French, very good, nice décor; *La Belle Epoque*, French, expensive; *Cric-Crac* (at *Hotel Beauregard*, Créole cooking, lovely atmosphere; *Le Snack Créole*, 17 rue Eboué; *Palmiste*, Place des Palmistes (downtown), good daily menu, US$17, central and spacious; *Frégate*, Av de Gaulle; *Le Traiteur de la Fôret*, Blvd Jubelin, friendly, good; *Marveen Snack Bar*, rue Ch Colombe, near Canal de L'Est, food and staff pleasant, the patrons are very helpful regarding air travel and excursions (the elder of the two is a pilot for the Guyane Flying Club). *Ko Fei*, 18 rue Lalouette, T 312888, good Chinese; *Apsara*, 95 rue Colombe, Chinese, good value. *La Rose d'Asie*, 20 rue Samuel Lubin, very good Vietnamese. *Hindu-Creol*, rue J Catayee, Indian, good. Along the Canal Laussant there are Javanese snack bars; try *bami* (spicy noodles) or *saté* (barbequed meat in a spicy peanut sauce). Also along the canal are small, cheap Créole restaurants, not very clean. Vans around Place des Palmistes in evenings sell cheap, filling sandwiches. *Bar Cayenne Palace*, 45 Av de Gaulle, disco 80F with first drink. *Delifrance*, Av de Gaulle at rue Catayée, hot chocolate and croissants; *Epi D'or*, Av Jubelin, good sweets and cakes, rec. Food is about 38% more expensive than Metropolitan France: it is hard to find a meal for under 50F (small Chinese restaurants charge 50-80F for a full meal).

● Bookshops

Librairie AJC, 31 Boulevard Jubelin, has some stock in English. Also old maps and prints. Current map sold at *Librairie Alain* Pion, Av de Gaulle and in most bookshops.

● Exchange

Banque Nacional de Paris-Guyane, 2 Place Schoelcher; no exchange facilities on Sat. Banque Française Commerciale, 2 Place des Palmistes (best bank exchange rates); Crédit Populaire Guyanais, 93 rue Lalouette. Most banks have ATMs for cash withdrawals on Visa, sometimes Mastercard, never Amex. *Cambio Caraïbe*, Av Gen de Gaulle mear Catayée (best rates for US$); *Guyane Change*, Av Gen de Gaulle nr rue F Eboué. The Post Office exchanges cash and TCs at good rates, but complicated and time-consuming. There are no exchange facilities at the airport; if in extreme need on Sat you may be able to change money at Air France office in Place des Palmistes. Central drugstore may help when banks closed. Almost impossible to change dollars outside Cayenne or Kourou. Buy francs before arrival if possible.

● Laundromat

Corner of rue Lalouette and rue Eboué, US$5 load all in; *Ros'in*, 87 Av Liberté, T 31-73-13.

● Main Post Office

Route de Baduel, 2 km out from town (15F by taxi or 20 mins on foot). Poste Restante letters are only kept for 2 weeks maximum. Also Poste Cayenne Cépéron, place L Heder.

● Tourist Office

Agence Régionale de Développement du Tourisme et des Loisirs de la Guyane (ARDTLG), 12 rue Lalouette (T 30-09-00), 0800-1200, 1500-1800. Free map and tourist guide (Guyane Poche). The SLM manager is reported to be very helpful with advice.

● Travel Agents

Takari Tour, Colline du Montabo, T 31-19-60 (BP 513) and at *Novotel*, rec for inland tours. *Guyane Excursions*, Centre Commercial Simarouba, Kourou, T 32-05-41, specializes in inland tours, particularly to the Maroni river, highly rec, US$700 for 5-6 days, but a wide variety of options. Also *JAL Voyages*, T 38-23-70, for a wide range of tours. *Somarig*, place L Héder, T 30-29-80, is reported to be good for South American and European airline tickets. It also sells boat tickets to Ile Royale as well as meal tickets for the Auberge which are rec.

Agence Sainte-Claire, 8 rue de Rémire, T 30-00-38, for travel outside Guyane (inc charters to Caracas and Cuba); *Havas*, 2 place du Marché, T 31-26-22/31-27-26.

● Transport

Bus terminal at corner of rue Molé and Av de la Liberté. Regular urban services. The only westbound bus is run by Raffinel & Cie, 8 Av Galmot, T 31-26-66 (Kourou US$12, St Laurent US$30) leaves 0530 (not Sun). Minibuses to St-Laurent du Maroni leave when full from the terminal, 0400-1200, 3 hrs, US$30. Service to **Mana** Mon and Thur only. To Kaw, Wed. Otherwise transport is by shared taxis (collectifs), which leave from Av de la Liberté, near the fish market early in the morning (Kourou US$12, St Laurent US$30).

WEST TO SURINAME

Kourou, 56 km W of Cayenne, where the main French space centre (Centre Spatial Guyanais), used for the European Space Agency's Ariane programme, is located, is referred to by the Guyanais as "white city" because of the number of metropolitan French families living there; its population is about 15,000. Tourist attractions include bathing, fishing, sporting and aero club, and a variety of organized excursions. The space centre occupies an area of about 4 km deep along some 30 km of coast, bisected by the Kourou river. Public guided tours are given Mon-Fri 0745-1130 and 1300-1630 (or some Fri am only). Phone 32-61-23 to reserve a place on a tour of the centre (in French only, max 40), often booked up days ahead; closed during Carnival. No public transport, take a taxi or hitch. Visits are free. If you book at least 3 days in advance you can ask Public Relations for an English-speaking guide for 2-3 people, minimum; for a group of 20-25, a full English-speaking tour can be arranged.

Local Information – Kourou
● Where To Stay

All hotels are overbooked and raise their prices when there is an Ariane rocket launch (about once a month). *Relais de Guyane* (*Hotel des Roches*), Av des Roches, T 32-00-66, F 32-03-

28, US$110, breakfast inc, a/c, not too good, pool, beach, good restaurants; *(Le Paradisier) Atlantis*, nr Lac Bois Diable, T 32-13-00, F 32-40-12, US$97, a/c, modern, pool, good restaurant, best value for business visitors; also at Lac Bois Diable, *Mercure*, T 32-07-00, US$188-132; *Studios Vercors*, place Newton, T 33-10-00/32-62-89, F 33-62-87, US$96, cooking facilities, old, not too good; better are *Studios Le Gros Bec*, T 32-56-10, rue Dr Floch, US$66, cooking facilities; *Espace Loisirs*, rue Berloiz, T 32-27-80, US$50, studios with 2 beds, cooking facilities; *Les Jardins D'Hermes*, 56 rue Duchense, T 32-01-83, F 32-09-17, US$74, in heart of old Kourou, a/c, modern, good; *Ballahou*, 1 rue Armet Martial, T 32-42-06, a/c, TV, nice, modern, friendly, good restaurant; *Mme Moutton*, rue Séraphin 56, studios with or without kitchen, friendly. Cheap hotels and rooms for US$20 on Av de Gaulle.

20 km S of Kourou on the road to Saramaca is *Les Maripas*, tourist camp, T 32-05-41, F 32-28-47, river and overland excursions available.

● **Where To Eat**

Many, esp on de Gaulle inc *Le Catouri*, *Cachiri Combo*, (No 3, T 32-44-64, 100-150F, also has basic rooms to let), *Auberge de Père Jean*, *La Perle Noire*, excellent, friendly (all Créole), *Vieux Montmartre*; *Espace Grill*, 2 place Europe (nr post office); *La Grillade*, Ave G Berloiz; *Le Provence*, 11 passage G Monnerville, best French, expensive; *Ballahou* (see **Hotels**), best for fish and seafood (try *Guyabaisse*); *Le Travelling*, place Moryse Bastié, good, French, friendly, 150F. *La Cage*, Av des Roches, good pizza, evening only, cheap for Kourou, 80F; pizza also at *Le Valentino*, place Galilé; *Le Saramaca*, place du Marché; *Relais de L'Europe*, 20m from post office, at 50F best value in town. Many cheap Chinese (also takeaway); many vans sell sandwiches filled with Créole food, good. **Bar** *Le Forban*, rue Dreyfus, district 205, worth seeing the murals (also for the lonely, many young Brazilian women). **Night Clubs:** *Saxo* (best) *3ème Dimension* (Créole style), *Le Vieux Montmartre*, all on de Gaulle; *Jupiter*, Av des Roches.

● **Exchange**

Banque National de Paris Guyane, Place Newton; Banque Française Commerciale, Place Jeanne d'Arc; Crédit Populaire Guyanais, Simarouba.

● **Post Office**

Avenue des Frères Kennedy.

● **Travel Agency**

Guyane Excursions, T 32-05-41 (see under Cayenne); *Havas Voyages Kourou*, T 32-55-77; *Agence Sainte Claire*, T 32-36-98, F 32-50-40; *Air France*, place Newton, T 32-10-50.

● **Transport**

Taxi in town US$10. To Cayenne leaves from Shell service station. Corner Av de France, Av Vermont Polycarpe, bus to St-Laurent du Maroni from same place, 0700, US$20; *taxis collectifs*, 0630 US$12 to Cayenne. Taxi to Cayenne or airport, US$60 (US$80 at night); to St-Laurent du Maroni US$25 by *taxi collectif* (irregular).

The *Iles du Salut* (many visitors at weekends), opposite Kourou, include the Ile Royale, the Ile Saint-Joseph, and the Ile du Diable. They were the scene of the notorious convict settlement built in 1852; the last prisoners left in 1953. The Ile du Diable ("Devil's Island"), a rocky palm-covered islet almost inaccessible from the sea, was where political prisoners, including Alfred Dreyfus, were held. There is a 60-bed hotel on Ile Royale, *Auberge Iles du Salut* (address Sothis, 97310 Kourou, T 32-11-00, F 32-42-23), US$54-71, also hammock space US$20 pp; former guard's bungalow, main meals (excellent), minimum US$36, breakfast US$8 (ex-mess hall for warders, with good food; bottled water sold); gift shop with high prices (especially when a cruise ship is in), good English guide book for sale. Camping is possible, but suitable sites are limited, the stronghearted may try the old prison barracks; take food and water (you can also sling a hammock in the open, take a plastic sheet to protect yourself from morning mist); bread and water (check bottle is sealed) can be bought from the hotel stall. You can see agoutis, turtles, humming birds and macaws, and there are many un-owned coconut palms. Beware the many open wells. Take a torch for visiting the ruins. Paintings of prison life are on show in the tiny church.

Points of interest include the children's graveyard, hospital, mental asylum and death cells. These, and the church, are not always open. Little is being done to prevent the deterioration of the buildings. Boat from Kourou's port at the end of Av General de Gaulle, 4 km from centre 180F return (children under 12 half price), leaves 0830 and 1030 daily, returns from island at 1600 and 1800 (check) additional sailing Sat 1600, 1 hour each way. Tickets may be obtained from Somarig Voyages, or Havas Voyages, addresses under Cayenne **Travel Agents**; Air Guyane Voyages, 2 rue Lallouette, T 31-72-00; in Kourou from au Carbet des Roches, cash only. There are no regular boats from Ile Royale to Ile Saint-Joseph, which is wilder and more beautiful, with a small beach (this island had solitary-confinement cells and the warders' graveyard). It may be possible to hire a private boat at the ferry dock, or ask for James on the Kourou-Ile Royale ferry. Surfing and swimming are possible between Ile Royale and Ile du Diable; strong currents at high tide. Boat owners are very reluctant to visit Ile du Diable except around July-August when the sea is calmer.

Between Kourou and Iracoubo, on the road W to St-Laurent, is *Sinnamary* (103 km from Cayenne), a pleasant town where Galibi Indians at a mission make artifical flowers from feathers, for sale to tourists. Scarlet ibis can be seen in numbers on the Sinnamary estuary at Iracoubo.

St-Laurent du Maroni, population 5,000, formerly a penal transportation camp, is now a quiet colonial town 250 km from Cayenne on the River Maroni, bordering Suriname. There are no gîtes in St-Laurent; those on a tight budget wanting a room or hammock space can try to make advance arrangements in Cayenne with: Fedération d'Oeuvres Laïques, Centre d'Hebergement de Saint-Louis, T 34-11-40; CAS EDF, cen-tre d'Hebergement, T 34-12-96/34-23-03; or Le Carbet du Balat, Mme Emille Lamtoukai, T 34-10-35. BNP opposite *Restaurant Le Saramaca* will change US$ TCs; both local banks give cash against Visa cards.

The old Camp de Transportation (the original penal centre) can be wandered round at will (an absolute must if visiting the country). Guided tours of Les Bagnes (prison camps) daily 0830-1230, 1500-1800, chilling. The Charbonière refugee camp, next to the ferry pier housed Surinamese Bush Negro refugees during that country's civil war. A few have remained or returned. (Nearby is St-Jean du Maroni, an Indian village.)

Local Information
● Where To Stay
Sinnamary *Sinnarive Motel*, T 34-55-55, US$52; *Eldo Grill*, T 34-51-41, F 34-50-90, US$55, a/c, TV, coffee, breakfast extra, rec; *Village Hotel*, T 34-56-18, F 34-56-18, US$52-108, or contact M Derain, T 34-53-09, who lets out rooms, US$15 pp; *Hotel du Fleuve*, expensive. *Restaurant Madras*, good Creole; ask for *Gaya Baru*, Indonesian restaurant in an Indonesian village. Wood carvings and jewellery are on sale here and the workshops can be visited. There are 3 to 5 day excursions up the Sinnamary river. **St-Laurent** *Hotel La Tentaire*, 12 Av Franklin Roosevelt, T 34-26-00, F 34-15-09, US$48, a/c, the best, breakfast extra; *Hotel Toucan*, Boulevard Republique, T 34-12-59, F 34-17-06, US$38, a/c, dirty, TV, poor value. *Star Hotel*, rue Thiers, T 34-10-84, US$36-60, a/c, pool, cheap restaurant, friendly, rec; *Chez Julienne*, Route des Malgaches, T 34-11-53, US$50, a/c, TV, shower, good. *Restaurant La Saramaca*, Av Felix Eboué, the best. *Restaurants Vietnam* and *Le Point d'Intérrogation* have been rec also *Loe*, nr hospital, Créole, excellent; many cheap Chinese.

● Tourist Office
rue August Boudinot Av de la Marne, T 342398.

● Transport
Minibuses to Cayenne meet the ferry from Suriname, leaving when full, 3 hrs, US$30. Bus to Cayenne, US$30, 0500 daily (not Sun); *taxis collectifs* to and from Cayenne, US$30 a head,

3½-hour trip. Freight *pirogues* sometimes take passengers inland along the Maroni River; alternatively a group can hire a *pirogue* at about US$200 a day. Avis has a car rental office in St-Laurent.

Excursions

About 3 km from St-Laurent, along the Paul Isnard Road, is Saint-Maurice, where the rum distillery of the same name can be visited, Mon-Thur 0630-1430, Fri 0630-1330. At Km 70 on the same dirt road is access to **Voltaire Falls**, 1½ hrs walk from the road. 7 km S of St-Laurent on the road to St-Jean is the Amerindian village of *Terre Rouge*; canoes can be hired for day trips up the Maroni River (see Maripasoula below).

Crossing to Suriname

Make sure you obtain proper entry stamps from immigration, not the police, to avoid problems when leaving. Customs and immigration close at 1900. Ferry for vehicles and passengers (free) to Albina Mon, Tues, Wed, Thur, 0900, 1100, 1300, 1500 (sometimes only once a day), ½ hr. Minibuses and taxis for Paramaribo meet the Albina ferry; many aggressive touts on the St-Laurent and Albina piers. It is best to change money in the Village Chinois in St-Laurent; although rates are lower than in Paramaribo, it is illegal to change money in Albina. Beware theft at St-Laurent's black market. GUM airways fly from St-Laurent to Paramaribo, 3 times a week, enquire at the *Star Hotel*.

● **Accommodation** In the countryside not far from St-Laurent are 2 *Auberge de brousse*, which are good places to stay for walking, or for trips to see turtles at Les Hattes (see below: *Auberge Bois Diable*, PK8 Acarouany, T 34-19-35, 1 bedroom, US$20, hammock space, US$6, meals, US$16, breakfast US$4, good food, hospitable, tours arranged; *Relais d'Acarouany*, T 34-17-20, 6 rooms, US$20-28, meals US$18, breakfast US$4.

40 km N of St-Laurent du Maroni is *Mana*, a delightful town with rustic architecture near the coast (*Gîte d'Etape*,

rooms OK, filthy kitchen, mosquitoes, disco next door; nuns next to the church rent beds and hammocks, US$10pp, clean and simple, T 34-17-29, Communauté des Soeurs de St-Joseph de Cluny, 1 rue Bourguignon; Mme Hidair, T 34-80-62, has rooms, US$25). 20 km W of Mana following the river along a single track access road is *Les Hattes*, or Awala-Yalimapo (*Gîte Rureau*, US$35, clean) an Amerindian village (ask M Daniel for permission to stay in the church); 4 km further on is Les Hattes beach where leatherback-turtles lay their eggs at night; season April-August with its peak in June-July (in July you can see both adults coming ashore to lay and hatchlings rushing to meet the high tide). No public transport to Les Hattes and its beach, but hitching possible at weekends; take food and water and mosquito repellent. In spite of the dryish climate Mana is a malaria region. The fresh water of the Maroni and Mana rivers makes sea bathing very pleasant. Very quiet during the week.

Aouara, an Amerindian village with hammock places, is a few kilometres S E of Les Hattes. It also has a beach where the leatherback turtles lay their eggs; they take about three hours over it. Take mosquito nets, hammock and insect repellent.

There are daily flights from Cayenne to*Maripasoula*, US$170 return, (*Auberge Chez Dedè*, Av Leonard, T 37-20-05, US$20, US$4 per extra person) up the Maroni from St-Laurent (2-4 day journey up river in *pirogue*). There may be freight canoes which take passengers (200F) or private boats (750F) which leave from St-Laurent; 5-6 day tours and other options with Guyane-Excursions or with Takari Tour (see under Cayenne *Travel Agents*). Maripasoula has 5,000 inhabitants in town and its surroundings. Many bush negros live here. If going up the Maroni, take malaria prophylaxis. 20 mins by canoe from Maripasoula is *Campement Touristique Lassort*, T 31-49-45.

CENTRAL MASSIF

Saül, a remote gold-mining settlement in the "central massif" is the geographical centre of Guyane. The main attractions are for the nature-loving tourist. Beautiful undisturbed tropical forests are accessible by a very well-maintained system of 90 km of marked trails, including several circular routes. The place has running water, a radiotelephone, and electricity. Ten-day expeditions are run by Christian Ball, "Vie Sauvage", 97314 Saül, US$70 (30% in advance) per day with meals, maps of local trails provided, own hammock and bedding useful but not essential. It can be cold at night. Another fascinating overland route goes from Roura (see below) up the Comte River to Belizon, followed by a 14 to 16-day trek through the jungle to Saül, visiting many villages en route, guide recommended. N of Saül is *Eden des Eaux Claires*, tourist camp, T 30-91-11. Air service Mon, Wed, Fri with Air Guyane from Cayenne (US$66 one way, US$124 return) or via Maripasoula; try at airport even if flight said to be full. By *pirogue* from Mana up Mana River, 9-12 days, then one day's walk to Saül, or from St-Laurent via Maripasoula along Moroni and Inini Rivers, 15 days and one day's walk to Saül, both routes expensive.

SOUTHEAST TO BRAZIL

43 km E of Cayenne is *Montisery*, with a zoo featuring Amazonian flora and fauna (open daily 1000-1900), an orchid and a walking trail, "Bagne des Annamites", through remains of a camp where prisoners from Indochina were interned in the 1930s.

28 km SE of Cayenne is the small town of **Roura** (*Hotel – restaurant Amazone River*, T 31-91-13, US$36, a/c, good restaurant, good views of the river; rooms to rent from Mme Luap, US$20, T 31-54-84), which has an interesting church; an excursion may be made to the Fourgassier Falls several km away (*L'Auberge des Cascades*, excellent restaurant). From Cayenne the road now crosses a new bridge over the River Comte. Excursions can be arranged along the Comte River. For information about the area contact the Syndicat D'Initiative de Roura, T 31-11-04. Nearby is Dacca, a Laotian village. 27 km from Roura is *Alberge du Camp Caiman*, T 31-96-64, tours arranged to watch caiman in the swamps.

From Roura an unpaved road runs SE towards the village of Kaw. At Km 36 from Cayenne is the *Hotel Relais de Patawa* (T 31-93-95), US$25, or sling your hammock for 30F, cheaper rates for longer stays, highly recommended. The owners, M and Mme Baloué, who are entomologists, will show you their collection, take you on guided tours of local sights and introduce you to their pet anaconda and boa constrictors. At Km 59 on the road to Régina is the turn-off to *Cacao* (a further 13 km), a small, quiet village, where Hmong refugees from Laos are settled; they are farmers and produce fine traditional handicrafts. (Accommodation: *Restaurant La Lan*, one room, US$25, good value, good food; *Quimbe-Kio*, hammock camp, US$7, breakfast US$3; M Levessier, T 30-51-22, US$10 has hammocks; best restaurant is *Chez By et David*, Laotian food; also good is *Degrad Cacao*). Minibus from Cayenne, Monday 1200; Friday 1800, return Mon 0730, Fri 1400. Halfway along the side road is the *Belle Vue* restaurant, which lives up to its name, because of the superb view over the tropical forest (hammock space available, US$5 pp, bring your own); the restaurant is open at weekends or when hammock-guests are there. SW of Cacao is the tourist camp *Carbet La Source*, T 31-96-64. *Kaw*, at Km 83, is on an island amid swamps which are home to much rare wildlife including caymans. The village is reached by dugout either from the Cayenne road or from Régina; basic accommodation available (Mme Musron, T 31-88-15), take insect repellent. Southwest of Kaw on the River

Approuague is *Régina*, linked with Cayenne by an unpaved road.

St-Georges de l'Oyapoc is 15 mins down river from Oiapoque (Brazil) US$4 pp by motorized canoe, bargain for a return fare. *Hotel Modestina*, US$10, restaurant, rooms to rent from M Carème; unnamed hotel to left of supermarket opposite town hall, US$15, a dump, no fan, no window; also *Theofila*, lunch US$3, other restaurants and a night club. Two supermarkets with French specialities. Immigration (*gendarmerie*) for entry/exit stamps at E end of town, follow signs, open daily 0700-1200, 1500-1800 (sometimes not open after early morning on Sun, in which case try the police at the airport); French and Portuguese spoken. One of the Livre Service supermarkets and *Hotel Modestina* will sometimes change dollars cash into francs at very poor rates; if entering the country here, change money before arriving in St-Georges. Note that nowhere in town accepts Visa cards. Post office; public telephone which takes phone card.

For Air Guyane flights to Cayenne see below, **Airport Information**. Air Guyane office at airport open 0700-0730, 1400-1430 for check in, open 0800-1100 for reservations. Flights are fully-booked several days in advance; you must check in at stated times. Extra flights are sometimes added. The police check that those boarding flights who have arrived from Brazil have obtained their entry stamp; also thorough baggage search. A small vessel, the *Sao Pedro*, normally runs a shipping service to Cayenne, deck passengers US$30, but check it is not under repair. A cargo ship, the *Normelia*, calls at St-Georges about twice a month and will sometimes take passengers to Cayenne, 12-14 hrs, US$30 inc meals. Speak directly to the captain. The Elf petrol station has details on ship arrivals.

A trail has been cut by the French army from St-Georges to the road-head at Régina, along which a road will eventually be built. It is 4 to 5 days of hard trekking with many rivers to be forded, impassable during the rainy season.

The **Saut Maripa** rapids (not too impressive with high water) are located about 30 mins upstream along the Oiapoc river, past the Brazilian towns of Oiapoque and Clevelândia do Norte. Hire a motorized *pirogue* (canoe) to take you to a landing downstream from the rapids. Then walk along the remains of a narrow gauge railway line (one of only two in Guyane, formerly used for gold mining) for 20 mins through the jungle, to reach a small tourist complex with restaurant, bar, and guest houses by the rapids. A pleasant day trip. There are more rapids further upstream.

INFORMATION FOR VISITORS

● Documents

Passport not required by nationals of France and most French-speaking African countries carrying identity cards. For EC visitors, documents are the same as for Metropolitan France (ie no visa, no exit ticket required – check with a consulate in advance). No visa (45F) required for most nationalities (except for those of Guyana, Australia, some Eastern European countries, and Asian—not Japan—and other African countries) for a stay of up to 3 months, but an exit ticket out of the country is essential (a ticket out of one of the other Guianas is not sufficient); a deposit is required otherwise. If one stays more than three months, income tax clearance is required before leaving the country. Inoculation against yellow-fever is officially required only for those staying in Guyane longer than 2 weeks, but advisable for all. Travel to certain Amerindian villages is restricted.

● How To Get There By Air

Air France flies 5 times a week direct to Guyane from Paris, 9 times a week from Pointe-à-Pitre (Guadeloupe) Fort-de-France (Martinique), and once a week from Santo Domingo, once a week from Miami. Air France operating jointly with Aeropostal flies once a week from Caracas. AOM French Airlines fly 3 times a week direct from Paris and are reported to be the cheapest from Europe (Paris T 40-74-00-

04). Surinam Airways flies to Belém and Paramaribo 3 times a week; Gonini Air flies 4 times a week to Paramaribo; for Georgetown you have to change in Paramaribo. Surinam Airways sells tickets for Cayenne-Paramaribo-Georgetown-Port of Spain (US$360 return late 1993). Taba flies to Macapá, Brazil, 3 times a week.

Airport Information

Cayenne-Rochambeau is 16 km from Cayenne, 20 mins by taxi. No exchange facilities. No public transport; only taxis (US$30 daytime, US$40 night, but you can probably bargain or share). The cheapest route to town is taxi to Matoury US$10, then bus to centre US$2. Cheapest method of return to airport is by collective taxi from corner of Av de la Liberté and rue Malouet to Matoury (10 km) for US$2.40, then hitch or walk. Air France, 13, rue L G Damas, Place des Palmistes, T 30-27-40; Air Guyane, 2 rue Lalouette, T 31-72-00/35-65-55; Surinam Airways, 2 place Schoelcher, T 31-72-98. Local air services: Air Guyane to all main centres. These flights are always heavily booked, so be prepared to wait or write or telephone Air Guyane in Cayenne (T 31-72-00). There are regular connections with Maripasoula, daily at 0930, 474F; St-Georges, daily at 0745 and usually one in early pm, 350F; Saül on Mon, Wed and Fri, at 0930, 364F; Régina, Mon, Wed, Fri at 0745, 165F. No services on Sun. Baggage allowance 10 kg; 6.45F per kg excess.

● Surface Transport To Guyane

The Compagnie Général Maritime runs a passenger service to France once a month via Martinique and a freight service every 3 months. To Brazil by motorized dugout from St Georges to Oiapoque, no custom or immigration post but foreigners are still sometimes returned to Guyane if their papers are not in order. Make sure you get an exit stamp from Gendarmerie in St-Georges. This journey is possible in reverse.

● Internal Surface Transport

There are about 1,000 km of road. The main road, narrow but now paved, runs for 130 km from Pointe Macouris, on the roadstead of Cayenne, to Iracoubo. Another 117 km takes it to Mana and St-Laurent. **Car Hire** There is a lack of public transport (details in the text above); car hire can be a great convenience. All types of car available, from economy to luxury to pick-ups and jeeps. Cheapest rates are US$20-30 a day for a Citroen AX or Fiat

Uno or Panda, to US$90 for luxury, a/c car; Santana 4x4 US$72 a day (rates EuroRent and Europcar. Gasoline/petrol costs 5.32F a litre; diesel 3.64F a litre. There are 15 companies inc both Hertz and Avis at airport. Full list available from ARDTLG (see **Tourist Office** below). An international driving licence is required. **Bicycle Hire** Takari Tour office at *Novotel*, US$24 per day, US$100 per week, also guided tours. **Hitching** is reported to be easy and widespread. One-to three-ton boats which can be hauled over the rapids are used by the gold-seekers, the forest workers, and the rosewood establishments. There is a twice-a-month shipping service which calls at nearly all the coastal towns of Guyane. Ferries are free. Trips by motor-canoe (*pirogue*) up-river from Cayenne into the jungle can be arranged.

● Accommodation

Details of hotels are given in the text. For information on *Gîtes* and *Chambres chez l'habitant* write to Agence Régionale de Développement du Tourisme et des Loisirs de la Guyane (ARDTLG), 12, rue Lalouette, 97338, Cayenne Cedex, T 30-09-00, Telex 910364 FG; also, for *Gîtes*, Association pour le Tourisme Vert en Guyane, 27, rue Justin Cataye, 97300 Cayenne, T 31-10-11.

● Food

Most is imported, except seafood; it is of very high quality but expensive.

● Currency

The currency is the French franc (5.50F = US$1 June 1994). These are bank rates; *cambios* offer higher rates for cash. Try to take francs with you as the exchange rate for dollars is low, many banks do not offer exchange facilities and most places demand cash. A better rate can be obtained by using Visa cards to withdraw cash from the Banque Nationale de Paris Guyane, Place Victor Schoelcher, Cayenne. Some report difficulties using cash dispensers (ATMs).

● Health

Tropical diseases, dysentery, malaria, etc, occur, but the country is fairly healthy. Malaria prophylaxis rec.

● Climate

Tropical with a very heavy rainfall. Average temperature at sea-level is 27°C, and fairly constant at that. Night and day temperatures vary more in the highlands. The rainy season is from November to July, with (sometimes) a short dry interruption in February and March. The great rains begin in May. The best months to visit are between August and November, which are the usual months for trips to the jungle.

● **Hours of Business**
Hours vary widely between different offices, shops and even between different branches of the same bank or supermarket. There seem to be different business hours for every day of the week, but they are usually posted.

● **Public Holidays**
Public holidays are the same as in Metropolitan France, with the addition of Slavery Day, 10 June.

Carnaval (February or March). Although not as famous as those of its neighbours in Brazil or the Caribbean, Guyane's Carnaval is joyous and interesting. It is principally a Créole event, but there is some participation by all the different cultural groups in the department (best known are the contributions of the Brazilian and Haitian communities). Celebrations begin in January, with festivities every weekend, and culminate in colourful parades, music, and dance during the four days preceding Ash Wednesday. Each day has its own motif and the costumes are very elaborate. On Saturday night, a dance called "Chez Nana – Au Soleil Levant" is held, for which the women disguise themselves beyond recognition as "Touloulous", and ask the men to dance. They are not allowed to refuse. On Sunday there are parades in downtown Cayenne. Lundi Gras (Fat Monday) is the day to ridicule the institution of marriage, with mock wedding parties featuring men dressed as brides and women as grooms. "Vaval", the devil and soul of Carnaval, appears on Mardi Gras (Fat Tuesday) with dancers sporting red costumes, horns, tails, pitch-forks, etc. He is burnt that night (in the form of a straw doll) on a large bonfire in the Place des Palmistes. Ash Wednesday is a time of sorrow, with participants in the final parades dressed in black and white.

● **Time Zone**
3 hours behind GMT.

● **Weights And Measures**
The metric system is in use.

● **Telecommunications**
International calls can be made direct to any country from any phone: dial 19 + country code. Public telephones are widely installed and used. They take phonecards of 50 or 120 units (35F or 80F), which can be bought at tobacconists, bookshops or supermarkets. How to use the phone is displayed in each phone booth in French, English, Italian and Spanish. To call the USA, 1 unit buys 3.6 seconds, to EC 2.5 seconds; discounts at weekends and between 1700 and 0700. The system is totally interconnected with the French system. International code for Guyane is 594.

● **Consulates**
British (Honorary), 16 Av Monnerville (BP 664, Cayenne 97300, T 31-10-34/30-42-42, F 30-40-94); Brazilian, 12 rue L Héder, at corner of Place des Palmistes, near Air France offices (closed Sat T 30-04-67). Suriname, 38 rue Christophe Colomb (T 30-04-61), Mon-Fri 0900-1200, visa 150F, 2 photos needed (takes 15 days; may be obtained same day, at extra cost in some cases).

● **Media**
La Presse de la Guyane is the daily paper (circulation 1,500). *France-Guyane-Antilles* is a weekly newspaper with a good information page for the tourist.

● **Tourist Information**
The French Government tourist offices generally have leaflets on Guyane; there is a special office in Paris, La Maison du Tourisme de la Guyane, 26 rue du 4 Septembre 75002, Paris, T 47-42-84-16, F 47-42-84-91. The Cayenne offices, called Agence Régionale de Développement du Tourisme et des Loisirs de la Guyane (ARDTLG) are at 12, rue Lalouette, Cayenne (Telex 910356, T 300900), free map and tourist guide *Guyane Poche*; Délégation Régionale, 10, rue L-Heder, 97307 Cayenne, T 31-84-91; Syndicat d'Initiative de Cayenne, Jardin Botanique, PO Box 702, 97338 Cayenne, T 31-29-19; Syndicat d'Initiative Rémire-Montjoly, Mairie de Rémire, 97305 Rémire, T 35-41-10.

THE VENEZUELAN ISLANDS

VENEZUELA has 2,800 kilometres of coastline on the Caribbean Sea. The country's total area is 912,050 square kilometres, and its population exceeds 20,227,000. It was given its name, "Little Venice", by the Spanish navigators, who saw in the Indian pile dwellings on Lake Maracaibo a dim reminder of the buildings along Venetian waterways.

When the Spaniards landed in E Venezuela in 1498, in the course of Columbus' third voyage, they found a poor country sparsely populated by Indians who had created no distinctive culture. Four hundred years later it was still poor, almost exclusively agrarian, exporting little, importing less. The miracle year which changed all that was 1914, when oil was discovered near Maracaibo. Today, Venezuela is said to be the richest country in Latin America and is one of the largest producers and exporters of oil in the world.

In the 1980s, the country faced economic difficulties resulting from a combination of falling oil prices and a large external debt. In consequence, the government has reappraised the potential of tourism as one of a number of means of earning foreign exchange. There is still much scope for improving every facet of tourist infrastructure.

Venezuela has 72 island possessions in the Caribbean, of which the largest and the most visited is Isla de Margarita. This island, and two close neighbours, Coche and Cubagua, form the state of Nueva Esparta. Most of the other islands are Federal Dependencies (whose capital is Los Roques) stretching in small groups of keys to the E of Bonaire. Two other sets of islands are incorporated in the national parks of Morrocoy (W of the country's capital, Caracas) and Mochima, E of Caracas.

ISLA DE MARGARITA

Isla de Margarita is in fact one island whose two sections are tenuously linked by the 18 kilometre sandspit which separates the sea from the Restinga lagoon. At its largest, Margarita is about 32 kilometres from N to S and 67 kilometres from E to W. Most of its people live in the developed E part, which has some wooded areas and fertile valleys. The W part, the Peninsula de Macanao, is hotter and more barren, with scrub, sand dunes and marshes. Wild deer, goats and hares roam the interior, but 4-wheel drive vehicles are needed to penetrate it. The entrance to the Peninsula de Macanao is a pair of hills known as Las Tetas de María Guevara, a national monument covering 1,670 hectares.

The climate is exceptionally good, but rain is scant. Water is piped from the mainland. The roads are good, and a bridge connects the two parts. Nueva

Esparta's population is over 200,000, of whom about 68,000 live in the main city, Porlamar (which is not the capital, that is La Asunción).

History

Christopher Columbus made landfall on the nearby Paria Peninsula in August 1498. Two years later, a settlement had been established at Santiago de Cubagua (later called Nueva Cádiz) to exploit the pearls which grew in its waters. Cubagua became a centre for pearling and for slavery, as the local Indians were used, under appalling duress, to dive into the oyster beds. By 1541, when Santiago was destroyed by an earthquake and tidal wave, the pearl beds had been almost exhausted, but the Greek word for pearl, *margarita*, was retained for the main island of the group.

Margarita, and the nearest town on the mainland, Cumaná, were strongholds of the forces for the independence of South America from Spain. Between 1810 and 1817, the island was the scene of revolts and harsh Spanish reprisals. The liberator Simón Bolívar declared the Third Republic, and was himself declared Commander in Chief of the Liberating Army, at Villa del Norte (now Santa Ana) in 1816. After the war, the name of Nueva Esparta (maintaining the Greek allusion) was conferred in recognition of the bravery of Margarita in the struggle. Subsequent events have been nothing like so heroic, with life revolving around fishing and small agriculture. After a regeneration of the the pearl industry at the end of the 19th century, it has gone into decline, the oyster beds having all but disappeared through disease.

The Economy

The island has enjoyed a boom since 1983, largely as a result of the fall in the value of the bolívar and the consequent tendency of Venezuelans to spend their holidays at home. Margarita's status as a

VENEZUELA : FACT FILE

Geographic

Land area	912,050 sq km
forested	34.5%
pastures	20.0%
cultivated	4.4%

Demographic

Population (1992)	20,184,000
annual growth rate (1987-92)	2.4%
urban	84.0%
rural	16.0%
density	22.1 per sq km
Religious affiliation	
Roman Catholic	91.7%
Birth rate per 1,000 (1990)	29.9
	(world av 27.1)
Death rate per 1,000 (1990)	4.7
	(world av 9.8)

Education and Health

Life expectancy at birth,	
male	67.0 years
female	73.3 years
Infant mortality rate	
per 1,000 live births (1990)	25.9
Physicians (1989)	1 per 576 persons
Hospital beds	1 per 370 persons
Calorie intake as %	
of FAO requirement	106%
Population age 10 and over	
with no formal schooling	9.5%
Literate males (over 15)	93.5%
Literate females (over 15)	91.1%

Economic

GNP (1990 market prices)	US$50,574mn
GNP per capita	US$2,560
Public external debt (1990)	US$26,027mn
Tourism receipts (1990)	US$359mn
Inflation (annual av 1986-91)	42.0%
Radio	1 per 2.4 persons
Television	1 per 5.3 persons
Telephone	1 per 10 persons

Employment

Population economically active (1990)	
	7,173,317
Unemployment rate	9.9%
% of labour force in	
agriculture	11.9
mining and petroleum	1.0
manufacturing	15.9
construction	9.0
Military forces	75,000

Source *Encyclopaedia Britannica*

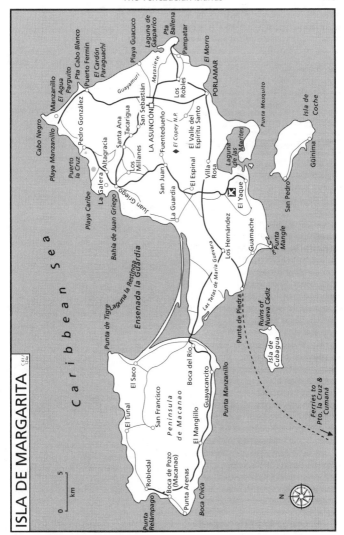

ISLA DE MARGARITA

duty-free zone also helps. Venezuelan shoppers go in droves for clothing, electronic goods and other consumer items. Gold and gems are good value, but many things are not. There has been extensive building in Porlamar, with new shopping areas and Miami-style hotels going up. A number of beaches are also being developed. The island's popularity means that various packages are on offer, sometimes at good value, especially off-season.

Local industries are fishing and fibre work, such as hammocks and straw hats. Weaving, pottery and sweets are being pushed as handicraft items for the tourists. An exhibition centre has been opened at El Cercado, near Santa Ana, on Calle Principal, near the church.

Flora and Fauna

Despite the property boom and frenetic building on much of the coast and in Porlamar, much of the island has been given over to natural parks. Of these the most striking is the Laguna La Restinga. Launches provide lengthy runs around the mangrove swamps, but they create a lot of wash and noise. The mangroves are fascinating, with shellfish clinging to the roots. The launch will leave you on a shingle and shell beach (don't forget to arrange with your boatman to collect you), and you can rummage for shellfish in the shallows (protection against the sun essential). Flamingoes live in the lagoon.

There are mangroves also in the Laguna de las Marites Natural Monument, W of Porlamar. Other parks are Las Tetas de María Guevara, Cerro el Copey, 7,130 hectares, and Cerro Matasiete y Guayamurí, 1,672 hectares (both reached from La Asunción). Details of Inparques, the National Parks office, are given in the **Information for Visitors.**

By boat from Porlamar you can go to the Isla de los Pájaros, or Morro Blanco, for both bird-spotting and underwater fishing. In Boca del Río there is a Museum of the Sea.

Beaches and Watersports

Apart from the shopping, what attracts the holidaymakers from Venezuela and abroad are the beaches: long white stretches of sand bordered by palms, but rather hot, with little shade (sunscreen essential). Topless bathing is not seen, but the tanga (*hilo dental*—dental floss) is fairly common.

In Porlamar, the beach by the *Concorde* hotel suffers from its popularity: calm shallow water, pedalos for hire, windsurf classes; but that by the *Bella Vista*, although crowded with foreign tourists, is kept clean. For a more Venezuelan atmosphere go NW to **Pampatar** (population 10,950), which is set around a bay favoured as a summer anchorage by foreign yachtsmen escaping the hurricane season. Jet skis can be hired on the beach. A scale model of Columbus' *Santa María* is used for taking tourists on trips. (*Hotel Flamingo Beach*, 5-star, US$100, all inclusive, food, drinks, entertainment, service, taxes and tips, price pp, casino, good value; *Residencial Don Juan*, US$15 for room with bath and fan; apartments sleeping 6 are available, negotiate over price. Beach restaurant *Antonio's*, recommended; also *Trimar*, good value.) Pampatar has the island's largest fort, San Carlos Borromeo, and the smaller La Caranta, where the cannon show signs of having been spiked. Visit also the church of Cristo del Buen Viaje, the Library/Museum and the customs house (now the offices of Fondene, the local development agency). The beach at Pampatar is not very good, but there are lots of fishing boats and fishermen mending their nets. A fishing boat can be hired for US$12 for 2½ hrs, 4-6 passengers; shop around for the best price. A fishing trip is good fun. New hotels are being built on this stretch. There is an amusement park to the SW of Pampatar, called Isla Aventura, with ferris wheel, roller coaster, water slide, dodgems, etc, open Friday and Saturday 1800-2400, Sunday 1700-2400 and more frequently in peak holiday season. Entrance in peak season is US$5 adults, US$3.85 children, all rides included; in low season entrance is US$0.50 and each ride is US$0.30-0.60.

A number of good beaches are being developed on the E side. These are divided into ocean and calm beaches, according to their location in relation to the open sea. The former tend to be rougher (good surfing and windsurfing) and colder. Water is uniformly clear and unpolluted. Not all the beaches have local services yet, such as restaurants, though these, *churuatas* (bars built like indian huts), sunshades and deckchairs are becoming more widespread. (Hire charges are about US$1.50 per item.) It is still possible, even in high season, to find practically deserted beaches.

On the E coast are Playa Guacuco, reached from La Asunción by a road through the Guayamurí reserve: a lot of surf, fairly shallow (beware cross current when you are about waist deep, it gets very strong and can quickly carry you out to sea), palm trees, restaurant and parking lot; excellent horseriding here or up into the hills, US$30 for 2 hrs, contact Harry Padrón at the ranch in Agua de Vaca, or phone travel agent on 611311. The liquor shop at La Sabana, 1 km before the beach, sells ice by the bucket, cheap. Parguito: long and open, best for surfing; Paraguachí: some *churuatas*. At **Playa del Agua** (45 mins by bus from Porlamar, US$0.45), the sea is very rough for children, but fairly shallow. The beach is 4 km long, free of stones, white sand, with many kiosks which have installed palm-leaf covered shade areas. Two sun chairs under one of these costs US$8, under an umbrella US$5. This is by far the most popular beach on the island and during Venezuelan holidays, such as Semana Santa, it gets overcrowded. At other times it is a beautiful beach for sunbathing and walking. The fashionable part is at the S end (interesting range of vendors on the beach— quail's eggs, caipirinha cocktails, coconuts, *cachapa* maize buns). Since the recent opening of the large, luxury *Playa El Agua Beach Resort* and *Miragua Club Resort* (about US$75), many of the beach restaurants stay open till 2100. Some that can be recommended are *Moisés* (Venezuelan owned), *Sueño Tropical* (French

owned and very popular with Germans) and *Tinajón del Agua* (on the main road near the entrance to the beach, small, very good, popular). The restaurants which aim for the German market tend to be priced very high. *Restaurant El Paradiso* rents out cabins, US$12, small but comfortable; *Kiosko El Agua*, helpful, English spoken; *Posada Shangri-Lá*, recommended, and many other good seafood restaurants such as *Casa Vieja*, most are pricey but *La Dorada* is good value. The N end is popular with younger people, is less touristy, with fewer facilities and less shade. It is possible to see the island by Ultralight from here at weekends. Contact Omar Contreras, T (095) 617632, or José-Antonio Fernández (095) 623519, English spoken, US$35 per flight. (Also possible from the old airport at Porlamar). *Residencias Miramar*, Av 31 de Julio—Carretera Manzanillo—esquina Calle Miragua, rooms from about US$25, 3 minutes from beach, 1 minute from supermarket, family-run, self-catering apartments, comfortable, clean, barbeque recommended; *Casa Trudel*, T/F 95-48-735, Apartado 106, 6301 Porlamar (Dan and Trudy O'Brien), small, US$36s-38d, bed and breakfast, no accommodation for small children, homely atmosphere and excellent breakfasts, German Dutch, Spanish and English spoken, snacks served, barbeque twice a week, car rental, 5 minutes' walk from beach, recommended; *Vacacional El Agua*, Calle Miragua, T (095) 48082, owned by Antonio J Sotillo, similar price range, friendly, minimum 3 days stay, cheaper for longer stays and for groups, clean bathroom, good beds, fan, fridge, laundry facilities, 4 minutes' walk from beach; also *Pelican Village*, N end, small group of bungalows, satellite TV, pool, restaurant, bar, German-run, quiet. An un-named chalet park next to the *Miragua Club Resort*, self-catering, all facilities, very welcoming, highly recommended (no price, but "usually cheaper than *Miramar*"). **Manzanillo** (population 2,000): water gets deep rather suddenly, fishing huts, fish sold on beach, new apartments under construction, expensive restaurant, Playa Escondida at the far end; Puerto Fermín/El Tirano (Lope de Aguirre, the infamous conquistador, landed here in 1561 on his flight from Peru), El Caserío handicrafts museum is nearby; Punta Cabo Blanco: attractive limestone outcrop; El Cardón: some development (*Pahayda Villas*, US$30, nice apartments, large rooms, 2 baths for 4 people, sign at main road; 100m further on towards Playa Azul is a beach house with rooms to let and German-owned restaurant, good food).

The coast road is interesting, with glimpses of the sea and beaches to one side, inland vistas on the other. There are a number of clifftop look-out points. The road improves radically beyond Manzanillo, winding from one beach to the next. Playa Puerto la Cruz adjoins **Pedro González** (population 3,700), another fashionable spot with a broad sweeping beach, running from a promontory (easy to climb) to scrub and brush that reach down almost to the water's edge (ask for Antonietta Luciani at *Restaurant Pedrogonzález*, she has an apartment to rent, US$40 per day, sleeps 6, well-equipped, recommended as is her restaurant). The next bay is accessible by scrambling over rocks (major building here). One advantage of Pedro González beach is that there is a large lagoon on the other side of the coast road, so it will be impossible to spoil the bay with speculative building. There are a lot of pelicans and sea urchins (harmless).

Further W is **Juan Griego** bay and town (population 8,300). The town is marred by a number of cheap clothing bazaars and the beach has little sand. The bays to the N, however, are worth the walk. *Hotel El Yare*, one block from beach, T 095-55835, rooms US$30-40, 2-bed suite with kitchen US$40, longer stays can be negotiated, owner speaks English, highly rec; *Hotel La Galera*, recommended; *Gran Sol*, La Marina, entrance in shopping arcade, T 55736, a/c, bath, TV, US$15; *Residencia Carmencita*, Guevara 20, T 55561, a/c, hot water, food, US$10; *Fortín*, about US$12, a/c, cold water, opposite beach, most rooms have good views, good restaurant, tables on the beach; several others; also cabins for 5 with cooking facilities for US$20. *Restaurant Mi Isla* is recommended on the beach, also Lebanese restaurant on the beach; *Viña del Mar*, opposite *Hotel Fortín*, a/c, attractive, excellent food; *Juan Griego Steak House*, same building as *Hotel El Yare*, good value, recommened; also *El Buho*; *Viejo Muelle*, next door, good restaurant, live music, outside beach bar. Playas Caribe (reported to be the best deserted beach) and Galera are less spoilt (*Posada del Sol*, under US$20, bedroom, bath, kitchen, sitting area, clean, fan, fridge). Fortín La Galera is worth a visit for the view of Juan Griego and Galera bays; children will breathlessly recite the epic siege fought here during the wars of independence.

South of Juan Griego, the road goes inland to **San Juan**, then to Punta de Piedra, the ferry dock, see below (a pleasant stretch through cultivated land and farms at regular intervals). Due S of San Juan is El Yaque, near the airport and the mouth of the Laguna de las Marites. This is said to be the best place for windsurfing. Near San Juan is Fuentedueño park which has special walks. A branch goes NW to **La Guardia** at the E end of La Restinga. The dyke of broken seashells stretches to the Península de Macanao: on its right a spotlessly clean beach, on its left the lagoon. At the far end is a cluster of fishermen's huts with landing stages from which the launches make trips into the labyrinth of canals in the lagoon (US$8 per boat taking 5 passengers; bus from Porlamar harbour front US$1, ask driver to drop you off).

The **Península de Macanao** is quite underdeveloped, although it is hardly an untouched paradise. Construction companies are extracting large amounts of ballast for the building boom in Porlamar, while urban waste is simply being dumped in large quantities along the roadside. Some of the beaches, however, are highly regarded: Manzanilla, Guayaconcito, Boca de Pozo, Macanao, Punta Arenas and El Manglillo.

Festivals on Margarita

6-13 January at Altagracia; 20-27 January at Tacarigua (San Sebastian); 16-26 March at Paraguachí (*Feria de San José*); 3-10 May at Los Robles; 24-30 May at La Guardia; 6 June at Tacarigua (Sagrado Corazón de Jesús); 25-26 July at Santa Ana; 27 July at Punta de Piedra; 31 July (Batalla de Matasiete) and 14-15 August (Asunción de la Virgen) at La Asunción; 30 August-8 September at Villa Rosa; 8-15 September at El Valle; 11-12 (Fiesta del Virgen del Pilar) and 28 October (San Juan Tadeo) at Los Robles; 4-11 November at Boca del Río, 4-30 November at Boca del Pozo; 5-6 December at Porlamar; 15 December at San Francisco de Macanao; 27 December-3 January at Juan Griego. See map for locations.

PORLAMAR

Most of the hotels are at *Porlamar*, 11 kilometres from the airport and about 28 kilometres from **Punta de Piedra**, where most of the ferries dock. It has a magnificent cathedral. At Igualdad y Díaz is the Museo de Arte Francisco Narváez. The main, and most expensive, shopping area is Avenida Santiago Mariño; better bargains and a wider range of shops are to be found on Gómez and Guevara. At night everything closes by 2300; women alone should avoid the centre after dark. Note that in Porlamar there is a Calle Mariño and an Avenida Santiago Mariño in the centre.

Ferries go to the Isla de Coche (11 kilometres by 6), which has over 5,000 inhabitants and one of the richest salt mines in the country. They also go, on hire only, to Isla de Cubagua, which is totally deserted, but you can visit the ruins of Nueva Cádiz (which have been excavated).

The capital, *La Asunción* (population 16,660), is a few kilometres inland from Porlamar. It has several colonial buildings, a cathedral, and the fort of Santa Rosa, with a famous bottle dungeon (open Monday 0800-1500, other days 0800-1800). There is a museum in the Casa Capitular, and a local market, good for handicrafts. Nearby are the Cerro Matasiete historical site and the Félix Gómez look out in the Sierra Copuy.

Between La Asunción and Porlamar are the Parque Francisco Fajardo, beside the Universidad de Oriente, and **El Valle del Espíritu Santo**. Here is the church of the Virgen del Valle, a picturesque building with twin towers, painted white and pink. The Madonna is richly dressed (one dress has pearls, the other diamonds); the adjoining museum opens at 1400, it displays costumes and presents for the Virgin, including the "milagro de la pierna de perla", a leg-shaped pearl. A pilgrimage is held in early September. Proper dress is requested to enter the church.

Throughout the island, the churches are attractive: fairly small, with baroque towers and adornments and, in many cases, painted pink.

Island Information—Isla de Margarita
● **How To Get There**

There are over 30 **flights** a day from **Caracas**, with Avensa, Servivensa and Aeropostal, 45 mins flight; tickets are much cheaper if purchased in Venezuela in local currency (about US$89 one way – Avensa, US$85 with the other 2). Reservations made from outside Venezuela are not always honoured. Daily Servivensa flight to **Ciudad Guyana**, also Aserca at 1815, and daily Aereotuy to **Ciudad Bolívar**. Daily flights from **Cumaná**, **Carúpano**, **Barcelona**, **Maturín**, **Valencia**. Twice a week from Barbados with Aeropostal; once a week with Viasa from Frankfurt, London, Miami and New York. Viasa, Av 4 de Mayo, Edif Banco Royal, Porlamar (T 32273,

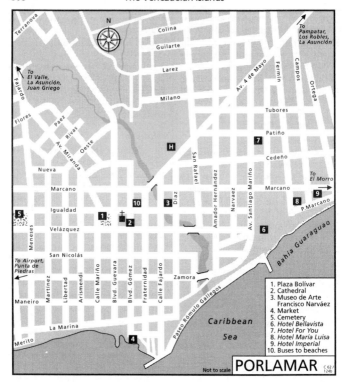

1. Plaza Bolívar
2. Cathedral
3. Museo de Arte Francisco Narváez
4. Market
5. Cemetery
6. Hotel Bellavista
7. Hotel For You
8. Hotel María Luisa
9. Hotel Imperial
10. Buses to beaches

Caribbean Sea

PORLAMAR   C 62 / 124b

Not to scale

airport 691137); Avensa and Aeropostal are both on Calle Fajardo, Porlamar, opposite each other (Aeropostal hours 0800-1200, 1400-1800, T 617064, airport 691128; Avensa T 617111, airport 691021). Airport: General Santiago Mariño, between Porlamar and Punta de Piedra; bus from Plaza Bolívar, Mariñoy Velázquez, US$0.70; taxi US$7.

Ferries (very busy at weekends and Mondays; in good condition, punctual): from **Puerto La Cruz**, Turismo Margarita, Los Boqueticos, T 87-683, Pto La Cruz to Margarita 0700 and 1300, 4 hrs (5-6 inc check-in), depart Margarita (**Punta de Piedra**) 1000 and 1800; Conferries, Los Cocos terminal, T 66-0389, and *Meliá Hotel*, Pto La Cruz to Margarita, 8 a day between 0300 and 2400 each way, 3½ hrs, passengers US$8.60 1st class, US$4.50 2nd (in enclosed middle deck with limited views), cars, US$16.50, jeeps, US$18.25. From

Cumaná, vehicle ferries of Naviarca at 0700 and 1600 daily, 3 hrs, cars US$10.50, jeeps US$13, passengers US$5.10, ferry terminal is almost at mouth of the river. Faster, more expensive launch, *Gran Cacique I* (Turismo Margarita) twice daily to Punta de Piedra, US$6.35. *Gran Cacique II* from Punta de Piedra to Cumaná at 1100, no cars, US$5.50 first class. Several bus companies in Caracas sell through tickets from Caracas to Porlamar, arriving about midday. By car from Caracas, it takes about 4 hrs, but will be reduced to 2½ when the Sucre motorway is opened (still under construction April 1993). A ferry from Punta de Piedra to Coche sails Mon-Fri, 1600, returns 1730, Sat and Sun, 0800 and 1730, returns 0530 and 1730.

A ferry sails from Mercado Viejo to Chacopata on the mainland at 1000 and 1200, also takes cars. Windward Lines (Global Steamship

Agencies Ltd, Mariner's Club, Wrightston Road, PO Box 966, Port of Spain, Trinidad, T (809) 624-2279, F 627-5091 sails to Pampatar alternate weeks from Trinidad, St Vincent, Barbados and St Lucia. Its other route is to Güiria. It leaves Trinidad Tues 1700 for its Venezuelan destination, arriving 2130, and leaves Güiria or Margarita at 2300 Wed, arriving back in Trinidad Thur 0300. Return fares: from Trinidad US$60, St Lucia, St Vincent or Barbados US$155. TCs can be changed on board at good rates. Go to the Puerto de Pescadores, El Guamache, near Punta de Piedra, and ask boat captains about taking a boat to the Leeward or Windward Islands (very difficult to find boats willing to take passengers).

NB August and September are the vacation months when flights and hotels are fully booked.

● **Public Transport**
Por Puestos serve most of the island, leaving mainly from the corners of Plaza Bolívar in Porlamar. Fares: to Punta de Piedra (from 4 blocks from Plaza Bolívar, towards sea-front), US$0.50, to the ferry terminal US$0.70; to la Asunción, US$0.25, from Calle Fajardo, half a block from Igualdad; to Pampatar, US$0.20; to La Restinga (from La Marina y Mariño), US$0.70, El Agua (from corner of Guevara and Marcano), US$0.40; Juan Griego, US$0.40. **Taxi** fares are published by the magazine *Mira* but are not uniformly applied by drivers. If you want to hire a taxi for a day you will be charged US$7-10 per hour. Always establish the fare before you get in the car. There is a 30% surcharge after 2100.

● **Car Hire**
An economic proposition for any number above one and probably the best way of getting around the island, from US$20 to US$50 per day depending on the make of car. To the cheapest rate add US$0.20-0.50/km and US$4.25 for each hour after the first day. With 200 km free rates are from US$40 to US$100, plus US$0.40-1 for each extra km and US$8.50 for each extra hour over the first day. Several competing offices at the airport, (*Beach* have been rec as cheap and reliable, US$30 a day for a jeep) also at *Hotel Bella Vista* (inc Hertz, reliable, Avis, and Lizmar, cheapest, but watch insurance excess), others on Av Santiago Mariño. In all cases check the brakes. Scooters can also be hired for about US$14 a day from Diversion Rentals, Calle Amador Hernández, Maruba Motor Rentals, La Mariña (English

spoken, good maps, highly rec, US$16 bike for 2, US$13 bike for 1), or Auto Camping Margarita (boats and bicycles also for rent). Motor cycles may not be ridden between 2000 and 0500; although this (apparently) should not apply to tourists, police officers have been known to confiscate tourists' machines and impose heavy fines. **NB** remember to keep an eye on the fuel gauge; there are service stations in towns, but a/c is heavy on fuel.

Driving on Isla Margarita: the roads are generally good and most are paved. Sign posts are often poorly-positioned (behind bushes, round corners), which adds to the nighttime hazard of vehicles with badly adjusted lights. It is best not to drive outside Porlamar after dark. Also beware of robbery of hired vehicles, several incidents reported. Check conditions and terms of hire very carefully for your liability.

● **Where To Stay At Porlamar**
Margarita Hilton, Calle Los Uveros, T (95) 61-5822/5054, F 61-4801, US$115d (+ 13% tax), new, health club, swimming pool, private beach with sailing dinghies for hire; other top class establishments: *Stauffer*, large rooms, excellent service and restaurant, small pool and bar on roof; *Concorde*, Balúa de El Morro, and *Bella Vista*, Av Santiago, swimming pool, beach. In the US$35-45 range: *For You*, Patiño y Av Santiago Mariño. *Marbella Mar*, Av Principal y Calle, Chipichipi, good service, clean rooms, friendly especially with children, bus to beach, rec; *Cabañas Turísticas*, Vía La Isleta, US$35 for a cabin sleeping 4, pool, restaurant. *Venus*, T (095) 23722, Calle Milano y San Rafael, clean, a/c, safe, under US$30. *Colibrí*, Av Santiago Mariño, T 616346, new rooms, cheaper in older rooms, both with bath, a/c, TV, rec; *Aguila Inn*, Narváez, clean, swimming pool, restaurant, rec. In the US$20-30 range: *Contemporáneo*, Calle Mariño entre Igualdad y Velázquez, modern, a/c, TV, clean, bar restaurant; *Italia*, San Nicolás, with bath, cold water, a/c, clean, safe, English spoken, rec, although area is a bit rough. Under US$20 a night: *Imperial*, Av Raúl Leoni, Via El Morro, T (095) 61-6420/4823, US$25, a/c, good showers, triple rooms available, clean, comfortable, safe, English spoken, rec, but restaurant only average; next door is *Tamá* (more with a/c, hot water, TV), excellent atmosphere and restaurant, bar is German-run, lots of languages spoken, highly rec, Vía El Morro, beach; *Garland*, Av Miranda, good restaurant, convenient for *por puestos*; *Porlamar*,

Igualdad y Fajardo, clean, hot water, good restaurant, and video bar *La Punta*, a/c or fan, friendly; *Marocco*, Mariño between San Nicolás y Zamora, a/c, TV, fridge, bath, but dark, windowless rooms. Under US$12d: on the Boulevard; *Chez Toni*, San Nicolás 14-56, clean, helpful, English spoken, cheap restaurant, rec; *Brasilia*, San Nicolás, quiet, clean, nice new rooms at back, rec; *Boston*, in the same block, US$7s with bath, fan, very clean; *Om*, San Nicholás, clean, friendly, a/c, cheaper with fan; *Residencia Paraíso*, near main square, basic but clean, fan; good value is *Rioja*, Fajardo, with fan and bath, clean, safe. *Los Duques*, Arismendi, shower, a/c, tv, rec; *España*, Mariño 6-35, T 612479, cold shower, very clean, friendly, good breakfast, fan, highly rec; *Palermo*, Igualdad opp Cathedral, friendly, clean, top floor rooms best with view of plaza; *Robaldar*, Igualdad nr Libertad, shower, a/c, TV, friendly, rec; *Domino*, La Libertad 7-40, fan or a/c, basic, friendly. Many others round Plaza Bolívar. Cheaper places on Maneiro.

● **Where To Eat**

La Gran Pirámide, Calle Malave and JM Patiño, superb food, very good service, cocktails worth trying, very good value, highly rec; *Doña Martha*, Velázquez nr Calle Hernández, Colombian food, good, inexpensive; *El Punto Criollo*, Igualdad nr *Hotel Porlamar*, good; *El Peñero*, Vía El Morro, service slow but good food; *Vecchia Marina*, Vía El Morro, good but more expensive; *Bahía* bar-restaurant, Av Raúl Leoni y Vía El Morro, excellent value, live music; good breakfast at *Panadería* at Av 4 de Mayo y Fermín; *Sadaka*, Calle Fajardo, Lebanese, reasonable prices, good food, rec; *Martín Pescador*, Av 4 de Mayo, lobsters and other seafood, friendly, rec; *Cheers*, Santiago Mariño, good bar, popular, rec; *Flamingo*, 4 de Mayo (in hotel), cheap, good, but small portion; *La Brada de Titti*, Av 4 de Mayo, good, rec; excellent pizzas (!) at *París Croissant* on Blvd Santiago Mariño; *Los 3 Delfines*, Cedeño 26-9, seafood, rec; *Guanaguanare*, pedestrian boulevard by sea, good food and service, reasonable prices. *La Isla*, Mariño y Cedeño, 8 fast food counters ranging from hamburgers to sausages from around the world. *El Rincón de Miguelacho*, Calle San Nicolás, friendly, inexpensive, good value. *La Cotorrera*, Av Santiago Mariño, steaks, rec, closed Sunday. Good afternoon tea at the *Hotel Concorde*. *Bella China*, Igualdad, good;

La Tapa Tasca, Marcano entre Narváez y Mariño, good seafood and atmosphere, expensive; *La Pilarica*, Ortega y Marcano, good service; *Pizzería Pida Pasta II*, *Da Giovanni*, 4 de Mayo nr Calle Carnevali, popular.

● **Shopping**

Besides all duty-free shops, *Del Bellorin*, Cedeño, near Santiago Mariño, is good for handicrafts. Good selection of jewellery at *Sonia Gems*, on Cedeño; *Ivan Joyería* and *Inter Gold*, both on 4 de Mayo (latter is between *Ivan* and *Hotel Flamingo*); many other places on the main street are overpriced. When purchasing jewellery, bargain hard, don't pay by credit card (surcharges are imposed), get a detailed guarantee of the item and, if unsure, get another jeweller to check its validity. Designer clothes are cheap in many places, especially on Blvd Guevara, Blvd Gómez, Calles Igualdad and Velázquez; cosmetics and perfumes also good value.

● **Entertainment**

Mosquito Coast Club, behind *Hotel Bella Vista*, disco with genuine Venezuelan feel, good *merengue* and rock music, bar outside; also does excellent Mexican meals (beware of overcharging on simple items like water). Discothèque for singles, *Village Club*, Av Santiago Mariño, recommended for good music with a variety of styles but expensive drinks, cover charge. *Doce 34*, Av 4 de Mayo, entrance US$3, 2 dance floors, highly rec. Nightlife is generally good, but at European prices.

● **Exchange**

Banco Mercantil for changing TCs; Banco Consolidado, Guevara y San Nicolás; banks generally slow with poor rates; best at Banco Construcción, Guevara or at *Hotel Contemporáneo* next to Banco Consolidado. *Casa de cambio* at Igualdad y Av Santiago Mariño. Amex office closed on Mon. Banks are open 0830-1130, 1400-1630. There are often long queues. Most shops accept credit cards.

● **Information**

An outspoken and well-informed English-language newspaper, *Mira*, is published on the island; the editor/publisher acts also as an inexpensive tour guide; Av Santiago Mariño, Ed Carcaleo Suites, Apartamento 2-A, Porlamar (T 095-61-3351). The best map is available from Corpoven.

● **Travel Agents**

Holiday Tours, based at *Hotel Concorde*, rec

for island tour, including very good lunch; *Turisol*, Calle Hernández, friendly and helpful (no island tours); *Supertours*, Calle Larez, Quinta Thaid, T 61-8781, F 61-7061, tours of the island and elsewhere; *Zuluoga Tours*, Calle San Nicolás entre Arismendi y Mariño No 16-40, helpful; *Tourismo Guaiquerí*, Santiago Mariño y Marcano, English spoken. Ask travel agents about excursions on the sailing catamaran, *Catatumbo*, rec.

ISLAS LOS ROQUES

Islas Los Roques lie 150 km due N of Caracas; the atoll, of about 340 islets and reefs, constitutes one of Venezuela's loveliest National Parks (225, 241 ha). There are long stretches of white beaches (beware of sunburn as there is no shade), miles of coral reef with crystal-clear water ideal for snorkelling (best at Francisqui and Cayo Agua) and many bird nesting sites (eg the huge gull colonies on Cayo Francés (Francisqui) and the pelicans, boobies and frigates on Selenqui). Small lizards, chameleons and iguanas, and cactus vegetation on some islets also add to the atoll's variety. Many of the islands' names seem strange because they are contractions of earlier names: eg 'Sarky' comes from Sister Key, 'Dos Mosquices' from Domus Key, where there are sea turtles and a Marine Biology Centre researching the coral reef and its ecology. For more information write to La Fundación Científica Los Roques, Apartado No 1, Av Carmelitas, Caracas 1010, T 32-6771.

Gran Roque is the main and only inhabited island; here flights land near the scattered fishing village (pop 900) which is Park Headquarters; average temp 27°C with coolish nights. Private accommodation is available, eg small *pensión* run by Sra Carmen Zambrano; *Posada Vora La Mar*, run by Marta Agustí, US$30 full board, T Caracas 238-5408; rooms rented by Maria, fiancée of Silvestre, cheap and friendly with excellent seafood, and others. You can negotiate with local fishermen for transport to other islands: you will need to take your own tent, food and (especially) water. "Eola" is a yacht, fully equipped, with cabins, chartered for US$100 per day, all inclusive, highly recommended as a worthwhile way of getting some shade on the treeless beaches. Run by Italians Gianni and Jaqueline, book direct by phone, T (5899) 216735. Nordisqui is very isolated while Madrisqui has many summer houses. Cayo Francés has an abandoned house and enough vegetation to provide shaded hammock sites, but otherwise there are no facilities. Warning to would-be campers: leave nothing out on the ground, the crabs eat everything! The *Pelicano Club* has accommodation and organizes excursions, boat trips, dives, recommended. Cayo Francés is two islands joined by a sandspit, with calm lagoon waters on the S and rolling surf on the N; May is nesting time at the gull colonies here. For solitude, Los Roques are a "must" midweek: Venezuelans swarm here on long weekends and at school holidays. Tiny but irritating biting insects in the calmer months can make camping miserable. Marta Agustí at *Posada Vora La Mar* can put you in touch with fisherman Andrés Ibarra, who can negotiate for transport to other islands; reasonable prices. If you are looking for solitude, ask Andrés to take you to Nordisqui or Isla Larga.

To get to Los Roques, take a SAN flight from Maiquetía airport, 4-5 flights a day, max 12 passengers (return fare US$100), or with Aereotuy (T 02-262-1966/71-6231), who fly to Gran Roque from Porlamar. Tours for 1 night, 3 meals, excursions and flight cost US$225.

OTHER VENEZUELAN ISLANDS

Also worth mentioning are the *Archipelago of Las Aves*, W of Los Roques, where fishing and diving are good. *La Tortuga* is Venezuela's second largest island, lying W of Margarita. Further out are *La Blan-*

quilla and *La Orchila*, both with coral reefs. About 500 kilometres N of Margarita, at the same latitude as Dominica, is *Isla de Aves*, 65 square kilometres of seabirds (sooty and brown noddy tern, frigate birds, gulls) surrounded by crystal clear water. The island is also a nesting site of the endangered green turtle. There is a Venezuelan coast guard station. For a full description of the island see *Audubon*, the magazine of the US National Audubon Society, January 1991, pages 72-81.

Much closer to the mainland are two areas of reefs and islands which have been designated national parks. There is no way to get to them other than by spending time in Venezuela itself.

The Morrocoy National Park

Was founded in 1974 to protect the large colonies of frigate birds, brown boobies and pelicans, and conserve the coral reefs and oyster beds in the mangrove swamps on the mainland coast between Tucacas and Chichiriviche. This region is 3½-4 hrs by road W of Caracas and is a popular place for spending the weekend away from the capital. There are marinas, dive shops and boat hire in Tucacas, boat hire in Chichiriviche, and plenty of possibilities for bathing, beachcombing and camping.

Tucacas (population 15,100) is a small, hot, busy, dirty and expensive town with lots on new building in progress, where bananas and other fruit are loaded for Curaçao and Aruba. Offshore is the national park of Morrocoy, where there are hundreds of coral reefs, palm-studded islets, small cosy beaches and calm water for water-skiing, snorkelling, and skindiving. (The Park is reached on foot from Tucacas; camping allowed, no facilities, no alcohol for sale, very crowded at weekends and, in the holiday season, with litter strewn all over the place.) With appropriate footwear it is possible to walk between some of the islands. The largest, cleanest and most popular of the islands is Cayo Sombrero (very busy at weekends). Even so it has some deserted beaches, with trees to sling hammocks. Playuela is equally beautiful and better for snorkelling, while Playa del Sol has no good beach and no palm trees. Bocaseca is more exposed to the open sea than other islands and thus has fewer mosquitoes. Boats are for hire (US$10-20 return to Cayo Sombrero, per boat, US$5.25 to nearer islands, ticket office to the left of the car entrance to the park; they will pick you up for the return journey, Pepe has been recommended). A more expensive way to organize a trip to any of the islands is through the travel agency Guili at Calle Sucre y Calle Silva No 1, T 84661, Freddy speaks English, French and Spanish, Valentine speaks German and Russian; if you want to spend several days they will come and check on you every 2 days, also trips to Los Roques. Venezuelan diving clubs come here for their contests. Scuba diving equipment can be hired from near the harbour for US$5 a day, but the diving is reported not very interesting. Try American-owned Submatur, Calle Ayacucho 6, T (042) 84082, 2 dives, lunch and gear US$65, for scuba diving and trips. This is one of the two main fishing grounds of Venezuela; the other is off Puerto La Cruz.

Local Information - Tucacas
● Where To Stay
Hotel Manaure-Tucacas, US$35, Av Silva, a/c, hot water, clean, restaurant; *Hotel Said*, at entrance, about US$15, swimming pool, good; *Palma*, US$10 without shower, fan, owner organizes boat trips; *Carlos*, US$10, basic, with fan, kitchen and laundry facilities, cheap and cheerful, tin roof noisy in the rain; *La Suerte* on main street, under US$7.50s, but bargain, clean. Cheap accommodation is difficult to find, especially in high season and at weekends, hotels are generally more expensive than elsewhere in Venezuela.

Restaurant Fruti Mar, very good; *Cervezería Tito*, good food; many good bakeries. Camping gas available in Tucacas for camping in the

Park. Bicycles can be hired in town. Banco Unión for exchange, Visa card and TCs accepted.

A few kilometres beyond, towards Coro, is the favourite beach resort of **Chichiriviche** (population 4,700); the town is filthy but offshore are numerous lovely islands and coral reefs. It is possible to hire a boat to any one of the islands; recommended for a weekend away from Caracas; note that prices posted on board, or on the jetty are per boat, not per person, from US$10 (take a snorkel, no hire facilities; snorkel and mask can be bought from a shop near *Hotel Capri*). All-day cruises, stopping at three islands, cost US$50 per boat. Prices are fixed, but bargaining may be possible on Paseo por la Bahía. You may camp on the islands, but there are no facilities or fresh water (three islands have beach restaurants serving simple fish dishes, clean, good), and you require a permit from Inparques (Instituto Nacional de Parques, address in **Information for Visitors**). Take precautions against rats. Nearby is a vast nesting area for scarlet ibis, flamingoes and herons, the Parque Nacional Cuare. Most of the flamingoes are in and around the estuary next to Chichiriviche, which is too shallow for boats, but you can walk there or take a taxi. Birds are best to watch early in the morning or late in the afternoon.

Local Information - Chichiriviche
● **Hotels and Restaurants**
Hotel Mario, over US$30 including 3 meals, swimming pool, upgraded; *La Garza*, US$10 without food, full board available, comfortable, pleasant meals at low prices, popular, pool; *Náutico*, T (099) 35866, over US$20, friendly, clean, good meals (breakfast and dinner inc in price), fans but no a/c, transport to nearest islands included, popular; *Villa Marina*, aparthotel, about US$10 pp, good, clean, safe, pool; *La Puerta*, out of town, US$25, next to port, clean, nice bar and restaurant, helpful owners, rec; *Gregoria*, Calle Mariño, US$15, with bath, clean, fan, laundry facilities, very friendly, Spanish run, highly rec; *Parador Manaure*, T 86236/86452, US$10 pp in apartments for 5, clean, small pool, poor restaurant; *Posada La Perrera*, Calle Riera, near centre, quiet, fan, clean, laundry facilities, patio, hammocks, helpful, firendly Italian owner, safe, cooking possible, free coffee, tours arranged, rec; *Capri*, near docks, US$15 (bargain), shower, fan or a/c, clean, pleasant Italian-owned, good restaurant and supermarket; bakery opposite has tiny rooms, similar price, fan, shared bathroom; *Casa Falcón*, Calle Falcón, 2 blocks from seafront on E side of town, US$15 or so, good, cheap, good coffee and juices, restaurant, Italian owner Sra Emanuela speaks French and English, friendly, tours arranged, bike rental, bird-watching, highly rec. Good fish at *Restaurant Veracruz*.

● **Exchange**
At banks on main street.

● **Diving**
Subma Tour, on main street; *Centro de Buceo Caribe*, Playa Sur.

Mochima

Venezuela's second Caribbean coastal National Park is **Mochima**, 55 kilometres from the port of Puerto la Cruz. This city is 320 kilometres, 5 hrs E of Caracas. It is the main commercial centre in this part of the country, but is also a popular holiday centre with good watersports and yachting facilities. The park itself also includes the mainland coast between Los Altos and Cumaná. The beaches and vistas of this stretch of the coast are beautiful (although see the note about litter, below). Since both Puerto La Cruz and Cumaná are ferry terminals for Margarita, Mochima can easily be incorporated into a visit to this part of Venezuela.

The easiest island to reach is **Isla de la Plata**, yet another supposed lair of the pirate Henry Morgan. It has a white sand beach, and clear waters which are ideal for snorkelling. There are food and drink stalls, but take drinking water as there is none on the island. Also take a hat and sunscreen. It's about 10 minutes by boat to the island, and the fare is about US$4 pp return. Further away, and larger, are the **Chimana islands** with

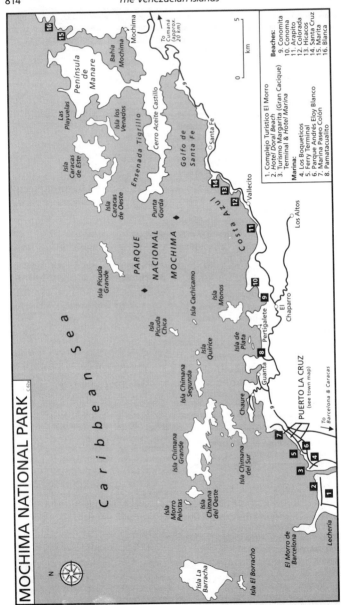

MOCHIMA NATIONAL PARK

Beaches:
9. Conomita
10. Conoma
11. Arapito
12. Colorada
13. Hicacos
14. Santa Cruz
15. Marita
16. Blanca

1. Complejo Turistico El Morro
2. *Hotel Doral Beach*
3. Turismo Margarita (Gran Cacique)
4. Terminal & *Hotel Marina*

Marina:
4. Los Boqueticos
5. Ferry Terminal
6. Parque Andrés Eloy Blanco
7. Marina Paseo Colón
8. Pamatacualito

PUERTO LA CRUZ

N

Caribbean
Sea

To
Ferry Dock

To
Cumaná & Parque
Nacional Mochima

Paseo Colón

Marina

Paseo Colón

Av Alberto Ravel

Guaraguao

Arismendi

Carabobo

Flores

Miranda

Freites

Av de Julio

Manejo

Bolívar

Libertad

Honduras

Giraldot

Anzoátegui

Sucre

Juncal

Buenos Aires

Democracia

Esperanza

Av Municipal

Nueva

To
Caracas &
Barcelona

Av de Julio

Simón Rodríguez

Ricaurte

1. Plaza Bolívar
2. Catholic Church
3. Post Office & Telephones
4. Restaurante El Parador
5. Restaurante Guatacarauzo
6. Hotel Meliá
7. Hotels Neptuno, Monte
   Carlo & Margelina
8. Hotel Riviera
9. Hotel Gaeta

beautiful beaches (Grande, Sur, del Oeste), in the waters around which there is snorkelling and good scuba diving (boat ride about US\$14 return). The islands are very popular and consequently are badly littered. All have restaurants and snack-bars, and thatched shelters can be hired for US\$1.80. Boats to the islands leave from the E end of Paseo Colón beach, next to the yacht club, Puerto La Cruz. Prices are fixed, payable in advance, arrange the time of return, reliable service.

Other islands in the vicinity are Monos (also good for scuba diving), La Borracha, El Borracho and Los Borrachitos, and Caracas de Oeste and Caracas del Este. All are in sheltered waters and are easy to explore by boat.

Further E from Puerto La Cruz is **Santa Fe**, a good place to relax; it is not (yet) a tourist town, but there is plenty of loud music, a golf course on the dark red,

sandy beach, and a market on Saturday.

● **Where to Stay and Services** *Hotel Cochaima*, run by Margot (US\$15 or so), is rec as clean, friendly, popular, noisy, meals available, fan, close to beach, dollars exchanged, ask for Diego who takes snorkelling or diving trips, US\$10 for 6 hrs snorkelling, all equipment provided; *Siete Delfines*, bath, fan, US\$9, dollars exchange, café and terrace where you can cook, excellent food available, warmly rec; 2 hotels on beach; private houses let rooms; *Salón de Jugos Chomena*, has one basic, cheap room for real budget travellers, owner changes travellers' cheques. Gasoline is available; *por puesto* at 0600 and bus to Cumaná (US\$1) and Puerto La Cruz (US\$0.80). It is sometimes difficult to get the bus from Puerto La Cruz to stop at Santa Fe; a *por puesto* may be a better bet, US\$2, or taxi, US\$13.30 including wait. Jeep, boat or diving tours are available. Boat trips to nearby beaches (Colorada, Blanca), US\$10; better to hire your own boat, US\$35 or hitch along the coast road.

● **Diving** Scuba diving is possible at Technosub, next to *Hotel Meliá*, US\$50 for 2 dives.

Hotel Meliá also offers diving: US$60 for 2 dives, US$250 for four day certification course. There are many other agencies, all charging about US$70-80 for 2 dives. Hotels and travel agents organize trips. The nearest recompression chamber is on Isla Margarita.

The sleepy and friendly village of Mochima, beyond Santa Fe, is 4 km off the main road, hitching difficult; bus to Cumaná at 1400, US$0.80; taxi from Puerto La Cruz US$25. Here Sra Cellita Día, Gaby, Mama Inés and Doña María let rooms, under US$6; houses to rent with kitchens and fans for US$12 per day depending on length of stay; eat at *Los Mochimeros*, good and friendly (try the *empanadas* with ice cold coconut milk), also *Don Quijote*, Av Bermúdez, very good. The restaurants and few shops are often closed. The sea is dirty near the town, but if you do swim, beware of the rusty ladder at the end of the pier. There is a lot of construction going on. Boats to nearby beaches (such as Playa Marita and Playa Blanca) and around the islands, fares negotiable, about US$10 to one island, US$20 for a 2-hour trip round the islands (up to 6 people). **NB** At holiday times this coast is very busy and, like many other beaches in the country, has become littered and polluted, especially at Santa Fe and on the islands.

INFORMATION FOR VISITORS

● **Documents**

Entry is by passport and visa, or by passport and tourist card. Tourist cards (*tarjetas de ingreso*) are valid only for those entering by air and are issued by most airlines to visitors from 25 countries including the USA, Canada, Japan and all Western European countries except Spain and Portugal. They are valid for 60 days with, theoretically, 2 extensions of 60 days each permissible, at a cost of US$25 each. On arrival in Venezuela your passport is stamped at immigration, but not necessarily with any indication of how long you can stay. Do not assume that if your visa is valid for one year you can stay that long. Overstaying your 60

days without an extension can lead to arrest and a fine when you try to depart. Renew at DIEX offices on Plaza Miranda in Caracas (many other DIEX offices do not offer extensions), take passport, tourist card and return ticket; opens 0800, passport with extension returned at the end of the day.

If you enter the country overland, you will be required to obtain a visa from a Venezuelan consulate prior to arrival; if not you may only be issued with a 72-hour transit visa which is hard to change into a full visa. Visas cost US$10 (£6 in UK), US$30 to New Zealanders and Germans, but US$3 to US citizens and US$1 to Swiss nationals; you will need your passport, return ticket and letter of reference from your employer and bank. You must fill in an application form and the visa will take about 3 working days to come through, sometimes longer if authorization has to come from Venezuela. It appears that you cannot get a visa in advance in the USA or Canada, so to apply for an overland visa in Colombia you need: passport, one photo and an onward ticket. A tourist card issued by Viasa in Bogotá is only valid for arriving in Caracas by air from Bogotá, not if you travel overland. To extend a visa for one month, in any city, costs about US$25; it is best to leave the country (eg to Curaçao) and get a new one free. To change a tourist visa to a business visa, to obtain or to extend the latter, costs US$50 (£31 in UK). Tourist visas are multiple entry within their specified period. Transit passengers to another country can stay only 72 hrs.

NB Carry your passport with you all the time you are in Venezuela as the police mount frequent spot checks and anyone found without identification is immediately detained (carrying a certified copy for greater safety is permissible, though not always accepted by officials). A press card as identification is reported to work wonders. Border searches are very thorough and there are many military checkpoints in military areas, at which all transport is stopped. Have your documents ready and make sure you know what entry permits you need; soldiers may be unfamiliar with regulations for foreigners. Do not lose the carbon copy of your visa as this has to be surrendered when leaving the country.

Information for business visitors is given in "Hints to Exporters: Venezuela", issued by the DTI Export Publications, PO Box 55, Stratford-upon-Avon, Warwickshire, CV37 9GE. Businessmen on short visits are strongly advised to enter the country as tourists, otherwise they will have to obtain a tax clearance certificate (*solvencia*) before they can leave.

● **How To Get There**

From Europe British Airways and Viasa fly from London to Simón Bolívar, the international airport for Caracas, the former twice a week direct. Viasa fly once direct, once via Porlamar. Viasa also serves Frankfurt, Lisbon, Madrid, Milan, Paris, Porto, Rome, Santiago de Compostela and Zurich. The cheapest route from Europe is with Air Portugal from Lisbon to Caracas. There are also services from Europe by Air France, KLM, Iberia, Alitalia and Lufthansa. There is a weekly flight from Amsterdam to Porlamar by Martinair, bookable in Holland and Germany, packages available.

From North America By air, passengers may reach Venezuela by American Airlines (New York, Orlando, Miami, Boston, Dallas, Detroit, Las Vegas, Raleigh/Durham), United Airlines (New York, Miami, Chicago, Phoenix, Seattle), Viasa (Houston, Miami, New York), Aeropostal (Orlando, Atlanta), Avensa (New York) and Servivensa (Miami, New York). Viasa and Air Canada (operated by Viasa) fly to Toronto; there are also many charters at holiday times.

Within the Caribbean Aeropostal and United have services to Port of Spain (daily from Caracas). Difficulties have been reported in entering Trinidad unless with a UK, US or Canadian passport. LIAT flies twice a week to St Lucia. Aeropostal—Air France joint operation to Guadeloupe twice a week. Viasa (4 times) and Aeropostal (twice a week) fly Caracas-Havana (Viasa's outward flights London-Caracas connect with this service). Ideal Tours, Centro Capriles, Plaza Venezuela, Caracas, T 793-0037/5738, offer trips to Cuba: US$406-497 low season, US$449-517 high, for 4 days (with all transfers etc included), US$500-640 low season, US$575-706 high for 8 days.

To The Netherlands Antilles To Aruba from Caracas: Servivensa and Aeropostal daily, Viasa 3 a week, Air Aruba daily except Sat, US$112 return; from Las Piedras/Punto Fijo on the Paranaguá Peninsula, Servivensa daily, US$90 return. To Curaçao from Caracas: ALM daily, Aeropostal and Servivensa daily; from Las Piedras, Servivensa daily (if you have no onward ticket from Curaçao, you must buy a return). Private flights from Coro airport to Curaçao

cost US$50 one way. The regular ferry service La Vela de Coro – Aruba – Curaçao has been suspended (1994).

Airport 28 km from Caracas, near the port of La Guaira: Maiquetía, for national flights, Simón Bolívar for international flights, adjacent to each other (5 mins' walk—taxis take a circular route, fare US$2.25; Viasa and Avensa have shuttle buses). The Tourist Office at the international airport has good maps, helpful; some English spoken, open 0600-2400, T 55-1060, passenger assistance T 55-2424; police T 55-2498. 3 *casas de cambio* open 24 hrs (Italcambio, good rates, outside duty-free area; best exchange rate with Banco Industrial, branch in International terminal and another, less crowded, in baggage re-claim area). If changing TCs, you may be asked for your purchase receipt. Check your change. There are cash machines for Visa, Amex and Mastercard. Pharmacy, bookshops, basement café (good value meals and snacks, open 0500-2400, hard to find; cafes and bars on 1st floor viewing terrace also good value); no seating in main terminal until you pass through security and check in. No official left luggage; ask for Paulo at the mini bar on the 1st floor of international terminal. Look after your belongings in both terminals. Direct dial phone calls to USA only, from AT&T booth in international departure lounge. At Simón Bolívar, airline offices are in the basement, hard to find: Viasa information and ticket desk open 0500-2400 daily, others at flight times. A Viasa lounge on the 1st floor of the International departure lounge, near to the viewing gallery, is open to transit passengers, serving free tea, coffee and soft drinks. If it is closed, transit facilities are poor.

Always allow plenty of time when going to the airport, whatever means of transport you are using: the route can be very congested and check-in procedures are very slow (2 hrs in daytime, but only 1/2 hr at 0430). Allow at least 2 hrs checking-in time before your flight, especially if flying Viasa. Taxi fares from airport to Caracas cost on average US$13.50-30, depending on part of city, or on the number of stars of your hotel, regardless of distance, overcharging is rife (fare in early am about US$15). Fares are supposedly controlled, but the system of the taxi office in the airport issuing tickets at the official fare seems to have been abandoned. There are official fares, but you still have to negotiate with the drivers; find out what the official fare is first. After 2200 and at weekends a surcharge of 20% may be added, you may get charged up to US$40. Drivers may only surcharge you for luggage (US$0.50 per large bag). If you think the taxi driver is overcharging you, make a complaint to Corpoturismo or tell him you will report him to the Departamento de Protección del Consumidor. The airport shuttle bus (blue and white with "Aeropuerto Internacional" on the side) leaves from E end of terminal, left out of exit for the city terminal (in the city, under the flyover at Bolívar and Av Sur 17, 250m from Bellas Artes metro, poorly lit at night, not rec to wait here in the dark), regular service from 0400 to 0030, bus leaves when there are enough passengers and may not stop at international terminal if no flights due; go to start of route at national terminal, fare US$1.15 (US$1.25 to international terminal). The bus is usually crowded so first time visitors may find a taxi good value. From city to airport at night, to avoid unsafe shuttle departure point, take local La Guaira bus from right hand side of exit from Nuevo Circo bus terminal to highway by airport. *Por puesto* airport—Caracas also US$1.35; from Caracas they are marked "Caracas Litoral", asked to be dropped off. Airport bus or *por puesto* to airport can be caught at Gato Negro metro station. When checking in, keep 10 bolívar bills handy to pay departure tax levied at most large airports.

● **Taxes**

All tourists and diplomats leaving the country, except nationals of Denmark and transit passengers, must pay US$25 approx, Bs2,800 at the airport or port of embarkation, payable in bolívares only. At Caracas airport this procedure is split between 2 desks; the form, or parts of it, may be required for up to 3 separate checks. Minors under twelve years of age do not pay the exit tax. Venezuelans, resident foreigners and holders of a *visa transeunte* have to pay Bs1,200 on departure. There is also an airport tax of US$0.30 Bs40 for those passengers on internal flights.

● **Customs**

You may bring into Venezuela, free of duty, 25 cigars and 200 cigarettes, 2 litres of alcoholic drinks, 4 small bottles of perfume, and gifts at the inspector's discretion.

● **Air Services**

Most places of importance are served by Avensa and/or Aeropostal. Some internal flights are also operated by Servivensa and Viasa, while Aerotuy serves a number of smaller destinations. Internal airlines offer special family discounts and student discounts, but this practice is variable (photocopies of ISTC card are useful as this allows officials to staple one to the ticket). Sometimes there is little difference between 1st class and tourist class fares. Beware of overbooking during holiday time, especially at Caracas airport; it is recommended that you check in 2 hrs before departure, particularly at Easter. Internal night-time flights are scarce, and there is no later hour discount. If you travel with Viasa or any other airline for which Viasa is agent, it is possible to check in the day before flying out of Caracas by taking baggage, ticket and passport to their office at Centro Comercial Tamanaco, Nivel C2, "Predespacho", between 1500 and 2100 (cost US$0.40); take bus from Chacaíto. To avoid overbooking the Government now obliges airlines to post a passenger list, but it is important to obtain clear instructions from the travel agent regarding confirmation of your flight and checking-in time. Passengers leaving Caracas on international flights must reconfirm their reservations not less than 72 hrs in advance, it is safer to do so in person than by telephone; not less than 24 hrs for national flights (if you fail to do this, you lose all rights to free accommodation, food, transport, etc if your flight is cancelled and you may lose your seat if the plane is fully booked). Beware of counterfeit tickets; buy only from agencies. If told by an agent that a flight is fully booked, try at the airport anyway. International passengers must check in 2 hrs before departure or they may lose their seat to someone on a waiting list. Viasa flights to Miami are often heavily overbooked. Venezuelans are prepared for this and check in during the morning before an evening flight. Read carefully any notice you see posted with the relevant instructions. Handling charge for your luggage US$0.50. All flights are subject to delays or cancellation. Avensa operates an air-pass system, open only to non-residents and purchasable only outside Venezuela: unlimited travel for 21 days for US$139. Passengers are issued with an MCO (Miscellaneous Charges Order) in the country of purchase, this is exchanged in Caracas at Pasajes Avensa, Esquina El Conde, 1 block W of Plaza Bolívar. At the same time ask for a timetable of all Avensa flights. (In view of the cheapness of internal flights, the pass may not be worth buying.) For independent charter flights try Rudi González at Carlota aiport in the city of Caracas.

● **Road Transport**

There are excellent (but slow) bus services between the major cities, but the colectivo taxis and minibuses, known in Venezuela as *por puesto*, seem to monopolize transport to and from smaller towns and villages. Outside Caracas, town taxis are relatively expensive.

● **Motoring**

All visitors to Venezuela can drive if they are over 18 and have a valid driving licence from their own country; an international driving licence is preferred. If you have an accident and someone is injured, you will be detained as a matter of routine, even if you are not at fault. Do not drive at night if you can help it (if you do have to, do not drive fast). Carry insect spray if you do; if you stop and get out, the car will fill with biting insects. Self-drive tours, and fly-drive are now being marketed, the latter through National Car Rental, which has a wide network of offices. Car rental rates are given under Porlamar.

There are 5 grades of gasoline: "normal", 83 octane; 87 octane; 89 octane; 91 octane ; and "alta", 95 octane. Gasoline costs on average Bs4-8/US$0.03-0.07 a litre; diesel costs US$0.03 a litre. Service stations are open 0500-2100, Mon-Sat, except those on highways which are open longer hours. Only those designated to handle emergencies are open on Sun. In the event of breakdown, Venezuelans are usually very helpful. There are many garages, even in rural areas; service charges are not high, nor are tyres, oil or accessories expensive, but being able to speak Spanish will greatly assist in sorting out problems. Carry spare battery water, fan belts, an obligatory breakdown triangle, a jack and spanners. Some cars have a security device to prevent the engine being started and this is recommended. The best road map is published by Lagoven, available from most service stations (not just Lagoven's), latest edition 1989. **Warning** There is an automatic US$20 fine for running out of fuel.

● **Hotel Reservations**

Fairmont International, Torre Capriles, Planta Baja, Plaza Venezuela, Caracas, T 782 8433, Telex 21232 SNRHO, F 782 4407, will book hotel rooms both in Caracas and in other towns, where they have 102 hotels on their books. All, except luxury class hotels charge officially controlled prices. In 1988 a 10% tourist tax was added to hotel prices, not for the benefit of hoteliers but for the construction and maintenance of tourist amenities.

● **Camping**

Camping in Venezuela is a popular recreation, for spending a weekend at the beach, on the islands, in the *llanos* and in the mountains. Camping is not however used by travellers as a substitute for hotels on the main highways, and no special camp sites are yet provided for this purpose. Wild camping is much easier with a car than with just a tent. If camping on the beach, for the sake of security, pitch your tent close to others, even though they play their radios loud.

● **Food And Drink**

There is excellent local fish (we recommend *pargo* or red snapper), crayfish, small oysters and prawns, though sole, trout and large oysters are imported. Of true Venezuelan food there is *sancocho* (a stew of vegetables, especially yuca, with meat, chicken or fish); *arepas*, a kind of white maize bread, very bland in flavour; toasted *arepas* served with a wide selection of relishes, fillings or the local somewhat salty white cheese are cheap, filling and nutritious; *cachapas*, a maize pancake (soft, not hard like Mexican *tortillas*) wrapped around white cheese; *pabellón*, made of shredded meat, beans, rice and fried plantains vegetarian versions available); and *empanadas*, maize-flour pies containing cheese, meat or fish. At Christmas only there are *hallacas*, maize pancakes stuffed with chicken, pork, olives, etc boiled in a plantain leaf (but don't eat the leaf). The nearest thing to a boiled egg in most places is a *huevo tibio*. It comes without the shell because there are no eggcups. A *muchacho* (boy) on the menu is not a sign of cannibalism; it is a cut of beef. *Ganso* is also not goose but beef. *Solomo* and *lomito* are other cuts of beef. *Hervido* is chicken or beef with vegetables. *Contorno* with a meat of fish dish is a choice of chips, boiled potatoes, rice or yuca. *Caraotas* are beans; *cachitos* are *croissants* of bread. *Pasticho* is what the Venezuelans call Italian *lasagne*. The main fruits are bananas, oranges, grapefruit, mangoes, pineapple and papaya. **NB** Some Venezuelan variants of names for fruit: *lechosa* is papaya, *patilla* is water melon, *parchita* passion fruit, and *cambur* a small banana. A delicious sweet is *huevos chimbos*—egg yolk boiled and bottled in sugar syrup. Venezuelans dine late.

Venezuelan rum is very good; recommended brands are Cacique, Pampero and Santa Teresa.

There are 4 good local beers: Polar (the most popular), Regional (with a strong flavour of hops), Cardenal and Nacional (a *lisa* is a glass of keg beer; for a bottle of beer ask for a *tercio*), mineral waters and gin. There is no good local wine though some foreign wines are bottled locally. Local wine is used only in cooking or in *sangría*. Liqueurs are cheap, try the local *ponche crema*. The coffee is very good (*café con leche* has a lot of milk, *café marrón* much less, *cafe negro* for black coffee, which, though obvious, is not common in the rest of Latin America); visitors should also try a *merengada*, a delicious drink made from fruit pulp, ice, milk and sugar; a *batido* is the same but with water and a little milk; *jugo* is the same but with water. A *plus-café* is an after-dinner liqueur. Water is free in all restaurants even if no food is bought. Bottled water in *cervecerías* is often from the tap; no deception is intended, bottles are simply used as convenient jugs. Insist on seeing the bottle opened if you do not want a mouthful of chlorine with your whisky. *Chicha de arroz* is a sweet drink made from milk, rice starch, sugar and vanilla; fruit juices are very good. Gin and rum at about US$2 and coffee beans at US$1.50 per kilo are good buys.

● **Value Added Tax**
IVA (VAT) at 10% was introduced on 1 January 1994, but was withdrawn for retailing by President Caldera in February. At the time of going to press IVA was not charged on anything, but a luxury goods tax was planned. There is 10% service in restaurants and 10% tourist tax in hotels.

● **Tipping**
Taxi drivers are tipped if the taxi has a meter (hardly anywhere), but not if you have agreed the fare in advance. Usherettes are not tipped. Hotel porters, Bs 2; airport porters Bs 2 per piece of baggage. Restaurants, between 5% and 10% of bill.

● **Shopping**
Goods in shops bear a label "PVP" followed by the price. This is the maximum authorized price; you may be able to negotiate a discount but should never pay more than the PVP price.

● **Currency**
The unit of currency is the bolívar, which is divided into 100 céntimos. There are nickel alloy coins for 25 and 50 céntimos and 1, 2 and 5 bolívares, and notes for 1, 2, 5, 10, 20, 50, 100, 500 and 1,000 bolívares. There is a shortage of small coinage: many shops round up prices unless you have small change and bars may refuse to serve you unless you produce the correct change. In 1989, the official and free rates of exchange were unified. Change travellers' cheques or US dollar notes in a *casa de cambio* for optimum rates (if travelling off the beaten track consider changing a considerable amount); of the banks, Banco Unión and Banco de Venezuela change cheques and cash, but the latter usually only changes money after 1500. The majority of banks do not cash travellers' cheques; in major towns, one or 2 banks may, but this varies from branch to branch. Bancos Unión, Consolidado, Mercantil and Provincial are usually good bets. American Express cheques are widely accepted (but proof of purchase is required for changing them into bolívares) as are Visa and Mastercard. Mastercard transactions offer good rates. Banco Consolidado is affiliated with American Express, no commission, some branches cash personal cheques from abroad on an Amex card; Banco Unión and Banco de Venuzuela Visa transactions, including cash advances and Banco Mercantil handles Mastercard. Thomas Cook Mastercard refund assistance point, Edif Cavendes, piso 7, of 706, Av Fco de Mirando, Los Palos Grandes, 1060 Caracas, T 284-3866/3255. When changing dollars cash in banks, it is best to go in the morning, queues can be very long. If changing money in hotels, do not take sterling or any other European currencies. Have money sent to you by telex and not by post, which can take weeks. Rates of exchange in hotels are generally poor.

NB It is quite common for tour companies not to accept credit cards, other than for flights, so you will need cash or travellers' cheques for buying tours.

Popular names for coins: Fuerte, Bs 5; Real, Bs 0.50; Medio, 0.25; Puya or Centavo, 0.05. The brown Bs 100 note is sometimes referred to as a *marrón*, or a *papel*, the Bs 500 note as an *orquidea*, because of its picture.

● **Security**
Cameras and other valuables should not be exposed prominently. The police may confiscate pocket knives as "concealed weapons" if they find them, although they are sold legally in the shops. In Caracas, carry handbags, cameras etc on the side away from the street as motor-cycle purse-snatchers are notorious. Hotel thefts are becoming more frequent.

● **Health**
Health conditions are good. Water in all main

towns is heavily chlorinated, so safe to drink, although most people drink bottled water. Medical attention is good. State health care is free and said to be good (the Clínica Metropolitana in Caracas has been recommended). On the coast from Cumaná E precautions against vampire bat bite are warranted since they can be rabies-carriers. Lights over hatches and windows are used by local fishermen to deter bats from entering boats and shore cabins. If bitten seek medical advice. Some rivers are infected with bilharzia and in some areas there are warning signs; check before bathing.

● **Climate**
Tropical, with little change between season.

● **Hours Of Business**
Banks are open from 0830 to 1130 and 1400 to 1630, Mon to Fri only. Government office hours vary, but 0800-1200 are usual morning hours. Government officials have fixed hours, usually 0900-1000 or 1500-1600, for receiving visitors. Business firms generally start work about 0800, and some continue until about 1800 with a midday break. Shops, 0900-1300, 1500-1900, Mon to Sat. Generally speaking, Venezuelans start work early, and by 0700 everything is in full swing. Most firms and offices close on Sat.

● **Holidays**
There are 2 sorts of holidays, those enjoyed by everybody and those taken by employees of banks and insurance companies. Holidays applying to all businesses include: 1 January, Carnival on the Monday and Tuesday before Ash Wednesday (everything shuts down Sat-Tues; make sure accommodation is booked in advance), Thursday-Saturday of Holy Week, 19 April, 1 May, 24 June (24 June is the feast day of San Juan Bautista, a particularly popular festival celebrated along the central coast where there were once large concentrations of plantation slaves who considered San Juan their special Saint. Some of the best-known events are in villages between Puerto Cabello and Chuspa, to the E, such as Chuao, Cata and Ocumane de la Costa), 5, 24 July, 12 October, 25 December. Holidays for banks and insurance companies include all the above and also: 19 March and the nearest Monday to 6 January, Ascension Day, 29 June, 15 August, 1 November and 8 December. There are also holidays applying to certain occupations such as Doctor's Day or Traffic Policeman's Day. From 24 December-1 January, most restaurants are closed and there is no long-distance public transport. On New Year's Eve, everything closes and does not open for a least a day. Queues for tickets, and traffic jams, are long. Business travellers should not visit during Holy week or Carnival.

Local: La Guaira: 10 March. Maracaibo: 24 October, 18 November.

● **Official Time**
Atlantic Standard Time, 4 hours behind GMT, 1 hour ahead of EST.

● **Weights And Measures**
are metric.

● **Electric Current**
110 volts, 60 cycles, throughout the country.

● **Postal Services**
The postal service can be extremely slow and unreliable. Air mail letters to the USA or Europe can take from one to 4 weeks and registered mail is no quicker. Important mail should be sent by air courier to a Venezuelan address. Internal mail also travels slowly, especially if there is no PO Box number. As in other countries, removing stamps from letters occurs; insist on seeing your letters franked, saying that you are a collector. Avoid the mail boxes in pharmacies as some no longer have collections. A private parcel delivery company, such as DHL, will charge around US$60 for parcels of up to 500g to Europe.

● **Telephone Service**
All international and long distance calls are operated by CANTV in Caracas in the S building, Centro Simón Bolívar (facing Plaza Caracas), T 41-8644, on the mezzanine of Centro Plaza on Francisco Miranda near US Embassy in E Caracas (corner of Andrés Bello between metros Parque del Este and Altamira), open 0800-2100, T 284-7932, phone cards (*tarjetas*—see below) sold here. Most major cities are now linked by direct dialling (*Discado Directo*), with a 3-figure prefix for each town in Venezuela. Otherwise CANTV offices deal with most long-distance and international calls in the cities outside Caracas. Collect calls are possible to some countries, at least from Caracas, though staff in offices may not be sure of this. Calls out of Venezuela are more expensive than calls into it and are subject to long delays. Local calls are troublesome and the connection is often cut in the middle of your conversation; calls are best made from hotels or CANTV offices, rather than from booths (of

which there are few). Many public phones operate with phonecards (*tarjetas*), available from CANTV or shops for many different values up to US$10 equivalent, though many small shops impose a 25% handling charge and *tarjetas* may be out of stock. International calls are cheaper with a *tarjeta*, minimum needed Bs500, for example you can make 3 one-minute calls to Europe for US$10 with a *tarjeta*, but you have to pay for 3 mins (at US$10) without one. To make an international call, dial 00 plus country code, etc. Many shops now offer fax services, set price to Europe US$8-12 per page.

● **Tourist Information**

may be obtained from Corpoturismo, Apartado 50.200, Caracas, main office for information is on floor 37, Torre Oeste, Parque Central. A useful publication is the *Guía Turística y Hoteles de Venezuela, Colombia y el Caribe*, published every July by Corpoturismo, which includes not only hotel details, but also road maps and tourist attractions. Also useful is the *Guía Progreso*, published by Seguros Progreso SA, available at the company offices and elsewhere, which is very detailed. The *Guide to Venezuela* (925 pages, updated and expanded 1989), by Janice Bauman, Leni Young and others, in English (freely available in Caracas) is a mine of information and maps, US$11.

For sailors, *A Sailor's Guide to a Venezuelan Cruise*, by Chris Doyle, is recommended, US$10 from Frances Punnett, PO Box 17, St Vincent, T (809) 458 4246; it gives information on all the small islands as well as Margarita.

For information on the **National Parks** system, and to obtain necessary permits to stay in the parks, go to Instituto Nacional de Parques (Inparques), Avenida Rómulo Gallegos, Parque del Este (opposite *Restaurante Carreta*), T 284-1956, Caracas, or to the local office of the *guardaparques* for each park. Further information can be had from the Ministerio del Ambiente y de los Recursos Naturales Renovables (MARNR) in Caracas. The book: *Guía de los Parques Nacionales y Monumentos Naturales de Venezuela*, is obtainable in Audubon headquarters (open 0900-1230, 1430-1800), Las Mercedes shopping centre, Las Mercedes, Caracas, in the La Cuadra sector next to the car parking area (it is difficult to find), T 91-3813. It is also available at Librería Noctúa, Villa Mediterránea, in the Centro Plaza Shopping Centre. The society will plan itineraries and make reservations.

We are deeply grateful to many travellers who wrote to *The South American Handbook* with updating material on the Venezuelan islands.

NETHERLANDS ANTILLES AND ARUBA THE ABCs

PAPIAMENTO GLOSSARY

Bon bini	Welcome
Con ta bai	How are you?
Mi ta bon	I am well
Bon dia	Good morning
Bon tardi	Good afternoon
Bon nochi	Good evening
Cuanti?	How much?
Danki	Thank you
Te aworo	See you later
A yo	Goodbye

THE NETHERLANDS AN-TILLES consist of the islands of (Aruba – autonomous, see below, Government) Bonaire and Curaçao (popularly known as the ABCs) 60-80 km off the coast of Venezuela, outside the hurricane belt; 880 km further N (in the hurricane belt) are the "3 S's": Sint Eustatius (Statia), Saba, and the S part of Sint Maarten (St-Martin) in what are generally known as the Leeward Islands. Because of the distance separating the N islands from the other Dutch possessions, the 3 S's are described in a separate section earlier in the Handbook. There is some confusion regarding which islands are Leeward and which Windward: locals refer to the ABCs as "Leeward Islands", and the other 3 as "Windward", a distinction adopted from the Spaniards, who still speak of the *Islas de Sotavento* and *de Barlovento* with reference to the trade winds. Each island is different from the others in size, physical features, the structure of the economy and the level of development and prosperity.

History

The first known settlers of the islands were the Caiquetios, a tribe of peaceful Arawak Indians, who lived in small communities under a chieftain or a priest. They survived principally on fish and shellfish and collected salt from the Charoma saltpan to barter with their mainland neighbours for supplements to their diet. There are remains of Indian villages on Curaçao at Westpunt, San

PAPIAMENTO - THE NETHERLANDS ANTILLES' ABC

Dutch is the official language, and many islanders also speak English or Spanish, but the *lingua franca* of the ABC islands is Papiamento, which originated with the Portuguese spoken by Jewish emigrants from Portugal, who were the most numerous settlers in the 17th century. Since then it has developed into a mixture of Portuguese, Dutch, Spanish, English, and some African and Indian dialects. Papiamento has been in existence since at least the early 18th century, but has no fixed spelling, though there is a committee seeking to establish a standard orthography. It is spoken by all social classes and is becoming prized as a symbol of cultural identity. The Aruban parliament now conducts its debates in Papiamento; poetry, plays and novels have been published in it; Curaçao has one Dutch-language newspaper but 7 in Papiamento. There are differences of accent and vocabulary between Aruba, Bonaire and Curaçao but speakers from the different islands have no difficulty understanding one another. There is more of a Dutch influence in Curaçao's Papiamentu and more of a Spanish influence in Aruba's Papiamento. There is a useful *Papiamentu Textbook* by E R Goilo (6th edition, published by De Wit Stores nv, Oranjestad, Aruba, also Dutch and Spanish versions). The most comprehensive dictionary by Sidney Joubert is available only in Papiamento/Dutch, 2 others in Papiamento/English are by Jossy M Mansur (published by Edicionnan Clasico Diario, Oranjestad, Aruba) and Betty Ratzlaff (TWR Dictionary Foundation, Bonaire).

Juan, de Savaan and Santa Barbara, and on Aruba near Hooiberg. On each of the ABC islands there are cave and rock drawings. The Arawaks in this area had escaped attack by the Caribs but soon after the arrival of the Spaniards most were forcibly transported from Curaçao to work on Hispaniola. Although some were later repatriated, more fled when the Dutch arrived. The remainder were absorbed into the black or white population, so that by 1795, only 5 full-blooded Indians were to be found on Curaçao. On Aruba and Bonaire the Indians maintained their identity until about the end of the 19th century, but there were no full-blooded Indians left by the 20th century.

The islands were discovered in 1499 by a Spaniard, Alonso de Ojeda, accompanied by the Italian, Amerigo Vespucci and the Spanish cartographer Juan de la Cosa. The Spanish retained control over the islands throughout the 16th century, but because there was no gold, they were declared "useless islands". After 1621, the Dutch became frequent visitors looking for wood and salt and later for a military foothold. Curaçao's strategic position between Pernambuco and New Amsterdam within the Caribbean setting made it a prime target. In 1634, a Dutch fleet took Curaçao, then in 1636 they took Bonaire, which was inhabited by a few cattle and 6 Indians, and Aruba which the Spanish and Indians evacuated. Curaçao became important as a trading post and as a base for excursions against the Spanish. After 1654, Dutch refugees from Brazil brought sugar technology, but the crop was abandoned by 1688 because of the very dry climate. About this time citrus fruits were introduced, and salt remained a valuable commodity.

Wars between England and the Netherlands in the second half of the 17th century led to skirmishes and conquests in the Caribbean. The Peace of Nijmegen in 1678 gave the Dutch Aruba, Curaçao, Bonaire and the 3 smaller islands in the Leeward group, St Eustatius, Saba and half of St Martin. Further conflicts in

Europe and the Americas in the 18th century led to Curaçao becoming a commercial meeting place for pirates, American rebels, Dutch merchants, Spaniards and créoles from the mainland. In 1800 the English took Curaçao but withdrew in 1803. They occupied it again from 1807 until 1816, when Dutch rule was restored, during when it was declared a free port. From 1828 to 1845, all Dutch West Indian colonies were governed from Surinam. In 1845 the Dutch Leeward Islands were joined to Willemstad in one colonial unit called Curaçao and Dependencies. The economy was still largely based on commerce, much of it with Venezuela, and there was a ship building industry, some phosphate mining and the salt pans, although the latter declined after the abolition of slavery in 1868.

In the 20th century the economy prospered with the discovery of oil in Venezuela and the subsequent decision by the Dutch-British Shell Oil Company to set up a refinery on Curaçao because of its political stability, its good port facilities and its better climate than around Lake Maracaibo. In 1924 another refinery was built on Aruba, which brought unprecedented wealth to that island and the population rose. The Second World War was another turning point as demand for oil soared and British, French and later US forces were stationed on the islands. The German invasion of Holland encouraged Dutch companies to transfer their assets to the Netherlands Antilles leading to the birth of the offshore financial centre. After the War, demands for autonomy from Holland began to grow.

Government

The organization of political parties began in 1936 and by 1948 there were four parties on Curaçao and others on Aruba and the other islands, most of whom endorsed autonomy. In 1948, the Dutch constitution was revised to allow

NETHERLANDS ANTILLES : FACT FILE

Geographic
Land area	800 sq km
Bonaire	288
Curaçao	444
Saba	13
Statia	21
Sint-Maarten	34

Demographic
Population (1992)	191,000
annual growth rate (1987-92)	0.2%
urban	92.4%
density	238.8 per sq km
Religious affiliation	
Roman Catholic	83.8%
Birth rate per 1,000 (1991)	18.3
	(world av 26.4)
Death rate per 1,000 (1991)	5.8
	(world av 9.2)

Education and Health
Life expectancy at birth, male	71.1 years
female	75.8 years
Infant mortality rate	
per 1,000 live births (1989)	6.3
Physicians (1992)	1 per 701 persons
Hospital beds	1 per 133 persons
Calorie intake as %	
of FAO requirement	111%
Population age 25 and over	
with no formal schooling	29.7%
Literate males (over 15)	94.2%
Literate females (over 15)	93.4%

Economic
GNP (1991 market prices)	US$1,490mn
GNP per capita	US$7,800
Public external debt (1991)	US$375mn
Tourism receipts (1991)	US$450mn
Inflation(annual av 1985-90)	3.0%
Radio	1 per 1.5 persons
Television	1 per 5.5 persons
Telephone	1 per 3.3 persons

Employment
Population economically active (1988)	
	72,906
Unemployment rate	20.4%
% of labour force in	
agriculture and mining	0.7
manufacturing	6.2
construction	7.4

Source *Encyclopaedia Britannica*

for the transition to complete autonomy of the islands. In 1954 they were granted full autonomy in domestic affairs and became an integral part of the Kingdom of the Netherlands. The Crown continued to appoint the Governor, although since the 1960s this has gone to a native-born Antillian. Nevertheless, a strong separatist movement developed on Aruba and the island finally withdrew from the Netherlands Antilles in 1986, becoming an autonomous member of the Kingdom of the Netherlands, the same status as the whole of the Netherlands Antilles. Aruba will gain complete independence in 1996 unless proposed constitutional changes come to fruition (see below).

The Netherlands Antilles now form two autonomous parts of the Kingdom of the Netherlands. The main part, comprising all the islands except Aruba, is a parliamentary federal democracy, the seat of which is in Willemstad, Curaçao, and each island has its own Legislative and Executive Council. Parliament (Staten) is elected in principle every four years, with 14 members from Curaçao, three from Bonaire, three from Sint Maarten and one each from Saba and St Eustatius.

Ms Maria Liberia-Peters was re-elected Prime Minister of the five-island federation in 1990, as head of a coalition led by the National People's Party (Partido Nashonal di Pueblo-PNP) with 10 of the Curaçao seats and the support of the five from Bonaire, Saba and St Eustatius in the 22-seat Parliament.

Mr Nelson Oduber became Prime Minister of Aruba in 1989, as head of a coalition led by the People's Electoral Movement with 12 seats in the 21-seat Parliament. The coalition remained in office following the January 1993 elections even though the MEP won fewer votes than the opposition Arubaanse Volkspartij (AVP). Both parties won nine seats and the three smaller parties of the coalition won one seat each. Mr Oduber initially governed with the support of the minority parties but when two of them left his coalition in April 1994 he was unable to reach agreement with the AVP on a new coalition and the government fell. A new general election was to be held on 29 July 1994.

Separate status for some or all of the islands has been a political issue with a breakaway movement in Curaçao and St Maarten. The Netherlands Government's previous policy of encouraging independence has been reversed. The Hague has been trying to draw up a new constitution governing relations between the Netherlands, the Antilles Federation and Aruba. A round-table conference was held in 1993 to establish the basis for future relations including financial support but ended without any decision on Aruba's desire to cancel proposals for independence in 1996, Curaçao's demand for *status aparte* and future relations of the islands with the Netherlands if the Federation collapses.

In November 1993 a referendum was held in Curaçao on its future status within the Federation. The Government was soundly defeated when the electorate unexpectedly voted to continue the island's present status as a member of the Antillean federation (73.6%), rejecting the other options of separate status (11.9%), incorporation in the Netherlands (8.0%) and independence (0.5%). Ms Liberia-Peters resigned and the Antillean Justice Minister, Suzy Romer, took over until late December, when Professor Alejandro Paula was sworn in pending elections.

General elections were held on 25 February 1994. A new party formed after the referendum, the Partido Antiya Restruktura (PAR - Antillean Restructuring Party), of Curaçao, won eight of the 22 seats. The PNP won only three of Curaçao's 14 seats, the Movimiento Antiyano Nobo (MAN- New Antillean Movement) won two and the Democratic Party (DP) one. In St Maarten, the St

Maarten People's Alliance (SPA) won two seats and the third was won by the Progressive Democratic Party (PDP). In Bonaire the DP won two seats and the Union Patriotico Bonairiano the third. The DP also won St Eustatius' single seat and the Windward Islands People's Movement retained its seat for Saba. On 31 March, Miguel Pourier, a former Prime Minister and leader of the PAR, was sworn in as federal Prime Minister, leading a coalition government. Mr Pourier advocates greater autonomy for the Antilles within the federation and has the support of 16 members of the Staten.

The new cabinet agreed that the other islands, Saba, Statia, St Maarten and Bonaire, should also hold referenda before September 1994, with the aim of restructuring the Antilles in a new form to go into effect in 1996. The position of the Netherlands has yet to be clarified, particularly, over higher financial super-vision for those islands which choose to remain part of the Federation but desire greater autonomy. The issues of good government, drugs trafficking and illegal immigration are high on the agenda.

Island governments seemed particularly unstable in 1994 as alliances collapsed. In Curaçao, the island government resigned on 1 June after three of the ten PNP island councillors resigned over education policy differences and the MAN declined an offer to join a new coalition. In St Maarten the leader of the governing PDP joined forces with the opposition SPA to vote through a motion of no confidence in the executive on 3 June. Two of the four commissioners on the executive council resigned, but the other two refused and had to face individual no-confidence motions. The SPA and PDP signed a coalition agreement on 20 June, their first since 1991 when a similar alliance collapsed after two months.

BONAIRE

BONAIRE, second largest of the five islands comprising the Netherlands Antilles, is 38 km long and $6^1/_2$-$11^1/_2$ km wide and 288 km square. It lies 80 km N of Venezuela, 50 km E of Curaçao, 140 km E of Aruba, at 12° 5' N and 86°25' W, outside the hurricane belt. The S part of the crescent-shaped island is flat and arid, much of it given over to the production of salt. The N end of the island is more hilly, the highest point being Mount Brandaris, and is a national park. There is little agriculture and most of the island is covered in scrub and a variety of cacti, many of which reach a height of 6m. Despite its lack of natural resources, it is, however, known as "Diver's Paradise", for its rich underwater life and is also valued by bird watchers. The windward coast is rough and windy, while the leeward coast is sheltered and calm.

Klein Bonaire, a small (608 hectares), flat, rocky and uninhabited islet one km off Bonaire's shores, is frequented by snorkellers and divers. It has sandy beaches but no natural shade and only a few shelters used by tour boats.

Bonaire is the least densely populated of the islands and the inhabitants, who number around 11,139 and are mostly of mixed Arawak, European and African descent, are a very friendly and hospitable people. The island is quiet, peaceful and very safe. As in Curaçao and Aruba, Dutch is the official language, Papiamento the colloquial tongue, and Spanish and English are both widely spoken.

The Economy

Bonaire has a fairly diversified economy with salt mining, oil trans-shipment, a textile factory, rice mill and radio communications industry. The Antilles International Salt Company has reactivated the long dormant salt industry, which benefits so greatly from the constant sunshine (with air temperatures averaging 27°C and water 26°C), scant rainfall (less than 560 mm a year), and refreshing trade winds. However, for foreign exchange, the island is overwhelmingly dependent on tourism, even if it is highly specialized. In 1993, tourist arrivals rose by 8.9% to 55,126 of which 41% came from the USA and 32% from Europe. An additional 5,443 excursionists stayed on the island for less than 24 hrs. Cruise ship passenger arrivals have risen sharply since the 1980s to about, 17,000 a year. Divers are the main category among stayover visitors, although their proportion of the total has fallen as the attractions of windsurfing and birdwatching have been publicized more widely. Accommodation for tourists is split fairly evenly between hotels and villas, amounting to about 1,000 rooms and still growing. Financial assistance for the development of tourism has been provided by the EU, which has financed the expansion of the airport and development of other infrastructure.

Flora and Fauna

The old salt pans of Pekelmeer, needed by the Salt Company, posed an ecological problem: Bonaire has one of the largest Caribbean flamingo colonies in the Western Hemisphere, and these birds build their conical mud nests in the salt pans. Pleas from wild-life conservationists convinced the company that it should set aside an area of 56 hectares for a flamingo sanctuary, with access strictly prohibited. The birds, initially rather startled by the sudden activity, have settled into a peaceful coexistence, so peaceful in fact that they have actually doubled

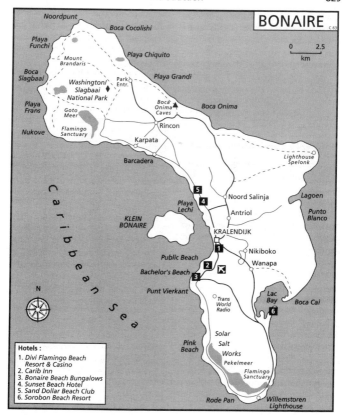

their output and are now laying two eggs a year instead of their previous one. There are said to be over 15,000 flamingoes on the island, and they can be seen wading in Goto Meer Bay in the NW, in the salt lake near Playa Grandi, and in Lac Bay on the SE coast of Bonaire, feeding on algae which give them their striking rose-pink colour. It is an impressive sight to witness the flamingoes rising from the water in the evening as they prepare to overnight in Venezuela.

There are also two smaller bird sanctuaries at the Solar Salt Works and Goto Meer. At Pos'i Mangel, in the National Park, thousands of birds gather in the late afternoon. Bronswinkel Well, also in the Park, is another good place to see hundreds of birds and giant cacti. The indigenous Bonaire Green Parrot can be seen in the Park and at Onima. About 130 species of birds have been found on Bonaire as well as the flamingoes. An annual Birdwatching Olympics and Nature Week is held in September, with prizes for those who spot the greatest number of species.

There are lots of iguanas and lizards of all shapes and sizes. The big blue lizards are endemic to Bonaire, while the

Anolis, a tree lizard with a yellow dewlap, is related to the Windward Islands Anolis species rather than to the neighbouring Venezuelan species. The interior has scant vegetation but the enormous cacti provide perching places for yellow-winged parrots. The most common mammal you are likely to see is the goat, herds of which roam the island eating everything in sight except the cacti.

Beaches and Watersports

Bonaire is not noted for its beaches; the sand is usually full of coral and gritty, which is rather hard on the feet, and those on the leeward coast are narrow. Beaches in front of some hotels have been helped with extra sand. However, they do offer peace and quiet, and you will not get pestered by people trying to sell you things. Recommended are Sorobon (a private, nudist resort where non-guests pay US$10 for admission), Lac Bay which has an area of mangroves at the N end of the bay, and in the NE Playa Chiquito. Be careful at Playa Chiquito, or Chikito, there is a memorial plaque there for good reason. The surf is strong and it is dangerous to swim but it is pleasant for sunbathing. There were a few huts for shade but they are in a poor state of repair. Another reasonable, but shadeless beach is Pink Beach, S of Kralendijk, past the Salt Pier, the water is shallow and good for swimming but the strip of sand is narrow and gritty. In the Washington-Slagbaai National Park are two attractive bays: Playa Funchi, which is good for snorkelling, but has no sand and no facilities so the area is very smelly, and Boca Slagbaai, which is popular with tour boats for snorkelling and you can see flamingoes wading in the salina behind the beach. At the latter, there are clean toilets and showers in a restored 19th century house and salt barn (ask the attendant to open them for you) and drinks and snacks are available. A very pleasant break in a hot and sweaty tour round the National Park. Fishing, sailing, windsurfing and waterskiing are all popular as an alternative to diving, which is what most people come to Bonaire to enjoy.

You can charter a fishing boat through your hotel and arrange half or full day trips with tackle and food included. Two independent charter companies are Piscatur, run by Captain Chris Morkos, T 8774, F 8380, half day US$275 for 4 people, US$425 full day in 30-foot diesel boat, or US$125 half day for 2 people, US$225 full day in 15-foot skiff; and *Slamdunk*, a 30-foot Topaz, T 5111 Captain Rich at the Marina, same rates but for 6 people. Captain Bob, T 7070, F 7071, also does fishing charters, half or full day, with his boat *Its About Time*. There is an annual Bonaire International Fishing Tournament, held at the end of March, which attracts participants from throughout the Americas.

The annual Bonaire Sailing Regatta is held in mid-October. This has grown into a world class event with races for seagoing yachts, catamarans, sunfishes, windsurfers and local fishing boats. The smaller craft compete in Kralendijk Bay, while the larger boats race round Bonaire and Klein Bonaire. Held over five days, the event attracts crowds and hotel reservations need to be made well in advance. For information call the Regatta office, T 5555, F 5576. There is also an annual Nautical Race in November for small boats. Speed races are held in Kralendijk Bay. The Marina at *Harbour Village* is the only facility of its kind in Bonaire. There are 60 slips for boats up to 110 feet with showers, laundry, fuel, waste disposal etc, and has a 120-ton syncrolift and supply shop for repairs. Sailing trips with snorkelling and beach barbeque, often on Klein Bonaire, or sunset booze cruises, from US$25.45 pp plus 10% service, are offered on *Samur* (PO Box 287, T 5433, F 5592), a 56-foot Siamese junk built in Bangkok in 1968, based at the *Sand Dollar Dive and Photo*, with pick up service from most resorts. Others include *Oscarina*, a 42' cutter, T 8290, 8819, and the *Bonaire Dream*, a glass bottom boat which sails out of Harbour Village Marina, tickets available in hotels, Bonaire Book Store, *La Sonrisa Soda Fountain*, Super Corner or T 8239, 4514, F 4536.

At Lac Bay on the windward side of the island where the water is calm and shallow, there is a constant onshore wind. The bay is about 3 miles long and 1½ miles wide but a coral reef just outside the bay breaks up the waves. However, the adventurous can get out of the bay at one end where long, high waves enable you to wave ride, jump or loop. Windsurfing Bonaire is based here, PO Box 301, T/F 5363, fax before 0830 for a free hotel pick up 0900 or 1300, instruction and board rental; windsurfing US$20 for 1 hour, US$50/day, lessons US$20, ocean kayaks US$10/hour, US$30/day. Windsurfing rentals and instruction are also available at Great Adventures Bonaire at the *Harbour Village Beach Resort*, T 7500, along with kayak, sunfish, mini speed boats, water skiing, sea biscuit rides and water taxi service to Klein Bonaire. *Sunset Beach Resort*, T 5300, F 8593, offers small hobie cat and sunfish rentals, waterscooters, waterskiing, hydrosliding and paddle boats. Waterskiing also from Goodlife Watersport, T 4588.

Diving and Marine Life

The least developed and least populated of the ABC islands, Bonaire has a special appeal to devotees of the sea, whose treasures are unsurpassed in the Caribbean. Surrounding the island, with submarine visibility up to 60m, are coral reefs harbouring over a thousand different species of marine creatures. Ranked as one of the three top dive spots in the world, and number one in the Caribbean (followed by Grand Cayman Island and Cozumel), Bonaire is a leader in the movement for preservation of underwater resources and the whole island is a protected marine park. Two areas have been designated marine reserves, with no diving allowed; along Playa Frans, N to Boca Slogbaai, and W of Karpata. Lac Bay may also become a protected area because of its mangroves and seagrass beds. Stringent laws passed in 1971 ban spearfishing and the removal of any marine life from Bonaire's waters. It is a serious offence to disturb the natural life of the coral reefs, and the local diving schools have set up permanent anchors in their dive spots to avoid doing any unwarranted damage. With about 600 dives a day, conservation is essential. You are requested not to touch the coral or other underwater life, such as sea horses; not to feed the fish, as it is not natural and encourages the more aggressive species; not to drop litter, particularly plastic which does not decompose and can be harmful to sea creatures, and not to kick up sand with your fins as it can choke and kill the coral. Advanced buoyancy courses are available free of charge and are highly recommended for divers to train you to keep horizontal along the reef and limit fin damage to coral. Several sea turtles can be seen around Bonaire but they are rare. If you see one, in the water or on a beach, report the sighting to the Sea Turtle Club Bonaire, c/o Tom van Eijck (Project Manager), *Sunset Beach Hotel*, T 5300 or contact the Bonaire Marine Park, T 8444.

On the E side of the island there is a shelf and a drop-off about 12m from the shore down to a 30m coral shelf and then another drop down to the ocean floor. The sea is rather rough for most of the year although it sometimes calms down in October or November. Along the W side of the island there are numerous dive sites of varying depths with wrecks as well as reefs. The most frequently dived sites include, Calabas Reef, Pink Beach, Salt City, Angel City and the Town Pier. There are also several sites for boat dives off Klein Bonaire, just 1½ km from

Kralendijk. The Bonaire Marine Park Guide is recommended and can be obtained from dive shops or from the environmental group, STINAPA.

Snorkelling is recommended at Nukove, Boca Slagbaai, Playa Funchi, Playa Benge, Windsock Steep and Klein Bonaire. Salt Pier, where the wooden support pilings give shelter to small fish, and the *Divi Flamingo Hotel* pier encrusted with coral, are also popular. Dive boats usually take snorkellers along when dive sites are close to shore, about US$12 for 2-hour trip with divers on one tank. The snorkelling trail was wiped out by bad weather several years ago but will be replaced when the reef has recovered.

Whether you dive or snorkel, you are certain to enjoy the underwater world of Bonaire. Most visitors are tempted to take at least the one-day "resort" or crash diving course. This enables you to decide if you'd like to continue, but one day will not make a diver of anyone. The main schools are Peter Hughes' Dive Bonaire (T 8285, F 8238, at the *Divi Flamingo Beach Resort*), Buddy Dive Resort (PO Box 231, T 5080, T/F 8647), Captain Don's Habitat (T 8290, F 8240, PO Box 88), *Carib Inn* (PO Box 68, T 8819, F 5295), Dive Inn Bonaire (PO Box 362, T 8761, F 8513, at the *Sunset Inn*), Sand Dollar Dive and Photo at the *Sand Dollar Beach Club* (T 5252, F 8760, also has photo shop), Sunset Beach Dive Centre (PO Box 362, T 5300 ext 278, F 8513) at the *Sunset Beach Hotel*, Great Adventures Bonaire (PO Box 312, T 7500, F 7507) at the *Harbour Village Beach Resort*, with instruction in several languages, Neal Watson's Underwater Adventures (PO Box 380, T 5580, F 5680) at the *Coral Regency Resort* and Bonaire Scuba Centre (T 8978, F 8846, at the harbour, next to the shopping mall and at *Black Durgon Inn*). Blue Divers Diveshop has been rec, Swiss and Belgian owned, English, German, Dutch, French and Spanish spoken, good value accommodation available, excellent guided dives with Bonairian Franklin Winklaar, who has been diving the reef for over 20 years, helping the likes of Jacques Cousteau, Kaya Grand; 60, Kralendijk, T 6860, F 6865. Prices are competitive, ranging from US$25-50 for a 2 tank dive if you have your own equipment. Add a 10% service charge on most diving. All packages include tank, air, weights and belt; equipment rental varies, US$6-11 for a BC jacket, US$6-11 for a regulator, US$6-7 for mask, snorkel and fins. Camera and other equipment rental widely available. Dive Inn and Carib Inn are among the cheapest. All dive operations are well equipped and well staffed with a good safety record. If booking a package deal check whether their week-long dive packages include nightly night dives, or only one a week. For less experienced divers it is worth choosing a dive boat which keeps staff on board while the leader is underwater, in case you get into difficulties. We have received reports that in the case of reasonably experienced divers, some dive masters do not always get into the water but stay on board. Shore diving is available nearly everywhere. Dive packages are available at the following hotels: *Captain Don's Habitat, Carib Inn, Coral Regency, Divi Flamingo, Harbour Village, Sand Dollar Beach Club, Sunset Beach Hotel, Sunset Inn, Sunset Oceanfront Apartments* and *Sunset Villas*. There is a US$10 pp levy for maintenance of the marine park which has to be paid only once a year.

Other Sports

There are tennis courts at the *Divi Flamingo Beach Resort*, open 0800-2200, T 8285; *Sand Dollar Beach Club*, open 0900-2100, T 8738; and at *Sunset Beach Hotel*, open 0800-1030, 1530-2100, T 5300. There is also horse riding but little else in the way of land based sports. Walking and birdwatching are popular in the Washington/Slagbaai National Park, particularly climbing up Mount

Brandaris. A bridge club, Ups and Downs, meets at the *Hotel Rochaline*, T 8286, welcomes guest players, enroll before 1400, play starts 1930.

KRALENDIJK

Kralendijk, meaning coral dike, the capital of Bonaire, is a small, sleepy town with colourful buildings one or two stories high. It is often referred to locally as simply 'Playa', because of its historic position as the main landing place. About 1,700 people live here and it is just a few blocks long with some streets projecting inland. Most of the shops are in the small Harbourside Shopping Mall and on the main street, the name of which changes from J A Abraham Boulevard to Kaya Grandi to Breedestraat. Places to visit include the Museum (Department of Culture), Sabana 14, T 8868, open weekdays 0800-1200, 1300-1700, folklore, archaeology and a shell collection; the small Fort Oranje, the plaza called Wilhelminaplein, and the fish market built like a Greek temple.

Excursions

Hire a car if you do not want to go on an organized tour. The island can be toured in a day if you start early but it is more pleasant to do a N tour on one day and a S tour another. Take food and drinks, there is rarely any available along the way, and aim to picnic somewhere you can swim to cool off. N of Kralendijk the road passes most of the hotels and planned developments, past the Water Distillation Plant along the "scenic" road, which offers several descents to the sea and some excellent spots for snorkelling or diving along the rocky coastline. The first landmark is the radio station which has masses of aerials. Note that the road is one way, do not turn round, but beware of pot holes and watch out for lizards sunbathing. At the National Parks Foundation building you can turn right on a better road to Rincon, climbing to the top of the hill for a steep descent and a good view of Rincon and the Windward coast. Alternatively, continue along to the Bonaire Petroleum Company where the road turns inland to Goto Meer Bay, the best place to see flamingoes, on another road to Rincon, Bonaire's oldest village where the slaves' families lived. Past Rincon is a side road to the Boca Onima caves with their Arawak Indian inscriptions. Indian inscriptions in several caves around the island can still be seen, but they have not been decyphered.

The road leading N from Rincon takes you to Washington/Slagbaai National Park, which occupies the N portion of the island, about 6,075 hectares, and contains more than 130 species of birds. The park is open to the public daily (entrance fee NAf 5, US$3, children up to 15 NAf 0.75) from 0800 to 1700 (no entry after 1500). There is a small museum of local historical items opposite the office and a room with geological explanations, bird pictures and a shell collection behind the office. Toilet at the entrance. Bring food and water. No hunting, fishing, 2-wheeled transport or camping is permitted. You can choose from a 34-km or a 24-km tour, the roads being marked by yellow or green arrows. You will get a route map when you pay to get in; a more detailed and attractively illustrated guidebook is available in English for NAf 10. The road is dirt, rough in parts, and the long route can be very hot and tiring unless you make several stops to swim and cool off. It is possible to drive round in an ordinary car but 4-wheel drive is preferable. Allow plenty of time as once you have chosen your route you have to stick to it. Even the short route takes a minimum of 2 hrs. Check your spare tyre before you start. Do not expect much variation in vegetation, the overall impression is of miles of scrub and cactus, broken only by rocks or salinjas. You can drive to Goto Meer on the longer route but you can get a better view from the observation point outside

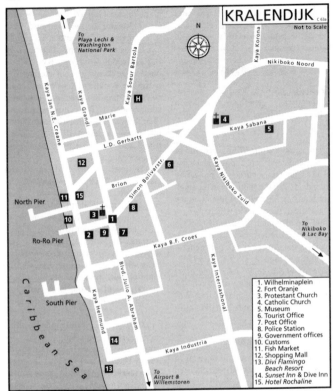

KRALENDIJK c 63a
Not to Scale

1. Wilhelminaplein
2. Fort Oranje
3. Protestant Church
4. Catholic Church
5. Museum
6. Tourist Office
7. Post Office
8. Police Station
9. Government offices
10. Customs
11. Fish Market
12. Shopping Mall
13. *Divi Flamingo Beach Resort*
14. *Sunset Inn* & *Dive Inn*
15. *Hotel Rochaline*

the Park. The return to Kralendijk is inland through the villages of Noord Salinja and Antriol. It is not well marked but you are unlikely to get lost for long.

The tour S passes the airport and Trans World Radio's towering 213-metre antenna which transmits 3 million watts, making it the hemisphere's most powerful radio station. Its shortwave broadcasts can be picked up in almost any part of the world. The coastal area S of Kralendijk is being heavily developed for tourism with construction of time share apartments, villas and hotels. The salt pier dominates the view along the coastal road and the salt pans are a stunning pink/purple colour. Further on are the snow-white salt piles and the three obelisks: blue, white, and orange, dating from 1838, with the tiny huts that sheltered the slaves who worked the saltpans. The roofs start at waist level and it is startling to think of men sharing one of these structures. Remember the flamingoes are easily frightened, so move quietly if near them.

At the S tip of the island is Willemstoren, Bonaire's lighthouse, which dates from 1837. Pass Sorobon Beach and the mangrove swamps to Boca Cai at landlocked Lac Bay, with its clear water excellent for underwater exploration. The extensive seagrass beds and surrounding mangroves are an important nursery for marine creatures; the Government plans to turn Lac into a protected area. What seem to be snow-capped hills from a distance are great piles of empty conch shells left by the local fishermen at Boca Cai. Near the Sorobon Resort is the Marcultura fish farming project (conch, lobster, shrimp etc), which you can tour by prior appointment; guided tours at 1000 and 1330, adults US$2, children under 12 US$1, T 8595 in advance. Take the road back to Kralendijk through the village of Nikiboko.

INFORMATION FOR VISITORS

● **Documents**
See below under Curaçao Information for Visitors.

● **How To Get There**
If you fly with ALM you are entitled to a free return flight to Curaçao as part of your ticket. KLM flies from Amsterdam twice a week direct. If you are a diver and it is specified on your airline ticket, KLM will allow you an extra 10kg baggage allowance for diving equipment (regular allowance 20kg tourist class, 30kg business class) without incurring overweight charges. ALM flies from Aruba, Curaçao, Atlanta, Georgia and Miami and there are flights from Aruba and New York with Air Aruba and from Caracas with Servivensa, KLM and ALM. ALM also flies weekly from Valencia, Venezuela. There is a departure tax of US$5.75 (NAf 10) on local flights and US$10 (NAf 18) on international flights.

● **Airlines**
ALM/KLM, T 8300 ext 220/1, after business hours, T 8500. Air Aruba, reservations, T 8300 ext 222, confirmations, T 7880, 7890. Avensa, T 8361.

● **Local Transport**
The best way of getting about is to hire a car. There are no public buses. Hitching is fairly easy. Bicycles are available to rent from most hotels' front desks. The roads in the S are flat and in good condition but there is no shade and you would need lots of water and sun screen. In the N it is more hilly and the roads are not so good. Either way cycling is hot, hard work.

● **Taxis**
There are taxis at the airport but they are difficult to find around the island. Taxis do not "cruise" so you must telephone for one, T 8100. Drivers carry list of officially approved rates, including touring and waiting time. The short trip from the airport to the *Divi Flamingo Beach Resort* is US$4; airport to *Sunset Beach Hotel*, US$8; fares increase by 25% 2000-midnight and by 50% from midnight- 0600. Taxis have TX on their licence plates.

● **Self-Drive Cars**
A B Car Rental at the airport, PO Box 339, T 8980 and in town, T 8667, also at *Divi Flamingo Beach Hotel*, T 8285 ext 32, check cars carefully, brake failure reported, poor service. Dollar Rent A Car at Kaya Grandi No 86, Kralendijk, T 8888 and at airport T 5588, F 7788, new cars in excellent condition. Budget at Kaya L D Gerharts No 22, Kralendijk, T 8300 ext 225, also at *Divi Flamingo Beach Hotel*, T 8300 ext 234, at Shopping Gallery, Kaya Grandi, T 8460, Airport, T 8315, *Sunset Beach Hotel, Harbour Village Beach Resort*, and *Captain Don's Habitat*, F 8865/8118. Sun-ray Car Rental, T 5600 ext 34. Trupial Car Rental, Kaya Grandi No 96, T 8487. Camel Rent A Car, Kaya Betico Croes 28, T 5120, airport, T 5124, low rates for Suzuki cars, jeeps and vans. Avis, J A Abraham Blvd, Kralendijk, T 8033, F 5791. Daily rates, unlimited mileage start at US$30 for a minibus (dive car), US$33 for a Toyota Starlet, US$40 for a Suzuki jeep, not including tax and insurance. At the busiest times of the year, it is best to reserve a car in advance. 4-wheel drive vehicles are not easy to find, there are not many on the island, and it is best to order one in advance. Some companies prohibit the use of ordinar} cars on unmade roads and in Washington/Slagbaai Park.

Small motorcycles can be rented from US$12 a day, contact Bonaire Motorcycle Rentals, Gouverneur Debrotweg 28, T 8488, Caribbean Touring Scooters on Kralendijk waterfront between *Raffles* and old fort, T 6877, US$15/half day, US$25/day, US$150/week, or Happy Chappy Rentals at *Dive Inn*, Kaya C E B Hellmund 27, T 8761. Prices are high compared with car rental and there are several inconveniences: the tanks are small and filling stations are few and far between, and you are not allowed into Washington/Slagbaai National Park.

The speed limit in built-up areas is 33 kph,

outside towns it is 60 kph unless otherwise marked. Many of the roads in Kralendijk and the N of the island are one way.

There are filling stations at Kralendijk, Antriol and Rincon, open Mon-Sat 0700-2100. The Kralendijk station is also open Sun 0900-1530.

● **Where To Stay**

High season rates (December 16 to 2 weeks after Easter) are roughly double low-season rates in the more expensive hotels; the cheaper ones tend to charge the same all year round. Dive packages are available at most resorts. A 5% or US$4.50 per person per night government tax and 10-15% service charge must be added. All the hotels with on site dive shops, and some others besides, offer dive packages which give better value than the summer-winter 1994 rack rates listed here.

On the leeward coast, S of Kralendijk are *Sunset Inn*, PO Box 115, T 8291/8448, F 8118/8865, only 7 rooms, US$80d, some rooms with kitchenettes, bicycle rental, across the road from the sea, use Sunset Beach Hotel facilities, within easy walking distance of town, next to Dive Inn dive shop; *Divi Flamingo Beach Resort & Casino*, T 8285, F 8238, 145 units, US$150-215d, standard rooms or more luxurious in the *Divi Club Flamingo*, is on a small artificial beach, snorkelling or diving just off the beach is excellent, Dive Bonaire and Photo Bonaire based here, tennis, pools, jacuzzi, dining is outdoors, some rooms in need of refurbishment, friendly staff but front office slow and inefficient, heavy tax and service charges, no food available after 2200 for late arrivals; next door is *Carib Inn*, T 8819, F 5295, PO Box 68, one-bedroomed apartments US$59-89d and 2 bedrooms US$109, a/c, cable TV, pool, dive shop.

Two cheaper hotels in Kralendijk are *Hotel Rochaline*, T 8286, 25 rooms, US$55d, functional, bar facing sea, restaurant, and *Leeward Inn*, T 5516, F 5517, 500m away at Kaya Grandi 60, 5 rooms, US$40s, US$50d, suite US$60d, US$75 triple inc tax, weekly rates cheaper, credit cards 5% extra, one room wheelchair accessible, *Harthouse Café* on site for all meals, clean, comfortable, very friendly, several recs. Also popular and often full is the lodge attached to *Blue Divers Diveshop* on Kaya Grandi, T 6860, F 6865, 4 rooms, US$35s, US$45d, common shower and kitchen, big garden, clean, cosy, rec for budget travellers/divers. The *Blue Iguana*, bed and breakfast, Kaya Prinses Marie 6, T/F 6855, 7 rooms,

US$75, walking distance of seafront and shops.

Going N out of Kralendijk are *Harbour Village Beach Resort and Marina* on Playa Lechi, PO Box 312, T 7500, F 7507, 72 rooms, US$165-235d, suites US$375-540, a/c, cable TV, restaurants, bars, fitness centre, tennis, pool, private beach, Great Adventures Bonaire dive shop, and non-motorized watersports, a growing, upmarket resort with more facilities coming on stream all the time, look out for promotional packages, also watch out for extra charges such as breakfast, or incoming phone calls. *Sunset Beach Hotel*, on Playa Lechi, T 8448, F 8593, 148 rooms US$75-100d, suites US$135, a/c, cable TV, tennis, watersports, dive shop, good breakfast, ideal for divers; *Sand Dollar Beach Club*, T 8738, F 8760, PO Box 175, 75 condominiums and 10 town houses US$125- 245, a/c, beach, tennis, pool, sailing, sport fishing, Sand Dollar Dive and Photo, restaurant and delicatessen; *Buddy Beach and Dive Resort*, PO Box 231, T 5080, F 8647, 22 apartments US$87-182, a/c, kitchen, pool, Buddy Watersports Center; *Coral Regency*, Kaya Gobernador N Debrot 91, PO Box 380, T 5580, F 5680, opened 1991, thirty-one 1-2 bedrooms, suites US$150-230 summer, US$190-315 winter, with kitchen, a/c, cable TV, pool, restaurant, Neal Watson Undersea Adventures Dive Center, more suites and entertainment complex planned; *Captain Don's Habitat*, PO Box 88, T 8290, F 8240, in USA T 800-327 6709, F 305-371 2337, rooms, US$145-185d, 11 cottages US$220 and 11 nice villas US$380-440 of differing standards with more under construction, well laid out seafront bar and restaurant, dive packages, family packages, special excursions for children during their family month every August, pool, dive shop with world's youngest snorkelling instructor; a little further along the coast is *Black Durgon Inn*, T 5736, F 8846, 1-bedroom apartments US$59, 2/3-bedroom villas US$130, with view of radio masts and oil storage tanks as well as the sea, a/c, cable TV, Bonaire Scuba Center dive shop; right by the radio masts is *Bonaire Caribbean Club*, T 7901, F 7900, from US$57, good view from *Hill Top Bar and Restaurant*, bicycles and snorkelling gear for rent, caves nearby, good walking.

On the windward coast are the *Sorobon Beach Resort*, at Lac Bay, T 8080, F 5363, clothes optional, 23 chalets US$90-150d, snack bar, 6% charge for credit cards, and *Lac*

Bay Resort, T 8198, F 5198, from US$80, in protected nature area, good seafood at *De Roode Pelikaan* restaurant.

The Tourist Office has a more extensive list, including apartments and villas, of properties approved by Bonhata.

● **Where To Eat**

International food at the major hotels varies on different nights of the week with barbeques or Indonesian nights, etc. Two good places to watch the fish are the **Green Parrot** at the *Sand Dollar Beach Club* and the **Chibi Chibi** at the *Divi Flamingo* (but do not feed them). Main courses in the upper- priced restaurants are about US$12- 20, but several restaurants do bar snacks if you want to economize. All food is imported, so even fruit and vegetables in the market are not cheap. Conch is rec, either fried or in a stew, as is goat stew. You may not want to try iguana soup, which may also be on the menu. If you want to eat lobster, check where the restaurant gets its supplies, some lobster fishermen are reported to be unauthorized and disapproved of by divers and conservationists.

In Kralendijk, *Rendez-Vous*, Kaya L D Gerharts 3, T 8454, is rec, seafood specials, vegetarian choice, good vegetables, small and friendly, closed Sun; *Bistro des Amis*, opposite, French style, good but pricey, the only member of the Chaine de Rôtisseurs on the island, T 4191, open Mon-Sat 1800-2300; cheaper is **Mona Lisa**, on Kaya Grandi, T 8718, closed Sun, bar and restaurant, interesting, imaginative food, Dutch chef enjoys discussing the menu, expect to pay NAf 25-35 for main course, friendly service, popular; *Beefeater*, Kaya Grandi 12, T 8773/8081, open 1830- 2300, closed Sun, steak and seafood, pricey, small; *Raffles*, at the harbourside, T 8617, open 1830- 2230, tiny, smokey dining room, nice terrace, reasonable prices at lunch, closed Mon, Indonesian and international; *Zeezicht*, on the waterfront, does breakfast, lunch and dinner, sandwiches and omelettes as well as fish and some Indonesian, food all right but service criticized; a cheap place to eat is *Ankertje*, but view nothing special, overlooks the small industrial harbour; *Restaurant Lisboa*, in *Hotel Rochaline*, outdoor dining on waterfront, T 8286, grills and seafood, lobster, also some more modestly priced dishes; in the new shopping mall upstairs is *Jardin Tropical Restaurant*, open 1800-2200, closed Mon, T 5718, 5716, downstairs there is a pizza bar, *Cozzoli's Pizza*, for fast food; S of town, just past *Carib Inn* is

Richard's waterfront dining, happy hour 1730-1830, dinner 1830- 2230, closed Mon, seafood specialities; *Den Laman Seafood Restaurant*, between the *Sunset Beach Hotel* and the *Sand Dollar Beach Club*, lots of fresh fish and lobster, 1800-2300, T 8955; *Toy's Grand Café*, on airport road opposite *Point Resort*, Indonesian, French or barbeque food, open from 1600, T 6666; *Twins Chicken Salad Bar*, in restored 19th century building on Kaya L D Gerharts, takeaway service available, lots of chicken dishes, lots of salads, open daily 1100-2400, T 4433.

There are a few good Chinese restaurants in town, the best of which is probably the *China Garden* in an old restored mansion on Kaya Grandi, which is open for lunch and dinner, T 8480, closed Tues. *Mentor's*, about 1½ miles from *Sunset Beach*, is rec, cheap, large portions of Chinese food. *Super Bon* vegetarian restaurant, open 0700-1800, closed Sat, good for snacks and juices, at Kaya Fraternan di Tilburg 2, T 8337. There are several snack bars in Kralendijk.

Water comes from a desalinization plant and is safe to drink. Take water with you on excursions. Do not, however, wash in or drink water from outside taps. This is *sushi* (dirty) water, treated sufficiently for watering plants but nothing more.

● **Camping**

Is possible on the beach, though fresh water is hard to obtain; there are no campsites.

● **Entertainment**

Nightlife is not well developed but there are a few places to go. Late night dancing takes place at the *E Wowo* and *Dynamite* discos and at the *Zeezicht Bar and Restaurant*. There is a casino at the *Divi Flamingo Beach Resort* (open 2000 except Sun). There is a modest cinema in Kralendijk.

● **Shops**

Open 0800-1200 and 1400-1800, Mon- Sat, or until 2100 on Fri, and for a few hours on Sun if cruise ships are in port. Bonaire is not a major shopping centre, though some shops do stock high quality low duty goods. The Harbourside Shopping Mall contains small boutiques and a 1- hr photo processing shop, Kodalux. Photo Bonaire at *Divi Flamingo* is good for underwater photographic equipment to buy or hire. Photo Tours on Kaya Grandi 68, T 8060, also offers full underwater facilities. Local arts and crafts are largely shell-work, coral jewellery and fabrics. The state owned Fundashon Arte Industri Bonairano and the privately owned Caribbean Arts and Crafts shop are both in Kralendijk for souvenirs. In Kralendijk there is a supermarket on Kaya L D Gerharts, just past the Exito bakery, well-stocked, good. Uncle Buddy's Sand Dollar Grocery, open daily, is located in a small plaza in from of the *Sand Dollar Beach Club* along with *Lovers Ice Cream Parlour*. Near the *Divi Flamingo* a turning opposite leads to Joke's grocery and mini-market. Health food or snacks from Je-Mar Health shop, Kaya Grandi 5.

● **Banks**
Open 0830- 1200, 1400- 1600, Mon- Fri. Algemene Bank Nederland NV, Kaya Grandi No 2, T 8429; Maduro & Curiel's Bank (Bonaire) NV, T 5520, with a branch in Rincon, T 6266; Bank van de Nederlandse Antillen, T 8507; Banco de Caribe NV, T 8295.

● **Public Holidays**
New Year's Day, Good Friday, Easter Monday, Queen's Birthday (30 April), Labour Day (1 May), Ascension Day, Bonaire Day (6 September), Christmas Day and Boxing Day.

● **Electric Current**
127 volts, 50 cycles.

● **Hospital**
The Hospital in Kralendijk has a decompression chamber, T 8900/8445. The emergency phone number for the hospital is T 14, and for Police, Fire and Ambulance T 11.

● **Post Office**
J A Abraham Blvd, Kralendijk, on the corner of Plaza Reina Wilhelmina opposite the ABN bank, open 0730- 1200, 1330- 1700 for stamps and postage, 1330- 1600 for money orders etc. Airmail to the USA and Canada is NAf1.75 for letters, NAf0.90 for postcards. There is also Express Mail and Federal Express Mail.

● **Telephones**
Direct dialling to the USA with a credit card is available at the airport and at Landsradio in town. The international code for Bonaire is 599-7, followed by a 4 digit local number.

● **Tour Agency**
Bonaire Sightseeing Tours, T 8778 or 8300 ext 212, F 8118, head office Kaya L D Gerharts 22 or at any Budget Rent A Car desk, 2- hour N or S tour US$13, half or full day Washington Park tour, day trip to Curaçao.

● **Religious Services**
Roman Catholic, San Bernardo Church, Kralendijk, T 8304, Our Lady of Coromoto, Antriol, T 4211, or San Ludovico Church, Rincon; United Protestant Church, T 8086; Evangelical Alliance Mission, T 6245; Jehova's Witnesses, Antriol; New Apostolic Church, Nikiboko, T 8483; Seventh Day Adventist Church, T 4254.

● **Tourist Office**
Kaya Simón Bolívar 12, Kralendijk, T 8322/8649, F 8408. Limited tourist information and leaflets, no maps. The Official Roadmap with Dive Sites is available in some shops and adequate for most purposes. It gives a good street plan of Kralendijk, dive sites and points of interest on Bonaire and Klein Bonaire, but tends to indicate as 'beach' areas which are rocky cliffs.

In the **USA**: Adams Unlimited, 444 Madison Avenue, Suite 2403, New York, NY 1002, T (212) 832-0779, F (212) 838-3407. In **Canada**: RMR Group Inc, Taurus House, 512 Duplex Avenue, Toronto, Ontario, M4R 2E3, T (416) 484-4864, F (416) 485-8256. In

Europe: Interreps BV, Visseringlaan 24, 2288 ER Rijswijk, The Netherlands, T (31) 070-395 4444, F (31) 070-3368333. In **Venezuela**: Organización Ebor CA, Torre Capriles, Piso 2, Oficina 202, Plaza Venezuela, PO Box 52031, Sabana Grande, Caracas, T 0602 782 3591, F 781 7445. In **Brazil**: Atomic Comunição E,

Marketing S/C Ltda, R Marconi, 31-6 andar, CEP 01047, São Paulo, T 5511-231 2583, F 258 1013.

Bonhata, the Bonaire Hotel and Tourist Association, also promotes the island, T 5134, F 8240, PO Box 358.

CURAÇAO

CURAÇAO, the largest of the five islands comprising the Netherlands Antilles, lies in the Caribbean Sea 60 km off the Venezuelan coast at a latitude of 12°N, outside the hurricane belt. It is 65 km long and 11 km at its widest, with an area of 448 square km. The landscape is barren, because of low rainfall (560 mm a year) which makes for sparse vegetation (consisting mostly of cactus thickets), and although it is not flat, the only significant hill is Mount Christoffel in the NW, which rises to a height of 375m. On a clear day you can see Aruba, Bonaire and Venezuela from the top. Deep bays indent the S coast, the largest of which, Schottegat, provides Willemstad with one of the finest harbours in the Caribbean. On the island cactus plants grow up to 6m high, and the characteristic wind-distorted divi divi trees reach 3m, with another 3m or so of branches jutting out away from the wind at right angles to the trunk.

The population of 160,000 (1993 est) is truly cosmopolitan, and 79 nationalities are represented, of whom 16% were born outside the Netherlands Antilles.

The Economy

Curaçao has a more diversified economy than the other islands, yet even so, it suffered severe recession in the 1980s and unemployment is around 21% of the labour force. The major industry is the oil refinery dating back to 1917, now one of the largest in the world, to which the island's fortunes and prosperity are tied. Imports of crude oil and petroleum products make up two thirds of total imports, while exports of the same are 95% of total exports. That prosperity was placed under threat when Shell pulled out of the refinery in 1985, but the operation was saved when the island government purchased the plant, and leased it to Venezuela for US$11mn a year. Its future is in the balance again because of the need for a US$270mn reconstruction, principally to reduce pollution. The Venezuelan company, PDVSA, would like the Dutch government and the Antilles to share the cost before renewing its lease in mid-1994. Bunkering has also become an important segment of the economy, and the terminal at Bullenbaai is one of the largest bunkering ports in the world. Besides oil, other exports include the famous Curaçao liqueur, made from the peel of the native orange. The island's extensive trade makes it a port of call for a great many shipping lines.

Coral reefs surrounding the island, constant sunshine, a mean temperature of 27°C (81°F), and refreshing trade winds lure visitors the year round, making tourism the second industry. Curaçao used to be a destination for tourists from Venezuela, but a devaluation of the bolívar in 1983 caused numbers to drop by 70% in just one year and several hotels had to be temporarily taken over by the Government to protect employment. A restructuring of the industry has led to a change of emphasis towards attracting US and European tourists, as well as South Americans, and numbers are now increasing, with further hotel expansion. Despite the recession in the North American market, tourism was not severely affected in 1991 with overall visitor numbers declining by only 1%, largely because of a 24% increase in the number of visitors from Europe. In 1992 numbers of visitors rose slightly but a healthy rate of growth was seen in 1993 when cruise ship passengers increased by 13% to 182,924 with 273 cruise ship calls, and stopover visitors rose by 3.5% to

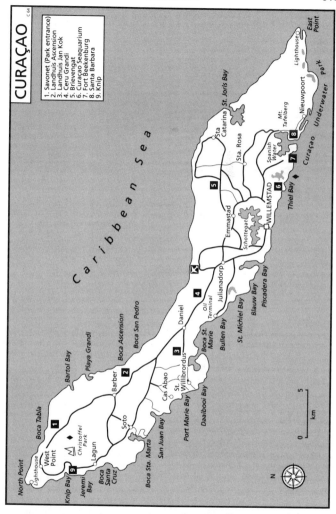

CURAÇAO C.64

1. Savonet (Park entrance)
2. Landhuis Ascension
3. Landhuis Jan Kok
4. Ceru Grandi
5. Brievengat
6. Curaçao Seaquarium
7. Fort Beekenburg
8. Santa Barbara
9. Knip

214,082. The fastest rate of growth was in the US market, which grew by 24%. Most rooms are in top grade hotels, with only a few in guest houses, but self-catering apartments, time share and condominiums are growing fast. In 1993 there were 1,815 hotel rooms, with another 3,000 planned to be built.

A third major foreign currency earner, the offshore financial sector, saw its operations severely curtailed in the 1980s. Once a centre for booking the issue of Eurobonds because of its favourable tax laws, the repeal of witholding tax in the USA in 1984 eliminated Curaçao's advantages and virtually wiped out the business. A second blow came with the cancellation by the USA, followed by similar action by the UK, of its double taxation treaty. These changes have led to greatly reduced income for the island's Government, although the offshore centre is actively seeking new areas of business, including captive insurance and mutual funds, in a highly competitive market. There are 61 banks, of which only 14 are licenced to carry out domestic business, the rest are offshore. After the crisis of the mid-1980s, assets in the offshore banks have risen steadily again.

Diving and Marine Life

The waters around Curaçao contain a wide variety of colourful fish and plant life and several wrecks (*Superior Producer*, near the water distillation plant, and a tugboat in Caracas Bay) which have foundered on the coral reef just offshore. The reef surrounds the island and consists generally of a gently sloping terrace to a depth of about 10m, then a drop off and a reef slope with an angle of about 45°. Underwater visibility averages 24m and water temperature varies between 24-27°C. Scuba diving is becoming increasingly popular in Curaçao and many of the large resort hotels have dive shops on site. They have been encouraged by the establishment in 1983 of the Curaçao Underwater Park managed by the Netherlands Antilles National Parks Foundation (Stinapa), which stretches from the *Princess Beach Hotel* to East Point. The Park extends out from the shore to a depth of 60m and covers 600 hectares of reef and 436 hectares of inner bays. There is an underwater trail for snorkellers (accessible by boat) between the Seaquarium and Jan Thiel Bay. Over 40 permanent mooring buoys for boats have been placed at dive sites along the coast as part of Stinapa's programme for sustained utilization of the reef. A few of the sites can be dived from the shore (West Point, Blauwbaa, Port Marie, Daaibooi, San Juan, Playa Kalki), but most of the coastal strip is private property and boat dives are necessary. The *Guide to the Curaçao Underwater Park*, by Jeffrey Sybesma & Tom van't Hof, published in 1989 by Stinapa and available in bookshops locally, describes the sites and discusses conservation. No harpoons or spear guns are allowed and make sure you do not damage or remove coral or any other sea creatures.

There are several dive operators, not all of which are mentioned here, and it is worth shopping around before booking a package deal. Most operators offer a single boat dive for around US$30-35 and snorkelling trips including equipment for about US$15-20, but check when booking whether 10% service is included in the quoted price. Underwater Curaçao (T 618131, F 657826) at the *Lions Dive Hotel* next to the Seaquarium is one of the larger operations with 2 dive boats for 24 divers each and 2 scheduled dives a day. It has a large air station with a capacity to fill 1,000 tanks daily, equipment rental, a retail shop and offers several courses. Princess Divers, a Peter Hughes diving operation, T 658991, F 655756, has 2 new dive boats and offers snorkelling, boat dives, shore dives, PADI courses at the *Princess Beach Resort and Casino*. *Curaçao Caribbean Hotel* has the Seascape Diving Shop on site, with 3 dive boats, a glass bottom boat, sailing boats and jet skis, T 625000 ext 6031, F 625846. Coral Cliff Diving at Santa Martha Bay (PO Box 3782, T 642822, F 642237) has a deliberately sunk airplane in shallow water just offshore for divers and also offers introductory or certification courses and package deals, also windsurfing US$10/hour, with sunfish, hobiecats and pedalboats available, prices not including 10% service. Sami Scuba Centre Dive School Wederfoort has been in operation since 1966, very friendly, reputable, mostly shore dives by van; a 6-day package including air, weights and no tank limit, costs US$120, a PADI open water course is US$257, contact Eric and Yolanda Wederfoort, T 684414, F 692062. Splash Diving, run by Chris Richards, T 616633, has very experienced staff and offers full certification for US$290. A smaller, more informal dive operation is at *Landhuis Daniel*. Dive Center Daniel (T 648600, F 648400) offers dive packages or individual dives from boat or car, photo equipment available, night diving on request, generally, however, you can do your own thing, take your tanks and a map and go where you want. For independent divers and snorkellers without a boat there is the *Complete Guide to Landside Diving and Snorkelling Locations in Curaçao*, by Jeffrey Sybesma and Suzanne Koelega, including a map with the sites and roads to them.

The Seaquarium, SE of Willemstad, just beyond the *Lions Dive Hotel*, has a collection of undersea creatures and plants found around the island, which live in channelled sea water to keep them as close as possible to their natural environment. Some tanks are incorrectly marked, the inhabitants have obviously been moved. The Seaquarium was built in 1984, the lagoons and marina being excavated so as to leave the original coastline untouched and do minimal damage to the reef offshore. Open 0900-2200, entrance US$6, children under 15 and adults over 63 half price, after 1800 US$3 and US$1.50 respectively, T 616666. Glass bottomed boat trips can also be arranged from the entrance, minimum 5 people, adults US$5.50, children and over 63 US$3. The water is frequently rough outside the marina, beware of seasickness. There is a restaurant, snack bar and shops selling shells and coral in marked contrast to the conservation efforts of the Underwater Park administration. The Seaquarium can be reached by bus marked Dominguito from the Post Office at 35 mins past the hour (except for 1335), which passes the *Avila Beach Hotel*.

Beaches and Watersports

There are several nice beaches on Curaçao. The NW coast is rugged and rough for swimming, but the W coast offers some sheltered bays and beaches with excellent swimming and snorkelling. Windsurfing, waterskiing, yachting and fishing are available at resorts. Many of the beaches are private and make a charge per car (amount depends on day of the week and popularity, US$3-6) but in return you usually get some changing facilities, toilets and refreshments. Public beaches are free but most have no facilities and some are rather dirty and smelly round the edges. Topless sunbathing is not recommended on public beaches but is tolerated on private beaches.

Heading S out of Willemstad is the small, artificial beach at the *Avila Beach Hotel*, where non-residents pay an entrance fee. The sand is very gritty at the water's edge and the sea is not calm enough to see much if you snorkel. You can get to the beach at Piscadera Bay near the *Curaçao Caribbean* or *Las Palmas* hotels by catching one of their shuttle buses from beside the Rif Fort in Otrabanda. SE of Willemstad, by the *Princess Beach Hotel*, the *Lions Dive Hotel* and the Seaquarium (see above), is a 450-metre, man-made beach and marina with all watersports available. Entrance to the beach is US$1.50. It can be crowded and noisy from music and motorized watersports. Showers and toilets. Past the Seaquarium is a residential area and private beach on Jan Thiel Bay, good swimming and snorkelling, entrance free for tourists, changing facilities, drinks and snacks, closed Tuesdays. Santa Barbara located at the mouth of Spanish Water Bay on the Mining Company property, is a favourite with locals and has changing rooms, toilets and snack bars, open 0800-

1800. Entrance free but US$3.33 per car. You can take a bus from the Post Office, get off at the Mining Company gate and hitchhike down to the beach, or take a taxi, it is too far to walk. Across the bay, which is one of the island's beauty spots, is the Curaçao Yacht Club, with a pleasant bar. There are four yacht clubs in Spanish Water.

Travelling NW from Willemstad heading towards Westpoint, there are lots of coves and beaches worth exploring. A left turn soon after leaving town will take you to Blauw Bay, good for snorkelling but closed in 1994 for construction of a Curasol development or to St Michiel's Bay, a fishing village and tanker clearing harbour (free). Daaibooibaai, S of St Willibrordus is a public beach and gets very crowded on a Sunday. Further up the coast, Port Marie (private, charge per car) is sandy but there is no shade. Cas Abao beach is pretty with good snorkelling and diving from shore in beautiful clear water, changing facilities, showers, shade huts, lounge chairs, US$3/car per day, US$5 at weekends and holidays, snacks and beverages. San Juan, a private beach with lots of coral is off to the left of the main Westpoint road down a poor track, entrance fee charged. Boca Sta Martha, where the *Coral Cliff Resort* is located, is quiet with nice sea, beach entrance US$4.50 for non-residents, no pets or food allowed on the beach, some shade provided. Lagun is a lovely secluded beach in a small cove with cliffs surrounding it and small fishing boats pulled up on the sand. It is safe for children and good for snorkelling, there are facilities and some shade from trees. Some buses pass only 50m from the beach. Jeremi, a private beach with a charge per car, is of the same design, slightly larger sandy beach with a steep drop to deep water and boats moored here, protected by the cliffs. Further up the coast, Knip is a more open, larger, sandy beach again with cliffs at either end. Many people rate this the best beach on the island. There are some facilities here and it is very popular at weekends when there is loud music and it gets crowded and noisy. A charge per car is being considered even though it is a public beach. Playa Abau is big, sandy, with beautiful clear water, surrounded by cliffs, some shade provided, toilets, well organized, popular at weekends and busy. Nearing the W tip, Playa Forti has dark sand and good swimming. There is a restaurant on the cliff top overlooking the sea which gets very busy at weekend lunchtimes. The beach at Westpoint below the church is stoney and littered, the only shade comes from the poisonous manchineel trees, but there is so much litter under them you would not be tempted to sit there. Fishing boats tie up at the pier but bathers prefer to go to Playa Forti. Beyond Westpoint is Kalki beach which is good for snorkelling and diving as well as bathing. Westpoint is the end of the road, about 45 mins by car or one hour by bus from Otrabanda, US$0.85.

Many charter boats and diving operators go to Klein Curaçao, a small, uninhabited island off East Point which has sandy beaches and is good for snorkelling and scuba diving, a nice day trip with lunch provided. The most popular and respected charter boats are *Mermaid* and *Something Special*, both operated by Bart Schoonen, T 601530, F 616569, he also does sunset trips, deep sea fishing, private parties etc, his sunset trips from Spanish Waters past *Princess Beach* and *Avila* hotels into St Anna Harbour are particularly recommended, US$25 with music, wine, beer, soft drinks and snacks, very good and fun. There are also day trips from Willemstad up the coast with barbeque lunches at, for example, Port Marie, for about US$45, and weekend sailing trips to Bonaire, accommodation on board, for about US$200. One such sailing ship is the 120-foot *Insulinde*, T 601340.

The Curaçao International Sailing

Regatta is held in March with competitions in three categories, short distance (windsurfers, hobie cats, sunfish etc), long distance (yachts race 112 km to Klein Curaçao and back) and open boat (trimarans, catamarans etc race 32 km to Spanish Water and back), all starting from the *Princess Beach Hotel*. For details, contact Timo Hilhorst at Uranusstraat 20, Curaçao, T 613433. The Yacht Club is at Brakkeput Ariba, z/n, T 673038 or contact Mr B van Eerten, T 675275. Sail Curaçao has sailing courses, rentals and boat trips, also surfing lessons, T 676003. They also own *Vira Cocha* at the Seaquarium, which does snorkelling, picnic and sunset trips (US$20-25).

Other Sports

Rancho Alegre, T 81181, does horse riding for US$15/hour, including transport. Ashari's Ranch offers horses for hire by the hour inland, or 1½ hrs including a swim at the beach, open 1000-1900, Groot Piscadera Kaya A-23, T 686254, beginners as well as experienced riders, playground for children. There is bowling on the island, Curaçao Bowling Club, Chuchubiweg 10, T 379275. The Curaçao Golf and Squash Club at Wilhelminalaan, Emmastad, has a 10-hole sand golf course open 0800-1230, green fee US$15 for 18-hole round, and 2 squash courts, US$7, open 0800-1800, T 373590. Santa Catharina Sport and Country Club, T 677028/677030, F 677026, has 6 hard tennis courts, a swimming pool, bar and restaurant. The large hotels have tennis courts: the *Curaçao Caribbean, Holiday Beach, Sonesta* and the *Princess Beach* have a pro, while *Las Palmas* is open 24 hrs.

Carnival

Curaçao, Aruba and Bonaire all hold the traditional pre-Lent carnival. Curaçao's main parade is on the Sunday at 1000 and takes three hrs to pass, starting at Otrabanda. The following Monday and Tuesday see most shops closed. On the Monday at 1500 there is a children's parade and there is a Farewell Grand Parade on the Tuesday evening when the Rey Momo is burned.

WILLEMSTAD

Willemstad, capital of the Netherlands Antilles and of the island of Curaçao (population about 140,000), is full of charm and colour. The architecture is a joyous tropical adaptation of 17th-century Dutch, painted in storybook colours. Pastel shades of all colours are used for homes, shops and government buildings alike. Fanciful gables, arcades, and bulging columns evoke the spirit of the Dutch colonial burghers.

The earliest buildings in Willemstad were exact copies of Dutch buildings of the mid-17th century, high-rise and close together to save money and space. Not until the first quarter of the 18th century did the Dutch adapt their northern ways to the tropical climate and begin building galleries on to the façades of their houses, to give shade and more living space. The chromatic explosion is attributed to a Governor-General of the islands, the eccentric Vice-Admiral Albert Kikkert ("Froggie" to his friends), who blamed his headaches on the glare of white houses and decreed in 1817 that pastel colours be used. Almost every point of interest in the city is in or within walking distance of the shopping centre in Punda, which covers about five blocks. Some of the streets here are only 5m wide, but attract many tourists with their myriad shops offering international goods at near duty-free prices. The numerous jewellery shops in Willemstad have some of the finest stones to be found anywhere.

The Floating Market, a picturesque string of visiting Venezuelan, Colombian and other island schooners, lines the small canal leading to the Waaigat, a small yacht basin. Fresh fish, tropical fruit, vegetables and a limited selection

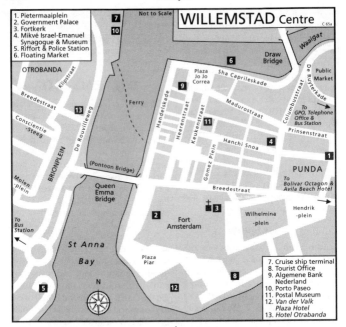

1. Pietermaaiplein
2. Government Palace
3. Fortkerk
4. Mikvé Israel-Emanuel
   Synagogue & Museum
5. Riffort & Police Station
6. Floating Market

7. Cruise ship terminal
8. Tourist Office
9. Algemene Bank
   Nederland
10. Porto Paseo
11. Postal Museum
12. Van der Valk
    Plaza Hotel
13. Hotel Otrabanda

WILLEMSTAD Centre

of handicrafts are sold with much haggling. Visit early in the morning.

In the circular, concrete, public market building nearby there are straw hats and bags, spices, butcheries, fruit and vegetables for sale, while in the old market building behind, local food is cooked over charcoal and sold to office workers at lunchtime.

Nearby on Hanchi Snoa, is one of the most important historical sites in the Caribbean, the Mikvé Israel-Emanuel synagogue, which dates back to 1732, making it the oldest in the Western Hemisphere. In the 1860s, several families broke away from the Mikvé Israel congregation to found a Sephardi Reform congregation which was housed in the Temple Emanuel (1867-1964) on the Wilhelminaplein. In 1964, however, they reunited to form the Mikvé Israel-Emanuel congregation, which is affiliated with both the Reconstructionist Foundation and the World Union for Progressive Judaism. Services are held Friday 1830 and Saturday 1000. Normally open 0900-1145 and 1430-1700, free. The big brass chandeliers are believed to be 300 years older than their synogogue, originating in Spain and Portugal, their candles are lit for Yom Kippur and special occasions. The names of the four mothers, Sara, Rebecca, Leah and Rachel are carved on the four pillars and there are furnishings of richly carved mahogany with silver ornamentation, blue stained glass windows and stark white walls. The traditional sand on the floor is sprinkled there daily, some say, to symbolize the wandering of the Israelites in the Egyptian desert during the Exodus. Others say it was meant to muffle the sound of the feet of those who had to worship secretly during the Inquisition period.

In the courtyard is the Jewish Mu-

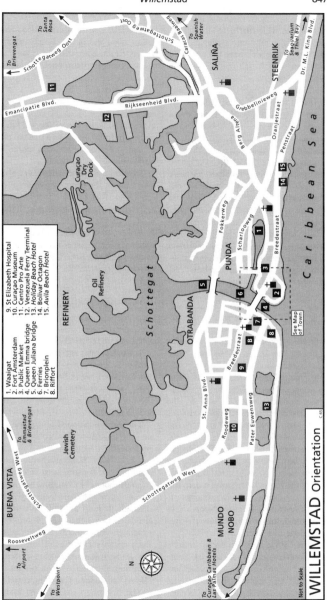

WILLEMSTAD Orientation

1. Waaigat
2. Fort Amsterdam
3. Public Market
4. Queen Emma bridge
5. Queen Juliana bridge
6. Ferries
7. Brionplein
8. Riffort
9. St Elizabeth Hospital
10. Curaçao Museum
11. Centro Pro Arte
12. Venezuela Ferry Terminal
13. Holiday Beach Hotel
14. Bolivar Octagon
15. Avila Beach Hotel

seum, occupying two restored 18th century houses, which harbours an excellent permanent exhibition of religious objects, most of which have been donated by local Jewish families. There are scrolls, silver, books, bibles, furniture, clothing and household items, many 18th century pieces and family bequeathments. Two circumcision chairs are still in use. Outside are some tombstones and a ritual bath excavated during restoration work. The Museum is open Monday-Friday 0900-1145, 1430-1700, closed Jewish and public holidays, entrance US$2, T 611633. A small shop sells souvenirs, the Synagogue Guide Book and *Our Snoa*, papiamento for Synagogue, produced for the 250th anniversary in 1982. *Sephardim: The Spirit That Has Withstood The Times*, by Piet Huisman (Huisman Editions, The Netherlands, 1986) is an interesting illustrated account of the Sephardic communities of the Caribbean and the Americas, setting them in their historical context. Available in the synagogue shop and bookshops in town. Unfortunately, for those who want deeper research of the Jewish families, the *History of the Jews of the Netherlands Antilles*, by Isaac S and Suzanne A Emmanuel, two volumes, is no longer in print. W of the city, on the Schottegatweg Nord, is one of the two Jewish cemeteries, Bet Chayim (or Beth Haim), consecrated in 1659 and still in use. There are more than 1,700 tombstones from the 17th and 18th centuries, with bas-relief sculpture and inscriptions, many still legible. It is a little out of the way but well worth a visit. It is also a fine example of what atmospheric pollution can do, as the tombstones have suffered from the fumes from the surrounding oil refinery.

The 18th century Protestant church, the **Fortkerk**, located at the back of the square behind **Fort Amsterdam**, the Governor's palace, still has a British cannonball embedded in its walls. It has recently been renovated, T 611139, open Monday-Friday 0800-1200, 1400-1700. Admission US$2/NAf3, children US$1, you get a guided tour of the church and the associated museum. It is not as large as the synagogue museum, but well laid out, with some interesting items, eg original church silver and reproductions of old maps and paintings of Curaçao. Note the clock in the ceiling of the church and make sure you are shown the still-functioning rain water cistern inside the church. It was once the main source of fresh water for the garrison.

Two forts, **Rif Fort** and **Water Fort** were built at the beginning of the 19th century to protect the harbour entrance and replace two older batteries. All that is left of Rif Fort is a guard house dating from about 1840 but you can walk on the walls and eat at the restaurants in the vaults. The Water Fort Arches have been converted to house shops, bars and restaurants and the Tourist Information Office is here.

The Philatelic Museum is on the corner of Keukenstraat and Kuiperstraat in a recently restored building which is the oldest in Punda (1693). There is a comprehensive permanent display of Dutch Caribbean stamps, plus temporary exhibitions. Open Monday-Friday, 0900-1800, Saturdays 0900-1500, admission US$2 or NAf3 for adults, US$1 for children, T 658010.

The Octagon, Simón Bolívar's sisters' house where Simón Bolívar stayed during his exile in Curaçao in 1812, is near the *Avila Beach Hotel* reached down a small road off Penstraat just before you get to the hotel. The building is in need of some repair work and looks neglected although there is an attendant (make sure his dogs are chained). There is one octagonal room downstairs, with some manuscripts, pictures and books, and a similar one upstairs, with a bed and some furniture; not much to see unless you are a Bolívar aficionado. Closed lunchtimes.

The swinging Queen Emma bridge spans St Anna Bay, linking the two parts of the city, Punda and Otrabanda (the latter means "the other side" in Papiamento, and people tend to refer to 'Punda' and 'Otrabanda' rather than 'Willemstad'). Built on sixteen great pontoons, it is swung aside some thirty times a day to let ships pass in and out of the harbour. The present bridge, the third on the site, was built in 1939. While the bridge is open, pedestrians are shuttled free by small ferry boats. The bridge is closed to vehicular traffic.

The new Queen Juliana fixed bridge vaults about 50m over the bay and connects Punda and Otrabanda by a 4-lane highway. Taxis will often offer to stop at the bridge so you can get a panoramic view and photo of Willemstad on one side and the oil refinery on the other. Although you can reach it on foot it is not recommended; the wind and the way it shakes will explain why.

Parts of Otrabanda are gradually being restored and there are many old houses here, both small, tucked away down alleys, and large mansions or town houses. The Belvedere, an Otrabanda landmark, was restored in 1992-93. Breedestraat is the main shopping street, the Basilica Santa Ana, founded in 1752 and made a Basilica in 1975 by Pope Paul VI, is just off here. The houses fronting on to the Pater Eeuwensweg, the highway heading W along the coast, once overlooked the Rifwater lagoon, now reclaimed land. Along St Anna Bay, past the ferry landing, is Porto Paseo, a restored area with bars and restaurants, popular on Friday evenings when there is music and dancing, or you can just sit and admire the view. The old hospital has been restored and is now the *Hotel and Casino Porto Paseo*.

On the outskirts of Otrabanda, on van Leeuwenhoekstraat, is the Curaçao Museum, founded in 1946 (housed in an old quarantine station built in 1853) with a small collection of artefacts of the Caiquetio Indian culture, as well as 19th and 20th century paintings, antique lo-cally-made furniture, and other items from the colonial era. Labels are inadequate and the hand-out leaflets only partly make up for this. In the basement there is a children's museum of science, but it is limited and rather outdated, almost a museum piece in itself. On the roof is a 47-bell carillon, named The Four Royal Children after the four daughters of Queen Juliana of the Netherlands, which was brought from Holland and installed in 1951. Lots of explanatory leaflets are given out at the museum, with a suggested route map. The museum is open daily, except Monday, admission US$2, US$1 for children under 14 (open 0900-1200 and 1400-1700, Sunday 1000-1600, T 623873).

Another area within walking distance of Punda and worth exploring, is Scharloo, across the Wilhelmina bridge from the floating market. A former Jewish merchant housing area, now under renovation, there are many substantial properties with all the typical architectural attributes; note the green house with white trimmings known as the Wedding Cake House. Under a 5-10 year plan to restore the buildings, companies or government departments take them over for use as offices in many cases. Reading matter of architectural enthusiasts includes the expensive but magnificently illustrated *Scharloo - a nineteenth century quarter of Willemstad, Curaçao: historical architecture and its background*, by Pauline Pruneti-Winkel (Edizioni Poligrafico Fiorentino, Florence 1987), and a more general collection of essays with illustrations, *Building up the Future from the Past: Studies on the Architecture and Historic Monuments of the Dutch Caribbean*, edited by Henry E Coomans and others (De Walburg Pers, Zutphen, the Netherlands, 1990).

Excursions

The restored country estate houses, or *landhuizen*, emerge here and there in the parched countryside. Not all of them are open to the public but it is worth visiting some of those that are. Set in 503 hectares in the E part of the island is **Brievengat**. Its exact date of construction is unknown, but it is believed to date from the early 18th century. It was used in the 19th century to produce cattle, cochineal and aloe, but a hurricane in 1877 devastated the plantation and the house which were gradually abandoned. Shell later took over the property to extract water from the subsoil, but in 1954 when it was in a state of ruin Shell donated it to the Government who restored it to its former grandeur. The windows and the roof are typical of the local style but unusual are the arches extending the length of the house and the two towers at either side, which were once used to incarcerate slaves. Open daily 0930-1230, 1500-1800, bar and snacks, live music on Wednesday and Friday and often on Sundays, check beforehand, open house last Sunday of the month 1000-1500 with folklore show, T 378344. Take the bus marked Punda-Hato from Punda at 15 mins past the hour and get off at the Sentro Deportivo Korsou, US$0.40.

Chobolobo, at Salinja, came into the Senior family in 1948 and Senior & Co make the Curaçao liqueur here, using a copper still dating from 1896 and the original Valencia orange known locally as Laraha. Open Monday-Friday 0800-1200, 1300-1700, visitors may taste the liqueur. The clear, orange, amber, red, green and blue are for cocktails and all taste the same; others are chocolate, coffee, rum raisin. Chobolobo is worth visiting, but if you resist the temptation to buy Senior & Co's products you will find them cheaper in the duty free lounge at Hato Airport. Entrance free, T 378459. Near the Hato international airport are the **Hato Caves** which contain stalactites and stalagmites. Guided tours every hour, the last one at 1600, closed Mondays.

Jan Kok is the oldest landhouse on the island, dating from 1654 and overlooking the salt flats where flamingoes gather. It is open for private tours by reservation only Monday-Friday, T 648087, open on Sundays 1100-2000, when local food and Dutch pancakes are served. Take the bus marked Lagun and Knip from the Riffort, Otrabanda, at half past the even hour in the morning or half past the odd hour in the afternoon, US$0.70. **Santa Martha**, built in 1700 and restored in 1979, is used as a day care centre for the physically and mentally handicapped but is open Monday-Thursday, 0900-1200, 1300-1500, Fridays 0900-1200, first Sunday in the month 0900-1300, T 641559. **Ascension**, built in 1672 and restored in 1963, is used by Dutch marines stationed on the island and is only open to the public the first Sunday of the month 1000-1400, with local music, handicrafts and snacks, T 641950. Take bus marked Westpunt from Otrabanda (see below). **Knip**, near the beach of the same name, is a restored 17th century landhouse where local handicrafts are on sale. On the same bus route as Jan Kok.

The **Christoffel Park** covers an area of 1,860 hectares in the W of the island, including Mount Christoffel at 375m, which was formerly 3 plantations. These plantations, Savonet, Zorgvlied and Zevenbergen, are the basis for a system of well-marked trails, blue (9km), green (7.5km or 12km) and yellow (11km), and there is a red walking trail up Mount Christoffel which takes about 3 hrs there and back. You can see a wide range of fauna and flora, including orchids, the indigenous _wayacá_ (_lignum vitae_) plant, acacias, aloe, many cacti, calabash and the tiny Curaçao deer. The ruins of the Zorgvlied landhouse can be seen off the green route. The Savonet route takes you to the coast and along to Amerindian rock drawings, painted between 500 and 2,000 years ago in terracotta, black and white. In this area there are also two caves (take a strong torch), one of which is about 125m long and you have to crawl in before you can stand up (lots of bats and lots of guano on the ground) and walk to the 'white chamber'(stalactites and stalagmites) and the 'cathedral'. The 17th century Savonet Plantation House is at the entrance to the Park on the Westpoint road, but it is not open to the public. However, several outbuildings are used; there is a small museum with archaeological exhibits, open Monday-Saturday 0800-1700, Sun 0600-1500, T 640363. The Park is also open from 0800 Monday-Saturday, US$5 pp, admission to the mountain side closes at 1400 and to the ocean side at 1500, although you can stay in until later. On Sundays the Park opens at 0600 and closes at 1500, no admittance after 1300 and 1400 for inland or sea routes. Guided tours are available, special walks at dawn or dusk are organized at random, check in the newspapers, evening walking tours to see the Curaçao deer, maximum 8 people, reservations essential, T 640363. Stinapa publishes an excellent *Excursion Guide to the Christoffel Park, Curaçao*, by Peer Reijns, 1984, which is available at the Park administration. A basic map of the trails is also provided. The bus Otrabanda-Westpunt passes the entrance to the Park.

Behind Spanish Water Bay on the S coast rises Mount Tafelberg, where phosphate mining used to take place. It can be visited on Tuesday and Friday when a special bus leaves the Mining Company entrance at 1400.

INFORMATION FOR VISITORS

● **Documents**

All visitors must have an onward ticket to a destination outside the Netherlands Antilles. US citizens do not need a passport; a birth certificate, alien registration card or naturalization papers are sufficient. Canadians must have a valid passport or birth certificate. Transit visitors and cruise ship visitors must have proof of identity for a 24-hour, or less, stay on the island. Immigration procedures at the airport are quick and easy.

● **How To Get There**

Curaçao is very well served by airlines from Europe, the USA, Central and South America and the Caribbean, but the companies and their routes change frequently so check the latest flight guide. KLM flies direct from Amsterdam several times a week and has connecting flights to Guayaquil, Quito, Lima, Guatemala City, Managua, Panama City and San José. TAP flies from Lisbon. There are flights from New York and Baltimore with Air Aruba, and from Miami with Air Aruba, American Airlines, and ALM. ALM also flies from Atlanta, Georgia. In high season there are more flights from the USA, eg American Airlines flies from Baltimore and San Juan, Puerto Rico and ALM flies from New York (JFK). Avianca flies from Barranquilla and Bogotá; ALM, Servivensa, Air Aruba and Aeropostal fly from Caracas; ALM also flies from Barquisimeto and Valencia and Servivensa from Las Piedras and Maracaibo, Venezuela. ALM and Surinam Airways fly from Paramaribo. ALM flies from Georgetown, Guyana. Caribbean island destinations include Aruba (Air Aruba, ALM), Bonaire (ALM), Havana (ALM), Kingston (ALM), Port au Prince (ALM) (suspended 1994), Port of Spain (ALM), Sint Maarten (ALM) and Santo Domingo in the Dominican Republic (ALM and Aeropostal). Getting to the Eastern Caribbean can be difficult without overnighting in Trinidad or long waits in Puerto Rico.

ALM (T 613033) has an office in Gomezplein in Punda where the staff are helpful and efficient. You can pay your departure tax here and avoid the queues at Hato Airport. There is also an ALM office in the International Trade Centre. ALM often has flights at rather unsociable hours and is jokingly known in Dutch as 'Altijd Laat Maatschappij', the Always Late Company. KLM (T 686747/636646) and BWIA (T 687835/613033) offices are also at Gomezplein; Avianca, T 680122; Aeropostal, Pietermaaiplein, T 616776; Servivensa, T 680500; Air Portugal, T 686241; Air Aruba, T 683777/683659, American Airlines, T 695707. Pelican Air, T 628155, does helicopter tours of the island.

There is an airport tax of US$6 on departure to the Netherlands Antilles or US$10 to Aruba or other destinations. This must be paid at a separate kiosk before you check in.

● Taxis

Taxis are easily identified by the signs on the roof and TX before the licence number. There are taxi stands at all hotels and at the airport, as well as in principal locations in Willemstad. It is not always possible to get a taxi to the airport early in the morning or late at night. Fares from the airport to *Las Palmas* or *Holiday Beach*, US$12, *Van der Valk Plaza* or *Avila Beach* US$15, *Lions Dive* US$18, *Coral Cliff* US$25, *Kadushi Cliffs* US$35. Airport displays taxi fares to main hotels. Taxi meters are to be installed. Fares for sightseeing trips should be established at beginning of trip, the usual price is US$20 for the first hour and US$5 for each subsequent 15 mins. Tipping is not strictly obligatory. The high price of taxis is a common complaint. There are collective taxis, called buses, and identified by an AC prefix on their licence plates. Taxis do not always go looking for business and it can be difficult to hail one. Best to telephone from a hotel lobby or restaurant/bar, one will arrive in a couple of minutes (Dispatch T 616711, complaints T 615577, main office T 690747/690752), or go to a taxi stand and just get into an empty car, the driver will then turn up. Drivers do not always know the area as well as they should, even restaurants can sometimes be tricky for them to find. The rear windows of many taxis do not work, which makes the car uncomfortable in the hot climate. Courtesy vans operated by the hotels can be more comfortable.

● Buses

Konvoois are big yellow buses which run to a schedule and serve outlying areas of Curaçao. There is a terminal at the Post Office in Punda and another at the Rif Fort in Otrabanda. To the airport get a bus marked Hato from Punda at 15 mins past the hour from 0615 to 2315, or from Otrabanda at 15 mins past the hour from 0615 to 2320, US$0.40. Buses to Westpunt leave from Otrabanda on the odd hour, last bus 2300, US$1, return on the even hour. Buses to Dominguito (the Seaquarium) and Caracas Bay run at 35 mins past the hour but minibuses also do this route. A bus marked Schottegat runs from Punda via the Octagon Bolívar Museum, the *Trupial Inn Hotel*, the Curaçao Golf and Squash Club, the Jewish cemetery and the Curaçao Museum to Otrabanda every 2 hrs from 0620-2320 at 20 mins past the hour in either direction. The Lagun and Knip bus route leaves Otrabanda at half past the even hour in the mornings and on the odd hour in the afternoons via the Curaçao Museum, the University, Landhuis Jan Kok, Santa Cruz beach, Jeremi beach, Lagun Beach and Bahia beach, returning from Knip on the alternate hour. The standard city bus fare is US$0.50; *autobuses* (ie colectivos) charge US$1. For more information T 684733.

● Self-Drive Cars

There are about 8 car rental agencies at the airport, all the offices are together so it is easy to pick up price lists for comparison. One or 2 companies usually have desks in each of the major hotels. Look in local tourist literature or newspapers for news of special deals on offer, there is lots of choice. There have been problems with unsafe cars, inadequate insurance and licensing. Those listed here are considered reputable. Companies include Budget, Love Car Rentals, Europcar/National, Avis, Caribe Rentals, U Save Car Rental, Dollar Rent a Car, Star Rent a Car, Visa Car Rental. Prices start at about US$35 daily, unlimited mileage, including insurance, deposits from US$250; jeeps, minimokes, buggies, scooters and bikes also available. At Landhuis Daniel you can rent Harley Davidson motor bikes, T 649000. Foreign and international driving licences are accepted. Traffic moves on the right.

● Where To Stay

There is a 7% government tax and 10% (sometimes 12-15%) service charge to be added to any quoted room rate and many hotels add an extra US$3 per day energy surcharge. In Willemstad, *Plaza Hotel and Casino* in the Van der Valk chain, on Punda seafront, very central, huge tower dominates the skyline by the fortress walls, T 612500, F 616543, US$100-140 per room all year, including service, tax, breakfast, bargain for a cheaper rate for several nights, popular with the Dutch, good food; *Otrabanda Hotel and Casino*, opened December 1990 and still rather sterile, on Breedestraat just by the bridge in Otrabanda, excellent location, good for business travellers, standard rooms small but comfortable US$105d, single rooms available, suites are larger rooms with sofas, coffee shop and restaurant with good view of Punda and floating bridge, excellent buffet breakfast in coffee shop, pleasant service, pool planned, T 627400, F 627299, or reservations through International Travel & Resorts, New York, T 800-223-9815, F 212-545-8467, or in Holland, Holland International, T 70-395 7957, F 70-395 7747; also very central is *Ho-*

tel and Casino Porto Paseo, de Rouvilleweg 47, US$120d room, US$200, 2-bedroom suite, inc breakfast, winter 1993/94, swimming pool, dive shop, in attractive restored old hospital, T 627878, F 627989; *Pelikaan Hotel*, T 623555, F 626063, in the heart of Otrabanda, newly rebuilt, small, comfortable, clean, 40 rooms, a/c, restaurant, US$48 all year; further W along the main road is the *Holiday Beach*, a concrete block on a man-made beach, but convenient and elegant inside, 10 mins walk to shops and restaurants, T 625400, F 624397, 200 rooms in need of decoration in 1994, US$140-155d plus 12% service, 7% tax, US$3 energy surcharge daily, a/c, phone, TV, casino and banks of gaming machines, mediocre food at high prices, pool, tennis, dive shop on site, US$125 for 5 dive package, conference rooms, reservations through ITR. 15 mins walk E of the centre is the family- owned *Avila Beach*, Penstraat 130, PO Box 791, T 614377, F 611493, built in 1811 as Governor's residence but most rooms in an old hospital wing, small and with no sea view, US$95-140d winter 1993/94, very popular, always full, cool reception area, service friendly but slow, no pool, lovely bar shaped like a ship's prow on the beach (rather gritty and painful on the feet at water's edge), great for evening cocktails, pleasant outdoor dining. A new extension has been built in an attractive colonial style, called *La Belle Alliance*, the other side of the pier (bar and restaurant, *Blues*) on another man-made beach, 40 hotel rooms, US$175d, and some apartments, US$230-395d, all rooms and suites with sea view, conference facilities and ballroom, tennis; *Trupial Inn*, Groot Davelaarweg 5, T 378200, F 371545, in residential area, 74 rooms, a/c, US$70, newly decorated, nice, pool, restaurant, tennis, open air bar, entertainment, shuttle bus to downtown, suites available.

The Tourist Board main office at Pietermaai 19 has a list of guesthouses and apartments (not all of which it recommends) including some cheap hotels such as *Stelaris* close to the *Otrabanda*, looking out over to the floating market, seedy, T 625337, from US$19 with fan, no bath, to US$37, a/c, with bath; *Estoril*, Breedestraat 181, Otrabanda, T 625244, US$29; in Scharloo, *Central*, Scharlooweg 2, T 613965, all rooms US$10; *Park*, on Frederikstraat 84, T 623112, US$35d inc tax, bath and fan, noise from road, fleas, not clean enough; *Bon Auberge*, Dutch owned, friendly, clean, conveniently located in Otrabanda close to

shops and transport, Hoogstraat 63- 65, T 627902/627540, F 627579, US$15s, US$25-50d, some rooms have a/c, others fans, only 2 rooms with private bath; *Motel La Creole*, Saliña 2, PO Box 878, T/F 613991, in Holland T 020- 910134, US$25, fan or a/c, large rooms sleep 4. A rec small hotel is *Buona Sera Inn*, T 618286/658565, Pietermaai 104, on the road to the Bolívar museum, 15 rooms, US$25s, US$40d, US$53 triple, US$70 quad, a/c, private bathroom, recently built seaview restaurant and bar, plans to create small beach, family-run, friendly, English, Dutch, Spanish, French and Papiamento spoken. Centrally located self- catering, *Pietersz Guesthouse & Apartments*, Roodeweg 1, in Otrabanda very near the hospital and easy walking distance from the Floating Bridge and Punda, T 625222 0800- 1900, T 82036 after 1900, clean, spacious rooms from US$48 with kitchenette, phone, a/c, TV, bathroom, 5 huge rooms also have sofabed and table for 4, coffee shop downstairs offers everything from pastechi to more substantial dishes, all cheap and filling; *Douglas Apartments*, Saliña 174, PO Box 3220, T 614549, F 614467, US$59s or d, a/c, cots available, towels and linen provided, kitchenettes, a/c, phone, fax facilities, on first floor of shopping gallery, bus stop outside; outside town, *Wayaca Apartments and Bungalows*, Gosieweg 153, T 375589, F 369797, US$37- 77, a/c, TV, phone, supermarket, launderette, tennis, min 1 week, car rental can be included; houses also available usually on weekly basis or longer.

East of Willemstad is the *Princess Beach Resort and Casino*, a Holiday Inn Crowne Plaza hotel, 600m from the Seaquarium on a narrow beach, US$95-225d, T 367888, F 614131, pools, restaurants, bars, shops, 341 rooms and suites make this the biggest resort on the island, popular but service poor, mediocre food at high prices, newly constructed conference centre, Princess Divers on site, dive packages available; next door is the *Lion's Dive*, attractive, not high rise, wooden balconies give it style, 72 rooms, TV, US$110-130d winter 1993/94, small pool, unlimited use of Seaquarium, dive shop on site, dive packages available, fitness centre, windsurfing, 3 restaurants, nice atmosphere, friendly staff, caters for hard-core diving fraternity, courtesy bus to town, T 618100, F 618200.

Heading W of Willemstad along the coast are *El Conde Hotel*, 15 rooms, a/c, US$48d all year, T 627611, F 627875; *Sonesta Beach Hotel and Casino*, 248 luxury rooms, very comfortable, from US$215d, suites US$300-770, 1993/94 winter rates, summer rates about 28% less, 12% service charge, 2 children under 12 sharing room free, this new, upmarket resort, built in Dutch colonial style is on a private beach and offers a freeform pool, whirlpools, tennis, watersports, casino, conference facilities and is next to the International Trade Centre, Piscadera Bay, PO Box 6003, T 368800, F 627502; 2 Golden Tulip resorts overlook Piscadera Bay: *Las Palmas*, rooms, US$125d, suites, US$145d, and villas, US$180d, winter 1993/94, free shuttle bus to town, telephone, a/c, TV, pool, tennis, diving and watersports, 400m walk to beach, restaurant, T 625200, F 625962, the hotel's future was uncertain in 1994, staff walked out when they were not paid; and *Curaçao Caribbean*, 200 rooms and suites in need of redecoration in 1994, upmarket facilities, executive floor, a/c, US$140-850d, casino, bar opening out on to terrace, good food, pleasant ambience, diving, watersports, tennis, energy surcharge, T 625000, F 625846; *Club Seru Coral*, a new resort in the E part of the island, in the middle of nowhere but great restaurant, nice pool, nice studios, apartments and villas, US$91-217, 3 miles from beach, 18 from airport, 9 miles from town, Koral Partier 10, T 678499, F 678256; 2 mins from the airport is *Holland*, 45 rooms, a/c, TV, phone, business services, restaurant, pool, car rental, US$79d inc tax, T 688044, F 688114; *Bulado Inn*, in Boca St Michiel fishing village, Red A'Weg, T/F 685960, family run, new, 17 rooms and 4 older apartments, all ocean view, restaurant, bar, pool, nicely landscaped, from US$65s or d, meal plan available; *Landhuis Cas Abao*, dates from 1751 rebuilt 1993, rooms vary but have good views, secluded beach, US$45-70 inc service, min stay 4 days, no credit cards, jeep rental available, beautiful area, T 649688, F 649460; in the centre of the island, at Weg naar Westpunt Z/N, is the 17th century *Landhuis Daniel*, a small, friendly hotel popular with Europeans, children welcome, family rooms, 5 rooms in the landhouse (best) US$50d with a/c, US$45d with fans, and 4 small cabin rooms, US$40d, by the pool, basic, being upgraded gradually, good food, diving trips arranged, good shore dive sites close by, car, jeep and motor bike rental, US$30/day, T/F 648400; *Coral Cliff*, a Golden Tulip resort on Santa Marta Bay, quiet beach, nice sea, some shade provided, entrance NAf8 for non-residents, sprawling, concrete block hotel, US$68-122d, PO Box 3782, T 641610, F 641781, good sea view from restaurant on hill, dive shop on premises, watersports, mini golf, horse riding, free airport pickup, shuttle service to town; *Bahia Inn*, near Lagun beach, small, basic, adequate, several beds in each room, US$42-51d, PO Box 3501, T 641000/84417, building work all along this coastal road; at Westpoint, *Jaanchie Christian's* is a popular restaurant with 4 rooms to let, US$40- 50d, a/c, bathroom, breakfast included, double beds, can fit extras in, usually full, phone for reservation, T 640126, 640354.

New hotel, villa or timeshare developments are springing up all over Curaçao. *Kadushi Cliff Resort*, at Westpoint is open although more building work is still being done, US$200-275, kitchenettes, pool, TV, scuba, T 640282; several huge resorts are planned around Knip beach, Lagun, Cas Abao, Piscadera, Parasasa, Cornelis Bay and Jan Thiel. Be prepared for construction work.

Camping at *Brakkeput*, adjoining Spanish Waters, Arowakenweg 41A, PO Box 3291, T 674428, school parties catered for, sports fields, showers and toilets, tents available, US$1.25 pp overnight with min charge US$18.75, cheaper for youth organizations. Camping is allowed on some beaches, but there are no facilities and you have to bring your own fresh water supplies.

● **Where To Eat**

10% service is added to the bill in restaurants but an extra 5% is appreciated. One of the most highly regarded restaurants in Willemstad is *The Wine Cellar* on Concordiastraat, T 612178/674909, owned by chef Nico Cornelisie, a master rotisseur, in small old house, only 8 tables, reservations rec, open for lunch Tues-Fri, dinner Tues-Sun; *Alouette*, in a restored house, Orionweg 12, T 618222, very popular, reservations rec, French-style food, low-calorie or vegetarian meals available, comparatively small menu but changed frequently, except for the goat cheese crêpe which is such a favourite it is a permanent fixture, excellent food and service, attractive decor, open 1200-1430, 1900-2200, later at weekends; *Larousse*, also in an old house on Penstraat 5, almost opposite the *Avila Beach*, T 655418, French menu with local and imported North Sea fish, quiet, open 1800-2400, closed Mon; *Fort Nassau* has a spectacular location with a panoramic view from the 200-year old fort, American-style menu using local ingredients, open Mon-Fri 1200-1400, Mon-Sun 1830-2300, reservations T 613086; *De Taveerne*, in an octagonal mansion, Landhuis Groot Davelaar, T 370669, beef and seafood, à la carte menu, antique furnishings, closed Sun; *Bistro Le Clochard*, in the Rif Fort walls overlooking the harbour, French and Swiss cuisine, T 625666/625667, open Mon-Fri 1200-1400, 1830 onwards, Sat evenings only, open Sun in December-March; *Down Town*, Da Costa Gomezplein 4, T 616722, nice place to eat; *Caribana*, De Rouvilleweg 9, Koral Agostini, near the ferry landing in Otrabanda, rec for seafood and local dishes, not cheap but good food, open 1200-1400, 1800-2300, T 623088; in the Waterfort Arches is *Seaview*, open air or indoors, bar and international restaurant, lunch 1200-1400, dinner 1800-2300 daily, T 616688; *Grill King*, also in the Waterfort Arches is friendly and has good international food, open 1200-1400, 1700-2300, later at weekends, T 616870. There are several restaurants in the Arches, nice variety, pleasant location, good for a meal or just drinks. Great fruit shakes at *Trax's*, a van at the Otrabanda side of the Queen Emma bridge. Some other moderately priced yet good restaurants include *Fort Waakzaamheid and Terrace Bistro Bon Bini*, T 623633, lovely sunset views from the terrace on top of the fort, which is on a hill above Otrabanda, closed Tues, open every other day from 1700, barbeque and salad bar from 1800, seafood, early bird special 1700-1900, 3 courses, US$14; *Green Mill*, Salinja Galleries, T 658821, lunches or dinners, happy hour Mon-Thur 1800-1900, Fri 1700-1830, menu with good variety; *Pinocchio Family Restaurant* at the Promenade Shopping Centre, T 376784/376 929; *Cactus Club* Tex Mex food, fun atmosphere, Van Staverenweg 6, T 371600, in the Mahaai area; *Hard Rock Society*, sandwiches, soups, salads, burgers or grills, rock music, outdoors under trees or indoors at the bar, open Mon-Thur 0930-0100, Fri and Sat 0930-0200, Sun 1530-0100, happy hour Thur-Fri 1730-1830, Sun 1700-1900, pool, darts and backgammon upstairs, Keuken Plein, Punda, T 656633.

For an Indonesian meal it is best to make up a party to get the maximum number of dishes but this is not essential. The *Indonesia*, Mercuriusstraat 13, wonderful Javanese food specializing in 16 or 25-dish rijstaffel, essential to book, often several days ahead, restaurant badly needed redecorating in 1994, T 612606/612999, open 1200-1400, 1800-2130 daily, dinner only on Sun; the *Garuda* at the *Curaçao Caribbean* is currently the best place for a rijstaffel, open air dining overlooking the sea, Indonesian owner uses old family recipes, nice atmosphere, good portions and prices, T 626519, open 1200-1400 daily except Sat, 1830-2200, closed Mon; *Surabaya* in the Waterfront Arches has good food but no hot plates to keep it warm, vegetarian menu too, T 617388, open Tues-Fri 1200-1400, Tues-Sun 1800-2300.

The best place to try local food in Willemstad is the old market building beyond the round concrete market tower by the floating market, here many cooks offer huge portions of good, filling local food cooked in huge pots on charcoal fires, at reasonable prices, choose what you want to eat and sit down at the closest bench or one of the nearby tables having first ordered, takeaway available, very busy at lunchtimes, the best dishes often run out, make sure you have the right money available; the best restaurant for local food is *The Golden Star*, Socratesstraat 2, T 54795/54865, informal, friendly, plastic table cloths and permanent Christmas decorations, tacky but fun, TV showing American sport, home cooking, very filling, goat stew washed down by a couple of Amstels rec, popular with locals and tourists, open daily 1100-0100; outside town, *Martha Koosje* on the left on the Westpoint road, Colombian and local specialities particularly seafood, outdoor dining, family run, open 1500-2300, the bar is open until 0200, T 648235; further along the same road, opp the entrance to the Christoffel Park, is *Oasis*, seafood and creole dishes but also offering chicken and ribs, open 1200-2400, weekends 1030-0300, dinner served until 2100, dancing afterwards, T 640085; *Playa Forti*, atop a cliff overlooking beach of same name, wonderful view, very popular lunchtime at weekends, Colombian and local dishes; further along the road in Westpoint is *Jaanchie's*, another weekend lunchtime favourite with local families although no sea view, huge, filling portions, see the bananaquits eating sugar, parties catered for, takeaway service, bus stops outside for return to Willemstad, T 640126; near the airport excellent local food at Chez Susenne, Blomonteweg 1, Santa Maria, cosy atmosphere, very popular, T 688545.

A good fish restaurant is *Pisces*, at the end of

Caracasbaaiweg, reservations rec, T 672181; *El Marinero*, moderately priced seafood dishes, lunch 1200-1500, dinner 1830-2330, Schottegatweg Noord 87B, T 379833; *Pirates Seafood Restaurant*, also reasonably priced and good food, open daily 1200-1500, 1830-2330, T 628500, located in *Caribbean Hotel*; *Villa Elizabeth Shellfish House*, M L King Blvd, opp *Princess Beach Hotel*, open 1800-2300, closed Tues, very good food, lovely atmosphere, European and South American cooking, T 657565; Italian food at *Baffo & Bretella*, in the Seaquarium, homemade pasta, seafood, open 1200-1400, 1900-2300, closed Tues, reservations required, T 618700; *La Pergola*, in the Waterfort Arches, also serves Italian food, fish, pizza, terrace or a/c dining, T 613482, open 1200-1400 Mon-Sat, 1830-2230 daily; Chinese food at *Ho Wah*, Saturnusstraat 93, T 615745; for drinks, snacks or cheap lunches, *Downtown Terrace*, also in Gomezplein, you can hear the chimes from the Spritzer and Fuhrmann bells; if you are touring the island, *Landhuis Daniel* is a pleasant place to stop for a drink, snack or light lunch. There is plenty of fast food to cater for most tastes, including pancake houses, and *Pizza Hut* prides itself on having won awards. Late night fast food, local fashion, can be found at truk'i pans, bread trucks which stay open until 0400-0500 and sell sandwiches filled with conch, goat stew, salt fish and other Antillean specialities.

● Food And Drink

Native food is filling and the meat dish is usually accompanied by several different forms of carbohydrate, one of which may be *funchi*, a corn meal bread in varying thickness but usually looking like a fat pancake (the same as *cou-cou* in the Eastern Caribbean). Goat stew (*stoba di kabritu*) is popular, slow cooked and mildly spicey (milder and tastier than Jamaican curry goat), rec. Soups (*sopi*) are very nourishing and can be a meal on their own, grilled fish or meat (*la paria*) is good although the fish may always be grouper, red snapper or conch (*karkó*), depending on the latest catch; meat, chicken, cheese or fish filled pastries (*pastechi*) are rather like the *empanadas* of South America or Cornish pasties.

While in the Netherlands Antilles, most visitors enjoy trying a *rijsttafel* (rice table), a sort of Asian *smørgasbørd* adopted from Indonesia, and delicious. Because *rijsttafel* consists of anywhere from 15 to 40 separate dishes, it is usually prepared for groups of diners, although some Curaçao restaurants will do a modified version of 10 or 15 dishes.

A selection of European, South American (mostly Chilean) and Californian wines is usually available in restaurants, although local waiters have little familiarity with them and it is advisable to examine your bottle well before allowing it to be opened. Curaçao's goldmedal-winning Amstel beer, the only beer in the world brewed from desalinated sea water, is very good indeed and available throughout the Netherlands Antilles. Amstel brewery tours are held on Tues and Thur at 1000, T 612944, 616922 for information. Some Dutch and other European beers can also be found. Fresh milk is difficult to get hold of and you are nearly always given evaporated milk with your tea or coffee. Curaçao's tap water is good; also distilled from the sea. Many hotels have no hot water taps, only cold. This is because the water pipes in Curaçao are laid overground, the water in them being warmed by the sun during the day and cold at night. Time your shower accordingly.

● Entertainment

For "night-owls", there are casinos. All the large hotels have them, with many gaming tables and rows and rows of fruit machines, open virtually all hours. There are many nightclubs and discothèques, several of which are in the Salinja area: *Façade* (Lindbergweg 32-34, T 614640, open 2200-0400 except Mon and Thur, happy hour on Fri from 1800) and *L'Aristocrat* (Lindbergweg, T 614353, open 0800-0200, Fri and Sat 2200-0400, closed Mon) are favoured by wealthy locals of all ages, you will not be let in wearing jeans or trainers and they have airport-style metal detectors at the door; *Infinity* is at Fort Nassau, open Fri and Sat, 2100-0200, T 613450; *The Pub*, Salinja, T 612190, open daily from 2100, happy hour 2100-2200, noisy, favoured by Dutch marines and their girlfriends, a youngish crowd; in Otrabanda, *Rum Runners* is rec for cocktails and harbour view; the *Lion's Dive Hotel* has a trendy bar and Sun evening happy hour is rec. The Centro Pro Arte presents concerts, ballets and plays. While on the subject of entertainment, one of the most bizarre sights of Curaçao, not dealt with in the tourist brochures, is the government-operated red-light area, aptly named Campo Alegre. Close to the airport, it resembles a prison camp and is even guarded by a policeman.

● **Shops**

Open on Sun morning and lunchtimes if cruise ships are in port. Weekday opening is 0800-1200 and 1400-1800. The main tourist shopping is in Punda (see above) where you can pick up all sorts of bargains in fashion, china etc. Willemstad's jewellery shops are noted for the quality of their stones.

● **Bookshops**

Boekhandel Mensing in Punda has a limited selection of guide books and maps. Larger and more well stocked bookshops are out of the centre of Willemstad. Boekhandel Salas in the Foggerweg has good maps and guide book section as has Mensings' Caminada in the Schottegatweg and Van Dorp in the Promenade Shopping Centre. The public Library is a modern building in Scharloo, cross the bridge by the floating market, turn right along the water and it is on your left. The Reading Room has books in Dutch, English, Spanish, French and Papiamento, T 617055.

● **Banks**

Algemene Bank Nederland, Banco Popular Antilliano, Banco Venezolano Antillano, McLaughlin's Bank, Maduro & Curiel Bank on Plaza Jojo Correa, T 611100, Banco di Caribe on Schottegatweg Oost, T 616588. Banking hours are 0800-1530 Mon to Fri. At the airport the bank is open 0800-2000 Mon-Sat, 0900-1600 Sun.

● **Currency**

The currency is the guilder, divided into 100 cents. There are coins of 1, 5, 10, 25, 50 cents and 1 and 2½ guilders, and notes of 5, 10, 25, 50, 100, 250 and 500 guilders. Old and new coins are in circulation. The older ones are bigger, the newer ½, 1 and 2½ guilder coins are gold coloured. The exchange rate is US$1=NAf1.77 for bank notes, NAf1.79 for cheques, although the rate of exchange offered by shops and hotels ranges from NAf1.75-1.80. Credit cards and US dollars are widely accepted.

● **Warning**

Beware of a tree with small, poisonous green apples that borders some beaches. This is the manchineel (*manzanilla*) and its sap causes burns on exposed skin.

● **Health**

The climate is healthy and non-malarial; epidemic incidence is slight. Rooms without air-conditioning or window and door screens may need mosquito nets during the wetter months of November and December and sometimes May and June, and, although some spraying is done in tourist areas, mosquitoes are a problem. Some anti-mosquito protection is rec if you are outdoors any evening. The 550-bed St Elisabeth Hospital is a well-equipped and modern hospital with good facilities including a coronary unit and a decompression chamber. For emergencies, T 624900 (hospital), 625822 (ambulance). The Sentro Mediko Santa Rosa, at Santa Rosaweg 329, is open 7 days a week, 0700-0000, laboratory on the premises, T 676666, 672300.

● **Emergency**

Emergency telephone numbers: Police and Fire Department T 114 or 44444, ambulance 112, 625822, 89337 or 89266.

● **National Holidays**

New Year's Day, Carnival Monday (February), Good Friday, Easter Monday, Queen's Birthday (30 April), Labour Day (1 May), Ascension Day, Flag Day (2 July), Christmas on 25 and 26 December.

● **Time Zone**

Atlantic Standard Time, 4 hours behind GMT,

1 ahead of EST.

● **Electric Current**

110/130 volts AC, 50 cycles.

● **Telecommunications**

All American Cables & Radio Inc, Keukenstraat; Kuyperstraat; Radio Holland NV, De Ruytergade 51; Sita, Curaçao Airport.

Telephone rates abroad are published in the telephone book, but beware if phoning from a hotel, you can expect a huge mark up, check their rates before you call. To Europe, US$3.05 a minute, to the USA US$1.60, to Australia and Africa US$5.55, to the Netherlands Antilles US$0.55, Central America US$3.90, Venezuela US$1.10, Leeward and Windward Islands US$1.75.

● **Places of Worship**

Curaçao has always had religious tolerance and as a result there are many faiths and denominations on the island. Details of services can be found in the official free guide, *Curaçao Holiday*, which lists Anglican, Catholic, Jewish, Protestant and other churches. Anglican Church, Leidenstraat, T 53251; Holy Family Church (Roman Catholic), Mgr Neiwindstraat, Otrabanda, T 62527; Methodist Church, Abr de Veerstraat 10, T 75834; Mikvé Israel – Emanuel Synagogue, Hanchi Snoa 29, Punda, T 611067; Ebenezer Church of the United Protestant Congregation, Oranjestraat, T 53121; Christian Heritage Ministries (Evangelical), Polarisweg 27, Zeelandia, T 615663; Church of Christ, 40 Schottegatweg West, T 627628; Church of God Prophecy (Ecumenical), Caricauweg 35, T 75306.

● **Tour Agencies**

The best island tour available is with Casper Tours, T 605442, 653010, informative, fun, covers E to W, 0900-1600 inc lunch at *Jaanchie's* (see above) for US$25 in a/c, mini buses, English, Dutch and Spanish spoken. Daltino Tours (a good travel agency conveniently located downtown Punda) do island coach tours eg to the E US$10, to the W US$16, day trips to Aruba, US$160, to Bonaire US$125, to

Caracas US$195, T 614888; Taber Tours do an E tour including the Seaquarium and glass bottomed boat trip for US$27.50 adults, US$17.50 children under 12, a W tour is US$12, children US$6, to Aruba US$135, Bonaire US$120. Old City Tours do a walking tour of Otrabanda, 1715-1900, US$5.55 including a drink, T 613554.

● **Tourist Office**

The main office of the Curaçao Tourism Development Bureau is at Pietermaai 19, Willemstad, PO Box 3266, T 616000, F 612305. The Curaçao Hotel and Tourism Association (CHATA) is at the International Trade Centre, Piscadera Bay, T 636260. However tourists should go to the offices at Waterfort Plaza, T 613397 and the airport, T 686789, offering helpful information, assistance in finding a hotel, brochures, maps, etc. There are also several Visitor Information Centres dotted round Willemstad and some booths sponsored by resort hotels, which have irregular hours. Members of Curaçao Hospitality Services look after the parking lots and are trained in first aid and how to give directions. Curoil nv publishes a good road map with a satellite photo of the island with superimposed information, town street plans and an excellent index, available in Mensing and other bookshops. *Curaçao Holiday* is a useful, free guide, the walking tour of Willemstad described in the brochure is recommended. For business travellers, *Business Curaçao* (monthly) is a useful source of information.

USA In New York: 400 Madison Avenue, suite 311, NY 10017, T 212-751 8266, F 486-3024.

Venezuela In Caracas: Avenida Francisco de Miranda, Centro Comercial Country, piso 2, T 713403.

Holland: Benelux—Eendrachtsweg 69-C, 3012 LG Rotterdam, T 010 414-2639.

We are very grateful to Nan Elisa, formerly resident in Curaçao, for her help in updating this section.

ARUBA

ARUBA, smallest and most W of the ABC group, lies 25 km N of Venezuela and 68 km W of Curaçao, at 12° 30′N, outside the hurricane belt. It is 31.5 km long, 10 km at its widest, with an area of 184 sq km. The average yearly temperature is 27.5°C, constantly cooled by NE trade winds, with the warmest months being August and September, the coolest January and February. Average annual rainfall is less than 510 mm, and the humidity averages 76%. Like Curaçao and Bonaire, Aruba has scant vegetation, its interior or *cunucu* is a dramatic landscape of scruffy bits of foliage, mostly cacti, the weird, wind-bent divi divi trees and tiny bright red flowers called *fioritas*, plus huge boulders, caves and lots of dust.

Aruba is one of the very few Caribbean islands on which the Indian population was not exterminated although there are no full-blooded Indians now. The Aruban today is a descendant of the indigenous Arawak Indians, with a mixture of Spanish and Dutch blood from the early colonizers. There was no plantation farming in Aruba, so African slaves were never introduced. Instead, the Indians supervised the raising of cattle, horses, goats and sheep, and their delivery to the other Dutch islands. They were generally left alone and maintained regular contact with the mainland Indians. They lived mostly in the N at Ceru Cristal and then at Alto Vista, where in 1750 the first Catholic church was founded. The last Indians to speak an Indian language were buried in urns about 1800; later Indians lost their language and culture. When Lago Oil came to Aruba many workers from the British West Indies came to work in the refinery in San Nicolas, leading to Caribbean English becoming the colloquial tongue there instead of Papiamento. Of the total population today of about 69,100, including some 40 different nationalities, only about two-thirds were actually born on the island. The official language here, as in the other Netherlands Antilles, is Dutch, but Papiamento is the colloquial tongue. English and Spanish are widely spoken and the people are extremely welcoming. The crime rate is low and there are very few attacks on tourists.

The Economy

Gold was discovered in 1825, but the mine ceased to be economic in 1916. In 1929, black gold brought real prosperity to Aruba when Lago Oil and Transport Co, a subsidiary of Exxon, built a refinery at San Nicolas at the E end of the island. At that time it was the largest refinery in the world, employing over 8,000 people. In March 1985 Exxon closed the refinery, a serious shock for the Aruban economy, and one which the Government has striven to overcome. In 1989, Coastal Oil of Texas signed an agreement with the Government to reopen part of the refinery by 1991, with an initial capacity of 150,000 barrels a day, but despite plans to increase it, present capacity is only about 140,000 b/d.

Aruba has three ports. San Nicolas is used for the import and transshipment of crude oil and materials for the refinery and for the export of oil products. There are also two sea-berths at San Nicolas capable of handling the largest tankers in the world. Oranjestad is the commercial port of Aruba, and it is open for day and night navigation. In 1962 the port of Barcadera was built to facilitate shipment of products from Aruba's new industrial zone on the leeward coast.

The economic crisis of 1985 forced the

ARUBA : FACT FILE

Geographic
Land area	193 sq km
farmland	43.3%

Demographic
Population (1992)	69,100
annual growth rate (1987-92)	2.8%
density	358 per sq km
Religious affiliation	
Roman Catholic	82%
Birth rate per 1,000 (1990)	17.3
	(world av 27.1)
Death rate per 1,000 (1990)	6.4
	(world av 9.8)

Education and Health
Life expectancy at birth,	
male	71.6 years
female	76.8 years
Infant mortality rate	
per 1,000 live births (1989)	9.6
Physicians (1990)	1 per 918 persons
Hospital beds	1 per 294 persons
Literacy (over 15)	95%

Economic
GDP (1989 market prices)	US$730mn
GDP per capita	US$11,840
Public external debt	na
Tourism receipts (1990)	US$353mn
Radio	1 per 1.6 persons
Television	1 per 3.4 persons
Telephone	1 per 1.8 persons

Employment
Population economically active (1981)	
	26,000
% of labour force in	
agriculture	0.2
mining, manufacturing	
and public utilities	10.6
construction	8.0
trade, hotels and restaurants	32.7

Source *Encyclopaedia Britannica*

have attracted investors and visitors from as far afield as Japan. By 1990 tourist accommodation in 15 major high rise and low rise hotels reached 3,326 rooms, with many more available in small hotels, guest houses and apartments. Today the number stands at a total of over 5,000 rooms. Nevertheless, by 1992 the Government was facing a financial crisis because of state guarantees totalling NG516mn for three hotel projects which had run into financial difficulties and on which work had ceased: the 466-room *Beta Hotel* (NG170mn), the 376-room *Eagle Beach Hotel* (NG186mn) and the 411-room *Plantation Bay Hotel* (NG160mn). Although the Dutch government provided a loan for the hotels' completion in 1992, the Aruban government now faces heavy interest and principal repayments for 15 years to banks. These will be funded by unpopular higher excise duties, petrol prices and import duties. In mid-1993, the *Plantation Bay Hotel* was sold to the Marriott chain.

The economy is now overwhelmingly dependent on tourism for income, with 562,034 stayover visitors in 1993, a rise of 4% over 1992. Over 56% of tourists came from the USA; the next largest country of origin was Venezuela. A further 251,104 passengers arrived on cruiseships in 1993, a rise of 16% over 1992.

Efforts are being made to diversify away from a single source of revenues into areas such as re-exporting through the free trade zone, and offshore finance. Aruba is still dependent on the Netherlands for budget support and the aim is to reduce the level of financial assistance. New legislation has been approved to encourage companies to register on the island by granting tax and other benefits. Regulations are generally flexible and unrestricting on offshore business, although efforts are being made to ensure an efficient level of supervision.

There is no unemployment on Aruba and labour is imported for large projects

Government to turn to the IMF for help. The Fund recommended that Aruba promote tourism and increase the number of hotel rooms by 50%. The Government decided, however, to triple hotel capacity to 6,000 rooms, which it was estimated would provide employment for 20% of the population. Hotel construction has expanded rapidly and marketing efforts

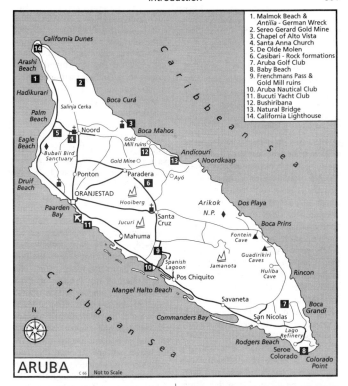

1. Malmok Beach &
   Antilia - German Wreck
2. Sereo Gerard Gold Mine
3. Chapel of Alto Vista
4. Santa Anna Church
5. De Olde Molen
6. Casibari - Rock formations
7. Aruba Golf Club
8. Baby Beach
9. Frenchmans Pass &
   Gold Mill ruins
10. Aruba Nautical Club
11. Bucuti Yacht Club
12. Bushiribana
13. Natural Bridge
14. California Lighthouse

ARUBA Not to Scale

such as the refinery and construction work. Turkish guest workers came to help get Coastal started and Philippinos work in the high rise hotels. The Government is encouraging skilled Arubans to return from Holland but is hampered by a housing shortage and a consequent boom in real estate prices.

Flora and Fauna

About 170 species of birds can be found on Aruba, and about 50 species breed on the island but if you include the migratory birds which come in November-January the total rises to around 300 species. The most common birds are the trupiaal (with its bright orange colours), the chuchubi, the prikichi (a little parrot)

and the barika geel (the little yellow-bellied bird you will find eating the sugar on the table in your hotel). An interesting site to see waterfowl is the Bubali Plassen, opposite the Olde Molen. Here you can often find cormorants, herons and fish eagle. Brown pelicans can be found along the S shore. As well as various kinds of lizards. Aruba has large iguanas. These animals are hunted to prepare a typical Arubian soup. Two kinds of snakes can be found on Aruba: the Santanero, a harmless little snake (however, be careful when you pick it up, because it defecates in your hand) and the not so harmless rattle snake. Aruba's rattle snake is a unique subspecies and does not use its rattle. Rattle snakes live in the triangular area between the Jamanota, Fontein and San Nicolas. The best place to go looking for rattle snakes, if you really want to, is the area S of the Yamanota mountain. In the unlikely event that you get a bite from a rattle snake, go immediately to the hospital. They have anti-serum.

Beaches and Watersports

Of the 3 ABC islands, Aruba stands out as having the best beaches, all of which are public and free. There are good, sandy beaches on both sides of the island although fewer on the E side which is rough and not so good for swimming. Travelling N along the W coast from Oranjestad an excellent road takes you to the main resort areas where nearly all the hotels are gathered. Druif beach starts at the *Tamarijn Aruba Beach Resort*, extending and widening along the coast to the sister hotel, the *Divi Aruba*, with good windsurfing. At the *Best Western Manchebo* there is a huge expanse of sand, often seen in advertisements; Caribasurf, *Manchebo Beach Resort*, T 23444, F 32446, windsurfing boards and instruction. N of here is Eagle Beach where the 'low rise' hotels are separated from the beach by the road, and then Palm Beach there the 'high rise' hotels front directly on to the beach. These three sandy beaches extend for several miles, the water is calm, clear and safe for children, although watch out for watersports and keep within markers where provided.

North of Palm Beach is an area of very shallow water with no hotels to break the wind, known as Fisherman's Huts, which is excellent for very fast windsurfing. Surfers from all over the world come here to enjoy their sport and professionals often come here for photo sessions. Although speeds are high and there is a strong offshore wind, surfing is quite safe and there are several rescue boats to get you back if the wind blows you to Pan-ama. This beach is called Malmok (S end) or Arashi (N end) and there are many villas and guesthouses across the road which cater for windsurfers. Windsurfing Aruba is a sympathetic small firm by the Heineken flags at the huts which rents equipment and gives lessons to beginners and intermediates at reasonable prices, T 33472, F 34407. There are other operators of high quality with higher prices: Roger's Windsurf Place, L G Smith Blvd 472, T/F 21918, windsurf packages available, boards and accommodation; Sailboard Vacation, L G Smith Blvd 462, T 21072, boards of different brands for rent. For information about the Aruba Hi-Winds Pro/Am boardsailing competitions, contact the B T A Group at L G Smith Boulevard 62, T 35454, F 37266. They usually take place around the same time as the Jazz and Latin Festival in June.

A residential area stretches up from Arashi to the lighthouse and the coast is indented with tiny rocky bays and sandy coves, the water is beautiful and good for snorkelling, while shallow and safe for children. It is also a fishing ground for the brown pelicans. At night they normally sleep in the shallow water close to the lighthouse. A little way after the lighthouse, if you follow the coastroad, there is a very spectacular place where high waves smash against the rocks at a small inlet. There is a blow hole, where water sometimes spouts up more than 5m.

At the other end of the island is Seroe Colorado, known as 'the colony', which used to be a residential area for Exxon staff but is currently used as temporary housing. You have to enter the zone through a guard post, but there is no entrance fee and no hindrance. There are two W facing beaches here worth visiting. Rodgers Beach has a snack bar, showers, yachts and is protected by a reef but is in full view of the refinery. Baby Beach, on the other hand, is round the corner, out of sight of the refinery, in a lovely sandy bay, protected by the reef, nice swimming and snorkelling, very busy on Sundays, with toilets but little shade. Sea Grape Grove and Boca Grandi, on the E coast of the S tip has good snorkelling and swimming, being protected by a reef, and is popular with tours who come to see the largest elkhorn coral. Experienced windsurfers come here to wave jump. The prison is near here, remarkable for the pleasant sea view from the cells. Other beaches on the E side of the island are Boca Prins, where there are sand dunes, and further N from there, reached by a poor road, is Dos Playa where there is good surf for body surfing. The landscape is hilly and barren because of serious overgrazing by herds of goats. Andicouri is also popular with surfers, note that if you approach it through the coconut grove you will be crossing private land, for which there used to be a charge but there is no longer any one around to collect the fee.

Virtually every type of watersport is available and most hotels provide extensive facilities. Activities which are not offered on site can be arranged through several tour agencies such as De Palm Tours, T 24545, Pelican Tours and Watersports, T 31228/24739, or ECO Destination Management. Caribbean Watersports, T 29118, open 1000-1630, rents jetskis US$35, waterskis US$20 and snorkelling equipment US$15. Mirto's Watersports at Eagle Beach, T 77188, has single or double waverunners (US$35 or US$45), banana boats (US$15), waterskiing (US$35). Watersports companies are too numerous to mention in further detail. Parasailing can be done from the high-rise hotels. Glass bottomed boat trips from various locations are around US$20-25, but can be more for a sunset cruise. Several yachts and catamarans offer cruises along the coast with stops for snorkelling and swimming. A morning cruise often includes lunch (about US$40-50), an afternoon trip will be drinks only – and then there are the sunset booze cruises (about US$20-30). *Pelican I* is a 50-foot catamaran running along the W coast from Pelican pier; *Balia*, a 53 foot racing catamaran operated by Red Sail Sports, does all the usual cruises and is available for private charter at US$450 an hour, minimum 2 hrs; *Wave Dancer*, another catamaran, departs from *Holiday Inn* beach, T 25520; *Octopus* is a 40 foot trimaran, departing from *Holiday Inn* pier, is also available for private charter, snorkelling and sailing cruises, US$20-35, T 33081; *Tranquilo*, a yacht, can be contacted through Mike, its captain T 47533, or Pelican Tours T 31228. *Mi Dushi* is an old sailing ship which starts cruises from the *Tamarijn Beach Resort*, morning and lunch US$35, snorkelling and sunset US$24, sunset booze cruise US$20, pirate sails and beach party US$40, T 25842 or De Palm Tours.

Near Spanish Lagoon is the Aruba Nautical Club complex, with pier facilities offering safe, all-weather mooring for almost any size of yacht, plus gasoline, diesel fuel, electricity and water. For information, write to PO Box 161. A short sail downwind from there is the Bucuti Yacht Club with clubhouse and stormproofed pier providing docking, electricity, water and other facilities. Write to PO Box 743.

Over a dozen charter boats are available for half or whole day deep sea fishing. The Tourist Office has a list so you can contact the captain direct, or else go through De Palm Tours or ECO Destination Management. Whole day trips including food and drinks range from US$350-480, depending on the number of people on board. Deep sea fishing tournaments are held in October and November at the Aruba Nautical Club and the Bucuti Yacht Club.

Diving and Marine Life

Visibility in Aruban waters is about 30m in favourable conditions and snorkelling and scuba diving is good, although not as spectacular as in the waters around Bonaire. A coral reef extends along the W side of the island from California reef in the N to Baby Beach reef in the S, with dives varying in depth from 5 to 45m. Organized boat trips regularly visit the two wrecks worth exploring, although they can get a bit crowded. One is a German freighter, the *Antilia*, which went down just after World War II was declared and is found in 20m of water off Malmok beach on the W coast. You can see quite a lot just snorkelling here as parts of the wreck stick up above the water. Snorkelling boat trips usually combine Malmok beach and the wreck. The other wreck is nearby in 10m of water, the *Pedernales*, a flat-bottomed oil tanker which was hit in a submarine attack in May 1941, while ferrying crude oil from Venezuela to Aruba. Be very careful not to touch anything underwater; not all the dive masters bother to warn you of the dangers of fire coral and hydroids.

There are several scuba diving operations and prices vary from US$30-40 for a single tank dive, US$35-45 for a night dive and US$55-80 for an introductory course and dive. Snorkelling from a dive boat varies from US$10-22. *The Talk of the Town* has a beach bar and pool opposite the hotel and across the road, in full view of the airport runway; Aruba Aqua Sports on the premises operates a set schedule of daily dives, T 23380 ext 254. Aruba Pro Dive is on the beach at *Playa Linda*, T 25520, F 37723. S E A Scuba, Charlie's Buddies, operates out of Seaport Market, T 34877, quite good on safety checks, instruction available in German, 40 foot boat, also deep sea fishing charters. Red Sail Sports, L G Smith Blvd 83, PO Box 218, T 31603, and at hotels, sailing, snorkelling, diving with certification courses, windsurfing, waterskiing, hobie cats etc, accommodation packages available, this is a large, reputable international operation and an expensive one. Mermaid

Sport Divers, between *Manchebo* and *Bucuti Beach Resorts*, T 35546, not very professional, few safety checks, boat smells of diesel. Scuba Aruba has a retail operation in Seaport Village selling all watersports equipment, open Mon-Sat, 0900-1900, T 34142.

The Atlantis Submarine has hourly dives 1000-1500 most days from the Seaport Village Marina. A catamaran takes you past the airport and the local garbage dump to where the submarine begins its 1-hour tour of the Barcadera reef to a depth of 50m, turning frequently so that both sides can see. Recommended for those who are interested in marine life but do not scuba dive, but not for anyone who is claustrophobic. The submarine takes 46 passengers and is nearly always full, particularly when a cruise ship is in port, so book beforehand, US$58 adults, Arubans and children aged 4-12 US$29, no children under 4 allowed, T 36090. Lunchtime is quite a good time to go, it is not so full then; Thursday is a bad day when a lot of cruise ships come in. Throwaway cameras with 400 ASA film, US$20, are available at the ticket office.

Other Sports

There is a 9-hole golf course with oiled sand greens and goats near San Nicolas, golf clubs for rent US$6, green fee US$10 for 18 holes, US$7.50 for 9 holes, T 42006, Saturday and Sunday members only, open daily 0800-1700. At the *Holiday Inn* is an 18-hole mini-golf course. A mini golf course called Adventure Golf has been built opposite *La Cabana*, close to Bubali, in a nice garden. A large golf course is planned near the lighthouse, but the need to import water and completely alter the barren landscape will prevent it coming into operation before the turn of the century. There are tennis courts at most major hotels. Horseriding at Rancho El Paso, Washington 44, near Santa Ana Church, T 73310, Paso Fino horses, daily rides except Sunday, 1 hour through countryside, US$15, or 2 hrs part beach, part *cunucu*, US$30. The Eagle Bowling Palace at Pos Abou has 12 lanes, of which 6 are for reservation, open 1000-0200, US$9 from 1000-1500, US$10.50 from 1500-0200, US$1.20 shoe rental; also 3 racquetball courts available. Wings Over Aruba, at the airport, T 37104, F 37124, has a pilot school, with sightseeing flights, aerial photography, aircraft rental; sightseeing in a seaplane US$130/half hour, trial flying lesson US$120/90 mins. Sailcarts available at a special rink not on the beach, Aruba Sailcart N V, Bushiri 213, T 36005, open 0900-sunset, US$15/30 mins for a single cart, US$20/30 mins for a double cart. Drag races are held several times a year at the Palo Margo circuit near San Nicolas. A 10-km mini-marathon is held annually in June, contact the Tourist Office for details.

Festivals

The most important festival of the year is Carnival, held from the Sunday two weeks preceding Lent, starting with Children's Carnival. There are colourful parades and competitions for best musician, best dancer, best costume etc. The culmination is the Grand Parade on the Sunday preceding Lent. Other festive occasions during the year include New Year, when fireworks are let off at midnight and musicians and singers go round from house to house (and hotel to hotel); National Anthem and Flag Day on 18 March, when there are displays of national dancing and other folklore, and St John's Day on 24 June, which is another folklore day: "Derramento di Gai". For visitors who do not coincide their trip with one of the annual festivals, there is a weekly Bonbini show in the courtyard of the Fort Zoutman museum on Tuesday 1830-2030, Afl 2, US$1.15, adults, Afl 1, US$0.55, children, music, singing and dancing, interesting but overenthusiastic MC, bartenders from hotels mix cocktails and special drinks. The programme is altered every week, so those on a 2-week holiday do not sit through the same thing twice. Local dance music, such as the fast, lively *tumba* is very influenced by Latin America. Arubans are fond of *merengue*. In June there is a well-attended and popular festival of jazz and Latin American music, with many famous musicians and bands playing. Contact the Aruba Tourism Authority, PO Box 1019, Oranjestad, T 23777, F 34702, for information on the programme and package tours available. The International Theatre Festival takes place annually; for information contact CCA, Vondellaan 2, T 21758. There is also a Dance Festival in October, for information T 24581.

ORANJESTAD

Oranjestad, the capital of Aruba, population about 17,000, is a bustling little freeport town where "duty-free" generally implies a discount rather than a bargain. The main shopping area is on Caya G F (Betico) Croes, formerly named Nassaustraat, and streets off it; also shops in the Port of Call Market Place, Seaport Village Mall, Harbour Town, The Galleries, Strada I and II and the Holland Aruba Mall. Many of the buildings in the colourful Antillean style are actually modern and do not date from colonial times as in Willemstad, Curaçao.

There is a small museum in the restored 17th century Fort Zoutman/Willem III Tower, Zoutmanstraat, T 26099, open Monday-Friday, 0900-1600, Saturday, 0900-1200, entrance Afl 1. Named the **Museo Arubano**, it contains items showing the island's history and geology, with fossils, shells, tools, furniture and products. It is not particularly well laid out, the displays are unimaginative and old-fashioned but it is still worth going if only to see the building. The fort, next to the Parliament buildings, opposite the police station, dates from 1796 and marks the beginning

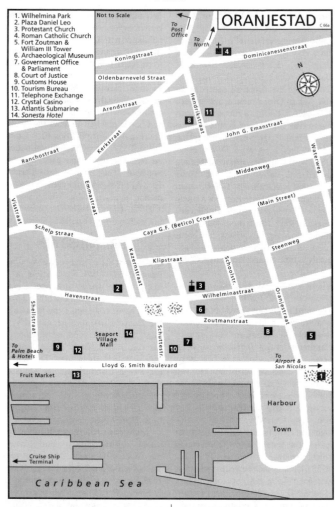

ORANJESTAD C 66a

1. Wilhelmina Park
2. Plaza Daniel Leo
3. Protestant Church
4. Roman Catholic Church
5. Fort Zoutman &
   William III Tower
6. Archaeological Museum
7. Government Office
   & Parliament
8. Court of Justice
9. Customs House
10. Tourism Bureau
11. Telephone Exchange
12. Crystal Casino
13. Atlantis Submarine
14. *Sonesta Hotel*

Not to Scale

To Post Office

To North

Koningstraat

Dominicanessenstraat

Oldenbarneveld Straat

Arendstraat

Hendrikstraat

John G. Emanstraat

Ranchostraat

Kerkstraat

Emmastraat

Middenweg

Waterweg

Visstraat

Schelp Straat

Caya G.F. (Betico) Croes

(Main Street)

Kazernstraat

Klipstraat

Schoolstr.

Steenweg

Havenstraat

Wilhelminastraat

Oranjestraat

Shellstraat

Seaport Village Mall

Schuttestr.

Zoutmanstraat

To Palm Beach & Hotels

Fruit Market

Lloyd G. Smith Boulevard

To Airport & San Nicolas

Harbour

Town

Cruise Ship Terminal

Caribbean Sea

of Oranjestad as a settlement. Built with four guns to protect commercial traffic, in 1810-1911 it sheltered the government offices. The tower was added around 1868 with the first public clock and a petrol lamp in the spire, which was first lit on King Willem III's birthday in 1869 and served as a lighthouse. The Fort was

restored in 1974 and the tower in 1980-83. The **Archaeological Museum** on Zoutmanstraat 1, T 28979, is open Monday-Friday 0800-1200, 1330-1630. Small, but cleverly laid out in three parts, Preceramic, Ceramic (from 500 AD) and Historic (from 1500-1800 AD when the Indians used European tools). The two main sites excavated are Canashitu and Malmok and most objects come from these. The descriptions are in English and Papiamento, easy to read and educational. There are some interesting publications available in English. Recommended, the best museum in the ABCs. A numismatic museum, **Mario's Worldwide Coin Collection**, also known as the Museo Numismatico, Zuidstraat 7, not far from Fort Zoutman and the Central Bank of Aruba (where it is possible to buy specimen sets of Aruba's extremely attractive coins) has a large collection of coins from over 400 countries and coins from ancient Greece, Rome, Syria and Egypt. A bit cramped, but with a lot of fascinating material, the museum is run by the daughter of the collector, Mario Odor; donations welcomed. Open Monday-Friday, 0900-1200, 1330-1730, Saturday 1000-1200, 1400-1700. There is an extensive collection of shells at De Man's Shell Collection, Morgenster 18, T 24246 for an appointment. The Cas di Cultura, Vondellaan 2, has concerts, ballet, folklore shows and art exhibitions, T 21010. *Gasparito* Restaurant/Art Gallery has an exhibition of Aruban art for sale and display, Gasparito 3, T 37044, open 0900-2300 daily.

Excursions

The landscape is arid, mostly scrub and cactus with wind blown divi divi (watapana) trees and very dusty. Traditional Aruban houses are often protected from evil spirits by 'hex' signs molded in cement around the doorways and are surrounded by cactus fences. Flashes of colour are provided by bougainvillea, oleanders, flamboyant, hibiscus and other tropical plants. You will need a couple of days to see everything on offer inland without rushing. The Esso Road Map marks all the sites worth seeing and it is best to hire a car (4 wheel drive if possible, but not essential) as you have to

go on dirt roads to many of them and there is no public transport. Tour agencies do excursions, about US$15-17 for a half day tour of the island, see **Information for Visitors**.

The village of Noord is known for the Santa Anna Church, founded in 1766, rebuilt in 1831 and 1886, the present stone structure was erected in 1916 by Father Thomas V Sadelhoff, whose portrait is on the twelfth station of the Cross. It has heavily carved neo-Gothic oak altar, pulpit and communion rails made by the Dutchman, Hendrik van der Geld, which were the prize work shown at the Vatican Council exhibition in 1870. They were then housed in St Anthony's Church at Scheveningen in Holland, before being given to Aruba in 1928. The church is popular for weddings, being light and airy with a high vaulted ceiling and stained glass windows. Services are held Mondays, Wednesdays and Fridays at 1830, Saturdays at 1900 and Sundays at 0730 and 1800. Not far from Noord on the N coast is the tiny Chapel of Alto Vista, dating from 1952 but on the site of the chapel built by the Spanish missionary, Domingo Antonio Silvester in 1750. It is in a spectacular location overlooking the sea and is so small that stone pews have been built in semi circles outside the Chapel.

Also on the N coast are the ruins of a gold mine at Seroe Gerard and a refinery at Bushiribana in a particularly bleak and sparsely vegetated area. The machinery at the mill, right on the coast, was damaged by sea spray and moved to Frenchman's Pass in 1824. A partly paved road leads to the natural bridge where long ago the roof of a cave collapsed, leaving only the entrance standing. It is actually fairly low and not as spectacular as tourist brochures would have you believe. There is a souvenir shop and you can get snacks here.

Inland, extraordinary rock formations can be seen at Casibari and Ayó, where huge, diorite boulders have been carved into weird shapes by the wind. At Casibari steps have been made so that you can climb to the top, from where you get a good view of the island and the Haystack. There is a snack bar and souvenir shop. Ayó does not have steps, you have to clamber up, but a wall is being built up around the rocks to keep out the goats. There are some Indian inscriptions. Toilets, a snack bar and souvenir shop are planned. The 541-foot **Hooiberg**, or Haystack, has steps all the way up. Very safe, even with children, the view is worth the effort.

At the village of **Santa Cruz**, just SE of the Haystack, a cross on top of a boulder marks the first mission on the island. Travelling E from here you pass the **Arikok National Park**, where there are some well laid out trails for easy, but hot, walking. The road leads to Boca Prins (dune sliding) and the **Fontein** cave. Admission to the cave is free, you can hire helmets and flashlights. There is a large chamber at the entrance, with natural pillars, and a 100-metre tunnel leading off, halfway down which are Indian paintings. Despite the desolation of the area, there is a well near the caves with brackish water, which a Japanese man uses to cultivate vegetables for the Chinese restaurants on the island. Further along the coast are the **Guadirikiri** caves, two large chambers lit by sunlight, connected by passages and pillars, with a 100-metre tunnel, for which you need a torch. Bats live in this cave system. The road around the coast here is very bumpy and dusty, being used by quarry trucks. A third cave, **Huliba**, is known as the Tunnel of Love. Again, no entry fee but helmets (US$2.50) and torches available. The walk through the tunnel takes 20-30 mins with a 10-minute return walk overground.

The road then takes you to *San Nicolas* where there is a strong smell of oil. After the closure of the oil refinery in 1985, San Nicolas was a ghost town, but now that Coastal Oil has taken over the refinery, activity is beginning to pick up. Old wooden houses are being demolished and new concrete houses built instead. A landmark is *Charlie's Bar*, which has been in operation since 1941; a good place to stop for refreshment to see the souvenirs hanging everywhere.

Returning NW towards Oranjestad you pass through Savaneta, where the Dutch marines have a camp. Turn off to the left to *Brisas del Mar*, a good seafood restaurant open to the sea, very popular. At Pos Chiquito, a walkway leads through mangroves to *Isla di Oro*, a restaurant built like a ship where there is dancing at weekends and pedalos and watersports. A little further on a bay with shallow water and mangroves is ideal for snorkelling beginners. The view is not spectacular but you can see many colourful fish. **Spanish Lagoon**, once a pirates' hideout, is a seawater channel, at the mouth of which is the Aruba Nautical Club and the water desalination plant. At the other end is a bird sanctuary where parakeets breed and the ruins of the Balashi gold mill dating from 1899, where the machinery is better preserved than at Bushiribana. There is quicksand in the area around the bird sanctuary, so it is not advisable to walk there. Nearby is **Frenchman's Pass** where the French attacked the Indians in 1700. From here you can turn E again to drive up **Jamanota**, at 188m the highest elevation on the island.

INFORMATION FOR VISITORS

● **Documents**

US and Canadian citizens only require proof of identity, such as birth certificate, certificate of naturalization or voter registration card. Other nationalities need a passport. A return or onward ticket and proof of adequate funds are also required. Dogs and cats are permitted entry if they have a valid rabies and health certificate. However, no pets are allowed from South or Central America. Check with your hotel to see if they are allowed to stay.

How To Get There
● By Air
KLM has direct flights from Amsterdam and some via Caracas; some continue to Lima. American Airlines (daily from JFK) and Air Aruba (daily from Newark) fly from New York; Air Aruba, American Airlines, and ALM fly from Miami; American Airlines from Baltimore, Hartford CT Springfield and San Juan, Puerto Rico; Viasa from Houston; Air Aruba from Baltimore; ALM and Aeropostal from Atlanta, Aeropostal from Orlando. Avianca and SAM fly from Barranquilla, SAM from Cali, SAM and Air Aruba from Medellín and Avianca and Air Aruba from Bogotá. Servivensa flies from Maracaibo and there are lots of flights from Caracas with Viasa, Servivensa, Aeropostal and Air Aruba; from Las Piedras on the Paraguaná Peninsula with Servivensa, from Barquisimeto with ALM and from Valencia with Valenciana de Aviación and ALM. VASP flies from Brasilia via São Paulo and Manaus, Air Aruba has a weekly flight from São Paulo.

Within the Caribbean, there are only flights from Santo Domingo with Aeropostal and San Juan with American Airlines, as well as frequent flights from Bonaire and Curaçao with ALM and Air Aruba.

Airport tax US$10. Airline offices: for all airport lines T 24800; American Airlines, T 22700; Aeropostal, T 31892/39040; Air Aruba, T 30005/23151 (also Vasp); ALM, T 38080; Avianca, T 23388; KLM, T 23546/7; LAV, T 31892; Avensa, T 27779.

If flying out to the USA, you will clear US immigration in Aruba, which saves you time at the other end. There is no in-transit facility, so if you are passing through (eg making a connection to Bonaire or Curaçao) you have to collect your luggage, clear customs and immigration, then walk (no trolleys) down to the queue for departure tax exemption and clear immigration again on your way out.

● By Sea
The harbour is 5 mins' walk from the town, there are a tourist information centre and some souvenir shops which open if a cruise ship is in. A fruit boat leaves once a week for Punto Fijo, Venezuela; check with Agencia Marítima La Confianza, Braziliëstraat 6 (T 23814), Oranjestad. There used to be a ferry to Venezuela, check with Rufo U Winterdaal, Eman Trading Co, LG Smith Blvd 108, Oranjestad (PO Box 384), T 21533/21156, F 22135, Telex: 5027.

● Taxis
Telephone the dispatcher at Alhambra Bazaar or Boulevard Centre, T 22116/21604. Drivers speak English, and individual tours can be arranged. Taxis do not have meters. Ask for flat rate tariffs. From the airport to Oranjestad is US$9, to the low rise hotels US$11 and to the high rise hotels US$12.

● Buses
The bus station is behind Parliament on Zoutmanstraat. Route 1 starts in San Nicolas and runs through Oranjestad via the hospital to Malmok, Mon-Sat, 0455-2255 hourly, returning from Malmok on the hour, journey time 55 mins. Route 2 also runs from San Nicolas on a slightly different route to Oranjestad and Palm Beach, more or less hourly, 0525-2200. Route 3 runs between Oranjestad and San Nicolas, 0550-2030 and Route 4 runs from Oranjestad through Noord to Palm Beach almost hourly on the half hour. There are also extra buses running between Oranjestad and the *Holiday Inn* (schedules available at the hotels and the Tourist Office). One way fare is US$0.90. Otherwise there are "jitney cars" which operate like colectivos; the fare is US$1.00. A jitney or bus from Oranjestad to San Nicolas will drop you at the airport.

● Self-Drive Cars
You must have a valid foreign or international driver's licence and be at least 21 to rent a car. Airways (T 21845/29112), Hertz (T 24545 24886), Avis (T 28787/25496), Budget (T 28600/25423), National (T 21967/25451), Dollar (T 22783/25651) and Thrifty (T 35300/35335) have offices in Oranjestad and at the airport. Many companies also have desks in the hotels. Prices begin at US$35 daily, US$215 weekly, with unlimited mileage. Often when you rent a 4WD vehicle (rec for getting to beaches like Dos Playa) you cannot take out all risks insurance. George Rental is the biggest 4WD rental company.

Motorcycles, mopeds, and bicycles can also be rented; a 50cc moped or scooter costs around US$14-25 a day, a 250cc motorcycle US$35, a Harley Davidson SP1100 US$80 and insurance is US$8-15 a day, depending on the size of engine. Melchor Cycle Rental has all sorts of motorbikes, T 23448, Tanki Leendert 170-A, driver's licence required, drivers must be 18 or over. Pablito's Bikes Rental, L G Smith Blvd 228, T 75010/78655/30623, at *La Quinta Beach Resort*, Eagle Beach, men's ladies, children's bikes, US$3/hr, US$8 until 1700,

US$12/24 hrs. The Tourist Office has a list of rental companies. Beware the local drivers, who are aggressive. Driving is on the right and all traffic, except bicycles, coming from the right should be given right of way, except at T junctions. Good maps are available at petrol stations, US$0.90.

● **Where To Stay**

A cluster of glittering luxury hotels has sprung up along Druif Bay, and Eagle and Palm beaches; decent, cheap accommodation is now very difficult to find. High season winter rates (16 December to 15 April) quoted here are roughly double low season rates. A 5% government tax and 10-15% service charge must be added; some hotels also add a US$3-5/day energy surcharge.

Closest to the airport, but only a 10-15 minute walk into town, is the *Best Western Talk of the Town*, L G Smith Blvd 2, T 23380, F 32446/33208, convenient for business travellers, 63 rooms and suites built round a pool, US$119-210d, children under 18 sharing free, large rooms, most with kitchenette, oceanside rooms are cheaper than pool side as they overlook the road but a/c reduces traffic noise, beach club and watersports centre across the road, guests may use facilities at the other Best Western hotels. In Oranjestad on the waterfront is the *Sonesta*, L G Smith Blvd 82, T 36000, F 34389, deluxe highrise, 300 rooms and 25 suites, US$195-610d, Seaport Village shops and Crystal casino on the premises, no beach at the hotel but guests may use a private island reached by motor launch from the hotel lobby which has watersports and all facilities, even a private honeymooners' beach, the only drawback being that the island is right at the end of the airport runway. A cheap hotel in town is *Central*, behind the main street, US$50, clean, basic, a/c, usually full of construction workers. Just outside town to the W in a rather unattractive industrial area immediately after the free zone, is the *Bushiri*, L G Smith Blvd 35, T 25216, F 26789, a 150-room hotel school and all-inclusive, often booked solid, reserve in advance, US$140-180pp, on man-made beach, gym, table tennis, lots of activities, good reputation for food.

The low-rise resort hotel development starts on Punta Brabo Beach, Druif Bay, all hotels are on the beach and offer swimming pools, tennis, watersports, shops, restaurants etc. *Tamarijn Aruba Beach Resort*, J E Irausquin Boulevard 41, T 24150, F 34002,

all-inclusive, rates fluctuate monthly, highest at Christmas, US$250 pp double occupancy inc tax, service, watersports, land sports, all meals, snacks, drinks etc, rates fall to US$140 the week before Christmas, children 2-11, US$50 pp, resort is next to Alhambra Bazaar and Casino; *Divi Aruba Beach Resort*, next along the beach at J E Irausquin Blvd 45, T 23300, F 34002, rooms and suites, highest rates US$275-600 per room, plus 16.55% tax and service, honeymoon and windsurfing packages available, tennis, pool. Next is the *Best Western Manchebo Beach Resort*, T 23444, F 32446/33667, 70 rooms with balcony or terrace, US$158-175d, dive shop (Mermaid Divers, see above) and windsurfing on huge expanse of beach; under same management with shared facilities is the *Bucuti Beach Resort*, same phone numbers, 63 rooms, some with kitchenette, some suites, balconies, sea view, US$170-220d. *Casa del Mar*, T 27000, F 26557, 147 luxury 2-bedroom (timeshare) apartments on the beach and 1-bedroom suites not on the beach, US$200-400 winter, children's playground, gamesroom, tennis, pool, minimarket, laundromats. The *Aruba Beach Club*, same phone numbers, shared facilities, 131 rooms with kitchenette, US$180-300d winter, US$120-195 summer for up to 4 people, 11% service, energy surcharge and 5.55% tax.

At Eagle Beach the road splits the hotels/timeshare from the beach, where it is prohibited to build. *La Cabana*, T 79000, F 75474, studios and suites, racquetball, squash, fitness centre, waterslide, children's pool and playground, casino and condominiums. *Amsterdam Manor*, T 71492, F 71463, 47 painted Dutch colonial style studios and apartments with sea view, kitchen, US$100-185 winter, pool, no restaurant. *Paradise Beach Villas*, T 34000, F 31662, 43 suites, US$150-230 winter, family oriented, pool, tennis, racquetball, watersports. *La Quinta*, T 74133, suites and rooms with kitchenette, from US$140 winter, pools, tennis, racquetball, expanding.

After the sewage treatment plant and Pos Chiquito the road curves round Palm Beach where all the high rise luxury hotels are. All have at least one smart restaurant and another informal bar/restaurant, some have about 5, all have shops, swimming pools, watersports, tennis and other sports facilities on the premises and can arrange anything else. Hotels with 300 rooms have casinos. The first one is the

Aruba Royal Resort, T 67000, F 69090, 300 rooms and suites, US$200-850d winter, squash courts, fitness centre, all luxury facilities. *Aruba Hilton and Casino*, T 64466/64470, F 68217, 481 rooms, US$170-680d winter, behind it is the restaurant *De Olde Molen*, an imported windmill around which a condominium resort *The Mill Resort* has been built, T 67700, US$155-500 winter, waterslide, racquetball. *Aruba Palm Beach*, T 63900, F 61941, 202 rooms and suites from US$155d, Olympic size swimming pool. The oldest hotel along here is the renewed and extended *Radisson Aruba Caribbean*, T 66555, F 63260, 378 rooms and suites, not all with sea view, from US$170d, golf putting, usual luxury facilities. *Americana Aruba*, T 64500, F 63191, recently renovated, 421 rooms and suites with sea view and balcony, US$140-175d winter, Red Sails diving and watersports on site. The next hotel along is the new and glittering *Hyatt Regency Aruba*, T 61234, 360 rooms and suites, US$240-365d, designed for a luxury holiday or for business meetings and incentive trips, built around a huge 3-level pool complex with waterfalls, slides and salt water lagoon, in beautiful gardens, health and fitness centre, Red Sail diving and watersports, very popular, great for children or business travellers, always full. *Playa Linda*, T 61000, F 65210, a timeshare resort of suites and efficiencies, US$200-600d winter, health club, games room. *Holiday Inn Aruba,*, T 63600, F 65165, 602 rooms with balcony, US$179-230d winter, refurbished and re-landscaped 1993-94, pools, tennis, diving, casino, lots of other facilities.

The Aruba Tourism Authority publishes a list of apartments and guesthouses. Weekly or monthly rates are more advantageous. If you arrive at a weekend the Tourist Office will be shut and you cannot get any help. In residential Oranjestad, *Aruba Apartments*, US$60, George Madurostraat 7, T 24736; *Aulga's Place*, US$30, Seroe Blanco 31, T 22717; *Camari Guesthouse*, US$25, Hospitaalstraat 10, T 28026; *Camacuri Apartments*, US$53-67, Fergusonstraat 46-B, T 26805. In the district of Noord, *Cactus Apartments*, US$40-50, Matadera 5, Noord, T 22903; *Coconut Inn*, US$35-50, Noord 31, T 66288, F 65433; *Turibana Plaza Apartments*, US$50-75, Noord 124, T 67292, F 62658; *Montaña Apartments*, US$25, Montaña 6-A, Noord, T 74981; *Roger's (windsurf) Place*, windsurfing packages only, L G Smith Blvd 472, PO Box 461, Malmok, T 61918, F 69045; *Boardwalk Vacation*, US$79-99, Bakval 20,

Noord, T/F 66654; *The Villas*, L G Smith Blvd 462, *The Boulevards*, L G Smith 486, and *The Edges Guesthouse*, L G Smith Blvd 458, all run by Sailboard Vacations Windsurf Villages, windsurfing packages only, T 62527, F 61870; *Vistalmar*, Bucutiweg 28, T 28579 daytime, T 47737 evenings, F 22200, 1-bedroom apartments run by Alby and Katy Yarzagaray, friendly, wooden jetty for swimming and sunbathing, near airport, laundry facilities, from US$70 with car. Mrs B de Blieck has some comfortable apartments within walking distance of Oranjestad and also the beach, shopping mall and laundromat, Dutch owners, hospitable, a/c, clean, US$25-45 depending on size of apartment, rec, Stadionweg 9, T 22560; also Mr and Mrs Kemp, Pagaaistraat 5, T 28963, fully-furnished a/c rooms with kitchenette, US$40, 10-15 mins walk from main shopping centre and public beach at *Bushiri Beach Hotel*.

● **Camping**

Permit needed from police station, on Arnold Schuttrstraat, Oranjestad, who will advise on locations. It can take 10 days to get a permit and you must have a local address (ie hotel room). The permit costs one Afl4 stamp and it appears you can camp anywhere.

● **Where To Eat**

With few exceptions, meals on Aruba are expensive and generally of the beef-and-seafood variety, but you can get some excellent food. Service charge on food and drinks is 15% at the hotels but at other places varies from 10% to 15%. Most tourists are on MAP at the hotels, many of which have a choice of formal or informal restaurants. Good wine is often difficult to find and always check that you get what you ordered, the waiter may not know that there is a difference between French and Californian wines which bear the same name.

For Aruban specialities, *Gasparito*, Gasparito 3, T 67044, Aruban and seafood, open daily 1800-2300, Art Gallery attached; *Mamas & Papas*, Dakota Shopping Centre, T 26537, open 1200-1400; *Mi Cushina*, Noord Cura Cabai 24, T 48335, Aruban and seafood, open 1200-1400, 1800-2200, closed Thur, rec, on road to San Nicolas, about 1 mile from San Nicolas; *Brisas del Mar*, Savaneta 222A, T 47718, seafood specialities, right on the sea, cool and airy, rec, reasonable prices, open 1200-1430, 1830-2200; *La Nueva Marina Pirata*, seafood and Aruban dishes at Spanish Lagoon, T 47150, open 1800-2300, Sun 1200-2300, closed Tues, follow the main road to

San Nicolas, turn right at *Drive Inn*. The hotels have some very good gourmet restaurants, but outside the hotels the best French restaurant is *Chez Mathilde*, Havenstraat 23, T 34968, open for lunch and dinner, expect to pay over US$25pp; *Boonoonoonoos*, Wilhelminastraat 18A, T 31888, open 1800-2300, has French and Caribbean specialities and the average price is around US$15; *Chalet Suisse*, J E Irausquin Blvd 246, T 75054, between low rise and high rise hotels, beef from New York, try the chocolate fondue, open Mon-Sat, 1800-2230, reservations advised. For US prime steak and seafood, *Cattle Baron*, L G Smith Blvd 228, T 22977, open 1200-1500, 1800-2400; *Twinkle Bone's*, Turibana Plaza, Noord 124, open 1800-2300, prices around US$18. Several Argentine restaurants serving steak, seafood and Argentine specialities, *El Gaucho*, Wilhelminastraat 80, T 23677, open 1130-1430, 1800-2300; *Buenos Aires*, Noord 41, T 27913, open 1800-2300; and *La Cabana Argentina*, Oude Schoolstraat 84, T 27913, open 1800-2400. *The Steamboat Buffet and Deli*, opposite the *Hyatt* has a good brunch buffet, 0600-1200, dinner buffet, 1800-2300, open 24hrs, no reservations, T 66700; *Qué Pasa?* is a good, cheap and intimate restaurant in the centre of Oranjestad.

Lots of Chinese restaurants, including the highly rec *Kowloon*, Emmastraat 11, T 24950, open 1100-2230, regional specialities; *Dragon Phoenix*, Havenstraat 31, T 21928, open 1100-2300; *Far East Restaurant*, Havenstraat 25, T 21349, good food, roast pork dish, rec; and *Astoria*, Crijnsenstraat 6, T 45132, open 0800-2100, indoor and outdoor dining, low prices; in the Harbourtown shopping centre there is the *Japanese & Thai Dynasty*, T 36288, open 1200-1430, 1800-2330, highly rec but rather expensive. *Warung Djawa*, Wilhelminastraat 2, T 34888, serves Indonesian and Surinamese food, open Mon-Fri, 1130-1400 for weekday rijstafel buffet lunch, and Wed-Mon 1800-2300, all you can eat, many recs; *Surindo Snackbar*, Zoutmanstraat 3, T 32040, has Indonesian snacks, 0800-2200, closed Tues nights.

There are plenty of Italian restaurants to choose from, *Cosa Nostra*, is on Scheopstraat 20, T 33872, pizza, salads and other Italian dishes, open Mon-Fri 1200-0300, Sat 1700-0100; *La Paloma*, Noord 39, T 74611, open 1800-2400, Mon-Fri, closed Tues, Northern Italian and seafood; *Porto Bello*, Harbourtown, T 35966, open 1130-2330, good for a cheap,

light meal of pasta or pizza, specializes in huge ice creams; *Pizza Pub*, L G Smith Blvd 54, T T 29061, open daily around the clock, 24 hour delivery service. At the Alhambra Bazaar, *Roseland Buffet*, a good buffet meal for US$11, they also serve good pizzas (munchies) at a reasonable price. The *New York Deli*, Alhambra Bazaar, serves soup and oversized sandwiches, open 0800-0200; *Charlie's Bar*, Zeppenfeldtstraat 56, San Nicholas, T 45086, is also good for Aruban light meals, open 1200-2130, bar until 2200. *Café The Paddock* on L G Smith Blvd near *Wendy's* has outside seating. Amstel on draught and the *daghap* (dish of the day) for Afl 14.50; *The Silver Skate*, Caya G F Croes 42, is a *broodjeszaak* (sandwich shop) with imported Dutch cheese, chocolate milk, draught Amstel and bottled Grolsch beer, all at reasonable prices. There is a wide array of fast food outlets, including *Burger King*, *Kentucky Fried Chicken*, *McDonalds*, *Wendy's*, *Taco Bell*, *Dunkin Donuts*, *Subway* and *Domino Pizza*. For night owls in need of food the white trucks (mobile restaurants) serve local food and snacks from 2100- 0500 at around US$5, located at Wilhelmina Park, the Post Office and the Courthouse.

● **Entertainment**

The major attraction is gambling and there are many casinos on the island. Hotels must have 300 rooms before they can build one; those that do usually start at 1000 and operate 2 shifts. Their open air bars close around that time. Arubans are allowed in to casinos only 4 times a month. Some casinos also offer dancing and live bands. The place to be for a disco night out is *Visage*, next to the *Pizza Pub* at L G Smith Blvd 54. Other discothèques include *Blue Wave* on Shellstraat, T 38856; *Chesterfield Night Club*, Zeppenfeldtstraat 57, San Nicolas, T 45109; *Club L'Atmosphère*, L G Smith Blvd 152A, T 36836; *Club Nouveau*, Wilhelminastraat 7, T 24544; *Exit Nightclub*, Caya G F (Betico) Croes 152, T 33839; *Isla de Oro*, Pos Chiquito; *Surfside Beach Club*, across the road from *Talk of the Town*, T 23380. *The Plaza* at the Harbour Town Shopping Centre has a nice terrace and you can get a good, reasonably priced meal there. The *Coca Plum* on Caya Betico Croes serves a good meal and refreshing fruit juices on a terrace.

● **Shopping**

A wide range of luxury items are imported from all over the world for re-sale to visitors at cut rate prices. Liquor rates are good, but prices for jewellery, silverware and crystal are only slightly lower than US or UK prices. There is no sales tax. There are also local handicrafts such as pottery and art work, try Artesanía Arubiano, on L G Smith Blvd 178, opposite *Tamarijn Hotel*, or ask the Institute of Culture, T 22185, or the Aruba Tourism Authority, T 23777, for more information.

● **Bookshops**

Van Dorp in Caya G F (Betico) Croes is the main town centre bookshop. The light and airy Captains Log in the new Harbour Town development has a few books and reading material but is mostly souvenirs. Many bookshops in the hotels have some paperbacks.

● **Banks**

Algemene Bank Nederland NV, Caya G F (Betico) Croes 89, T 21515, F 21856, also a branch on van Zeppen Feldstraat, San Nicolas and at the Port of Call shopping centre (close to the harbour where the cruise ships come in) on L G Smith Blvd. Aruba Bank NV, Caya G F (Betico) Croes 41, T 21550, F 29152, and at L G Smith Blvd 108, T 31318; Banco di Caribe NV, L G Smith Blvd 90-92, T 32168, F 34222; Caribbean Mercantile Bank NV, Caya G F (Betico) Croes 53, T 23118, F 24373; Interbank, Caya G F (Betico) Croes 38, T 31080, F 24058; First National Bank, Caya G F (Betico) Croes 67, T 33221, F 21756. American Express representative for refunds, exchange or replacement of cheques or cards is SEL Maduro & Sons, Rockefellerstraat 1, T 23888, open Mon-Fri 0800-1200, 1300-1700. Aruba Bank, Caribbean Mercantile Bank and Interbank are Visa/Mastercard representatives with cash advance.

● **Currency**

Aruba has its own currency, the Aruban florin, not to be confused with the Antillean guilder, which is not accepted in shops and can only be exchanged at banks. The exchange rate is Afl1.77=US$1, but shops' exchange rate is Afl1.80. US dollars and credit cards are widely accepted and the Venezuelan bolívar is also used.

● **Health**

All the major hotels have a doctor on call. There is a well-equipped, 280-bed hospital (Dr Horacio Oduber Hospital, L G Smith Blvd, T 74300) near the main hotel area with modern facilities and well-qualified surgeons and dentists. The emergency telephone number for the Ambulance and Fire Department is 115. Also for ambulance in Oranjestad, T 21234 and in San Nicolas, T 45050. Drinking water is distilled from sea water and consequently is safe. The main health hazard for the visitor is over-exposure to the sun. Be very careful from 1100-1430, and use plenty of high factor suntan lotion.

● **Climate**

Aruba is out of the hurricane belt and the climate is dry. The hottest months are August-October and the coolest are December-February, but the temperature rarely goes over 90°F or below 80°F. A cooling trade wind can make the temperature deceptive. Average rainfall is 20 inches a year, falling in short showers during October-December.

● **Laundromat**

Wash 'n Dry Laundromat, Turibana Plaza, Noord; Hop Long Laundromat, Grensweg 7, San Nicolas.

● **Clothing**

Swim suits are not permitted in the shopping area. Most casinos require men to wear jackets and smart clothes are expected at expensive restaurants, otherwise casual summer clothes worn all year.

● **Hours Of Business**

Banks are open 0800-1200, 1330-1530, Mon-Fri, although some banks remain open during lunch. Shops are open 0800-1830, Mon-Sat, although some shut for lunch. Some shops open on Sun or holidays when cruise ships are in port. Late night shopping at the Alhambra Bazaar 1700-2400.

● **National Holidays**

New Year's Day, Carnival Monday (beginning of February), Flag Day (18 March), Good Friday, Easter Monday, Queen's Birthday (30 April), Labour Day (1 May), Ascension Day (May), Christmas Day, Boxing Day.

● **Time Zone**

Atlantic Standard Time, 4 hrs behind GMT, 1 ahead of EST.

● **Telecommunications**

Modern telephone services with direct dialling are available. Aruba's country and area code is 2978. Hotels add a service charge on to international calls. The ITT office is on Boecoetiweg 33, T 21458. Phone calls, telex, telegrams, electronic mailgram and mariphone calls at Servicio di Telecommunicacion di Aruba (Setar), next to the Post Office Building at Irausquinplein, Oranjestad. There are

Teleshops in Oranjestad (Leoplein) and San Nicolas (Post Office), from where you can make international calls. The Post Office at J E Irausquinplein is open 0730-1200, 1300-1630. Postal rates to the USA, Canada and the Netherlands are Afl 0.40, for letters, and Afl0.60, for post cards. The local television station is Tele-Aruba, but US programmes are also received.

● **Religion**

A wide range of churches is represented in Aruba, including Catholic, Jewish and Protestant. There are Methodists, Baha'i, Baptists, Church of Christ, Evangelical, Jehovah's Witnesses and 7th Day Adventists. Check at your hotel for the times of services and the language in which they are conducted.

● **Electric Current**

110 volts, 60 cycles AC.

● **Consulates**

Brazil: E Pory Ierlandstraat 19, T 21994; **Chile:** H de Grootstraat 1, T 21085; **Costa Rica:** Savaneta 235-B, T 47193; **Denmark:** L G Smith Blvd 82, T 24622; **Dominican Republic:** J G Emanstraat 79, T 36928; **Germany:** Scopetstraat 13, T 21767; **Honduras:** Bilderdijkstraat 13, T 21187; **Italy:** Caya G F Betico Croes 7, T 22621; **Liberia:** Windstraat 20, T 21171; **Panama:** Weststraat 15, T 22908; **Peru:** Waterweg 3, T 25355; **Portugal:** Seroe Colorado 73, T 46178; **El Salvador:** H de Grootstraat 1, T 21085; **Spain:** Madurostraat 9, T 23163; **Sweden:** Havenstraat 33, T 21821; **Venezuela:** Adriane Lacle Blvd 8, T 21078.

● **Travel Agents**

Pelican Tours PO Box 1194, T 24739/31228, F 32655, lobby desks in many hotels, also at Pelican Pier, Palm Beach, between *Holiday Inn* and *Playa Linda*, sightseeing trips, cruises, watersports. De Palm Tours, L G Smith Blvd 142, PO Box 656, T 24400, F 23012, also with offices in many hotels, sightseeing tours of the

island and excursions to nearby islands or Venezuela. Their Mar-Lab Biological Tour, US$25 includes a visit to Seroe Colorado, and snorkelling at Boca Grandi. ECO Destination Management, T 26034, for watersports, boating and excursions. Aruba Transfer Tours and Taxi, PO Box 723, L G Smith Blvd 82, T 22116. Julio Maduro, Corvalou Tours, T 21149, specializes in archaeological, geological, architectural, botanical and wildlife tours, a mine of information on anything to do with Aruba, strongly rec. For a combination 6-hour tour with lunch, US$35, call archaeologist E Boerstra, T 41513, or Julio Maduro, or Private Safaris educational tour, T 34869. There are lots of companies offering tours of the island by minibus with a swimming and snorkelling stop at Baby Beach, about US$30 pp.

● **Tourist Office**

L G Smith Boulevard 172, Oranjestad, PO Box 1019, near the harbour, T 23777, F 34702. Also at airport and cruise dock. Staff are friendly and efficient.

USA: 199 Fourteenth Street, N E Suite 1506, Atlanta, GA 30309-3686, T (404) 89 ARUBA, F (404) 873-2193; 2344 Salzedo Street, Miami, Florida 33134-5033, T (305) 567-2720, F (305) 567-2721; 1000 Harbor Blvd, Ground level, Weehawken, N J 07087, T (201) 330-0800, F 330-8758, toll free (800) to ARUBA. **Canada**: 86 Bloor Street West, Suite 204, Toronto, Ontario M5S 1M5, T (416) 975 1950, F (416) 975 1947, toll free 800-268 3042. **Venezuela**: Centro Ciudad Comercial Tamanaco, Torre C, Piso 8, Oficina C-805, Chuao, Caracas, T 959 1256. **Colombia**: Calle 100, No. 8A-49, Torre B, Edificio World Trade Center, Bogotá, T 226 9013, F 226 9038. **The Netherlands**: Amaliastraat 16, 2514 JC, Den Haag, T (70) 3566220, F 3604877. **Germany**: Viktoriastrasse 28, D-6100, Darmstadt, T 6151-23068, F 6151-22854.

ISLANDS OF THE WESTERN CARIBBEAN

CLOSE TO THE CARIBBEAN coast of Central America are several groups of islands which we describe below, from S to N. In most cases they can only be reached by air from the country to which they belong: Panama for the San Blas archipelago, Nicaragua for the Corn Islands and Belize for its Cayes. The exceptions are San Andrés, belonging to Colombia, which is a regular stop-over on flights from Miami or Central America to Colombia, the Bay Islands of Honduras, to which there are direct flights from three US cities, and Cancún and Cozumel, which are Mexican points of entry for flights originating in the USA and for package holidays. Sailors, of course, have greater flexibility in travelling to these islands.

These islands' close geographical and political links with Latin America have not eradicated their Caribbean nature. In fact, the mainland seaboard is invariably distinct from the countries' interior and Pacific regions. A strong English influence persists, the black population is larger, the island atmosphere is often un-Hispanic. Moreover, the San Blas islands, and the Nicaraguan and Honduran Mosquito Coast, are largely indigenous Indian areas. Unlike the Lesser and Greater Antilles, though, these island groups are not part of a chain, so they either retain a stronger sense of individuality, or they look to the mainland for their identity.

In view of the necessity of travelling to these islands via a South or Central American country, selective details on the points of access are given and a detailed Information for Visitors section is provided in each case.

SAN BLAS ISLANDS, PANAMA

The S-shaped isthmus of Panama, 80 km at its narrowest and no more than 193 km at its widest, is one of the great crossroads of the world. Its destiny has been entirely shaped by that fact. To it Panama owes its national existence, the make-up of its population and their distribution: two-fifths of the people are concentrated in the two cities which control the entry and exit of the canal.

The history of Panama is the history of its pass-route; its fate was determined on that day in 1513 when Balboa first glimpsed the Pacific. Panama City was of paramount importance for the Spaniards: it was the focus of conquering expeditions N and S along the Pacific coasts. All trade to and from these Pacific countries passed across the isthmus. Panama City was founded in 1519 after a trail had been discovered between it and the Caribbean. The trail became an established road to accommodate the Spanish traders; it was the route Henry Morgan took when he sacked Panama City in 1671; and it was the "road to hell" for the forty-niners on their way to the Californian goldfields. The goldrush brought a railway to the isthmus, which was superseded by the Panama Canal. On 15 August 1914, the first passage was made, by the ship *Ancón*.

The Canal Area, formerly Zone, is being gradually incorporated into Panamanian jurisdiction; this long process began in 1964, when Panama secured the right to fly its flag in the Zone alongside that of the USA, and is due for completion, with Panamanian operation of the Canal, by 2000.

Alongside this unique development and the vast influx of people that has accompanied it, only three Indian tribes have survived out of the 60 who inhabited the isthmus at the time of the Spanish Conquest. These are the Cuna of the San Blas Islands, the Guaymíes of the W provinces and the Chocóes of Darién.

SAN BLAS ISLANDS

We are concerned here with the San Blas Islands, an archipelago, which has 365 islands ranging in size from tiny ones with a few coconut palms to islands on which hundreds of Cuna Indians live. About 50 are inhabited. The islands vary in distance from the shore from 100m to several kilometres. They lie off the coast E of the Caribbean landfall for the passage of the Panama Canal, which is made at the twin cities of Cristóbal and Colón.

The Cuna are the most sophisticated and politically organized of the country's three major groups. They run the San Blas Territory virtually on their own terms, with internal autonomy and, uniquely among Panama's Indians, send their representative to the National Assembly. They have their own language, but Spanish is widely spoken. The women wear gold nose- and ear-rings, and costumes with unique designs based on local themes, geometric patterns, stylized flora and fauna, and pictorial representations of current events or political propaganda. They are outside the Panamanian tax zone and have negotiated a treaty perpetuating their long-standing trade with small craft from Colombia. Many men work on the mainland, but live on the islands.

Photographers need plenty of small change, as the set price for a Cuna to pose is US$0.25. *Molas* (decorative handsewn appliqué for blouse fronts) are very popular purchases; they cost upwards of US$10 each (also obtainable in many Panama City and Colón shops). You can also try the San Blas perfume, Kantule, similarly available in the city shops.

All Panamanian agencies run trips to El Porvenir, the island where the planes land; from there boats go to other islands, eg Wichub Huala, Nalunega and Corbisky, all close to each other (about 20 mins by boat). There are hotels on the first three. A one-day tour costs US$120 inclusive of food and sightseeing (a recommended agent is Chadwick Travel, at the YMCA building in Balboa, T 52-28-63-29, fluent English spoken). One night at *Hotel Hanay Kantule* (also spelt *Anai Katule*) on Wichub Huala (T 20-0746) costs US$55, bookable at the major Panama hotels (ask for Israel Fernández on arrival at El Porvenir). Other hotels near El Porvenir are *San Blas* on Nalunega Island, 2 daily tours included in the price (T 62-1606/5410) and *Residencial Turístico Yeri* (T 62-3402); both charge US$25 a night. At Narganá (airport) there is a basic hotel (under US$7) and one restaurant, *El Caprichito*, serving good crab dishes. Take your own drinks, because they are expensive on the islands (beer costs US$1). You can go to any island in the San Blas group, just ask to be dropped off by the pilot. The beaches and sea are inviting, but you must arrange when you will be collected and bear in mind that there is no water or food available.

The nearest city on the Caribbean is Colón (population 122,500), the second largest in Panama. It was established in 1852 as the terminus of the railway across the isthmus and was originally called Aspinwall, after one of the founders of the railway. Despite its fine public buildings and well-stocked shops, it has some of the nastiest slums in Latin America, and is generally dirty. There are plans to revitalize and improve the city. There is a curfew in Colón from 2100 to 0500 for all under the age of 18. Cristóbal, Colón's twin city, came into being as the port of entry for the supplies used in building the Canal. The two cities merge into one another almost imperceptibly on Manzanillo Island at the entrance of the Canal; the island has now been connected with the mainland.

There are occasional boats to the San Blas islands from Colón or Portobelo (48 km NE of Colón, 9 hrs to San Blas), but there is no scheduled service and the trip can be rough. One ship that goes from time to time is the *Almirante*, try to find the captain, Figueres Cooper, who charges US$30 for the trip. The port captain's office at Coco Solo may have information on boat departures, T 41-5231, although most boats "are not keen on being landed with potentially stranded gringos".

Isla Grande

Isla Grande is a favourite with international visitors because of its relaxed lifestyle, fishing, scuba diving and snorkelling, windsurfing and dazzling white palm-fringed beaches. The island's 300 black inhabitants make a living from fishing and coconut cultivation, and a powerful French-built lighthouse crowns the small island's N point. There are a number of colourful African-tinged festivals held here throughout the year, particularly on 24 June, 16 July and the pre-Lenten Carnival with *Congos*, part of a slowly enfolding ritual which lasts from Epiphany (6 January) to Easter. Isla Grande is reached by *panga*, US$1, from the car park in La Guaira, a coastal town on a narrow gravel road which runs along the Caribbean shore NE from Portobelo. Portobelo itself, a fascinating historical site (see *Mexico and Central American Handbook*) is 34 km NE of Colón (US$2, 1 hr by bus).

Island Information
● **Where to Stay**
Popular on holidays and dry season weekends,

make reservations in advance, prices often double during high season. *Isla Grande*, T 64-3046, F 64-0646, bungalows scattered along an excellent sandy beach; boat, snorkel and jet ski hire, restaurant, mini zoo (toucans, crocodiles, monkeys, etc), the most expensive, US$50-70, reduced tariffs on weekdays, rec; *Posada Villa Ensueño*, T 68-2926/1445, US$30-40, good café/bar; *La Cholita*, similar prices; *Candy Rose*; *Cabañas Jackson*, T 41-6472, US$20-30, many huts/bungalows available; *Posada Guayaco*. All have bars and simple restaurants, *Candy Rose* serves drinks with a special octopus cooked in coconut milk.

The Panama Canal

It would be unusual, if in Panama, not to visit the Canal. Since the regular excursions to San Blas leave from Panama City's Paitilla airport, it would be simplest to travel through the Canal from there. Eco-Tours de Panamá (T 36-3675-3076, F 36-3550) offer a day-long full transit through the canal on a luxury yacht for US$109. Agencia Giscomes, T 64-0111, also offers trips through the canal every 2nd and 4th Saturday of the month. Partial boat trips are also offered on the canal, through Miraflores locks as for Pedro Miguel locks. They go about twice monthly (eg Argo Tours, T 28-4348, F 28-1234, every other Saturday from pier 17, Balboa, US$40, children under 12 US$20, refreshments and snacks on sale); enquire at any travel agent. Otherwise, since the Panama City-Colón train journey is no longer running (and does not afford full views when it does), travellers are advised to take a bus to the Miraflores Locks (open 0900-1700, best between 0600-1000 for photographs and 1430-1800 for viewing, the sun is against you in the afternoon) if you want to see shipping. The viewing gallery is free. A detailed model of the canal is here and there is also a free slide show given throughout the day, with explanations in English. About 250m past the entrance to the Locks is a road (left) to the filtration plant and observatory, behind which is a picnic area and viewing point. Or-

ange bus from Panama City to Miraflores Locks leaves from the bus station next to Plaza 5 de Mayo (direction Paraíso or Gamboa), 15 mins, US$0.35. Ask the driver to let you off at the stop for "Esclusas de Miraflores", from where it's a 10-min walk to the Locks. Another good way to see the Panama Canal area is to rent a car.

The very best way to see the Canal, though, is by boat. It is possible to traverse it as a linehandler (no experience necessary) on a yacht; the journey takes 2 days. Note that more boats pass through from N to S than the other way around. Yachts are allowed into the canal on Tuesday and Thursday only. The yacht owners need four linehandlers. Go a couple of days in advance to the Panama Canal Yacht Club in Colón, or the Yacht Clubs in Cristóbal (downstairs from the building next to the wharf), or in Balboa (the port with the Canal Administration at the Pacific end), and ask people hanging around the bar. The Balboa Club offers good daily lunch special; a good place to watch canal traffic. 50m right of the Club is a small white booth which has a list of boat departures for the next day; ask here if you can go to the dock and take the motor boat which shuttles out to yachts preparing for passage. Ask to speak to captains from the launch and see if they'll let you "transit". At Cristóbal you can approach boats directly at their moorings. They have to book their passage through the canal 48 hrs in advance. However, don't expect too much, at times less than one private boat a week goes through the Canal.

PANAMA : FACT FILE

Geographic

Land area	75,517 sq km
forested	43.9%
pastures	20.4%
cultivated	7.6%

Demographic

Population (1992)	2,515,000
annual growth rate (1987-92)	2.0%
urban	52.9%
rural	47.1%
density	33.3 per sq km
Religious affiliation	
Roman Catholic	84.0%
Birth rate per 1,000 (1991)	26.0
	(world av 26.4)
Death rate per 1,000 (1991)	
	(world av 9.2)

Education and Health

Life expectancy at birth,	
male	72.0 years
female	76.0 years
Infant mortality rate	
per 1,000 live births (1991)	21.0
Physicians (1990)	1 per 880 persons
Hospital beds	1 per 330 persons
Calorie intake as %	
of FAO requirement	110%
Population age 25 and over	
with no formal schooling	17.4%
Literate males (over 15)	88.1%
Literate females (over 15)	88.2%

Economic

GNP (1990 market prices)	US$4,414mn
GNP per capita	US$1,830
Public external debt (1990)	US$3,758mn
Tourism receipts (1990)	US$167mn
Inflation (annual av 1986-91)	5.9%
Radio	1 per 5.5 persons
Television	1 per 12 persons
Telephone	1 per 9.4 persons

Employment

Population economically active (1989)	
	820,042
Unemployment rate (1992)	28.0%
% of labour force in	
agriculture	25.4
manufacturing	9.8
construction	3.9
National Police force	11,000

Source *Encyclopaedia Britannica*

INFORMATION FOR VISITORS

● Documents

Visitors must have a passport, together with a tourist card (issued for 30 days and renewable for another 60 in the Immigration Office, Panama City, see below) or a visa (issued for 30 days, extendable to 90 days in Panama). Tourist cards are available at borders, from Panamanian consulates, Ticabus or airlines. To enter Panama you must have an onward flight ticket, travel agent confirmation of same, or, if entering by land, sufficient funds to cover your stay (US$550; US$300 may be asked for if you have an onward ticket). "Sufficient funds" do not have to be in cash; traveller's cheques or credit card accepted. Once in Panama, you cannot get a refund for an onward flight ticket unless you have another exit ticket. Copa tickets can be refunded at any office in any country (in the currency of that country). **Customs at Paso Canoas**, at the border with Costa Rica, have been known to run out of tourist cards. If not entering Panama at the main entry points (Tocumen airport, Paso Canoas), expect more complicated arrangements.

Neither visas nor tourist cards are required by nationals of Austria, Costa Rica, Finland, Germany, Honduras, Spain, Switzerland and the UK.

Citizens of the following countries need a visa which is free: USA, The Netherlands, Norway, Denmark, Colombia and Mexico. Before visiting Panama it is advisable to enquire at a Panamanian consulate whether you need a visa stamped in your passport, or whether a tourist card will suffice. Citizens of the United States, for example, may buy a tourist card at a border for US$5 instead of a visa. A visa costing the local equivalent of £10 (US$10 in Central American capitals) must be obtained by citizens of Australia, New Zealand, Canada, Japan, France, Italy, Sweden, Israel, El Salvador, Dominican Republic. Visas for citizens of many African, Eastern European and Asian countries require authorization from Panama, which takes 3 days (this includes Hong Kong, India, Poland, the former Soviet republics, and also Cuba and South Africa).

Immigration in Panama City is at Av Cuba (2 Sur) y Calle 28E, T 25-8925 (take 2 passport photos, exit ticket and a letter explaining why you wish to extend your visit; sufficient funds may be asked for); the Ministerio de Hacienda y Tesoro (for exit permits, if required) is at Calles 35 y 36, entre Avs Perú y Cuba, T 27-4879.

● **How To Get There By Air**

From London: British Airways, American, Delta, Continental or Virgin Atlantic to Miami, then by American, United, Copa, or LAB to Panama City. From elsewhere in North America: New York City, Continental via Houston, or American or United, change planes in Miami; from Los Angeles, Aviateca (4 stops), Continental (via Houston), American (via Miami) or Lacsa (via San José); from San Francisco, Taca and Continental; from Houston, Continental, Taca. From Mexico, Aeroperú, Copa, or connections with Lacsa via San José, Taca via San Salvador, or American via Miami. From Central America, Copa, Lacsa (to San José, to connect with its Central American network and Los Angeles/Mexico/Miami/New Orleans/ San Juan-Puerto Rico routes), Taca (including to Belize) and Nica. There are no direct flights to Tegucigalpa, only Lacsa with connection in San José or Taca in San Salvador, but Copa flies direct to San Pedro Sula. Copa also flies to Kingston and Santo Domingo. From South America, Lacsa (Barranquilla, Caracas, Lima, Santiago de Chile), Copa (Barranquilla, Bogotá, Cartagena, Cali, Medellín, Quito, Guayaquil). Note that one-way tickets are not available from Colombia to Panama, on SAM, or Copa, but a refund on an unused return portion is possible, less 17% taxes, on SAM. To Bogotá direct with Avianca and Copa, be at airport very early because it can leave before time; also to Cali with Avianca. To Guayaquil, Continental (also to Quito), Aerolíneas Argentinas and AeroPerú. Cubana flies direct to Havana on Thur, from Havana on Wed. Other carriers are Avianca, Servivensa, Lloyd Aéreo Boliviano, SAM, Aerolíneas Argentinas, AeroPerú. From Europe, Iberia (Madrid via Santo Domingo), KLM (from Amsterdam via Curaçao), Aeroflot from Moscow and Shannon.

● **Taxes**

An airport tax of US$20 has to be paid by all passengers. There is a 5.5% tax on air tickets purchased in Panama.

● **Airport**

Tocumen, 27 km from Panama City. Taxi fares to/from city about US$20, colectivo US$8 pp (if staying for only a couple of days, it is cheaper to rent a car at the airport). There is a 24-hr left-luggage office near the Avis car rental desk

for US$1 per article per day (worth it, since theft in the departure lounge is common). There are duty-free shops at the airport but more expensive than those downtown.

The national airport is at La Paitilla, on the N side of Punta Paitilla, near *Hotel Marriott* and Atlapa Convention Centre, Panama City (take a number 2 bus going to Boca La Caja, from Av Balboa at Calle 40, US$0.30).

● **Customs**

Even if you only change planes in Panama you must have the necessary papers for the airport officials. Cameras, binoculars, etc, 500 cigarettes or 500 grams of tobacco and 3 bottles of alcoholic drinks for personal use are taken in free. The Panamanian Customs are strict; drugs without a doctor's prescription are confiscated. **NB**: Passengers leaving Panama by land are *not* entitled to any duty-free goods, which are delivered only to ships and aircraft.

● **Shipping Services**

From Panama there are frequent shipping services with the principal European and North American ports; with the Far East, New Zealand, and Australia, with both the E and W coast ports of South America and Central America, regularly with some, irregularly with others. For full information on shipping lines which carry passengers, contact Strand Cruise and Travel Centre, Charing Cross Shopping Concourse, The Strand, London WC2N 4HZ, T 071-836 6363, F 071-497 0078.

● **Internal Flights To San Blas Islands**

The flights arranged by agencies leave Paitilla airport between 0600 and 0630, returning next day between 0700 and 0730 Mon to Sat. If you can collect 9 people to fill the plane, you can leave at 0800 and return next day at 1600. Sun flights must be booked privately. The airline serving the islands are Transpasa (T 26-0932 or 26-0843), with single-engine, 6-seater Cessnas, and Ansa (T 26-7891 or 26-6881) with twin-engine Islanders. Both companies fly to any of the 20 airports in San Blas province (mainland and islands). A one-way fare to El Porvenir island is US$25 (including 5% tax), to Puerto Obaldía on the mainland US$40. Passports must be taken on these flights since every so often someone tries to hijack a flight to Colombia.

There are local flights to most parts of Panama by the national airlines Ansa (T 26-7891, F 26-4070), Aeroperlas (T 69-4555, F 23-0606), Alas Chiricanas (T 64-7759, F 64-

7190), Parsa (T 26-3803, F 26-3422), Aerotaxi (T64-8644), and others.

● **Rail**

No passenger trains run between Panama City and Colón since the track, and especially the rolling stock, are in a very poor state. For information, T 52-7720.

● **Local Transport**

Taxis have no meters; charges are according to how many "zones" in town are traversed (about US$1 per zone): ask driver to show you the zone map and settle fare beforehand if you can. Note that there are large taxis (*grandes*) and cheaper small ones (*chicos*). Taxis out of town charge US$10 per hour for tours to Miraflores locks and the Canal Area.

There are numerous small town buses nicknamed *chivas* (goats), gradually being replaced. These charge US$0.05 per zone, are not very comfortable but are very colourful, and run along the major streets of the capital. The number of fingers held up by the conductor indicates the fare in 5-cents, or *reales* (eg 3 fingers = 15 cents). Travel into the suburbs costs more. Yell "*parada*" to stop the bus.

Buses to all Canal Area destinations (Balboa, Miraflores, Paraíso, Kobbe, etc) leave from Canal Area bus station (SACA), on Plaza 5 de Mayo. Panamá-Colón under 2 hrs, US$2.20, from Calle 26 Oeste y Av Central in Panamá City, opposite San Miguel church, 2 blocks N of Plaza 5 de Mayo.

● **Car Rental**

At the airport (Hertz—T 38-4081, Avis—T 38-4069, National—T 38-4144; also International, Budget and Dollar). Other offices in El Cangrejo: Avis, Calle 55, T 64-0722; International, Calle 55, T 64-4540; Barriga, Edif Wonaga 1 B, Calle D, T 69-0221; Gold, Calle 55, T 64-1711. Hertz, Vía España 130, T 64-1729; Budget T 63-8777; Discount, T 23-6111. Rates vary from company to company and from model to model: on average they start at US$24/day for a small saloon to US$65 for 4WD jeep, free mileage, insurance US$8/day, 5% tax, US$500 deposit (can be paid by credit card), minimum age 23, home driver's licence acceptable. In general 4WDs must be booked 5 days in advance.

● **Where To Stay**

Some information on hotels on the San Blas islands is given above.

In Panama City there are many hotels to choose from in all price ranges. For instance:

El Marriott Caesar Park, Vía Israel y Calle 17, T 26-4077, F 26-4262, US$132 for a double room; *Plaza Paitilla Inn* (former *Holiday Inn*), Punta Paitilla, PO Box 1807, T 69-1122, F 23-1470, US$99d, US$95s (not inc tax), cheaper weekends rates available, restaurant, café, nightclub, swimming pool; a number on Vía España: *El Panamá*, Vía España y Calle 55, T 69-5000, F 69-5990, US$125, vast rooms, Art Deco style, charming; *Riande Continental*, Vía España, T 63-9999, F 69-4599, US$99d; *Europa*, Vía España y Calle 42, T 63-6911, F 63-6749, US$45d; *California*, Vía España y Calle 43, T 63-7844, US$27.50, a/c, TV, restaurant (breakfast US$1.75); *Gran Hotel Soloy*, Av Perú, T 27-1133, F 27-0884, US$35d; nearby are *Acapulco*, Calle 30 Este, T 25-3832, between Avs Perú and Cuba, US$20, a/c, clean, comfortable, TV, private bath, restaurant, conveniently located, rec; *Aramo*, Vía Brasil y Abel Bravo, T 69-0174, F 69-2406, US$55, a/c, restaurant; around corner from *Soloy*, *Residencia Turístico Volcán*, Calle 29, between Avs Perú y Cuba, T 25-5263, with shower, under US$20, fan, a/c extra, clean. *Central*, Plaza Catedral (T 62-8044), US$12 with bath, under US$10 with shared bath, safe motorcycle parking, reasonably clean and friendly, rooms on plaza have balcony, run down; *Ideal*, Calle 17 just off Av Central, T 62-2400, US$18, good location between Plazas Santa Ana and 5 de Mayo.

Cheaper accommodation can be found in *pensiones*: *Colonial*, Plaza Bolívar y Calle 4, Casco Viejo, T 62-3858, with bath, some balconies overlooking plaza, faded but enjoyable; *Las Palmeras*, Av Cuba between Calles 38-39, T 25-0811, US$10-12, safe, clean; *Vásquez*, Av A, 2-47, opp Santo Domingo, T 28-8453, quiet, friendly, nice rooms, one or two with view of ocean and sand, US$9; *Herrera*, Plaza Herrera y Calle 9, T 28-8994, variety of prices up to US$12, some with a/c more expensive, TV, fridge, nice location, restaurant; *Residencial Primavera*, Av Cuba y Calle 42, on edge of Bella Vista, 1 block E of Av España, T 25-1195, with bath and fan, quiet residential area; many more, for example on Av México.

In Colón, the best is *Washington*, Av del Frente final, T 41-1870, Art Deco style, a guarded enclave, followed by the *Carlton*, Calle 10 y Av Meléndez, T 45-0717, *Andros*, Av Herrera, between Calles 9 and 10, T 41-0477/41-7923, US$15-20, safe, clean, fan or a/c, bath, TV, good; at the cheaper end, *Pensión Plaza*, Av Central, T 41-3216, is clean, in the US$10-15 range.

NB There is a 10% tax on all hotel prices. All hotels are a/c (but not necessarily _pensiones_). It may not be easy to find accommodation just before Christmas, as Central Americans tend to invade the capital to do their shopping, nor during Carnival. In the higher parts of Panama City, water shortages are common in summer, and electricity cuts are common in late summer everywhere.

● **Camping**

The Panamanian Embassy in London advises that it is not safe for female travellers to camp in Panama. There are no official sites but it is possible to camp on some beaches or, if in great need (they agree, but don't like it much) in the Balboa Yacht Club car park. Outside Panama City, camping requires prior arrangement.

● **What To Eat**

Best hors d'oeuvre is _carimañola_, cooked mashed yuca wrapped round a savoury filling of chopped seasoned fried pork and fried a golden brown. The traditional stew, _sancocho_, made from chicken, yuca, dasheen, cutup corn on the cob, plantain, potatoes, onions, flavoured with salt, pepper and coriander. _Ropa vieja_, shredded beef mixed with fried onions, garlic, tomatoes and green peppers and served with white rice, baked plantain or fried yuca. _Sopa borracha_, a rich sponge cake soaked in rum and garnished with raisins and prunes marinated in sherry. Panama is famous for its seafood: lobsters, corvina, shrimp, tuna, etc. Piquant _ceviche_ is usually corvina or white fish seasoned with tiny red and yellow peppers, thin slices of onion and marinated in lemon juice; it is served very cold and has a bite. _Arroz con coco y tití_ is rice with coconut and tiny dried shrimp. Plain coconut rice is also delicious. For low budget try _comida corriente_ or _del día_ (US$1.50 or so). Corn (maize) is eaten in various forms, depending on season, eg _tamales_ (or _bollos_), made of corn meal mash filled with cooked chicken or pork, olives and prunes; or _empanadas_, toothsome meat pies fried crisp. Plantain, used as a vegetable, appears in various forms. A fine dessert is made from green plantain flour served with coconut cream. Other desserts are _arroz con cacao_, chocolate rice pudding; _buñuelos de viento_, a puffy fritter served with syrup; _sopa de gloria_, sponge cake soaked in cooked cream mixture with rum added; _guanábana_ ice cream is made from sweet ripe soursop.

● **Tipping**

At hotels, restaurants: 10% of bill. Porters, 15 cents per item, but US$1 expected at the airport. Cloakroom, 25 cents. Hairdressers, 25 cents. Cinema usherettes, nothing. Taxi drivers don't expect tips; rates should be arranged before the trip.

● **Festivals**

The _fiestas_ in the towns are well worth seeing. That of Panama City at Carnival time, held on the 4 days before Ash Wednesday, is the best. During carnival women who can afford it wear the _pollera_ dress, with its "infinity of diminutive gathers and its sweeping skirt finely embroidered", a shawl folded across the shoulders, satin slippers, tinkling pearl hair ornaments in spirited shapes and colours. The men wear a _montuno_ outfit: native straw hats, embroidered blouses and trousers sometimes to below the knee only, and carry the _chácara_, or small purse. There is also a splendid local Carnival at Las Tablas, W of Panama City.

At the Holy Week ceremonies at Villa de Los Santos the farces and acrobatics of the big devils – with their debates and trials in which the main devil accuses and an angel defends the soul – the dance of the "dirty little devils" and the dancing drama of the Montezumas are all notable. The ceremonies at Pesé (near Chitré) are famous all over Panama. At Portobelo, near Colón, there is a procession of little boats in the canals of the city and the ritual of the _congos_ from Epiphany to Easter.

There are, too, the folk-tunes and dances. The music is cheerful, combining the rhythms of Africa with the melodic tones and dancesteps of Andalucía, to which certain characteristics of the Indian pentatonic scale have been added. The _tamborito_ is the national dance. Couples dance separately and the song – which is sung by the women only, just as the song part of the _mejorana_ or _socavón_ is exclusively for male voices – is accompanied by the clapping of the audience and 3 kinds of regional drums. The _mejorana_ is danced to the music of native guitars and in the interior are often heard the laments known as the _gallo_ (rooster), _gallina_ (hen), _zapatero_ (shoemaker), or _mesano_. Two other dances commonly seen at _fiestas_ are the _punto_, with its promenades and foot tapping, and the _cumbia_, of African origin, in which the dancers carry lighted candles and strut high.

● **Currency**

Panama is one of the few countries in the world

which issues no paper money; US banknotes are used exclusively, being called balboas instead of dollars. There are "silver" coins of 50c (called a *peso*), 25c, 10c, nickel of 5c (called a *real*) and copper of 1c. All the "silver" money is used interchangeably with US currency; each coin is the same size and material as the US coin of equivalent value. You can take in or out any amount of foreign or Panamanian currency. Visa ATMs are available at branches of Telered (T 001-800-111-0016 if card is lost or stolen). Mastercard/Cirrus ATMs are available at 24 locations at branches of Chase Manhattan and Banco del Istmo.

● **Security**

Panama City and Colón are not safe cities, particularly after dark. While most Panamanians are friendly and helpful, it is wise to take full precautions to protect your valuables.

● **Health**

No particular precautions, water in Panama City and Colón is safe to drink.

● **Climate**

The Isthmus is only 9° N of the equator, but prevailing winds reduce the discomfort, especially in the cool evenings of the dry season (January-April), though the humidity is high (the wet season is called *invierno* – winter, the dry *verano* – summer). Heavy rain falls sometimes in October and November.

The rate of deforestation in Panama has accelerated in the 1980s and early 1990s. Although more of the country is forested than any other Central American republic except Belize, the loss of forest in 1990 was estimated at 220,000 acres, against felling of up to 154,000 acres per year between 1985 and 1989. Deforestation is affecting the pattern of rainfall upon which depend not only the birds (over 800 species), animals, insects and plants, but also the Panama Canal. A further threat to the Canal is silting as a result of soil erosion.

● **Clothing**

Lightweight tropical clothes for men, light cotton or linen dresses or trousers for women.

● **Hours Of Business**

Government departments, 0800-1200, 1230-1630 (Mon to Fri). Banks: open and close at different times, but are usually open all morning, but not on Sat. Shops and most private enterprises: 0700 or 0800-1200 and 1400-1800 or 1900 every day, including Sat.

● **Public Holidays**

New Year's Day, National Mourning (9 January), Carnival (Shrove Tuesday), Good Friday, Labour Day (1 May: Republic), 15 August (Panama City only), National Revolution Day (11 October), National Anthem Day (1 November), All Souls (2 November), Independence Day (3 November), Flag Day (4 November), Independence Day (5 November: Colón only), First Call of Independence (10 November), Independence from Spain (28 November), Mothers' Day (8 December), Christmas Day. Many others are added at short notice.

● **Time Zone**

Eastern Standard Time, 5 hrs behind GMT.

● **Embassies And Consulates**

Costa Rican, Calle Gilberto Ortega 7, Edif Miramar, T 64-2980 (open 0800-1330); **Nicaraguan**, Av Federico Boyd y Calle 50, T 23-0981 (0900-1300, 1500-1800); **Salvadorean**, Vía España, Edif Citibank, piso 4, T 23-3020, (0900-1300); **Guatemalan**, Calle 55, El Congrejo, Condominio Abir, piso 6, T 69-3475, open 0800-1300; **Honduran**, Av Justo Arosemena y Calle 31, Edif Tapia, piso 2, T 25-8200, (0900-1400); **Mexican**, Ed Bank of America, piso 5, Calle 50 y 53, T 63-5021 (0830-1300); **Venezuelan**, Banco Unión Building, Av Samuel Lewis, T 69-1244 (0830-1230), visa takes 24 hrs; **Colombian**, Calle M M Icaza 12, Edif Grobman, 6th floor, T 64-9266, open 0800-1300; the **Chilean** and **Ecuadorean** embassies are housed in the same building, T 23-8488 and 64-7820 respectively, neither is open in pm.

US, Av Balboa and 40, Edif Macondo, piso 3, PO Box 6959 (Zona 5), T 27-1777, F 27-1964 (0800- 1700); **Canadian**, Calle MM Icaza, Ed Aeroperú, piso 5, T 64-7014 (0800-1100). **British**, Torre Swiss Bank, Calle 53, Zona 1, T 69-0866, F (507) 230730, Apartado 889 (0800-1200); **French**, Plaza Francia, T 28-7835 (0830-1230); **German**, Edif Bank of America, Calle 50 y 53, T 63-7733 (0900-1200); **Netherlands**, Altos de Algemene Bank, Calle MM Icaza, 4, T 64-7257 (0830-1300, 1400-1630); **Swedish**, Vía José Agustín Arango/Juan Díaz, T 33-5883 (0900-1200, 1400-1600); **Swiss**, Av Samuel Lewis y Calle Gerardo Ortega, Ed Banco Central Cancellería, piso 4, T 64-9731, PO Box 499 (Zona 9A), open 0845-1145; **Italian**, Calle 1, Parque Lefevre 42, T 26-3111, open 0900-1200; **Danish**, Calle Ricardo Arias, Ed Ritz Plaza, piso 2, T 63-5872, open 0800- 1200, 1330-1630; **Spanish**, entre Av Cuba y Av Perú, Calle 33A, T 27-5122 (0900-1300); **Norwegian**, Av Justo Arosemena y Calle 35, T 25-8217 (0900-1300, 1400-1630). **Japanese**, Calle 50 y 61, Ed Don Camilo, T 63-6155 (0830-1200, 1400-1700); **Israeli Embassy**, Ed Grobman, Calle MM Icaza, 5th floor, PO Box 6357, T 64-8022/8257.

● **Weights And Measures**
Both metric and the US system of weights and measures are used.

● **Electric Current**
In modern homes and hotels, 220 volts. Otherwise 110 volt 3 phase, 60 cycles AC.

● **Foreign Postage**
Great care should be taken to address all mail as "Republic of Panama" or "RP", otherwise it is returned to sender. Air mail takes 3-10 days, sea mail 3-5 weeks from Britain. Rates (examples) for air mail (up to 15 grams) are as follows: Central, North and South America and Caribbean, 30c; Europe, 37c up to 10 grams, 5c for every extra 5 grams; Africa, Asia, Oceania, 44c; all air letters require an extra 2c stamp. Parcels to Europe can only be sent from the post office in the El Dorado shopping centre in Panama City (bus from Calle 12 to Tumba Muerta).

● **Telecommunications**
Telex is available at the airport, the cable companies and many hotels. Rate for a 3-min call to Britain is US$14.40, and US$4.80 for each minute more. Telephone calls can be made between the UK and Panama any time, day or night. Collect calls are possible, 3 min minimum charge: US$10 station to station, but person to person, US$16 on weekdays, US$12 on Sun plus tax of US$1 per call. To the USA the charge is US$4 for 3 mins. Phone to Australia US$16 for 3 mins (US$13 on Sun).

Inter-continental contact by satellite is laid on by the Pan-American Earth Satellite Station. The local company is Intercomsa.

● **Tourist Bureau**
Information office of the Instituto Panameño de Turismo (IPAT), in the Atlapa Convention Centre, Vía Israel opposite *Hotel Marriott* (0900 to 1600) issues good list of hotels, *pensiones*, motels and restaurants, and a free *Focus on Panama* guide (available at all major hotels, and airport). IPAT's address: aptdo 4421, Panama 5, RP; T 26-7000/3544, ask for "información", helpful, English spoken. In USA: Laura Haayen, 1110 Brickell Ave, Suite 103, Miami, FL 33131, T (305) 579-2001, F 579-0910. *Getting to Know Panama*, by Michelle Labrut, published by Focus Publications (Apdo 6-3287, El Dorado, Panamá, RP, F 25-0466, US$12) has been recommended as very informative.

Best **maps** from Instituto Geográfico Nacional Tommy Guardia (IGNTG), on Vía Simón Bolívar, opposite the National University (footbridge nearby, fortunately), take Transístmica bus from Calle 12 in Santa Ana: physical map of the country in 2 sheets, US$3.50 each; Panama City map in many sheets, US$1.50 per sheet (travellers will only need 3 or so). At the back of the Panama Canal Commission telephone books are good maps of the Canal Area, Panama City and Colón.

CORN ISLANDS (ISLAS DEL MAIZ), NICARAGUA

NICARAGUA, the largest Central American republic (128,000 square km) has a Caribbean coastline of 541 km. The zone inland from the coast is a wide belt of lowland through which a number of rivers flow from the central mountains into the Atlantic. Wet, warm winds off the Caribbean pour heavy rain onto this region, especially between May and December, with more than 6m annually.

Because of this heavy rainfall and the consequent unhealthiness, the forested E lowlands, together with about half the coastal area of Honduras, was never colonized by Spain. From 1687 to 1894 it was a British Protectorate known as the Miskito kingdom. It was populated then, as now, by Miskito Indians (some 75,000), but today there is strong African influence. The Afro-Nicaraguan people call themselves creoles (*criollos*). Other groups are Sumu (5,000), Rama, of whom only a few hundred remain, and Garifuna. The largest number of inhabitants of this zone are Spanish-speaking *mestizos*. English is widely spoken. The Sandinista revolution, like most other political developments in the Spanish-speaking part of Nicaragua, was met with mistrust, and many Indians engaged in fighting for self-determination. About half the Miskito population fled as refugees to Honduras, but most returned after 1985 when a greater understanding grew between the Sandinista government and the people of the East Coast. The Caribbean Coast, divided into the North and South Autonomous Atlantic Regions, was given the status of a self-governing region in 1987.

The British established several colonies of Jamaicans in the 18th century at Bluefields and San Juan del Norte (Greytown). But early this century the United Fruit Company of America (now United Brands) opened banana plantations inland from Puerto Cabezas, worked by blacks from Jamaica. Other companies followed suit along the coast, but the bananas were later attacked by Panama disease and exports today are small. A plan to re-establish banana plantations was announced in 1991. The local economy is now based on timber, fishing and mining.

THE CORN ISLANDS

The Corn Islands (Islas del Maíz) are two small beautiful islands fringed with white coral and slender coconut trees, though many were blown down on the larger island by Hurricane Joan in October, 1988. They are approximately 70 km out into the Caribbean, opposite Bluefields, Nicaragua's main Caribbean port. The language of the islands is English. Local industries are the manufacture of coconut oil (devastated by the Hurricane), lobster fishing and shrimp-freezing plants.

The larger island is a popular Nicaraguan holiday resort; its surfing and bathing facilities make it ideal for tourists (best months March and April). Plans for developing the islands for larger-scale tourism before the Revolution never came to fruition. The best beach for swimming is Long Beach on Long Bay; walk across the island from Playa Coco. If you climb the mountain, wear long trousers, as there are many ticks. For fishing (barracuda, etc), contact Ernie Jenkie (about US$5/hour). It is possible to dive off the Corn Islands although locally available equipment "looks like leftovers from World War II". The reef is good, however, and dives are very cheap.

The smaller of the two islands escaped serious hurricane damage; it can be visited by boat from the larger island, but there are no facilities for tourists.

The atmosphere is very relaxed. On the larger Corn Island some hotels survived Hurricane Joan, but visitors must be prepared for basic conditions and food shortages. There is a also a shortage of water and most drinks (except rum). Furthermore, you can expect power cuts and electricity generators to be turned off before midnight (pack a torch and/or candles). In general, the islands are expensive because everything has to be brought over from the mainland (except seafood, that is). Dollars are widely used and there is a Almacen Internacional for the purchase of Western-style goods which are not available in normal Nicaraguan shops. The main market area is near Will Bowers wharf. There is no bank, so take the cash you need with you. The local craftsmen work red and black coral, pearls, and tortoiseshell, but this and the black coral are prohibited imports in some countries, so think carefully before buying. The islanders are very friendly, but petty thievery has been reported, even clothes stolen off a washing line.

Bluefields

Bluefields, from where some transport goes to the Corn Islands, gets its name from the Dutch pirate Abraham Blaauwveld. It stands on a lagoon behind the bluff at the mouth of the Bluefields river (Río Escondido), which is navigable as far as Rama (96 km). From Rama a paved highway runs to the Nicaraguan capital, Managua, 290 km away, through Santo Tomás and Juigalpa. There are also flights (lasting 1 hr) to the capital.

Bananas, cabinet woods, frozen fish, shrimps and lobsters were the main ex-

NICARAGUA : FACT FILE

Geographic

Land area	130,682 sq km
forested	28.5%
pastures	45.5%
cultivated	10.7%

Demographic

Population (1992)	4,131,000
annual growth rate (1987-92)	3.4%
urban	59.8%
rural	40.2%
density	34.3 per sq km
Religious affiliation	
Roman Catholic	90.7%
Birth rate per 1,000 (1991)	37.0
	(world av 26.4)
Death rate per 1,000 (1991)	7.0
	(world av 9.2)

Education and Health

Life expectancy at birth,	
male	60 years
female	65 years
Infant mortality rate	
per 1,000 live births (1991)	60.0
Physicians (1988)	1 per 2,024 persons
Hospital beds	1 per 761 persons
Calorie intake as %	
of FAO requirement	110%
Population age 25 and over	
with no formal schooling	53.9%
Literacy (over 15)	74.0%

Economic

GNP (1988 market prices)	US$1,661mn
GNP per capita	US$460
Public external debt (1990)	US$7,920mn
Tourism receipts (1990)	US$12mn
Inflation (annual av 1988-91)	6,350%
Radio	1 per 4.5 persons
Television	1 per 19 persons
Telephone	1 per 82 persons

Employment

Population economically active (1991)	
	1,386,300
Unemployment rate (1992)	60.0%
% of labour force in	
agriculture	32.4
mining	0.3
manufacturing	8.0
construction	1.5
Military forces	14,700
Source *Encyclopaedia Britannica*	

ports until, tragically, in October 1988, Hurricane Joan destroyed virtually all of Bluefields. The rebirth is well under way. Information on the region can be found at the Cidca office. Local bands practice above the Ivan Dixon Cultural Centre, beside the Library. There are several bars, a couple of reggae clubs, *comedores* and restaurants (2 with a/c) and a dollar-tienda. The atmosphere has become tense and grasping (1994), with many "guides" offering their services and leading visitors to buy things at inflated prices.

INFORMATION FOR VISITORS

● **Documents**
Visitors must have a passport with 6 months' validity (at least), an onward ticket and proof of US$500 (or equivalent in córdobas) in cash or cheques for their stay in the country. Credit cards may be accepted as proof of adequate funds. No visa is required by nationals of Guatemala, El Salvador, Honduras, Argentina, Chile, Bolivia, USA, Belgium, Denmark, Finland, Greece, Hungary, Ireland, Liechtenstein, Luxembourg, Netherlands, Norway, Spain, Sweden, Switzerland or the United Kingdom for a 90-day stay. Citizens of all other countries need a visa, which should be bought before arriving at the border, is valid for arrival within 30 days, and for a stay of up to 30 days, it costs US$25; 2 passport photographs are required. In most cases a visa takes 48 hrs to process; in some instances consultation with Managua is needed and this takes 1 week. Nationalities for whom consultation is necessary: Libya, Cuba, Hong Kong and the People's Republic of China. An air ticket can be cashed if not used, especially if issued by a large company, but bus tickets are sometimes difficult to encash. It is reported, however, that the Nicaraguan Embassy in a neighbouring country is empowered to authorize entry without the outward ticket, if the traveller has enough money to buy the ticket. Also, if you have a visa to visit another Central American country, you are unlikely to be asked to show an outward ticket.

● **How To Get There By Air**
From London: British Airways, Virgin Atlantic, American Airlines, Continental or Delta to Miami and connect to American, Nica, Central American Airlines, Lacsa, Iberia, or Taca via San Salvador. Continental flies from Houston 4 times a week. From other US cities: Chicago with Aviateca (change in Guatemala City); Los Angeles and San Francisco, Continental (change in Houston), Aviateca; New York, Continental via Houston. Nica flies daily to Guatemala City, San José, San Salvador and Panama City; Taca flies to Tegucigalpa daily; Copa flies to Guatemala City, San José, San Salvador and Panama. From Europe, with Iberia to Managua Thur and Sun from Madrid via Miami (connections from other European cities). Aeroflot flies on Wed from Moscow via Shannon and Havana. All flight tickets purchased by non-residents must be paid in US dollars.

All passengers have to pay a sales tax of US$5 on all tickets issued in and paid for in Nicaragua; a transport tax of 1% on all tickets issued in Nicaragua to any destination; and an airport tax of US$10, payable in US dollars, on all departing passengers.

● **Transport To The Corn Islands**
The local airlines, Nica and La Costeña, fly from Managua to Bluefields, US$45 one way, US$90 return plus US$1.50 internal departure tax. Managua offices of both airlines are in the domestic terminal at the airport: Nica, T 663136; La Costeña, T 631228. Bring passport, it is sometimes asked for in the departure lounge. There is a customs check on return to Managua. This advice applies to flights by La Costeña from Managua to the Corn Islands, US$60 one way, US$120 return (US$40 one way from Bluefields). Air services are suspended from time to time because of the poor state of the Corn Islands runway. Air services between Bluefields and the Corn Islands should be booked well in advance and return booked immediately on arrival.

Passenger-carrying cargo boats leave Bluefields for the Corn Islands from the docks of Copesnica, N of town, around a small bay and past the ruined church. There is usually a boat from Bluefields via El Bluff on Wed at 0900, 8 hrs, but there is no guarantee. The water around Bluefields is dirty, muddy brown, soon becoming a clear, sparkling blue. Boats back to Bluefields leave from Will Bowers Wharf on Thur; tickets available in advance from nearby office, US$4.50 one way. It is possible to hitch a lift on a fishing boat, enquire at Inpesca at the port. It is also possible to hitch lifts on boats to Puerto Cabezas, N of Bluefields, and San

Juan del Norte, to the S. There is an irregular boat service to and from Jamaica.

● **Airport**
César Augusto Sandino, 12 km E of Managua, near Lake Managua. Take any bus marked "Tipitapa" from Mercado Huembes, Mercado San Miguel or Mercado Oriental, US$0.16. Alternatively take a taxi for no more than US$5. Be early for international flights since formalities can take 2 hrs.

● **Airlines**
Around Plaza España in the capital: Nica (international and internal flight information, T 663136), Aeroflot, Iberia, KLM (300m E), Lufthansa and Continental; in Colonia Los Robles (Carretera a Masaya), Copa, Taca, Cubana (E of Plaza 19 de Julio, turn right on road opposite *Restaurant Lacmiel*, T 73976).

● **Customs**
Duty-free import of $^1/_2$ kg of tobacco products, 3 litres of alcoholic drinks and 1 large bottle (or 3 small bottles) of perfume is permitted.

● **From Managua To Bluefields Overland**
Take a bus from Mercado San Miguel (Terminal Atlántico), on Pista José Angel Benavides, in the E of Managua to Rama, along the paved road (in poor condition), 7-8 hrs, leaves 2300, Mon, Wed, Fri to connect with boat to Bluefields at 1130, Tues, Thur, Sat (check in advance, bus US$5.85, boat US$5, combined ticket US$10.85, buy the ticket at the reservation office at the terminal, preferably one day in advance. Food and soft drinks are sold on the ferry. Fast boats (*pangas*) can be hired in Roma for US$12-15 to Bluefields (taking 1$^1/_2$ hr) or hitch on a fishing boat. Return from Bluefields: boat at 0530 Tues, Thur, Sat, bus to Managua 1030 (combined tickets available, ticket office at Encab, near dock). There is also one boat each way on Sun, departs Roma 1130, departs Bluefields 0530. Or take your car and park it in the compound at the Chinaman's store at Rama (opposite *Hotel Amy*) for US$0.50 a day.

● **Internal Transport**
Hitchhiking is widely accepted, but is difficult because everyone does it and there is little traffic, offer to pay ("pedir un ride"). Local buses are the cheapest in Central America, but are extremely crowded owing to a lack of vehicles and fuel. Better equipment is being introduced. Baggage that is loaded on to the roof or in the luggage compartment is charged

for, usually half the rate for passengers.

● **Car Hire**
Hertz, Avis and Budget. Targa at the airport (T 31176) and *Hotel Intercontinental* (T 24875) in Managua. Rates are US$45 per day plus US$0.25 per km, not including tax and insurance. Only foreign exchange or credit cards accepted; special weekend rates available. Given the poor public transport and the decentralized layout of Managua, renting a car is often the best way to get around. Alternatively hire a taxi for long-distance trips out of Managua, US$10 per hour from an office opposite *Hotel Intercontinental* (opens 0930).

● **Motoring**
Low octane gasoline costs US$2 a US gallon, super US$2.20 (shortages frequent, diesel US$1.20). Cars will be fumigated on entry, for which there is a US$1 charge. For motorcyclists, the wearing of crash helmets is compulsory. Service stations close at 1700-1800. Beware when driving at night, the national shortage of spare parts means that many cars have no lights. Unless left securely, unattended cars may be broken into.

● **Where To Stay And Eat On The Corn Islands**
A 15% tax is levied on all hotel and restaurant bills, nevertheless, outside Managua, hotel accommodation is extremely cheap. An extra 10% service charge is often added to restaurant bills.

There are 4 hotels: *Hospedaje Miramar*, rec, meals served; *Hospedaje Playa Coco* also serves meals; *Brisas del Mar*, with restaurant, US$5 pp; one other. One can find rooms for about US$2 (Miss Florence's house, *Casa Blanca*, although it is blue, at Playa Coco is rec, US$10d). The chief problem in all the hotels is rats, which may not be dangerous, but neither are they pleasant. For eating: *Comedor Blackstone*; *Mini Café*; ice cream parlour; several bars and reggae clubs. Ask around where meals are available; the restaurants serve mainly chicken and chop suey, but in private houses the fare is much better. Try banana porridge and sorrel drink (red, ginger flavoured).

Where To Stay In Bluefields *South Atlantic*, near the central square, next to Telcor telephone office, run by Fanny and Hubert Chambers (native language English), with bath, safe, a/c, cable TV, fridge, clean, friendly, excellent food, room prices from US$40; *Costa*

Sur, about US$25 pp; *Caribbean*, under US$20 with bath, a/c, near centre of town, good cook (Angela), friendly, rec; *El Dorado,* may offer floor space to late arrivals; *Marda Maus*, one of the nicer places in its price range, with bath and fan, dark, not too clean, no restaurant, soft drinks available, near market; *Hollywood*, has its own well and generator, all about US$10. Cheaper is *Cuento*, showers, intermittent water. *Café Central* provides accommodation, has colour TV, good value meals. Everywhere can be full if you arrive late, or are last off the ferry.

● **Where To Stay In Managua**
There is a shortage of accommodation. Try to choose a central hotel (ie near *Intercontinental* or Plaza España) since transport to the outskirts is very difficult. 15% tax is added to hotel rates. There are, however, 2 good hotels near the airport: *Camino Real*, T 31410, Apartado Postal C118, 2 km from terminal, about US$80 (low season), shuttlebus to the airport, free, good, no English spoken, restaurant, live music; and *Las Mercedes*, T 32121/9, opposite the airport, 4 mins walk (US$35-60), pleasant, but service generally slow, good food in expensive, charming open-air restaurant, 3 swimming pools, beware mosquitoes after dark, tennis court, barber shop, all rooms have cable TV, a/c, bath, fridge, phone. There is regular water rationing and most hotels do not have large enough water tanks. The government stipulates a small additional charge for rooms with a telephone (whether used or not).

Intercontinental, 101 Octava Calle 50, T (505-2) 23531/9, F 25208, Apartado Postal 3278, is the city's major luxury hotel and a prominent landmark, US$110s or d (corporate rates available) service door, sauna, use of swimming pool for non-residents on Sun, US$3, bookshop, handicrafts, buffet breakfast and lunch (see below), Amex and Visa cards accepted. There are a number of other hotels with rooms priced at US$20d or over, eg *Estrella*, Pista de la Solidaridad (over US$45), a/c, swimming pool, with breakfast, long way from centre, book in advance, very popular; *Hotel Magut*, 1 block W of *Intercontinental*, US$30, with restaurant *La Fragata*; *Las Cabañas*, near Plaza 19 de Julio, good, helpful, pool, decent restaurant next door; *Casa de Fiedler*, 8a Calle Sur-Oeste 1320, with bath and a/c or fan, comfortable, soft mattresses, clean, friendly,

cold Victoria beer sold, good breakfasts; *Palace*, Av Pedro A Flores, US$30, with a/c and bath (US$23 without a/c), cold shower, run down, no restaurant, helpful, TV lounge, quiet; *Guest House Tres Laureles*, a few blocks W of *Intercontinental*, about 3 S of Cine Cabrera, under US$20, with bath, fan, laundry facilities, only 3 rooms, friendly, filtered water, English spoken; *Jardín de Italia*, W of *Intercontinental*, 3 blocks E and ½ block N of Cine Dorado, with bath, new.

For cheaper accommodation, US$12 or below: *Royal*, near railway station, shared shower and toilet, nice family, always full; *Sultana* (basic), noisy, clean, rec, if full, staff will arrange for you to stay at *Mi Siesta* on the other side of town (with bath and a/c, less without a/c), good, friendly, laundry facilities. Many hotels W of *Intercontinental Hotel* in the Barrio Martha Quezada and near the Cine Dorado; apart from those listed above, cheaper places usually have very thin walls and are therefore noisy. This district, which also has a number of good eating places, is where many gringos congregate. For instance, on street leading to *Intercontinental Hotel*, *Casa de Huéspedes Santos* and, on same street, *Hospedaje Meza* (T 22046); and many others.

● **Where To Eat In Managua**
The *Hotel Intercontinental* serves enormous breakfasts (0600-1100) for US$8 (plus 15% tax and service charge), and an excellent lunch between 1200 and 1500, US$12 for as much as you can eat (best to dress smartly). Bill is made out in dollars, major credit cards accepted.

In the *Intercontinental*/Plaza España / Barrio Martha Quezada area there is a variety of eating places, including: *Antojitos*, opp *Intercontinental*, Mexican, a bit overpriced, interesting photos of Managua pre-earthquake, good food and garden (open at 1200); a good piano bar next door; *Costa Brava*, N of Plaza España, excellent seafood; opposite German Embassy, 200m N from Plaza España, is *Bavaria Haus*, German and European specialities, German beer, food and service highly rec, only Spanish spoken, open Mon-Sat 1200-2300; *Cipitio* is a Salvadorean restaurant in this area, 2½ blocks S of Ciné Cabrera.

On Carretera a Masaya: *La Carreta* (Km 12), rec; *Sacuanjoche* (Km 8), international cuisine; *Lacmiel* (Km 4.5), good value, a/c, real ice cream; *Los Gauchos*, steaks; *Nerja*, on the highway a few hundred metres from the bypass, good; *La Marseillaise*, Colonia Los Robles, French, excellent. *Sandy's* is the bad local version of MacDonalds, one on Carretera a Masaya, about Km 5, and 2 other branches. Vegetarian: *Soya Restaurant*, just off the Carretera on Pista de la Resistencia; *Licuado Ananda*, just E of Estatua Montoya, open for breakfast and lunch. On Carretera Sur, Km 8½, *César*, specializes in European food and Swiss desserts; at Km 6½ is *The Lobster's Inn*, very good seafood but beware overcharging.

● **Tipping**
10% of bill in hotels and restaurants (many restaurants add 10% service; 15% tax is added compulsorily); US$0.50 per bag for porters; no tip for taxi drivers.

● **Cost Of Living**
In 1993/94 Nicaragua was a relatively expensive country as far as hotel accommodation was concerned, but public transport was fairly cheap. For food, as a rough guide a *comida corrida* costs about US$2-2.50 (meals in restaurants US$6-10, breakfasts US$3-4); a beer US$0.60-1, a coke US$0.30-50 (depending on the establishment) and a newspaper US$0.33.

● **Currency**
The unit is the córdoba oro (C$), divided into 100 centavos. It was introduced in July, 1990, at a par with the US dollar. The córdoba oro was devalued to 5 = US$1 in March 1991 and the old córdoba was withdrawn from circulation on 30 April 1991; a further devaluation in January 1993 set the dollar at 6 córdobas oro, to be followed by continuous mini-devaluations. The black market rate in the first half of 1994 was about 3% higher than the official rate (see **Exchange Rates** at the end of the book for latest official rate). Notes in circulation are for ½, 1, 5, 10, 20, 50 and 100 córdobas oro. A decree, passed on 22 March 1991, permitted private banks to operate (the financial system was nationalized in 1979). The import and export of foreign and local currencies are unrestricted. Visa and Mastercard are accepted in nearly all restaurants and hotels and in many shops. This applies to a lesser extent to Amex, Cred-o-Matic and Diners Club. Do not rely exclusively on credit cards.

Changing TCs is difficult outside Managua; while the situation is improving, it is best to carry US dollar notes and sufficient local currency away from the bigger towns.

● **Security**
Visitors to Nicaragua must carry their passports (or a photocopy) with them at all times. There are police checkpoints on roads and in outlying districts; the police search for firearms. Border officials do not like army-type clothing on travellers, and may confiscate green or khaki rucksacks (backpacks), parkas, canteens. They usually inspect all luggage thoroughly on entering and leaving Nicaragua. Do not photograph any military personnel or installations.

Pickpocketing and bagslashing has increased greatly in Managua, especially in crowded places, and on buses throughout the country. Do not leave the beaten track, especially in N Nicaragua, without enquiring about local conditions first.

● **Health**
Take the usual tropical precautions about food and drink. Tap water is not rec for drinking generally and avoid uncooked vegetables and peeled fruit. Intestinal parasites abound; if requiring treatment, take a stool sample to a government laboratory before going to a doctor. Malaria risk exists especially in the wet season; take regular prophylaxis. Treatment in Centros de Salud, medical laboratories and dispensaries is free, although foreigners may have to pay. You may be able to get prescribed medicines free. Private dentists are better-equipped than those in the national health service (but no better trained). Medicines are in short supply, so you are advised to bring what you need from home.

● **Climate And Dress**
There is a wide range of climates. Details of Atlantic conditions are given above, but note that it can get quite cold, especially after rain, in the Caribbean lowlands. Mid-day temperatures at Managua range from 30° to 36°C, but readings of 38° are not uncommon from March to May. Maximum daily humidity ranges from 90% to 100%.

Dress is informal; business men often shed jackets and wear sports shirts, but shorts are never worn. The wearing of trousers is perfectly OK for women.

● **Hours Of Business**
0800-1200, 1430-1730 or 1800. Banks: 0830-1200, 1400-1600, but 0830-1130 on Sat. Government offices are not normally open on Sat in Managua, or in the afternoon anywhere.

● **Public Holidays**
New Year's Day, Thursday of Holy Week and Good Friday (March or April), Labour Day (1 May), Revolution of 1979 (19 July), Battle of

San Jacinto (14 September), Independence Day (15 September), All Souls' Day (Día de los Muertos, 2 November), Immaculate Conception (Purísima, 7 and 8 December), Christmas Day.

Businesses, shops and restaurants all close for most of Holy Week; many companies also close down during the Christmas-New Year period. Holidays which fall on a Sunday are taken the following Monday.

● **Time Zone**

Eastern Standard Time, 5 hrs behind GMT, since the beginning of 1992.

● **Immigration**

Pista de la Resistencia, Managua, about 1 km from Km 7 Carretera del Sur, bus No 118, open till 1400. **Customs** Km 5 Carretera del Norte, bus No 108.

● **Embassies**

All in Managua: **USA**, Km 4½ Carretera del Sur (T 666010, F 663865); **Canada**, consul, 208/c del Triunfo, Frente Plazoleta Telcor Central, T 24541; **German**, 200m N of Plaza España, T 663917/8, open Mon-Fri 0900-1200; **French**, Km 12 Carretera del Sur, T 26210, F 621057; **British**, El Reparto, "Los Robles", Primera Etapa, Entrada Principal de la Carretera a Masaya, Cuarta Casa a la mano derecha, T 780014, F 784085, Telex 2166, Apdo Aéreo 169, it is located on a right-turn off Carretera a Masaya; **Dutch**, del Terraza 1 cuadra al norte, 1 cuadra al oeste, Apartado 3534, T (010-505-2) 666175, F 660364; **Swiss**, c/o Cruz Lorena SA, Km 6.5 Carretera Norte entrada de la Tona, Apartado postal 166, T 492671; **Swedish**, from Plaza España, 1 block W (Abajo), 2 blocks to the Lake, ½ block W (Abajo), Apartado Postal 2307, T 60085; **Danish** Consulate General, Iglesia del Carmen, 2 cuadras al Oeste No 1610, T 23189; **Panamanian** Consulate, from *Lacmiel* restaurant on Carretera a Masaya turn left and then the 4th street on the right, it is 200m on the left, T 670154, F 74223, 0800-1300; **Honduran** Consulate, Carretera del Sur, Km 15, Colonia Barcelona, open Mon-Fri, 0800-1400 (bus 118 from *Hotel Intercontinental*), Embassy, Planes de Altamira 29, T 670182, F 670184; **Venezuelan**, about Km 10.5 on the road to Masaya. International fax service is available in all major cities, US$4.50 per page to Europe.

● **Weights And Measures**

The metric system is official, but in domestic trade local terms are in use; for example, the *medio*, which equals a peck (2 dry gallons), and the *fanega*, of 24 *medios*. These are not used in foreign trade. The principal local weight is the *arroba*=25 lb and the *quintal* of 101.417 English lb. A random variety of other measures in use include US gallon for petrol, US quart and pint for liquids; *vara* (33 ins) for short distances and the lb for certain weights.

● **Electric Current**

110 volts AC, 60 cycles.

● **Postal Services**

Airmail to Europe takes 2-4 weeks (US$0.80), from Europe 7-10 days.

● **Telecommunications**

There are wireless transmitting stations at Managua, Bluefields and Cabo Gracias a Dios, and private stations at Puerto Cabezas, El Gallo, and Río Grande.

Phone lines are owned by the Government (Telcor). Automatic national and international telephone calls are possible from any private or public phone. Quality is now of the highest international standard. Card phones were due to be introduced in 1994. International or national calls can be made at any Telcor office, open 0700-2200. All phone calls can be paid for in córdobas. Rates in early 1994 were: US$10 for 3 mins to USA, US$11.50 to Europe. You may have to wait a long time for a line, except for early in the morning on weekdays. You have to say in advance how long you want to talk for. Collect calls to the USA are easy ("a pagarse allá"), also possible to Europe.

● **Tourist Information**

Inturismo in Managua 1 block W of *Hotel Intercontinental*, enter by side door. Standard information available, inc on all types of transport in the country. Apartado postal 122, T 22498/27423, F 25314. Maps of Managua (almost up-to-date), with insets of León and Granada and whole country on reverse, US$4. Inturismo will help with finding accommodation with families, with full board. Turnica, Av 11 SO, 300m, or 2 mins from Plaza España, T 661387/660406, sells maps of Managua and of the country, and organizes tours of the capital, US$15 pp, and other cities, from US$30-50 pp (min 2 people, payable in dollars only).

SAN ANDRES AND PROVIDENCIA, COLOMBIA

COLOMBIA'S Caribbean islands of the San Andrés and Providencia archipelago are 480 km N of the South American coast, 400 km SW of Jamaica, and 180 km E of Nicaragua. This proximity has led Nicaragua to claim them from Colombia in the past. They are small and attractive, but very expensive by South American standards. Nevertheless, with their surrounding islets and cays, they are a popular holiday and shopping resort.

Colombia itself encompasses a number of distinct regions, the most marked difference being between the sober peoples of the Andean highlands (in which the capital, Bogotá, is built) and the more light-hearted *costeños*, or people of the coast. The islands belong in the latter category, but, owing to their location, have more in common with the Caribbean's history of piracy, planters and their slaves than with Colombia's rich imperial past. The original inhabitants, mostly black, speak some English, but the population has swollen with unrestricted immigration from Colombia. There are also Chinese and Middle Eastern communities. The population in 1992 was about 41,580.

History and Economy

Before the European explorers and pirates came upon the islands, Miskito fisherman from Central America are known to have visited them. The date of European discovery is subject to controversy; some say Columbus found them in 1502, others that Alonso de Ojedo's landing in 1510 was the first. The earliest mention is on a 1527 map. Although the Spaniards were uninterested in them, European navies and pirates recognized the group's strategic importance. The first permanent settlement, called Henrietta, was not set up until 1629, by English puritans. The first slaves were introduced in 1633, to extract timber and plant cotton, but in that century, pirates held sway. Henry Morgan had his headquarters at San Andrés; the artificial Aury channel between Providencia and Santa Catalina is named after another pirate of that time. Although more planters arrived in the eighteenth century from Jamaica, England agreed in 1786 that the islands should be included in the Dominions of Spain. In 1822 they became Colombian possessions. After the abolition of slavery in 1837, coconut production replaced cotton and remained the mainstay of the economy until disease ruined the trade in the 1920s. In 1953, San Andrés was declared a freeport, introducing its present activities of tourism and commerce.

The main problem is deteriorating water and electricity supplies (in most hotels the water is salty). Being a customs-free zone, San Andrés is very crowded with Colombian shoppers looking for foreign-made bargains. Although alcoholic drinks are cheap, essential goods are extremely costly, and electronic goods are more expensive than in the UK.

Culture

San Andrés and Providencia are famous in Colombia for their music, whose styles include the local form of calypso, soca, reggae and church music. A number of good local groups perform on the islands and in Colombia. Concerts are held at the Old Coliseum (every Saturday at

COLOMBIA : FACT FILE

Geographic
Land area	1,141,748 sq km
forested	48.4%
pastures	38.9%
cultivated	5.2%

Demographic
Population (1992)	33,392,000
annual growth rate (1987-92)	2.0%
urban	67.2%
rural	32.8%
density	29.2 per sq km
Religious affiliation	
Roman Catholic	93.8%
Birth rate per 1,000 (1988)	27.9
	(world av 27.1)
Death rate per 1,000 (1988)	7.4
	(world av 9.8)

Education and Health
Life expectancy at birth,	
male	66.4 years
female	72.3 years
Infant mortality rate	
per 1,000 live births (1990-95)	37.0
Physicians (1988)	1 per 1,079 persons
Hospital beds (1983)	1 per 612 persons
Calorie intake as %	
of FAO requirement	106%
Population age 25 and over	
with no formal schooling	15.3%
Literate males (over 15)	87.5%
Literate females (over 15)	85.9%

Economic
GNP (1990 market prices)	US$40,805mn
GNP per capita	US$1,240
Public external debt (1990)	US$15,637mn
Tourism receipts (1990)	US$362mn
Inflation (annual av 1986-91)	27.3%
Radio	1 per 7.3 persons
Television	1 per 6.1 persons
Telephone	1 per 11 persons

Employment
Population economically active (1985)	
	9,558,000
Unemployment rate	4.3%
% of labour force in	
agriculture	28.5
mining	0.6
manufacturing	13.4
construction	2.9
Military forces	139,000

Source *Encyclopaedia Britannica*

2100 in the high season); the Green Moon Festival is held in May. There is a cultural centre at Punta Hansa in San Andrés town (T 25518).

Marine Life and Watersports

Diving off San Andrés is very good; depth varies from 10 to 100 feet, visibility from 30 to 100 feet. There are 3 types of site: walls of sea-weed and minor coral reefs, large groups of different types of coral, and underwater plateaux with much marine life. 70% of the insular platform is divable. Names of some of the sites are: The Pyramid, Big Channel, Carabela Blue, Blue Hole, Blowing Hole, The Cove and Small Mountain/La Montañita.

Diving trips to the reef cost US$60 with Pedro Montoya at Aquarium diving shop, Punta Hansa, T 26649; also Buzos del Caribe, Centro Comercial Dann, T 23712; both offer diving courses and equipment hire.

For the less-adventurous, take a morning boat (20 mins, none in the afternoon) to the so-called Aquarium (US$3 return), off Haynes Key, where, using a mask and wearing sandals as protection against sea-urchins, you can see colourful fish. Snorkelling equipment can be hired on San Andrés for US$4-5, but it is better and cheaper on the shore than on the island.

Pedalos can be rented for US$4 per hour. Windsurfing and sunfish sailing rental and lessons are available from Bar Boat, road to San Luis (opposite the naval base), 1000-1800 daily (also has floating bar, English and German spoken), and Windsurf Spot, *Hotel Isleño*, T 23990; water-skiing at Water Spot, *Hotel Aquarium*, T 23117, and Jet Sky. From Tominos Marina there are boat trips around the island. Bay trips for 2 hrs cost US$8.75, for 4 hrs US$17.50, including 3 free rum-and-cokes.

Beaches and Cays

Boats go in the morning from San Andrés

to Johnny Key with a white beach and parties all day Sunday (US$3 return, you can go in one boat and return in another). Apart from those already mentioned, other cays and islets in the archipelago are Bolívar, Albuquerque, Algodón/Cotton (included in the Sunrise Park development in San Andrés), Rocky, the Grunt, Serrana, Serranilla and Quitasueño.

On San Andrés the beaches are in town and on the E coast (some of the most populated ones have been reported dirty). Perhaps the best is at San Luis and Bahía Sonora/Sound Bay.

On Providencia the 3 main beaches are Bahía Manzanillo/Manchineal Bay, the largest, most attractive and least developed, Bahía del Suroeste/South West Bay and Bahía Agua Dulce/Freshwater Bay, all in the SW.

Festivals

20 July: independence celebrations on San Andrés with various events. Providencia holds its carnival in June.

SAN ANDRES

San Andrés is of coral, some 11 km long, rising at its highest to 104m. The town, commercial centre, major hotel sector and airport are at the N end. A picturesque road circles the island. Places to see, besides the beautiful cays and beaches on the E side, are the Hoyo Soplador (South End), a geyser-like hole through which the sea spouts into the air most surprisingly when the wind is in the right direction. The W side is less spoilt, but there are no beaches on this side. Instead there is The Cove, the island's deepest anchorage, and Morgan's Cave (Cueva de Morgan, yet another reputed hiding place for the pirate's treasure) which is penetrated by the sea through an underwater passage. At The Cove, the road either continues round the coast, or crosses the centre of the island back to town over La Loma, on which is a Baptist Church, built in 1847.

Island Information – San Andrés
● **Island Travel**
Buses cover the E side of the island all day (15 mins intervals), US$0.25 (more at night and on holidays). A "tourist train" (suitably converted tractor and carriages) tours the island in 3 hrs for US$3. **Taxis** round the island, US$8; to airport, US$3.50; in town, US$0.60; *colectivo* to airport, US$0.50.

SAN ANDRÉS C 67 / MAC 98a

Not to Scale

Punta Norte
Johnny Cay
Bahía Sardinas
Punta Hansa
Roca del Pescador
SAN ANDRES
Punta Paraíso
Bahía de San Andrés
Bahía Baja
El Acuario
L o m a   A l t a
Haynes Cay
Cueva de Morgan
Lagoon
Cayo Rocoso
Punta Evans
San Luis
Sound Bay
Bahía El Cove
Smith Channel
Monte Derecho
La Piscinita
Elsie Bay Channel
N
Hoyo Soplador
Punta Sur

Boat transport: Cooperativa de Lancheros, opposite *Hotel Abacoa*.

● **Vehicle Rental**

Bicycles are a popular way of getting around on the island and are easy to hire, eg opp *El Dorado Hotel* – usually in poor condition, choose your own bike and check all parts thoroughly (US$1.10 per hour, US$6 per day);

motorbikes also easy to hire, US$3.50 per hour. Cars can be hired for US$15 for 2 hrs, with US$6 for every extra hour.

● **Where To Stay**

In the upper bracket (over US$60), *Aquarium*, Av Colombia 1-19, T 23120, F 26174, US$61-100 suites; *Bahía Marina*, road to San Luis Km 5, T 23539, 1st class resort; *Cacique Toné*, Av

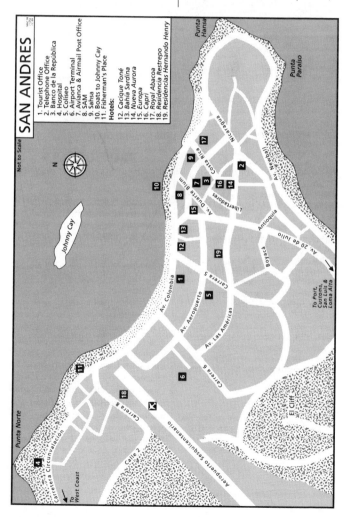

SAN ANDRES

Not to Scale

1. Tourist Office
2. Telephone Office
3. Banco de la Republica
4. Hospital
5. Coliseo
6. Airport Terminal
7. Avianca & Airmail Post Office
8. SAM
9. Sahsa
10. Boats to Johnny Cay
11. Fisherman's Place

Hotels:
12. Cacique Toné
13. Bahía Sardina
14. Nueva Aurora
15. Europa
16. Capri
17. Royal Abacoa
18. Residencia Restrepo
19. Residencias Hernando Henry

Colombia, No 5-02, T 24251, deluxe, a/c, pool, on sea-front, US$75; *Casablanca*, Av Colombia y Costa Rica, T 25950, central, good, US$73-80; *Casa Dorada*, Av Las Américas, T 24008, reasonable food, salt-water washing, US$83; *Decameron*, road to San Luis Km 15, book through Decameron Cartagena, T 655-4400, F 653-738, all-inclusive, pool, a/c, TV, good restaurant, rec; *El Isleño*, Av de la Playa 3-59, T 23990, F 23126, 2 blocks from airport, in palm grove, sea views, US$67; *Tiuna*, Av Colombia No 3-59, T 23235, a/c, swimming pool, US$60; *Royal Abacoa*, Av Colombia No 2-41, good restaurant, T 24043, US$75. *Verde Mar*, Av 20 de Julio, T 25525, quiet and friendly, a/c, rec.

Up to US$60: *Nueva Aurora*, Av de las Américas No. 3-46, T 23811, fan and private bath, pool, restaurant, US$21; *Abacoa*, Av Colombia, T 24133/4, with bath and a/c, US$33; *Bahía Sardinas*, Av Colombia No 4-24, T 23793, across the street from the beach, a/c, TV, fridge, good service, comfortable, clean, no swimming pool, US$46; *Capri*, Av Costa Rica No 1A-64, T 24315, with bath and a/c, good value, US$42; *El Dorado*, Av Colombia No 1A-25, T 24057, a/c, restaurant, casino, swimming pool, US$56; *Coliseo*, Av Colombia No 1-59, T 3330, friendly, noisy, good restaurant, US$18. *Mediterráneo*, Av Los Libertadores, T 26722, US$20, clean, friendly, poor water supply.

Residencias Hernando Henry, Av Américas 4-84, T 26416, under US$20, restaurant, fan, clean, good value, often full, on road from airport; *Residencia Restrepo*, "gringo hotel", Av 8 near airport, noisy ("share a room with a Boeing 727" – till midnight), much cheaper than others, about US$5, or less for a hammock in the porch, but you get what you pay for, the accommodation is in a poor state and the grounds are a junkyard. On the way to *Restrepo* you pass a good food shop, breakfast, juices, snacks. Campsite at South End said to be dirty and mosquito-ridden.

● **Where To Eat**
Oasis (good), Av Colombia No 4-09; *Sea Food House*, Av 20 de Julio at Parque Bolívar, good food, not expensive, second floor terrace; *Popular*, on Av Bogotá, good square meal; *El Pimentón*, Av de las Américas, good and cheap; *El Zaguán de los Arrieros*, Av 20 de Julio (50m after cinema), good food and value; *Bahía*, good food; *Fonda Antioqueña Nos 1 and 2*, on Av Colombia near the main beach,

and Av Colombia at Av Nicaragua, best value for fish; excellent fruit juices at *Jugolandia*, Calle 20 de Julio; *Jugosito*, Av Colombia, 1½ blocks from tourist office towards centre, cheap meals; *Nueva China*, next to *Restrepo*, reasonable Chinese; *Fisherman's Place*, in the fishing cooperative at N end of main beach, very good, simple. Fish meals for US$2.50 can be bought at San Luis beach.

● **Exchange**
Banco Industrial Colombiano, Av Costa Rica, will exchange dollars and TCs; Banco de Bogotá will advance pesos on a Visa card. Aerodisco shop at airport will change dollars cash anytime at rates slightly worse than banks, or try the Photo Shop on Av Costa Rica. Many shops will change US$ cash; it is impossible to change TCs at weekends. (Airport employees will exchange US$ cash at a poor rate.)

PROVIDENCIA

Providencia, commonly called Old Providence (3,000 inhabitants), 80 km back to the N-NE from San Andrés, is 7 km long and is more mountainous than San Andrés, rising to 610m. There are waterfalls, and the land drops steeply into the sea in places. Superb views can be had by climbing from Casabaja/Bottom House or Aguamansa/Smooth Water to the peak. There are relics of the fortifications built on the island during its disputed ownership. Horse riding is available, and boat trips can be made to neighbouring islands such as Santa Catalina (an old pirate lair separated from Providencia by a channel cut for their better defence), and to the NE, Cayo Cangrejo/Crab Cay (beautiful swimming and snorkelling) and Cayos Hermanos/Brothers Cay. Trips from 1000-1500 cost about US$7 pp. On the W side of Santa Catalina is a rock formation called Morgan's Head; seen from the side it looks like a man's profile.

Like San Andrés, it is an expensive island. The sea food is good, water and fresh milk are generally a problem.

Island Information – Providencia

● **How to Get There**

Day tours are arranged by the Providencia office in San Andrés, costing US$35 inclusive. SAM fly from San Andrés, US$30, 25 mins, up to 6 times a day, bookable only in San Andrés. (Return flight has to be confirmed at the airport, where there is a tourist office.) There are no flights from anywhere else. Boat trips from San Andrés take 8 hrs, but are not regular.

● **Where To Stay**

Most of the accommodation is at Freshwater (Playa Agua Dulce): *Cabañas El Recreo* (Captain Brian's), T 48010, US$30; *Cabañas El Paraíso*, T 26330, a/c, TV, fridge, US$82; *Cabañas Aguadulce*, T 48160, US$40. *Miss Elma's* rec for cheap food; also *Morgan's Bar*, for fish meals and a good breakfast for US$2. On Santa Catalina island, is German-owned *Cabañas Santa Catalina*, friendly, use of small kitchen. Several houses take in guests. Camping is possible at Freshwater Bay. Truck drivers who provide transport on the island may be able to advise on accommodation.

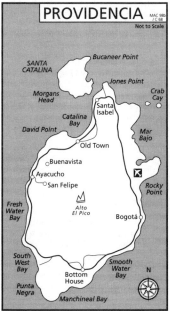

PROVIDENCIA MAC 98b / C 68
Not to Scale

SANTA CATALINA
Bucaneer Point
Morgans Head
Jones Point
Crab Cay
Catalina Bay
Santa Isabel
David Point
Mar Bajo
Old Town
Buenavista
Ayacucho
San Felipe
Rocky Point
Fresh Water Bay
Alto El Pico
Bogotá
South West Bay
Smooth Water Bay
Bottom House
Punta Negra
Manchineal Bay
N

Cartagena and Barranquilla

Mention should be made here of the two Caribbean cities on the mainland to which access is made from San Andrés, Cartagena and Barranquilla.

Cartagena, old and steeped in history, is one of the most interesting towns in South America, and should not be missed if you are taking this route. As well as the historical sites, Cartagena also has a popular beach resort at Bocagrande, a 10-min bus ride from the city centre. Cartagena de Indias, to give it its full name, was founded on 13 January 1533, as one of the storage points for merchandise sent out from Spain and for treasure collected from the Americas to be sent back to Spain. A series of forts protecting the approaches from the sea, and the formidable walls built around the city, made it almost impregnable. All the same, it was challenged again and again by enemies. Sir Francis Drake, with 1,300 men, broke in successfully in 1586. The Frenchmen Baron de Pointis and Ducasse, with 10,000 men, sacked the city in 1697. But the strongest attack of all, by Sir Edward Vernon with 27,000 men and 3,000 pieces of artillery, failed in 1741 after besieging the city for 56 days. It was defended by the one-eyed, one-armed, one-legged hero Blas de Lezo.

A full description of the city, with its churches, forts, colonial streets and other attractions, is given in *The South American Handbook*.

Barranquilla (also described in detail in *The South American Handbook*) is Colombia's fourth city, with almost 2 million people. It is a modern, industrial sea and river port on the W bank of the Magdalena, one of the country's main waterways. The 4-day Carnival in February is undoubtedly the best in Colombia.

INFORMATION FOR VISITORS

● **Documents**

A passport is always necessary; an onward ticket is officially necessary, but is not always asked for at land borders. Visitors are sometimes asked to prove that they have US$20 for each day of their stay (US$10 for students). You are given 90 days permission to stay on entry. Extensions (*salvoconducto*) for 15-day periods can be applied for at the DAS office in any major city up to a maximum of 6 months (including the first 90 days). Application must be made within 3 weeks of the expiry of the first 90 days and 2 weeks are needed for authorization from the Ministerio de Relaciones Exteriores in Bogotá. The 30-day extension runs from the day authorization is received by the DAS office (so if you apply on the last of your 90 days you could get 30 days more). Leaving the country and re-entering to get a new permit is not always allowed. To visit Colombia as a tourist, nationals of only China, Taiwan and Haiti need a visa (this information was correct according to the Colombian consulate in London, May 1994). You must check regulations before leaving your home country. Visas are issued only by Colombian consulates. When a visa is required you must be prepared to show 3 photographs, police clearance and medical certificates, an application form (£11 or equivalent), as well as a passport (allow 48 hrs). Various business and temporary visas are needed for foreigners who have to reside in Colombia for a length of time. Fees range from £54 (or equivalent) for a student visa, £90 for a business visa, to £131 for a working visa. You may find that your onward ticket, which you must show before you can obtain a visa, is stamped "non-refundable". If you do not receive an entry card when flying in, the information desk will issue one, and restamp your passport for free. Note that to leave Colombia you must get an exit stamp from the DAS (security police). They often do not have offices at the small frontier towns, so try to get your stamp in a main city, and save time.

NB It is highly recommended that you have your passport photocopied, and witnessed by a notary. This is a valid substitute (although some travellers report difficulties with this variant) and your passport can then be put into safe-keeping. Also, photocopy your travellers' cheques, airline ticket and any other essential documents. For more information, check with your consulate.

● **How To Get There By Air**

San Andrés is a popular stopover on the routes from Central America to Colombia. By changing planes in San Andrés you can save money on flight fares. SAM flies to Guatemala City, Panama City and San José, Costa Rica, Aero Costa Rica also flies to San José. Note that Panama, Costa Rica and Honduras all require onward tickets which cannot be bought on San Andrés, but can be in Cartagena. SAM office in San Andrés town will not issue one way tickets to Central America (although the airport office is reported to do so). You buy a return and the SAM office on the mainland will refund once you show an onward ticket. The refund (less 15%) may not be immediate. Avianca and SAM have flights to most major Colombian cities: SAM to Barranquilla, Bogotá, Bucaramanga, Cali, Cartagena, Cúcuta, Medellín; Avianca to Bogotá with connections to many other cities; Aces flies to Bogotá and Medellín; Intercontinental de Aviación to Cali and Medellín; Aerorepública to Cali. With SAM you can arrange a stop-over in Cartagena, which is good value; the onward flight from Cartagena to Bogotá, Cali and Medellín does not cost much more than the bus fare and saves a lot of time. Providencia is served only by SAM from San Andrés.

● **Airport Information**

San Andrés airport is 15 mins' walk to town (taxi US$3 pp). All airline offices are in town (Avianca and SAM on Av Duarte Blum), except Aces at the airport. Improvement of the airport was undertaken in 1992/93. There is a customs tax of 15% on some items purchased if you are continuing to mainland Colombia.

On arrival all visitors have to pay an entry tax of US$15 (on it is stamped "Welcome Home"!). There is a Colombian airport exit tax of US$18 (in cash, dollars or pesos), from which only travellers staying less than 24 hrs are exempt. When you arrive, ensure that all necessary documentation bears a stamp for your date of arrival; without it you will have to pay double the exit tax on leaving (with the correct stamp, you will only be charged half the exit tax if you have been in the country less than 60 days). Visitors staying more than 60 days have to pay an extra US$12 tax, which can only be avoided by bona-fide tourists who can produce the card given them on entry. There is a 17% tax on all international air tickets bought in Colombia for flights out of the country (7.5% on international return flights). Do not buy tickets for domestic flights to or from San Andrés island outside Colombia; they are much more expensive. When getting an onward ticket from Avianca for entry into Colombia, reserve a seat only and ask for confirmation in writing, otherwise you will pay twice as much as if purchasing the ticket inside Colombia.

Sunday flights are always heavily booked. In July and August, December and January, it is very difficult to get on flights into and out of San Andrés; book in advance if possible. If wait-listed for a flight, do not give up, most passengers get on a plane. Checking in for flights can be difficult because of queues of shoppers with their goods.

If flying from Guatemala to Colombia with SAM, via San Andrés, you have to purchase a round-trip ticket, refundable only in Guatemala. To get around this (if you are not going back to Guatemala) you will have to try to arrange a ticket swap with a traveller going in the other direction on San Andrés. There is, however, no difficulty in exchanging a round-trip ticket for a San Andrés-Colombian ticket with the airline, but you have to pay extra.

● **Flights To Colombia**
British Airways has a twice-weekly service from London to **Bogotá**, via Caracas. Airlines with services from continental Europe are Air France, Iberia, Alitalia, and Lufthansa. Avianca, Aces, Continental, the Colombian national airline, flies from Frankfurt, Paris and Madrid. Frequent services to and from the USA by Avianca, Aces, Continental and American.

Avianca flies from Miami and Newark to **Cartagena**; the same airline flies to **Barranquilla** from Miami (as does American, daily), New York, JFK (also Continental from La Guardia and Newark via Houston), Aruba (also SAM) and Curaçao.

● **Customs**
Duty-free admission is granted for portable typewriters, radios, binoculars, personal and ciné cameras, but all must show use; 200 cigarettes or 50 cigars or 250 grams of tobacco or up to 250 grams of manufactured tobacco in any form, 2 bottles of liquor or wine per person.

● **How To Get There By Sea**
Cruise ships and tours go to San Andrés; there are no other, official passenger services by sea.

Cargo ships are not supposed to carry passengers to the mainland, but many do. If you want to leave by sea, speak only to the ship's captain. (Any other offer of tickets on ships to/from San Andrés, or of a job on a ship, may be a con trick.) Sometimes the captain may take you for free, otherwise he will charge anything between US$10-25; the sea crossing takes 3-4 days, depending on the weather. In Cartagena, ships leave from the Embarcadero San Andrés, opposite the Plaza de la Aduana.

● **Car Rental**
National driving licences may be used by foreigners in Colombia, but must be accompanied by an official translation if in a language other than Spanish. International drivers licences are also accepted. Carry driving documents with you at all times. Even if you are paying in cash, a credit card may be asked for as proof of identity (Visa, Mastercard, American Express), in addition to passport and driver's licence (**see also p 900**).

● **Where To Stay**
There is a tourist tax of 5% on rooms and an insurance charge, but no service charge, and tipping is at discretion. The Colombian tourist office has lists of authorized prices for all hotels which are usually at least a year out of date. If you are overcharged the tourist office will arrange a refund. Most hotels in Colombia charge US$1 to US$6 for extra beds for children, up to a maximum (usually) of 4 beds per room.

● **Food**
Colombia's food is very regional; it is quite difficult to buy in one area a dish you particularly liked in another. If you are economizing, ask for the "*plato del dia*" or "*plato corriente*" (dish of the day). Of the Caribbean dishes, Cartagena's rice with coconut can be compared with rice *a la valenciana*; an egg *empanada*, consists of 2 layers of corn (maize) dough that open like an oyster-shell, fried with eggs in the middle, and try the *patacón*, a cake of mashed and baked plantain (green banana). *Huevos pericos*, eggs scrambled with onions and tomatoes, are a popular, cheap and nourishing snack for the impecunious – available almost anywhere. Throughout the country there is an abundance of fruits: bananas, oranges, mangoes, avocado pears, and (at least in the tropical zones) *chirimoyas, papayas*, and the delicious *pitahaya*, taken either as an appetizer or dessert and, for the wise, in modera-

tion, because even a little of it has a laxative effect. Other fruits such as the *guayaba* (guava), *guanábana* (soursop), *maracuyá* (passion fruit), *lulo* (naranjilla), *mora* (blackberry) and *curuba* make delicious juices, sometimes with milk added to make a *sorbete* – satisfy yourself, though, that the milk is fresh. Fruit yoghurts are nourishing and cheap (try *Alpina* brand; *crema* style is best).

● **Drink**

Tinto, the national small cup of black coffee, is taken ritually at all hours. Colombian coffee is always mild. (Coffee with milk is called *café perico*; *café con leche* is a mug of milk with coffee added.) *Agua de panela* (hot water with unrefined sugar), also made with limes, milk, or cheese. Many acceptable brands of beer are produced. The local rum is good and cheap; ask for *ron*, not *aguardiente*, because in Colombia the latter word is used for a popular drink containing aniseed (*aguardiente anisado*).

● **Warning**

Great care should be exercised when buying imported spirits in shops. It has been reported that bottles bearing well-known labels have often been "recycled" and contain a cheap and poor imitation of the original contents. This can be dangerous to the health, and travellers are warned to stick to beer and rum. Also note that ice is usually not made from potable water.

● **Tipping**

Hotels and restaurants 10%. Porters, cloakroom attendants, hairdressers and barbers, US$0.05-0.25. Taxi-drivers are not tipped.

● **Shopping**

Local handicrafts are made from coral and coconut. Otherwise shopping is concentrated on the duty-free items so readily available. Typical Colombian products which are good buys: emeralds, leatherwork and handworked silver.

● **Currency**

The monetary unit is the peso, divided into 100 centavos. There are coins of 5, 10, 20 and 50 pesos; there are notes of 100, 200, 500, 1,000, 2,000, 5,000 and 10,000 pesos. Large notes of over 1,000 pesos are often impossible to spend on small purchases as change is in short supply, especially in small cities, and in the morning. There is a limit of US$25,000 import of foreign currency, with the export limit set at

the equivalent of the amount brought in. Travellers' cheques can in theory be exchanged in any bank, except the Banco de la República which, since June 1991, no longer undertakes exchange transactions. There are some legitimate *casas de cambio*, which are quicker to use than banks. Always check which rate of exchange is being offered. Hotels may give very poor rates of exchange, especially if you are paying in dollars, but practice varies. Owing to the quantity of counterfeit American Express TCs in circulation, travellers may experience difficulty in cashing these cheques, but the procedure is always slow, involving finger printing and photographs. A photocopy of your passport will be taken; you may have to provide your own, so take a supply. It is also very difficult, according to our correspondents, to get reimbursement for lost American Express TCs. Take Thomas Cook's or a US bank's dollar TCs in small denominations, but better still take a credit card (see below). Sterling TCs are practically impossible to change in Colombia.

As it is unwise to carry large quantities of cash, **credit cards** are widely used, especially Mastercard and Visa; Diner's Club is also used, while American Express is only accepted in high-priced establishments in Bogotá. Branches of Banco de Colombia and Banco Popular advance pesos against Visa, and Banco Industrial de Colombia give cash advances against Mastercard (Cajeo BIC for ATMs). In 1993-94 cash advances against credit cards gave the best rates of exchange. American Express cards are rarely accepted for cash advances.

Note In 1993-94, there were so many dollars in circulation (as a result of drugs trafficking) that it was very difficult to change dollars into pesos. Banks were reluctant to do so for anyone but account holders. The official rate of exchange was much higher than the street rate. In general, the best option was to use a Visa or Mastercard credit card.

● **Security**

Carry your passport (or photocopy) at all times.

Avoid money changers on the street who offer over-favourable rates of exchange. They often short-change you or run off with your money, pretending that the police are coming. Beware of counterfeit dollars and pesos.

Colombia is part of a major drug-smuggling route. Police and customs activities have greatly intensified and smugglers increasingly try to use innocent carriers. Travellers are warned against carrying packages for other people without checking the contents (even taking your own boxes, packages or gift-wrapped parcels through customs may cause problems). Penalties run up to 12 years in none too comfortable jails. Be very polite if approached by policemen. If your hotel room is raided by police looking for drugs, try, if possible, to get a witness to prevent drugs being planted on you. Colombians who offer you drugs may well be setting you up for the police, who are very active on the N coast and San Andrés island.

If someone accosts you on the street, saying he's a plain-clothes policeman or drugs officer, and asks you to go to his office, offer to go with him to the nearest policeman (the tourist police where possible) or police station. He may well be a "confidence man" (if he doesn't ask to see your passport, he almost certainly is). These conmen usually work in pairs.

● **Health**

Emergency medical treatment is given in hospitals: if injured in a bus accident, for example, you will be covered by insurance and treatment will be free. Take water sterilizer with you, or boil the water, or use the excellent mineral waters, when travelling outside the capital. Choose your food and eating places with care everywhere. Hepatitis is common; get protection before your trip. There is some risk of malaria and yellow fever in the coastal areas; prophylaxis is advised.

● **Climate And Clothing**

Tropical clothing is needed in the hot and humid climate of the coast. Average temperature on the islands is 27-31°C.

● **Tourist Seasons**

On the Caribbean coast and San Andrés and Providencia, high season is 15 December-30 April, 15 June-31 August.

● **Working Hours**

Mon to Fri, commercial firms work 0800-1200 and from 1400-1730 or 1800. Government offices follow the same hours on the whole as the commercial firms, but generally prefer to do business with the public in the afternoon only. Embassy hours for the public are from 0900-1200 and from 1400-1700 (weekdays). Bank hours in San Andrés are 0800-1100, 1400-1500 Mon to Fri, Sat am only. Shopping hours are 0900-1230 and 1430-1830, including Sat.

● **Public Holidays**

Circumcision of our Lord (1 January), Epiph-

any* (6 January), St Joseph* (19 March), Maundy Thur, Good Fri, Labour Day (1 May), Ascension Day*, Corpus Christi*, Sacred Heart*, SS Peter and Paul* (29 June), Independence Day (20 July), Battle of Boyacá (7 August), Assumption* (15 August), Discovery of America* (12 October), All Saints' Day* (1 November), Independence of Cartagena* (11 November), Immaculate Conception (8 December), Christmas Day (25 December).

When those marked with an asterisk do not fall on a Mon, or when they fall on a Sun, they will be moved to the following Mon.

● **Time Zone**

Eastern Standard Time, 5 hrs behind GMT.

● **Useful Addresses**

DAS (immigration authorities) are at the San Andrés airport, T 25540. (In Cartagena, DAS is just beyond Castillo San Felipe, behind the church-ask, helpful, T 664649. San Andrés Police, T 14; Red Cross, T 3333; Panamanian Consulate, Av Atlántico No 1A-60, T 26545. Other diplomatic representation in Barranquilla, Cartagena, or Bogotá.

● **Weights And Measures**

Metric; weights should always be quoted in kilograms. Litres are used for liquid measures but US gallons are standard for the petroleum industry. Linear measures are usually metric, but the inch is quite commonly used by engineers and the yard on golf courses. For land measurement the hectare and cubic metre are officially employed but the traditional measures *vara* (80 centimetres) and *fanegada* (1,000 square *varas*) are still in common use. Food etc is often sold in *libras* (pounds), which are equivalent to 1/2 kilo.

● **Electric Current**

120 volts AC Transformer must be 110-150 volt AC, with flat-prong plugs (all of same size). Be careful with electrically heated showers.

● **Postal Services**

Send all letters by airmail. Avianca controls all airmail services and has offices in provincial cities (Catalina Building, Av Duarte Blum in San Andrés). Correspondence with UK is reported to be good. It costs US$0.35 to send a letter or postcard to the US or Europe; a 1 kg package to Europe costs US$13 by air (Avianca).

● **Telecommunications**

Systems have been automated; the larger towns are interconnected. Inter-city calls and cables must be made from Telecom offices unless you have access to a private phone (Telecom in San Andrés: Av Américas No 2A-23). Long-distance pay 'phones are located outside most Telecom offices, also at bus stations and airports. They take 50-peso coins (at San Andrés airport, advice and exchange for phone usage is available). 5-peso coins are needed for ordinary phones which also take 20-peso coins. From the larger towns it is possible to telephone to Canada, the USA, the UK, and to several of the Latin American republics. International phone charges are high about US$6 a minute to USA, US$8 to Europe, US$12 to Australia), but there is a 20% discount on Sun. A deposit is required before the call is made which can vary between US$18 and US$36 (try bargaining it down), US$1 is charged if no reply, for person-to-person add an extra min's charge to Canada, 2 mins' to UK; all extra mins' conversation cost ¹/₃ more. The best value is to purchase a phone card and dial direct yourself. AT&T's USA Direct service can be dialled on 980-11-0010. Canada Direct is 980-19-0057; UK Direct 980-44-0057. Collect, or reversed-charge, telephone calls are only possible from private telephones; make sure the operator understands what is involved or you may be billed in any case. It is also possible that the operator, once you have got through to him/her, may not call you back. The surest way of contacting home, assuming the facilities are available at each end, is to fax your hotel phone number to home and ask them to call you.

● **Tourist Information**
In San Andrés, Corporación Nacional de Turismo (CNT), Avenida Colombia No 5-117, English spoken, maps, friendly. CNT has its headquarters at Calle 28, No 13A-59, **Bogotá** (T 284-3761); it has branches in every departmental capital and other places of interest (in **Cartagena**, Av Blas de Lezo, Ed Muelle de los Pegasos, Empresa Promotora de Turismo de Cartagena, or CNT, Calle de la Factoría, Cra 3, No 36-57; in **Barranquilla**, Carrera 54 No 75-45, T 454458). They should be visited as early as possible not only for information on accommodation and transport, but also for details on areas which are dangerous to visit.

CNT also has offices in **New York**: 140 East 57th St, T 688-0151; **Caracas**: Planta Baja 5 Av Urdaneta Ibarras a Pelota, T 561-3592/5805; **Madrid**: Calle Princesa No 17 Tercero Izquierda, T 248-5090/5690; and **Paris**: 9, Boulevard de la Madeleine, 75001 Paris, T 260-3565.

BAY ISLANDS, HONDURAS

The Central American republic of Honduras (capital Tegucigalpa) has a Caribbean coastline of 640 kilometres. Much of the country is mountainous: a rough plateau covered with volcanic ash and lava in the S, rising to peaks of over 2,000m in the Celaque range, but with intermont basins at between 900 and 1,800m. The volcanic detritus disappears to the N, revealing saw-toothed ranges which approach the coast at an angle; the one in the extreme NW, along the border with Guatemala, disappears under the sea and shows itself again in an island group called the Bay Islands (Islas de la Bahía).

There are three main islands, Utila, Roatán and Guanaja, lying in an arc which curves away NE from a point 32 km N of the port of La Ceiba. At the E end of Roatán are three small ones: Morat, Santa Elena and Barbareta; there are other islets and 52 cays. Today only Utila rests on the continental shelf, a deep trench separates it from Roatán.

Honduras possesses a number of other islands and cays: the Cayos Cochinos (Hog Cays), two islands and 13 cays 17 km from the Caribbean coast; Cayos Zapotillos, comprising Grass and Hunting Cays and one other, 42 km from the coast; the Swan Islands (Great Swan, Little Swan and Bobby Cay – Islas del Cisne, or Santanilla), 150 km NE of Honduras; and 130 islets, cays and rocks off the swampy, densely-forested Mosquito coast, collectively called the Cayos Misquitos.

The total population of the Bay Islands is estimated at 30,000. There are English-speaking blacks who constitute the majority of the population, particularly on Roatán. Utila has a population which is roughly half black and half white, the latter of British stock descended mainly from settlers from Grand Cayman who arrived in 1830. Latin Hondurans have been moving to the islands from the mainland in recent years. There are also some Black Caribs, 5,000 of whom were deported from St Vincent in 1797 to Roatán. Many moved on to the mainland at a later date. The culture is very un-Latin American even though the government schools teach in Spanish. The population is bilingual.

The main industry is fishing, mostly for shellfish. Trade is also done in coconuts, bananas and plantains. Boat-building, once the principal occupation, is now dying.

Some of the things that you will *not* find on the Bay Islands are shopping centres, fast food, cruise ships, or crowds of tourists, and there are only two small stretches of paved road (on Roatán and Utila). There are telephones and television, including cable, now. Until 1988, wealthy Hondurans and the international and diplomatic community took most advantage of the islands' underwater potential, but the expansion of Roatán's airport to accommodate jets, will bring in many more visitors. If landing rights are granted to overseas carriers, the flow of tourists will increase further.

History

Columbus anchored off Guanaja in 1502, on his fourth voyage, but the islands had been inhabited for a long time before. Archaeologists have been busy on the islands but their findings are very confusing. The relationship between the Paya Indians who lived there and mainland groups has not been fully established. Clay vessels and figurines, articles of jade and stone, pendants, necklaces and amulets have been uncovered. In the 18th century European buccaneers, in the name of England or Spain,

HONDURAS : FACT FILE

Geographic
Land area	112,088 sq km
forested	29.9%
pastures	22.8%
cultivated	16.2%

Demographic
Population (1992)	4,996,000
annual growth rate (1987-92)	3.3%
urban	41.1%
rural	58.9%
density	44.6 per sq km
Religious affiliation	
Roman Catholic	85.0%
Birth rate per 1,000 (1991)	39.0
	(world av 26.4)
Death rate per 1,000 (1991)	8.0
	(world av 9.2)

Education and Health
Life expectancy at birth,	
male	63 years
female	67 years
Infant mortality rate	
per 1,000 live births (1991)	48.0
Physicians (1990)	1 per 1,586 persons
Hospital beds	1 per 818 persons
Calorie intake as %	
of FAO requirement	99%
Population age 25 and over	
with no formal schooling	33.4%
Literate males (over 15)	75.5%
Literate females (over 15)	70.6%

Economic
GNP (1990 market prices)	US$3,023mn
GNP per capita	US$590
Public external debt (1990)	US$2,992mn
Tourism receipts (1990)	US$29mn
Inflation (annual av 1986-91)	14.2%
Radio	1 per 2.6 persons
Television	1 per 24 persons
Telephone	1 per 46 persons

Employment
Population economically active (1991)	
	1,523,300
Unemployment rate (1990)	40%
% of labour force in	
agriculture	46.1
mining	0.3
manufacturing	11.8
construction	5.8
Military forces	17,500

Source *Encyclopaedia Britannica*

disputed the ownership of the islands. The ubiquitous Henry Morgan had a lair at Port Royal, Roatán and, according to local mythology, is buried on Utila. The British held the group for over a century before ceding the islands to Honduras in 1859.

Fauna

The Bay Islands' separation from the mainland permitted the development of a number of endemic animal species. Of the 106 species of sea bird reported on the islands, 20 (species and subspecies) are endemic, as are two lizards, the Roatán coral snake (poisonous) and a local type of *garrobo* (a reptile). The agouti found on Roatán is different from that found on the continent. The white-tailed deer is set to follow the islands' wild pig into extinction following indiscriminate hunting and the burning of vegetation. The Bay Islands Conservation Association (BICA) can be contacted through Charles George, "Vegas", Edificio Cooper, Calle Principal, Coxen Hole, Roatán, T (504) 45-14-24, or Shelby McNab, c/o Robinson Crusoe Tours, or Troy Bodden, Troy's Dive Shop, Utila. Port Royal Park and Wildlife Refuge on Roatán is a highland reserve and unique Bay Island ecosystem. It contains the largest tract of the pine *pinus caribaea, var. hondurensis* and is home to many endemic species of flora and fauna (opossum, spiny lizard, coral snake, agouti, and a rare parrot). It also has precolumbian archaeological sites, and Port Royal harbour with its historical associations. BICA is seeking financial assistance to manage the Park and Refuge. At Sandy Bay, Roatán, is Carambola Botanical Gardens (Bill and Irma Brady, T 45-11-17), open daily 0700-1700, with flowering plants, ferns, spices, fruit trees, an orchid collection and archaeological sites. A 20-min walk from the garden goes to the top of the Monte Carambola past the Iguana Wall, a breeding ground for iguana and parrots.

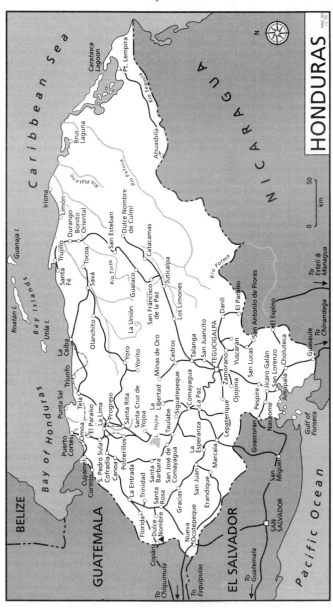

Diving and Marine Life

The underwater environment is rich and extensive. Reefs surround the islands, often within swimming distance of the shore. They are a continuation of one of the largest barrier reefs in the world, stretching from reefs off Belize. Caves and caverns are a common feature, with a wide variety of sponges and the best collection of pillar coral in the Caribbean. 95% of the region's known corals can, it is claimed, be found in these waters. Snorkellers and divers are strongly recommended not to touch or stand on the coral reefs; the slightest contact, even the turbulence of a fin, will kill the delicate organisms. There is also great diversity in the fish, crustacea, turtles and other creatures. This wealth of marine life (and the dry land it surrounds) has inspired the Asociación Hondureña de Ecología (Honduran Ecology Association) to designate the following areas as sanctuaries or natural parks: all of Utila, except the island's settlements; the National Marine Park of Barbareta (comprising the islands of Barbareta, Morat, Santa Elena, mangrove swamps, the only remaining humid tropical forest (on Diamond Rock), unsurpassed coral reefs, and the E end of Roatán); West End, Roatán; 90% of Guanaja and its surrounding reefs. BICA manages the Sandy Bay Marine Reserve on West End, Roatán. The reserve contains coral reef ecosystems, which divers and snorkellers are permitted to visit under the control of BICA and local operators. Plans are under way to extend the reserve.

In addition, Honduras' other islands have been declared marine sanctuaries (Swan Islands, Cayos Cochinos) or biological reserves (Cayos Zapotillos and Misquitos), to protect the bird and aquatic life. (For more information, contact the Asociación Hondureña de Ecología, T 32-38-62/32-18-00, Tegucigalpa, or at its office ½ block N of Farmacia Tegucigalpa, Parque Finlay, near *Hotel Granada*, street has no sign, but the house displays the AHE plaque).

The islands are a major diving centre. Each of the three main islands offers a fascinating range of diving environments, from shallow, flat-bottomed dives to dramatic sheer reef walls. Jorge Valle-Aguiluz writes: "The reef area is so extensive and the dive resorts so few that there is very little chance that you will see another dive boat during your visit. Where the best diving is to be found is strictly a matter of opinion.

"Bay Islands coral formations are mostly close-fringing reefs with deeper areas near the shore creating extensive drop-offs, or walls, a short distance from the reef crest. A few areas near Utila, Cayos Cochinos and Pigeon Cays have a variety of patch, platform and bank reefs. An impressive feature of most Bay Islands reefs is the dramatic spur and groove systems associated with modern and ancient river drainage and local tide channels.

"Variations on this theme result in the development of numerous clefts, fissures, ledges, undercuts, overhangs, swim throughs, tunnels, caves, holes, and sizeable cathedral effects. Perhaps the most memorable example of this characteristic is Mary's Place on the S side of Roatán. Most island dive operations feature a number of special dive sites through wide or narrow cracks, with divers surrounded by huge masses of coral."

Snorkelling and diving equipment can be rented, and many of the hotels and resorts offer dive packages. Information on diving can be obtained from Jorge Valle-Aguiluz at his *Café Allegro*, Av República de Chile 360-B, Colonia Palmira, Tegucigalpa. For more details of diving and boating possibilities, see text below.

Recompression Chamber and Ambulance are situated at "Cornerstone", at the entrance to *Anthony's Key Resort*, Sandy Bay, T 45-15-15.

UTILA

Utila (41 sq km, population 1,515) is only 32 km from La Ceiba and is low lying, with only two hills, Pumpkin, and the smaller Stewarts with an aerial. The latter is nearer the main town, which is known locally as East Harbour. There are caves to which you can hike, one of them being reputed locally to have been a hideout for Henry Morgan. There is some evidence of Paya Indian culture. Utila is the cheapest and least developed of the islands to visit; there are no big resorts, but rather simpler dwellings where you can rent rooms.

You can hike to Pumpkin Hill (45 mins beyond *Bucket of Blood Bar*, on E side of the island) where there are some fresh water caves and a beach nearby (watch out for sharp coral), with a bar open in season. It can be very muddy after rain. Another 40-min hike goes to the N part of the island along a forested path. There are good views and a beach at the end, but it is rocky so sandals are needed. Take plenty of insect repellent; you will need to protect against sandflies on dry days when there is no breeze. Coconut oil or Avon "Skin-so-Soft" helps to keep them off. Sunbathing and swimming are not particularly good, but there is a swimming hole near the airport. At the left-hand end of the airstrip (from the town) is one of the best places for coral and quantity of fish. Snorkelling and diving equipment for hire. Snorkelling gear costs US$3 per day. See below, **Diving**.

A 20-min motorboat ride from East Harbour are the Cays, a chain of small islands populated by fisherfolk off the SW coast of Utila. On the main Cay, a few families live; they are very friendly to foreigners, but there is nowhere to put a tent. Three islands further out is Water Cay, one of the few places where you can camp, sling a hammock or, in emergency, sleep in, or under, the house of the caretaker; take food and fresh water. The caretaker collects a US$1 pp fee for land-ing. There are no facilities, but children sell cheap *pasteles de carne*. It is a coconut island with "white holes" (sandy areas with wonderful hot bathing in the afternoon) and some of the most beautiful underwater reefs in the world. The best snorkelling is off the S shore, a short walk from the beach, shallow water all around. To hire a *dory* (big motorized canoe) costs US$30 for up to 8; many boatmen go and will collect you in the evening, recommended.

Island Information – Utila
● **Where To Stay**
The best hotel on the island is *Utila Lodge*, T 45-31-43, usually booked through US agent T (904) 588-4131, an all-wooden building with decks and balconies, harbour view, US$50-67d, a/c, 8 rooms, clean and modern, run by Americans Shirley and Tom, meals only when they have guests; *Bay View*, 100m from *Utila Lodge*, with bath, spotlessly clean, private pier, great location with sea views, highly rec; *Harbour View*, a few 100m past the bank on the left, US$15d, clean, fans, bathrooms clean, restaurant downstairs, owner takes diving and snorkelling trips; *Blue Bayou*, 25 mins out of town, opp end from airport (1 hr away), a beautiful spot for diving off the reef, US$10d, may be closed out of season, snacks and drinks available, restaurant only in high season, hammocks on the porch in the day, breeze usually keeps the mosquitoes away, bike rental US$2/day (take torch for night-time riding), rents canoes; *Trudy's*, 5 mins from airport, US$4.60-6.50 pp with and without bath, comfortable, good breakfast and evening meals (expensive, may be little room for non-residents), US satellite TV, diving equipment and boats for hire; opp, cheaper, is *Laguna del Mar*, T 45-31-03, terrace, clean, fan, mosquito net, diving offered with Underwater Vision (see below); also *Spencer*, Main St, T 45-31-62, and *Sea Side*, on Sand Beach Road, pleasant, clean, private pier and garden, helpful owner; *Palm Villa*, cabins at US$15 for 4, cooking facilities, good value, run by Willis Bodden; *Cross Creek* (see also **Diving** below), US$4.50, clean rooms, basic bathrooms, house rental US$40 for 2, US$45 for 3 and US$50 for 4; *Monkey Tail Inn*, US$1.30 pp, noisy, wooden building, you may share your room with bats!, cooking facilities, water all the time (beyond the *Bucket of Blood Bar*); *Coopers Inn*, under US$7d, very clean and friendly, rec.

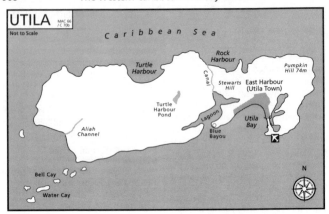

Cheap and basic rooms at *Blueberry Hill* (run by Norma and Will, very friendly, clothes washing facilities), opposite *Bucket of Blood*, and *Dolores*; plenty of other houses and rooms for rent.

● Restaurants

Mis Delicias, small, go early, good fish, good breakfasts, but slow service and not that clean; *Tropical Sunset and Bar*, pleasant atmosphere, good food and cheap drinks; *Orma's*, simple but good food in nice little thatched bar overlooking the harbour; *Sea Side Inn*, see above under **Where to Stay**, offers good food; *Comedor El Teleño*, good food, meeting point; *Nolan's Place*, run by Dorothy, popular with locals, good food; *Selly's*, up the hill beyond *Bucket of Blood*, the best food, cheap, self-service, popular with travellers, cable TV. *Mermaid's Corner Souvenir Shoppe* has good pastries when open. *Underground*, on Main St, Caribbean-style food, pleasant, good value; *Utila* for ice-cream, lemonade and food. Good yoghurt at Henderson's store; *Green Ribbon* store has cakes and sandwiches to order.

● Bars

Bucket of Blood, owned by Mr Woods, a mine of information on the history of Utila and the Cays; on the same side of the road is *Tompsons*, good breakfasts; *The Lost Soles* (sic), *07* and *Casino* are both lively, as is *Captain Roy's*, next to the airport. *Bahia del Mar*, bar with pier and swimming; *Sea Breaker*, on waterfront behind *Orma's*.

● Arts and Crafts

Günther Kordovsky is a painter and sculptor with a gallery at his house (up the hill, near *Selly's* restaurant), good map of Utila, paintings, cards, wood carving and black coral jewellery (remember that black coral is protected); another sculptor is Bill Green, ask for him at *Casino Bar*.

● Facilities

There is a bank for changing dollars (Bancahsa) and you can get cash against a Visa card, but not Mastercard. Dollars are accepted on the island. There is a post office, a Hondutel office near *Utila Lodge*, and a good clinic. A paved road runs through the town and there is a 60m concrete pier.

● Tours

Shelby McNab, who runs Robinson Crusoe Tours, takes visitors on half-day tours around the island (US$10 pp) explaining his theory that Daniel Defoe based his famous book on Robinson Crusoe on Utila (not Alexander Selkirk off Chile), fascinating. He also runs Gables Health Club, keep-fit, weight machines, steam bath and massages.

● Diving

All 8 schools offer similar prices and include accommodation. If planning to do a diving course, take a passport-sized photograph with you for the PADI certificate. **NB** It may be difficult to pay by credit card. *Bay Islands Divers* give instruction to PADI certification level; prices start at US$145 for individually structured courses. *Cross Creek*, run by Ronald

Janssen, T 45-31-34, F 45-32-34, scuba trips for beginners and certified divers, US$30 for 2 dives in one day, free accommodation for that day; 4-day beginner course (PADI, open water), 4 nights' accommodation, US$175; advanced open water, 2 days, 5 dives US$150; rescue and dive master, 3 weeks, US$750; snorkel equipment (mask, snorkel and fins) US$2.50, 2-3 instructors, new equipment. Gunter Kordovsky teaches a range of PADI courses, including instructor training, with 26 years' diving experience on Utila, at his dive school, T 45-31-13/31-30, based at Sea Side Inn, also video and photographic services (and arts and crafts, see above). *Utila Watersports*, excellent equipment, popular with travellers (but pay in dollars), run by Troy Bodden, who also owns Bell Cay, a tiny immaculately-kept cay next to Water Cay (2 houses, fully self-contained, usually booked by groups, up to 14 people, US$50 per day pp, bookings through Caribbean Travel Agency in La Ceiba, T 43-13-60/1), Troy also hires out snorkel equipment and takes boat trips and one of his scuba instructors, Chris Watto, has been highly rec, he has an underwater video camera and you can have your dives transferred onto VHS to take home, US$35 for each video. Also recommended is Chris Phillips from the Utila Dive Centre, who is patient with beginners and speaks English, PADI certificates, dive trips. Linda Geraci of *Underwater Vision* is rec, English speaking, good equipment and good ratio of students/instructors. *Sea-Eye* (Danish run) also rec, Peder is a thorough instructor and equipment is good.

ROATAN

It is a few hours' sail to ***Roatán***, the largest of the islands (127 sq km, population 10,245). It has a paved road running from West End to just beyond French Harbour, continuing unpaved to Oak Ridge, Punta Gorda and Wilkes Point; there are other, unmade roads. Renting a car or scooter gives access to many places that public transport does not reach. The capital of the department, Coxen Hole, or Roatán City, is on the SW shore. Besides being the seat of the local government, it has immigration, customs and the law courts. Port Royal, towards the E end of the island, and famous in the annals of buccaneering, is now just a community of private homes with no public facilities.

From Coxen Hole to Sandy Bay, with the Sandy Bay Reserve and the Carambola Botanical Gardens, is a 2-hr walk, or a US$1 bus ride (airport employees try to charge US$12; it should only be US$2 from the airport). West End, a further 5 mins by road beyond Sandy Bay, is a quiet community at the W tip of the island. There are several good restaurants as well as hotels with bungalows and rooms to rent. You can take a small motor boat from *Foster and Vivian's Restaurant* for a 10-min ride to West Bay (US$1). West Bay is a beautiful, clean, unspoilt beach with excellent snor-

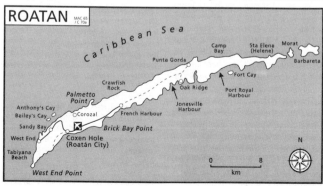

kelling at the far end; there are a couple of jetties where you can escape the sand-flies which lurk in the powdery white sand (use coconut oil or Avon Skin-so-Soft as protection; latter is sold in Coxen Hole Supermarket). Take your own food and drinks, and insect repellent, because there are no facilities there. It is a stiff walk from Coxen Hole over the hills (3 hrs) to West End, or take the bus on the paved road for US$1, 20 mins; they run till 1700.

There are many minibuses which wait on Calle Principal in Coxen Hole, going to points E and W; they usually leave on the hour or half-hour. Mi Esperanza has a bus service every 30 mins to French Harbour and Oak ridge (US$1.50). French Harbour, with its shrimping and lobster fleet, is the main fishing port of Roatán. There are 2 seafood packing plants: Mariscos Agua Azul and Mariscos Hybour. The road passes *Coleman's Midway Bakery*, where you can buy freshly-baked products.

The main road goes across the mountain ridge to Wilkes Point, with side roads to Jonesville, Punta Gorda and Oak Ridge. Taking a bus on this route is the best way to see the island's hilly interior, with beautiful views from coast to coast. Jonesville is known for its mangrove canal, which is best reached by hiring a taxi boat in Oak Ridge. In Punta Gorda on the N coast, the oldest established community on Roatán, Black Caribs retain their own language, music, dance, food, crafts and religion. Carib Week, 8-12 April, is a good time to experience their customs. Bus from Coxen's Hole costs US$1. There are also boat tours which include Punta Gorda (information from the Kiwi woman at the secondhand bookstore in West End). Oak Ridge, situated on a cay (US$0.40 crossing in a dory from the bus stop), is built around a deep inlet. It is a charming little fishing port, with rows of dwellings on stilts built on the water's edge (bus Coxen Hole-Oak, 1 hr, US$1.60). You can hire a taxi boat to show you round. As well as its hotels, there is a grocery store and a couple of good restaurants.

Hire a boat for an hour's sail up the coast to Port Royal; old British gun emplacements on Fort Cay. No bus from Port Royal to Oak Ridge, and it's a tough 3-hr walk. Note the Black Carib village of Punta Gorda on the N coast (probably the first non-Indian settlement on the islands). Beaches excellent; the best is said to be Camp Bay on the N coast at the E end (road sometimes too muddy to get there by land). Roatán is expensive, twice as dear as the mainland.

Dennis, at *Foster and Vivian's Restaurant*, West End, sails his glass-bottomed boat to Hottest Sparrow Bay, beyond *Anthony's Key Resort*, where the boat anchors for snorkelling, about US$4 pp in a group of 16, 4½ hrs. He also takes charters and cruises all along the coast. Horseriding available with Sharky, find him by *Brewster's Place* (restaurant in West End), 2-3 hr rides to Flowers Bay, US$10, experienced riders only.

Island Information – Roatán
● Where To Stay And Eat

At West End: *Roberts-Hill*, T 45-11-76, US$20 with bath and fan, more basic rooms with shared bath US$10, snorkelling, friendly, good value; *Lost Paradise*, T 45-13-06, F 45-13-88, US$70, full board only, delicious meals (open to non-residents, book in advance), snorkelling equipment, transport back to airport, dollars exchange; *Sunrise Resort*, T 45-12-65, dive shop offers packages with diving, full board etc, good value, under US$70; not so expensive is *Keifitos Plantation Resort*, bungalows on private beach, beautiful setting, friendly owners, rec; similar price range; *Seagrape Plantation*, T 45-14-28, cabins, family atmosphere, friendly; *Coconut Tree Hotel and Restaurant*, owner Vince, US$35, private cabins (3 double beds), hot water, fan, fridge, clean, friendly; *Half Moon Bay Cabins*, T 45-10-80/13-82, US$25, bungalows and cabins with bath, restaurant with excellent seafood (same owner as *Coral* at Coxen Hole); *Seaside Cottages*, US$25, individual cabins, pleasant owner, Rudy, coffee shop with good cookies and breakfasts, T 45-12-05; *Jimmy's Lodge*, US$7, very friendly, hammocks, cheap meals, snorkelling gear and horseriding available, it is very cheap to sling a hammock here, but very exposed and the tin roof is not waterproof, you'll be bitten by sandflies, hosepipe for shower; similar price at *Mario's Rooms*, friendly, on beach, water; also *Stass' Place*, cheap rooms. *Sam's*, at the far end near *Jimmy's*, very cheap, but hot rooms, no water, popular with travellers, cheap food. Other rooms for rent, about US$5d, some rather dingy. At Gibson Bight, on the road to West End, are *Alexander's Cabins*, T 45-15-01.

Places to eat at West End: *Foster and Vivian's Restaurant* is on the beach, good atmosphere and seafood, not cheap, built over the water, no sandflies, owned by Foster Diaz, his wife Vivian is the cook (they are Texans and jointly own a duplex on the beach, enquire at the restaurant, or to the other partner Robert Beels in Mount Dora, Florida, T 904-383-7424). *Sea View Restaurant*, go early since it's small and often runs out of food, large portions, home cooking, band dances on Fri; *Luna's Bay Café*, good for breakfast, downstairs at *Lucy's Minimart* for basic foodstuffs; *Bite on the Beach*, open Tues-Sun, daily menu, 5 mins from beach, excellent fresh seafood at reasonable prices, run by Dian and Gene, formerly backpackers. *Rudy's* has good pancakes and cookies for breakfast; next door is *Bamboo Hut*, breakfasts and snacks, film shows in evening, US$1. Try the coconut bread which can be bought from the local women. There is a good gift shop, *Joanna's* next to *Robert's-Hill*, with some good quality products.

At Sandy Bay: *Anthony's Key Resort*, T 45-10-03, F 45-13-27 (US$75 full board), glorious situation, accommodation in small wooden cabins, launch and diving facilities (US$20, US$40 non-residents, the owner, Julio Galindo, is very serious about helping the environment and local community, the resort's own cay, Bailey's, has a small wildlife reserve (parrots, cockatoo, toucan, monkeys, agoutis, turtles), it has an interesting museum of some archaeological and colonial history, natural history laboratory, A-V lecture hall (entry for non-guests US$2); it also has a dolphin enclosure in a natural pool, guests can swim with the dolphins for US$45, non-guests US$50); *Oceanside Inn*, T 45-15-52, F 45-15-32, clean, comfortable, friendly owners Joseph and Jenny, nice deck with view of bay, full board, superb restaurant, diving packages offered, highly rec (under US$70 pp). *Quinn's*, reasonable.

At French Harbour: *French Harbour Yacht Club*, T 45-14-78, F 45-14-59, US$35,

cable TV in every room, reasonable rates, good food (especially lunch), friendly; *Buccaneer*, T 45-10-32, F 45-12-89 (Tegucigalpa T 36-90-03, F 36-98-00, San Pedro Sula T 52-62-42, F 52-62-39), from US$55 to US$195 pp for a 3-day, 2-night package, good food, rec; *Fantasy Island Beach Resort*, T 45-12-22 (USA 813-251-5771, F 45-12-68), 80 a/c rooms, on a 15-acre cay, US$90-150, up to US$390 for package, pool, diving, many other watersports; *Coco View Resort*, T 45-10-11, about US$60; *Coral Reef Inn*; *Caribinn*, both US$15-20 range; *Hotelito*, US$10, sometimes no water, in the village; *Brito's* (no sign, green) just before *Buccaneer Inn*, US$6-7, with fan, very good value; a bit dearer, *Isabel*, comfortable, restaurant, free transport to airport;. *Dixon's Plaza*, past the *Buccaneer*, good; *Romeo's Restaurant*, T 45-15-18, good for seafood. *Celebrations*, is a good a/c nightclub, entrance US$1.50, drinks expensive, with restaurant and marina, open evenings, T 45-15-44.

At Brick Bay: *Caribbean Sailing Club*, modern hotel, US$55, with breakfast; *Romeo's Resort Dive and Yacht Club*, T 45-11-27, F 45-15-94, US$30 and up, dedicated dive resort, good.

At Oak Ridge: *Reef House Resort*, T 45-21-42/22-97, F 45-21-42, in USA (512) 681-2888, 1-800-328-8897, F (512) 341-7942, US$130d, inc meals, various packages, inc diving, offered, wooden cabins with seaview balconies, seaside bar, private natural pool, good snorkelling from the shore, manager Carlos Acosta. *San José Hotel*, US$10, with bath (2 rooms), US$8 without (3 rooms), clean, pleasant, good value, good food, English-speaking owner, Louise Solórzano. There is a *pizzería* and, next door, a supermarket.

At Port Royal: *Camp Bay Resort*, over US$50; *Roatán Lodge*, luxury accommodation in cabins, hosts Brian and Lisa Blancher provide scuba diving and snorkelling expeditions; *Miss Merlee's Guest House*.

At Coxen Hole: *Coral*, T 45-10-80, owner Dr Jackeline Bush, US$10d, shared bath, clean, comfortable, Peace Corps favourite; *Airport View*, T 45-10-74, US$25 (less without bath or a/c); *Cay View*, Calle Principal, T 45-12-02, F 45-11-79, 15 rooms, US$16d, a/c, phone, laundry, restaurant, bar, fishing, snorkelling, diving, cable TV; *El Paso*, T 45-10-59, US$10, shared bath, restaurant (not cheap). Many of the cheaper hotels have water shortages.

Comedor Ray Monty, very cheap, set meal

US$1.50 but avoid the meat, fish good; *Burger Hut*, opp *Hotel Coral*, clean, good, chicken and fish, not expensive; *Hungry Diver*, pizzas and expensive seafood. *El Punto*, bar with one basic dish, very cheap. *H B Warren*, large well-stocked supermarket with cafetería, mainly lunch and snacks, open 0700-1800. *Hibiscus Sweet Shop*, homemade fruit pies, cakes and biscuits. There is also good food at *DJ's Bar and Grill* on Osgood Cay, a few mins by free water-taxi from the wharf.

There are other, cheaper, places to stay, for example, Miss Effie's (near *Anthony's Key Resort*) and houses to let (at West End, Half Moon Bay, or Punta Gorda).

● **Facilities**
At Coxen Hole are a post office, tourist information, *VIPs* duty free shop, groceries and several souvenir shops.

● **Discothèques**
2 informal ones which come alive about midnight, *Paraguas* and *Harbour View*. They play mostly reggae, punta, calypso, salsa, punta and some rock.

● **Banks**
Banco Atlántida and Bancahsa in Coxen Hole and French Harbour; also Banco Sogerín and Banffaa. Bancahsa in Oak Ridge, T 45-22-10, Mastercard for cash advances. No banks in West End, but TCs will be changed by *Bamboo Hut*.

● **Car Rental**
National, *Hotel Fantasy Island*, T 45-11-28; Amigo at the airport. Tokio Motorbike Rental, attached to *Chino's* at West End, US$21 pp per day.

● **Information**
Tourist office at the airport, T 45-15-59. Excellent map of the island at about 1:50,000 supplied by Antonio E Rosales, T 45-15-59. The local tourist magazine is *Coconut Telegraph*.

● **Travel Agents**
Bay Islands Tour and Travel Center, in Coxen Hole and French Harbour. *Tropical Travel*, in *Hotel Cay View*, T 45-11-46; *Columbia Tours*, Barrio El Centro, T 45-11-60.

● **Diving**
West End: Tyll Sass, T 45-1314 or in USA (813) 593-1259, one-tank dive US$20, windsurfing US$4 per hour, resort courses in both sports and charters available; Seagrape does PADI courses for US$150; Ocean Divers diving and snorkel hire, mask, snorkel and fin rental US$5 per day. Roatán Divers, Half Moon Bay,

West End, T 45-12-65, Tino and Alejo Monterrosa, experienced, Spanish and English spoken, US$20 package dives, US$25 single dives, night dives, rec. French Harbour: John Davis, Green House on pier below Yachting Club, US$300 for 4 days (less pp for groups); at the *Yacht Club* itself, Off the Wall Divers. The *Bay Islands Aggressor* operates out of Roatán, US$1,395 for a 6-day cruise; contact The Aggressor Fleet, PO Drawer K, Morgan City, LA 70381, T (504) 385-2416, F (504) 384-0817 (1-800-348-2628). The most popular dive sites have permanent mooring buoys; most dive shops hold briefings on diving in the Reserve to minimize ecological damage.

GUANAJA

Columbus called Guanaja, the easternmost of the group, the Island of Pines, and the tree is still abundant. The locals call the island Bonacca, and it is also known as Isla Grande. The island's origins are both volcanic and coraline, so it has a variety of aspects. Marble Hill cave can be visited. Good (but sweaty) clambering on the island gives splendid views of the jungle and the sea. There are several attractive waterfalls. Much of Guanaja town, covering a small cay off the coast, is built on stilts above sea water: hence its nick-name, the "Venice of Honduras". Many other cays surround the coast and launches go to West End, Pine Ridge Bight, Michael Rock, Sandy Bay and Los Cayos. The island's population is 4,000; its area is 56 sq km. Bathing is made somewhat unpleasant by the many sandflies. These and mosquitoes cannot be escaped on the island, all the beaches are infected (coconut oil will help to ward off sandflies and doubles as sun protection). The cays are better, including Guanaja town. South West Caye is specially recommended. The diving and snorkelling in the clear waters compensates for any discomfort on the shore.

Island Information – Guanaja
● **Where To Stay**
Alexander, US$25, T 45-43-26, US$100 in 3-bed, 3-bathroom apartment; *Bayman Bay Club* (beautiful location on the N coast, T 45-

41-79) and *Posada del Sol* (on an outlying cay, beach, pool, tennis, fitness studio, T 45-43-11), both have diving facilities and are in the US$120-150 range; *Miller*, US$25 (cheaper without air conditioning or bath, TV, restaurant, T 45-43-27); *Harry Carter*, US$15, ask for a fan, clean however. *El Rosari*, US$25, with bath and a/c. *Club Guanaja Este*, full board available, many aquatic activities, and horseriding and hiking, reservations and information PO Box 40541, Cincinnati, Ohio 45240 or travel agents. *Casa Sobre El Mar*, on Bound Cay, T 45-42-69 (31-05-95 in Tegucigalpa), offers all-inclusive packages for US$75 per person. *Day Inn*, hotel and restaurant.

● **Where To Eat**
Harbour Light, through *Mountain View* discothèque, good food reasonably priced for the island; *The Nest*, T 45-42-90, good eating in the evening; *Glenda's*, good standard meals for under US$1, small sandwiches.

● **Facilities**
There are 3 banks, including Bancahsa and Banco Atlántida.

● **Sailing and Diving**
SV Railovy, T (504) 45-41-35, F (504) 45-42-74, is a 40 foot yacht running local cruises and excursion packages; also sailing, diving and snorkelling services, and PADI courses. Ask for Hans on VHF radio channel 70.

CAYOS COCHINOS

The Cayos Cochinos (Hog Islands), with lovely primeval hardwood forests, are 17 km NE of La Ceiba (two small islands and thirteen palm-fringed cays): privately owned with reserved accommodation at Cayos del Sol. On the Isla de Cochino Grande is a dive resort; very beautiful. The owner of the largest island, Bobby Griffith, permits camping, especially if you can give him a news magazine or two. See above on trips from Utila.

● **Tours** *Sea Safaris*, Ocean Club, 14 de Julio, Calle 1, PO Box 601, La Ceiba, T/F 43-22-72, offer trips to the Cayos Cochinos (Sandy Island), one-day, or sleeping the night in thatched hut or hammock; they also do trips to other destinations around La Ceiba, have a book exchange (several European languages) and a travellers' message desk.

INFORMATION FOR VISITORS

● **Documents**
A visa is not required, nor tourist card, for nationals of all West European countries, USA, Canada, Australia, New Zealand, or Japan. Citizens of other countries need either a tourist card which can be bought from Honduran consulates for US$2-3, occasionally less, or a visa, and they should enquire at a Honduran consulate in advance to see which they need. The price of a visa seems to vary per nationality, and according to where bought. It is imperative to check entry requirements in advance at a consulate.

Extensions of 30 days are easy to obtain (up to a maximum of 6 months' stay, cost US$5). There are immigration offices for extensions at La Ceiba, San Pedro Sula and other towns, and all are more helpful than the Tegucigalpa office. A valid International Certificate of Vaccination against smallpox is required only from visitors coming from the Indian subcontinent, Indonesia and the countries of Southern Africa. A ticket out of the country is necessary for air travellers (if coming from USA, you won't be allowed on the plane without one); onward tickets must be bought outside the country. It is not impossible to cash in the return half of the ticket in Honduras, but there is no guarantee and plenty of time is required.

There are no Customs duties on personal effects; 200 cigarettes or 100 cigars, or $^1/_2$ kg of tobacco, and 2 quarts of spirit are allowed in free.

● **How To Get There**
Taca has direct flights once a week, each to Roatán from Houston, Miami and New Orleans. Taca/Isleña connection from Miami via San Pedro Sula, daily in season. Alternatively, the best flight connections from the USA are to San Pedro Sula, the second city, from Miami (American, Iberia, Taca), then fly Taca or Isleña to the islands; or else go Isleña or Lacsa to La Ceiba from Tegucigalpa and on from there (see **Transport to Roatán** below). There may be irregular boat connections with the Cayman Islands (see below). Flights to all 3 main islands originate in La Ceiba, with interconnection flights between Roatán and Guanaja only. Alternatively, you can go overland from either city (taking in some of mainland Honduras's sights on the way – see *The Mexico and Central American Handbook*) to the main port of ac-

cess, La Ceiba, or to Puerto Cortés (which has a less frequent service).

There are no direct flights to Tegucigalpa from Europe, but connecting flights can be made via Guatemala (with KLM or Iberia) or Miami, then American Airlines, or Taca. To Tegucigalpa from New Orleans with Lacsa, or with Continental (via Houston); from Houston, besides Continental, Taca flies daily via San Salvador. Iberia flies to San Pedro Sula via Miami from Madrid twice a week. Lacsa flies to San Pedro Sula from New York (also Continental and American), New Orleans, Los Angeles, Cancún and Mexico City. Taca and American fly direct Miami-San Pedro Sula. Taca and Lacsa fly from Tegucigalpa to all Central American capitals; Lacsa and Aero Costa Rica fly to San José from San Pedro Sula direct; Taca also flies to Mexico City. Copa flies from Panama City and Mexico City to San Pedro Sula. Connections with Curaçao are made at Guatemala City (KLM/Taca).

There is an airport tax and hospital tax of 3% on all tickets sold for domestic journeys, and a 10% tax on airline tickets for international journeys. There is an airport departure tax of US$18 and a customs tax of 20 lempiras (neither charged if in transit less than 9 hrs). Note that the border offices close at 1700, not 1800 as in most other countries; there may be a fee charged after that time.

La Ceiba is reached by bus in 3-4 hrs from San Pedro Sula (Tupsa, 2 Avenida N, 1-2 Calle, hourly from 0530, US$2); Puerto Cortés is 45 mins by bus from San Pedro Sula (eg Impala, 2 Avenida, 4-5 Calle S O, No 23, several each hour, US$0.75). If going from the capital there is a direct Traliasa bus to La Ceiba for US$5, or you have to go to San Pedro Sula and change buses there: take a Hedmán Alas bus (the best, US$4, or luxury service US$8.90, 4½ hrs, address in Tegucigalpa: 13-14 Calle, 11 Avenida, Comayagüela district, T 37-71-43; in San Pedro Sula: 7-8 Avenida N O, 3 Calle, Casa 51, T 53-13-61); other services between Tegucigalpa and San Pedro are cheaper at US$2.50.

Transport to Utila Isleña and Sosa fly from La Ceiba for US$9 one way. Flights leave at 0600, 1500 and 1600, 15 mins. Fare to Tegucigalpa US$25. Check all flight times in advance, flight information and ticket sales at *Salon 07*. Always reserve flights and make onward reservations in advance. Sosa in La Ceiba, T 43-13-99, Isleña T 43-01-97 (downtown), 43-23-26 (airport). There are no flights to the other islands. Local transport between airport and hotels.

Boats MV *Starfish* goes from the new harbour in Utila to **La Ceiba** Mon 0400 returning from La Ceiba Tues 1200, US$4.50 each way (information from *Green Ribbon* store). There are irregular boats to **Puerto Cortés**, times posted in main street, 7 hrs, US$7.50, ask at public dock. Fishing boats from La Ceiba charge US$10 to Utila.

Boats from Utila to Roatán can be chartered for about US$70; with enough passengers this can work out cheaper than flying back to La Ceiba and out to Roatán. Occasional freight boats, eg *Utila Tom*, take passengers from Utila to Roatán. It's a 3-hr journey between the 2 islands and you and your possessions are liable to get soaked.

Transport to Roatán Take a plane to Coxen Hole (airport is 20 mins walk from town, taxi US$1.50) and launch up coast to French Harbour and Oak Ridge. Isleña and Taca fly from **La Ceiba** several times a day, US$16 one way (fewer on Sun); flights also to and from **Tegucigalpa** and **San Pedro Sula**, frequency varies according to season. From the USA, Taca flies on Sat from **Houston** via San Pedro Sula, on Sun from **Miami**, and on Fri from **New Orleans**; Taca/Isleña connection from Miami via San Pedro Sula, daily in season, Sosa fly from La Ceiba to Roatán 0700 and 1300 Mon-Sat, continuing to **Guanaja** (US$15 one way) about 10 mins after arrival in Roatán. Roatán airport takes jets. Airlines: Taca, Edificio Shop and Save, Coxen Hole, T 45-12-36, at airport T 45-13-87; Isleña, airport T 45-10-88.

Boats go irregularly from Puerto Cortés to Roatán, US$5 plus US$0.50 dock charge for tourists. Boats occasionally from the new harbour 5 km E of La Ceiba, US$20; from Roatán enquire at the wharf for boats to La Ceiba. Fishing boats to La Ceiba for US$10 pp.

Transport to Guanaja An airport on Bonacca Island, boat to Guanaja, US$1; Isleña has flights daily except Sun from La Ceiba, leaving at 1430, 30 mins, US$20 each way. Flights from San Pedro Sula leave at 1500, US$62 return. Other, non-scheduled flights are available.

The *Suyapa* sails between Guanaja, La Ceiba and Puerto Cortés. The *Miss Sheila* also does the same run and goes on to George Town (Grand Cayman). Cable Doly Zapata, Guanaja, for monthly sailing dates to Grand Cayman (US$75 one way). Irregular sailings from Guanaja to Trujillo, twice a week, 5 hrs, US$10. Irregular but frequent sailings in lobster boats for next to nothing to Puerto Lempira in Caratasco Lagoon, Mosquitia, or more likely, only as far as the Río Plátano.

Transport to Cayos Cochinos Take a bus from the stop 1 block from La Ceiba market to Nueva Armenia (US$1.50), then try to hitch on a dugout, or charter one (about US$10). See also *Sea Safaris*, above.

● **Where To Stay On The Mainland**

Accommodation on the islands is given above.

If you have to spend the night in Tegucigalpa or San Pedro Sula, there are many hotels in each city in all price ranges. In Tegucigalpa, the cheaper ones tend to be in the Comayagüela district, which is most convenient for the bus terminals. The most expensive is the *Honduras Maya* in Colonia Palmira. In San Pedro Sula, the best is the *Gran Hotel Sula*, in the city; cheaper ones can be found between the bus terminals and the downtown market.

Accommodation is more limited in **La Ceiba**: the cheapest are beside the railway line leading from the central square to the pier; middle range hotels can be found on Avenida San Isidro (eg *Ceiba*, *Iberia*, *El Caribe*, all reasonable); *Príncipe*, on 7 Calle between Av 14 de Julio and Av San Isidro, US$10 with bath and a/c, cheaper with fan, clean, rec; the best in town is probably the *Colonial*, Av 14 de Julio, 6a y 7a Calle, T 43-19-53, F 43-19-55, over US$20 a night, a/c, jacuzzi, nice atmosphere, or *Gran Hotel París*, Parque Central. *Hotel San Carlos* and its cafeteria (near *Hotel Iberia*) is an information point for travel to the Bay Islands (cheap rooms).

Hotels in **Puerto Cortés** tend to be more basic, but in the US$30-40 range *International Mr Ggeerr* (9 Calle, 2 Av E, T 55-04-44, F 55-07-50) has been rec; also *Costa Azul*, Playa El Faro, T 55-22-60, F 55-22-62, with restaurant, sports including horse riding, first class. Rec at the cheaper end is *Formosa*, friendly Chinese owners, good food and value.

● **Tipping**

Normally 10% of the bill.

● **Currency**

The Honduran unit is the lempira, divided into 100 centavos. It was floated against the US dollar in 1990, having been fixed at a value of half the dollar since 1926. The exchange rate is given in the Exchange Rate tables at the end of the book.

● **Credit Cards**

Mastercard and Visa are accepted in major hotels and most restaurants in cities and larger towns. Cash advances from Credomatic, Blvd Morazán, Tegucigalpa, and branches of Ban-

cahsa, Ficensa and Futuro throughout the country. Cash advances using Mastercard costs US$10 in banks. Mastercard/Cirrus ATMs at branches of Credomatic, Banco de Occidente or Ficensa at 11 locations, including Tegucigalpa, La Ceiba, Puerto Cortés, Roatán, San Pedro Sula and Tela.

● **Health**

Dysentery and stomach parasites are common and malaria is endemic in coastal regions, where a prophylactic regime should be undertaken and mosquito nets carried. Inoculate against typhoid and tetanus. Cholera is on the increase on the mainland, so eating on the street or at market stalls can no longer be recommended. Water is definitely not safe; drink bottled water. Salads and raw vegetables must be sterilized under personal supervision. There are hospitals at Tegucigalpa and all the larger towns.

Although the islands' climate is cooled by the trade winds, the sun is very strong (the locals bathe in T-shirts). Sandflies and other insects are common, especially away from the resorts.

● **Climate**

Average temperature is about 27°C, with E trade winds blowing all year. The wettest months are October to February; little rain falls March to May.

● **Public Holidays In Honduras**

Most of the feast days of the Roman Catholic religion and also New Year's Day (1 January), Day of the Americas (14 April), Holy Week: Thursday, Friday, and Saturday before Easter Sunday, Labour Day (1 May), Independence Day (15 September), Francisco Morazán (3 October), Columbus' arrival in America (12 October), Army Day (21 October).

● **Time Zone**

Local standard time is 6 hrs behind GMT, 1 hr behind EST.

● **Weights And Measures**

The metric system is in use.

● **Tourist Information**

Instituto Hondureño de Turismo, Edificio Europa, Av Ramón E Cruz y Calle Principal Clínicas Médicas, above Lloyds Bank, Colonia San Carlos, T 22-40-02, F 38-21-02 (offices at Toncontin airport, or SECTUR, Edificio Inmosa, 4 Calle No, 3-4 Avenida, San Pedro Sula, and Ramón Villeda Morales airport, San Pedro Sula). See above for the address of the Asociación Hondureña de Ecología.

THE BELIZE CAYES

BELIZE, formerly known as British Honduras, borders on Mexico and Guatemala, and has a land area of about 8,900 square miles, including numerous small islands, called cayes. Its greatest length (N-S) is 174 miles and its greatest width (E-W) is 68 miles. The capital is Belmopan, but the main commercial centre is Belize City on the coast.

The coastlands are low and swampy with much mangrove, many salt and fresh water lagoons and some sandy beaches. In the N the land is low and flat, but in the SW there is a heavily forested mountain massif with a general elevation of between 2,000 and 3,000 feet. In the E part are the Maya Mountains, not yet wholly explored, and the Cockscomb Range which rises to a height of 3,675 feet at Victoria Peak. To the W are some 250 square miles of the Mountain Pine Ridge, with large open spaces and some of the best scenery in the country.

The most fertile areas of the country are in the N foothills of the Maya Mountains: citrus fruit is grown in the Stann Creek valley, while in the valley of the Mopan, or upper Belize river, cattle raising and mixed farming are successful. The N area of the country has long proved suitable for sugar cane production. In the S bananas and mangoes are cultivated. The lower valley of the Belize river is a rice-growing area as well as being used for mixed farming and citrus cultivation.

The population is estimated at 196,000 (1992). About 40% of them are of mixed ancestry, the so-called Creoles. They predominate in Belize City and along the coast, and on the navigable rivers. 33% of the population as mestizo; 10% are Indians, mostly Mayas, who predominate in the N between the Hondo and New rivers and in the extreme S and W. About 8% of the population are Garifuna (Black Caribs), descendants of the Black Caribs deported from St Vincent in 1797; they have a distinct language, and can be found in the villages and towns along the S coast. They are good linguists, many speaking Mayan languages as well as Spanish and "Creole" English. They also brought much of their culture and customs from the West Indies, including religious practices and ceremonies, for example Yankanu (John Canoe) dancing at Christmas time. The remainder are of unmixed European ancestry (the majority Mennonites, who speak a German dialect, and are friendly and helpful) and a rapidly growing group of North Americans.

English is the official language, although about 75% speak mostly "Creole" English. Spanish is the mother tongue for about 15%. About 30% are bilingual, and 10% trilingual (see above). Spanish is widely spoken in the N and W areas.

History

Throughout the country, especially in the forests of the centre and S are many ruins of the Classic Maya Period, which flourished here and in neighbouring Guatemala from the 4th to the 9th century and then somewhat mysteriously emigrated to Yucatán. It has been estimated that the population then was ten times what it is now.

The first settlers were Englishmen and their black slaves from Jamaica who came about 1640 to cut logwood, then the source of textile dyes. The British Government made no claim to the territory but tried to secure the protection of the wood-cutters by treaties with Spain. Even after 1798, when a strong Spanish force was decisively beaten off at St

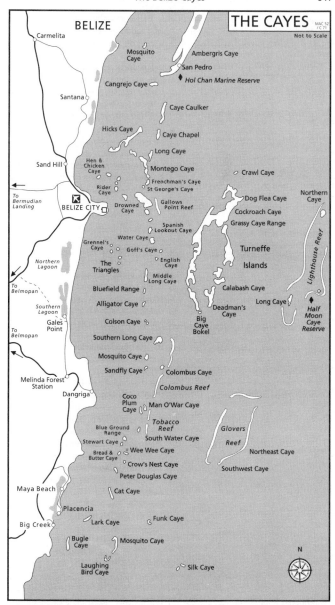

George's Cay, the British Government still failed to claim the territory, though the settlers maintained that it had now become British by conquest.

When they achieved independence from Spain in 1821, both Guatemala and Mexico laid claim to sovereignty over Belize as successors to Spain, but these claims were rejected by Britain. Long before 1821, in defiance of Spain, the British settlers had established themselves as far S as the river Sarstoon, the present S boundary. Independent Guatemala claimed that these settlers were trespassing and that Belize was a province of the new republic. By the middle of the 19th century Guatemalan fears of an attack by the United States led to a *rapprochement* with Britain. In 1859, a Convention was signed by which Guatemala recognized the boundaries of Belize while, by Article 7, the United Kingdom undertook to contribute to the cost of a road from Guatemala City to the sea "near the settlement of Belize"; an undertaking which was never carried out.

Heartened by what it considered a final solution of the dispute, Great Britain declared Belize, still officially a settlement, a Colony in 1862, and a Crown Colony nine years later. Mexico, by treaty, renounced any claims it had on Belize in 1893, but Guatemala, which never ratified the 1859 agreement, renews its claims periodically.

Belize became independent on 21 September 1981, following a United Nations declaration to that effect. Guatemala refused to recognize the independent state, but in 1986, President Cerezo of Guatemala announced an intention to drop his country's claim to Belize. A British military force was maintained in Belize from independence until 1993, when the British government announced that the defence of Belize would be handed over to the government on 1 January 1994. The 1,200-strong garrison was reduced to about 100 soldiers who organize jungle-training facilities.

Belize was admitted into the OAS in 1991 following negotiations between Belize, Guatemala and Britain. As part of Guatemala's recognition of Belize as an independent nation (ratified by Congress in 1992) Britain will recompense Guatemala by providing financial and technical assistance to construct road, pipeline and port facilities that will guarantee Guatemala access to the Atlantic. In Belize there will be a referendum to decide whether to accept the proposed Maritime Areas Bill which will delimit Belize's S maritime borders in such a manner as to allow Guatemala uncontested and secure access to the high seas.

Mr George Price, of the People's United Party, who had been reelected continuously as Prime Minister since internal self-government was instituted in 1964, was defeated by Mr Manuel Esquivel, of the United Democratic Party (UDP), in general elections held in December 1984 (the first since independence), but was returned as Prime Minister in 1989. The National Alliance for Belizean Rights (NABR) was created in 1992 by a defector from the UDP. General elections were held early, in 1993, and contrary to forecasts, the PUP was defeated. The UDP, in alliance with the NABR, won 16 of the 29 seats, many by a very narrow margin, and Mr Esquivel took office as Prime Minister with the additional portfolios of Finance and Defence. In the months following the elections, a corruption scandal rocked Belizean politics. Several PUP members, including the former Foreign Minister were arrested on charges of offering bribes to two UDP members of the House of Representatives to persuade them to cross the floor.

Government

Belize is a constitutional monarchy; the British monarch is the Chief of State, represented by a Governor-General, who is Belizean. The head of government is

BELIZE : FACT FILE

Geographic

Land area	22,965 sq km
forested	44.4%
pastures	2.1%
cultivated	2.5%

Demographic

Population (1992)	196,000
annual growth rate (1987-92)	2.5%
urban	51.6%
rural	48.4%
density	8.5 per sq km
Religious affiliation	
Roman Catholic	62.0%
Protestant	30.6%
Birth rate per 1,000 (1990)	38.1
	(world av 27.1)
Death rate per 1,000 (1990)	5.0
	(world av 9.8)

Education and Health

Life expectancy at birth (1991),	
male	67 years
female	72 years
Infant mortality rate	
per 1,000 live births (1991)	35
Physicians (1990)	1 per 1,543 persons
Hospital beds	1 per 309 persons
Calorie intake as %	
of FAO requirement	118%
Population age 25 and over	
with no formal schooling	10.7%
Literacy (over 15)	93%

Economic

GNP (1990 market prices)	US$373mn
GNP per capita	US$1,970
Public external debt (1990)	US$142.8mn
Tourism receipts (1990)	US$91mn
Inflation (annual av 1987-92)	3.5%
Radio	1 per 1.9 persons
Television	1 per 16 persons
Telephone	1 per 12 persons

Employment

Population economically active (1983-84)	
	47,325
Unemployment rate	na
% of labour force in	
agriculture	27.6
mining	0.2
manufacturing	8.9
construction	4.2
Military forces	665

Source *Encyclopaedia Britannica*

the Prime Minister. There is a National Assembly, with a House of Representatives of 28 members (not including the speaker) elected by universal adult suffrage, and a Senate of 8: 5 appointed by the advice of the Prime Minister, 2 on the advice of the Leader of the Opposition, 1 by the Governor-General after consultation. General elections are held at intervals of not more than 5 years.

Flora and Fauna

Nature Conservation has become a high priority, with nature reserves sponsored by the Belize Audubon Society, the Government and various international agencies. "Nature tourism" is Belize's fastest growing industry. By 1992 18 national parks and reserves had been established, including: Half Moon Caye, Cockscomb Basin Wildlife Sanctuary (the world's only jaguar reserve), Crooked Tree Wildlife Sanctuary (swamp forests and lagoons with wildfowl), Community Baboon Sanctuary, Blue Hole National Park, Guanacaste Park, Society Hall Nature Reserve (a research area with Maya presence), Bladen Nature Reserve (watershed and primary forest), Hol Chan Marine Reserve (reef eco-system), Rio Bravo Conservation Area (managed by the Programme for Belize, 1 King Street, Belize City, T 02-75616/7, or John Burton, Old Mission Hall, Sibton Green, Saxmundham, Suffolk, IP17 2JY), the Shipstern Nature Reserve (butterfly breeding, forest, lagoons, mammals and birds: contact PO Box 1694, Belize City, T 08-22149 via BCL Radio phone, or International Tropical Conservation Foundation, Box 31, CH-2074 Marin-Ne, Switzerland). Five Blue Lakes National Park, based on an unusually deep karst lagoon in the far S near Guatemala was designated in April 1991. On 8 December 1991 the government created three new forest reserves and national parks: the Vaca Forest Reserve (52,000 acres), Chiquibul National Park (containing the Maya ruins of Caracol, 265,894 acres), both in Cayo District, and Laughing Bird Caye National Park (off Placencia). The first 8 listed are managed by the Belize Audubon Society, 29 Regent Street, Belize City (PO Box 1001), T 02-77369/78239. Glovers Reef was declared a marine reserve in 1993.

Belize Enterprise for Sustained Technology (BEST) is a non-profit organization committed to the sustainable development of Belize's disadvantaged communities and community-based ecotourism, eg Gales Point and Hopkins Village; PO Box 35, Forest Drive, Belmopan, T 08-23043, F 08-22563.

NB A wildlife protection Act was introduced in 1982, which forbids the sale, exchange or dealings in wildlife, or parts thereof, for profit; the import, export, hunting or collection of wildlife is not allowed without a permit; only those doing scientific research or for educational purposes are eligible for exporting or collecting permits. Also prohibited are removing or exporting black coral, picking orchids, exporting turtle or turtle products, and spear fishing in certain areas or while wearing scuba gear.

Bird watchers are recommended to take Petersen's *Field Guide to Mexican Birds.*

THE CAYES

From 10 to 40 miles off the coast an almost continuous, 150-mile line of reefs and cayes (meaning islands, pronounced "keys") provides shelter from the Caribbean and forms the longest barrier reef in the Western Hemisphere (the fifth-longest in the world). The overall area of the cayes is 212 square miles. Most of the cayes are quite tiny, but some have been developed as tourist resorts. Many have beautiful sandy beaches with clear, clean water, where swimming and diving are excellent. They are popular destinations, especially from February to May and in August.

The larger ones are the Turneffe Islands and Ambergris and Caulker Cayes. Fishermen live on some cayes, coconuts are grown on others, but many are uninhabited swamps. The smaller cayes do not have much shade, so be careful if you go bathing on them. Sandflies infest some cayes (eg Caulker), the sandfly season is December to beginning of February; mosquito season is June, July, sometimes October.

Travel by boat to and between the islands is becoming increasingly regulated. Boats can only be hired for diving, fishing or sightseeing if they are licensed for the specific purpose by the government. This is intended to ensure that tourists travel on safe, reliable vessels and also to prevent the proliferation of self-appointed guides. The new licensing requirements will probably drive the cheaper boats out of business. In general, it is easier to arrange travel between the islands once there, than from Belize City. All authorized boats leave from Jan's Shell (A and R) Station on North Front Street, Belize City. Cargo boats are no longer allowed to carry passengers, too many have capsized with tourists on board, causing loss of life.

Fishing

The sea provides game fish such as sailfish, marlin, wahoo, barracuda and tuna. Tarpon, permit, grouper and snapper are also popular for sport fishing. On the flats, the most exciting fish for light tackle, the bonefish, are found in great abundance. In addition to the restrictions on turtle and coral extraction noted above, the following regulations apply: no person may take, buy or sell crawfish (lobster) between 15 March and 14 July, shrimp from 15 April to 14 August, or conch between 1 July and 30 September.

Fishing seasons: Billfish: blue marlin, all year (best November-March); white marlin, November-May; sailfish, March-May. Oceanic: yellowfin tuna, all year;

blackfin tuna, all year; bonito, all year; wahoo, November-February; sharks, all year. Reef: kingfish, March-June; barracuda, all year; jackfish, all year; mackerel, all year; grouper, all year; snapper, all year; permit, all year; bonefish, November-April; tarpon, June-August River: tarpon, February-August; snook, February-August; snapper, year round.

Operators In Belize City: **Blackline Marine**, PO Box 332, Mile 2, Western Highway, T 02-44155, F 02-31975; **Sea Masters Company Ltd**, PO Box 59, T 02-33185, F 026-2028; **Caribbean Charter Services**, PO Box 752, Mile 5, Northern Highway, T 02-45814 (have guarded car and boat park), fishing, diving and sightseeing trips to the Cayes. **Belize River Lodge**, PO Box 459, T 025-2002, F 025-2298, excellent reputation.

Diving

The shores are protected by the longest barrier reef in the Western Hemisphere. Old wrecks and other underwater treasures are protected by law and cannot be removed. Spear fishing, as a sport, is discouraged in the interests of conservation. The beautiful coral formation is a great attraction for scuba diving, with canyons, coves, overhangs, ledges and walls. There are endless possibilities for underwater photography: schools of fishes amid the hard and soft coral, sponges and fans. Try to see that the boat which is taking you to see the reef does not damage this attraction by dropping its anchor on, or in any other way destroying, the coral. The coral reefs around the N, most touristy cayes are dying. There are decreasing numbers of small fishes as a necessary part of the coral lifecycle in more easily accessible reefs, including the underwater parks.

We describe the islands from N to S.

AMBERGRIS CAYE

This island (pronounced Am*bergris*), with its town of San Pedro, population 1,527, has grown rapidly over the last couple of years, with 50 hotels and guest houses registered on the island. Buildings are still restricted to no more than three storeys in height and the many wooden structures retain an authentic village atmosphere. It should be noted that, although sand is in abundance, there are few excellent beach areas around San Pedro town. The emphasis is on snorkelling on the nearby barrier reef and Hol Chan Marine Park, as well as the fine scuba diving, sailing, fishing and board sailing. In fact it can be dangerous to swim near San Pedro as there have been serious accidents with boats. A short distance to the N and S of San Pedro lie miles of deserted beach front, where picnic barbeques are popular for day-tripping snorkellers and birders who have visited nearby small cayes hoping to glimpse flamingoes or scarlet ibis. The British Ordnance Survey has published a Tourist Map of Ambergris Caye, scale 1:50,000, with a plan of San Pedro, 1:5,000.

Just S of Ambergris Caye, and not far from Caye Caulker, is the ***Hol Chan Marine Park***, an underwater natural park. Divided into three zones, zone A is the reef, where fishing is prohibited. Entry US$1.50. Zone B is the seagrass beds, where fishing can only be done with a special licence; the Boca Ciega blue hole is here. Zone C is mangroves where fishing also requires a licence. Only certified scuba divers may dive in the reserve. Contact the Reserve Manager in San Pedro for further information. Several boatmen in San Pedro offer snorkelling trips to the park, US$15 (not including entry fee), 2 hrs. You can see shark, manta ray, many other fish and coral; a highly recommended trip. Fish feeding is prohibited. Only very experienced snorkellers should attempt to swim in the cutting between the reef and the open sea; seek advice on the tides.

Island Information – Ambergris Caye

● Transport

Several flights daily to and from Belize City municipal airport with Tropic, Island and Maya Air, US$35 return (about US$10 more from international airport). Universal Travel at San Pedro airfield helpful. More interesting than going by air are the boats from Shell station, Belize City, US$10-15, non-stop. From Southern Foreshore jetty boats leave for San Pedro Mon-Fri 1600, return 0700, Sat 1300, return 0800, none on Sun, US$10, 1¹/₂ hrs. *Triple J* boat leaves fron N end of swing bridge, daily round trip to Caye Caulker and San Pedro leaving Belize City 0900, return 1500, to San Pedro US$10 one way, US$17.50 return, fast, dependable, rec. Boats, irregular, between Ambergris and Caye Caulker, no set fare. Remember, pay on arrival. Bikes can be rented for US$2/hour. One cannot in practice walk N along the beach from San Pedro to Xcalak, Mexico.

● Where To Stay

Ramon's Village Resort, San Pedro Village, T 026-2071/2213, F 2214, or USA 601-649-1990, F 601-425-2411 (PO Drawer 4407, Laurel, MS 39441), from US$110 to 225d, agree on which currency you are paying in, 61 rooms, a diving and beach resort, all meals and all diving, highly rec even for non-divers (fishing, swimming, boating, snorkelling), very efficient, comfortable rooms, pool with beach club atmosphere; *Belize Yacht Club*, San Pedro town, PO Box 1, T 026-2005/2060, F 026-2331, all rooms are suites with fully-furnished kitchens, under US$200d, pool, docking facilities. The following 3 are under US$125d: *Sun Breeze*, San Pedro Town, T 026-2347/2191/2345, F 026-2346, near airport, Mexican style building, a/c, comfortable, all facilities, excellent restaurant, good dive shop, rec; *Paradise Resort Hotel*, San Pedro, T 026-2083, F 026-2232, wide selection of rooms and villas, good location, villas better value, cheaper summer rates, all water sports; *Coral Beach*, San Pedro, T 026-2013, F 026-2001, central location, slightly run down but good local feel and excellent water sports facilities inc dive boat charter, tours for fishing and scuba available. *San Pedro Holiday Hotel*, PO Box 1140, Belize City, T 026-2014/2103, F 026-2295, 16 rooms in good central location, US$63-90d, fun atmosphere with good facilities, reasonable value; *Spindrift Hotel*, San Pedro, T 026-2018, F 026-2251, 24

rooms, 4 apartments, about US$60, unattractive block but central location, good bar and restaurant, popular meeting place, trips up the Belize River, a/c, comfortable; *Rock's Inn Apartments*, San Pedro Town, T 026-2326, F 026-2358, good value and service, over US$70d.

Just outside San Pedro: *El Pescador*, on Punta Arena beach 3 miles N, PO Box 793, Belize City, T/F 026-2398, over US$125, access by boat, specialist fishing lodge with good reputation, a/c, good food and service; *Journey's End*, PO Box 13, San Pedro, T 026-2173, F 026-2028, 4¹/₂ miles N, about US$150, excellent resort facilities inc diving, resort club theme; *Captain Morgan's Retreat*, 3 miles N of town, T 026-2567, F 026-2616, similar price range, access by boat, thatched roofed cabañas with private facilities, pool, dock, secluded, rec; *Victoria House*, PO Box 22, San Pedro, T 026-2067/2240, F 026-2429, inc meals, 1 mile from town, 3 different types of room, from about US$75-150, excellent facilities, good dive shop and water sports, windsurfing US$15/hour, highly rec; *Royal Palm*, PO Box 18, San Pedro, T 026-2148/2244, F 026-2329, good location near *Victoria House*, a little cheaper, 12 new villas with pool and full facilities just completed; *House of the Rising Sun*, T 026-2336/2505, F 026-2349, about US$50, nice location, reasonable rooms and value.

Other, cheaper hotels: *San Pedrano*, San Pedro, T 026-2054/2093, over US$40, clean and good value. In the US$30-40 price range: *Conch Shell Inn*, facing sea, some rooms with kitchenette, T 026-2062; *Hide Away Lodge*, PO Box 484, Belize City, T 026-2141/2269, good value but a bit run down; *Lily's*, rooms with sea view, fan, clean, T 026-2059, US$45; *Rubie's*, San Pedro Town on the beach, fan, private bath, good views, beach cabaña, central, rec as best value in town, T 026-2063/2434, US$35; *Martha's Hotel* (cheaper in low season), PO Box 27, San Pedro, T 026-2054, F 026-2589, good value, rec; *La Joya del Caribe*, San Pedro T 026-2050/2385, F 026-2316, nice location just out of town, rec; *Casa Blanca*, San Pedro town, T 026-2630; *Pirate's Lantern*, in town, T 026-2146; *Thomas*, airy rooms, fan, bath (tub, not shower), drinking water, clean, friendly, US$25; *Milo's*, comfortable, clean, hot water, T 026-2033, US$10; *Seven Seas*, T 026-2382/2137. At Coral Beach, the Forman, Gómez, González and Paz families provide rooms and meals for US$9 each. At Sea Breeze, the Paz and Núñez families offer the same accommodation at the same price.

● **Where To Eat**

The *San Pedro Grill* is a good place to meet other travellers and swap information on boats, etc. Other eating places are: *Elvi's Kitchen*, popular, newly upmarket; one block N is *Ambergris Delight*, pleasant, inexpensive, clean; one block S of *Elvi's* is *Marinos*, excellent food, good prices, popular with locals, erratic service; *Lily's Restaurant*, best seafood in town, friendly, good breakfast; *Jade Garden Restaurant*, Chinese, sweet and sour everything, drinks expensive; *The Hut*, Mexican, friendly; *Estel's*, on the beach, good food and '40s-'50s music. In the same building complex as the *Spindrift* is the *Pier Restaurant*, very Mexican, dinners from US$10, also a branch of the Atlantic Bank, a post office and a chemist. *Big Daddy's Disco*, rec.

● **Diving**

Instruction to PADI open water widely available, from US$400 at Coral Beach to US$350 at Amigos del Mar, opp *Lily's*; freelance instructor Lynne Stevens can be contacted through *Marinos* restaurant.

● **Vehicle Rental**

Golf carts US$10/hour, make sure battery is fully charged before hiring; gives quick access to S, quieter end. Bicycles US$5/hour, try negotiating for long-term rates, good way to get around.

CAYE CAULKER

A lobster-fishing island, which used to be relatively unspoilt, Caye Caulker, Corker or Cayo Hicaco is now popular with tourists. The houses are of wood, the majority built on stilts. It has been allowed to run down and the main landing jetty has been closed. It is said to be a drug centre. Some services are reported to have deteriorated, and theft and unpleasantness from some mainlanders who go to the caye with tourists occurs; on the other hand the islanders are friendly. The atmosphere seems to be much more relaxed out of the high tourist season; nevertheless, women should take care if alone at night. There are no beaches, but

you can swim at the channel ("cutting", formed by a recent hurricane) or off one of the many piers. Diving is excellent because the caye is above one of the largest underwater cave systems in the world.

A reef museum has opened with enlarged photos of reef fish, free for school parties, tourists are asked for a US$2 donation to help expansion. There are only 2 vehicles on the island one of which is used solely to transport Belikin beer. Sandflies are ferocious in season (December-February), take trousers and a good repellent. Make sure you fix prices before going on trips or hiring equipment and clarify whether you are talking US$ or BZ$. Do not pay the night before.

A walk S along the shore takes you to the new airstrip, a gash across the island, and to mangroves where the rare black catbird (*melanoptila glabirostris*) can be seen and its sweet song heard. In this area there are lots of mosquitoes. A campaign to make the black catbird's habitat and the associated reef a Nature Reserve (called Siwa-Ban, after the catbird's Maya name) can be contacted at *Hiriarco Giftshop* (Ellen McCrea, near *Tropical Paradise*), or 143 Anderson, San Francisco, California.

Watersports and Diving

Reef trips (see also below, under Where to Stay), US$7.50-12.50 each (sometimes less) for 3-7 hrs as long as there are 4 or more in a group. It is almost impossible to arrange boat trips the evening before; just wander down the main street at 1000, ask around for names of boat men, and you can not fail. Hol Chan gets very crowded and the earlier you get there the better. Try to ascertain that the boat operator is reliable. We have received reports of theft of valuables left on board while snorkelling and even of swimmers being left in the water while the boat man went off to pick up another group. Protect against sunburn on reef trips, even while snorkelling. Mervin, a local man, is reliable for snorkelling trips, he will also take you to Belize City. Try "Bongo" for yacht trips to the reefs, "first mate" Donna (a Canadian) will guide first time snorkellers. Another is Ignacio; also Gamoosa and his wife Tina, who may spend all day with you on the reef and then sometimes invites you to his house to eat the fish and lobster you have caught, prepared deliciously by his wife; she also offers a healthy breakfast of banana, yoghurt, granola and honey for US$2.50. Also recommended is Alfonso Rosardo, a Mexican, reef trips for up to 6 people, 5-6 hrs, sometimes offers meals at his house afterwards. Also recommended is Lawrence (next to *Riva's Guest House*), Obdulio Lulu (a man) at *Tom's Hotel* goes to Hol Chan and San Pedro for a full day (if he catches a barracuda on the return, he will barbeque it at the hotel for US$0.75), Raoul and Charles, also from *Tom's Hotel*, US$12.50; also Harrison (ask around for him, rec). Lobster fishing and diving for conch is also possible. "Island Sun", near the "cutting", local husband and American wife, very conscientious; day tours to reef, plus snorkel hire (1000-1400); day tour to San Pedro and Hol Chan, plus snorkel hire, plus entry fee for reserve, rec. Snorkel Equipment Rental and Pastries Shop, do tour, rental gear, on same route 1015-1630, boat has sunshade. Capt Jim Novelo, of *Sunrise* boat, does daily trips to Hol Chan and San Pedro, 1000-1600, and snorkelling excursions to the Turneffe Islands, Half Moon Caye and Blue Hole, 0630-1700, every Tues, December-April, July-August, or on request, T 022-2195, F 022-2239. A sailing boat also goes to Hol Chan, but the trip takes a long time, leaving only a short while for snorkelling, departs 1000, US$12 for a day. Mask, snorkel and fins for US$2.50, cheapest (for instance at the post office, or *Sammie's Pastry Shop*). Benji, owner of a small sailboat and Joe Joe, his Rasta captain, will take you to Placencia or the Cayes, fun.

Diving Frank and Janie Bounting of Belize Diving Service (PO Box 667, T 44307, ext 143 mainland side, past the football pitch) charge US$55 for 2 scuba dives, day and night, good equipment, good value; they also offer a 4-day PADI certificate course for US$300, rec, also 2 and 3-day trips to Lighthouse Reef on the *Reef Roamer*, highly rec; the 3-day trip comprises 7 dives, including the Blue Hole, a visit to a bird reserve, good food and crew, US$290. Frenchie's Diving Service, T 022-2234, charges US$330 for a 4-day PADI course, friendly and effective, 2-tank dive US$60, also advanced PADI instruction.

For **sailing** charters, Jim and Dorothy Beveridge, "Seaing is Belizing", who also run scuba trips to Goff's Caye Park and the Turneffe Islands (5-10 days). They arrange slide shows of the reefs and the Jaguar Reserve (Cockscomb) at 2000, from time to time, US$2, excellent photography, personally narrated (they, too, have a book exchange); PO Box 374, Belize City, T 022-2189. Ask Chocolate for all-day trips to the manatee reserve in the S of Belize, about US$25 pp for a group of at least 8. There is a sailing school, charging US$30 for a 5-hr, solo beginner's course. It may be possible to hire a boat for 6-8 people to Chetumal. There are also boats leaving for Placencia and Honduras from Caye Caulker, but be sure to get exit stamps and other documentation in Belize City first if going to Honduras.

Wind-surfing equipment hire from Orlando, US$10/hour, poor quality, bring your own or go to San Pedro. Canoes for hire from Salvador, at painted house behind *Marin's* restaurant, US$10 a day. Go fishing with Rolly Rosardo, 4 hrs, US$45, up to 5 people, equipment, fresh bait and instruction provided.

Island Information – Caye Caulker
● **Transport**
Boats leave from behind A & R Shell Station on North Front Street, Belize City, for Caye Caulker, at 0630, then from 0900 until afternoon daily (US$6-7.50pp, US$5 on "sunrise boat", payable only on arrival at Caye Caulker,

otherwise you'll be swindled), 45 mins one way (boats depend on weather and number of passengers, can be "exciting" if it's rough), return boats from 0630 till pm (if booked in advance at some places, inc *Edith's Hotel*, US$6). You can sometimes catch a boat as late as 1600, but do not rely on it. Jerry Pacheco's *Blue Wave* (rec as fast and good, also snorkelling trips), Emilio Novelo's *Ocean Star* (good, cheaper than others) and "Chocolate's" *Soledad* are the currently authorized boats, but there are many others (including *Rainbow Runner*, 0830 from Belize City via Caye Chapel, boat in good condition, 2 motors, *Good Grief*, mixed reports, and *C Train*). Boats from San Pedro en route to Belize City 0700-0800, US$7.50. Incidentally, "Chocolate" is white, over 50 years old and has a white moustache. Anyone else introducing himself as Chocolate is an imposter! *Triple J* (see above, San Pedro) boat, rec, US$6 one way, US$11 round trip, daily service.

The airstrip has been newly constructed; Tropic Air, Island Air and Maya Air US$30 return from municipal airport (add US$10 from International airport). Flying is rec if you have a connection to make.

You can rent golf carts, US$5/hr, popular, the locals rent them to take the family for a drive.

● **Where To Stay**

The cheapest end of town is the S, but it is a long way from the "cutting" for swimming or snorkelling. A map which can be bought on arrival lists virtually everything on the island. Camping on the beach is forbidden. *Rainbow Hotel*, on the beach, T 022-2123, 10 small bungalows, with shower, rooms also, US$25-35, hot water. Beach houses can also be rented for US$50-150 a month. *Tropical Paradise*, T 022-2124, F 022-2225 (PO Box 1206 Belize City), cabins, rooms US$22-35, restaurant (see below), good excursions; *CB's*, further S than *Tropical Paradise*, T 022-2176, US$32 with bath, clean 12 beds, no advance bookings, good, small beds, restaurant; *Reef* or *Martínez Hotel*, (T 022-2196), US$25, small rooms, smelly recycled shower water, basic, but reasonable for the caye; *Jimenez's Cabins*, delightful, self-contained huts, friendly staff, similar prices; *Shirley's Guest House*, T 022-2145, US$20, S end of village, very relaxing, rec; *Marin*, T 022-44307 (also private hut) with bath, US$15, clean, helpful, rec (the proprietor, John Marin, will take you out for a

snorkelling trip on the reef); *Vega's Far Inn* rents 7 rooms, all doubles, T 022-2142, US$15, with ceiling fan and fresh linen, flush toilets and showers (limited hot water) shared with camping ground, which is guarded, has drinking water, hot water, clean toilets, barbeque, can rent out camping gear (camping costs US$6 pp, overpriced); much the same price is *Anchorage Hotel*, near *Ignacio's*, basic, large cabañas with cold showers, no fan, discounts for stays over 4 days, pleasant atmosphere, friendly family, breakfast and drinks served under shade on the beach.

Mira Mar, T 022-44307, US$10s-US$20d, 2nd floor rooms best, clean showers, rec, bargain if staying longer, helpful owner Melvin Badillo, he owns liquor store, his family runs a pastry shop and grocery store; *Deisy's*, T 022-2150, US$15 with shower, toilet and fan, reductions for longer stays, cheaper rooms downstairs, cash travellers' cheques, rooms with communal bathroom not good value, cold water only; *Edith's*, US$8 per bed in room (whether occupied or not), good; *Hideaway*, round corner from *Deisy's*, US$10, clean, quiet, shared toilets and shower (cold, unpotable water), rec; *Ignacio Beach Cabins*, T 022-2212 (PO Box 1169, Belize City), small huts or hammocks just outside town, for double room, US$15 for a hut for 3-4, rec, camping space US$6, plus US$1, cheap lobster tails and free coconuts for luggage store, toilet and shower facilities in private cabins only (Ignacio runs reef trips and he has equipment; he is principally a lobster fisherman); *Riva's Guest House*, T 022-2127, US$10, basic accommodation, their reef trips in an attractive schooner are the longest, snorkelling equipment hire, US$2.50; *Sandy Lane Hotel*, T 022-2217, one block back from main street, bungalow-type accommodation, US$10, clean, shared toilet and hot showers, run by Rico and Elma Novelo, rec; *Tom's Hotel*, T 022-2102, US$12, with shared bath and fan, up to US$25 in cabin with 3 beds, basic, clean, friendly, cold water, long walk from beach, laundry service US$5, safe deposit, barbeque. Tom's boat trips go to various destinations, including Hol Chan and coral gardens, and to Belize City. In all accommodation take precautions against theft.

● **Where To Eat**

Rodriguez for dinner at 1800 onwards for US$3.50-4, US$5 for lobster, very good (limited accommodation available). *Melvin's*, excellent lobster meals (opp *Riva's*); *Tropical*

Paradise for excellent seafood, slightly more expensive than others (also the only place selling ice cream); *The Sandbox*, run by American couple, one of the Caye's social centres. Cakes and pastries can be bought at houses displaying the sign, rec are *Deisy's, Jessie's*, open 0830-1300, 1500-1700, behind *Riva's*; *Glenda's*, near *Hotel Marin*, try the delicious lobster, or chicken "burritos", chicken, vegetables, chile and sauce wrapped in a tortilla for US$0.50, also good breakfast with cinnamon rolls, closed evenings; also good for "Burritos", *Claudette*, next to Fishermen's Wharf, US$1.25, delicious. *Pinx Diner*, good value breakfasts, lunches and dinners, good waffles, rec; *Marin's*, good seafood in evening at reasonable prices; *Syd's* home cooking, big portions. Many private houses serve food. Buy lobster or fish from the cooperative and cook up at the barbeque on the beach; beer is sold by the crate at the wholesaler on the dock by the generator; ice for sale at *Tropical Paradise*.

● **Services**

There are at least 4 small "markets" on the island where a variety of food can be bought; prices are 20-50% higher than the mainland. Better to buy food in Belize City beforehand, but rates for changing cash and TCs are reasonable; there is a bank and many places for exchange including the Post Office. Gift shops will charge a commission on TCs.

International telephone and fax connections available on Caye Caulker (telephone exchange is open till 1600; fax number at telephone exchange is 501-22-2239). The island also boasts 2 book swaps, including *Seaing is Belizing* (see **Diving** above) and Belize Diving Service. Bookstore on opposite side of island to ferries has many different magazines, inc *Time* and *Newsweek*. Dolphin Bay is a helpful travel agency on the island.

CAYE CHAPEL

40 mins by boat from Belize City, this caye is free of sandflies and mosquitoes and there are several beaches, cleaned daily. It also has a landing strip used by local airlines. Be careful if you hire a boat for a day to visit Caye Chapel: the boatmen enjoy the bar on the island and your return journey can be unreasonably exciting. Also, there are very few fish now round this caye. On Caye Chapel is the

Pyramid Island Resort, which owns the island (prices over US$50, credit cards not accepted), it has an excellent beach and diving courses (PADI).

LONG CAYE

Long Caye is S of Caye Chapel, reached by boat from Jan's Shell Station in Belize City, US$7.50. The island is quiet, relaxing, with bird watching, snorkelling, fishing, although it gets a bit busy at the weekend when fishermen drop in for a drink and chat. There is birdwatching, snorkelling, alligator spotting and fishing, and a good supply of books in the one guesthouse. They charge US$45 double, or US$35 single, full board, superb food, clean, very friendly. If it is full, ask Bob and he will try and fit you in somewhere.

ST GEORGE'S CAYE

Nine miles NE of Belize City, St George's Caye was the capital of British Honduras from 1650 to 1784. It was the scene of the battle between Britain and Spain in 1798 which established British possession. *Cottage Colony*, PO Box 428, Belize City, T 02-77051, F 02-73253, colonial style cabañas with dive facilities, price varies according to season (US$65-105, not inc tax), easy access from Belize City. *St George's Island Cottages*, PO Box 625, Belize City, 6 rooms. Boat fare is US$15, day trips are possible.

ENGLISH CAYE

This beautiful island, 12 miles off Belize City, has no facilities (apart from a lighthouse); take a day trip only. It is part of the reef so you can snorkel right off the beach. Sunrise Travel, Belize City, T 72051/32670, can help arrange a trip, book in advance, US$15.

Small caye resorts within easy reach of Belize City: *Moonlight Shadows Lodge*, Middle Long Caye, T 08-22587, still in early stages of development. *Ricardo's*

Beach Huts, Blue Field Range (59 North Front St, PO Box 55, Belize City, T 02-44970), recommended, charming and knowledgeable host, rustic, authentic fish camp feel, overnight camps to Rendez-vous Caye, English Caye and Sargeants Caye can be arranged with Ricardo, excellent food, snorkelling. *Spanish Bay Resort*, PO Box 35, Belize City, T 02-77288, also in early stages of development, dive facilities. *The Wave*, Gallows Point Caye (9 Regent St, Belize City, T 02-73054), 6 rooms, water sports facilities and diving.

TURNEFFE ISLANDS

The Turneffe Islands are one of Belize's three atolls. On **Big Caye Bokel**, at the S end of the group, is *Turneffe Islands Lodge*, PO Box 480, Belize City, which can accommodate 16 guests for week-long fishing and scuba packages. *Turneffe Flats*, 56 Eve St, Belize City, T 02-45634, in a lovely location, also offers week-long packages, for fishing and scuba; it can take 12 guests, but is soon to expand. *Blackbird Caye Resort*, 81 West Collet Canal St, Belize City, T 02-77670, F 02-73092, is a new, ecologically-oriented resort on this 4,000 acre island used by the Oceanic Society and is a potential site for a Biosphere Reserve 2 underwater project. Reservations in the USA, T (713) 658-1142, F (713) 658-0379. Diving or fishing packages available, no bar, take your own alcohol.

HALF MOON CAYE AT LIGHTHOUSE REEF

Lighthouse Reef is the outermost of the 3 N-S reef systems off Belize, some 45 miles E of Belize City. Half Moon Caye is the site of the Red-Footed Booby Sanctuary, the first national reserve established in Belize (1982). Besides the booby, which is unusual in that almost all the individuals have the white colour phase (normally they are dull brown), magnificent frigate birds nest on the island. The seabirds nest on the W side, which has dense vegetation (the E side is covered mainly in coconut palms). Of the 98 other bird species recorded on Half Moon Caye, 77 are migrants. Iguana, the wish willy (smaller than the iguana) and the *anolis allisoni* lizard inhabit the caye, and hawksbill and loggerhead turtles lay their eggs on the beaches. The Belize Audubon Society, 29 Regent Street, maintains the sanctuary; there is a lookout tower and trail. A lighthouse on the caye gives fine views of the reef. Around sunset you can watch the boobies from the lookout as they return from fishing. They land beside their waiting mates at the rate of about 50 a minute. They seem totally unbothered by humans.

There are no facilities; take all food, drink and fuel. On arrival you must register with the warden near the lighthouse (the warden will provide maps and tell you where you can camp).

Twelve miles N of Half Moon Caye is the **Blue Hole**, an almost circular sinkhole 1,000 feet across and with depths exceeding 400 feet. It was studied by Jacques Cousteau in 1984. Stalagmites and stalactites can be found in the underwater cave. Scuba diving is outstanding at Lighthouse Reef, including two walls which descend almost vertically from 30-40 feet to several thousand.

Bobby takes passengers by sailing boat from Caye Caulker to Half Moon Caye and the Blue Hole for US$25 pp including food (bring your own tent and sleeping bag). To charter a motor boat in Belize City costs about US$50 pp if 10 people are going (6-hr journey). Bill Hinkis, in San Pedro Town, Ambergris Caye, offers 3-day sailing cruises to Lighthouse Reef for US$150 (you provide food, ice and fuel). Bill and his boat *Yanira* can be found beside the lagoon off Back Street, just N of the football field. Out Island Divers, San Pedro, do various 2-3 day trips. Other sailing vessels charge US$150-250 per day. Speed boats charge

US$190 pp for a day trip including lunch and 3 dives, recommended. The main dive in the Blue Hole is very deep, at least 130 feet (almost 50 metres). Check your own qualifications as the dive operator probably will not. It is well worth doing if you are qualified. Keep an eye on your computer or dive charts if doing subsequent dives.

THE SOUTHERN CAYES

Further S, the reef and cayes stretch down towards Guatemala and Honduras. There is a concentration of islets between the town of Dangriga and the Placencia/Mango Creek area. Among these are the Tobacco Range and Man of War Caye (a nesting site for frigate, or man of war, birds and boobies). *South Water Caye* is a private island, small, sandy, with snorkelling off the beach. It is partly taken up by *Blue Marlin Lodge* (PO Box 21, Dangriga, T 05-22243, F 05-22296), an excellent dive lodge which offers 8 day/7 night dive packages for about US$1,000 pp (less for non-divers, or 5 day/4 nights), or similar length fishing packages for US$1,300. It has a restaurant, runs tours to Twin Cayes (where manatees may be seen), the Smithsonian Marine Biology Institute Laboratory on Carrie Bow Caye, and mainland sites. *Leslie Cottages*, 2 rooms, US contact T 800-548-5843 or 508-655-1461. Also based on South Water Caye is Coral Cay Conservation Ltd – Belize 90/95, a scientific survey of the reef ecosystem designed to establish a marine reserve. Expeditions are manned by volunteers who should apply to 154 Clapham Park Road, London, SW4 7DE, T 071-498 6248, F 071-498 8447. CCC is undertaking a 5-year survey of the reef on behalf of the Belizean government in order to develop a management plan for protecting the barrier reef.

Volunteers usually spend from one to 3 months (or longer) working a 12-hr day, 5 days a week; 2 survey dives a day, with leisure diving on Thursday evenings and Saturday. Every fourth weekend is a free long weekend. Accommodation is basic in communal dormitories, and food is Youth Hostel style and quality, but South Water Caye is a tropical Paradise, a few minutes' swim from the reef, white sand and palm-fringed. All inclusive costs from the UK are £1725 for one month, £2678 for 2 months and £3296 for 3 months. This is no holiday, you have to work hard, if you consider privileged diving hard work, but is a wonderful way of spending part of a year off. There is nothing to stop you spending time on the project then starting your Central or South American travels afterwards. Not much use contacting on spec in Belize as everything tends to be pre-arranged, but can be contacted by radio link via *Pelican Beach Resort* in Dangriga on 05-22044 (with thanks to Neil McAllister).

Tobacco Caye 1 hr by speedboat from Dangriga (US$12.50), this tiny island, quite heavily populated, has lots of local flavour and fishing camp charm. It is becoming a little commercialised, but still has an authentic feel. It sits right on the reef; you can snorkel from the beach although there are no large schools of fish. No sandflies on the beach; snorkelling equipment for rent. Boats go daily, enquire at *The Hub* or *Rio Mar* restaurants, Dangriga, Captain Buck or Anthony charge US$12-15 pp. *Reefs End Lodge*, PO Box 10, Dangriga, basic, small rooms, excellent host and food, boat transfer on request from Dangriga; *Island Camps*, PO Box 174 (51 Regent St, Belize City, T 02-72109), owner Mark Bradley will pick up guests in Dangriga, neat, spacious campground, meals on request, reef excursions, friendly; *Ellwood Fairweather and Friends*, US$15-20, friendly, good seafood, tax not inc, check the bill, "not very serious". Several families on the island take guests; accommodation very basic and grubby, 3 meals are usually provided. A dive camp is scheduled to open on Tobacco Caye, in the meanwhile scuba dives can be taken from nearby *Blue Marlin Lodge* on South Water Caye. There is no electricity on the island.

Still further S is *Wee Wee Caye*, a mangrove islet used as a field station by the Northeast Marine Environmental Institution, Inc (NEMEII, PO Box 660, Monument Beach, MA 02553, USA, T 508-759 4055; it also has a station up the Sittee River, at Possum Point).

Outside the Barrier Reef in this area is *Glover's Reef*, about 45 miles off-shore, an atoll with beautiful diving and a Marine Reserve since 1993. *Manta Reef Resort*, Glover's Reef Atoll, PO Box 215, 3 Eyre St, Belize City, T 02-31895/12767, F 02-31764; 9 individual cabins with full facilities, in perfect desert island setting, one week packages available only, reservations essential; excellent diving and fishing, good food, highly recommended (E6 photo lab available). On 15-acre Long Cay is *Glover's Atoll Resort* (Gilbert, Marsha-Jo and Madeleine Lomont and Becky and Breeze Cabral, PO Box 563, Belize City, T 08-23505/22149, F 08-23505/23235, no reservations needed) with cabins for 2, US$55 pp a week, discounts for longer stays, with cooking facilities, cold shower, rainwater for drinking, basic groceries, meals available at advance notice. On 9-acre North East Cay there are unfurnished cabins with wood burning stoves, US$15/night. Camping on either island US$30 pp a week. The resort also comprises Lomont Caye and Cabral Cayeabral Caye, both of 1 acre and within swimming distance. Boats for hire, with or without guide, also canoes, rowboats, windsurfer; snorkel and scuba rental, tank of air US$12; 4-day NAUI certification course US$250. Contact the Lomonts in advance to obtain a full breakdown of all services and costs. To get there take any bus for Punta Gorda, Placencia or Hopkins-Sittee River or 0800 Z-Line bus from Venus terminal in Belize City (US$8); ask the driver to stop 1½ miles past the Sittee River road (about 5 hrs) at Kendal Village G & G Cool Spot. For US$10 (share the fare) a truck takes you to *Glover's Atoll Guest House* at Sittee River Village, (on river bank, 5 rooms, camping, restaurant, jungle river trips, run by Lomont-Cabral family), T 08-22505/22149. At 0800 Sunday a boat leaves for the Reef 5 hrs, US$20 pp one way, returns Saturday. At other times, charter a boat (skiff or sailing boat, US$200 one way, up to 8 people, diesel sloop US$350, up to 30 people).

POINTS OF ACCESS

Belize City is the old capital and chief town. Most of the houses are built of wood, often of charming design, with galvanized iron roofs; they stand for the most part on piles about 7 feet above the ground, which is often swampy and flooded. Ground-floor rooms are used as kitchens, or for storage. Note the vast water butts outside many houses, with pipes leading to the domestic supply. Humidity is high, but the summer heat is tempered by the NE trades. The population (43,621) is just under a quarter of the total population, with the African strain predominating.

Haulover Creek divides the city; the swing bridge across the river is opened at 1730 daily to let boats pass. Among the commonest craft are sandlighters, whose lateen sails can be seen off Belize City. Three canals further divide the city. The main commercial area is either side of the swing bridge, although most of the shops are on the S side, many being located on Regent and Albert streets. The area around Central Park is always busy, but it is no distance to Southern Foreshore with its views of the rivermouth, harbour and out to sea. At the S end of Regent Street, the Anglican Cathedral and Government House nearby are interesting; both were built in the early 19th century. In the days before the foundation of the Crown Colony the kings of the Mosquito Coast were crowned in the Cathedral. In the Cathedral, note the 19th century memorial plaques which give a harrowing account of early death from "country fever" (yellow fever) and other tropical diseases.

On the N side of the swing bridge, turn left up North Front Street for some of the cheaper hotels and the A and R Station, from which most boats leave for the Cayes. Turn right for the Post Office, Tourist Office and roads which lead to Marine Parade (also with sea views). At the junction of Cork Street at Marine Parade is the *Fort George Hotel* whose new Club Wing, a copper-coloured glass tower, is a considerable landmark. Memorial Park on Marine Parade has a small obelisk, two cannon, concrete benches, and is peppered with the holes of landcrabs. The small park by the Fort George Lighthouse has a children's play area and is a popular meeting place.

Coming in by sea, after passing the barrier reef, Belize City is approached by a narrow, tortuous channel. This and the chain of mangrove cayes give shelter to what would otherwise be an open roadstead.

Some 48 miles from Belize City, near Belmopan, the narrow 52-mile Hummingbird Highway branches off SE from the Western Highway, through beautiful jungle scenery to *Dangriga* (chief town of the Stann Creek District), some 105 miles from Belize City and 1¾-2½ hrs drive from Belmopan. Dangriga's population is 6,838. In this, the most fertile area in the country, are grown citrus fruits, bananas, cassava, and general food crops. The town is on the seashore, and has an airstrip and cinema. Houses are built of wood, on piles. Mosquitoes and sand flies are a nuisance.

● **Local Holiday**

18-19 November, Garifuna, or Settlement Day, re-enacting the landing of the Black Caribs in 1823; there is dancing all night and next day. It's a very popular festival. All transport to Dangriga is booked up a week in advance and hotel rooms impossible to find.

Placencia is a little resort 30 miles S of Dangriga, reached by dugout, US$5 each way, 3 hrs, or, now that the road from Dangriga is finished, by bus (leaves Dangriga in the afternoon 4 times a week, 1½ hrs, US$3.50, returns at 0600 to connect with 0900 bus to Belize City). There are no streets, just a concrete footpath and wooden houses under the palms. Electricity and lighting on the main path have been installed. The atmosphere has been described as good, with lots of Jamaican music and lots of substances to make it tolerable for over 1 hr's listening. There is a police station. The people are very friendly and it's a good place for making excursions to the coral reef, 10 miles offshore (US$75-100 for 6 people). The only telephone is at the post office (good source of information on boats). The nearest bank in *Mango Creek* (Bank of Nova Scotia) open Friday only 0900-1200, but shops and market change travellers' cheques. Visa extensions obtainable in Mango Creek, which is a banana exporting port, 20 miles S of Dangriga.

Details of mainland excursions to Maya archaeological sites and the Mountain Pine Ridge area, near San Ignacio, are given in *The Mexico and Central American Handbook*. Most of the large hotels on the cayes and the mainland run tours to these places.

INFORMATION FOR VISITORS

● **Documents**

All nationalities need passports, as well as sufficient funds and, officially, an onward ticket. Visas are usually not required from nationals of all the countries of the EEC, some Commonwealth countries eg Australia, New Zealand, most Caribbean states (citizens of India, Austria and Switzerland do need a visa), USA, Canada, Liechtenstein, Mexico, Norway, Finland, Panama, Sweden, Turkey, Uruguay, Venezuela. Visas must be obtained from a consulate before arriving in the country; they cost US$10. They are not available at borders. It is possible that a visa may not be required if you have an onward ticket, but check all details at a consulate before arriving at the airport or border. Those going to other countries after leaving Belize should get any necessary visas in their home country. Visitors are initially granted 30 days' stay in Belize; this may be extended every 30 days up to 6 months at the Immigration Office, 115 Barrack Road, Belize City. At the end of 6 months, visitors must leave the country for at least 24 hrs. Visitors must not engage in any type of employment, paid or unpaid, without first securing a work permit from the Department of Labour; if caught, the penalty for both the employer and the employee is severe. There have been reports that tourists carrying less than US$30 for each day of intended stay have been refused entry.

If arriving by boat, you must submit to the Customs Boarding Officer the vessel's certificate of registration, clearance from the last port of call, 4 copies of the crew and passenger list and of the stores list.

● **Customs**
Clothing and articles for personal use are allowed in without payment of duty, but a deposit may be required to cover the duty payable on typewriters, dictaphones, cameras and radios. The duty, if claimed, is refunded when the visitor leaves the country. Import allowances are: 200 cigarettes or $1/2$ lb of tobacco; 20 fluid ozs of alcohol; 1 bottle of perfume. Visitors can take in an unspecified amount of other currencies (a maximum amount may now be set). No fruit or vegetables may be brought into Belize; searches are very thorough. Firearms may be imported only with prior arrangements. Pets must have proof of rabies inoculations and a vet's certificate of good health. CB radios are held by customs until a licence is obtained from Belize Communications Ltd.

● **How To Get There By Air**
There is a first-class airport, 10 miles from Belize, served by American, Sahsa and Taca International from Miami. Flights from London (Virgin and British Airways), Frankfurt (Lufthansa), Toronto (Delta and Air Canada), Montreal (Air Canada), and several US cities connect with the daily Taca flight from Miami. Other US points served direct: New Orleans (Taca), Dallas, Chicago, Detroit, Cleveland and Denver (Continental), Houston (Continental, Taca), New York (Continental and American) and Los Angeles (Taca). Also daily flights to San

Pedro Sula (Taca), San Salvador, San José, and Panama (all Taca). Flights to Flores (Guatemala), with Aviateca, TropicAir and AeroCaribe, to Guatemala City (Taca, Aviateca). In 1993 the Mexican airline, Bonanza, began a Mon/Wed/Fri service, Mérida-Belize via Chetumal, 0700-0925, US$100 one way.

● **Departure Tax**
US$12 on leaving from the international airport, but not for transit passengers who have spent less than 24 hrs in the country. There is also a security screening charge of US$1.25.

● **Airport**
There is a 10-mile tarmac road from Belize City to the Phillip SW Goldson International Airport. Modern check-in facilities, a/c, toilets, restaurant, viewing deck and duty-free shop. Collective taxi US$15; make sure your taxi is legitimate. Any bus going up the Northern Highway passes the airport junction (US$0.75), then $1^1/2$ mile walk. There is a municipal airstrip for local flights. Taxi from Belize City US$7.50, no bus.

● **Airline Offices**
Local: Tropic Air, Belize City T 02-45671, San Pedro T 026-2012/2117/2029, F 026-2338; Island Air, Belize City T 02-31140, International airport T 025-2219, San Pedro T 026-2435/2484, F 026-2192; Maya Air, 6 Fort St, Belize City T 02-72312, municipal airport T 02-44234/44032, International T 025-2336, San Pedro T 026-2611, F 02-30585.

Taca (Belize Global Travel), 41 Albert St (T 02-77363/77185, F 75213), International T 025-2163, F 025-2453, also British Airways, T 77363. American, Valencia Building (T 02-32522/3/4) and Continental Airlines, 32 Albert St, T 02-78309/78463/78223, International T 025-2263/2488. Aerovías, in *Mopan Hotel*, 55 Regent St, T 02-75383/75445/6, F 75383, for Flores/Guatemala; Belize Trans Air, T 02-77666, for Miami;

● **How To Get There By Sea**
The only regular boat service to Belize is from Punta Gorda, S of Mango Creek, to Puerto Barrios (and possibly Livingston), Guatemala (Tues and Fri at 1400, 3 hrs, US$5.40). Obtain all necessary exit stamps and visas before sailing. To Puerto Cortés, Honduras, from Belize City, you must charter a boat for US$360, 2-4 days, for 8 people. Motorized canoes go from Mango Creek to Puerto Cortés, Honduras, with no fixed schedule, but mostly Thur-Sun (Antonio Zabaneh at his store, T 06-

22011, knows when boats will arrive), US$50 one way, 7-9 hrs (rubber protective sheeting is provided, hang on to it, usually not enough to go round, nor lifejackets, but you will still get wet unless wearing waterproofs, or just a swimming costume on hot days; it can be dangerous in rough weather. Remember to get an exit stamp (preferably in Belize City), obtainable at the police station in Mango Creek, not Placencia (the US$10 departure tax demanded here is not official).

● **Internal Travel**

Air services to San Pedro, Caye Chapel and Caye Caulker with Tropic Air, Island Air and Maya Air, flights every hour 0700 to 1630, US$35 municipal airport to San Pedro return, US$30 to Caye Chapel and Caye Caulker (flights to these cayes from International airport cost about US$10 more). Flights also to Big Creek for Placencia, Dangriga, Punta Gorda with Maya Air and Tropic Air, 5 flights daily from 0700, last return flight 1705 (one way fares).

Passenger transport between the main towns is by colectivo or bus. By law, buses are not allowed to carry standing passengers; some companies are stricter than others. Hitch hiking is very difficult as there is little traffic.

Bus If going overland to Mexico, take a bus to Chetumal, several daily each way between 0400 and 1800 (there is an express Batty Bus at 1400 stopping at Orange Walk and Corozal only), US$5, 3-4 hrs, with 2 companies: Batty Bus, 54 East Collet Canal, T 72025, and Venus, Magazine Rd, T 73354. Bus Belize City to Dangriga, via Belmopan and the Hummingbird Highway, Z-line (T 73937), from Venus bus station, daily, 0800, 1000, 1100, 1500, 1600, plus Mon 0600, US$9.50 to Dangriga; James Bus Line, Pound Yard Bridge (Collet Canal), unreliable, slow, 10-12 hrs, US$9.50, to Punta Gorda via Dangriga and Mango Creek, daily 0800 and 1500 (insect repellent imperative).

Taxis have green licence plates (drivers must also have identification card); within Belize City, US$2.50 for one person; for 2 or more passengers, US$1.75 pp. There is a taxi stand on Central Park opposite Barclays, another on the corner of Collet Canal Street and Cemetery Road. Outside Belize City, US$1.75 per mile, regardless of number of passengers. Check fare before setting off. No meters. No tips necessary.

● **Car Hire**

Car hire cost is high in Belize owing to heavy wear and tear on the vehicles. You can expect to pay between US$65 for a Suzuki Samuri to US$125 for an Isuzu Trooper per day. Cautious driving is advised in Belize as road conditions are generally poor except for the Northern and Western Highways and there is no street lighting in rural areas. Emory King's *Drivers Guide to Belize* is helpful when driving to the more remote areas.

Budget, PO Box 863, 771 Bella Vista (near International Airport, can pick up and drop off car at airport, office almost opposite *Biltmore Plaza Hotel*), T 32435, good service, well-maintained vehicles, good deals (Suzukis and Isuzu Troopers); **Crystal**, Mile 1.5 Northern Highway, T 31600, Jay Crofton, cheapest deals in town, but not always most reliable, wide selection of vehicles including 30-seater bus, will release insurance papers for car entry to Guatemala and Mexico; **Pancho's**, 5747 Lizarraga Ave, T 45554; **National**, International, Airport, T 31586 (Cherokee Chiefs); **Avis**, at *Fort George Hotel*, T 78637, largest fleet, well-maintained, Daihatsus and Isuzu Troopers. **Smith & Sons**, 125 Cemetery Road, T 73779 (less reliable than in the past); **Gilly's**, 31 Regent St, T 77613; **Lewis**, 23 Cemetery Rd, T 74461. CDW ranges from US$10 to US$20 per day.

Motorists should carry their own driving licence and certificate of vehicle ownership. Third party insurance is mandatory, and can be purchased at any border (US$25 a week). There may be no one to collect it after 1900 or on Sun. Valid International Driving Licences are accepted in place of Belize driving permits. Fuel costs US$4.50 for a US gallon. There is no unleaded gasoline in Belize.

Traffic drives on the right. When making a left turn, it is the driver's responsibility to ensure clearance of both oncoming traffic and vehicles behind; generally, drivers pull over to the far right, allow traffic from behind to pass, then make the left turn. Many accidents are caused by failure to observe this procedure. All major roads have been, or are being, improved.

● **Where To Stay On The Mainland**

Accommodation on the **Cayes** is given above.

In Belize City Unless otherwise indicated, preface Belize City phone numbers with 02 (2 from outside Belize). All hotels are subject to 6% government tax (on room rate only). The following is a selection; there are many others: *Radisson Fort George Hotel*, 2 Marine Parade (PO Box 321, T 77400, F 73820), in 2 wings (Club Wing and Colonial Section), each with excellent rooms, US$115-165, a/c, helpful staff, reservations should be made, safe parking, good restaurant, good pool (non-residents may use pool for US$10), rec. *Ramada Royal Reef and Marina*, Newtown Barracks (PO Box 1248), T 32670, F 32660, US$149, on sea front (but not central), a/c, good food and service in restaurant and bar (a/c with sea views, expensive), pool; *Holiday Inn Villa*, 13 Cork St, T 32800, F 30276, a/c, TV, good restaurant (local and Lebanese), excellent rooftop bar with views of cayes and harbour, pool, nice gardens. *Belize Biltmore Plaza*, Mile 3 Northern Highway, T 32962, F 32962, US$100-160, comfortable rooms, a/c, restaurant (nice atmosphere, a/c, good selection), excellent English pub-style bar with Karaoke most evenings, pool, conference facilities, a long way from town (US$3.50 or more by taxi); *Bellevue*, 5 Southern Foreshore (T 77051, F 73253), US$83, a/c, private bath, good laundry service, restaurant (nice atmosphere, good lunches with live music, steaks), leafy courtyard pool, nice bar with live music Fri and Sat nights, good entertainment, rec; *Chateau Caribbean*, 6 Marine Parade, by *Fort George* (T 30800, F 30900), US$79, a/c, with good bar, restaurant (excellent Chinese and seafood, sea view, good service) and discothèque, parking, rec. *Belize International*, at Ladyville, 9 miles on Northern Highway, T 52150 or 44001, 1½ miles from airport, tennis court, restaurant and bar; *Bakadeer Inn*, 74 Cleghorn Street, T 31286, F 31963, US$50-55 (low-high season), private bath, breakfast US$4, a/c, TV, fridge, friendly, rec, also has bicycle hire; *Bliss*, 1 Water Lane (T 72552), over US$30 with bath and a/c, cheaper with fan, good value; *El Centro*, 4 Bishop St, T 72413, a/c, restaurant, good value; *Mopan*, 55 Regent Street (T 77351), US$31.50 with bath, breakfast, a/c, in historic house, has restaurant and bar (owners Tom and Jean Shaw), nice but pricey, helpful with information and travel arrangements.

Four Fort Street (address as name, T 30116, F 78808), 6 rooms, all with 4-poster beds and shared bath, charming, excellent restaurant, rec; *Belize River Lodge*, Ladyville, PO Box 459 Belize City, T 025-2002, F 025-2298, 10 miles from airport on Belize River, excellent accommodation, food and fishing (from lodge or cruises), also scuba facilities, numerous packages. *Isabel Guest House*, 3 Albert St, above Matus Store, PO Box 362,

T 73139, 3 double rooms, 1 huge triple, quiet, private shower, clean, friendly, safe, Spanish spoken, highly rec, US$15. *Sea Side Guest House*, 3 Prince Street, T 78339, US$14, US$5 in bunk room, comfortable, quiet, very popular, very helpful American owners, German spoken, 6 rooms, breakfast only (good), repeatedly rec; *Freddie's*, 86 Eve St, T 44396, US$15 with shower and toilet, fan, hot water, clean, very nice, secure, very small. *North Front Street Guest House*, T 77595, 1 block N of Post Office, 15 mins walk from Batty bus station, 124 North Front St, US$12.50, US$5 pp in dormitory, no hot water, fan, book exchange, TV, friendly, laundry, mice, French spoken, good information, keep windows closed at night and be sure to lock your door; *Bell's Hotel*, 140 North Front St, T 31083, US$12.50, US$5 pp, owner Richard Clarke-Bell has a boat and can provide transport to the Cayes. *Bon Aventure*, 122 North Front St, T 44248 (cheaper in dormitory), purified water available, a bit run down, but Hong Kong Chinese owners helpful, Spanish spoken, laundry service, good meals at reasonable prices, a few rooms rented by 'working girls'; opp are *Mira Rio*, 59 North Front Street, similar prices, fan, toilet, clean, covered verandah overlooking Haulover Creek, rec, and *Riverside*, T 32397, 61 North Front St, Chinese run, same prices.

If going to the Southern Cayes and you want to stay on the mainland: hotels in Dangriga *Pelican Beach*, on the beach 15 mins walk N of town, or taxi US$2.50 (PO Box 14, T 05-22044, F 05-22570), from US$60, with private bath and a/c, expensive restaurant, in need of investment; *Bonefish*, Mahogany Street, T 025-22165, on seafront on outskirts of town, US$50, a/c, colour TV with US cable, hot water, takes Visa, good; *Riverside*, 5 Commerce St, T 05-22168, F 05-22296,not always clean, US$15-20; *Hub Guest House*, 573 South Riverside, T 05-22397, F 05-22813, US$15-20 with bath, meals, helpful; *Cameleon*, 119 Commerce St, T 05-22008, US$11, shared cold showers, fans, cramped but reasonably safe and friendly; *Sofie's Hotel and Restaurant*, Chatuye St, unimpressive but pleasant, US$15; *Catalina*, 37 Cedar St, T 05-22390, US$7.50, very small, dirty, but friendly, luggage store; *Rio Mar*, 977 Southern Foreshore, US$15, friendly, good, music piped to all rooms, you will hear your neighbours even if yours is turned off; also in private homes (basic), eg Miss Caroline's. Unfurnished houses are rented out for US$20-30 a month.

Accommodation **in Placencia** (note that rooms may be hard to find in afternoon, eg after arrival of the bus from Dangriga) *Ranguana Lodge*, T 06-23112, approx US$60, wooden cabins on the ocean, very clean; same range, **Cove Resort**, PO Box 007, T 06-22024; **Paradise Vacation Resort**, US$25-30, full board extra (single meals available), créole cooking, run by Dalton Eiley and Jim Lee; they offer reef fishing, snorkelling, excursions to the jungle, Pine Ridge, Mayan ruins and into the mountains. If arriving by air at Big Creek, first contact Hubert Eiley, T 06-23118 who will arrange for a boat to take you to Placencia. *Ran's Travel Lodge*, T 06-22027, US$5, no meals, shared shower, toilet, friendly, fresh coconut bread baked next door (1000-1100); **Conrad and Lydia's Rooms**, 5 double rooms with shared toilet and shower, on quiet part of the beach, US$17.50, good meals, rec, Conrad is a boat owner, ask for his prices; **Julia's Budget Hotel**, US$10, no private bath, central, friendly, reliable, wake-up call for bus; also good value are **Lucille's Rooms**, clean, fans, meals by arrangement. Ask at *Jennie's Restaurant*, or T 06-23148, for lodgings at **Seaspray**, with bath, good value, very nice, bar. **Kitty's Place**, T 06-22027, beach apartment, US$45 per day, US$135 per week, rooms US$20, camping US$5, hot showers, bar, restaurant and Placencia Dive Shop; Mrs Leslie at the Post Office rents houses at US$20 per day (4-6 people, fridge and cooker); she also has hammock space for 3, US$2.50 per night (noisy). The *Galley* restaurant is a good place to eat (order meals 2-3 hrs in advance) and has information on lodging, fishing and snorkelling. There are other hotels and rooms for rent. Camping on the beach or under the coconut palms.

● **Where To Eat**

Eating places on the Cayes are given above. In Belize City there are plenty of places to eat, with Creole, or Chinese food, burgers and sandwiches. *Golden Dragon*, Queen St, good, reasonably priced, rec for Chinese food; *Four Fort Street* (at that address), near Memorial Park, nice atmosphere, sit out on the verandah, desserts a speciality, rec, also has 6 rooms (see above); *Macy's*, 18 Bishop Street (T 73419), rec for well-prepared local range, Creole cooking, different fixed menu daily, charming host; *Barracks Restaurant and Bar*, 136 Barrack Rd, excellent value, much frequented by expatriot community and Be-

lizeans alike, Chinese and Far Eastern cuisine; *Grill*, 164 Newtown Barracks (a short taxi ride from major hotels), English owner Richard Price, new, considered by many as best restaurant in the city, varied menu, T 45020; *DIT's*, 50 King St, good, cheap; *GG's Café and Patio*, 2-3 King St, popular for lunches, good quality and service. *King's*, St Thomas St, good value; *Big Daddy's*, Church St, good, cheap vegetarian food available; *Pearl's*, Handyside St, Italian and pizza, good value, friendly host Bill (ex-Placencia), no bar; *Pizza House*, King St, closed Mon, large pizzas, inexpensive, good also for juices and shakes. *Marlin*, 11 Regent St West, overlooking Belize River, T 73913, varied menu, good seafood. Several good Chinese restaurants.

Outside Belize City the restaurants tend to be simpler, but you can usually find good fare, especially the seafood.

Try the local drink, anise and peppermint, known as "A and P"; also the powerful "Old Belizeno" rum. The local beer, Belikin, is good, as is the "stout", strong and free of gas.

● **Camping**

Camping on the beaches, in forest reserves, or in any other public place is not allowed. There are no tent camp sites. **NB** Butane gas in trailer/coleman stove size storage bottles is available in Belize.

● **Shopping**

Handicrafts, woodcarvings, straw items, are all good buys. The Belize Chamber of Commerce has opened a Belize crafts sales room on Fort St, opp *Four Fort Street* restaurant, to be a showcase and promote the efforts of crafts people from all over Belize, come here first. *Admiral Burnaby's Coffee Shop*, Regent St, combination art gallery, book and craft shop, serving also coffee and juices. *The Holy Redeemer Book Centre*, North Front St, close to bridge and Catholic church, very good, has secondhand books and back issues of US magazines, front of shop sells T-shirts and souvenirs. *Belize Bookshop*, Regent St (opp *Mopan Hotel*), ask at counter for "racy" British greetings cards. *Angelus Press*, 10 Queen Street, excellent selection of stationery supplies, books, cards, etc. *Go Tees*, 23 Regent St, T 74082, excellent selection of T-shirts (printed on premises), arts and crafts from Belize, Guatemala and Mexico: jewellery, silver, wood carvings, clothes, paintings, etc; also has a branch at Belize Zoo, good zoo T-shirts and cuddly animals. Zericote (or Xericote) wood carvings can be bought in Belize City, for example at **Brodies Department Store** (Central Park end of Regent St), which also sells postcards, the *Fort George Hotel*, the small gift shop at *Four Fort Street*, or from Egbert Peyrefitte, 11a Cemetery Road. Such wood carvings are the best buy, but to find a carver rather than buy the tourist fare in shops, ask a taxi driver. (At the Art Centre, near Government House, the wood sculpture of Charles Gabb, who introduced carving into Belize, can be seen.) Wood carvers sell their work in front of the *Fort George* and *Holiday Inn Villa* hotels. A new craft centre at the S end of the swing bridge, on the site of the old market, should be open by 1993. The market is by the junction of North Front St and Fort St. *Ro-Macs*, 27 Albert St, excellent supermarket including wide selection of imported foods and wines.

● **Exchange**
All banks have facilities to arrange cash advance on Visa card. If you want US dollars against a credit card or travellers' cheques, you will be sent to get permission from the Central Bank, 2 Bishop Street, alternatively you may show proof that you are leaving the country; 3% commission is charged. The Belize Bank is particularly efficient and modern, US$0.50 commission on Amex cheques, gives cash on Visa and Mastercard; also Barclays Bank International, with some country branches, slightly better rates, 2% commission. Atlantic Bank, 6 Albert Street, or 16 New Road, quick efficient service, smaller queues than in others. Bank of Nova Scotia. It is easy to have money telexed to Belize City. American Express at Global Travel, 41 Albert Street, Belize City (T 77185/77363/4). Money changers at Batty Bus terminal just before departure of bus to Chetumal (the only place to change Mexican pesos, except the border).

● **Currency**
The monetary unit is the Belizean dollar, stabilized at BZ$2=US$1. Currency notes (Monetary Authority of Belize) are issued in the denominations of 100, 50, 20, 10, 5, 2, and 1 dollars, and coinage of 1 dollar, 50, 25, 10, 5 and 1 cent is in use. Notes marked Government of Belize, or Government of British Honduras, are only redeemable at a bank. The American expressions Quarter (25c), Dime (10c) and Nickel (5c) are common, although 25c is sometimes referred to as a shilling.

● **Security**
Take good care of your possessions in Belize City. Do not trust the many self-appointed "guides" who also sell hotel rooms, boat trips to the Cayes, drugs, etc. Local advice is not even to say "no"; just shake your head and wag your finger if approached by a stranger. Street money changers are not to be trusted either. Recent government measures have increased the security presence in Belize City. It is wise to avoid small, narrow side streets and stick to major thoroughfares, although even on main streets of Belize City you can be victim to unprovoked and violent threats and racial abuse. Travel by taxi is cheap and advisable at night and in the rain, but you can get mugged even in broad daylight. Outside the city the visitor should feel at no personal risk.

● **Health**
The climate is generally pleasant and healthy. Malaria is reportedly under control, but you are advised to take precautions when in Belize. It is advisable to use mosquito repellent. Inoculation against yellow fever and tetanus is advisable but not obligatory. Tap water in Belize City is said to be safe to drink but bottled water is preferable. Out-patients' medical attention is free of charge.

● **Climate**
Shade temperature is not often over 32°C on the coast, even in the hotter months of February to May (the "dry" season). Inland, in the W, day temperatures can exceed 38°C, but the nights are cooler. Between November and February there are cold spells during which the temperature at Belize City may fall to 13°C. Humidity is high, making it "sticky" most of the time in the lowlands.

There are sharp annual variations of rainfall, there is even an occasional drought, but the average at Belize City is 65 inches, with about 50 inches in the N and a great increase to 170 inches in the S. Generally the driest months are April and May; in June and July there are heavy showers followed by blue skies; September and October tend to be overcast and there are lots of insects. Hurricanes can threaten the country from June to November, but there have been only 4 in the past thirty years. An efficient warning system has been established and there are hurricane shelters in most towns and large villages.

● **Clothing**
The business dress for men is a short-sleeved

cotton or poplin shirt or *guayabera* (ties not often worn) and trousers of some tropical weight material. Formal wear may include ties and jackets, but long-sleeved embroidered *guayaberas* are commoner. Women should not wear shorts in the cities and towns; acceptable only on the cayes and at resorts.

● **Business Hours**

Retail shops are open 0800-1200, 1300-1600 and Fri 0900-2100, with a half day from 1200 on Wed. Small shops open additionally most late afternoons and evenings, and some on Sun 0800-1000.

Government and commercial office hours are 0800-1200 and 1300-1600 Mon to Fri. Banking hours in Belize City: 0800-1300 Mon-Thur, 0800-1300, 1500-1800 Fri (some variations elsewhere in the country).

● **Public Holidays**

New Year's Day (1 January), Baron Bliss Day (9 March), Good Friday and Saturday; Easter Monday, Labour Day (1 May), Commonwealth Day (24 May), St George's Caye Day (10 September), Belize Independence Day (21 September), Pan American Day (12 October), Garifuna Settlement Day (19 November), Christmas and Boxing Day.

● **Note**

Most services throughout the country close down Good Friday to Easter Monday: banks close at 1130 on the Thursday, buses run limited services Holy Saturday to Easter Monday, and boats to the Cayes are available. St George's Caye Day celebrations in September start 2 or 3 days in advance and require a lot of energy.

● **Time Zone**

6 hrs behind GMT, 1 behind EST.

● **Consulates**

Mexico, 20 North Park St, T 30193/4 (open 0900-1300, Mon-Fri; if going to Mexico and requiring a visa, get it here, not at the border, tourist card given on the spot, long queues are normal, arrive early, get visa the afternoon before departure; **Honduras**, 91 North Front St, T 45889; **El Salvador**, 120 New Road, T 44318; **Panama**, 5481, Princess Margaret Drive, T 44940. **Guatemala**, 6A Saint Matthew St, near municipal airstrip, T 33150, open 0900-1300, advisable to obtain visas or tourist cards here rather than leave it till you reach the border. **Jamaica**, 26 corner Hyde's Lane and New Road, T 45926, F 23312. **USA**, 29 Ga-

bourel Lane, T 77161/2, consulate is round corner on Hutson Street; **Canada**, c/o Vogue Ltd, corner Queen and North Front Street, T 45773/45769, PO Box 216; **Belgium**, Marcelo Ltd, Queen St, T 45769; **The Netherlands**, 14 Central American Blvd, T 75936; **Denmark**, 13 Southern Foreshore, T 72172; **Sweden**, 13 Queen St, T 77234; **Italy**, 18 Albert St, T 77777; **Israel**, 4 Albert St, T 30749/ F 30750. **France**, 10 Queen Street, T 45777; **German Honorary Consul**, 2 Cork Street, T 77316.

● **Electric Current**

110/220 volts single phase, 60 cycles for domestic supply.

● **Weights And Measures**

Imperial and US standard weights and measures. The US gallon is used for gasoline and motor oil.

● **Telecommunications**

There is a direct-dialling system between the major towns and to Mexico and USA. Belize Telecommunications Ltd, 1 Church Street, Belize City, open 0800-2100 Mon-Sat, 0800-1200 Sun and holidays, has an international telephone, telegraph and telex service. Also public fax service and booths for credit card and charge calls to USA, UK. To make an international call from Belize costs far less than from neighbouring countries. US$12 for 3 mins to UK and Europe (a deposit of US$15 required first); US$6.40 to USA and Canada; US$16 elsewhere. Collect calls to USA, Canada, Australia and UK only. Fax US$4.80 min, plus US$2.50 service charge.

● **Airmail Postage**

To UK 4-5 days, US$0.38 for a letter, US$0.20 for a postcard, US$0.30 for a letter to USA, US$0.15 for a post card , US$0.30 postcard, US$0.50 letter to Australia, takes 4-6 weeks. **Post Office in Belize City**: letters, Queen Street and North Front Street; parcels, beside main Post Office. Letters held for one month. Beautiful stamps sold.

● **Press**

Belize Times; Amandala, People's Pulse, Reporter (weekly). Monthlies *Belize Today* and *Belize Review*; bi-monthly *Belize Currents*.

Belize First, published 5 times a year in the USA, has articles on travel, life, news and history in the country. Equator Travel Publications Inc, 280 Beaverdam Rd, Candler, NC 28715, USA, F (704) 667-1717 (US$27 a year in Belize, USA, Canada, Mexico, US$37 elsewhere).

● **Tourist Information**

Belize Tourist Bureau, 83 North Front Street, Belize City, PO Box 325, T 02-77213/73255, F 02-77490 (open 0800-1200, 1300-1700 Mon- Thur, and till 1630 Fri), provides complete bus schedule as well as list of hotels and their prices. Also has a list of recommended taxi guides and tour operators, and free publications on the country and its Maya ruins, practical and informative. Excellent maps of the country for US$3 (postage extra). In the **USA**, 15 Penn Plaza, 415 Seventh Avenue, 18th floor, New York, NY 10001, T 800-624-0686, 212-268-8798, F 212-695-3018; **Canada**, Belize High Commission, 273 Patricia Avenue, Ottawa, K1Y V6C, T 613-722-7187; **Germany**, Belize Tourist Board/WICRG, Lomenstr.-28, 2000 Hamburg 70, T 49-40-695-8846, F 49-40-380-0051.

Belize Tourism Industry Association, private sector body for hotels, tour companies, etc, 99 Albert Street, T 75717, F 78710, brochures and information on all members throughout Belize. Enquire for details on all tour operators.

● **Recommended Reading**

Suggested reading is *Hey Dad, this is Belize*, by Emory King, a collection of anecdotes, available in bookshops. Also *Warlords and Maize Men, a Guide to the Mayan Sites of Belize*, published by the Association for Belize Archaeology. Maps (US$3), books on Belizean fauna etc available at Angelus Press, Queen St. Above the Post Office is the Survey Office selling maps, 2-sheet, 1:250,000, US$8, dated, or more basic map US$2.

CANCUN, ISLA MUJERES AND COZUMEL, MEXICO

OFF THE EASTERN, Caribbean coast of the Yucatán Peninsula, there are three Mexican islands which have been developed for tourism. All in the state of Quintana Roo, these are Cancún, the most recent and grandest of the resorts, Isla Mujeres and Cozumel (the largest island of the three). The islands are in fact a very small part of what the Yucatán has to offer the visitor. In Quintana Roo and the neighbouring state of Yucatán there are other beaches, magnificent archaeological sites in the form of Maya cities, and the important Spanish colonial city of Mérida. If visiting the region, you are strongly advised to make at least one excursion away from the beach. For an extended coverage of the whole area, consult *The Mexico and Central American Handbook*.

The proximity of all these attractions has helped Quintana Roo to become the largest tourist area in Mexico, with most tourists staying at the three island resorts. Since so many of the tourists coming to the coastal resorts know no Spanish, price hikes and short-changing have become very common there, making those places very expensive if one is not careful. In the peak, winter season, prices are increased anyway.

The peninsula of Yucatán is a flat land of tangled scrub in the drier NW, merging into exuberant jungle and tall trees in the wetter SE. There are no surface streams. The underlying geological foundation is a horizontal bed of limestone in which rainwater has dissolved enormous caverns. Here and there their roofs have collapsed, disclosing deep holes or *cenotes* in the ground, filled with water. Today this water is raised to surface-level by wind-pumps: a typical feature of the landscape. It is hot during the day but cool after sunset. Humidity is often high. All round the peninsula are splendid beaches fringed with palm groves and forests of coconut palms. The best time for a visit is from October to March.

The people are divided into two groups: the Maya Indians, the minority, and the *mestizos*, of mixed blood. The Maya women wear *huipiles*, or white cotton tunics (silk for *fiestas*) which may reach the ankles and are embroidered round the square neck and bottom hem. Ornaments are mostly gold. A few of the men still wear straight white cotton (occasionally silk) jackets and pants, often with gold or silver buttons, and when working protect this dress with aprons.

History

The Maya arrived in Yucatán from what is now Guatemala and Belize about AD 600 and later rebuilt their cities, but along different lines from those found further S, probably because of the arrival of Toltecs in the ninth and tenth centuries. Each city was autonomous, and in rivalry with other cities. Before the Spaniards arrived the Maya had developed a writing in which the hieroglyphic was somewhere between the pictograph and the letter. Bishop Landa collected their books, wrote a very poor summary, the *Relación de las Cosas de Yucatán*, and with Christian but unscholar like zeal burnt all his priceless sources.

In 1511 some Spanish adventurers were shipwrecked on the coast. Two survived. One of them, Juan de Aguilar, taught a Maya girl Spanish. She became interpreter for Cortés after he had landed

MEXICO : FACT FILE

Geographic

Land area	1,958,201 sq km
forested	22.3%
pastures	39.0%
cultivated	13.0%

Demographic

Population (1992)	84,439,000
annual growth rate (1987-92)	1.6%
urban	71.3%
rural	28.7%
density	43.1 per sq km
Religious affiliation	
Roman Catholic	89.7%
Birth rate per 1,000 (1990)	31.2
	(world av 27.1)
Death rate per 1,000 (1990)	5.0
	(world av 9.8)

Education and Health

Life expectancy at birth,	
male	66.5 years
female	73.1 years
Infant mortality rate	
per 1,000 live births (1988)	46.6
Physicians (1987)	1 per 600 persons
Hospital beds (1990)	1 per 1,298 persons
Calorie intake as %	
of FAO requirement	131%
Population age 25 and over	
with no formal schooling	13.4%
Literate males (over 15)	90.2%
Literate females (over 15)	84.8%

Economic

GNP (1990 market prices)	US$214,500mn
GNP per capita	US$2,490
Public external debt (1992)	US$76,087mn
Tourism receipts (1992)	US$6,641mn
Inflation (annual av 1986-91)	56.1%
Radio	1 per 5.1 persons
Television	1 per 6.7 persons
Telephone	1 per 7.6 persons

Employment

Population economically active (1990)	
	24,063,283
Unemployment rate	2.7%
% of labour force in	
agriculture	22.0
mining	1.1
manufacturing	18.7
construction	6.6
Military forces	175,000

Source *Encyclopaedia Britannica*

in 1519. The Spaniards found little to please them: no gold, no concentration of natives, but Mérida was founded in 1542 and the few natives handed over to the conquerors in *encomiendas*. The Spaniards found them difficult to exploit: even as late as 1847 there was a major revolt, mainly arising from the inhuman conditions in the *henequén* (sisal) plantations. In Yucatán and Quintana Roo, the economy has long been dependent on the export of *henequén* and chicle (for chewing gum), but both are facing heavy competition from substitutes and tourism is becoming ever more important.

Culture

Carnival is the year's most joyous occasion, with concerts, dances, processions. Yucatán's folk dance is the Jarana, the man dancing with his hands behind his back, the woman raising her skirts a little, and with interludes when they pretend to be bullfighting. During pauses in the music the man, in a high falsetto voice, sings *bambas* (compliments) to the woman.

The Maya are a courteous, gentle, strictly honest and scrupulously clean people. They drink little, except on feast days, speak Mayan, and profess Christianity laced with a more ancient nature worship.

Diving and Watersports

Quintana Roo (and especially Cozumel) is the main area for Diving and Watersports in the Yucatán Peninsula. The text below gives information on some of the options available, with addresses of dive shops, etc. It should be noted that watersports in Quintana Roo are expensive and touristy, but operators are generally helpful; snorkelling is often organized for large groups. On the more accessible reefs the coral is dying and there are no small coral fishes as a necessary part of the coral life cycle. Further from the shore, though, there is still much reef life to enjoy.

NB The Yucatán peninsula falls

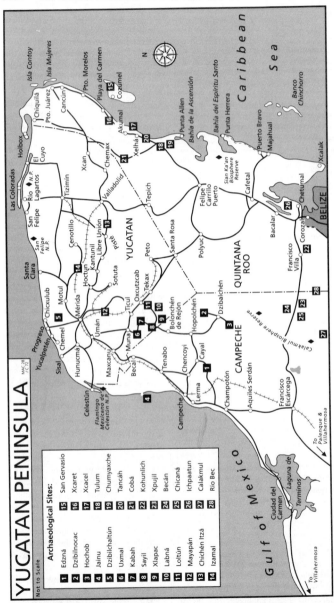

within the hurricane zone, and was most recently affected in September 1988, when Hurricane Gilbert caused extensive damage on the E coast (especially on Isla Mujeres).

CANCUN

Isla Mujeres, Cancún and the port of Puerto Juárez are all close to each other at the NE tip of the Yucatán Peninsula. *Cancún* is a thriving holiday resort and town. The town is on the mainland; the resort, usually known simply as the Zona Hotelera (Hotel Zone), is on an island shaped like the number 7, encompassing the Laguna Nichupté. The population is about 30,000, almost all dedicated to servicing the tourist industry. A bridge at each end of the island links the hotel zone with the mainland in a seamless ribbon, not yet developed along its entire length, but not far off. Beaches stretch all along the seaward side of the Zona Hotelera; both sand and sea are clean and beautiful. Watersports take place on the Caribbean and on the Laguna, but when bathing, watch out for the warning flags at intervals along the shore.

The scale of the Zona Hotelera is huge, with skyscraper hotels and sprawling resorts between the beach and Bulevar Kukulkán, which runs the length of the island. At the N end are shopping malls and an archaeological museum with local finds, next to the Convention Centre (a new Convention Centre has been constructed opposite the *Fiesta Americana Coral Beach*.) There are vestiges of Maya occupation here, San Miguelito and El Rey towards the S of the island, a small temple in the grounds of the *Sheraton* and Pok-ta-Pok on a peninsula at the N of the Laguna, but they are virtually lost in the midst of the modern concrete and the architectural fantasies. Near El Rey (open 0800-1630), land is being reclaimed for the construction of a golf course, marina, hotel and commercial centre. Prices are higher on Cancún than elsewhere in Mexico because everything is brought in from miles outside. Buses, marked "Hoteles", run every 5 mins for US$0.80 from the S end of the Zona Hotelera to the town and back. At busy times they are packed with holidaymakers trying to locate where they should get off.

It is about 4 km from the Zona Hotelera to the town, which is full of tourist shops, restaurants and a variety of hotels which are cheaper than on the island. The town is divided into "supermanzanas", indicated by SM in addresses, each block being divided further by streets and avenues. The two main avenues are Tulum and Yaxchilán, the former having most of the shops, exchange facilities, many restaurants and hotels. Its busiest sector runs from the roundabout at the junction with Bulevar Kukulkán to the roundabout by the bus station.

Local Information – Cancún
● Buses
Local bus ("Hoteles" Route), US$0.80 (taxis are exorbitant); to Puerto Juárez for Isla Mujeres from Av Tulum, marked "Puerto Juárez or "Colonia Lombardo", US$0.55.

Cancún bus terminal, at the junction of Avs Tulum and Uxmal, is the hub for routes W to Mérida and S to Tulum and Chetumal. The station is neither large nor very well organized. It is open 24 hrs.

Inter Playa Express every 30 mins to **Playa del Carmen** for Cozumel, US$2.25 and Tulum, US$4. Other services to Playa del Carmen and Tulum are more expensive, eg 1st class Caribe Inter to Playa del Carmen US$3, 2nd class US$2.35 to Playa del Carmen and US$4.75 to Tulum. Last bus to Playa del Carmen at 2000. These services are en route to **Chetumal** near the Belize border (US$33 1st class, US$15-17.75 2nd). Several other services to Chetumal, including Caribe Express, deluxe service with a/c. Many services to **Mérida**, 4 hrs, ranging from *plus* with TV, a/c, etc, US$20, to 1st class US$14; to **Chichén Itzá**, Expreso de Oriente 1st class en route to Mérida, US$6.20.

● Boat Services
The Playa Linda boat dock is at the mainland side of the bridge across Canal Nichupté, about

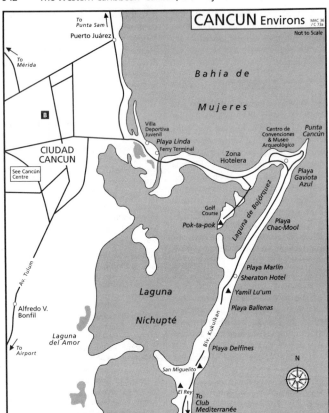

CANCUN Environs MAC 36 /C 73a
Not to Scale

To Punta Sam
Puerto Juárez
To Mérida

Bahía de Mujeres

B

CIUDAD CANCUN

See Cancún Centre

Villa Deportiva Juvenil
Playa Linda
Ferry Terminal

Centro de Convenciones & Museo Arqueológico

Zona Hotelera

Punta Cancún

Playa Gaviota Azul

Golf Course
Pok-ta-pok

Laguna de Bojórquez

Playa Chac-Mool

Av. Tulum

Playa Marlín
Sheraton Hotel
Yamil Lu'um
Playa Ballenas

Alfredo V. Bonfil

Laguna

Nichupté

Blv. Kukulkan

Playa Delfines

Laguna del Amor

To Airport

San Miguelito

El Rey
To Club Mediterranée

N

4 km from centre, opposite the *Calinda Quality Cancún Beach*. It has shops, agencies for boat trips, a snack bar and Computel. Trips to Isla Mujeres, with snorkelling, bar, shopping, start at US$27.50, or US$35 with meal; ferry to Isla Mujeres 0900, 1100, 1330, returning 1600 and 2000, US$6.65 one way. Cheaper ferries go from Puerto Juárez, see below.

Trips to Isla Contoy (see under Isla Mujeres) were suspended in mid-1993 owing to excessive disturbance of bird habitats. *Nautibus*, a vessel with seats below the waterline, makes trips to the reefs, 1½ hrs, a good way to see fish, Playa Linda dock, T 83-35-52. There are a number of other cruises on offer.

● **Car Hire**
Budget Rent-a-Car in Cancún has been rec

for good service. **Avis**, Plaza Caracol, cheapest but still expensive. There are many car hire agencies, with offices on Av Tulum, in the Zona Hotelera and at the airport; look out for special deals, but check vehicles carefully. Rates vary enormously, from US$40 to US$80 a day for a VW Golf (VW Beetles are cheaper), larger cars and jeeps available.

● **Where To Stay**
Hotels fall roughly into 2 categories: those in the Zona Hotelera, which are expensive and tend to cater for package tours, but which have all the facilities associated with a beach holiday; those in the town are less pricey and more functional. The list below gives more detail on the latter.

In the Zona Hotelera: *Camino Real*, T 83-

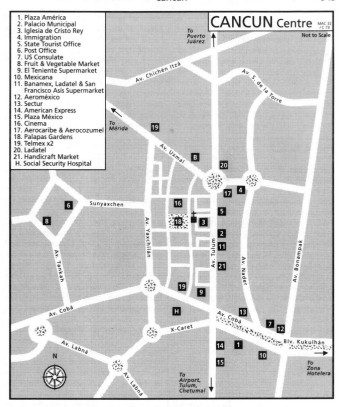

CANCUN Centre MAC 32 / C 73
Not to Scale

1. Plaza América
2. Palacio Municipal
3. Iglesia de Cristo Rey
4. Immigration
5. State Tourist Office
6. Post Office
7. US Consulate
8. Fruit & Vegetable Market
9. El Teniente Supermarket
10. Mexicana
11. Banamex, Ladatel & San
    Francisco Asís Supermarket
12. Aeroméxico
13. Sectur
14. American Express
15. Plaza México
16. Cinema
17. Aerocaribe & Aerocozumel
18. Palapas Gardens
19. Telmex x2
20. Ladatel
21. Handicraft Market
H. Social Security Hospital

01-00, F 83-17-30; *Sheraton Cancún Resort and Towers*, US$230 lagoon view, US$240 ocean view (PO Box 834, Cancún, T 83-19-88, F 85-02-02); *Hyatt Cancún Caribe*, T 83-00-44, F 83-15-14 (from US$130), and *Hyatt Regency*, T 83-09-66, F 83-13-49 (from US$115, high season); *Stouffer Presidente*, T 83-02-00, F 83-25-15, *Miramar Misión Park Plaza*, T 83-17-55, F 83-11-36. *Playa Blanca*, Av Kukulkán Km 3.5, T 83-00-71, F 83-09-04, resort facilities; and *Krystal*, T 83-11-33, F 83-17-90. Slightly less expensive: *Aristos*, T 83-00-11, F 83-00-78, *Calinda Quality Cancún Beach*, T 83-08-00, F 83-18-57, and *Calinda Viva*, same phone, F 83-20-87; *Club Lagoon Marina*, T 83-11-01, F 83-13-26. Also represented are hotels in the *Fiesta Americana* chain (3 in all), *Days Inn*, *Holiday Inn*

(*Crowne Plaza*, T 85-10-22, F 85-17-07, US$120; and *Centro*, Av Náder 1 SM2, T 87-44-55, F 84-79-54, US$90, high season), *Marriott*, *Meliá* (2), *Radisson* (also 2), and many more hotels, suites and villas. At the S end of the island is the *Club Méditerranée* with its customary facilities (T 85-29-00, F 85-22-90).

Youth hostel, *Villa Deportiva Juvenil*, is at Km 3.2 Av Kukulkán, T 83-13-37, on the beach, 5 mins walk from the bridge towards Cancún town, next to *Club Verano Beat*, dormitory style, US$10 per person, US$10 deposit, 25% discount with membership card, 12 people per room, basic, dirty, plumbing unreliable, sketchy locker facilities, meals at set times, small shop, camping US$5.

Hotels in Cancún town: most are to be found on Av Tulum and Av Yaxchilán and the streets off them. In Cancún town you will be lucky to find a double under US$20; many do not serve meals. **Best Western Plaza Caribe**, Av Tulum y Uxmal, T 84-13-77, F 84-63-52, US$60-96, opposite bus terminal; **Caribe Internacional**, at the junction of Yaxchilán and Sunyaxchén, T 84-34-99, F 84-19-93, US$52; **Plaza del Sol**, Yaxchilán y Gladiolas, T 84-38-88, F 84-43-93, modern, comfortable. Up to US$50: **Antillano**, Av Tulum y Claveles, T 84-15-32, F 84-11-32, a/c, TV, phone, pool; **Cancún Rosa**, Margaritas 2, local 10, T 84-28-73, F 84-06-23, close to bus terminal, a/c, TV, phone, comfortable rooms; **El Alux**, Av Uxmal 21, T 84-06-62, 2 blocks from bus terminal; **El Rey del Caribe**, Av Uxmal y Náder, T 84-20-28, F 84-98-57, a/c, kitchenettes, pool, garden with hammocks, parking, older style, rec; **Hacienda**, Sunyaxchén 38-40, a/c, TV; **Margarita**, Yaxchilán y Jazmines, T 84-93-33, F 84-92-09, US$50; **María de Lourdes**, Av Yaxchilán SM 22, T 84-47-44, F 84-12-42; **Parador**, Av Tulum 26, T 84-13-10, F 84-97-12, close to bus terminal, US$45, inefficient a/c, TV, phone, pool, restaurant attached, clean, quite good. Under US$30: **Colonial**, Tulipanes 22 y Av Tulum, T 84-15-35, a/c, cheaper with fan, quiet, TV, phone; **Coral**, Sunyaxchén 30 (towards post office), T 84-29-01; **Cotty**, Av Uxmal 44, T 84-05-50, near bus station, a/c, TV, reports vary on cleanliness; **Lucy**, Gladiolas 25, between Tulum and Yaxchilán, T 84-41-65, a/c, kitchenettes, takes credit cards; **María Isabel**, Palmera 595, T 84-90-15, near bus station and Av Tulum, fan and a/c, hot water, TV, small and clean, friendly, helpful; **Novotel**, Av Tulum y Azucenas, T 84-29-99, F 84-31-62, close to bus station, rooms start at under US$30 with fan, but rise to US$40 with a/c, popular, noisy on Av Tulum side; **Rivemar**, Av Tulum 49-51 y Crisantemas, T 84-17-08, a/c, phone, TV; **Villa Maya Cancún**, Uxmal 20 y Rubia, T 84-28-29, F 84-17-62, a/c, pool, *La Francesa* bakery next door; **Villa Rossana**, Yaxchilán, opposite *Plaza del Sol*. Cheaper still: **Piña**, US$15, hot showers, fan, clean, rec; similar price, **Tropical Caribe**, Cedro 10 SM 23, T 41-14-42, bath and fan, quiet, secure, not too clean (walk N up Av Tulum from junction with Uxmal for about 5 blocks, turn left at Disco Salsa and hotel is on the right).

Camping is not permitted in Cancún town except at the Villa Deportiva youth hostel. There is a trailer park, *Rainbow*, just S of the airport.

● **Where To Eat**

There is a huge variety of restaurants, ranging from hamburger stands to 5-star, gourmet places. Just about every type of cuisine can be found. The best buys are on the side streets of Cancún town, while the largest selection can be found on Avs Tulum and Yaxchilán. The ones on the island are of slightly higher price and quality and are scattered along Blv Kukulkán, with a high concentration in the shopping centres (of which there are about ten). If you are in no hurry to eat, look at what the restaurants are offering in the way of dishes, prices and drinks specials, then decide, if you can resist the pressurized selling.

The best is said to be **100% Natural**, opposite *Hotel Caribe Internacional* on Yaxchilán y Sunyaxchén, freshly-prepared food, friendly staff, "invigorating eating"; **Los Braceritos**, Yaxchilán 35, open 24 hrs; **La Estancia**, Gladiolas 25 next to *Hotel Lucy*, good; **Los Huaraches**, on Uxmal opposite Yaxchilán, fast food, cheap empanada specials after 1300; many others on Av Uxmal, not too expensive. **Los Almendros**, Av Bonampak y Sayil, Lote 60, 61 and 62, good local food. **La Bodeguita del Medio**, Tulipanes SM 22 y Av Tulum, good food and service, "Cuban"; **El Pescador**, Tulipanes 28, good seafood but expensive; **Pop**, next to *Hotel Parador*, for quicker-type food; **Bing**, Av Tulum y Uxmal, close to Banpais bank, best ice cream. **Jaguari**, Zona Hotelera, Brazilian, opens 1700, US$15.95 + tax, set price, has been rec. **Piemonte Pizzería**, Av Yaxchilán 52, good food and value, appetizing aperitifs on the house, rec; **Las Tejas**, Av Tulum, central end, good food at reasonable prices; also on Av Tulum, **Olé Olé**, good meat, friendly. **Tacolote**, Av Cobá 19, good food and excellent value, cheerful, popular; taco stands can be found each evening on and around the squares between Avs Tulum and Yaxchilán, good family atmosphere. **Comida Casera**, Av Uxmal, opp bus terminal, good coffee. The native Mexican restaurants in the workers' colonies are cheapest. Best bet is to buy food and beer in a store and take it to the beach, spending the day on a lounger.

● **Shopping**

The market, at Av Tulum 23, is basically a handicrafts market, with jewellery, clothing, hats, etc. Downtown there are several supermarkets, big and small, for food and drink, eg **Comercial Mexicana**, near Ladatel; **San Francisco de Asís**. Next to *Hotel Caribe Internacional*, on Yaxchilán, are 2 24-hr *farmacias*. **Bookshop** *Fama*, Av Tulum 105, international books and magazines, English, French, German.

● **Entertainment**

Ballet Folclórico de México, nightly dinner shows at 1900 at *Continental Villas Plaza Hotel*, Zona Hotelera, T 85-14-44, ext 5706. *La Boom* disco, almost opposite Playa Linda dock, near the youth hostel, US$7 for all you can drink. Salsa club *Batachá* in *Miramar Misión* hotel, US$5 entry charge, popular with locals, good music. Crococun crocodile ranch, 30 km on road to Playa del Carmen.

● **Sports**

Parasailing from beaches on Zona Hotelera; sailing; many other water sports; bungee jumping also available, from a crane hoist.

● **Exchange**

Many Mexican banks. Many small *casas de cambio*, which change cash and travellers' cheques (latter at poorer rates) until 2100; rec is *Cunex*, Av Tulum 13, close to Av Cobá. Rates are better in town than at the airport. It is possible to change dollar TCs into dollars cash, but not one-for-one.

● **Consulates**

Downtown, unless stated otherwise, most open am only: **Costa Rica**, Calle Mandinga, manzana 11, SM 30, T 84-48-69; **USA**, Av Náder 40, T 84-24-11, 0900-1400, 1500-1800; **Canada**, Plaza México 312, 2nd floor, T 84-37-16, 1100-1300; **Germany**, Punta Conoco 36, SM 24, T 84-18-98; **Sweden**, Av Náder 34, SM 2-A, T 84-72-71, 0800-1300, 1700-2000; **Spain**, Cielo 17, Depto 10, SM 4, T 84-18-95; **Italy**, La Mansión Costa Blanca Shopping Center, Zona Hotelera, T 83-21-84; **France**, Instituto Internacional de Idiomas, Av Xel-Há 113, SM 25, T 84-60-78, 0800-1100, 1700-1900.

● **Post Office**

At end of Av Sunyaxchen, a short distance from Av Yaxchilán. **Telephones** Telmex *caseta* just off Av Cobá on Alcatraces; another *caseta* on Av Uxmal next to *Los Huaraches* restaurant. Ladatel phones in Plaza América, at San Francisco de Asís shopping centre and opp the bus station on the end wall of a supermarket at Tulum y Uxmal. Computel phone and fax, more expensive, at Yaxchilán 49 and other locations.

● **Tourist Information**

State Tourist Office, Av Tulum, between Comermex and city hall; Sectur Federal Tourist Office, corner of Av Cobá and Av Náder, closed weekends, but kiosk on Av Tulum at Tulipanes is open sometimes at weekends. There are

kiosks in the Zona Hotelera, too, eg at Mayfair Plaza. Downtown and in the Zona Hotelera closest to downtown most street corners have a map. See free publication, *Cancún Tips*, issued twice a year, and *Cancún Tips Magazine*, quarterly, from Av Tulum 29, Cancún, QR 77500, Mexico.

ISLA MUJERES

Isla Mujeres (which got its name from the large number of female idols first found by the Spaniards) once epitomized the Caribbean island: long silver beaches (beware sandflies), palm trees and clean blue water at the N end (although the large *Del Prado* hotel dominates the view there) away from the beach pollution of the town, and the naval airstrip to the SW of the town. There are limestone (coral) cliffs and a rocky coast at the S end. A lagoon on the W side is now fouled up. The island has suffered from competition from Cancún and although it is touristy, it is worth a visit. A disease destroyed practically all the palms which used to shade the houses and beach, but new, disease-resistant varieties have been planted and are growing to maturity. There was considerable damage from hurricane Gilbert. The main activity in the evening takes place in the square near the church, where there are also a supermarket and a cinema. Between 1-8 December there is a fiesta for the Virgin of the island, fireworks, dances until 0400 in the Plaza. In October there is a festival of music, with groups from Mexico and the USA performing in the main square. The Civil Guard patrol the beaches at night.

At *El Garrafón*, 7 km (entry US$2, and the same for a locker with an extra US$3.35 key deposit), there is a tropical fish reserve (fishing forbidden) on a small coral reef. Take snorkel (rental US$2.65 a day for mask and snorkel, same again for fins, US$5 for underwater camera, plus deposit of US$30, passport, driver's licence, credit card or hotel key, from shops in the park) and swim among a variety of multicoloured tropical fish – they aren't at all shy, but the coral is dead and not colourful. Reef trips by boat cost US$11.65 without equipment hire, US$15 with hire. El Garrafón is a very popular excursion on the island and from Cancún; the water is usually full of snorkellers between 1100 and 1400. It is open 0800-1630; there are showers, toilets, expensive restaurants and bars, reasonable snackbar, shops and a small museum-cum-aquarium.

Taxi from the town to El Garrafón costs about US$6, maybe more for the return. It is cheaper to take a taxi from El Garrafón to the Casa Mundaca (see below), US$2.65, then another back to town, US$1.65. There is a bus which goes half-way to El Garrafón, the end of the line being at the bend in the road by the entrances to Casa Mundaca and Playa Paraíso (bus fare US$0.35). This beach, and its neighbour, Lancheros, is quite clean, has palms, restaurants and toilets. The area of sand is quite small. Sadly, there are pens at the shore containing nurse sharks, which swim up and down their cages like big cats in a zoo. If so moved, you can join them in the water. Playa Indios, S of Lancheros, towards El Garrafón, has similar facilities and "entertainment".

The curious remains of a pirate's domain, called Casa de Mundaca, is in the centre of the island; a big, new arch gate marks its entrance. Paths have been laid out among the large trees, but all that remains of the estate (called Vista Alegre) are one small building and a circular garden with raised beds, a well and a gateway. Fermín Mundaca, more of a slave-trader than a buccaneer, built Vista Alegre for the teenage girl he loved. She rejected him and he died, broken-hearted, in Mérida. His epitaph there reads "Como eres, yo fui; como soy, tu serás" (what you are I was; what I am you shall be). See the poignant little carving on the garden side of the gate, "La entrada de La Trigueña" (the girl's nickname). At the S tip is a small, ruined Mayan lighthouse or shrine of Ixtel, just beyond a modern lighthouse. The lighthouse keeper sells coca-cola for US$1, hammocks and conch shells. The view from the Maya shrine is beautiful, with a pale turquoise channel running away from the island to the mainland, deep blue water surrounding it, and the high-rise hotels of Cancún in the distance. Looking N from the temple you see both coasts of the island stretching away from you.

The town is at the NW end of the island; at the end of the N-S streets is the N beach (Playa Coco), the widest area of dazzling white sand on the island (watersport equipment is rented at very high prices). The island is best visited April to November, off-season (although one can holiday here the year round). **NB** Bathing on the Caribbean side of the island can be unsafe because of strong undertows and cross-currents.

Trip to *Isla Contoy* (bird and wildlife sanctuary), while suspended from Cancún, are still possible from Isla Mujeres, US$40, 9 hrs, with excellent lunch, 2 hrs of fishing, snorkelling (equipment hire extra, US$2.50) and relaxing. Boats from the cooperative at the town pier may not leave until full. From the same point boat trips go to the lighthouse at the entrance to the harbour, Isla Tiburón, El Garrafón and Playa Lancheros for lunch, 3-4 hrs, US$16.65 pp. You will be approached by boatmen on the boat from Puerto Juárez, and on arrival.

Local Information – Isla Mujeres
● **Public transport**
There is public transport on Isla Mujeres, ie taxis at fixed prices, and the bus service mentioned above. You can walk from one end of the island to the other in 2½ hrs. At the top of the rise before El Garrafón, by the speed humps and the houses for rent, is a point where you can see both sides of the island. A track leads from the road to the Caribbean coast, a couple of minutes stroll. You can then walk down the E coast to the S tip. Worth hiring a bicycle, US$5 a day (about US$7 deposit, eg *Sport Bike*, Av Juárez y Morelos), or a moped (US$5/hr, US$20-25 all day, US$35-40/24 hrs,

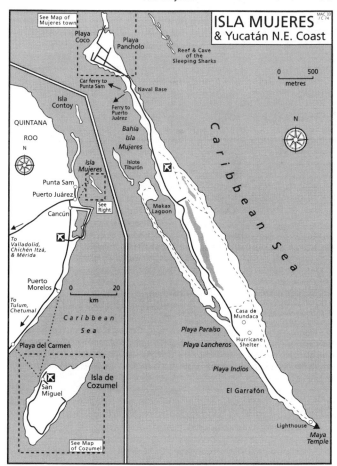

ISLA MUJERES MAC 33
& Yucatán N.E. Coast /C 74

See Map of Mujeres town

Playa Coco

Playa Pancholo

Reef & Cave of the Sleeping Sharks

Car ferry to Punta Sam

Naval Base

Isla Contoy

QUINTANA

ROO

N

Ferry to Puerto Juárez

Bahia Isla Mujeres

Isla Mujeres

Islote Tiburón

Punta Sam

Puerto Juárez

See Right

Cancún

To Valladolid, Chichén Itzá, & Mérida

Makax Lagoon

Puerto Morelos

0   20

km

To Tulum, Chetumal

Caribbean Sea

Casa de Mundaca

Playa Paraíso

Hurricane Shelter

Playa Lancheros

Playa del Carmen

Playa Indios

El Garrafón

San Miguel

Isla de Cozumel

Lighthouse

Maya Temple

See Map of Cozumel

Caribbean Sea

N

0   500
metres

---

credit card, passport or money deposit, helmet not required), to explore the island in about 2 hrs. Do check if there is any damage to the bicycle *before* you hire. Bicycles for hire from several hotels. Try Ciro's Motorrentor by *Hotel Caribe* for good motorbikes.

● **Where To Stay**

At Christmas hotel prices are increased steeply and the island can heave with tourists, esp in January. The island has several costly hotels and others, mainly in the US$13-25 range; food,

especially fresh fruit, is generally expensive.

Reasonable hotels to stay at on Isla Mujeres are *Posada del Mar*, Alte Rueda 15, T 20212 (including meals) has pleasant drinks terrace but expensive drinks, restaurant for residents only; *Las Perlas del Caribe*, Caribbean side of town, US$58 with a/c, US$44 with fan, clean, pool, rec; *Belmar*, Av Hidalgo 110 entre Madero y Abasolo, T 70430, F 70429, US$75 (luxury) to US$35, a/c, TV, restaurant *Pizza Rolandi* downstairs; *El Mesón del Bucanero*, Hidalgo 11, T 20210, F 20126, all rooms with fan,

ISLA MUJERES TOWN

Not to Scale

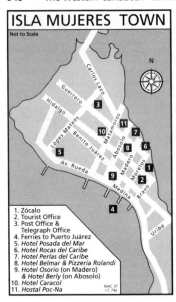

1. Zócalo
2. Tourist Office
3. Post Office & Telegraph Office
4. Ferries to Puerto Juárez
5. Hotel Posada del Mar
6. Hotel Rocas del Caribe
7. Hotel Perlas del Caribe
8. Hotel Belmar & Pizzería Rolandi
9. Hotel Osorio (on Madero) & Hotel Berly (on Abosolo)
10. Hotel Caracol
11. Hostal Poc-Na

MAC 37 / C 74a

US$50 (junior suite) to US$23; in the US$25-30 range: *Berny*, Juárez y Abasolo, T 20025, with bath and fan, basic, swimming pool, long-distance calls possible, residents only, but does not even honour confirmed reservations if a deposit for one night's stay has not been made. *El Paso*, Morelos 13, with bath, clean, facing the pier, 2nd floor; *Rocas del Caribe*, Madero 2, 100m from ocean, cool rooms, big balcony, clean, good service; *Vistalmar*, on promenade about 300m left from ferry dock (under US$20: for longer stays – negotiate), ask for rooms on top floor, bath, balcony, fan, insect screens, good value; *Isla Mujeres*, next to church, with bath, renovated, run by pleasant Englishman; *María José*, Madero 25, T 20130, US$13.50, clean, fans, friendly, scooter hire; *Caracol*, Matamaros 5, T 70150, F 70547, US$23 with a/c, US$20 with fan, hot water, terrace balcony, stoves for guests' use, bar, coffee shop, laundry, central, clean, good value. Under US$20: *Caribe Maya*, Madero 9, central, modern, a/c, cheaper than *Rocas del Caribe*, comfy and comfy; *Carmelina*, Guerrero 4, T 70006, US$25, central with bath and a/c, clean, comfortable, safe, rec, rents bikes and snorkelling gear, advance payment for room required daily; *Las Palmas*, central, Guerrero 20, 2 blocks from N beach,

good, clean; *Osorio*, Madero, 1 block from waterfront, clean, fan, with bath and hot water, rec, *La Reina* bakery nearby; *Xul-Ha*, on Hidalgo towards N beach, US$17 with fan. *Isleñas*, US$15 with bath, cheaper without, very clean, helpful; *Poc-Na Hostal*, US$4.50 pp, is cheapest, dormitories, try for central section where there are fans, clean, everything works, no bedding, but linen is included in the price, gringo hang-out, good and cheap café, video, take insect repellent (San Jorge laundry is just 1 block away, US$2 per kg). There is a trailer park on the island, with a restaurant. At Playa Indios is *Camping Los Indios* where you can put up your hammock. **NB** If you arrive late, book into any hotel the first night and set out to find what you want by 0700-0800, when the first ferries leave the next morning.

● **Where To Eat**

Many beach restaurants close just before sunset. *El Limbo* at Roca Mar Hotel (Nicolás Bravo y Guerrero), excellent seafood, good view, reasonable prices; *Miriti*, opp ferry, quite good value; *Pizza Rolandi*, see above, good breakfast, popular. *Gomar*, Madero y Hidalgo, expensive, possible to eat outside on veranda or in the colonial-style interior, popular; *Chen Huayo*, Hidalgo, excellent Mexican food, cheap; *Las Gemelas*, also on Hidalgo, US-owned, vegetarian options, good value; *Mano de Dios*, near the beach, probably cheapest on island, quite good. *Eric's*, very good inexpensive Mexican snacks; *Tropicana*, 1 block from pier, simple, popular, cheap; *Cielito Lindo*, waterfront, open air, good service; good fish restaurant 50m to left of jetty, US$3-4; *Peña*, overlooks beach, good pizzas, nice atmosphere; *La Langosta*, good Mexican dishes, lovely view; *Bucanero*, downtown, steak, seafood, prime rib, classy for Islas Mujeres. *Sergio's* on main square, expensive, very good; also *Robert's*, on square, cheap and good. *Giltri*, in town, good value; *Café Cito* on B Juárez, 1 Block W of *Tequila*, best breakfast, good health food, rec. *Ciro's* lobster house, not too good but *Napolito's*, opp, is excellent. Small restaurants round market are good value. Daily fish barbeque at El Paraíso beach. At Garrafón Beach: *El Garrafón*, *El Garrafón de Castilla*, catering for tour boats from Cancún; between Playa Indios and El Garrafón, *María's Kankin Hotel and Restaurant*, French cuisine.

● **Shopping**

Opposite the restaurant *Gomar* are several souvenir shops, selling good stone Maya carvings (copies), macramé hangings and colourful wax crayon "Maya" prints. *El Paso Boutique*, opp ferry, trades a small selection of English novels.

● **Disco-bars**

Tequila, on Hidalgo, video bar and restaurant. *Bad Bones* has live rock-and-roll.

● **Watersports**

You can rent skin and scuba diving equipment, together with guide, on the waterfront N of the public pier, a boat and equipment costs about US$50 pp for ¹/₂ day, check how many tanks of air are included and shop around. They can set up group excursions to the Cave of the Sleeping Sharks; English spoken. It is no cheaper to hire snorkel gear in town than on the beach. Deep sea fishing for 10 in a boat from *Aguamundo*. Diving is not in the class of Cozumel.

● **Services**

Exchange Banco del Atlántico, Av Juárez 5, 1% commission. **Telephones** Ladatel cards are sold at *Artesanía Yamily*, Hidalgo, just N of the square. **Tourist Information** Tourist office on square, opposite the basketball pitch.

Puerto Juárez

Puerto Juárez is about 3 km N of Cancún. It is the dock for the cheaper ferry services to Isla Mujeres; there is also a bus terminal, but services are more frequent from Cancún. There are many buses between Cancún and Puerto Juárez, eg No 8 opposite bus terminal (US$0.65), but when the ferries arrive from Isla Mujeres there are many more taxis than buses (taxi fare should be US$3, beware overcharging).

Local Information – Puerto Juárez
● **Where To Stay And Eat**

Hotel Caribel, resort complex, with bath and fan, over US$50, in the same price range is *San Marcos*; other hotels include *Kah Che*, first hotel on right coming from Cancún, US$25 in room for 3, fan, clean, swimming pool on beach, good value; *Posada Hermanos Sánchez*, 100m from bus terminal, on road to Cancún; under US$20, *Fuente Azul* opp the dock. *Restaurants Natz Ti Ha* and *Mandinga* by the ferry dock, serve breakfast. *Cabañas Punta Sam*, clean, comfortable, on the beach,

with bath (over US$20 in high season). Possible to camp, with permission, on the beach near the restaurant next door. A big trailer park is being built opp *Punta Sam*. Irregular bus service there, or hitchhike from Puerto Juárez. Check to see if restaurant is open evenings. No shops nearby. Take mosquito repellent.

● **Ferries**

Passenger ferry to Isla Mujeres leaves from the jetty opposite the bus terminal at Puerto Juárez 16 times a day between 0600 and 2100, returning 0500-1930; sometimes leaves early, last boat back may not sail at all (US$1.50, 1 hr, 5 vessels; *Caribbean Queen* is faster, US$3.35; *Caribbean Express* is faster still). There are also small water taxis, but these are much more expensive (US$6 at least to the town or El Garrafón). At the jetty is a luggage store (0800-1800) and a tourist information desk. Car ferry from Punta Sam to Isla Mujeres (about 75 cars carried), 5 km by bus from Cancún via Puerto Juárez (facilities to store luggage), US$1.50 pp and US$6-7 per car; 6 times a day between 0830 and 2200, returning between 0715 and 2200 (45-min journey).

● **Buses**

On the whole it is better to catch outgoing buses in Cancún rather than in Puerto Juárez: there are more of them.

COZUMEL

Cozumel island is not only a marvellous place for snorkelling and scuba diving, but is described as a "jewel of nature, possessing much endemic wildlife including pygmy species of coati and raccoon; the bird life has a distinctly Caribbean aspect and many endemic forms also" – Jeffrey L White, Tucson, Arizona. A brief visit does not afford much opportunity to see the flora and fauna on land; the forested centre of the island is not easy to visit, except at the Maya ruins of San Gervasio (see below), and there are few vantage points. On the other hand, the island has a great deal to offer the tourist. The name derives from the Maya "Cuzamil", land of swallows. Maya pilgrims hoped to visit once in their lifetime the shrine to Ix-Chel (goddess of the moon, pregnancy, childbirth, all things feminine, but also floods, tides and destructive waters), which was located on the island. By the 14th century AD, Cozumel had also become an important trading centre. The Spaniards first set foot on the island on 1 May 1518 when Juan de Grijalva arrived with a fleet from Cuba. Spanish dominance came in 1520. By the 18th century, the island was deserted. In all, there are some 32 archaeological sites on Cozumel, those on the E coast mostly single buildings (lookouts, navigational aids?). The easiest to see are the restored ruins of the Maya-Toltec period at *San Gervasio* in the N (7 km from Cozumel town, then 6 km to the left up a paved road, toll US$1). Entry to the site is US$4.35; guides are on hand, or you can buy a self-guiding booklet at the *librería* on the square in San Miguel, or at the *Flea Market*, for US$1. It is an interesting site, quite spread out, with *sacbes* (Maya roads) between the groups of buildings. There are no large structures, but a nice plaza, an arch, and pigment can be seen in places. It is also a pleasant place to listen to birdsong, see butterflies, animals (if lucky), lizards and landcrabs (and insects). Castillo Real is one of many sites on the NE coast, but the road to this part of the island is in very bad condition. *El Cedral* in the SW (3 km from the main island road) is a 2-room temple, overgrown with trees, in the centre of the village of the same name. Behind it is a ruin, and next to it a modern church with a green and white façade (an incongruous pairing). In the village are large, permanent shelters for agricultural shows, rug sellers, and locals who pose with *iguanas doradas*. El Caracol, where the sun, in the form of a shell, was worshipped is 1 km from the southernmost Punta Celarain. At Punta Celarain is an old lighthouse.

The main town is *San Miguel de Cozumel*, on the sheltered W coast. Here the ferries from the mainland and the cruise ships dock. The waterfront, Av Rafael Melgar, and a couple of streets behind it are dedicated to the shoppers and restaurant-goers, but away from this area the atmosphere is quite Mexican. Fishermen sell their catch by the passenger ferry pier, which is in the centre of town. It is a friendly town, with a good range of hotels (both in town and in zones to the N and S) and eating places. The best public beaches are some way from San Miguel town: in the N of the island they are sandy and wide, although those at the Zona Hotel Norte were damaged in 1989 and are smaller than they used to be. (At the end of the paved road, walk up the unmade road until it becomes "dual carriageway"; turn left for the narrow beach, which is a bit dirty. Cleaner beaches are accessible only through the hotels.) South of San Miguel, San Francisco is good if narrow (clean, very popular, lockers at *Pancho's*, expensive restaurants), but others are generally narrower still and rockier. All the main hotels are on the sheltered W coast. The E Caribbean coast is rockier still, but very picturesque; swimming and diving on the unprotected side is very dangerous owing to ocean underflows. The only safe place is at a sheltered bay at Chen Río.

A circuit of the island on paved roads can easily be done in a day (see **Local Transport** below). Head due E out of San Miguel (take the continuation of Av Benito Juárez). Make the detour to San Gervasio before continuing to the Caribbean coast at *Mescalito's* restaurant. Here, turn left for the N tip (road unsuitable for ordinary vehicles), or right for the S, passing Punta Moreno, Chen Río, Punta Chiqueros (restaurant, bathing), El Mirador (a low viewpoint with sea-worn rocks, look out for holes) and Paradise Cove. At this point, the paved road heads W while an unpaved road continues S to Punta Celarain. On the road W, opposite the turnoff to El Cedral, is a sign to *Restaurante Mac y Cía*, an excellent fish restaurant on a lovely beach, popular with dive groups for lunch. Next is Playa San Francisco (see above). A few more

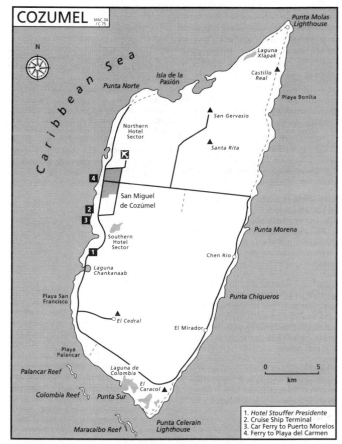

COZUMEL MAC 34 / C 75

Caribbean Sea

Punta Molas Lighthouse

N

Laguna Xlapak

Castillo Real

Isla de la Pasión

Punta Norte

Playa Bonita

San Gervasio

Northern Hotel Sector

Santa Rita

San Miguel de Cozúmel

Punta Morena

Southern Hotel Sector

Chen Río

Laguna Chankanaab

Playa San Francisco

Punta Chiqueros

El Cedral

El Mirador

Playa Palancar

Laguna de Colombia

0   5
km

Palancar Reef

El Caracol

Colombia Reef   Punta Sur

Maracaibo Reef

Punta Celerain Lighthouse

1. *Hotel Stouffer Presidente*
2. Cruise Ship Terminal
3. Car Ferry to Puerto Morelos
4. Ferry to Playa del Carmen

km lead to the former *Holiday Inn*, the last big hotel S of San Miguel. Just after this is Parque Chankanab, which used to be an idyllic lagoon behind the beach (9 km from San Miguel). After it became totally spoilt, it was restored as a National Park, with the lagoon, crystal clear again, a botanical garden with local and imported plants, a "Maya Area" (rather artificial), swimming (ideal for families with young children), snorkelling, dive shops, souvenirs, expensive but good restaurants and lockers (US$2). Entry costs

US$4, snorkelling mask and fins US$5, use of underwater camera US$25, open 0800-1600. Soon the road enters the S hotel zone at the *Stouffer Presidente*, coming to the cruise ship dock and car ferry port on the outskirts of town.

Diving The island is famous for the beauty of its underwater environment. The best reef for scuba-diving is Palancar, reached only by boat. Also highly recommended are Santa Rosa and Colombia. There are at least 20 major dive sites. There are also over 20 dive operators. PADI, NAUI or SSI certification are all available; most trips are 2-tank dives, but one-tank and nighttime dives are easily arranged. The better establishments have more dive masters accompanying reef trips. There are 2 hyperbaric chambers on the island. A resort course costs on average US$60, a 3-4 certification course US$350, including equipment. Lots of packages are available. The following operators have been recommended: *Chino's Scuba Shop*, T/F 24487, ask for Ruben Maldonado; *Caribbean Divers*, T 21080, F 21426; there are many others, shop around.

Local Information – Cozumel

● Local Transport

The main road around Cozumel is paved, but public buses serve only the expensive hotels N of town. It is best to hire a bicycle (quiet) when touring around the island so one can see wildlife – iguanas, turtles, birds. Rental charges are US$5 for 12 hrs, US$8 for 24 hrs, eg from *Splash*, on Calle 6 Norte, T 20502, 0800-2000.
Vehicle rental Many agencies for cars, jeeps and mopeds. Eg Avis, Budget, Hertz, National, and local companies. Car hire ranges from about US$55 a day for a VW Beetle to US$70 minimum for a jeep. Scooter rental is US$27 a day high season, US$22 low. One Pemex filling station, at Av Juárez y Av 30; beware overcharging. If taking a moped be aware of traffic laws, helmets must be worn, illegal parking is subject to fines, etc (single women should not ride alone on the E side of the island).

● Taxis

All carry an official price list. Downtown fare US$1.15; to N or S hotel zones US$2.35; San Francisco beach US$10; Maya ruins US$30; island tour including San Gervasio US$50.

● Ferries

See under Playa del Carmen for passenger ferries. Car ferry goes from Puerto Morelos twice a day: US$27 for a car, US$4 per passenger; the entrance to the car ferry on Cozumel is just past the cruise ship dock.

● Hotels

(prices rise 50% around Christmas) *Meliá Mayan Cozumel*, in N hotel zone, 5 km from airport, T 20072, F 21599, US$115 low season, US$152 high season; *El Cozumeleño*, also in N zone, T 20149, F 20381, good, but like all hotels in this area, a bit inconvenient. South of San Miguel are *Stouffer Presidente*, T 20322, F 21360, first class, but some distance from town; *Fiesta Americana*, T 22900, F 21301, linked to beach by tunnel; *La Ceiba*, T 20844, F 20065, and others (all in the US$100-200 range).

Hotels in San Miguel town: *Bahía*, Av Rafael Melgar y Calle 3 Sur (above *Kentucky Fried Chicken*), a/c, phone, cable TV, fridge, even numbered rooms have balcony, US$60, T 20209, F 21387, rec; also above US$45: *Barracuda*, Av Rafael Melgar 628, T 20002, F 20884, popular with divers; *Mesón San Miguel*, on the plaza, T 20233, F 21820; *Plaza Cozumel*, Calle 2 Norte 3, T 22711, F 20066, a/c, TV, phone, pool, restaurant, car hire, laundry. Under US$45: *Maya Cozumel*, Calle 5 Sur 4, T 20011, F 20781, a/c, pool; *Safari*, T 20101, F 20661, a/c; *Soberanis*, Av Rafael Melgar 471, T 20246, a/c, restaurant terrace bar; and *Vista del Mar*, Av R Melgar 45, T 20545, a/c, restaurant, parking. Under US$30: *Al Marestal*, Calle 10 y 25 Av Norte, T 20822, spacious, clean rooms, fan or a/c, cool showers, swimming pool, very good; *Elizabeth*, Adolfo Rosado Salas 44, T 20330, with a/c (cheaper with fan), suites with fridge and stove, also has villas at Calle 3 Sur con Av 25 Sur; 2 doors away is *Flores*, a/c, cheaper with fan; *Flamingo*, Calle 6 Norte 81, T 21264, showers, fan, clean, good value; *López*, on Plaza, Calle Sur 7-A, T 20108, hot showers, clean, no meals; *Marqués*, 5 Av Sur between 1 Sur and A R Salas, T 20677, with a/c, cheaper with fan, rec; close by are *Mary Carmen* and *El Pirata*, both cheaper with fan; *Pepita's*, 15 Av Sur 120, T 20098, same price range, a/c, fan, fridge, owner, Eduardo Ruiz, speaks English, Spanish, French, Italian, German and Mayan, highly rec as best value on island; also *Posada Cozumel*, Calle 4 Norte 3, T 20314, pool, showers, a/c, cheaper with fan, clean. Under US$20: *Blanquita*, 10 Norte, T 21190, comfortable, clean, friendly, owner speaks English, rents snorkelling gear and motor-scooters, rec. *José de León*, Av Pedro J Coldwell y 17 Calle Sur, fairly clean, showers; *Posada del Charro*, one block E of *José de León*, same owner, same facilities; *Kary*, 25 Av Sur y A R Salas, T 22011, a/c, showers, pool, clean; *Paraíso Caribe*, 15 Av Norte y 10 Calle, fan, showers, clean; *Saolima*, A R Salas 260, T 20886, US$13.50, clean, fan, showers, cold water, rec; *Posada Letty*, Calle 1 Sur y Av 15 Sur, clean, hot water, good value.

Camping is not permitted although there are 2 suitable sites on the S shore. Try asking for permission at the army base.

● Restaurants

In general, it is much cheaper to eat in town than at the resort hotels to the N or S. Very few hotels in town have restaurants since there are so many other places to eat. *Las Palmeras*, at the pier (people-watching spot), rec, very

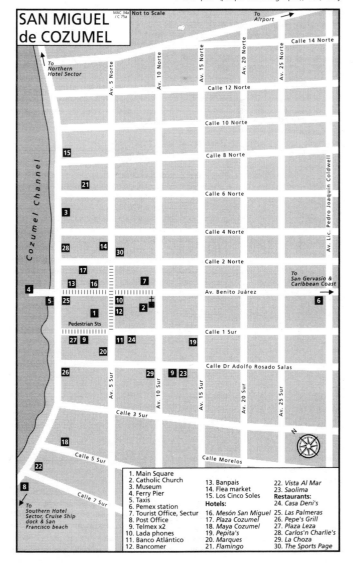

SAN MIGUEL de COZUMEL
MAC 34a / C 75a **Not to Scale**

1. Main Square
2. Catholic Church
3. Museum
4. Ferry Pier
5. Taxis
6. Pemex station
7. Tourist Office, Sectur
8. Post Office
9. Telmex x2
10. Lada phones
11. Banco Atlántico
12. Bancomer
13. Banpais
14. Flea market
15. Los Cinco Soles
Hotels:
16. *Mesón San Miguel*
17. *Plaza Cozumel*
18. *Maya Cozumel*
19. *Pepita's*
20. *Marques*
21. *Flamingo*
22. *Vista Al Mar*
23. *Saolima*
Restaurants:
24. *Casa Deni's*
25. *Las Palmeras*
26. *Pepe's Grill*
27. *Plaza Leza*
28. *Carlos'n Charlie's*
29. *La Choza*
30. *The Sports Page*

popular for breakfast, opens 0700, always busy; *Morgans*, main square, elegant, expensive, good; *Plaza Leza*, main square, excellent and reasonable; *La Choza*, A R Salas 198, reasonable, Mexico City food, rec; *Karen's Pizza and Grill*, Av 5 Norte between Av B Juárez and Calle 2 Norte, pizza cheap, good; *Gatto Pardo*, 10 Av Sur 121, good pizzas and try their "tequila slammers"; *Café del Puerto*, 2nd floor by pier, South Seas style; *El Moro*, 75 Bis Norte 124, between 4 y 2, good, closed Thur; *Santiago's Grill*, 15 Av Sur y A R Salas, excellent, medium price-range, popular with divers; also popular with divers is *Las Tortugas*, 10 Av Norte, just N of square, good in the evening; *El Capi Navegante*, 2 locations: by market for lunch, and C 3 y 10 Av Sur, more up market, seafood at each; *La Yucatequita*, 9 C Sur y 10 Av Sur, genuine Mayan food, closes at 2130, best to go day before and discuss menu; *La Misión*, Av Benito Juárez y 10 Av Norte, good food, friendly atmosphere; *Pepe's Grill*, waterfront, 2 blocks S of pier, expensive and excellent, service not always courteous; *Acuario*, on beach 6 blocks S of pier, famous for seafood, aquarium in restaurant (ask to see the tanks at the back). *Carlos and Charlie's* restaurant/bar, popular, 2nd floor on waterfront 2 blocks N of pier. *Pancho's Backyard*, Rafael Melgar 27, in *Los Cinco Soles* shopping complex, Mexican food and wine elegantly served, good food. *Mi Chabalita*, 10 Av Sur between Calle 1 Sur and Calle Salas, friendly, good Mexican food. *Casa Deni's*, Calle 1 Sur 164, close to Plaza, open air restaurant, very good, moderate prices. *The Sports Page*, Calle 2 Norte y Av 5, US-style, breakfasts, burgers, steaks, lobster, satellite TV, money exchange, phones for USA; US-style breakfasts also at *Los Cocos*, next to ProDive on A R Salas.

Naked Turtle, on E side (has basic rooms to let); *Mescalito's*, see above, another place, like *The Sports Page*, to write a message on your T-shirt and leave it on the ceiling; several other bar restaurants on the E side.

● **Nightclubs**
Joman's (very seedy), *Scaramouche* (the best, Av R Melgar y Calle A R Salas), *Neptuno* (Av R Melgar y Calle 11, S of centre, these 2 state-of-the-art discos), as well as hotel nightclubs.

● **Exchange**
4 banks on the main square, all exchange money in am only, but not at same hours; BancomerhasATMmachines.*Casas de cambio* on Av 5 Norte (eg next to Banco Atlántida) and around square, 3.5% commission, open longer hours.

● **Museum**
On waterfront between Calles 4 and 6, history of the island, well laid-out (entry US$3). Bookshop, art gallery, rooftop restaurant has excellent food and views of sunset, good for breakfast, too, from 0700 ("The Quick" is excellent value). Recommended.

● **Film**
Two shops develop film, both quite expensive (about US$20 for 36 prints). Best to wait till you get home.

● **Laundry**
On A R Salas between Avs 5 and 10, coin op or service wash.

● **Post Office**
Av Rafael Melgar y Calle 7 Sur. **Telephones** Credit card LADA phones on main square at corner of Av Juárez y Av 5, or on A R Salas, just up from Av 5 Sur, opp *Roberto's Black Coral Studio* (if working). For calls to the USA go to *The Sports Page*. Telmex phone offices on the main square next to *Restaurant Plaza Leza*, open 0800-2300, and on A R Salas between Avs 10 and 15. There are also expensive Computel offices in town, eg at the cruise ship dock.

● **Tourist Information**
Sectur tourist office in Plaza Cozumel on Av Juárez, between 5 Av and 10 Av, 1st floor, English-speaking service in am, opens 1800 in pm. On arrival, cross the road from the pier to the square where lots of information kiosks give maps, tour information, etc. A good map (*The Brown Map*), including reef locations, is available from stores and shops. *The Blue Guide*, free, has maps and practical details, available everywhere. Booklets on archaeological sites and the region, and Mexico City newspapers are available at the *papelería* on the E side of the square.

PLAYA DEL CARMEN

On the mainland, opposite Cozumel, *Playa del Carmen* is a fast growing beach centre, with many new hotels and restaurants. In Maya times it was a departure point for boats to Cozumel; modern services have resumed with the development of Playa del Carmen as a resort. This has only happened more-or-less concurrently with the expansion of Cancún. "Playa", as it is usually known, has several kilometres of white sand beaches, which are relatively clean; those to the N of town are the most pleasant (there are sandflies, though). Avenida Juárez runs from Highway 307 to the park which fronts the sea. One block S of the park is the ferry terminal. All along Avenida 5, the street which parallels the beach, are restaurants and shops, with hotels on the streets running back from the beach. Playa is conveniently placed between Cancún and Tulum, giving easy access to these and other tourist sites on the coast and inland.

Local information
● Transport
Ferry for **Cozumel**, 2 companies, *Mexico I* and *Mexico II* waterjets, US$8.35 one way, minimum 30 mins journey, and Caribe Tours, which has 2 classes of boat, US$8.35 5 times a day, and US$5 3 times (40 mins). Each company has 8-9 a day from 0530-2045, returning 0400-2000 (schedules change frequently).

Buses: to/from **Cancún**, 1 hr 15 mins, Playa Express (Av Juárez, between Avs 5 y 10) goes every 30 mins, US$2.25; also Caribe (Av Juárez, by *Posada Lily*) to Cancún luxury bus at 1215, 1st class 3 times a day. To Cancún international airport, take a 2nd class bus to the crossroads (US$2.50) and walk, or take a taxi (US$1.65) the 4 km to the terminal. Taxi from Cancún airport to Playa del Carmen, US$50 per vehicle. Caribe luxury buses to **Mérida**, US$25.30, and **Chetumal** US$16.50, also 1st and 2nd class to Chetumal, 2nd class calls at **Tulum**, US$2.20. Expreso Oriente (Av Juárez y Av 5) has luxury, 1st and 2nd class buses to Mérida via Cancún, many a day, US$17.50, US$14.30 and US$12 respectively; also 2nd class Tulum (US$1.80) and **Cobá** (US$3.30). In all, several buses a day to Tulum between 0500 and 2130, 1 hr.

Tours to Tulum and Xel-Há from kiosk by boat dock US$30; taxi tours to Tulum, Xel-Há and Xcaret, 5-6 hrs, US$60; taxi to Xcaret US$6.65. Taxis congregate on the Av Juárez side of the square (Sindicato Lázaro Cárdenas del Río, T 30032/30414).

● Car Hire
Continental Car Rental, Av Juárez; car and motorcycle hire on Av Juárez, opp bus office,

beside Caribe Express. *Playa*, at Plaza Marina Playacar; *National* at *Hotel Molcas*, near ferry pier.

● Hotels
Hotels fill up early; cheaper rooms are hard to find in January. Outside town are: at Km 297/8, N of Playa del Carmen, *Cabañas Capitán Lafitte*, very good, pool, excellent cheap restaurant on barren beach; under same ownership is *Shangri-Lá Caribe*, T 22888, 7 km S, closer to town (at N end of the bay N of Playa), US$100 in cabins, equally good, excellent beach with diving (Cyan-Ha, PADI) and snorkelling, sailing, easy birdwatching beside hotel; beside *Shangri-Lá* is *Las Palapas*, breakfast and dinner included, cabins with hammocks outside, US$125, good, T 22977, F 41668 (F Mexico City 379-8641); at Km 296, *El Marlín Azul*, swimming pool, good food.

Most luxurious is *Continental Plaza Playacar*, T 30100, F 30105, a huge new development just S of the ferry terminal; in the same development as this 5-star hotel is the 5-star *Diamond Resort*, Apdo Postal 149, T 30340, F 30348, and the 4-star *Caribbean Villages*, T 30434, F 30437, both all-inclusive club resorts, the latter in the middle of a golf course; there are also villas for rent from US$65 to US$280, PO Box 139, Playa del Carmen, T/F 30148. At the N end of town, on a popular stretch of beach between Calles 12 and 14, is *Blue Parrot*, T 30083, F 44564 (reservations in USA 904- 775 6660, toll free 800-634 3547), US$20-90, price depends on type of room and facilities, has bungalows, with excellent bar (Happy Hour 2200) and café, volley ball court, deep sea fishing expeditions, highly rec; *Rosa Mirador*, behind the *Blue Parrot*, hot showers, fan, best views from 3rd floor, owner Alberto speaks English, rec. *Azul Profundo*, next to *Blue Parrot*, with bath and balcony. *Costa del Mar*, on little road between Calles 10 and 12, T 30058, US$40, restaurant and bar, pool; *Cabañas Alejari*, Calle 6 going down to beach, T 30374, US$45, very nice, shop has long distance phones; next to *Alejari* on the beach is *Albatros*, US$25, and *Albatros Royale*, T 30001, clean, very good, no pool, US$30-35, *Mom's*, Av 30 y Calle 4, T 30315, about 5 blocks from bus station or beach, US$35, clean, comfortable, small pool, good restaurant with US home cooking and plenty of vegetables, good value. *Yax-Ha* cabins, on the beach, via Av 5 by Calle 10, US$25-50 (price depending on size and season), excellent. *Cabañas Banana*, Av 5 entre Calles 6 y 8, T 30036, cabins (US$23) and rooms (US$18-25), kitchenettes; *Casa de Gopala*, Calle 2 Norte and Av 10 Norte (PO Box 154), T/F 30054, with bath and fan, quiet and central, pool, American/Mexican owned, large rooms, quiet and comfortable, rec, US$40 (high season); *Cabañas Tuxatah*, 2 mins from sea, 2 blocks S from Av Juárez (Apdo 45, T 30025), German owner, Maria Weltin speaks English and French, with bath, clean, comfortable, hot water, laundry service, beautiful gardens, rec, breakfast US$4. *Nuevo Amanecer*, Calle 4 W of Av 5, very attractive, fans, hot water, hammocks, mosquito nets, clean, laundry area, pool room, helpful, rec; *Maya Bric*, Av 5, between Calles 8 and 10, T 30011, hot water, clean, friendly, pool, Tank-Ha dive shop (see below). *Sian Ka'an*, Av 5 y Calle 2, T 30203, 100m from bus station, modern rooms with balcony, US$20, clean, rec. *Posada Fernández*, Av 5 opp Calle 1, US$15, with bath hot water and fan, friendly, rec; *Posada Lily*, US$17, with shower, fan, safe, clean, rec, but noisy in am and cell-like rooms, Av Juárez at Caribe bus stop; under same ownership *Dos Hermanos*, 3 blocks W and 2 blocks N of *Posada Lily*, clean, hot showers, fan, quiet. *Cabañas Tucan*, Av 5 beyond Calle 14, new, clean, good, mosquito net, highly rec; *Cabañas La Ruina*, at the beach end of Calle 2, popular, noisy, clean, well-organized, rec, lots of options and prices, from 2- to 3-bedded cabins (US$8.50-16.50), hammock space under *palapa* (US$2.50 plus US$8 deposit) with or without security locker, hammock in open air (US$2 plus US$8 deposit), camping, space for vehicles and camper vans (US$4-11), linen rental, bath extra, cooking facilities; *Mi Casa* (unmarked), Av 5 opp *Maya Bric*, US$11.50, with bath and fan, cold water, clean, friendly manager speaks English, mosquito coils necessary. Lots of new places going up, none under US$10 a night. Youth Hostel *Villa Deportiva Juvenil*, from US$5 in dormitory to US$20 for up to 4 in cabin with fan and private shower, comfortable, with basketball court and good café, rec, but difficult to find, especially after dark, but it is signposted—it's 5 blocks up from Av 5, on Calle 8 (T 525-2548). **Camping** See above under *La Ruina*; also *Camping Las Brisas* at the beach end of Calle 4.

● **Restaurants**

Belvedere, on square between ferry and bus station, good pasta. *Máscaras*, on square, highly rec; also on the square, *El Tacolote*, tacos, etc, and *Las Piñatas*. *Da Gabi*, just up Calle 12 from *Blue Parrot*, good pastas, Mexican dishes, breakfast buffet, also has rooms for US$25. Next to *Cabañas Yax-Ha* is *El Pescador*, fish, has a variety of beers. On or near Av 5: *Pez Vela* Av 5 y Calle 2, good atmosphere, food, drinks and music (closed 1500-1700); *Nuestra Señora del Carmen*, Av 5 y Calle 2, family-run, cheap, generous portions, rec; *Playa Caribe*, 1 block up Av 5 from plaza, fish and seafood specialities, good breafast, nice atmosphere, cheap, and popular with budget minded travellers; *Karen's Pizza*, Av 5 entre Calles 2 y 4, pizzas, Mexican dishes, cable TV, popular; *El Capitán*, Calle 4 just off Av 5, good meals and music, popular; next door is *Sabor* for sandwiches, juices, breakfast. In Playa Plaza on Av 5 entre Calles 4 y 6, *Restaurante y Tropical Bar*, good service. *Limones*, Av 5 y Calle 6, good food, popular, reasonable prices; opposite is *Chicago*, steakhouse, American-owned, also serves seafood and breakfast (US$2.50 on terrace with seaview), good, CNN TV; across Calle 6, still on Av 5 is *Flippers*, good atmosphere, good food especially fish, moderately priced. *Bip Bip*, Av 5 between Calles 4 and 6, best pizza in town; *La Hueva del Coronado*, same block, seafood and local dishes, reasonable; *El Correo*, just beyond *Posada Fernández*, Mexican, cheap, rec; *Panadería del Caribe*, Av 5 entre Calles 4 y 2, for breads and cakes; *Zermat Bakery*, at extreme end of pedestrian Calle Norte, 5 blocks from bus station, rec for pastries. Various places serve breakfast close to Post Office. Many places have "happy hour", times vary, shop around.

● **Entertainment**

La Opción, Av 5 beside *Bip Bip*, upstairs, shows video films, usually 2 a night. *Ziggy's Bar and Disco* on the square, very busy Fri/Sat night, expensive drinks; live music in a number of places at night, look for notices. *Pez Vela*, has live music at about 2000 followed by Happy Hour.

● **Diving**

Tank-Ha Dive Center, at *Maya Bric Hotel*, resort course US$60 (diving lesson in the hotel pool before first dive), 1-tank dive US$35, 2-tank US$50, packages from US$90-395, PDIC certification course US$350. Dive shop at Yax-Ha *Cabañas*. Also *El Oasis Dive Shop*, Calle 4 between Avs 5 and 10; *Albatros Water Sports*; *Costa del Mar Dive Shop*, beside *Blue Parrot*; and others.

● **Bank**

Banco del Atlántico on Av Juárez y Av 10, 2 blocks up from plaza; **Bancomer**, Av Juárez 5 blocks W of Av 5; *casa de cambio* on Av 5 opp tourist information booth, reasonable rates for US$ cash, no commission.

● **Post Office**

Av Juárez y Av 15, open 0800-1700 Mon-Fri, 0900-1300 Sun and holidays. **Telephones** Computel next to bus station on Av Juárez. Long distance phones at shop at *Cabañas Alejari*. International fax service at Turquoise Reef Realty, in same block as *Hotel Playa del Carmen*, cost of phone call plus US$3.65 for first sheet, US$1.65 for second.

● **Launderette**

Av Juárez, 2 blocks from bus station; another on Av 5.

● **Tourist Information**

Tourist kiosk on square, with information and leaflets, books guided tours to Tulum and Cobá, US$30 including transport, entry to site, and English-speaking guide, Mon and Fri, 0930. *Destination Playa del Carmen* bulletin gives details of many of the services in town, plus map.

ON THE MAINLAND

Xcaret, a turnoff left on Route 307 S of Playa del Carmen, was once an undeveloped spot, with the unrestored ruins of Pole near three linked *cenotes* and sea water lagoons. Pole was the Maya departure point for Cozumel. It has now been redesigned as a clean, well-tended park, catering exclusively for day-trippers, which costs US$17 to enter. This entitles you to visit the small ruins, the beach, lagoon and inlet, to take an underground river trip (life vest included) and to use all chairs, hammocks and *palapas*. Everything else is extra: food and drink (none may be brought in), snorkel rental (US$7), snorkel lessons, reef trips (US$10), diving, horse riding (US$30) and lockers (for which you have to pay US$1 each time you lock the door). There are also dolphins in pens with which you may swim for US$50. No sun tan lotion may be worn in the sea, but there is a film of oils in the sea nonetheless. Buses from

Playa del Carmen leave you at the turnoff (US$0.65), a 1 km walk from the entrance. The alternative is to take a taxi, or a tour from Playa del Carmen or Cancún (in a multicoloured bus).

The frequently mentioned *Tulum* is on the route between the NE Yucatán resorts and the Mexico/Belize border. It is a spectacular Maya-Toltec ruined city, dating from the 12th century, 131 km S of Cancún, 1 km off the main road. The city walls of white stone stand atop coastal cliffs (frescoes are still visible on the interior walls of temples). The temples were dedicated to the worship of the Falling God, or the Setting Sun, represented as a falling character over nearly all the W-facing doors (Cozumel was the home of the Rising Sun). The same idea is reflected in the buildings, which are wider at the top than at the bottom. Open 0700-1700, about 2 hrs are needed to view the city at leisure (entry US$4.35, Sun free). Tulum is these days crowded with tourists (even at 0800 on some days). Take towel and swimsuit if you wish to scramble down from the ruins to one of the two beaches for a swim. The reef is from 600 to 1,000m from the shore, so if you wish to snorkel you must either be a strong swimmer, or take a boat trip.

Tulum village, 4 km S of the turnoff, is not very large and has a post office, but no bank. When arriving by bus, alight at the turnoff, El Crucero, not the village, for the ruins and accommodation. There are two hotels at El Crucero, and a number of *cabañas* and camping places on the coast road that runs S from the car park outside the ruins.

There is a road linking Tulum with the large city of *Cobá*, which flourished in the 8th and 9th centuries AD (open 0800-1630, entry US$4.35, free on Sun). The present day village of Cobá lies on either side of Lago Cobá, at the end of which is the entrance to the ruins. A second lake, Lago Macanxoc, is within the 70 sq km of the site. Both lakes and their surrounding forest can be seen from the summit of the Iglesia, the tallest structure in the Cobá group. There are three other groups of buildings to visit: Macanxoc, Las Pinturas and Nohoch Mul, which contains the tallest pyramid in the N Yucatán. The delight of the place is the architecture in the jungle, with birds, butterflies, spiders and lizards, and the many uncovered structures which hint at the vastness of the city in its heyday. An unusual feature is the network of ancient roads, known as *sacbes* (white roads), which connect the groups in the site and are known to have extended across the entire Maya Yucatán.

Another interesting place near Tulum is the beautiful clear lagoon, **Laguna Xelhá**, which is full of fish, but no fishing allowed as it is a national park (open 0800-1700), entry US$5 – get a receipt if you want to leave and come back next day (12 km N, 45 mins by bus from Playa del Carmen). Snorkelling gear can be rented at US$7 for a day, but it is often in poor repair; better to rent from your hotel. Arrive as early as possible to see fish as later buses full of tourists arrive from Cancún (you need to dive down about a metre because above that level the water is cold and fresh with few fish; below it is the warm, fish-filled salt water – watch out for sting-rays). There is a marvellous jungle path to one of the lagoon bays. Xelhá ruins (known also as Los Basadres) are located across the road from the beach of the same name. Entry US$3.35, few tourists but not much to see. You may have to jump the fence to visit; there is a beautiful *cenote* at the end of the ruins where you can have a lovely swim. The small ruins of Ak are near Xelhá. Closer to Tulum, at Tancáh, are newly-discovered bright post-classical Maya murals but they are sometimes closed to the public.

20 km N of Tulum is the luxury resort of Akumal.

Chetumal, the capital of the state of Quintana Roo and border town with Belize, is now being developed for tourism (albeit slowly). It is a free port, 240 km S of Tulum, with clean wide streets, and a pleasant waterfront with parks and trees. Accommodation may be a problem at holiday times, but in general there are plenty of places to stay and eat. Tourist information can be found on Boulevard Bahía and 5 de Mayo; also a small kiosk on the plaza at Avenida Héroes and Aguilar.

● **Buses** The main bus station is 2-3 km out of town at the intersection of Insurgentes y Belice (clean facilities, reasonable café); colectivo taxi from town US$1.60. Many buses go to the border, US$0.30; taxi from Chetumal to border, 20 mins, US$6 for 2.

To Belize Batty Bus from bus terminal to Belize City, several daily, schedules change frequently, taking 4-5 hrs on a paved road, US$6 in pesos, US or Belize dollars. Venus Bus to Belize City leaves from the square by Mercado Nuevo on Calzada Veracruz, 3 blocks from main terminal (US$1 taxi ride), again frequent schedule changes. Be there in good time; they sometimes leave early if full.

Excursions from Chetumal

From Chetumal you can make excursions into the lagoons which lie just N of the town. You can also visit the fascinating ruins that lie on the way to Francisco Escárcega (a town on the W side of the Yucatán): Kohunlich, Xpujil, Becán, and Chicanna. Across the bay from Chetumal, at the very tip of Quintana Roo is **Xcalak**, which may be reached from Chetumal by private launch (2 hrs) or by a long, scenic unpaved road from Cafetal to Majahual, then turning S for 55 km (186 km from Chetumal, suitable for passenger cars but needs skilled driver). Daily colectivos from 0700-1900 from 16 de Septiembre y Mahatma Ghandi, but the only one back is at 1300. Bus runs Fri 1600 and Sun 0600, returning Sat morning and Sun afternoon (details from Chetumal tourist office). Xcalak is a fishing village (250 pop) with a few shops with beer and basic supplies and one small restaurant serving Mexican food. A few km N of Xcalak are 2 hotels, *Costa de Cocos* and *Villa Caracol*, both American run, latter is good, comfortable *cabañas*, expensive. From here trips can be arranged to the Banco Chinchorro or to San Pedro, Belize. *Villa Caracol* has sport fishing and diving facilities. In the village you may be able to rent a boat to explore Chetumal Bay and the unspoiled islands of Banco Chinchorro. Do *not* try to walk from Xcalak along the coast to San Pedro, Belize; the route is virtually impassable.

If you are travelling from Belize into the Yucatán, or if you are staying at one of the coastal resorts, an excursion to some of the peninsula's other sites is recommended. These include **Mérida**, capital of Yucatán state. It was founded in 1542 on the site of the city of Tihoo. There are many colonial buildings, museums, parks and a good market where traditional crafts can be bought. The two most extensively excavated and restored cities in the region are Chichén Itzá, 120 km SE of Mérida, and Uxmal, 74 km S. Each deserves a day's exploration. Many other smaller sites can be visited, or, if you are tired of archaeology, you can investigate the N and W coasts. Our map shows them and other points of interest in the Yucatán; for more detail, see the International Travel Map of the region (1:1,000,000), ITM No 205, prepared by Kevin Healey (International Travel Map Productions, PO Box 2290, Vancouver BC, V6Z 1G3, Canada). For a succinct introduction to Maya culture, read *The Maya*, by Michael D Coe (Pelican Books, 1971).

INFORMATION FOR VISITORS

● **Documents**

A passport is necessary, but US and Canadian citizens need only show birth certificate (or for US, a naturalization certificate). Tourists need the free **tourist card**, which can be obtained from any Mexican Consulate or Tourist Commission office, at the Mexican airport on entry, from the offices or on the aircraft of airlines operating into Mexico. Ask for at least 30 days (maximum 180 days); if you say you are in transit you may be charged US$8, with resulting paper work. NB Not all Mexican consuls in

USA are aware of exact entry requirements; it is best to confirm details with airlines which fly to Mexico. Some nationalities appear no longer to need a tourist card. Best to say you are going to an inland destination. (Airlines may issue cards only to citizens of West European countries, most Latin American countries – not Cuba, Chile or Haiti – the USA, Canada, Australia, Japan and the Philippines.) There is a multiple entry card valid for all visits within 6 months for US nationals. The normal validity for other nationals is 90 days, but sometimes only 30 days are granted at border crossings; insist you want more if wishing to stay longer.

Renewal of entry cards or visas must be done at the Secretaría de Gobernación, Dirección General de Servicios Migratorios, Albañiles 19, esquina Eduardo Molina, Colonia 20 de Noviembre, Mexico City, 1st floor, 1st door on right, takes 15 mins, only 60 days given, open 0830-1500, T 795-6685 (Metro San Lázaro or Morelos) or at international airports. To renew a tourist card by leaving the country, you must stay outside Mexico for 72 hrs. If you have proof of US$500 to cover each month of your intended stay, you may renew tourist cards at any immigration office. Take travellers' cheques as proof of finance. Travellers not carrying tourist cards need **visas** (Israelis and French need a visa); multiple entry not permitted, visa must be renewed before re-entry.

At border crossings make sure the immigration people don't con you to pay a dollar for the card or visa. It is free and the man typing it out is only doing his job. We would warn travellers that there have been several cases of tourist cards not being honoured, or a charge being imposed, or the validity being changed arbitrarily to 60 days or less. In this case, complaint should be made to the authorities in Mexico City. Some border stations do not issue tourist cards; you are therefore strongly advised, if travelling by land, to obtain a card before arriving at the border. If, on leaving Mexico, your tourist card is not taken from you, post it to the Mexico City address above. Above all, do not lose your tourist card – you cannot leave the country without it and it can take up to a week to replace. If you want to return to Mexico after leaving there to visit Belize or Guatemala, remember that you will need a new visa/tourist card if yours is not marked for multiple entry.

At the land frontiers with Belize and Guatemala, you may be refused entry into Mexico if you have less than US$200 (or US$350 for each month of intended stay, up to a maximum of 180 days). This restriction does not officially apply to North American and European travellers. *Everyone* entering Mexico from Belize and Guatemala is given only 30 days entry, possibly renewable for up to 60 days.

● **Customs Regulations**
The luggage of tourist-card holders is often passed unexamined. If flying into Mexico from South America, expect to be thoroughly searched (body and luggage) at the airport. US citizens can take in their own clothing and equipment without paying duty, but all valuable and non-US-made objects (diamonds, cameras, binoculars, typewriters, etc) should be registered at the US Customs office or the port of exit so that duty will not be charged on returning. Radios and television sets must be registered and taken out when leaving.

Anyone entering Mexico is allowed to bring in: clothing, footwear and personal cleaning items suitable for the length of stay; camera, or video recorder, and 12 rolls of film, or video-cassettes; books and magazines; one used article of sporting equipment; 20 packs of cigarettes, or 50 cigars, or 250 grams of tobacco; medicines for personal use. Foreigners who reside legally outside Mexico are also allowed: a portable TV, stereo, 20 records or audio cassettes, a musical instrument, 5 used toys, fishing tackle, tennis racket, a pair of skis, a boat up to 5m without an engine, camping equipment, a tent. Those entering by trailer, private plane or yacht may also bring a videocassette recorder, bicycle, motorbike and kitchen utensils. Anything additional to this list with a value of over US$300, if entering by land, air or sea, is taxable and must be declared as such (for Mexicans returning by land the value is US$50). There are no restrictions on the import or export of money apart from gold, but foreign gold coins are allowed into the US only if they are clearly made into jewellery (perforated or otherwise worked on). Archaeological relics may not be taken out of Mexico. US tourists should remember that the US Endangered Species Act, 1973, prohibits importation into the States of products from endangered species, eg tortoise shell. The Department of the Interior issues a leaflet about this. The UK also forbids the import of products from endangered species.

● **How To Get There By Air**
There are international airports at Cancún (16 km S of town, very expensive shops and restaurant) and Cozumel, and a domestic airfield at Isla Mujeres. On arrival at Cancún, make sure you fill in documents correctly, or else you will be sent back to the end of the long, slow queue. At customs, press a button for random bag search. Colectivo taxi buses run from the airport to Cancún town via the Zona Hotelera, US$7; taxis on the same route charge US$25.35. Only taxis go to the airport, US$8 minimum, usually US$11.50 (beware of overcharging; even if you take a "Hotelera" bus to the last hotel, the taxi fare remains the same. Irregular bus from Cancún to the airport 4 times a day, US$3, allow 1 hr. From Cancún by Aeroméxico to Miami, Mérida, Mexico City, and other Mexican destinations. Continental flies to Houston, New York and Chicago. To Los Angeles daily with Mexicana (less frequent out of high season). Cheap flights to USA and Canada can be found. Flights to Mexico City are heavily booked; try stand-by at the airport, or go instead to Mérida. From Amsterdam direct, once a week with Martin Air. Nouvelles Frontières fly charter Zürich-Cancún, 66 Blvd St Michel, 75006 Paris, France. Many charters from North America.

Flight **Cozumel**-Mexico City with Mexicana, daily; this airline also flies to Miami from Cozumel. Continental goes to Houston direct and makes connections with other US cities. Aero Caribe has several flights daily to Cancún, Mérida (as does Mexicana) and Playa del Carmen.

● **To Cuba**
Return flight from Mexico City to Cuba, Sun and Wed, with stop at Mérida if plane is not fully booked (Mexicana); Mexicana direct on Mon, Thur and Fri, Cubana Wed and Sat (US$165 return). Cuba package tours with Mexicana start at US$383 (Wed-Sun) to US$425 (Sun-Sun) depending on hotel category and season, visa (US$18) included, but not tax, staying in Havana; "Sun, sea and sand" packages cost from US$510. There are other packages available. In all cases, tours starting in Mérida cost US$157 less. High season is mid-Dec to early Jan, mid- to end-March and mid-July to mid-August. *Cuba-Mex SA* (reliable), Calle 63, No 500, Depto D, Edificio La Literaria, Mérida, Yucatán (Apdo Postal 508, CP 97000, Telex 753806 Cumeme, T 23-91-99/97-25, F 28-33-68), with branch at Manzanillo 123, D 104, esq Baja California, Colonia Roma Sur, T 574-0813/584-2465, F 584-

6814, México, DF. Also *Cubana Tours*, Reforma 400 C, local "B", Av Colón, Mérida, T 25-79-91, Telex 75-36-22, or Baja California 255, Edif, "B" Despacho 103, Col Hipódromo Condesa, México DF, Casilla Postal 06100, T 564-7839/5208, F 264-2865, Telex 176-1240. Ask around Hamburgo in Mexico City for cheap tickets: might pick them up for as little as US$120 or so. If you pay in dollars make sure the fact is noted on the ticket; if you pay in new pesos and use the ticket later you may be surcharged if the peso price has risen meanwhile. Visas for Cuba available through *Viñales Tours*, Oaxaca 80, Colonia Roma, T 208-99-00/564 4417 (metro Insurgentes, very helpful), or other travel agencies; you have to show your return ticket for Cuba. Tourist visas only are issued in Mexico, valid for the length of your tour. To extend a tourist visa in Cuba will cost US$120. The Cuban consulate in Mexico City does not give visas to individual travellers. Once in Cuba, check with the Mexican Embassy (Calle 12, No 518, between 5 y 7, Miramar, T 33-2142/2489, Mon-Fri 0900-1200) on procedures for reentering Mexico.

● **Tax**

US$12 airport departure tax on international flights; US$6.50 on internal flights. VAT is payable on domestic plane tickets bought in Mexico. Domestic tax on Mexican flights is 10%, on international flights 3.75%.

● **Airline Addresses**

All in Cancún: AeroMéxico, Av Cobá 80, T 84-11-86; Mexicana, Av Cobá 13, T 87-14-44; American Airlines, Aeropuerto, T 86-00-55. Mexicana in Cozumel, Avenida General Rafael E Melgar Sur 17, T 20263, Aeropuerto 20405. Continental, T 20487.

● **Airport Taxis**

To avoid overcharging, the Government has taken control of taxi services from airports to cities and only those with government licences are allowed to carry passengers from the airport. Sometimes one does not pay the driver but purchases a ticket from a booth on leaving the airport. No further tipping is then required, except when the driver handles luggage for you. The same system has been applied at bus stations but it is possible to pay the driver direct.

● **Travel In Mexico**

Promotional packages for local tourism exist, with 30-40% discount, operated by hoteliers, restaurateurs, hauliers and Aeroméxico and Mexicana (the latter is more punctual). Their tickets are not interchangeable. Mexicana offer MexiPass tickets, which are 2-, or 4-coupon tickets for 5 zones of the country (Colonial, Maya, Pleasure, Golden and Central, which includes Guatemala); the pass is eligible only to those arriving on international flights, valid 2-45 days. Fares range from US$124 to US$683; extra coupons may be bought. Mexicana also has 50% discounts on flights between 2300 and 0600.

● **Motoring**

British AA and Dutch ANWB members are reminded that there are ties with the American Automobile Association (AAA), which extends cover to the US and entitles AA members to free travel information including a very useful book and map on Mexico. Holders of 180-day tourist cards can keep their cars in Mexico for that time.

Gasoline is either unleaded, 85 and 90 octane, called *magna sin*, which costs US$0.43/litre, and *nova*, leaded, 80 octane, US$0.39/litre. Unleaded petrol is supposed to be available every 80 km or so. It is signed on major roads, but filling stations sometimes run out, which is not much use for rental cars which often require it. Always fill up when you can. Make sure you are given full value when you tank up, that the pump is set to zero before your tank is filled, that both they and you know what money you've proffered, that your change is correct, that the pump is correctly calibrated, and that your filler cap is put back on. The Free Assistance Service of the Mexican Tourist Department's green jeeps ("*ángeles verdes*") patrol most of Mexico's main roads. The drivers speak English, are trained to give first aid and to make minor auto repairs and deal with flat tyres. They carry gasoline and have radio connection. All help is completely free. Gasoline at cost price. Every state has an Angeles Verdes Hotline.

When entering Mexico from Belize by car point out to the authorities that you have a car with you, otherwise they may not note it and you could be arrested for illegally importing a car.

Tourists' cars cannot, *by law*, be sold in Mexico. This is very strictly applied. You may not leave the country without the car you entered in, except with written government permission with the car in bond.

● **Car Rental**

It is cheaper to rent a car by arrangement in the USA or Europe than to do it in Mexico.

● **Where To Stay**

Accommodation on the islands and neighbouring towns is given above.

Hotel rates were freed from government control in early 1993; some establishments raised prices above the rate of inflation, so some bargaining, or shopping around, may be required to find the best value. Complaints about violations must be reported to the Department of Tourism, Presidente Masaryk 172, Colonia Polanco, Mexico City, T 250-1964 and 250-8555. English is spoken at the best hotels.

Casas de huéspedes are usually the cheapest places to stay, although they are often dirty with poor plumbing. Usually a flat rate for a room is charged, so sharing works out cheaper, say US$3-5 pp. There are very few places with double beds (*matrimonial*) under US$9 double. Sleeping out is possible anywhere, but is not advisable in urban areas. Choose a secluded, relatively invisible spot. Mosquito netting (*pabellón*) is available by the metre in textile shops and, sewn into a sheet sleeping bag, is ample protection against insects.

Beware of "helpfuls" who try to find you a hotel, as prices quoted at the hotel desk rise to give them a commission. If backpacking, it is best for one of you to watch over luggage while the other goes to book a room and pay for it; some hotels are put off by backpacks. During peak season (November-April), it may be hard to find a room and clerks do not always check to see whether a room is vacant. Insist, or if desperate, provide a suitable tip. The week after Semana Santa is normally a holiday, so prices remain high, but resorts are not as crowded as the previous week. When using a lift, remember PB (*Planta Baja*) stands for ground floor. Discounts on hotel prices can often be arranged in the low season (May-October), but this is more difficult in Yucatán. There is not a great price difference between single and double rooms in lower-priced establishments. When checking into a hotel, always ask if the doors are locked at night, preventing guests from entering if no nightguard is posted. Always check the room before paying in advance.

Motels and Auto-hotels are not usually places where guests stay the whole night (you can recognise them by curtains over the garage and red and green lights above the door to show if the room is free). If driving, and wishing to avoid a night on the road, they can be quite acceptable (clean, some have hot water, in the Yucatán they have a/c), and they tend to be cheaper than respectable establishments.

● **Camping**

Most sites are called Trailer Parks, but tents are usually allowed. Beware of people stealing clothes, especially when you hang them up after washing. Paraffin oil (kerosene) for stoves is called *petróleo para lámparas* in Mexico; it is not a very good quality (dirty) and costs about US$0.05 per litre. It is available from an *expendio*, or *despacho de petróleo*, or from a *tlalalpería*, but not from gas stations. Calor gas is widely available. *Gasolina blanca* may be bought in *ferreterías* (ironmongers), prices vary widely; also for Coleman fuel. *Alcohol* for heating the burner can be obtained from supermarkets.

● **Youth Hostels**

21 *albergues* (*Villas Deportivas Juveniles*) exist in Mexico, mostly in small towns, and generally of poor quality. The hostels take YHA members and non-members, who have to pay more. You have to pay a deposit for sheets, pillow and towel; make sure that this is written in the ledger or else you may not get your deposit back. Hostels have lockers for valuables; take good care of your other possessions.

● **Food**

Usual meals are a light breakfast, and a heavy lunch between 1400 and 1500. Dinner, between 1800 and 2000, is light. Many restaurants give foreigners the menu without the *comida corrida* (set meals), and so forcing them to order *à la carte* at double the price; watch this! Try to avoid eating in restaurants which don't post a menu. Meals in modest establishments cost about US$2.25-3.25 for breakfast, US$2.65-4 for lunch (*comida corrida*, US$5.25-8 for a special *comida corrida*) and US$8.35-12 for dinner (generally no set menu). *A la carte* meals at modest establishments cost about US$10; a very good meal can be had for US$16.50 at a middle level establishment. Much higher prices are charged by the classiest restaurants. The best value is undoubtedly in small, family-run places. For those who are self-catering the cost of food in markets and supermarkets is not high. In resort areas the posh hotels include breakfast and dinner in many cases.

● **What To Eat**

Tamales, or meat wrapped in maize and then banana leaves and boiled. Turkey, chicken and pork with exotic sauces – *mole de guajolote* and *mole poblano* (*chile* and chocolate sauce with grated coconut) are famous. *Tacos* (without *chiles*) and *enchiladas* (with all too many of them) are meat or chicken and beans rolled in *tortillas* (maize pancakes) and fried in oil; they are delicious. Try also spring onions with salt and lime juice in *taquerías*. Indian food is found everywhere: for instance, *tostadas* (toasted fried tortillas with chicken, beans and lettuce), or *gorditas*, fried, extra-thick tortillas with sauce and cheese. Black kidney beans (*frijoles*) appear in various dishes. Red snapper (*huachinango*), Veracruz style, is a famous fish dish, sautéed with *pimientos* and spices. Another excellent fish is the sea bass (*róbalo*). Fruits include a vast assortment of tropical types – avocados, bananas, pineapples, *zapotes*, pomegranates, guavas, limes and *mangos de Manila*, which are delicious. Don't eat fruit unless you peel it yourself, and avoid raw vegetables. Try *higos rebanados* (delicious fresh sliced figs), *guacamole* (a mashed avocado seasoned with tomatoes, onions, coriander and *chiles*) and of course, *papaya*, or pawpaw. Mexico has numerous elaborate regional cuisines. Some Maya dishes are *sopa de lima* (chicken, rice, *tostada* and lime), *pok chuk* (pork in achiote sauce), *pibil* (a mild sauce on meat or chicken, cooked in banana leaves), *longanizo* (sausage from Valladolid). Chinese restaurants, present in most towns, generally give clean and efficient service. Fried eggs are known as *huevos estrellados*. On 6 January, Epiphany, the traditional *rosca*, a ring-shaped sweet bread with dried fruit and little plastic baby Jesuses inside, is eaten. The person who finds a baby Jesus in his piece must make a crib and clothes for Him, and invite everyone present to a *fiesta* on 2 February, Candelaria.

● **Drink**

The beer is quite good. Brands include Dos Equis-XX, Montejo, Bohemia, Sol and Superior (the last 2 not as good). Negra Modelo is a dark beer, it has the same alcohol content as the other beers. Local wine, some of it quite good, is cheap. The native drinks are *pulque*, the fermented juice of the agave plant (those unaccustomed to it should not overindulge), *tequila*, made mostly in Jalisco and *mescal* from Oaxaca; the last 2 are distilled from agave plants. Mescal usually has a "gusano de maguey" (a worm) in the bottle, considered by Mexicans to be a particular speciality. Tequila and mescal rarely have an alcoholic content above 40-43%. Also available is the Spanish aniseed spirit, *anís*, which is made locally. Imported whiskies and brandies are expensive.

Rum is cheap and good. There are always plenty of non-alcoholic soft drinks (*refrescos*) – try the *paletas*, safe and refreshing (those of Michoacán are everywhere) – and mineral water. Fresh juices, as long as not mixed with water, and milk shakes (*licuados*) are good and usually safe. If you don't like to drink out of a glass, ask for a straw (*popote*). Herbal teas, eg camomile, are available. There are few outdoor drinking places in Mexico except in tourist spots.

● **Tipping**

More or less on a level of 10-15%; the equivalent of US$0.25 per bag for porters, the equivalent of US$0.20 for bell boys, theatre usherettes, and nothing for a taxi driver unless he gives some extra service. It is not necessary to tip the drivers of hired cars.

● **Cost Of Living**

Budget travellers should note that there is a definite tourist economy, with high prices and, on occasion, unhelpful service. This can be avoided by seeking out those places used by locals; an understanding of Spanish is useful. For travellers, Mexico is in some respects cheaper than the USA in that 1st class bus travel is less, there are local bus services which many US cities lack, and cheap hotel accommodation exists in city centres where, in the USA, there is little more than YMCAs and youth hostels. In other respects, though, Mexico can be more expensive than the USA. In comparison with most Western European countries, Mexico is considerably cheaper. The only areas in which travellers will find Mexico more expensive than the UK are luxury hotels, coffee, beer, long-distance and international phone calls, international postage, theatres and especially car hire. Doctors and dentists provide good quality care at high prices (taking appropriate insurance is highly rec). Film is reasonably cheap, but developing is expensive and of poor quality.

● **Exchange**

Travellers' cheques from any well-known bank can be cashed in most towns if drawn in US dollars; TCs in terms of sterling are harder to cash, and certainly not worth trying to change outside the largest of cities. The free rate of exchange changes daily and varies from bank to bank. Until the new day's rate is posted, at any time between 1000 and 1100, yesterday's rate prevails. Many banks only change foreign currency during a limited period (often between 1000 and 1200, but sometimes also 1600-1800 in Banamex), which should be remembered, especially on Fri. *Casas de cambio* are generally quicker than banks for exchange transactions, but their rates are often not as good. Beware of short-changing at all times. American Express, Mastercard and Visa are generally accepted in Mexico and cash is obtainable with these credit cards at certain banks. Automatic Teller Machines (ATM, *cajero automático*) of Banamex accept Visa, Mastercard and ATM cards of the US Cirrus ATM network for withdrawals up to 300 new pesos. ATM withdrawals on Visa can also be made at branches of Bancomer and Cajeros RED throughout the country. Many banks are affiliated to Mastercard but locations of ATMs should be checked with Mastercard in advance. There have been repeated instances of Banamex ATMs stating that cash cannot be given, "try again later", only for the cardholder to find that his/her account has been debited anyway. If you get a receipt saying no cash dispensed, keep it. NB An American Express card issued in Mexico states "valid only in Mexico", and is used only for peso transactions. All other American Express cards are transacted in US dollars even for employees living in Mexico. Amex TCs are readily accepted. There is a 6% tax on the use of credit cards.

● **Currency**

Until 1 January 1993, the monetary unit was the Mexican peso (represented by an 'S' crossed with one vertical line – unlike 2 vertical lines on the US dollar sign), divided into 100 centavos. On that date 3 zeros were eliminated from the peso, so that 1,000 peso now equals 1 new peso. The new symbol is N$. The smallest note is for 2 new pesos, 2,000 pesos, then 5/5,000, 10/10,000, 20/20,000, 50/50,000 and 100/100,000 pesos (2 and 5 peso notes are disappearing fast). Colours of notes to remain the same. New coins: 5C, 10C, 20C (dodecagonal), 50C (notched dodecagonal), N$1, 2, 5 and 10, all circular except those indicated. It is wise to check the number on coins. Local cheques are easier to cash in the issuing branch. There is a charge for cashing a cheque in a different city; if you can take someone along as a guarantor who has an account in the branch it helps.

● **Health**

The Social Security hospitals are restricted to members, but will take visitors in emergencies;

they are more up to date than the Centros de Salud and Hospitales Civiles found in most centres, which are very cheap and open to everyone. There are many homeopathic physicians in all parts of Mexico. You are recommended to use bottled or mineral water for drinking, except in hotels which normally provide purified drinking water free. Ice is usually made from *agua purificada*. Coffee water is not necessarily boiled. Bottled water is available everywhere. Tehuacán mineral water is sold all over Mexico; both plain and flavoured are first class. Water-sterilizing tablets and water purification solution, Microdyn, can be bought at pharmacies. Milk is only safe when in sealed containers marked *pasteurizado*. Raw salads and vegetables, and food sold on the streets and in cheap cafés, may be dangerous. It is advisable to vaccinate against typhoid, paratyphoid and poliomyelitis if visiting the low-lying tropical zones, where there is also some risk of malaria.

● **Language**

Speaking Spanish is a great asset in avoiding rip-offs for gringos and for making the most of cheap *comedores* and market shopping.

● **Best Season**

For pleasure visits, between October and early April, when it hardly ever rains in most of the country. August is not a good time because it is a holiday month throughout Central America and most internal flights and other transport are heavily booked.

● **Clothing**

Four musts are good walking shoes, sun hats, dark glasses, and flip-flops for the hot sandy beaches. Men may need a jacket and tie in some restaurants. Topless bathing: ask first, or do as others do.

● **National Holidays**

Sunday is a statutory holiday. Saturday is also observed as a holiday, except by the shops. There is no early-closing day. National holidays are as follows: New Year (1 January), Constitution Day (5 February), Birthday of Benito Juárez (21 March), Holy Thursday, Good Friday and Easter Saturday, Labour Day (1 May), Battle of Puebla (5 May), President's Annual Message (1 September), Independence Day (16 September), Discovery of America (12 October), Day of the Revolution (20 November), Christmas Day (25 December).

All Souls' Day (2 November), and Our Lady of Guadalupe (12 December), are not national holidays, but are widely celebrated.

● **Time Zone**
Central Standard Time, 6 hrs behind GMT, 1 behind EST.

● **Weights And Measures**
The metric system is compulsory.

● **Postal Services**
Rates are raised periodically in line with the peso's devaluation against the dollar. They are posted next to the windows where stamps are sold. Air mail letters to the USA take about 6 days, and to the UK via the USA one to 2 weeks. Rates in March 1994 were: to North and Central America and the Caribbean: letters N$2 (20g), N$3.70 (50g), N$5.50 (100g), postcards N$1.50; South America and Europe N$2.50, 4.40, 7.70, postcards N$1.80; Asia and Africa N$2.80, 5.20, 8.60, postcards N$2.10 (an increase was due later in 1994). *Poste restante* ("general delivery" in the USA) functions quite reliably, but you may have to ask under each of your names; if you wish to use this facilty it is known as *lista de correos*; mail is sent back after ten days. Address "*favor de retener hasta llegada*" on envelope. Should it be necessary to send anything swiftly and safely (in Mexico and to other countries), there are many courier firms; the best known is DHL, but it is about twice the cost of Estrella Blanca or Federal Express.

● **Telecommunications**
Pay telephones (black) for local calls take coins, or *fichas*, also for collect long-distance calls. Follow local procedures, then dial 02 for calls inside Mexico and 09 for international calls, and be patient. AT&T's USA Direct service is available, for information in Mexico dial 412-553-7458, ext 359. From LADA phones (see below), dial **01, similar for AT&T credit cards. To use calling cards to Canada, T 95-800-010-1990. 1994 rates for phone and fax: Europe N$9.30, cheap rate 6.20; USA/New York N$5.60, cheap rate 3.73; Australia N$11.85, cheap rate 7.90; plus 10% VAT. Commercially-run *casetas*, or booths (eg Computel), where you pay after phoning, are 2-3 times more expensive, and charges vary from place to place. It is better to call collect from private phones, but better still to use the LADA system. Collect calls on LADA can be made from any blue public phone, silver phones for local and direct long distance calls, some take coins. Others take foreign credit cards (Visa, Mastercard, not Amex – "a slot machine scenario",

not all phones that say they take cards accept them, others that say they don't do), still others take plastic cards worth from 5 to 50 new pesos, purchasable from phone company offices, supermarkets, etc. LADA numbers are: 91 long distance within Mexico, add city code and number (half-price Sunday); 92 long distance in Mexico, person to person; 95 long distance to USA and Canada, add area code and number; 96 to USA and Canada person to person for collect calls; 98 to rest of the world, add country code, city code and number; 99 to rest of the world, person to person; it is not possible to call collect to Germany, but it is possible to Israel. Cheap rates vary according to the country called. For information dial 07 or 611-1100. Foreign calls (through the operator, at least) cannot be made from 1230 on 24 December until the end of Christmas Day. The *Directorio Telefónico Nacional Turístico* is full of useful information, including LADA details, federal tourist offices, time zones, yellow pages for each state, places of interest and maps. Fax services are common in main post offices.

● **Press**
The more important journals are in Mexico City. The most influential dailies are: *Excelsior, Novedades, El Día* (throughout Mexico), *Uno más Uno; The News* (in English, now available in all main cities); *El Universal* (*El Universal Gráfico*); *El Financiero*, the financial newspaper; *La Jornada* (more to the left); *La Prensa*, a popular tabloid, has the largest circulation. *El Nacional* is the mouthpiece of the Government. There are weekly magazines: *Epoca, Proceso*, and *Siempre*. The political satirical weekly is *Los Agachados*.

● **Local Information**
All Mexican Government tourist agencies are now grouped in the Department of Tourism building at Avenida Masaryk 172, near corner of Reforma, Mexico City. A few cities run municipal tourist offices to help travellers. Offices in Cancún, Isla Mujeres and Cozumel are given above.

The Mexican Automobile Association (AMA) is at Orizaba 7, 06700 México DF, T 208-8329, F 511-6285; it sells an indispensable road guide, with good maps and very useful lists of hotels, with current prices. The ANA (Asociación Nacional Automobilística) sells similar but not such good material; offices in Insurgentes (Metro Glorieta) and Avenida Jalisco 27, México 18 DF. For road conditions consult the AMA, which is quite reliable. A calendar of *fiestas* is published by *Mexico This Month*.

There is a series of telephone numbers that tourists can call to clarify problems. In USA, phone Mexican Turismo, Miami, 1-800-446-8277. In Houston T 1-800-44-639-420, for English information for US and Canadian citizens. There is another Houston number which anyone can call, 1-713-880-8772 for information on surface tourism. In Mexico, tourists can call 91-800-00148 and in Mexico City 604-1240. The Secretaría de Turismo has an emergency hot line, open 24 hrs a day: (05) 250-0123/0151.

If you have any complaints about faulty goods or services, go to the Procuraduría Federal de Protección del Consumidor of which there is a branch in every city (head office in Mexico City, José Vasconcelos 208, CP 06720, México DF, T 761-3801/11). Major cities also have a Procurador del Turista. The Tourist Office may also help with these, or criminal matters, while the Agente del Ministro Público (Federal or State District Attorney) will also deal with criminal complaints.

● **Maps**

The Mexican Government Tourist Highway map is available free of charge at tourist offices (when in stock). If driving from the USA you get a free map if you buy your insurance at AAA or at Sanborn's in the border cities. The official map printers, Detenal, produce the only good large-scale maps of the country.

The Dirección General de Oceanografía in Calle Medellín 10, near Insurgentes underground station (Mexico City), sells excellent maps of the entire coastline of Mexico. Good detailed maps of the states of Mexico and the country itself from Dirección General de Geografía y Meteorología, Avenida Observatorio 192, México 18, DF, T 515-15-27. The best road maps of Mexican states, free, on polite written request, are available from Ing Daniel Díaz Díaz, Director General de Programación, Xola 1755, 8° Piso, México 12 DF. Maps are also available from Instituto Nacional de Estadística, Geografía e Informática (INEGI), which has branches in Mexico City (Insurgentes Sur 795, planta baja, PO Box 03810, T 687-4691/687-2911 ext 289) and 40 other cities around the country; in Quintana Roo: Lázaro Cárdenas 91, Chetumal; in Yucatán: Paseo Montejo 442, Edificio Oasis, Mérida (PO Box 97100).

● **Guidebooks**

Travellers wanting more information than we have space to provide, on archaeological sites for instance, would do well to use the widely available Easy Guides written by Richard Bloomgarden, with plans and good illustrations. *A Field Guide to Mexican Birds*, Peterson and Chalif, Houghton Mifflin, 1973, has been recommended. For ornithologists: *Finding Birds in Mexico*, by Ernest P Edwards, Box AQ, Sweet Briar, Virginia 24595, USA, recommended as detailed and thorough. Highly recommended, practical and entertaining is *The People's Guide to Mexico* by Carl Franz (John Muir Publications, Santa Fe, NM), now in its 8th edition, 1990, *Back Country Mexico, A Traveller's Guide and Phrase Book*, by Bob Burlison and David H Riskind (University of Texas Press, Box 7819, Austin, Texas, 78713-7819) has been recommended. Also *Hidden Mexico* by Rebecca Brüns, and *Mexico from the Driver's Seat*, by Mike Nelson (Sanborn's).

Recommended reading for the Maya archaeological area: *The Maya*, by M D Coe (Pelican Books, or large format edition, Thames and Hudson); C Bruce Hunter, *A Guide to Ancient Mayan Ruins* (University of Oklahoma Press, 1986); Joyce Kelly, *An Archaeological Guide to Mexico's Yucatán Peninsula* (the states of Yucatán, Quintana Roo and Campeche) (University of Oklahoma Press, Norman and London, 1993, with maps, photos, 364 pp, accessible, informative and very good). For the Puuc region, *Guide to Puuc Region*, Prof Gualberto Zapata Alonzo (US$7.30), has been recommended. The Panorama series of guide books to the Maya sites is always good, but not always available. Bloomgarden guides also cover the major sites. For a contemporary account of travel in the Maya region, see *Time among the Maya*, by Ronald Wright. Perhaps the most descriptive of travel in the region is John L Stephens, *Incidents of Travel in Central America, Chiapas and Yucatán*, with illustrations by Frederick Catherwood (several editions exist).

We should like to thank all the correspondents who sent information to *The Mexico and Central American Handbook* for information on the Mexican islands.

CLIMATIC TABLES

The following table has been very kindly furnished by Mr. R.K. Headland, the notes by Mark Wilson. Each weather station is given with its altitude in metres (m). Temperatures (Centigrade) are given as averages for each month; the first line is the maximum and the second the minimum. The third line is the average number of wet days encountered in each month.

	Jan	Feb	Mar	Apr	May	June	July	Aug	Sept	Oct	Nov	Dec
Havana	26	27	28	29	30	31	31	32	31	29	27	26
49m.	18	18	19	21	22	23	24	24	24	23	21	19
	6	4	4	4	7	10	9	10	11	11	7	6
Kingston	30	29	30	30	31	31	32	32	32	31	31	30
7m.	22	22	23	24	25	25	26	26	25	25	24	23
	3	2	3	3	5	6	3	6	6	12	5	3
Nassau	25	25	27	28	29	31	31	32	31	29	28	26
10m.	17	17	18	20	22	23	24	24	24	22	20	18
	6	5	5	6	9	12	14	14	15	13	9	6
Port-au-Prince	31	31	32	33	33	35	35	35	34	33	32	31
41m.	23	22	22	23	23	24	25	24	24	24	23	22
	3	5	7	11	13	8	7	11	12	12	7	3
Port of Spain	30	32	31	32	32	31	31	31	32	31	31	30
12m.	20	21	21	21	23	23	23	23	23	22	22	21
	11	8	2	8	9	19	23	17	16	13	17	16
San Juan, PR	27	27	27	28	29	29	29	29	30	30	28	27
14m.	21	21	22	22	23	24	24	24	24	24	23	22
	13	7	8	10	15	14	18	15	14	12	13	14
Santo Domingo	28	28	29	29	30	30	31	31	31	31	30	29
14m.	20	19	20	21	22	23	23	23	23	23	22	21
	7	6	5	7	11	12	11	11	11	11	10	8
Willemstad	28	29	29	30	30	31	31	31	32	31	30	29
23m.	24	23	23	24	25	26	25	26	26	26	24	24
	14	8	7	4	4	7	9	8	6	9	15	16

Use these tables with caution; variations within islands can be dramatic. On the mountainous islands, such as the Windwards, rainfall is generally about 3000 mm (120 inches) in the interior, but only 1500mm (60 inches) in coastal rain shadow areas. Rain falls in intense showers, so even on a wet day there may be plenty of sunshine too. In most of the Caribbean, the wet season is from June to November, but there is plenty of fine weather at this time of year, and it is quite likely to rain in the dry season too. June to November is also the hurricane season, but most islands experience a hurricane on average only two or three times per century.

Temperatures are generally very steady. Nights are much warmer than in (for example) a Mediterranean summer. It generally feels much cooler on the windward (east) coasts; and it actually *is* a lot cooler in the mountains, where temperatures may fall to around 16°C (60°F). At high altitudes, there may be an almost continuous cover of low cloud at certain times of year. The winter season (January to March) is generally dry and not too hot. A possible hazard at this time of year are cold fronts or "northers", which can bring surprisingly cold winds and heavy rain to Jamaica and the northern Caribbean. Don't worry too much about the weather, the Caribbean's reputation is well deserved, and on most islands at most times of year, you can't go too far wrong.

EXCHANGE RATES
(July 1994)

Country	Currency	Abbreviation	Exchange rate/US$
Anguilla	East Caribbean dollar	EC$	2.70
Antigua & Barbuda	East Caribbean dollar	EC$	2.70
Aruba	Aruban florin	Afl	1.77
Bahamas	Bahamian dollar	B$	1.00
Barbados	Barbados dollar	B$	2.00
Belize	Belize dollar	Bz$	2.00
Bermuda	Bermuda dollar	Bd$	1.00
Bonaire	Guilder	Naf	1.79
British Virgin Islands	US dollar	US$	1.00
Cayman Islands	Cayman dollar	CI$	0.80
Cuba	Cuban peso		0.76
	(Black market 130 pesos = US$1)		
Curaçao	Guilder	Naf	1.79
Dominica	East Caribbean dollar	EC$	2.70
Dominican Rep	Dominican peso	RD$	13.08
Grenada	East Caribbean dollar	EC$	2.70
Guadeloupe	French franc	F	5.34
Guyana	Guyanese dollar	G$	140.75
Guyane	French franc	F	5.34
Haiti	Gourde		12.00
Honduras	Lempira	L	8.59
Jamaica	Jamaican dollar	J$	33.04
Martinique	French franc	F	5.34
Mexico	New peso	N$	3.40
Montserrat	East Caribbean dollar	EC$	2.70
Nicaragua	Córdoba Oro	C$	6.74
Panama	US dollar	US$	1.00
Puerto Rico	US dollar	US$	1.00
Saba	Guilder	Naf	1.79
St Barthélémy	French franc	F	5.34
St Kitts & Nevis	East Caribbean dollar	EC$	2.70
St Lucia	East Caribbean dollar	EC$	2.70
St Martin	French franc	F	5.34
St Vincent & the Grenadines	East Caribbean dollar	EC$	2.70
Sint Eustatius	Guilder	Naf	1.79
Sint Maarten	Guilder	Naf	1.79
Suriname	Suriname guilder	Sf	183.05
Trinidad & Tobago	Trinidad dollar	TT$	5.97
Turks & Caicos	US dollar	US$	1.00
US Virgin Islands	US dollar	US$	1.00
Venezuela	Bolívar	Bs	170.00

INDEX

INDEX TO TOWN AND ISLAND MAPS

TRADE & TRAVEL
Handbooks
1995

Award-winning guidebooks for all independently minded travellers. This annually updated series of impeccable accuracy and authority now covers over 120 countries, dependencies and dominions from Latin America and the Caribbean across the globe to Africa, India and Southeast Asia.

Practical, pocket sized and excellent value - **Handbooks** take you further.

South American Handbook

Mexico & Central American Handbook

Caribbean Islands Handbook

India Handbook (formerly *South Asian Handbook*)

Thailand & Burma Handbook

Vietnam, Laos & Cambodia Handbook

Indonesia, Malaysia & Singapore Handbook

North African Handbook
includes Andalucía (Moorish southern Spain)

East African Handbook
includes Zanzibar, Madagascar and the Seychelles

Write for our latest catalogue
Trade & Travel, 6 Riverside Court, Lower Bristol Road,
Bath BA2 3DZ, England.
Tel 0225 469141   Fax 0225 469461

"More information - less blah!"